GREAT POEMS
OF THE
ENGLISH LANGUAGE

GREAT POEMS
OF THE
ENGLISH LANGUAGE

GREAT POEMS

of the

English Language

❧❧❧❧❧❧❧❧❧❧❧❧❧❧❧❧❧❧❧❧❧❧❧❧❧❧❧❧❧❧❧❧❧❧❧❧❧

AN ANTHOLOGY

❧❧❧❧❧❧❧❧❧❧❧❧❧❧❧❧❧❧❧❧❧❧❧❧❧❧❧❧❧❧❧❧❧❧❧❧❧

Compiled by

WALLACE ALVIN BRIGGS

WITH A SUPPLEMENT of RECENT POETRY

Selected by

WILLIAM ROSE BENÉT

New York

TUDOR PUBLISHING COMPANY

MCMXLVIII

GREAT POEMS OF THE ENGLISH LANGUAGE

PRINTED IN THE UNITED STATES OF AMERICA

In Memory of
ELLA PARDEE BRIGGS
NEL CIEL CHE PIU DELLA SUA LUCE
PRENDE FU' IO

THE PORTRAIT

O Lord of all compassionate control,
O Love! let this my lady's picture glow
Under my hand to praise her name, and show
Even of her inner self the perfect whole:
That he who seeks her beauty's furthest goal,
Beyond the light that the sweet glances throw
And refluent wave of the sweet smile, may know
The very sky and sea-line of her soul.

.   .   .   .

—DANTE GABRIEL ROSSETTI

PREFACE

I sing of brooks, of blossoms, birds and bowers,
Of April, May, of June, and July flowers;
I sing of May-poles, hock-carts, wassails, wakes,
Of bridegrooms, brides, and of their bridal cakes.
I write of Youth, of Love, and have access
By these, to sing of cleanly wantonness;
I sing of dews, of rains, and, piece by piece,
Of balm, of oil, of spice, and ambergris.
I sing of times trans-shifting; and I write
How roses first came red, and lilies white;
I write of groves, of twilights, and I sing
The court of Mab, and of the Fairy King.
I write of Hell; I sing, and ever shall,
Of Heaven, and hope to have it after all.

—ROBERT HERRICK.

Give Beauty all her right,
    She's not to one form tied;
Each shape yields fair delight,
    Where her perfections bide.

. . . .

—THOMAS CAMPION.

In the preparation of "Great Poems of the English Language," I am greatly indebted to Mrs. Garret W. McEnerney for many selections and for sympathetic and helpful criticism.

W. A. B.

PUBLISHER'S NOTE

The ambition of the anthologist, in compiling *Great Poems of the English Language,* has been to bring together representative selections of the work of every important English poet from the beginnings of poetry in our language down to the present time. In this he has been, for the greater part, successful—although it has been necessary to omit selections from the works of certain modern poets where permissions to reprint could not be obtained.

Naturally, then, the anthology is composed of poems by English, Irish, Scottish, Welsh and American writers—men and women; and it has been found desirable to arrange them in chronological order. This brings together the contemporary poets of the several countries and aids the reader in obtaining a comprehensive view of the development of English as a poetic language.

To avoid the controversy likely to arise from conflicting claims of nationality—country of birth *versus* country of naturalization—*Great Poems of the English Language* follows the rule of stating the country of birth. In most cases this clearly indicates nationality, and in some may show the influence of environment on the poet's work. Among the younger writers there are, of necessity, quite a few cases where no biographical data are available. However, many of these have produced work that deserves—actually demands—admission to an anthology of this scope. We have included these men and women, feeling that information regarding a poet's nationality or age is of secondary importance.

An interesting feature of the book is the inclusion of numerous selections from longer poems which could not be printed in full in a work of one volume—each excerpt being in itself, and entirely apart from the context, an entity, a complete picture or thought. Thus, we believe, *Great Poems of the English Language* will fill most satisfactorily the gap between the ordinary anthology and the complete works of the poets.

PUBLISHER'S NOTE

Because of the characteristics just discussed, the index has been made exceptionally full. Not only are given the titles of the complete poems—as, for instance, Shakespeare's plays—but a glance will show whether or not a favorite passage is included: the source or location of each selection is indicated. Also in the case of long poems whose excerpts have individual titles, as in Sir Philip Sidney's "Astrophel and Stella," proper credit is given at the end of each part of the work cited.

For her intelligent appreciation of the problems involved in this arrangement and in the indexing, and for her pains-taking accuracy in carrying out the actual work, the publishers are grateful to Miss Julie M. Eidesheim without whose expert services they would have been seriously handicapped.

ACKNOWLEDGMENTS

ACKNOWLEDGMENTS

Before turning to the formal, though deeply sincere, acknowledgments so reasonably required of every anthologist, I wish, as compiler, here to express my personal thanks to those who have assisted in preparing this volume for publication: to Miss Florence Abegglen, for patient and meticulous typing; to Mr. George Platt and Mr. Winsor Josselyn, who have worked with me, here in Sacramento, upon the several drafts of the manuscript; to Mr. Kenneth Fuessle, my advisor and representative, and his associates—Miss Julie M. Eidesheim, Mr. John R. Brown, Mr. Philip Emerson Wood; and to the House of Robert M. McBride and Company, Publishers.

Every anthologist, of course, assumes two major obligations: the one, to make sure that his selections are scrupulously faithful to the original texts, or, as the case may be, to the authorized revisions of these texts; the other, to make due acknowledgment to all those who have so generously permitted him to reprint the selections in any form whatsoever. Through careful research and proof-reading I am confident that the first obligation has been fulfilled; in the case of the second obligation, if, in the following acknowledgments, I have failed to mention some poet, publisher, or executor, or if I have otherwise erred or offended, I trust that the individual involved will appreciate that the error has not been intentional. In some cases, among the hundreds of poems selected, it has been almost impossible to locate authorized holders of copyrights; the enormous bulk of our correspondence is tangible proof of the repeated efforts made. I believe that we have covered all sources, and every possible effort has been made properly to establish our rights to reprint material. In spite of all this care certain mistakes may have been made; if so, upon notification, such errors will be rectified at the earliest opportunity.

It is greatly to be regretted that, for reasons quite aside from their merit, selections from several modern poets had to be omitted. In other instances it has been necessary to reduce the number of selections. On the whole, however, my requests to use copyrighted material have been met with great

ACKNOWLEDGMENTS

courtesy and friendliness; thus, with hearty thanks, I wish to make specific acknowledgment to:

D. APPLETON & COMPANY for permission to use "Thanatopsis," "To a Waterfowl," "The Fringed Gentian" and "O, Fairest of the Rural Maids" by William Cullen Bryant, taken from his volume *Poems*;

THE ATLANTIC MONTHLY COMPANY for permission to use "On a Subway Express" by Chester Firkins, taken from the February, 1908, issue of *The Atlantic Monthly*; and "Invocation" by Wendell Phillips Stafford, taken from the May, 1915, issue;

G. BELL & SONS, LTD., for permission to use Coventry Patmore's "Preludes" (from *The Angel in the House*), "The Married Lover," "The Toys," "Departure," and "Magna Est Veritas";

ERNEST BENN, LTD., for permission to use Michael Field's "The Tragic Mary Queen of Scots";

BASIL BLACKWELL, PUBLISHER, for permission to use Aldous Huxley's "Doors of the Temple" and "Villiers de L'Isle-Adam";

WILLIAM BLACKWOOD & SONS, LTD., for permission to use George Eliot's "Two Lovers" and William Canton's "The Comrades," "Moonlight" and "This Grace Vouchsafe Me";

THE BOBBS-MERRILL COMPANY for special permission to use James Whitcomb Riley's "A Parting Guest" from *Morning*, copyright 1907, and "When She Comes Home" from *Poems Here at Home*, copyright 1893; John Erskine's "Valentine to One's Wife" from *Sonata and Other Poems*, copyright 1925; and Hilaire Belloc's "Duncton Hill" from *The Four Men*, copyright 1912;

BONI & LIVERIGHT for permission to use H. D.'s "Loss"; George O'Neil's "Where It Is Winter" from *White Rooster*; and Robinson Jeffers' "Joy" from *Roan Stallion, Tamar and Other Poems*;

BRANDT & BRANDT for permission to use Edna St. Vincent Millay's "Autumn Chant," "Feast" and "Euclid Alone Has Looked" from *The Harp Weaver and Other Poems*, published by Harper and Brothers, copyright 1920-1921-1922-1923;

BRENTANO'S for permission to use Harry Kemp's "Blind," "God, the Architect," "The Hummingbird" and "The Passing Flower"; and Oscar Wilde's "Ballad of Reading Gaol";

BURNS OATES & WASHBOURNE, LTD., for permission to use G. K. Chesterton's "The Sword of Surprise"; Francis Thompson's "Dream Tryst," "Correlated Greatness" and "Messages"; and Alice Meynell's "The Visiting Sea," "Parted," "In Early Spring," "Renouncement," "The Shepherdess," "The Lady Poverty," "Maternity," "A Poet of One Mood," "Rivers Unknown to Song," "I Am the Way" and "To Silence";

ACKNOWLEDGMENTS

JONATHAN CAPE, LTD., for permission to use Samuel Butler's "Not on Sad Stygian Shore" and William H. Davies' "Happy Wind," "Sweet Stay-at-Home," "Leisure," "The Kingfisher," "The Example," "Thunderstorms," "A Great Time," "The Moon," "A Thought," "The Two Children" and "Early Spring";

MRS. KATHERINE M. CARRUTH for permission to use William Carruth's "Each in His Own Tongue";

THE CENTURY COMPANY for permission to use David Morton's "When There Is Music" and John Henry Boner's "Poe's Cottage at Fordham" from *The Century Magazine*; Will Thompson's "The High Tide at Gettysburg" and S. Weir Mitchell's "Evening"; and "When the Wind Is Low" by Cale Young Rice, taken from *Selected Plays and Poems*;

R. COBDEN-SANDERSON, PUBLISHER, for permission to use J. Middleton Murry's "Serenity" from *Poems, 1916-20*;

CONTEMPORARY VERSE for permission to use Ralph M. Jones' "Bed-Time" and George Brandon Saul's "Elizabeth";

J. M. DENT & SONS, LTD., for permission to use "Dagonet's Canzonet" and "Lost in France" by Ernest Rhys; and Eleanor Farjeon's "The Night Will Never Stay";

THE DIAL PRESS for permission to use "The Rosary" from *The Poems of Robert Cameron Rogers*;

P. J. AND A. E. DOBELL for permission to use James Thomson's "Art" (Three Lyrics);

DODD, MEAD & COMPANY, INC., for permission to use "A Hymn," "Music," "To F. C. in Memoriam Palestine," "The Donkey" and "The Praise of Dust" by G. K. Chesterton; "1914," "Sonnet" and "The Treasure" by Rupert Brooke; "The Ballad of a Nun" by John Davidson; "Last Memory," "The Return," "Memory" and "Modern Beauty" by Arthur Symons; "To a Lost Love" by Stephen Phillips; "They Are Not Long," "In Tempore Senectutis," "Non Sum Qualis Eram Bonæ sub Regno Cynaræ" and "Vain Resolves" by Ernest Dowson; "Epilogue" by Lascelles Abercrombie; "Daisy," "To a Snowflake" and "The Hound of Heaven" by Francis Thompson; and "Spirit of Sadness," "The Passionate Reader to His Poet," "Song," "The Lonely Dancer," "Flos Ævorum" and "To a Bird at Dawn" by Richard Le Gallienne;

GEORGE H. DORAN COMPANY for permission to use Aline Kilmer's "Prevision," "Olim Meminisse Juvabit," "Haunted," "Hill Country," "To a Young Aviator" and "My Mirror" from *Candles That Burn*, copyright 1919; "Atonement" from *Vigils*, copyright 1921; and "To Aphrodite: With a Mirror" from *The Poor King's Daughter*, copyright 1925; Joyce Kilmer's "Trees," "Martin" and "Poets" from *Trees and Other Poems*, copyright 1914; J. C. Squire's "The March," "In a Chair," "Tree-tops" and "The

ACKNOWLEDGMENTS

Lake" from *Poems: First Series*, copyright 1919 by Alfred A. Knopf, Inc.; Elinor Wylie's "Let No Charitable Hope" from *Black Armour*, copyright 1923, and "Don Quixote" from *The Selected Poems of Arthur Davison Ficke*, copyright 1926;

DOUBLEDAY, PAGE & COMPANY for permission to use Walt Whitman's "Joy, Shipmate, Joy," "O Captain, My Captain," "Out of the Cradle Endlessly Rocking," "To the Man-of-War-Bird," "A Noiseless, Patient Spider" and "When Lilacs Last in the Dooryard Bloomed," taken from *Leaves of Grass*; and Rudyard Kipling's "Rebirth," "Recessional," "Cities and Thrones and Powers" and "Sussex";

DUCKWORTH & COMPANY, LTD., for permission to use Hilaire Belloc's "The South Country";

DUFFIELD & COMPANY for permission to use Eugene Lee-Hamilton's "O, Bless the Law," "The Ring of Faustus" and "What the Sonnet Is," and Fiona MacLeod's (William Sharp) "The Washer of the Ford" and "The Wasp";

E. P. DUTTON & COMPANY for permission to use six of Clement Wood's "Eagle Sonnets" from *The Tide Comes In*; and Leonora Speyer's "The Ladder" and "A Note from the Pipes" from *A Canopic Jar*;

GOOD HOUSEKEEPING for permission to use "A Prayer After Illness" by Violet Alleyn Storey;

HARCOURT, BRACE & COMPANY, INC., for permission to use "How Much of Godhood," "Caliban in the Coal Mines," "Feuerzauber," "Prayer" and "Mockery" by Louis Untermeyer, taken from his volume *Challenge*; Elinor Wylie's "The Eagle and the Mole" from *Nets to Catch the Wind*, copyright 1921; and "Beauty" from *Poems by J. E. Spingarn*, copyright 1924;

HARPER & BROTHERS for permission to use "Yet Do I Marvel," "A Song of Praise," "Simon the Cyrenian Speaks," "The Shroud of Color" and "Fruit of the Flower" by Countee Cullen, taken from his volume *Color*; Edward Davison's sonnets "O Thou in the Darkness" and "Now That the Moonlight" from *Harvest of Youth*; and Arthur Guiterman's "The Idol-Maker Prays";

HARVARD UNIVERSITY PRESS for permission to use Robert Hillyer's "To a Scarlatti Passepied";

WILLIAM HEINEMANN, LTD., for permission to use Edmund Gosse's "The Fear of Death" and "Revelation," and Algernon Charles Swinburne's "Chorus from Atalanta," "Itylus," "Rondel," "A Forsaken Garden," "Ave Atque Vale," "Christopher Marlowe," "William Shakespeare," "Beaumont and Fletcher," "Ben Jonson," "In Memory of Walter Savage Landor," "On Lamb's Specimens of Dramatic Poets," "By the North Sea," "The Garden of Proserpine" and "The Triumph of Time";

xviii

ACKNOWLEDGMENTS

HENRY HOLT & COMPANY for permission to use Arthur Colton's
"Sometime It May Be" from *Harps Hung Up in Babylon;* Mar-
garet Widdemer's "Greek Folk Song" and "The Masters" from
Factories and "The Dark Cavalier" from *The Old to Paradise;*
Walter de la Mare's "The Miracle," "All That's Past," "The
Stranger" and "Arabia" from *Lyrical Poems,* "The Listeners,"
"The Linnet," "The Sunken Garden," "An Epitaph" and "The
Ghost" from *The Listeners,* "Music" from *Motley,* and "A Song
of Enchantment" from *Peacock Pie;* Robert Frost's "Mending
Wall" and "My November Guest" from *North of Boston,* "Mow-
ing" and "Fire and Ice" from *A Boy's Will,* "The Aim Was
Song" and "The Oft-Repeated Dream" from *New Hampshire;*
and "The Road Not Taken" from *Mountain Interval;* and
"Cyrano's Presentation of Cadets" from Brian Hooker's transla-
tion of Rostand's *Cyrano de Bergerac;*

HOUGHTON MIFFLIN COMPANY for permission to use all poems in
the anthology by Ralph Waldo Emerson, Henry Wadsworth Long-
fellow, John Greenleaf Whittier, James Russell Lowell, Oliver
Wendell Holmes and Francis Bret Harte; John Burroughs'
"Waiting," Richard Watson Gilder's "On the Life-Mask of
Abraham Lincoln," Edgar Fawcett's "To an Oriole," Thomas
Wentworth Higginson's "The Trumpeter," Edmund Clarence
Stedman's "Voice of the Western Wind," Edith M. Thomas'
"Patmos," Conrad Aiken's "Music I Heard" and Anna Hemp-
stead Branch's "To a New York Shop-Girl Dressed for Sunday";
Amy Lowell's "Crowned" and "Venus Transiens"; Jessie B. Rit-
tenhouse's "Debt" and "Transformation"; John Drinkwater's
"Last Confessional" and "Invocation"; and Edward Rowland
Sill's "The Fool's Prayer," "Truth at Last" and "Wordsworth";

EDITH M. HOWE for permission to use Edith M. Thomas' "A Chant
of the Fought Field," "The Courage of the Lost," "Evoe!" and
"The Security of Desolation";

MITCHELL KENNERLEY for permission to use Shaemas O'Sheel's "He
Whom a Dream Hath Possessed" and "They Went Forth to
Battle but They Always Fell"; Theodosia Garrison's "Tears of
Harlequin" from *The Joy of Life;* and Arthur Davison Ficke's
sonnets "This Is the Burden" and "In the Fair Picture" (Sonnet
XXIX);

ALFRED A. KNOPF, INC., for permission to use Leonora Speyer's
"Duet" and "Pioneers" from *Fiddler's Farewell;* an excerpt (first
fourteen lines) from Witter Bynner's *The New World;* and Ed-
mund Blunden's "Almswomen" (held jointly with Sidgwick &
Jackson, Ltd.);

ACKNOWLEDGMENTS

John Lane the Bodley Head, Ltd., for permission to use John Bannister Tabb's "Beethoven and Angelo," "Father Damien," "To Shelley" and "Fraternity," from *Poems*;

Little, Brown, & Company for permission to use Emily Dickinson's "Autumn," "Chartless," "Choice," "Parting," "Peace," "Suspense," "Simplicity" and "Pedigree";

Longmans, Green & Company for permission to use "The Odyssey" and "Scythe Song" from *The Poetical Works of Andrew Lang*; and William Morris' "Love Is Enough" from *Poems by the Way & Love Is Enough*;

Longmans, Green & Company, Limited, for permission to use William E. H. Lecky's "Homeward Bound," "To ——" and "Unconscious Cerebration";

The Macmillan Company for permission to use all poems in the anthology by Matthew Arnold; George W. Russell's "Carrowmore," "The Twilight of Earth" and "A Dream of Defeated Beauty"; Laurence Binyon's "Nothing Is Enough," "To Women," "Thinking of Shores" and "Song"; Padraic Colum's "An Old Woman of the Roads" and "The Furrow and the Hearth"; Thomas Hardy's "The Darkling Thrush" and "Shelley's Skylark"; Hermann Hagedorn's "Doors" and "Broadway"; Ralph Hodgson's "Eve"; Nicholas Vachel Lindsay's "The Dreamer"; John Masefield's "A Consecration," "Sea-Fever," "The Passing Strange" and "On Growing Old"; Scudder Middleton's "Wisdom" and "The Journey"; John G. Neihardt's "Let Me Live Out My Years" and "Prayer for Pain"; Edwin Arlington Robinson's "Flammonde," "The Gift of God" and "The Master"; James Stevens' "Hate," "What Tomas an Buile Said in a Pub" and "The Waste Places"; Sara Teasdale's "Peace," "The Lamp" and "Foreknown"; William Butler Yeats' "The Lake Isle of Innisfree," "The Land of Heart's Desire" and "The Lover Tells of the Rose in His Heart"; and Percy MacKaye's "France";

Macmillan and Co., Ltd., for permission to use the desired poems by Alfred, Lord Tennyson;

Robert M. McBride & Company for permission to use Hilaire Belloc's "The South Country," "To the Balliol Men Still in Africa" and "Song"; and James Branch Cabell's "Garden-Song";

Elkins Mathews, Ltd., for permission to use Lionel Johnson's "By the Statue of King Charles at Charing Cross," "A Friend," "Beyond" and "Glories";

Methuen & Company, Ltd., for permission to use May Doney's "Ruth" from *The Way of Wonder*, and "Requiescat" from *Poems by Oscar Wilde*;

T. S. Moore for permission to use Michael Field's "Gold" and "Beloved, My Glory";

xx

ACKNOWLEDGMENTS

THOMAS B. MOSHER, PUBLISHER, for permission to use Arthur Upson's "Ex Libris" from *Sonnets and Songs;*

SIR HENRY NEWBOLT for permission to use "A Huguenot" from *Poems by Mary E. Coleridge,* from his collection, published by Elkins Mathews, Ltd.;

HUMPHREY MILFORD, manager of the Oxford University Press, and MR. A. T. A. DOBSON, trustee for the author, for permission to use Austin Dobson's "Urceus Exit," "For a Charity Annual," "For a Copy of Theocritus," "In After Days," "The Song of the Sea Wind," "A Greeting" and "Henry Wadsworth Longfellow";

L. C. PAGE & COMPANY, INC., for permission to use Bliss Carman's "Lord of My Heart's Elation," "The Unreturning" and "Daphne"; and Frederick Lawrence Knowles' "Laus Mortis," "To Mother Nature," "Nature: the Artist," "Love Triumphant," and "On a Fly Leaf of Burns' Songs," taken from his volume *On Life's Stairway,* copyright 1905;

A. D. PETERS for permission to use "In the Train" by Clifford Bax;

MRS. GRACE PLUNKETT for permission to use Joseph Mary Plunkett's "I See His Blood upon the Rose";

POETRY for permission to use Frances Wells Shaw's "Who Loves the Rain";

G. P. PUTNAM'S SONS for permission to use David Morton's "Fields at Evening" from *Harvest,* "Who Walks with Beauty" from *Ships in Harbour,* and "Lover to Lover"; William Carruth's "Each in His Own Tongue" from *Each in His Own Tongue and Other Poems;* Herbert S. Gorman's "The Last Fire" from *The Barcarole of James Smith and Other Poems;* and Colonel John McCrae's "In Flanders Fields" from *In Flanders Fields and Other Poems;*

A. M. ROBERTSON for permission to use George Sterling's "Mirage," "Spring in Carmel" and "The Lost Nymph" from *Sails and Mirage;* "The Black Vulture" from *The House of Orchids;* "The Master-Mariner," "The Last Days" and "Omnia Exeunt in Mysterium";

CHARLES SCRIBNER'S SONS for permission to use Sidney Lanier's "The Song of the Chattahoochee," "Ballad of Trees and the Master," "The Marshes of Glynn," "Evening Song" and selections from "Acknowledgments"; Alice Meynell's "The Visiting Sea," "Parted," "In Early Spring," "Renouncement," "The Shepherdess," "The Lady Poverty," "Maternity," "A Poet of One Mood," "Rivers Unknown to Song," "I Am the Way," and "To Silence"; Robert Louis Stevenson's "My Wife," "The Celestial Surgeon," "Requiem," "In the Highlands," "Romance," and "Envoy"; Alan Seeger's "I Have a Rendezvous with Death"; John Hall Wheelock's "The Lion-House," "To the Modern Man,"

ACKNOWLEDGMENTS

"Panther! Panther!", "Earth," "I Do Not Love to See Your Beauty Fire," "The Poet Tells of His Love" and "Plaint"; George Meredith's "Marion," "When I Would Image," "Lucifer in the Starlight," "Love in the Valley," "Song in the Songless" and "Song"; and Francis Thompson's "Envoy";

MARTIN, SECKER, LTD., for permission to use "A Ship, an Isle, a Sickle Moon," "To a Poet a Thousand Years Hence" and "In Phæacia," by J. E. Flecker, taken from his *Collected Poems*;

SELWYN & BLOUNT, LTD., for permission to use Robin Flower's "Say Not That Beauty" and John Freeman's "Caterpillars";

SIDGWICK & JACKSON, LTD., for permission to use Ivor Gurney's "To the Poet Before Battle" from *Severn and Somme*; and Edmund Blunden's "Almswomen" from *The Waggoner*; also for permission, in conjunction with his literary executor, to use A. H. Bullen's "By Avon Stream" from *Weeping Cross*;

SMALL, MAYNARD & COMPANY, INC., for permission to use Bliss Carman's "Roadside Flowers," and Richard Hovey's "The Sea Gypsy," "Love in the Winds" and "Envoy";

FREDERICK A. STOKES COMPANY for permission to use Alfred A. Noyes' "In Memory of Swinburne" from his *Collected Poems, volume II*, copyright 1910, "A Forest Song" from *Collected Poems, volume III*, copyright 1915, and "Epilogue" from *Collected Poems, volume I*, copyright 1907;

TOWN TOPICS for permission to use Mary Carolyn Davies' "The Gown";

D. P. TRENCH for permission to use Herbert Trench's "Come, Let Us Make Love Deathless" and "I Heard a Soldier";

THE VIKING PRESS for permission to use James Joyce's "Strings in the Earth" from *Chamber Music*, copyright 1918; also William Ellery Leonard's "The Insulting Letter" from *The Vaunt of Man*, copyright 1912, and "Indian Summer" from *Tutankhamen and After*, copyright 1924.

A. P. WATT & SON for permission to use Rudyard Kipling's "Cities and Thrones and Powers," "Rebirth," "Sussex" and "Recessional"; and Alfred Noyes' "On Rembrandt's Portrait of a Rabbi";

YALE UNIVERSITY PRESS for permission to use Karle Wilson Baker's "I Shall Be Loved As Quiet Things" from *Burning Bush*, and "Creeds" and "Days" from *Blue Smoke*; William Rose Benét's "The Falconer of God" from *The Falconer of God and Other Poems*, and "Mad Blake" from *The Burglar of the Zodiac*; Brian Hooker's "Ballade of the Dreamland Rose" from his *Poems*; Harold Vinal's "Earth Lover" from *White April*; and William Alexander Percy's "Overtones" and "A Volunteer's Grave" from *In April Once*, and "The Unloved to His Beloved" from *Enzio's Kingdom*.

ACKNOWLEDGMENTS

Acknowledgment is also due these authors who, either independently or supplementing the permissions given by their publishers, have kindly allowed their works to be included:

LAURENCE BINYON, for "Nothing Is Enough," "A Song," "Thinking of Shores" and "To Women";

EDMUND BLUNDEN, for "Almswomen";

GORDON BOTTOMLEY, for "In Memoriam A. M. W.";

JOSEPH CAMPBELL, for "The Old Woman";

FRANCIS CARLIN, for "Perfection," "Her Reverie," "The Parish Bard" and "Under an Irish Lark";

WILLA SIBERT CATHER, for "The Palatine";

JOHN JAY CHAPMAN, for "No Pilots We";

LORD CREWE, for "A Harrow Grave in Flanders";

MARY CAROLYN DAVIES, for "Door-Mats," "Reminiscences," "Rust," "The Dead Make Rules," "The Day Before April" and "The Dream-Bearer";

ELEANOR FARJEON, for "The Night Will Never Stay";

FORD MADOX FORD, for "Footsloggers";

HAMLIN GARLAND, for "To a Captive Crane," "Do You Fear the Wind?" and "The Mountains Are a Lonely Folk";

HERBERT S. GORMAN, for "The Last Fire";

GERALD L. GOULD, for "Fallen Cities";

IVOR GURNEY, for "To the Poet Before Battle";

HERMANN HAGEDORN, for "Doors" and "Broadway";

GEORGE R. HAMILTON, for "Multiplicity";

THOMAS S. JONES, JR., for "Sometimes" and "Joyous-Gard," taken from his volume *The Rose-Jar*, published by Thomas B. Mosher;

EDWIN MARKHAM, for "A Prayer," "How to Go and Forget," "Your Tears," "Night Moths," "The Man with the Hoe," "Lincoln, the Man of the People," "The Invisible Bride," "The Testing" and "Virgilia," taken from his *Collected Poems*, copyrighted by himself.

DAVID MORTON, for "Fields at Evening," "Lover to Lover" and "Who Walks with Beauty";

J. MIDDLETON MURRY, for "Serenity" from *Poems, 1916-20*;

SIR HENRY NEWBOLT, for "Admiral Death" and "St. George's Day— Ypres 1915," taken from his volume *Poems New and Old*, published by John Murray;

ALFRED NOYES, for "In Memory of Swinburne," "A Forest Song," "Epilogue," "On Rembrandt's Portrait of a Rabbi";

JOHN MYERS O'HARA, for "A Faun in Wall Street";

SIEGFRIED SASSOON, for "Aftermath";

CLINTON SCOLLARD, for "As I Came Down from Lebanon" and "Bag-Pipes at Sea";

ACKNOWLEDGMENTS

FRANCES WELLS SHAW, for "Who Loves the Rain";

CLARK ASHTON SMITH, for "Impression," "Recompense" and "Transcendence";

VIOLET ALLEYN STOREY, for "A Prayer After Illness";

LOUIS UNTERMEYER, for "Only of Thee and Me";

SIR WILLIAM WATSON, for "Song," "Invention," "In Laleham Churchyard," "Leavetaking" and "The Sovereign Poet."

WALLACE ALVIN BRIGGS.

Sacramento, California.
April, 1927.

SUPPLEMENT

For permission to reprint the Additional Poems in this volume, the editor, William Rose Benét, wishes to thank not only the poets themselves, but also the following publishers and agents:

COVICI, FRIEDE, INC., for "Through Streets Where Crooked Wicklow Flows" from *Chorus for Survival* by Horace Gregory;

THE JOHN DAY COMPANY, INC., for "The River in the Meadows" from *High Falcon* by Léonie Adams, and for "Text" from *Bright Ambush* by Audrey Wurdemann;

THE DIAL PRESS, INC., for "The Zebras" from *Adamastor* by Roy Campbell;

DOUBLEDAY, DORAN AND COMPANY, INC., for the following poems reprinted by their permission: "Elegy for Mr. Goodbeare" from *England Reclaimed* by Osbert Sitwell; "Mary" from *American Song* by Paul Engle, copyright 1933, 1934; "The Soldier I" and "The High Song" from *Requiem* by Humbert Wolfe, copyright 1927; "Lovers Relentlessly" from *Intellectual Things* by Stanley J. Kunitz, copyright 1929, 1930; "Spring-Fraternity" from *Collected Poems*, by V. Sackville-West, copyright 1934;

FARRAR & RINEHART, INC., for the following poem reprinted by their permission: "Tears" from *The Selected Poems of Lizette Woodworth Reese*, copyright 1926;

HARCOURT, BRACE & COMPANY, INC., for the following poem reprinted by their permission: "Sweeney Among the Nightingales" from *Poems 1909-1925* by T. S. Eliot, copyright 1932;

HARPER & BROTHERS, for "Steel" from *Cyclops' Eye* by Joseph Auslander, "XXVII" from *Animula Vagula* by Leonard Bacon,

ACKNOWLEDGMENTS

(here used under the title of "Io Ritornai Dalla Santissima Onda"), "Try Tropic" from *Not Mine To Finish* by Genevieve Taggard, and "Ecstatic Ode" from *An Omnibus* by Richard Hughes;

HENRY HOLT AND COMPANY, INC., for "Prayers of Steel" from *Cornhuskers* by Carl Sandburg and "Four Little Foxes" from *Slow Smoke* by Lew Sarett;

HOUGHTON MIFFLIN COMPANY, for the following poems reprinted by their permission: "The Brute" from *Selected Poems of William Vaughn Moody*, copyright 1931; "The Kings" from *Happy Ending* by Louise Imogen Guiney, copyright 1927; "You, Andrew Marvell" from *Poems 1924-1933* by Archibald MacLeish, copyright 1933; "Colonel Fantock" from *The Collected Poems of Edith Sitwell*, copyright 1930; "Songs from Cyprus IV," from *Red Roses for Bronze* by H. D., copyright 1931.

ALFRED A. KNOPF, INC., for the following poems reprinted by their permission: "Python" from *Flying Fish* by Grace Hazard Conkling, copyright 1926; "The Worms at Heaven's Gate" from *Harmonium* by Wallace Stevens, copyright 1923, 1931; "Here Lies a Lady" from *Chills and Fever* by John Crowe Ransom, copyright 1924;

LIVERIGHT PUBLISHING CORPORATION, for passage from "Powhatan's Daughter—The Dance," from *The Bridge* by Hart Crane;

THE MACMILLAN COMPANY, for the following poems reprinted by their permission: "A Catch for Singing" from *Collected Poems 1905-1925* by Wilfrid Wilson Gibson copyright 1926, 1929; "Eye-Witness" from *Hesperides* by Ridgely Torrence, copyright 1925; "The Swan" from *The Black Rock* by John Gould Fletcher, copyright 1928; "Crystal Moment" from *The Yoke of Thunder* by Robert P. Tristram Coffin, copyright 1932; "Wit" from *A Winter Diary* by Mark Van Doren, copyright 1935; "Essay on Deity" from *Thing of Sorrow* by Elder Olson, copyright 1934.

RANDOM HOUSE, for "30," "I Think Continually—," from *Poems* by Stephen Spender;

CHARLES SCRIBNER'S SONS, for "Medusa" from *Dark Summer* by Louise Bogan;

THE VIKING PRESS, INC., for the following poems reprinted by their permission: "Apologia pro Poemate Meo" from *The Poems of Wilfred Owen*; "Silver for Midas" from *This Delicate Love* by Winifred Welles, copyright, 1929; "Réveille" from *Sun-Up* by Lola Ridge, copyright, 1920;

ACKNOWLEDGMENTS

BRANDT AND BRANDT, INC., for "The Ballad of William Sycamore" from *Ballads and Poems 1915-1930* by Stephen Vincent Benét;

MR. EDWARD DORO, for his poem "The Boar and Shibboleth" from his volume of that title.

INTRODUCTION

To those who particularly love literature in its highest expression, it is unnecessary to plead the cause of poetry; but to the average reader, at this particular time in the world's history, it may be appropriate to say a few words in its behalf. Presumably you are looking at this large collection of the world's best poetry because you feel it well to become acquainted with one of the fine arts, and yet you are somewhat dubious of its value in a world today so full of the thunder and fury of war and of the immediate demands of what is known as the "practical." Yet I venture to say that, as never before in the world's history, poetry is necessary to the world.

Of course if you think of poetry as something merely pretty pretty and sentimental, something like those old-fashioned lace valentines one used to buy, something that is a mere extraneous decoration of actual life, you will not regard this book as especially valuable. But also you will have a most incorrect idea of what poetry actually is. What it actually is is no less than a condensation, in the most striking language, of the highest ideals of civilization, ideals that today are being challenged by all the forces of barbarism. You have only to turn at random to page 389, for instance, to find in one of the noblest of Wordsworth's sonnets words most extraordinarily appropriate to the issues of the day. That sonnet speaks like a trumpet of British freedom, and spurns the thought that it should perish "and to evil and to good be lost forever." It thrills us with the ringing lines:

> We must be free or die, who speak the tongue
> That Shakespeare spake; the faith and morals hold
> Which Milton held—

Americans *do* speak the same tongue that Shakespeare spake, though they speak it with differing accents and a modern vocabulary. The finest usage of that tongue is to be found in poetry, both ancient and modern, English and American. Not only that, but the whole range of English and American history may be learned from such poetry, just as the deepest comments on the deepest emotions and most vital interests of the human race reside in the great poems of the English language.

INTRODUCTION

The scope of the volume you hold in your hand is extraordinary. From the narratives of Geoffrey Chaucer, which were really the first novels in English, English poetry embraces the plays of Shakespeare, the unforgettable singing of the Seventeenth Century, down through the beauties of Milton, Byron, Shelley and Keats, to the modernity of the Sitwells. And the American tradition flows from the great Walt Whitman to the living Carl Sandburg and Edna St. Vincent Millay. Here are over a thousand pages, packed with the best selections from English-speaking poetry of all kinds, lyric, epic, introspective or objectively narrative! The finest sonnets in the English language are here, expressing the most intimate human feelings—and, on the other hand, the greatest stories in verse. The craftsmanship of great artists waits your recognition, and the vital things they have to say will move you deeply. This is veritably the heart of the world, beating—and what you hear is the voice that will inevitably destroy all tyranny over the human spirit. In this time that tries men's souls, the great poems of the English language are a resource and a spiritual stay that cannot be overestimated.

"For all things change," as a great modern poet has sung, one who today is the Poet Laureate of England, "the darkness changes, the wandering spirits change their ranges . . . the rhythms change, they do not close . . ." So we may be sure that the evil things of today will pass, but that the great things of life will remain—remain in the heritage of great English verse for the inheritors of the English language, so that, as the same poet tells us in this volume:

> —those who follow feel behind
> Their backs, when all before is blind,
> Our joy, a rampart to the mind.

Yes, as never before, this is the time for poetry, for the living word that is, in the end, more potent than bombing planes or panzer divisions, or all the cruel armory of war and slavery! So when we put this book into your hand, we give you a spiritual weapon you cannot afford to be without, as well as a great and permanent solace for the darker hours.

WILLIAM ROSE BENÉT.

New York City,
June 5, 1941.

INTRODUCTION
AND
PROLOGUE

INTRODUCTION

One morn as through Hyde Park we walk'd,
My friend and I, by chance we talk'd
Of Lessing's famed Laocoön;
And after we awhile had gone
In Lessing's track, and tried to see
What painting is, what poetry—
Diverging to another thought,
"Ah," cries my friend, "but who hath taught
Why music and the other arts
Oftener perform aright their parts
Than poetry? why she, than they,
Fewer fine successes can display?

"For 'tis so, surely! Even in Greece,
Where best the poet framed his piece,
Even in that Phœbus-guarded ground
Pausanias on his travels found
Good poems, if he look'd, more rare
(Though many) than good statues were—
For these, in truth, were everywhere.
Of bards full many a stroke divine
In Dante's, Petrarch's, Tasso's line,
The land of Ariosto show'd;
And yet, e'en there, the canvas glow'd
With triumphs, a yet ampler brood,
Of Raphael and his brotherhood.
And nobly perfect, in our day
Of haste, half-work, and disarray,
Profound yet touching, sweet yet strong,
Hath risen Goethe's, Wordsworth's song;
Yet even I (and none will bow
Deeper to these) must needs allow,
They yield us not, to soothe our pains,
Such multitude of heavenly strains
As from the kings of sound are blown,
Mozart, Beethoven, Mendelssohn."

While thus my friend discoursed, we pass
Out of the path, and take the grass.
The grass hath still the green of May,
And still the unblacken'd elms were gay;
The kine were resting in the shade,
The flies a summer-murmur made.
Bright was the morn and south the air;
The soft-couch'd cattle were as fair
As those which pastured by the sea,
That old-world morn, in Sicily,
When on the beach the Cyclops lay,
And Galatea from the bay
Mock'd her poor lovelorn giant's lay.
"Behold," I said, "the painter's sphere!
The limits of his art appear.
The passing group, the summer-morn,
The grass, the elms, that blossom'd thorn—
Those cattle couched, or, as they rise,
Their shining flanks, their liquid eyes—
These, or much greater things, but caught
Like these, and in one aspect brought!
In outward semblance he must give
A moment's life of things that live;
Then let him choose his moment well,
With power divine its story tell."

Still we walk'd on, in thoughtful mood,
And now upon the bridge we stood.
Full of sweet breathings was the air,
Of sudden stirs and pauses fair.
Down o'er the stately bridge the breeze
Came rustling from the garden-trees
And on the sparkling waters play'd;
Light-plashing waves an answer made,
And mimic boats their haven near'd.
Beyond, the Abbey-towers appear'd,
By mist and chimneys unconfined,
Free to the sweep of light and wind;
While through their earth-moor'd nave below
Another breath of wind doth blow,
Sound as of wandering breeze—but sound
In laws by human artists bound.

2

INTRODUCTION

"The world of music!" I exclaim'd—
"This breeze that rustles by, that famed
Abbey recall it! what a sphere
Large and profound, hath genius here!
The inspired musician what a range,
What power of passion, wealth of change!
Some source of feeling he must choose
And its lock'd fount of beauty use,
And through the stream of music tell
Its else unutterable spell;
To choose it rightly is his part,
And press into its inmost heart.

"*Miserere, Domine!*
The words are utter'd, and they flee.
Deep is their penitential moan,
Mighty their pathos, but 'tis gone.
They have declared the spirit's sore
Sore load, and words can do no more.
Beethoven takes them then—those two
Poor, bounded words—and makes them new;
Infinite makes them, makes them young;
Transplants them to another tongue,
Where they can now, without constraint,
Pour all the soul of their complaint,
And roll adown a channel large
The wealth divine they have in charge.
Page after page of music turn,
And still they live and still they burn,
Eternal, passion-fraught, and free—
Miserere, Domine!"

Onward we moved, and reach'd the Ride
Where gaily flows the human tide.
Afar, in rest the cattle lay;
We heard, afar, faint music play;
But agitated, brisk, and near,
Men, with their stream of life, were here.
Some hang upon the rails, and some
On foot behind them go and come.
This through the Ride upon his steed
Goes slowly by, and this at speed.

3

INTRODUCTION

The young, the happy, and the fair,
The old, the sad, the worn, were there;
Some vacant, and some musing went,
And some in talk and merriment.
Nods, smiles, and greetings, and farewells!
And now and then, perhaps, there swells
A sigh, a tear—but in the throng
All changes fast, and hies along.
Hies, ah, from whence, what native ground?
And to what goal, what ending, bound?
"Behold at last the poet's sphere!
But who," I said, "suffices here?

"For, ah! so much he has to do;
Be painter and musician too!
The aspect of the moment show,
The feeling of the moment know!
The aspect not, I grant, express
Clear as the painter's art can dress;
The feeling not, I grant, explore
So deep as the musician's lore—
But clear as words can make revealing,
And deep as words can follow feeling.
But, ah! then comes his sorest spell
Of toil—he must life's *movement* tell!
The thread which binds it all in one
And not its separate parts alone.
The *movement* he must tell of life,
Its pain and pleasure, rest and strife;
His eye must travel down, at full,
The long, unpausing spectacle;
With faithful unrelaxing force
Attend it from its primal source.
From change to change and year to year
Attend it of its mid career,
Attend it to the last repose
And solemn silence of its close.

"The cattle rising from the grass
His thought must follow where they pass;
The penitent with anguish bow'd
His thought must follow through the crowd.

INTRODUCTION

Yes! all this eddying, motley throng
That sparkles in the sun along,
Girl, statesman, merchant, soldier bold,
Master and servant, young and old,
Grave, gay, child, parent, husband, wife,
He follows home and lives their life.

"And many, many are the souls
Life's movement fascinates, controls;
It draws them on, they cannot save
Their feet from its alluring wave;
They cannot leave it, they must go
With its unconquerable flow.
But ah! how few, of all that try
This mighty march, do aught but die!
For ill-endow'd for such a way,
Ill-stored in strength, in wits, are they.
They faint, they stagger to and fro,
And wandering from the stream they go;
In pain, in terror, in distress,
They see, all round, a wilderness.
Sometimes a momentary gleam
They catch of the mysterious stream;
Sometimes, a second's space, their ear
The murmur of its waves doth hear.
That transient glimpse in song they say,
But not as painter can portray—
That transient sound in song they tell,
But not, as the musician, well.
And when at last their snatches cease,
And they are silent and at peace,
The stream of life's majestic whole
Hath ne'er been mirror'd on their soul.

"Only a few the life-stream's shore
With safe unwandering feet explore;
Untired its movement bright attend,
Follow its windings to the end.
Then from its brimming waves their eye
Drinks up delighted ecstasy,
And its deep-toned, melodious voice
Forever makes their ear rejoice.

INTRODUCTION

They speak! the happiness divine
They feel, runs o'er in every line;
Its spell is round them like a shower—
It gives them pathos, gives them power.
No painter yet hath such a way,
Nor no musician made, as they,
And gather'd on immortal knolls
Such lovely flowers for cheering souls.
Beethoven, Raphael, cannot reach
The charm which Homer, Shakespeare, teach.
To these, to these, their thankful race
Gives, then, the first, the fairest place;
And brightest is their glory's sheen,
For greatest hath their labor been."

—MATTHEW ARNOLD.

PROLOGUE

The wedded light and heat,
Winnowing the witless space,
Without a let,
What are they till they beat
Against the sleepy sod, and there beget
Perchance the violet!

—COVENTRY PATMORE.

That son of Italy who tried to blow,
Ere Dante came, the trump of sacred song,
In his light youth amid a festal throng
Sate with his bride to see a public show.

Fair was the bride, and on her front did glow
Youth like a star; and what to youth belong—
Gay raiment, sparkling gauds, elation strong.
A prop gave way! crash fell a platform! lo,

'Mid struggling sufferers, hurt to death, she lay!
Shuddering, they drew her garments off—and found
A robe of sackcloth next the smooth, white skin.

Such, poets, is your bride, the Muse! young, gay,
Radiant, adorn'd outside; a hidden ground
Of thought and of austerity within.
—MATTHEW ARNOLD.

Loving in truth, and fain in verse my love to show,
That She, dear She! might take some pleasure of my pain;
Pleasure might cause her read, reading might make her know,
Knowledge might pity win, and pity grace obtain:
I sought fit words to paint the blackest face of woe,
Studying inventions fine, her wits to entertain;
Oft turning others' leaves, to see if thence would flow
Some fresh and fruitful showers upon my sunburnt brain:

7

PROLOGUE

But words came halting forth, wanting Invention's stay.
Invention, Nature's child, fled step-dame Study's blows;
And others' feet still seemed but strangers in my way.
Thus, great with child to speak, and helpless in my throes,
    Biting my truant pen, beating myself for spite:
        "Fool!" said my Muse to me, "look in thy heart, and
            write!"

                            —SIR PHILIP SIDNEY.

He sits above the clang and dust of Time,
With the world's secret trembling on his lip.
He asks not converse nor companionship
In the cold starlight where thou canst not climb.

The undelivered tidings in his breast
Suffer him not to rest.
He sees afar the immemorable throng,
And binds the scattered ages with a song.

The glorious riddle of his rhythmic breath,
His might, his spell, we know not what they be:
We only feel, whate'er he uttereth,
This savours not of death,
This hath a relish of eternity.

                            —WILLIAM WATSON.

I hung my verses in the wind,
Time and tide their faults may find.
All were winnowed through and through,
Five lines lasted sound and true;
Five were smelted in a pot
Than the South more fierce and hot;
These the siroc could not melt,
Fire their fiercer flaming felt,
And the meaning was more white
Than July's meridian light.
Sunshine cannot bleach the snow,
Nor time unmake what poets know.
Have you eyes to find the five
Which five hundred did survive?

                            —RALPH WALDO EMERSON.

8

PROLOGUE

(O Earth-and-Autumn of the Setting Sun,
She is not by, to know my task is done!)

In the brown grasses slanting with the wind,
Lone as a lad whose dog's no longer near,
Lone as a mother whose only child has sinned,
Lone on the loved hill . . . and below me here
The thistle-down in tremulous atmosphere
Along red clusters of the sumach streams;
The shriveled stalks of golden-rod are sere,
And crisp and white their flashing old racemes.
(. . . forever . . . forever . . . forever . . .)
This is the lonely season of the year,
This is the season of our lonely dreams.

(O Earth-and-Autumn of the Setting Sun,
She is not by, to know my task is done!)

The corn-shocks westward on the stubble plain
Show like an Indian village of dead days;
The long smoke trails behind the crawling train,
And floats atop the distant woods ablaze
With orange, crimson, purple. The low haze
Dims the scarped bluffs above the inland sea,
Whose wide and slaty waters in cold glaze
Await yon full-moon of the night-to-be,
(. . . far . . . and far . . . and far . . .)
These are the solemn horizons of man's ways,
These the horizons of solemn thought to me.

(O Earth-and-Autumn of the Setting Sun,
She is not by, to know my task is done!)

And this the hill she visited, as friend;
And this the hill she lingered on, as bride—
Down in the yellow valley is the end:
They laid her . . . in no evening autumn tide . . .
Under fresh flowers of that May morn, beside
The queens and cave-women of ancient earth. . . .

This is the hill . . . and over my city's towers,
Across the world from sunset, yonder in air,
Shines, through its scaffoldings, a civic dome

PROLOGUE

Of pilèd masonry, which shall be ours
To give, completed, to our children there. . . .
And yonder far roof of my abandoned home
Shall house new laughter. . . . Yet I tried . . . I tried . . .
And, ever wistful of the doom to come,
I built her many a fire for love . . . for mirth. . . .
(When snows were falling on our oaks outside,
Dear, many a winter fire upon the hearth) . . .
(. . . farewell . . . farewell . . . farewell . . .)

—WILLIAM ELLERY LEONARD.

GREAT POEMS
OF THE
ENGLISH LANGUAGE

John Barbour

FREEDOM

A! Fredome is a noble thing!
Fredome mayse man to haif liking;
Fredome all solace to man giffis,
He livis at ese that frely livis!
A noble hart may haif nane ese,
Na ellys nocht that may him plese,
Gif fredome fail'th; for fre liking
Is yharnit ouer all othir thing.
Na he that ay has livit fre
May nocht knaw well the propertè,
The anger, na the wretchit doom
That is couplit to foul thraldome.
But gif he had assayit it,
Then all perquer he suld it wit;
And suld think fredome mar to prise
Than all the gold in warld that is.
Thus contrar thingis evermar
Discoweringis of the tothir are.

Geoffrey Chaucer

A DREAM OF FAIR WOMEN

I read, before my eyelids dropt their shade,
  "The Legend of Good Women," long ago
Sung by the morning star of song, who made
  His music heard below;

Dan Chaucer, the first warbler, whose sweet breath
  Preluded those melodious bursts, that fill
The spacious times of great Elizabeth
  With sounds that echo still.

12

And, for a while, the knowledge of his art
Held me above the subject, as strong gales
Hold swollen clouds from raining, tho' my heart,
Brimful of those wild tales,

Charged both mine eyes with tears. In every land
I saw, wherever light illumineth,
Beauty and anguish walking hand in hand
The downward slope to death.

. . . .

—ALFRED, LORD TENNYSON.

CAPTIVITY

Your eyën two wol slee me sodenly,
    I may the beautè of hem not sustene,
So woundeth hit through-out my herte kene.
And but your word wol helen hastily
My hertes wounde, whyl that hit is grene,
    Your eyën two wol slee me sodenly,
    I may the beautè of hem not sustene.

Upon my trouthe I sey yow feithfully,
That ye ben of my lyf and deeth the quene;
For with my deeth the trouthe shal be sene.
    Your eyën two wol slee me sodenly,
    I may the beautè of hem not sustene,
    So woundeth hit through-out my herte kene.
                —MERCILES BEAUTE.

BALADE

Hyd, Absolon, thy gilte tresses clere;
Ester, ley thou thy meknesse al a-doun;
Hyd, Jonathas, al thy frendly manere;
Penalopee, and Marcia Catoun,
Mak of your wyfhod no comparisoun;
Hyde ye your beautes, Isoude and Eleyne,
My lady cometh, that al this may disteyne.

GEOFFREY CHAUCER

Thy faire body, lat hit nat appere,
Lavyne; and thou, Lucresse of Rome toun,
And Polixene, that boghten love so dere,
And Cleopatre, with al thy passioun,
Hyde ye your trouthe of love and your renoun;
And thou, Tisbe, that hast of love swich peyne;
My lady cometh, that al this may disteyne.

Herro, Dido, Laudomia, alle y-fere,
And Phyllis, hanging for thy Demophoun,
And Canace, espyed by thy chere,
Ysiphile, betraysed with Jasoun,
Maketh of your trouthe neyther boost ne soun;
Nor Ypermistre or Adriane, ye tweyne;
My lady cometh, that al this may disteyne.
    —THE LEGEND OF GOOD WOMEN.

PROLOGUE TO THE CANTERBURY TALES

Whan that Aprille with his shoures sote
The droghte of Marche hath perced to the rote,
And bathed every veyne in swich licour,
Of which vertu engendred is the flour;
Whan Zephirus eek with his swete breeth
Inspired hath in every holt and heeth
The tendre croppes, and the yonge sonne
Hath in the Ram his halfe cours y-ronne,
And smale fowles maken melodye,
That slepen al the night with open yë,
(So priketh hem nature in hir corages):
Than longen folk to goon on pilgrimages
(And palmers for to seken straunge strondes)
To ferne halwes, couthe in sondry londes;
And specially, from every shires ende
Of Engelond, to Caunterbury they wende,
The holy blisful martir for to seke,
That hem hath holpen, whan that they were seke.

A Knight ther was, and that a worthy man,
That fro the tyme that he first bigan
To ryden out, he loved chivalrye,
Trouthe and honour, fredom and curteisye.
Ful worthy was he in his lordes werre,
And therto hadde he riden (no man ferre)
As wel in Cristendom as hethenesse,
And ever honoured for his worthinesse.

    .   .   .

And though that he were worthy, he was wys,
And of his port as meke as is a mayde.
He never yet no vileinye ne sayde
In al his lyf, un-to no maner wight.
He was a verray parfit gentil knight.

    .   .   .   .   .   .

Ther was also a Nonne, a Prioresse,
That of hir smyling was ful simple and coy;
Hir gretteste ooth was but by sëynt Loy;
And she was cleped madame Eglentyne.
Ful wel she song the service divyne,
Entuned in hir nose ful semely;
And Frensh she spak ful faire and fetisly,
After the scole of Stratford atte Bowe,
For Frensh of Paris was to hir unknowe.

    .   .   .

She was so charitable and so pitous,
She wolde wepe, if that she sawe a mous
Caught in a trappe, if it were deed or bledde.
Of smale houndes had she, that she fedde
With rosted flesh, or milk and wastel-breed.
But sore weep she if oon of hem were deed,
Or if men smoot it with a yerde smerte:
And al was conscience and tendre herte.
Ful semely hir wimpel pinched was;
Hir nose tretys; hir eyën greye as glas;
Hir mouth ful smal, and ther-to softe and reed;
But sikerly she hadde a fair forheed;
It was almost a spanne brood, I trowe;
For, hardily, she was nat undergrowe.

16

Ful fetis was hir cloke, as I was war.
Of smal coral aboute hir arm she bar
A peir of bedes, gauded al with grene;
And ther-on heng a broche of gold ful shene,
On which ther was first write a crowned A,
And after, *Amor vincit omnia.*

. . . .

A Clerk ther was of Oxenford also,
That un-to logik hadde longe y-go.
As lene was his hors as is a rake,
And he nas nat right fat, I undertake;
But loked holwe, and ther-to soberly.
Ful thredbar was his overest courtepy;
For he had geten him yet no benefyce,
Ne was so worldly for to have offyce.
For him was lever have at his beddes heed
Twenty bokes, clad in blak or reed,
Of Aristotle and his philosophye,
Than robes riche, or fithele, or gay sautrye.
But al be that he was a philosophre,
Yet hadde he but litel gold in cofre;
But al that he mighte of his freendes hente,
On bokes and on lerninge he it spente,
And bisily gan for the soules preye
Of hem that yaf him wher-with to scoleye.
Of studie took he most cure and most hede.
Noght o word spak he more than was nede,
And that was seyd in forme and reverence,
And short and quik, and ful of hy sentence.
Souninge in moral vertu was his speche,
And gladly wolde he lerne, and gladly teche.

. . . .

With us ther was a Doctour of Phisyk,
In al this world ne was ther noon him lyk
To speke of phisik and of surgerye;
For he was grounded in astronomye.
He kepte his pacient a ful greet del
In houres, by his magik naturel.

17

Wel coude he fortunen the ascendent
Of his images for his pacient.
He knew the cause of everich maladye,
Were it of hoot or cold, or moiste, or drye,
And where engendred, and of what humour;
He was a verray parfit practisour.

.   .   .   .   .   .

A good man was ther of religioun,
And was a povre Persoun of a toun;
But riche he was of holy thoght and werk.
He was also a lerned man, a clerk,
That Cristes gospel trewely wolde preche;
His parisshens devoutly wolde he teche.
Benigne he was, and wonder diligent,
And in adversitee ful pacient;
And swich he was y-preved ofte sythes.
Ful looth were him to cursen for his tythes,
But rather wolde he yeven, out of doute,
Un-to his povre parisshens aboute
Of his offring, and eek of his substaunce.
He coude in litel thing han suffisaunce.

He sette nat his benefice to hyre,
And leet his sheep encombred in the myre,
And ran to London, un-to sëynt Poules,
To seken him a chaunterie for soules,
Or with a bretherhed to been withholde;
But dwelte at hoom, and kepte wel his folde,
So that the wolf ne made it nat miscarie;
He was a shepherde and no mercenarie.

.   .   .

A bettre preest, I trowe that nowher noon is.
He wayted after no pompe and reverence,
Ne maked him a spyced conscience,
But Cristes lore, and his apostles twelve,
He taughte, and first he folwed it himselve.

.   .   .   .   .

Walter Kennedy

THE PRAISE OF AGE

At matin hour, in middis of the night,
Wakenèd ot sleep, I saw beside me soon,
Ane aged man, seemèd sixty years of sight,
This sentence set, and sung it in good tune—
Omnipotent, and eterne God in trone!
To be content and love thee I have cause
That my light youth-head is opprest and done,
　Honour with age to every virtue draws.

Green youth, to age thou mon obey and bow,
They folly lustis lastis scant ane May;
That then was wit, is natural folly now,
As worldly honour, riches, or fresh array,
Defy the devil, dread God and doomisday.
For all shall be accusèd as thou knawis;
Blessed be God, my youth-head is away;
　Honour with age to every virtue drawis.

O bitter youth! that seemis so delicious;
O holy age! that sometimes seemèd sour,
O restless youth! hie, hait, and vicious;
O honest age! fulfillèd with honour;
O froward youth! fruitless and feedand flowr,
Contrar to conscience, both to God and lawis
Of all vain glore the lamp and the mirrour:
　Honour with age till every virtue drawis.

This world is set for to deceive us even,
Pride is the net, and covetous the train;
For no reward, except the joy of heaven,
Would I be young into this world again.
The ship of faith, tempestuous wind and rain
Drives in the sea of Lolledry, that blawis;
My youth is gane, and I am glad and fain:
　Honour with age to every virtue drawis.

19

Law, love, and lawtie, graven low they lie;
Dissimulance has borrowed conscience clais;
Aithis, writ, wax nor seals are nought set by;
Flattery is fostered both with friends and faes.
The son, to bruik it that his father has,
Would see him dead: Sathanus sic seed sawis
Youth-head, adieu! ane of my mortal faes:
    Honour with age to every virtue drawis.

Earl of Surrey

GIVE PLACE, YE LOVERS

Give place, ye lovers, here before
That spent your boasts and brags in vain;
My lady's beauty passeth more
The best of yours, I dare well sayen,
Than doth the sun the candle light
Of brightest day the darkest night.

And thereto hath a troth as just
As had Penelope the fair;
For what she saith, ye may it trust,
As it by writing sealed were:
And virtues hath she many moe
Than I with pen have skill to show.

I could rehearse, if that I would,
The whole effect of Nature's plaint,
When she had lost the perfect mould,
The like to whom she could not paint:
With wringing hands, how she did cry,
And what she said, I know it, I

I know she swore with raging mind,
Her kingdom only set apart,
There was no loss by law of kind
That could have gone so near her heart;
And this was chiefly all her pain;
"She could not make the like again."

20

Sith Nature thus gave her the praise,
To be the chiefest work she wrought;
In faith, methinks! some better ways
On your behalf might well be sought,
Than to compare, as ye have done,
To match the candle with the sun.

George Turberville

THE LOVER TO HIS LADY

My Girl, thou gazest much
Upon the golden skies:
Would I were Heaven, I would behold
Thee then with all mine eyes.

John Skelton

TO MISTRESS MARGERY WENTWORTH

Merry Margaret,
As midsummer flower,
Gentle as falcon,
Or hawk of the tower;
With solace and gladness,
Much mirth and no madness,
All good and no badness;
So joyously,
So maidenly,
So womanly,
Her demeaning,
In everything,
Far, far passing
That I can indite,
Or suffice to write,
Of merry Margaret,
As midsummer flower,

21

Gentle as falcon,
Or hawk of the tower;
As patient and as still,
And as full of goodwill,
As fair Isiphil,
Coliander,
Sweet Pomander,
Good Cassander;
Stedfast of thought,
Well made, well wrought,
Far may be sought,
Ere you can find
So courteous, so kind,
As merry Margaret,
This midsummer flower,
Gentle as falcon,
Or hawk of the tower.

Nicholas Breton

A SWEET PASTORAL

Good Muse, rock me asleep
    With some sweet harmony;
The weary eye is not to keep
    Thy wary company.

Sweet Love, begone awhile,
    Thou knowest my heaviness;
Beauty is born but to beguile
    My heart of happiness.

See how my little flock,
    That loved to feed on high,
Do headlong tumble down the rock,
    And in the valley die.

The bushes and the trees
    That were so fresh and green,
Do all their dainty colour leese,
    And not a leaf is seen

The blackbird and the thrush
  That made the woods to ring,
With all the rest are now at hush,
  And not a note they sing.

Sweet Philomel, the bird
  That hath the heavenly throat,
Doth now, alas! not once afford
  Recording of a note.

The flowers have had a frost,
  Each herb hath lost her savour,
And Phyllida the fair hath lost
  The comfort of her favour.

Now all these careful sights
  So kill me in conceit,
That how to hope upon delights,
  It is but mere deceit.

And therefore, my sweet Muse,
  Thou knowest what help is best;
Do now thy heavenly cunning use,
  To set my heart at rest.

And in a dream bewray
  What fate shall be my friend,
Whether my life shall still decay,
  Or when my sorrow end.

PHILLIDA AND CORIDON

In the merry month of May,
In a morn by break of day,
Forth I walked by the wood-side
When as May was in his pride:
There I spièd all alone
Phillida and Coridon.
Much ado there was, God wot!
He would love and she would not.

23

She said, Never man was true;
He said, None was false to you.
He said, He had loved her long;
She said, Love should have no wrong.
Coridon would kiss her then;
She said, Maids must kiss no men
Till they did for good and all;
Then she made the shepherd call
All the heavens to witness truth
Never loved a truer youth.
Thus with many a pretty oath,
Yea and nay, and faith and troth,
Such as silly shepherds use
When they will not Love abuse,
Love, which had been long deluded,
Was with kisses sweet concluded;
And Phillida, with garlands gay,
Was made the Lady of the May.

Sir Thomas Wyatt

BLAME NOT MY LUTE

Blame not my Lute! for he must sound
  Of this or that as liketh me;
For lack of wit the Lute is bound
    To give such tunes as pleaseth me;
Though my songs be somewhat strange,
And speak such words as touch thy change,
        Blame not my Lute!

My Lute, alas! doth not offend,
    Though that perforce he must agree
To sound such tunes as I intend
    To sing to them that heareth me;
Then though my songs be somewhat plain,
And toucheth some that use to feign,
        Blame not my Lute!

24

SIR THOMAS WYATT

My Lute and strings may not deny,
  But as I strike they must obey;
Break not them then so wrongfully,
  But wreak thyself some other way;
And though the songs which I indite
Do quit thy change with rightful spite,
      Blame not my Lute!

.   .   .   .

Blame but thyself that hast misdone,
  And well deservèd to have blame;
Change thou thy way, so evil begun,
  And then my Lute shall sound that same;
But if till then my fingers play,
By thy desert their wontèd way,
      Blame not my Lute!

FORGET NOT YET

Forget not yet the tried intent
Of such a truth as I have meant;
My great travail so gladly spent
      Forget not yet!

Forget not yet when first began
The weary life ye know, since whan
The suit, the service none tell can;
      Forget not yet!

Forget not yet the great assays,
The cruel wrong, the scornful ways,
The painful patience in delays,
      Forget not yet!

Forget not! oh! forget not this,
How long ago hath been, and is
The mind that never meant amiss—
      Forget not yet!

Forget not then thine own approved,
The which so long hath thee so loved,
Whose steadfast faith yet never moved—
      Forget not this!

25

MY LUTE, AWAKE

My lute, awake, perform the last
Labour that thou and I shall waste,
And end that I have now begun,
And, when this song is sung and past,
My lute, be still, for I have done!

As to be heard where ear is none,
As lead to grave in marble stone,
My song may pierce her heart as soon:
Should we, then, sigh or sing or moan?
No, no, my lute, for I have done!

The rocks do not so cruelly
Repulse the waves continually,
As she my suit and affection:
So that I am past remedy:
Whereby my lute and I have done!

Proud of the spoil that thou hast got
Of simple hearts thorough Love's shot,
By whom unkind thou hast them won,
Think not he hath his bow forgot,
Although my lute and I have done!

Vengeance shall fall on thy disdain,
That mak'st but game of earnest pain,
Trow not alone under the sun
Unquit to cause thy lover's plain,
Although my lute and I have done.

Now cease, my lute, this is the last
Labour that thou and I shall waste,
And ended is that we begun:
Now is this song both sung and past—
My lute, be still, for I have done.

Sir Edward Dyer

MY MIND TO ME A KINGDOM IS

My mind to me a kingdom is,
  Such present joys therein I find,
That it excels all other bliss
  That earth affords or grows by kind:
Though much I want which most would have,
Yet still my mind forbids to crave.

No princely pomp, no wealthy store,
  No force to win the victory,
No wily wit to salve a sore,
  No shape to feed a loving eye;
To none of these I yield as thrall:
For why? My mind doth serve for all.

I see how plenty surfeits oft,
  And hasty climbers soon do fall;
I see that those which are aloft
  Mishap doth threaten most of all,
They get with toil, they keep with fear;
Such cares my mind could never bear.

Content to live, this is my stay;
  I seek no more than may suffice;
I press to bear no haughty sway;
  Look, what I lack my mind supplies:
Lo, thus I triumph like a king,
Content with that my mind doth bring.

Some have too much, yet still do crave;
  I little have, and seek no more.
They are but poor, though much they have,
  And I am rich with little store;
They poor, I rich; they beg, I give;
They lack, I leave; they pine, I live.

27

I laugh not at another's loss;
　　I grudge not at another's pain;
No worldly waves my mind can toss;
　　My state at one doth still remain:
I fear no foe, I fawn no friend;
I loathe not life, nor dread my end.

Some weigh their pleasure by their lust,
　　Their wisdom by their rage of will;
Their treasure is their only trust;
　　A cloaked craft their store of skill:
But all the pleasure that I find
Is to maintain a quiet mind.

My wealth is health and perfect ease:
　　My conscience clear my chief defence;
I neither seek by bribes to please,
　　Nor by deceit to breed offence:
Thus do I live; thus will I die;
Would all did so as well as I!

Edmund Spenser

AMORETTI

XXXIV

Like as a ship, that through the ocean wide,
By conduct of some star doth make her way,
Whenas a storm hath dimmed her trusty guide,
Out of her course doth wander far astray;
So I, whose star, that wont with her bright ray
Me to direct, with clouds is overcast,
Do wander now, in darkness and dismay,
Through hidden perils round about me placed;
Yet hope I well that, when this storm is past,
My Helicè, the lodestar of my life,
Will shine again, and look on me at last,
With lovely light to clear my cloudy grief:
　　Till then I wander care-full, comfortless,
　　In secret sorrow, and sad pensiveness.

EDMUND SPENSER

LXXII

Oft when my spirit doth spread her bolder wings,
In mind to mount up to the purest sky,
It down is weighed with thought of earthly things,
And clogged with burden of mortality;
Where when that sovereign beauty it doth spy,
Resembling heaven's glory in her light,
Drawn with sweet pleasure's bait it back doth fly,
And unto heaven forgets her former flight.
There my frail fancy, fed with full delight,
Doth bathe in bliss, and mantleth most at ease;
Me thinks of other heaven but how it might
Her heart's desire with most contentment please.
   Heart need not wish none other happiness
   But here on earth to have such heaven's bliss.

LXXV

One day I wrote her name upon the strand,
But came the waves and washèd it away:
Again I wrote it with a second hand,
But came the tide and made my pains his prey.
"Vain man," said she, "that dost in vain essay
A mortal thing so to immortalize;
For I myself shall like to this decay,
And eke my name be wipèd out likewise."
"Not so," quoth I; "let baser things devise
To die in dust, but you shall live by fame;
My verse your virtues rare shall eternize,
And in the heavens write your glorious name:
   Where, whenas Death shall all the world subdue,
   Our love shall live, and later life renew."

LXXXI

Fair is my Love, when her fair golden hairs
With the loose wind ye waving chance to mark;
Fair, when the rose in her red cheeks appears;
Or in her eyes the fair of love does spark.
Fair, when her breast, like a rich laden bark,

29

With precious merchandise she forth doth lay;
Fair, when that cloud of pride, which oft doth dark
Her goodly light, with smiles she drives away.
But fairest she, when so she doth display
The gate with pearls and rubies richly dight;
Through which her words so wise do make their way
To bear the message of her gentle spright.
  The rest be works of Nature's wonderment;
  But this the work of heart's astonishment.

PROTHALAMION

Calm was the day, and through the trembling air
Sweet-breathing Zephyrus did softly play
A gentle spirit, that lightly did delay
Hot Titan's beams, which then did glister fair;
When I (whom sullen care,
Through discontent of my long fruitless stay
In Prince's Court, and expectation vain
Of idle hopes, which still do fly away,
Like empty shadows, did afflict my brain),
Walked forth to ease my pain
Along the shore of silver streaming Thames;
Whose rutty bank, the which his river hems,
Was painted all with variable flowers,
And all the meads adorned with dainty gems,
Fit to deck maidens' bowers,
And crown their paramours
Against the bridal day, which is not long:
  Sweet Thames! run softly, till I end my song.

There, in a meadow, by the river's side,
A flock of nymphs I chancèd to espy,
All lovely daughters of the flood thereby,
With goodly greenish locks, all loose untied,
As each had been a bride:
And each one had a little wicker basket,
Made of fine twigs, entrailèd curiously,
In which they gathered flowers to fill their flasket,
And, with fine fingers, cropped full feateously

The tender stalks on high.
Of every sort, which in that meadow grew,
They gathered some; the violet, pallid blue,
The little daisy, that at evening closes,
The virgin lily, and the primrose true,
With a store of vermeil roses,
To deck their bridegroom's posies
Against the bridal day, which was not long:
   Sweet Thames! run softly, till I end my song.

With that I saw two swans of goodly hue
Come softly swimming down along the Lee;
Two fairer birds I yet did never see;
The snow, which doth the top of Pindus strew,
Did never whiter shew,
Nor Jove himself, when he a swan would be
For love of Leda, whiter did appear;
Yet Leda was, they say, as white as he,
Yet not so white as these, nor nothing near;
So purely white they were,
That even the gentle stream, the which them bare,
Seemed foul to them, and bade his billows spare
To wet their silken feathers, lest they might
Soil their fair plumes with water not so fair,
And mar their beauties bright,
That shone as heaven's light,
Against their bridal day, which was not long:
   Sweet Thames! run softly, till I end my song.

Eftsoons the nymphs, which now had flowers their fill,
Ran all in haste to see that silver brood,
As they came floating on the crystal flood;
Whom when they saw, they stood amazèd still,
Their wondering eyes to fill;
Them seemed they never saw a sight so fair
Of fowls so lovely, that they sure did deem
Them heavenly born, or to be that same pair
Which through the sky draw Venus' silver team;
For sure they did not seem
To be begot of any earthly seed,
But rather angels, or of angels' breed;

31

Yet were they bred of summer's heat, they say,
In sweetest season, when each flower and weed
The earth did fresh array;
So fresh they seemed as day,
Even as their bridal day, which was not long:
   Sweet Thames! run softly, till I end my song.

Then forth they all out of their baskets drew
Great store of flowers, the honour of the field,
That to the sense did fragrant odours yield,
All which upon those goodly birds they threw
And all the waves did strew,
That like old Peneus' waters they did seem,
When down along by pleasant Tempe's shore,
Scattered with flowers, through Thessaly they stream,
That they appear, through lilies' plenteous store,
Like a bride's chamber floor:
Two of those nymphs, meanwhile, two garlands bound
Of freshest flowers which in that mead they found,
The which presenting all in trim array,
Their snowy foreheads therewithal they crowned,
Whilst one did sing this lay,
Prepared against that day,
Against their bridal day, which was not long:
   Sweet Thames! run softly, till I end my song.

"Ye gentle birds! the world's fair ornament,
And heaven's glory whom this happy hour
Doth lead unto your lover's blissful bower,
Joy may you have, and gentle hearts' content
Of your love's complement;
And let fair Venus, that is queen of love,
With her heart-quelling son upon you smile,
Whose smile, they say, hath virtue to remove
All love's dislike, and friendship's faulty guile
For ever to assoil;
Let endless peace your steadfast hearts accord,
And blessèd plenty wait upon your board;
And let your bed with pleasures chaste abound,
That fruitful issue may to you afford,

Which may your foes confound,
And make your joys redound
Upon your bridal day, which is not long":
  Sweet Thames! run softly, till I end my song.

So ended she: and all the rest around
To her redoubled that her undersong,
Which said their bridal day should not be long:
And gentle Echo from the neighbour-ground
Their accents did resound.
So forth those joyous birds did pass along,
Adown the Lee, that to them murmured low,
As he would speak, but that he lacked a tongue,
Yet did by signs his glad affection show,
Making his stream run slow.
And all the fowl which in his flood did dwell
'Gan flock about these twain, that did excel
The rest, so far as Cynthia doth shend
The lesser stars. So they, enrangèd well,
Did on those two attend,
And their best service lend
Against their wedding day, which was not long:
  Sweet Thames! run softly, till I end my song.

At length they all to merry London came,
To merry London, my most kindly nurse,
That to me gave this life's first native source;
Though from another place I take my name,
An house of ancient fame:
There when they came, whereas those bricky towers
The which on Thames' broad, aged back do ride,
Where now the studious lawyers have their bowers,
There whilom wont the Templar Knights to bide,
Till they decayed through pride:
Next whereunto there stands a stately place,
Where oft I gainèd gifts and goodly grace
Of that great lord, which therein wont to dwell,
Whose want too well now feels my friendless case;
But ah! here fits not well
Old woes, but joys, to tell
Against the bridal day, which is not long:
  Sweet Thames! run softly, till I end my song.

Yet therein now doth lodge a noble peer,
Great England's glory, and the world's wide wonder,
Whose dreadful name late through all Spain did thunder,
And Hercules' two pillars standing near
Did make to quake and fear:
Fair branch of honour, flower of chivalry!
That fillest England with thy triumph's fame,
Joy have thou of thy noble victory,
And endless happiness of thine own name,
That promiseth the same;
That through thy prowess, and victorious arms,
Thy country may be freed from foreign harms;
And great Elisa's glorious name may ring
Through all the world, filled with thy wide alarms,
Which some brave muse may sing
To ages following,
Upon the bridal day, which is not long:
    Sweet Thames! run softly, till I end my song.

From those high towers this noble lord issuing,
Like radiant Hesper, when his golden hair
In the ocean billows he hath bathèd fair,
Descended to the river's open viewing,
With a great train ensuing.
Above the rest were goodly to be seen
Two gentle knights of lovely face and feature
Beseeming well the bower of any queen,
With gifts of wit, and ornaments of nature,
Fit for so goodly stature,
That like the twins of Jove they seemed in sight,
Which deck the baldrick of the heavens bright;
They two, forth pacing to the river's side,
Received those two fair brides, their love's delight;
Which, at the appointed tide,
Each one did make his bride
Against their bridal day, which is not long:
    Sweet Thames! run softly, till I end my song.

34

Sir Walter Raleigh

HIS PILGRIMAGE

Give me my scallop-shell of quiet,
  My staff of faith to walk upon,
My scrip of joy, immortal diet,
  My bottle of salvation,
My gown of glory, hope's true gage;
And thus I'll take my pilgrimage.

Blood must be my body's balmer;
  No other balm will there be given;
Whilst my soul, like quiet palmer,
  Travelleth towards the land of heaven;
Over the silver mountains,
Where spring the nectar fountains;
  There will I kiss
  The bowl of bliss;
And drink mine everlasting fill
Upon every milken hill.

Then by that happy blissful day,
  More peaceful pilgrims I shall see,
That have cast off their rags of clay,
  And walk apparelled fresh like me,
  I'll take them first
  To quench their thirst
  At those clear wells
  Where sweetness dwells.

From thence to heaven's bribeless hall
Where no corrupted voices brawl;
No conscience molten into gold,
No forged accuser bought or sold,
No cause deferred, no vain-spent journey,
For there Christ is the king's Attorney,
Who pleads for all without degrees,
And He hath angels, but no fees.

35

And when the grand twelve-million jury
Of our sins, with direful fury,
Against our souls black verdicts give,
Christ pleads his death, and then we live.

THE SILENT LOVER

Passions are liken'd best to floods and streams:
   The shallow murmur, but the deep are dumb;
So, when affection yields discourse, it seems
   The bottom is but shallow whence they come
They that are rich in words, in words discover
That they are poor in that which makes a lover.

Wrong not, sweet empress of my heart,
   The merit of true passion,
With thinking that he feels no smart,
   That sues for no compassion.

Silence in love bewrays more woe
   Than words, though ne'er so witty:
A beggar that is dumb, you know,
   May challenge double pity.

Then wrong not, dearest to my heart,
   My true, though secret passion;
He smarteth most that hides his smart,
   And sues for no compassion.

THE LIE

Go, Soul, the Body's guest,
   Upon a thankless arrant;
Fear not to touch the best;
   The truth shall be thy warrant:
Go, since I needs must die,
And give the World the lie.

36

SIR WALTER RALEIGH

Say to the Court, it glows
   And shines like rotten wood.
Say to the Church, it shows
   What's good, and doth no good:
If Court and Church reply
Then give them both the lie.

Tell Potentates, they live
   Acting by others' action,
Not loved unless they give,
   Not strong but by a faction:
If Potentates reply,
Give Potentates the lie.

Tell men of high condition
   That manage the Estate,
Their purpose is ambition,
   Their practice, only hate:
And if they once reply,
Then give them all the lie.

Tell them that brave it most,
   They beg for more by spending,
Who, in their greatest cost,
   Seek nothing but commending:
And if they make reply,
Then give them all the lie.

Tell Zeal it wants devotion;
   Tell Love it is but lust;
Tell Time it is but motion;
   Tell Flesh it is but dust:
And wish them not reply,
For thou must give the lie.

Tell Age it daily wasteth;
   Tell Honour how it alters;
Tell Beauty how she blasteth;
   Tell Favour how it falters:
And as they shall reply,
Give every one the lie.

Tell Wit how much it wrangles
   In tickle points of niceness;
Tell Wisdom she entangles
   Herself in over-wiseness:
And when they do reply,
Straight give them both the lie.

Tell Physic of her boldness;
   Tell Skill it is pretension;
Tell Charity of coldness;
   Tell Law it is contention:
And as they do reply,
So give them still the lie.

Tell Fortune of her blindness;
   Tell Nature of decay;
Tell Friendship of unkindness;
   Tell Justice of delay:
And if they will reply,
Then give them all the lie.

Tell Arts they have no soundness,
   But vary by esteeming;
Tell Schools they want profoundness,
   And stand too much on seeming:
If Arts and Schools reply,
Give Arts and Schools the lie.

Tell Faith it's fled the City;
   Tell how the Country erreth,
Tell Manhood shakes off pity;
   Tell Virtue least preferreth:
And if they do reply,
Spare not to give the lie.

So when thou hast, as I
   Commanded thee, done blabbing,—
Although to give the lie
   Deserves no less than stabbing,—
Yet, stab at thee that will,
No stab the soul can kill!

SIR WALTER RALEIGH

THE CONCLUSION

Even such is Time, that takes in trust
   Our youth, our joys, our all we have,
And pays us but with earth and dust;
   Who in the dark and silent grave,
When we have wander'd all our ways,
Shuts up the story of our days;
But from this earth, this grave, this dust,
My God shall raise me up, I trust.

THE NYMPH'S REPLY

If all the world and love were young,
And truth in every shepherd's tongue,
These pretty pleasures might me move
To live with thee, and be thy Love.

But Time drives flocks from field to fold;
When rivers rage and rocks grow cold;
And Philomel becometh dumb;
The rest complains of cares to come.

The flowers do fade, and wanton fields
To wayward Winter reckoning yields:
A honey tongue, a heart of gall,
Is fancy's spring, but sorrow's fall.

Thy gowns, thy shoes, thy beds of roses,
Thy cap, thy kirtle, and thy posies,
Soon break, soon wither,—soon forgotten,
In folly ripe, in reason rotten.

Thy belt of straw and ivy-buds,
Thy coral clasps and amber studs,—
All these in me no means can move
To come to thee and be thy Love.

But could youth last, and love still breed,
Had joys no date, nor age no need,
Then these delights my mind might move
To live with thee and be thy Love.

A VISION UPON SPENSER'S "FAERY QUEEN"

Methought I saw the grave where Laura lay,
Within that temple where the vestal flame
Was wont to burn; and passing by that way,
To see that buried dust of living fame,
Whose tomb fair Love and fairer Virtue kept;
All suddenly I saw the Faery Queen;
At whose approach the soul of Petrarch wept;
And from thenceforth those Graces were not seen,
For they this Queen attended: in whose stead
Oblivion laid him down on Laura's hearse:
Hereat the hardest stones were seen to bleed,
And groans of buried ghosts the heavens did pierce,
    Where Homer's sprite did tremble all for grief,
    And cursed th' access of that celestial thief.

Sir Philip Sidney

TO THE MOON

With how sad steps, O Moon, thou climb'st the skies!
How silently, and with how wan a face!
What! may it be that even in heavenly place
That busy archer his sharp arrows tries?
Sure, if that long-with-love-acquainted eyes
Can judge of love, thou feel'st a lover's case;
I read it in thy looks. Thy languished grace
To me, that feel the like, thy state descries.
Then, even of fellowship, O Moon, tell me,
Is constant love deemed there but want of wit?
Are beauties there as proud as here they be?
Do they above love to be loved, and yet

40

SIR PHILIP SIDNEY

Those lovers scorn whom that love doth possess?
Do they call virtue there ungratefulness?

—ASTROPHEL AND STELLA.

SLEEP

Come Sleep! O Sleep, the certain knot of peace,
The baiting-place of wit, the balm of woe,
The poor man's wealth, the prisoner's release,
The indifferent judge between the high and low!
With shield of proof, shield me from out the press
Of those fierce darts Despair at me doth throw:
O make in me those civil wars to cease!
I will good tribute pay if thou do so.
Take thou of me, smooth pillows, sweetest bed,
A chamber deaf to noise and blind to light,
A rosy garland, and a weary head:
And if these things, as being thine in right,
    Move not thy heavy grace, thou shalt in me,
    Livelier than elsewhere, Stella's image see.

—ASTROPHEL AND STELLA.

NO MORE, MY DEAR

No more, my Dear, no more these counsels try;
O give my passions leave to run their race!
Let Fortune lay on me her worst disgrace;
Let folk o'ercharged with brain, against me cry;
Let clouds bedim my face, break in mine eye;
Let me no steps but of lost labour trace;
Let all the earth with scorn recount my case;
But do not will me from my love to fly!
I do not envy Aristotle's wit;
Nor do aspire to Cæsar's bleeding fame;
Nor aught do care, though some above me sit;
Nor hope, nor wish another course to frame,
    But that which once may win thy cruel heart:
    Thou art my Wit, and thou my Virtue art.

—ASTROPHEL AND STELLA.

41

O HAPPY THAMES

O happy Thames that didst my Stella bear!
I saw thee with full many a smiling line
Upon thy cheerful face, Joy's livery wear,
While those fair planets on thy streams did shine.
The boat for joy could not to dance forbear;
While wanton winds, with beauties so divine,
Ravished, stayed not, till in her golden hair
They did themselves (O sweetest prison!) twine.
And fain those Æol's youths there would their stay
Have made, but forced by Nature still to fly,
First did with puffing kiss those locks display.
She so dishevelied, blushed. From window, I,
    With sight thereof, cried out, "O fair disgrace!
    Let Honour's self to thee grant highest place!"
                              —ASTROPHEL AND STELLA.

INSPIRATION

I never drank of Aganippe well,
Nor ever did in shade of Tempe sit,
And Muses scorn with vulgar brains to dwell;
Poor layman I, for sacred rites unfit.
Some do I hear of poets' fury tell,
But, God wot, wot not what they mean by it;
And this I swear by blackest brook of hell,
I am no pick-purse of another's wit.
How falls it then, that with so smooth an ease
My thoughts I speak; and what I speak doth flow
In verse, and that my verse best wits doth please?
Guess we the cause! What, is it thus? Fie, no.
Or so? Much less. How then? Sure thus it is,
My lips are sweet, inspired with Stella's kiss.
                              —ASTROPHEL AND STELLA.

SIR PHILIP SIDNEY

DOUBT YOU TO WHOM MY MUSE

Doubt you to whom my Muse these notes intendeth,
Which now my breast, o'ercharged, to music lendeth?
   To you! to you! all song of praise is due;
Only in you my song begins and endeth.

Who hath the eyes which marry state with pleasure?
Who keeps the key of Nature's chiefest treasure?
   To you! to you! all song of praise is due;
Only for you the heaven forgat all measure.

Who hath the lips where wit in fairness reigneth?
Who womankind at once both decks and staineth?
   To you! to you! all song of praise is due;
Only by you Cupid his crown maintaineth.

Who hath the feet, whose step all sweetness planteth?
Who else, for whom Fame worthy trumpets wanteth?
   To you! to you! all song of praise is due;
Only to you her sceptre Venus granteth.

Who hath the breast, whose milk doth passions nourish?
Whose grace is such, that when it chides doth cherish?
   To you! to you! all song of praise is due;
Only through you the tree of life doth flourish.

Who hath the hand, which without stroke subdueth?
Who long-dead beauty with increase reneweth?
   To you! to you! all song of praise is due;
Only at you all envy hopeless rueth.

Who hath the hair, which loosest fastest tieth?
Who makes a man live then glad when he dieth?
   To you! to you! all song of praise is due;
Only of you the flatterer never lieth.

Who hath the voice, which soul from senses sunders?
Whose force but yours the bolts of beauty thunders?
   To you! to you! all song of praise is due;
Only with you not miracles are wonders.

Doubt you to whom my Muse these notes intendeth,
Which now my breast, o'ercharged, to music lendeth?
   To you! to you! all song of praise is due;
Only in you my song begins and endeth.
               —ASTROPHEL AND STELLA.

PHILOMELA

The nightingale, as soon as April bringeth
   Unto her rested sense a perfect waking,
While late bare earth, proud of new clothing, springeth,
   Sings out her woes, a thorn her song-book making,
   And mournfully bewailing,
Her throat in tunes expresseth
What grief her breast oppresseth,
   For Tereus' force on her chaste will prevailing.
O Philomela fair, O take some gladness,
That here is juster cause of plaintful sadness:
Thine earth now springs, mine fadeth;
Thy thorn without, my thorn my heart invadeth.

O FAIR! O SWEET!

O fair! O sweet! when I do look on thee,
   In whom all joys so well agree,
Heart and soul do sing in me,
   Just accord all music makes;
In thee just accord excelleth,
Where each part in such peace dwelleth,
   One of other beauty takes,
Since, then, truth to all minds telleth
   That in thee lives harmony,
   Heart and soul do sing in me.

A DIRGE

Ring out your bells, let mourning shews be spread;
For Love is dead:
44

All Love is dead, infected
With plague of deep disdain:
   Worth, as nought worth, rejected,
And Faith fair scorn doth gain.
   From so ungrateful fancy,
   From such a female frenzy,
   From them that use men thus,
   Good Lord, deliver us!

Weep, neighbours, weep; do you not hear it said
That Love is dead?
   His death-bed, peacock's folly;
His winding-sheet is shame;
   His will, false-seeming wholly;
His sole executor, blame.
   From so ungrateful fancy,
   From such a female frenzy,
   From them that use men thus,
   Good Lord, deliver us!

Let dirge be sung, and trentals rightly read,
For Love is dead;
   Sir Wrong his tomb ordaineth
My mistress' marble heart;
   Which epitaph containeth,
"Her eyes were once his dart."
   From so ungrateful fancy,
   From such a female frenzy,
   From them that use men thus,
   Good Lord, deliver us!

Alas, I lie: rage hath this error bred;
Love is not dead;
   Love is not dead, but sleepeth
In her unmatchèd mind,
   Where she his counsel keepeth,
Till due deserts she find.
   Therefore from so vile fancy,
   To call such wit a frenzy,
   Who Love can temper thus,
   Good Lord, deliver us!

45

THE IMPATIENT LOVER

Be your words made, good Sir, of Indian ware,
That you allow me them by so small rate?
Or do you curted Spartans imitate?
Or do you mean my tender ears to spare,
That to my questions you so total are?
When I demand of Phœnix-Stella's state,
You say, forsooth, you left her well of late:
O God, think you that satisfies my care?
I would know whether she did sit or walk;
How clothed; how waited on; sighed she, or smiled;
Whereof,—with whom,—how often did she talk;
With what pastimes Time's journey she beguiled;
If her lips deigned to sweeten my poor name:
Say all; and all well said, still say the same.

—ASTROPHEL AND STELLA.

EPITAPH ON ARGALUS AND PARTHENIA

His being was in her alone;
And he not being, she was none.
They joy'd one joy, one grief they griev'd;
One love they lov'd, one life they liv'd.
The hand was one, one was the sword
That did his death, her, death afford.
As all the rest, so now the stone
That tombs the two is justly one.

—ARCADIA—BOOK III.

MY TRUE-LOVE HATH MY HEART

My true-love hath my heart, and I have his,
By just exchange one for the other given:
I hold his dear, and mine he cannot miss;
There never was a bargain better driven.
His heart in me keeps me and him in one,
My heart in him his thoughts and senses guides;

46

JOHN LYLY

He loves my heart for once it was his own;
I cherish his because in me it bides.
His heart his wound received from my sight;
My heart was wounded with his wounded heart;
For as from me on him his hurt did light,
So still methought in me his hurt did smart:
Both equal hurt, in this change sought our bliss,
My true love hath my heart, and I have his.

—ARCADIA—BOOK III.

OFT HAVE I MUSED

Oft have I mused, but now at length I find
    Why those that die, men say they do depart:
Depart! a word so gentle to my mind,
    Weakly did seem to paint Death's ugly dart.
But now the stars, with their strange course, do bind
    Me one to leave, with whom I leave my heart;
I hear a cry of spirits faint and blind
    That parting thus, my chiefest part I part.
Part of my life, the loathèd part to me,
    Lives to impart my weary clay some breath;
But that good part wherein all comforts be,
    Now dead, doth shew departure is a death;
Yea, worse than death; death parts both woe and joy,
From joy I part, still living in annoy.

—SIDERA.

John Lyly

HYMN TO APOLLO

Sing to Apollo, god of day,
Whose golden beams with morning play
And make her eyes so brightly shine,
Aurora's face is called divine;

47

Sing to Phœbus and that throne
Of diamonds which he sits upon.
  Io, pæans let us sing
  To Physic's and to Poesy's king!

Crown all his altars with bright fire,
Laurels bind about his lyre,
A Daphnean coronet for his head,
The Muses dance about his bed;
When on his ravishing lute he plays,
Strew his temple round with bays.
  Io, pæans let us sing
  To the glittering Delian king!

CUPID AND MY CAMPASPE PLAYED

Cupid and my Campaspe played
At cards for kisses, Cupid paid;
He stakes his quiver, bow, and arrows,
His mother'd doves and team of sparrows:
Loses them too; then down he throws
The coral of his lip, the rose
Growing on 's cheek (but none knows how);
With these the crystal of his brow,
And then the dimple of his chin—
All these did my Campaspe win.
At last he set her both his eyes.
She won, and Cupid blind did rise.
O Love, has she done this to thee?
What shall, alas! become of me?

APOLLO'S SONG

My Daphne's hair is twisted gold,
Bright stars apiece her eyes do hold,
My Daphne's brow enthrones the Graces,
My Daphne's beauty stains all faces,
On Daphne's cheek grow rose and cherry,
On Daphne's lip a sweeter berry.

48

Daphne's snowy hand but touched does melt,
And then no heavenlier warmth is felt,
My Daphne's voice tunes all the spheres,
My Daphne's music charms all ears.
Fond am I thus to sing her praise;
These glories now are turned to bays.

Thomas Lodge

FAIR ROSALYND

Like to the clear in highest sphere,
    Where all imperial glory shines,
Of self-same colour is her hair,
    Whether unfolded or in twines;
        Heigh ho, fair Rosalynd!

Her eyes are sapphires set in snow,
    Refining heaven by every wink;
The gods do fear whenas they glow,
    And I do tremble when I think:
        Heigh ho, would she were mine!

Her cheeks are like the blushing cloud
    That beautifies Aurora's face,
Or like the silver-crimson shroud
    That Phœbus' smiling looks doth grace;
        Heigh ho, fair Rosalynd!

Her lips are like two budded roses,
    Whom ranks of lilies neighbour nigh,
Within whose bounds she balm encloses
    Apt to entice a deity.
        Heigh ho, would she were mine!

Her neck like to a stately tower,
    Where Love himself imprisoned lies,
To watch for glances every hour,
    From her divine and sacred eyes;
        Heigh ho, fair Rosalynd!

Her paps are centres of delight,
  Her paps are orbs of heavenly frame,
Where nature moulds the dew of light
  To feed perfection with the same:
    Heigh ho, would she were mine!

With orient pearl, with ruby red,
  With marble white, with sapphire blue,
Her body every way is fed,
  Yet soft to touch, and sweet in view:
    Heigh ho, fair Rosalynd!

Nature herself her shape admires,
  The gods are wounded in her sight,
And Love forsakes his heavenly fires,
  And at her eyes his brand doth light:
    Heigh ho, would she were mine!

Then muse not, Nymphs, though I bemoan
  The absence of fair Rosalynd,
Since for a fair there is fairer none,
  Nor for her virtues so divine:
    Heigh ho! fair Rosalynd!
Heigh ho! my heart! would God that she were mine!

PHILLIS

My Phillis hath the morning sun
  At first to look upon her;
And Phillis hath morn-waking birds
  Her risings still to honour.
My Phillis hath prime-feather'd flowers,
  That smile when she treads on them;
And Phillis hath a gallant flock,
  That leaps since she doth own them.
But Phillis hath too hard a heart,
  Alas, that she should have it!
It yields no mercy to desert,
  Nor grace to those that crave it.

Robert Greene

THE SHEPHERD'S WIFE'S SONG

Ah, what is love? It is a pretty thing,
As sweet unto a shepherd as a king,
    And sweeter, too:
For kings have cares that wait upon a crown,
And cares can make the sweetest love to frown:
    Ah then, ah then,
If country loves such sweet desires do gain,
What lady would not love a shepherd swain?

His flocks are folded; he comes home at night
As merry as a king in his delight,
    And merrier, too:
For kings bethink them what the state require,
Where shepherds, careless, carol by the fire:

He kisseth first, then sits as blithe to eat
His cream and curds, as doth a king his meat,
    And blither, too:
For kings have often fears when they do sup,
Where shepherds dread no poison in their cup:

To bed he goes, as wanton then, I ween,
As is a king in dalliance with a queen;
    More wanton, too:
For kings have many griefs, affects to move,
Where shepherds have no greater grief than love:

Upon his couch of straw he sleeps as sound
As doth the king upon his bed of down;
    More sounder, too:
For cares cause kings full oft their sleep to spill,
Where weary shepherds lie and snort their fill:

Thus, with his wife, he spends the year as blithe
As doth the king at every tide or sithe,
    And blither, too:

51

For kings have wars and broils to take in hand,
Where shepherds laugh and love upon the land:
  Ah then, ah then,
Since country loves such sweet desires do gain,
What lady would not love a shepherd swain?

SAMELA

Like to Diana in her summer weed,
Girt with a crimson robe of brightest dye,
  Goes fair Samela;
Whiter than be the flocks that straggling feed,
When washed by Arethusa's Fount they lie,
  Is fair Samela.

As fair Aurora in her morning-gray,
Decked with the ruddy glister of her love,
  Is fair Samela;
Like lovely Thetis on a calmèd day,
Whenas her brightness Neptune's fancy move,
  Shines fair Samela.

Her tresses gold, her eyes like glassy streams,
Her teeth are pearl, the breasts are ivory
  Of fair Samela;
Her cheeks like rose and lily yield forth gleams;
Her brows bright arches framed of ebony:
  Thus far Samela

Passeth fair Venus in her bravest hue,
And Juno in the show of majesty,
  For she's Samela;
Pallas, in wit,—all three, if you well view,
For beauty, wit, and matchless dignity
  Yield to Samela.

George Chapman

HER COMING

See where she issues in her beauty's pomp,
As Flora to salute the morning sun;
Who when she shakes her tresses in the air,
Rains on the earth dissolvèd pearl in showers,
Which with his beams the sun exhales to heaven:
She holds the spring and summer in her arms,
And every planet puts on his freshest robes,
To dance attendance on her princely steps,
Springing and fading as she comes and goes.

Samuel Daniel

TO DELIA

When men shall find thy flower, thy glory pass,
And thou, with careful brow, sitting alone,
Receivèd hast this message from thy glass,
That tells the truth, and says that *all is gone;*
Fresh shalt thou see in me the wounds thou madest,
Though spent thy flame, in me the heat remaining:
I that have loved thee thus before thou fadest,
My faith shall wax, when thou art in thy waning!
The world shall find this miracle in me,
That fire can burn when all the matter's spent:
Then what my faith hath been, thyself shalt see,
And that thou wast unkind, thou may'st repent!
 Thou may'st repent that thou hast scorned my tears,
 When Winter snows upon thy golden hairs.

 . . . .

I must not grieve my Love, whose eyes would read
Lines of delight, whereon her youth might smile!
Flowers have a time, before they come to seed;
And she is young, and now must sport the while.

53

And sport, Sweet Maid, in season of these years,
And learn to gather flowers before they wither!
And where the sweetest blossom first appears,
Let Love and Youth conduct thy pleasures thither!
Lighten forth smiles to clear the clouded air,
And calm the tempest which my sighs do raise!
Pity and smiles do best become the fair;
Pity and smiles shall yield thee lasting praise.
   I hope to say, when all my griefs are gone,
   "Happy the heart that sighed for such a one!"

     .   .   .   .

Let others sing of Knights and Paladines
In agèd accents and untimely words,
Paint shadows in imaginary lines,
Which well the reach of their high wit records:
But I must sing of Thee, and those fair eyes!
Authentic shall my verse in time to come,
When the yet unborn shall say, *Lo, where she lies!*
Whose beauty made him speak, that else was dumb!
These are the arks, the trophies I erect,
That fortify thy name against old age;
And these thy sacred virtues must protect
Against the Dark, and Time's consuming rage.
   Though the error of my youth in them appear,
   Suffice, they showed I lived, and loved thee dear.

     .   .   .   .

Care-charmer Sleep, son of the sable Night,
Brother to Death, in silent darkness born:
Relieve my languish, and restore the light;
With dark forgetting of my care, return!
And let the day be time enough to mourn
The shipwreck of my ill-adventured youth:
Let waking eyes suffice to wail their scorn,
Without the torment of the night's untruth.
Cease, dreams, the images of day-desires,
To model forth the passions of the morrow;

Never let rising sun approve you liars,
To add more grief to aggravate my sorrow.
   Still let me sleep, embracing clouds in vain;
   And never wake to feel the day's disdain.

Michael Drayton

A SUMMER'S EVE

Clear had the day been from the dawn,
   All chequer'd was the sky,
Thin clouds, like scarfs of cobweb lawn,
   Veil'd heaven's most glorious eye.

The wind had no more strength than this,
   That leisurely it blew,
To make one leaf the next to kiss,
   That closely by it grew.

The flowers, like brave embroidered girls,
   Look'd as they most desired,
To see whose head with orient pearls
   Most curiously was tyred.

The rills, that on the pebbles played,
   Might now be heard at will;
This world the only music made,
   Else every thing was still.

And to itself the subtle air
   Such sovereignty assumes,
That it receives too large a share
   From nature's rich perfumes.

IMMORTALITY IN SONG

How many paltry, foolish, painted things,
That now in coaches trouble every street,
Shall be forgotten, whom no poet sings,
Ere they be well wrapped in their winding-sheet?

55

Where I to thee eternity shall give,
When nothing else remaineth of these days,
And queens hereafter shall be glad to live
Upon the alms of thy superfluous praise;
Virgins and matrons reading these my rhymes,
Shall be so much delighted with thy story,
That they shall grieve they lived not in these times,
To have seen thee, their sex's only glory:
   So shalt thou fly above the vulgar throng,
   Still to survive in my immortal song.

                        —IDEA.

SINCE THERE'S NO HELP

Since there's no help, come, let us kiss and part,—
Nay I have done, you get no more of me;
And I am glad, yea glad with all my heart,
That thus so cleanly I myself can free;
Shake hands for ever, cancel all our vows,
And when we meet at any time again,
Be it not seen in either of our brows
That we one jot of former love retain.
Now at the last gasp of Love's latest breath,
When his pulse failing, Passion speechless lies,
When Faith is kneeling by his bed of death,
And Innocence is closing up his eyes,—
   Now if thou would'st, when all have given him over,
   From death to life thou might'st him yet recover!

                        —IDEA.

SOME ATHEIST IN LOVE

Some atheist or vile infidel in love,
When I do speak of thy divinity,
May blaspheme thus, and say I flatter thee,
And only write my skill in verse to prove.
See miracles, ye unbelieving! see
A dumb-born Muse made to express the mind,
A cripple hand to write, yet lame by kind,
56

One by thy name, the other touching thee.
Blind were my eyes, till they were seen of thine,
And mine ears deaf by thy fame healèd be;
My vices cured by virtues sprung from thee,
My hopes revived, which long in grave had lyne:
    All unclean thoughts, foul spirits, cast out in me
    By thy great power, and by strong faith in thee.

Joshua Sylvester

CONSTANCY

Were I as base as is the lowly plain,
And you, my Love, as high as heaven above,
Yet should the thoughts of me your humble swain
Ascend to heaven, in honour of my Love.

Were I as high as heaven above the plain,
And you, my Love, as humble and as low
As are the deepest bottoms of the main,
Whereso'er you were, with you my love should go.

Were you the earth, dear Love, and I the skies,
My love should shine on you like to the sun,
And look upon you with ten thousand eyes
Till heaven wax'd blind, and till the world were done.

Whereso'er I am, below, or else above you,
Whereso'er you are, my heart shall truly love you.

THE GLORIOUS STARS OF HEAVEN

I'll ne'er believe that the Arch-Architect
With all these fires the heavenly arches decked
Only for show, and with their glistening shields
To amaze poor shepherds watching in the fields:
I'll ne'er believe that the least flower that pranks
Our garden borders, or the common banks,

57

And the least stone that in her warming lap
Our kind nurse Earth doth covetously wrap
Hath some peculiar virtue of its own,
And that the glorious stars of Heaven have none,
But shine in vain, and have no charge precise,
But to be walking in Heaven's galleries,
And through the palace up and down to clamber
As golden gulls about a presence-chamber.

Christopher Marlowe

MARLOWE

Next Marlowe, bathed in the Thespian springs,
Had in him those brave translunary things
That the first poets had; his raptures were
All air and fire, which made his verses clear;
For that fine madness still he did retain
Which rightly should possess a poet's brain.
                    —MICHAEL DRAYTON.

THE PASSIONATE SHEPHERD TO HIS LOVE

Come live with me and be my Love,
And we will all the pleasures prove
That hills and valleys, dales and fields,
Or woods or steepy mountain yields.

And we will sit upon the rocks,
And see the shepherds feed their flocks
By shallow rivers, to whose falls
Melodious birds sing madrigals.

And I will make thee beds of roses
And a thousand fragrant posies;
A cap of flowers, and a kirtle
Embroidered all with leaves of myrtle.

CHRISTOPHER MARLOWE

A gown made of the finest wool
Which from our pretty lambs we pull;
Fair-lined slippers for the cold,
With buckles of the purest gold.

A belt of straw and ivy-buds
With coral clasps and amber studs:
And if these pleasures may thee move,
Come live with me and be my Love.

The shepherd swains shall dance and sing
For thy delight each May morning:
If these delights thy mind may move,
Then live with me and be my Love.

TAMBURLAINE THE GREAT

If all the pens that ever poets held
Had fed the feeling of their masters' thoughts,
And every sweetness that inspir'd their hearts,
Their minds, and muses on admirèd themes;
If all the heavenly quintessence they still
From their immortal flowers of poesy,
Wherein, as in a mirror, we perceive
The highest reaches of a human wit;
If these had made one poem's period,
And all combin'd in beauty's worthiness,
Yet should there hover in their restless heads
One thought, one grace, one wonder, at the least,
Which into words no virtue can digest.
                    —ACT V, SCENE I.

FAUSTUS

Was this the face that launch'd a thousand ships,
And burnt the topless towers of Ilium?—
Sweet Helen, make me immortal with a kiss.—
Her lips suck forth my soul: see, where it flies!—
Come, Helen, come, give me my soul again.

59

Here will I dwell, for heaven is in these lips,
And all is dross that is not Helena.
I will be Paris, and for love of thee,
Instead of Troy, shall Wittenberg be sack'd;
And I will combat with weak Menelaus,
And wear thy colours on my plumèd crest;
Yea, I will wound Achilles in the heel,
And then return to Helen for a kiss.
O, thou art fairer than the evening air
Clad in the beauty of a thousand stars;
Brighter art thou than flaming Jupiter
When he appear'd to hapless Semele;
More lovely than the monarch of the sky
In wanton Arethusa's azur'd arms;
And none but thou shalt be my paramour!

—Scene XIV.

O Faustus,
Now hast thou but one bare hour to live,
And then thou must be damn'd perpetually!
Stand still, you ever-moving spheres of heaven,
That time may cease, and midnight never come;
Fair Nature's eye, rise, rise again, and make
Perpetual day; or let this hour be but
A year, a month, a week, a natural day,
That Faustus may repent and save his soul!
O lente, lente currite, noctis equi!
The stars move still, time runs, the clock will strike,
The devil will come, and Faustus must be damn'd.
O, I'll leap up to heaven!—Who pulls me down?—
See, where Christ's blood streams in the firmament!
One drop of blood will save me: O my Christ!—
Rend not my heart for naming of my Christ;
Yet will I call on him: O, spare me, Lucifer!—
Where is it now? 'tis gone:
And, see, a threatening arm, an angry brow!
Mountains and hills, come, come, and fall on me,
And hide me from the heavy wrath of heaven!
No!
Then will I headlong run into the earth:
Gape, earth! O, no, it will not harbour me!
60

CHRISTOPHER MARLOWE

You stars that reign'd at my nativity,
Whose influence hath allotted death and hell,
Now draw up Faustus, like a foggy mist,
Into the entrails of yon labouring cloud,
That, when you vomit forth into the air,
My limbs may issue from your smoky mouths;
But let my soul mount and ascend to heaven!
O, half the hour is past! 'twill all be past anon.
O, if my soul must suffer for my sin,
Impose some end to my incessant pain;
Let Faustus live in hell a thousand years,
A hundred thousand, and at last be sav'd!
No end is limited to damnèd souls.
Why wert thou not a creature wanting soul?
Or why is this immortal that thou hast?
O, Pythagoras' metempsychosis, were that true,
This soul should fly from me, and I be chang'd
Into some brutish beast! all beasts are happy,
For, when they die,
Their souls are soon dissolv'd in elements;
But mine must live still to be plagu'd in hell.
Curs'd be the parents that engender'd me!
No, Faustus, curse thyself, curse Lucifer
That hath depriv'd thee of the joys of heaven.
It strikes, it strikes! Now, body, turn to air,
Or Lucifer will bear thee quick to hell!
O soul, be chang'd into small water-drops,
And fall into the ocean, ne'er be found!
                              —Scene XVI.

HERO AND LEANDER

It lies not in our power to love or hate,
For will in us is over-rul'd by fate.
When two are stript long ere the course begin,
We wish that one should lose, the other win;
And one especially do we affect
Of two gold ingots, like in each respect:
The reason no man knows; let it suffice,
What we behold is censur'd by our eyes.

Where both deliberate, the love is slight:
Who ever lov'd, that lov'd not at first sight?

. . . .

Nor heaven nor thou were made to gaze upon:
As heaven preserves all things, so save thou one
A stately-builded ship, well-rigg'd and tall,
The ocean maketh more majestical:
Why vow'st thou, then, to live in Sestos here,
Who on Love's seas more glorious wouldst appear?
Like untun'd golden strings all women are,
Which long time lie untouch'd, will harshly jar.
Vessels of brass, oft handled, brightly shine:
What difference betwixt the richest mine
And basest mould, but use? for both, not us'd,
Are of like worth. Then treasure is abus'd,
When misers keep it: being put to loan,
In time it will return us two for one.
Rich robes themselves and others do adorn;
Neither themselves nor others, if not worn.
Who builds a palace, and rams up the gate,
Shall see it ruinous and desolate:
Ah, simple Hero, learn thyself to cherish!
Lone women, like to empty houses, perish.

—FIRST SESTIAD

William Shakespeare

SHAKESPEARE

Others abide our question. Thou art free.
We ask and ask—Thou smilest and art still,
Out-topping knowledge. For the loftiest hill,
Who to the stars uncrowns his majesty,

Planting his steadfast footsteps in the sea,
Making the heaven of heavens his dwelling-place,
Spares but the cloudy border of his base
To the foil'd searching of mortality;

62

WILLIAM SHAKESPEARE

And thou, who didst the stars and sunbeams know,
Self-school'd, self-scann'd, self-honour'd, self-secure,
Didst tread on earth unguess'd at.—Better so!

All pains the immortal spirit must endure,
All weakness which impairs, all griefs which bow,
Find their sole speech in that victorious brow.
                                    —MATTHEW ARNOLD.

THE TEMPEST

Come unto these yellow sands,
    And then take hands:
Curtsied when you have, and kiss'd,—
    The wild waves whist,—

Foot it featly here and there;
And, sweet sprites, the burden bear.
        Hark, hark!
    The watch-dogs bark:
    Hark, hark!   I hear
The strain of strutting Chanticleer.
                    —ACT I, SCENE II.

Our revels now are ended.   These our actors,
As I foretold you, were all spirits and
Are melted into air, into thin air:
And, like the baseless fabric of this vision,
The cloud-capp'd towers, the gorgeous palaces,
The solemn temples, the great globe itself,
Yea, all which it inherit, shall dissolve
And, like this insubstantial pageant faded,
Leave not a rack behind.   We are such stuff
As dreams are made on, and our little life
Is rounded with a sleep.
                    —ACT IV, SCENE I.

Where the bee sucks, there suck I
In a cowslip's bell I lie;
There I couch when owls do cry.

63

On the bat's back I do fly
After summer merrily:
Merrily, merrily shall I live now
Under the blossom that hangs on the bough.
                                    —Act V, Scene I.

THE TWO GENTLEMEN OF VERONA

Who is Silvia? what is she?
    That all our swains commend her?
Holy, fair, and wise is she;
    The heaven such grace did lend her,
That she might admired be.

Is she kind as she is fair?
    For beauty lives with kindness:
Love doth to her eyes repair,
    To help him of his blindness;
And, being help'd, inhabits there.

Then to Silvia let us sing,
    That Silvia is excelling;
She excels each mortal thing
    Upon the dull earth dwelling;
To her let us garlands bring.
                                    —Act IV, Scene II.

MEASURE FOR MEASURE

                        But man, proud man,
Drest in a little brief authority,
Most ignorant of what he's most assur'd,
His glassy essence, like an angry ape,
Plays such fantastic tricks before high heaven
As make the angels weep.
                                    —Act II, Scene II.

Ay, but to die, and go we know not where;
    To lie in cold obstruction and to rot;

WILLIAM SHAKESPEARE

This sensible warm motion to become
A kneaded clod; and the delighted spirit
To bathe in fiery floods, or to reside
In thrilling region of thick-ribbed ice;
To be imprison'd in the viewless winds,
And blown with restless violence round about
The pendant world; or to be worse than worst
Of those that lawless and incertain thoughts
Imagine howling: 'tis too horrible!
The weariest and most loathed worldly life
That age, ache, penury and imprisonment
Can lay on nature is a paradise
To what we fear of death.
> —ACT III, SCENE I.

Take, O take those lips away,
    That so sweetly were forsworn;
And those eyes, the break of day,
    Lights that do mislead the morn:
But my kisses bring again,
                bring again,
Seals of love, but seal'd in vain,
                seal'd in vain.
> —ACT IV, SCENE I.

MUCH ADO ABOUT NOTHING

Sigh no more, ladies, sigh no more,
    Men were deceivers ever;
One foot in sea, and one on shore,
    To one thing constant never.
        Then sigh not so,
        But let them go,
And be you blithe and bonny,
Converting all your sounds of woe
Into Hey nonny, nonny.

Sing no more ditties, sing no mo
    Of dumps so dull and heavy;
The fraud of men was ever so,
    Since summer first was leavy.

65

Then sigh not so,
But let them go,
And be you blithe and bonny,
Converting all your sounds of woe
Into Hey nonny, nonny.
—ACT II, SCENE III.

LOVE'S LABOUR'S LOST

On a day, alack the day!
Love, whose month is ever May,
Spied a blossom passing fair
Playing in the wanton air:
Through the velvet leaves the wind,
All unseen, 'gan passage find;
That the lover, sick to death,
Wish'd himself the heaven's breath.
Air, quoth he, thy cheeks may blow;
Air, would I might triumph so!
But alack! my hand is sworn
Ne'er to pluck thee from thy thorn:
Vow, alack! for youth unmeet,
Youth so apt to pluck a sweet.
Do not call it sin in me,
That I am forsworn for thee;
Thou for whom e'en Jove would swear
Juno but an Ethiop were;
And deny himself for Jove,
Turning mortal for thy love.
—ACT IV, SCENE III

When daisies pied and violets blue
    And lady-smocks all silver-white
And cuckoo-buds of yellow hue
    Do paint the meadows with delight,
The cuckoo then, on every tree,
Mocks married men; for thus sings he,
                        Cuckoo;
Cuckoo, cuckoo: O, word of fear,
    Unpleasing to a married ear!

66

WILLIAM SHAKESPEARE

When shepherds pipe on oaten straws,
    And merry larks are ploughmen's clocks,
When turtles tread, and rooks, and daws,
    And maidens bleach their summer smocks,
The cuckoo then, on every tree,
Mocks married men; for thus sings he,
                    Cuckoo;
Cuckoo, cuckoo: O, word of fear,
Unpleasing to a married ear!

   .   .   .   .

When icicles hang by the wall,
    And Dick the shepherd blows his nail,
And Tom bears logs into the hall,
    And milk comes frozen home in pail,
When blood is nipp'd, and ways be foul,
Then nightly sings the staring owl,
                    Tu-who;
Tu-whit, tu-who—a merry note,
While greasy Joan doth keel the pot.

When all aloud the wind doth blow,
    And coughing drowns the parson's saw,
And birds sit brooding in the snow,
    And Marian's nose looks red and raw,
When roasted crabs hiss in the bowl,
Then nightly sings the staring owl,
                    Tu-who;
Tu-whit, tu-who—a merry note,
While greasy Joan doth keel the pot.
                  —ACT V, SCENE II

A MIDSUMMER-NIGHT'S DREAM

Swift as a shadow, short as any dream,
Brief as the lightning in the collied night,
That, in a spleen, unfolds both heaven and earth,
And ere a man hath power to say, "Behold!"
The jaws of darkness do devour it up:
So quick bright things come to confusion.
                  —ACT I, SCENE I

You spotted snakes with double tongue,
  Thorny hedge-hogs, be not seen;
Newts, and blind-worms, do no wrong;
  Come not near our fairy queen.
    Philomel, with melody,
    Sing in our sweet lullaby;
Lulla, lulla, lullaby; lulla, lulla, lullaby:
    Never harm,
    Nor spell, nor charm,
    Come our lovely lady nigh;
    So, good night, with lullaby.

Weaving spiders come not here;
  Hence, you long-legg'd spinners, hence!
Beetles black, approach not near;
  Worm nor snail, do no offence.
    Philomel, with melody,
    Sing in our sweet lullaby;
Lulla, lulla, lullaby; lulla, lulla, lullaby:
    Never harm,
    Nor spell, nor charm,
    Come our lovely lady nigh;
    So, good night, with lullaby.

—ACT II, SCENE II.

        I never may believe
These antique fables, nor these fairy toys.
Lovers and madmen have such seething brains,
Such shaping fantasies, that apprehend
More than cool reason ever comprehends.
The lunatic, the lover, and the poet,
Are of imagination all compact:
One sees more devils than vast hell can hold,
That is, the madman; the lover, all as frantic,
Sees Helen's beauty in a brow of Egypt:
The poet's eye, in a fine frenzy rolling,
Doth glance from heaven to earth, from earth to heaven;
And, as imagination bodies forth
The forms of things unknown, the poet's pen
Turns them to shapes, and gives to airy nothing
A local habitation and a name.
68

WILLIAM SHAKESPEARE

Such tricks hath strong imagination,
That, if it would but apprehend some joy,
It comprehends some bringer of that joy;
Or in the night, imagining some fear,
How easy is a bush suppos'd a bear!

—ACT V, SCENE I.

Now the hungry lion roars,
    And the wolf behowls the moon;
Whilst the heavy ploughman snores,
    All with weary task fordone.
Now the wasted brands do glow,
    Whilst the screech-owl, screeching loud,
Puts the wretch that lies in woe
    In remembrance of a shroud.
Now it is the time of night
    That the graves, all gaping wide,
Every one lets forth his sprite,
    In the church-way paths to glide:
And we fairies, that do run
    By the triple Hecate's team,
From the presence of the sun,
    Following darkness like a dream,
Now are frolic; not a mouse
Shall disturb this hallow'd house:
I am sent with broom before,
To sweep the dust behind the door.

—ACT V, SCENE II.

THE MERCHANT OF VENICE

Tell me where is fancy bred,
Or in the heart or in the head?
How begot, how nourished?
    Reply, reply.

It is engender'd in the eyes,
With gazing fed; and fancy dies
In the cradle where it lies.

69

Let us all ring fancy's knell:
I'll begin it,—Ding, dong, bell.
                    —ACT III, SCENE II.

The quality of mercy is not strain'd,
It droppeth as the gentle rain from heaven
Upon the place beneath: it is twice bless'd;
It blesseth him that gives and him that takes:
'Tis mightiest in the mightiest; it becomes
The throned monarch better than his crown;
His sceptre shows the force of temporal power,
The attribute to awe and majesty,
Wherein doth sit the dread and fear of kings;
But mercy is above this sceptred sway,
It is enthroned in the hearts of kings,
It is an attribute to God himself,
And early power doth then show likest God's
When mercy seasons justice.
                    —ACT IV, SCENE I.

How sweet the moonlight sleeps upon this bank!
Here will we sit, and let the sounds of music
Creep in our ears: soft stillness and the night
Become the touches of sweet harmony.
Sit, Jessica: look, how the floor of heaven
Is thick inlaid with patines of bright gold:
There's not the smallest orb which thou behold'st
But in his motion like an angel sings,
Still quiring to the young-eyed cherubins;
Such harmony is in immortal souls;
But, whilst this muddy vesture of decay
Doth grossly close it in, we cannot hear it.

          .   .   .   .

The man that hath no music in himself,
Nor is not mov'd with concord of sweet sounds,
Is fit for treasons, stratagems, and spoils;
The motions of his spirit are dull as night,
And his affections dark as Erebus:
Let no such man be trusted.
                    —ACT V. SCENE I.

WILLIAM SHAKESPEARE

AS YOU LIKE IT

Under the greenwood tree
Who loves to lie with me,
And turn his merry note
Unto the sweet bird's throat,
Come hither, come hither, come hither:
Here shall he see
No enemy
But winter and rough weather.

.   .   .   .

Who doth ambition shun,
And loves to live i' the sun,
Seeking the food he eats,
And pleas'd with what he gets,
Come hither, come hither, come hither:
Here shall he see
No enemy
But winter and rough weather.
—ACT II, SCENE V

All the world's a stage,
And all the men and women merely players:
They have their exits and their entrances;
And one man in his time plays many parts,
His acts being seven ages. At first the infant,
Mewling and puking in the nurse's arms.
And then the whining school-boy, with his satchel,
And shining morning face, creeping like snail
Unwillingly to school. And then the lover,
Sighing like furnace, with a woful ballad
Made to his mistress' eyebrow. Then a soldier,
Full of strange oaths, and bearded like the pard,
Jealous in honour, sudden and quick in quarrel,
Seeking the bubble reputation
Even in the cannon's mouth. And then the justice,
In fair round belly with good capon lin'd,
With eyes severe, and beard of formal cut,

71

Full of wise saws and modern instances;
And so he plays his part. The sixth age shifts
Into the lean and slipper'd pantaloon,
With spectacles on nose and pouch on side,
His youthful hose well sav'd, a world too wide
For his shrunk shank; and his big manly voice,
Turning again toward childish treble, pipes
And whistles in his sound. Last scene of all,
That ends this strange eventful history,
Is second childishness and mere oblivion,
Sans teeth, sans eyes, sans taste, sans everything.

.   .   .   .

      Blow, blow, thou winter wind,
      Thou art not so unkind
        As man's ingratitude;
      Thy tooth is not so keen,
      Because thou art not seen,
        Although thy breath be rude.
Heigh-ho! sing, heigh-ho! unto the green holly:
Most friendship is feigning, most loving mere folly.
      Then heigh-ho! the holly!
        This life is most jolly.

      Freeze, freeze, thou bitter sky,
      That dost not bite so nigh
        As benefits forgot:
      Though thou the waters warp,
      Thy sting is not so sharp
        As friend remember'd not.
Heigh-ho! sing, heigh-ho! unto the green holly:
Most friendship is feigning, most loving mere folly.
      Then heigh-ho! the holly!
        This life is most jolly.
                —ACT II, SCENE VII

      Why should this a desert be?
        For it is unpeopled? No;
    Tongues I'll hang on every tree,
        That shall civil sayings show.

Some, how brief the life of man
   Runs his erring pilgrimage,
That the stretching of a span
   Buckles in his sum of age;
Some, of violated vows
   'Twixt the souls of friend and friend:
But upon the fairest boughs,
   Or at every sentence' end,
Will I Rosalinda write;
   Teaching all that read to know
The quintessence of every sprite
   Heaven would in little show.
Therefore Heaven Nature charg'd
   That one body should be fill'd
With all graces wide enlarg'd:
   Nature presently distill'd
Helen's cheek, but not her heart,
   Cleopatra's majesty,
Atalanta's better part,
   Sad Lucretia's modesty.
Thus Rosalind of many parts
   By heavenly synod was devis'd
Of many faces, eyes, and hearts,
   To have the touches dearest priz'd.
Heaven would that she these gifts should have,
   And I to live and die her slave.
                —ACT III, SCENE II.

It was a lover and his lass,
   With a hey, and a ho, and a hey nonino,
That o'er the green corn-field did pass,
   In the spring time, the only pretty ring time,
When birds do sing, hey ding a ding, ding;
Sweet lovers love the spring.

Between the acres of the rye,
   With a hey, and a ho, and a hey noninq
These pretty country folks would lie.

This carol they began that hour,
   With a hey, and a ho, and a hey nonino,
How that a life was but a flower.

73

And therefore take the present time,
    With a hey, and a ho, and a hey nonino;
For love is crowned with the prime.
            —ACT V, SCENE III.

TWELFTH-NIGHT

If music be the food of love, play on;
Give me excess of it, that, surfeiting,
The appetite may sicken, and so die.
That strain again! it had a dying fall:
O! it came o'er my ear like the sweet sound
That breathes upon a bank of violets,
Stealing and giving odour. Enough! no more:
'Tis not so sweet now as it was before.
O spirit of love! how quick and fresh art thou,
That, notwithstanding thy capacity
Receiveth as the sea, nought enters there,
Of what validity and pitch soe'er,
But falls into abatement and low price,
Even in a minute: so full of shapes is fancy,
That it alone is high fantastical.
            —ACT I, SCENE I.

O mistress mine! where are you roaming?
O! stay and hear; your true love's coming,
    That can sing both high and low.
Trip no further, pretty sweeting;
Journeys end in lovers meeting,
    Every wise man's son doth know.
            —ACT II, SCENE III

Come away, come away, death,
    And in sad cypress let me be laid;
Fly away, fly away, breath;
    I am slain by a fair cruel maid.
My shroud of white, stuck all with yew,
    O! prepare it.
My part of death, no one so true
    Did share it.

WILLIAM SHAKESPEARE

Not a flower, not a flower sweet,
   On my black coffin let there be strown;
Not a friend, not a friend greet
   My poor corse, where my bones shall be thrown.
A thousand thousand sighs to save,
   Lay me, O! where
Sad true lover never find my grave,
   To weep there.

. . . .

       . . . She never told her love,
But let concealment, like a worm i' the bud,
Feed on her damask cheek: she pin'd in thought,
And with a green and yellow melancholy,
She sat like Patience on a monument,
Smiling at grief.
                   —ACT II, SCENE IV.

THE WINTER'S TALE

        . . . O Proserpina!
For the flowers now that frighted thou let'st fall
From Dis's waggon! daffodils,
That come before the swallow dares, and take
The winds of March with beauty; violets dim,
But sweeter than the lids of Juno's eyes
Or Cytherea's breath; pale prime-roses,
That die unmarried, ere they can behold
Bright Phœbus in his strength, a malady
Most incident to maids; bold oxlips and
The crown imperial; lilies of all kinds,
The flower-de-luce being one.

  .   .   .   .

    Lawn as white as driven snow;
    Cyprus black as e'er was crow;
    Gloves as sweet as damask roses;
    Masks for faces and for noses;

Bugle-bracelet, necklace-amber,
Perfume for a lady's chamber;
Golden quoifs and stomachers,
For my lads to give their dears;
Pins and poking-sticks of steel;
What maids lack from head to heel:
Come buy of me, come; come buy, come
   buy;
Buy, lads, or else your lasses cry:
Come buy.
                    —Act IV, Scene III.

KING JOHN

To gild refinèd gold, to paint the lily,
To throw a perfume on the violet,
To smooth the ice, or add another hue
Unto the rainbow, or with taper-light
To seek the beauteous eye of heaven to garnish,
Is wasteful and ridiculous excess.
                    —Act IV, Scene II.

KING RICHARD THE SECOND

O! who can hold a fire in his hand
By thinking on the frosty Caucasus?
Or cloy the hungry edge of appetite
By bare imagination of a feast?
Or wallow naked in December snow
By thinking on fantastic summer's heat?
O, no! the apprehension of the good
Gives but the greater feeling to the worse:
Fell sorrow's tooth doth never rankle more
Than when it bites, but lanceth not the sore.
                    —Act I, Scene III.

This royal throne of kings, this scepter'd isle,
This earth of majesty, this seat of Mars,
This other Eden, demi-paradise,
76

This fortress built by Nature for herself
Against infection and the hand of war,
This happy breed of men, this little world,
This precious stone set in the silver sea,
Which serves it in the office of a wall,
Or as a moat defensive to a house,
Against the envy of less happier lands,
This blessed plot, this earth, this realm, this England.

—ACT II, SCENE I.

. . . Know'st thou not
That when the searching eye of heaven is hid
Behind the globe, and lights the lower world,
Then thieves and robbers range abroad unseen,
In murders and in outrage bloody here;
But when, from under this terrestrial ball
He fires the proud tops of the eastern pines
And darts his light through every guilty hole,
Then murders, treasons, and detested sins,
The cloak of night being pluck'd from off their backs,
Stand bare and naked, trembling at themselves?

.   .   .   .

. . . Of comfort no man speak:
Let's talk of graves, of worms, and epitaphs;
Make dust our paper, and with rainy eyes
Write sorrow on the bosom of the earth;
Let's choose executors and talk of wills:
And yet not so—for what can we bequeath
Save our deposed bodies to the ground?
Our lands, our lives, and all are Bolingbroke's,
And nothing can we call our own but death,
And that small model of the barren earth
Which serves as paste and cover to our bones.
For God's sake, let us sit upon the ground
And tell sad stories of the death of kings:
How some have been depos'd, some slain in war,
Some haunted by the ghosts they have depos'd,
Some poison'd by their wives, some sleeping kill'd;
All murder'd: for within the hollow crown

77

That rounds the mortal temples of a king
Keeps Death his court, and there the antick sits,
Scoffing his state and grinning at his pomp;
Allowing him a breath, a little scene,
To monarchize, be fear'd, and kill with looks,
Infusing him with self and vain conceit
As if this flesh which walls about our life
Were brass impregnable; and humour'd thus
Comes at the last, and with a little pin
Bores through his castle wall, and farewell king!
Cover your heads, and mock not flesh and blood
With solemn reverence: throw away respect,
Tradition, form, and ceremonious duty,
For you have but mistook me all this while:
I live with bread like you, feel want,
Taste grief, need friends: subjected thus,
How can you say to me I am a king?

—ACT III, SCENE II.

KING HENRY THE FOURTH

. . . O sleep! O gentle sleep!
Nature's soft nurse, how have I frighted thee,
That thou no more wilt weigh my eyelids down
And steep my senses in forgetfulness?
Why rather, sleep, liest thou in smoky cribs,
Upon uneasy pallets stretching thee,
And hush'd with buzzing night-flies to thy slumber,
Than in the perfum'd chambers of the great,
Under the canopies of costly state,
And lull'd with sound of sweetest melody?
O thou dull god! why liest thou with the vile
In loathsome beds, and leav'st the kingly couch
A watch-case or a common 'larum bell?
Wilt thou upon the high and giddy mast
Seel up the ship-boy's eyes, and rock his brains
In cradle of the rude imperious surge,
And in the visitation of the winds,
Who take the ruffian billows by the top,
Curling their monstrous heads, and hanging them
78

WILLIAM SHAKESPEARE

With deaf'ning clamour in the slippery clouds,
That with the hurly death itself awakes?
Canst thou, O partial sleep! give thy repose
To the wet sea-boy in an hour so rude,
And in the calmest and most stillest night,
With all appliances and means to boot,
Deny it to a king? Then, happy low, lie down!
Uneasy lies the head that wears a crown.

—Second Part: Act III, Scene I

KING HENRY THE FIFTH

       . . . So work the honey-bees,
Creatures that by a rule in nature teach
The act of order to a peopled kingdom.
They have a king and officers of sorts;
Where some, like magistrates, correct at home,
Others, like merchants, venture trade abroad,
Others, like soldiers, armed in their stings,
Make boot upon the summer's velvet buds:
Which pillage they with merry march bring home
To the tent-royal of their emperor:
Who, busied in his majesty, surveys
The singing masons building roofs of gold,
The civil citizens kneading up the honey,
The poor mechanic porters crowding in
Their heavy burdens at his narrow gate,
The sad-ey'd justice, with his surly hum,
Delivering o'er to executors pale
The lazy yawning drone.

—Act I, Scene II.

I am not covetous for gold,
Nor care I who doth feed upon my cost;
It yearns me not if men my garments wear;
Such outward things dwell not in my desires:
But if it be a sin to covet honour,
I am the most offending soul alive.

. . . .

We few, we happy few, we band of brothers;
For he to-day that sheds his blood with me
Shall be my brother; be he ne'er so vile
This day shall gentle his condition:
And gentlemen in England, now a-bed
Shall think themselves accurs'd they were not here,
And hold their manhoods cheap whiles any speaks
That fought with us upon Saint Crispin's day.

—ACT IV, SCENE III.

KING RICHARD THE THIRD

Now is the winter of our discontent
Made glorious summer by this sun of York;
And all the clouds that lour'd upon our house
In the deep bosom of the ocean buried.
Now are our brows bound with victorious wreaths;
Our bruised arms hung up for monuments;
Our stern alarums changed to merry meetings;
Our dreadful marches to delightful measures.
Grim-visag'd war hath smooth'd his wrinkled front;
And now,—instead of mounting barbed steeds,
To fright the souls of fearful adversaries,—
He capers nimbly in a lady's chamber
To the lascivious pleasing of a lute.

—ACT I, SCENE I

Methought what pain it was to drown:
What dreadful noise of water in mine ears!
What sights of ugly death within mine eyes!
Methought I saw a thousand fearful wracks;
A thousand men that fishes gnaw'd upon;
Wedges of gold, great anchors, heaps of pearl,
Inestimable stones, unvalu'd jewels,
All scatter'd in the bottom of the sea.
Some lay in dead men's skulls; and in those holes
Where eyes did once inhabit, there were crept,
As 'twere in scorn of eyes, reflecting gems,
That woo'd the slimy bottom of the deep,
And mock'd the dead bones that lay scatter'd by.

—ACT I, SCENE IV.

WILLIAM SHAKESPEARE

KING HENRY THE EIGHTH

Orpheus with his lute made trees,
And the mountain tops that freeze,
　　Bow themselves, when he did sing:
To his music plants and flowers —
Ever sprung; as sun and showers
　　There had made a lasting spring.

Every thing that heard him play,
Even the billows of the sea,
　　Hung their heads, and then lay by.
In sweet music is such art,
Killing care and grief of heart
　　Fall asleep, or hearing, die.
　　　　　　　—ACT III, SCENE I.

Farewell! a long farewell, to all my greatness!
This is the state of man: to-day he puts forth
The tender leaves of hopes; to-morrow blossoms,
And bears his blushing honours thick upon him;
The third day comes a frost, a killing frost;
And, when he thinks, good easy man, full surely
His greatness is a-ripening, nips his root,
And then he falls, as I do. I have ventur'd,
Like little wanton boys that swim on bladders,
This many summers in a sea of glory,
But far beyond my depth: my high-blown pride
At length broke under me, and now has left me,
Weary and old with service, to the mercy
Of a rude stream, that must for ever hide me.
Vain pomp and glory of this world, I hate ye:
I feel my heart new open'd. O! how wretched
Is that poor man that hangs on princes' favours!
There is, betwixt that smile we would aspire to,
That sweet aspect of princes, and their ruin,
More pangs and fears than wars or women have;
And when he falls, he falls like Lucifer,
Never to hope again.

　　·　　·　　·　　·　　·　　·　　·　　·

Love thyself last: cherish those hearts that hate thee;
Corruption wins not more than honesty.
Still in thy right hand carry gentle peace,
To silence envious tongues: be just, and fear not.
Let all the ends thou aim'st at be thy country's,
Thy God's, and truth's; then if thou fall'st, O
    Cromwell!
Thou fall'st a blessed martyr.

—ACT III, SCENE II.

ROMEO AND JULIET

She is the fairies' midwife, and she comes
In shape no bigger than an agate-stone
On the fore-finger of an alderman,
Drawn with a team of little atomies
Athwart men's noses as they lie asleep:
Her waggon-spokes made of long spinners' legs;
The cover, of the wings of grasshoppers;
The traces, of the smallest spider's web;
The collars, of the moonshine's watery beams;
Her whip, of cricket's bone; the lash, of film;
Her waggoner, a small grey-coated gnat,
Not half so big as a round little worm
Prick'd from the lazy finger of a maid;
Her chariot is an empty hazel-nut,
Made by the joiner squirrel or old grub,
Time out o' mind the fairies' coach-makers.
And in this state she gallops night by night
Through lovers' brains, and then they dream of love;
O'er courtiers' knees, that dream on curtsies straight;
O'er lawyers' fingers, who straight dream on fees;
O'er ladies' lips, who straight on kisses dream;
Which oft the angry Mab with blisters plagues,
Because their breaths with sweetmeats tainted are.
Sometimes she gallops o'er a courtier's nose,
And then dreams he of smelling out a suit;
And sometimes comes she with a tithe-pig's tail,
Tickling a parson's nose as a' lies asleep,
Then dreams he of another benefice;

Sometime she driveth o'er a soldier's neck,
And then dreams he of cutting foreign throats,
Of breaches, ambuscadoes, Spanish blades,
Of healths five fathom deep; and then anon
Drums in his ear, at which he starts and wakes;
And, being thus frighted, swears a prayer or two,
And sleeps again.

—ACT I, SCENE IV.

He jests at scars, that never felt a wound.
But, soft! what light through yonder window breaks?
It is the east, and Juliet is the sun!
Arise, fair sun, and kill the envious moon,
Who is already sick and pale with grief,
That thou her maid art far more fair than she:
Be not her maid, since she is envious;
Her vestal livery is but sick and green,
And none but fools do wear it; cast it off.
It is my lady; O! it is my love:
O! that she knew she were.
She speaks, yet she says nothing: what of that?
Her eye discourses; I will answer it.
I am too bold, 'tis not to me she speaks:
Two of the fairest stars in all the heaven,
Having some business, do entreat her eyes
To twinkle in their spheres till they return.
What if her eyes were there, they in her head?
The brightness of her cheek would shame those stars
As daylight doth a lamp; her eyes in heaven
Would through the airy region stream so bright
That birds would sing and think it were not night.
See! how she leans her cheek upon her hand:
O! that I were a glove upon that hand,
That I might touch that cheek.

—ACT II, SCENE II.

JULIUS CÆSAR

I know that virtue to be in you, Brutus,
As well as I do know your outward favour.

83

Well, honour is the subject of my story.
I cannot tell what you and other men
Think of this life; but, for my single self,
I had as lief not be as live to be
In awe of such a thing as I myself.
I was born free as Cæsar; so were you:
We both have fed as well, and we can both
Endure the winter's cold as well as he:
For once, upon a raw and gusty day,
The troubled Tiber chafing with her shores,
Cæsar said to me, "Dar'st thou, Cassius, now
Leap in with me into this angry flood,
And swim to yonder point?" Upon the word,
Accoutred as I was, I plunged in
And bade him follow; so, indeed he did.
The torrent roar'd, and we did buffet it
With lusty sinews, throwing it aside
And stemming it with hearts of controversy;
But ere we could arrive the point propos'd,
Cæsar cried, "Help me, Cassius, or I sink!"
I, as Æneas, our great ancestor,
Did from the flames of Troy upon his shoulder
The old Anchises bear, so from the waves of Tiber
Did I the tired Cæsar. And this man
Is now become a god, and Cassius is
A wretched creature and must bend his body
If Cæsar carelessly but nod on him.
He had a fever when he was in Spain,
And when the fit was on him, I did mark
How he did shake; 'tis true, this god did shake;
His coward lips did from their colour fly,
And that same eye whose bend doth awe the world
Did lose his lustre; I did hear him groan;
Ay, and that tongue of his that bade the Romans
Mark him and write his speeches in their books,
Alas! it cried, "Give me some drink, Titinius,"
As a sick girl. Ye gods, it doth amaze me,
A man of such a feeble temper should
So get the start of the majestic world,
And bear the palm alone.

—ACT I, SCENE II.

WILLIAM SHAKESPEARE

Friends, Romans, countrymen, lend me your ears;
I come to bury Cæsar, not to praise him.
The evil that men do lives after them,
The good is oft interred with their bones;
So let it be with Cæsar. The noble Brutus
Hath told you Cæsar was ambitious;
If it were so, it was a grievous fault,
And grievously hath Cæsar answer'd it.
Here, under leave of Brutus and the rest,—
For Brutus is an honourable man;
So are they all, all honourable men.
He hath brought many captives home to Rome,
Whose ransoms did the general coffers fill:
Did this in Cæsar seem ambitious?
When that the poor have cried, Cæsar hath wept;
Ambition should be made of sterner stuff:
Yet Brutus says he was ambitious;
And Brutus is an honourable man.
You all did see that on the Lupercal
I thrice presented him a kingly crown,
Which he did thrice refuse: was this ambition?
Yet Brutus says he was ambitious;
And, sure, he is an honourable man.
I speak not to disprove what Brutus spoke,
But here I am to speak what I do know.
You all did love him once, not without cause:
What cause withholds you then to mourn for him?
O judgment! thou art fled to brutish beasts,
And men have lost their reason. Bear with me;
My heart is in the coffin there with Cæsar,
And I must pause till it come back to me.
                              —ACT III, SCENE II.

There is a tide in the affairs of men,
Which, taken at the flood, leads on to fortune;
Omitted, all the voyage of their life
Is bound in shallows and in miseries.
On such a full sea are we now afloat;
And we must take the current when it serves,
Or lose our ventures.
                              —ACT IV, SCENE III

This was the noblest Roman of them all;
All the conspirators save only he
Did that they did in envy of great Cæsar;
He only, in a general honest thought
And common good to all, made one of them.
His life was gentle, and the elements
So mix'd in him that Nature might stand up
And say to all the world, "This was a man!"
—Act V, Scene V.

MACBETH

If it were done when 'tis done, then 'twere well
It were done quickly; if the assassination
Could trammel up the consequence, and catch
With his surcease success; that but this blow
Might be the be-all and the end-all here,
But here, upon this bank and shoal of time,
We'd jump the life to come.   But in these cases
We still have judgment here; that we but teach
Bloody instructions, which, being taught, return
To plague the inventor; this even-handed justice
Commends the ingredients of our poison'd chalice
To our own lips.   He's here in double trust:
First, as I am his kinsman and his subject,
Strong both against the deed; then, as his host,
Who should against his murderer shut the door,
Not bear the knife myself.   Besides, this Duncan
Hath borne his faculties so meek, hath been
So clear in his great office, that his virtues
Will plead like angels trumpet-tongu'd against
The deep damnation of his taking-off;
And pity, like a naked new-born babe,
Striding the blast, or heaven's cherubin, hors'd
Upon the sightless couriers of the air,
Shall blow the horrid deed in every eye,
That tears shall drown the wind.   I have no spur
To prick the sides of my intent, but only
Vaulting ambition, which o'er-leaps itself
And falls on the other.—
                                    —Act I, Scene VII.

WILLIAM SHAKESPEARE

Is this a dagger which I see before me,
The handle toward my hand?   Come, let me clutch thee:
I have thee not, and yet I see thee still.
Art thou not, fatal vision, sensible
To feeling as to sight? or art thou but
A dagger of the mind, a false creation,
Proceeding from the heat-oppressed brain?
I see thee yet, in form as palpable
As this which now I draw.
Thou marshall'st me the way that I was going;
And such an instrument I was to use.
Mine eyes are made the fools o' the other senses,
Or else worth all the rest: I see thee still;
And on thy blade and dudgeon gouts of blood,
Which was not so before.   There's no such thing:
It is the bloody business which informs
Thus to mine eyes.   Now o'er the one half-world
Nature seems dead, and wicked dreams abuse
The curtain'd sleep; witchcraft celebrates
Pale Hecate's offerings; and wither'd murder,
Alarum'd by his sentinel, the wolf,
Whose howl's his watch, thus with his stealthy pace,
With Tarquin's ravishing strides, toward his design
Moves like a ghost.   Thou sure and firm-set earth,
Hear not my steps, which way they walk, for fear
Thy very stones prate of my whereabout,
And take the present horror from the time,
Which now suits with it.   Whiles I threat he lives:
Words to the heat of deeds too cold breath gives.
I go, and it is done; the bell invites me.
Hear it not, Duncan; for it is a knell
That summons thee to heaven or to hell.

—Act II, Scene I.

        . . . Better be with the dead,
Whom we, to gain our peace, have sent to peace,
Than on the torture of the mind to lie
In restless ecstasy.   Duncan is in his grave;
After life's fitful fever he sleeps well;
Treason has done his worst: nor steel, nor poison,

Malice domestic, foreign levy, nothing
Can touch him further.

—Act III, Scene II.

Canst thou not minister to a mind diseas'd,
Pluck from the memory a rooted sorrow,
Raze out the written troubles of the brain,
And with some sweet oblivious antidote
Cleanse the stuff'd bosom of that perilous stuff
Which weighs upon the heart?

—Act V, Scene II.

To-morrow, and to-morrow, and to-morrow,
Creeps in this petty pace from day to day,
To the last syllable of recorded time;
And all our yesterdays have lighted fools
The way to dusty death. Out, out, brief candle!
Life's but a walking shadow, a poor player
That struts and frets his hour upon the stage,
And then is heard no more; it is a tale
Told by an idiot, full of sound and fury,
Signifying nothing.

—Act V, Scene V.

HAMLET

O! that this too too solid flesh would melt,
Thaw and resolve itself into a dew;
Or that the Everlasting had not fix'd
His canon 'gainst self-slaughter! O God! O God!
How weary, stale, flat, and unprofitable
Seem to me all the uses of this world.

.   .   .   .

. . . Frailty, thy name is woman!
A little month; or ere those shoes were old
With which she follow'd my poor father's body,
Like Niobe, all tears.

—Act I, Scene II.

88

WILLIAM SHAKESPEARE

The chariest maid is prodigal enough
If she unmask her beauty to the moon;
Virtue herself 'scapes not calumnious strokes;
The canker galls the infants of the spring
Too oft before their buttons be disclos'd,
And in the morn and liquid dew of youth
Contagious blastments are most imminent.
Be wary then; best safety lies in fear:
Youth to itself rebels, though none else near.

. . . .

I shall th' effect of this good lesson keep,
As watchman to my heart.   But, good my brother,
Do not, as some ungracious pastors do,
Show me the steep and thorny way to heaven,
Whiles, like a puff'd and reckless libertine,
Himself the primrose path of dalliance treads,
And recks not his own rede.

. . . .

. . . Give thy thoughts no tongue,
Nor any unproportion'd thought his act.
Be thou familiar, but by no means vulgar;
The friends thou hast, and their adoption tried,
Grapple them to thy soul with hoops of steel;
But do not dull thy palm with entertainment
Of each new-hatch'd, unfledg'd comrade.   Beware
Of entrance to a quarrel, but, being in,
Bear 't that th' opposed may beware of thee.
Give every man thine ear, but few thy voice;
Take each man's censure, but reserve thy judgment.
Costly thy habit as thy purse can buy,
But not express'd in fancy; rich, not gaudy;
For the apparel oft proclaims the man,
And they in France of the best rank and station
Are most select and generous, chief in that.
Neither a borrower, nor a lender be;
For loan oft loses both itself and friend,
And borrowing dulls the edge of husbandry.

89

This above all: to thine own self be true,
And it must follow, as the night the day,
Thou canst not then be false to any man.
—ACT I, SCENE III.

But to my mind,—though I am native here
And to the manner born,—it is a custom
More honour'd in the breach than the observance.
This heavy-headed revel east and west
Makes us traduc'd and tax'd of other nations;
They clepe us drunkards, and with swinish phrase
Soil our addition; and indeed it takes
From our achievements, though perform'd at height,
The pith and marrow of our attribute.
So, oft it chances in particular men,
That for some vicious mole of nature in them,
As, in their birth,—wherein they are not guilty,
Since nature cannot choose his origin,—
By the o'ergrowth of some complexion,
Oft breaking down the pales and forts of reason,
Or by some habit that too much o'er-leavens
The form of plausive manners; that these men,
Carrying, I say, the stamp of one defect,
Being nature's livery, or fortune's star,
Their virtues else, be they as pure as grace,
As infinite as man may undergo,
Shall in the general censure take corruption
From that particular fault: the dram of eale
Doth all the noble substance of a doubt
To his own scandal.

.   .   .   .

Angels and ministers of grace defend us!
Be thou a spirit of health or goblin damn'd,
Bring with thee airs from heaven or blasts from hell,
Be thy intents wicked or charitable,
Thou com'st in such a questionable shape
That I will speak to thee: I'll call thee Hamlet,
King, father; royal Dane, O! answer me:
Let me not burst in ignorance; but tell

WILLIAM SHAKESPEARE

Why thy canoniz'd bones, hearsed in death,
Have burst their cerements; why the sepulchre,
Wherein we saw thee quietly inurn'd,
Hath op'd his ponderous and marble jaws,
To cast thee up again. What may this mean,
That thou, dead corse, again in complete steel
Revisit'st thus the glimpses of the moon,
Making night hideous; and we fools of nature
So horridly to shake our disposition
With thoughts beyond the reaches of our souls?
                                —ACT I, SCENE IV.

            I am thy father's spirit;
Doom'd for a certain term to walk the night,
And for the day confin'd to fast in fires,
Till the foul crimes done in my days of nature
Are burnt and purg'd away. But that I am forbid
To tell the secrets of my prison-house,
I could a tale unfold whose lightest word
Would harrow up thy soul, freeze thy young blood,
Make thy two eyes, like stars, start from their spheres,
Thy knotted and combined locks to part,
And each particular hair to stand on end,
Like quills upon the fretful porpentine:
But this eternal blazon must not be
To ears of flesh and blood.
                                —ACT I, SCENE V.

O! what a rogue and peasant slave am I:
Is it not monstrous that this player here,
But in a fiction, in a dream of passion,
Could force his soul so to his own conceit
That from her working all his visage wann'd,
Tears in his eyes, distraction in 's aspect,
A broken voice, and his whole function suiting
With forms to his conceit? and all for nothing!
For Hecuba!
What's Hecuba to him or he to Hecuba
That he should weep for her? What would he do
Had he the motive and the cue for passion
That I have? He would drown the stage with tears,

And cleave the general ear with horrid speech,
Make mad the guilty and appal the free,
Confound the ignorant, and amaze indeed
The very faculties of eyes and ears.
Yet I,
A dull and muddy-mettled rascal, peak,
Like John-a-dreams, unpregnant of my cause,
And can say nothing; no, not for a king,
Upon whose property and most dear life
A damn'd defeat was made. Am I a coward?
Who calls me villain? breaks my pate across?
Plucks off my beard and blows it in my face?
Tweaks me by the nose? gives me the lie i' the throat,
As deep as to the lungs? Who does me this?
Ha!
Swounds, I should take it, for it cannot be
But I am pigeon-liver'd, and lack gall
To make oppression bitter, or ere this
I should have fatted all the region kites
With this slave's offal. Bloody, bawdy villain!
Remorseless, treacherous, lecherous, kindless villain!
O! vengeance!
Why, what an ass am I! This is most brave
That I, the son of a dear father murder'd,
Prompted to my revenge by heaven and hell,
Must, like a whore, unpack my heart with words,
And fall a-cursing, like a very drab,
A scullion!

—Act II, Scene II.

To be, or not to be: that is the question:
Whether 'tis nobler in the mind to suffer
The slings and arrows of outrageous fortune,
Or to take arms against a sea of troubles,
And by opposing end them? To die: to sleep;
No more; and, by a sleep to say we end
The heart-ache and the thousand natural shocks
That flesh is heir to, 'tis a consummation
Devoutly to be wish'd. To die, to sleep;
To sleep: perchance to dream: ay, there's the rub;
For in that sleep of death what dreams may come

WILLIAM SHAKESPEARE

When we have shuffled off this mortal coil,
Must give us pause. There's the respect
That makes calamity of so long life;
For who would bear the whips and scorns of time,
The oppressor's wrong, the proud man's contumely,
The pangs of dispriz'd love, the law's delay,
The insolence of office, and the spurns
That patient merit of the unworthy takes,
When he himself might his quietus make
With a bare bodkin? who would fardels bear,
To grunt and sweat under a weary life,
But that the dread of something after death,
The undiscover'd country from whose bourn
No traveller returns, puzzles the will,
And makes us rather bear those ills we have
Than fly to others that we know not of?
Thus conscience does make cowards of us all;
And thus the native hue of resolution
Is sicklied o'er with the pale cast of thought,
And enterprises of great pith and moment
With this regard their currents turn awry,
And lose the name of action.
                              —Act III, Scene I

Since my dear soul was mistress of her choice
And could of men distinguish, her election
Hath seal'd thee, for herself; for thou hast been
As one, in suffering all, that suffers nothing,
A man that fortune's buffets and rewards
Hast ta'en with equal thanks; and bless'd are those
Whose blood and judgment are so well comingled
That they are not a pipe for fortune's finger
To sound what stop she please. Give me that man
That is not passion's slave, and I will wear him
In my heart's core, ay, in my heart of heart,
As I do thee.
                              —Act III, Scene II.

See, what a grace was seated on this brow;
Hyperion's curls, the front of Jove himself,
An eye like Mars, to threaten and command,

A station like the herald Mercury
New-lighted on a heaven-kissing hill,
A combination and a form indeed,
Where every god did seem to set his seal,
To give the world assurance of a man.

—Act III, Scene IV.

Sure he that made us with such large discourse,
Looking before and after, gave us not
That capability and god-like reason
To fust in us unus'd. Now, whe'r it be
Bestial oblivion, or some craven scruple
Of thinking too precisely on the event,
A thought, which, quarter'd, hath but one part wisdom,
And ever three parts coward, I do not know
Why yet I live to say "This thing's to do";
Sith I have cause and will and strength and means
To do 't. Examples gross as earth exhort me·
Witness this army of such mass and charge
Led by a delicate and tender prince,
Whose spirit with divine ambition puff'd
Makes mouths at the invisible event,
Exposing what is mortal and unsure
To all that fortune, death and danger dare,
Even for an egg-shell. Rightly to be great
Is not to stir without great argument,
But greatly to find quarrel in a straw
When honour's at the stake.

—Act IV, Scene IV.

KING LEAR

How fearful
And dizzy 'tis to cast one's eyes so low!
The crows and choughs that wing the midway air
Show scarce so gross as beetles; half way down
Hangs one that gathers samphire, dreadful trade!
Methinks he seems no bigger than his head.
The fishermen that walk upon the beach·
Appear like mice, and yond tall anchoring bark
94

WILLIAM SHAKESPEARE

Diminish'd to her cock, her cock a buoy
Almost too small for sight. The murmuring surge,
That on the unnumber'd idle pebbles chafes,
Cannot be heard so high. I'll look no more,
Lest my brain turn, and the deficient sight
Topple down headlong.
—ACT IV, SCENE VI.

OTHELLO

Most potent, grave, and reverend signiors,
My very noble and approv'd good masters,
That I have ta'en away this old man's daughter,
It is most true; true, I have married her:
The very head and front of my offending
Hath this extent, no more. Rude am I in my speech,
And little bless'd with the soft phrase of peace;
For since these arms of mine had seven years' pith,
Till now some nine moons wasted, they have us'd
Their dearest action in the tented field;
And little of this great world can I speak,
More than pertains to feats of broil and battle;
And therefore little shall I grace my cause
In speaking for myself. Yet, by your gracious patience,
I will a round unvarnish'd tale deliver
Of my whole course of love.

　·　·　·　·　·　·　·　·　·

Her father lov'd me; oft invited me;
Still question'd me the story of my life
From year to year, the battles, sieges, fortunes
That I have pass'd.
I ran it through, even from my boyish days
To the very moment that he bade me tell it;
Wherein I spake of most disastrous chances,
Of moving accidents by flood and field,
Of hair-breadth 'scapes i' the imminent deadly breach,
Of being taken by the insolent foe
And sold to slavery, of my redemption thence

95

And portance in my travel's history;
Wherein of antres vast and desarts idle,
Rough quarries, rocks and hills whose heads touch heaven,
It was my hint to speak, such was the process;
And of the Cannibals that each other eat,
The Anthropophagi, and men whose heads
Do grow beneath their shoulders. This to hear
Would Desdemona seriously incline;
But still the house-affairs would draw her thence;
Which ever as she could with haste dispatch,
She'd come again, and with a greedy ear
Devour up my discourse. Which I observing,
Took once a pliant hour, and found good means
To draw from her a prayer of earnest heart
That I would all my pilgrimage dilate,
Whereof by parcels she had something heard,
But not intentively: I did consent;
And often did beguile her of her tears,
When I did speak of some distressful stroke
That my youth suffer'd. My story being done,
She gave me for my pains a world of sighs:
She swore, in faith, 'twas strange, 'twas passing strange;
'Twas pitiful, 'twas wondrous pitiful:
She wish'd she had not heard it, yet she wish'd
That heaven had made her such a man; she thank'd me,
And bade me, if I had a friend that lov'd her,
I should but teach him how to tell my story,
And that would woo her. Upon this hint I spake:
She lov'd me for the dangers I had pass'd,
And I lov'd her that she did pity them.
This only is the witchcraft I have us'd.

—ACT I, SCENE III.

She that was ever fair and never proud,
Had tongue at will and yet was never loud,
Never lack'd gold and yet went never gay,
Fled from her wish and yet said, "Now I may,"
She that being anger'd, her revenge being nigh,
Bade her wrong stay and her displeasure fly,
She that in wisdom never was so frail
To change the cod's head for the salmon's tail,
96

She that could think and ne'er disclose her mind,
See suitors following and not look behind,
She was a wight, if ever such wight were,—
To suckle fools and chronicle small beer.

—ACT II, SCENE I.

Good name in man and woman, dear my lord,
Is the immediate jewel of their souls:
Who steals my purse steals trash; 'tis something, nothing;
'Twas mine, 'tis his, and has been slave to thousands;
But he that filches from me my good name
Robs me of that which not enriches him,
And makes me poor indeed.

.   .   .   .

Farewell the tranquil mind; farewell content!
Farewell the plumed troop and the big wars
That make ambition virtue!   O, farewell!
Farewell the neighing steed, and the shrill trump,
The spirit-stirring drum, the ear-piercing fife,
The royal banner, and all quality,
Pride, pomp, and circumstance of glorious war!
And, O you mortal engines, whose rude throats
The immortal Jove's dread clamours counterfeit,
Farewell!   Othello's occupation's gone!

.   .   .   .

Like to the Pontick sea,
Whose icy current and compulsive course
Ne'er feels retiring ebb, but keeps due on
To the Propontic and the Hellespont,
Even so my bloody thoughts, with violent pace,
Shall ne'er look back, ne'er ebb to humble love,
Till that a capable and wide revenge
Swallow them up.

—ACT III, SCENE III.

I have done the state some service, and they know't;
No more of that.   I pray you, in your letters,

When you shall these unlucky deeds relate,
Speak of me as I am; nothing extenuate,
Nor set down aught in malice: then, must you speak
Of one that lov'd not wisely but too well;
Of one not easily jealous, but, being wrought,
Perplex'd in the extreme; of one whose hand,
Like the base Indian, threw a pearl away
Richer than all his tribe; of one whose subdu'd eyes
Albeit unused to the melting mood,
Drop tears as fast as the Arabian trees
Their med'cinable gum.

       —ACT V, SCENE II.

CYMBELINE

Hark! hark! the lark at heaven's gate sings,
 And Phœbus 'gins arise,
His steeds to water at those springs
 On chalic'd flowers that lies;
And winking Mary-buds begin
 To ope their golden eyes:
With every thing that pretty is,
 My lady sweet, arise:
  Arise, arise!

       —ACT II, SCENE III

Fear no more the heat o' the sun,
 Nor the furious winter's rages;
Thou thy worldly task hast done,
 Home art gone, and ta'en thy wages;
Golden lads and girls all must,
As chimney-sweepers, come to dust.

Fear no more the frown o' the great,
 Thou art past the tyrant's stroke:
Care no more to clothe and eat;
 To thee the reed is as the oak:
The sceptre, learning, physic, must
All follow this, and come to dust.

WILLIAM SHAKESPEARE

Fear no more the lightning-flash,
   Nor the all-dreaded thunder-stone;
Fear not slander, censure rash;
   Thou hast finish'd joy and moan:
All lovers young, all lovers must
Consign to thee, and come to dust.

               —Act IV, Scene II

PERICLES

Thou God of this great vast, rebuke these surges,
Which wash both heaven and hell; and thou, that hast
Upon the winds command, bind them in brass,
Having call'd them from the deep. O! still
Thy deafening, dreadful thunders; gently quench
Thy nimble, sulphurous flashes. O! how Lychorida,
How does my queen? Thou stormest venomously;
Wilt thou spit all thyself? The seaman's whistle
Is as a whisper in the ears of death,
Unheard. Lychorida! Lucina, O!
Divinest patroness, and midwife gentle
To those that cry by night, convey thy deity
Aboard our dancing boat; make swift the pangs
Of my queen's travails!

  .   .   .   .

A terrible child-bed hast thou had, my dear;
No light, no fire: the unfriendly elements
Forgot thee utterly; nor have I time
To give thee hallow'd to thy grave, but straight
Must cast thee, scarcely coffin'd, in the ooze;
Where, for a monument upon thy bones,
And aye-remaining lamps, the belching whale
And humming water must o'erwhelm thy corpse,
Lying with simple shells!

               —Act III, Scene I

VENUS AND ADONIS

.   .   .   .

"Hard-favour'd tyrant, ugly, meagre, lean,
Hateful divorce of love,"—thus chides she Death,—
Grim-grinning ghost, earth's worm, what dost thou mean
To stifle beauty and to steal his breath,
    Who when he liv'd, his breath and beauty set
    Gloss on the rose, smell to the violet?

.   .   .   .

Hadst thou but bid beware, then he had spoke,
And, hearing him, thy power had lost his power.
The Destinies will curse thee for this stroke;
They bid thee crop a weed, thou pluck'st a flower
    Love's golden arrow at him should have fled,
    And not Death's ebon dart, to strike him dead.

.   .   .   .

SONNETS

XII

When I do count the clock that tells the time,
And see the brave day sunk in hideous night;
When I behold the violet past prime,
And sable curls, all silver'd o'er wi h white;
When lofty trees I see barren of le ves,
Which erst from heat did canopy t e herd,
And summer's green all girded up n sheaves,
Borne on the bier with white and bi istly beard,
Then of thy beauty do I question make,
That thou among the wastes of time must go,
Since sweets and beauties do themselves forsake
And die as fast as they see others grow;
    And nothing 'gainst Time's scythe can make defence
    Save breed, to brave him when he takes thee hence.
100

WILLIAM SHAKESPEARE

XV

When I consider every thing that grows
Holds in perfection but a little moment,
That this huge stage presenteth nought but shows
Whereon the stars in secret influence comment;
When I perceive that men as plants increase,
Cheered and check'd e'en by the self-same sky,
Vaunt in their youthful sap, at height decrease,
And wear their brave state out of memory;
Then the conceit of this inconstant stay
Sets you most rich in youth before my sight,
Where wasteful Time debateth with Decay,
To change your day of youth to sullied night;
   And, all in war with Time for love of you,
   As he takes from you, I engraft you new.

XVII

Who will believe my verse in time to come,
If it were fill'd with your most high deserts?
Though yet, heaven knows, it is but as a tomb
Which hides your life and shows not half your parts.
If I could write the beauty of your eyes
And in fresh numbers number all your graces,
The age to come would say, "This poet lies;
Such heavenly touches ne'er touch'd earthly faces."
So should my papers, yellow'd with their age,
Be scorn'd, like old men of less truth than tongue,
And your true rights be term'd a poet's rage
And stretched metre of an antique song:
   But were some child of yours alive that time,
   You should live twice,—in it and in my rime.

XVIII

Shall I compare thee to a summer's day?
Thou art more lovely and more temperate:
Rough winds do shake the darling buds of May,
And summer's lease hath all too short a date:

Sometime too hot the eye of heaven shines,
And often is his gold complexion dimm'd;
And every fair from fair sometime declines,
By chance, or nature's changing course untrimm'd;
But thy eternal summer shall not fade,
Nor lose possession of that fair thou ow'st,
Nor shall death brag thou wander'st in his shade,
When in eternal lines to time thou grow'st;
   So long as men can breathe, or eyes can see,
   So long lives this, and this gives life to thee.

XXIX

When, in disgrace with fortune and men's eyes,
I all alone beweep my outcast state,
And trouble deaf heaven with my bootless cries,
And look upon myself, and curse my fate,
Wishing me like to one more rich in hope,
Featur'd like him, like him with friends possess'd,
Desiring this man's art, and that man's scope,
With what I most enjoy contented least;
Yet in these thoughts myself almost despising,
Haply I think on thee,—and then my state,
Like to the lark at break of day arising
From sullen earth, sings hymns at heaven's gate;
   For thy sweet love remember'd such wealth brings
   That then I scorn to change my state with kings.

XXX

When to the sessions of sweet silent thought
I summon up remembrance of things past,
I sigh the lack of many a thing I sought,
And with old woes new wail my dear times' waste:
Then can I drown an eye, unus'd to flow,
For precious friends hid in death's dateless night,
And weep afresh love's long since cancell'd woe,
And moan the expense of many a vanish'd sight:
Then can I grieve at grievances forgone,
And heavily from woe to woe tell o'er

WILLIAM SHAKESPEARE

The sad account of fore-bemoaned moan,
Which I new pay as if not paid before.
　But if the while I think on thee, dear friend,
　All losses are restor'd and sorrows end.

XXXI

Thy bosom is endeared with all hearts,
Which I by lacking have supposed dead;
And there reigns Love, and all Love's loving parts,
And all those friends which I thought buried.
How many a holy and obsequious tear
Hath dear religious love stol'n from mine eye,
As interest of the dead, which now appear
But things remov'd that hidden in thee lie!
Thou art the grave where buried love doth live,
Hung with the trophies of my lovers gone,
Who all their parts of me to thee did give,
That due of many now is thine alone:
　Their images I lov'd I view in thee,
　And thou—all they—hast all the all of me.

XXXIII

Full many a glorious morning have I seen
Flatter the mountain-tops with sovereign eye,
Kissing with golden face the meadows green,
Gilding pale streams with heavenly alchymy;
Anon permit the basest clouds to ride
With ugly rack on his celestial face,
And from the forlorn world his visage hide,
Stealing unseen to west with this disgrace:
Even so my sun one early morn did shine,
With all-triumphant splendour on my brow;
But, out! alack! he was but one hour mine,
The region cloud hath mask'd him from me now.
　Yet him for this my love no whit disdaineth;
　Suns of the world may stain when heaven's sun staineth.

XXXIX

O! how thy worth with manners may I sing,
When thou art all the better part of me?
What can mine own praise to mine own self bring?
And what is 't but mine own when I praise thee?
Even for this let us divided live,
And our dear love lose name of single one,
That by this separation I may give
That due to thee, which thou deserv'st alone.
O absence; what a torment wouldst thou prove,
Were it not thy sour leisure gave sweet leave
To entertain the time with thoughts of love,
Which time and thoughts so sweetly doth deceive,
   And that thou teachest how to make one twain,
   By praising him here who doth hence remain.

LIV

O! how much more doth beauty beauteous seem
By that sweet ornament which truth doth give!
The rose looks fair, but fairer we it deem
For that sweet odour which doth in it live.
The canker-blooms have full as deep a dye
As the perfumed tincture of the roses,
Hang on such thorns, and play as wantonly
When summer's breath their masked buds discloses:
But, for their virtue only is their show,
They live unwoo'd, and unrespected fade;
Die to themselves. Sweet roses do not so;
Of their sweet deaths are sweetest odours made:
   And so of you, beauteous and lovely youth,
   When that shall vade, my verse distils your truth.

LV

Not marble, nor the gilded monuments
Of princes, shall outlive this powerful rime;
But you shall shine more bright in these contents
Than unswept stone, besmear'd with sluttish time.

WILLIAM SHAKESPEARE

When wasteful war shall statues overturn,
And broils root out the work of masonry,
Nor Mars his sword nor war's quick fire shall burn
The living record of your memory.
'Gainst death and all-oblivious enmity
Shall you pace forth; your praise shall still find room
Even in the eyes of all posterity
That wear this world out to the ending doom.
So, till the judgment that yourself arise,
You live in this, and dwell in lovers' eyes.

LVII

Being your slave, what should I do but tend
Upon the hours and times of your desire?
I have no precious time at all to spend,
Nor services to do, till you require.
Nor dare I chide the world-without-end hour
Whilst I, my sovereign, watch the clock for you,
Nor think the bitterness of absence sour
When you have bid your servant once adieu;
Nor dare I question with my jealous thought
Where you may be, or your affairs suppose,
But, like a sad slave, stay and think of nought,
Save, where you are how happy you make those.
So true a fool is love that in your will,
Though you do anything, he thinks no ill.

LX

Like as the waves make towards the pebbled shore,
So do our minutes hasten to their end;
Each changing place with that which goes before,
In sequent toil all forwards do contend.
Nativity, once in the main of light,
Crawls to maturity, wherewith being crown'd,
Crooked eclipses 'gainst his glory fight,
And Time that gave doth now his gift confound.
Time doth transfix the flourish set on youth
And delves the parallels in beauty's brow,

Feeds on the rarities of nature's truth,
And nothing stands but for his scythe to mow:
    And yet to times in hope my verse shall stand,
    Praising thy worth, despite his cruel hand.

LXI

Is it thy will thy image should keep open
My heavy eyelids to the weary night?
Dost thou desire my slumbers should be broken,
While shadows, like to thee, do mock my sight?
Is it thy spirit that thou send'st from thee
So far from home, into my deeds to pry,
To find out shames and idle hours in me,
The scope and tenour of thy jealousy?
O, no! thy love, though much, is not so great:
It is my love that keeps mine eye awake;
Mine own true love that doth my rest defeat,
To play the watchman ever for thy sake:
    For thee watch I whilst thou dost wake elsewhere,
    From me far off, with others all too near.

LXV

Since brass, nor stone, nor earth, nor boundless sea,
But sad mortality o'er sways their power,
How with this rage shall beauty hold a plea,
Whose action is no stronger than a flower?
O! how shall summer's honey breath hold out
Against the wrackful siege of battering days,
When rocks impregnable are not so stout,
Nor gates of steel so strong, but Time decays?
O fearful meditation! where, alack,
Shall Time's best jewel from Time's chest lie hid?
Or what strong hand can hold his swift foot back?
Or who his spoil of beauty can forbid?
    O! none, unless this miracle have might,
    That in black ink my love may still shine bright.

WILLIAM SHAKESPEARE

LXXI

No longer mourn for me when I am dead
Than you shall hear the surly sullen bell
Give warning to the world that I am fled
From this vile world, with vilest worms to dwell:
Nay, if you read this line, remember not
The hand that writ it; for I love you so,
That I in your sweet thoughts would be forgot,
If thinking on me then should make you woe.
O! if,—I say, you look upon this verse,
When I perhaps compounded am with clay,
Do not so much as my poor name rehearse,
But let your love even with my life decay;
    Lest the wise world should look into your moan,
    And mock you with me after I am gone.

LXXII

O! lest the world should task you to recite
What merit lived in me, that you should love
After my death,—dear love, forget me quite,
For you in me can nothing worthy prove;
Unless you would devise some virtuous lie,
To do more for me than mine own desert,
And hang more praise upon deceased I
Than niggard truth would willingly impart:
O! lest your true love may seem false in this,
That you for love speak well of me untrue,
My name be buried where my body is,
And live no more to shame nor me nor you.
    For I am sham'd by that which I bring forth,
    And so should you, to love things nothing worth.

LXXIII

That time of year thou may'st in me behold
When yellow leaves, or none, or few, do hang
Upon those boughs which shake against the cold,
Bare ruin'd choirs, where late the sweet birds sang.

107

In me thou see'st the twilight of such day
As after sunset fadeth in the west;
Which by and by black night doth take away,
Death's second self, that seals up all in rest.
In me thou see'st the glowing of such fire,
That on the ashes of his youth doth lie,
As the death-bed whereon it must expire
Consum'd with that which it was nourish'd by.
   This thou perceiv'st, which makes thy love more strong,
   To love that well which thou must leave ere long.

LXXVI

Why is my verse so barren of new pride,
So far from variation or quick change?
Why with the time do I not glance aside
To new-found methods and to compounds strange?
Why write I still all one, ever the same,
And keep invention in a noted weed,
That every word doth almost tell my name,
Showing their birth, and where they did proceed?
O! know, sweet love, I always write of you,
And you and love are still my argument;
So all my best is dressing old words new,
Spending again what is already spent:
   For as the sun is daily new and old,
   So is my love still telling what is told.

LXXXI

Or I shall live your epitaph to make,
Or you survive when I in earth am rotten;
From hence your memory death cannot take,
Although in me each part will be forgotten.
Your name from hence immortal life shall have,
Though I, once gone, to all the world must die:
The earth can yield me but a common grave,
When you entombed in men's eyes shall lie.
Your monument shall be my gentle verse,
Which eyes not yet created shall o'er-read;

108

And tongues to be your being shall rehearse,
When all the breathers of this world are dead;
  You still shall live,   such virtue hath my pen,—
  Where breath most breathes,—even in the mouths
    men.

LXXXIV

Who is it that says most? which can say more
Than this rich praise,—that you alone are you?
In whose confine immured is the store
Which should example where your equal grew.
Lean penury within that pen doth dwell
That to his subject lends not some small glory;
But he that writes of you, if he can tell
That you are you, so dignifies his story,
Let him but copy what in you is writ,
Not making worse what nature made so clear,
And such a counterpart shall fame his wit,
Making his style admired everywhere.
  You to your beauteous blessings add a curse,
  Being fond on praise, which makes your praises worse.

LXXXVI

Was it the proud full sail of his great verse,
Bound for the prize of all too precious you,
That did my ripe thoughts in my brain inhearse,
Making their tomb the womb wherein they grew?
Was it his spirit, by spirits taught to write
Above a mortal pitch, that struck me dead?
No, neither he, nor his compeers by night
Giving him aid, my verse astonished.
He, nor that affable familiar ghost
Which nightly gulls him with intelligence,
As victors of my silence cannot boast;
I was not sick of any fear from thence:
  But when your countenance fill'd up his line,
  Then lack'd I matter; that enfeebled mine.

109

LXXXVII

Farewell! thou art too dear for my possessing,
And like enough thou know'st thy estimate:
The charter of thy worth gives thee releasing;
My bonds in thee are all determinate.
For how do I hold thee but by thy granting?
And for that riches where is my deserving?
The cause of this fair gift in me is wanting,
And so my patent back again is swerving.
Thyself thou gav'st, thy own worth then not knowing,
Or me, to whom thou gav'st it, else mistaking;
So thy great gift, upon misprision growing,
Comes home again, on better judgment making.
   Thus have I had thee, as a dream doth flatter,
   In sleep a king, but, waking, no such matter.

LXXXIX

Say that thou didst forsake me for some fault,
And I will comment upon that offence:
Speak of my lameness, and I straight will halt,
Against thy reasons making no defence.
Thou canst not, love, disgrace me half so ill,
To set a form upon desired change,
As I'll myself disgrace; knowing thy will,
I will acquaintance strangle, and look strange;
Be absent from thy walks; and in my tongue
Thy sweet beloved name no more shall dwell,
Lest I, too much profane, should do it wrong,
And haply of our old acquaintance tell.
   For thee, against myself I'll vow debate,
   For I must ne'er love him whom thou dost hate.

XCVII

How like a winter hath my absence been
From thee, the pleasure of the fleeting year!
What freezings have I felt, what dark days seen!
What old December's bareness every where!

And yet this time remov'd was summer's time;
The teeming autumn, big with rich increase,
Bearing the wanton burden of the prime,
Like widow'd wombs after their lords' decease:
Yet this abundant issue seem'd to me
But hope of orphans and unfather'd fruit;
For summer and his pleasures wait on thee,
And, thou away, the very birds are mute:
　　Or, if they sing, 'tis with so dull a cheer,
　　That leaves look pale, dreading the winter's near.

XCVIII

From you have I been absent in the spring,
When proud-pied April, dress'd in all his trim,
Hath put a spirit of youth in every thing,
That heavy Saturn laugh'd and leap'd with him.
Yet nor the lays of birds, nor the sweet smell
Of different flowers in odour and in hue,
Could make me any summer's story tell,
Or from their proud lap pluck them where they grew:
Nor did I wonder at the lily's white,
Nor praise the deep vermilion in the rose;
They were but sweet, but figures of delight,
Drawn after you, you pattern of all those.
　　Yet seem'd it winter still, and, you away,
　　As with your shadow I with these did play.

XCIX

The forward violet thus did I chide:
Sweet thief, whence didst thou steal thy sweet that smells,
If not from my love's breath?　The purple pride
Which on thy soft cheek for complexion dwells
In my love's veins thou hast too grossly dy'd.
The lily I condemned for thy hand,
And buds of marjoram had stol'n thy hair;
The roses fearfully on thorns did stand,
One blushing shame, another white despair;
A third, nor red nor white, had stol'n of both,

III

And to his robbery had annex'd thy breath;
But, for his theft, in pride of all his growth
A vengeful canker eat him up to death.
  More flowers I noted, yet I none could see
  But sweet or colour it had stol'n from thee.

CIV

To me, fair friend, you never can be old,
For as you were when first your eye I ey'd,
Such seems your beauty still. Three winters cold
Have from the forests shook three summers' pride,
Three beauteous springs to yellow autumn turn'd
In process of the seasons have I seen,
Three April perfumes in three hot Junes burn'd,
Since first I saw you fresh, which yet are green.
Ah! yet doth beauty, like a dial-hand,
Steal from his figure, and no pace perceiv'd;
So your sweet hue, which methinks still doth stand,
Hath motion, and mine eye may be deceiv'd:
  For fear of which, hear this, thou age unbred:
  Ere you were born was beauty's summer dead.

CVI

When in the chronicle of wasted time
I see descriptions of the fairest wights,
And beauty making beautiful old rime,
In praise of ladies dead and lovely knights,
Then, in the blazon of sweet beauty's best,
Of hand, of foot, of lip, of eye, of brow,
I see their antique pen would have express'd
Even such a beauty as you master now.
So all their praises are but prophecies
Of this our time, all you prefiguring;
And, for they look'd but with divining eyes,
They had not skill enough your worth to sing:
  For we, which now behold these present days,
  Have eyes to wonder, but lack tongues to praise.

WILLIAM SHAKESPEARE

CXVI

Let me not to the marriage of true minds
Admit impediments. Love is not love
Which alters when it alteration finds,
Or bends with the remover to remove:
O, no! it is an ever-fixed mark,
That looks on tempests and is never shaken;
It is the star to every wandering bark,
Whose worth's unknown, although his height be taken.
Love's not Time's fool, though rosy lips and cheeks
Within his bending sickle's compass come;
Love alters not with his brief hours and weeks,
But bears it out even to the edge of doom.
   If this be error, and upon me prov'd,
   I never writ, nor no man ever lov'd.

CXXIX

The expense of spirit in a waste of shame
Is lust in action; and till action, lust
Is perjur'd, murderous, bloody, full of blame,
Savage, extreme, rude, cruel, not to trust;
Enjoy'd no sooner but despised straight;
Past reason hunted; and no sooner had,
Past reason hated, as a swallow'd bait,
On purpose laid to make the taker mad:
Mad in pursuit, and in possession so;
Had, having, and in quest to have, extreme;
A bliss in proof,—and prov'd, a very woe;
Before, a joy propos'd; behind, a dream.
   All this the world well knows; yet none knows well
   To shun the heaven that leads men to this hell.

CRABBÈD AGE AND YOUTH

Crabbèd Age and Youth cannot live together:
   Youth is full of pleasure, age is full of care;
Youth like summer morn, age like winter weather,
   Youth like summer brave, age like winter bare:

Youth is full of sport, age's breath is short;
  Youth is nimble, age is lame:
Youth is hot and bold, age is weak and cold,
  Youth is wild, and age is tame.
Age, I do abhor thee, youth, I do adore thee;
  O! my love, my love is young:
Age, I do defy thee: O! sweet shepherd, hie thee,
  For methinks thou stay'st too long.
                        —THE PASSIONATE PILGRIM.

Thomas Campion

WHEN TO HER LUTE CORINNA SINGS

When to her lute Corinna sings,
Her voice revives the leaden strings,
And doth in highest notes appear,
As any challenged echo clear:
But when she doth of mourning speak,
E'en with her sighs, the strings do break.

And as her lute doth live or die,
Led by her passion, so must I;
For when of pleasure she doth sing,
My thoughts enjoy a sudden spring,
But if she doth of sorrow speak,
E'en from my heart the strings do break.

FOLLOW THY FAIR SUN

Follow thy fair sun, unhappy shadow,
  Though thou be black as night,
  And she made all of light;
Yet follow thy fair sun, unhappy shadow!

Follow her, whose light thy light depriveth!
  Though here thou livest disgraced,
  And she in heaven is placed;
Yet follow her whose light the world reviveth!

THOMAS CAMPION

Follow those pure beams, whose beauty burneth!
  That so have scorched thee;
  As thou still black must be,
Till her kind beams thy black to brightness turneth!

Follow her, while yet her glory shineth!
  There comes a luckless night
  That will dim all her light;
And this the black unhappy shade divineth.

Follow still, since so thy Fates ordained!
  The sun must have his shade,
  Till both at once do fade;
The sun still proved, the shadow still disdained!

NOW WINTER NIGHTS ENLARGE

Now winter nights enlarge
  The number of their hours,
And clouds their storms discharge
  Upon the airy towers.
Let now the chimneys blaze
  And cups o'erflow with wine;
Let well-tuned words amaze
  With harmony divine.
Now yellow waxen lights
  Shall wait on honey love,
While youthful revels, masques, and courtly sights
  Sleep's leaden spells remove.
This time doth well dispense
  With lovers' long discourse;
Much speech hath some defence,
  Though beauty no remorse.
All do not all things well;
  Some measures comely tread,
Some knotted riddles tell,
  Some poems smoothly read.
The summer hath his joys,
  And winter his delights;
Though love and all his pleasures are but toys,
  They shorten tedious nights.

115

THE CHARM

Thrice toss these oaken ashes in the air,
Thrice sit thou mute in this enchanted chair,
Then thrice-three times tie up this true love's knot,
And murmur soft "She will or she will not."

Go, burn these poisonous weeds in yon blue fire,
These screech-owl's feathers and this prickling briar,
This cypress gathered at a dead man's grave,
That all thy fears and cares an end may have.

Then come, you Fairies! dance with me a round!
Melt her hard heart with your melodious sound!
In vain are all the charms I can devise:
She hath an art to break them with her eyes.

CHERRY-RIPE

There is a garden in her face
    Where roses and white lilies blow;
A heavenly paradise is that place,
    Wherein all pleasant fruits do grow;
There cherries grow that none may buy,
Till cherry-ripe themselves do cry.

Those cherries fairly do enclose
    Of orient pearl a double row,
Which when her lovely laughter shows,
    They look like rose-buds filled with snow:
Yet them no peer nor prince may buy,
Till cherry-ripe themselves do cry.

Her eyes like angels watch them still;
    Her brows like bended bows do stand,
Threat'ning with piercing frowns to kill
    All that approach with eye or hand
These sacred cherries to come nigh—
Till Cherry-ripe themselves do cry!

THOMAS CAMPION

FOLLOW YOUR SAINT

Follow your saint. Follow, with accents sweet!
Haste you, sad notes, fall at her flying feet!
There, wrapped in cloud of sorrow, pity move,
And tell the ravisher of my soul I perish for her love.
But if she scorns my never-ceasing pain,
Then burst with sighing in her sight, and ne'er return again!
All that I sang, still to her praise did tend.
Still she was first, still she my songs did end;
Yet she my love and music both doth fly,
The music that her echo is, and beauty's sympathy:
Then let my notes pursue her scornful flight!
It shall suffice that they were breathed and died for her
    delight.

THE MAN OF LIFE UPRIGHT

The man of life upright,
    Whose guiltless heart is free
From all dishonest deeds,
    Or thought of vanity;

The man whose silent days
    In harmless joys are spent,
Whom hopes cannot delude
    Nor sorrow discontent:

That man needs neither towers
    Nor armour for defence,
Nor secret vaults to fly
    From thunder's violence:

He only can behold
    With unaffrighted eyes
The horrors of the deep
    And terrors of the skies.

Thus scorning all the cares
    That fate or fortune brings,
He makes the heaven his book,
    His wisdom heavenly things;

Good thoughts his only friends,
    His wealth a well-spent age,
The earth his sober inn
    And quiet pilgrimage.

THE MEASURE OF BEAUTY

Give Beauty all her right,
    She's not to one form tied;
Each shape yields fair delight,
    Where her perfections bide:
Helen, I grant, might pleasing be,
And Ros'mond was as sweet as she.

Some the quick eye commends,
    Some swelling lips and red;
Pale looks have many friends,
    Through sacred sweetness bred:
Meadows have flowers that pleasure move,
Though roses are the flowers of love.

Free beauty is not bound
    To one unmoved clime;
She visits every ground
    And favours every time.
Let the old loves with mine compare,
My sovereign is as sweet and fair.

KIND ARE HER ANSWERS

Kind are her answers,
But her performance keeps no day;
    Breaks time, as dancers
    From their own music when they stray.
All her free favours and smooth words,
    Wing my hopes in vain.
O did ever voice so sweet but only feign?
    Can true love yield such delay,
    Converting joy to pain?

Lost is our freedom,
When we submit to women so:
Why do we need them
When, in their best they work our woe?
There is no wisdom
Can alter ends, by Fate prefixed.
O why is the good of man with evil mixed?
Never were days yet called two,
But one night went betwixt.

JACK AND JOAN

Jack and Joan they think no ill,
But loving live, and merry still;
Do their week-days' work, and pray
Devoutly on the holy day:
Skip and trip it on the green,
And help to choose the Summer Queen;
Lash out, at a country feast,
Their silver penny with the best.

Well can they judge of nappy ale,
And tell at large a winter tale;
Climb up to the apple loft,
And turn the crabs till they be soft.
Tib is all the father's joy,
And little Tom the mother's boy.
All their pleasure is Content;
And care, to pay their yearly rent.

Joan can call by name her cows,
And deck her window with green boughs;
She can wreaths and tutties make,
And trim with plums a bridal cake.
Jack knows what brings gain or loss;
And his long flail can stoutly toss:
Makes the hedge, which others break;
And ever thinks what he doth speak.

Now, you courtly dames and knights,
That study only strange delights;

Though you scorn the homespun grey,
And revel in your rich array:
Though your tongues dissemble deep,
And can your heads from danger keep;
Yet, for all your pomp and train,
Securer lives the silly swain.

WHEN THOU MUST HOME

When thou must home to shades of underground,
And there arrived, a new admired guest,
The beauteous spirits do engirt thee round,
White Iope, blithe Helen, and the rest,
To hear the stories of thy finished love
From that smooth tongue whose music hell can move;

Then wilt thou speak of banqueting delights,
Of masques and revels which sweet youth did make,
Of tourneys and great challenges of knights,
And all these triumphs for thy beauty's sake:
When thou hast told these honours done to thee,
Then tell, O tell, how thou didst murder me.

Sir Henry Wotton

ELIZABETH OF BOHEMIA

You meaner beauties of the night,
    That poorly satisfy our eyes
More by your number than your light,
    You common people of the skies;
    What are you when the moon shall rise?

You curious chanters of the wood,
    That warble forth Dame Nature's lays,
Thinking your passions understood
    By your weak accents; what's your praise
    When Philomel her voice shall raise?

SIR HENRY WOTTON

You violets that first appear,
  By your pure purple mantles known
Like the proud virgins of the year,
  As if the spring were all your own;
  What are you when the rose is blown?

So, when my mistress shall be seen
  In form and beauty of her mind,
By virtue first, then choice, a Queen,
  Tell me, if she were not designed
  Th' eclipse and glory of her kind.

THE CHARACTER OF A HAPPY LIFE

How happy is he born and taught
  That serveth not another's will;
Whose armor is his honest thought,
  And simple truth his utmost skill!

Whose passions not his masters are;
  Whose soul is still prepared for death,
Not tied unto the world by care
  Of public fame or private breath;

Who envies none that chance doth raise,
  Nor vice; who never understood
How deepest wounds are given by praise;
  Nor rules of state, but rules of good;

Who hath his life from rumors freed;
  Whose conscience is his strong retreat;
Whose state can neither flatterers feed,
  Nor ruin make oppressors great;

Who God doth late and early pray
  More of His grace than gifts to lend;
And entertains the harmless day
  With a well-chosen book or friend;

—This man is freed from servile bands
  Of hope to rise, or fear to fall:
Lord of himself, though not of lands,
  And having nothing, yet hath all.

Thomas Dekker

SWEET CONTENT

Art thou poor, yet hast thou golden slumbers?
  O sweet content!
Art thou rich, yet is thy mind perplexed?
  O punishment!
Dost thou laugh to see how fools are vexed
To add to golden numbers golden numbers?
  O sweet content! O sweet, O sweet content!

Canst drink the waters of the crispèd spring?
  O sweet content!
Swimm'st thou in wealth, yet sink'st in thine own tears?
  O punishment!
Then he that patiently want's burden bears,
No burden bears, but is a king, a king!
O sweet content! O sweet, O sweet content!
  Work apace, apace, apace, apace;
  Honest labour bears a lovely face!
                    —PATIENT GRISSEL.

Thomas Heywood

YE LITTLE BIRDS THAT SIT AND SING

Ye little birds that sit and sing
  Amidst the shady valleys,
And see how Phillis sweetly walks
  Within her garden-alleys;

Go, pretty birds, about her bower;
Sing, pretty birds, she may not lower;
Ah, me! methinks I see her frown!
    Ye pretty wantons, warble.

Go, tell her through your chirping bills,
    As you by me are bidden,
To her is only known my love,
    Which from the world is hidden.
Go, pretty birds, and tell her so;
See that your notes strain not too low,
For still, methinks, I see her frown;
    Ye pretty wantons, warble.

Go, tune your voices' harmony,
    And sing, I am her lover;
Strain loud and sweet, that every note
    With sweet content may move her:
And she that hath the sweetest voice,
Tell her I will not change my choice;
Yet still, methinks, I see her frown!
    Ye pretty wantons, warble.

Oh, fly! make haste! see, see, she falls
    Into a pretty slumber!
Sing round about her rosy bed,
    That waking, she may wonder.
Say to her, 'tis her lover true
That sendeth love to you, to you!
And when you hear her kind reply,
    Return with pleasant warblings.
          —THE FAIR MAID OF THE EXCHANGE.

PSYCHE

But Psyche lives, and on her breath attend
Delights that far surmount all earthly joy;
Music, sweet voices, and ambrosian fare;
Winds, and the light-winged creatures of the air;
Clear channeled rivers, springs, and flowery meads,

Are proud when Psyche wantons on their streams,
When Psyche on their rich embroidery treads,
When Psyche gilds their crystal with her beams.
We have but seen our sister, and, behold!
She sends us with our laps full brimmed with gold.

PACK, CLOUDS, AWAY!

Pack, clouds, away! and welcome, day!
   With night we banish sorrow.
Sweet air, blow soft; mount, lark, aloft
   To give my Love good-morrow!
Wings from the wind to please her mind,
   Notes from the lark I'll borrow:
Bird, prune thy wing! nightingale, sing!
   To give my Love good-morrow!
   To give my Love good-morrow,
   Notes from them all I'll borrow.

Wake from thy nest, robin red-breast!
   Sing, birds, in every furrow!
And from each bill let music shrill
   Give my fair Love good-morrow!
Blackbird and thrush in every bush,
   Stare, linnet, and cock-sparrow,
You pretty elves, amongst yourselves,
   Sing my fair Love good-morrow!
   To give my Love good-morrow!
   Sing, birds, in every furrow!
      —THE RAPE OF LUCRECE

Ben Jonson

BEN JONSON

Broad-based, broad-fronted, bounteous, multiform,
  With many a valley impleached with ivy and vine,
  Wherein the springs of all the streams run wine,
And many a crag full-faced against the storm,

BEN JONSON

The mountain where thy Muse's feet made warm
Those lawns that revelled with her dance divine,
Shines yet with fire as it was wont to shine
From tossing torches round the dance a-swarm.

Nor less, high-stationed on the grey grave heights,
High-thoughted seers with heaven's heart-kindling lights
Hold converse: and the herd of meaner things
Knows or by fiery scourge or fiery shaft
When wrath on thy broad brows has risen, and laughed,
Darkening thy soul with shadow of thunderous wings.
—ALGERNON CHARLES SWINBURNE.

TO THE MEMORY OF MY BELOVED MASTER WILLIAM SHAKESPEARE, AND WHAT HE HATH LEFT US

                     . . . Soul of the age!
The applause, delight, the wonder of our stage!
My Shakespeare, rise! I will not lodge thee by
Chaucer, or Spenser, or bid Beaumont lie
A little further, to make thee a room:
Thou art a monument without a tomb,
And art alive still while thy book doth live
And we have wits to read and praise to give.
That I not mix thee so, my brain excuses,
I mean with great, but disproportioned Muses;
For if I thought my judgment were of years,
I should commit thee surely with thy peers,
And tell how far thou didst our Lyly outshine,
Or sporting Kyd, or Marlowe's mighty line.
And though thou hadst small Latin and less Greek,
From thence to honour thee, I would not seek
For names; but call forth thundering Æschylus,
Euripides, and Sophocles to us;
Pacuvius, Accius, him of Cordova dead,
To life again, to hear thy buskin tread,
And shake a stage; or, when thy socks were on,
Leave thee alone for the comparison
Of all that insolent Greece or haughty Rome
Sent forth, or since did from their ashes come.

Triumph, my Britain, thou hast one to show
To whom all scenes of Europe homage owe.
He was not of an age, but for all time!
And all the Muses still were in their prime,
When, like Apollo, he came forth to warm
Our ears, or like a Mercury to charm!
Nature herself was proud of his designs
And joyed to wear the dressing of his lines!
Which were so richly spun, and woven so fit,
As, since, she will vouchsafe no other wit.
The merry Greek, tart Aristophanes,
Neat Terence, witty Plautus, now not please;
But antiquated and deserted lie,
As they were not of Nature's family.
Yet must I not give Nature all; thy Art
My gentle Shakespeare, must enjoy a part.
For though the poet's matter nature be,
His art doth give the fashion; and, that he
Who casts to write a living line, must sweat,
(Such as thine are) and strike the second heat
Upon the Muses' anvil; turn the same
(And himself with it) that he thinks to frame,
Or, for the laurel, he may gain a scorn;
For a good poet's made, as well as born.
And such wert thou!   Look how the father's face
Lives in his issue, even so the race
Of Shakespeare's mind and manners brightly shines
In his well-turnèd, and true-filèd lines;
In each of which he seems to shake a lance,
As brandished at the eyes of ignorance.

.   .   .   .

EPITAPH ON ELIZABETH L. H.

Wouldst thou hear what man can say
In a little? Reader, stay.

Underneath this stone doth lie
As much beauty as could die;
Which in life did harbour give
To more virtue than doth live.

If at all she had a fault,
Leave it buried in this vault.
One name was Elizabeth,
The other, let it sleep with death:
Fitter, where it died, to tell
Than that it lived at all.   Farewell.

ON THE PORTRAIT OF SHAKESPEARE

This figure that thou here seest put,
It was for gentle Shakespeare cut,
Wherein the graver had a strife
With Nature, to outdo the life.
    Oh, could he but have drawn his wit
As well in brass, as he has hit
His face, the print would then surpass
All that was ever writ in brass.
    But, since he cannot, reader, look
Not on his picture, but his book.

THE TRIUMPH

Have you seen but a bright lily grow
    Before rude hands have touch'd it?
Have you mark'd but the fall of the snow
    Before the soil hath smutch'd it?
Have you felt the wool of beaver,
        Or swan's down ever?
Or have smelt of the bud of the brier,
        Or the nard in the fire?
Or have tasted the bag of the bee?
O so white, O so soft, O so sweet is she!
                —A Celebration of Charis

TRUTH

Truth is the trial of itself,
    And needs no other touch;
And purer than the purest gold,
    Refine it ne'er so much.

It is the life and light of love,
　The sun that ever shineth,
And spirit of that special grace,
　That faith and love defineth.

It is the warrant of the word,
　That yields a scent so sweet,
As gives a power to faith to tread
　All falsehood under feet.

THE PICTURE OF THE MIND

A mind so pure, so perfect fine,
As 'tis not radiant, but divine;
　And so disdaining any trier,
　'Tis got where it can try the fire.

Whose notions when it will express
In speech, it is with that excess
　Of grace, and music to the ear,
　As what it spoke it planted there.

The voice so sweet, the words so fair,
As some soft chime had stroked the air,
　And though the sound were parted thence,
　Still left an echo in the sense.

But that a mind so rapt, so high,
So swift, so pure, should yet apply
　Itself to us, and come so nigh
　Earth's grossness; there's the how and why.

Hath she here, upon the ground,
Some Paradise or palace found,
　In all the bounds of Beauty, fit
　For her t' inhabit?　There is it.

Thrice happy house, that hast receipt
For this so lofty form, so straight,
　So polish'd, perfect, round, and even,
　As it slid moulded off from heaven.

BEN JONSON

Smooth, soft, and sweet, in all a flood
Where it may run to any good;
   And where it stays, it there becomes
   A nest of odorous spice and gums.

In action, wingèd as the wind;
In rest like spirits left behind
   Upon a bank, or field of flowers,
   Begotten by the wind and showers.

SIMPLEX MUNDITIIS

Still to be neat, still to be dressed
As you were going to a feast;
Still to be powdered, still perfumed:
Lady, it is to be presumed,
Though art's hid causes are not found,
All is not sweet, all is not sound.

Give me a look, give me a face,
That makes simplicity a grace;
Robes loosely flowing, hair as free:
Such sweet neglect more taketh me
Than all the adulteries of art;
They strike mine eyes, but not my heart.
          —THE SILENT WOMAN.

SONG: TO CYNTHIA

Queen and huntress, chaste and fair,
Now the sun is laid to sleep,
Seated in thy silver chair,
State in wonted manner keep:
   Hesperus entreats thy light,
   Goddess excellently bright.

Earth, let not thy envious shade
Dare itself to interpose;
Cynthia's shining orb was made
Heaven to clear, when day did close:

129

Bless us then with wishèd sight,
Goddess excellently bright.

Lay thy bow of pearl apart,
And thy crystal-shining quiver;
Give unto the flying hart
Space to breathe, how short soever:
  Thou that mak'st a day of night,
  Goddess excellently bright.
                    —CYNTHIA'S REVELS.

THE NOBLE NATURE

It is not growing like a tree
  In bulk, doth make man better be;
Or standing long an oak, three hundred year,
To fall a log at last, dry, bald, and sear:
    A lily of a day
    Is fairer far in May,
Although it fall and die that night,—
It was the plant and flower of Light.
In small proportions we just beauties see,
And in short measures life may perfect be.

SONG—TO CELIA

Drink to me only with thine eyes,
  And I will pledge with mine;
Or leave a kiss but in the cup,
  And I'll not look for wine.
The thirst that from the soul doth rise,
  Doth ask a drink divine;
But might I of Jove's nectar sup,
  I would not change for thine.

I sent thee late a rosy wreath,
  Not so much honouring thee,
As giving it a hope, that there
  It could not withered be;

But thou thereon didst only breathe,
   And sent'st it back to me;
Since when it grows, and smells, I swear,
   Not of itself, but thee.

LOVE FREED FROM IGNORANCE AND FOLLY

.   .   .   .

How near to good is what is fair!
   Which we no sooner see,
But with the lines and outward air
   Our senses taken be.
We wish to see it still, and prove
   What ways we may deserve;
We court, we praise, we more than love:
   We are not grieved to serve.

.   .   .   .   .   .

SLOW, SLOW, FRESH FOUNT

Slow, slow, fresh fount, keep time with my salt tears;
Yet slower, yet, O faintly gentle springs:
List to the heavy part the music bears,
   Woe weeps out her division, when she sings.
   Droop herbs, and flowers;
   Fall grief in showers;
   Our beauties are not ours:
                  O, I could still
(Like melting snow upon some craggy hill),
   drop, drop, drop, drop,
Since nature's pride is, now, a wither'd daffodill.
                —CYNTHIA'S REVELS.

John Donne

THE DREAM

Dear love, for nothing less than thee
Would I have broke this happy dream;
   It was a theme
For reason, much too strong for fantasy.
Therefore thou waked'st me wisely; yet
My dream thou brokest not, but continued'st it.
Thou art so true that thoughts of thee suffice
To make dreams truths, and fables histories;
Enter these arms, for since thou thought'st it best,
Not to dream all my dream, let's act the rest.

As lightning, or a taper's light,
Thine eyes, and not thy noise waked me;
   Yet I thought thee
—For thou lov'st truth—an angel, at first sight;
But when I saw thou saw'st my heart,
And knew'st my thoughts beyond an angel's art,
When thou knew'st what I dreamt, when thou knew'st when
Excess of joy would wake me, and camest then,
I must confess, it could not choose but be
Profane, to think thee any thing but thee.

Coming and staying show'd thee, thee,
But rising makes me doubt, that now
   Thou art not thou.
That love is weak where fear's as strong as he;
'Tis not all spirit, pure and brave,
If mixture it of fear, shame, honour have;
Perchance as torches, which must ready be,
Men light and put out, so thou deal'st with me;
Thou cam'st to kindle, go'st to come; then I
Will dream that hope again, but else would die.

JOHN DONNE

HOLY SONNETS

. . . .

Death, be not proud, though some have callèd thee
Mighty and dreadful, for thou art not so:
For those whom thou think'st thou dost overthrow
Die not, poor Death; nor yet canst thou kill me.
From Rest and Sleep, which but thy Picture be,
Much pleasure, then from thee much more must flow;
And soonest our best men with thee do go——
Rest of their bones and souls' delivery!
Thou'rt slave to fate, chance, kings, and desperate men,
And dost with poison, war, and sickness dwell;
And poppy or charms can make us sleep as well
And better than thy stroke.   Why swell'st thou then?
   One short sleep past, we wake eternally,
   And Death shall be no more: Death, thou shalt die!

. . . .

THE GOOD MORROW

I wonder, by my troth, what thou and I
   Did till we loved!   Were we not weaned till then,
But sucked on country pleasures childishly?
   Or snorted we in the Seven Sleepers' den?
'Twas so; but thus all pleasures fancies be.
If ever any beauty I did see,
Which I desired and got,——'twas but a dream of thee

And, now, good morrow to our waking souls,
   Which watch not one another out of fear;
For Love all love of other sights controls,
   And makes one little room an everywhere.
Let sea-discoverers to new worlds be gone;
Let maps to other worlds our world have shown;
Let us possess one world; each hath one, and is one.

My face in thine eye, thine in mine appears,
   And true plain hearts do in the faces rest.
Where can we find two fitter hemispheres,
   Without sharp North, without declining West?

133

Whatever dies was not mixed equally;
If our two loves be one, or thou and I
Love so alike that none do slacken, none can die.

ABSENCE

Absence, hear thou my protestation
  Against thy strength,
  Distance and length:
Do what thou canst for alteration,
  For hearts of truest mettle
  Absence doth join and Time doth settle.

Who loves a mistress of such quality,
  His mind hath found
  Affection's ground
Beyond time, place, and all mortality.
  To hearts that cannot vary
  Absence is prest, Time doth tarry.

My senses want their outward motion
  Which now within
  Reason doth win,
Redoubled by her secret notion:
  Like rich men that take their pleasure
  In hiding more than handling treasure.

By Absence this good means I gain,
  That I can catch her
  Where none can watch her,
In some close corner of my brain:
  There I embrace and kiss her,
  And so enjoy her and none miss her.

A VALEDICTION FORBIDDING MOURNING

As virtuous men pass mildly away,
  And whisper to their souls to go:
Whilst some of their sad friends do say,
  The breath goes now—and some say, no;

JOHN DONNE

So let us melt, and make no noise,
No tear-floods, nor sigh-tempests move;
'Twere profanation of our joys
To tell the laity our love.

Moving of th' earth brings harms and fears,
Men reckon what it did, and meant;
But trepidation of the spheres,
Though greater far, is innocent.

Dull, sublunary lovers' love—
Whose soul is sense—cannot admit
Absence, because it doth remove
Those things which alimented it.

But we're by love so much refined,
That ourselves know not what it is;
Inter-assurèd of the mind,
Careless eyes, lips, and hands to miss.

Our two souls, therefore, (which are one)
Though I must go, endure not yet
A breach, but an expansion,
Like gold to airy thinness beat.

If they be two, they are two so
As stiff thin compasses are two;
Thy soul, the fix'd foot, makes no show
To move, but doth, if th' other do.

And though it in the centre sit,
Yet when the other far doth roam,
It leans, and hearkens after it,
And grows erect as that comes home.

Such wilt thou be to me, who must
Like th' other foot, obliquely run;
Thy firmness makes my circles just,
And makes me end where I begun.

THE UNDERTAKING

I have done one braver thing,
　　Than all the worthies did;
And yet a braver thence doth spring,
　　Which is, to keep that hid.

It were but madness now to impart
　　The skill of specular stone,
When he, which can have learned the **art**
　　To cut it, can find none.

So, if I now should utter this,
　　Others (because no more
Such stuff to work upon there is)
　　Would love but as before.

Be he, who loveliness within
　　Hath found, all outward loathes:
For he, who colour loves and skin,
　　Loves but their oldest clothes.

If, as I have, you also do
　　Virtue in woman see,
And dare love that, and say so too,
　　And forget the he and she;

And if this love, though placèd so,
　　From profane men you hide,
Which will no faith on this bestow,
　　Or, if they do, deride:

Then you have done a braver thing,
　　Than all the worthies did,
And a braver thence will spring,
　　Which is, to keep that hid.

Richard Barnefield

AN ODE

As it fell upon a day
In the merry month of May,
Sitting in a pleasant shade
Which a grove of myrtles made,
Beasts did leap and birds did sing,
Trees did grow and plants did spring;
Every thing did banish moan
Save the Nightingale alone.
She, poor bird, as all forlorn,
Lean'd her breast up-till a thorn,
And there sung the dolefull'st ditty
That to hear it was great pity.
"*Fie, fie, fie*," now would she cry;
"*Teru, teru*," by and by:
That to hear her so complain
Scarce I could from tears refrain,
For her griefs so lively shown
Made me think upon mine own.
—Ah, thought I, thou mourn'st in vain,
None takes pity on thy pain:
Senseless trees, they cannot hear thee,
Ruthless beasts, they will not cheer thee;
King Pandion, he is dead,
All thy friends are lapp'd in lead:
All thy fellow birds do sing
Careless of thy sorrowing.

Francis Beaumont and John Fletcher

BEAUMONT AND FLETCHER

An hour ere sudden sunset fired the west,
Arose two stars upon the pale deep east.
The hall of heaven was clear for night's high feast,
Yet was not yet day's fiery heart at rest.

137

Love leapt up from his mother's burning breast
To see those warm twin lights, as day decreased,
Wax wider, till when all the sun had ceased
As suns they shone from evening's kindled crest.
Across them and between, a quickening fire,
Flamed Venus, laughing with appeased desire.
  Their dawn, scarce lovelier for the gleam of tears,
Filled half the hollow shell 'twixt heaven and earth
With sound like moonlight, mingling moan and mirth
  Which rings and glitters down the darkling years.
                    —ALGERNON CHARLES SWINBURNE.

John Fletcher

MAN HIS OWN STAR

Man is his own star; and the soul that can
Render an honest and a perfect man
Commands all light, all influence, all fate;
Nothing to him falls early, or too late.
Our acts our angels are, or good or ill,
Our fatal shadows that walk by us still.

                    —THE HONEST MAN'S FORTUNE.

SWEETEST MELANCHOLY

Hence, all you vain delights,
As short as are the nights
    Wherein you spend your folly!
There's nought in this life sweet
If man were wise to see't,
    But only melancholy;
    O sweetest melancholy!

Welcome, folded arms and fixèd eyes,
A sigh that piercing mortifies,
A look that's fastened to the ground,
A tongue chained up without a sound!

JOHN FLETCHER

Fountain heads and pathless groves,
Places which pale passion loves!
Moonlight walks, when all the fowls
Are warmly housed save bats and owls!

A midnight bell, a parting groan,
These are the sounds we feed upon;
Then stretch our bones in a still gloomy valley;
Nothing's so dainty sweet as lovely melancholy.
—THE NICE VALOUR—ACT III, SCENE III.

SLEEP

Come, Sleep, and with thy sweet deceiving
    Lock me in delight awhile;
    Let some pleasing dreams beguile
    All my fancies; that from thence
    I may feel an influence
All my powers of care bereaving!

Though but a shadow, but a sliding,
    Let me know some little joy!
    We that suffer long annoy
    Are contented with a thought
    Through an idle fancy wrought:
O let my joys have some abiding!
—THE WOMAN-HATER.

GOD LYÆUS

God Lyæus, ever young,
Ever honoured, ever sung;
Stained with blood of lusty grapes,
In a thousand lusty shapes
Dance upon the mazer's brim,
In the crimson liquor swim;
From thy plenteous hand divine
Let a river run with wine;
    God of Youth, let this day here
    Enter neither care nor fear.
—VALENTINIAN.

139

Francis Beaumont

ON THE TOMBS IN WESTMINSTER ABBEY

. . . .

Mortality, behold, and fear,
What a change of flesh is here!
Think how many royal bones
Sleep within this heap of stones;
Here they lie, had realms and lands,
Who now want strength to stir their hands;
Where from their pulpits seal'd with dust,
They preach, "In greatness is no trust!"
Here's an acre sown indeed
With the richest, royal'st seed,
That the earth did e'er suck in
Since the first man died for sin;
Here the bones of birth have cried,
"Though gods they were, as men they died";
Here are sands, ignoble things
Dropt from the ruin'd sides of kings.
Here's a world of pomp and state
Buried in dust, once dead by fate!

MR. FRANCIS BEAUMONT'S LETTER TO BEN JONSON

. . . What things have we seen
Done at the Mermaid! heard words that have been
So nimble, and so full of subtile flame,
As if that everyone from whence they came
Had meant to put his whole wit in a jest,
And had resolved to live a fool the rest
Of his dull life; then when there hath been thrown
Wit able enough to justify the town
For three days past; wit that might warrant be
For the whole city to talk foolishly
Till that were cancell'd; and when that was gone,
We left an air behind us, which alone
Was able to make the two next companies
Right witty; though but downright fools, mere wise!

William Basse

ELEGY ON MR. WILLIAM SHAKESPEARE

Renownèd Spenser, lie a thought more nigh
To learnèd Chaucer, and rare Beaumont lie
A little nearer Spenser, to make room
For Shakespeare in your threefold, fourfold tomb.
To lodge all four in one bed, make a shift
Until Doomsday, for hardly will a fift
Betwixt this day and that by Fate be slain,
For whom your curtains may be drawn again.
If your precédency in death doth bar
A fourth place in your sacred sepulchre,
Under this carvèd marble of thine own,
Sleep, rare tragedian, Shakespeare, sleep alone;
Thy unmolested peace, unsharèd cave
Possess as lord, not tenant of thy grave,
   That unto us and others it may be
   Honour hereafter to be laid by thee.

William Drummond

MADRIGAL

My thoughts hold mortal strife;
I do detest my life,
And with lamenting cries
Peace to my soul to bring
Oft call that prince which here doth monarchize:
—But he, grim grinning King,
Who caitiffs scorns, and doth the blest surprise,
Late having deck'd with beauty's rose his tomb,
Disdains to crop a weed, and will not come.

SONNET: REPENT, REPENT!

The last and greatest herald of heaven's King,
Girt with rough skins, hies to the deserts wild,
Among that savage brood the woods forth bring,
Which he than man more harmless found and mild:
His food was locusts, and what young doth spring,
With honey that from virgin hives distilled;
Parched body, hollow eyes, some uncouth thing
Made him appear, long since from earth exiled.
There burst he forth: "All ye, whose hopes rely
On God, with me amidst these deserts mourn;
Repent, repent, and from old errors turn."
Who listened to his voice, obeyed his cry?
　Only the echoes, which he made relent,
　Rung from their marble caves, "Repent, repent."

I KNOW THAT ALL THE MOON DECAYS

I know that all the moon decays,
And what by mortals in this world is brought
In Time's great periods, shall return to nought;
The fairest states have fatal nights and days.
I know that all the Muse's heavenly lays
With toil of sprite which are so dearly bought,
As idle sounds, of few or none are sought,
That there is nothing lighter than vain praise.
I know frail beauty like the purple flower,
To which one morn oft birth and death affords,
That love a jarring is of mind's accords,
Where sense and will bring under Reason's power:
Know what I list, all this cannot me move,
But that alas! I both must write and love.

SOLITUDE

Thrice happy he who by some shady grove,
Far from the clamorous world, doth live his own:

WILLIAM DRUMMOND

Though solitary, who is not alone,
But doth converse with that eternal love.
O! how more sweet is birds' harmonious moan,
Or the hoarse sobbings of the widowed dove,
Than those smooth whisperings near a prince's throne,
Which good make doubtful, do the evil approve!
O! how more sweet is zephyr's wholesome breath,
And sighs embalmed, which new born flowers unfold,
Than that applause vain honour doth bequeath!
How sweet are streams, to poison drunk in gold!
    The world is full of horrors, troubles, slights:
    Woods' harmless shades have only true delights.

TO HIS LUTE

My lute, be as thou wert when thou didst grow
With thy green mother in some shady grove,
When immelodious winds but made thee move,
And birds their ramage did on thee bestow.

Since that dear Voice which did thy sounds approve,
Which wont in such harmonious strains to flow,
Is reft from Earth to tune those spheres above,
What art thou but a harbinger of woe?

Thy pleasing notes be pleasing notes no more,
But orphans' wailings to the fainting ear;
Each stroke a sigh, each sound draws forth a tear;
For which be silent as in woods before:

Or if that any hand to touch thee deign,
Like widow'd turtle still her loss complain.

PHŒBUS, ARISE

Phœbus, arise,
And paint the sable skies
With azure, white, and red;
Rouse Memnon's mother from her Tithon's bed,

That she thy càreer may with roses spread:
The nightingales thy coming each where sing,
Make an eternal spring!
Give life to this dark world which lieth dead;
Spread forth thy golden hair
In larger locks than thou wast wont before,
And, emperor-like, decore
With diadem of pearl thy temples fair:
Chase hence the ugly night,
Which serves but to make dear thy glorious light.

. . . .

THE LESSONS OF NATURE

Of this fair volume which we World do name
If we the sheets and leaves could turn with care,
Of Him who it corrects, and did it frame,
We clear might read the art and wisdom rare:

Find out His power which wildest powers doth tame,
His providence extending everywhere,
His justice which proud rebels doth not spare,
In every page, no period of the same.

But silly we, like foolish children, rest
Well pleased with colour'd vellum, leaves of gold,
Fair dangling ribbands, leaving what is best,
On the great Writer's sense ne'er taking hold;

Or if by chance we stay our minds on aught,
It is some picture on the margin wrought.

. . . .

Doth then the World go thus, doth all thus move?
Is this the justice which on Earth we find?
Is this that firm decree which all doth bind?
Are these your influences, Powers above?

Those souls which vice's moody mists most blind,
Blind Fortune, blindly, most their friend doth prove;
And they who thee, poor idol Virtue! love,
Ply like a feather toss'd by storm and wind.

Ah! if a Providence doth sway this all
Why should best minds groan under most distress?
Or why should pride humility make thrall,
And injuries the innocent oppress?

Heavens! hinder, stop this fate; or grant a time
When good may have, as well as bad, their prime!

George Wither

LILIES WITHOUT, LILIES WITHIN

Can I think the Guide of Heaven
Hath so bountifully given
Outward features, 'cause He meant
To have made less excellent
Your divine part?   Or suppose
Beauty, goodness doth oppose;
Like those fools, who do despair
To find any, good and fair?
Rather there I seek a mind
Most excelling, where I find
God hath to the body lent
Most-beseeming ornament,
And I do believe it true,
That, as we the body view
Nearer to perfection grow;
So, the soul herself doth show:
Others more and more excelling
In her powers; as in her dwelling.

FOR ANNIVERSARY MARRIAGE-DAYS

Lord, living, here are we
As fast united, yet
As when our hands and hearts by Thee
Together first were knit.

And, in a thankful song,
Now sing we will Thy praise,
For, that Thou dost as well prolong
Our loving as our days.

Together we have now
Begun another year;
But how much time Thou wilt allow
Thou mak'st it not appear.
We, therefore, do implore
That live and love we may,
Still so, as if but one day more
Together we should stay.

Let each of other's wealth
Preserve a faithful care,
And of each other's joy and health,
As if one soul we were.
Such conscience let us make,
Each other not to grieve,
As if we, daily, were to take
Our everlasting-leave.

The frowardness that springs
From our corrupted kind,
Or from those troublous outward things,
Which may distract the mind,
Permit Thou not, O Lord,
Our constant love to shake;
Or to disturb our true accord,
Or make our hearts to ache.

But let these frailties prove
Affection's exercize;
And that discretion teach our love
Which wins the noblest prize.
So Time which wears away
And ruins all things else
Shall fix our love on Thee for aye
In Whom perfection dwells.

GEORGE WITHER

THE MARYGOLD

When with a serious musing I behold
The grateful and obsequious marygold,
How duly, every morning, she displays
Her open breast, when Titan spreads his rays
How she observes him in his daily walk,
Still bending tow'rds him her small slender stalk;
How, when he down declines, she droops and mourns,
Bedewed, as 'twere with tears, till he returns;
And how she veils her flowers when he is gone,
As if she scornèd to be lookèd on
By an inferior eye; or did contemn
To wait upon a meaner light than him:
—When this I meditate, methinks the flowers
Have spirits far more generous than ours,
And give us fair examples, to despise
The servile fawning and idolatries
Wherewith we court these earthly things below,
Which merit not the service we bestow.
   But O my God! though grovelling I appear
Upon the ground, and have a rooting here
Which pulls me downward, yet in my desire
To that which is above me I aspire;
And all my best affections I profess
To Him that is the Sun of Righteousness.
Oh! keep the morning of His incarnation,
The burning noontide of His bitter passion,
The night of His descending, and the height
Of His ascension—ever in my sight!
That, imitating Him in what I may,
I never follow an inferior way.

SHALL I, WASTING IN DESPAIR

Shall I, wasting in despair,
Die because a woman's fair?
Or make pale my cheeks with care
'Cause another's rosy are?

Be she fairer than the day,
Or the flowery meads in May,
　If she be not so to me
　What care I how fair she be?

Should my heart be grieved or pined
'Cause I see a woman kind?
Or a well-disposèd nature
Joinèd with a lovely feature?
Be she meeker, kinder than
Turtle-dove, or pelican,
　If she be not so to me,
　What care I how kind she be?

Shall a woman's virtues move
Me to perish for her love?
Or her well-deserving, known,
Make me quite forget my own?
Be she with that goodness blest
Which may gain her name of best,
　If she be not such to me
　What care I how good she be?

'Cause her fortune seems too high,
Shall I play the fool, and die?
Those that bear a noble mind,
Where they want of riches find,
Think what with them they would do
That without them dare to woo;
　And unless that mind I see,
　What care I though great she be?

Great, or good, or kind, or fair,
I will ne'er the more despair:
If she love me, this believe
I will die ere she shall grieve:
If she slight me when I woo,
I can scorn and let her go;
　For if she be not for me,
　What care I for whom she be?

GEORGE WITHER

THE MUSE

She doth tell me where to borrow
Comfort in the midst of sorrow:
Makes the desolatest place
To her presence be a grace;
And the blackest discontents
Be her fairest ornaments,
In my former days of bliss,
Her divine skill taught me this,
That from everything I saw,
I could some invention draw,
And raise pleasure to her height,
Through the meanest object's sight;
By the murmur of a spring,
Or the least bough's rustlëing.
By a daisy, whose leaves spread,
Shut when Titan goes to bed;
Or a shady bush or tree,
She could more infuse in me,
Than all Nature's beauties can
In some other wiser man.
By her help I also now
Make this churlish place allow
Some things that may sweeten gladness,
In the very gall of sadness.
The dull loneness, the black shade,
That these hanging vaults have made;
The strange music of the waves,
Beating on these hollow caves;
This black den which rocks emboss,
Overgrown with eldest moss:
The rude portals that give light
More to terror than delight;
This my chamber of neglect,
Walled about with disrespect.
From all these, and this dull air,
A fit object for despair,
She hath taught me by her might
To draw comfort and delight.

Therefore, thou best earthly bliss,
I will cherish thee for this.
Poesy, thou sweet'st content
That e'er heaven to mortals lent:
Though they as a trifle leave thee,
Whose dull thoughts cannot conceive thee,
Though thou be to them a scorn,
That to nought but earth are born,
Let my life no longer be
Than I am in love with thee,
Though our wise ones call thee madness,
Let me never taste of gladness,
If I love not thy madd'st fits
Above all their greatest wits.
And though some, too seeming holy,
Do account thy raptures folly,
Thou dost teach me to contemn
What makes knaves and fools of them.

Robert Herrick

TO VIOLETS

Welcome, maids of honour,
    You do bring
    In the spring;
And wait upon her.

She has virgins many,
    Fresh and fair;
    Yet you are
More sweet than any.

Y' are the maiden posies,
    And so graced,
    To be placed,
'Fore damask roses.

Yet though thus respected,
   By and by
   Ye do lie,
Poor girls, neglected.

UPON A CHILD

Here a pretty baby lies
Sung asleep with lullabies;
Pray be silent, and not stir
The easy earth that covers her.

THE LITANY

In the hour of my distress,
When temptations me oppress,
And when I my sins confess,
      Sweet Spirit, comfort me!

When I lie within my bed,
Sick in heart and sick in head,
And with doubts discomforted,
      Sweet Spirit, comfort me!

When the house doth sigh and weep,
And the world is drown'd in sleep,
Yet mine eyes the watch do keep,
      Sweet Spirit, comfort me!

When the artless doctor sees
No one hope, but of his fees,
And his skill runs on the lees,
      Sweet Spirit, comfort me!

When his potion and his pill,
His, or none, or little skill,
Meet for nothing, but to kill,
      Sweet Spirit, comfort me!

151

When the passing bell doth toll,
And the Furies in a shoal
Come to fright a parting soul,
   Sweet Spirit, comfort me!

When the tapers now burn blue,
And the comforters are few,
And that number more than true,
   Sweet Spirit, comfort me!

When the priest his last hath prayed,
And I nod to what is said
'Cause my speech is now decayed,
   Sweet Spirit, comfort me!

When, God knows, I'm toss'd about,
Either with despair or doubt;
Yet, before the glass be out,
   Sweet Spirit, comfort me!

When the tempter me pursu'th
With the sins of all my youth,
And half damns me with untruth,
   Sweet Spirit, comfort me!

When the flames and hellish cries
Fright mine ears and fright mine eyes,
And all terrors me surprise,
   Sweet Spirit, comfort me!

When the Judgment is revealed,
And that opened which was sealed;
When to Thee I have appealed,
   Sweet Spirit, comfort me!

THE NIGHT-PIECE

Her eyes the glow-worm lend thee,
The shooting stars attend thee;
  And the elves also,
  Whose little eyes glow
Like the sparks of fire, befriend thee.

ROBERT HERRICK

No Will-o'-th'-Wisp mislight thee,
Nor snake or slow-worm bite thee;
    But on, on thy way,
    Not making a stay,
Since ghost there's none to affright thee.

Let not the dark thee cumber;
What though the moon does slumber?
    The stars of the night
    Will lend thee their light
Like tapers clear, without number.

Then, Julia, let me woo thee,
Thus, thus to come unto me;
    And when I shall meet
    Thy silvery feet,
My soul I'll pour into thee.

THE PRIMROSE

Ask me why I send you here
This sweet Infanta of the year?
Ask me why I send to you
This primrose, thus bepearl'd with dew?
I will whisper to your ears:—
The sweets of love are mix'd with tears.

Ask me why this flower does show
So yellow-green, and sickly too?
Ask me why the stalk is weak
And bending (yet it doth not break)?
I will answer:—These discover
What fainting hopes are in a lover.

A MEDITATION FOR HIS MISTRESS

You are a tulip seen to-day,
But, dearest, of so short a stay
That where you grew scarce man can say.

153

You are a lovely July-flower,
Yet one rude wind or ruffling shower
Will force you hence, and in an hour.

You are a sparkling rose i' th' bud,
Yet lost ere that chaste flesh and blood
Can show where you or grew or stood.

You are a full-spread, fair-set vine,
And can with tendrils love entwine,
Yet dried ere you distil your wine.

You are like balm enclosèd well
In amber or some crystal shell,
Yet lost ere you transfuse your smell.

You are a dainty violet,
Yet wither'd ere you can be set
Within the virgin's coronet.

You are the queen all flowers among;
But die you must, fair maid, ere long,
As he, the maker of this song.

TO DAISIES

Shut not so soon; the dull-eyed night
   Has not as yet begun
To make a seizure on the light,
   Or to seal up the sun.

No marigolds yet closèd are,
   No shadows great appear;
Nor doth the early shepherd's star
   Shine like a spangle here.

Stay but till my Julia close
   Her life-begetting eye,
And let the whole world then dispose
   Itself to live or die.

ROBERT HERRICK

COMFORT

What needs complaints,
When she a place
Has with the race
    Of saints?

In endless mirth
She thinks not on
What's said or done
    In Earth.

She sees no tears,
Or any tone
Of thy deep groan
    She hears:

Nor does she mind
Or think on't now
That ever thou
    Wast kind;

But changed above,
She likes not there,
As she did here,
    Thy love.

Forbear therefore,
And lull asleep
Thy woes, and weep
    No more.

TO MUSIC, TO BECALM HIS FEVER

Charm me asleep, and melt me so
    With thy delicious numbers;
That being ravished, hence I go
    Away in easy slumbers.

155

Ease my sick head,
And make my bed,
Thou power that canst sever
From me this ill,
And quickly still,
Though thou not kill
My fever.

Thou sweetly canst convert the same
From a consuming fire
Into a gentle-licking flame,
And make it thus expire.
Then make me weep
My pains asleep,
And give me such reposes
That I, poor I,
May think, thereby,
I live and die
'Mongst roses.

Fall on me like the silent dew,
Or like those maiden showers,
Which, by the peep of day, do strew
A baptism o'er the flowers.
Melt, melt my pains
With thy soft strains;
That having ease me given,
With full delight
I leave this light,
And take my flight
For Heaven.

CORINNA'S GOING A-MAYING

Get up, get up for shame! The blooming morn
Upon her wings presents the god unshorn.
See how Aurora throws her fair
Fresh-quilted colours through the air:
Get up, sweet slug-a-bed, and see
The dew bespangling herb and tree!

Each flower has wept, and bowed toward the east
Above an hour since, yet you not dressed;
  Nay! not so much as out of bed?
  When all the birds have matins said
  And sung their thankful hymns, 'tis sin,
  Nay, profanation to keep in,
Whenas a thousand virgins on this day
Spring sooner than the lark, to fetch in May.

Rise, and put on your foliage, and be seen
To come forth, like the spring-time, fresh and green,
  And sweet as Flora. Take no care
  For jewels for your gown, or hair:
  Fear not, the leaves will strew
  Gems in abundance upon you:
Besides, the childhood of the day has kept,
Against you come, some orient pearls unwept.
  Come, and receive them while the light
  Hangs on the dew-locks of the night:
  And Titan on the eastern hill
  Retires himself, or else stands still
Till you come forth! Wash, dress, be brief in praying;
Few beads are best, when once we go a-Maying.

Come, my Corinna, come; and coming, mark
How each field turns a street, each street a park
  Made green, and trimmed with trees! see how
  Devotion gives each house a bough
  Or branch! each porch, each door, ere this,
  An ark, a tabernacle is,
Made up of white-thorn neatly interwove;
As if here were those cooler shades of love.
  Can such delights be in the street,
  And open fields, and we not see 't?
  Come, we'll abroad; and let's obey
  The proclamation made for May,
And sin no more, as we have done, by staying;
But, my Corinna, come, let's to a-Maying.

There's not a budding boy or girl, this day,
But is got up, and gone to bring in May.

A deal of youth, ere this, is come
Back, and with white-thorn laden home.
Some have dispatched their cakes and cream,
Before that we have left to dream:
And some have wept and wooed, and plighted troth,
And chose their priest, ere we can cast off sloth:
    Many a green-gown has been given,
    Many a kiss, both odd and even:
    Many a glance, too, has been sent
    From out the eye, love's firmament:
Many a jest told of the key's betraying
This night, and locks picked: yet we're not a-Maying!

Come, let us go, while we are in our prime,
And take the harmless folly of the time!
    We shall grow old apace, and die
    Before we know our liberty.
    Our life is short, and our days run
    As fast away as does the sun.
And as a vapour, or a drop of rain
Once lost, can ne'er be found again,
    So when or you or I are made
    A fable, song, or fleeting shade,
    All love, all liking, all delight
    Lies drowned with us in endless night.
Then while time serves, and we are but decaying,
Come, my Corinna, come, let's go a-Maying.

DELIGHT IN DISORDER

    A sweet disorder in the dress
    Kindles in clothes a wantonness;
    A lawn about the shoulders thrown
    Into a fine distraction;
    An erring lace, which here and there
    Enthrals a crimson stomacher;
    A cuff neglectful, and thereby
    Ribands to flow confusedly;
    A winning wave, deserving note,
    In the tempestuous petticoat;

A careless shoe-string, in whose tie
I see a wild civility;
Do more bewitch me, than when art
Is too precise in every part.

TO DIANEME

Sweet, be not proud of those two eyes
Which starlike sparkle in their skies;
Nor be you proud, that you can see
All hearts your captives; yours yet free:
Be you not proud of that rich hair
Which wantons with the lovesick air;
Whenas that ruby which you wear,
Sunk from the tip of your soft ear,
Will last to be a precious stone
When all your world of beauty's gone.

TO ANTHEA

Now is the time, when all the lights wax dim;
And thou, Anthea, must withdraw from him
Who was thy servant: Dearest, bury me
Under that holy-oak, or gospel-tree;
Where, though thou see'st not, thou mayst think upon
Me, when thou yearly go'st procession;
Or for mine honour, lay me in that tomb
In which thy sacred reliques shall have room;
For my embalming, Sweetest, there will be
No spices wanting when I'm laid by thee.

TO BLOSSOMS

Fair pledges of a fruitful tree,
    Why do ye fall so fast?
    Your date is not so past
But you may stay yet here awhile
    To blush and gently smile,
        And go at last.

What! were ye born to be
   An hour or half's delight,
   And so to bid good-night?
'Twas pity Nature brought you forth
   Merely to show your worth
   And lose you quite.

But you are lovely leaves, where we
   May read how soon things have
   Their end, though ne'er so brave:
And after they have shown their pride
   Like you awhile, they glide
   Into the grave.

TO MEADOWS

Ye have been fresh and green;
   Ye have been filled with flowers;
And ye the walks have been
   Where maids have spent their hours.

Ye have beheld how they
   With wicker arks did come
To kiss and bear away
   The richer cowslips home.

Ye've heard them sweetly sing,
   And seen them in a round,
Each virgin, like a Spring,
   With honeysuckles crowned.

But now we see none here
   Whose silvery feet did tread,
And with dishevelled hair
   Adorned this smoother mead.

Like unthrifts, having spent
   Your stock, and needy grown,
Ye're left here to lament
   Your poor estates, alone.

ROBERT HERRICK

WHENAS IN SILKS MY JULIA GOES

Whenas in silks my Julia goes,
Then, then, me thinks, how sweetly flows
That liquefaction of her clothes.
Next, when I cast mine eyes and see
That brave vibration each way free,
O how that glittering taketh me!

AN ODE FOR BEN JONSON

Ah Ben!
  Say how or when
  Shall we, thy guests,
Meet at those lyric feasts,
  Made at the Sun,
The Dog, the Triple Tun;
Where we such clusters had,
As made us nobly wild, not mad?
And yet each verse of thine
Out-did the meat, out-did the frolic wine.

  My Ben!
  Or come again,
  Or send to us
Thy wit's great overplus;
  But teach us yet
Wisely to husband it,
Lest we that talent spend;
And having once brought to an end
That precious stock,—the store
Of such a wit the world should have no more.

TO DAFFODILS

Fair Daffodils, we weep to see
  You haste away so soon;
As yet the early-rising sun
  Has not attained his noon.

Stay, stay,
Until the hasting day
Has run
But to the even-song;
And, having prayed together, we
Will go with you along.

We have short time to stay, as you;
We have as short a spring;
As quick a growth to meet decay,
As you, or any thing.
We die
As your hours do, and dry
Away,
Like to the summer's rain;
Or as to the pearls of morning's dew,
Ne'er to be found again.

TO THE VIRGINS

Gather ye rosebuds while ye may,
Old Time is still a-flying:
And this same flower that smiles to-day
To-morrow will be dying.

The glorious lamp of heaven, the sun,
The higher he's a-getting,
The sooner will his race be run,
And nearer he's to setting.

That age is best which is the first,
When youth and blood are warmer;
But being spent, the worse, and worst
Times still succeed the former.

Then be not coy, but use your time,
And while ye may, go marry:
For having lost but once your prime,
You may for ever tarry.

WILLIAM BROWNE

CHERRY-RIPE

Cherry-ripe, ripe, ripe, I cry,
Full and fair ones; come and buy.
If so be you ask me where
They do grow, I answer: There
Where my Julia's lips do smile;
There's the land, or cherry-isle,
Whose plantations fully show
All the year where cherries grow.

TO THE ROSE

Go, happy rose, and interwove
With other flowers, bind my love.
Tell her, too, she must not be
Longer flowing, longer free,
That so oft has fettered me.

Say, if she's fretful, I have bands
Of pearl and gold, to bind her hands;
Tell her, if she struggle still,
I have myrtle rods at will,
For to take, though not to kill.

Take thou my blessing thus, and go
And tell her this,—but do not so!
Lest a handsome anger fly
Like a lightning from her eye,
And burn thee up, as well as I.

William Browne

A WELCOME

Welcome, welcome, do I sing,
Far more welcome than the spring;
He that parteth from you never
Shall enjoy a spring forever.

163

He that to the voice is near,
　Breaking from your ivory pale,
Need not walk abroad to hear
　The delightful nightingale.

He that looks still on your eyes,
　Though the winter have begun
To benumb our arteries,
　Shall not want the summer's sun.

He that still may see your cheeks,
　Where all rareness still reposes,
Is a fool if e'er he seeks
　Other lilies, other roses.

He to whom your soft lip yields,
　And perceives your breath in kissing,
All the odours of the fields
　Never, never shall be missing.

He that question would anew
　What fair Eden was of old,
Let him rightly study you,
　And a brief of that behold.

Welcome, welcome, then I sing,
Far more welcome than the spring;
He that parteth from you never,
Shall enjoy a spring forever.

EPITAPH ON THE COUNTESS OF PEMBROKE

Underneath this sable hearse,
Lies the subject of all verse,
Sidney's sister, Pembroke's mother;
Death! ere thou hast slain another,
Fair and learn'd, and good as she,
Time shall throw a dart at thee.

WILLIAM BROWNE

AN ELEGY ON THE COUNTESS DOWAGER
OF PEMBROKE

.   .   .   .

I, hapless soul, that never knew a friend
But to bewail his too untimely end;
Whose hopes, cropp'd in the bud, have never come,
But to sit weeping on a senseless tomb,
That hides not dust enough to count the tears,
Which I have fruitless spent, in so few years;

I, that have trusted those that would have given
For our dear Saviour and the Son of Heaven,
Ten times the value Judas had of yore,
Only to sell him for three pieces more,
I that have lov'd and trusted thus in vain,
Yet weep for thee.

IN OBITUM. M. S.

May!   Be thou never graced with birds that sing,
    Nor Flora's pride!
In thee all flowers and roses spring,
    Mine only died.

SONG

    Hearken then awhile to me;
And if such a woman move,
    As I now shall versify:
Be assur'd, 'tis she, or none
    That I love, and love alone.

    Nature did her so much right,
    As she scorns the help of Art;
In as many virtues dight
    As e'er yet embraced a heart.
So much good so truly tried,
    Some for less were deified.

165

Wit she hath without desire
　To make known how much she hath;
And her anger flames no higher
　Than may fitly sweeten wrath.
Full of pity as may be,
　Though perhaps not so to me.

Reason masters every sense,
　And her virtues grace her birth;
Lovely as all excellence,
　Modest in her most of mirth;
Likelihood enough to prove,
　Only worth could kindle love.

Such she is; and if you know
　Such a one as I have sung:
Be she brown, or fair, or so,
　That she be but somewhile young:
Be assur'd, 'tis she, or none
　That I love and love alone.

Francis Quarles

RESPICE FINEM

My soul, sit thou a patient looker-on;
Judge not the play before the play is done:
Her plot hath many changes; every day
Speaks a new scene; the last act crowns the play.

ON THE LIFE AND DEATH OF MAN

The world's a theatre. The earth, a stage
Placed in the midst: where both prince and page,
Both rich and poor, fool, wise man, base and high,
All act their parts in life's short tragedy.
　Our life's a tragedy. Those secret rooms,
Wherein we 'tire us, are our mothers' wombs.
166

The music ushering in the play is mirth
To see a man-child brought upon the earth.
That fainting gasp of breath which first we vent,
Is a dumb show; presents the argument.
Our new-born cries, that new-born griefs bewray,
Are the sad prologue of the ensuing play.
False hopes, true fears, vain joys, and fierce distracts,
Are like the music that divides the Acts.
Time holds the glass, and when the hour's outrun,
Death strikes the epilogue, and the play is done.

Henry King

SIC VITA

Like to the falling of a star,
Or as the flights of eagles are,—
Or like the fresh spring's gaudy hue,
Or silver drops of morning dew;
Or like a wind that chafes the flood,
Or bubbles which on water stood:
Even such is man, whose borrowed light
Is straight called in, and paid to night.
The wind blows out, the bubble dies;
The spring entombed in autumn lies;
The dew dries up, the star is shot;
The flight is past—and man forgot.

A DIRGE

What is the existence of man's life,
But open war, or slumbered strife;
Where sickness to his sense presents
The combat of the elements;
And never feels a perfect peace
Till Death's cold hand signs his release?

It is a weary interlude—
Which doth short joys, long woes, include,
The world the stage, the prologue tears,
The acts vain hopes and varied fears;
The scene shuts up with loss of breath,
And leaves no epilogue but death.

A CONTEMPLATION UPON FLOWERS

Brave flowers—that I could gallant it like you,
   And be as little vain!
You come abroad, and make a harmless show,
   And to your beds of earth again.
You are not proud: you know your birth:
For your embroidered garments are from earth.

You do obey your months and times, but I
   Would have it ever Spring:
My fate would know no Winter, never die,
   Nor think of such a thing.
O that I could my bed of earth but view
And smile, and look as cheerfully as you!

O teach me to see Death and not to fear,
   But rather to take truce!
How often have I seen you at a bier,
   And there look fresh and spruce!
You fragrant flowers. Then teach me, that my breath
Like yours may sweeten and perfume my death.

AN ELEGY

Thus kiss I your fair hands, taking my leave,
As prisoners at the bar their doom receive.
All joys go with you: let sweet peace attend
You on the way, and wait your journey's end.
But let your discontents and sourer fate
Remain with me, borne off in my retrait.

168

HENRY KING

Might all your crosses, in that sheet of lead
Which folds my heavy heart, lie burièd:
'Tis the last service I would do you, and the best
My wishes ever meant, or tongue profest.
Once more I take my leave. And once for all
Our parting shows so like a funeral,
It strikes my soul, which hath most right to be
Chief mourner at this sad solemnity.

And think not, dearest, 'cause this parting knell
Is rung in verses, that at your farewell
I only mourn in poetry and ink:
No, my pen's melancholy plummets sink
So low, they dive where th' hid affections sit,
Blotting that paper where my mirth was writ.

Believ't, that sorrow truest is, which lies
Deep in the breast, not floating in the eyes:
And he with saddest circumstance doth part,
Who seals his farewell with a bleeding heart.

EXEQUY ON HIS WIFE

Accept, thou shrine of my dead saint,
   Instead of dirges this complaint:
And for sweet flowers to crown thy hearse
   Receive a strew of weeping verse
From thy grieved friend, whom thou might'st see
Quite melted into tears for thee.
   Dear loss! since thy untimely fate,
My task hath been to meditate
On thee, on thee! Thou art the book,
The library whereon I look,
Tho' almost blind. For thee, loved clay,
I languish out, not live, the day . . .
Thou hast benighted me; thy set
This eve of blackness did beget,
Who wast my day (tho' overcast
Before thou had'st thy noontide past):
And I remember must in tears
Thou scarce had'st seen so many years

169

As day tells hours.   By thy clear sun
My love and fortune first did run;
But thou wilt never more appear
Folded within my hemisphere,
Since both thy light and motion,
Like a fixed star, is fall'n and gone,
And 'twixt me and my soul's dear wish
The earth now interposèd is.

    I could allow thee for a time
To darken me and my sad clime;
Were it a month, a year, or ten,
I would thy exile live till then,
And all that space my mirth adjourn—
So thou would'st promise to return,
And putting off thy ashy shroud
At length disperse this sorrow's cloud.

    But woe is me! the longest date
Too narrow is to calculate
These empty hopes: never shall I
Be so much blest as to descry
A glimpse of thee, till that day come
Which shall the earth to cinders doom,
And a fierce fever must calcine
The body of this world—like thine,
My little world!   That fit of fire
Once off, our bodies shall aspire
To our souls' bliss: then shall we rise
And view ourselves with clearer eyes
In that calm region where no night
Can hide us from each other's sight.

    Meantime thou hast her, earth: much good
May my harm do thee!   Since it stood
With Heaven's will I might not call
Her longer mine, I will give thee all
My short-lived right and interest
In her whom living I loved best.
Be kind to her, and prithee look
Thou write into thy Doomsday book
Each parcel of this rarity
Which in thy casket shrined doth lie,

As thou wilt answer Him that lent—
Not gave—thee my dear monument.
So close the ground, and 'bout her shade
Black curtains draw: my bride is laid.

Sleep on, my Love, in thy cold bed
Never to be disquieted!
My last good-night!   Thou wilt not wake
Till I thy fate shall overtake:
Till age, or grief, or sickness must
Marry my body to that dust
It so much loves; and fill the room
My heart keeps empty in thy tomb.
Stay for me there: I will not fail
To meet thee in that hollow vale,
And think not much of my delay:
I am already on the way,
And follow thee with all the speed
Desire can make, or sorrows breed.
Each minute is a short degree
And every hour a step towards thee . . .

'Tis true—with shame and grief I yield—
Thou, like the van, first took'st the field;
And gotten hast the victory
In thus adventuring to die
Before me, whose more years might crave
A just precèdence in the grave.
But hark!   My pulse, like a soft drum,
Beats my approach, tells thee I come:
And slow howe'er my marches be,
I shall at last sit down by thee.

The thought of this bids me go on
And wait my dissolutiòn
With hope and comfort.   Dear—forgive
The crime—I am content to live
Divided, with but half a heart,
Till we shall meet and never part.

171

George Herbert

THE QUIP

The merry World did on a day
   With his train-bands and mates agree
To meet together, where I lay,
   And all in sport to jeer at me.

First, Beauty crept into a rose,
   Which when I plucked not, "Sir," said she,
"Tell me, I pray, whose hands are those?"—
   But Thou shalt answer, Lord, for me.

Then Money came, and clinking still,
   "What tune is this, poor man?" said he:
"I heard in Music you had skill."
   But Thou shalt answer, Lord, for me.

Then came brave Glory puffing by
   In silks that whistled—who but he?
He scarce allowed me half an eye—
   But Thou shalt answer, Lord, for me.

Then came quick Wit and Conversation,
   And he would needs a comfort be,
And, to be short, make an oration—
   But Thou shalt answer, Lord, for me.

Yet when the hour of Thy design
   To answer these fine things shall come,
Speak not at large, say, I am Thine,
   And then they have their answer home.

THE PULLEY

   When God at first made man,
Having a glass of blessings standing by,
"Let us," said He, "pour on him all we can:
Let the world's riches, which dispersèd lie
   Contract into a span."

GEORGE HERBERT

So strength first made a way,
Then beauty flowed, then wisdom, honour, pleasure;
When almost all was out, God made a stay,
Perceiving that, alone of all His treasure,
    Rest in the bottom lay.

"For if I should," said He,
"Bestow this jewel also on My creature,
He would adore My gifts instead of Me,
And rest in Nature, not the God of Nature:
    So both should losers be.

"Yet let him keep the rest,
But keep them with repining restlessness;
Let him be rich and weary, that at least,
If goodness lead him not, yet weariness
    May toss him to My breast."

DISCIPLINE

Throw away Thy rod,
Throw away Thy wrath;
    O my God,
Take the gentle path!

For my heart's desire
Unto Thine is bent:
    I aspire
To a full consent.

Not a word or look
I affect to own,
    But by book,
And Thy Book alone.

Though I fail, I weep;
Though I halt in pace,
    Yet I creep
To the throne of grace.

Then let wrath remove;
Love will do the deed;
   For with love
Stony hearts will bleed.

Love is swift of foot;
Love's a man of war,
   And can shoot,
And can hit from far.

Who can 'scape his bow?
That which wrought on Thee,
   Brought Thee low,
Needs must work on me.

Throw away Thy rod;
Though man frailties hath,
   Thou art God:
Throw away Thy wrath.

VIRTUE

Sweet day, so cool, so calm, so bright!
The bridal of the earth and sky—
The dew shall weep thy fall to-night;
   For thou must die.

Sweet rose, whose hue angry and brave
Bids the rash gazer wipe his eye,
Thy root is ever in its grave,
   And thou must die.

Sweet spring, full of sweet days and roses,
A box where sweets compacted lie,
My music shows ye have your closes,
   And all must die.

Only a sweet and virtuous soul,
Like seasoned timber, never gives;
But though the whole world turn to coal
   Then chiefly lives.

THE COLLAR

I struck the board and cried, No more;
    I will abroad.
What, shall I ever sigh and pine?
My lines and life are free, free as the road,
Loose as the wind, as large as store.
    Shall I be still in suit?
Have I no harvest but a thorn
To let me blood, and not restore
What I have lost with cordial fruit?
    Sure there was wine
Before my sighs did dry it; there was corn
Before my tears did drown it.
Is the year only lost to me?
Have I no bays to crown it?
No flowers, no garlands gay? All blasted?
    All wasted?
Not so, my heart; but there is fruit,
    And thou hast hands.

Recover all thy sigh-blown age
On double pleasure: leave thy cold dispute
Of what is fit and not; forsake thy cage,
    Thy rope of sands
Which petty thoughts have made, and made to thee
Good cable to enforce and draw
    And be thy law,
While thou dost wink and would'st not see.
    Away: take heed,
    I will abroad.
Call in thy death's-head there: tie up thy fears.
    He that forbears
    To suit and serve his need
    Deserves his load.
But as I raved and grew more fierce and wild
    At every word,
Methought I heard one calling "Child!"
    And I replied "My Lord."

Thomas Carew

SONG

Ask me no more where Jove bestows,
When June is past, the fading rose;
For in your beauty's orient deep
These flowers, as in their causes, sleep.

Ask me no more whither do stray
The golden atoms of the day;
For in pure love heaven did prepare
Those powders to enrich your hair.

Ask me no more whither doth haste
The nightingale when May is past;
For in your sweet dividing throat
She winters and keeps warm her note.

Ask me no more where those stars 'light
That downwards fall in dead of night;
For in your eyes they sit, and there
Fixed become as in their sphere.

Ask me no more if east or west
The Phœnix builds her spicy nest;
For unto you at last she flies,
And in your fragrant bosom dies.

THE COMPLIMENT

I do not love thee for that fair
Rich fan of thy most curious hair;
Though the wires thereof be drawn
Finer than the threads of lawn,
And are softer than the leaves
On which the subtle spider weaves.

THOMAS CAREW

I do not love thee for those flowers
Growing on thy cheeks,—love's bowers;
Though such cunning them hath spread,
None can paint them white and red:
Love's golden arrows thence are shot,
Yet for them I love thee not.

I do not love thee for those soft
Red coral lips I've kissed so oft;
Nor teeth of pearl, the double guard
To speech whence music still is heard,
Though from those lips a kiss being taken
Mighty tyrants melt, and death awaken.

I do not love thee, O my fairest,
For that richest, for that rarest
Silver pillar, which stands under
Thy sound head, that globe of wonder;
Though that neck be whiter far
Than towers of polished ivory are.

DISDAIN RETURNED

He that loves a rosy cheek,
    Or a coral lip admires,
Or from starlike eyes doth seek
    Fuel to maintain his fires;
As old Time makes these decay,
So his flames must waste away.

But a smooth and steadfast mind,
    Gentle thoughts, and calm desires,
Hearts with equal love combined,
    Kindle never-dying fires:—
Where these are not, I despise
Lovely cheeks or lips or eyes.

James Shirley

THE GLORIES OF OUR BLOOD AND STATE

The glories of our blood and state
  Are shadows, not substantial things;
There is no armour against fate;
  Death lays his icy hand on kings:
    Sceptre and Crown
    Must tumble down,
And in the dust be equal made
With the poor crookèd scythe and spade.

Some men with swords may reap the field,
  And plant fresh laurels where they kill:
But their strong nerves at last must yield;
  They tame but one another still:
    Early or late
    They stoop to fate,
And must give up their murmuring breath,
When they, pale captives, creep to death.

The garlands wither on your brow,
  Then boast no more your mighty deeds;
Upon Death's purple altar now
  See, where the victor-victim bleeds:
    Your heads must come
    To the cold tomb;
Only the actions of the just
Smell sweet, and blossom in their dust.

VICTORIOUS MEN OF EARTH

Victorious men of earth, no more
  Proclaim how wide your empires are;
Though you bind in every shore,
  And your triumphs reach as far
    As night or day,
  Yet you, proud monarchs, must obey
And mingle with forgotten ashes, when
Death calls ye to the crowd of common men.

SIR WILLIAM DAVENANT

Devouring Famine, Plague, and War,
  Each able to undo mankind,
Death's servile emissaries are;
  Nor to these alone confined,
    He hath at will
  More quaint and subtle ways to kill;
A smile or kiss, as he will use the art,
Shall have the cunning skill to break a heart.

ON HER DANCING

I stood and saw my Mistress dance,
Silent, and with so fixed an eye,
Some might suppose me in a trance:
  But being askèd why,
By one who knew I was in love,
  I could not but impart
My wonder, to behold her move
So nimbly with a marble heart.

Sir William Davenant

MORNING SONG

The lark now leaves his watery nest,
  And climbing shakes his dewy wings,
He takes your window for the east,
  And to implore your light, he sings;
Awake, awake! the morn will never rise,
Till she can dress her beauty at your eyes.

The merchant bows unto the seaman's star,
  The ploughman from the sun his season takes;
But still the lover wonders what they are,
  Who look for day before his mistress wakes;
Awake, awake! break through your veils of lawn!
Then draw your curtains and begin the dawn!

179

PRAISE AND PRAYER

Praise is devotion fit for mighty minds,
   The diff'ring world's agreeing sacrifice;
Where Heaven divided faiths united finds:
   But Prayer in various discord upward flies.

For Prayer the ocean is where diversely
   Men steer their course, each to a sev'ral coast;
Where all our interests so discordant be
   That half beg winds by which the rest are lost.

By Penitence when we ourselves forsake,
   'Tis but in wise design on piteous Heaven;
In Praise we nobly give what God may take,
   And are, without a beggar's blush, forgiven.

Edmund Waller

ENGLISH VERSE

Poets may boast, as safely vain,
Their works shall with the world remain;
Both bound together, live or die,
The verses and the prophecy.

But who can hope his line should long
Last in a daily changing tongue?
While they are new, envy prevails;
And, as that dies, our language fails.

When architects have done their part,
The matter may betray their art:
Time, if we use ill-chosen stone,
Soon brings a well-built palace down.

Poets, that lasting marble seek,
Must carve in Latin or in Greek:
We write in sand: our language grows,
And, like the tide, our work o'erflows.

189

EDMUND WALLER

TO A LADY SINGING

Chloris, yourself you so excel,
   When you vouchsafe to breathe my thought,
That like a spirit, with this spell
   Of my own teaching I am caught.

That eagle's fate and mine is one,
   Which, on the shaft that made him die
Espied a feather of his own,
   Wherewith he wont to soar so high.

Had Echo, with so sweet a grace,
   Narcissus' loud complaints returned;
Not for reflection of his face,
   But of his voice, the boy had mourned.

ON A GIRDLE

That which her slender waist confined
Shall now my joyful temples bind:
No monarch but would give his crown
His arms might do what this has done.

It was my heaven's extremest sphere,
The pale which held that lovely dear:
My joy, my grief, my hope, my love,
Did all within this circle move.

A narrow compass! and yet there
Dwelt all that's good, and all that's fair:
Give me but what this riband bound,
Take all the rest the sun goes round.

OLD AGE

The seas are quiet when the winds give o'er;
So calm are we when passions are no more;

For then we know how vain it was to boast
Of fleeting things so certain to be lost.
Clouds of affection from our younger eyes
Conceal that emptiness which age descries.

The soul's dark cottage, battered and decayed,
Lets in new light through chinks that time hath made;
Stronger by weakness, wiser men become
As they draw near to their eternal home:
Leaving the Old, both worlds at once they view
That stand upon the threshold of the New.

SONG

Go, lovely Rose!
Tell her, that wastes her time and me,
That now she knows,
When I resemble her to thee,
How sweet, and fair, she seems to be.

Tell her that's young,
And shuns to have her graces spy'd,
That had'st thou sprung
In deserts where no men abide,
Thou must have uncommended dy'd.

Small is the worth
Of beauty from the light retir'd;
Bid her come forth,
Suffer herself to be desir'd,
And not blush so to be admir'd.

Then die! that she
The common fate of all things rare
May read in thee;
How small a part of time they share
That are so wondrous sweet and fair!

JOHN MILTON

John Milton

ON MILTON

Three poets, in three distant ages born,
Greece, Italy and England did adorn.
The first in loftiness of thought surpassed;
The next in majesty; in both the last.
The force of nature could no further go;
To make a third, she joined the former two.
— JOHN DRYDEN.

PARADISE LOST

Of Man's first disobedience, and the fruit
Of that forbidden tree, whose mortal taste
Brought death into the world, and all our woe,
With loss of Eden, till one greater Man
Restore us, and regain the blissful seat,
Sing, heavenly Muse, that on the secret top
Of Oreb, or of Sinai, didst inspire
That shepherd, who first taught the chosen seed,
In the beginning how the heavens and earth
Rose out of chaos: or if Sion hill
Delight thee more, and Siloa's brook that flowed
Fast by the oracle of God; I thence
Invoke thy aid to my adventurous song,
That with no middle flight intends to soar
Above the Aonian mount, while it pursues
Things unattempted yet in prose or rhyme,
And chiefly thou, O Spirit, that dost prefer
Before all temples the upright heart and pure,
Instruct me, for Thou knowest; Thou from the first
Wast present, and with mighty wings outspread
Dove-like sat'st brooding on the vast Abyss
And mad'st it pregnant: what in me is dark
Illumine, what is low raise and support;
That to the height of this great argument

I may assert Eternal Providence,
And justify the ways of God to men.

—Book I.

Hail, holy Light! offspring of heaven first-born!
Or of the Eternal Co-eternal beam,
May I express thee unblamed? since God is light,
And never but in unapproachèd light
Dwelt from eternity, dwelt then in thee,
Bright effluence of bright essence increate.

. . . .

                        With the year
Seasons return; but not to me returns
Day, or the sweet approach of even or morn,
Or sight of vernal bloom, or summer's rose,
Or flocks, or herds, or human face divine;
But cloud instead, and ever-during dark
Surrounds me, from the cheerful ways of men
Cut off, and for the book of knowledge fair
Presented with a universal blank
Of Nature's works, to me expunged and rased,
And wisdom at one entrance quite shut out.
So much the rather thou, celestial light,
Shine inward, and the mind through all her powers
Irradiate: there plant eyes, all mist from thence
Purge and disperse, that I may see and tell
Of things invisible to mortal sight.

—Book III.

O Thou, that with surpassing glory crowned,
Look'st from thy sole dominion like the god
Of this new world; at whose sight all the stars
Hide their diminished heads; to thee I call,
But with no friendly voice, and add thy name,
O sun! to tell thee how I hate thy beams,
That bring to my remembrance from what state
I fell, how glorious once above thy sphere,
Till pride and worse ambition threw me down
Warring in heaven against heaven's matchless king.
184

JOHN MILTON

Ah, wherefore? He deserved no such return
From me, whom He created what I was
In that bright eminence, and with his good
Upbraided none; nor was his service hard.

.   .   .   .

Me miserable! which way shall I fly
Infinite wrath and infinite despair?
Which way I fly is hell; myself am hell;
And, in the lowest deep, a lower deep
Still threatening to devour me opens wide,
To which the hell I suffer seems a heaven.
—Book IV.

These are thy glorious works, Parent of good,
Almighty, Thine this universal frame,
Thus wondrous fair: Thyself how wondrous then!
Unspeakable, who sitt'st above these heavens
To us invisible, or dimly seen
In these thy lowest works; yet these declare
Thy goodness beyond thought, and power divine.
Speak, ye who best can tell, ye sons of light,
Angels, for ye behold Him, and with songs
And choral symphonies, day without night,
Circle His throne rejoicing, ye, in heaven,
On earth join all ye creatures to extol
Him first, Him last, Him midst, and without end.

.   .   .   .

Join voices, all ye living souls: ye birds,
That, singing, up to heaven-gate ascend,
Bear on your wings and in your notes His praise.
Ye that in waters glide, and ye that walk
The earth, and stately tread, or lowly creep;
Witness if I be silent, morn or even,
To hill, or valley, fountain, or fresh shade,
Made vocal by my song, and taught His praise.
Hail! universal Lord! be bounteous still
To give us only good; and if the night

185

Have gathered aught of evil or concealed,
Disperse it, as now light dispels the dark!

   .   .   .   .   .   ∘   .   .   ι

      The seraph Abdiel, faithful found,
Among the faithless, faithful only he;
Among innumerable false, unmoved,
Unshaken, unseduced, unterrified,
His loyalty he kept, his love, his zeal;
Nor number, nor example with him wrought
To swerve from truth, or change his constant mind,
Though single.

                           —Book V

COMUS

   .   .   .   .   .   ∘   .   .   .

Sweet Echo, sweetest Nymph that liv'st unseen
      Within thy airy shell
      By slow Meander's margent green,
And in the violet-embroidered vale
      Where the love-lorn nightingale
Nightly to thee her sad song mourneth well:
Canst thou not tell me of a gentle pair
      That likest thy Narcissus are?
      O, if thou have
      Hid them in some flowery cave,
      Tell me but where,
      Sweet queen of parley, daughter of the sphere!
      So may'st thou be translated to the skies,
And give resounding grace to all Heaven's harmonies!

   .   .   .   .   .   ∘   .   .   ∘

    Sabrina fair,
      Listen where thou art sitting
    Under the glassy, cool, translucent wave,
      In twisted braids of lilies knitting
      The loose train of thy amber-dropping hair;

JOHN MILTON

Listen for dear honour's sake,
   Goddess of the silver lake,
   Listen and save!

    .   .   .   .

To the Ocean now I fly,
And those happy climes that lie
Where day never shuts his eye,
Up in the broad fields of the sky;
There I suck the liquid air
All amidst the Gardens fair
Of Hesperus, and his daughters three
That sing about the golden tree:
Along the crisped shades and bowers
Revels the spruce and jocund Spring,
The Graces, and the rosy-bosomed Hours,
Thither all their bounties bring,
That there eternal Summer dwells,
And West winds, with musky wing
About the cedarn alleys fling
Nard, and Cassia's balmy smells.
Iris there, with humid bow,
Waters the odorous banks that blow
Flowers of more mingled hue
Than her purfled scarf can show,
And drenches with Elysian dew
(List, mortals, if your ears be true)
Beds of hyacinth, and roses
Where young Adonis oft reposes,
Waxing well of his deep wound
In slumber soft, and on the ground
Sadly sits the Assyrian Queen.

    .   .   .   .

LYCIDAS

A LAMENT FOR A FRIEND DROWNED IN HIS PASSAGE FROM
CHESTER ON THE IRISH SEAS, 1637

Yet once more, O ye Laurels, and once more
Ye Myrtles brown, with Ivy never sere,
I come to pluck your Berries harsh and crude,
And with forced fingers rude,
Shatter your leaves before the mellowing year.
Bitter constraint, and sad occasion dear,
Compels me to disturb your season due:
For Lycidas is dead, dead ere his prime,
Young Lycidas, and hath not left his peer:
Who would not sing for Lycidas? he knew
Himself to sing, and build the lofty rhyme.
He must not float upon his watery bier
Unwept, and welter to the parching wind,
Without the meed of some melodious tear.
  Begin, then, Sisters of the sacred well,
That from beneath the seat of Jove doth spring;
Begin, and somewhat loudly sweep the string.
Hence with denial vain, and coy excuse,
So may some gentle Muse
With lucky words favor my destined Urn,
And as he passes turn,
And bid fair peace be to my sable shroud.
For we were nursed upon the self-same hill,
Fed the same flock, by fountain, shade, and rill;
Together both, ere the high Lawns appeared
Under the opening eye-lids of the Morn,
We drove a-field, and both together heard
What time the Grey-fly winds her sultry horn,
Battening our flocks with the fresh dews of night,
Oft till the Star that rose, at Evening, bright
Toward Heaven's descent had sloped his westering wheel.
Meanwhile the Rural ditties were not mute,
Tempered to the Oaten Flute;
Rough Satyrs danced, and Fauns with cloven heel,

From the glad sound would not be absent long,
And old Damætas loved to hear our song.

But O the heavy change, now thou art gone,
Thee, Shepherd, thee the Woods, and desert Caves,
With wild Thyme and the gadding Vine o'ergrown,
And all their echoes mourn.
The Willows, and the Hazel Copses green,
Shall now no more be seen,
Fanning their joyous Leaves to thy soft lays.
As killing as the Canker to the Rose,
Or Taint-worm to the weanling Herds that graze,
Or Frost to Flowers, that their gay wardrobe wear,
When first the White-thorn blows;
Such, Lycidas, thy loss to Shepherd's ear.

Where were ye, Nymphs, when the remorseless deep
Closed o'er the head of your loved Lycidas?
For neither were ye playing on the steep,
Where your old Bards, the famous Druids, lie,
Nor on the shaggy top of Mona high,
Nor yet where Deva spreads her wizard stream:
Ay me, I fondly dream!
Had ye been there—for what could that have done?
What could the Muse herself that Orpheus bore,
The Muse herself, for her enchanting son
Whom Universal nature did lament,
When, by the rout that made the hideous roar,
His gory visage down the stream was sent,
Down the swift Hebrus to the Lesbian shore?

Alas! What boots it with uncessant care
To tend the homely slighted Shepherd's trade,
And strictly meditate the thankless Muse,
Were it not better done, as others use,
To sport with Amaryllis in the shade,
Or with the tangles of Neæra's hair?
Fame is the spur that the clear spirit doth raise
(That last infirmity of Noble mind)
To scorn delights, and live laborious days;
But the fair Guerdon when we hope to find,
And think to burst out into sudden blaze,
Comes the blind Fury with the abhorrèd shears,
And slits the thin-spun life. "But not the praise,"

Phœbus replied, and touched my trembling ears;
"Fame is no plant that grows on mortal soil,
Nor in the glistering foil
Set off to the world, nor in broad rumor lies,
But lives and spreads aloft by those pure eyes,
And perfect witness of all-judging Jove;
As he pronounces lastly on each deed,
Of so much fame in Heaven expect thy meed."
   O fountain Arethuse, and thou honored flood,
Smooth-sliding Mincius, crowned with vocal reeds,
That strain I heard was of a higher mood:
But now my Oat proceeds,
And listens to the Herald of the Sea
That came in Neptune's plea.
He asked the Waves, and asked the Felon winds,
What hard mishap hath doomed this gentle swain?
And questioned every gust of rugged wings
That blows from off each beakèd Promontory.
They knew not of his story,
And sage Hippotades their answer brings,
That not a blast was from his dungeon strayed,
The Air was calm, and on the level brine,
Sleek Panope with all her sisters played.
It was that fatal and perfidious Bark
Built in the eclipse, and rigged with curses dark,
That sunk so low that sacred head of thine.
   Next Camus, reverend Sire, went footing slow,
His Mantle hairy, and his Bonnet sedge,
Inwrought with figures dim, and on the edge
Like to that sanguine flower inscribed with woe.
"Ah, who hath reft," (quoth he) "my dearest pledge?"
Last come, and last did go,
The Pilot of the Galilean Lake.
Two massy Keys he bore of metals twain,
(The Golden opes, the Iron shuts amain).
He shook his Mitred locks, and stern bespake,
"How well could I have spared for thee, young swain.
Enow of such as, for their bellies' sake,
Creep and intrude, and climb into the fold!
Of other care they little reckoning make,
Than how to scramble at the shearers' feast,
   190

And shove away the worthy bidden guest.
Blind mouths! that scarce themselves know how to hold
A Sheep-hook, or have learned aught else the least
That to the faithful Herdman's art belongs!
What recks it them? What need they? They are sped;
And when they list, their lean and flashy songs
Grate on their scrannel Pipes of wretched straw,
The hungry Sheep look up, and are not fed,
But swoln with wind, and the rank mist they draw,
Rot inwardly, and foul contagion spread:
Besides what the grim Wolf with privy paw
Daily devours apace, and nothing said.
But that two-handed engine at the door,
Stands ready to smite once, and smite no more."
    Return Alpheus, the dread voice is past,
That shrunk thy streams; return Sicilian Muse,
And call the Vales, and bid them hither cast
Their Bells, and Flowerets of a thousand hues.
Ye valleys low, where the mild whispers use,
Of shades and wanton winds, and gushing brooks,
On whose fresh lap the swart Star sparely looks,
Throw hither all your quaint enamelled eyes,
That on the green turf suck the honied showers,
And purple all the ground with vernal flowers.
Bring the rathe Primrose that forsaken dies,
The tufted Crow-toe, and pale Jessamine,
The white Pink, and the Pansy freaked with jet,
The glowing Violet,
The Musk-rose, and the well-attired Woodbine,
With Cowslips wan that hang the pensive head,
And every flower that sad embroidery wears:
Bid Amaranthus all his beauty shed,
And Daffadillies fill their cups with tears,
To strew the Laureate Hearse where Lycid lies.
For so to interpose a little ease,
Let our frail thoughts dally with false surmise.
Ay me! Whilst thee the shores, and sounding Seas
Wash far away, where e'er thy bones are hurled,
Whether beyond the stormy Hebrides,
Where thou perhaps under the whelming tide
Visit'st the bottom of the monstrous world;

Or whether thou, to our moist vows denied,
Sleep'st by the fable of Bellerus old,
Where the great vision of the guarded Mount
Looks toward Namancos and Bayona's hold;
Look homeward, Angel, now, and melt with ruth:
And, O ye Dolphins, waft the hapless youth.
    Weep no more, woful Shepherds, weep no more,
For Lycidas your sorrow is not dead,
Sunk though he be beneath the watery floor.
So sinks the day-star in the Ocean bed,
And yet anon repairs his drooping head,
And tricks his beams, and with new-spangled Ore,
Flames in the forehead of the morning sky:
So Lycidas sunk low, but mounted high,
Through the dear might of Him that walked the waves
Where, other groves and other streams along,
With Nectar pure his oozy Locks he laves,
And hears the unexpressive nuptial Song,
In the blest Kingdoms meek of joy and love.
There entertain him all the Saints above,
In solemn troops, and sweet Societies,
That sing, and singing in their glory move,
And wipe the tears for ever from his eyes.
Now, Lycidas, the Shepherds weep no more;
Henceforth thou art the Genius of the shore,
In thy large recompense, and shalt be good
To all that wander in that perilous flood.
    Thus sang the uncouth Swain to the Oaks and rills,
While the still morn went out with Sandals grey,
He touched the tender stops of various Quills,
With eager thought warbling his Doric lay:
And now the Sun had stretched out all the hills,
And now was dropt into the Western bay;
At last he rose, and twitched his Mantle blue:
To-morrow to fresh Woods, and Pastures new.

JOHN MILTON

IL PENSEROSO

Hence vain deluding Joys,
  The brood of Folly without father bred!
How little you bestead,
  Or fill the fixèd mind with all your toys;
Dwell in some idle brain,
  And fancies fond with gaudy shapes possess,
As thick and numberless
  As the gay motes t'at people the sun-beams,
Or likest hovering dreams
  The fickle Pensioners of Morpheus' train.
But hail, thou Goddess, sage and holy,
Hail, divinest Melancholy!
Whose Saintly visage is too bright
To hit the Sense of human sight;
And therefore to our weaker view,
O'er-laid with black, staid Wisdom's hue.
Black, but such as in esteem,
Prince Memnon's sister might beseem,
Or that Starred Ethiope Queen that strove
To set her beauty's praise above
The Sea Nymphs, and their powers offended.
Yet thou art higher far descended:
Thee bright-haired Vesta long of yore,
To solitary Saturn bore;
His daughter she (in Saturn's reign,
Such mixture was not held a stain).
Oft in glimmering Bowers, and glades
He met her, and in secret shades
Of woody Ida's inmost grove,
Whilst yet there was no fear of Jove.
Come, pensive Nun, devout and pure,
Sober, steadfast, and demure,
All in a robe of darkest grain,
Flowing with majestic train,
And sable stole of Cypress Lawn,
Over thy decent shoulders drawn.
Come, but keep thy wonted state,
With even step, and musing gait,

192

And looks commercing with the skies,
Thy rapt soul sitting in thine eyes:
There, held in holy passion still,
Forget thy self to Marble, till
With a sad Leaden downward cast,
Thou fix them on the earth as fast.
And join with thee calm Peace, and Quiet,
Spare Fast, that oft with gods doth diet,
And hears the Muses in a ring,
Aye round about Jove's Altar sing.
And add to these retirèd Leisure,
That in trim Gardens takes his pleasure;
But first, and chiefest, with thee bring,
Him that yon soars on golden wing,
Guiding the fiery-wheelèd throne,
The Cherub Contemplation,
And the mute Silence hist along,
'Less Philomel will deign a Song,
In her sweetest, saddest plight,
Smoothing the rugged brow of Night,
While Cynthia checks her Dragon yoke,
Gently o'er th' accustomed Oak;
Sweet Bird, that shunn'st the noise of folly,
Most musical, most melancholy!
Thee, Chauntress, oft the Woods among,
I woo to hear thy even-song;
And missing thee, I walk unseen
On the dry smooth-shaven Green,
To behold the wandering Moon,
Riding near her highest noon,
Like one that had been led astray
Through the Heaven's wide pathless way;
And oft, as if her head she bowed,
Stooping through a fleecy cloud.
Oft on a Plat of rising ground,
I hear the far-off Curfew sound,
Over some wide-watered shore,
Swinging slow with sullen roar;
Or if the Air will not permit,
Some still removèd place will fit,

JOHN MILTON

Where glowing Embers through the room
Teach light to counterfeit a gloom,
Far from all resort of mirth,
Save the Cricket on the hearth,
Or the Bellman's drowsy charm,
To bless the doors from nightly harm:
Or let my Lamp, at midnight hour,
Be seen in some high lonely Tower,
Where I may oft out-watch the Bear,
With thrice great Hermes, or unsphere
The spirit of Plato to unfold
What Worlds, or what vast Regions hold
The immortal mind that hath forsook
Her mansion in this fleshly nook:
And of those Dæmons that are found
In fire, air, flood, or under ground,
Whose power hath a true consent
With Planet, or with Element.
Some time let Gorgeous Tragedy
In Sceptred Pall come sweeping by,
Presenting Thebes, or Pelops' line,
Or the tale of Troy divine,
Or what (though rare) of later age,
Ennoblèd hath the Buskined stage.
   But, O sad Virgin, that thy power
Might raise Musæus from his bower,
Or bid the soul of Orpheus sing
Such notes as, warbled to the string,
Drew Iron tears down Pluto's cheek,
And made Hell grant what Love did seek.
Or call up him that left half told
The story of Cambuscan bold,
Of Camball, and of Algarsife,
And who had Canace to wife,
That owned the virtuous Ring and Glass,
And of the wondrous Horse of Brass,
On which the Tartar King did ride;
And if aught else great Bards beside,
In sage and solemn tunes have sung,
Of Tourneys and of Trophies hung;

Of Forests, and enchantments drear,
Where more is meant than meets the ear.
Thus, Night, oft see me in thy pale career,
Till civil-suited Morn appear,
Not tricked and frounced as she was wont,
With the Attic Boy to hunt,
But Kerchiefed in a comely Cloud,
While rocking Winds are Piping loud,
Or ushered with a shower still,
When the gust hath blown his fill,
Ending on the rustling Leaves,
With minute-drops from off the Eaves.
And when the Sun begins to fling
His flaring beams, me, Goddess, bring
To archèd walks of twilight groves,
And shadows brown, that Sylvan loves,
Of Pine, or monumental Oak,
Where the rude Ax with heavèd stroke,
Was never heard the Nymphs to daunt,
Or fright them from their hallowed haunt
There in close covert by some Brook,
Where no profaner eye may look,
Hide me from Day's garish eye,
While the Bee with Honied thigh,
That at her flowery work doth sing,
And the Waters murmuring
With such consort as they keep,
Entice the dewy-feathered Sleep;
And let some strange mysterious dream,
Wave at his Wings, in Airy stream
Of lively portraiture displayed,
Softly on my eye-lids laid.
And as I wake, sweet music breathe
Above, about, or underneath,
Sent by some Spirit to mortals good,
Or th' unseen Genius of the Wood.
  But let my due feet never fail,
To walk the studious Cloister's pale,
And love the high embowèd Roof,
With antique Pillars massy proof,

And storied Windows richly dight
Casting a dim religious light.
There let the pealing Organ blow,
To the full voiced choir below,
In Service high, and Anthems clear,
As may with sweetness, through mine ear,
Dissolve me into ecstasies,
And bring all Heaven before mine eyes.
And may at last my weary age
Find out the peaceful hermitage,
The Hairy Gown and Mossy Cell,
Where I may sit and rightly spell
Of every Star that Heaven doth shew,
And every Herb that sips the dew;
Till old experience do attain
To something like Prophetic strain.
These pleasures, Melancholy, give,
And I with thee will choose to live.

L'ALLEGRO

Hence loathèd Melancholy,
　Of Cerberus and blackest Midnight born,
In Stygian cave forlorn,
　'Mongst horrid shapes, and shrieks, and sights unholy!
Find out some uncouth cell,
　Where brooding Darkness spreads his jealous wings,
And the night-raven sings;
　There under ebon shades, and low-browed rocks,
As ragged as thy locks,
　In dark Cimmerian desert ever dwell.
But come, thou goddess fair and free,
In heaven yclept Euphrosyne,
And by men heart-easing Mirth;
Whom lovely Venus, at a birth,
With two sister Graces more,
To ivy-crownèd Bacchus bore:
Or whether (as some sager sing)
The frolic wind that breathes the spring,

Zephyr, with Aurora playing,
As he met her once a-Maying;
There on beds of violets blue,
And fresh-blown roses washed in dew,
Filled her with thee, a daughter fair,
So buxom, blithe, and debonair.
    Haste thee, nymph, and bring with thee
Jest, and youthful jollity,
Quips, and cranks, and wanton wiles,
Nods, and becks, and wreathèd smiles,
Such as hang on Hebe's cheek,
And love to live in dimple sleek;
Sport that wrinkled Care derides,
And Laughter holding both his sides.
Come, and trip it as you go,
On the light fantastic toe;
And in thy right hand lead with thee
The mountain-nymph, sweet Liberty;
And, if I give thee honour due,
Mirth, admit me of thy crew,
To live with her, and live with thee,
In unreprovèd pleasures free;
To hear the lark begin his flight,
And singing startle the dull night,
From his watch-tower in the skies,
Till the dappled dawn doth rise;
Then to come, in spite of sorrow,
And at my window bid good-morrow,
Through the sweet-briar, or the vine,
Or the twisted eglantine:
While the cock, with lively din,
Scatters the rear of darkness thin,
And to the stack, or the barn-door,
Stoutly struts his dames before:
Oft listening how the hounds and horn
Cheerly rouse the slumbering morn,
From the side of some hoar hill,
Through the high wood echoing shrill.
    Sometime walking, not unseen,
By hedgerow elms, on hillocks green,

JOHN MILTON

Right against the eastern gate,
Where the great sun begins his state,
Robed in flames and amber light,
The clouds in thousand liveries dight;
While the ploughman, near at hand,
Whistles o'er the furrowed land,
And the milkmaid singeth blithe,
And the mower whets his scythe,
And every shepherd tells his tale,
Under the hawthorn in the dale.
  Straight mine eye hath caught new pleasures,
While the landskip round it measures;
Russet lawns, and fallows grey,
Where the nibbling flocks do stray;
Mountains, on whose barren breast
The labouring clouds do often rest;
Meadows trim, with daisies pied,
Shallow brooks, and rivers wide;
Towers and battlements it sees
Bosomed high in tufted trees,
Where perhaps some beauty lies,
The cynosure of neighbouring eyes.
  Hard by, a cottage chimney smokes
From betwixt two aged oaks,
Where Corydon and Thyrsis met,
Are at their savoury dinner set
Of herbs, and other country messes,
Which the neat-handed Phillis dresses;
And then in haste her bower she leaves,
With Thestylis to bind the sheaves;
Or, if the earlier season lead,
To the tanned haycock in the mead.
  Sometimes with secure delight
The upland hamlets will invite,
When the merry bells ring round,
And the jocund rebecks sound
To many a youth and many a maid,
Dancing in the chequered shade,
And young and old come forth to play
On a sunshine holiday,

Till the livelong daylight fail:
Then to the spicy nut-brown ale,
With stories told of many a feat:
How faery Mab the junkets eat;
She was pinched, and pulled, she said;
And he, by friar's lantern led,
Tells how the drudging goblin sweat
To earn his cream-bowl duly set,
When in one night, ere glimpse of morn,
His shadowy flail hath threshed the corn,
That ten day-labourers could not end;
Then lies him down, the lubber fiend,
And, stretched out all the chimney's length,
Basks at the fire his hairy strength;
And crop-full out of doors he flings,
Ere the first cock his matin rings.
Thus done the tales, to bed they creep,
By whispering winds soon lulled asleep.
    Towered cities please us then,
And the busy hum of men,
Where throngs of knights and barons bold,
In weeds of peace, high triumphs hold,
With store of ladies, whose bright eyes
Rain influence, and judge the prize
Of wit or arms, while both contend
To win her grace whom all commend.
There let Hymen oft appear
In saffron robe, with taper clear,
And pomp, and feast, and revelry,
With mask and antique pageantry;
Such sights as youthful poets dream
On summer eves by haunted stream.
Then to the well-trod stage anon,
If Jonson's learned sock be on,
Or sweetest Shakespeare, Fancy's child,
Warble his native wood-notes wild.
    And ever, against eating cares,
Lap me in soft Lydian airs,
Married to immortal verse,
Such as the meeting soul may pierce,

JOHN MILTON

In notes with many a winding bout
Of linkèd sweetness long drawn out,
With wanton heed and giddy cunning;
The melting voice through mazes running,
Untwisting all the chains that tie
The hidden soul of harmony;
That Orpheus' self may heave his head
From golden slumber on a bed
Of heaped Elysian flowers, and hear
Such strains as would have won the ear
Of Pluto, to have quite set free
His half-regained Eurydice. .
   These delights if thou canst give,
Mirth, with thee I mean to live.

ARCADES

.   .   .   .

O'er the smooth enamelled green,
Where no print of step hath been,
   Follow me, as I sing
   And touch the warbled string;
Under the shady roof
Of branching elm star-proof
      Follow me.
I will bring you where she sits,
Clad in splendour as befits
      Her deity.
Such a rural Queen
All Arcadia hath not seen.

.   .   .   .

ON THE MORNING OF CHRIST'S NATIVITY

This is the month, and this the happy morn
Wherein the Son of Heaven's Eternal King,
Of wedded maid and virgin mother born,
Our great redemption from above did bring;

For so the holy sages once did sing
That he our deadly forfeit should release,
And with his Father work us a perpetual peace.

That glorious Form, that Light unsufferable,
And that far-beaming blaze of Majesty
Wherewith he wont at Heaven's high council-ta
To sit the midst of Trinal Unity,
He laid aside; and, here with us to be,
Forsook the courts of everlasting day,
And chose with us a darksome house of mortal clay.

Say, Heavenly Muse, shall not thy sacred vein
Afford a present to the Infant God?
Hast thou no verse, no hymn, or solemn strain
To welcome him to this his new abode,
Now while the heaven, by the sun's team untrod,
Hath took no print of the approaching light,
And all the spangled host keep watch in squadrons bright?

See how from far, upon the eastern road,
The star-led wizards haste with odours sweet!
O run, prevent them with thy humble ode
And lay it lowly at his blessed feet;
Have thou the honour first thy Lord to greet,
And join thy voice unto the angel choir
From out his secret altar touched with hallowed fire.

THE HYMN

It was the winter wild
While the heaven-born Child
All meanly wrapped in the rude manger lies;
Nature in awe to Him
Had doffed her gaudy trim,
With her great Master so to sympathize:
It was no season then for her
To wanton with the sun, her lusty paramour.

Only with speeches fair
She woos the gentle air
202

JOHN MILTON

To hide her guilty front with innocent snow;
And on her naked shame,
Pollute with sinful blame,
The saintly veil of maiden white to throw;
Confounded, that her Maker's eyes
Should look so near upon her foul deformities.

But he, her fears to cease,
Sent down the meek-eyed Peace;
She, crowned with olive green, came softly sliding
Down through the turning sphere,
His ready harbinger,
With turtle wing and amorous clouds dividing;
And waving wide her myrtle wand,
She strikes a universal peace through sea and land.

.   .   .   .

ON MAY MORNING

Now the bright morning star, day's harbinger,
Comes dancing from the east, and leads with her
The flow'ry May, who from her green lap throws
The yellow cowslip, and the pale primrose.
   Hail, bounteous May, that dost inspire
   Mirth, and youth, and warm desire;
   Woods and groves are of thy dressing,
   Hill and dale doth boast thy blessing.
Thus we salute thee with our early song,
And welcome thee, and wish thee long.

ON SHAKESPEARE, 1630

What needs my Shakespeare for his honoured bones,
The labour of an age in pilèd stones,
Or that his hallowed relics should be hid
Under a star-ypointing pyramid?
Dear son of memory, great heir of Fame,
What need'st thou such weak witness of thy name?

203

Thou in our wonder and astonishment
Hast built thyself a livelong monument.
For whilst to the shame of slow-endeavouring art,
Thy easy numbers flow, and that each heart
Hath from the leaves of thy unvalued book,
Those Delphic lines with deep impression took,
Then thou our fancy of itself bereaving,
Dost make us marble with too much conceiving;
And so sepulchred in such pomp dost lie,
That kings for such a tomb would wish to die.

THE NIGHTINGALE

O Nightingale, that on yon bloomy spray
Warbl'st at eve, when all the woods are still,
Thou with fresh hope the Lover's heart dost fill,
While the jolly hours lead on propitious May,
Thy liquid notes that close the eye of Day,
First heard before the shallow Cuckoo's bill
Portend success in love; O if Jove's will
Have linked that amorous power to thy soft lay,
Now timely sing, ere the rude Bird of Hate
Foretell my hopeless doom in some grove nigh:
As thou from year to year hast sung too late
For my relief; yet hadst no reason why,
Whether the Muse or Love call thee his mate,
Both them I serve, and of their train am I.

TO THE LADY MARGARET LEY

Daughter to that good Earl, once President
    Of England's Council, and her Treasury,
        Who liv'd in both, unstain'd with gold or fee,
        And left them both, more in himself content,
Till sad the breaking of that Parliament
        Broke him, as that dishonest victory
        At Chæronea, fatal to liberty,
    Kill'd with report that old man eloquent.

204

JOHN MILTON

Though later born than to have known the days
    Wherein your father flourish'd, yet by you,
    Madam, methinks I see him living yet;
So well your words his noble virtues praise,
    That all both judge you to relate them true,
    And to possess them, honour'd Margaret.

TO THE LORD GENERAL CROMWELL

Cromwell, our chief of men, who through a cloud
Not of war only, but detractions rude,
Guided by faith and matchless fortitude
To peace and truth thy glorious way hast ploughed,
And on the neck of crownèd Fortune proud
Hast reared God's trophies, and His work pursued,
While Darwen stream with blood of Scots imbrued
And Dunbar field resounds thy praises loud,
And Worcester's laureate wreath; yet much remains
To conquer still; peace hath her victories
No less renowned than war, new foes arise
Threatening to bind our souls with secular chains:
Help us to save free conscience from the paw
Of hireling wolves whose gospel is their maw.

ON HIS BLINDNESS

When I consider how my light is spent,
Ere half my days, in this dark world and wide,
And that one talent which is death to hide,
Lodged with me useless, though my soul more bent
To serve therewith my Maker, and present
My true account, lest He returning chide,
Doth God exact day-labour, light denied?
I fondly ask; but Patience, to prevent
That murmur, soon replies, God doth not need
Either man's work or His own gifts: who best
Bear his mild yoke, they serve Him best; His state
Is kingly. Thousands at His bidding speed
And post o'er land and ocean without rest:
They also serve who only stand and wait.

ON HIS DECEASED WIFE

Methought I saw my late espousèd saint
  Brought to me like Alcestis from the grave,
  Whom Jove's great son to her glad husband gave,
Rescued from Death by force, though pale and faint.
Mine, as whom washed from spot of child-bed taint
  Purification in the Old Law did save,
  And such as yet once more I trust to have
Full sight of her in Heaven without restraint,
Came vested all in white, pure as her mind.
  Her face was veiled; yet to my fancied sight
  Love, sweetness, goodness, in her person shined
So clear as in no face with more delight.
  But, oh! as to embrace me she inclined,
  I waked, she fled, and day brought back my night.

Sir John Suckling

A BALLAD UPON A WEDDING

I tell thee, Dick, where I have been,
Where I the rarest things have seen,
  Oh, things beyond compare!
Such sights again cannot be found
In any place on English ground,
  Be it at wake or fair.

At Charing Cross, hard by the way
Where we (thou know'st) do sell our hay,
  There is a house with stairs;
And there did I see coming down
Such folk as are not in our town,
  Forty at least, in pairs.

Amongst the rest, one pestilent fine
  (His beard no bigger, though, than thine!)

206

SIR JOHN SUCKLING

Walked on before the rest.
Our landlord looks like nothing to him;
The king (God bless him!), 'twould undo him,
    Should he go still so dressed.

.   .   .   .

But wot you what?   The youth was going
To make an end of all his wooing;
    The Parson for him stayed.
Yet, by his leave, for all his haste,
He did not so much wish all passed,
    Perchance, as did the maid.

The maid (and thereby hangs a tale)
For such a maid no Whitsun ale
    Could ever yet produce;
No grape that's kindly ripe could be
So round, so plump, so soft, as she;
    Nor half so full of juice!

Her finger was so small, the ring
Would not stay on; which they did bring.
    It was too wide a peck!
And to say truth, for out it must,
It looked like the great collar (just)
    About our young colt's neck.

Her feet, beneath her petticoat,
Like little mice stole in and out,
    As if they feared the light:
But oh! she dances such a way,
No sun, upon an Easter Day,
    Is half so fine a sight!

.   .   .   .

Her cheeks so rare a white was on;
No daisy makes comparison,
    Who sees them is undone.
For streaks of red were mingled there,
Such as are on a Katherine pear
    (The side that's next the sun).

Her lips were red, and one was thin
Compared to that was next her chin

(Some bee had stung it newly).
But, Dick, her eyes so guard her face,
I durst no more upon them gaze,
    Than on the sun in July.

Her mouth so small, when she does speak
Thou'dst swear her teeth her words did break,
    That they might passage get:
But she so handled still the matter,
They came as good as ours or better,
    And are not spent a whit!

.   .   .   .

Passion o' me! how I run on;
There's that that would be thought upon,
    I trow, besides the bride:
The business of the kitchen's great
For it is fit that men should eat;
    Nor was it there denied.

Just in the nick, the cook knocked thrice,
And all the waiters, in a trice,
    His summons did obey.
Each serving-man, with dish in hand,
Marched boldly up like our trained band,
    Presented, and away!

When all the meat was on the table
What man of knife or teeth was able
    To stay to be entreated?
And this the very reason was,
Before the Parson could say grace
    The company was seated.

The business of the kitchen's great,
For it is fit that men should eat;
    Nor was it there denied.
(Passion o' me, how I run on!
There's that, that would be thought upon,
    I trow, beside the bride).

Now hats fly off; and youths carouse:
Healths first go round, and then the house.

SIR JOHN SUCKLING

The bride's came thick and thick.
And when 'twas named another's health,
Perhaps he made it hers by stealth.
    (And who could help it, Dick?)

O' th' sudden, up they rise and dance:
Then sit again and sigh and glance,
    Then dance again and kiss.
Thus several ways the time did pass;
Whilst every woman wished her place,
    And every man wished his!

HAST THOU SEEN THE DOWN IN THE AIR

Hast thou seen the down in the air,
When wanton blasts have tossed it?
Or the ship on the sea,
When ruder winds have crossed it?

Hast thou marked the crocodile's weeping,
Or the fox's sleeping?
Or hast thou viewed the peacock in his pride,
Or the dove by his bride? . . .
O so fickle, O so vain, O so false, so false is 'she!

I PRITHEE SEND ME BACK MY HEART

I prithee send me back my heart,
    Since I cannot have thine;
For if from yours you will not part,
    Why, then, shouldst thou have mine?

Yet now I think on't, let it lie,
    To find it were in vain;
For thou hast a thief in either eye
    Would steal it back again.

Why should two hearts in one breast lie,
    And yet not lodge together?
O Love! where is thy sympathy,
    If thus our breasts thou sever?

209

But love is such a mystery,
    I cannot find it out;
For when I think I'm best resolved,
    I then am in most doubt.

Then farewell care, and farewell woe;
    I will no longer pine;
For I'll believe I have her heart,
    As much as she hath mine.

THE CONSTANT LOVER

Why so pale and wan, fond lover?
    Prithee, why so pale?
Will, when looking well can't move her,
    Looking ill prevail?
    Prithee, why so pale?

Why so dull and mute, young sinner?
    Prithee, why so mute?
Will, when speaking well can't win her,
    Saying nothing do't?
    Prithee, why so mute?

Quit, quit, for shame! this will not move,
    This cannot take her;
If of herself she will not love,
    Nothing can make her:
    The Devil take her!

WHEN, DEAREST, I BUT THINK OF THEE

When, dearest, I but think of thee,
Methinks all things that lovely be
    Are present, and my soul delighted:
For beauties that from worth arise
Are like the grace of deities,
    Still present with us, though unsighted.

Thus while I sit and sigh the day
With all his borrowed lights away,
   Till night's black wings do overtake me,
Thinking on thee, thy beauties then,
As sudden lights do sleepy men,
   So they by their bright rays awake me.

Thus absence dies, and dying proves
No absence can subsist with loves
   That do partake of fair perfection:
Since in the darkest night they may
By love's quick motion find a way
   To see each other by reflection.

The waving sea can with each flood
Bathe some high promont that hath stood
   Far from the main up in the river:
O think not then but love can do
As much! for that's an ocean too,
   Which flows not every day, but ever!

Richard Crashaw

SAINT TERESA

O thou undaunted daughter of desires!
By all thy dower of lights and fires;
By all the eagle in thee, all the dove;
By all thy lives and deaths of love;
By thy large draughts of intellectual day,
And by thy thirsts of love more large than they;
By all thy brim-filled bowls of fierce desire,
By thy last morning's draught of liquid fire;
By the full kingdom of that final kiss
That seized thy parting soul, and sealed thee His;
By all the Heaven thou hast in Him
(Fair sister of the seraphim!);

By all of Him we have in thee;
Leave nothing of myself in me.
Let me so read thy life, that I
Unto all life of mine may die!

IN THE TEMPLE

Two went to pray? oh, rather say
One went to brag, the other to pray.

One stands up close, and treads on high,
Where the other dares not send his eye.

One nearer to God's altar trod;
The other to the altar's God.

WISHES FOR THE SUPPOSED MISTRESS

Whoe'er she be,
That not impossible She
That shall command my heart and me;

Where'er she lie,
Lock'd up from mortal eye
In shady leaves of destiny:

Till that ripe birth
Of studied Fate stand forth,
And teach her fair steps to our earth;

Till that divine
Idea take a shrine
Of crystal flesh, through which to shine:

—Meet you her, my Wishes,
Bespeak her to my blisses,
And be ye call'd, my absent kisses.

I wish her beauty
That owes not all its duty
To gaudy tire, or glist'ring shoe-tie:

RICHARD CRASHAW

Something more than
Taffata or tissue can,
Or rampant feather, or rich fan.

A face that's best
By its own beauty drest,
And can alone command the rest:

A face made up
Out of no other shop
Than what Nature's white hand sets ope.

Sidneian showers
Of sweet discourse, whose powers
Can crown old Winter's head with flowers.

Whate'er delight
Can make day's forehead bright
Or give down to the wings of night.

Soft silken hours,
Open suns, shady bowers;
'Bove all, nothing within that lowers.

Days, that need borrow
No part of their good morrow
From a fore-spent night of sorrow:

Days, that in spite
Of darkness, by the light
Of a clear mind are day all night.

Life, that dares send
A challenge to his end,
And when it comes, say, "Welcome, friend."

I wish her store
Of worth may leave her poor
Of wishes; and I wish—no more.

—Now, if Time knows
That Her, whose radiant brows
Weave them a garland of my vows;

Her that dares be
What these lines wish to see:
I seek no further, it is She.

'Tis She, and here,
Lo! I unclothe and clear
My wishes' cloudy character.

Such worth as this is
Shall fix my flying wishes,
And determine them to kisses.

Let her full glory,
My fancies, fly before ye;
Be ye my fictions:—but her story.

EUTHANASIA

Wouldst see blithe looks, fresh cheeks beguile
Age? wouldst see December smile?
Wouldst see nests of new roses grow
In a bed of reverend snow?
Warm thoughts, free spirits, flattering
Winter's self into a spring?
In sum wouldst see a man that can
Live to be old, and still a man?
Whose latest and most leaden hours,
Fall with soft wings stuck with soft flowers;
And, when life's sweet fable ends,
Soul and body part like friends;
No quarrels, murmurs, no delay—
A kiss, a sigh, and so away.
This rare one, reader, wouldst thou see?
Hark hither!—and thyself be he.

Richard Lovelace

TO ALTHEA, FROM PRISON

When Love with unconfinèd wings
    Hovers within my gates,
And my divine Althea brings
    To whisper at the grates;
When I lie tangled in her hair
    And fettered to her eye,
The birds that wanton in the air
    Know no such liberty.

When flowing cups run swiftly round
    With no allaying Thames,
Our careless heads with roses bound,
    Our hearts with loyal flames;
When thirsty grief in wine we steep,
    When healths and draughts go free—
Fishes that tipple in the deep
    Know no such liberty.

When, like committed linnets, I
    With shriller throat shall sing
The sweetness, mercy, majesty,
    And glories of my King;
When I shall voice aloud how good
    He is, how great should be,
Enlargèd winds, that curl the flood,
    Know no such liberty.

Stone walls do not a prison make,
    Nor iron bars a cage;
Minds innocent and quiet take
    That for an hermitage;
If I have freedom in my love
    And in my soul am free,
Angels alone, that soar above,
    Enjoy such liberty.

TO LUCASTA, GOING TO THE WARS

Tell me not, Sweet, I am unkind,
    That from the nunnery
Of thy chaste breast and quiet mind
    To war and arms I fly.

True, a new mistress now I chase,
    The first foe in the field;
And with a stronger faith embrace
    A sword, a horse, a shield.

Yet this inconstancy is such
    As thou too shalt adore;
I could not love thee, Dear, so much,
    Loved I not Honour more.

Sir John Denham

O COULD I FLOW

O could I flow like thee, and make thy stream
My great example, as it is my theme!
Though deep, yet clear; though gentle, yet not dull;
Strong without rage, without o'erflowing full.

Abraham Cowley

DRINKING

The thirsty earth soaks up the rain,
And drinks, and gapes for drink again.
The plants suck in the earth, and are
With constant drinking fresh and fair;
The sea itself—which one would think
Should have but little need of drink—

Drinks ten thousand rivers up,
So filled that they o'erflow the cup.
The busy sun—and one would guess
By's drunken fiery face no less—
Drinks up the sea, and when he's done,
The moon and stars drink up the sun:
They drink and dance by their own light;
They drink and revel all the night.
Nothing in nature's sober found,
But an eternal health goes round.
Fill up the bowl then, fill it high,
Fill up the glasses there; for why
Should every creature drink but I;
Why, man of morals, tell me why?

ON THE DEATH OF MR. CRASHAW

Poet and Saint! to thee alone are given
The two most sacred names of earth and heaven,
The hard and rarest union which can be,
Next that of Godhead with humanity.
Long did the Muses banished slaves abide,
And built vain pyramids to mortal pride:
Like Moses, thou (though spells and charms withstand)
Hast brought them nobly home back to their Holy Land.
    Ah, wretched we, poets of earth! but thou
Wert living the same poet which thou'rt now.
Whilst angels sing to thee their airs divine,
And joy in an applause so great as thine.
Equal society with them to hold,
Thou need'st not make new songs, but say the old.
And they (kind spirits!) shall all rejoice to see
How little less than they exalted man may be.

   •   •   •   •   •   •   •   •   •

SPORT

The merry waves dance up and down and play,
Sport is granted to the sea;

Birds are the quiristers of the empty air,
    Sport is never wanting there;
The ground doth smile at the spring's flowery birth,
    Sport is granted to the earth;
The fire its cheering flame on high doth rear,
    Sport is never wanting there.
If all the elements, the earth, the sea,
    Air, and fire, so merry be,
Why is man's mirth so seldom and so small,
    Who is compounded of them all?

THE WISH

Well then, I now do plainly see
This busy world and I shall ne'er agree.
The very honey of all earthly joy
Does, of all meats, the soonest cloy;
    And they, methinks, deserve my pity
Who for it can endure the stings,
The crowd and buzz and murmurings
    Of this great hive, the city!

Ah yet, ere I descend to the grave,
May I a small house and large garden have;
And a few friends, and many books, both true,
Both wise, and both delightful too!
    And since Love ne'er will from me flee,—
A Mistress moderately fair,
And good as guardian angels are,
    Only beloved, and loving me!

O founts! Oh, when in you shall I
Myself eased of unpeaceful thoughts espy?
O fields! O woods! when, when shall I be made
The happy tenant of your shade?
    Here's the spring-head of Pleasure's flood!
Here's wealthy Nature's treasury,
Where all the riches lie that she
    Has coined and stamped for good.

228

ABRAHAM COWLEY

Pride and ambition here
Only in far-fetched metaphors appear;
Here naught but winds can hurtful murmurs scatter,
And naught but echo flatter.
   The gods, when they descended, hither
From heaven did always choose their way;
And therefore we may boldly say
   That 'tis the way to thither.

How happy here should I
And one dear She live, and embracing die!
She who is all the world, and can exclude
In deserts solitude.
   I should have then this only fear:
Lest men, when they my pleasures see,
Should hither throng to live like me,
   And so make a city here.

IN DEFENSE OF THE ROYAL SOCIETY

The things which these proud men despise, and call
   Impertinent, and vain, and small,
Those smallest things of nature let me know,
Rather than all their greatest actions do!
Whoever would deposèd Truth advance
   Into the throne usurped from it,
Must feel at first the blows of Ignorance,
   And the sharp points of envious Wit.
So, when, by various turns of the celestial dance,
   In many thousand years
   A star, so long unknown, appears,
Though heaven itself more beauteous by it grow,
It troubles and alarms the world below;
Does to the wise a star, to fools a meteor, show.

ON THE DEATH OF MR. WILLIAM HERVEY

.   .   .   .

   Say, for you saw us, ye immortal lights,
   How oft unwearied have we spent the nights,

Till the Ledæan stars, so famed for Jove,
  Wonder'd at us from above!
We spent them not in toys, in lusts, or wine;
  But search of deep Philosophy,
  Wit, Eloquence, and Poetry,—
Arts which I lov'd, for they, my friend, were thine.

Ye fields of Cambridge, our dear Cambridge, say
Have ye not seen us walking every day?
Was there a tree about which did not know
  The love betwixt us two?
Henceforth, ye gentle trees, for ever fade;
  Or you sad branches thicker join
  And into darksome shades combine,
Dark as the grave wherein my friend is laid!

HYMN TO LIGHT

. . . .

Thou, Scythian-like, dost round thy lands above
  The sun's gilt tents for ever move,
  And still, as thou in pomp dost go,
The shining pageants of the world attend thy show;

Nor amidst all these triumphs dost thou scorn
  The humble glow-worms to adorn,
  And with those living spangles gild—
O greatness without pride!—the bushes of the field;

. . . .

When, Goddess! thou lift'st up thy waken'd head,
  Out of the morning's purple bed,
  Thy quire of birds about thee play,
And all the joyful world salutes the rising day.

. . . .

All the world's bravery that delights our eyes,
  Is but thy several liveries.
  Thou the rich dye on them bestow'st,
Thy nimble pencil paints this landscape as thou go'st.

A crimson garment in the rose thou wear'st;
  A crown of studded gold thou bear'st;
220

ANDREW MARVELL

The virgin lilies in their white
Are clad but with the lawn of almost naked light.

The violet, Spring's little infant, stands
   Girt in thy purple swaddling bands;
   On the fair tulip thou dost doat;
Thou cloath'st it in a gay and party-colour'd coat.

LIFE

     Life's a name
That nothing here can truly claim;
This wretched inn, where we scarce stay to bait,
   We call our dwelling-place!
   And mighty voyages we take,
   And mighty journeys seem to make,
O'er sea and land, the little point that has no space.
   Because we fight and battles gain,
Some captives call, and say, "the rest are slain";
Because we heap up yellow earth, and so
Rich, valiant, wise, and virtuous seem to grow;
Because we draw a long nobility
From hieroglyphic proofs of heraldry,
And impudently talk of a posterity—
We grow at last by Custom to believe,
   That really we Live;
Whilst all these Shadows, that for Things we take,
Are but the empty Dreams which in Death's sleep we make

Andrew Marvell

BERMUDAS

Where the remote Bermudas ride
In the ocean's bosom unespied,
From a small boat that rowed along
The listening winds received this song:

"What should we do but sing His praise
That led us through the watery maze
Unto an isle so long unknown,
And yet far kinder than our own?
Where He the huge sea-monsters wracks,
That lift the deep upon their backs,
He lands us on a grassy stage,
Safe from the storms' and prelates' rage:
He gave us this eternal Spring
Which here enamels everything,
And sends the fowls to us in care
On daily visits through the air:
He hangs in shades the orange bright
Like golden lamps in a green night,
And does in the pomegranates close
Jewels more rich than Ormus shows:
He makes the figs our mouths to meet
And throws the melons at our feet;
But apples plants of such a price,
No tree could ever bear them twice.
With cedars chosen by His hand
From Lebanon He stores the land;
And makes the hollow seas that roar
Proclaim the ambergris on shore.
He cast (of which we rather boast)
The Gospel's pearl upon our coast;
And in these rocks for us did frame
A temple where to sound His name.
O, let our voice His praise exalt
Till it arrive at Heaven's vault,
Which thence (perhaps) rebounding may
Echo beyond the Mexique bay!"

Thus sung they in the English boat
A holy and a cheerful note:
And all the way, to guide their chime,
With falling oars they kept the time.

ANDREW MARVELL

THE NYMPH COMPLAINING FOR THE DEATH
OF HER FAWN

The wanton troopers riding by
Have shot my fawn, and it will die.

. . . .

With sweetest milk and sugar first
I it at mine own fingers nursed;
And as it grew, so every day,
It waxed more white and sweet than they;
It had so sweet a breath! and oft
I blushed to see its foot more soft,
And white, shall I say? than my hand—
Nay, any lady's of the land!
It was a wondrous thing how fleet
'Twas on those little silver feet.
With what a pretty skipping grace
It oft would challenge me the race;
And when't had left me far away,
'Twould stay, and run again, and stay;
For it was nimbler much than hinds,
And trod as if on the four winds.

I have a garden of my own,
But so with roses overgrown,
And lilies, that you would it guess
To be a little wilderness;
And all the spring-time of the year
It lovèd only to be there.
Among the beds of lilies I
Have sought it oft, where it should lie,
Yet could not, till itself would rise,
Find it, although before mine eyes;
For in the flaxen lilies' shade,
It like a bank of lilies laid.
Upon the roses it would feed,
Until its lips e'en seemed to bleed;
And then to me 'twould boldly trip,
And print those roses on my lip.

But all its chief delight was still
On roses thus itself to fill;
And its pure virgin lips to fold
In whitest sheets of lilies cold.
Had it lived long, it would have been
Lilies without, roses within.

O help! O help! I see it faint
And die as calmly as a saint!
See how it weeps! the tears do come
Sad, slowly, dropping like a gum.
So weeps the wounded balsam; so
The holy frankincense doth flow;
The brotherless Heliades
Melt in such amber tears as these.

I in a golden vial will
Keep these two crystal tears, and fill
It, till it doth overflow, with mine,
Then place it in Diana's shrine.

. . . .

First my unhappy statue shall
Be cut in marble; and withal
Let it be weeping too; but there
The engraver sure his art may spare;
For I so truly thee bemoan
That I shall weep though I be stone,
Until my tears, still dropping, wear
My breast, themselves engraving there;
Then at my feet shalt thou be laid,
Of purest alabaster made;
For I would have thine image be
White as I can, though not as thee.

AN EPITAPH

Enough; and leave the rest to fame;
'Tis to commend her, but to name.
Courtship, which, living, she declined,
When dead, to offer were unkind.

ANDREW MARVELL

Where never any could speak ill,
Who would officious praises spill?
Nor can the truest wit, or friend,
Without detracting, her commend;
To say, she lived a virgin chaste
In this age loose and all unlaced,
Nor was, when vice is so allowed,
Of virtue or ashamed or proud;
That her soul was on heaven so bent,
No minute but it came and went;
That, ready her last debt to pay,
She summed her life up every day;
Modest as morn, as mid-day bright,
Gentle as evening, cool as night;
'Tis true; but all too weakly said:
'Twas more significant, she's dead.

THE GARDEN

How vainly men themselves amaze
To win the palm, the oak, or bays,
And their incessant labours see
Crowned from some single herb or tree,
Whose short and narrow-vergèd shade
Does prudently their toils upbraid;
While all the flowers and trees do close
To weave the garlands of repose!

Fair Quiet, have I found thee here,
And Innocence, thy sister dear?
Mistaken long, I sought you then
In busy companies of men:
Your sacred plants, if here below,
Only among the plants will grow;
Society is all but rude
To this delicious solitude.

No white nor red was ever seen
So amorous as this lovely green.
Fond lovers, cruel as their flame,
Cut in these trees their mistress' name:

Little, alas! they know or heed
How far these beauties hers exceed!
Fair trees! where'er your barks I wound,
No name shall but your own be found.

When we have run our passions' heat,
Love hither makes his best retreat:
The gods, that mortal beauty chase,
Still in a tree did end their race;
Apollo hunted Daphne so
Only that she might laurel grow;
And Pan did after Syrinx speed,
Not as a nymph, but for a reed.

What wondrous life is this I lead!
Ripe apples drop about my head;
The luscious clusters of the vine
Upon my mouth do crush their wine;
The nectarine and curious peach
Into my hands themselves do reach;
Stumbling on melons, as I pass,
Ensnared with flowers, I fall on grass.

Meanwhile the mind, from pleasure less,
Withdraws into its happiness;
The mind, that ocean where each kind
Does straight its own resemblance find;
Yet it creates, transcending these,
Far other worlds, and other seas;
Annihilating all that's made
To a green thought in a green shade.

Here at the fountain's sliding foot,
Or at some fruit-tree's mossy root,
Casting the body's vest aside,
My soul into the boughs does glide;
There, like a bird, it sits and sings,
Then whets and combs its silver wings,
And, till prepared for longer flight,
Waves in its plumes the various light.

Such was that happy Garden-state
While man there walked without a **mate:**
After a place so pure and sweet,
What other help could yet be meet!
But 'twas beyond a mortal's share
To wander solitary there:
Two paradises 'twere in one,
To live in Paradise alone.

How well the skilful gardener drew
Of flowers and herbs this dial new!
Where, from above, the milder sun
Does through a fragrant zodiac run:
And, as it works, the industrious bee
Computes its time as well as we.
How could such sweet and wholesome hours
Be reckoned, but with herbs and flowers!

A GARDEN

See how the flowers, as at parade,
Under their colors stand displayed:
Each regiment in order grows,
That of the tulip, pink, and rose.
But when the vigilant patrol
Of stars walks round about the pole,
Their leaves, that to the stalks are curled,
Seem to their staves the ensigns furled,
Then in some flower's belovèd hut
Each bee, as sentinel, is shut,
And sleeps so too; but if once stirred,
She runs you through, nor asks the word.

O thou, that dear and happy Isle,
The garden of the world erewhile,
Thou Paradise of the four seas
Which Heaven planted us to please,
But, to exclude the world, did guard
With watery if not flaming sword;
What luckless apple did we taste

227

To make us mortal and thee waste!
Unhappy! shall we never more
That sweet militia restore,
When gardens only had their towers,
And all the garrisons were flowers;
When roses only arms might bear,
And men did rosy garlands wear?

CROMWELL IN DEATH

. . . .

I saw him dead: a leaden slumber lies,
And mortal sleep over those wakeful eyes;
Those gentle rays under the lids were fled,
Which through his looks that piercing sweetness shed;
That port, which so majestic was and strong,
Loose, and deprived of vigour, stretched along;
All withered, all discoloured, pale and wan,
How much another thing, no more that man!
O, human glory vain! O, Death! O, wings!
O, worthless world! O, transitory things!
Yet dwelt that greatness in his shape decayed,
That still though dead, greater than death he laid,
And in his altered face you something feign
That threatens Death, he yet will live again.

THE FAIR SINGER

To make a final conquest of all me,
Love did compose so sweet an enemy,
In whom both beauties to my death agree,
Joining themselves in fatal harmony;
That, while she with her eyes my heart does bind,
She with her voice might captivate my mind.

I could have fled from one but singly fair:
My disentangled soul itself might save,
Breaking the curled trammels of her hair.
But how should I avoid to be her slave,

228

ANDREW MARVELL

Whose subtle art invisibly can wreathe
My fetters of the very air I breathe?

It had been easy fighting in some plain,
Where victory might hang in equal choice,
But all resistance against her is vain,
Who has the advantage both of eyes and voice;
And all my forces needs must be undone,
She having gained both the wind and sun.

TO HIS COY MISTRESS

Had we but world enough, and time,
This coyness, lady, were no crime.
We would sit down, and think which way
To walk, and pass our long love's day.
Thou by the Indian Ganges' side
Shouldst rubies find: I by the tide
Of Humber would complain. I would
Love you ten years before the flood,
And you should, if you please, refuse
Till the conversion of the Jews;
My vegetable love should grow
Vaster than empires and more slow;
An hundred years should go to praise
Thine eyes, and on thy forehead gaze;
Two hundred to adore each breast,
But thirty thousand to the rest;
An age at least to every part,
And the last age should show your heart.
For, lady, you deserve this state,
Nor would I love at lower rate.
    But at my back I always hear
Time's wingèd chariot hurrying near,
And yonder all before us lie
Deserts of vast eternity.
Thy beauty shall no more be found,
Nor, in thy marble vault, shall sound
My echoing song; then worms shall try
That long-preserved virginity,

And your quaint honour turn to dust,
And into ashes all my lust:
The grave's a fine and private place,
But none, I think, do there embrace.
    Now therefore, while the youthful hue
Sits on thy skin like morning dew,
And while thy willing soul transpires
At every pore with instant fires,
Now let us sport us while we may,
And now, like amorous birds of prey,
Rather at once our time devour,
Than languish in his slow-chapt power,
Let us roll all our strength and all
Our sweetness up into one ball,
And tear our pleasures with rough strife
Thorough the iron gates of life;
Thus, though we cannot make our sun
Stand still, yet we will make him run.

THE MOWER, TO GLOW-WORMS

Ye living lamps, by whose dear light
The nightingale does sit so late,
And, studying all the summer night,
Her matchless songs does meditate;

Ye country comets, that portend
No war nor prince's funeral,
Shining unto no higher end
Than to presage the grass's fall;

Ye glow-worms, whose officious flame
To wandering mowers shows the way,
That in the night have lost their aim
And after foolish fires do stray;

Your courteous lights in vain you waste,
Since JULIANA here is come,
For she my mind hath so displaced,
That I shall never find my home.

230

ANDREW MARVELL

THE PICTURE OF LITTLE T. C.

See with what simplicity
This nymph begins her golden days!
In the green grass she loves to lie,
And there with her fair aspect tames
The wilder flowers and gives them names,
But only with the roses plays,
   And them does tell
What colour best becomes them and what smell.

Who can foretell for what high cause
This darling of the Gods was born?
Yet this is she whose chaster laws
The wanton Love shall one day fear,
And under her command severe
See his bow broke and ensigns torn.
   Happy who can
Appease this virtuous enemy of man!

O then let me in time compound
And parley with those conquering eyes,
Ere they have tried their force to wound;
Ere with their glancing wheels they drive
In triumph over hearts that strive,
And them that yield but more despise:
   Let me be laid
Where I may see the glories from some shade.

Meantime, whilst every verdant thing
Itself does at thy beauty charm,
Reform the errors of the spring;
Make that the tulips may have share
Of sweetness, seeing they are fair;
And roses of their thorns disarm;
   But most procure
That violets may a longer age endure.

But O, young beauty of the woods,
Whom Nature courts with fruit and flowers,

Gather the flowers, but spare the buds,
Lest FLORA, angry at thy crime
To kill her infants in their prime,
Do quickly make the example yours;
      And ere we see
Nip in the blossom all our hopes and thee.

Henry Vaughan

BEYOND THE VEIL

They are all gone into the world of light,
   And I alone sit lingering here;
Their very memory is fair and bright,
      And my sad thoughts doth clear.

It glows and glitters in my cloudy breast,
   Like stars upon some gloomy grove,
Or those faint beams in which this hill is dressed,
      After the sun's remove.

I see them walking in an air of glory,
   Whose light doth trample on my days;
My days, which are at best but dull and hoary,
      Mere glimmerings and decays.

O holy Hope, and high Humility,
   High as the heavens above!
These are your walks, and you have showed them me,
      To kindle my cold love.

Dear, beauteous Death, the jewel of the just,
   Shining nowhere but in the dark,
What mysteries do lie beyond thy dust,
      Could Man outlook that mark!

He that hath found some fledged bird's nest, may know
   At first sight, if the bird be flown;
But what fair well or grove he sings in now,
      That is to him unknown.

And yet, as angels in some brighter dreams
    Call to the soul when man doth sleep,
So some strange thoughts transcend our wonted themes,
       And into glory peep.

If a star were confined into a tomb,
    Her captive flames must needs burn there;
But when the hand that locked her up, gives room,
       She'll shine through all the sphere.

O Father of Eternal Life, and all
    Created glories under Thee!
Resume Thy spirit from this world of thrall
       Into true liberty.

Either disperse these mists, which blot and fill
    My perspective still, as they pass;
Or else remove me hence unto that hill
       Where I shall need no glass.

A SONG TO AMORET

If I were dead, and, in my place,
    Some fresher youth designed
To warm thee, with new fires; and grace
    Those arms I left behind:

Were he as faithful as the Sun,
    That's wedded to the Sphere;
His blood as chaste and temperate run,
    As April's mildest tear;

Or were he rich; and, with his heap
    And spacious share of earth,
Could make divine affection cheap,
    And court his golden birth;

For all these arts, I'd not believe
    (No! though he should be thine!),
The mighty Amorist could give
    So rich a heart as mine!

233

Fortune and beauty thou might'st find,
    And greater men than I;
But my true resolvèd mind
    They never shall come nigh.

For I not for an hour did love,
    Or for a day desire,
But with my soul had from above
    This endless holy fire.

ANGUISH

My God and King! to Thee
    I bow my knee;
I bow my troubled soul, and greet
With my foul heart thy holy feet.
Cast it, or tread it! it shall do
Even what thou wilt, and praise thee too.

My God, could I weep blood,
    Gladly I would,
Or if thou wilt give me that art,
Which through the eyes pours out the heart,
I will exhaust it all, and make
Myself all tears, a weeping lake.

O! 'tis an easy thing
    To write and sing;
But to write true, unfeigned verse
Is very hard! O God, disperse
These weights, and give my spirit leave
To act as well as to conceive!

            O my God, hear my cry;
                Or let me die!

THE WORLD

I saw Eternity the other night,
    Like a great ring of pure and endless light,
    All calm, as it was bright;
234

And round beneath it Time in hours, days, years,
   Driven by the spheres
Like a vast shadow moved; in which the world
   And all her train were hurled.

THE RETREAT

Happy those early days, when I
Shin'd in my angel infancy!
Before I understood this place
Appointed for my second race,
Or taught my soul to fancy ought
But a white celestial thought;
When yet I had not walked above
A mile or two from my first Love,
And looking back—at that short space—
Could see a glimpse of His bright face;
When on some gilded cloud or flow'r,
My gazing soul would dwell an hour,
And in those weaker glories spy
Some shadows of eternity;
Before I taught my tongue to wound
My conscience with a sinful sound,
Or had the black art to dispense
A sev'ral sin to ev'ry sense,
But felt through all this fleshly dress
Bright shoots of everlastingness.

O how I long to travel back,
And tread again that ancient track!
That I might once more reach that plain,
Where first I left my glorious train;
From whence th' enlighten'd spirit sees
That shady City of palm-trees.
But ah! my soul with too much stay
Is drunk, and staggers in the way!
Some men a forward motion love,
But I by backward steps would move;
And when this dust falls to the urn,
In that state I came, return.

John Dryden

LIFE A CHEAT

When I consider life, 'tis all a cheat;
Yet, fooled with hope, men favour the deceit;
Trust on, and think to-morrow will repay:
To-morrow's falser than the former day;
Lies worse; and while it says, we shall be blessed
With some new joys, cuts off what we possessed.
Strange cozenage! none would live past years again,
Yet all hope pleasure in what yet remain;
And, from the dregs of life, think to receive
What the first sprightly running could not give.
I'm tired with waiting for this chemic gold,
Which fools us young, and beggars us when old.

O SOULS, IN WHOM NO HEAVENLY FIRE

O souls, in whom no heavenly fire is found,
Fat minds, and ever grovelling on the ground!
We bring our manners to the blest abodes,
And think what pleases us must please the Gods.

THE POWER OF MUSIC

'Twas at the royal feast for Persia won
By Philip's warlike son—
Aloft in awful state
The godlike hero sate
On his imperial throne;
His valiant peers were placed around,
Their brows with roses and with myrtles bound
(So should desert in arms be crown'd);
The lovely Thais by his side
Sate like a blooming eastern bride
In flower of youth and beauty's pride:—

236

Happy, happy, happy pair!
None but the brave
None but the brave
None but the brave deserves the fair!

Timotheus placed on high
Amid the tuneful quire
With flying fingers touch'd the lyre:
The trembling notes ascend the sky
And heavenly joys inspire.
The song began from Jove
Who left his blissful seats above—
Such is the power of mighty love!
A dragon's fiery form belied the god;
Sublime on radiant spires he rode
When he to fair Olympia prest,
And while he sought her snowy breast,
Then round her slender waist he curl'd,
And stamp'd an image of himself, a sovereign of the world
—The listening crowd admire the lofty sound!
A present deity! they shout around:
A present deity! the vaulted roofs rebound!
With ravish'd ears
The monarch hears,
Assumes the god;
Affects to nod
And seems to shake the spheres.

The praise of Bacchus then the sweet musician sung,
Of Bacchus ever fair and ever young:
The jolly god in triumph comes!
Sound the trumpets, beat the drums!
Flush'd with a purple grace
He shows his honest face:
Now give the hautboys breath; he comes, he comes!
Bacchus, ever fair and young,
Drinking joys did first ordain;
Bacchus' blessings are a treasure,
Drinking is the soldier's pleasure:
Rich the treasure,

Sweet the pleasure,
Sweet is pleasure after pain.

Soothed with the sound, the king grew vain
Fought all his battles o'er again,
And thrice he routed all his foes, and thrice he slew the slain!
The master saw the madness rise,
His glowing cheeks, his ardent eyes;
And while he Heaven and Earth defied
Changed his hand and check'd his pride.
He chose a mournful Muse
Soft pity to infuse:
He sung Darius great and good,
By too severe a fate
Fallen, fallen, fallen, fallen,
Fallen from his high estate,
And weltering in his blood;
Deserted, at his utmost need,
By those his former bounty fed;
On the bare earth exposed he lies
With not a friend to close his eyes.
—With downcast looks the joyless victor sate,
Revolving in his alter'd soul
The various turns of Chance below;
And now and then a sigh he stole,
And tears began to flow.

The mighty master smiled to see
That love was in the next degree;
'Twas but a kindred sound to move,
For pity melts the mind to love.
Softly sweet, in Lydian measures
Soon he soothed his soul to pleasures.
War, he sung, is toil and trouble,
Honour but an empty bubble;
Never ending, still beginning,
Fighting still, and still destroying;
If the world be worth thy winning,
Think, O think, it worth enjoying:
Lovely Thais sits beside thee,
Take the good the gods provide thee!

238

—The many rend the skies with loud applause;
So Love was crown'd, but Music won the cause.
The prince, unable to conceal his pain,
Gazed on the fair
Who caused his care,
And sigh'd and look'd, sigh'd and look'd,
Sigh'd and look'd, and sigh'd again:
At length with love and wine at once opprest
The vanquish'd victor sunk upon her breast.

    Now strike the golden lyre again:
A louder yet, and yet a louder strain!
Break his bands of sleep asunder
And rouse him like a rattling peal of thunder.
Hark, hark! the horrid sound
Has raised up his head:
As awaked from the dead
And amazed he stares around.
Revenge, revenge, Timotheus cries,
See the Furies arise!
See the snakes that they rear
How they hiss in their hair,
And the sparkles that flash from their eyes!
Behold a ghastly band,
Each a torch in his hand!
Those are Grecian ghosts, that in battle were slain
And unburied remain
Inglorious on the plain:
Give the vengeance due
To the valiant crew!
Behold how they toss their torches on high,
How they point to the Persian abodes
And glittering temples of their hostile gods.
—The princes applaud with a furious joy:
And the King seized a flambeau with zeal to destroy;
Thais led the way
To light him to his prey,
And like another Helen, fired another Troy!

—Thus, long ago,
Ere heaving bellows learn'd to blow,

While organs yet were mute,
Timotheus, to his breathing flute
And sounding lyre
Could swell the soul to rage, or kindle soft desire.
At last divine Cecilia came,
Inventress of the vocal frame;
The sweet enthusiast from her sacred store
Enlarged the former narrow bounds,
And added length to solemn sounds,
With Nature's mother-wit, and arts unknown before.
—Let old Timotheus yield the prize
Or both divide the crown;
He raised a mortal to the skies;
She drew an angel down!

ABSALOM AND ACHITOPHEL

.   .   .   .

Of these the false Achitophel was first;
A name to all succeeding ages curst;
For close designs, and crooked councils fit;
Sagacious, bold, and turbulent of wit;
Reckless, unfix'd in principles and place;
In power unpleas'd, impatient of disgrace;
A fiery soul, which, working out its way,
Fretted the pigmy-body to decay,
And o'er-informed the tenement of clay.
A daring pilot in extremity;
Pleas'd with the danger, when the waves went high
He sought the storms; but for a calm unfit,
Would steer too nigh the sands to boast his wit.
Great wits are sure to madness near allied,
And thin partitions do their bounds divide;
Else why should he with wealth and honour blest,
Refuse his age the needful hours of rest?
Punish a body which he could not please;
Bankrupt of life, yet prodigal of ease?
And all to leave what with his toil he won,
To that unfeather'd two-legg'd thing, a son;

JOHN DRYDEN

Got while his soul did huddled notions try;
And born a shapeless lump, like anarchy.
In friendship false, implacable in hate;
Resolv'd to ruin or to rule the state.
To compass this the triple bond he broke;
The pillars of the public safety shook;
And fitted Israel for a foreign yoke:
Then sciz'd with fear, yet still affecting fame,
Usurp'd a patriot's all-atoning name.
So easy still it proves in factious times
With public zeal to cancel private crimes.
How safe is treason, and how sacred ill,
Where none can sin against the people's will?
Where crowds can wink, and no offence be known,
Since in another's guilt they find their own.
Yet fame deserv'd no enemy can grudge;
The statesman we abhor, but praise the judge.
In Israel's courts ne'er sat an Abethdin
With more discerning eyes, or hands more clean,
Unbrib'd, unsought, the wretched to redress,
Swift of dispatch, and easy of access.
Oh! had he been content to serve the crown,
With virtues only proper to the gown;
Or had the rankness of the soil been freed
From cockle, that oppress'd the noble seed;
David for him his tuneful harp had strung,
And heaven had wanted one immortal song.

. . . .

A man so various, that he seemed to be
Not one, but all mankind's epitome:
Stiff in opinions, always in the wrong;
Was everything by starts, and nothing long;
But, in the course of one revolving moon,
Was chemist, fiddler, statesman, and buffoon;
Then all for women, painting, rhyming, drinking,
Beside ten thousand freaks that died in thinking.
Blest madman, who could every hour employ,
With something new to wish, or to enjoy!

241

Railing and praising were his usual themes,
And both, to show his judgement, in extremes;
So over violent, or over civil,
That every man with him was God or Devil.
In squandering wealth was his peculiar art;
Nothing went unrewarded but desert.
Beggared by fools, whom still he found too late;
He had his jest, and they had his estate.

.   .   .   .

TO THE MEMORY OF MRS. ANNE KILLIGREW

Thou youngest Virgin-Daughter of the skies,
    Made in the last promotion of the blest;
Whose palms, new plucked from Paradise,
In spreading branches more sublimely rise,
    Rich with immortal green above the rest:
Whether, adopted to some neighbouring star,
Thou roll'st above us in thy wandering race,
    Or, in procession fixed and regular,
Moved with the heavens' majestic pace;
    Or, called to more superior bliss,
Thou tread'st, with seraphims, the vast abyss:
Whatever happy region is thy place,
Cease thy celestial song a little space;
(Thou wilt have time enough for hymns divine,
Since Heaven's eternal year is thine.)
Hear then a mortal muse thy praise rehearse
        In no ignoble verse;
But such as thy own voice did practice here,
When thy first fruits of poesie were given,
To make thyself a welcome inmate there;
    While yet a young probationer,
        And candidate of Heaven.

If by traduction came thy mind,
    Our wonder is the less to find
A soul so charming from a stock so good;
Thy father was transfused into thy blood·

JOHN DRYDEN

So wert thou born into the tuneful strain,
(An early, rich, and inexhausted vein.)
   But if thy pre-existing soul
Was formed, at first, with myriads more,
   It did through all the mighty poets roll
Who Greek or Latin laurels wore,
And was that Sappho last, which once it was before.
   If so, then cease thy flight, O Heaven-born mind!
Thou hast no dross to purge from thy rich ore:
   Nor can thy soul a fairer mansion find
   Than was the beauteous frame she left behind:
Return, to fill or mend the choir of thy celestial kind.

   May we presume to say, that at thy birth
New joy was sprung in Heaven as well as here on earth?
For sure the milder planets did combine
On thy auspicious horoscope to shine,
And even the most malicious were in trine.
Thy brother-angels at thy birth
   Strung each his lyre, and tuned it high,
   That all the people of the sky
Might know a poetess was born on earth.
   And then if ever, mortal ears
   Had heard the music of the spheres!
   And if no clustering swarm of bees
On thy sweet mouth distilled their golden dew,
   'Twas that, such vulgar miracles
   Heaven had not leisure to renew:
   For all the blest fraternity of love
Solemnized there thy birth, and kept thy holyday above.

   O gracious God! How far have we
Profaned thy Heavenly gift of poesy!
Made prostitute and profligate the muse,
Debased to each obscene and impious use,
Whose harmony was first ordained above,
For tongues of angels and for hymns of love!
Oh wretched we! why were we hurried down
This lubrique and adulterate age,
(Nay, added fat pollutions of our own)
To increase the steaming ordures of the stage?

243

What can we say to excuse our second fall?
Let this thy vestal, Heaven, atone for all:
   Her Arethusian stream remains unsoiled,
   Unmixed with foreign filth and undefiled,
Her wit was more than man, her innocence a child.

   Art she had none, yet wanted none,
     For nature did that want supply:
   So rich in treasures of her own,
     She might our boasted stores defy:
Such noble vigour did her verse adorn,
That it seemed borrowed, where 'twas only born.
Her morals too were in her bosom bred
   By great examples daily fed,
What in the best of books, her father's life, she read.
   And to be read her self she need not fear;
   Each test, and every light, her muse will bear,
   Though Epictetus with his lamp were there.
   E'en love (for love sometimes her muse expressed),
Was but a lambent-flame which played about her breast:
Light as the vapours of a morning dream,
   So cold herself, whilst she such warmth expressed,
   'Twas Cupid bathing in Diana's stream.

Born to the spacious empire of the Nine,
One would have thought, she should have been content
To manage well that mighty government;
But what can young ambitious souls confine?
   To the next realm she stretched her sway,
   For painting near adjoining lay,
A plenteous province, and alluring prey.
A chamber of dependences was framed,
(As conquerors will never want pretence,
   When armed, to justify the offence),
And the whole fief, in right of poetry she claimed.
   The country open lay without defence;
For poets frequent inroads there had made,
   And perfectly could represent
   The shape, the face, with every lineament;
And all the large domains which the dumb-sister swayed;

244

JOHN DRYDEN

All bowed beneath her government,
Received in triumph wheresoe'er she went.
Her pencil drew whate'er her soul designed
And oft the happy draught surpassed the image in her mind.
The sylvan scenes of herds and flocks
And fruitful plains and barren rocks,
Of shallow brooks that flowed so clear,
The bottom did the top appear;
Of deeper too and ampler floods
Which as in mirrors, showed the woods;
Of lofty trees, with sacred shades
And perspectives of pleasant glades,
Where nymphs of brightest form appear,
And shaggy satyrs standing near,
Which them at once admire and fear.
The ruins too of some majestic piece,
Boasting the power of ancient Rome or Greece,
Whose statues, friezes, columns, broken lie,
And, though defaced, the wonder of the eye;
What nature, art, bold fiction, e'er durst frame,
Her forming hand gave feature to the name.
So strange a concourse ne'er was seen before,
But when the peopled ark the whole creation bore.

The scene then changed; with bold erected look
Our martial King the sight with reverence strook:
For, not content to express his outward part,
Her hand called out the image of his heart,
His warlike mind, his soul devoid of fear,
His high-designing thoughts were figured there,
As when, by magic, ghosts are made appear.
Our phœnix Queen was portrayed too so bright,
Beauty alone could beauty take so right:
Her dress, her shape, her matchless grace,
Were all observed, as well as heavenly face.
With such a peerless majesty she stands,
As in that day she took the crown from sacred hands:
Before a train of heroines was seen,
In beauty foremost, as in rank, the Queen!
Thus nothing to her genius was denied,

But like a ball of fire, the farther thrown,
Still with a greater blaze she shone,
   And her bright soul broke out on every side.
What next she had designed, Heaven only knows:
To such immoderate growth her conquest rose
That Fate alone its progress could oppose.

Now all those charms, that blooming grace,
The well-proportioned shape and beauteous **face,**
Shall never more be seen by mortal eyes;
In earth the much-lamented virgin lies!
   Not wit nor piety could Fate prevent;
   Nor was the cruel destiny content
   To finish all the murder at a blow,
   To sweep at once her life and beauty too;
But, like a hardened felon, took a pride
   To work more mischievously slow,
And plundered first, and then destroyed.
O double sacrilege on things divine,
To rob the relique, and deface the shrine!
   But thus Orinda died:
Heaven, by the same disease, did both translate,
As equal were their souls, so equal was their fate.

Mean time, her warlike brother on the seas
His waving streamers to the winds displays,
And vows for his return, with vain devotion, pays.
Ah, generous youth! that wish forbear,
   The winds too soon will waft thee here!
   Slack all thy sails, and fear to come,
Alas, thou know'st not, thou art wrecked at home!
No more shalt thou behold thy sister's face,
Thou hast already had her last embrace.
But look aloft, and if thou ken'st from **far,**
Among the Pleiads, a new-kindled star,
If any sparkles than the rest more bright,
'Tis she that shines in that propitious light.

When in mid-air the golden trump shall **sound,**
   To raise the nations under ground;

JOHN DRYDEN

When in the valley of Jehosaphat
The judging God shall close the book of Fate;
  And there the last assizes keep
  For those who wake and those who sleep;
  When rattling bones together fly
  From the four corners of the sky,
When sinews o'er the skeletons are spread,
Those clothed with flesh, and life inspires the dead;
The sacred poets first shall hear the sound,
And foremost from the tomb shall bound:
For they are covered with the lightest ground;
And straight, with in-born vigour, on the wing,
Like mounting larks to the New Morning sing.
There thou, sweet Saint, before the choir shalt go,
As harbinger of Heaven, the way to show,
The way which thou so well hast learned below.

SONG TO A FAIR YOUNG LADY

Ask not the cause why sullen Spring
  So long delays her flowers to bear;
Why warbling birds forget to sing,
  And winter storms invert the year:
Chloris is gone; and fate provides
To make it Spring where she resides.

Chloris is gone, the cruel fair;
  She cast not back a pitying eye:
But left her lover in despair
  To sigh, to languish, and to die:
Ah! how can those fair eyes endure
To give the wounds they will not cure?

Great God of Love, why hast thou made
  A face that can all hearts command,
That all religions can invade,
  And change the laws of every land?
Where thou hadst placed such power before,
Thou shouldst have made her mercy more.

When Chloris to the temple comes,
   Adoring crowds before her fall;
She can restore the dead from tombs
   And every life but mine recall,
I only am by Love designed
To be the victim for mankind.

SONG FOR SAINT CECILIA'S DAY, 1687

From harmony, from heavenly harmony,
   This universal frame began:
   When Nature underneath a heap
     Of jarring atoms lay,
   And could not heave her head,
The tuneful voice was heard from high,
   Arise, ye more than dead!
Then cold, and hot, and moist, and dry
In order to their stations leap,
   And Music's power obey.
From harmony, from heavenly harmony
   This universal frame began:
   From harmony to harmony
Through all the compass of the notes it ran,
The diapason closing full in Man.

What passion cannot Music raise and quell?
   When Jubal struck the chorded shell
   His listening brethren stood around,
    And, wondering, on their faces fell
   To worship that celestial sound.
Less than a god they thought there could not dwell
   Within the hollow of that shell,
   That spoke so sweetly and so well.
What passion cannot Music raise and quell?

   The trumpet's loud clangour
    Excites us to arms,
   With shrill notes of anger
    And mortal alarms.

JOHN DRYDEN

The double double double beat
  Of the thundering drum
Cries "Hark! the foes come;
Charge, charge, 'tis too late to retreat!"

The soft complaining flute
In dying notes discovers
The woes of hopeless lovers,
Whose dirge is whispered by the warbling lute.

  Sharp violins proclaim
Their jealous pangs and desperation,
Fury, frantic indignation,
Depth of pains, and height of passion,
  For the fair disdainful dame.

But oh! what art can teach,
What human voice can reach
  The sacred organ's praise?
Notes inspiring holy love,
Notes that wing their heavenly ways
  To mend the choirs above.

Orpheus could lead the savage race,
And trees uprooted left their place
  Sequacious of the lyre;
But bright Cecilia raised the wonder higher:
When to her organ vocal breath was given,
An angel heard, and straight appeared—
  Mistaking earth for heaven!

Grand Chorus
  As from the power of sacred lays
    The spheres began to move,
  And sung the great Creator's praise
    To all the blest above;
So when the last and dreadful hour
This crumbling pageant shall devour,
The trumpet shall be heard on high,
The dead shall live, the living die,
And Music shall untune the sky.

MANKIND

Men are but children of a larger growth;
Our appetites are apt to change as theirs,
And full as craving too, and full as vain;
And yet the soul, shut up in her dark room,
Viewing so clear abroad, at home sees nothing;
But, like a mole in earth, busy and blind,
Works all her folly up, and casts it outward
To the world's open view.

DREAMS

Dreams are but interludes which Fancy makes;
When monarch Reason sleeps, this mimic wakes:
Compounds a medley of disjointed things,
A mob of cobblers, and a court of kings:
Light fumes are merry, grosser fumes are sad:
Both are the reasonable soul run mad;
And many monstrous forms in sleep we see,
That neither were, nor are, nor e'er can be.
Sometimes forgotten things long cast behind
Rush forward in the brain, and come to mind.
The nurse's legends are for truths received,
And the man dreams but what the boy believed.
Sometimes we but rehearse a former play,
The night restores our actions done by day;
As hounds in sleep will open for their prey.
In short, the farce of dreams is of a piece,
Chimeras all; and more absurd, or less.

Sir Charles Sedley

LOVE STILL HAS SOMETHING OF THE SEA

Love still has something of the sea
From whence his mother rose;
No time his slaves from doubt can free,
Nor give their thoughts repose.

SIR CHARLES SEDLEY

They are becalmed in clearest days,
  And in rough weather tossed;
They wither under cold delays,
  Or are in tempests lost.

One while they seem to touch the port:
  Then straight into the main,
Some angry wind, in cruel sport,
  Their vessel drives again.

.   .   .   .

CHILD AND MAIDEN

Ah, Chloris! could I now but sit
  As unconcern'd as when
Your infant beauty could beget
  No happiness or pain!
When I the dawn used to admire,
  And praised the coming day,
I little thought the rising fire
  Would take my rest away.

Your charms in harmless childhood lay
  Like metals in a mine;
Age from no face takes more away
  Than youth conceal'd in thine.
But as your charms insensibly
  To their perfection prest,
So love as unperceived did fly,
  And centred in my breast.

My passion with your beauty grew,
  While Cupid at my heart,
Still as his mother favour'd you,
  Threw a new flaming dart:
Each gloried in their wanton part;
  To make a lover, he
Employ'd the utmost of his art—
  To make a beauty, she.

251

PHYLLIS

Phyllis is my only joy,
  Faithless as the winds or seas,
Sometimes cunning, sometimes coy,
  Yet she never fails to please:
    If with a frown
    I am cast down,
    Phyllis, smiling
    And beguiling,
Makes me happier than before.

Though alas! too late I find
  Nothing can her fancy fix;
Yet the moment she is kind
  I forgive her all her tricks,
    Which though I see,
    I can't get free:
    She deceiving,
    I believing,
What need lovers wish for more?

John Wilmot

EPITAPH ON CHARLES II

Here lies our Sovereign Lord the King,
  Whose word no man relies on,
Who never said a foolish thing,
  Nor ever did a wise one.

CONSTANCY

I cannot change, as others do,
  Though you unjustly scorn;
Since that poor swain that sighs for you,
  For you alone was born.

JOHN WILMOT

No, Phillis, no! your heart to move,
   A surer way I'll try,
And to revenge my slighted love,
Will still love on, will still love on, and die!

  When killed with grief Amyntas lies,
    And you to mind shall call
.The sighs that now unpitied rise,
    The tears that vainly fall:
That welcome hour, that ends this smart,
    Will then begin your pain,
For such a faithful, tender heart
Can never break, can never break, in vain.

MY LIGHT THOU ART

My light thou art, without thy glorious sight
My eyes are darkened with eternal night;
My Love, thou art my way, my life, my light.

Thou art my way, I wander if thou fly;
Thou art my light, if hid, how blind am I!
Thou art my life, if thou withdraw'st I die.

Thou art my life; if thou but turn away,
My life's a thousand deaths. Thou art my way;
Without thee, Love, I travel not, but stray.

A SONG

My dear mistress has a heart
   Soft as those kind looks she gave me;
When with love's resistless art,
   And her eyes, she did enslave me.
But her constancy's so weak,
   She's so wild and apt to wander,
That my jealous heart would break
   Should we live one day asunder.

Melting joys about her move,
  Killing pleasures, wounding blisses;
She can dress her eyes in love,
  And her lips can arm with kisses.
Angels listen when she speaks;
  She's my delight, all mankind's wonder;
But my jealous heart would break
  Should we live one day asunder.

Matthew Prior

THE DYING ADRIAN TO HIS SOUL

Poor, little, pretty, fluttering thing,
  Must we no longer live together?
And dost thou prune thy trembling wing,
  To take thy flight thou know'st not whither?
Thy humorous vein, thy pleasing folly,
  Lies all neglected, all forgot:
And pensive, wavering, melancholy,
  Thou dread'st and hop'st thou know'st not what.

THE MERCHANT, TO SECURE HIS TREASURE

The merchant, to secure his treasure,
  Conveys it in a borrowed name:
Euphelia serves to grace my measure,
  But Chloe is my real flame.

My softest verse, my darling lyre,
  Upon Euphelia's toilet lay—
When Chloe noted her desire
  That I should sing, that I should play.

My lyre I tune, my voice I raise,
  But with my numbers mix my sighs;
And whilst I sing Euphelia's praise,
  I fix my soul on Chloe's eyes.

Fair Chloe blushed: Euphelia frowned:
  I sung, and gazed; I played, and trembled:
And Venus to the Loves around
  Remarked how ill we all dissembled.

William Douglas

ANNIE LAURIE

Maxwelton banks are bonnie,
  Where early fa's the dew;
Where me and Annie Laurie
  Made up the promise true;
Made up the promise true,
  And never forget will I;
And for bonnie Annie Laurie
  I'll lay me down and die.

She's backit like the peacock,
  She's breistit like the swan,
She's jimp about the middle,
  Her waist ye weel micht span;
Her waist ye weel micht span,
  And she has a rolling eye;
And for bonnie Annie Laurie
  I'll lay me down and die.

Joseph Addison

CATO

, ...

    . . . Plato, thou reason'st well,
Else whence this pleasing hope, this fond desire,
This longing after immortality?
Or whence this secret dread and inward horror
Of falling into nought? Why shrinks the soul

255

Back on herself and startles at destruction?
—'Tis the Divinity that stirs within us,
'Tis Heaven itself that points out an hereafter,
And intimates Eternity to man.
Eternity!—thou pleasing-dreadful thought!
Through what variety of untried being—
Through what new scenes and changes must we pass!
The wide, the unbounded prospect lies before me;
But shadows, clouds, and darkness rest upon it.
Here will I hold:—If there's a Power above us
(And that there is, all nature cries aloud
Through all her works), he must delight in Virtue;
And that which he delights in must be happy:
But—when?—or where?—*This* world was made for Cæsar
I'm weary of conjectures:—This must end them.
Thus I am doubly armed; my death and life,
My bane and antidote are both before me.
This in a moment brings me to an end,
But this informs me I shall never die.
The soul, secured in her existence, smiles
At the drawn dagger and defies its point.
The stars shall fade away, the sun himself
Grow dim with age, and nature sink in years;
But thou shalt flourish in immortal youth,
Unhurt amidst the war of elements,
The wrecks of matter, and the crush of worlds.

．　．　．　．　．　．　．　．　．

Isaac Watts

ODE TO A SCHOOLMASTER

Custom, that Tyranness of Fools
   That leads the Learned round the Schools
In magic Chains of Forms and Rules!
   My Genius storms her Throne:
No more, ye Slaves, with Awe profound
Beat the dull Track, nor dance the Round;
Loose Hands, and quit th' inchanted Ground
Knowledge invites us each alone.

AMBROSE PHILIPS

I hate these Shackles of the mind
  Forg'd by the haughty wise;
Souls were not born to be confin'd,
And led like Sampson blind and bound;
But when his native Strength he found
  He well aveng'd his Eyes.
I love thy gentle Influence, Rowe,
Thy gentle Influence like the Sun
Only dissolves the frozen Snow,
Then bids our Thoughts like Rivers flow,
And chuse the Channels where they run.

Thoughts should be free as Fire or Wind;
The Pinions of a single Mind
  Will thro' all Nature fly:
But who can drag up to the Poles
Long fetter'd Ranks of Leaden Souls?
My Genius which no Chain controls
Roves with Delight, or deep or high:
Swift I survey the Globe around,
Dive to the Centre thro' the solid Ground,
  Or travel o'er the Sky.

TRUE GREATNESS

Were I so tall to reach the pole
Or grasp the ocean with my span,
I must be measured by my soul:
The mind's the standard of the man.

Ambrose Philips

TO MISS CHARLOTTE PULTENEY

Little gossip, blithe and hale,
Tattling many a broken tale,
Singing many a tuneless song,
Lavish of a heedless tongue,

257

Simple maiden void of art,
Babbling out the very heart,
Sleeping, waking, still at ease,
Pleasing without skill to please;
Yet abandon'd to thy will,
Yet imagining no ill,
Yet too innocent to blush;
Like the linnet in the bush,
To the mother-linnet's note
Moduling her slender throat;
Chirping forth thy petty joys,
Wanton in the change of toys;
Like the linnet green in May
Flitting to each bloomy spray;
Wearied then, and glad of rest,
Like the linnet in the nest.

Edward Young

NIGHT THOUGHTS

.   .   .   .   c

Tired Nature's sweet restorer, balmy Sleep!
He, like the world, his ready visit pays
Where fortune smiles; the wretched he forsakes,
Swift on his downy pinions flies from woe,
And lights on lids unsullied by a tear!

.   .   .   .

All promise is poor dilatory man,
And that through every state: when young, indeed.
In full content we, sometimes, nobly rest,
Unanxious for ourselves; and only wish,
As duteous sons, our fathers were more wise.
At thirty man suspects himself a fool;
Knows it at forty, and reforms his plan;
At fifty chides his infamous delay,
Pushes his prudent purpose to resolve;

JOHN GAY

In all the magnanimity of thought
Resolves; and re-resolves; then, dies the same.

.   .   .   .

AUTHORS AND CRITICS

With fame in just proportion envy grows;
The man that makes a character makes foes;
Slight peevish insects round a genius rise,
As a bright day awakes the world of flies;
With hearty malice, but with feeble wing,
To show they live, they flutter and they sting:
But as by depredations wasps proclaim
The fairest fruit, so these the fairest fame.

—EPISTLE TO POPE

John Gay

ACIS AND GALATEA

AIR

Love in her eyes sits playing,
    And sheds delicious death;
Love on her lips is straying,
    And warbling in her breath;
Love on her breast sits panting,
    And swells with soft desire;
Nor grace nor charm is wanting
    To set the heart on fire.

AIR

O ruddier than the cherry!
O sweeter than the berry!
    O Nymph more bright
    Than moonshine night,
Like kidlings blithe and merry!

259

Ripe as the melting cluster!
No lily has such lustre;
Yet hard to tame
As raging flame,
And fierce as storms that bluster.

BLACK-EYED SUSAN

All in the Downs the fleet was moored,
The streamers waving in the wind,
When black-eyed Susan came aboard.
"Oh! where shall I my true love find?
Tell me, ye jovial sailors, tell me true,
If my sweet William sails among the crew."

William, who high upon the yard
Rocked with the billow to and fro,
Soon as her well-known voice he heard,
He sighed, and cast his eyes below:
The cord slides swiftly through his glowing hands,
And (quick as lightning) on the deck he stands.

So the sweet lark, high poised in air,
Shuts close his pinions to his breast,
If chance his mate's shrill call he hear,
And drops at once into her nest:—
The noblest captain in the British fleet
Might envy William's lip those kisses sweet.

"O Susan, Susan, lovely dear,
My vows shall ever true remain,
Let me kiss off that falling tear;
We only part to meet again.
Change, as ye list, ye winds; my heart shall be
The faithful compass that still points to thee.

"Believe not what the landmen say,
Who tempt with doubts thy constant mind.
They'll tell thee, sailors, when away,
In every port a mistress find:
Yes, yes, believe them when they tell thee so,
For thou art present wheresoe'er I go.

260

ALEXANDER POPE

"If to far India's coast we sail
  Thy eyes are seen in diamonds bright,
Thy breath is Afric's spicy gale,
  Thy skin is ivory so white.
Thus every beauteous object that I view
Wakes in my soul some charm of lovely Sue.

"Though battle call me from thy arms
  Let not my pretty Susan mourn;
Though cannons roar, yet safe from harms
  William shall to his Dear return.
Love turns aside the balls that round me fly,
Lest precious tears should drop from Susan's eye."

The boatswain gave the dreadful word,
  The sails their swelling bosom spread;
No longer must she stay aboard;
  They kissed, she sighed, he hung his head.
Her lessening boat unwilling rows to land;
"Adieu!" she cries; and waved her lily hand.

Alexander Pope

ODE ON SOLITUDE

Happy the man, whose wish and care
  A few paternal acres bound,
Content to breathe his native air
      In his own ground.

Whose herds with milk, whose fields with bread,
  Whose flocks supply him with attire,
Whose trees in summer yield him shade,
      In winter fire.

Blest, who can unconcern'dly find
  Hours, days, and years, slide soft away,
In health of body, peace of mind,
      Quiet by day,

261

Sound sleep by night; study and ease,
Together mixt; sweet recreation;
And innocence, which most does please
With meditation.

Thus let me live, unseen, unknown;
Thus unlamented let me die,
Steal from the world, and not a stone
Tell where I lie.

AN ESSAY ON CRITICISM

A *little learning* is a dangerous thing;
Drink deep, or taste not the Pierian spring:
There shallow draughts intoxicate the brain,
And drinking largely sobers us again.
Fired at first sight with what the Muse imparts,
In fearless youth we tempt the heights of arts,
While from the bounded level of our mind,
Short views we take, nor see the lengths behind;
But more advanced, behold with strange surprise
New distant scenes of endless science rise!
So pleased at first the towering Alps we try,
Mount o'er the vales and seem to tread the sky,
The eternal snows appear already pass'd,
And the first clouds and mountains seem the last:
But, those attain'd, we tremble to survey
The growing labours of the lengthen'd way,
The increasing prospect tires our wandering eyes,
Hills peep o'er hills, and Alps on Alps arise!

．　．　．　．　．　．　．　．　．

But most by numbers judge a poet's song,
And smooth or rough, with them, is right or wrong:
In the bright Muse, though thousand charms conspire,
Her voice is all these tuneful fools admire;
Who haunt Parnassus but to please their ear,
Not mend their minds; as some to church repair,
Not for the doctrine, but the music there.

ALEXANDER POPE

These equal syllables alone require,
Though oft the ear the open vowels tire;
While expletives their feeble aid do join;
And ten low words oft creep in one dull line:
While they ring round the same unvaried chimes,
With sure returns of still expected rhymes:
Where'er you find "the cooling western breeze,"
In the next line, it "whispers through the trees":
If crystal streams "with pleasing murmurs creep,"
The reader's threaten'd (not in vain) with "sleep":
Then, at the last and only couplet fraught
With some unmeaning thing they call a thought,
A needless Alexandrine ends the song,
That, like a wounded snake, drags its slow length along.
Leave such to tune their own dull rhymes, and know
What's roundly smooth, or languishingly slow;
And praise the easy vigour of a line,
Where Denham's strength and Waller's sweetness join.
True ease in writing comes from art, not chance,
As those move easiest who have learn'd to dance.

—PART II.

THE RAPE OF THE LOCK

And now, unveil'd, the toilet stands display'd,
Each silver vase in mystic order laid.
First, robed in white, the nymph intent adores,
With head uncover'd, the cosmetic powers.
A heavenly image in the glass appears,
To that she bends, to that her eyes she rears;
The inferior priestess, at her altar's side,
Trembling begins the sacred rites of pride.
Unnumber'd treasures ope at once, and here
The various offerings of the world appear;
From each she nicely culls with curious toil,
And decks the goddess with the glittering spoil.
This casket India's glowing gems unlocks,
And all Arabia breathes from yonder box.
The tortoise here and elephant unite,
Transform'd to combs, the speckled, and the white.

263

Here files of pins extend their shining rows,
Puffs, powders, patches, bibles, billets-doux.
Now awful beauty puts on all its arms;
The fair each moment rises in her charms,
Repairs her smiles, awakens every grace,
And calls forth all the wonders of her face;
Sees by degrees a purer blush arise,
And keener lightnings quicken in her eyes.
The busy sylphs surround their darling care,
These set the head, and those divide the hair,
Some fold the sleeve, whilst others plait the gown;
And Betty's praised for labours not her own.

—Canto I.

On her white breast a sparkling cross she wore,
Which Jews might kiss, and Infidels adore.
Her lively looks a sprightly mind disclose,
Quick as her eyes, and as unfix'd as those:
Favours to none, to all she smiles extends;
Oft she rejects, but never once offends.
Bright as the sun, her eyes the gazers strike,
And like the sun, they shine on all alike.
Yet graceful ease, and sweetness void of pride,
Might hide her faults, if belles had faults to hide:
If to her share some female errors fall,
Look on her face, and you'll forget 'em all.

—Canto II.

ELEGY

TO THE MEMORY OF AN UNFORTUNATE LADY

.   .   .   .

What can atone (O ever-injured shade!)
Thy fate unpitied, and thy rites unpaid?
No friend's complaint, no kind domestic tear
Pleased thy pale ghost, or graced thy mournful bier.
By foreign hands thy dying eyes were closed,
By foreign hands thy decent limbs composed,

264

ALEXANDER POPE

By foreign hands thy humble grave adorn'd,
By strangers honour'd, and by strangers mourn'd!
What though no friends in sable weeds appear,
Grieve for an hour, perhaps, then mourn a year,
And bear about the mockery of woe
To midnight dances, and the public show?
What though no weeping loves thy ashes grace,
Nor polish'd marble emulate thy face?
What though no sacred earth allow thee room,
Nor hallow'd dirge be mutter'd o'er thy tomb?
Yet shall thy grave with rising flowers be drest,
And the green turf lie lightly on thy breast:
There shall the morn her earliest tears bestow,
There the first roses of the year shall blow;
While angels with their silver wings o'ershade
The ground, now sacred by thy reliques made.

.   .   .   .

PROLOGUE

TO MR. ADDISON'S TRAGEDY OF CATO

To wake the soul by tender strokes of art,
To raise the genius, and to mend the heart,
To make mankind, in conscious virtue bold,
Live o'er each scene, and be what they behold:
For this the Tragic Muse first trod the stage,
Commanding tears to stream through every age;
Tyrants no more their savage nature kept,
And foes to virtue wonder'd how they wept.
Our author shuns by vulgar springs to move
The hero's glory, or the virgin's love;
In pitying love, we but our weakness show,
And wild ambition well deserves its woe.
Here tears shall flow from a more generous cause,
Such tears as patriots shed for dying laws:
He bids your breasts with ancient ardour rise,
And calls forth Roman drops from British eyes.
Virtue confess'd in human shape he draws,
What Plato thought, and godlike Cato was:

No common object to your sight displays,
But what with pleasure Heaven itself surveys,
A brave man struggling in the storms of fate,
And greatly falling with a falling state.

.   .   .   .

Your scene precariously subsists too long
On French translation, and Italian song.
Dare to have sense yourselves; assert the stage,
Be justly warm'd with your own native rage:
Such plays alone should win a British ear,
As Cato's self had not disdain'd to hear.

AN ESSAY ON MAN

Heaven from all creatures hides the book of fate,
All but the page prescribed, their present state:
From brutes what men, from men what spirits know:
Or who could suffer being here below?
The lamb thy riot dooms to bleed to-day,
Had he thy reason, would he skip and play?
Pleased to the last, he crops the flowery food,
And licks the hand just raised to shed his blood.
Oh blindness to the future! kindly given,
That each may fill the circle mark'd by Heaven:
Who sees with equal eye, as God of all,
A hero perish, or a sparrow fall,
Atoms or systems into ruin hurl'd,
And now a bubble burst, and now a world.

.   .   .   .

Lo, the poor Indian! whose untutor'd mind
Sees God in clouds, or hears him in the wind;
His soul, proud science never taught to stray
Far as the solar walk, or milky way;
Yet simple nature to his hope has given,
Behind the cloud-topp'd hill, an humbler heaven;
Some safer world, in depth of woods embraced,
Some happier island in the watery waste,

ALEXANDER POPE

Where slaves once more their native land behold,
No fiends torment, no Christians thirst for gold:
To be, contents his natural desire,
He asks no angel's wing, no seraph's fire;
But thinks, admitted to that equal sky,
His faithful dog shall bear him company.

.   .   .   .

If plagues or earthquakes break not Heav'n's design,
Why then a Borgia, or a Catiline?
Who knows but He, whose hand the lightning forms,
Who heaves old ocean, and who wings the storms:
Pours fierce ambition in a Cæsar's mind,
Or turns young Ammon loose to scourge mankind?

.   .   .   .

All are but parts of one stupendous whole,
Whose body nature is, and God the soul;
That, changed through all, and yet in all the same;
Great in the earth, as in the ethereal frame;
Warms in the sun, refreshes in the breeze,
Glows in the stars, and blossoms in the trees,
Lives through all life, extends through all extent,
Spreads undivided, operates unspent;
Breathes in our soul, informs our mortal part,
As full, as perfect, in a hair as heart;
As full, as perfect, in vile man that mourns,
As the rapt seraph, that adores and burns:
To Him no high, no low, no great, no small;
He fills, He bounds, connects, and equals all.
                                        —Epistle I.

Know then thyself, presume not God to scan,
The proper study of mankind is Man.
Placed on this isthmus of a middle state,
A being darkly wise, and rudely great;
With too much knowledge for the sceptic side,
With too much weakness for the stoic's pride,
He hangs between; in doubt to act or rest;
In doubt to deem himself a god, or beast;

261

In doubt his mind or body to prefer;
Born but to die, and reasoning but to err;
Alike in ignorance, his reason such,
Whether he thinks too little, or too much;
Chaos of thought and passion, all confused;
Still by himself abused, or disabused;
Created half to rise, and half to fall;
Great lord of all things, yet a prey to all;
Sole judge of truth, in endless error hurl'd:
The glory, jest, and riddle of the world!

. . . .

Self-love, the spring of motion, acts the soul;
Reason's comparing balance rules the whole.
Man, but for that, no action could attend,
And but for this, were active to no end;
Fix'd like a plant on his peculiar spot,
To draw nutrition, propagate, and rot;
Or, meteor-like, flame lawless through the void,
Destroying others, by himself destroy'd.

. . . .

Self-love and reason to one end aspire,
Pain their aversion, pleasure their desire;
But greedy That, its object would devour,
This taste the honey, and not wound the flower.
Pleasure, or wrong or rightly understood,
Our greatest evil, or our greatest good.

. . . .

In lazy apathy let stoics boast
Their virtue fix'd; 'tis fix'd as in a frost;
Contracted all, retiring to the breast;
But strength of mind is exercise, not rest:
The rising tempest puts in act the soul,
Parts it may ravage, but preserves the whole.
On life's vast ocean diversely we sail,
Reason the card, but passion is the gale;

Nor God alone in the still calm we find,
He mounts the storm, and walks upon the wind.

.   .   .   .

This light and darkness in our chaos join'd,
What shall divide?   The God within the mind.
Extremes in nature equal ends produce,
In man they join to some mysterious use;
Though each by turns the other's bound invade,
As, in some well-wrought picture, light and shade,
And oft so mix, the difference is too nice
Where ends the virtue, or begins the vice.
Fools! who from hence into the notion fall,
That vice or virtue there is none at all.
If white and black blend, soften, and unite
A thousand ways, is there no black or white?
Ask your own heart, and nothing is so plain;
'Tis to mistake them costs the time and pain

.   .   .   .

Vice is a monster of so frightful mien,
As, to be hated, needs but to be seen;
Yet seen too oft, familiar with her face,
We first endure, then pity, then embrace.

.   .   .   .

Behold the child, by nature's kindly law,
Pleased with a rattle, tickled with a straw:
Some livelier plaything gives his youth delight,
A little louder, but as empty quite:
Scarfs, garters, gold, amuse his riper stage,
And beads and prayer-books are the toys of age:
Pleased with this bauble still, as that before,
Till tired he sleeps, and life's poor play is o'er.
                                        —Epistle II

Say, where full instinct is the unerring guide,
What pope or council can they need beside?

Reason, however able, cool at best,
Cares not for service, or but serves when prest,
Stays till we call, and then not often near;
But honest instinct comes a volunteer,
Sure never to o'ershoot, but just to hit;
While still too wide or short is human wit;

.   .   .   .

For forms of government let fools contest;
Whate'er is best adminster'd is best:
For modes of faith let graceless zealots fight;
His can't be wrong whose life is in the right.
In faith and hope the world will disagree,
But all mankind's concern is charity:
All must be false that thwart this one great end;
And all of God, that bless mankind or mend.

—EPISTLE III.

O Happiness! our being's end and aim!
Good, pleasure, ease, content! whate'er thy name:
That something still which prompts the eternal sigh,
For which we bear to live, or dare to die,
Which still so near us, yet beyond us lies,
O'erlook'd, seen double, by the fool, and wise.
Plant of celestial seed! if dropp'd below,
Say, in what mortal soil thou deign'st to grow?
Fair opening to some court's propitious shrine,
Or deep with diamonds in the flaming mine?
Twined with the wreaths Parnassian laurels yield,
Or reap'd in iron harvests of the field?
Where grows?—where grows it not? If vain our toil,
We ought to blame the culture, not the soil:
Fix'd to no spot is happiness sincere,
'Tis no where to be found, or every where:
'Tis never to be bought, but always free,
And fled from monarchs, St. John! dwells with thee.

.   .   .   .

Shall burning Etna, if a sage requires,
Forget to thunder, and recall her fires?

On air or sea new motions be imprest,
O blameless Bethel, to relieve thy breast?
When the loose mountain trembles from on high,
Shall gravitation cease, if you go by?
Or some old temple, nodding to its fall,
For Chartres' head reserve the hanging wall?

. . . .

What nothing earthly gives, or can destroy,
The soul's calm sunshine, and the heartfelt joy,
Is virtue's prize: A better would you fix,
Then give Humility a coach and six,
Justice a conqueror's sword, or Truth a gown,
Or Public Spirit its great cure, a crown.

. . . .

Honour and shame from no condition rise;
Act well your part, there all the honour lies.
Fortune in men has some small difference made,
One flaunts in rags, one flutters in brocade;
The cobbler apron'd, and the parson gown'd,
The friar hooded, and the monarch crown'd.
"What differ more (you cry) than crown and cowl?"
I'll tell you, friend! a wise man and a fool.
You'll find, if once the monarch acts the monk,
Or, cobbler-like, the parson will be drunk,
Worth makes the man, and want of it the fellow;
The rest is all but leather or prunella.

. . . .

If parts allure thee, think how Bacon shined,
The wisest, brightest, meanest of mankind:
Or ravish'd with the whistling of a name,
See Cromwell, damn'd to everlasting fame!

. . . .

See the sole bliss Heaven could on all bestow!
Which who but feels can taste, but thinks can know:

271

Yet poor with fortune, and with learning blind,
The bad must miss; the good, untaught, will find;
Slave to no sect, who takes no private road,
But looks through Nature up to Nature's God;
Pursues that chain which links the immense design,
Joins heaven and earth, and mortal and divine;
Sees, that no being any bliss can know,
But touches some above, and some below;
Learns from this union of the rising whole,
The first, last purpose of the human soul;
And knows where faith, law, morals, all began,
All end, in Love of God, and Love of Man.

—EPISTLE IV.

MORAL ESSAYS

That each from other differs, first confess;
Next that he varies from himself no less:
Add nature's, custom's, reason's, passion's strife,
And all opinion's colours cast on life.
Our depths who fathoms, or our shallows finds,
Quick whirls, and shifting eddies, of our minds?

. . . .

In vain sedate reflections we would make,
When half our knowledge we must snatch, not take.
Oft, in the passions' wide rotation toss'd,
Our spring of action to ourselves is lost;
Tired, not determined, to the last we yield,
And what comes then is master of the field.
As the last image of the troubled heap,
When sense subsides, and fancy sports in sleep,
(Though past the recollection of the thought)
Becomes the stuff of which our dream is wrought.

. . . .

In life's low vale, the soil the virtues like,
They please as beauties, here as wonders strike.

ALEXANDER POPE

Though the same sun with all-diffusive rays
Blush in the rose, and in the diamond blaze,
We prize the stronger effort of his power,
And justly set the gem above the flower.

. . . .

And you, brave Cobham! to the latest breath,
Shall feel your ruling passion strong in death:
Such in those moments as in all the past;
"Oh, save my country, Heaven!" shall be your last.
—Epistle I.

Come then, the colours and the ground prepare!
Dip in the rainbow, trick her off in air;
Choose a firm cloud, before it fall, and in it
Catch, ere she change, the Cynthia of this minute.

. . . .

But what are these to great Atossa's mind?
Scarce once herself, by turns all womankind!
Who, with herself, or others, from her birth
Finds all her life one warfare upon earth:
Shines in exposing knaves, and painting fools,
Yet is, whate'er she hates and ridicules.
No thought advances, but her eddy brain
Whisks it about, and down it goes again.
Full sixty years the world has been her trade,
The wisest fool much time has ever made.
From loveless youth to unrespected age,
No passion gratified, except her rage.
So much the fury still outran the wit,
The pleasure miss'd her, and the scandal hit.

. . . .

Oh! blest with temper, whose unclouded ray
Can make to-morrow cheerful as to-day;
She who can love a sister's charms, or hear
Sighs for a daughter with unwounded ear;

273

She, who ne'er answers till a husband cools,
Or, if she rules him, never shows she rules;
Charms by accepting, by submitting sways,
Yet has her humour most, when she obeys;
Let fops or fortune fly which way they will;
Disdains all loss of tickets or codille;
Spleen, vapours, or small-pox, above them all,
And mistress of herself, though china fall.

—EPISTLE II.

But all our praises why should lords engross?
Rise, honest muse! and sing the Man of Ross:
Pleased Vaga echoes through her winding bounds,
And rapid Severn hoarse applause resounds.
Who hung with woods yon mountain's sultry brow?
From the dry rock who bade the waters flow?
Not to the skies in useless columns toss'd,
Or in proud falls magnificently lost,
But clear and artless, pouring through the plain
Health to the sick, and solace to the swain.
Whose causeway parts the vale with shady rows?
Whose seats the weary traveller repose?
Who taught that heaven-directed spire to rise?
"The Man of Ross!" each lisping babe replies.
Behold the market-place with poor o'erspread!
The Man of Ross divides the weekly bread;
He feeds yon alms-house, neat, but void of state,
Where age and want sit smiling at the gate:
Him portion'd maids, apprenticed orphans bless'd,
The young who labour, and the old who rest.
Is any sick? the Man of Ross relieves,
Prescribes, attends, the medicine makes, and gives.
Is there a variance? enter but his door,
Balk'd are the courts, and contest is no more.
Despairing quacks with curses fled the place,
And vile attorneys, now a useless race.

.   .   .   .

In the worst inn's worst room, with mat half-hung,
The floors of plaster, and the walls of dung,

274

ALEXANDER POPE

On once a flock-bed, but repair'd with straw,
With tape-tied curtains, never meant to draw,
The George and Garter dangling from that bed
Where tawdry yellow strove with dirty red,
Great Villiers lies—alas! how changed from him,
That life of pleasure, and that soul of whim!
Gallant and gay, in Cliefden's proud alcove,
The bower of wanton Shrewsbury and love;
Or just as gay, at council, in a ring
Of mimic statesmen, and their merry king.
No wit to flatter, left of all his store!
No fool to laugh at, which he valued more.
There, victor of his health, of fortune, friends,
And fame; this lord of useless thousands ends.

—EPISTLE III.

"Statesman, yet friend to truth! of soul sincere,
In action faithful, and in honour clear;
Who broke no promise, served no private end,
Who gain'd no title, and who lost no friend;
Ennobled by himself, by all approved,
And praised, unenvied, by the muse he loved."

—EPISTLE V.

PROLOGUE TO THE SATIRES

Shut, shut the door, good John! fatigued I said,
Tie up the knocker, say I'm sick, I'm dead.
The Dog-star rages! nay, 'tis past a doubt,
All Bedlam, or Parnassus, is let out:
Fire in each eye, and papers in each hand,
They rave, recite, and madden round the land.
What walls can guard me, or what shades can hide?
They pierce my thickets, through my grot they glide,
By land, by water, they renew the charge,
They stop the chariot, and they board the barge.
No place is sacred, not the church is free,
Even Sunday shines no Sabbath-day to me:
Then from the Mint walks forth the man of rhyme,
Happy! to catch me, just at dinner-time.

275

Is there a parson much be-mused in beer,
A maudlin poetess, a rhyming peer,
A clerk, foredoom'd his father's soul to cross,
Who pens a stanza, when he should engross?
Is there, who, lock'd from ink and paper, scrawls
With desperate charcoal round his darken'd walls?
All fly to Twic'nam, and in humble strain
Apply to me, to keep them mad or vain.
Arthur, whose giddy son neglects the laws,
Imputes to me and my damn'd works the cause:
Poor Cornus sees his frantic wife elope,
And curses wit, and poetry, and Pope.

    .   .   .   .

Why did I write? what sin to me unknown
Dipp'd me in ink, my parents', or my own?
As yet a child, nor yet a fool to fame,
I lisp'd in numbers, for the numbers came.
I left no calling for this idle trade,
No duty broke, no father disobey'd.
The muse but served to ease some friend, not wife,
To help me through this long disease, my life.

    .   .   .   .

Were there one whose fires
True genius kindles, and fair fame inspires;
Blest with each talent and each art to please,
And born to write, converse, and live with ease:
Should such a man, too fond to rule alone,
Bear, like the Turk, no brother near the throne,
View him with scornful, yet with jealous eyes,
And hate for arts that caused himself to rise;
Damn with faint praise, assent with civil leer,
And without sneering, teach the rest to sneer;
Willing to wound, and yet afraid to strike,
Just hint a fault, and hesitate dislike;
Alike reserved to blame, or to commend,
A timorous foe, and a suspicious friend;
Dreading e'en fools, by flatterers besieged,
And so obliging, that he ne'er obliged;
276

ALEXANDER POPE

Like Cato, give his little senate laws,
And sit attentive to his own applause;
While wits and templars every sentence raise,
And wonder with a foolish face of praise—
Who but must laugh, if such a man there be?
Who would not weep, if Atticus were he?

. . . .

EPILOGUE TO THE SATIRES

. . . .

Yes, I am proud; I must be proud to see
Men, not afraid of God, afraid of me:
Safe from the bar, the pulpit, and the throne,
Yet touched and shamed by ridicule alone.
  O sacred weapon! left for truth's defence,
Sole dread of folly, vice, and insolence!
To all but Heaven-directed hands denied,
The muse may give thee, but the gods must guide.
Reverent I touch thee! but with honest zeal;
To rouse the watchman of the public weal,
To virtue's work provoke the tardy hall,
And goad the prelate slumbering in his stall.
Ye tinsel insects! whom a court maintains,
That counts your beauties only by your stains.
Spin all your cobwebs o'er the eye of day!
The Muse's wing shall brush you all away:
All his grace preaches, all his lordship sings,
All that makes saints of queens, and gods of kings;
All, all but truth, drops dead-born from the press,
Like the last gazette, or the last address.

. . . .

Robert Crawford

THE BUSH ABOON TRAQUAIR

Hear me, ye nymphs, and every swain,
    I'll tell how Peggy grieves me;
Tho' thus I languish, thus complain,
    Alas! she ne'er believes me.
My vows and sighs, like silent air,
    Unheeded never move her;
At the bonny bush aboon Traquair,
    'Twas there I first did love her.

That day she smiled, and made me glad,
    No maid seem'd ever kinder;
I thought myself the luckiest lad,
    So sweetly there to find her.
I tried to soothe my amorous flame
    In words that I thought tender;
If more there pass'd, I'm not to blame,
    I meant not to offend her.

Yet now she scornful flees the plain,
    The fields we then frequented;
If e'er we meet, she shows disdain,
    She looks as ne'er acquainted.
The bonny bush bloom'd fair in May,
    Its sweets I'll aye remember;
But now her frowns make it decay,
    It fades as in December.

Ye rural powers, who hear my strains,
    Why thus should Peggy grieve me?
Oh! make her partner in my pains,
    Then let her smiles relieve me.
If not, my love will turn despair,
    My passion no more tender,
I'll leave the bush aboon Traquair,
    To lonely wilds I'll wander.

Henry Carey

SALLY IN OUR ALLEY

Of all the girls that are so smart,
There's none like pretty Sally;
She is the darling of my heart,
And she lives in our alley.
There is no lady in the land
Is half so sweet as Sally;
She is the darling of my heart,
And she lives in our alley.

Her father he makes cabbage-nets,
And through the streets does cry 'em;
Her mother she sells laces long
To such as please to buy 'em:
But sure such folks could ne'er beget
So sweet a girl as Sally!
She is the darling of my heart,
And she lives in our alley.

When she is by I leave my work,
I love her so sincerely;
My master comes like any Turk,
And bangs me most severely—
But let him bang his bellyful,
I'll bear it all for Sally;
She is the darling of my heart,
And she lives in our alley.

Of all the days that's in the week
I dearly love but one day,
And that's the day that comes betwixt
A Saturday and Monday;
For then I'm drest all in my best,
To walk abroad with Sally;
She is the darling of my heart,
And she lives in our alley.

My master carries me to Church,
And often I am blamed
Because I leave him in the lurch
As soon as text is named;
I leave the Church in sermon-time,
And slink away to Sally;
She is the darling of my heart,
And she lives in our alley.

When Christmas comes about again,
O then I shall have money;
I'll hoard it up, and box it all,
I'll give it to my honey:
I would it were ten thousand pound,
I'd give it all to Sally;
She is the darling of my heart,
And she lives in our alley.

My master and the neighbours all
Make game of me and Sally,
And, but for her, I'd better be
A slave and row a galley;
But when my seven long years are out,
O then I'll marry Sally,—
O then we'll wed, and then we'll bed . . .
But not in our alley!

Samuel Johnson

POVERTY

Has Heaven reserved, in pity to the poor,
No pathless waste, or undiscovered shore?
No secret island in the boundless main?
No peaceful desert yet unclaimed by Spain?
Quick let us rise, the happy seats explore,
And bear oppression's insolence no more.
This mournful truth is everywhere confessed,
Slow rises worth by poverty depressed.

—LONDON.

280

SAMUEL JOHNSON

CHARLES XII

On what foundation stands the warrior's pride,
How just his hopes let Swedish Charles decide.
A frame of adamant, a soul of fire,
No dangers fright him, and no labours tire;
O'er love, o'er fear, extends his wide domain,
Unconquered lord of pleasure and of pain;
No joys to him pacific sceptres yield,
War sounds the trump, he rushes to the field.
Behold surrounding kings their powers combine,
And one capitulate, and one resign:
Peace courts his hand, but spreads her charms in vain:
"Think nothing gained," he cries, "till naught remain,
On Moscow's walls till Gothic standards fly,
And all be mine beneath the polar sky."
The march begins, in military state,
And nations on his eye suspended wait;
Stern famine guards the solitary coast,
And Winter barricades the realms of frost;
He comes, nor want nor cold his course delay!—
Hide, blushing glory, hide Pultowa's day:
The vanquished hero leaves his broken bands,
And shows his miseries in distant lands;
Condemned a needy supplicant to wait,
While ladies interpose, and slaves debate.
But did not chance at length her error mend?
Did no subverted empire mark his end?
Did rival monarchs give the fatal wound?
Or hostile millions press him to the ground?
His fall was destined to a barren strand,
A petty fortress, and a dubious hand:
He left the name at which the world grew pale,
To point a moral, or adorn a tale.

—THE VANITY OF HUMAN WISHES.

Sir Charles Wyndham

THE FAIR THIEF

Before the urchin well could go,
She stole the whiteness of the snow;
And more, that whiteness to adorn,
She stole the blushes of the morn;
Stole all the sweetness ether sheds
On primrose buds and violet beds.

Still to reveal her artful wiles
She stole the Graces' silken smiles;
She stole Aurora's balmy breath;
And pilfered orient pearl for teeth;
The cherry, dipped in morning dew,
Gave moisture to her lips, and hue.

These were her infant spoils, a store;
And she, in time, still pilfered more!
At twelve, she stole from Cyprus' queen
Her air and love-commanding mien;
Stole Juno's dignity; and stole
From Pallas sense to charm the soul.

Apollo's wit was next her prey;
Her next, the beam that lights the day;
She sang;—amazed, the Sirens heard,
And to assert their voice appeared.
She played;—the Muses from their hill,
Wondered who thus had stole their skill.

Great Jove approved her crimes and art;
And, t'other day, she stole my heart!
If lovers, Cupid, are thy care,
Exert thy vengeance on this Fair:
To trial bring her stolen charms,
And let her prison be my arms!

William Shenstone

WRITTEN AT AN INN AT HENLEY

To thee, fair freedom! I retire
    From flattery, cards, and dice, and din;
Nor art thou found in mansions higher
    Than the low cot, or humble inn.

'Tis here with boundless power I reign;
    And every health which I begin,
Converts dull port to bright champagne;
    Such freedom crowns it, at an inn.

I fly from pomp, I fly from plate!
    I fly from falsehood's specious grin!
Freedom I love, and form I hate,
    And choose my lodgings at an inn.

Here, waiter! take my sordid ore,
    Which lackeys else might hope to win;
It buys, what courts have not in store;
    It buys me freedom at an inn.

Whoe'er has travelled life's dull round,
    Where'er his stages may have been,
May sigh to think he still has found
    The warmest welcome, at an inn.

Thomas Gray

ON A DISTANT PROSPECT OF ETON COLLEGE

Ye distant spires, ye antique towers,
    That crown the watery glade,
Where grateful Science still adores
    Her Henry's holy shade;
And ye, that from the stately brow
Of Windsor's heights the expanse below

Of grove, of lawn, of mead survey,
Whose turf, whose shade, whose flowers among
Wanders the hoary Thames along
    His silver-winding way:

Ah, happy hills! ah, pleasing shade!
    Ah, fields beloved in vain!
Where once my careless childhood strayed,
    A stranger yet to pain!
I feel the gales that from ye blow
A momentary bliss bestow,
    As waving fresh their gladsome wing,
My weary soul they seem to soothe,
And, redolent of joy and youth,
    To breathe a second spring.

Say, Father Thames, for thou hast seen
    Full many a sprightly race
Disporting on thy margent green
    The paths of pleasure trace;
Who foremost now delight to cleave,
With pliant arm, thy glassy wave?
    The captive linnet which enthral?
What idle progeny succeed
To chase the rolling circle's speed,
    Or urge the flying ball?

While some on earnest business bent
    Their murmuring labours ply
'Gainst graver hours, that bring constraint
    To sweeten liberty:
Some bold adventurers disdain
The limits of their little reign,
    And unknown regions dare descry:
Still as they run they look behind,
They hear a voice in every wind,
    And snatch a fearful joy.

Gay Hope is theirs by fancy fed,
    Less pleasing when possessed;
The tear forgot as soon as shed,
    The sunshine of the breast:

284

Theirs buxom Health, of rosy hue,
Wild Wit, Invention ever new,
  And lively Cheer, of Vigour born;
The thoughtless day, the easy night,
The spirits pure, the slumbers light
  That fly the approach of morn.

Alas! regardless of their doom
  The little victims play;
No sense have they of ills to come,
  Nor care beyond to-day:
Yet see, how all around them wait
The ministers of human fate
  And black Misfortune's baleful train!
Ah, show them where in ambush stand,
To seize their prey, the murderous band!
  Ah, tell them they are men!

These shall the fury Passions tear,
  The vultures of the mind,
Disdainful Anger, pallid Fear,
  And Shame that sculks behind;
Or pining Love shall waste their youth,
Or Jealousy, with rankling tooth,
  That inly gnaws the secret heart,
And Envy wan, and faded Care,
Grim-visaged comfortless Despair,
  And Sorrow's piercing dart.

Ambition this shall tempt to rise,
  Then whirl the wretch from high,
To bitter Scorn a sacrifice,
  And grinning Infamy.
The stings of Falsehood those shall try
And hard Unkindness' altered eye,
  That mocks the tear it forced to flow;
And keen Remorse with blood defiled,
And moody Madness laughing wild
  Amid severest woe.

Lo! in the Vale of Years beneath
   A grisly troop are seen,
The painful family of Death,
   More hideous than their Queen:
This racks the joints, this fires the veins,
That every labouring sinew strains,
   Those in the deeper vitals rage:
Lo! Poverty, to fill the band,
That numbs the soul with icy hand,
   And slow-consuming Age.

To each his sufferings: all are men,
   Condemned alike to groan;
The tender for another's pain,
   The unfeeling for his own.
Yet, ah! why should they know their fate,
Since sorrow never comes too late,
   And happiness too swiftly flies?
Thought would destroy their paradise!
No more;—where ignorance is bliss,
   'Tis folly to be wise.

AN ODE ON THE SPRING

Lo! where the rosy-bosomed Hours,
   Fair Venus' train, appear,
Disclose the long-expecting flowers,
   And wake the purple year!
The Attic warbler pours her throat
Responsive to the cuckoo's note,
   The untaught harmony of spring:
While, whispering pleasure as they fly,
Cool Zephyrs through the clear blue sky
   Their gathered fragrance fling.

Where'er the oak's thick branches stretch
   A broader browner shade,
Where'er the rude and moss-grown beech
   O'er-canopies the glade,

286

THOMAS GRAY

Beside some water's rushy brink
With me the Muse shall sit, and think
    (At ease reclined in rustic state)
How vain the ardour of the crowd,
How low, how little are the proud,
    How indigent the great!

Still is the toiling hand of Care:
    The panting herds repose:
Yet, hark, how through the peopled air
    The busy murmur glows!
The insect-youth are on the wing,
Eager to taste the honied spring
    And float amid the liquid noon;
Some lightly o'er the current skim,
Some show their gaily-gilded trim
    Quick-glancing to the sun.

To Contemplation's sober eye
    Such is the race of Man:
And they that creep, and they that fly,
    Shall end where they began.
Alike the Busy and the Gay
But flutter through life's little day,
    In Fortune's varying colours dressed:
Brushed by the hand of rough Mischance,
Or chilled by Age, their airy dance
    They leave, in dust to rest.

Methinks I hear, in accents low,
    The sportive kind reply:
Poor moralist! and what art thou?
    A solitary fly!
Thy joys no glittering female meets,
No hive hast thou of hoarded sweets,
    No painted plumage to display;
On hasty wings thy youth is flown;
Thy sun is set, thy spring is gone—
    We frolic, while 'tis May.

ELEGY WRITTEN IN A COUNTRY CHURCHYARD

The curfew tolls the knell of parting day,
    The lowing herd winds slowly o'er the lea,
The plowman homeward plods his weary way,
    And leaves the world to darkness and to me.

Now fades the glimmering landscape on the sight,
    And all the air a solemn stillness holds,
Save where the beetle wheels his droning flight,
    And drowsy tinklings lull the distant folds:

Save that from yonder ivy-mantled tower
    The moping owl does to the moon complain
Of such as, wandering near her secret bower,
    Molest her ancient solitary reign.

Beneath those rugged elms, that yew-tree's shade,
    Where heaves the turf in many a mouldering heap,
Each in his narrow cell for ever laid,
    The rude forefathers of the hamlet sleep.

The breezy call of incense-breathing morn,
    The swallow twittering from the straw-built shed,
The cock's shrill clarion, or the echoing horn,
    No more shall rouse them from their lowly bed.

For them no more the blazing hearth shall burn,
    Or busy housewife ply her evening care:
No children run to lisp their sire's return,
    Or climb his knees the envied kiss to share.

Oft did the harvest to their sickle yield,
    Their furrow oft the stubborn glebe has broke:
How jocund did they drive their team afield!
    How bowed the woods beneath their sturdy stroke!

Let not Ambition mock their useful toil,
    Their homely joys, and destiny obscure;
Nor Grandeur hear with a disdainful smile
    The short and simple annals of the poor.

THOMAS GRAY

The boast of heraldry, the pomp of power,
   And all that beauty, all that wealth e'er gave.
Await alike the inevitable hour:
   The paths of glory lead but to the grave.

Nor you, ye proud, impute to these the fault
   If Memory o'er their tomb no trophies raise,
Where through the long-drawn aisle and fretted vault
   The pealing anthem swells the note of praise.

Can storied urn or animated bust
   Back to its mansion call the fleeting breath?
Can Honour's voice provoke the silent dust,
   Or Flattery soothe the dull cold ear of death?

Perhaps in this neglected spot is laid
   Some heart once pregnant with celestial fire;
Hands, that the rod of empire might have swayed,
   Or waked to ecstasy the living lyre.

But Knowledge to their eyes her ample page
   Rich with the spoils of time did ne'er unroll;
Chill Penury repressed their noble rage,
   And froze the genial current of the soul.

Full many a gem of purest ray serene
   The dark unfathomed caves of ocean bear:
Full many a flower is born to blush unseen,
   And waste its sweetness on the desert air.

Some village Hampden that, with dauntless breast,
   The little tyrant of his fields withstood,
Some mute inglorious Milton here may rest,
   Some Cromwell guiltless of his country's blood.

The applause of listening senates to command,
   The threats of pain and ruin to despise,
To scatter plenty o'er a smiling land,
   And read their history in a nation's eyes,

Their lot forbade: nor circumscribed alone,
Their growing virtues, but their crimes confined;
Forbade to wade through slaughter to a throne,
And shut the gates of mercy on mankind;

The struggling pangs of conscious truth to hide,
To quench the blushes of ingenuous shame,
Or heap the shrine of Luxury and Pride
With incense kindled at the Muse's flame.

Far from the madding crowd's ignoble strife,
Their sober wishes never learned to stray;
Along the cool, sequestered vale of life
They kept the noiseless tenor of their way.

Yet even these bones from insult to protect
Some frail memorial still erected nigh,
With uncouth rhymes and shapeless sculpture decked,
Implores the passing tribute of a sigh.

Their name, their years, spelt by the unlettered Muse,
The place of fame and elegy supply:
And many a holy text around she strews,
That teach the rustic moralist to die.

For who, to dumb Forgetfulness a prey,
This pleasing anxious being e'er resigned,
Left the warm precincts of the cheerful day,
Nor cast one longing lingering look behind?

On some fond breast the parting soul relies,
Some pious drops the closing eye requires;
E'en from the tomb the voice of Nature cries,
E'en in our ashes live their wonted fires.

For thee, who, mindful of the unhonoured dead,
Dost in these lines their artless tale relate;
If chance, by lonely contemplation led,
Some kindred spirit shall inquire thy fate,—

Haply some hoary-headed swain may say,
  "Oft have we seen him at the peep of dawn
Brushing with hasty steps the dews away
  To meet the sun upon the upland lawn.

"There at the foot of yonder nodding beech
  That wreathes its old fantastic roots so high,
His listless length at noontide would he stretch,
  And pore upon the brook that babbles by.

"Hard by yon wood, now smiling as in scorn,
  Muttering his wayward fancies he would rove,
Now drooping, woeful-wan, like one forlorn,
  Or crazed with care, or crossed in hopeless love.

"One morn I missed him on the 'customed hill,
  Along the heath, and near his favourite tree;
Another came; nor yet beside the rill,
  Nor up the lawn, nor at the wood was he:

"The next, with dirges due in sad array,
  Slow through the church-way path we saw him borne.
Approach and read (for thou canst read) the lay
  Graved on the stone beneath yon aged thorn":

THE EPITAPH

Here rests his head upon the lap of Earth
  A Youth, to Fortune and to Fame unknown.
Fair Science frowned not on his humble birth,
  And Melancholy marked him for her own.

Large was his bounty, and his soul sincere,
  Heaven did a recompense as largely send:
He gave to Misery (all he had) a tear,
  He gained from Heaven ('twas all he wished) a friend.

No farther seek his merits to disclose,
  Or draw his frailties from their dread abode,
(There they alike in trembling hope repose,)
  The bosom of his Father and his God.

THE PROGRESS OF POESY

A PINDARIC ODE

Awake, Æolian lyre, awake,
And give to rapture all thy trembling strings.
From Helicon's harmonious springs
A thousand rills their mazy progress take:
The laughing flowers, that round them blow,
Drink life and fragrance as they flow.
Now the rich stream of music winds along
Deep, majestic, smooth and strong,
Through verdant vales, and Ceres' golden reign:
Now rolling down the steep amain,
Headlong, impetuous, see it pour;
The rocks and nodding groves rebellow to the roar.

O Sovereign of the willing soul,
Parent of sweet and solemn-breathing airs,
Enchanting shell! the sullen Cares
And frantic Passions hear thy soft control.
On Thracia's hills the Lord of War
Has curbed the fury of his car,
And dropped his thirsty lance at thy command.
Perching on the sceptred hand
Of Jove, thy magic lulls the feathered king
With ruffled plumes and flagging wing:
Quenched in dark clouds of slumber lie
The terror of his beak, and lightnings of his eye.

Thee the voice, the dance, obey,
Tempered to thy warbled lay.
O'er Idalia's velvet-green
The rosy-crowned Loves are seen
On Cytherea's day,
With antic Sports, and blue-eyed Pleasures,
Frisking light in frolic measures;
Now pursuing, now retreating,
Now in circling troops they meet:
To brisk notes in cadence beating,
Glance their many-twinkling feet.

292

THOMAS GRAY

Slow melting strains their Queen's approach declare:
  Where'er she turns, the Graces homage pay.
With arms sublime, that float upon the air,
  In gliding state she wins her easy way:
O'er her warm cheek and rising bosom move
The bloom of young Desire and purple light of Love.

  Man's feeble race what ills await!
Labour, and Penury, the racks of Pain,
Disease, and Sorrow's weeping train,
  And Death, sad refuge from the storms of fate!
The fond complaint, my song, disprove,
And justify the laws of Jove.
Say, has he given in vain the heavenly Muse?
Night, and all her sickly dews,
Her spectres wan, and birds of boding cry,
He gives to range the dreary sky:
Till down the eastern cliffs afar
Hyperion's march they spy, and glittering shafts of war.

In climes beyond the solar road,
Where shaggy forms o'er ice-built mountains roam,
The Muse has broke the twilight gloom
  To cheer the shivering native's dull abode.
And oft, beneath the odorous shade
Of Chili's boundless forests laid,
She deigns to hear the savage youth repeat
In loose numbers wildly sweet
Their feather-cinctured chiefs, and dusky loves.
Her track, where'er the Goddess roves,
Glory pursue and generous Shame,
The unconquerable Mind, and Freedom's holy flame.

Woods, that wave o'er Delphi's steep,
Isles, that crown the Ægean deep,
  Fields, that cool Ilissus laves,
  Or where Mæander's amber waves
In lingering labyrinths creep,
  How do your tuneful echoes languish,
  Mute, but to the voice of anguish?

293

Where each old poetic mountain
    Inspiration breathed around:
Every shade and hallowed fountain
    Murmured deep a solemn sound:
Till the sad Nine, in Greece's evil hour,
    Left their Parnassus for the Latian plains.
Alike they scorn the pomp of tyrant Power,
    And coward Vice, that revels in her chains.
When Latium had her lofty spirit lost,
They sought, O Albion! next thy sea-encircled coast.

    Far from the sun and summer gale,
In thy green lap was Nature's darling laid,
What time, where lucid Avon strayed,
    To him the mighty mother did unveil
Her awful face: the dauntless child
Stretched forth his little arms, and smiled.
This pencil take (she said), whose colours clear
Richly paint the vernal year:
Thine too these golden keys, immortal boy!
This can unlock the gates of joy;
Of horror that, and thrilling fears,
Or ope the sacred source of sympathetic tears.

    Nor second he, that rode sublime
Upon the seraph-wings of Ecstasy,
The secrets of the abyss to spy.
    He passed the flaming bounds of place and time:
The living Throne, the sapphire-blaze,
Where Angels tremble while they gaze,
He saw; but, blasted with excess of light,
Closed his eyes in endless night.
Behold, where Dryden's less presumptuous car,
Wide o'er the fields of glory bear
Two coursers of ethereal race,
With necks in thunder clothed, and long-resounding pace

Hark, his hands the lyre explore!
Bright-eyed Fancy, hovering o'er,
    Scatters from her pictured urn
    Thoughts that breathe, and words that burn.
294

But ah, 'tis heard no more!
  O Lyre divine! what daring Spirit
  Wakes thee now?   Though he inherit
Nor the pride, nor ample pinion,
  That the Theban Eagle bear,
Sailing with supreme dominion
  Through the azure deep of air:
Yet oft before his infant eyes would run
  Such forms as glitter in the Muse's ray,
With orient hues, unborrowed of the Sun:
  Yet shall he mount, and keep his distant way
Beyond the limits of a vulgar fate,
Beneath the Good how far—but far above the Great.

William Collins

HOW SLEEP THE BRAVE

How sleep the brave, who sink to rest
By all their country's wishes blest!
When Spring, with dewy fingers cold,
Returns to deck their hallowed mould,
She there shall dress a sweeter sod
Than Fancy's feet have ever trod.

By fairy hands their knell is rung;
By forms unseen their dirge is sung;
There Honour comes, a pilgrim grey,
To bless the turf that wraps their clay;
And Freedom shall awhile repair
To dwell, a weeping hermit, there!

ODE TO EVENING

If aught of oaten stop, or pastoral song,
May hope, chaste Eve, to soothe thy modest ear,
    Like thy own solemn springs,
    Thy springs and dying gales;

295

O Nymph reserved, while now the bright-haired sun
Sits in yon western tent, whose cloudy skirts,
    With brede ethereal wove,
    O'erhang his wavy bed:

Now air is hushed, save where the weak-eyed bat
With short shrill shriek flits by on leathern wing,
    Or where the beetle winds
    His small but sullen horn,

As oft he rises, 'midst the twilight path
Against the pilgrim borne in heedless hum:
    Now teach me, maid composed,
    To breathe some softened strain,

Whose numbers, stealing through thy darkening vale,
May not unseemly with its stillness suit,
    As, musing slow, I hail
    Thy genial loved return!

For when thy folding-star arising shows
His paly circlet, at his warning lamp
    The fragrant Hours, and Elves
    Who slept in buds the day,

And many a Nymph who wreathes her brows with sedge,
And sheds the freshening dew, and, lovelier still,
    The pensive Pleasures sweet,
    Prepare thy shadowy car:

Then lead, calm votaress, where some sheety lake
Cheers the lone heath, or some time-hallowed pile,
    Or upland fallows grey
    Reflect its last cool gleam.

Or, if chill blustering winds, or driving rain,
Prevent my willing feet, be mine the hut
    That, from the mountain's side,
    Views wilds and swelling floods,

WILLIAM COLLINS

And hamlets brown, and dim-discovered spires,
And hears their simple bell, and marks o'er all
    Thy dewy fingers draw
    The gradual dusky veil.

While Spring shall pour his showers, as of the wont,
And bathe thy breathing tresses, meekest Eve!
    While Summer loves to sport
    Beneath thy lingering light;

While sallow Autumn fills thy lap with leaves,
Or Winter, yelling through the troublous air,
    Affrights thy shrinking train,
    And rudely rends thy robes:

So long, regardful of thy quiet rule,
Shall Fancy, Friendship, Science, smiling Peace,
    Thy gentlest influence own,
    And hymn thy favourite name!

THE PASSIONS

AN ODE FOR MUSIC

When Music, heavenly maid, was young,
While yet in early Greece she sung,
The Passions oft, to hear her shell,
Throng'd around her magic cell.
Exulting, trembling, raging, fainting,
Possest beyond the Muse's painting;
By turns they felt the glowing mind
Disturb'd, delighted, raised, refined:
'Til once, 'tis said, when all were fired,
Fill'd with fury, rapt, inspired,
From the supporting myrtles round
They snatch'd her instruments of sound,
And, as they oft had heard apart
Sweet lessons of her forceful art,
Each, for Madness ruled the hour,
Would prove his own expressive power.

First Fear his hand, its skill to try,
    Amid the chords bewilder'd laid,
And back recoil'd, he knew not why,
    E'en at the sound himself had made.

Next Anger rush'd, his eyes on fire,
    In lightnings own'd his secret stings;
In one rude clash he struck the lyre
    And swept with hurried hand the strings.

With woeful measures wan Despair—
    Low sullen sounds his grief beguiled,
A solemn, strange, and mingled air,
    'Twas sad by fits, by starts 'twas wild.

But thou, O Hope, with eyes so fair,
    What was thy delightful measure?
Still it whisper'd promised pleasure
    And bade the lovely scenes at distance hail!
Still would her touch the strain prolong;
    And from the rocks, the woods, the vale
She call'd on Echo still through all the song;
    And, where her sweetest theme she chose,
    A soft responsive voice was heard at every close;
And Hope enchanted smiled, and waved her golden hair;—

And longer had she sung:—but with a frown
    Revenge impatient rose:
He threw his blood-stain'd sword in thunder down;
    And with a withering look
    The war-denouncing trumpet took
And blew a blast so loud and dread,
Were ne'er prophetic sounds so full of woe!
    And ever and anon he beat
    The doubling drum with furious heat;
And, though sometimes, each dreary pause between,
    Dejected Pity at his side
    Her soul-subduing voice applied,
    Yet still he kept his wild unalter'd mien,
While each strain'd ball of sight seem'd bursting from his
    head.

Thy numbers, Jealousy, to nought were fix'd:
  Sad proof of thy distressful state!
Of differing themes the veering song was mix'd;
  And now it courted Love, now raving call'd on Hate.

With eyes up-raised, as one inspired,
Pale Melancholy sat retired;
  And from her wild sequester'd seat,
  In notes by distance made more sweet,
Pour'd through the mellow horn her pensive soul:
    And dashing soft from rocks around,
    Bubbling runnels join'd the sound;
Through glades and glooms the mingled measure stole,
  Or, o'er some haunted stream, with fond delay,
    Round an holy calm diffusing,
    Love of peace, and lonely musing,
In hollow murmurs died away.

But O! how alter'd was its sprightlier tone
When Cheerfulness, a nymph of healthiest hue,
  Her bow across her shoulder flung,
  Her buskins gemm'd with morning dew,
Blew an inspiring air, that dale and thicket rung,
  The hunter's call to Faun and Dryad known!
The oak-crown'd Sisters and their chaste-eyed Queen,
  Satyrs and Sylvan Boys, were seen
  Peeping from forth their alleys green:
Brown Exercise rejoiced to hear;
  And Sport leapt up, and seized his beechen spear.

Last came Joy's ecstatic trial:
He, with viny crown advancing,
  First to the lively pipe his hand addrest:
But soon he saw the brisk awakening viol,
  Whose sweet entrancing voice he loved the best:
They would have thought who heard the strain
    They saw, in Tempe's vale, her native maids
    Amidst the festal-sounding shades
To some unwearied minstrel dancing;
While, as his flying fingers kiss'd the strings,
  Love framed with Mirth a gay fantastic round:

Loose were her tresses seen, her zone unbound;
And he, amidst his frolic play,
As if he would the charming air repay,
Shook thousand odours from his dewy wings.

O Music! sphere-descended maid,
Friend of Pleasure, Wisdom's aid!
Why, goddess, why, to us denied,
Lay'st thou thy ancient lyre aside?
As, in that loved Athenian bower
You learn'd an all-commanding power,
Thy mimic soul, O nymph endear'd!
Can well recall what then it heard.
Where is thy native simple heart
Devote to Virtue, Fancy, Art?
Arise, as in that elder time,
Warm, energic, chaste, sublime!
Thy wonders, in that god-like age,
Fill thy recording Sister's page;—
'Tis said, and I believe the tale,
Thy humblest reed could more prevail,
Had more of strength, diviner rage,
Than all which charms this laggard age,
E'en all at once together found
Cecilia's mingled world of sound:—
O bid our vain endeavours cease:
Revive the just designs of Greece:
Return in all thy simple state!
Confirm the tales her sons relate!

DIRGE IN CYMBELINE

. . . . . .

The redbreast oft, at evening hours,
Shall kindly lend his little aid,
With hoary moss, and gather'd flowers,
To deck the ground where thou art laid.

When howling winds and beating rain
In tempests shake the sylvan cell;
Or 'midst the chase, on every plain,
The tender thought on thee shall dwell;

Each lovely scene shall thee restore;
  For thee the tear be duly shed;
Beloved till life can charm no more,
  And mourn'd till Pity's self be dead.

ODE TO FEAR

Thou, to whom the world unknown
With all its shadowy shapes, is shown;
Who seest, appalled, the unreal scene,
While fancy lifts the veil between:
    Ah fear! ah frantic fear!
    I see, I see thee near.
I know thy hurried step, thy haggard eye!
Like thee I start; like thee disordered fly.
For, lo, what monsters in thy train appear!
Danger, whose limbs of giant mould
What mortal eye can fixed behold?
Who stalks his round, an hideous form,
Howling amidst the midnight storm;
Or throws him on the ridgy steep
Of some loose hanging rock to sleep:
And with him thousand phantoms joined,
Who prompt to deeds accursed the mind:
And those, the fiends, who, near allied,
O'er nature's wounds, the wrecks, preside;
Whilst vengeance, in the lurid air,
Lifts her red arm, exposed and bare:
On whom that ravening brood of fate,
Who lap the blood of sorrow, wait:
Who, fear, this ghastly train can see,
And look not madly wild, like thee?

EPODE

In earliest Greece, to thee, with partial choice,
  The grief-full muse addrest her infant tongue;
The maids and matrons, on her awful voice,
  Silent and pale, in wild amazement hung.

Yet he, the bard who first invoked thy name,
  Disdained in Marathon its power to feel:
For not alone he nursed the poet's flame,
  But reached from virtue's hand the patriot's steel.

But who is he whom later garlands grace,
  Who left awhile o'er Hybla's dews to rove,
With trembling eyes thy dreary steps to trace,
  Where thou and furies shared the baleful grove?

Wrapt in thy cloudy veil, the incestuous queen
  Sighed the sad call her son and husband heard,
When once alone it broke the silent scene,
  And he, the wretch of Thebes, no more appeared.

O fear, I know thee by my throbbing heart:
  Thy withering power inspired each mournful line:
Though gentle pity claim her mingled part,
  Yet all the thunders of the scene are thine!

ANISTROPHE

Thou who such weary lengths hast past,
Where wilt thou rest, mad nymph, at last?
Say, wilt thou shroud in haunted cell,
Where gloomy rape and murder dwell?
  Or, in some hollowed seat,
  'Gainst which the big waves beat,
Hear drowning seamen's cries, in tempests brought?
Dark power, with shuddering meek submitted thought,
Be mine to read the visions old
Which thy awakening bards have told:
And, lest thou meet my blasted view,
Hold each strange tale devoutly true;
Ne'er be I found, by thee o'erawed,
In that thrice hallowed eve. abroad,
When ghosts, as cottage maids believe,
Their pebbled beds permitted leave;
And goblins haunt, from fire, or fen,
Or mine, or flood, the walks of men!

O thou, whose spirit most possest
The sacred seat of Shakespeare's breast!
By all that from thy prophet broke,
In thy divine emotions spoke;
Hither again thy fury deal,
Teach me but once more like him to feel:
His cypress wreath my meed decree,
And I, O fear, will dwell with thee!

Oliver Goldsmith

THE DESERTED VILLAGE

Sweet Auburn! loveliest village of the plain,
Where health and plenty cheered the labouring swain,
Where smiling spring its earliest visit paid,
And parting summer's lingering blooms delayed:
Dear lovely bowers of innocence and ease,
Seats of my youth, when every sport could please:
How often have I loitered o'er thy green,
Where humble happiness endeared each scene!
How often have I paused on every charm,
The sheltered cot, the cultivated farm,
The never-failing brook, the busy mill,
The decent church that topped the neighboring hill,
The hawthorn-bush, with seats beneath the shade,
For talking age and whispering lovers made!
How often have I blessed the coming day,
When toil remitting lent its turn to play,
And all the village train, from labour free,
Led up their sports beneath the spreading tree:
While many a pastime circled in the shade,
The young contending as the old surveyed;
And many a gambol frolicked o'er the ground,
And sleights of art and feats of strength went round:
And still, as each repeated pleasure tired,
Succeeding sports the mirthful band inspired;
The dancing pair that simply sought renown,
By holding out, to tire each other down;

The swain mistrustless of his smutted face,
While secret laughter tittered round the place;
The bashful virgin's sidelong looks of love,
The matron's glance that would those looks reprove,—
These were thy charms, sweet village! sports like these,
With sweet succession, taught e'en toil to please;
These, round thy bowers their cheerful influence shed,
These were thy charms,—but all these charms are fled!

Sweet smiling village, loveliest of the lawn,
Thy sports are fled, and all thy charms withdrawn;
Amidst thy bowers the tyrant's hand is seen,
And desolation saddens all thy green;
One only master grasps the whole domain,
And half a tillage stints thy smiling plain;
No more thy glassy brook reflects the day,
But, choked with sedges, works its weedy way;
Along thy glades, a solitary guest,
The hollow-sounding bittern guards its nest;
Amidst thy desert-walks the lapwing flies,
And tires their echoes with unvaried cries.
Sunk are thy bowers in shapeless ruin all,
And the long grass o'ertops the mouldering wall,
And, trembling, shrinking from the spoiler's hand,
Far, far away thy children leave the land.

Ill fares the land, to hastening ills a prey,
Where wealth accumulates, and men decay:
Princes and lords may flourish, or may fade;
A breath can make them, as a breath has made;
But a bold peasantry, their country's pride,
When once destroyed, can never be supplied.

A time there was, ere England's griefs began,
When every rood of ground maintained its man;
For him light Labour spread her wholesome store,
Just gave what life required, but gave no more:
His best companions, innocence and health;
And his best riches, ignorance of wealth.

But times are altered: trade's unfeeling train
Usurp the land and dispossess the swain;

OLIVER GOLDSMITH

Along the lawn, where scattered hamlets rose,
Unwieldy wealth and cumbrous pomp repose,
And every want to luxury allied,
And every pang that folly pays to pride.
Those gentle hours that plenty bade to bloom,
Those calm desires that asked but little room,
Those healthful sports that graced the peaceful scene,
Lived in each look, and brightened all the green,—
These, far departing, seek a kinder shore,
And rural mirth and manners are no more.

Sweet Auburn! parent of the blissful hour,
Thy glades forlorn confess the tyrant's power.
Here, as I take my solitary rounds,
Amidst thy tangling walks and ruined grounds,
And, many a year elapsed, return to view
Where once the cottage stood, the hawthorn grew,
Remembrance wakes, with all her busy train,
Swells at my breast, and turns the past to pain.

In all my wanderings round this world of care,
In all my griefs—and God has given my share—
I still had hopes my latest hours to crown,
Amidst these humble bowers to lay me down;
To husband out life's taper at the close,
And keep the flame from wasting by repose;
I still had hopes—for pride attends us still—
Amidst the swains to show my book-learned skill,
Around my fire an evening group to draw,
And tell of all I felt and all I saw;
And, as a hare, whom hounds and horns pursue,
Pants to the place from whence at first she flew,
I still had hopes, my long vexations past,
Here to return,—and die at home at last.

O blest retirement! friend to life's decline,
Retreats from care, that never must be mine,
How blest is he who crowns in shades like these
A youth of labour with an age of ease;
Who quits a world where strong temptations try,
And, since 'tis hard to combat, learns to fly!

305

For him no wretches, born to work and weep,
Explore the mine, or tempt the dangerous deep;
No surly porter stands in guilty state,
To spurn imploring famine from the gate:
But on he moves to meet his latter end,
Angels around befriending virtue's friend;
Sinks to the grave with unperceived decay,
While Resignation gently slopes the way;
And, all his prospects brightening to the last,
His heaven commences ere the world be past.

Sweet was the sound, when oft, at evening's close,
Up yonder hill the village murmur rose;
There, as I passed with careless steps and slow,
The mingling notes came softened from below;
The swain responsive as the milkmaid sung,
The sober herd that lowed to meet their young;
The noisy geese that gabbled o'er the pool,
The playful children just let loose from school;
The watch-dog's voice that bayed the whispering wind,
And the loud laugh that spoke the vacant mind,—
These all in sweet confusion sought the shade,
And filled each pause the nightingale had made.
But now the sounds of population fail,
No cheerful murmurs fluctuate in the gale,
No busy steps the grass-grown foot-way tread,
But all the bloomy flush of life is fled.
All but yon widowed, solitary thing,
That feebly bends beside the plashy spring;
She, wretched matron, forced in age, for bread,
To strip the brook with mantling cresses spread,
To pick her wintry fagot from the thorn,
To seek her nightly shed, and weep till morn;
She only left of all the harmless train,
The sad historian of the pensive plain.

Near yonder copse, where once the garden smiled,
And still where many a garden-flower grows wild;
There, where a few torn shrubs the place disclose,
The village preacher's modest mansion rose.

A man he was to all the country dear,
And passing rich with forty pounds a year;
Remote from towns he ran his godly race,
Nor e'er had changed, nor wished to change, his place;
Unskilful he to fawn, or seek for power,
By doctrines fashioned to the varying hour;
Far other aims his heart had learned to prize,
More skilled to raise the wretched than to rise.
His house was known to all the vagrant train.
He chid their wanderings, but relieved their pain;
The long-remembered beggar was his guest,
Whose beard descending swept his aged breast;
The ruined spendthrift, now no longer proud,
Claimed kindred there, and had his claims allowed;
The broken soldier, kindly bade to stay,
Sate by his fire, and talked the night away;
Wept o'er his wounds, or, tales of sorrow done,
Shouldered his crutch, and showed how fields were won.
Pleased with his guests, the good man learned to glow,
And quite forgot their vices in their woe;
Careless their merits or their faults to scan,
His pity gave ere charity began.

  Thus to relieve the wretched was his pride,
And e'en his failings leaned to Virtue's side;
But in his duty prompt at every call,
He watched and wept, he prayed and felt for all;
And, as a bird each fond endearment tries,
To tempt its new-fledged offspring to the skies,
He tried each art, reproved each dull delay,
Allured to brighter worlds, and led the way.

  Beside the bed where parting life was laid,
And sorrow, guilt, and pain, by turns dismayed,
The reverend champion stood. At his control,
Despair and anguish fled the struggling soul;
Comfort came down the trembling wretch to raise,
And his last faltering accents whispered praise.

  At church, with meek and unaffected grace,
His looks adorned the venerable place;

307

Truth from his lips prevailed with double sway,
And fools, who came to scoff, remained to pray.
The service past, around the pious man,
With steady zeal, each honest rustic ran;
E'en children followed, with endearing wile,
And plucked his gown, to share the good man's smile.
His ready smile a parent's warmth expressed,
Their welfare pleased him, and their cares distressed;
To them his heart, his love, his griefs were given,
But all his serious thoughts had rest in heaven.
As some tall cliff, that lifts its awful form,
Swells from the vale, and midway leaves the storm,
Though round its breast the rolling clouds are spread,
Eternal sunshine settles on its head.

Beside yon straggling fence that skirts the way,
With blossomed furze unprofitably gay,
There, in his noisy mansion, skilled to rule,
The village master taught his little school;
A man severe he was, and stern to view;
I knew him well, and every truant knew:
Well had the boding tremblers learned to trace
The day's disasters in his morning face;
Full well they laughed, with counterfeited glee,
At all his jokes, for many a joke had he;
Full well the busy whisper, circling round,
Conveyed the dismal tidings when he frowned;
Yet he was kind, or, if severe in aught,
The love he bore to learning was in fault.
The village all declared how much he knew;
'Twas certain he could write, and cipher too;
Lands he could measure, terms and tides presage,
And e'en the story ran that he could gauge;
In arguing, too, the parson owned his skill,
For, e'en though vanquished, he could argue still,
While words of learnèd length and thundering sound
Amazed the gazing rustics ranged around;
And still they gazed, and still the wonder grew
That one small head could carry all he knew.

308

OLIVER GOLDSMITH

But past is all his fame. The very spot
Where many a time he triumphed, is forgot.—
Near yonder thorn, that lifts its head on high,
Where once the sign-post caught the passing eye,
Low lies that house where nut-brown draughts inspired,
Where greybeard mirth and smiling toil retired,
Where village statesmen talked with looks profound,
And news much older than their ale went round.
Imagination fondly stoops to trace
The parlour splendours of that festive place,—
The whitewashed wall; the nicely sanded floor;
The varnished clock that ticked behind the door;
The chest, contrived a double debt to pay,
A bed by night, a chest of drawers by day;
The pictures placed for ornament and use;
The twelve good rules; the royal game of goose;
The hearth, except when winter chilled the day,
With aspen boughs and flowers and fennel gay;
While broken teacups, wisely kept for show,
Ranged o'er the chimney, glistened in a row.

Vain, transitory splendours! could not all
Reprieve the tottering mansion from its fall?
Obscure it sinks, nor shall it more impart
An hour's importance to the poor man's heart;
Thither no more the peasant shall repair
To sweet oblivion of his daily care;
No more the farmer's news, the barber's tale,
No more the woodman's ballad shall prevail;
No more the smith his dusky brow shall clear,
Relax his ponderous strength, and lean to hear;
The host himself no longer shall be found
Careful to see the mantling bliss go round;
Nor the coy maid, half willing to be pressed,
Shall kiss the cup to pass it to the rest.

Yes! let the rich deride, the proud disdain,
These simple blessings of the lowly train;
To me more dear, congenial to my heart,
One native charm, than all the gloss of art.
Spontaneous joys, where nature has its play,
The soul adopts, and owns their first-born sway;

309

Lightly they frolic o'er the vacant mind,
Unenvied, unmolested, unconfined:
But the long pomp, the midnight masquerade,
With all the freaks of wanton wealth arrayed,—
In these, ere triflers half their wish obtain,
The toiling pleasure sickens into pain;
And, e'en while fashion's brightest arts decoy,
The heart, distrusting, asks if this be joy.

Ye friends to truth, ye statesmen, who survey
The rich man's joys increase, the poor's decay,
'Tis yours to judge, how wide the limits stand
Between a splendid and a happy land.
Proud swells the tide with loads of freighted ore,
And shouting Folly hails them from her shore;
Hoards e'en beyond the miser's wish abound,
And rich men flock from all the world around.
Yet count our gains. This wealth is but a name
That leaves our useful products still the same.
Not so the loss. The man of wealth and pride
Takes up a space that many poor supplied;
Space for his lake, his park's extended bounds,
Space for his horses, equipage, and hounds:
The robe that wraps his limbs in silken sloth
Has robbed the neighbouring fields of half their growth;
His seat, where solitary sports are seen,
Indignant spurns the cottage from the green;
Around the world each needful product flies,
For all the luxuries the world supplies:
While thus the land, adorned for pleasure all,
In barren splendour feebly waits the fall.

As some fair female, unadorned and plain,
Secure to please while youth confirms her reign,
Slights every borrowed charm that dress supplies,
Nor shares with art the triumph of her eyes,
But when those charms are past,—for charms are frail,—
When time advances, and when lovers fail,
She then shines forth, solicitous to bless,
In all the gleaming impotence of dress;
Thus fares the land, by luxury betrayed,
In nature's simplest charms at first arrayed,

But verging to decline, its splendours rise,
Its vistas strike, its palaces surprise;
While, scourged by famine from the smiling land,
The mournful peasant leads his humble band;
And while he sinks, without one arm to save,
The country blooms,—a garden and a grave.

Where then, ah! where shall poverty reside,
To 'scape the pressure of contiguous pride?
If to some common's fenceless limits strayed,
He drives his flock to pick the scanty blade,
Those fenceless fields the sons of wealth divide,
And e'en the bare-worn common is denied.
If to the city sped,—what waits him there?
To see profusion that he must not share;
To see ten thousand baneful arts combined
To pamper luxury and thin mankind;
To see each joy the sons of pleasure know
Extorted from his fellow-creature's woe.
Here while the courtier glitters in brocade,
There the pale artist plies the sickly trade;
Here while the proud their long-drawn pomps display,
There the black gibbet glooms beside the way.
The dome where Pleasure holds her midnight reign,
Here, richly decked, admits the gorgeous train;
Tumultuous grandeur crowds the blazing square,
The rattling chariots clash, the torches glare.
Sure scenes like these no troubles e'er annoy!
Sure these denote one universal joy!
Are these thy serious thoughts?—Ah, turn thine eyes
Where the poor houseless shivering female lies.
She once, perhaps, in village plenty blest,
Has wept at tales of innocence distressed;
Her modest looks the cottage might adorn,
Sweet as the primrose peeps beneath the thorn;
Now lost to all, her friends, her virtue fled,
Near her betrayer's door she lays her head,
And, pinched with cold, and shrinking from the shower,
With heavy heart deplores that luckless hour,
When idly first, ambitious of the town,
She left her wheel and robes of country brown.

Do thine, sweet Auburn, thine, the loveliest train,
Do thy fair tribes participate her pain?
E'en now, perhaps, by cold and hunger led,
At proud men's doors they ask a little bread!

Ah, no!   To distant climes, a dreary scene,
Where half the convex world intrudes between,
Through torrid tracts with fainting steps they go,
Where wild Altama murmurs to their woe.
Far different there from all that charmed before,
The various terrors of that horrid shore,—
Those blazing suns that dart a downward ray,
And fiercely shed intolerable day;
Those matted woods where birds forget to sing,
But silent bats in drowsy clusters cling;
Those poisonous fields with rank luxuriance crowned,
Where the dark scorpion gathers death around;
Where at each step the stranger fears to wake
The rattling terrors of the vengeful snake;
Where crouching tigers wait their hapless prey,
And savage men more murderous still than they;
While oft in whirls the mad tornado flies,
Mingling the ravaged landscape with the skies.
Far different these from every former scene,
The cooling brook, the grassy-vested green,
The breezy covert of the warbling grove,
That only sheltered thefts of harmless love.

Good Heaven! what sorrows gloomed that parting day
That called them from their native walks away;
When the poor exiles, every pleasure past,
Hung round the bowers, and fondly looked their last,
And took a long farewell, and wished in vain
For seats like these beyond the western main;
And, shuddering still to face the distant deep,
Returned and wept, and still returned to weep.
The good old sire the first prepared to go
To new-found worlds, and wept for others' woe;
But for himself, in conscious virtue brave,
He only wished for worlds beyond the grave.

OLIVER GOLDSMITH

His lovely daughter, lovelier in her tears,
The fond companion of his helpless years,
Silent went next, neglectful of her charms,
And left a lover's for a father's arms.
With louder plaints the mother spoke her woes,
And blessed the cot where every pleasure rose;
And kissed her thoughtless babes with many a tear,
And clasped them close, in sorrow doubly dear;
Whilst her fond husband strove to lend relief
In all the silent manliness of grief.

O Luxury! thou cursed by Heaven's decree,
How ill exchanged are things like these for thee!
How do thy potions, with insidious joy,
Diffuse their pleasures only to destroy!
Kingdoms by thee, to sickly greatness grown,
Boast of a florid vigour not their own.
At every draught more large and large they grow,
A bloated mass of rank, unwieldy woe;
Till, sapped their strength, and every part unsound,
Down, down they sink, and spread a ruin round.

E'en now the devastation is begun,
And half the business of destruction done;
Even now, methinks, as pondering here I stand,
I see the rural virtues leave the land.
Down where yon anchoring vessel spreads the sail
That idly waiting flaps with every gale,
Downward they move, a melancholy band,
Pass from the shore, and darken all the strand.
Contented toil, and hospitable care,
And kind connubial tenderness, are there;
And piety with wishes placed above,
And steady loyalty, and faithful love.
And thou, sweet Poetry, thou loveliest maid,
Still first to fly where sensual joys invade;
Unfit, in these degenerate times of shame,
To catch the heart, or strike for honest fame;
Dear charming nymph, neglected and decried,
My shame in crowds, my solitary pride;

Thou source of all my bliss and all my woe,
That found'st me poor at first, and keep'st me so;
Thou guide, by which the nobler arts excel,
Thou nurse of every virtue, fare thee well!
Farewell; and oh, where'er thy voice be tried,
On Torno's cliffs, on Pambamarca's side,
Whether where equinoctial fervours glow,
Or winter wraps the polar world in snow,
Still let thy voice, prevailing over time,
Redress the rigours of the inclement clime;
Aid slighted truth with thy persuasive strain;
Teach erring man to spurn the rage of gain;
Teach him, that states of native strength possessed,
Though very poor, may still be very blest;
That trade's proud empire hastes to swift decay,
As ocean sweeps the laboured mole away;
While self-dependent power can time defy,
As rocks resist the billows and the sky.

THE TRAVELLER

Remote, unfriended, melancholy, slow,
Or by the lazy Scheld, or wandering Po;
Or onward, where the rude Carinthian boor
Against the houseless stranger shuts the door;
Or where Campania's plain forsaken lies,
A weary waste expanding to the skies;
Where'er I roam, whatever realms to see,
My heart untravell'd fondly turns to thee;
Still to my brother turns, with ceaseless pain,
And drags at each remove a lengthening chain.
Eternal blessings crown my earliest friend,
And round his dwelling guardian saints attend;
Blest be that spot, where cheerful guests retire
To pause from toil, and trim their evening fire;
Blest that abode, where want and pain repair,
And every stranger finds a ready chair;
Blest be those feasts with simple plenty crown'd,
Where all the ruddy family around

314

OLIVER GOLDSMITH

Laugh at the jests or pranks that never fail,
Or sigh with pity at some mournful tale;
Or press the bashful stranger to his food,
And learn the luxury of doing good.

But me, not destined such delights to share,
My prime of life in wandering spent and care;
Impell'd, with steps unceasing, to pursue
Some fleeting good, that mocks me with the view;
That, like the circle bounding earth and skies,
Allures from far, yet, as I follow flies;
My fortune leads to traverse realms alone,
And find no spot of all the world my own.

Even now, where Alpine solitudes ascend,
I sit me down a pensive hour to spend;
And, placed on high above the storm's career,
Look downward where a hundred realms appear;
Lakes, forests, cities, plains, extending wide,
The pomp of kings, the shepherd's humbler pride.

When thus Creation's charms around combine,
Amidst the store should thankless pride repine?
Say, should the philosophic mind disdain
That good which makes each humbler bosom vain?
Let school-taught pride dissemble all it can,
These little things are great to little man;
And wiser he, whose sympathetic mind
Exults in all the good of all mankind.
Ye glittering towns, with wealth and splendour crown'd;
Ye fields, where summer spreads profusion round;
Ye lakes, whose vessels catch the busy gale;
Ye bending swains, that dress the flowery vale;
For me your tributary stores combine:
Creation's heir, the world, the world is mine!

. . . .

THE CAPTIVITY

. . . .

Fatigued with life, yet loth to part,
 On Hope the wretch relies;
And every blow that sinks the heart
 Bids expectation rise.

Hope, like the taper's gleamy light,
    Adorns the wretch's way;
And still, as darker grows the night,
    Emits a brighter ray.

RETALIATION

Here lies our good Edmund, whose genius was such,
We scarcely can praise it, or blame it too much;
Who, born for the universe, narrow'd his mind,
And to party gave up what was meant for mankind.
Though fraught with all learning, yet straining his throat,
To persuade Tommy Townshend to lend him a vote;
Who, too deep for his hearers, still went on refining,
And thought of convincing, while they thought of dining:
Though equal to all things, for all things unfit,
Too nice for a statesman, too proud for a wit;
For a patriot, too cool; for a drudge, disobedient,
And too fond of the right, to pursue the expedient.

Here lies David Garrick, describe me who can,
An abridgement of all that was pleasant in man;
As an actor, confess'd without rival to shine;
As a wit, if not first, in the very first line:
Yet, with talents like these, and an excellent heart,
The man had his failings, a dupe to his art.
Like an ill-judging beauty, his colours he spread,
And beplaster'd with rouge his own natural red.
On the stage he was natural, simple, affecting;
'Twas only that when he was off he was acting.

Here Reynolds is laid, and, to tell you my mind,
He has not left a wiser or better behind;
His pencil was striking, resistless, and grand;
His manners were gentle, complying and bland;

316

Still born to improve us in every part,
His pencil our faces, his manners our heart:
To coxcombs averse, yet most civilly steering,
When they judged without skill, he was still hard of hearing:
When they talk'd of their Raphaels, Correggios, and stuff,
He shifted his trumpet, and only took snuff.

. . . .

William Cowper

CHARITY

. . . .

When one, that holds communion with the skies,
Has filled his urn where these pure waters rise,
And once more mingles with us meaner things,
'Tis even as if an angel shook his wings;
Immortal fragrance fills the circuit wide,
That tells us whence his treasures are supplied.
So, when a ship well-freighted with the stores
The sun matures on India's spicy shores,
Has dropped her anchor and her canvas furled
In some safe haven of our western world,
'Twere vain inquiry to what port she went;
The gale informs us, laden with the scent.
Some seek, when queasy conscience has its qualms,
To lull the painful malady with alms;
But charity, not feigned, intends alone
Another's good—theirs centres in their own;
And, too short-lived to reach the realms of peace,
Must cease for ever when the poor shall cease.
Flavia, most tender of her own good name,
Is rather careless of her sister's fame:
Her superfluity the poor supplies,
But, if she touch a character, it dies.
The seeming virtue weighed against the vice,
She deems all safe, for she has paid the price:
No charity but alms aught values she,
Except in porcelain on her mantel-tree.

317

How many deeds, with which the world has rung,
From pride, in league with ignorance, have sprung!
But God o'errules all human follies still,
And bends the tough materials to His will.
A conflagration or a wintry flood
Has left some hundreds without home or food;
Extravagance and avarice shall subscribe,
While fame and self-complacence are the bribe.
The brief proclaimed, it visits every pew,
But first the squire's—a compliment but due.
With slow deliberation he unties
His glittering purse—that envy of all eyes!
And, while the clerk just puzzles out the psalm,
Slides guinea behind guinea in his palm;
Till, finding (what he might have found before)
A smaller piece amidst the precious store,
Pinched close between his finger and his thumb,
He half exhibits, and then drops the sum.
Gold, to be sure!—Throughout the town 'tis told
How the good squire gives never less than gold.
From motives such as his, though not the best,
Springs in due time supply for the distressed;
Not less effectual than what love bestows—
Except that office clips it as it goes.

.   .   .   .

BOADICEA.   AN ODE

When the British Warrior Queen,
    Bleeding from the Roman rods,
Sought, with an indignant mien,
    Counsel of her country's gods,

Sage beneath a spreading oak
    Sat the druid, hoary chief,
Every burning word he spoke
    Full of rage and full of grief:

"Princess! if our aged eyes
　Weep upon thy matchless wrongs,
'Tis because resentment ties
　All the terrors of our tongues.

"Rome shall perish,—write that word
　In the blood that she has spilt;
Perish hopeless and abhorred,
　Deep in ruin as in guilt.

"Rome, for empire far renowned,
　Tramples on a thousand states,
Soon her pride shall kiss the ground,—
　Hark! the Gaul is at her gates.

"Other Romans shall arise,
　Heedless of a soldier's name,
Sounds, not arms, shall win the prize,
　Harmony the path to fame.

"Then the progeny that springs
　From the forests of our land,
Armed with thunder, clad with wings,
　Shall a wider world command.

"Regions Cæsar never knew
　Thy posterity shall sway,
Where his eagles never flew,
　None invincible as they."

Such the bard's prophetic words,
　Pregnant with celestial fire,
Bending as he swept the chords
　Of his sweet but awful lyre.

She, with all a monarch's pride,
　Felt them in her bosom glow,
Rushed to battle, fought and died,
　Dying, hurled them at the foe.

"Ruffians, pitiless as proud,
　Heaven awards the vengeance due;
Empire is on us bestowed,
　Shame and ruin wait for you!"

A COMPARISON

The lapse of time and rivers is the same,
Both speed their journey with a restless stream;
The silent pace, with which they steal away,
No wealth can bribe, no prayers persuade to stay;
Alike irrevocable both when past,
And a wide ocean swallows both at last.
Though each resemble each in every part,
A difference strikes at length the musing heart;
Streams never flow in vain; where streams abound,
How laughs the land with various plenty crown'd!
But time, that should enrich the nobler mind,
Neglected leaves a dreary waste behind.

ANOTHER

ADDRESSED TO A YOUNG LADY

Sweet stream, that winds through yonder glade,
Apt emblem of a virtuous maid—
Silent and chaste she steals along,
Far from the world's gay busy throng;
With gentle yet prevailing force,
Intent upon her destined course;
Graceful and useful all she does,
Blessing and blest where'er she goes,
Pure bosom'd as that watery glass,
And heaven reflected in her face.

MY MARY

The twentieth year is wellnigh past
Since first our sky was overcast;
Ah, would that this might be the last!
My Mary!

Thy spirits have a fainter flow,
I see thee daily weaker grow;
'Twas my distress that brought thee low,
  My Mary!

Thy needles, once a shining store,
For my sake restless heretofore,
Now rust disused, and shine no more;
  My Mary!

For though thou gladly wouldst fulfil
The same kind office for me still,
Thy sight now seconds not thy will,
  My Mary!

But well thou play'dst the housewife's part,
And all thy threads with magic art
Have wound themselves about this heart,
  My Mary!

Thy indistinct expressions seem
Like language utter'd in a dream;
Yet me they charm, whate'er the theme,
  My Mary!

Thy silver locks, once auburn bright,
Are still more lovely in my sight
Than golden beams of orient light,
  My Mary!

For could I view nor them nor thee,
What sight worth seeing could I see?
The sun would rise in vain for me,
  My Mary!

Partakers of thy sad decline,
Thy hands their little force resign;
Yet, gently pressed, press gently mine,
  My Mary!

And then I feel that still I hold
A richer store ten thousandfold
Than misers fancy in their gold,
      My Mary!

Such feebleness of limbs thou prov'st
That now at every step thou mov'st
Upheld by two; yet still thou lov'st,
      My Mary!

And still to love, though pressed with ill,
In wintry age to feel no chill,
With me is to be lovely still,
      My Mary!

But oh! by constant heed I know
How oft the sadness that I show
Transforms thy smiles to looks of woe,
      My Mary!

And should my future lot be cast
With much resemblance of the past,
Thy worn-out heart will break at last,
      My Mary!

TO MARY UNWIN

Mary! I want a lyre with other strings;
Such aid from Heaven as some have feigned they drew!
An eloquence scarce given to mortals, new,
And undebased by praise of meaner things!
That, ere through age or woe I shed my wings,
I may record thy worth, with honour due,
In verse as musical as thou art true,—
Verse, that immortalises whom it sings!
But thou hast little need: there is a book,
By seraphs writ with beams of heavenly light,
On which the eyes of God not rarely look;
A chronicle of actions just and bright!
   There all thy deeds, my faithful Mary, shine,
   And since thou own'st that praise, I spare thee mine.

322

WILLIAM COWPER

THE TASK

Now stir the fire, and close the shutters fast,
Let fall the curtains, wheel the sofa round,
And, while the bubbling and loud-hissing urn
Throws up a steamy column, and the cups,
That cheer but not inebriate, wait on each,
So let us welcome peaceful evening in.
Not such his evening who, with shining face,
Sweats in the crowded theatre, and, squeezed
And bored with elbow-points through both his sides,
Outscolds the ranting actor on the stage:
Nor his, who patient stands till his feet throb,
And his head thumps, to feed upon the breath
Of patriots, bursting with heroic rage,
Or placemen, all tranquillity and smiles.

.   .   .   .

Come, Evening, once again, season of peace;
Return, sweet Evening, and continue long!
Methinks I see thee in the streaky west,
With matron-step slow-moving, while the night
Treads on thy sweeping train; one hand employed
In letting fall the curtain of repose
On bird and beast, the other charged for man
With sweet oblivion of the cares of day:
Not sumptuously adorned, nor needing aid,
Like homely-featured night, of clustering gems
A star or two, just twinkling on thy brow,
Suffices thee; save that the moon is thine
No less than hers, not worn indeed on high
With ostentatious pageantry, but set
With modest grandeur in thy purple zone,
Resplendent less, but of an ampler round.

—Book IV

Books are not seldom talismans and spells,
By which the magic art of shrewder wits
Holds an unthinking multitude enthralled.
Some to the fascination of a name

323

Surrender judgement, hoodwinked. Some the style
Infatuates, and through labyrinths and wilds
Of error leads them by a tune entranced.
While sloth seduces more, too weak to bear
The insupportable fatigue of thought,
And swallowing, therefore, without pause or choice,
The total grist unsifted, husks and all.

. . . .

. . . One spirit, His
Who wore the platted thorns with bleeding brows,
Rules universal nature. Not a flower
But shows some touch, in freckle. streak, or stain,
Of His unrival'd pencil. He inspires
Their balmy odours, and imparts their hues,
And bathes their eyes with nectar, and includes,
In grains as countless as the seaside sands,
The forms with which He sprinkles all the earth.

. . . .

E'en in the spring and playtime of the year,
That calls the unwonted villager abroad
With all her little ones, a sportive train,
To gather kingcups in the yellow mead,
These shades are all my own. The timorous hare,
Grown so familiar with her frequent guest,
Scale shuns me; and the stockdove unalarm'd
Sits cooing in the pine tree, nor suspends
His long love-ditty for my near approach.
Drawn from his refuge in some lonely elm,
That age or injury has hollow'd deep,
Where, on his bed of wool and matted leaves,
He has outslept the winter, ventures forth
To frisk awhile, and bask in the warm sun,
The squirrel, flippant, pert, and full of play;
He sees me, and at once, swift as a bird,
Ascends the neighbouring beech; there whisks his brush,
And perks his ears, and stamps, and cries aloud,
With all the prettiness of feign'd alarm,
And anger insignificantly fierce.

—Book VI.

324

Anna Letitia Aikin

LIFE

Life! we've been long together,
Through pleasant and through cloudy weather;
  'Tis hard to part when friends are dear;
  Perhaps 'twill cost a sigh, a tear;
Then steal away, give little warning,
  Choose thine own time,
Say not "Good-night," but in some brighter clime
  Bid me "Good-morning."

Sir William Jones

WHAT CONSTITUTES A STATE?

What constitutes a State?
Not high-raised battlement or laboured mound,
  Thick wall or moated gate;
Not cities proud with spires and turrets crowned;
  Not bays and broad-armed ports,
Where, laughing at the storm, rich navies ride;
  Not starred and spangled courts,
Where low-browed baseness wafts perfume to pride.
  No:—men, high-minded men,
With powers as far above dull brutes endued
  In forest, brake, or den,
As beasts excel cold rocks and brambles rude,—
  Men who their duties know,
But know their rights, and, knowing, dare maintain,
  Prevent the long-aimed blow,
And crush the tyrant while they rend the chain;
  These constitute a State;
And sovereign law, that State's collected will,
  O'er thrones and globes elate
Sits empress, crowning good, repressing ill.

Smit by her sacred frown,
The fiend, Dissension, like a vapour sinks,
    And e'en the all-dazzling crown
Hides his faint rays, and at her bidding shrinks.
    Such was this heaven-loved isle,
Than Lesbos fairer and the Cretan shore!
    No more shall freedom smile?
Shall Britons languish, and be men no more?
    Since all must life resign,
Those sweet rewards which decorate the brave
    'Tis folly to decline,
And steal inglorious to the silent grave.

John Logan

TO THE CUCKOO

Hail, beauteous stranger of the grove!
    Thou messenger of Spring!
Now Heaven repairs thy rural seat,
    And woods thy welcome ring.

What time the daisy decks the green,
    Thy certain voice we hear:
Hast thou a star to guide thy path,
    Or mark the rolling year?

Delightful visitant! with thee
    I hail the time of flowers
And hear the sound of music sweet
    From birds among the bowers.

The school-boy, wandering through the wood
    To pull the primrose gay,
Starts, the new voice of Spring to hear,
    And imitates thy lay.

What time the pea puts on the bloom,
    Thou fli'st thy vocal vale,
An annual guest in other lands,
    Another Spring to hail.

326

Sweet bird! thy bower is ever green,
Thy sky is ever clear;
Thou hast no sorrow in thy song,
No Winter in thy year!

O could I fly, I'd fly with thee!
We'd make, with joyful wing,
Our annual visit o'er the globe,
Companions of the Spring.

Thomas Chatterton

SONG FROM ÆLLA

O sing unto my roundelay,
O drop the briny tear with me;
Dance no more at holyday,
Like a running river be:
My love is dead,
Gone to his death-bed,
All under the willow-tree.

Black his locks as the winter night,
White his robe as the summer snow,
Red his face as the morning light,
Cold he lies in the grave below:
My love is dead,
Gone to his death-bed,
All under the willow-tree.

Sweet his tongue as the throstle's note,
Quick in dance as thought can be,
Deft his tabor, cudgel stout;
O! he lies by the willow-tree:
My love is dead,
Gone to his death-bed,
All under the willow-tree.

Hark! the raven flaps his wing
In the briered dell below;
Hark! the death-owl loud doth sing
To the night-mares as they go:
My love is dead,
Gone to his death-bed,
All under the willow-tree.

See! the white moon shines on high;
Whiter is my true love's shroud,
Whiter than the morning sky,
Whiter than the evening cloud:
My love is dead,
Gone to his death-bed,
All under the willow-tree.

Here upon my true love's grave
Shall the barren flowers be laid,
Not one holy Saint to save
All the coldness of a maid:
My love is dead,
Gone to his death-bed,
All under the willow-tree.

With my hands I'll dent the briers
Round his holy corse to gree;
Ouph and fairy, light your fires—
Here my body still shall be:
My love is dead,
Gone to his death-bed,
All under the willow-tree.

Come, with acorn-cup and thorn,
Drain my hearte's blood away;
Life and all its goods I scorn,
Dance by night, or feast by day:
My love is dead,
Gone to his death-bed,
All under the willow-tree.

Water-witches, crowned with reytes,
    Bear me to your deadly tide.
I die—I come—my true-love waits.
    Thus the damsel spake, and died.

George Crabbe

LATE WISDOM

We've trod the maze of error round,
    Long wandering in the winding glade;
And now the torch of truth is found,
    It only shows us where we strayed:
Light for ourselves, what is it worth,
    When we no more our way can choose?
For others when we hold it forth,
    They, in their pride, the boon refuse.

By long experience taught, we now
    Can rightly judge of friends and foes,
Can all the worth of these allow,
    And all their faults discern in those.
Relentless hatred, erring love,
    We can for sacred truth forgo;
We can the warmest friend reprove,
    And bear to praise the fiercest foe:
To what effect? Our friends are gone
    Beyond reproof, regard or care;
And of our foes remains there one
    The mild relenting thoughts to share?

Now 'tis our boast that we can quell
    The wildest passions in their rage;
Can their destructive force repel,
    And their impetuous wrath assuage:
Ah! Virtue, dost thou arm, when now
    This bold rebellious race are fled;
When all these tyrants rest, and thou
    Art warring with the mighty dead?

William Blake

MAD BLAKE

Blake saw a tree-ful of angels at Peckham Rye,
And his hands could lay hold of the tiger's terrible heart.
Blake knew how deep is Hell, and Heaven how high,
And could build the Universe from one tiny part.
Blake heard the asides of God, as with furrowed brow
He sifts the star-streams between the Then and the Now,
In vast infant sagacity brooding—an infant's grace
Shining serene on His simple benignant face.

Blake, they say, was mad; and Space's Pandora-box
Loosed its secrets upon him, devils—and angels, indeed!
I, they say, am sane; but no key of mine unlocks
One lock of one gate wherethrough Heaven's glory is
freed.
And I hark and I hold my breath daylong, yearlong,
Out of comfort and easy dreaming evermore starting
awake,
Yearning beyond all sanity for some echo of that song
Of songs that was sung to the soul of the madman, Blake!
—William Rose Benét.

TO SPRING

O Thou with dewy locks, who lookest down
Through the clear windows of the morning, turn
Thine angel eyes upon our western isle,
Which in full choir hails thy approach, O Spring!

The hills tell each other, and the list'ning
Valleys hear; all our longing eyes are turned
Up to thy bright pavilions: issue forth,
And let thy holy feet visit our clime.

Come o'er the eastern hills, and let our winds
Kiss thy perfumèd garments; let us taste
330

Thy morn and evening breath; scatter thy pearls
Upon our love-sick land that mourns for thee.

O deck her forth with thy fair fingers; pour
Thy soft kisses on her bosom; and put
Thy golden crown upon her languished head,
Whose modest tresses were bound up for thee.

LOVE'S PRISONER

How sweet I roamed from field to field,
   And tasted all the summer's pride,
Till I the Prince of Love beheld
   Who in the sunny beams did glide.

He showed me lilies for my hair,
   And blushing roses for my brow:
He led me through his gardens fair
   Where all his golden pleasures grow.

With sweet May-dews my wings were wet,
   And Phœbus fired my vocal rage;
He caught me in his silken net,
   And shut me in his golden cage.

He loves to sit and hear me sing,
   Then laughing, sports and plays with me;
Then stretches out my golden wing,
   And mocks my loss of liberty.

SONG

My silks and fine array,
   My smiles and languished air,
By love are driven away;
   And mournful lean Despair
Brings me yew to deck my grave:
Such end true lovers have.

His face is fair as heaven
  When springing buds unfold;
Oh, why to him was't given,
  Whose heart is wintry cold?
His breast is love's all-worshipped tomb,
Where all love's pilgrims come.

Bring me an axe and spade,
  Bring me a winding-sheet;
When I my grave have made,
  Let winds and tempests beat:
Then down I'll lie, as cold as clay.
True love doth pass away!

MEMORY, HITHER COME

Memory, hither come,
  And tune your merry notes:
And, while upon the wind
  Your music floats,
I'll pore upon the stream
Where sighing lovers dream,
And fish for fancies as they pass
Within the watery glass.

I'll drink of the clear stream,
  And hear the linnet's song,
And there I'll lie and dream
  The day along:
And, when night comes, I'll go
To places fit for woe,
Walking along the darkened valley
With silent Melancholy.

TO THE MUSES

Whether on Ida's shady brow,
  Or in the chambers of the East,
The chambers of the Sun, that now
  From ancient melody have ceased;

WILLIAM BLAKE

Whether in heaven ye wander fair,
  Or the green corners of the earth,
Or the blue regions of the air
  Where the melodious winds have birth;

Whether on crystal rocks ye rove,
  Beneath the bosom of the sea,
Wandering in many a coral grove;
  Fair Nine, forsaking Poetry;

How have you left the ancient love
  That bards of old enjoyed in you!
The languid strings do scarcely move,
  The sound is forced, the notes are few!

THE DIVINE IMAGE

To Mercy, Pity, Peace, and Love,
  All pray in their distress,
And to these virtues of delight
  Return their thankfulness.

For Mercy, Pity, Peace, and Love,
  Is God our Father dear;
And Mercy, Pity, Peace, and Love,
  Is man, his child and care.

For Mercy has a human heart;
  Pity, a human face;
And Love, the human form divine;
  And Peace, the human dress.

Then every man, of every clime,
  That prays in his distress,
Prays to the human form divine:
  Love, Mercy, Pity, Peace.

And all must love the human form,
  In heathen, Turk, or Jew.
Where Mercy, Love, and Pity dwell,
  There God is dwelling too.

THE CLOD AND THE PEBBLE

"Love seeketh not itself to please,
  Nor for itself hath any care,
But for another gives its ease,
  And builds a heaven in hell's despair."

So sang a little clod of clay,
  Trodden with the cattle's feet.
But a pebble of the brook
  Warbled out these metres meet:

"Love seeketh only *Self* to please,
  To bind another to its delight,
Joys in another's loss of ease,
  And builds a hell in heaven's despite."

THE TIGER

Tiger, tiger, burning bright
In the forests of the night,
What immortal hand or eye
Could frame thy fearful symmetry?

In what distant deeps or skies
Burnt the fire of thine eyes?
On what wings dare he aspire?
What the hand dare seize the fire?

And what shoulder and what art
Could twist the sinews of thy heart?
And, when thy heart began to beat,
What dread hand and what dread feet?

What the hammer? what the chain?
In what furnace was thy brain?
What the anvil? what dread grasp
Dare its deadly terrors clasp?

When the stars threw down their spears,
And watered heaven with their tears,
Did He smile his work to see?
Did He who made the lamb make thee?

Tiger, tiger, burning bright
In the forests of the night,
What immortal hand or eye
Dare frame thy fearful symmetry?

AH, SUNFLOWER

Ah, Sunflower, weary of time,
  Who countest the steps of the sun;
Seeking after that sweet golden clime
  Where the traveller's journey is done;

Where the Youth pined away with desire,
  And the pale virgin shrouded in snow,
Arise from their graves, and aspire
  Where my Sunflower wishes to go!

IDEAS OF GOOD AND EVIL

To see a world in a grain of sand,
  And a heaven in a wild flower;
Hold infinity in the palm of your hand,
  And eternity in an hour.

.   .   .   .

Every night and every morn
Some to misery are born;
Every morn and every night
Some are born to sweet delight;
Some are born to sweet delight,
Some are born to endless night.
Joy and woe are woven fine,
A clothing for the soul divine:

335

Under every grief and pine
Runs a joy with silken twine.
It is right it should be so:
Man was made for joy and woe;
And when this we rightly know
Safely through the world we go.

—AUGURIES OF INNOCENCE.

To find the Western path,
Right through the Gates of Wrath
    I urge my way;
Sweet Mercy leads me on
With soft repentant moan:
    I see the break of day.

The war of swords and spears,
Melted by dewy tears,
    Exhales on high;
The Sun is freed from fears,
And with soft grateful tears
    Ascends the sky.

—DAYBREAK

MILTON

And did those feet in ancient time
Walk upon England's mountains green:
And was the holy Lamb of God
On England's pleasant pastures seen?

And did the Countenance Divine
Shine forth upon our clouded hills?
And was Jerusalem builded here,
Among these dark Satanic Mills?

Bring me my Bow of burning gold:
Bring me my Arrows of desire:
Bring me my Spear: O clouds unfold:
Bring me my Chariot of fire!

WILLIAM BLAKE

I will not cease from Mental Fight,
Nor shall my Sword sleep in my hand:
Till we have built Jerusalem,
In England's green and pleasant Land.

LOVE'S SECRET

Never seek to tell thy love,
    Love that never told can be;
For the gentle wind doth move
    Silently, invisibly.

I told my love, I told my love,
    I told her all my heart,
Trembling, cold, in ghastly fears,
    Ah! she did depart!

Soon after she was gone from me,
    A traveller came by,
Silently, invisibly:
    He took her with a sigh.

LONDON

I wander through each chartered street,
    Near where the chartered Thames does flow,
A mark in every face I meet,
    Marks of weakness, marks of woe.

In every cry of every man,
    In every infant's cry of fear,
In every voice, in every ban,
    The mind-forged manacles I hear:

How the chimney-sweeper's cry
    Every blackening church appals,
And the hapless soldier's sigh
    Runs in blood down palace-walls.

337

But most, through midnight streets I hear
How the youthful harlot's curse
Blasts the new-born infant's tear,
And blights with plagues the marriage-hearse.

THE WILD-FLOWER'S SONG

I wandered in the forest
The green leaves among,
I heard a wild-flower
Singing a song:

"I slept in the earth
In the silent night;
I murmured my thoughts,
And I felt delight.

"In the morning I went,
As rosy as morn,
To seek for new joy,
But I met with scorn."

THE GREY MONK

. . . . . .

But vain the Sword and vain the Bow,
They never can work War's overthrow.
The Hermit's prayer and the Widow's Tear
Alone can free the World from fear.

For a Tear is an Intellectual Thing,
And a Sigh is the Sword of an Angel King,
And the bitter groan of the Martyr's woe
Is an arrow from the Almightie's bow.

ROBERT BURNS

Robert Burns

ON A FLY-LEAF OF BURNS' SONGS

These are the best of him,
Pathos and jest of him;
Earth holds the rest of him.

Passions were strong in him,—
Pardon the wrong in him;
Hark to the song in him!—

Each little lyrical
Grave or satirical
Musical miracle!
—FREDERIC LAWRENCE KNOWLES.

THE BIRKS OF ABERFELDY

Bonie lassie, will ye go,
Will ye go, will ye go;
Bonie lassie, will ye go,
To the birks of Aberfeldy?

Now simmer blinks on flowery braes,
And o'er the crystal streamlet plays;
Come, let us spend the lightsome days
In the birks of Aberfeldy.

While o'er their heads the hazels hing,
The little birdies blithely sing,
Or lightly flit on wanton wing
In the birks of Aberfeldy.

The braes ascend, like lofty wa's,
The foaming stream deep-roaring fa's,
O'erhung wi' fragrant spreading shaws
The birks of Aberfeldy.

339

The hoary cliffs are crown'd wi' flowers,
White o'er the linns the burnie pours,
And rising, weets wi' misty showers
    The birks of Aberfeldy.

Let fortune's gifts at random flee,
They ne'er shall draw a wish frae me,
Supremely blest wi' love and thee,
    In the birks of Aberfeldy.

    Bonie lassie, will ye go,
    Will ye go, will ye go;
    Bonie lassie, will ye go
        To the birks of Aberfeldy?

THE COTTER'S SATURDAY NIGHT

My lov'd, my honour'd, much respected friend!
  No mercenary bard his homage pays;
With honest pride, I scorn each selfish end,
  My dearest meed, a friend's esteem and praise:
  To you I sing, in simple Scottish lays,
The lowly train in life's sequester'd scene;
  The native feelings strong, the guileless ways;
What Aiken in a cottage would have been;
Ah! tho' his worth unknown, far happier there I ween!

November chill blaws loud wi' angry sugh;
  The short'ning winter-day is near a close;
The miry beasts retreating frae the pleugh;
  The black'ning trains o' craws to their repose:
  The toil-worn Cotter frae his labour goes—
This night his weekly moil is at an end,
  Collects his spades, his mattocks, and his hoes,
Hoping the morn in ease and rest to spend,
And weary, o'er the moor, his course does hameward bend.

At length his lonely cot appears in view,
  Beneath the shelter of an aged tree;
Th' expectant wee-things, toddlin, stacher through
  To meet their dad, wi' flichterin' noise and glee.

340

ROBERT BURNS

His wee bit ingle, blinkin bonilie,
His clean, hearth-stane, his thrifty wifie's smile,
   The lisping infant, prattling on his knee,
Does a' his weary kiaugh and care beguile,
And makes him quite forget his labour and his toil.

Belyve, the elder bairns come drapping in,
   At service out, amang the farmers roun';
Some ca' the pleugh, some herd, some tentie rin
   A cannie errand to a neebour town:
   Their eldest hope, their Jenny, woman grown,
In youthfu' bloom, love sparkling in her e'e,
   Comes hame; perhaps, to shew a braw new gown,
Or deposite her sair-won penny-fee,
To help her parents dear, if they in hardship be.

With joy unfeign'd, brothers and sisters meet,
   And each for other's weelfare kindly spiers:
The social hours, swift-wing'd, unnotic'd fleet;
   Each tells the uncos that he sees or hears.
   The parents partial eye their hopeful years;
Anticipation forward points the view;
   The mother, wi' her needle and her sheers,
Gars auld claes look amaist as weel's the new;
The father mixes a' wi' admonition due.

Their master's and their mistress's command
   The younkers a' are warnèd to obey;
And mind their labours wi' an eydent hand,
   And ne'er, tho' out o' sight, to jauk or play:
   "And O! be sure to fear the Lord alway,
And mind your duty, duly, morn and night;
   Lest in temptation's path ye gang astray,
Implore His counsel and assisting might:
They never sought in vain that sought the Lord aright."

But hark! a rap comes gently to the door;
   Jenny, wha kens the meaning o' the same,
Tells how a neebour lad came o'er the moor,
   To do some errands, and convoy her hame.
   The wily mother sees the conscious flame

341

Sparkle in Jenny's e'e, and flush her cheek;
  With heart-struck anxious care, enquires his name,
While Jenny hafflins is afraid to speak;
  Weel-pleas'd the mother hears, it's nae wild, worthless rake.

With kindly welcome, Jenny brings him ben;
  A strappin' youth, he takes the mother's eye;
Blythe Jenny sees the visit's no ill taen;
  The father cracks of horses, pleughs, and kye.
The youngster's artless heart o'erflows wi' joy,
But blate and laithfu', scarce can weel behave;
  The mother, wi' a woman's wiles, can spy
What makes the youth sae bashfu' and sae grave;
Weel-pleas'd to think her bairn's respected like the lave.

O happy love! where love like this is found:
  O heart-felt raptures! bliss beyond compare!
I've pacèd much this weary, mortal round,
  And sage experience bids me this declare:—
  "If Heaven a draught of heavenly pleasure spare,
One cordial in this melancholy vale,
  'Tis when a youthful, loving, modest pair,
In other's arms, breathe out the tender tale
Beneath the milk-white thorn that scents the ev'ning gale."

Is there, in human form, that bears a heart,
  A wretch! a villain! lost to love and truth!
That can, with studied, sly, ensnaring art,
  Betray sweet Jenny's unsuspecting youth?
  Curse on his perjur'd arts! dissembling, smooth!
Are honour, virtue, conscience, all exil'd?
  Is there no pity, no relenting ruth,
Points to the parents fondling o'er their child?
Then paints the ruin'd maid, and their distraction wild?

But now the supper crowns their simple board,
  The healsome parritch, chief o' Scotia's food;
The soupe their only hawkie does afford,
  That 'yont the hallan snugly chows her cood;
  The dame brings forth, in complimental mood,

To grace the lad, her weel-hain'd kebbuck, fell;
   And aft he's prest, and aft he ca's it guid;
The frugal wifie, garrulous, will tell,
How 'twas a towmond auld, sin' lint was i' the bell.

The chearfu' supper done, wi' serious face,
   They, round the ingle, form a circle wide;
The sire turns o'er, wi' patriarchal grace,
   The big ha'-Bible, ance his father's pride.
His bonnet rev'rently is laid aside,
His lyart haffets wearing thin and bare;
   Those strains that once did sweet in Zion glide,
He wales a portion with judicious care,
And "Let us worship God!" he says, with solemn air.

They chant their artless notes in simple guise,
   They tune their hearts, by far the noblest aim;
Perhaps *Dundee's* wild-warbling measures rise,
   Or plaintive *Martyrs*, worthy of the name;
   Or noble *Elgin* beets the heaven-ward flame,
The sweetest far of Scotia's holy lays:
   Compar'd with these, Italian trills are tame;
The tickl'd ears no heart-felt raptures raise;
Nae unison hae they, with our Creator's praise.

The priest-like father reads the sacred page,
   How Abram was the friend of God on high;
Or, Moses bade eternal warfare wage
   With Amalek's ungracious progeny;
   Or, how the royal Bard did groaning lie
Beneath the stroke of Heaven's avenging ire;
   Or Job's pathetic plaint, and wailing cry;
Or rapt Isaiah's wild, seraphic fire;
Or other holy Seers that tune the sacred lyre.

Perhaps the Christian volume is the theme:
   How guiltless blood for guilty man was shed;
How He, who bore in Heaven the second name,
   Had not on earth whereon to lay His head;
   How His first followers and servants sped;

The precepts sage they wrote to many a land:
  How he, who lone in Patmos banishèd,
Saw in the sun a mighty angel stand,
And heard great Bab'lon's doom pronounc'd by Heaven's com-
    mand.

Then kneeling down to Heaven's Eternal King,
  The saint, the father, and the husband prays:
Hope "springs exulting on triumphant wing,"
  That thus they all shall meet in future days,
  There, ever bask in uncreated rays,
No more to sigh or shed the bitter tear,
  Together hymning their Creator's praise,
In such society, yet still more dear;
While circling Time moves round in an eternal sphere.

Compar'd with this, how poor Religion's pride,
  In all the pomp of method, and of art;
When men display to congregations wide
  Devotion's ev'ry grace, except the heart,
  The Power, incens'd, the pageant will desert,
The pompous strain, the sacerdotal stole;
  But haply, in some cottage far apart,
May hear, well-pleas'd, the language of the soul,
And in His Book of Life the inmates poor enroll.

Then homeward all take off their sev'ral way;
  The youngling cottagers retire to rest:
The parent-pair their secret homage pay,
  And proffer up to Heaven the warm request,
  That He who stills the raven's clam'rous nest,
And decks the lily fair in flow'ry pride,
  Would, in the way His wisdom sees the best,
For them and for their little ones provide;
But, chiefly, in their hearts with Grace Divine preside.

From scenes like these, old Scotia's grandeur springs,
  That makes her lov'd at home, rever'd abroad:
Princes and lords are but the breath of kings,
  "An honest man's the noblest work of God";
  And certes, in fair Virtue's heavenly road,

The cottage leaves the palace far behind;
  What is a lordling's pomp? a cumbrous load,
Disguising oft the wretch of human kind,
Studied in arts of Hell, in wickedness refin'd!

O Scotia! my dear, my native soil!
  For whom my warmest wish to Heaven is sent!
Long may thy hardy sons of rustic toil
  Be blest with health, and peace, and sweet content!
And O! may Heaven their simple lives prevent
From Luxury's contagion, weak and vile!
  Then, howe'er crowns and coronets be rent,
A virtuous populace may rise the while,
And stand a wall of fire around their much-lov'd Isle.

O Thou! who pour'd the patriotic tide,
  That stream'd thro' Wallace's undaunted heart,
Who dar'd to, nobly, stem tyrannic pride,
  Or nobly die, the second glorious part:
  (The patriot's God, peculiarly Thou art,
His friend, inspirer, guardian, and reward!)
  O never, never Scotia's realm desert;
But still the patriot, and the patriot-bard
In bright succession raise, her ornament and guard!

TO A MOUSE

*(On Turning Her Up in Her Nest With the Plough,
November, 1785.)*

    Wee, sleekit, cowrin, tim'rous beastie,
    O, what a panic's in thy breastie!
    Thou need na start awa sae hasty
          Wi' bickering brattle!
    I wad be laith to rin an' chase thee,
          Wi' murdering pattle!

    I'm truly sorry man's dominion
    Has broken Nature's social union,

An' justifies that ill opinion
        Which makes thee startle
At me, thy poor, earth-born companion
        An' fellow mortal!

I doubt na, whyles, but thou may thieve;
What then? poor beastie, thou maun live
A daimen icker in a thrave
        'S a sma' request;
I'll get a blessin wi' the lave,
        An' never miss't!

Thy wee-bit housie, too, in ruin!
Its silly wa's the win's are strewin!
An' naething, now, to big a new ane,
        O' foggage green!
An' bleak December's win's ensuin,
        Baith snell an' keen!

Thou saw the fields laid bare an' waste,
An' weary winter comin fast,
An' cozie here, beneath the blast,
        Thou thought to dwell,
Till crash! the cruel coulter past
        Out thro' thy cell.

That wee bit heap o' leaves an' stibble,
Has cost thee monie a weary nibble!
Now thou's turned out, for a' thy trouble,
        But house or hald,
To thole the winter's sleety dribble,
        An' cranreuch cauld!

But Mousie, thou art no thy lane,
In proving foresight may be vain:
The best-laid schemes o' mice an' men
        Gang aft agley,
An' lea's us nought but grief an' pain,
        For promis'd joy!

Still thou art blest, compared wi' me!
The present only toucheth thee:
But och! I backward cast my e'e,
    On prospects drear!
An' forward, tho' I canna see,
    I guess an' fear!

TO A MOUNTAIN DAISY

Wee, modest, crimson-tippèd flow'r,
Thou's met me in an evil hour;
For I maun crush amang the stoure
    Thy slender stem:
To spare thee now is past my pow'r,
    Thou bonie gem.

Alas! it's no thy neebour sweet,
The bonie lark, companion meet,
Bending thee 'mang the dewy weet,
    Wi' spreckl'd breast!
When upward-springing, blythe, to greet
    The purpling east.

Cauld blew the bitter-biting north
Upon thy early, humble birth;
Yet cheerfully thou glinted forth
    Amid the storm,
Scarce rear'd above the parent-earth
    Thy tender form.

The flaunting flow'rs our gardens yield,
High shelt'ring woods and wa's maun shield:
But thou, beneath the random bield
    O' clod or stane,
Adorns the histie stibble-field,
    Unseen, alane.

There, in thy scanty mantle clad,
Thy snawie bosom sun-ward spread,

347

Thou lifts thy unassuming head
        In humble guise;
But now the share uptears thy bed,
        And low thou lies!

Such is the fate of artless maid,
Sweet flow'ret of the rural shade!
By love's simplicity betray'd,
        And guileless trust;
Till she, like thee, all soil'd, is laid
        Low i' the dust.

Such is the fate of simple Bard,
On Life's rough ocean luckless starr'd!
Unskilful he to note the card
        Of prudent lore,
Till billows rage, and gales blow hard,
        And whelm him o'er!

Such fate to suffering Worth is giv'n,
Who long with wants and woes has striv'n,
By human pride, or cunning driv'n
        To mis'ry's brink;
Till, wrench'd of ev'ry stay but Heav'n,
        He, ruin'd, sink!

Ev'n thou who mourn'st the Daisy's fate,
That fate is thine—no distant date;
Stern Ruin's plough-share drives elate,
        Full on thy bloom,
Till crush'd beneath the furrow's weight
        Shall be thy doom!

ADDRESS TO THE UNCO GUID

.   .   .   .

Then gently scan your brother man,
    Still gentler sister woman;
Tho' they may gang a kennin wrang,
    To step aside is human:

One point must still be greatly dark,
 The moving why they do it;
And just as lamely can ye mark
 How far perhaps they rue it.

Who made the heart, 'tis He alone
 Decidedly can try us:
He knows each chord, its various tone,
 Each spring, its various bias:
Then at the balance let's be mute,
 We never can adjust it;
What's done we partly may compute,
 But know not what's resisted.

THE DAY RETURNS

The day returns, my bosom burns,
 The blissful day we twa did meet!
Tho' winter wild in tempest toil'd,
 Ne'er summer sun was half sae sweet.
Than a' the pride that loads the tide,
 And crosses o'er the sultry line,
Than kingly robes, than crowns and globes,
 Heav'n gave me more—it made thee mine!

While day and night can bring delight,
 Or Nature aught of pleasure give,
While joys above my mind can move,
 For thee, and thee alone, I live!
When that grim foe of Life below
 Comes in between to make us part,
The iron hand that breaks our band,
 It breaks my bliss, it breaks my heart!

MY BONIE MARY

Go fetch to me a pint o' wine,
 An' fill it in a silver tassie,
That I may drink, before I go,
 A service to my bonie lassie.

349

The boat rocks at the pier o' Leith,
 Fu' loud the wind blaws frae the ferry,
The ship rides by the Berwick-law,
 And I maun leave my bonie Mary.

The trumpets sound, the banners fly,
 The glittering spears are rankèd ready;
The shouts o' war are heard afar,
 The battle closes thick and bloody;
It's no the roar o' sea or shore
 Wad mak me langer wish to tarry;
Nor shout o' war that's heard afar—
 It's leaving thee, my bonie Mary!

JEAN

Of a' the airts the wind can blaw,
 I dearly like the west,
For there the bonie lassie lives,
 The lassie I lo'e best:
There wild woods grow, and rivers row,
 And monie a hill between;
But day and night my fancy's flight
 Is ever wi' my Jean.

I see her in the dewy flowers,
 I see her sweet and fair:
I hear her in the tunefu' birds,
 I hear her charm the air:
There's not a bonie flower that springs
 By fountain, shaw, or green;
There's not a bonie bird that sings,
 But minds me o' my Jean.

JOHN ANDERSON, MY JO

John Anderson, my jo, John,
 When we were first acquent,
Your locks were like the raven,
 Your bonie brow was brent;

But now your brow is beld, John,
   Your locks are like the snaw;
But blessings on your frosty pow,
   John Anderson, my jo!

John Anderson, my jo, John,
   We clamb the hill thegither;
And monie a canty day, John,
   We've had wi' ane anither:
Now we maun totter down, John,
   But hand in hand we'll go,
And sleep thegither at the foot,
   John Anderson, my jo.

AE FOND KISS

Ae fond kiss, and then we sever!
Ae farewell, and then forever!
Deep in heart-wrung tears I'll pledge thee,
Warring sighs and groans I'll wage thee.
Who shall say that Fortune grieves him,
While the star of hope she leaves him?
Me, nae cheerfu' twinkle lights me,
Dark despair around benights me.

I'll ne'er blame my partial fancy:
Naething could resist my Nancy!
But to see her was to love her,
Love but her, and love for ever.
Had we never lov'd sae kindly,
Had we never lov'd sae blindly,
Never met—or never parted—
We had ne'er been broken-hearted.

Fare-the-weel, thou first and fairest!
Fare-the-weel, thou best and dearest!
Thine be ilka joy and treasure,
Peace, Enjoyment, Love and Pleasure!

Ae fond kiss, and then we sever!
Ae farewell, alas, for ever!
Deep in heart-wrung tears I'll pledge thee,
Warring sighs and groans I'll wage thee.

THE BANKS O' DOON

Ye banks and braes o' bonie Doon,
   How can ye bloom sae fresh and fair?
How can ye chant, ye little birds,
   And I sae weary fu' o' care!
Thou'll break my heart, thou warbling bird
   That wantons thro' the flowering thorn!
Thou minds me o' departed joys,
   Departed never to return.

Aft hae I rov'd by bonie Doon
   To see the rose and woodbine twine,
And ilka bird sang o' its luve,
   And fondly sae did I o' mine.
Wi' lightsome heart I pu'd a rose,
   Fu' sweet upon its thorny tree!
And my fause luver staw my rose—
   But ah! he left the thorn wi' me.

A RED, RED ROSE

O, my luve is like a red, red rose,
   That's newly sprung in June.
O, my luve is like the melodie,
   That's sweetly play'd in tune.

As fair art thou, my bonie lass,
   So deep in luve am I,
And I will luve thee still, my dear,
   Till a' the seas gang dry.

Till a' the seas gang dry, my dear,
   And the rocks melt wi' the sun!
And I will luve thee still, my dear,
   While the sands o' life shall run.

And fare thee weel, my only luve,
   And fare thee weel a while!
And I will come again, my luve,
   Tho' it were ten thousand mile!

AULD LANG SYNE

*   For auld lang syne, my dear,*
For auld lang syne,
*   We'll tak a cup o' kindness yet*
*   For auld lang syne!*

Should auld acquaintance be forgot,
   And never brought to mind?
Should auld acquaintance be forgot,
   And auld lang syne!

And surely ye'll be your pint-stowp,
   And surely I'll be mine,
And we'll tak a cup o' kindness yet
   For auld lang syne!

We twa hae run about the braes,
   And pou'd the gowans fine,
But we've wander'd monie a weary fit
   Sin' auld lang syne.

We twa hae paidl'd in the burn
   Frae morning sun till dine,
But seas between us braid hae roar'd
   Sin' auld lang syne.

And there's a hand, my trusty fiere,
   And gie's a hand o' thine,
And we'll tak a right guid-willie waught
   For auld lang syne!

   For auld lang syne, my dear,
     For auld lang syne,
   We'll tak a cup o' kindness yet
     For auld lang syne!

353

MALLY'S MEEK, MALLY'S SWEET

Mally's meek, Mally's sweet,
Mally's modest and discreet,
Mally's rare, Mally's fair,
Mally's ev'ry way complete.

As I was walking up the street,
  A barefit maid I chanc'd to meet;
But O, the road was very hard
  For that fair maiden's tender feet!

It were mair meet that those fine feet
  Were weel laced up in silken shoon!
An' 't were more fit that she should sit
  Within yon chariot gilt aboon!

Her yellow hair, beyond compare,
  Comes tumbling down her swan-white neck,
And her twa eyes, like stars in skies,
  Would keep a sinking ship frae wreck!

SAW YE BONIE LESLEY

O, saw ye bonie Lesley,
  As she gaed o'er the Border?
She's gane, like Alexander,
  To spread her conquests farther!

To see her is to love her,
  And love but her for ever;
For Nature made her what she is,
  And never made anither!

Thou art a queen, fair Lesley—
  Thy subjects, we before thee!
Thou art divine, fair Lesley—
  The hearts o' men adore thee.

354

The Deil he could na skaith thee,
  Or aught that wad belang thee:
He'd look into thy bonie face,
  And say:—"I canna wrang thee!"

The Powers aboon will tent thee,
  Misfortune sha' na steer thee
Thou'rt like themsel' sae lovely,
  That ill they'll ne'er let near thee.

Return again, fair Lesley,
  Return to Caledonie!
That we may brag we hae a lass
  There's nane again sae bonie.

BRUCE'S ADDRESS AT BANNOCKBURN

Scots, wha hae wi' Wallace bled,
Scots, wham Bruce has aften led,
Welcome to your gory bed
      Or to victorie!

Now's the day, and now's the hour:
See the front o' battle lour,
See approach proud Edward's power—
      Chains and slaverie!

Wha will be a traitor knave?
Wha can fill a coward's grave?
Wha sae base as be a slave?—
      Let him turn, and flee!

Wha for Scotland's King and Law
Freedom's sword will strongly draw,
Freeman stand or freeman fa',
      Let him follow me!

By Oppression's woes and pains,
By your sons in servile chains,
We will drain our dearest veins
      But they shall be free!

Lay the proud usurpers low!
Tyrants fall in every foe!
Liberty's in every blow!
   Let us do, or die!

HIGHLAND MARY

Ye banks and braes and streams around
 The castle o' Montgomery,
Green be your woods, and fair your flowers,
 Your waters never drumlie!
There Summer first unfald her robes,
 And there the langest tarry!
For there I took the last fareweel
 O' my sweet Highland Mary!

How sweetly bloom'd the gay, green birk,
 How rich the hawthorn's blossom,
As underneath their fragrant shade
 I clasp'd her to my bosom!
The golden hours on angel wings
 Flew o'er me and my dearie:
For dear to me as light and life
 Was my sweet Highland Mary.

Wi' monie a vow and lock'd embrace
 Our parting was fu' tender;
And, pledging aft to meet again,
 We tore oursels asunder.
But O, fell Death's untimely frost,
 That nipt my flower sae early!
Now green's the sod, and cauld's the clay,
 That wraps my Highland Mary!

O, pale, pale now, those rosy lips
 I aft hae kiss'd sae fondly;
And clos'd for ay, the sparkling glance
 That dwalt on me sae kindly;

356

And mouldering now in silent dust
   That heart that lo'ed me dearly!
But still within my bosom's core
   Shall live my Highland Mary.

CA' THE YOWES TO THE KNOWES

Hark, the mavis' e'ening sang
Sounding Clouden's woods amang;
Then a-faulding let us gang,
   My bonie dearie!

We'll gae down by Clouden side,
Thro' the hazels, spreading wide
O'er the waves that sweetly glide
   To the moon sae clearly.

Yonder Clouden's silent towers
Where, at moonshine's midnight hours,
O'er the dewy bending flowers
   Fairies dance sae cheery.

Ghaist nor bogle shalt thou fear—
Thou'rt to Love and Heav'n sae dear
Nocht of ill may come thee near,
   My bonie dearie.

Chorus
Ca' the yowes to the knowes,
Ca' them where the heather grows,
Ca' them where the burnie rowes,
   My bonie dearie.

IS THERE FOR HONEST POVERTY

Is there for honest poverty
   That hings his head, an' a' that?
The coward slave, we pass him by—
   We dare be poor for a' that!

For a' that, an' a' that,
  Our toils obscure, an' a' that,
The rank is but the guinea's stamp,
  The man's the gowd for a' that.

What though on hamely fare we dine,
  Wear hoddin grey, an' a' that?
Gie fools their silks, and knaves their wine—
  A man's a man for a' that.
For a' that, an' a' that,
  Their tinsel show, an' a' that,
The honest man, tho' e'er sae poor,
  Is king o' men for a' that.

Ye see yon birkie ca'd "a lord,"
  Wha struts, an' stares, an' a' that?
Tho' hundreds worship at his word,
  He's but a cuif for a' that.
For a' that, an' a' that,
  His ribband, star, an' a' that,
The man o' independent mind,
  He looks an' laughs at a' that.

A prince can mak a belted knight,
  A marquis, duke, an' a' that!
But an honest man's aboon his might—
  Guid faith, he mauna fa' that!
For a' that, an' a' that,
  Their dignities, an' a' that,
The pith o' sense an' pride o' worth
  Are higher rank than a' that.

Then let us pray that come it may
  (As come it will for a' that)
That Sense and Worth o'er a' the earth
  Shall bear the gree an' a' that!
For a' that, an' a' that,
  It's comin yet for a' that,
That man to man the world o'er
  Shall brithers be for a' that.

WILLIAM LISLE BOWLES

O, WERE MY LOVE

O, were my love yon lilac fair
  Wi' purple blossoms to the spring,
And I a bird to shelter there,
  When wearied on my little wing,
How I wad mourn when it was torn
  By Autumn wild and Winter rude!
But I wad sing on wanton wing,
  When youthfu' May its bloom renew'd.

O, gin my love were yon red rose,
  That grows upon the castle wa',
And I mysel a drap o' dew
  Into her bonie breast to fa',
O, there, beyond expression blest,
  I'd feast on beauty a' the night,
Seal'd on her silk-saft faulds to rest,
  Till fley'd awa by Phœbus' light!

THE TRUE PATHOS

. . . . .

To make a happy fireside clime
    To weans and wife,
That's the true pathos and sublime
    Of human life.
      —Epistle to Dr. Blacklock

William Lisle Bowles

TIME AND GRIEF

O Time! who know'st a lenient hand to lay
Softest on Sorrow's wound, and slowly thence
(Lulling to sad repose the weary sense)
The faint pang stealest unperceived away;

359

On thee I rest my only hope at last,
And think, when thou hast dried the bitter tear
That flows in vain o'er all my soul held dear,
I may look back on every sorrow past,
And meet life's peaceful evening with a smile:
As some lone bird, at day's departing hour,
Sings in the sunbeam, of the transient shower
Forgetful, though its wings are wet the while:—
    Yet ah! how much must that poor heart endure,
    Which hopes from thee, and thee alone, a cure!

Samuel Rogers

A WISH

Mine be a cot beside the hill;
A beehive's hum shall soothe my ear;
A willowy brook, that turns a mill,
With many a fall shall linger near.

The swallow oft, beneath my thatch,
Shall twitter from her clay-built nest;
Oft shall the pilgrim lift the latch,
And share my meal, a welcome guest.

Around my ivied porch shall spring
Each fragrant flower that drinks the dew;
And Lucy, at her wheel, shall sing
In russet gown and apron blue.

The village church, among the trees,
Where first our marriage-vows were given,
With merry peals shall swell the breeze,
And point with taper spire to heaven.

AN ITALIAN SONG

Dear is my little native vale,
  The ring-dove builds and murmurs there;

SAMUEL ROGERS

Close by my cot she tells her tale
To every passing villager:
The squirrel leaps from tree to tree,
And shells his nuts at liberty.

In orange groves and myrtle bowers,
That breathe a gale of fragrance round,
I charm the fairy-footed hours
With my loved lute's romantic sound;
Or crowns of living laurel weave,
For those that win the race at eve.

The shepherd's horn at break of day,
The ballet danced in twilight glade,
The canzonet and roundelay
Sung in the silent greenwood shade:
These simple joys, that never fail,
Shall bind me to my native vale.

TO . . .

Go—you may call it madness, folly;
You shall not chase my gloom away.
There's such a charm in melancholy,
I would not, if I could, be gay.

Oh, if you knew the pensive pleasure
That fills my bosom when I sigh,
You would not rob me of a treasure
Monarchs are too poor to buy.

AN EPITAPH ON A ROBIN REDBREAST

Tread lightly here, for here, 'tis said,
When piping winds are hushed around,
A small note wakes from underground,
Where now his tiny bones are laid.

361

No more in lone and leafless groves,
With ruffled wing and faded breast,
His friendless, homeless spirit roves;
—Gone to the world where birds are blest!
Where never cat glides o'er the green,
Or schoolboy's giant form is seen;
But Love, and Joy, and smiling Spring
Inspire their little souls to sing!

WRITTEN IN WESTMINSTER ABBEY

Whoe'er thou art, approach, and, with a sigh,
Mark where the small remains of greatness lie.
There sleeps the dust of Fox for ever gone;
How near the place where late his glory shone!
And, tho' no more ascends the voice of prayer,
Tho' the last footsteps cease to linger there,
Still, like an awful dream that comes again,
Alas, at best, as transient and as vain,
Still do I see (while thro' the vaults of night
The funeral-song once more proclaims the rite)
The moving pomp along the shadowy aisle,
That, like a darkness, filled the solemn pile;
The illustrious line, that in long order led,
Of those, that loved Him living, mourned Him dead;
Of those the few, that for their country stood
Round Him who dared be singularly good;
All, of all ranks, that claimed him for their own;
And nothing wanting—but Himself alone!
    Oh, say, of Him now rests there but a name;
Wont, as He was, to breathe ethereal flame?
Friend of the Absent, Guardian of the Dead!
Who but would here their sacred sorrows shed?
(Such as He shed on NELSON's closing grave;
How soon to claim the sympathy He gave!)
In Him, resentful of another's wrong,
The dumb were eloquent, the feeble strong.
Truth from his lips a charm celestial drew—
Ah, who so mighty and so gentle too?

What tho' with war the madding nations rung,
"Peace," when He spoke, was ever on his tongue!
Amid the frowns of Power, the tricks of State,
Fearless, resolved, and negligently great!
In vain malignant vapours gathered round;
He walked, erect, on consecrated ground.
The clouds, that rise to quench the orb of day,
Reflect its splendour, and dissolve away!
　　When in retreat He laid his thunder by,
For lettered ease and calm philosophy,
Blest were his hours within the silent grove,
Where still his god-like spirit deigns to rove;
Blest by the orphan's smile, the widow's prayer,
For many a deed long done in secret there.
There shone his lamp on Homer's hallowed page,
There, listening, sate the hero and the sage;
And they, by virtue and by blood allied,
Whom most He loved, and in whose arms He died.
　　Friend of all humankind! not here alone
(The voice, that speaks, was not to Thee unknown)
Wilt Thou be missed.—O'er every land and sea
Long, long shall England be revered in Thee!
And, when the storm is hushed—in distant years—
Foes on Thy grave shall meet, and mingle tears!

PÆSTUM

They stand between the mountains and the sea;
Awful memorials, but of whom we know not!
The seaman, passing, gazes from the deck;
The buffalo-driver, in his shaggy cloak,
Points to the work of magic and moves on.
Time was they stood along the crowded street,
Temples of Gods! and on their ample steps
What various habits, various tongues beset
The brazen gates for prayer and sacrifice!
Time was perhaps the third was sought for Justice;
And here the accuser stood, and there the accused;
And here the judges sate, and heard, and judged.
All silent now!—as in the ages past,

363

Trodden under foot and mingled, dust with dust.
How many centuries did the sun go round
From MOUNT ALBURNUS to the TYRRHENE sea,
While, by some spell rendered invisible,
Or, if approached, approached by him alone
Who saw as though he saw not, they remained
As in the darkness of a sepulchre,
Waiting the appointed time!   All, all within
Proclaims that Nature had resumed her right,
And taken to herself what man renounced;
No cornice, triglyph, or worn abacus,
But with thick ivy hung or branching fern;
Their iron-brown o'erspread with brightest verdure.
From my youth upward have I longed to tread
This classic ground—And am I here at last?
Wandering at will through the long porticoes,
And catching, as through some majestic grove,
Now the blue ocean, and now, chaos-like,
Mountains and mountain-gulfs, and, half-way up,
Towns like the living rock from which they grew?
A cloudy region, black and desolate,
Where once a slave withstood a world in arms.
The air is sweet with violets, running wild
Mid broken friezes and fallen capitals;
Sweet as when TULLY, writing down his thoughts,
Those thoughts so precious and so lately lost,
(Turning to thee, divine Philosophy,
Ever at hand to calm his troubled soul,)
Sailed slowly by, two thousand years ago,
For ATHENS; when a ship, if north-east winds
Blew from the PÆSTAN gardens, slacked her course.
On as he moved along the level shore,
These temples, in their splendour eminent
Mid arcs and obelisks, and domes and towers,
Reflecting back the radiance of the west,
Well might he dream of Glory!—Now, coiled up,
The serpent sleeps within them; the she-wolf
Suckles her young: and, as alone I stand
In this, the nobler pile, the elements
Of earth and air its only floor and roof,
How solemn is the stillness!   Nothing stirs
Save the shrill-voiced cicala flitting round

On the rough pediment to sit and sing;
Or the green lizard rustling through the grass,
And up the fluted shaft with short quick spring,
To vanish in the chinks that Time has made.
      In such an hour as this, the sun's broad disk
Seen at his setting, and a flood of light
Filling the courts of these old sanctuaries,
(Gigantic shadows, broken and confused,
Athwart the innumerable columns flung,)
In such an hour he came, who saw and told,
Led by the mighty Genius of the Place.
      Walls of some capital city first appeared,
Half raised, half sunk, or scattered as in scorn;
—And what within them? what but in the midst
These Three in more than their original grandeur,
And, round about, no stone upon another?
As if the spoiler had fallen back in fear,
And, turning, left them to the elements.
      'Tis said a stranger in the days of old
(Some say a DORIAN, some a SYBARITE;
But distant things are ever lost in clouds),—
'Tis said a stranger came, and, with his plough,
Traced out the site; and POSIDONIA rose,
Severely great, NEPTUNE the tutelar God;
A HOMER's language murmuring in her streets
And in her haven many a mast from TYRE.
Then came another, an unbidden guest.
He knocked and entered with a train in arms;
And all was changed, her very name and language!
The TYRIAN merchant, shipping at his door
Ivory and gold, and silk, and frankincense,
Sailed as before, but, sailing, cried "For PÆSTUM!"
And now a VIRGIL, now an OVID sung
PÆSTUM's twice-blowing roses; while, within,
Parents and children mourned—and, every year
('Twas on the day of some old festival),
Met to give way to tears, and once again
Talk in the ancient tongue of things gone by.
At length an Arab climbed the battlements,
Slaying the sleepers in the dead of night;
And from all eyes the glorious vision fled!
Leaving a place lonely and dangerous,

Where whom the robber spares, a deadlier foe
Strikes at unseen—and at a time when joy
Opens the heart, when summer skies are blue,
And the clear air is soft and delicate;
For then the demon works—then with that air
The thoughtless wretch drinks in a subtle poison
Lulling to sleep; and, when he sleeps, he dies.
    But what are These still standing in the midst?
The Earth has rocked beneath; the Thunderbolt
Passed thro' and thro', and left its traces there;
Yet still they stand as by some Unknown Charter!
Oh, they are Nature's own! and, as allied
To the vast Mountains and the eternal Sea,
They want no written history; theirs a voice
For ever speaking to the heart of Man!

NATURE'S GIFT

    Nature denied him much,
But gave him at his birth what most he values:
A passionate love for music, sculpture, painting,
For poetry, the language of the gods,
For all things here, or grand or beautiful,
A setting sun, a lake among the mountains,
The light of an ingenuous countenance,
And, what transcends them all, a noble action.

ITALY—A FAREWELL.

THE SLEEPING BEAUTY

Sleep on, and dream of Heaven awhile—
Though shut so close thy laughing eyes,
Thy rosy lips still wear a smile
And move, and breathe delicious sighs!

Ah, now soft blushes tinge her cheeks
And mantle o'er her neck of snow:
Ah, now she murmurs, now she speaks
What most I wish—and fear to know!

366

She starts, she trembles, and she weeps!
Her fair hands folded on her breast:
—And now, how like a saint she sleeps!
A seraph in the realms of rest!

Sleep on secure! Above control
Thy thoughts belong to Heaven and thee:
And may the secret of thy soul
Remain within its sanctuary!

William Robert Spencer

TO——

Too late I stayed—forgive the crime;
Unheeded flew the hours;
How noiseless falls the foot of Time,
That only treads on flowers!

What eye with clear account remarks
The ebbing of the glass,
When all its sands are diamond sparks,
That dazzle as they pass!

Oh, who to sober measurement
Time's happy swiftness brings,
When birds of Paradise have lent
Their plumage for his wings!

James Hogg

A BOY'S SONG

Where the pools are bright and deep,
Where the grey trout lies asleep,
Up the river and over the lea,
That's the way for Billy and me.

367

Where the blackbird sings the latest,
Where the hawthorn blooms the sweetest,
Where the nestlings chirp and flee,
That's the way for Billy and me.

Where the mowers mow the cleanest,
Where the hay lies thick and greenest,
There to track the homeward bee,
That's the way for Billy and me.

Where the hazel bank is steepest,
Where the shadow falls the deepest,
Where the clustering nuts fall free,
That's the way for Billy and me.

Why the boys should drive away
Little sweet maidens from the play,
Or love to banter and fight so well,
That's the thing I never could tell.

But this I know, I love to play
Through the meadow, among the hay;
Up the water and over the lea,
That's the way for Billy and me.

THE SKYLARK

Bird of the wilderness,
Blithesome and cumberless,
Sweet be thy matin o'er moorland and lea!
Emblem of happiness,
Blest is thy dwelling-place—
Oh, to abide in the desert with thee!

Wild is thy lay and loud,
Far in the downy cloud;
Love gives it energy, love gave it birth.
Where, on thy dewy wing,
Where art thou journeying?
Thy lay is in heaven, thy love is on earth.

368

O'er fell and fountain sheen,
O'er moor and mountain green,
O'er the red streamer that heralds the day,
Over the cloudlet dim,
Over the rainbow's rim,
Musical cherub, soar, singing, away!

Then, when the gloaming comes,
Low in the heather blooms,
Sweet will thy welcome and bed of love be!
Emblem of happiness,
Blest is thy dwelling-place—
Oh, to abide in the desert with thee!

William Wordsworth

WORDSWORTH

A moonlit desert's yellow sands,
Where, dimmer than its shadow, stands
A motionless palm-tree here and there,
And the great stars through amber air
Burn calm as planets, and the face
Of earth seems lifting into space:—

A tropic ocean's starlit rest,
Along whose smooth and sleeping breast
Slow swells just stir the mirrored gleams,
Like faintest sighs in placid dreams;
All overhead the night, so high
And hollow that there seems no sky,
But the unfathomed deeps, among
The worlds down endless arches swung:—

On moonlit plain, and starlit sea,
Is life's lost charm, tranquillity.

A poet found it once, and took
It home, and hid it in a book,

369

As one might press a violet.
There still the odor lingers yet.
Delicious; from your treasured tomes
Reach down your Wordsworth, and there comes

That fragrance which no bard but he
E'er caught, as if the plain and sea
Had yielded their serenity.
                              —EDWARD ROWLAND SILL.

THE REVERIE OF POOR SUSAN

At the corner of Wood Street, when daylight appears,
Hangs a Thrush that sings loud, it has sung for three years:
Poor Susan has passed by the spot, and has heard
In the silence of morning the song of the Bird.

'Tis a note of enchantment; what ails her?   She sees
A mountain ascending, a vision of trees;
Bright volumes of vapour through Lothbury glide,
And a river flows on through the vale of Cheapside.

Green pastures she views in the midst of the dale,
Down which she so often has tripped with her pail;
And a single small cottage, a nest like a dove's,
The one only dwelling on earth that she loves.

She looks, and her heart is in heaven: but they fade,
The mist and the river, the hill and the shade:
The stream will not flow, and the hill will not rise,
And the colours have all passed away from her eyes!

LINES WRITTEN IN EARLY SPRING

I heard a thousand blended notes,
While in a grove I sate reclined,
In that sweet mood when pleasant thoughts
Bring sad thoughts to the mind.

WILLIAM WORDSWORTH

To her fair works did Nature link
The human soul that through me ran;
And much it grieved my heart to think
What man has made of man.

Through primrose tufts, in that green bower,
The periwinkle trailed its wreaths;
And 'tis my faith that every flower
Enjoys the air it breathes.

The birds around me hopped and played,
Their thoughts I cannot measure:—
But the least motion which they made
It seemed a thrill of pleasure.

The budding twigs spread out their fan,
To catch the breezy air;
And I must think, do all I can,
That there was pleasure there.

If this belief from heaven be sent,
If such be Nature's holy plan,
Have I not reason to lament
What man has made of man?

LINES

COMPOSED A FEW MILES ABOVE TINTERN ABBEY

Five years have past; five summers, with the length
Of five long winters! and again I hear
These waters, rolling from their mountain-springs
With a soft inland murmur.—Once again
Do I behold these steep and lofty cliffs,
That on a wild secluded scene impress
Thoughts of more deep seclusion; and connect
The landscape with the quiet of the sky.
The day is come when I again repose
Here, under this dark sycamore, and view
These plots of cottage-ground, these orchard-tufts,

371

Which at this season, with their unripe fruits,
Are clad in one green hue, and lose themselves
'Mid groves and copses. Once again I see
These hedge-rows, hardly hedge-rows, little lines
Of sportive wood run wild: these pastoral farms,
Green to the very door; and wreaths of smoke
Sent up, in silence, from among the trees!
With some uncertain notice, as might seem
Of vagrant dwellers in the houseless woods,
Or of some Hermit's cave, where by his fire
The Hermit sits alone.

                These beauteous forms,
Through a long absence, have not been to me
As is a landscape to a blind man's eye:
But oft, in lonely rooms, and 'mid the din
Of towns and cities, I have owed to them
In hours of weariness, sensations sweet,
Felt in the blood, and felt along the heart;
And passing even into my purer mind,
With tranquil restoration:—feelings too
Of unremembered pleasure: such, perhaps,
As have no slight or trivial influence
On that best portion of a good man's life,
His little, nameless, unremembered, acts
Of kindness and of love. Nor less, I trust,
To them I may have owed another gift,
Of aspect more sublime; that blessed mood,
In which the burthen of the mystery,
In which the heavy and the weary weight
Of all this unintelligible world,
Is lightened:—that serene and blessed mood,
In which the affections gently lead us on,—
Until, the breath of this corporeal frame
And even the motion of our human blood
Almost suspended, we are laid asleep
In body, and become a living soul:
While with an eye made quiet by the power
Of harmony, and the deep power of·joy,
We see into the life of things.

                      If this
Be but a vain belief, yet, oh! how oft—

WILLIAM WORDSWORTH

In darkness and amid the many shapes
Of joyless daylight; when the fretful stir
Unprofitable, and the fever of the world,
Have hung upon the beatings of my heart—
How oft, in spirit, have I turned to thee,
O sylvan Wye! thou wanderer thro' the woods,
How often has my spirit turned to thee!

    And now, with gleams of half-extinguished thought,
With many recognitions dim and faint,
And somewhat of a sad perplexity,
The picture of the mind revives again:
While here I stand, not only with the sense
Of present pleasure, but with pleasing thoughts
That in this moment there is life and food
For future years.   And so I dare to hope,
Though changed, no doubt, from what I was when first
I came among these hills; when like a roe
I bounded o'er the mountains, by the sides
Of the deep rivers, and the lonely streams,
Wherever nature led: more like a man
Flying from something that he dreads, than one
Who sought the thing he loved.   For nature then
(The coarser pleasures of my boyish days,
And their glad animal movements all gone by)
To me was all in all.—I cannot paint
What then I was.   The sounding cataract
Haunted me like a passion: the tall rock,
The mountain, and the deep and gloomy wood,
Their colours and their forms, were then to me
An appetite; a feeling and a love,
That had no need of a remoter charm,
By thought supplied, nor any interest
Unborrowed from the eye.—That time is past,
And all its aching joys are now no more,
And all its dizzy raptures.   Not for this
Faint I, nor mourn nor murmur; other gifts
Have followed; for such loss, I would believe,
Abundant recompence.   For I have learned
To look on nature, not as in the hour
Of thoughtless youth; but hearing oftentimes
The still, sad music of humanity,

Nor harsh nor grating, though of ample power
To chasten and subdue. And I have felt
A presence that disturbs me with the joy
Of elevated thoughts; a sense sublime
Of something far more deeply interfused,
Whose dwelling is the light of setting suns,
And the round ocean and the living air,
And the blue sky, and in the mind of man;
A motion and a spirit, that impels
All thinking things, all objects of all thought,
And rolls through all things. Therefore am I still
A lover of the meadows and the woods,
And mountains; and of all that we behold
From this green earth; of all the mighty world
Of eye, and ear,—both what they half create,
And what perceive; well pleased to recognise
In nature and the language of the sense,
The anchor of my purest thoughts, the nurse,
The guide, the guardian of my heart, and soul
Of all my moral being.
                    Nor perchance,
If I were not thus taught, should I the more
Suffer my genial spirits to decay:
For thou art with me here upon the banks
Of this fair river; thou my dearest Friend,
My dear, dear Friend; and in thy voice I catch
The language of my former heart, and read
My former pleasures in the shooting lights
Of thy wild eyes. Oh! yet a little while
May I behold in thee what I was once,
My dear, dear Sister! and this prayer I make,
Knowing that Nature never did betray
The heart that loved her; 'tis her privilege,
Through all the years of this our life, to lead
From joy to joy: for she can so inform
The mind that is within us, so impress
With quietness and beauty, and so feed
With lofty thoughts, that neither evil tongues,
Rash judgements, nor the sneers of selfish men,
Nor greetings where no kindness is, nor all
The dreary intercourse of daily life,

374

Shall e'er prevail against us, or disturb
Our cheerful faith, that all which we behold
Is full of blessings. Therefore let the moon
Shine on thee in thy solitary walk;
And let the misty mountain-winds be free
To blow against thee: and, in after years,
When these wild ecstasies shall be matured
Into a sober pleasure; when thy mind
Shall be a mansion for all lovely forms,
Thy memory be as a dwelling-place
For all sweet sounds and harmonies; oh then,
If solitude, or fear, or pain, or grief,
Should be thy portion, with what healing thoughts
Of tender joy wilt thou remember me,
And these my exhortations! Nor, perchance—
If I should be where I no more can hear
Thy voice, nor catch from thy wild eyes these gleams
Of past existence—wilt thou then forget
That on the banks of this delightful stream
We stood together; and that I, so long
A worshipper of Nature, hither came
Unwearied in that service: rather say
With warmer love—oh! with far deeper zeal
Of holier love. Nor wilt thou then forget,
That after many wanderings, many years
Of absence, these steep woods and lofty cliffs,
And this green pastoral landscape, were to me
More dear, both for themselves and for thy sake!

SHE DWELT AMONG THE UNTRODDEN WAYS

She dwelt among the untrodden ways
    Beside the springs of Dove,
A Maid whom there were none to praise
    And very few to love:

A violet by a mossy stone
    Half hidden from the eye!
—Fair as a star, when only one
    Is shining in the sky.

375

She lived unknown, and few could know
    When Lucy ceased to be;
But she is in her grave, and, oh,
    The difference to me!

I TRAVELLED AMONG UNKNOWN MEN

I travelled among unknown men,
    In lands beyond the sea;
Nor, England! did I know till then
    What love I bore to thee.

'Tis past, that melancholy dream!
    Nor will I quit thy shore
A second time; for still I seem
    To love thee more and more.

Among thy mountains did I feel
    The joy of my desire;
And she I cherished turned her wheel
    Beside an English fire.

Thy mornings showed, thy nights concealed
    The bowers where Lucy played;
And thine too is the last green field
    That Lucy's eyes surveyed.

THREE YEARS SHE GREW IN SUN AND SHOWER

Three years she grew in sun and shower,
Then Nature said, "A lovelier flower
On earth was never sown;
This Child I to myself will take;
She shall be mine, and I will make
A Lady of my own.

"Myself will to my darling be
Both law and impulse: and with me
The Girl, in rock and plain,

WILLIAM WORDSWORTH

In earth and heaven, in glade and bower,
Shall feel an overseeing power
To kindle or restrain.

"She shall be sportive as the fawn
That wild with glee across the lawn,
Or up the mountain springs;
And hers shall be the breathing balm,
And hers the silence and the calm
Of mute insensate things.

"The floating clouds their state shall lend
To her; for her the willow bend;
Nor shall she fail to see
Even in the motions of the Storm
Grace that shall mould the Maiden's form
By silent sympathy.

"The stars of midnight shall be dear
To her; and she shall lean her ear
In many a secret place
Where rivulets dance their wayward round,
And beauty born of murmuring sound
Shall pass into her face.

"And vital feelings of delight
Shall rear her form to stately height,
Her virgin bosom swell;
Such thoughts to Lucy I will give
While she and I together live
Here in this happy dell."

Thus Nature spake—The work was done—
How soon my Lucy's race was run!
She died, and left to me
This heath, this calm, and quiet scene;
The memory of what has been,
And never more will be.

A SLUMBER DID MY SPIRIT SEAL

A slumber did my spirit seal;
    I had no human fears:
She seemed a thing that could not feel
    The touch of earthly years.

No motion has she now, no force;
    She neither hears nor sees;
Rolled round in earth's diurnal course,
    With rocks, and stones, and trees.

A POET'S EPITAPH

.   .   .   .   .

But who is He, with modest looks,
And clad in homely russet brown?
He murmurs near the running brooks
A music sweeter than their own.

He is retired as noontide dew,
Or fountain in a noon-day grove;
And you must love him, ere to you
He will seem worthy of your love.

The outward shows of sky and earth,
Of hill and valley, he has viewed;
And impulses of deeper birth
Have come to him in solitude.

In common things that round us lie
Some random truths he can impart,—
The harvest of a quiet eye
That broods and sleeps on his own heart.

But he is weak; both Man and Boy,
Hath been an idler in the land;
Contented if he might enjoy
The things which others understand.

WILLIAM WORDSWORTH

—Come hither in thy hour of strength;
Come, weak as is a breaking wave!
Here stretch thy body at full length;
Or build thy house upon this grave.

MY HEART LEAPS UP

My heart leaps up when I behold
    A rainbow in the sky:
So was it when my life began;
So is it now I am a man;
So be it when I shall grow old,
    Or let me die!
The Child is father of the Man;
And I could wish my days to be
Bound each to each by natural piety.

TO THE SMALL CELANDINE

Pansies, lilies, kingcups, daisies,
Let them live upon their praises;
Long as there's a sun that sets,
Primroses will have their glory;
Long as there are violets,
They will have a place in story:
There's a flower that shall be mine,
'Tis the little Celandine.

Eyes of some men travel far
For the finding of a star;
Up and down the heavens they go,
Men that keep a mighty rout!
I'm as great as they, I trow,
Since the day I found thee out,
Little Flower!—I'll make a stir,
Like a sage astronomer.

Modest, yet withal an Elf
Bold, and lavish of thyself;

Since we needs must first have met
I have seen thee, high and low,
Thirty years or more, and yet
'Twas a face I did not know;
Thou hast now, go where I may,
Fifty greetings in a day.

Ere a leaf is on a bush,
In the time before the thrush
Has a thought about her nest,
Thou wilt come with half a call,
Spreading out thy glossy breast
Like a careless Prodigal;
Telling tales about the sun,
When we've little warmth, or none.

Poets, vain men in their mood!
Travel with the multitude:
Never heed them; I aver
That they all are wanton wooers;
But the thrifty cottager,
Who stirs little out of doors,
Joys to spy thee near her home;
Spring is coming, Thou art come!

Comfort have thou of thy merit,
Kindly unassuming Spirit!
Careless of thy neighbourhood,
Thou dost show thy pleasant face
On the moor, and in the wood,
In the lane;—there's not a place,
Howsoever mean it be,
But 'tis good enough for thee.

Ill befall the yellow flowers,
Children of the flaring hours!
Buttercups, that will be seen,
Whether we will see or no;
Others, too, of lofty mien;
They have done as worldlings do,
Taken praise that should be thine,
Little, humble Celandine!

WILLIAM WORDSWORTH

Prophet of delight and mirth,
Ill-requited upon earth;
Herald of a mighty band,
Of a joyous train ensuing,
Serving at my heart's command,
Tasks that are no tasks renewing,
I will sing, as doth behove,
Hymns in praise of what I love!

TO THE SAME FLOWER

Pleasures newly found are sweet
When they lie about our feet:
February last, my heart
First at sight of thee was glad;
All unheard of as thou art,
Thou must needs, I think, have had,
Celandine! and long ago,
Praise of which I nothing know.

I have not a doubt but he,
Whosoe'er the man might be,
Who the first with pointed rays
(Workman worthy to be sainted)
Set the sign-board in a blaze,
When the rising sun he painted,
Took the fancy from a glance
At thy glittering countenance.

Soon as gentle breezes bring
News of winter's vanishing,
And the children build their bowers,
Sticking 'kerchief-plots of mould
All about with full-blown flowers,
Thick as sheep in shepherd's fold!
With the proudest thou art there,
Mantling in the tiny square.

Often have I sighed to measure
By myself a lonely pleasure,

Sighed to think, I read a book
Only read, perhaps, by me;
Yet I long could overlook
Thy bright coronet and Thee,
And thy arch and wily ways,
And thy store of other praise.

Blithe of heart, from week to week
Thou dost play at hide-and-seek;
While the patient primrose sits
Like a beggar in the cold,
Thou, a flower of wiser wits,
Slipp'st into thy sheltering hold;
Liveliest of the vernal train
When ye all are out again.

Drawn by what peculiar spell,
By what charm of sight or smell,
Does the dim-eyed curious Bee,
Labouring for her waxen cells,
Fondly settle upon Thee
Prized above all buds and bells
Opening daily at thy side,
By the season multiplied?

RESOLUTION AND INDEPENDENCE

There was a roaring in the wind all night;
The rain came heavily and fell in floods;
But now the sun is rising calm and bright;
The birds are singing in the distant woods;
Over his own sweet voice the Stock-dove broods;
The Jay makes answer as the Magpie chatters;
And all the air is filled with pleasant noise of waters.

All things that love the sun are out of doors;
The sky rejoices in the morning's birth;
The grass is bright with rain-drops;—on the moors
The hare is running races in her mirth;
And with her feet she from the plashy earth

382

Raises a mist, that, glittering in the sun,
Runs with her all the way, wherever she doth run.

I was a Traveller then upon the moor,
I saw the hare that raced about with joy;
I heard the woods and distant waters roar;
Or heard them not, as happy as a boy:
The pleasant season did my heart employ:
My old remembrances went from me wholly;
And all the ways of men, so vain and melancholy.

But, as it sometimes chanceth, from the might
Of joy in minds that can no further go,
As high as we have mounted in delight
In our dejection do we sink as low;
To me that morning did it happen so;
And fears and fancies thick upon me came;
Dim sadness—and blind thoughts, I knew not, nor could
    name.

I heard the sky-lark warbling in the sky;
And I bethought me of the playful hare:
Even such a happy Child of earth am I;
Even as these blissful creatures do I fare;
Far from the world I walk, and from all care;
But there may come another day to me—
Solitude, pain of heart, distress, and poverty.

My whole life I have lived in pleasant thought,
As if life's business were a summer mood;
As if all needful things would come unsought
To genial faith, still rich in genial good;
But how can He expect that others should
Build for him, sow for him, and at his call
Love him, who for himself will take no heed at all?

I thought of Chatterton, the marvellous Boy,
The sleepless Soul that perished in his pride;
Of Him who walked in glory and in joy
Following his plough, along the mountainside:
By our own spirits are we deified:

383

We Poets in our youth begin in gladness;
But thereof come in the end despondency and madness.

Now, whether it were by peculiar grace,
A leading from above, a something given,
Yet it befell, that, in this lonely place,
When I with these untoward thoughts had striven,
Beside a pool bare to the eye of heaven
I saw a Man before me unawares:
The oldest man he seemed that ever wore grey hairs.

As a huge stone is sometimes seen to lie
Couched on the bald top of an eminence;
Wonder to all who do the same espy,
By what means it could thither come, and whence;
So that it seems a thing endued with sense:
Like a sea-beast crawled forth, that on a shelf
Of rock or sand reposeth, there to sun itself;

Such seemed this Man, not all alive nor dead,
Nor all asleep—in his extreme old age:
His body was bent double, feet and head
Coming together in life's pilgrimage;
As if some dire constraint of pain, or rage
Of sickness felt by him in times long past,
A more than human weight upon his frame had cast.

Himself he propped, limbs, body, and pale face,
Upon a long grey staff of shaven wood:
And, still as I drew near with gentle pace,
Upon the margin of that moorish flood
Motionless as a cloud the old Man stood,
That heareth not the loud winds when they call
And moveth all together, if it move at all.

At length, himself unsettling, he the pond
Stirred with his staff, and fixedly did look
Upon the muddy water, which he conned,
As if he had been reading in a book:
And now a stranger's privilege I took;
And, drawing to his side, to him did say,
"This morning gives us promise of a glorious day."

384

A gentle answer did the old Man make,
In courteous speech which forth he slowly drew:
And him with further words I thus bespake,
"What occupation do you there pursue?
This is a lonesome place for one like you."
Ere he replied, a flash of mild surprise
Broke from the sable orbs of his yet-vivid eyes,

His words came feebly, from a feeble chest,
But each in solemn order followed each,
With something of a lofty utterance drest—
Choice word and measured phrase, above the reach
Of ordinary men; a stately speech;
Such as grave Livers do in Scotland use,
Religious men, who give to God and man their dues.

He told, that to these waters he had come
To gather leeches, being old and poor:
Employment hazardous and wearisome!
And he had many hardships to endure:
From pond to pond he roamed, from moor to moor;
Housing, with God's good help, by choice or chance,
And in this way he gained an honest maintenance.

The old Man still stood talking by my side;
But now his voice to me was like a stream
Scarce heard; nor word from word could I divide;
And the whole body of the Man did seem
Like one whom I had met with in a dream;
Or like a man from some far region sent,
To give me human strength, by apt admonishment.

My former thoughts returned: the fear that kills;
And hope that is unwilling to be fed;
Cold, pain, and labour, and all fleshly ills;
And mighty Poets in their misery dead.
—Perplexed, and longing to be comforted,
My question eagerly did I renew,
"How is it that you live, and what is it you do?"

385

He with a smile did then his words repeat;
And said, that, gathering leeches, far and wide
He travelled; stirring thus about his feet
The waters of the pools where they abide.
"Once I could meet with them on every side;
But they have dwindled long by slow decay;
Yet still I persevere, and find them where I may.'

While he was talking thus, the lonely place,
The old Man's shape, and speech—all troubled me:
In my mind's eye I seemed to see him pace
About the weary moors continually,
Wandering about alone and silently.
While I these thoughts within myself pursued,
He, having made a pause, the same discourse renewed.

And soon with this he other matter blended,
Cheerfully uttered, with demeanour kind,
But stately in the main; and when he ended,
I could have laughed myself to scorn to find
In that decrepit Man so firm a mind.
"God," said I, "be my help and stay secure;
I'll think of the Leech-gatherer on the lonely moor!"

COMPOSED UPON WESTMINSTER BRIDGE

(September 3, 1802)

Earth has not anything to show more fair:
Dull would he be of soul who could pass by
A sight so touching in its majesty:
This City now doth, like a garment, wear
The beauty of the morning; silent, bare,
Ships, towers, domes, theatres, and temples lie
Open unto the fields, and to the sky;
All bright and glittering in the smokeless air.
Never did sun more beautifully steep
In his first splendour, valley, rock, or hill;
Ne'er saw I, never felt, a calm so deep!
The river glideth at his own sweet will:
Dear God! the very houses seem asleep;
And all that mighty heart is lying still!

386

WILLIAM WORDSWORTH

IT IS A BEAUTEOUS EVENING

It is a beauteous evening, calm and free,
The holy time is quiet as a Nun
Breathless with adoration; the broad sun
Is sinking down in its tranquillity;
The gentleness of heaven broods o'er the Sea;
Listen! the mighty Being is awake,
And doth with his eternal motion make
A sound like thunder-everlastingly.
Dear Child! dear Girl! that walkest with me here,
If thou appear untouched by solemn thought,
Thy nature is not therefore less divine:
Thou liest in Abraham's bosom all the year;
And worship'st at the Temple's inner shrine,
God being with thee when we know it not.

ON THE EXTINCTION OF THE VENETIAN REPUBLIC

Once did She hold the gorgeous east in fee;
And was the safeguard of the west: the worth
Of Venice did not fall below her birth,
Venice, the eldest Child of Liberty.
She was a maiden City, bright and free;
No guile seduced, no force could violate;
And, when she took unto herself a Mate,
She must espouse the everlasting Sea.
And what if she had seen those glories fade,
Those titles vanish, and that strength decay;
Yet shall some tribute of regret be paid
When her long life hath reached its final day:
Men are we, and must grieve when even the Shade
Of that which once was great, is passed away.

TO TOUSSAINT L'OUVERTURE

Toussaint, the most unhappy man of men!
Whether the whistling Rustic tend his plough
Within thy hearing, or thy head be now
Pillowed in some deep dungeon's earless den;—

O miserable Chieftain! where and when
Wilt thou find patience? Yet die not; do thou
Wear rather in thy bonds a cheerful brow:
Though fallen thyself, never to rise again,
Live, and take comfort. Thou hast left behind
Powers that will work for thee; air, earth, and skies;
There's not a breathing of the common wind
That will forget thee; thou hast great allies;
Thy friends are exultations, agonies,
And love, and man's unconquerable mind.

WRITTEN IN LONDON

(September, 1802)

O Friend! I know not which way I must look
For comfort, being, as I am, opprest,
To think that now our life is only drest
For show; mean handy-work of craftsman, cook,
Or groom!—We must run glittering like a brook
In the open sunshine, or we are unblest:
The wealthiest man among us is the best:
No grandeur now in nature or in book
Delights us. Rapine, avarice, expense,
This is idolatry; and these we adore:
Plain living and high thinking are no more:
The homely beauty of the good old cause
Is gone; our peace, our fearful innocence,
And pure religion breathing household laws.

LONDON, 1802

Milton! thou should'st be living at this hour:
England hath need of thee: she is a fen
Of stagnant waters: altar, sword, and pen,
Fireside, the heroic wealth of hall and bower,
Have forfeited their ancient English dower
Of inward happiness. We are selfish men;
Oh! raise us up, return to us again;
And give us manners, virtue, freedom, power.
388

WILLIAM WORDSWORTH

Thy soul was like a Star, and dwelt apart:
Thou hadst a voice whose sound was like the sea:
Pure as the naked heavens, majestic, free,
So didst thou travel on life's common way,
In cheerful godliness; and yet thy heart
The lowliest duties on herself did lay.

GREAT MEN HAVE BEEN AMONG US

Great men have been among us; hands that penned
And tongues that uttered wisdom—better none:
The later Sidney, Marvell, Harrington,
Young Vane, and others who called Milton friend.
These moralists could act and comprehend:
They knew how genuine glory was put on;
Taught us how rightfully a nation shone
In splendour: what strength was, that would not bend
But in magnanimous meekness. France, 'tis strange,
Hath brought forth no such souls as we had then.
Perpetual emptiness! unceasing change!
No single volume paramount, no code,
No master spirit, no determined road;
But equally a want of books and men!

IT IS NOT TO BE THOUGHT OF

It is not to be thought of that the Flood
Of British freedom, which, to the open sea
Of the world's praise, from dark antiquity
Hath flowed, "with pomp of waters, unwithstood,"
Roused though it be full often to a mood
Which spurns the check of salutary bands
That this most famous Stream in bogs and sands
Should perish; and to evil and to good
Be lost for ever. In our halls is hung
Armoury of the invincible Knights of old:
We must be free or die, who speak the tongue
That Shakspeare spake; the faith and morals hold
Which Milton held.—In everything we are sprung
Of Earth's first blood, have titles manifold.

389

WHEN I HAVE BORNE IN MEMORY

When I have borne in memory what has tamed
Great Nations, how ennobling thoughts depart
When men change swords for ledgers, and desert
The student's bower for gold, some fears unnamed
I had, my Country!—am I to be blamed?
Now, when I think of thee, and what thou art,
Verily, in the bottom of my heart,
Of those unfilial fears I am ashamed.
For dearly must we prize thee; we who find
In thee a bulwark for the cause of men:
And I by my affection was beguiled:
What wonder if a Poet now and then,
Among the many movements of his mind,
Felt for thee as a lover or a child!

TO H. C.

SIX YEARS OLD

O Thou! whose fancies from afar are brought;
Who of thy words dost make a mock apparel,
And fittest to unutterable thought
The breeze-like motion and the self-born carol;
Thou faery voyager! that dost float
In such clear water, that thy boat
May rather seem
To brood on air than on an earthly stream;
Suspended in a stream as clear as sky,
Where earth and heaven do make one imagery;
O blessed vision! happy child!
Thou art so exquisitely wild,
I think of thee with many fears
For what may be thy lot in future years.
  I thought of times when Pain might be thy guest,
Lord of thy house and hospitality;
And Grief, uneasy lover! never rest
But when she sate within the touch of thee.

390

WILLIAM WORDSWORTH

O too industrious folly!
O vain and causeless melancholy!
Nature will either end thee quite;
Or, lengthening out thy season of delight,
Preserve for thee, by individual right,
A young lamb's heart among the full-grown flocks.
What hast thou to do with sorrow,
Or the injuries of to-morrow?
Thou art a dew-drop, which the morn brings forth
Ill fitted to sustain unkindly shocks,
Or to be trailed along the soiling earth;
A gem that glitters while it lives,
And no forewarning gives;
But, at the touch of wrong, without a strife
Slips in a moment out of life.

TO THE DAISY

In youth from rock to rock I went,
From hill to hill in discontent
Of pleasure high and turbulent,
    Most pleased when most uneasy;
But now my own delights I make,—
My thirst at every rill can slake,
And gladly Nature's love partake,
    Of Thee, sweet Daisy!

Thee Winter in the garland wears
That thinly decks his few grey hairs;
Spring parts the clouds with softest airs,
    That she may sun thee;
Whole Summer-fields are thine by right;
And Autumn, melancholy Wight!
Doth in thy crimson head delight
    When rains are on thee.

In shoals and bands, a morrice train,
Thou greet'st the traveller in the lane;
Pleased at his greeting thee again;
    Yet nothing daunted,

Nor grieved if thou be set at nought:
And oft alone in nooks remote
We meet thee, like a pleasant thought,
   When such are wanted.

Be violets in their secret mews
The flowers the wanton Zephyrs choose;
Proud be the rose, with rains and dews
   Her head impearling,
Thou liv'st with less ambitious aim,
Yet hast not gone without thy fame;
Thou art indeed by many a claim
   The Poet's darling.

If to a rock from rains he fly,
Or, some bright day of April sky,
Imprisoned by hot sunshine lie
   Near the green holly,
And wearily at length should fare;
He needs but look about, and there
Thou art!—a friend at hand, to scare
   His melancholy.

A hundred times, by rock or bower,
Ere thus I have lain couched an hour,
Have I derived from thy sweet power
   Some apprehension;
Some steady love; some brief delight;
Some memory that had taken flight;
Some chime of fancy wrong or right;
   Or stray invention.

If stately passions in me burn,
And one chance look to Thee should turn,
I drink out of an humbler urn
   A lowlier pleasure;
The homely sympathy that heeds
The common life, our nature breeds;
A wisdom fitted to the needs
   Of hearts at leisure.

WILLIAM WORDSWORTH

Fresh-smitten by the morning ray,
When thou art up, alert and gay,
Then, cheerful Flower! my spirits play
   With kindred gladness:
And when, at dusk, by dews opprest
Thou sink'st, the image of thy rest
Hath often eased my pensive breast
   Of careful sadness.

And all day long I number yet,
All seasons through, another debt,
Which I, wherever thou art met,
   To thee am owing;
An instinct call it, a blind sense;
A happy, genial influence,
Coming one knows not how, nor whence,
   Nor whither going.

Child of the Year! that round dost run
Thy pleasant course,—when day's begun
As ready to salute the sun
   As lark or leveret,
Thy long-lost praise thou shalt regain;
Nor be less dear to future men
Than in old time;—thou not in vain
   Art Nature's favourite.

TO THE SAME FLOWER

With little here to do or see
Of things that in the great world be,
Daisy! again I talk to thee,
   For thou art worthy,
Thou unassuming Common-place
Of Nature, with that homely face,
And yet with something of a grace,
   Which Love makes for thee!

Oft on the dappled turf at ease
I sit, and play with similies,

393

Loose types of things through all degrees,
  Thoughts of thy raising:
And many a fond and idle name
I give to thee, for praise or blame,
As is the humour of the game,
  While I am gazing.

A nun demure of lowly port;
Or sprightly maiden, of Love's court,
In thy simplicity the sport
  Of all temptations;
A queen in crown of rubies drest;
A starveling in a scanty vest;
Are all, as seems to suit thee best,
  Thy appellations.

A little cyclops, with one eye
Staring to threaten and defy,
That thought comes next—and instantly
  The freak is over,
The shape will vanish—and behold
A silver shield with boss of gold,
That spreads itself, some faery bold
  In fight to cover!

I see thee glittering from afar—
And then thou art a pretty star;
Not quite so fair as many are
  In heaven above thee!
Yet like a star, with glittering crest,
Self-poised in air thou seem'st to rest;—
May peace come never to his nest,
  Who shall reprove thee!

Bright Flower! for by that name at last,
When all my reveries are past,
I call thee, and to that cleave fast,
  Sweet silent creature!
That breath'st with me in sun and air,
Do thou, as thou art wont, repair
My heart with gladness, and a share
  Of thy meek nature!

WILLIAM WORDSWORTH

THE GREEN LINNET

Beneath these fruit-tree boughs that shed
Their snow-white blossoms on my head,
With brightest sunshine round me spread
　Of spring's unclouded weather,
In this sequestered nook how sweet
To sit upon my orchard-seat!
And birds and flowers once more to greet,
　My last year's friends together.

One have I marked, the happiest guest
In all this covert of the blest:
Hail to Thee, far above the rest
　In joy of voice and pinion!
Thou, Linnet! in thy green array,
Presiding Spirit here to-day,
Dost lead the revels of the May;
　And this is thy dominion.

While birds, and butterflies, and flowers,
Make all one band of paramours,
Thou, ranging up and down the bowers,
　Art sole in thy employment:
A Life, a Presence like the Air,
Scattering thy gladness without care,
Too blest with any one to pair;
　Thyself thy own enjoyment.

Amid yon tuft of hazel trees,
That twinkle to the gusty breeze,
Behold him perched in ecstasies,
　Yet seeming still to hover;
There! where the flutter of his wings
Upon his back and body flings
Shadows and sunny glimmerings,
　That cover him all over.

My dazzled sight he oft deceives,
A Brother of the dancing leaves;

Then flits, and from the cottage-eaves
   Pours forth his song in gushes;
As if by that exulting strain
He mocked and treated with disdain
The voiceless Form he chose to feign,
   While fluttering in the bushes.

TO A HIGHLAND GIRL

Sweet Highland Girl, a very shower
Of beauty is thy earthly dower!
Twice seven consenting years have shed
Their utmost bounty on thy head:
And these grey rocks; that household lawn;
Those trees, a veil just half withdrawn;
This fall of water that doth make
A murmur near the silent lake;
This little bay; a quiet road
That holds in shelter thy Abode—
In truth together do ye seem
Like something fashioned in a dream;
Such Forms as from their covert peep
When earthly cares are laid asleep!
But, O fair Creature! in the light
Of common day, so heavenly bright,
I bless Thee, Vision as thou art,
I bless thee with a human heart;
God shield thee to thy latest years!
Thee, neither know I, nor thy peers;
And yet my eyes are filled with tears.
   With earnest feeling I shall pray
For thee when I am far away:
For never saw I mien, or face,
In which more plainly I could trace
Benignity and home-bred sense
Ripening in perfect innocence.
Here scattered, like a random seed,
Remote from men, Thou dost not need
The embarrassed look of shy distress,
And maidenly shamefacedness:

WILLIAM WORDSWORTH

Thou wear'st upon thy forehead clear
The freedom of a Mountaineer:
A face with gladness overspread!
Soft smiles, by human kindness bred!
And seemliness complete, that sways
Thy courtesies, about thee plays;
With no restraint, but such as springs
From quick and eager visitings
Of thoughts that lie beyond the reach
Of thy few words of English speech:
A bondage sweetly brooked, a strife
That gives thy gestures grace and life!
So have I, not unmoved in mind,
Seen birds of tempest-loving kind—
Thus beating up against the wind.

   What hand but would a garland cull
For thee who art so beautiful?
O happy pleasure! here to dwell
Beside thee in some healthy dell;
Adopt your homely ways, and dress,
A Shepherd, thou a Shepherdess!
But I could frame a wish for thee
More like a grave reality:
Thou art to me but as a wave
Of the wild sea; and I would have
Some claim upon thee, if I could,
Though but of common neighbourhood.
What joy to hear thee, and to see!
Thy elder Brother I would be,
Thy Father—anything to thee!

   Now thanks to Heaven! that of its grace
Hath led me to this lonely place.
Joy have I had; and going hence
I bear away my recompense.
In spots like these it is we prize
Our Memory, feel that she hath eyes:
Then, why should I be loth to stir?
I feel this place was made for her;
To give new pleasure like the past,
Continued long as life shall last.

Nor am I loth, though pleased at heart,
Sweet Highland Girl! from thee to part:
For I, methinks, till I grow old,
As fair before me shall behold,
As I do now, the cabin small,
The lake, the bay, the waterfall;
And Thee, the Spirit of them all!

THE SOLITARY REAPER

Behold her, single in the field,
Yon solitary Highland Lass!
Reaping and singing by herself;
Stop here, or gently pass!
Alone she cuts and binds the grain,
And sings a melancholy strain;
O listen! for the Vale profound
Is overflowing with the sound.

No Nightingale did ever chaunt
More welcome notes to weary bands
Of travellers in some shady haunt,
Among Arabian sands:
A voice so thrilling ne'er was heard
In spring-time from the Cuckoo-bird,
Breaking the silence of the seas
Among the farthest Hebrides.

Will no one tell me what she sings?—
Perhaps the plaintive numbers flow
For old, unhappy, far-off things,
And battles long ago:
Or is it some more humble lay,
Familiar matter of to-day?
Some natural sorrow, loss, or pain,
That has been, and may be again?

Whate'er the theme, the Maiden sang
As if her song could have no ending;
I saw her singing at her work,
And o'er the sickle bending;—

I listened, motionless and still;
And, as I mounted up the hill
The music in my heart I bore,
Long after it was heard no more.

YARROW UNVISITED

From Stirling castle we had seen
The mazy Forth unravelled;
Had trod the banks of Clyde, and Tay,
And with the Tweed had travelled;
And when we came to Clovenford,
Then said my "winsome Marrow,"
"Whate'er betide, we'll turn aside,
And see the Braes of Yarrow."

"Let Yarrow folk, frae Selkirk town,
Who have been buying, selling,
Go back to Yarrow, 'tis their own;
Each maiden to her dwelling!
On Yarrow's banks let herons feed,
Hares couch, and rabbits burrow!
But we will downward with the Tweed,
Nor turn aside to Yarrow.

"There's Galla Water, Leader Haughs,
Both lying right before us;
And Dryborough, where with chiming Tweed
The lintwhites sing in chorus;
There's pleasant Tiviot-dale, a land
Made blithe with plough and harrow:
Why throw away a needful day
To go in search of Yarrow?

"What's Yarrow but a river bare,
That glides the dark hills under?
There are a thousand such elsewhere
As worthy of your wonder."
—Strange words they seemed of slight and scorn
My True-love sighed for sorrow;
And looked me in the face, to think
I thus could speak of Yarrow!

"Oh! green," said I, "are Yarrow's holms,
And sweet is Yarrow flowing!
Fair hangs the apple frae the rock,
But we will leave it growing.
O'er hilly path, and open Strath,
We'll wander Scotland thorough;
But, though so near, we will not turn
Into the dale of Yarrow.

"Let beeves and home-bred kine partake
The sweets of Burn-mill meadow;
The swan on still St. Mary's Lake
Float double, swan and shadow!
We will not see them; will not go,
To-day, nor yet to-morrow,
Enough if in our hearts we know
There's such a place as Yarrow.

"Be Yarrow stream unseen, unknown!
It must, or we shall rue it:
We have a vision of our own;
Ah! why should we undo it?
The treasured dreams of times long past,
We'll keep them, winsome Marrow!
For when we're there, although 'tis fair,
'Twill be another Yarrow!

"If Care with freezing years should come,
And wandering seem but folly,—
Should we be loth to stir from home,
And yet be melancholy;
Should life be dull, and spirits low,
'Twill soothe us in our sorrow,
That earth has something yet to show,
The bonny holms of Yarrow!"

TO THE CUCKOO

O blithe New-comer! I have heard,
I hear thee and rejoice,
O Cuckoo! shall I call thee Bird,
Or but a wandering Voice?

While I am lying on the grass
Thy twofold shout I hear,
From hill to hill it seems to pass,
At once far off, and near.

Though babbling only to the Vale,
Of sunshine and of flowers,
Thou bringest unto me a tale
Of visionary hours.

Thrice welcome, darling of the Spring!
Even yet thou art to me
No bird, but an invisible thing,
A voice, a mystery;

The same whom in my school-boy days
I listened to; that Cry
Which made me look a thousand ways
In bush, and tree, and sky.

To seek thee did I often rove
Through woods and on the green;
And thou wert still a hope, a love;
Still longed for, never seen.

And I can listen to thee yet;
Can lie upon the plain
And listen, till I do beget
That golden time again.

O blessèd Bird! the earth we pace
Again appears to be
An unsubstantial, faery place;
That is fit home for Thee!

SHE WAS A PHANTOM OF DELIGHT

She was a Phantom of delight
When first she gleamed upon my sight;
A lovely Apparition, sent
To be a moment's ornament;

Her eyes as stars of Twilight fair;
Like Twilight's, too, her dusky hair;
But all things else about her drawn
From May-time and the cheerful Dawn;
A dancing Shape, an Image gay,
To haunt, to startle, and way-lay.

I saw her upon nearer view,
A Spirit, yet a Woman too!
Her household motions light and free,
And steps of virgin-liberty;
A countenance in which did meet
Sweet records, promises as sweet;
A Creature not too bright or good
For human nature's daily food;
For transient sorrows, simple wiles,
Praise, blame, love, kisses, tears, and smiles.

And now I see with eyes serene
The very pulse of the machine;
A Being breathing thoughtful breath,
A Traveller between life and death;
The reason firm, the temperate will,
Endurance, foresight, strength, and skill;
A perfect Woman, nobly planned,
To warn, to comfort, and command;
And yet a Spirit still, and bright
With something of angelic light.

I WANDERED LONELY AS A CLOUD

I wandered lonely as a cloud
That floats on high o'er vales and hills,
When all at once I saw a crowd,
A host, of golden daffodils;
Beside the lake, beneath the trees,
Fluttering and dancing in the breeze.

Continuous as the stars that shine
And twinkle on the milky way,
They stretched in never-ending line
Along the margin of a bay:

Ten thousand saw I at a glance,
Tossing their heads in sprightly dance.

The waves beside them danced; but they
Out-did the sparkling waves in glee:
A poet could not but be gay,
In such a jocund company:
I gazed—and gazed—but little thought
What wealth the show to me had brought:

For oft, when on my couch I lie
In vacant or in pensive mood,
They flash upon that inward eye
Which is the bliss of solitude;
And then my heart with pleasure fills,
And dances with the daffodils.

THE SMALL CELANDINE

There is a Flower, the lesser Celandine,
That shrinks, like many more, from cold and rains;
And, the first moment that the sun may shine,
Bright as the sun himself, 'tis out again!

When hailstones have been falling, swarm on swarm,
Or blasts the green field and the trees distrest,
Oft have I seen it muffled up from harm,
In close self-shelter, like a Thing at rest.

But lately, one rough day, this Flower I passed
And recognised it, though an altered form,
Now standing forth an offering to the blast,
And buffeted at will by rain and storm.

I stopped, and said with inly-muttered voice,
"It doth not love the shower, nor seek the cold:
This neither is its courage nor its choice,
But its necessity in being old.

"The sunshine may not cheer it, nor the dew;
It cannot help itself in its decay;
Stiff in its members, withered, changed of hue."
And, in my spleen, I smiled that it was grey.

To be a Prodigal's Favourite—then, worse truth,
A Miser's Pensioner—behold our lot!
O Man, that from thy fair and shining youth
Age might but take the things Youth needed not!

ODE TO DUTY

Stern Daughter of the Voice of God!
O Duty! if that name thou love
Who art a light to guide, a rod
To check the erring, and reprove;
Thou, who art victory and law
When empty terrors overawe;
From vain temptations dost set free;
And calm'st the weary strife of frail humanity! .

There are who ask not if thine eye
Be on them; who, in love and truth,
Where no misgiving is, rely
Upon the genial sense of youth:
Glad Hearts! without reproach or blot
Who do thy work, and know it not:
Oh! if through confidence misplaced
They fail, thy saving arms, dread Power! around them cast

Serene will be our days and bright,
And happy will our nature be,
When love is an unerring light,
And joy its own security.
And they a blissful course may hold
Even now, who, not unwisely bold,
Live in the spirit of this creed;
Yet seek thy firm support, according to their need.

I, loving freedom, and untried;
No sport of every random gust,
Yet being to myself a guide,
Too blindly have reposed my trust:
And oft, when in my heart was heard
Thy timely mandate, I deferred
The task, in smoother walks to stray;
But thee I now would serve more strictly, if I may.

404

WILLIAM WORDSWORTH

Through no disturbance of my soul,
Or strong compunction in me wrought,
I supplicate for thy control;
But in the quietness of thought:
Me this unchartered freedom tires;
I feel the weight of chance-desires:
My hopes no more must change their name,
I long for a repose that ever is the same.

Stern Lawgiver! yet thou dost wear
The Godhead's most benignant grace;
Nor know we anything so fair
As is the smile upon thy face:
Flowers laugh before thee on their beds
And fragrance in thy footing treads;
Thou dost preserve the stars from wrong;
And the most ancient heavens, through
Thee, are fresh and strong.

To humbler functions, awful Power!
I call thee: I myself commend
Unto thy guidance from this hour;
Oh, let my weakness have an end!
Give unto me, made lowly wise,
The spirit of self-sacrifice;
The confidence of reason give;
And in the light of truth thy Bondman let me live!

TO A SKY-LARK

Up with me! up with me into the clouds!
    For thy song, Lark, is strong;
Up with me, up with me into the clouds!
        Singing, singing,
With clouds and sky about thee ringing,
    Lift me, guide me till I find
That spot which seems so to thy mind!

I have walked through wildernesses dreary
And to-day my heart is weary;

Had I now the wings of a Faery,
Up to thee would I fly.
There is madness about thee, and joy divine
In that song of thine;
Lift me, guide me high and high
To thy banqueting-place in the sky.

    Joyous as morning
Thou art laughing and scorning;
Thou hast a nest for thy love and thy rest,
And, though little troubled with sloth,
Drunken Lark! thou would'st be loth
To be such a traveller as I.
Happy, happy Liver,
With a soul as strong as a mountain river
Pouring out praise to the Almighty Giver,
  Joy and jollity be with us both!

Alas! my journey, rugged and uneven,
Through prickly moors or dusty ways must wind;
But hearing thee, or others of thy kind,
As full of gladness and as free of heaven,
I, with my fate contented, will plod on,
And hope for higher raptures, when life's day is done.

TO A YOUNG LADY

Dear Child of Nature, let them rail!
—There is a nest in a green dale,
A harbour and a hold;
Where thou, a Wife and Friend, shalt see
Thy own heart-stirring days, and be
A light to young and old.

There, healthy as a shepherd boy,
And treading among flowers of joy
Which at no season fade,
Thou, while thy babes around thee cling,
Shalt show us how divine a thing
A Woman may be made.

406

Thy thoughts and feelings shall not die,
Nor leave thee, when grey hairs are nigh,
A melancholy slave;
But an old age serene and bright,
And lovely as a Lapland night,
Shall lead thee to thy grave.

THE PRELUDE

.   .   .   .

Thus while the days flew by, and years passed on,
From Nature and her overflowing soul,
I had received so much, that all my thoughts
Were steeped in feeling; I was only then
Contented, when with bliss ineffable
I felt the sentiment of Being spread
O'er all that moves and all that seemeth still;
O'er all that, lost beyond the reach of thought
And human knowledge, to the human eye
Invisible, yet liveth to the heart;
O'er all that leaps and runs, and shouts and sings,
Or beats the gladsome air; o'er all that glides
Beneath the wave, yea, in the wave itself,
And mighty depth of waters. Wonder not
If high the transport, great the joy I felt,
Communing in this sort through earth and heaven
With every form of creature, as it looked
Towards the Uncreated with a countenance
Of adoration, with an eye of love.
One song they sang, and it was audible,
Most audible, then, when the fleshly ear,
O'ercome by humblest prelude of that strain,
Forgot her functions, and slept undisturbed.

If this be error, and another faith
Find easier access to the pious mind,
Yet were I grossly destitute of all
Those human sentiments that make this earth
So dear, if I should fail with grateful voice
To speak of you, ye mountains, and ye lakes

And sounding cataracts, ye mists and winds
That dwell among the hills where I was born.
If in my youth I have been pure in heart,
If, mingling with the world, I am content
With my own modest pleasures, and have lived
With God and Nature communing, removed
From little enmities and low desires—
The gift is yours; if in these times of fear,
This melancholy waste of hopes o'erthrown,
If, 'mid indifference and apathy,
And wicked exultation when good men
On every side fall off, we know not how,
To selfishness, disguised in gentle names
Of peace and quiet and domestic love
Yet mingled not unwillingly with sneers
On visionary minds; if, in this time
Of dereliction and dismay, I yet
Despair not of our nature, but retain
A more than Roman confidence, a faith
That fails not, in all sorrow my support,
The blessing of my life—the gift is yours,
Ye winds and sounding cataracts! 'tis yours,
Ye mountains! thine, O Nature! Thou hast fed
My lofty speculations; and in thee,
For this uneasy heart of ours, I find
A never-failing principle of joy
And purest passion.

—Book II.

Her pealing organ was my neighbour too;
And from my pillow, looking forth by light
Of moon or favouring stars, I could behold
The antechapel where the statue stood
Of Newton with his prism and silent face,
The marble index of a mind for ever
Voyaging through strange seas of Thought, alone.

        .   .   .   .

As if awakened, summoned, roused, constrained,
I looked for universal things; perused

108

The common countenance of earth and sky:
Earth, nowhere unembellished by some trace
Of that first Paradise whence man was driven;
And sky, whose beauty and bounty are expressed
By the proud name she bears—the name of Heaven.
I called on both to teach me what they might;
Or, turning the mind in upon herself,
Pored, watched, expected, listened, spread my thoughts
And spread them with a wider creeping; felt
Incumbencies more awful, visitings
Of the Upholder of the tranquil soul,
That tolerates the indignities of Time,
And, from the centre of Eternity
All finite motions overruling, lives
In glory immutable. But peace! enough
Here to record that I was mounting now
To such community with highest truth—
A track pursuing, not untrod before,
From strict analogies by thought supplied
Or consciousnesses not to be subdued.
To every natural form, rock, fruits, or flower,
Even the loose stones that cover the highway,
I gave a moral life: I saw them feel,
Or linked them to some feeling: the great mass
Lay bedded in a quickening soul, and all
That I beheld respired with inward meaning.
Add that whate'er of Terror or of Love
Or Beauty, Nature's daily face put on
From transitory passion, unto this
I was as sensitive as waters are
To the sky's influence in a kindred mood
Of passion; was obedient as a lute
That waits upon the touches of the wind.
Unknown, unthought of, yet I was most rich—
I had a world about me—'twas my own;
I made it, for it only lived to me,
And to the God who sees into the heart.

—Book III.

O Soul of Nature! excellent and fair!
That didst rejoice with me, with whom I, too,

Rejoiced through early youth, before the winds
And roaring waters, and in lights and shades
That marched and countermarched about the hills
In glorious apparition, Powers on whom
I daily waited, now all eye and now
All ear; but never long without the heart
Employed, and man's unfolding intellect.

—Book XII

CHARACTER OF THE HAPPY WARRIOR

Who is the happy Warrior? Who is he
That every man in arms should wish to be?
—It is the generous Spirit, who, when brought
Among the tasks of real life, hath wrought
Upon the plan that pleased his boyish thought:
Whose high endeavours are an inward light
That makes the path before him always bright:
Who, with a natural instinct to discern
What knowledge can perform, is diligent to learn;
Abides by this resolve, and stops not there,
But makes his moral being his prime care;
Who, doomed to go in company with Pain,
And Fear, and Bloodshed, miserable train!
Turns his necessity to glorious gain;
In face of these doth exercise a power
Which is our human nature's highest dower;
Controls them and subdues, transmutes, bereaves
Of their bad influence, and their good receives:
By objects, which might force the soul to abate
Her feeling, rendered more compassionate;
Is placable—because occasions rise
So often that demand such sacrifice;
More skilful in self-knowledge, even more pure,
As tempted more; more able to endure,
As more exposed to suffering and distress;
Thence, also, more alive to tenderness.
—'Tis he whose law is reason; who depends
Upon that law as on the best of friends;
410

Whence, in a stage where men are tempted still
To evil for a guard against worse ill,
And what in quality or act is best
Doth seldom on a right foundation rest,
He labours good on good to fix, and owes
To virtue every triumph that he knows:
—Who, if he rise to station of command,
Rises by open means; and there will stand
On honourable terms, or else retire,
And in himself possess his own desire;
Who comprehends his trust, and to the same
Keeps faithful with a singleness of aim;
And therefore does not stoop, nor lie in wait
For wealth, or honours, or for worldly state;
Whom they must follow, on whose head must fall,
Like showers of manna, if they come at all:
Whose power shed round him in the common strife,
Or mild concerns of ordinary life,
A constant influence, a peculiar grace;
But who, if he be called upon to face
Some awful moment to which Heaven has joined
Great issues, good or bad for human kind,
Is happy as a Lover; and attired
With sudden brightness, like a Man inspired;
And, through the heat of conflict, keeps the law
In calmness made, and sees what he foresaw;
Or if an unexpected call succeed,
Come when it will, is equal to the need:
—He who, though thus endued as with a sense
And faculty for storm and turbulence,
Is yet a Soul whose master-bias leans
To homefelt pleasures and to gentle scenes;
Sweet images! which, wheresoe'er he be,
Are at his heart; and such fidelity
It is his darling passion to approve;
More brave for this, that he hath much to love:—
'Tis, finally, the Man, who, lifted high,
Conspicuous object in a Nation's eye,
Or left unthought-of in obscurity,—
Who, with a toward or untoward lot,
Prosperous or adverse, to his wish or not—

411

Plays in the many games of life, that one
Where what he most doth value must be won:
Whom neither shape of danger can dismay,
Nor thought of tender happiness betray;
Who, not content that former worth stand fast,
Looks forward, persevering to the last,
From well to better, daily self-surpast:
Who, whether praise of him must walk the earth
For ever, and to noble deeds give birth,
Or he must fall, to sleep without his fame,
And leave a dead unprofitable name—
Finds comfort in himself and in his cause;
And, while the mortal mist is gathering, draws
His breath in confidence of Heaven's applause:
This is the happy Warrior; this is He
That every Man in arms should wish to be.

YES, IT WAS THE MOUNTAIN ECHO

Yes, it was the mountain Echo,
Solitary, clear, profound,
Answering to the shouting Cuckoo,
Giving to her sound for sound!

Unsolicited reply
To a babbling wanderer sent;
Like her ordinary cry,
Like—but oh, how different!

Hears not also mortal Life?
Hear not we, unthinking Creatures!
Slaves of folly, love, or strife—
Voices of two different natures?

Have not we too?—yes, we have
Answers, and we know not whence;
Echoes from beyond the grave,
Recognised intelligence!

WILLIAM WORDSWORTH

Such rebounds our inward ear
Catches sometimes from afar—
Listen, ponder, hold them dear;
For of God,—of God they are.

NUNS FRET NOT AT THEIR CONVENT'S
NARROW ROOM

Nuns fret not at their convent's narrow room;
And hermits are contented with their cells;
And students with their pensive citadels;
Maids at the wheel, the weaver at his loom,
Sit blithe and happy; bees that soar for bloom,
High as the highest Peak of Furness-fells,
Will murmur by the hour in foxglove bells:
In truth the prison, unto which we doom
Ourselves, no prison is: and hence for me,
In sundry moods, 'twas pastime to be bound
Within the Sonnet's scanty plot of ground;
Pleased if some Souls (for such there needs must be)
Who have felt the weight of too much liberty,
Should find brief solace there, as I have found.

THE WORLD IS TOO MUCH WITH US

The world is too much with us; late and soon,
Getting and spending, we lay waste our powers:
Little we see in Nature that is ours;
We have given our hearts away, a sordid boon!
The Sea that bares her bosom to the moon;
The winds that will be howling at all hours,
And are up-gathered now like sleeping flowers;
For this, for everything, we are out of tune;
It moves us not.—Great God! I'd rather be
A Pagan suckled in a creed outworn;
So might I, standing on this pleasant lea,
Have glimpses that would make me less forlorn;
Have sight of Proteus rising from the sea;
Or hear old Triton blow his wreathèd horn.

413

ODE

INTIMATIONS OF IMMORTALITY FROM RECOLLECTIONS OF EARLY CHILDHOOD

There was a time when meadow, grove, and stream,
The earth, and every common sight,
    To me did seem
    Apparelled in celestial light,
The glory and the freshness of a dream.
It is not now as it hath been of yore;—
    Turn wheresoe'er I may,
    By night or day,
The things which I have seen I now can see no more.

    The Rainbow comes and goes,
    And lovely is the Rose,
    The Moon doth with delight
Look round her when the heavens are bare,
    Waters on a starry night
    Are beautiful and fair;
    The sunshine is a glorious birth;
    But yet I know, where'er I go,
That there hath past away a glory from the earth.

Now, while the birds thus sing a joyous song,
    And while the young lambs bound
    As to the tabor's sound,
To me alone there came a thought of grief:
A timely utterance gave that thought relief,
    And I again am strong:
The cataracts blow their trumpets from the steep;
No more shall grief of mine the season wrong;
I hear the Echoes through the mountains throng,
The Winds come to me from the fields of sleep,
    And all the earth is gay;
    Land and sea
    Give themselves up to jollity,
    And with the heart of May

Doth every Beast keep holiday;—
　　Thou Child of Joy,
Shout round me, let me hear thy shouts, thou happy
　　　　Shepherd-boy!

Ye blessèd Creatures, I have heard the call
　　Ye to each other make; I see
The heavens laugh with you in your jubilee;
　　My heart is at your festival,
　　My head hath its coronal,
The fulness of your bliss, I feel—I feel it all.
　　Oh evil day! if I were sullen
　　While Earth herself is adorning,
　　　　This sweet May-morning,
　　And the Children are culling
　　　　On every side,
　　In a thousand valleys far and wide,
　　Fresh flowers; while the sun shines warm,
And the Babe leaps up on his Mother's arm:—
　　I hear, I hear, with joy I hear!
　　—But there's a Tree, of many, one,
A single Field which I have looked upon,
Both of them speak of something that is gone:
　　The Pansy at my feet
　　Doth the same tale repeat:
Whither is fled the visionary gleam?
Where is it now, the glory and the dream?

Our birth is but a sleep and a forgetting:
The Soul that rises with us, our life's Star,
　　Hath had elsewhere its setting,
　　　　And cometh from afar:
　　Not in entire forgetfulness,
　　And not in utter nakedness,
But trailing clouds of glory do we come
　　From God, who is our home:
Heaven lies about us in our infancy!
Shades of the prison-house begin to close
　　Upon the growing Boy,
But He beholds the light, and whence it flows,
　　He sees it in his joy;

The Youth, who daily farther from the east
   Must travel, still is Nature's Priest,
    And by the vision splendid
    Is on his way attended;
At length the Man perceives it die away,
And fade into the light of common day.

Earth fills her lap with pleasures of her own;
Yearnings she hath in her own natural kind,
And, even with something of a Mother's mind,
    And no unworthy aim,
    The homely Nurse doth all she can
To make her Foster-child, her Inmate Man,
   Forget the glories he hath known,
And that imperial palace whence he came.

Behold the Child among his new-born blisses,
A six years' Darling of a pigmy size!
See, where 'mid work of his own hand he lies,
Fretted by sallies of his mother's kisses,
With light upon him from his father's eyes!
See, at his feet, some little plan or chart,
Some fragment from his dream of human life,
Shaped by himself with newly-learned art;
    A wedding or a festival,
    A mourning or a funeral;
      And this hath now his heart,
    And unto this he frames his song:
      Then will he fit his tongue
To dialogues of business, love, or strife;
    But it will not be long
    Ere this be thrown aside,
    And with new joy and pride
The little Actor cons another part;
Filling from time to time his "humorous stage"
With all the Persons, down to palsied Age,
That Life brings with her in her equipage;
    As if his whole vocation
    Were endless imitation.

Thou, whose exterior semblance doth belie
    Thy Soul's immensity;
Thou best Philosopher, who yet dost keep
Thy heritage, thou Eye among the blind,
That, deaf and silent, read'st the eternal deep,
Haunted for ever by the eternal mind,—
    Mighty Prophet! Seer blest!
    On whom those truths do rest,
Which we are toiling all our lives to find,
In darkness lost, the darkness of the grave;
Thou, over whom thy Immortality
Broods like the Day, a Master o'er a Slave,
A Presence which is not to be put by;
Thou little Child, yet glorious in the might
Of heaven-born freedom on thy being's height,
Why with such earnest pains dost thou provoke
The years to bring the inevitable yoke,
Thus blindly with thy blessedness at strife?
Full soon thy Soul shall have her earthly freight,
And custom lie upon thee with a weight,
Heavy as frost, and deep almost as life!

    O joy! that in our embers
    Is something that doth live,
    That nature yet remembers
    What was so fugitive!
The thought of our past years in me doth breed
Perpetual benediction: not indeed
For that which is most worthy to be blest—
Delight and liberty, the simple creed
Of Childhood, whether busy or at rest,
With new-fledged hope still fluttering in his breast:—
    Not for these I raise
    The song of thanks and praise;
   But for those obstinate questionings
   Of sense and outward things,
   Fallings from us, vanishings;
   Blank misgivings of a Creature
Moving about in worlds not realised,
High instincts before which our mortal Nature
Did tremble like a guilty Thing surprised:

But for those first affections,
Those shadowy recollections,
 Which, be they what they may,
Are yet the fountain light of all our day,
Are yet a master light of all our seeing;
 Uphold us, cherish, and have power to make
Our noisy years seem moments in the being
Of the eternal Silence: truths that wake,
 To perish never;
Which neither listlessness, nor mad endeavour,
 Nor Man nor Boy,
Nor all that is at enmity with joy,
Can utterly abolish or destroy!
 Hence in a season of calm weather
 Though inland far we be,
Our Souls have sight of that immortal sea
 Which brought us hither,
 Can in a moment travel thither,
And see the Children sport upon the shore,
And hear the mighty waters rolling evermore.

Then sing, ye Birds, sing, sing a joyous song!
 And let the young Lambs bound
 As to the tabor's sound!
We in thought will join your throng,
 Ye that pipe and ye that play,
 Ye that through your hearts to-day
 Feel the gladness of the May!
What though the radiance which was once so bright
Be now for ever taken from my sight,
 Though nothing can bring back the hour
Of splendour in the grass, of glory in the flower;
 We will grieve not, rather find
 Strength in what remains behind;
 In the primal sympathy
 Which having been must ever be;
 In the soothing thoughts that spring
 Out of human suffering;
 In the faith that looks through death,
In years that bring the philosophic mind.

And O, ye Fountains, Meadows, Hills, and Groves,
Forbode not any severing of our loves!
Yet in my heart of hearts I feel your might;
I only have relinquished one delight
To live beneath your more habitual sway.
I love the Brooks which down their channels fret,
Even more than when I tripped lightly as they;
The innocent brightness of a new-born Day
   Is lovely yet;
The Clouds that gather round the setting sun
Do take a sober colouring from an eye
That hath kept watch o'er man's mortality;
Another race hath been, and other palms are won.
Thanks to the human heart by which we live,
Thanks to its tenderness, its joys, and fears,
To me the meanest flower that blows can give
Thoughts that do often lie too deep for tears.

THOUGHT OF A BRITON ON THE SUBJUGATION OF SWITZERLAND

Two Voices are there; one is of the sea,
One of the mountains; each a mighty Voice:
In both from age to age thou didst rejoice,
They were thy chosen music, Liberty!
There came a Tyrant, and with holy glee
Thou fought'st against him; but hast vainly striven:
Thou from thy Alpine holds at length art driven,
Where not a torrent murmurs heard by thee.
Of one deep bliss thine ear hath been bereft:
Then cleave, O cleave to that which still is left;
For, high-souled Maid, what sorrow would it be
That Mountain floods should thunder as before,
And Ocean bellow from his rocky shore,
And neither awful Voice be heard by thee!

O NIGHTINGALE! THOU SURELY ART

O Nightingale! thou surely art
A creature of a "fiery heart":—
These notes of thine—they pierce and pierce;
Tumultuous harmony and fierce!
Thou sing'st as if the God of wine
Had helped thee to a Valentine;
A song in mockery and despite
Of shades, and dews, and silent night;
And steady bliss, and all the loves
Now sleeping in these peaceful groves.

I heard a Stock-dove sing or say
His homely tale, this very day;
His voice was buried among trees,
Yet to be come at by the breeze:
He did not cease; but cooed—and cooed;
And somewhat pensively he wooed:
He sang of love, with quiet blending,
Slow to begin, and never ending;
Of serious faith, and inward glee;
That was the song—the song for me!

SURPRISED BY JOY

Surprised by joy—impatient as the Wind
I turned to share the transport—Oh! with whom
But Thee, deep buried in the silent tomb,
That spot which no vicissitude can find?
Love, faithful love, recalled thee to my mind—
But how could I forget thee? Through what power,
Even for the least division of an hour,
Have I been so beguiled as to be blind
To my most grievous loss?—That thought's return
Was the worst pang that sorrow ever bore,
Save one, one only, when I stood forlorn,
Knowing my heart's best treasure was no more;
That neither present time, nor years unborn
Could to my sight that heavenly face restore.

WILLIAM WORDSWORTH

THE THREE COTTAGE GIRLS

How blest the Maid whose heart—yet free
From Love's uneasy sovereignty—
Beats with a fancy running high,
Her simple cares to magnify;
Whom Labour, never urged to toil,
Hath cherished on a healthful soil;
Who knows not pomp, who heeds not pelf;
Whose heaviest sin it is to look
Askance upon her pretty Self
Reflected in some crystal brook;
Whom grief hath spared—who sheds no tear
But in sweet pity; and can hear
Another's praise from envy clear.

Such (but O lavish Nature! why
That dark unfathomable eye,
Where lurks a Spirit that replies
To stillest mood of softest skies,
Yet hints at peace to be o'erthrown,
Another's first, and then her own?)
Such, haply, yon Italian Maid,
Our Lady's laggard Votaress,
Halting beneath the chestnut shade
To accomplish there her loveliness:
Nice aid maternal fingers lend;
A Sister serves with slacker hand;
Then, glittering like a star, she joins the festal band.

How blest (if truth may entertain
Coy fancy with a bolder strain)
The Helvetian Girl—who daily braves,
In her light skiff, the tossing waves,
And quits the bosom of the deep
Only to climb the rugged steep!
—Say whence that modulated shout!
From Wood-nymph of Diana's throng?
Or does the greeting to a rout
Of giddy Bacchanals belong?

Jubilant outcry! rock and glade
Resounded—but the voice obeyed
The breath of an Helvetian Maid.

Her beauty dazzles the thick wood;
Her courage animates the flood;
Her steps the elastic greensward meets
Returning unreluctant sweets;
The mountains (as ye heard) rejoice
Aloud, saluted by her voice!
Blithe Paragon of Alpine grace,
Be as thou art—for through thy veins
The blood of Heroes runs its race!
And nobly wilt thou brook the chains
That, for the virtuous, Life prepares;
The fetters which the Matron wears;
The patriot Mother's weight of anxious cares!

"Sweet Highland Girl! a very shower
Of beauty was thy earthly dower,"
When thou didst flit before mine eyes,
Gay Vision under sullen skies,
While Hope and Love around thee played,
Near the rough falls of Inversneyd!
Have they, who nursed the blossom, seen
No breach of promise in the fruit?
Was joy, in following joy, as keen
As grief can be in grief's pursuit?
When youth had flown did hope still bless
Thy goings—or the cheerfulness
Of innocence survive to mitigate distress?

But from our course why turn—to tread
A way with shadows overspread;
Where what we gladliest would believe
Is feared as what may most deceive?
Bright Spirit, not with amaranth crowned
But heath-bells from thy native ground,
Time cannot thin thy flowing hair,
Nor take one ray of light from Thee;
For in my Fancy thou dost share

WILLIAM WORDSWORTH

The gift of immortality;
And there shall bloom, with Thee allied,
The Votaress by Lugano's side;
And that intrepid Nymph, on Uri's steep descried!

AFTER-THOUGHT

I thought of Thee, my partner and my guide,
As being past away.—Vain sympathies!
For, backward, Duddon, as I cast my eyes,
I see what was, and is, and will abide;
Still glides the Stream, and shall for ever glide;
The Form remains, the Function never dies;
While we, the brave, the mighty, and the wise,
We Men, who in our morn of youth defied
The elements, must vanish;—be it so!
Enough, if something from our hands have power
To live, and act, and serve the future hour;
And if, as toward the silent tomb we go,
Through love, through hope, and faith's transcendent
    dower,
We feel that we are greater than we know.

TO A SKY-LARK

Ethereal minstrel! pilgrim of the sky!
Dost thou despise the earth where cares abound?
Or, while the wings aspire, are heart and eye
Both with thy nest upon the dewy ground?
Thy nest which thou canst drop into at will,
Those quivering wings composed, that music still!

Leave to the nightingale her shady wood;
A privacy of glorious light is thine;
Whence thou dost pour upon the world a flood
Of harmony, with instinct more divine;
Type of the wise who soar, but never roam;
True to the kindred points of Heaven and Home!

423

SCORN NOT THE SONNET

Scorn not the Sonnet; Critic, you have frowned,
Mindless of its just honours; with this key
Shakspeare unlocked his heart; the melody
Of this small lute gave ease to Petrarch's wound;
A thousand times this pipe did Tasso sound;
With it Camoëns soothed an exile's grief;
The Sonnet glittered a gay myrtle leaf
Amid the cypress with which Dante crowned
His visionary brow: a glow-worm lamp,
It cheered mild Spenser, called from Faeryland
To struggle through dark ways; and, when a damp
Fell round the path of Milton, in his hand
The Thing became a trumpet; whence he blew
Soul-animating strains—alas, too few!

YARROW REVISITED

The gallant Youth, who may have gained,
    Or seeks, a "winsome Marrow,"
Was but an Infant in the lap
    When first I looked on Yarrow;
Once more, by Newark's Castle-gate
    Long left without a warder,
I stood, looked, listened, and with Thee,
    Great Minstrel of the Border!

Grave thoughts ruled wide on that sweet day,
    Their dignity installing
In gentle bosoms, while sere leaves
    Were on the bough, or falling;
But breezes played, and sunshine gleamed—
    The forest to embolden;
Reddened the fiery hues, and shot
    Transparence through the golden.

For busy thoughts the Stream flowed on
    In foamy agitation;

And slept in many a crystal pool
  For quiet contemplation:
No public and no private care
  The freeborn mind enthralling,
We made a day of happy hours,
  Our happy days recalling.

Brisk Youth appeared, the Morn of youth,
  With freaks of graceful folly,—
Life's temperate Noon, her sober Eve,
  Her Night not melancholy;
Past, present, future, all appeared
  In harmony united,
Like guests that meet, and some from far,
  By cordial love invited.

And if, as Yarrow, through the woods
  And down the meadow ranging,
Did meet us with unaltered face,
  Though we were changed and changing;
If, then, some natural shadows spread
  Our inward prospect over,
The soul's deep valley was not slow
  Its brightness to recover.

Eternal blessings on the Muse,
  And her divine employment!
The blameless Muse, who trains her Sons
  For hope and calm enjoyment;
Albeit sickness, lingering yet,
  Has o'er their pillow brooded;
And Care waylays their steps—a Sprite
  Not easily eluded.

For thee, O Scott! compelled to change
  Green Eildon-hill and Cheviot
For warm Vesuvio's vine-clad slopes;
  And leave thy Tweed and Tiviot
For mild Sorento's breezy waves;
  May classic Fancy, linking
With native Fancy her fresh aid,
  Preserve thy heart from sinking!

Oh! while they minister to thee,
    Each vying with the other,
May Health return to mellow Age
    With Strength, her venturous brother;
And Tiber, and each brook and rill
    Renowned in song and story,
With unimagined beauty shine,
    Nor lose one ray of glory!

For Thou, upon a hundred streams,
    By tales of love and sorrow,
Of faithful love, undaunted truth,
    Hast shed the power of Yarrow;
And streams unknown, hills yet unseen,
    Wherever they invite Thee,
At parent Nature's grateful call,
    With gladness must requite Thee.

A gracious welcome shall be thine,
    Such looks of love and honour
As thy own Yarrow gave to me
    When first I gazed upon her;
Beheld what I had feared to see,
    Unwilling to surrender
Dreams treasured up from early days,
    The holy and the tender.

And what, for this frail world, were all
    That mortals do or suffer,
Did no responsive harp, no pen,
    Memorial tribute offer?
Yea, what were mighty Nature's self?
    Her features, could they win us,
Unhelped by the poetic voice
    That hourly speaks within us?

Nor deem that localised Romance
    Plays false with our affections;
Unsanctifies our tears—made sport
    For fanciful dejections:

WILLIAM WORDSWORTH

Ah, no! the visions of the past
 Sustain the heart in feeling
Life as she is—our changeful Life,
 With friends and kindred dealing.

Bear witness, Ye, whose thoughts that day
 In Yarrow's groves were centred;
Who through the silent portal arch
 Of mouldering Newark entered;
And clomb the winding stair that once
 Too timidly was mounted
By the "last Minstrel," (not the last!)
 Ere he his Tale recounted.

Flow on for ever, Yarrow Stream!
 Fulfil thy pensive duty,
Well pleased that future Bards should chant
 For simple hearts thy beauty;
To dream-light dear while yet unseen,
 Dear to the common sunshine,
And dearer still, as now I feel,
 To memory's shadowy moonshine!

A POET

A Poet!—He hath put his heart to school,
Nor dares to move unpropped upon the staff
Which Art hath lodged within his hand—must laugh
By precept only, and shed tears by rule.
Thy Art be Nature; the live current quaff,
And let the groveller sip his stagnant pool,
In fear that else, when Critics grave and cool
Have killed him, Scorn should write his epitaph.
How does the Meadow-flower its bloom unfold?
Because the lovely little flower is free
Down to its root, and, in that freedom, bold;
And so the grandeur of the Forest-tree
Comes not by casting in a formal mould,
But from its own divine vitality.

427

Sir Walter Scott

ON THE DEPARTURE OF SIR WALTER SCOTT

A trouble, not of clouds, or weeping rain,
Nor of the setting sun's pathetic light
Engendered, hangs o'er Eildon's triple height:
Spirits of Power, assembled there, complain
For kindred Power departing from their sight;
While Tweed, best pleased in chanting a blithe strain,
Saddens his voice again, and yet again.
Lift up your hearts, ye Mourners! for the might
Of the whole world's good wishes with him goes;
Blessings and prayers, in nobler retinue
Than sceptred king or laurelled conqueror knows
Follow this wondrous Potentate. Be true,
Ye winds of ocean, and the midland sea,
Wafting your Charge to soft Parthenope!

—WILLIAM WORDSWORTH.

THE LAY OF THE LAST MINSTREL

The way was long, the wind was cold,
The Minstrel was infirm and old;
His withered cheek, and tresses grey,
Seemed to have known a better day;
The harp, his sole remaining joy,
Was carried by an orphan boy.
The last of all the Bards was he,
Who sung of Border chivalry;
For, welladay! their date was fled,
His tuneful brethren all were dead;
And he, neglected and oppressed,
Wished to be with them, and at rest.
No more, on prancing palfrey borne,
He carolled, light as lark at morn;
No longer courted and caressed,
High placed in hall, a welcome guest,

He poured to lord and lady gay
The unpremeditated lay:
Old times were changed, old manners gone;
A stranger filled the Stuarts' throne;
The bigots of the iron time
Had called his harmless art a crime.
A wandering Harper, scorned and poor,
He begged his bread from door to door,
And tuned, to please a peasant's ear,
The harp a king had loved to hear.

—INTRODUCTION

If thou would'st view fair Melrose aright,
Go visit it by the pale moonlight;
For the gay beams of lightsome day
Gild, but to flout, the ruins grey.
When the broken arches are black in night,
And each shafted oriel glimmers white;
When the cold light's uncertain shower
Streams on the ruined central tower;
When buttress and buttress, alternately,
Seem framed of ebon and ivory;
When silver edges the imagery,
And the scrolls that teach thee to live and die;
When distant Tweed is heard to rave,
And the owlet to hoot o'er the dead man's grave,
Then go—but go alone the while—
Then view St. David's ruined pile;
And home returning, soothly swear,
Was never scene so sad and fair!

—CANTO II.

Breathes there the man, with soul so dead,
Who never to himself hath said,
    This is my own, my native land!
Whose heart hath ne'er within him burned,
As home his footsteps he hath turned,
    From wandering on a foreign strand!
If such there breathe, go, mark him well;
For him no Minstrel raptures swell;

High though his titles, proud his name,
Boundless his wealth as wish can claim;
Despite those titles, power, and pelf,
The wretch, concentred all in self,
Living, shall forfeit fair renown,
And, doubly dying, shall go down
To the vile dust, from whence he sprung,
Unwept, unhonoured, and unsung.

O Caledonia! stern and wild,
Meet nurse for a poetic child!
Land of brown heath and shaggy wood,
Land of the mountain and the flood,
Land of my sires! what mortal hand
Can e'er untie the filial band,
That knits me to thy rugged strand!
Still as I view each well-known scene,
Think what is now, and what hath been,
Seems as, to me, of all bereft,
Sole friends thy woods and streams were left;
And thus I love them better still,
Even in extremity of ill.

.   .   .   .

O'er Roslin all that dreary night
    A wondrous blaze was seen to gleam;
'Twas broader than the watch-fire's light,
    And redder than the bright moon-beam.

It glared on Roslin's castled rock,
    It ruddied all the copse-wood glen,
'Twas seen from Dryden's groves of oak,
    And seen from cavern'd Hawthornden.

Seem'd all on fire that chapel proud,
    Where Roslin's chiefs uncoffin'd lie,
Each Baron, for a sable shroud,
    Sheathed in his iron panoply.

430

Seem'd all on fire, within, around,
  Deep sacristy, and altar's pale,
Shone every pillar foliage-bound,
  And glimmer'd all the dead men's mail.

Blazed battlement and pinnet high,
  Blazed every rose-carved buttress fair—
So still they blaze, when fate is nigh
  The lordly line of high St. Clair.

There are twenty of Roslin's barons bold
  Lie buried within that proud chapelle:
Each one the holy vault doth hold—
  But the sea holds lovely Rosabelle!

—Canto VI.

MARMION

With more than mortal powers endow'd,
How high they soar'd above the crowd!
Theirs was no common party race,
Jostling by dark intrigue for place;
Like fabled gods, their mighty war
Shook realms and nations in its jar;
Beneath each banner proud to stand,
Locked up the noblest of the land,
Till through the British world were known
The names of Pitt and Fox alone.
Spells of such force no wizard grave
E'er framed in dark Thessalian cave.
These spells are spent, and, spent with these,
The wine of life is on the lees;
Genius, and taste, and talent gone,
For ever tomb'd beneath the stone,
Where—taming thought to human pride!—
The mighty chiefs sleep side by side.
Drop upon Fox's grave the tear,
'Twill trickle to his rival's bier;

431

O'er Pitt's the mournful requiem sound,
And Fox's shall the notes rebound.
The solemn echo seems to cry—
"Here let their discord with them die.
Speak not for these a separate doom,
Whom Fate made Brothers in the tomb;
But search the land of living men.
Where wilt thou find their like again?"

—INTRODUCTION TO CANTO I.

They close, in clouds of smoke and dust,
With sword-sway, and with lance's thrust:
    And such a yell was there,
Of sudden and portentous birth,
As if men fought upon the earth,
    And fiends in upper air;
O life and death were in the shout,
Recoil and rally, charge and rout,
    And triumph and despair.
At length the freshening western blast
Aside the shroud of battle cast;
And, first, the ridge of mingled spears
Above the brightening cloud appears;
And in the smoke the pennons flew,
As in the storm the white seamew;
Then mark'd they, dashing broad and far,
The broken billows of the war,
And plumèd crests of chieftains brave,
Floating like foam upon the wave;
    But nought distinct they see.
Wide raged the battle on the plain;
Spears shook, and falchions flash'd amain;
Fell England's arrow-flight like rain;
Crests rose, and stoop'd, and rose again,
    Wild and disorderly.

· · · · · · · ·

O Woman! in our hours of ease
Uncertain, coy, and hard to please,

SIR WALTER SCOTT

And variable as the shade
By the light quivering aspen made;
When pain and anguish wring the brow,
A ministering angel thou!

—Canto VI.

THE LADY OF THE LAKE

SONG

Soldier, rest! thy warfare o'er,
  Sleep the sleep that knows not breaking;
Dream of battled fields no more,
  Days of danger, nights of waking.
In our isle's enchanted hall,
  Hands unseen thy couch are strewing,
Fairy strains of music fall,
  Every sense in slumber dewing.
Soldier, rest! thy warfare o'er,
Dream of fighting fields no more;
Sleep the sleep that knows not breaking,
Morn of toil, nor night of waking.

No rude sound shall reach thine ear,
  Armour's clang, or war-steed champing,
Trump nor pibroch summon here
  Mustering clan or squadron tramping.
Yet the lark's shrill fife may come
  At the daybreak from the fallow,
And the bittern sound his drum,
  Booming from the sedgy shallow.
Ruder sounds shall none be near,
Guards nor warders challenge here,
Here's no war-steed's neigh and champing,
Shouting clans or squadrons stamping.

Huntsman, rest! thy chase is done;
  While our slumbrous spells assail ye,
Dream not, with the rising sun,
  Bugles here shall sound reveille.

433

Sleep! the deer is in his den;
   Sleep! thy hounds are by thee lying:
Sleep! nor dream in yonder glen
   How thy gallant steed lay dying.
Huntsman, rest! thy chase is done;
Think not of the rising sun,
For at dawning to assail ye
Here no bugles sound reveille.

                            —CANTO I.

CORONACH

He is gone on the mountain,
   He is lost to the forest,
Like a summer-dried fountain,
   When our need was the sorest.
The font, reappearing,
   From the rain-drops shall borrow,
But to us comes no cheering,
   To Duncan no morrow!

The hand of the reaper
   Takes the ears that are hoary,
But the voice of the weeper
   Wails manhood in glory.
The autumn winds rushing
   Waft the leaves that are searest,
But our flower was in flushing
   When blighting was nearest.

Fleet foot on the correi,
   Sage counsel in cumber,
Red hand in the foray,
   How sound is thy slumber!
Like the dew on the mountain,
   Like the foam on the river,
Like the bubble on the fountain,
   Thou art gone and for ever!

                            CANTO III.

434

Wild as the scream of the curlew,
From crag to crag the signal flew.
Instant, through copse and heath, arose
Bonnets and spears and bended bows;
On right, on left, above, below,
Sprung up at once the lurking foe;
From shingles grey their lances start,
The bracken bush sends forth the dart,
The rushes and the willow-wand
Are bristling into axe and brand,
And every tuft of broom gives life
To plaided warrior arm'd for strife.
That whistle garrison'd the glen
At once with full five hundred men.
Watching their leader's back and will,
All silent there they stood, and still.

—Canto V.

Harp of the North, farewell! The hills grow dark,
    On purple peaks a deeper shade descending;
In twilight copse the glow-worm lights her spark,
    The deer, half-seen, are to the covert wending.
Resume thy wizard elm! the fountain lending,
    And the wild breeze, thy wilder minstrelsy;
Thy numbers sweet with nature's vespers blending,
    With distant echo from the fold and lea,
And herd-boy's evening pipe, and hum of housing bee.

Yet, once again, farewell, thou Minstrel Harp!
    Yet, once again, forgive my feeble sway,
And little reck I of the censure sharp
    May idly cavil at an idle lay.
Much have I owed thy strains on life's long way,
    Through secret woes the world has never known,
When on the weary night dawned wearier day,
    And bitterer was the grief devoured alone.—
That I o'erlive such woes, Enchantress! is thine own.

Hark! as my lingering footsteps slow retire,
    Some spirit of the Air has waked thy string!
'Tis now a seraph bold, with touch of fire,
    'Tis now the brush of Fairy's frolic wing.

435

Receding now, the dying numbers ring
  Fainter and fainter down the rugged dell;
And now the mountain breezes scarcely bring
  A wandering witch-note of the distant spell—
And now, 'tis silent all!—Enchantress, fare thee well!
          —CANTO VI.

ROKEBY

SONG

O Brignal banks are wild and fair,
  And Greta woods are green,
And you may gather garlands there
  Would grace a summer queen.
And as I rode by Dalton-hall
  Beneath the turrets high,
A maiden on the castle-wall
  Was singing merrily,—
"O, Brignal Banks are fresh and fair,
  And Greta woods are green;
I'd rather rove with Edmund there,
  Than reign our English queen."

"If, maiden, thou wouldst wend with me,
  To leave both tower and town,
Thou first must guess what life lead we,
  That dwell by dale and down.
And if thou canst that riddle read,
  As read full well you may,
Then to the greenwood shalt thou speed,
  As blithe as Queen of May."
Yet sung she, "Brignal banks are fair,
  And Greta woods are green;
I'd rather rove with Edmund there,
  Than reign our English queen.

"I read you, by your bugle-horn,
  And by your palfrey good,
I read you for a ranger sworn
  To keep the king's greenwood."

436

"A ranger, lady, winds his horn,
  And 'tis at peep of light;
His blast is heard at merry morn,
  And mine at dead of night."
Yet sung she, "Brignal banks are fair,
  And Greta woods are gay;
I would I were with Edmund there,
  To reign his Queen of May!

"With burnished brand and musketoon,
  So gallantly you come,
I read you for a bold dragoon
  That lists the tuck of drum."
"I list no more the tuck of drum,
  No more the tumpet hear;
But when the beetle sounds his hum,
  My comrades take the spear.
And O! though Brignal banks be fair,
  And Greta woods be gay,
Yet mickle must the maiden dare
  Would reign my Queen of May!

"Maiden! a nameless life I lead,
  A nameless death I'll die;
The fiend, whose lantern lights the mead,
  Were better mate than I!
And when I'm with my comrades met
  Beneath the greenwood bough,
What once we were we all forget,
  Nor think what we are now.
Yet Brignal banks are fresh and fair,
  And Greta woods are green,
And you may gather garlands there
  Would grace a summer queen."

SONG

"A weary lot is thine, fair maid,
  A weary lot is thine!
To pull the thorn thy brow to braid,
  And press the rue for wine!

A lightsome eye, a soldier's mien,
 A feather of the blue,
A doublet of the Lincoln green,—
 No more of me you knew,
    My Love!
No more of me you knew.

"This morn is merry June, I trow,
 The rose is budding fain;
But she shall bloom in winter snow,
 Ere we two meet again."
He turned his charger as he spake,
 Upon the river shore,
He gave his bridle-reins a shake,
 Said, "Adieu for evermore,
    My Love!
And adieu for evermore."

       —Canto III.

THE LORD OF THE ISLES

Rushing, ten thousand horsemen came,
With spears in rest, and hearts on flame,
 That panted for the shock!
With blazing crests and banners spread,
And trumpet-clang and clamour dread,
The wide plain thunder'd to their tread,
 As far as Stirling rock.
Down! Down! in headlong overthrow,
Horsemen and horse, the foremost go,
 Wild floundering on the field!
The first are in destruction's gorge,
Their followers wildly o'er them urge:—
The knightly helm and shield,
The mail, the acton, and the spear,
Strong hand, high heart, are useless here!
Loud from the mass confused the cry
Of dying warriors swells on high,
And steeds that shriek in agony!

438

They came like mountain-torrent red,
That thunders o'er its rocky bed;
They broke like that same torrent's wave,
When swallowed by a darksome cave.
Billows on billows burst and boil,
Maintaining still the stern turmoil,
And to their wild and tortured groan
Each adds new terrors of his own!

—CANTO VI.

JOCK OF HAZELDEAN

"Why weep ye by the tide, ladie?
    Why weep ye by the tide?
I'll wed ye to my youngest son,
    And ye sall be his bride;
And ye sall be his bride, ladie,
    Sae comely to be seen"—
But aye she loot the tears down fa'
    For Jock of Hazeldean.

"Now let this wilfu' grief be done,
    And dry that cheek so pale;
Young Frank is chief of Errington,
    And lord of Langley-dale;
His step is first in peaceful ha',
    His sword in battle keen"—
But aye she loot the tears down fa'
    For Jock of Hazeldean.

"A chain of gold ye sall not lack,
    Nor braid to bind your hair;
Nor mettled hound, nor managed hawk,
    Nor palfrey fresh and fair;
And you, the foremost o' them a',
    Shall ride our forest queen"—
But aye she loot the tears down fa'
    For Jock of Hazeldean.

439

The kirk was decked at morning-tide,
    The tapers glimmered fair;
The priest and bridegroom wait the bride,
    And dame and knight are there.
They sought her baith by bower and ha';
    The ladie was not seen!
She's o'er the Border, and awa'
    Wi' Jock of Hazeldean.
                    —GUY MANNERING.

TIME

"Why sit'st thou by that ruined hall,
    Thou aged carle so stern and grey?
Dost thou its former pride recall,
    Or ponder how it passed away?"

"Know'st thou not me?" the Deep Voice cried:
    "So long enjoyed, so oft misused—
Alternate, in thy fickle pride,
    Desired, neglected, and accused!

"Before my breath, like blazing flax,
    Man and his marvels pass away!
And changing empires wane and wax,
    Are founded, flourish, and decay.

"Redeem mine hours—the space is brief—
    While in my glass the sand-grains shiver,
And measureless thy joy or grief,
    When Time and thou shalt part forever!"
                    —THE ANTIQUARY

440

SIR WALTER SCOTT

OLD MORTALITY

. . . .

Sound, sound the clarion, fill the fife!
To all the sensual world proclaim,
One crowded hour of glorious life
Is worth an age without a name

. . . .

The sun upon the Weirdlaw Hill
In Ettrick's vale is sinking sweet;
The westland wind is hush and still,
The lake lies sleeping at my feet.
Yet not the landscape to mine eye
Bears those bright hues that once it bore,
Though evening with her richest dye
Flames o'er the hills of Ettrick's shore.

With listless look along the plain
I see Tweed's silver current glide,
And coldly mark the holy fane
Of Melrose rise in ruined pride.
The quiet lake, the balmy air,
The hill, the stream, the tower, the tree—
Are they still such as once they were,
Or is the dreary change in me?

Alas! the warped and broken board,
How can it bear the painter's dye?
The harp of strained and tuneless chord,
How to the minstrel's skill reply?
To aching eyes each landscape lowers,
To feverish pulse each gale blows chill;
And Araby's or Eden's bowers
Were barren as this moorland hill.

. . . .

PROUD MAISIE

Proud Maisie is in the wood,
  Walking so early;
Sweet Robin sits on the bush,
  Singing so rarely.

"Tell me, thou bonny bird,
  When shall I marry me?"
"When six braw gentlemen
  Kirkward shall carry ye."

"Who makes the bridal bed,
  Birdie, say truly?"
"The grey-headed sexton
  That delves the grave duly."

"The glow-worm o'er grave and stone
  Shall light thee steady.
The owl from the steeple sing
  'Welcome, proud lady.' "
                    —THE HEART OF MIDLOTHIAN.

CLAUD HALCRO'S SONG

Farewell to Northmaven,
  Grey Hillswicke, farewell!
To the calms of thy haven,
  The storms on thy fell—
To each breeze that can vary
  The mood of thy main,
And to thee, bonny Mary!
  We meet not again!

Farewell the wild ferry,
  Which Hacon could brave,
When the peaks of the Skerry
  Were white in the wave.

SIR WALTER SCOTT

There's a maid may look over
   These wild waves in vain,—
For the skiff of her lover—
   He comes not again!

The vows thou hast broke,
   On the wild currents fling them;
On the quicksand and rock
   Let the mermaidens sing them.
New sweetness they'll give her
   Bewildering strain;
But there's one who will never
   Believe them again.

O were there an island,
   Though ever so wild,
Where woman could smile, and
   No man be beguiled—
Too tempting a snare
   To poor mortals were given;
And the hope would fix there,
   That should anchor in heaven.
                —The Pirate

ONE HOUR WITH THEE

An hour with thee!—When earliest day
Dapples with gold the eastern grey,
Oh, what can frame my mind to bear
The toil and turmoil, cark and care,
New griefs, which coming hours unfold,
And sad remembrance of the old?
           One hour with thee!

One hour with thee!—When burning June
Waves his red flag at pitch of noon;
What shall repay the faithful swain,
His labour on the sultry plain;
And more than cave or sheltering bough,
Cool feverish blood, and throbbing brow?—
           One hour with thee!

443

One hour with thee!—When sun is set,
O, what can teach me to forget
The thankless labours of the day;
The hopes, the wishes, flung away;
The increasing wants and lessening gains,
The master's pride, who scorns my pains?—
One hour with thee!

—WOODSTOCK.

REBECCA'S HYMN

When Israel, of the Lord beloved,
    Out from the land of bondage came,
Her fathers' God before her moved,
    An awful guide in smoke and flame.
By day, along the astonished lands
    The cloudy pillar glided slow;
By night, Arabia's crimsoned sands
    Returned the fiery column's glow.

There rose the choral hymn of praise,
    And trump and timbrel answered keen,
And Zion's daughters poured their lays
    With priest's and warrior's voice between.
No portents now our foes amaze,
    Forsaken Israel wanders lone:
Our fathers would not know Thy ways,
    And Thou hast left them to their own.

But present still, though now unseen!
    When brightly shines the prosperous day,
Be thoughts of Thee a cloudy screen
    To temper the deceitful ray.
And oh, when stoops on Judah's path
    In shade and storm the frequent night,
Be Thou, long-suffering, slow to wrath,
    A burning and a shining light!

Our harps we left by Babel's streams,
    The tyrant's jest, the Gentile's scorn;
No censer round our altar beams,
    And mute are timbrel, harp, and horn.

444

But Thou hast said, The blood of goat,
  The flesh of rams I will not prize;
A contrite heart, a humble thought,
  Are Mine accepted sacrifice.

—IVANHOE.

James Montgomery

PRAYER

Prayer is the soul's sincere desire,
  Uttered or unexpressed;
The motion of a hidden fire,
  That trembles in the breast.

Prayer is the burden of a sigh;
  The falling of a tear;
The upward glancing of an eye,
  When none but God is near.

Prayer is the simplest form of speech
  That infant lips can try;
Prayer, the sublimest strains that reach
  The Majesty on high.

THE FALLING LEAF

Were I a trembling leaf
  On yonder stately tree,
After a season gay and brief,
  Condemned to fade and flee;

I should be loath to fall
  Beside the common way,
Weltering in mire, and spurned by all,
  Till trodden down to clay.

445

Nor would I like to spread
My thin and withered face
In hortus siccus, pale and dead,
A mummy of my race.

No—on the wings of air
Might I be left to fly,
I know not and I heed not where,
A waif of earth and sky!

Samuel Taylor Coleridge

SONG OF THE PIXIES

.   .   .   .

Hence! thou lingerer, light!
Eve saddens into night.
Mother of wildly-working dreams! we view
The sombre hours, that round thee stand
With down-cast eyes (a duteous band!)
Their dark robes dripping with the heavy dew.
Sorceress of the ebon throne!
Thy power the Pixies own,
When round thy raven brow
Heaven's lucent roses glow,
And clouds, in wat'ry colours drest,
Float in light drapery o'er thy sable vest;
What time the pale moon sheds a softer day,
Mellowing the woods beneath its pensive beam:
For mid the quiv'ring light 'tis ours to play,
Aye dancing to the cadence of the stream.

.   .   .   .

REFLECTIONS ON HAVING LEFT A PLACE OF RETIREMENT

Low was our pretty Cot: our tallest rose
Peeped at the chamber-window. We could hear

At silent noon, and eve, and early morn,
The sea's faint murmur. In the open air
Our myrtles blossom'd; and across the porch
Thick jasmines twined: the little landscape round
Was green and woody, and refreshed the eye.
It was a spot which you might aptly call
The Valley of Seclusion! Once I saw
(Hallowing his Sabbath-day by quietness)
A wealthy son of commerce saunter by,
Bristowa's citizen: methought, it calmed
His thirst of idle gold, and made him muse
With wiser feelings: for he paused, and looked
With a pleased sadness, and gazed all around,
Then eyed our Cottage, and gazed round again,
And sighed, and said, it was a Blessed Place.
And we *were* blessed. Oft with patient ear
Long-listening to the viewless sky-lark's note
(Viewless, or haply for a moment seen
Gleaming on sunny wings) in whispered tones
I've said to my beloved, "Such, sweet girl!
The inobtrusive song of Happiness,
Unearthly minstrelsy! then only heard
When the soul seeks to hear; when all is hushed,
And the heart listens!"
But the time, when first
From that low dell, steep up the stony mount
I climbed with perilous toil and reached the top,
Oh! what a goodly scene! *Here* the bleak mount,
The bare bleak mountain speckled thin with sheep;
Grey clouds, that shadowing spot the sunny fields:
And river, now with bushy rocks o'er browed,
Now winding bright and full, with naked banks;
And seats, and lawns, the abbey and the wood,
And cots, and hamlets, and faint city-spire;
The Channel *there*, the Islands and white sails,
Dim coasts, and cloud-like hills and shoreless Ocean—
It seem'd like Omnipresence! God, methought,
Had built him there a Temple: the whole World
Seemed imaged in its vast circumference:
No *wish* profaned my overwhelmed heart.
Blest hour! It was a luxury,—to be!

447

Ah! quiet dell! dear cot, and mount sublime!
I was constrained to quit you. Was it right,
While my unnumbered brethren toiled and bled,
That I should dream away the entrusted hours
On rose-leaf beds, pampering the coward heart
With feelings all too delicate for use?
Sweet is the tear that from some Howard's eye
Drops on the cheek of one he lifts from earth:
And he that works me good with unmoved face,
Does it but half: he chills me while he aids
My benefactor, not my brother man!
Yet even this, this cold beneficence
Praise, praise it, O my Soul! oft as thou scann'st
The sluggard Pity's vision-weaving tribe!
Who sigh for wretchedness, yet shun the wretched,
Nursing in some delicious solitude
Their slothful loves and dainty sympathies!
I therefore go, and join head, heart, and hand,
Active and firm, to fight the bloodless fight
Of science, freedom, and the truth in Christ.

Yet oft when after honourable toil
Rests the tired mind, and waking loves to dream,
My spirit shall revisit thee, dear Cot!
Thy jasmine and thy window-peeping rose,
And myrtles fearless of the mild sea-air.
And I shall sigh fond wishes—sweet abode!
Ah!—had none greater! And that all had such!
It might be so—but the time is not yet.
Speed it, O Father! Let thy Kingdom come!

TIME, REAL AND IMAGINARY

On the wide level of a mountain's head,
(I knew not where, but 'twas some faery place)
Their pinions, ostrich-like, for sails outspread,
Two lovely children run an endless race,
    A sister and a brother!
      That far outstripp'd the other;

448

Yet ever runs she with reverted face,
And looks and listens for the boy behind:
   For he, alas! is blind!
O'er rough and smooth with even step he pass'd,
And knows not whether he be first or last.

THE RIME OF THE ANCIENT MARINER

PART I

It is an ancient Mariner,
And he stoppeth one of three.
"By thy long grey beard and glittering eye,
Now wherefore stopp'st thou me?

"The Bridegroom's doors are opened wide,
And I am next of kin;
The guests are met, the feast is set:
May'st hear the merry din."

He holds him with his skinny hand,
"There was a ship," quoth he.
"Hold off! unhand me, grey-beard loon!"
Eftsoons his hand dropped he.

He holds him with his glittering eye—
The Wedding-Guest stood still,
And listens like a three years' child:
The Mariner hath his will.

The Wedding-Guest sat on a stone:
He cannot choose but hear;
And thus spake on that ancient man,
The bright-eyed Mariner.

"The ship was cheered, the harbour cleared,
Merrily did we drop
Below the kirk, below the hill,
Below the lighthouse top.

"The Sun came up upon the left,
Out of the sea came he!
And he shone bright, and on the right
Went down into the sea.

"Higher and higher every day,
Till over the mast at noon—"
The Wedding-Guest here beat his breast,
For he heard the loud bassoon.

The bride hath paced into the hall,
Red as a rose is she;
Nodding their heads before her goes
The merry minstrelsy.

The Wedding-Guest he beat his breast,
Yet he cannot choose but hear;
And thus spake on that ancient man,
The bright-eyed Mariner.

"And now the Storm-blast came, and he
Was tyrannous and strong:
He struck with his o'ertaking wings,
And chased us south along.

"With sloping masts and dipping prow,
As who pursued with yell and blow
Still treads the shadow of his foe,
And forward bends his head,
The ship drove fast, loud roared the blast,
And southward aye we fled.

"And now there came both mist and snow,
And it grew wondrous cold:
And ice, mast-high, came floating by,
As green as emerald.

"And through the drifts the snowy clifts
Did send a dismal sheen:
Nor shapes of men, nor beasts we ken—
The ice was all between.

450

SAMUEL TAYLOR COLERIDGE

"The ice was here, the ice was there,
The ice was all around:
It cracked and growled, and roared and howled,
Like noises in a swound!

"At length did cross an Albatross,
Through the fog it came;
As if it had been a Christian soul,
We hailed it in God's name.

"It ate the food it ne'er had eat,
And round and round it flew.
The ice did split with a thunder-fit;
The helmsman steered us through!

"And a good south wind sprung up behind;
The Albatross did follow,
And every day, for food or play,
Came to the mariners' hollo!

"In mist or cloud, on mast or shroud,
It perched for vespers nine;
Whiles all the night, through fog-smoke white,
Glimmered the white moonshine."

"God save thee, ancient Mariner,
From the fiends, that plague thee thus!—
Why look'st thou so?" "With my crossbow
I shot the Albatross.

PART II

"The Sun now rose upon the right:
Out of the sea came he,
Still hid in mist, and on the left
Went down into the sea.

"And the good south wind still blew behind,
But no sweet bird did follow,
Nor any day for food or play
Came to the mariners' hollo!

451

"And I had done a hellish thing,
And it would work 'em woe:
For all averred I had killed the bird
That made the breeze to blow.
Ah wretch! said they, the bird to slay,
That made the breeze to blow!

"Nor dim nor red, like God's own head,
The glorious Sun uprist:
Then all averred I had killed the bird
That brought the fog and mist.
'Twas right, said they, such birds to slay,
That bring the fog and mist.

"The fair breeze blew, the white foam flew,
The furrow followed free;
We were the first that ever burst
Into that silent sea.

"Down dropped the breeze, the sails dropped down,
'Twas sad as sad could be;
And we did speak only to break
The silence of the sea!

"All in a hot and copper sky,
The bloody Sun, at noon,
Right up above the mast did stand,
No bigger than the Moon.

"Day after day, day after day,
We stuck, nor breath nor motion;
As idle as a painted ship
Upon a painted ocean.

"The very deep did rot: O Christ!
That ever this should be!
Yea, slimy things did crawl with legs
Upon the slimy sea.

"About, about, in reel and rout
The death-fires danced at night;
The water, like a witch's oils,
Burnt green, and blue, and white.

"And some in dreams assurèd were
Of the Spirit that plagued us so;
Nine fathom deep he had followed us
From the land of mist and snow.

"And every tongue, through utter drought,
Was withered at the root;
We could not speak, no more than if
We had been choked with soot.

"Ah! well-a-day! what evil looks
Had I from old and young!
Instead of the cross, the Albatross
About my neck was hung.

PART III

"There passed a weary time. Each throat
Was parched, and glazed each eye.
A weary time! a weary time!
How glazed each weary eye!
When looking westward, I beheld
A something in the sky.

"At first it seemed a little speck,
And then it seemed a mist;
It moved and moved, and took at last
A certain shape, I wist.

"A speck, a mist, a shape, I wist!
And still it neared and neared:
As if it dodged a water-sprite,
It plunged, and tacked, and veered.

"With throats unslaked, with black lips baked,
We could nor laugh nor wail;
Through utter drought all dumb we stood!
I bit my arm, I sucked the blood,
And cried, A sail! a sail!

"With throats unslaked, with black lips baked,
Agape they heard me call:
Gramercy! they for joy did grin,
And all at once their breath drew in,
As they were drinking all.

"See! see! (I cried) she tacks no more
Hither to work us weal—
Without a breeze, without a tide,
She steadies with upright keel!

"The western wave was all aflame,
The day was wellnigh done!
Almost upon the western wave
Rested the broad, bright Sun;
When that strange shape drove suddenly
Betwixt us and the Sun.

"And straight the Sun was flecked with bars
(Heaven's Mother send us grace!),
As if through a dungeon-grate he peered
With broad and burning face.

"Alas! (thought I, and my heart beat loud)
How fast she nears and nears!
Are those her sails that glance in the Sun,
Like restless gossameres?

"Are those her ribs through which the Sun
Did peer, as through a grate?
And is that Woman all her crew?
Is that a Death? and are there two?
Is Death that Woman's mate?

"Her lips were red, her looks were free,
Her locks were yellow as gold:
Her skin was as white as leprosy,
The Nightmare Life-in-Death was she,
Who thicks man's blood with cold.

454

"The naked hulk alongside came,
And the twain were casting dice;
'The game is done! I've won! I've won!'
Quoth she, and whistles thrice.

"The Sun's rim dips; the stars rush out
At one stride comes the dark;
With far-heard whisper, o'er the sea,
Off shot the spectre-bark.

"We listened and looked sideways up!
Fear at my heart, as at a cup,
My life-blood seemed to sip!
The stars were dim, and thick the night,
The steersman's face by his lamp gleamed white;
From the sails the dew did drip—
Till clomb above the eastern bar
The hornèd Moon, with one bright star
Within the nether tip.

"One after one, by the star-dogged Moon,
Too quick for groan or sigh,
Each turned his face with a ghastly pang,
And cursed me with his eye.

"Four times fifty living men
(And I heard nor sigh nor groan),
With heavy thump, a lifeless lump,
They dropped down one by one.

"The souls did from their bodies fly—
They fled to bliss or woe!
And every soul, it passed me by
Like the whizz of my crossbow!"

PART IV

"I fear thee, ancient Mariner!
I fear thy skinny hand!
And thou art long, and lank, and brown,
As is the ribbed sea-sand.

455

"I fear thee and thy glittering eye,
And thy skinny hand so brown."—
"Fear not, fear not, thou Wedding-Guest!
This body dropped not down.

"Alone, alone, all, all alone,
Alone on a wide, wide sea!
And never a saint took pity on
My soul in agony.

"The many men, so beautiful!
And they all dead did lie:
And a thousand thousand slimy things
Lived on; and so did I.

"I looked upon the rotting sea,
And drew my eyes away;
I looked upon the rotting deck,
And there the dead men lay.

"I looked to heaven, and tried to pray;
But or ever a prayer had gushed,
A wicked whisper came, and made
My heart as dry as dust.

"I closed my lids, and kept them close,
And the balls like pulses beat;
For the sky and the sea, and the sea and the sky,
Lay like a load on my weary eye,
And the dead were at my feet.

"The cold sweat melted from their limbs,
Nor rot nor reek did they:
The look with which they looked on me
Had never passed away.

"An orphan's curse would drag to hell
A spirit from on high;
But oh! more horrible than that
Is a curse in a dead man's eye!
Seven days, seven nights, I saw that curse,
And yet I could not die.

SAMUEL TAYLOR COLERIDGE

"The moving Moon went up the sky,
And nowhere did abide;
Softly she was going up,
And a star or two beside—

"Her beams bemocked the sultry main,
Like April hoar-frost spread;
But where the ship's huge shadow lay,
The charmèd water burnt alway
A still and awful red.

"Beyond the shadow of the ship,
I watched the water-snakes:
They moved in tracks of shining white,
And when they reared, the elfish light
Fell off in hoary flakes.

"Within the shadow of the ship
I watched their rich attire:
Blue, glossy green, and velvet black,
They coiled and swam; and every track
Was a flash of golden fire.

"O happy living things! no tongue
Their beauty might declare:
A spring of love gushed from my heart,
And I blessed them unaware:
Sure my kind saint took pity on me,
And I blessed them unaware.

"The selfsame moment I could pray;
And from my neck so free
The Albatross fell off, and sank
Like lead into the sea.

PART V

"O sleep! it is a gentle thing,
Beloved from pole to pole!
To Mary Queen the praise be given!
She sent the gentle sleep from Heaven,
That slid into my soul.

"The silly buckets on the deck,
That had so long remained,
I dreamt that they were filled with dew;
And when I awoke, it rained.

"My lips were wet, my throat was cold,
My garments all were dank;
Sure I had drunken in my dreams,
And still my body drank.

"I moved, and could not feel my limbs:
I was so light—almost
I thought that I had died in sleep,
And was a blessed ghost.

"And soon I heard a roaring wind:
It did not come anear;
But with its sound it shook the sails,
That were so thin and sere.

"The upper air burst into life;
And a hundred fire-flags sheen;
To and fro they were hurried about;
And to and fro, and in and out,
The wan stars danced between.

"And the coming wind did roar more loud,
And the sails did sigh like sedge;
And the rain poured down from one black cloud;
The Moon was at its edge.

"The thick black cloud was cleft, and still
The Moon was at its side;
Like waters shot from some high crag,
The lightning fell with never a jag,
A river steep and wide.

"The loud wind never reached the ship,
Yet now the ship moved on!
Beneath the lightning and the Moon
The dead men gave a groan.

"They groaned, they stirred, they all uprose,
Nor spake, nor moved their eyes;
It had been strange, even in a dream,
To have seen those dead men rise.

"The helmsman steered, the ship moved on;
Yet never a breeze up-blew;
The mariners all 'gan work the ropes,
Where they were wont to do;
They raised their limbs like lifeless tools—
We were a ghastly crew.

"The body of my brother's son
Stood by me, knee to knee:
The body and I pulled at one rope,
But he said naught to me."

"I fear thee, ancient Mariner!"
"Be calm, thou Wedding-Guest:
'Twas not those souls that fled in pain,
Which to their corses came again,
But a troop of spirits blest:

"For when it dawned—they dropped their arms,
And clustered round the mast;
Sweet sounds rose slowly through their mouths,
And from their bodies passed.

"Around, around, flew each sweet sound,
Then darted to the Sun;
Slowly the sounds came back again,
Now mixed, now one by one.

"Sometimes a-dropping from the sky
I heard the skylark sing;
Sometimes all little birds that are,
How they seemed to fill the sea and air
With their sweet jargoning!

"And now 'twas like all instruments,
Now like a lonely flute;
And now it is an angel's song,
That makes the Heavens be mute.

459

"It ceased: yet still the sails made on
A pleasant noise till noon,
A noise like of a hidden brook
In the leafy month of June,
That to the sleeping woods all night
Singeth a quiet tune.

"Till noon we quietly sailed on,
Yet never a breeze did breathe:
Slowly and smoothly went the ship,
Moved onward from beneath.

"Under the keel nine fathom deep,
From the land of mist and snow
The Spirit slid: and it was he
That made the ship to go.
The sails at noon left off their tune,
And the ship stood still also.

"The Sun, right up above the mast,
Had fixed her to the ocean:
But in a minute she 'gan stir,
With a short uneasy motion—
Backwards and forwards half her length
With a short uneasy motion.

"Then like a pawing horse let go,
She made a sudden bound:
It flung the blood into my head,
And I fell down in a swound.

"How long in that same fit I lay,
I have not to declare;
But ere my living life returned,
I heard, and in my soul discerned
Two voices in the air.

" 'Is it he?' quoth one, 'is this the man?
By Him who died on cross,
With his cruel bow he laid full low
The harmless Albatross.

" 'The Spirit who bideth by himself
In the land of mist and snow,
He loved the bird that loved the man
Who shot him with his bow.'

"The other was a softer voice,
As soft as honey-dew:
Quoth he, 'The man hath penance done,
And penance more will do.'

PART VI

First Voice:
" 'But tell me, tell me! speak again,
What makes that ship drive on so fast?
Thy soft response renewing—
What is the Ocean doing?'

Second Voice:
" 'Still as a slave before his lord,
The Ocean hath no blast;
His great bright eye most silently
Up to the Moon is cast—

" 'If he may know which way to go;
For she guides him smooth or grim.
See, brother, see! how graciously
She looketh down on him.'

First Voice:
" 'But why drives on that ship so fast,
Without or wave or wind?'

Second Voice:
" 'The air is cut away before,
And closes from behind.

" 'Fly, brother, fly! more high, more high!
Or we shall be belated:
For slow and slow that ship will go;
When the Mariner's trance is abated.'

461

"I woke, and we were sailing on
As in a gentle weather:
'Twas night, calm night, the Moon was high;
The dead men stood together.

"All stood together on the deck,
For a charnel-dungeon fitter:
All fixed on me their stony eyes,
That in the Moon did glitter.

"The pang, the curse, with which they died,
Had never passed away:
I could not draw my eyes from theirs,
Nor turn them up to pray.

"And now this spell was snapped: once more
I viewed the ocean green,
And looked far forth, yet little saw
Of what had else been seen—

"Like one that on a lonesome road
Doth walk in fear and dread,
And having once turned round, walks on,
And turns no more his head;
Because he knows a frightful fiend
Doth close behind him tread.

"But soon there breathed a wind on me,
Nor sound nor motion made:
Its path was not upon the sea,
In ripple or in shade.

"It raised my hair, it fanned my cheek
Like a meadow-gale of spring—
It mingled strangely with my fears,
Yet it felt like a welcoming.

"Swiftly, swiftly flew the ship,
Yet she sailed softly too:
Sweetly, sweetly blew the breeze—
On me alone it blew.

462

"O dream of joy! is this indeed
The lighthouse top I see
Is this the hill? is this the kirk?
Is this mine own countree?

"We drifted o'er the harbour-bar,
And I with sobs did pray—
O let me be awake, my God!
Or let me sleep alway.

"The harbour-bay was clear as glass,
So smoothly it was strewn!
And on the bay the moonlight lay,
And the shadow of the Moon.

"The rock shone bright, the kirk no less,
That stands above the rock:
The moonlight steeped in silentness
The steady weathercock.

"And the bay was white with silent light
Till rising from the same,
Full many shapes, that shadows were,
In crimson colours came.

"A little distance from the prow
Those crimson shadows were;
I turned my eyes upon the deck—
O Christ! what saw I there!

"Each corse lay flat, lifeless and flat,
And, by the holy rood!
A man all light, a seraph-man,
On every corse there stood.

"This seraph-band, each waved his hand:
It was a heavenly sight!
They stood as signals to the land,
Each one a lovely light;

463

"This seraph-band, each waved his hand,
No voice did they impart—
No voice; but O, the silence sank
Like music on my heart.

"But soon I heard the dash of oars,
I heard the Pilot's cheer;
My head was turned perforce away,
And I saw a boat appear.

"The Pilot and the Pilot's boy,
I heard them coming fast:
Dear Lord in Heaven! it was a joy
The dead men could not blast.

"I saw a third—I heard his voice:
It is the Hermit good!
He singeth loud his godly hymns
That he makes in the wood.
He'll shrive my soul, he'll wash away
The Albatross's blood.

PART VII

"This Hermit good lives in that wood
Which slopes down to the sea.
How loudly his sweet voice he rears!
He loves to talk with marineres
That come from a far countree.

"He kneels at morn, and noon, and eve—
He hath a cushion plump:
It is the moss that wholly hides
The rotted old oak-stump.

"The skiff-boat neared: I heard them talk,
'Why, this is strange, I trow!
Where are those lights so many and fair,
That signal made but now?'

464

" 'Strange, by my faith!' the Hermit said—
'And they answered not our cheer!
The planks look warped! and see those sails,
How thin they are and sere!
I never saw aught like to them,
Unless perchance it were

" 'Brown skeletons of leaves that lag
My forest-brook along;
When the ivy-tod is heavy with snow,
And the owlet whoops to the wolf below,
That eats the she-wolf's young.'

" 'Dear Lord! it hath a fiendish look—
(The Pilot made reply)
I am a-feared.'—'Push on, push on!'
Said the Hermit cheerily.

"The boat came closer to the ship,
But I nor spake nor stirred;
The boat came close beneath the ship,
And straight a sound was heard.

"Under the water it rumbled on,
Still louder and more dread:
It reached the ship, it split the bay;
The ship went down like lead.

"Stunned by that loud and dreadful sound,
Which sky and ocean smote,
Like one that hath been seven days drowned
My body lay afloat;
But swift as dreams, myself I found
Within the Pilot's boat.

"Upon the whirl, where sank the ship,
The boat spun round and round;
And all was still, save that the hill
Was telling of the sound.

"I moved my lips—the Pilot shrieked
And fell down in a fit;
The holy Hermit raised his eyes,
And prayed where he did sit.

"I took the oars: the Pilot's boy,
Who now doth crazy go,
Laughed loud and long, and all the while
His eyes went to and fro.
'Ha! ha!' quoth he, 'full plain I see
The Devil knows how to row.'

"And now, all in my own countree,
I stood on the firm land!
The Hermit stepped forth from the boat,
And scarcely he could stand.

" 'O shrieve me, shrieve me, holy man!'
The Hermit crossed his brow,
'Say quick,' quoth he, 'I bid thee say—
What manner of man art thou?'

"Forthwith this frame of mind was wrenched
With a woeful agony,
Which forced me to begin my tale;
And then it left me free.

"Since then, at an uncertain hour,
That agony returns:
And till my ghastly tale is told,
This heart within me burns.

"I pass, like night, from land to land;
I have strange power of speech;
That moment that his face I see,
I know the man that must hear me:
To him my tale I teach.

"What loud uproar bursts from that door!
The wedding-guests are there:
But in the garden-bower the bride

And bride-maids singing are:
And hark, the little vesper bell,
Which biddeth me to prayer!

"O Wedding-Guest! this soul hath been
Alone on a wide, wide sea:
So lonely 'twas, that God Himself
Scarce seemèd there to be.

"O sweeter than the marriage-feast,
'Tis sweeter far to me,
To walk together to the kirk
With a goodly company!—

"To walk together to the kirk,
And all together pray,
While each to his great Father bends,
Old men, and babes, and loving friends,
And youths and maidens gay!

"Farewell, farewell! but this I tell
To thee, thou Wedding-Guest!
He prayeth well, who loveth well
Both man and bird and beast.

"He prayeth best, who loveth best
All things both great and small;
For the dear God, who loveth us,
He made and loveth all."

The Mariner, whose eye is bright,
Whose beard with age is hoar,
Is gone: and now the Wedding-Guest
Turned from the bridegroom's door.

He went like one that hath been stunned,
And is of sense forlorn:
A sadder and a wiser man
He rose the morrow morn.

CHRISTABEL

. . . . °

Alas! they had been friends in youth;
But whispering tongues can poison truth;
And constancy lives in realms above;
And life is thorny; and youth is vain;
And to be wroth with one we love,
Doth work like madness in the brain.
And thus it chanced, as I divine,
With Roland and Sir Leoline.
Each spake words of high disdain
And insult to his heart's best brother:
They parted—ne'er to meet again!
But never either found another
To free the hollow heart from paining—
They stood aloof, the scars remaining,
Like cliffs which had been rent asunder;
A dreary sea now flows between,
But neither heat, nor frost, nor thunder,
Shall wholly do away, I ween,
The marks of that which once hath been.

. . . .

LOVE

All thoughts, all passions, all delights,
Whatever stirs this mortal frame,
All are but ministers of Love,
    And feed his sacred flame.

Oft in my waking dreams do I
Live o'er again that happy hour,
When midway on the mount I lay,
    Beside the ruined tower.

The moonshine, stealing o'er the scene,
Had blended with the lights of eve;
And she was there, my hope, my joy,
    My own dear Genevieve!

She leaned against the armèd man,
The statue of the armèd Knight;
She stood and listened to my lay,
    Amid the lingering light.

Few sorrows hath she of her own,
My hope! my joy! my Genevieve!
She loves me best whene'er I sing
    The songs that make her grieve.

I played a soft and doleful air;
I sang an old and moving story—
An old rude song, that suited well
    That ruin wild and hoary.

She listened with a flitting blush,
With downcast eyes, and modest grace;
For well she knew I could not choose
    But gaze upon her face.

I told her of the Knight that wore
Upon his shield a burning brand;
And that for ten long years he wooed
    The Lady of the Land.

I told her how he pined: and ah!
The deep, the low, the pleading tone
With which I sang another's love,
    Interpreted my own.

She listened with a flitting blush,
With downcast eyes, and modest grace;
And she forgave me, that I gazed
    Too fondly on her face!

But when I told the cruel scorn
That crazed that bold and lovely Knight,
And that he crossed the mountain-woods,
    Nor rested day nor night;

That sometimes from the savage den,
And sometimes from the darksome shade,
And sometimes starting up at once
   In green and sunny glade—

There came and looked him in the face
An angel beautiful and bright;
And that he knew it was a Fiend,
   This miserable Knight!

And that, unknowing what he did,
He leaped amid a murderous band,
And saved from outrage worse than death
   The Lady of the Land;—

And how she wept and clasped his knees;
And how she tended him in vain—
And ever strove to expiate
   The scorn that crazed his brain;—

And that she nursed him in a cave;
And how his madness went away,
When on the yellow forest-leaves
   A dying man he lay;—

His dying words—but when I reached
That tenderest strain of all the ditty,
My faltering voice and pausing harp
   Disturbed her soul with pity!

All impulses of soul and sense
Had thrilled my guileless Genevieve;
The music and the doleful tale,
   The rich and balmy eve;

And hopes, and fears that kindle hope,
An undistinguishable throng,
And gentle wishes long subdued,
   Subdued and cherished long!

She wept with pity and delight,
She blushed with love and virgin-shame;
And like the murmur of a dream,
    I heard her breathe my name.

Her bosom heaved—she stepped aside,
As conscious of my look she stepped—
Then suddenly, with timorous eye
    She fled to me and wept.

She half enclosed me with her arms,
She pressed me with a meek embrace;
And bending back her head, looked up
    And gazed upon my face.

'Twas partly love, and partly fear,
And partly 'twas a bashful art,
That I might rather feel, than see,
    The swelling of her heart.

I calmed her fears, and she was calm,
And told her love with virgin pride;
And so I won my Genevieve,
    My bright and beauteous Bride.

KUBLA KHAN

In Xanadu did Kubla Khan
  A stately pleasure-dome decree:
Where Alph, the sacred river, ran
Through caverns measureless to man
  Down to a sunless sea.
So twice five miles of fertile ground
With walls and towers were girdled round:
And there were gardens bright with sinuous rills,
Where blossomed many an incense-bearing tree;
And here were forests ancient as the hills,
Enfolding sunny spots of greenery.

471

But O! that deep romantic chasm which slanted
Down the green hill athwart a cedarn cover!
A savage place! as holy and enchanted
As e'er beneath a waning moon was haunted
By woman wailing for her demon-lover!
And from this chasm, with ceaseless turmoil seething,
As if this Earth in fast thick pants were breathing,
A mighty fountain momently was forced,
Amid whose swift half-intermitted burst
Huge fragments vaulted like rebounding hail,
Or chaffy grain beneath the thresher's flail:
And 'mid these dancing rocks at once and ever
It flung up momently the sacred river.
Five miles meandering with a mazy motion
Through wood and dale the sacred river ran,
Then reached the caverns measureless to man,
And sank in tumult to a lifeless ocean:
And 'mid this tumult Kubla heard from far
Ancestral voices prophesying war!

    The shadow of the dome of pleasure
    Floated midway on the waves;
    Where was heard the mingled measure
    From the fountain and the caves.
It was a miracle of rare device,
A sunny pleasure-dome with caves of ice!

    A damsel with a dulcimer
    In a vision once I saw:
    It was an Abyssinian maid,
    And on her dulcimer she played,
    Singing of Mount Abora.
    Could I revive within me
    Her symphony and song,
    To such a deep delight 'twould win me
That with music loud and long,
I would build that dome in air,
That sunny dome! those caves of ice!
And all who heard should see them there,
And all should cry, Beware! Beware!
His flashing eyes, his floating hair!

472

Weave a circle roun'd him thrice,
And close your eyes with holy dread,
For he on honey-dew hath fed,
And drunk the milk of Paradise.

WORK WITHOUT HOPE

All Nature seems at work. Slugs leave their lair—
The bees are stirring—birds are on the wing—
And Winter, slumbering in the open air,
Wears on his smiling face a dream of Spring!
And I, the while, the sole unbusy thing,
Nor honey make, nor pair, nor build, nor sing.

Yet well I ken the banks where amaranths blow,
Have traced the fount whence streams of nectar flow.
Bloom, O ye amaranths! bloom for whom ye may,
For me ye bloom not! Glide, rich streams, away!
With lips unbrighten'd, wreathless brow, I stroll:
And would you learn the spells that drowse my soul?
Work without Hope draws nectar in a sieve,
And Hope without an object cannot live.

YOUTH AND AGE

Verse, a breeze 'mid blossoms straying,
    Where Hope clung feeding like a bee,—
Both were mine! Life went a-maying
    With Nature, Hope, and Poesy
                    When I was young!
When I was young?—Ah, woeful When!
Ah, for the change 'twixt Now and Then!
This breathing house not built with hands,
This body that does me grievous wrong,
O'er aery cliffs and glittering sands,
How lightly *then* it flashed along:—
Like those trim skiffs, unknown of yore,
On winding lakes and rivers wide,
That ask no aid of sail or oar,
That fear no spite of wind or tide!

473

Naught cared this body for wind or weather
When Youth and I lived in't together.

Flowers are lovely; Love is flower-like;
Friendship is a sheltering tree;
Oh! the joys that came down shower-like,
Of Friendship, Love, and Liberty
                      Ere I was old!
Ere I was old? Ah, woeful Ere,
Which tells me, Youth's no longer here!
O Youth! for years so many and sweet,
'Tis known that Thou and I were one.
I'll think it but a fond conceit—
It cannot be that Thou art gone!
Thy vesper-bell hath not yet tolled:—
And thou wert aye a masker bold!
What strange disguise hast now put on
To *make believe* that thou art gone?
I see these locks in silvery slips,
This drooping gait, this altered size:
But Springtide blossoms on thy lips,
And tears take sunshine from thine eyes!
Life is but thought: so think I will
That Youth and I are house-mates still.

Dewdrops are the gems of morning,
But the tears of mournful eve!
Where no hope is, life's a warning
That only serves to make us grieve
                   When we are old:
That only serves to make us grieve
With oft and tedious taking-leave,
Like some poor nigh-related guest,
That may not rudely be dismissed,
Yet hath outstayed his welcome while,
And tells the jest without the smile.

ROBERT SOUTHEY

FANCY IN NUBIBUS

O, it is pleasant, with a heart at ease,
Just after sunset, or by moonlight skies,
To make the shifting clouds be what you please,
Or let the easily persuaded eyes
Own each quaint likeness issuing from the mould
Of a friend's fancy; or, with head bent low,
And cheek aslant, see rivers flow of gold,
'Twixt crimson banks; and then a traveller go
From mount to mount, through Cloudland, gorgeous land!
Or, listening to the tide with closèd sight,
Be that blind Bard, who on the Chian strand,
By those deep sounds possessed with inward light,
Beheld the Iliad and the Odyssey,
Rise to the swelling of the voiceful sea.

Robert Southey

MY DAYS AMONG THE DEAD ARE PASSED

My days among the Dead are passed,
  Around me I behold,
Where'er these casual eyes are cast,
  The mighty minds of old:
My never-failing friends are they,
With whom I converse day by day.

With them I take delight in weal,
  And seek relief in woe;
And while I understand and feel
  How much to them I owe,
My cheeks have often been bedewed
With tears of thoughtful gratitude.

My thoughts are with the Dead; with them
  I live in long-past years,
Their virtues love, their faults condemn,
  Partake their hopes and fears;

And from their lessons seek and find
Instruction with an humble mind.

My hopes are with the Dead; anon
  My place with them will be,
And I with them shall travel on
  Through all Futurity;
Yet leaving here a name, I trust,
That will not perish in the dust.

THALABA

.   .   .   .

  How beautiful is night!
A dewy freshness fills the silent air;
No mist obscures, nor cloud, nor speck, nor stain,
  Breaks the serene of heaven;
In full-orbed glory yonder moon divine
  Rolls through the dark blue depths.
    Beneath her steady ray
    The desert-circle spreads,
Like the round ocean, girdled with the sky.
  How beautiful is night!

.   .   .   .

THE CURSE OF KEHAMA

.   .   .   .

They sin who tell us Love can die.
With life all other passions fly,
  All others are but vanity.
In Heaven Ambition cannot dwell,
Nor Avarice in the vaults of Hell;
Earthly these passions of the Earth,
They perish where they have their birth;
  But Love is indestructible.
Its holy flame for ever burneth,
From Heaven it came, to Heaven returneth;
Too oft on Earth a troubled guest,
At times deceived, at times opprest,

476

It here is tried and purified,
Then hath in Heaven its perfect rest;
It soweth here with toil and care
But the harvest time of Love is there.

Walter Savage Landor

IN MEMORY OF WALTER SAVAGE LANDOR

Back to the flower-town, side by side,
    The bright months bring,
New-born, the bridegroom and the bride,
    Freedom and spring.

The sweet land laughs from sea to sea,
    Filled full of sun;
All things come back to her, being free;
    All things but one.

In many a tender wheaten plot
    Flowers that were dead
Live, and old suns revive; but not
    That holier head.

By this white wandering waste of sea,
    Far north, I hear
One face shall never turn to me
    As once this year:

Shall never smile and turn and rest
    On mine as there,
Nor one most sacred hand be pressed
    Upon my hair.

I came as one whose thoughts half linger,
    Half run before;
The youngest to the eldest singer
    That England bore.

477

I found him whom I shall not find
  Till all grief end,
In holiest age our mightiest mind,
  Father and friend.

But thou, if anything endure,
  If hope there be,
O spirit that man's life left pure,
  Man's death set free,

Not with disdain of days that were
  Look earthward now;
Let dreams revive the reverend hair,
  The imperial brow;

Come back in sleep, for in the life
  Where thou art not
We find none like thee. Time and strife
  And the world's lot

Move thee no more; but love at least
  And reverent heart
May move thee, royal and released
  Soul, as thou art.

And thou, his Florence, to thy trust
  Receive and keep,
Keep safe his dedicated dust,
  His sacred sleep.

So shall thy lovers, come from far,
  Mix with thy name
As morning-star with evening-star
  His faultless fame.
            —ALGERNON CHARLES SWINBURNE

DEATH

Death stands above me, whispering low
  I know not what into my ear;
Of his strange language all I know
  Is, there is not a word of fear.

WALTER SAVAGE LANDOR

TWENTY YEARS HENCE

Twenty years hence my eyes may grow,
If not quite dim, yet rather so,
Yet yours from others they shall know
                Twenty years hence.

Twenty years hence, tho' it may hap
That I be call'd to take a nap
In a cool cell where thunder clap
                Was never heard,

There breathe but o'er my arch of grass
A not too-sadly sigh'd *Alas;*
And I shall catch, ere you can pass,
                That winged word.

ROSES AND THORNS

Why do our joys depart
For cares to seize the heart?
I know not. Nature says,
Obey; and man obeys,
I see, and know not why
Thorns live and roses die.

SYMPATHY

The maid I love ne'er thought of me
Amid the scenes of gaiety;
But when her heart or mine sank low,
Ah, then it was no longer so.

From the slant palm she raised her head,
And kiss'd the cheek whence youth had fled,
Angels! some future day for this,
Give her as sweet and pure a kiss.

THE ONE GREY HAIR

The wisest of the wise
Listen to pretty lies,
    And love to hear them told;
Doubt not that Solomon
Listened to many a one,—
Some in his youth, and more when he grew old.

I never sat among
The choir of Wisdom's song,
    But pretty lies loved I
As much as any king,—
When youth was on the wing,
And (must it then be told?) when youth had quite gone by

Alas! and I have not
The pleasant hour forgot,
    When one pert lady said,—
"O Landor! I am quite
Bewildered with affright;
I see (sit quiet now!) a white hair on your head!"

Another, more benign,
Drew out that hair of mine,
    And in her own dark hair
Pretended she had found
That one, and twirled it round.—
Fair as she was, she never was so fair.

ROSE AYLMER

Ah, what avails the sceptred race,
    Ah, what the form divine!
What every virtue, every grace!
    Rose Aylmer, all were thine.

Rose Aylmer, whom these wakeful eyes
    May weep, but never see,
A night of memories and of sighs
    I consecrate to thee.

480

WALTER SAVAGE LANDOR

SEPARATION

There is a mountain and a wood between us,
   Where the lone shepherd and late bird have seen us
Morning and noon and eventide repass.
Between us now the mountain and the wood
Seem standing darker than last year they stood,
   And say we must not cross—alas! alas!

ON CATULLUS

   Tell me not what too well I know
      About the bard of Sirmio.
     Yes, in Thalia's son
Such stains there are—as when a Grace
Sprinkles another's laughing face
     With nectar, and runs on.

IANTHE

From you, Ianthe, little troubles pass
   Like little ripples down a sunny river;
Your pleasures spring like daisies in the grass,
   Cut down, and up again as blithe as ever.

RESIGNATION

Why, why repine, my pensive friend,
   At pleasures slipped away?
Some the stern Fates will never lend,
   And all refuse to stay.

I see the rainbow in the sky,
   The dew upon the grass;
I see them, and I ask not why
   They glimmer or they pass.

With folded arms I linger not
   To call them back; 'twere vain:
In this, or in some other spot,
   I know they'll shine again.

CHILD OF A DAY

Child of a day, thou knowest not
   The tears that overflow thine urn,
The gushing eyes that read thy lot,
   Nor, if thou knewest, couldst return!

And why the wish? the pure and blest
   Watch like thy mother o'er thy sleep
O peaceful night!   O envied rest!
   Thou wilt not ever see her weep.

ON SUNIUM'S HEIGHT

   Wearers of rings and chains,
   Pray do not take the pains
   To set me right.
   In vain my faults ye quote:
   I write as others wrote
   On Sunium's height.

PLAYS

How soon, alas, the hours are over,
Counted us out to play the lover!
And how much narrower is the stage,
Allotted us to play the sage!
But when we play the fool, how wide
The theatre expands; beside,
How long the audience sits before us!
How many prompters! what a chorus!

WALTER SAVAGE LANDOR

SWEET WAS THE SONG THAT YOUTH SANG ONCE

Sweet was the song that Youth sang once,
And passing sweet was the response;
But there are accents sweeter far
When Love leaps down our evening star,

Holds back the blighting wings of Time,
Melts with his breath the crusty rime,
And looks into our eyes, and says,
"Come, let us talk of former days."

TO YOUTH

Where art thou gone, light-ankled Youth?
   With wing at either shoulder,
And smile that never left thy mouth
   Until the Hours grew colder:

Then somewhat seem'd to whisper near
   That thou and I must part;
I doubted it; I felt no fear,
   No weight upon the heart:

If aught befell it, Love was by
   And roll'd it off again;
So, if there ever was a sigh,
   'Twas not a sigh of pain.

I may not call thee back; but thou
   Returnest when the hand
Of gentle Sleep waves o'er my brow
   His poppy-crested wand;

Then smiling eyes bend over mine,
   Then lips once prest invite;
But sleep hath given a silent sign,
   And both, alas! take flight.

VERY TRUE, THE LINNETS SING

Very true, the linnets sing
Sweetest in the leaves of spring;
You have found in all these leaves
That which changes and deceives,
And, to pine by sun or star,
Left them, false ones as they are.
But there be who walk beside
Autumn's till they all have died,
And who lend a patient ear
To low notes from branches sere.

Charles Lamb

ON LAMB'S SPECIMENS OF DRAMATIC POETS

If all the flowers of all the fields on earth
  By wonder-working summer were made one,
  Its fragrance were not sweeter in the sun,
Its treasure-house of leaves were not more worth
Than those wherefrom thy light of musing mirth
  Shone, till each leaf whereon thy pen would run
  Breathed life, and all its breath was benison.
Beloved beyond all names of English birth,
More dear than mightier memories; gentlest name
That ever clothed itself with flower-sweet fame,
Or linked itself with loftiest names of old
  By right and might of loving; I, that am
Less than the least of those within thy fold,
  Give only thanks for them to thee, Charles Lamb.

So many a year had borne its own bright bees
  And slain them since thy honey-bees were hived,
  John Day, in cells of flower-sweet verse contrived
So well with craft of moulding melodies,
484

CHARLES LAMB

Thy soul perchance in amaranth fields at ease
  Though not to hear the sound on earth revived
  Of summer music from the spring derived
When thy song sucked the flower of flowering trees.
But thine was not the chance of every day:
  Time, after many a darkling hour, grew sunny,
  And light between the clouds ere sunset swam,
Laughing, and kissed their darkness all away,
  When, touched and tasted and approved, thy honey
  Took subtler sweetness from the lips of Lamb.
                    —ALGERNON CHARLES SWINBURNE.

THE OLD FAMILIAR FACES

I have had playmates, I have had companions,
In my days of childhood, in my joyful school-days,
All, all are gone, the old familiar faces.

I have been laughing, I have been carousing,
Drinking late, sitting late, with my bosom cronies,
All, all are gone, the old familiar faces.

I loved a love once, fairest among women;
Closed are her doors on me, I must not see her—
All, all are gone, the old familiar faces.

I have a friend, a kinder friend has no man;
Like an ingrate, I left my friend abruptly;
Left him, to muse on the old familiar faces.

Ghost-like I paced round the haunts of my childhood.
Earth seemed a desert I was bound to traverse,
Seeking to find the old familiar faces.

Friend of my bosom, thou more than a brother,
Why wert not thou born in my father's dwelling?
So might we talk of the old familiar faces—

How some they have died, and some they have left me,
And some are taken from me; all are departed;
All, all are gone, the old familiar faces.

485

HESTER

When maidens such as Hester die,
Their place ye may not well supply,
Though ye among a thousand try,
    With vain endeavour.

A month or more hath she been dead,
Yet cannot I by force be led
To think upon the wormy bed,
    And her together.

A springy motion in her gait,
A rising step, did indicate
Of pride and joy no common rate,
    That flushed her spirit.

I know not by what name beside
I shall it call:—if 'twas not pride,
It was a joy to that allied,
    She did inherit.

Her parents held the Quaker rule,
Which doth the human feeling cool,
But she was trained in Nature's school,
    Nature had blest her.

A waking eye, a prying mind,
A heart that stirs, is hard to bind,
A hawk's keen sight ye cannot blind,
    Ye could not Hester.

My sprightly neighbour, gone before
To that unknown and silent shore,
Shall we not meet, as heretofore,
    Some summer morning,

When from thy cheerful eyes a ray
Hath struck a bliss upon the day,
A bliss that would not go away,
    A sweet forewarning?

Joseph Blanco White

TO NIGHT

Mysterious Night! when our first parent knew
Thee from report divine, and heard thy name,
Did he not tremble for this lovely frame,
This glorious canopy of light and blue?
Yet 'neath the curtain of translucent dew,
Bathed in the rays of the great setting flame,
Hesperus with the host of heaven came,
And lo! creation widened on man's view.
Who could have thought such darkness lay concealed
Within thy beams, O Sun! or who could find,
While fly, and leaf, and insect stood revealed,
That to such countless orbs thou mad'st us blind!
 Why do we, then, shun Death with anxious strife?—
If Light can thus deceive, wherefore not Life?

Thomas Campbell

HALLOWED GROUND

What's hallowed ground? Has earth a clod
Its Maker meant not should be trod
By man, the image of his God,
 Erect and free,
Unscourged by Superstition's rod
 To bow the knee?

That's hallowed ground where, mourned and missed,
The lips repose our love has kissed;—
But where's their memory's mansion? Is't
 Yon churchyard's bowers?
No! in ourselves their souls exist,
 A part of ours.

487

A kiss can consecrate the ground
Where mated hearts are mutual bound:
The spot where love's first links were wound,
   That ne'er are riven,
Is hallowed down to earth's profound,
   And up to Heaven!

For time makes all but true love old;
The burning thoughts that then were told
Run molten still in memory's mould;
   And will not cool
Until the heart itself be cold
   In Lethe's pool.

What hallows ground where heroes sleep?
'Tis not the sculptured piles you heap!
In dews that heavens far distant weep
   Their turf may bloom;
Or Genii twine beneath the deep
   Their coral tomb.

But strew his ashes to the wind
Whose sword or voice has served mankind,—
And is he dead, whose glorious mind
   Lifts thine on high?—
To live in hearts we leave behind
   Is not to die.

Is't death to fall for Freedom's right?
He's dead alone that lacks her light!
And murder sullies in Heaven's sight
   The sword he draws:—
What can alone ennoble fight?
   A noble cause!

Give that!—and welcome War to brace
Her drums! and rend Heaven's reeking space!
The colours planted face to face,
   The charging cheer,
Though Death's pale horse lead on the chase
   Shall still be dear.

488

And place our trophies where men kneel
To Heaven!—but Heaven rebukes my zeal
The cause of Truth and human weal,
  O God above!
Transfer it from the sword's appeal
  To Peace and Love.

Peace, Love! the cherubim, that join
Their spread wings o'er Devotion's shrine,
Prayers sound in vain, and temples shine,
  Where they are not,—
The heart alone can make divine
  Religion's spot.

To incantations dost thou trust,
And pompous rites in domes august?
See mouldering stones and metal's rust
  Belie the vaunt,
That man can bless one pile of dust
  With chime or chaunt.

The ticking wood-worm mocks thee, man!
Thy temples,—creeds themselves grow wan!
But there's a dome of nobler span,
  A temple given
Thy faith, that bigots dare not ban,—
  Its space is Heaven!

Its roof, star-pictured Nature's ceiling,
Where, trancing the rapt spirit's feeling,
And God himself to man revealing,
  The harmonious spheres
Make music, though unheard their pealing
  By mortal ears.

Fair stars! are not your beings pure?
Can sin, can death, your worlds obscure?
Else why so swell the thoughts at your
  Aspect above?
Ye must be Heavens that make us sure
  Of heavenly love!

And in your harmony sublime
I read the doom of distant time:
That man's regenerate soul from crime
   Shall yet be drawn,
And reason on his mortal clime
   Immortal dawn.

What's hallowed ground? 'Tis what gives birth
To sacred thoughts in souls of worth!—
Peace! Independence! Truth! go forth
   Earth's compass round;
And your high-priesthood shall make earth
   All hallowed ground.

HOHENLINDEN

On Linden, when the sun was low,
All bloodless lay the untrodden snow;
And dark as winter was the flow
   Of Iser, rolling rapidly.

But Linden saw another sight,
When the drum beat at dead of night
Commanding fires of death to light
   The darkness of her scenery.

By torch and trumpet fast array'd,
Each horseman drew his battle-blade,
And furious every charger neigh'd
   To join the dreadful revelry.

Then shook the hills with thunder riven;
Then rush'd the steed, to battle driven;
And louder than the bolts of Heaven
   Far flash'd the red artillery.

But redder yet that light shall glow
On Linden's hills of stainèd snow;
And bloodier yet the torrent flow
   Of Iser, rolling rapidly.

'Tis morn; but scarce yon level sun
Can pierce the war-clouds, rolling dun,
Where furious Frank and fiery Hun
    Shout in their sulphurous canopy.

The combat deepens. On, ye Brave
Who rush to glory, or the grave!
Wave, Munich, all thy banners wave,
    And charge with all thy chivalry!

Few, few shall part, where many meet!
The snow shall be their winding-sheet,
And every turf beneath their feet
    Shall be a soldier's sepulchre.

Thomas Moore

OH! BREATHE NOT HIS NAME

Oh! breathe not his name, let it sleep in the shade,
Where cold and unhonour'd his relics are laid:
Sad, silent, and dark, be the tears that we shed,
As the night-dew that falls on the grass o'er his head.

But the night-dew that falls, though in silence it weeps,
Shall brighten with verdure the grave where he sleeps;
And the tear that we shed, though in secret it rolls,
Shall long keep his memory green in our souls.

THE HARP THAT ONCE THROUGH TARA'S HALLS

The harp that once through Tara's halls
    The soul of beauty shed,
Now hangs as mute on Tara's walls,
    As if that soul were fled.—
So sleeps the pride of former days,
    So glory's thrill is o'er,
And hearts that once beat high for praise,
    Now feel that pulse no more.

491

No more to chiefs and ladies bright
  The harp of Tara swells;
The chord alone, that breaks at night,
  Its tale of ruin tells.
Thus Freedom now so seldom wakes,
  The only throb she gives,
Is when some heart indignant breaks,
  To show that still she lives.

BELIEVE ME, IF ALL THOSE ENDEARING YOUNG CHARMS

Believe me, if all those endearing young charms,
  Which I gaze on so fondly to-day,
Were to change by to-morrow, and fleet in my arms,
  Like fairy-gifts fading away,
Thou wouldst still be adored, as this moment thou art,
  Let thy loveliness fade as it will,
And around the dear ruin each wish of my heart
  Would entwine itself verdantly still.

It is not while beauty and youth are thine own,
  And thy cheeks unprofaned by a tear,
That the fervour and faith of a soul can be known,
  To which time will but make thee more dear;
No, the heart that has truly loved never forgets,
  But as truly loves on to the close,
As the sun-flower turns on her god, when he sets,
  The same look which she turned when he rose.

THE LAST ROSE OF SUMMER

'Tis the last rose of summer
  Left blooming alone;
All her lovely companions
  Are faded and gone;
No flower of her kindred,
  No rosebud is nigh,
To reflect back her blushes,
  To give sigh for sigh.

I'll not leave thee, thou lone one!
　　To pine on the stem;
Since the lovely are sleeping,
　　Go, sleep thou with them.
Thus kindly I scatter
　　Thy leaves o'er the bed,
Where thy mates of the garden
　　Lie scentless and dead.

So soon may I follow,
　　When friendships decay,
And from Love's shining circle
　　The gems drop away.
When true hearts lie withered
　　And fond ones are flown,
Oh! who would inhabit
　　This bleak world alone?

SHE IS FAR FROM THE LAND

She is far from the land where her young hero sleeps,
　　And lovers are round her, sighing:
But coldly she turns from their gaze, and weeps,
　　For her heart in his grave is lying.

She sings the wild songs of her dear native plains,
　　Every note which he loved awaking;—
Ah! little they think, who delight in her strains,
　　How the heart of the minstrel is breaking.

He had lived for his love, for his country he died,
　　They were all that to life had entwined him;
Nor soon shall the tears of his country be dried,
　　Nor long will his love stay behind him.

Oh! make her a grave where the sunbeams rest,
　　When they promise a glorious morrow;
They'll shine o'er her sleep, like a smile from the West,
　　From her own loved island of sorrow.

493

AS SLOW OUR SHIP

As slow our ship her foamy track
    Against the wind was cleaving,
Her trembling pennant still looked back
    To that dear isle 'twas leaving.
So loth we part from all we love,
    From all the links that bind us;
So turn our hearts, where'er we rove,
    To those we've left behind us!

When round the bowl of vanished years
    We talk, with joyous seeming,—
With smiles, that might as well be tears,
    So faint, so sad their beaming;
While memory brings us back again
    Each early tie that twined us,
Oh, sweet's the cup that circles then
    To those we've left behind us!

And when, in other climes, we meet
    Some isle or vale enchanting,
Where all looks flowery, wild, and sweet,
    And nought but love is wanting,
We think how great had been our bliss,
    If Heaven had but assigned us
To live and die in scenes like this,
    With some we've left behind us!

As travellers oft look back, at eve,
    When eastward darkly going,
To gaze upon that light they leave
    Still faint behind them glowing,—
So, when the close of pleasure's day
    To gloom hath near consigned us,
We turn to catch one fading ray
    Of joy that's left behind us.

THOMAS MOORE

OFT IN THE STILLY NIGHT

Oft in the stilly night,
  Ere Slumber's chain has bound me,
Fond Memory brings the light
  Of other days around me;
    The smiles, the tears,
    Of boyhood's years,
  The words of love then spoken;
    The eyes that shone,
    Now dimmed and gone,
  The cheerful hearts now broken!
Thus in the stilly night,
  Ere Slumber's chain has bound me,
Sad Memory brings the light
  Of other days around me.

When I remember all
  The friends, so linked together,
I've seen around me fall,
  Like leaves in wintry weather;
    I feel like one
    Who treads alone
  Some banquet-hall deserted,
    Whose lights are fled,
    Whose garlands dead,
  And all but he departed!
Thus in the stilly night,
  Ere Slumber's chain has bound me,
Sad Memory brings the light
  Of other days around me.

495

James Henry Leigh Hunt

ABOU BEN ADHEM

Abou Ben Adhem (may his tribe increase!)
Awoke one night from a deep dream of peace,
And saw within the moonlight in his room,
Making it rich and like a lily in bloom,
An angel writing in a book of gold:
Exceeding peace had made Ben Adhem bold,
And to the presence in the room he said,
"What writest thou?" The vision raised its head,
And, with a look made of all sweet accord,
Answered, "The names of those who love the Lord."
"And is mine one?" said Abou. "Nay, not so,"
Replied the angel. Abou spoke more low,
But cheerily still; and said, "I pray thee, then,
Write me as one that loves his fellow-men."

The angel wrote, and vanished. The next night
It came again, with a great wakening light,
And showed the names whom love of God had blessed,—
And, lo! Ben Adhem's name led all the rest!

DIRGE

Blest is the turf, serenely blest,
Where throbbing hearts may sink to rest,
Where life's long journey turns to sleep,
Nor ever pilgrim wakes to weep.
A little sod, a few sad flowers,
A tear for long-departed hours,
Is all that feeling hearts request
To hush their weary thoughts to rest.
There shall no vain ambition come
To lure them from their quiet home;
Nor sorrow lift, with heart-strings riven,
The meek imploring eye to heaven;

496

ALLAN CUNNINGHAM

Nor sad remembrance stoop to shed
His wrinkles on the slumberer's head;
And never, never love repair
To breathe his idle whispers there!

THE GRASSHOPPER AND THE CRICKET

Green little vaulter in the sunny grass,
Catching your heart up at the feel of June,
Sole voice that's heard amidst the lazy noon,
When even the bees lag at the summoning brass;
And you, warm little housekeeper, who class
With those who think the candles come too soon,
Loving the fire, and with your tricksome tune
Nick the glad silent moments as they pass.

O sweet and tiny cousins, that belong,
One to the fields, the other to the hearth,
Both have your sunshine; both, though small, are strong
At your clear hearts; and both seem given to earth
To ring in thoughtful ears this natural song—
Indoors and out, summer and winter, Mirth.

Allan Cunningham

A WET SHEET AND A FLOWING SEA

A wet sheet and a flowing sea,
  A wind that follows fast,
And fills the white and rustling sail,
  And bends the gallant mast;
And bends the gallant mast, my boys,
  While, like the eagle free,
Away the good ship flies, and leaves
  Old England on the lee.

O for a soft and gentle wind!
  I heard a fair one cry;

497

But give to me the snoring breeze
    And white waves heaving high;
And white waves heaving high, my boys,
    The good ship tight and free—
The world of waters is our home,
    And merry men are we.

There's tempest in yon hornèd moon,
    And lightning in yon cloud;
And hark the music, mariners!
    The wind is piping loud;
The wind is piping loud, my boys,
    The lightning flashes free—
While the hollow oak our palace is,
    Our heritage the sea.

Thomas Love Peacock

THE WAR SONG OF DINAS VAWR

The mountain sheep are sweeter,
But the valley sheep are fatter;
We therefore deemed it meeter
To carry off the latter.
We made an expedition;
We met a host and quelled it;
We forced a strong position,
And killed the men who held it.

On Dyfed's richest valley,
Where herds of kine were browsing,
We made a mighty sally,
To furnish our carousing.
Fierce warriors rushed to meet us;
We met them, and o'erthrew them:
They struggled hard to beat us;
But we conquered them, and slew them.

As we drove our prize at leisure,
The king marched forth to catch us:
His rage surpassed all measure,
But his people could not match us.
He fled to his hall-pillars;
And, ere our force we led off,
Some sacked his house and cellars,
While others cut his head off.

We there, in strife bewildering,
Spilt blood enough to swim in:
We orphaned many children,
And widowed many women.
The eagles and the ravens
We glutted with our foemen;
The heroes and the cravens,
The spearmen and the bowmen.

We brought away from battle,
And much their land bemoaned them,
Two thousand head of cattle,
And the head of him who owned them:
Ednyfed, King of Dyfed,
His head was borne before us;
His wine and beasts supplied our feasts,
And his overthrow, our chorus.

Eaton Stannard Barrett

WOMAN

Not she with traitorous kiss her Saviour stung,
Not she denied him with unholy tongue;
She, while apostles shrank, could dangers brave,
Last at the cross and earliest at the grave.

499

Lord Byron

STANZAS FOR MUSIC

There be none of Beauty's daughters
   With a magic like thee;
And like music on the waters
   Is thy sweet voice to me:
When, as if its sound were causing
The charmed ocean's pausing
The waves lie still and gleaming,
And the lulled winds seem dreaming.

And the midnight moon is weaving
   Her bright chain o'er the deep;
Whose breast is gently heaving,
   As an infant's asleep:
So the spirit bows before thee,
To listen and adore thee;
With a full but soft emotion,
Like the swell of Summer's ocean.

ODE FROM THE FRENCH

.   .   .   .

There, where death's brief pang was quickest,
And the battle's wreck lay thickest,
Strewed beneath the advancing banner
   Of the eagle's burning crest—
(There with thunder-clouds to fan her,
   Who could then her wing arrest—
   Victory beaming from her breast?)
While the broken line enlarging
   Fell, or fled along the plain;
There be sure was Murat charging!
   There he ne'er shall charge again!

LORD BYRON

SHE WALKS IN BEAUTY

She walks in beauty, like the night
   Of cloudless climes and starry skies;
And all that's best of dark and bright
   Meet in her aspect and her eyes:
Thus mellow'd to that tender light
   Which heaven to gaudy day denies.

One shade the more, one ray the less,
   Had half impair'd the nameless grace
Which waves in every raven tress,
   Or softly lightens o'er her face;
Where thoughts serenely sweet express
   How pure, how dear their dwelling-place.

And on that cheek, and o'er that brow,
   So soft, so calm, yet eloquent,
The smiles that win, the tints that glow,
   But tell of days in goodness spent,
A mind at peace with all below,
   A heart whose love is innocent!

OH! SNATCHED AWAY IN BEAUTY'S BLOOM

Oh! snatched away in beauty's bloom,
On thee shall press no ponderous tomb;
But on thy turf shall roses rear;
Their leaves, the earliest of the year;
And the wild cypress wave in tender gloom:

And oft by yon blue gushing stream
Shall Sorrow lean her drooping head,
And feed deep thought with many a dream,
And lingering pause and lightly tread;
Fond wretch! as if her step disturbed the dead!

501

Away! we know that tears are vain,
That Death nor heeds nor hears distress:
Will this unteach us to complain?
Or make one mourner weep the less?
And thou,—who tell'st me to forget,
Thy looks are wan, thine eyes are wet.

CHILDE HAROLD'S PILGRIMAGE

There was a sound of revelry by night,
And Belgium's capital had gathered then
Her Beauty and her Chivalry, and bright
The lamps shone o'er fair women and brave men;
A thousand hearts beat happily; and when
Music arose with its voluptuous swell,
Soft eyes looked love to eyes which spake again,
And all went merry as a marriage-bell;
But hush! hark! a deep sound strikes like a rising knell!

Did ye not hear it?—No; 'twas but the wind,
Or the car rattling o'er the stony street;
On with the dance! let joy be unconfined;
No sleep till morn, when Youth and Pleasure meet
To chase the glowing Hours with flying feet—
But hark!—that heavy sound breaks in once more
As if the clouds its echo would repeat;
And nearer, clearer, deadlier than before!
Arm! Arm! it is—it is—the cannon's opening roar!

Within a windowed niche of that high hall
Sate Brunswick's fated chieftain; he did hear
That sound the first amidst the festival,
And caught its tone with Death's prophetic ear.
And when they smiled because he deemed it near,
His heart more truly knew that peal too well
Which stretched his father on a bloody bier,
And roused the vengeance blood alone could quell:
He rushed into the field, and, foremost fighting, fell.

502

Ah! then and there was hurrying to and fro,
And gathering tears, and tremblings of distress,
And cheeks all pale, which but an hour ago
Blushed at the praise of their own loveliness;
And there were sudden partings, such as press
The l'fe from out young hearts, and choking sighs
Which ne'er might be repeated; who could guess
If ever more should meet those mutual eyes,
Since upon night so sweet such awful morn could rise!

And there was mounting in hot haste: the steed,
The mustering squadron, and the clattering car,
Went pouring forward with impetuous speed,
And swiftly forming in the ranks of war;
And the deep thunder peal on peal afar;
And near, the beat of the alarming drum
Roused up the soldier ere the morning star;
While thronged the citizens with terror dumb,
Or whispering, with white lips—"The foe! They come!
    They come!"

And wild and high the "Cameron's gathering" rose!
The war-note of Lochiel, which Albyn's hills
Have heard, and heard, too, have her Saxon foes:—
How in the noon of night that pibroch thrills,
Savage and shrill! But with the breath which fills
Their mountain-pipe, so fill the mountaineers
With the fierce native daring which instils
The stirring memory of a thousand years,
And Evan's, Donald's fame rings in each clansman's ears!

And Ardennes waves above them her green leaves,
Dewy with nature's tear-drops, as they pass,
Grieving, if aught inanimate e'er grieves,
Over the unreturning brave,—alas!
Ere evening to be trodden like the grass
Which now beneath them, but above shall grow
In its next verdure, when this fiery mass
Of living valour, rolling on the foe
And burning with high hope, shall moulder cold and low.

Last noon beheld them full of lusty life,
Last eve in Beauty's circle proudly gay,
The midnight brought the signal-sound of strife,
The morn the marshalling in arms,—the day
Battle's magnificently-stern array!
The thunder-clouds close o'er it, which when rent
The earth is covered thick with other clay,
Which her own clay shall cover, heaped and pent,
Rider and horse,—friend, foe,—in one red burial blent!

. . . .

The castled crag of Drachenfels
Frowns o'er the wide and winding Rhine,
Whose breast of waters broadly swells
Between the banks which bear the vine,
And hills all rich with blossomed trees,
And fields which promise corn and wine,
And scattered cities crowning these,
Whose far white walls along them shine,
Have strewed a scene, which I should see
With double joy wert *thou* with me.

And peasant girls, with deep blue eyes,
And hands which offer early flowers,
Walk smiling o'er this paradise;
Above, the frequent feudal towers
Through green leaves lift their walls of grey,
And many a rock which steeply lowers,
And noble arch in proud decay,
Look o'er this vale of vintage-bowers;
But one thing want these banks of Rhine,—
Thy gentle hand to clasp in mine!

. . . .

Clear, placid Leman! thy contrasted lake,
With the wild world I dwelt in, is a thing
Which warns me, with its stillness, to forsake
Earth's troubled waters for a purer spring.

504

LORD BYRON

This quiet sail is as a noiseless wing
To waft me from distraction; once I loved
Torn ocean's roar, but thy soft murmuring
Sounds sweet as if a Sister's voice reproved,
That I with stern delights should e'er have been so moved.

.   .   .   .

The sky is changed!—and such a change! Oh night,
And storm, and darkness, ye are wondrous strong,
Yet lovely in your strength, as is the light
Of a dark eye in woman! Far along,
From peak to peak, the rattling crags among
Leaps the live thunder! Not from one lone cloud,
But every mountain now hath found a tongue,
And Jura answers, through her misty shroud,
Back to the joyous Alps, who call to her aloud!

And this is in the night:—Most glorious night!
Thou wert not sent for slumber! let me be
A sharer in thy fierce and far delight,—
A portion of the tempest and of thee!
How the lit lake shines, a phosphoric sea,
And the big rain comes dancing to the earth!
And now again 'tis black,—and now, the glee
Of the loud hills shakes with its mountain-mirth,
As if they did rejoice o'er a young earthquake's birth.
                              —Canto III.

Oh Rome! my country! city of the soul!
The orphans of the heart must turn to thee,
Lone mother of dead empires! and control
In their shut breasts their petty misery.
What are our woes and sufferance? Come and see
The cypress, hear the owl, and plod your way
O'er steps of broken thrones and temples, Ye!
Whose agonies are evils of a day—
A world is at our feet as fragile as our clay.

The Niobe of nations! there she stands,
Childless and crownless, in her voiceless woe;
An empty urn within her withered hands,
Whose holy dust was scattered long ago;
The Scipios' tomb contains no ashes now;
The very sepulchres lie tenantless
Of their heroic dwellers: dost thou flow,
Old Tiber! through a marble wilderness?
Rise with thy yellow waves, and mantle her distress.

.   .   .   .

Simple, erect, severe, austere, sublime—
Shrine of all saints and temple of all gods
From Jove to Jesus—spared and blest by time;
Looking tranquillity, while falls or nods
Arch, empire, each thing round thee, and man plods
His way through thorns to ashes—glorious dome!
Shalt thou not last?   Time's scythe and tyrant's rods
Shiver upon thee—sanctuary and home
Of art and piety—Pantheon!—pride of Rome!

Relic of nobler days, and noblest arts!
Despoiled yet perfect, with thy circle spreads
A holiness appealing to all hearts—
To art a model; and to him who treads
Rome for the sake of ages, Glory sheds
Her light through thy sole aperture; to those
Who worship here are altars for their beads;
And they who feel for genius may repose
Their eyes on honoured forms, whose busts around them close

.   .   .   .

There is a pleasure in the pathless woods,
There is a rapture on the lonely shore,
There is society, where none intrudes,
By the deep Sea, and music in its roar:
I love not Man the less, but Nature more,

LORD BYRON

From these our interviews, in which I steal
From all I may be, or have been before,
To mingle with the Universe, and feel
What I can ne'er express, yet cannot all conceal.

    Roll on, thou deep and dark blue Ocean—roll!
Ten thousand fleets sweep over thee in vain;
Man marks the earth with ruin—his control
Stops with the shore;—upon the watery plain
The wrecks are all thy deed, nor doth remain
A shadow of man's ravage, save his own,
When, for a moment, like a drop of rain,
He sinks into thy depths with bubbling groan,
Without a grave, unknelled, uncoffined, and unknown.

    His steps are not upon thy paths,—thy fields
Are not a spoil for him,—thou dost arise
And shake him from thee; the vile strength he wields
For earth's destruction thou dost all despise,
Spurning him from thy bosom to the skies,
And send'st him, shivering in thy playful spray
And howling, to his Gods, where haply lies
His petty hope in some near port or bay,
And dashest him again to earth:—there let him lay.

   · · · · · · · · ·

    Thy shores are empires, changed in all save thee—
Assyria, Greece, Rome, Carthage, what are they?
Thy waters washed them power while they were free,
And many a tyrant since; their shores obey
The stranger, slave, or savage; their decay
Has dried up realms to deserts:—not so thou,
Unchangeable save to thy wild waves' play—
Time writes no wrinkle on thine azure brow—
Such as creation's dawn beheld, thou rollest now.

    Thou glorious mirror, where the Almighty's form
Glasses itself in tempests; in all time,
Calm or convulsed—in breeze, or gale, or storm,
Icing the pole, or in the torrid clime

Dark-heaving;—boundless, endless, and sublime—
The image of Eternity—the throne
Of the Invisible; even from out thy slime
The monsters of the deep are made; each zone
Obeys thee; thou goest forth, dread, fathomless, alone.

And I have loved thee, Ocean! and my joy
Of youthful sports was on thy breast to be
Borne, like thy bubbles, onward: from a boy
I wantoned with thy breakers—they to me
Were a delight; and if the freshening sea
Made them a terror—'twas a pleasing fear,
For I was as it were a child of thee,
And trusted to thy billows far and near,
And laid my hand upon thy mane—as I do here.

—Canto IV.

THE GIAOUR

. . . .

Clime of the unforgotten brave!
Whose land from plain to mountain-cave
Was Freedom's home or Glory's grave!
Shrine of the mighty! can it be,
That this is all remains of thee?
Approach, thou craven crouching slave:
    Say, is not this Thermopylæ?
These waters blue that round you lave,
    Oh servile offspring of the free—
Pronounce what sea, what shore is this?
The gulf, the rock of Salamis!
These scenes, their story not unknown,
Arise, and make again your own;
Snatch from the ashes of your sires
The embers of their former fires;
And he who in the strife expires
Will add to theirs a name of fear
That Tyranny shall quake to hear,
And leave his sons a hope, a fame,
They too will rather die than shame:

508

LORD BYRON

For Freedom's battle once begun,
Bequeathed by bleeding Sire to Son,
Though baffled oft is ever won.
Bear witness, Greece, thy living page,
Attest it many a deathless age!
While kings, in dusty darkness hid,
Have left a nameless pyramid,
Thy heroes, though the general doom
Hath swept the column from their tomb,
A mightier monument command,
The mountains of their native land!
These points thy Muse to stranger's eye
The graves of those that cannot die!
'Twere long to tell, and sad to trace,
Each step from splendour to disgrace;
Enough—no foreign foe could quell
Thy soul, till from itself it fell;
Yes! Self-abasement paved the way
To villain-bonds and despot sway.

What can he tell who treads thy shore?
  No legend of thine olden time,
No theme on which the muse might soar
High as thine own in days of yore,
  When man was worthy of thy clime.
The hearts within thy valleys bred,
The fiery souls that might have led
  Thy sons to deeds sublime,
Now crawl from cradle to the grave,
Slaves—nay, the bondsmen of a slave,
  And callous, save to crime.

     . . . .

  As rising on its purple wing
The insect queen of eastern spring
O'er emerald meadows of Kashmeer
Invites the young pursuer near,
And leads him on from flower to flower
A weary chase and wasted hour,

Then leaves him, as it soars on high,
With panting heart and tearful eye:
So Beauty lures the full-grown child,
With hue as bright, and wing as wild;
A chase of idle hopes and fears,
Begun in folly, closed in tears.
If won, to equal ills betrayed,
Woe waits the insect and the maid;
A life of pain, the loss of peace,
From infant's play, and man's caprice:
The lovely toy so fiercely sought
Hath lost its charm by being caught,
For every touch that wooed its stay
Hath brushed its brightest hues away,
Till charm, and hue, and beauty gone,
'Tis left to fly or fall alone.
With wounded wing, or bleeding breast,
Ah! where shall either victim rest?
Can this with faded pinion soar
From rose to tulip as before?
Or Beauty, blighted in an hour,
Find joy within her broken bower?
No: gayer insects fluttering by
Ne'er droop the wing o'er those that die,
And lovelier things have mercy shown
To every failing but their own,
And every woe a tear can claim
Except an erring sister's shame.

.   .   .   .

SONNET ON CHILLON

Eternal Spirit of the chainless Mind!
Brightest in dungeons, Liberty! thou art,
For there thy habitation is the heart—
The heart which love of thee alone can bind;
And when thy sons to fetters are consigned——
To fetters, and the damp vault's dayless gloom,
Their country conquers with their martyrdom,
And Freedom's fame finds wings on every wind.

510

LORD BYRON

Chillon! thy prison is a holy place,
  And thy sad floor an altar—for 'twas trod,
Until his very steps have left a trace
Worn, as if thy cold pavement were a sod,
By Bonnivard!—May none those marks efface!
  For they appeal from tyranny to God.

DON JUAN

Man's love is of man's life a thing apart,
  'Tis woman's whole existence; man may range
The court, camp, church, the vessel, and the mart,
  Sword, gown, gain, glory, offer in exchange
Pride, fame, ambition, to fill up his heart,
  And few there are whom these can not estrange;
Men have all these resources, we but one,
To love again, and be again undone.
                                    —CANTO I.

Alas! the love of women! it is known
  To be a lovely and a fearful thing;
For all of theirs upon that die is thrown,
  And if 'tis lost, life hath no more to bring
To them but mockeries of the past alone.
                                    —CANTO II

Round her she made an atmosphere of life,
  The very air seemed lighter from her eyes,
They were so soft and beautiful, and rife
  With all we can imagine of the skies,
And pure as Psyche e'er she grew a wife—
  Too pure even for the purest human ties;
Her overpowering presence made you feel
It would not be idolatry to kneel.

  .   .   .   .

The isles of Greece, the isles of Greece!
  Where burning Sappho loved and sung,
Where grew the arts of war and peace,—
  Where Delos rose, and Phœbus sprung!

511

Eternal summer gilds them yet,
But all, except their sun, is set.

The Scian and the Teian muse,
  The hero's harp, the lover's lute,
Have found the fame your shores refuse;
  Their place of birth alone is mute
To sounds which echo further west
Than your sires' "Islands of the Blest."

The mountains look on Marathon—
  And Marathon looks on the sea;
And musing there an hour alone,
  I dreamed that Greece might still be free;
For standing on the Persians' grave,
I could not deem myself a slave.

A king sate on the rocky brow
  Which looks o'er sea-born Salamis;
And ships, by thousands, lay below,
  And men in nations;—all were his!
He counted them at break of day—
And when the sun set where were they?

And where are they? and where art thou
  My country? On thy voiceless shore
The heroic lay is tuneless now—
  The heroic bosom beats no more!
And must thy lyre, so long divine,
Degenerate into hands like mine?

'Tis something, in the dearth of fame,
  Though linked among a fettered race,
To feel at least a patriot's shame,
  Even as I sing, suffuse my face;
For what is left the poet here?
For Greeks a blush—for Greece a tear.

Must we but weep o'er days more blest?
  Must we but blush?—Our fathers bled.
Earth! render back from out thy breast
  A remnant of our Spartan dead!

Of the three hundred grant but three,
To make a new Thermopylæ!

What, silent still? and silent all?
    Ah! no;—the voices of the dead
Sound like a distant torrent's fall,
    And answer, "Let one living head,
But one arise,—we come, we come!"
'Tis but the living who are dumb.

In vain—in vain: strike other chords;
    Fill high the cup with Samian wine!
Leave battles to the Turkish hordes,
    And shed the blood of Scio's vine!
Hark! rising to the ignoble call—
How answers each bold Bacchanal!

You have the Pyrrhic dance as yet,
    Where is the Pyrrhic phalanx gone?
Of two such lessons, why forget
    The nobler and the manlier one?
You have the letters Cadmus gave—
Think ye he meant them for a slave?

Fill high the bowl with Samian wine!
    We will not think of themes like these!
It made Anacreon's song divine:
    He served—but served Polycrates—
A tyrant; but our masters then
Were still, at least, our countrymen.

The tyrant of the Chersonese
    Was freedom's best and bravest friend;
That tyrant was Miltiades!
    Oh! that the present hour would lend
Another despot of the kind!
Such chains as his were sure to bind.

Fill high the bowl with Samian wine!
    On Suli's rock, and Parga's shore,
Exists the remnant of a line
    Such as the Doric mothers bore;

And there, perhaps, some seed is sown,
The Heracleidan blood might own.

Trust not for freedom to the Franks—
    They have a king who buys and sells:
In native swords, and native ranks,
    The only hope of courage dwells;
But Turkish force, and Latin fraud,
Would break your shield, however broad.

Fill high the bowl with Samian wine!
    Our virgins dance beneath the shade—
I see their glorious black eyes shine;
    But gazing on each glowing maid,
My own the burning tear-drop laves,
To think such breasts must suckle slaves.

Place me on Sunium's marbled steep,
    Where nothing, save the waves and I,
May hear our mutual murmurs sweep;
    There, swan-like, let me sing and die:
A land of slaves shall ne'er be mine—
Dash down yon cup of Samian wine!

.   .   .   .

Ave Maria! blessed be the hour!
    The time, the clime, the spot, where I so oft
Have felt that moment in its fullest power
    Sink o'er the earth so beautiful and soft,
While swung the deep bell in the distant tower,
    Or the faint dying day-hymn stole aloft,
And not a breath crept through the rosy air,
And yet the forest leaves seemed stirred with prayer.

Ave Maria! 'tis the hour of prayer!
    Ave Maria! 'tis the hour of love!
Ave Maria! may our spirits dare
  Look up to thine and to thy Son's above!
Ave Maria! oh that face so fair!
    Those downcast eyes beneath the Almighty dove—
What though 'tis but a pictured image?—strike—
That painting is no idol,—'tis too like.

—CANTO III.

LORD BYRON

ON THIS DAY I COMPLETE MY THIRTY-SIXTH YEAR

'Tis time this heart should be unmoved,
  Since others it hath ceased to move:
Yet, though I cannot be beloved,
      Still let me love!

My days are in the yellow leaf;
  The flowers and fruits of love are gone;
The worm, the canker, and the grief
      Are mine alone!

The fire that on my bosom preys
  Is lone as some volcanic isle;
No torch is kindled at its blaze—
      A funeral pile.

The hope, the fear, the jealous care,
  The exalted portion of the pain
And power of love, I cannot share,
      But wear the chain.

But 'tis not *thus*—and 'tis not *here*—
  Such thoughts should shake my soul, nor *now*,
Where glory decks the hero's bier,
      Or binds his brow.

The sword, the banner, and the field,
  Glory and Greece, around me see!
The Spartan, borne upon his shield,
      Was not more free.

Awake! (not Greece—she *is* awake!)
  Awake, my spirit! Think through *whom*
Thy life-blood tracks its parent lake,
      And then strike home!

Tread those reviving passions down,
  Unworthy manhood!—unto thee
Indifferent should the smile or frown
      Of beauty be,

515

If thou regrett'st thy youth, *why live?*
  The land of honourable death
Is here:—up to the field, and give
    Away thy breath!

Seek out—less often sought than found—
  A soldier's grave, for thee the best;
Then look around, and choose thy ground,
    And take thy rest.

Charles Wolfe

TO MARY

If I had thought thou couldst have died,
  I might not weep for thee;
But I forgot, when by thy side
  That thou couldst mortal be:
It never through my mind had past
  The time would e'er be o'er,
And I on thee should look my last,
  And thou shouldst smile no more!

And still upon that face I look,
  And think 'twill smile again;
And still the thought I will not brook,
  That I must look in vain.
But when I speak—thou dost not say
  What thou ne'er left'st unsaid;
And now I feel, as well I may,
  Sweet Mary, thou art dead!

If thou wouldst stay, e'en as thou art,
  All cold and all serene—
I still might press thy silent heart,
  And where thy smiles have been.
While e'en thy chill, bleak corpse I have,
  Thou seemest still mine own;
But there—I lay thee in thy grave,
  And I am now alone!

CHARLES WOLFE

I do not think, where'er thou art,
 Thou hast forgotten me;
And I, perhaps, may soothe this heart
 In thinking too of thee:
Yet there was round thee such a dawn
 Of light ne'er seen before,
As fancy never could have drawn,
 And never can restore!

THE BURIAL OF SIR JOHN MOORE AFTER CORUNNA

Not a drum was heard, not a funeral note,
 As his corpse to the rampart we hurried;
Not a soldier discharged his farewell shot
 O'er the grave where our hero we buried.

We buried him darkly at dead of night,
 The sods with our bayonets turning;
By the struggling moonbeam's misty light
 And the lantern dimly burning.

No useless coffin enclosed his breast,
 Not in sheet nor in shroud we wound him;
But he lay like a warrior taking his rest
 With his martial cloak around him.

Few and short were the prayers we said,
 And we spoke not a word of sorrow;
But we steadfastly gazed on the face that was dead,
 And we bitterly thought of the morrow.

We thought, as we hollowed his narrow bed
 And smoothed down his lonely pillow,
That the foe and the stranger would tread o'er his head,
 And we far away on the billow!

Lightly they'll talk of the spirit that's gone
 And o'er his cold ashes upbraid him,—
But little he'll reck, if they let him sleep on
 In the grave where a Briton has laid him.

But half of our heavy task was done
    When the clock struck the hour for retiring:
And we heard the distant and random gun
    That the foe was sullenly firing.

Slowly and sadly we laid him down,
    From the field of his fame fresh and gory;
We carved not a line, and we raised not a stone,
    But we left him alone with his glory.

Percy Bysshe Shelley

SHELLEY

Midst others of less note, came one frail Form,
A phantom among men; companionless
As the last cloud of an expiring storm
Whose thunder is its knell; he, as I guess,
Had gazed on Nature's naked loveliness,
Actæon-like, and now he fled astray
With feeble steps o'er the world's wilderness,
And his own thoughts, along that rugged way,
Pursued, like raging hounds, their father and their prey.

A pardlike Spirit beautiful and swift—
A love in desolation masked;—a Power
Girt round with weakness;—it can scarce uplift
The weight of the superincumbent hour;
It is a dying lamp, a falling shower,
A breaking billow;—even whilst we speak
Is it not broken? On the withering flower
The killing sun smiles brightly: on a cheek
The life can burn in blood, even while the heart may
    break.

His head was bound with pansies overblown,
And faded violets, white, and pied, and blue;
And a light spear topped with a cypress cone,
Round whose rude shaft dark ivy-tresses grew
518

PERCY BYSSHE SHELLEY

Yet dripping with the forest's noonday dew,
Vibrated, as the ever-beating heart
Shook the weak hand that grasped it; of that crew
He came the last, neglected and apart;
A herd-abandoned deer struck by the hunter's dart.

—ADONAIS.

ALASTOR

Earth, ocean, air, belovèd brotherhood!
If our great Mother has imbued my soul
With aught of natural piety to feel
Your love, and recompense the boon with mine;
If dewy morn, and odorous noon, and even,
With sunset and its gorgeous ministers,
And solemn midnight's tingling silentness;
If autumn's hollow sighs in the sere wood,
And winter robing with pure snow and crowns
Of starry ice the grey grass and bare boughs;
If spring's voluptuous pantings when she breathes
Her first sweet kisses, have been dear to me;
If no bright bird, insect, or gentle beast
I consciously have injured, but still loved
And cherished these my kindred; then forgive
This boast, belovèd brethren, and withdraw
No portion of your wonted favour now!

Mother of this unfathomable world!
Favour my solemn song, for I have loved
Thee ever, and thee only; I have watched
Thy shadow, and the darkness of thy steps,
And my heart ever gazes on the depth
Of thy deep mysteries. I have made my bed
In charnels and on coffins, where black death
Keeps record of the trophies won from thee,
Hoping to still these obstinate questionings
Of thee and thine, by forcing some lone ghost
Thy messenger, to render up the tale
Of what we are. In lone and silent hours,
When night makes a weird sound of its own stillness,
Like an inspired and desperate alchymist

519

Staking his very life on some dark hope,
Have I mixed awful talk and asking looks
With my most innocent love; until strange tears
Uniting with those breathless kisses, made
Such magic as compels the charmèd night
To render up thy charge: . . . and, though ne'er yet
Thou hast unveiled thy inmost sanctuary,
Enough from incommunicable dream,
And twilight phantasms, and deep noon-day thought,
Has shone within me, that serenely now
And moveless, as a long-forgotten lyre
Suspended in the solitary dome
Of some mysterious and deserted fane,
I wait thy breath, Great Parent, that my strain
May modulate with murmurs of the air,
And motions of the forests and the sea,
And voice of living beings, and woven hymns
Of night and day, and the deep heart of man.

.   .   .   .

THE REVOLT OF ISLAM

TO MARY——

So now my summer task is ended, Mary,
    And I return to thee, mine own heart's home;
As to his Queen some victor Knight of Faery,
    Earning bright spoils for her enchanted dome;
    Nor thou disdain, that ere my fame become
A star among the stars of mortal night,
    If it indeed may cleave its natal gloom,
Its doubtful promise thus I would unite
With thy beloved name, thou Child of love and light.

The toil which stole from thee so many an hour,
    Is ended,—and the fruit is at thy feet!
No longer where the woods to frame a bower
    With interlacèd branches mix and meet,
    Or where with sound like many voices sweet,
520

Waterfalls leap among wild islands green,
    Which framed for my lone boat a lone retreat
Of moss-grown trees and weeds, shall I be seen:
But beside thee, where still my heart has ever been.

    Thoughts of great deeds were mine, dear Friend, when first
      The clouds which wrap this world from youth did pass.
I do remember well the hour which burst
      My spirit's sleep: a fresh May-dawn it was,
      When I walked forth upon the glittering grass,
And wept, I knew not why; until there rose
      From the near schoolroom, voices, that, alas!
Were but one echo from a world of woes—
The harsh and grating strife of tyrants and of foes.

    And then I clasped my hands and looked around—
      —But none was near to mock my streaming eyes,
Which poured their warm drops on the sunny ground—
      So, without shame, I spake:—"I will be wise,
      And just, and free, and mild, if in me lies
Such power, for I grow weary to behold
      The selfish and the strong still tyrannise
Without reproach or check."   I then controlled
My tears, my heart grew calm, and I was meek and bold.

    And from that hour did I with earnest thought
      Heap knowledge from forbidden mines of lore,
Yet nothing that my tyrants knew or taught
      I cared to learn, but from that secret store
      Wrought linkèd armour for my soul, before
It might walk forth to war among mankind;
      Thus power and hope were strengthened more and more
Within me, till there came upon my mind
A sense of loneliness, a thirst with which I pined.

    Alas, that love should be a blight and snare
      To those who seek all sympathies in one!—
Such once I sought in vain; then black despair,
      The shadow of a starless night, was thrown
      Over the world in which I moved alone:—

Yet never found I one not false to me,
  Hard hearts, and cold, like weights of icy stone
Which crushed and withered mine, that could not be
Aught but a lifeless clod, until revived by thee.

Thou Friend, whose presence on my wintry heart
  Fell, like bright Spring upon some herbless plain;
How beautiful and calm and free thou wert
  In thy young wisdom, when the mortal chain
  Of Custom thou didst burst and rend in twain,
And walked as free as light the clouds among,
  Which many an envious slave then breathed in vain
From his dim dungeon, and my spirit sprung
To meet thee from the woes which had begirt it long!

No more alone through the world's wilderness,
  Although I trod the paths of high intent,
I journeyed now: no more companionless,
  Where solitude is like despair, I went.—
  There is the wisdom of a stern content
When Poverty can blight the just and good,
  When Infamy dares mock the innocent,
And cherished friends turn with the multitude
To trample: this was ours, and we unshaken stood!

Now has descended a serener hour,
  And with inconstant fortune, friends return;
Though suffering leaves the knowledge and the power
  Which says:—Let scorn be not repaid with scorn.
  And from thy side two gentle babes are born
To fill our home with smiles, and thus are we
  Most fortunate beneath life's beaming morn;
And these delights, and thou, have been to me
The parents of the Song I consecrate to thee.

Is it, that now my inexperienced fingers
  But strike the prelude of a loftier strain?
Or, must the lyre on which my spirit lingers
  Soon pause in silence, ne'er to sound again,
  Though it might shake the Anarch Custom's reign,
522

PERCY BYSSHE SHELLEY

And charm the minds of men to Truth's own sway
  Holier than was Amphion's?   I would fain
Reply in hope—but I am worn away,
And Death and Love are yet contending for their prey.

And what art thou?   I know, but dare not speak:
  Time may interpret to his silent years.
Yet in the paleness of thy thoughtful cheek,
  And in the light thine ample forehead wears,
  And in thy sweetest smiles, and in thy tears,
And in thy gentle speech, a prophecy
  Is whispered, to subdue my fondest fears:
And through thine eyes, even in thy soul I see
A lamp of vestal fire burning internally.

They say that thou wert lovely from thy birth,
  Of glorious parents, thou aspiring Child.
I wonder not—for One then left this earth
  Whose life was like a setting planet mild,
  Which clothed thee in the radiance undefiled
Of its departing glory; still her fame
  Shines on thee, through the tempests dark and wild
Which shake these latter days; and thou canst claim
The shelter, from thy Sire, of an immortal name.

One voice came forth from many a mighty spirit,
  Which was the echo of three thousand years;
And the tumultuous world stood mute to hear it,
  As some lone man who in a desert hears
  The music of his home:—unwonted fears
Fell on the pale oppressors of our race,
  And Faith, and Custom, and low-thoughted cares,
Like thunder-stricken dragons, for a space
Left the torn human heart, their food and dwelling-place.

Truth's deathless voice pauses among mankind!
  If there must be no response to my cry—
If men must rise and stamp with fury blind
  On his pure name who loves them,—thou and I,
  Sweet friend! can look from our tranquillity

523

Like lamps into the world's tempestuous night,—
Two tranquil stars, while clouds are passing by
Which wrap them from the foundering seaman's sight,
That burn from year to year with unextinguished light.

. . . .

PROMETHEUS UNBOUND

On a poet's lips I slept
Dreaming like a love-adept
In the sound his breathing kept;
Nor seeks nor finds he mortal blisses,
But feeds on the aëreal kisses
Of shapes that haunt thought's wildernesses.
He will watch from dawn to gloom
The lake-reflected sun illume
The yellow bees in the ivy-bloom,
Nor heed nor see, what things they be;
But from these create he can
Forms more real than living man,
Nurslings of immortality!

—Act I.

Life of Life! thy lips enkindle
   With their love the breath between them;
And thy smiles before they dwindle
   Make the cold air fire; then screen them
In those looks, where whoso gazes
Faints, entangled in their mazes.

Child of Light! thy limbs are burning
   Through the vest which seems to hide them;
As the radiant lines of morning
   Through the clouds ere they divide them;
And this atmosphere divinest
Shrouds thee wheresoe'er thou shinest.

Fair are others; none beholds thee,
   But thy voice sounds low and tender
Like the fairest, for it folds thee
   From the sight, that liquid splendour,

524

And all feel, yet see thee never,
As I feel now, lost for ever!

Lamp of Earth! where'er thou movest
    Its dim shapes are clad with brightness,
And the souls of whom thou lovest
    Walk upon the winds with lightness,
Till they fail, as I am failing,
Dizzy, lost, yet unbewailing!

—Act II, Scene V.

ADONAIS

I weep for Adonais—he is dead!
Oh, weep for Adonais! though our tears
Thaw not the frost which binds so dear a head!
And thou, sad Hour, selected from all years
To mourn our loss, rouse thy obscure compeers,
And teach them thine own sorrow, say: "With me
Died Adonais; till the Future dares
Forget the Past, his fate and fame shall be
An echo and a light unto eternity!"

Where wert thou, mighty Mother, when he lay,
When thy Son lay, pierced by the shaft which flies
In darkness? where was lorn Urania
When Adonais died? With veilèd eyes,
'Mid listening Echoes, in her Paradise
She sate, while one, with soft enamoured breath
Rekindled all the fading melodies,
With which, like flowers that mock the corse beneath,
He had adorned and hid the coming bulk of Death.

Oh, weep for Adonais—he is dead!
Wake, melancholy Mother, wake and weep!
Yet wherefore? Quench within their burning bed
Thy fiery tears, and let thy loud heart keep

525

Like his, a mute and uncomplaining sleep;
For he is gone, where all things wise and fair
Descend;—oh, dream not that the amorous Deep
Will yet restore him to the vital air;
Death feeds on his mute voice, and laughs at our despair.

Most musical of mourners, weep again!
Lament anew, Urania!—He died,
Who was the Sire of an immortal strain,
Blind, old, and lonely, when his country's pride,
The priest, the slave, and the liberticide,
Trampled and mocked with many a loathèd rite
Of lust and blood; he went, unterrified,
Into the gulf of death; but his clear Sprite
Yet reigns o'er earth; the third among the sons of light.

Most musical of mourners, weep anew!
Not all to that bright station dared to climb;
And happier they their happiness who knew,
Whose tapers yet burn through that night of time
In which suns perished; others more sublime,
Struck by the envious wrath of man or god,
Have sunk, extinct in their refulgent prime;
And some yet live, treading the thorny road,
Which leads, through toil and hate, to Fame's serene abode

But now, thy youngest, dearest one, has perished—
The nursling of thy widowhood, who grew,
Like a pale flower by some sad maiden cherished,
And fed with true-love tears, instead of dew;
Most musical of mourners, weep anew!
Thy extreme hope, the loveliest and the last.
The bloom, whose petals nipped before they blew
Died on the promise of the fruit, is waste;
The broken lily lies—the storm is overpast.

To that high Capital, where kingly Death
Keeps his pale court in beauty and decay,
He came; and bought, with price of purest breath,
A grave among the eternal.—Come away!

Haste, while the vault of blue Italian day
Is yet his fitting charnel-roof! while still
He lies, as if in dewy sleep he lay;
Awake him not! surely he takes his fill
Of deep and liquid rest, forgetful of all ill.

He will awake no more, oh, never more!—
Within the twilight chamber spreads apace
The shadow of white Death, and at the door
Invisible Corruption waits to trace
His extreme way to her dim dwelling-place;
The eternal Hunger sits, but pity and awe
Soothe her pale rage, nor dares she to deface
So fair a prey, till darkness, and the law
Of change, shall o'er his sleep the mortal curtain draw.

Oh, weep for Adonais!—The quick Dreams,
The passion-wingèd Ministers of thought,
Who were his flocks, whom near the living streams
Of his young spirit he fed, and whom he taught
The love which was its music, wander not,—
Wander no more, from kindling brain to brain,
But droop there, whence they sprung; and mourn their lot
Round the cold heart, where, after their sweet pain,
They ne'er will gather strength, or find a home again.

And one with trembling hands clasps his cold head,
And fans him with her moonlight wings, and cries;
"Our love, our hope, our sorrow, is not dead;
See, on the silken fringe of his faint eyes,
Like dew upon a sleeping flower, there lies
A tear some Dream has loosened from his brain."
Lost Angel of a ruined Paradise!
She knew not 'twas her own; as with no stain
She faded, like a cloud which had outwept its rain.

One from a lucid urn of starry dew
Washed his light limbs as if embalming them;
Another clipped her profuse locks, and threw
The wreath upon him, like an anadem,

527

Which frozen tears instead of pearls begem;
Another in her wilful grief would break
Her bow and winged reeds, as if to stem
A greater loss with one which was more weak;
And dull the barbèd fire against his frozen cheek.

Another Splendour on his mouth alit,
That mouth, whence it was wont to draw the breath
Which gave it strength to pierce the guarded wit,
And pass into the panting heart beneath
With lightning and with music: the damp death
Quenched its caress upon his icy lips;
And, as a dying meteor stains a wreath
Of moonlight vapour, which the cold night clips,
It flushed through his pale limbs, and passed to its eclipse.

And others came . . . Desires and Adorations,
Wingèd Persuasions and veiled Destinies,
Splendours, and Glooms, and glimmering Incarnations
Of hopes and fears, and twilight Phantasies;
And Sorrow, with her family of Sighs,
And Pleasure, blind with tears, led by the gleam
Of her own dying smile instead of eyes,
Came in slow pomp;—the moving pomp might seem
Like pageantry of mist on an autumnal stream.

All he had loved, and moulded into thought,
From shape, and hue, and odour, and sweet sound,
Lamented Adonais. Morning sought
Her eastern watch-tower, and her hair unbound,
Wet with the tears which should adorn the ground,
Dimmed the aëreal eyes that kindle day;
Afar the melancholy thunder moaned,
Pale Ocean in unquiet slumber lay,
And the wild Winds flew round, sobbing in their dismay.

Lost Echo sits amid the voiceless mountains,
And feeds her grief with his remembered lay,
And will no more reply to winds or fountains,
Or amorous birds perched on the young green spray,

528

Or herdsman's horn, or bell at closing day;
Since she can mimic not his lips, more dear
Than those for whose disdain she pined away
Into a shadow of all sounds:—a drear
Murmur, between their songs, is all the woodmen hear.

Grief made the young Spring wild, and she threw down
Her kindling buds, as if she Autumn were,
Or they dead leaves; since her delight is flown,
For whom should she have waked the sullen year?
To Phœbus was not Hyacinth so dear
Nor to himself Narcissus, as to both
Thou, Adonais: wan they stand and sere
Amid the faint companions of their youth,
With dew all turned to tears; odour, to sighing ruth.

Thy spirit's sister, the lorn nightingale
Mourns not her mate with such melodious pain;
Not so the eagle, who like thee could scale
Heaven, and could nourish in the sun's domain
Her mighty youth with morning, doth complain,
Soaring and screaming round her empty nest,
As Albion wails for thee: the curse of Cain
Light on his head who pierced thy innocent breast,
And scared the angel soul that was its earthly guest!

Ah, woe is me! Winter is come and gone,
But grief returns with the revolving year;
The airs and streams renew their joyous tone;
The ants, the bees, the swallows reappear;
Fresh leaves and flowers deck the dead Seasons' bier;
The amorous birds now pair in every brake,
And build their mossy homes in field and brere;
And the green lizard, and the golden snake,
Like unimprisoned flames, out of their trance awake.

Through wood and stream and field and hill and Ocean
A quickening life from the Earth's heart has burst
As it has ever done, with change and motion,
From the great morning of the world when first

529

God dawned on Chaos; in its stream immersed,
The lamps of Heaven flash with a softer light;
All baser things pant with life's sacred thirst;
Diffuse themselves; and spend in love's delight,
The beauty and the joy of their renewèd might.

The leprous corpse, touched by this spirit tender,
Exhales itself in flowers of gentle breath;
Like incarnations of the stars, when splendour
Is changed to fragrance, they illumine death
And mock the merry worm that wakes beneath;
Nought we know, dies. Shall that alone which knows
Be as a sword consumed before the sheath
By sightless lightning?—the intense atom glows
A moment, then is quenched in a most cold repose.

Alas! that all we loved of him should be,
But for our grief, as if it had not been,
And grief itself be mortal! Woe is me!
Whence are we, and why are we? of what scene
The actors or spectators? Great and mean
Meet massed in death, who lends what life must borrow.
As long as skies are blue, and fields are green,
Evening must usher night, night urge the morrow,
Month follow month with woe, and year wake year to sorrow.

He will awake no more, oh, never more!
"Wake thou," cried Misery, "childless Mother, rise
Out of thy sleep, and slake, in thy heart's core,
A wound more fierce than his, with tears and sighs."
And all the Dreams that watched Urania's eyes,
And all the Echoes whom their sister's song
Had held in holy silence, cried: "Arise!"
Swift as a Thought by the snake Memory stung,
From her ambrosial rest the fading Splendour sprung.

She rose like an autumnal Night, that springs
Out of the East, and follows wild and drear
The golden Day, which, on eternal wings,
Even as a ghost abandoning a bier,

530

Had left the Earth a corpse. Sorrow and fear
So struck, so roused, so rapped Urania;
So saddened round her like an atmosphere
Of stormy mist; so swept her on her way
Even to the mournful place where Adonais lay.

Out of her secret Paradise she sped,
Through camps and cities rough with stone, and steel,
And human hearts, which to her aëry tread
Yielding not, wounded the invisible
Palms of her tender feet where'er they fell:
And barbèd tongues, and thoughts more sharp than they,
Rent the soft Form they never could repel,
Whose sacred blood, like the young tears of May,
Paved with eternal flowers that undeserving way.

In the death-chamber for a moment Death,
Shamed by the presence of that living Might,
Blushed to annihilation, and the breath
Revisited those lips, and Life's pale light
Flashed through those limbs, so late her dear delight.
"Leave me not wild and drear and comfortless,
As silent lightning leaves the starless night!
Leave me not!" cried Urania: her distress
Roused Death: Death rose and smiled, and met her vain caress

"Stay yet awhile! speak to me once again;
Kiss me, so long but as a kiss may live;
And in my heartless breast and burning brain
That word, that kiss, shall all thoughts else survive,
With food of saddest memory kept alive,
Now thou art dead, as if it were a part
Of thee, my Adonais! I would give
All that I am to be as thou now art!
But I am chained to Time, and cannot thence depart!

"O gentle child, beautiful as thou wert,
Why didst thou leave the trodden paths of men
Too soon, and with weak hands though mighty heart
Dare the unpastured dragon in his den?

531

Defenceless as thou wert, oh, where was then
Wisdom the mirrored shield, or scorn the spear?
Or hadst thou waited the full cycle, when
Thy spirit should have filled its crescent sphere,
The monsters of life's waste had fled from thee like deer.

"The herded wolves, bold only to pursue;
The obscene ravens, clamorous o'er the dead;
The vultures to the conqueror's banner true
Who feed where Desolation first has fed,
And whose wings rain contagion;—how they fled,
When, like Apollo, from his golden bow
The Pythian of the age one arrow sped
And smiled!—The spoilers tempt no second blow,
They fawn on the proud feet that spurn them lying low.

"The sun comes forth, and many reptiles spawn;
He sets, and each ephemeral insect then
Is gathered into death without a dawn,
And the immortal stars awake again;
So is it in the world of living men:
A godlike mind soars forth, in its delight
Making earth bare and veiling heaven, and when
It sinks, the swarms that dimmed or shared its light
Leave to its kindred lamps the spirit's awful night."

Thus ceased she: and the mountain shepherds came,
Their garlands sere, their magic mantles rent;
The Pilgrim of Eternity, whose fame
Over his living head like Heaven is bent,
An early but enduring monument,
Came, veiling all the lightnings of his song
In sorrow; from her wilds Ierne sent
The sweetest lyrist of her saddest wrong,
And Love taught Grief to fall like music from his tongue.

Midst others of less note, came one frail Form,
A phantom among men; companionless
As the last cloud of an expiring storm
Whose thunder is its knell; he, as I guess,

Had gazed on Nature's naked loveliness,
Actæon-like, and now he fled astray
With feeble steps o'er the world's wilderness,
And his own thoughts, along that rugged way,
Pursued, like raging hounds, their father and their prey.

A pardlike Spirit beautiful and swift—
A Love in desolation masked;—a Power
Girt round with weakness;—it can scarce uplift
The weight of the superincumbent hour;
It is a dying lamp, a falling shower,
A breaking billow;—even whilst we speak
Is it not broken?   On the withering flower
The killing sun smiles brightly: on a cheek
The life can burn in blood, even while the heart may break.

His head was bound with pansies overblown,
And faded violets, white, and pied, and blue;
And a light spear topped with a cypress cone,
Round whose rude shaft dark ivy-tresses grew
Yet dripping with the forest's noonday dew,
Vibrated, as the ever-beating heart
Shook the weak hand that grasped it; of that crew
He came the last, neglected and apart;
A herd-abandoned deer struck by the hunter's dart.

All stood aloof, and at his partial moan
Smiled through their tears; well knew that gentle band
Who in another's fate now wept his own,
As in the accents of an unknown land
He sung new sorrow; sad Urania scanned
The Stranger's mien, and murmured: "Who art thou?"
He answered not, but with a sudden hand
Made bare his branded and ensanguined brow,
Which was like Cain's or Christ's—oh! that it should be so!

What softer voice is hushed over the dead?
Athwart what brow is that dark mantle thrown?
What form leans sadly o'er the white death-bed,
In mockery of monumental stone,

533

The heavy heart heaving without a moan?
If it be He, who, gentlest of the wise,
Taught, soothed, loved, honoured the departed one,
Let me not vex, with inharmonious sighs,
The silence of that heart's accepted sacrifice.

Our Adonais has drunk poison—oh!
What deaf and viperous murderer could crown
Life's early cup with such a draught of woe?
The nameless worm would now itself disown:
It felt, yet could escape, the magic tone
Whose prelude held all envy, hate, and wrong,
But what was howling in one breast alone,
Silent with expectation of the song,
Whose master's hand is cold, whose silver lyre unstrung.

Live thou, whose infamy is not thy fame!
Live! fear no heavier chastisement from me,
Thou noteless blot on a remembered name!
But be thyself, and know thyself to be!
And ever at thy season be thou free
To spill the venom when thy fangs o'erflow:
Remorse and Self-contempt shall cling to thee;
Hot Shame shall burn upon thy secret brow,
And like a beaten hound tremble thou shalt—as now.

Nor let us weep that our delight is fled
Far from these carrion kites that scream below;
He wakes or sleeps with the enduring dead;
Thou canst not soar where he is sitting now—
Dust to the dust! but the pure spirit shall flow
Back to the burning fountain whence it came,
A portion of the Eternal, which must glow
Through time and change, unquenchably the same,
Whilst thy cold embers choke the sordid hearth of shame.

Peace, peace! he is not dead, he doth not sleep—
He hath awakened from the dream of life—
'Tis we, who lost in stormy visions, keep
With phantoms an unprofitable strife,

534

And in mad trance, strike with our spirit's knife
Invulnerable nothings.—We decay
Like corpses in a charnel; fear and grief
Convulse us and consume us day by day,
And cold hopes swarm like worms within our living clay.

He has outsoared the shadow of our night;
Envy and calumny and hate and pain,
And that unrest which men miscall delight,
Can touch him not and torture not again;
From the contagion of the world's slow stain
He is secure, and now can never mourn
A heart grown cold, a head grown grey in vain;
Nor, when the spirit's self has ceased to burn,
With sparkless ashes load an unlamented urn.

He lives, he wakes—'tis Death is dead, not he;
Mourn not for Adonais.—Thou young Dawn,
Turn all thy dew to splendour, for from thee
The spirit thou lamentest is not gone;
Ye caverns and ye forests, cease to moan!
Cease, ye faint flowers and fountains, and thou Air,
Which like a mourning veil thy scarf hadst thrown
O'er the abandoned Earth, now leave it bare
Even to the joyous stars which smile on its despair!

He is made one with Nature: there is heard
His voice in all her music, from the moan
Of thunder, to the song of night's sweet bird;
He is a presence to be felt and known
In darkness and in light, from herb and stone,
Spreading itself where'er that Power may move
Which has withdrawn his being to its own;
Which wields the world with never-wearied love,
Sustains it from beneath, and kindles it above.

He is a portion of the loveliness
Which once he made more lovely: he doth bear
His part, while the one Spirit's plastic stress
Sweeps through the dull dense world, compelling there,

535

All new successions to the forms they wear;
Torturing th' unwilling dross that checks its flight
To its own likeness, as each mass may bear;
And bursting in its beauty and its might
From trees and beasts and men into the Heaven's light.

The splendours of the firmament of time
May be eclipsed, but are extinguished not;
Like stars to their appointed height they climb,
And death is a low mist which cannot blot
The brightness it may veil. When lofty thought
Lifts a young heart above its mortal lair,
And love and life contend in it, for what
Shall be its earthly doom, the dead live there
And move like winds of light on dark and stormy air.

The inheritors of unfulfilled renown
Rose from their thrones, built beyond mortal thought,
Far in the Unapparent. Chatterton
Rose pale,—his solemn agony had not
Yet faded from him; Sidney, as he fought
And as he fell and as he lived and loved
Sublimely mild, a Spirit without spot,
Arose; and Lucan, by his death approved:
Oblivion as they rose shrank like a thing reproved.

And many more, whose names on Earth are dark,
But whose transmitted effluence cannot die
So long as fire outlives the parent spark,
Rose, robed in dazzling immortality.
"Thou art become as one of us," they cry,
"It was for thee yon kingless sphere has long
Swung blind in unascended majesty,
Silent alone amid an Heaven of Song.
Assume thy wingèd throne, thou Vesper of our throng!"

Who mourns for Adonais? Oh, come forth,
Fond wretch! and know thyself and him aright.
Clasp with thy panting soul the pendulous Earth;
As from a centre, dart thy spirit's light
536

Beyond all worlds, until its spacious might
Satiate the void circumference: then shrink
Even to a point within our day and night;
And keep thy heart light lest it make thee sink
When hope has kindled hope, and lured thee to the brink.

Or go to Rome, which is the sepulchre,
Oh, not of him, but of our joy: 'tis nought
That ages, empires, and religions there
Lie buried in the ravage they have wrought;
For such as he can lend,—they borrow not
Glory from those who made the world their prey;
And he is gathered to the kings of thought
Who waged contention with their time's decay,
And of the past are all that cannot pass away.

Go thou to Rome,—at once the Paradise,
The grave, the city, and the wilderness;
And where its wrecks like shattered mountains rise,
And flowering weeds, and fragrant copses dress
The bones of Desolation's nakedness
Pass, till the spirit of the spot shall lead
Thy footsteps to a slope of green access
Where, like an infant's smile, over the dead
A light of laughing flowers along the grass is spread;

And grey walls moulder round, on which dull Time
Feeds, like slow fire upon a hoary brand;
And one keen pyramid with wedge sublime,
Pavilioning the dust of him who planned
This refuge for his memory, doth stand
Like flame transformed to marble; and beneath,
A field is spread, on which a newer band
Have pitched in Heaven's smile their camp of death,
Welcoming him we lose with scarce extinguished breath.

Here pause: these graves are all too young as yet
To have outgrown the sorrow which consigned
Its charge to each; and if the seal is set,
Here, on one fountain of a mourning mind,

537

Break it not thou! too surely shalt thou find
Thine own well full, if thou returnest home,
Of tears and gall. From the world's bitter wind
Seek shelter in the shadow of the tomb.
What Adonais is, why fear we to become?

The One remains, the many change and pass;
Heaven's light forever shines, Earth's shadows fly;
Life, like a dome of many-coloured glass,
Stains the white radiance of Eternity,
Until Death tramples it to fragments.—Die,
If thou wouldst be with that which thou dost seek!
Follow where all is fled!—Rome's azure sky,
Flowers, ruins, statues, music, words, are weak
The glory they transfuse with fitting truth to speak.

Why linger, why turn back, why shrink, my Heart?
Thy hopes are gone before: from all things here
They have departed; thou shouldst now depart!
A light is passed from the revolving year,
And man, and woman; and what still is dear
Attracts to crush, repels to make thee wither.
The soft sky smiles,—the low wind whispers near:
'Tis Adonais calls! oh, hasten thither,
No more let Life divide what Death can join together.

That Light whose smile kindles the Universe,
That Beauty in which all things work and move,
That Benediction which the eclipsing Curse
Of birth can quench not, that sustaining Love
Which through the web of being blindly wove
By man and beast and earth and air and sea,
Burns bright or dim, as each are mirrors of
The fire for which all thirst; now beams on me,
Consuming the last clouds of cold mortality.

The breath whose might I have invoked in song
Descends on me; my spirit's bark is driven,
Far from the shore, far from the trembling throng
Whose sails were never to the tempest given;

538

PERCY BYSSHE SHELLEY

The massy earth and spherèd skies are riven!
I am borne darkly, fearfully, afar;
Whilst, burning through the inmost veil of Heaven,
The soul of Adonais, like a star,
Beacons from the abode where the Eternal are.

HELLAS

*   *   *   *   *   *   *   °

In the great morning of the world,
The Spirit of God with might unfurled
The flag of Freedom over Chaos,
   And all its banded anarchs fled,
Like vultures frighted from Imaus,
   Before an earthquake's tread.—
So from Time's tempestuous dawn
Freedom's splendour burst and shone:—
Thermopylæ and Marathon
Caught, like mountains beacon-lighted,
   The springing Fire.—The wingèd glory
On Philippi half-alighted,
   Like an eagle on a promontory.
Its unwearied wings could fan
The quenchless ashes of Milan.
From age to age, from man to man,
   It lived; and lit from land to land
   Florence, Albion, Switzerland.

Then night fell; and, as from night,
Reassuming fiery flight,
From the West swift Freedom came,
   Against the course of Heaven and doom,
A second sun arrayed in flame,
   To burn, to kindle, to illume.
From far Atlantis its young beams
Chased the shadows and the dreams.
France, with all her sanguine steams,
   Hid, but quenched it not; again
   Through clouds its shafts of glory rain
   From utmost Germany to Spain.

As an eagle fed with morning
Scorns the embattled tempest's warning,
When she seeks her aerie hanging
    In the mountain-cedar's hair,
And her brood expect the clanging
    Of her wings through the wild air,
Sick with famine:—Freedom, so
To what of Greece remaineth now
Returns; her hoary ruins glow
Like Orient mountains lost in day;
    Beneath the safety of her wings
Her renovated nurslings prey,
    And in the naked lightenings
Of truth they purge their dazzled eyes.
Let Freedom leave—where'er she flies,
A Desert, or a Paradise:
    Let the beautiful and the brave
    Share her glory, or a grave.

.   .   .   .

The world's great age begins anew,
    The golden years return,
The earth doth like a snake renew
    Her winter weeds outworn:
Heaven smiles, and faiths and empires gleam,
Like wrecks of a dissolving dream.

A brighter Hellas rears its mountains
    From waves serener far;
A new Peneus rolls his fountains
    Against the morning star.
Where fairer Tempes bloom, there sleep
Young Cyclads on a sunnier deep.

A loftier Argo cleaves the main,
    Fraught with a later prize;
Another Orpheus sings again,
    And loves, and weeps, and dies.
A new Ulysses leaves once more
Calypso for his native shore.

Oh, write no more the tale of Troy,
  If earth Death's scroll must be!
Nor mix with Laian rage the joy
  Which dawns upon the free:
Although a subtler Sphinx renew
Riddles of death Thebes never knew.

Another Athens shall arise,
  And to remoter time
Bequeath, like sunset to the skies,
  The splendour of its prime;
And leave, if nought so bright may live,
All earth can take or Heaven can give.

Saturn and Love their long repose
  Shall burst, more bright and good
Than all who fell, than One who rose,
  Than many unsubdued:
Not gold, not blood, their altar dowers,
But votive tears and symbol flowers.

Oh, cease! must hate and death return?
  Cease! must men kill and die?
Cease! drain not to its dregs the urn
  Of bitter prophecy.
The world is weary of the past,
Oh, might it die or rest at last!

STANZAS—APRIL, 1814

Away! the moor is dark beneath the moon,
  Rapid clouds have drank the last pale beam of even:
Away! the gathering winds will call the darkness soon,
  And profoundest midnight shroud the serene lights of
    heaven.

Pause not! The time is past! Every voice cries, Away!
  Tempt not with one last tear thy friend's ungentle mood:
Thy lover's eye, so glazed and cold, dares not entreat thy
    stay:
  Duty and dereliction guide thee back to solitude.

Away, away! to thy sad and silent home;
  Pour bitter tears on its desolated hearth;
Watch the dim shades as like ghosts they go and come,
  And complicate strange webs of melancholy mirth.

The leaves of wasted autumn woods shall float around thine
    head:
  The blooms of dewy spring shall gleam beneath thy feet:
But thy soul or this world must fade in the frost that binds
    the dead,
  Ere midnight's frown and morning's smile, ere thou and
    peace may meet.

The cloud shadows of midnight possess their own repose,
  For the weary winds are silent, or the moon is in the
    deep:
Some respite to its turbulence unresting ocean knows;
  Whatever moves, or toils, or grieves, hath its appointed
    sleep.

Thou in the grave shalt rest—yet till the phantoms flee
  Which that house and heath and garden made dear to thee
    erewhile,
Thy remembrance, and repentance, and deep musings are not
    free
  From the music of two voices and the light of one sweet
    smile.

MUTABILITY

We are as clouds that veil the midnight moon;
  How restlessly they speed, and gleam, and quiver,
Streaking the darkness radiantly!—yet soon
  Night closes round, and they are lost for ever:

Or like forgotten lyres, whose dissonant strings
  Give various response to each varying blast,
To whose frail frame no second motion brings
  One mood or modulation like the last.

542

PERCY BYSSHE SHELLEY

We rest.—A dream has power to poison sleep;
    We rise.—One wandering thought pollutes the day;
We feel, conceive or reason, laugh or weep;
    Embrace fond woe, or cast our cares away:

It is the same!—For, be it joy or sorrow,
    The path of its departure still is free:
Man's yesterday may ne'er be like his morrow;
    Nought may endure but Mutability.

TO WORDSWORTH

Poet of Nature, thou hast wept to know
That things depart which never may return:
Childhood and youth, friendship and love's first glow,
Have fled like sweet dreams, leaving thee to mourn.
These common woes I feel. One loss is mine
Which thou too feel'st, yet I alone deplore.
Thou wert as a lone star, whose light did shine
On some frail bark in winter's midnight roar:
Thou hast like to a rock-built refuge stood
Above the blind and battling multitude:
In honoured poverty thy voice did weave
Songs consecrate to truth and liberty,—
Deserting these, thou leavest me to grieve,
Thus having been, that thou shouldst cease to be.

HYMN TO INTELLECTUAL BEAUTY

The awful shadow of some unseen Power
    Floats though unseen among us,—visiting
    This various world with as inconstant wing
As summer winds that creep from flower to flower,—
Like moonbeams that behind some piny mountain shower,
    It visits with inconstant glance
    Each human heart and countenance;
Like hues and harmonies of evening,—
    Like clouds in starlight widely spread,—
    Like memory of music fled,—

543

> Like aught that for its grace may be
Dear, and yet dearer for its mystery.

Spirit of Beauty, that dost consecrate
  With thine own hues all thou dost shine upon
  Of human thought or form,—where art thou gone?
Why dost thou pass away and leave our state,
This dim vast vale of tears, vacant and desolate?
    Ask why the sunlight not for ever
    Weaves rainbows o'er yon mountain-river,
Why aught should fail and fade that once is shown,
    Why fear and dream and death and birth
    Cast on the daylight of this earth
    Such gloom,—why man has such a scope
For love and hate, despondency and hope?

No voice from some sublimer world hath ever
  To sage or poet these responses given—
  Therefore the names of Demon, Ghost, and Heaven,
Remain the records of their vain endeavour,
Frail spells—whose uttered charm might not avail to sever,
    From all we hear and all we see,
    Doubt, chance, and mutability.
Thy light alone—like mist o'er mountains driven,
    Or music by the night-wind sent
    Through strings of some still instrument,
    Or moonlight on a midnight stream,
Gives grace and truth to life's unquiet dream.

Love, Hope, and Self-esteem, like clouds depart
  And come, for some uncertain moments lent.
  Man were immortal, and omnipotent,
Didst thou, unknown and awful as thou art,
Keep with thy glorious train firm state within his heart.
    Thou messenger of sympathies,
    That wax and wane in lovers' eyes—
Thou—that to human thought art nourishment,
    Like darkness to a dying flame!
    Depart not as thy shadow came,
    Depart not—lest the grave should be,
Like life and fear, a dark reality.

544

PERCY BYSSHE SHELLEY

While yet a boy I sought for ghosts, and sped
 Through many a listening chamber, cave and ruin,
 And starlight wood, with fearful steps pursuing
Hopes of high talk with the departed dead.
I called on poisonous names with which our youth is fed;
  I was not heard—I saw them not—
  When musing deeply on the lot
Of life, at that sweet time when winds are wooing
  All vital things that wake to bring
  News of birds and blossoming,—
  Sudden, thy shadow fell on me;
I shrieked, and clasped my hands in ecstasy!

I vowed that I would dedicate my powers
 To thee and thine—have I not kept the vow?
 With beating heart and streaming eyes, even now
I call the phantoms of a thousand hours
Each from his voiceless grave: they have in visioned bowers
  Of studious zeal or love's delight
  Outwatched with me the envious night—
 They know that never joy illumed my brow
  Unlinked with hope that thou wouldst free
  This world from its dark slavery,
  That thou—O awful Loveliness,
Wouldst give whate'er these words cannot express.

The day becomes more solemn and serene
 When noon is past—there is a harmony
 In autumn, and a lustre in its sky,
Which through the summer is not heard or seen,
As if it could not be, as if it had not been!
  Thus let thy power, which like the truth
  Of nature on my passive youth
Descended, to my onward life supply
  Its calm—to one who worships thee,
  And every form containing thee,
  Whom, Spirit fair, thy spells did bind
To fear himself, and love all human kind.

A FRAGMENT: TO MUSIC

Silver key of the fountain of tears,
  Where the spirit drinks till the brain is wild;
Softest grave of a thousand fears,
  Where their mother, Care, like a drowsy child,
    Is laid asleep in flowers.

· OZYMANDIAS

I met a traveller from an antique land
Who said: Two vast and trunkless legs of stone
Stand in the desert . . . Near them, on the sand,
Half sunk, a shattered visage lies, whose frown,
And wrinkled lip, and sneer of cold command,
Tell that its sculptor well those passions read
Which yet survive, stamped on these lifeless things,
The hand that mocked them, and the heart that fed:
And on the pedestal these words appear:
"My name is Ozymandias, king of kings:
Look on my works, ye Mighty, and despair!"
Nothing beside remains. Round the decay
Of that colossal wreck, boundless and bare
The lone and level sands stretch far away.

LINES WRITTEN AMONG THE EUGANEAN HILLS

Many a green isle needs must be
In the deep wide sea of Misery,
Or the mariner, worn and wan,
Never thus could voyage on—
Day and night, and night and day,
Drifting on his dreary way,
With the solid darkness black
Closing round his vessel's track:
Whilst above the sunless sky,
Big with clouds, hangs heavily,
And behind the tempest fleet
Hurries on with lightning feet,

Riving sail, and cord, and plank,
Till the ship has almost drank
Death from the o'er-brimming deep;
And sinks down, down, like that sleep
When the dreamer seems to be
Weltering through eternity;
And the dim low line before
Of a dark and distant shore
Still recedes, as ever still
Longing with divided will,
But no power to seek or shun,
He is ever drifted on
O'er the unreposing wave
To the haven of the grave.
What, if there no friends will greet;
What, if there no heart will meet
His with love's impatient beat;
Wander wheresoe'er he may,
Can he dream before that day
To find refuge from distress
In friendship's smile, in love's caress?
Then 'twill wreak him little woe
Whether such there be or no:
Senseless is the breast, and cold,
Which relenting love would fold;
Bloodless are the veins and chill
Which the pulse of pain did fill;
Every little living nerve
That from bitter words did swerve
Round the tortured lips and brow,
Are like sapless leaflets now
Frozen upon December's bough.

On the beach of a northern sea
Which tempests shake eternally,
As once the wretch there lay to sleep,
Lies a solitary heap,
One white skull and seven dry bones,
On the margin of the stones,
Where a few grey rushes stand,
Boundaries of the sea and land:

Nor is heard one voice of wail
But the sea-mews, as they sail
O'er the billows of the gale;
Or the whirlwind up and down
Howling, like a slaughtered town,
When a king in glory rides
Through the pomp of fratricides:
Those unburied bones around
There is many a mournful sound;
There is no lament for him,
Like a sunless vapour, dim,
Who once clothed with life and thought
What now moves nor murmurs not.

Ay, many flowering islands lie
In the waters of wide Agony:
To such a one this morn was led,
My bark by soft winds piloted:
'Mid the mountains Euganean
I stood listening to the pæan
With which the legioned rooks did hail
The sun's uprise majestical;
Gathering round with wings all hoar,
Through the dewy mist they soar
Like grey shades, till the eastern heaven
Bursts, and then, as clouds of even,
Flecked with fire and azure, lie
In the unfathomable sky,
So their plumes of purple grain,
Starred with drops of golden rain,
Gleam above the sunlight woods,
As in silent multitudes
On the morning's fitful gale
Through the broken mist they sail,
And the vapours cloven and gleaming
Follow, down the dark steep streaming,
Till all is bright, and clear, and still,
Round the solitary hill.

Beneath is spread like a green sea
The waveless plain of Lombardy,

PERCY BYSSHE SHELLEY

Bounded by the vaporous air,
Islanded by cities fair;
Underneath Day's azure eyes
Ocean's nursling, Venice lies,
A peopled labyrinth of walls,
Amphitrite's destined halls,
Which her hoary sire now paves
With his blue and beaming waves.
Lo! the sun upsprings behind,
Broad, red, radiant, half-reclined
On the level quivering line
Of the waters crystalline;
And before that chasm of light,
As within a furnace bright,
Column, tower, and dome, and spire,
Shine like obelisks of fire,
Pointing with inconstant motion
From the altar of dark ocean
To the sapphire-tinted skies;
As the flames of sacrifice
From the marble shrines did rise,
As to pierce the dome of gold
Where Apollo spoke of old.

Sun-girt City, thou hast been
Ocean's child, and then his queen;
Now is come a darker day,
And thou soon must be his prey,
If the power that raised thee here
Hallow so thy watery bier.
A less drear ruin then than now,
With thy conquest-branded brow
Stooping to the slave of slaves
From thy throne, among the waves
Wilt thou be, when the sea-mew
Flies, as once before it flew,
O'er thine isles depopulate,
And all is in its ancient state,
Save where many a palace gate
With green sea-flowers overgrown
Like a rock of Ocean's own,

549

Topples o'er the abandoned sea
As the tides change sullenly.
The fisher on his watery way,
Wandering at the close of day,
Will spread his sail and seize his oar
Till he pass the gloomy shore,
Lest thy dead should, from their sleep
Bursting o'er the starlight deep,
Lead a rapid masque of death
O'er the waters of his path.

Those who alone thy towers behold
Quivering through aëreal gold,
As I now behold them here,
Would imagine not they were
Sepulchres, where human forms,
Like pollution-nourished worms,
To the corpse of greatness cling,
Murdered, and now mouldering:
But if Freedom should awake
In her omnipotence, and shake
From the Celtic Anarch's hold
All the keys of dungeons cold,
Where a hundred cities lie
Chained like thee, ingloriously,
Thou and all thy sister band
Might adorn this sunny land,
Twining memories of old time
With new virtues more sublime;
If not, perish thou and they!—
Clouds which stain truth's rising day
By her sun consumed away—
Earth can spare ye; while like flowers,
In the waste of years and hours,
From your dust new nations spring
With more kindly blossoming.

Perish—let there only be
Floating o'er thy hearthless sea
As the garment of thy sky
Clothes the world immortally,

PERCY BYSSHE SHELLEY

One remembrance, more sublime
Than the tattered pall of time,
Which scarce hides thy visage wan;—
That a tempest-cleaving Swan
Of the songs of Albion,
Driven from his ancestral streams
By the might of evil dreams,
Found a nest in thee; and Ocean
Welcomed him with such emotion
That its joy grew his, and sprung
From his lips like music flung
O'er a mighty thunder-fit,
Chastening terror:—what though yet
Poesy's unfailing River,
Which through Albion winds forever
Lashing with melodious wave
Many a sacred Poet's grave,
Mourn its latest nursling fled?
What though thou with all thy dead
Scarce can for this fame repay
Aught thine own? oh, rather say
Though thy sins and slaveries foul
Overcloud a sunlike soul?
As the ghost of Homer clings
Round Scamander's wasting springs;
As divinest Shakespeare's might
Fills Avon and the world with light
Like omniscient power which he
Imaged 'mid mortality;
As the love from Petrarch's urn,
Yet amid yon hills doth burn,
A quenchless lamp by which the heart
Sees things unearthly;—so thou art,
Mighty spirit—so shall be
The City that did refuge thee.

Lo, the sun floats up the sky
Like thought-wingèd Liberty,
Till the universal light
Seems to level plain and height;

From the sea a mist has spread,
And the beams of morn lie dead
On the towers of Venice now,
Like its glory long ago.
By the skirts of that grey cloud
Many-domèd Padua proud
Stands, a peopled solitude,
'Mid the harvest-shining plain,
Where the peasant heaps his grain
In the garner of his foe,
And the milk-white oxen slow
With the purple vintage strain,
Heaped upon the creaking wain,
That the brutal Celt may swill
Drunken sleep with savage will;
And the sickle to the sword
Lies unchanged, though many a lord,
Like a weed whose shade is poison,
Overgrows this region's foison,
Sheaves of whom are ripe to come
To destruction's harvest-home:
Men must reap the things they sow,
Force from force must ever flow,
Or worse; but 'tis a bitter woe
That love or reason cannot change
The despot's rage, the slave's revenge.

Padua, thou within whose walls
Those mute guests at festivals,
Son and Mother, Death and Sin,
Played at dice for Ezzelin,
Till Death cried, "I win, I win!"
And Sin cursed to lose the wager,
But Death promised, to assuage her,
That he would petition for
Her to be made Vice-Emperor,
When the destined years were o'er,
Over all between the Po
And the eastern Alpine snow,
Under the mighty Austrian.
Sin smiled so as Sin only can,

And since that time, ay, long before,
Both have ruled from shore to shore,—
That incestuous pair, who follow
Tyrants as the sun the swallow,
As Repentance follows Crime,
And as changes follow Time.

In thine halls the lamp of learning,
Padua, now no more is burning;
Like a meteor, whose wild way
Is lost over the grave of day,
It gleams betrayed and to betray:
Once remotest nations came
To adore that sacred flame,
When it lit not many a hearth
On this cold and gloomy earth:
Now new fires from antique light
Spring beneath the wide world's might;
But their spark lies dead in thee,
Trampled out by Tyranny.
As the Norway woodman quells,
In the depth of piny dells,
One light flame among the brakes,
While the boundless forest shakes,
And its mighty trunks are torn
By the fire thus lowly born:
The spark beneath his feet is dead,
He starts to see the flames it fed
Howling through the darkened sky
With a myriad tongues victoriously,
And sinks down in fear: so thou,
O Tyranny, beholdest now
Light around thee, and thou hearest
The loud flames ascend, and fearest:
Grovel on the earth; ay, hide
In the dust thy purple pride!

Noon descends around me now:
'Tis the noon of autumn's glow,
When a soft and purple mist
Like a vaporous amethyst,

553

Or an air-dissolvèd star
Mingling light and fragrance, far
From the curved horizon's bound
To the point of Heaven's profound,
Fills the overflowing sky;
And the plains that silent lie
Underneath the leaves unsodden
Where the infant Frost has trodden
With his morning-wingèd feet,
Whose bright print is gleaming yet;
And the red and golden vines,
Piercing with their trellised lines
The rough, dark-skirted wilderness;
The dun and bladed grass no less,
Pointing from this hoary tower
In the windless air; the flower
Glimmering at my feet; the line
Of the olive-sandalled Apennine
In the south dimly islanded;
And the Alps, whose snows are spread
High between the clouds and sun;
And of living things each one;
And my spirit which so long
Darkened this swift stream of song,—
Interpenetrated lie
By the glory of the sky:
Be it love, light, harmony,
Odour, or the soul of all
Which from Heaven like dew doth fall,
Or the mind which feeds this verse
Peopling the lone universe.

Noon descends, and after noon
Autumn's evening meets me soon,
Leading the infantine moon,
And that one star, which to her
Almost seems to minister
Half the crimson light she brings
From the sunset's radiant springs:
And the soft dreams of the morn
(Which like wingèd winds had borne

PERCY BYSSHE SHELLEY

To that silent isle, which lies
Mid remembered agonies,
The frail bark of this lone being)
Pass, to other sufferers fleeing,
And its ancient pilot, Pain,
Sits beside the helm again.

Other flowering isles must be
In the sea of Life and Agony:
Other spirits float and flee
O'er that gulf: even now, perhaps,
On some rock the wild wave wraps,
With folded wings they waiting sit
For my bark, to pilot it
To some calm and blooming cove,
Where for me, and those I love,
May a windless bower be built,
Far from passion, pain, and guilt,
In a dell mid lawny hills,
Which the wild sea-murmur fills,
And soft sunshine, and the sound
Of old forests echoing round,
And the light and smell divine
Of all flowers that breathe and shine:
We may live so happy there,
That the Spirits of the Air,
Envying us, may even entice
To our healing Paradise
The polluting multitude;
But their rage would be subdued
By that clime divine and calm,
And the winds whose wings rain balm
On the uplifted soul, and leaves
Under which the bright sea heaves;
While each breathless interval
In their whisperings musical
The inspired soul supplies
With its own deep melodies;
And, the love which heals all strife
Circling, like the breath of life,

555

All things in that sweet abode
With its own mild brotherhood,
They, not it, would change; and soon
Every sprite beneath the moon
Would repent its envy vain,
And the earth grow young again.

INVOCATION TO MISERY

Come, be happy!—sit near me,
Shadow-vested Misery:
Coy, unwilling, silent bride,
Mourning in thy robe of pride,
Desolation—deified!

Come, be happy!—sit near me:
Sad as I may seem to thee,
I am happier far than thou,
Lady, whose imperial brow
Is endiademed with woe.

Misery! we have known each other,
Like a sister and a brother
Living in the same lone home,
Many years—we must live some
Hours or ages yet to come.

'Tis an evil lot, and yet
Let us make the best of it;
If love can live when pleasure dies,
We two will love, till in our eyes
This heart's Hell seem Paradise.

Come, be happy!—lie thee down
On the fresh grass newly mown,
Where the Grasshopper doth sing
Merrily—one joyous thing
In a world of sorrowing!

There our tent shall be the willow,
And mine arm shall be thy pillow;
Sounds and odours, sorrowful
Because they once were sweet, shall lull
Us to slumber, deep and dull.

Ha! thy frozen pulses flutter
With a love thou darest not utter.
Thou art murmuring—thou art weeping—
Is thine icy bosom leaping
While my burning heart lies sleeping?

Kiss me;—oh! thy lips are cold:
Round my neck thine arms enfold—
They are soft, but chill and dead;
And thy tears upon my head
Burn like points of frozen lead.

Hasten to the bridal bed—
Underneath the grave 'tis spread:
In darkness may our love be hid,
Oblivion be our coverlid—
We may rest, and none forbid.

Clasp me till our hearts be grown
Like two shadows into one;
Till this dreadful transport may
Like a vapour fade away,
In the sleep that lasts alway.

We may dream, in that long sleep,
That we are not those who weep;
E'en as Pleasure dreams of thee,
Life-deserting Misery,
Thou mayst dream of her with me.

Let us laugh, and make our mirth,
At the shadows of the earth,
As dogs bay the moonlight clouds,
Which, like spectres wrapped in shrouds,
Pass o'er night in multitudes.

All the wide world, beside us,
Show like multitudinous
Puppets passing from a scene;
What but mockery can they mean,
Where I am—where thou hast been?

STANZAS

WRITTEN IN DEJECTION, NEAR NAPLES

The sun is warm, the sky is clear,
    The waves are dancing fast and bright,
Blue isles and snowy mountains wear
    The purple noon's transparent might,
    The breath of the moist earth is light,
Around its unexpanded buds;
    Like many a voice of one delight,
The winds, the birds, the ocean floods,
The City's voice itself, is soft like Solitude's.

I see the Deep's untrampled floor
    With green and purple seaweeds strown;
I see the waves upon the shore,
    Like light dissolved in star-showers, thrown:
    I sit upon the sands alone,—
The lightning of the noontide ocean
    Is flashing around me, and a tone
Arises from its measured motion,
How sweet! did any heart now share in my emotion.

Alas! I have nor hope nor health,
    Nor peace within nor calm around,
Nor that content surpassing wealth
    The sage in meditation found,
    And walked with inward glory crowned—
Nor fame, nor power, nor love, nor leisure.
    Others I see whom these surround—
Smiling they live, and call life pleasure;—
To me that cup has been dealt in another measure.

558

Yet now despair itself is mild,
  Even as the winds and waters are;
I could lie down like a tired child,
  And weep away the life of care
  Which I have borne and yet must bear,
Till death like sleep might steal on me,
  And I might feel in the warm air
My cheek grow cold, and hear the sea
Breathe o'er my dying brain its last monotony.

Some might lament that I were cold,
  As I, when this sweet day is gone,
Which my lost heart, too soon grown old,
  Insults with this untimely moan;
  They might lament—for I am one
Whom men love not,—and yet regret,
  Unlike this day, which, when the sun
Shall on its stainless glory set,
Will linger, though enjoyed, like joy in memory yet.

SONNET

Lift not the painted veil which those who live
Call Life: though unreal shapes be pictured there,
And it but mimic all we would believe
With colours idly spread,—behind, lurk Fear
And Hope, twin Destinies; who ever weave
Their shadows, o'er the chasm, sightless and drear.
I knew one who had lifted it—he sought,
For his lost heart was tender, things to love,
But found them not, alas! nor was there aught
The world contains, the which he could approve.
Through the unheeding many he did move,
A splendour among shadows, a bright blot
Upon this gloomy scene, a Spirit that strove
For truth, and like the Preacher found it not.

559

SONG TO THE MEN OF ENGLAND

Men of England, wherefore plough
For the lords who lay ye low?
Wherefore weave with toil and care
The rich robes your tyrants wear?

Wherefore feed, and clothe, and save,
From the cradle to the grave,
Those ungrateful drones who would
Drain your sweat—nay, drink your blood?

Wherefore, Bees of England, forge
Many a weapon, chain, and scourge,
That these stingless drones may spoil
The forced produce of your toil?

Have ye leisure, comfort, calm,
Shelter, food, love's gentle balm?
Or what is it ye buy so dear
With your pain and with your fear?

The seed ye sow, another reaps;
The wealth ye find, another keeps;
The robes ye weave, another wears;
The arms ye forge, another bears.

Sow seed,—but let no tyrant reap;
Find wealth,—let no impostor heap;
Weave robes,—let not the idle wear;
Forge arms,—in your defence to bear.

Shrink to your cellars, holes, and cells;
In halls ye deck another dwells.
Why shake the chains ye wrought?   Ye see
The steel ye tempered glance on ye.

With plough and spade, and hoe and loom,
Trace your grave, and build your tomb,
And weave your winding-sheet, till fair
England be your sepulchre.

PERCY BYSSHE SHELLEY

ODE TO THE WEST WIND

O wild West Wind, thou breath of Autumn's being,
Thou, from whose unseen presence the leaves dead
Are driven, like ghosts from an enchanter fleeing,

Yellow, and black, and pale, and hectic red,
Pestilence-stricken multitudes: O thou,
Who chariotest to their dark wintry bed

The wingèd seeds, where they lie cold and low,
Each like a corpse within its grave, until
Thine azure sister of the Spring shall blow

Her clarion o'er the dreaming earth, and fill
(Driving sweet buds like flocks to feed in air)
With living hues and odours plain and hill:

Wild Spirit, which art moving everywhere;
Destroyer and preserver; hear, oh, hear!

Thou on whose stream, mid the steep sky's commotion,
Loose clouds like earth's decaying leaves are shed,
Shook from the tangled boughs of Heaven and Ocean,

Angels of rain and lightning: there are spread
On the blue surface of thine aëry surge,
Like the bright hair uplifted from the head

Of some fierce Mænad, even from the dim verge
Of the horizon to the zenith's height,
The locks of the approaching storm. Thou dirge

Of the dying year, to which this closing night
Will be the dome of a vast sepulchre,
Vaulted with all thy congregated might

Of vapours, from whose solid atmosphere
Black rain, and fire, and hail will burst: oh, hear!

Thou who didst waken from his summer dreams
The blue Mediterranean, where he lay,
Lulled by the coil of his crystalline streams,

Beside a pumice isle in Baiæ's bay,
And saw in sleep old palaces and towers
Quivering within the wave's intenser day,

All overgrown with azure moss and flowers
So sweet, the sense faints picturing them! Thou
For whose path the Atlantic's level powers

Cleave themselves into chasms, while far below
The sea-blooms and the oozy woods which wear
The sapless foliage of the ocean, know

Thy voice, and suddenly grow grey with fear,
And tremble and despoil themselves: oh, hear!

If I were a dead leaf thou mightest bear;
If I were a swift cloud to fly with thee;
A wave to pant beneath thy power, and share

The impulse of thy strength, only less free
Than thou, O uncontrollable! If even
I were as in my boyhood, and could be

The comrade of thy wanderings over Heaven,
As then, when to outstrip thy skiey speed
Scarce seemed a vision; I would ne'er have striven

As thus with thee in prayer in my sore need.
Oh, lift me as a wave, a leaf, a cloud!
I fall upon the thorns of life! I bleed!

A heavy weight of hours has chained and bowed
One too like thee: tameless, and swift, and proud.

Make me thy lyre, even as the forest is:
What if my leaves are falling like its own!
The tumult of thy mighty harmonies

Will take from both a deep, autumnal tone,
Sweet though in sadness. Be thou, Spirit fierce,
My spirit! Be thou me, impetuous one!

Drive my dead thoughts over the universe
Like withered leaves to quicken a new birth!
And, by the incantation of this verse,

Scatter, as from an unextinguished hearth
Ashes and sparks, my words among mankind!
Be through my lips to unawakened earth

The trumpet of a prophecy! O Wind,
If Winter comes, can Spring be far behind?

THE INDIAN SERENADE

I arise from dreams of thee
In the first sweet sleep of night,
When the winds are breathing low,
And the stars are shining bright;
I arise from dreams of thee,
And a spirit in my feet
Hath led me—who knows how?
To thy chamber window, Sweet!

The wandering airs they faint
On the dark, the silent stream—
The Champak odours fail
Like sweet thoughts in a dream;
The nightingale's complaint,
It dies upon her heart;—
As I must on thine,
Oh, belovèd as thou art!

Oh lift me from the grass!
I die! I faint! I fail!
Let thy love in kisses rain
On my lips and eyelids pale.

My cheek is cold and white, alas!
My heart beats loud and fast;—
Oh! press it to thine own again,
Where it will break at last.

LOVE'S PHILOSOPHY

The fountains mingle with the river
    And the rivers with the Ocean,
The winds of Heaven mix for ever
    With a sweet emotion;
Nothing in the world is single;
    All things by a law divine
In one spirit meet and mingle.
    Why not I with thine?—

See the mountains kiss high Heaven
    And the waves clasp one another;
No sister-flower would be forgiven
    If it disdained its brother;
And the sunlight clasps the earth
    And the moonbeams kiss the sea:
What is all this sweet work worth
    If thou kiss not me?

FRAGMENT: WEDDED SOULS

                    I am as a spirit who has dwelt
Within his heart of hearts, and I have felt
His feelings, and have thought his thoughts, and known
The inmost converse of his soul, the tone
Unheard but in the silence of his blood,
When all the pulses in their multitude
Image the trembling calm of summer seas.
I have unlocked the golden melodies
Of his deep soul, as with a master-key.
And loosened them and bathed myself therein—
Even as an eagle in a thunder-mist
Clothing his wings with lightning.

PERCY BYSSHE SHELLEY

THE CLOUD

I bring fresh showers for the thirsting flowers,
    From the seas and the streams;
I bear light shade for the leaves when laid
    In their noonday dreams.
From my wings are shaken the dews that waken
    The sweet buds every one,
When rocked to rest on their mother's breast,
    As she dances about the sun.
I wield the flail of the lashing hail,
    And whiten the green plains under,
And then again I dissolve it in rain,
    And laugh as I pass in thunder.

I sift the snow on the mountains below,
    And their great pines groan aghast;
And all the night 'tis my pillow white,
    While I sleep in the arms of the blast.
Sublime on the towers of my skiey bowers,
    Lightning my pilot sits;
In a cavern under is fettered the thunder,
    It struggles and howls at fits;
Over earth and ocean, with gentle motion,
    This pilot is guiding me,
Lured by the love of the genii that move
    In the depths of the purple sea;
Over the rills, and the crags, and the hills.
    Over the lakes and the plains,
Wherever he dream, under mountain or stream,
    The Spirit he loves remains;
And I all the while bask in Heaven's blue smile,
    Whilst he is dissolving in rains.

The sanguine Sunrise, with his meteor eyes,
    And his burning plumes outspread,
Leaps on the back of my sailing rack,
    When the morning star shines dead;

As on the jag of a mountain crag,
  Which an earthquake rocks and swings,
An eagle alit one moment may sit
  In the light of its golden wings.
And when Sunset may breathe, from the lit sea beneath,
  Its ardours of rest and of love,
And the crimson pall of eve may fall
  From the depth of Heaven above,
With wings folded I rest, on mine aëry nest,
  As still as a brooding dove.

That orbèd maiden with white fire laden,
  Whom mortals call the Moon,
Glides glimmering o'er my fleece-like floor,
  By the midnight breezes strewn;
And wherever the beat of her unseen feet,
  Which only the angels hear,
May have broken the woof of my tent's thin roof,
  The stars peep behind her and peer;
And I laugh to see them whirl and flee,
  Like a swarm of golden bees,
When I widen the rent in my wind-built tent,
  Till the calm rivers, lakes, and seas,
Like strips of the sky fallen through me on high,
  Are each paved with the moon and these.

I bind the Sun's throne with a burning zone,
  And the Moon's with a girdle of pearl;
The volcanoes are dim, and the stars reel and swim,
  When the whirlwinds my banner unfurl.
From cape to cape, with a bridge-like shape,
  Over a torrent sea,
Sunbeam-proof, I hang like a roof,—
  The mountains its columns be.
The triumphal arch through which I march
  With hurricane, fire, and snow,
When the Powers of the air are chained to my chair,
  Is the million-coloured bow;
The sphere-fire above its soft colours wove,
  While the moist Earth was laughing below.

566

PERCY BYSSHE SHELLEY

I am the daughter of Earth and Water,
  And the nursling of the Sky;
I pass through the pores of the ocean and shores;
  I change, but I cannot die.
For after the rain when with never a stain
  The pavilion of Heaven is bare,
And the winds and sunbeams with their convex gleams
  Build up the blue dome of air,
I silently laugh at my own cenotaph,
  And out of the caverns of rain,
Like a child from the womb, like a ghost from the tomb,
  I arise and unbuild it again.

TO A SKYLARK

Hail to thee, blithe Spirit!
  Bird thou never wert,
That from Heaven, or near it,
  Pourest thy full heart
In profuse strains of unpremeditated art.

Higher still and higher
  From the earth thou springest
Like a cloud of fire;
  The blue deep thou wingest,
And singing still dost soar, and soaring ever singest.

In the golden lightning
  Of the sunken sun,
O'er which clouds are bright'ning,
  Thou dost float and run;
Like an unbodied joy whose race is just begun.

The pale purple even
  Melts around thy flight;
Like a star of Heaven,
  In the broad daylight
Thou art unseen, but yet I hear thy shrill delight,

Keen as are the arrows
    Of that silver sphere,
Whose intense lamp narrows
    In the white dawn clear
Until we hardly see—we feel that it is there.

All the earth and air
    With thy voice is loud,
As, when night is bare,
    From one lonely cloud
The moon rains out her beams, and Heaven is overflowed.

What thou art we know not;
    What is most like thee?
From rainbow clouds there flow not
    Drops so bright to see
As from thy presence showers a rain of melody.

Like a Poet hidden
    In the light of thought,
Singing hymns unbidden,
    Till the world is wrought
To sympathy with hopes and fears it heeded not:

Like a high-born maiden
    In a palace-tower,
Soothing her love-laden
    Soul in secret hour
With music sweet as love, which overflows her bower:

Like a glow-worm golden
    In a dell of dew,
Scattering unbeholden
    Its aëreal hue
Among the flowers and grass, which screen it from the view!

Like a rose embowered
    In its own green leaves,
By warm winds deflowered,
    Till the scent it gives
Makes faint with too much sweet those heavy-wingèd thieves:

568

PERCY BYSSHE SHELLEY

Sound of vernal showers
    On the twinkling grass,
Rain-awakened flowers,
    All that ever was
Joyous and clear, and fresh, thy music doth surpass:

Teach us, Sprite or Bird,
    What sweet thoughts are thine:
I have never heard
    Praise of love or wine
That panted forth a flood of rapture so divine.

Chorus Hymeneal,
    Or triumphal chant,
Matched with thine would be all
    But an empty vaunt,
A thing wherein we feel there is some hidden want.

What objects are the fountains
    Of thy happy strain?
What fields, or waves, or mountains?
    What shapes of sky or plain?
What love of thine own kind? what ignorance of pain?

With thy clear keen joyance
    Languor cannot be:
Shadow of annoyance
    Never came near thee:
Thou lovest—but ne'er knew love's sad satiety.

Waking or asleep,
    Thou of death must deem
Things more true and deep
    Than we mortals dream,
Or how could thy notes flow in such a crystal stream?

We look before and after,
    And pine for what is not:
Our sincerest laughter
    With some pain is fraught;
Our sweetest songs are those that tell of saddest thought.

Yet if we could scorn
    Hate, and pride, and fear;
If we were things born
    Not to shed a tear,
I know not how thy joy we ever should come near.

Better than all measures
    Of delightful sound,
Better than all treasures
    That in books are found,
Thy skill to poet were, thou scorner of the ground!

Teach me half the gladness
    That thy brain must know,
Such harmonious madness
    From my lips would flow
The world should listen then—as I am listening now.

HYMN OF APOLLO

The sleepless Hours who watch me as I lie,
    Curtained with star-inwoven tapestries
From the broad moonlight of the sky,
    Fanning the busy dreams from my dim eyes,—
Waken me when their Mother, the grey Dawn,
Tells them that dreams and that the moon is gone.

Then I arise, and climbing Heaven's blue dome,
    I walk over the mountains and the waves,
Leaving my robe upon the ocean foam;
    My footsteps pave the clouds with fire; the caves
Are filled with my bright presence, and the air
Leaves the green Earth to my embraces bare.

The sunbeams are my shafts, with which I kill
    Deceit, that loves the night and fears the day;
All men who do or even imagine ill
    Fly me, and from the glory of my ray
Good minds and open actions take new might,
Until diminished by the reign of Night.

570

I feed the clouds, the rainbows and the flowers
  With their æthereal colours; the moon's globe
And the pure stars in their eternal bowers
  Are cinctured with my power as with a robe;
Whatever lamps on Earth or Heaven may shine
Are portions of one power, which is mine.

I stand at noon upon the peak of Heaven,
  Then with unwilling steps I wander down
Into the clouds of the Atlantic even;
  For grief that I depart they weep and frown:
What look is more delightful than the smile
With which I soothe them from the western isle?

I am the eye with which the Universe
  Beholds itself and knows itself divine;
All harmony of instrument or verse,
  All prophecy, all medicine is mine,
All light of art or nature;—to my song
Victory and praise in its own right belong.

HYMN OF PAN

From the forests and highlands
  We come, we come;
From the river-girt islands,
  Where loud waves are dumb
    Listening to my sweet pipings.
The wind in the reeds and the rushes,
  The bees on the bells of thyme,
The birds on the myrtle bushes,
  The cicale above in the lime,
And the lizards below in the grass,
Were as silent as ever old Tmolus was,
  Listening to my sweet pipings.

Liquid Peneus was flowing,
  And all dark Tempe lay
In Pelion's shadow, outgrowing
  The light of the dying day,

Speeded by my sweet pipings.
The Sileni, and Sylvans, and Fauns,
  And the Nymphs of the woods and the waves,
To the edge of the moist river-lawns,
  And the brink of the dewy caves,
And all that did then attend and follow,
Were silent with love, as you now, Apollo,
  With envy of my sweet pipings.

I sang of the dancing stars,
  I sang of the dædal Earth,
And of Heaven—and the giant wars,
  And Love, and Death, and Birth,—
    And then I changed my pipings,—
Singing how down the vale of Mænalus
  I pursued a maiden and clasped a reed.
Gods and men, we are all deluded thus!
  It breaks in our bosom and then we bleed:
All wept, as I think both ye now would,
If envy or age had not frozen your blood,
  At the sorrow of my sweet pipings.

THE QUESTION

I dreamed that, as I wandered by the way,
  Bare Winter suddenly was changed to Spring,
And gentle odours led my steps astray,
  Mixed with a sound of waters murmuring
Along a shelving bank of turf, which lay
  Under a copse, and hardly dared to fling
Its green arms round the bosom of the stream,
But kissed it and then fled, as thou mightest in dream.

There grew pied wind-flowers and violets,
  Daisies, those pearled Arcturi of the earth,
The constellated flower that never sets;
  Faint oxslips; tender bluebells, at whose birth
The sod scarce heaved; and that tall flower that wets—
  Like a child, half in tenderness and mirth—
Its mother's face with Heaven's collected tears,
When the low wind, its playmate's voice, it hears.

572

And in the warm hedge grew lush eglantine,
   Green cowbind and the moonlight-coloured may,
And cherry-blossoms, and white cups, whose wine
   Was the bright dew, yet drained not by the day;
And wild roses, and ivy serpentine,
   With its dark buds and leaves, wandering astray;
And flowers azure, black, and streaked with gold,
Fairer than any wakened eyes behold.

And nearer to the river's trembling edge
   There grew broad flag-flowers, purple pranked with white,
And starry river buds among the sedge,
   And floating water-lilies, broad and bright,
Which lit the oak that overhung the hedge
   With moonlight beams of their own watery light;
And bulrushes, and reeds of such deep green
As soothed the dazzled eye with sober sheen.

Methought that of these visionary flowers
   I made a nosegay, bound in such a way
That the same hues, which in their natural bowers
   Were mingled or opposed, the like array
Kept these imprisoned children of the Hours
   Within my hand,—and then, elate and gay,
I hastened to the spot whence I had come,
That I might there present it!—Oh! to whom?

THE TWO SPIRITS

FIRST SPIRIT

O thou, who plumed with strong desire
   Wouldst float above the earth, beware!
A Shadow tracks thy flight of fire—
   Night is coming!
Bright are the regions of the air,
And among the winds and beams
   It were delight to wander there—
   Night is coming!

SECOND SPIRIT

The deathless stars are bright above;
　　If I would cross the shade of night,
Within my heart is the lamp of love,
　　　　And that is day!
And the moon will smile with gentle light
On my golden plumes where'er they move;
　　The meteors will linger round my flight,
　　　　And make night day.

FIRST SPIRIT

But if the whirlwinds of darkness waken
　　Hail, and lightning, and stormy rain;
See, the bounds of the air are shaken—
　　　　Night is coming!
The red swift clouds of the hurricane
Yon declining sun have overtaken,
　　The clash of the hail sweeps over the plain—
　　　　Night is coming!

SECOND SPIRIT

I see the light, and I hear the sound;
　　I'll sail on the flood of the tempest dark,
With the calm within and the light around
　　　　Which makes night day:
And thou, when the gloom is deep and stark,
Look from thy dull earth, slumber-bound,
　　My moon-like flight thou then mayst mark
　　　　On high, far away.

· · · ·

Some say there is a precipice
　　Where one vast pine is frozen to ruin
O'er piles of snow and chasms of ice
　　　　Mid Alpine mountains;
And that the languid storm pursuing
That wingèd shape, for ever flies
　　Round those hoar branches, aye renewing
　　　　Its aëry fountains.

PERCY BYSSHE SHELLEY

Some say when nights are dry and clear,
   And the death-dews sleep on the morass,
Sweet whispers are heard by the traveller,
      Which make night day:
And a silver shape like his early love doth pass
Upborne by her wild and glittering hair,
   And when he awakes on the fragrant grass,
      He finds night day.

TO THE MOON

   Art thou pale for weariness
Of climbing heaven and gazing on the earth,
   Wandering companionless
Among the stars that have a different birth?

.   .   .   .

THE WORLD'S WANDERERS

Tell me, thou Star, whose wings of light
Speed thee in thy fiery flight,
In what cavern of the night
      Will thy pinions close now?

Tell me, Moon, thou pale and grey
Pilgrim of Heaven's homeless way,
In what depth of night or day
      Seekest thou repose now?

Weary Wind, who wanderest
Like the world's rejected guest,
Hast thou still some secret nest
      On the tree or billow?

TIME LONG PAST

Like the ghost of a dear friend dead
   Is Time long past.
A tone which is now forever fled,
A hope which is now forever past,

A love so sweet it could not last,
    Was Time long past.

There were sweet dreams in the night
    Of Time long past:
And, was it sadness or delight,
Each day a shadow onward cast
Which made us wish it yet might last—
    That Time long past.

There is regret, almost remorse,
    For Time long past.
'Tis like a child's beloved corse
A father watches, till at last
Beauty is like remembrance, cast
    From Time long past.

DIRGE FOR THE YEAR

Orphan Hours, the Year is dead,
    Come and sigh, come and weep!
Merry Hours, smile instead,
    For the Year is but asleep.
See, it smiles as it is sleeping,
Mocking your untimely weeping.

As an earthquake rocks a corse
    In its coffin in the clay,
So White Winter, that rough nurse,
    Rocks the death-cold Year today;
Solemn Hours! wail aloud
For your mother in her shroud.

As the wild air stirs and sways
    The tree-swung cradle of a child,
So the breath of these rude days
    Rocks the Year:—be calm and mild,
Trembling Hours, she will arise
With new love within her eyes.

PERCY BYSSHE SHELLEY

January grey is here,
  Like a sexton by her grave;
February bears the bier,
  March with grief doth howl and rave,
And April weeps—but, O ye Hours!
Follow with May's fairest flowers.

TO NIGHT

Swiftly walk o'er the western wave,
    Spirit of Night!
Out of the misty eastern cave,
Where, all the long and lone daylight,
Thou wovest dreams of joy and fear,
Which make thee terrible and dear,—
    Swift be thy flight!

Wrap thy form in a mantle grey,
    Star-inwrought!
Blind with thine hair the eyes of Day;
Kiss her until she be wearied out,
Then wander o'er city, and sea, and land,
Touching all with thine opiate wand—
    Come, long-sought!

When I arose and saw the dawn,
    I sighed for thee;
When light rode high, and the dew was gone,
And noon lay heavy on flower and tree,
And the weary Day turned to his rest,
Lingering like an unloved guest,
    I sighed for thee.

Thy brother Death came, and cried,
    Wouldst thou me?
Thy sweet child Sleep, the filmy-eyed,
Murmured like a noontide bee,
Shall I nestle near thy side?
Wouldst thou me?—and I replied,
    No, not thee!

Death will come when thou art dead,
  Soon, too soon—
Sleep will come when thou art fled;
Of neither would I ask the boon
I ask of thee, belovèd Night—
Swift be thine approaching flight,
  Come soon, soon!

TIME

Unfathomable Sea! whose waves are years,
 Ocean of Time, whose waters of deep woe
Are brackish with the salt of human tears!
 Thou shoreless flood, which in thy ebb and flow
Claspest the limits of mortality,
And sick of prey, yet howling on for more,
Vomitest thy wrecks on its inhospitable shore;
 Treacherous in calm, and terrible in storm,
  Who shall put forth on thee,
  Unfathomable Sea?

TO ——

Music, when soft voices die,
Vibrates in the memory—
Odours, when sweet violets sicken,
Live within the sense they quicken.

Rose leaves, when the rose is dead,
Are heaped for the belovèd's bed;
And so thy thoughts, when thou art gone,
Love itself shall slumber on.

SONG

Rarely, rarely, comest thou,
 Spirit of Delight!
Wherefore hast thou left me now
 Many a day and night?
Many a weary night and day
'Tis since thou art fled away.

How shall ever one like me
   Win thee back again?
With the joyous and the free
   Thou wilt scoff at pain.
Spirit false! thou hast forgot
All but those who need thee not.

As a lizard with the shade
   Of a trembling leaf,
Thou with sorrow art dismayed;
   Even the sighs of grief
Reproach thee, that thou art not near,
And reproach thou wilt not hear.

Let me set my mournful ditty
   To a merry measure;
Thou wilt never come for pity,
   Thou wilt come for pleasure;
Pity then will cut away
Those cruel wings, and thou wilt stay.

I love all that thou lovest,
   Spirit of Delight!
The fresh Earth in new leaves dressed,
   And the starry night;
Autumn evening, and the morn
When the golden mists are born.

I love snow, and all the forms
   Of the radiant frost;
I love waves, and winds, and storms,
   Everything almost
Which is Nature's, and may be
Untainted by man's misery.

I love tranquil solitude,
   And such society
As is quiet, wise, and good;
   Between thee and me
What difference? but thou dost possess
The things I seek, not love them less.

I love Love—though he has wings,
   And like light can flee,
But above all other things,
   Spirit, I love thee—
Thou art love and life! Oh, come,
Make once more my heart thy home.

A LAMENT

O world! O life! O time!
On whose last steps I climb,
   Trembling at that where I had stood before;
When will return the glory of your prime?
    No more—Oh, never more!

Out of the day and night
A joy has taken flight;
   Fresh spring, and summer, and winter hoar,
Move my faint heart with grief, but with delight
    No more—Oh, never more!

REMEMBRANCE

Swifter far than summer's flight—
Swifter far than youth's delight—
Swifter far than happy night,
   Art thou come and gone—
As the earth when leaves are dead,
As the night when sleep is sped,
As the heart when joy is fled,
   I am left lone, alone.

The swallow summer comes again—
The owlet night resumes her reign—
But the wild-swan youth is fain
   To fly with thee, false as thou.—
My heart each day desires the morrow;
Sleep itself is turned to sorrow;
Vainly would my winter borrow
   Sunny leaves from any bough.

PERCY BYSSHE SHELLEY

Lilies for a bridal bed—
Roses for a matron's head—
Violets for a maiden dead—
   Pansies let *my* flowers be:
On the living grave I bear
Scatter them without a tear—
Let no friend, however dear,
   Waste one hope, one fear for me.

TO ——

One word is too often profaned
   For me to profane it,
One feeling too falsely disdained
   For thee to disdain it;
One hope is too like despair
   For prudence to smother,
And pity from thee more dear
   Than that from another.

I can give not what men call love,
   But wilt thou accept not
The worship the heart lifts above
   And the Heavens reject not,—
The desire of the moth for the star,
   Of the night for the morrow,
The devotion to something afar
   From the sphere of our sorrow?

TO ——

When passion's trance is overpast,
If tenderness and truth could last,
Or live, whilst all wild feelings keep
Some mortal slumber, dark and deep,
I should not weep, I should not weep!

It were enough to feel, to see,
Thy soft eyes gazing tenderly,

And dream the rest—and burn and be
The secret food of fires unseen,
Couldst thou but be as thou hast been.

After the slumber of the year
The woodland violets reappear;
All things revive in field or grove,
And sky and sea, but two, which move
And form all others, life and love.

MUSIC

I pant for the music which is divine,
  My heart in its thirst is a dying flower;
Pour forth the sound like enchanted wine,
  Loosen the notes in a silver shower;
Like a herbless plain, for the gentle rain,
I gasp, I faint, till they wake again.

Let me drink of the spirit of that sweet sound,
  More, oh more,—I am thirsting yet;
It loosens the serpent which care has bound
  Upon my heart to stifle it;
The dissolving strain, through every vein,
Passes into my heart and brain.

As the scent of a violet withered up,
  Which grew by the brink of a silver lake,
When the hot noon has drained its dewy cup,
  And mist there was none its thirst to slake—
And the violet lay dead while the odour flew
On the wings of the wind o'er the waters blue—

As one who drinks from a charmèd cup
  Of foaming, and sparkling, and murmuring wine,
Whom, a mighty Enchantress filling up.
  Invites to love with her kiss divine . . .

WHEN THE LAMP IS SHATTERED

When the lamp is shattered
The light in the dust lies dead—
When the cloud is scattered
The rainbow's glory is shed.
When the lute is broken,
Sweet tones are remembered not;
When the lips have spoken,
Loved accents are soon forgot.

As music and splendour
Survive not the lamp and the lute,
The heart's echoes render
No song when the spirit is mute:—
No song but sad dirges,
Like the wind through a ruined cell,
Or the mournful surges
That ring the dead seaman's knell.

When hearts have once mingled
Love first leaves the well-built nest;
The weak one is singled
To endure what it once possessed.
O Love! who bewailest
The frailty of all things here,
Why choose you the frailest
For your cradle, your home, and your bier?

Its passions will rock thee
As the storms rock the ravens on high;
Bright reason will mock thee,
Like the sun from a wintry sky.
From thy nest every rafter
Will rot, and thine eagle home
Leave thee naked to laughter,
When leaves fall and cold winds come.

TO JANE: THE INVITATION

Best and brightest, come away!
Fairer far than this fair Day,
Which, like thee to those in sorrow,
Comes to bid a sweet good-morrow
To the rough Year just awake
In its cradle on the brake.
The brightest hour of unborn Spring,
Through the winter wandering,
Found, it seems, the halcyon Morn
To hoar February born.
Bending from Heaven, in azure mirth,
It kissed the forehead of the Earth,
And smiled upon the silent sea,
And bade the frozen streams be free,
And waked to music all their fountains,
And breathed upon the frozen mountains,
And like a prophetess of May
Strewed flowers upon the barren way,
Making the wintry world appear
Like one on whom thou smilest, dear.

Away, away, from men and towns,
To the wild wood and the downs—
To the silent wilderness
Where the soul need not repress
Its music lest it should not find
An echo in another's mind,
While the touch of Nature's art
Harmonises heart to heart.
I leave this notice on my door
For each accustomed visitor:—
"I am gone into the fields
To take what this sweet hour yields;—
Reflection, you may come to-morrow,
Sit by the fireside with Sorrow.—
You with the unpaid bill, Despair,—
You, tiresome verse-reciter, Care,—
I will pay you in the grave,—
Death will listen to your stave.

PERCY BYSSHE SHELLEY

Expectation too, be off!
To-day is for itself enough;
Hope, in pity mock not Woe
With smiles, nor follow where I go;
Long having lived on thy sweet food,
At length I find one moment's good
After long pain—with all your love,
This you never told me of."

Radiant Sister of the Day,
Awake! arise! and come away!
To the wild woods and the plains,
And the pools where winter rains
Image all their roof of leaves,
Where the pine its garland weaves
Of sapless green and ivy dun
Round stems that never kiss the sun;
Where the lawns and pastures be,
And the sandhills of the sea;—
Where the melting hoar-frost wets
The daisy-star that never sets,
And wind-flowers, and violets,
Which yet join not scent to hue,
Crown the pale year weak and new;
When the night is left behind
In the deep east, dun and blind,
And the blue noon is over us,
And the multitudinous
Billows murmur at our feet,
Where the earth and ocean meet,
And all things seem only one
In the universal sun.

TO JANE: THE RECOLLECTION

Now the last day of many days,
  All beautiful and bright as thou,
    The loveliest and the last, is dead,

Rise, Memory, and write its praise!
    Up,—to thy wonted work! come, trace
    The epitaph of glory fled,—
For now the Earth has changed its face,
    A frown is on the Heaven's brow.

We wandered to the Pine Forest
    That skirts the Ocean's foam,
The lightest wind was in its nest,
    The tempest in its home.
The whispering waves were half asleep,
    The clouds were gone to play,
And on the bosom of the deep
    The smile of Heaven lay;
It seemed as if the hour were one
    Sent from beyond the skies,
Which scattered from above the sun
    A light of Paradise.

We paused amid the pines that stood
    The giants of the waste,
Tortured by storms to shapes as rude
    As serpents interlaced;
And, soothed by every azure breath,
    That under Heaven is blown,
To harmonies and hues beneath,
    As tender as its own,
Now all the tree-tops lay asleep,
    Like green waves on the sea,
As still as in the silent deep
    The ocean woods may be.

How calm it was!—the silence there
    By such a chain was bound
That even the busy woodpecker
    Made stiller by her sound
The inviolable quietness;
    The breath of peace we drew
With its soft motion made not less
    The calm that round us grew.

586

There seemed from the remotest seat
  Of the white mountain waste,
To the soft flower beneath our feet,
  A magic circle traced,—
A spirit interfused around,
  A thrilling, silent life,—
To momentary peace it bound
  Our mortal nature's strife;
And still I felt the centre of
  The magic circle there
Was one fair form that filled with love
  The lifeless atmosphere.

We paused beside the pools that lie
  Under the forest bough,—
Each seemed as 'twere a little sky
  Gulfed in a world below;
A firmament of purple light
  Which in the dark earth lay,
More boundless than the depth of night,
  And purer than the day—
In which the lovely forests grew,
  As in the upper air,
More perfect both in shape and hue
  Than any spreading there.
There lay the glade and neighbouring lawn,
  And through the dark green wood
The white sun twinkling like the dawn
  Out of a speckled cloud.
Sweet views which in our world above
  Can never well be seen,
Were imaged by the water's love
  Of that fair forest green.
And all was interfused beneath
  With an Elysian glow,
An atmosphere without a breath,
  A softer day below.
Like one beloved the scene had lent
  To the dark water's breast,
Its every leaf and lineament
  With more than truth expressed;

Until an envious wind crept by,,
    Like an unwelcome thought,
Which from the mind's too faithful eye
    Blots one dear image out.
Though thou art ever fair and kind,
    The forests ever green,
Less oft is peace in Shelley's mind,
    Than calm in waters, seen.

WITH A GUITAR, TO JANE

Ariel to Miranda:—Take
This slave of Music, for the sake
Of him who is the slave of thee,
And teach it all the harmony
In which thou canst, and only thou,
Make the delighted spirit glow,
Till joy denies itself again,
And, too intense, is turned to pain;
For by permission and command
Of thine own Prince Ferdinand,
Poor Ariel sends this silent token
Of more than ever can be spoken;
Your guardian spirit, Ariel, who,
From life to life, must still pursue
Your happiness;—for thus alone
Can Ariel ever find his own.
From Prospero's enchanted cell,
As the mighty verses tell,
To the throne of Naples, he
Lit you o'er the trackless sea,
Flitting on, your prow before,
Like a living meteor.
When you die, the silent Moon,
In her interlunar swoon,
Is not sadder in her cell
Than deserted Ariel.
When you live again on earth,
Like an unseen star of birth,
Ariel guides you o'er the sea
Of life from your nativity.

PERCY BYSSHE SHELLEY

Many changes have been run
Since Ferdinand and you begun
Your course of love, and Ariel still
Has tracked your steps, and served your will;
Now, in humbler, happier lot,
This is all remembered not;
And now, alas! the poor sprite is
Imprisoned, for some fault of his,
In a body like a grave;—
From you he only dares to crave,
For his service and his sorrow,
A smile to-day, a song to-morrow.

The artist who this idol wrought,
To echo all harmonious thought,
Felled a tree, while on the steep
The woods were in their winter sleep,
Rocked in that repose divine
On the wind-swept Apennine;
And dreaming, some of Autumn past,
And some of Spring approaching fast,
And some of April buds and showers,
And some of songs in July bowers,
And all of love; and so this tree,—
O that such our death may be!—
Died in sleep, and felt no pain,
To live in happier form again:
From which, beneath Heaven's fairest star,
The artist wrought this loved Guitar,
And taught it justly to reply,
To all who question skilfully,
In language gentle as thine own;
Whispering in enamoured tone
Sweet oracles of woods and dells,
And summer winds in sylvan cells;
For it had learned all harmonies
Of the plains and of the skies,
Of the forests and the mountains,
And the many-voicèd fountains;
The clearest echoes of the hills,
The softest notes of falling rills,

The melodies of birds and bees,
The murmuring of summer seas,
And pattering rain, and breathing dew,
And airs of evening; and it knew
That seldom-heard mysterious sound,
Which, driven on its diurnal round,
As it floats through boundless day,
Our world enkindles on its way.—
All this it knows, but will not tell
To those who cannot question well
The Spirit that inhabits it;
It talks according to the wit
Of its companions; and no more
Is heard than has been felt before,
By those who tempt it to betray
These secrets of an elder day:
But, sweetly as its answers will
Flatter hands of perfect skill,
It keeps its highest, holiest tone
For our belovèd Jane alone.

TO JANE: THE KEEN STARS WERE TWINKLING

The keen stars were twinkling,
And the fair moon was rising among them,
    Dear Jane!
The guitar was tinkling,
But the notes were not sweet till you sung them
    Again.

As the moon's soft splendour
O'er the faint cold starlight of Heaven
    Is thrown,
So your voice most tender
To the strings without soul had then given
    Its own.

The stars will awaken,
Though the moon sleep a full hour later,
    To-night;

No leaf will be shaken
Whilst the dews of your melody scatter
   Delight.

Though the sound overpowers,
Sing again, with your dear voice revealing
   A tone
Of some world far from ours,
Where music and moonlight and feeling
   Are one.

A DIRGE

Rough wind, that moanest loud
   Grief too sad for song;
Wild wind, when sullen cloud
   Knells all the night long;
Sad storm, whose tears are vain,
Bare woods, whose branches strain,
Deep caves and dreary main,—
   Wail, for the world's wrong!

QUEEN MAB

.   .   .   .

How wonderful is Death,
   Death and his brother Sleep!
One, pale as yonder waning moon
   With lips of lurid blue;
The other, rosy as the morn
   When throned on ocean's wave
   It blushes o'er the world:
Yet both so passing wonderful!
   Hath then the gloomy Power
Whose reign is in the tainted sepulchres
   Seized on her sinless soul?
   Must then that peerless form
Which love and admiration cannot view
Without a beating heart, those azure veins

591

Which steal like streams along a field of snow,
   That lovely outline, which is fair
     As breathing marble, perish?
     Must putrefaction's breath
   Leave nothing of this heavenly sight
   But loathsomeness and ruin?
   Spare nothing but a gloomy theme,
On which the lightest heart might moralise?
   Or is it only a sweet slumber
     Stealing o'er sensation,
   Which the breath of roseate morning
     Chaseth into darkness?
     Will Ianthe wake again,
   And give that faithful bosom joy
   Whose sleepless spirit waits to catch
Light, life and rapture from her smile?

  •   •   •   •   •   •   •

Felicia Dorothea Hemans

THE GRAVES OF A HOUSEHOLD

They grew in beauty, side by side,
   They filled one home with glee;
Their graves are severed, far and wide,
   By mount, and stream, and sea.

The same fond mother bent at night
   O'er each fair sleeping brow;
She had each folded flower in sight—
   Where are those dreamers now?

One, 'midst the forests of the west,
   By a dark stream is laid—
The Indian knows his place of rest,
   Far in the cedar shade.

The sea, the blue lone sea, hath one,
   He lies where pearls lie deep;
He was the loved of all, yet none
   O'er his low bed may weep.

FELICIA DOROTHEA HEMANS

One sleeps where southern vines are dressed
    Above the noble slain:
He wrapt his colours round his breast,
    On a blood-red field of Spain.

And one—o'er her the myrtle showers
    Its leaves, by soft winds fanned;
She faded 'midst Italian flowers—
    The last of that bright band.

And parted thus they rest, who played
    Beneath the same green tree;
Whose voices mingled as they prayed
    Around one parent knee!

They that with smiles lit up the hall,
    And cheered with song the hearth—
Alas! for love, if *thou* wert all,
    And nought beyond, oh earth!

ENGLAND'S DEAD

    Son of the ocean isle!
    Where sleep your mighty dead?
Show me what high and stately pile
    Is reared o'er Glory's bed.

    Go, stranger! track the deep,
    Free, free, the white sail spread!
Wave may not foam, nor wild wind sweep,
    Where rest not England's dead.

    On Egypt's burning plains,
    By the pyramid o'erswayed,
With fearful power the noonday reigns,
    And the palm-trees yield no shade.

    But let the angry sun
    From heaven look fiercely red,
Unfelt by those whose task is done!—
    There slumber England's dead!

The hurricane hath might
Along the Indian shore,
And far by Ganges' banks at night
Is heard the tiger's roar.

But let the sound roll on!
It hath no tone of dread
For those that from their toils are gone;—
There slumber England's dead!

Loud rush the torrent-floods
The western wilds among,
And free in green Columbia's woods
The hunter's bow is strung.

But let the floods rush on!
Let the arrow's flight be sped!
Why should they reck whose task is done?—
There slumber England's dead!

The mountain-storms rise high
In the snowy Pyrenees,
And toss the pine-boughs through the sky
Like rose-leaves on the breeze.

But let the storm rage on!
Let the forest-wreaths be shed:
For the Roncesvalles' field is won,—
There slumber England's dead.

On the frozen deep's repose,
'Tis a dark and dreadful hour,
When round the ship the ice-fields close,
To chain her with their power.

But let the ice drift on!
Let the cold-blue desert spread!
Their course with mast and flag is done,—
Even *there* sleep England's dead.

The warlike of the isles,
The men of field and wave!
Are not the rocks their funeral piles,
The seas and shores their grave?

Go, stranger! track the deep,
Free, free, the white sail spread!
Wave may not foam, nor wild wind sweep,
Where rest not England's dead.

William Cullen Bryant

THANATOPSIS

To him who in the love of Nature holds
Communion with her visible forms, she speaks
A various language; for his gayer hours
She has a voice of gladness, and a smile
And eloquence of beauty, and she glides
Into his darker musings, with a mild
And healing sympathy, that steals away
Their sharpness, ere he is aware. When thoughts
Of the last bitter hour come like a blight
Over thy spirit, and sad images
Of the stern agony, and shroud, and pall,
And breathless darkness, and the narrow house,
Make thee to shudder and grow sick at heart;—
Go forth, under the open sky, and list
To Nature's teachings, while from all around—
Earth and her waters, and the depths of air—
Comes a still voice:—
                        Yet a few days, and thee
The all-beholding sun shall see no more
In all his course; nor yet in the cold ground,
Where thy pale form was laid, with many tears,
Nor in the embrace of ocean, shall exist
Thy image. Earth, that nourished thee, shall claim
Thy growth, to be resolved to earth again,
And, lost each human trace, surrendering up

595

Thine individual being, shalt thou go
To mix forever with the elements,
To be a brother to the insensible rock
And to the sluggish clod, which the rude swain
Turns with his share, and treads upon. The oak
Shall send his roots abroad, and pierce thy mould.

    Yet not to thine eternal resting-place
Shalt thou retire alone, nor couldst thou wish
Couch more magnificent. Thou shalt lie down
With patriarchs of the infant world—with kings,
The powerful of the earth—the wise, the good,
Fair forms, and hoary seers of ages past,
All in one mighty sepulchre. The hills
Rock-ribbed and ancient as the sun,—the vales
Stretching in pensive quietness between;
The venerable woods—rivers that move
In majesty, and the complaining brooks
That make the meadows green; and, poured round all,
Old Ocean's gray and melancholy waste,—
Are but the solemn decorations all
Of the great tomb of man. The golden sun,
The planets, all the infinite host of heaven,
Are shining on the sad abodes of death
Through the still lapse of ages. All that tread
The globe are but a handful to the tribes
That slumber in its bosom.—Take the wings
Of morning, pierce the Barcan wilderness,
Or lose thyself in the continuous woods
Where rolls the Oregon, and hears no sound,
Save his own dashings—yet the dead are there:
And millions in those solitudes, since first
The flight of years began, have laid them down
In their last sleep—the dead reign there alone.
So shalt thou rest, and what if thou withdraw
In silence from the living, and no friend
Take note of thy departure? All that breathe
Will share thy destiny. The gay will laugh
When thou art gone, the solemn brood of care
Plod on, and each one as before will chase
His favorite phantom; yet all these shall leave

Their mirth and their employments, and shall come
And make their bed with thee. As the long train
Of ages glides away, the sons of men—
The youth in life's fresh spring, and he who goes
In the full strength of years, matron and maid,
The speechless babe, and the gray-headed man—
Shall one by one be gathered to thy side,
By those, who in their turn shall follow them.

So live, that when thy summons comes to join
The innumerable caravan, which moves
To that mysterious realm, where each shall take
His chamber in the silent halls of death,
Thou go not, like the quarry-slave at night,
Scourged to his dungeon, but, sustained and soothed
By an unfaltering trust, approach thy grave
Like one who wraps the drapery of his couch
About him, and lies down to pleasant dreams.

TO A WATERFOWL

Whither, midst falling dew,
While glow the heavens with the last steps of day,
Far, through their rosy depths, dost thou pursue
Thy solitary way?

Vainly the fowler's eye
Might mark thy distant flight to do thee wrong,
As, darkly painted on the crimson sky,
Thy figure floats along.

Seek'st thou the plashy brink
Of weedy lake, or marge of river wide,
Or where the rocking billows rise and sink
On the chafed ocean-side?

There is a Power whose care
Teaches thy way along that pathless coast,—
The desert and illimitable air,—
Lone wandering, but not lost.

597

All day thy wings have fanned
At that far height, the cold, thin atmosphere,
Yet stoop not, weary, to the welcome land,
Though the dark night is near.

And soon that toil shall end;
Soon shalt thou find a summer home, and rest,
And scream among thy fellows; reeds shall bend,
Soon, o'er thy sheltered nest.

Thou'rt gone, the abyss of heaven
Hath swallowed up thy form; yet, on my heart
Deeply hath sunk the lesson thou hast given,
And shall not soon depart.

He who, from zone to zone,
Guides through the boundless sky thy certain flight,
In the long way that I must tread alone,
Will lead my steps aright.

TO THE FRINGED GENTIAN

Thou blossom bright with autumn dew,
And colored with the heaven's own blue,
That openest when the quiet light
Succeeds the keen and frosty night,

Thou comest not when violets lean
O'er wandering brooks and springs unseen,
Or columbines, in purple dressed,
Nod o'er the ground-bird's hidden nest.

Thou waitest late and com'st alone,
When woods are bare and birds are flown,
And frost and shortening days portend
The aged year is near his end.

Then doth thy sweet and quiet eye
Look through its fringes to the sky,
Blue—blue—as if that sky let fall
A flower from its cerulean wall.

WILLIAM CULLEN BRYANT

I would that thus, when I shall see
The hour of death draw near to me,
Hope, blossoming within my heart,
May look to heaven as I depart.

O, FAIREST OF THE RURAL MAIDS

O, fairest of the rural maids!
Thy birth was in the fairest shades;
Green boughs and glimpses of the sky
Were all that met thine infant eye.

Thy sports, thy wanderings when a child,
Were ever in the sylvan wild;
And all the beauty of the place
Is in thy heart and on thy face.

The twilight of the trees and rocks
Is in the light shade of thy locks;
Thy step is as the wind that weaves
Its playful way among the leaves.

Thine eyes are springs, in whose serene
And silent waters Heaven is seen;
Their lashes are the herbs that look
On their young figures in the brook.

The forest depths by foot impressed
Are not more sinless than thy breast;
The holy peace that fills the air
Of those calm solitudes, is there.

John Keats

FRAGMENT ON KEATS

"Here lieth One whose name was writ on water."
 But, ere the breath that could erase it blew,
Death, in remorse for that fell slaughter,
 Death, the immortalising winter, flew
 Athwart the stream,—and time's printless torrent grew
A scroll of crystal, blazoning the name
 Of Adonais!

—PERCY BYSSHE SHELLEY.

DEDICATION. TO LEIGH HUNT, ESQ.

"Glory and loveliness have pass'd away";
 For if we wander out in early morn,
 No wreathed incense do we see upborne
Into the east, to meet the smiling day:
No crowd of nymphs soft voic'd and young, and gay,
 In woven baskets bringing ears of corn,
 Roses, and pinks, and violets, to adorn
The shrine of Flora in her early May.
But there are left delights as high as these,
 And I shall ever bless my destiny,
That in a time, when under pleasant trees
 Pan is no longer sought, I feel a free,
A leafy luxury, seeing I could please
 With these poor offerings, a man like thee.

TO ONE WHO HAS BEEN LONG IN CITY PENT

To one who has been long in city pent,
 'Tis very sweet to look into the fair
 And open face of heaven,—to breathe a prayer
Full in the smile of the blue firmament.
600

JOHN KEATS

Who is more happy, when, with heart's content,
  Fatigued he sinks into some pleasant lair
  Of wavy grass, and reads a debonair
And gentle tale of love and languishment?
Returning home at evening, with an ear
  Catching the notes of Philomel,—an eye
Watching the sailing cloudlet's bright career,
  He mourns that day so soon has glided by:
E'en like the passage of an angel's tear
  That falls through the clear ether silently.

ON FIRST LOOKING INTO CHAPMAN'S HOMER

Much have I travell'd in the realms of gold,
  And many goodly states and kingdoms seen;
  Round many western islands have I been
Which bards in fealty to Apollo hold.
Oft of one wide expanse had I been told
  That deep-brow'd Homer ruled as his demesne;
  Yet did I never breathe its pure serene
Till I heard Chapman speak out loud and bold:
Then felt I like some watcher of the skies
  When a new planet swims into his ken;
Or like stout Cortez when with eagle eyes
  He star'd at the Pacific—and all his men
Look'd at each other with a wild surmise—
  Silent, upon a peak in Darien.

ENDYMION

A thing of beauty is a joy for ever:
Its loveliness increases; it will never
Pass into nothingness; but still will keep
A bower quiet for us, and a sleep
Full of sweet dreams, and health, and quiet breathing.
Therefore, on every morrow, are we wreathing
A flowery band to bind us to the earth,
Spite of despondence, of the inhuman dearth
Of noble natures, of the gloomy days,
Of all the unhealthy and o'er-darkened ways

Made for our searching: yes, in spite of all,
Some shape of beauty moves away the pall
From our dark spirits. Such the sun, the moon,
Trees old, and young, sprouting a shady boon
For simple sheep; and such are daffodils
With the green world they live in; and clear rills
That for themselves a cooling covert make
'Gainst the hot season; the mid forest brake,
Rich with a sprinkling of fair musk-rose blooms:
And such too is the grandeur of the dooms
We have imagined for the mighty dead;
All lovely tales that we have heard or read:
An endless fountain of immortal drink,
Pouring unto us from the heaven's brink.

    Nor do we merely feel these essences
For one short hour; no, even as the trees
That whisper round a temple become soon
Dear as the temple's self, so does the moon,
The passion poesy, glories infinite,
Haunt us till they become a cheering light
Unto our souls, and bound to us so fast,
That, whether there be shine, or gloom o'ercast,
They always must be with us, or we die.

                         —BOOK I.

     O Sorrow,
       Why dost borrow
The natural hue of health, from vermeil lips?—
       To give maiden blushes
       To the white rose bushes?
Or is't thy dewy hand the daisy tips?

     O Sorrow,
       Why dost borrow
The lustrous passion from a falcon-eye?—
       To give the glow-worm light?
       Or, on a moonless night,
To tinge, on syren shores, the salt sea-spry?

602

O Sorrow,
Why dost borrow
The mellow ditties from a mourning tongue?—
To give at evening pale
Unto the nightingale,
That thou mayst listen the cold dews among?

O Sorrow,
Why dost borrow
Heart's lightness from the merriment of May?—
A lover would not tread
A cowslip on the head,
Though he should dance from eve till peep of day—
Nor any drooping flower
Held sacred for thy bower,
Wherever he may sport himself and play.

To Sorrow,
I bade good-morrow,
And thought to leave her far away behind;
But cheerly, cheerly,
She loves me dearly;
She is so constant to me, and so kind:
I would deceive her
And so leave her,
But ah! she is so constant and so kind.

Beneath my palm trees, by the river side,
I sat a weeping: in the whole world wide
There was no one to ask me why I wept,—
And so I kept
Brimming the water-lilly cups with tears
Cold as my fears.

Beneath my palm trees, by the river side,
I sat a weeping: what enamour'd bride,
Cheated by shadowy wooer from the clouds,
But hides and shrouds
Beneath dark palm trees by a river side?

And as I sat, over the light blue hills
There came a noise of revellers: the rills

603

Into the wide stream came of purple hue—
  'Twas Bacchus and his crew!
The earnest trumpet spake, and silver thrills
From kissing cymbals made a merry din—
  'Twas Bacchus and his kin!
Like to a moving vintage down they came,
Crown'd with green leaves, and faces all on flame;
All madly dancing through the pleasant valley,
  To scare thee, Melancholy!

O then, O then, thou wast a simple name!
And I forgot thee, as the berried holly
By shepherds is forgotten, when, in June,
Tall chestnuts keep away the sun and moon:—
  I rush'd into the folly!

Within his car, aloft, young Bacchus stood,
Trifling his ivy-dart, in dancing mood,
  With sidelong laughing;
And little rills of crimson wine imbrued
His plump white arms, and shoulders, enough white
  For Venus' pearly bite:
And near him rode Silenus on his ass,
Pelted with flowers as he on did pass
  Tipsily quaffing.

Whence came ye, merry Damsels! whence came ye!
So many, and so many, and such glee?
Why have ye left your bowers desolate,
  Your lutes, and gentler fate?—
"We follow Bacchus! Bacchus on the wing,
  A conquering!
Bacchus, young Bacchus! good or ill betide,
We dance before him thorough kingdoms wide:—
Come hither, lady fair, and joined be
  To our wild minstrelsy!"

Whence came ye, jolly Satyrs! whence came ye!
So many, and so many, and such glee?
Why have ye left your forest haunts, why left
  Your nuts in oak-tree cleft?—

JOHN KEATS

"For wine, for wine we left our kernel tree;
For wine we left our heath, and yellow brooms,
　　　And cold mushrooms;
For wine we follow Bacchus through the earth;
Great God of breathless cups and chirping mirth!—
Come hither, lady fair, and joined be
　　　To our mad minstrelsy!"

Over wide streams and mountains great we went,
And, save when Bacchus kept his ivy tent,
Onward the tiger and the leopard pants,
　　　With Asian elephants:
Onward these myriads—with song and dance,
With zebras striped, and sleek Arabians' prance,
Web-footed alligators, crocodiles,
Bearing upon their scaly backs, in files,
Plump infant laughers mimicking the coil
Of seamen, and stout galley-rowers' toil:
With toying oars and silken sails they glide,
　　　Nor care for wind and tide.

Mounted on panthers' furs and lions' manes,
From rear to van they scour about the plains;
A three days' journey in a moment done:
And always, at the rising of the sun,
About the wilds they hunt with spear and horn,
　　　On spleenful unicorn.

I saw Osirian Egypt kneel adown
　　　Before the vine-wreath crown!
I saw parch'd Abyssinia rouse and sing
　　　To the silver cymbals' ring!
I saw the whelming vintage hotly pierce
　　　Old Tartary the fierce!
The kings of Inde their jewel-sceptres vail,
And from their treasures scatter pearled hail;
Great Brahma from his mystic heaven groans,
　　　And all his priesthood moans;
Before young Bacchus' eye-wink turning pale.—
Into these regions came I following him,
Sick hearted, weary—so I took a whim

To stray away into these forests drear
    Alone, without a peer:
And I have told thee all thou mayest hear.

    Young stranger!
    I've been a ranger
In search of pleasure throughout every clime:
    Alas, 'tis not for me!
    Bewitch'd I sure must be,
To lose in grieving all my maiden prime.

    Come then, Sorrow!
    Sweetest Sorrow!
Like an own babe I nurse thee on my breast:
    I thought to leave thee
    And deceive thee,
But now of all the world I love thee best.

    There is not one,
    No, no, not one
But thee to comfort a poor lonely maid;
    Thou art her mother,
    And her brother,
Her playmate, and her wooer in the shade.

—BOOK IV.

THE EVE OF ST. AGNES

St. Agnes' Eve—Ah, bitter chill it was!
The owl, for all his feathers, was a-cold;
The hare limp'd trembling through the frozen grass,
And silent was the flock in woolly fold:
Numb were the Beadsman's fingers, while he told
His rosary, and while his frosted breath,
Like pious incense from a censer old,
Seem'd taking flight for heaven, without a death,
Past the sweet Virgin's picture, while his prayer he saith.

His prayer he saith, this patient, holy man;
Then takes his lamp, and riseth from his knees,
And back returneth, meagre, barefoot, wan,
Along the chapel aisle by slow degrees:
The sculptur'd dead, on each side, seem to freeze,
Emprison'd in black, purgatorial rails:
Knights, ladies, praying in dumb orat'ries,
He passeth by; and his weak spirit fails
To think how they may ache in icy hoods and mails.

Northward he turneth through a little door,
And scarce three steps, ere Music's golden tongue
Flatter'd to tears this aged man and poor;
But no—already had his deathbell rung:
The joys of all his life were said and sung:
His was harsh penance on St. Agnes' Eve:
Another way he went, and soon among
Rough ashes sat he for his soul's reprieve,
And all night kept awake, for sinners' sake to grieve.

That ancient Beadsman heard the prelude soft;
And so it chanc'd, for many a door was wide,
From hurry to and fro.   Soon, up aloft,
The silver, snarling trumpets 'gan to chide:
The level chambers, ready with their pride,
Were glowing to receive a thousand guests:
The carved angels, ever eager-eyed,
Star'd, where upon their heads the cornice rests,
With hair blown back, and wings put cross-wise on their
        breasts.

At length burst in the argent revelry,
With plume, tiara, and all rich array,
Numerous as shadows haunting faerily
The brain, new stuff'd, in youth, with triumphs gay
Of old romance.   These let us wish away,
And turn, sole-thoughted, to one Lady there,
Whose heart had brooded, all that wintry day,
On love, and wing'd St. Agnes' saintly care,
As she had heard old dames full many times declare.

They told her how, upon St. Agnes' Eve,
Young virgins might have visions of delight,
And soft adorings from their loves receive
Upon the honey'd middle of the night,
If ceremonies due they did aright;
As, supperless to bed they must retire,
And couch supine their beauties, lilly white;
Nor look behind, nor sideways, but require
Of Heaven with upward eyes for all that they desire.

Full of this whim was thoughtful Madeline:
The music, yearning like a God in pain,
She scarcely heard: her maiden eyes divine,
Fix'd on the floor, saw many a sweeping train
Pass by—she heeded not at all: in vain
Came many a tiptoe, amorous cavalier,
And back retir'd; not cool'd by high disdain,
But she saw not: her heart was otherwhere:
She sighed for Agnes' dreams, the sweetest of the year.

She danc'd along with vague, regardless eyes,
Anxious her lips, her breathing quick and short:
The hallow'd hour was near at hand: she sighs
Amid the timbrels, and the throng'd resort
Of whisperers in anger, or in sport;
'Mid looks of love, defiance, hate, and scorn,
Hoodwink'd with faery fancy; all amort,
Save to St. Agnes and her lambs unshorn,
And all the bliss to be before to-morrow morn.

So, purposing each moment to retire,
She linger'd still. Meantime, across the moors,
Had come young Porphyro, with heart on fire
For Madeline. Beside the portal doors,
Buttress'd from moonlight, stands he, and implores
All saints to give him sight of Madeline,
But for one moment in the tedious hours,
That he might gaze and worship all unseen;
Perchance speak, kneel, touch, kiss—in sooth such things have
    been.

608

He ventures in: let no buzz'd whisper tell:
All eyes be muffled, or a hundred swords
Will storm his heart, Love's fev'rous citadel:
For him, those chambers held barbarian hordes,
Hyena foemen, and hot-blooded lords,
Whose very dogs would execrations howl
Against his lineage: not one breast affords
Him any mercy, in that mansion foul,
Save one old beldame, weak in body and in soul.

Ah, happy chance! the aged creature came,
Shuffling along with ivory-headed wand,
To where he stood, hid from the torch's flame,
Behind a broad hall-pillar, far beyond
The sound of merriment and chorus bland:
He startled her; but soon she knew his face,
And grasp'd his fingers in her palsied hand,
Saying, "Mercy, Porphyro! hie thee from this place:
"They are all here to-night, the whole blood-thirsty race!

"Get hence! get hence! there's dwarfish Hildebrand;
"He had a fever late, and in the fit
"He cursed thee and thine, both house and land:
"Then there's that old Lord Maurice, not a whit
"More tame for his grey hairs—Alas me! flit!
"Flit like a ghost away."—"Ah, Gossip dear,
"We're safe enough; here in this arm-chair sit,
"And tell me how"—"Good Saints! not here, not here;
"Follow me, child, or else these stones will be thy bier."

He follow'd through a lowly arched way,
Brushing the cobwebs with his lofty plume,
And as she mutter'd "Well-a—well-a-day!"
He found him in a little moonlight room,
Pale, lattic'd, chill, and silent as a tomb.
"Now tell me where is Madeline," said he,
"O tell me, Angela, by the holy loom
"Which none but secret sisterhood may see,
"When they St. Agnes' wool are weaving piously."

"St. Agnes! Ah! it is St. Agnes' Eve—
"Yet men will murder upon holy days:
"Thou must hold water in a witch's sieve,
"And be liege-lord of all the Elves and Fays,
"To venture so: it fills me with amaze
"To see thee, Porphyro!—St. Agnes' Eve!
"God's help! my lady fair the conjuror plays
"This very night: good angels her deceive!
"But let me laugh awhile, I've mickle time to grieve."

Feebly she laugheth in the languid moon,
While Porphyro upon her face doth look,
Like puzzled urchin on an aged crone
Who keepeth clos'd a wond'rous riddle-book,
As spectacled she sits in chimney nook.
But soon his eyes grew brilliant, when she told
His lady's purpose; and he scarce could brook
Tears, at the thought of those enchantments cold,
And Madeline asleep in lap of legends old.

Sudden a thought came like a full-blown rose,
Flushing his brow, and in his pained heart
Made purple riot: then doth he propose
A stratagem, that makes the beldame start:
"A cruel man and impious thou art:
"Sweet lady, let her pray, and sleep, and dream
"Alone with her good angels, far apart
"From wicked men like thee. Go, go!—I deem
"Thou canst not surely be the same that thou didst seem."

"I will not harm her, by all saints I swear,"
Quoth Porphyro: "O may I ne'er find grace
"When my weak voice shall whisper its last prayer,
"If one of her soft ringlets I displace,
"Or look with ruffian passion in her face:
"Good Angela, believe me by these tears;
"Or I will, even in a moment's space,
"Awake, with horrid shout, my foemen's ears,
"And beard them, though they be more fang'd than wolves
        and bears."
610

"Ah! why wilt thou affright a feeble soul?
"A poor, weak, palsy-stricken, churchyard thing,
"Whose passing-bell may ere the midnight toll;
"Whose prayers for thee, each morn and evening,
"Were never miss'd."—Thus plaining, doth she bring
A gentler speech from burning Porphyro;
So woeful, and of such deep sorrowing,
That Angela gives promise she will do
Whatever he shall wish, betide her weal or woe.

Which was, to lead him, in close secrecy,
Even to Madeline's chamber, and there hide
Him in a closet, of such privacy
That he might see her beauty unespied,
And win perhaps that night a peerless bride,
While legion'd faeries pac'd the coverlet,
And pale enchantment held her sleepy-eyed.
Never on such a night have lovers met,
Since Merlin paid his Demon all the monstrous debt.

"It shall be as thou wishest," said the Dame:
"All cates and dainties shall be stored there
"Quickly on this feast-night: by the tambour frame
"Her own lute thou wilt see: no time to spare,
"For I am slow and feeble, and scarce dare
"On such a catering trust my dizzy head.
"Wait here, my child, with patience; kneel in prayer
"The while: Ah! thou must needs the lady wed,
"Or may I never leave my grave among the dead."

So saying, she hobbled off with busy fear.
The lover's endless minutes slowly pass'd;
The dame return'd, and whisper'd in his ear
To follow her; with aged eyes aghast
From fright of dim espial. Safe at last,
Through many a dusky gallery, they gain
The maiden's chamber, silken, hush'd, and chaste;
Where Porphyro took covert, pleas'd amain.
His poor guide hurried back with agues in her brain.

Her falt'ring hand upon the balustrade,
Old Angela was feeling for the stair,
When Madeline, St. Agnes' charmed maid,
Rose, like a mission'd spirit, unaware:
With silver taper's light, and pious care,
She turn'd, and down the aged gossip led
To a safe level matting. Now prepare,
Young Porphyro, for gazing on that bed;
She comes, she comes again, like ring-dove fray'd and fled.

Out went the taper as she hurried in;
Its little smoke, in pallid moonshine, died:
She clos'd the door, she panted, all akin
To spirits of the air, and visions wide:
No uttered syllable, or, woe betide!
But to her heart, her heart was voluble,
Paining with eloquence her balmy side;
As though a tongueless nightingale should swell
Her throat in vain, and die, heart-stifled, in her dell.

A casement high and triple-arch'd there was,
All garlanded with carven imag'ries
Of fruits, and flowers, and bunches of knot-grass,
And diamonded with panes of quaint device,
Innumerable of stains and splendid dyes,
As are the tiger-moth's deep-damask'd wings;
And in the midst, 'mong thousand heraldries,
And twilight saints, and dim emblazonings,
A shielded scutcheon blush'd with blood of queens and kings.

Full on this casement shone the wintry moon,
And threw warm gules on Madeline's fair breast,
As down she knelt for heaven's grace and boon;
Rose-bloom fell on her hands, together prest,
And on her silver cross soft amethyst,
And on her hair a glory, like a saint:
She seem'd a splendid angel, newly drest,
Save wings, for heaven:—Porphyro grew faint:
She knelt, so pure a thing, so free from mortal taint.

JOHN KEATS

Anon his heart revives: her vespers done,
Of all its wreathed pearls her hair she frees;
Unclasps her warmed jewels one by one;
Loosens her fragrant boddice; by degrees
Her rich attire creeps rustling to her knees:
Half-hidden, like a mermaid in sea-weed,
Pensive awhile she dreams awake, and sees,
In fancy, fair St. Agnes in her bed,
But dares not look behind, or all the charm is fled.

Soon, trembling in her soft and chilly nest,
In sort of wakeful swoon, perplex'd she lay,
Until the poppied warmth of sleep oppress'd
Her soothed limbs, and soul fatigued away;
Flown, like a thought, until the morrow-day;
Blissfully haven'd both from joy and pain;
Clasp'd like a missal where swart Paynims pray;
Blinded alike from sunshine and from rain,
As though a rose should shut, and be a bud again.

Stol'n to this paradise, and so entranced,
Porphyro gazed upon her empty dress,
And listen'd to her breathing, if it chanced
To wake into a slumberous tenderness;
Which when he heard, that minute did he bless,
And breath'd himself: then from the closet crept,
Noiseless as fear in a wide wilderness,
And over the hush'd carpet, silent, stept,
And 'tween the curtains peep'd, where, lo!—how fast she
    slept.

Then by the bed-side, where the faded moon
Made a dim, silver twilight, soft he set
A table, and, half anguish'd, threw thereon
A cloth of woven crimson, gold, and jet:—
O for some drowsy Morphean amulet!
The boisterous, midnight, festive clarion,
The kettle-drum, and far-heard clarinet,
Affray his ears, though but in dying tone:—
The hall door shuts again, and all the noise is gone.

And still she slept an azure-lidded sleep,
In blanched linen, smooth, and lavender'd,
While he from forth the closet brought a heap
Of candied apple, quince, and plum, and gourd;
With jellies soother than the creamy curd,
And lucent syrops, tinct with cinnamon;
Manna and dates, in argosy transferr'd
From Fez; and spiced dainties, every one,
From silken Samarcand to cedar'd Lebanon.

These delicates he heap'd with glowing hand
On golden dishes and in baskets bright
Of wreathed silver: sumptuous they stand
In the retired quiet of the night,
Filling the chilly room with perfume light.—
"And now, my love, my seraph fair, awake!
"Thou art my heaven, and I thine eremite:
"Open thine eyes, for meek St. Agnes' sake,
"Or I shall drowse beside thee, so my soul doth ache."

Thus whispering, his warm, unnerved arm
Sank in her pillow. Shaded was her dream
By the dusk curtains:—'twas a midnight charm
Impossible to melt as iced stream:
The lustrous salvers in the moonlight gleam;
Broad golden fringe upon the carpet lies:
It seem'd he never, never could redeem
From such a stedfast spell his lady's eyes;
So mus'd awhile, entoil'd in woofed phantasies.

Awakening up, he took her hollow lute,—
Tumultuous,—and, in chords that tenderest be,
He play'd an ancient ditty, long since mute,
In Provence call'd, "La belle dame sans mercy":
Close to her ear touching the melody;—
Wherewith disturb'd, she utter'd a soft moan:
He ceased—she panted quick—and suddenly
Her blue affrayed eyes wide open shone:
Upon his knees he sank, pale as smooth-sculptured stone.

614

Her eyes were open, but she still beheld,
Now wide awake, the vision of her sleep:
There was a painful change, that nigh expell'd
The blisses of her dream so pure and deep
At which fair Madeline began to weep,
And moan forth witless words with many a sigh;
While still her gaze on Porphyro would keep;
Who knelt, with joined hands and piteous eye,
Fearing to move or speak, she look'd so dreamingly.

"Ah, Porphyro!" said she, "but even now
"Thy voice was at sweet tremble in mine ear,
"Made tuneable with every sweetest vow;
"And those sad eyes were spiritual and clear:
"How chang'd thou art! how pallid, chill, and drear!
"Give me that voice again, my Porphyro,
"Those looks immortal, those complainings dear!
"Oh leave me not in this eternal woe,
"For if thou diest, my Love, I know not where to go."

Beyond a mortal man impassion'd far
At these voluptuous accents, he arose,
Ethereal, flush'd, and like a throbbing star
Seen mid the sapphire heaven's deep repose;
Into her dream he melted, as the rose
Blendeth its odour with the violet,—
Solution sweet: meantime the frost-wind blows
Like Love's alarum pattering the sharp sleet
Against the window-panes; St. Agnes' moon hath set.

'Tis dark: quick pattereth the flaw-blown sleet:
"This is no dream, my bride, my Madeline!"
'Tis dark: the iced gusts still rave and beat:
"No dream, alas! alas! and woe is mine!
"Porphyro will leave me here to fade and pine.—
"Cruel! what traitor could thee hither bring?
"I curse not, for my heart is lost in thine,
"Though thou forsakest a deceived thing;—
"A dove forlorn and lost with sick unpruned wing."

615

"My Madeline! sweet dreamer! lovely bride!
"Say, may I be for aye thy vassal blest?
"Thy beauty's shield, heart-shap'd and vermeil dyed?
"Ah, silver shrine, here will I take my rest
"After so many hours of toil and quest,
"A famish'd pilgrim,—sav'd by miracle.
"Though I have found, I will not rob thy nest
"Saving of thy sweet self; if thou think'st well
"To trust, fair Madeline, to no rude infidel.

"Hark! 'tis an elfin-storm from faery land,
"Of haggard seeming, but a boon indeed:
"Arise—arise! the morning is at hand;—
"The bloated wassaillers will never heed:—
"Let us away, my love, with happy speed;
"There are no ears to hear, or eyes to see,—
"Drown'd all in Rhenish and the sleepy mead:
"Awake! arise! my love, and fearless be,
"For o'er the southern moors I have a home for thee."

She hurried at his words, beset with fears,
For there were sleeping dragons all around,
At glaring watch, perhaps, with ready spears—
Down the wide stairs a darkling way they found.—
In all the house was heard no human sound.
A chain-droop'd lamp was flickering by each door;
The arras, rich with horseman, hawk, and hound,
Flutter'd in the besieging wind's uproar;
And the long carpets rose along the gusty floor.

They glide, like phantoms, into the wide hall;
Like phantoms, to the iron porch, they glide;
Where lay the Porter, in uneasy sprawl,
With a huge empty flaggon by his side:
The wakeful bloodhound rose, and shook his hide,
But his sagacious eye an inmate owns:
By one, and one, the bolts full easy slide:—
The chains lie silent on the footworn stones;—
The key turns, and the door upon its hinges groans.

616

And they are gone: aye, ages long ago
These lovers fled away into the storm.
That night the Baron dreamt of many a woe,
And all his warrior-guests, with shade and form
Of witch, and demon, and large coffin-worm,
Were long be-nightmar'd.   Angela the old
Died palsy-twitch'd, with meagre face deform;
The Beadsman, after thousand aves told,
For aye unsought for slept among his ashes cold.

ODE TO A NIGHTINGALE

My heart aches, and a drowsy numbness pains
  My sense, as though of hemlock I had drunk,
Or emptied some dull opiate to the drains
  One minute past, and Lethe-wards had sunk:
'Tis not through envy of thy happy lot,
  But being too happy in thine happiness,—
    That thou, light-winged Dryad of the trees,
      In some melodious plot
  Of beechen green, and shadows numberless,
    Singest of summer in full-throated ease.

O, for a draught of vintage! that hath been
  Cool'd a long age in the deep-delved earth,
Tasting of Flora and the country green,
  Dance, and Provençal song, and sunburnt mirth!
O, for a beaker full of the warm South,
  Full of the true, the blushful Hippocrene,
    With beaded bubbles winking at the brim,
      And purple-stained mouth;
  That I might drink, and leave the world unseen,
    And with thee fade away into the forest dim:

Fade far away, dissolve, and quite forget
  What thou among the leaves hast never known,
The weariness, the fever, and the fret
  Here, where men sit and hear each other groan;

Where palsy shakes a few, sad, last grey hairs,
   Where youth grows pale, and spectre-thin, and dies;
     Where but to think is to be full of sorrow
       And leaden-eyed despairs,
   Where Beauty cannot keep her lustrous eyes,
     Or new Love pine at them beyond to-morrow.

Away! away! for I will fly to thee,
   Not charioted by Bacchus and his pards,
But on the viewless wings of Poesy,
   Though the dull brain perplexes and retards:
Already with thee! tender is the night,
   And haply the Queen-Moon is on her throne,
     Cluster'd around by all her starry Fays;
       But here there is no light,
   Save what from heaven is with the breezes blown
     Through verdurous glooms and winding mossy ways.

I cannot see what flowers are at my feet,
   Nor what soft incense hangs upon the boughs,
But, in embalmed darkness, guess each sweet
   Wherewith the seasonable month endows
The grass, the thicket, and the fruit-tree wild;
   White hawthorn, and the pastoral eglantine;
     Fast fading violets cover'd up in leaves;
       And mid-May's eldest child,
   The coming musk-rose, full of dewy wine,
     The murmurous haunt of flies on summer eves.

Darkling I listen; and, for many a time
   I have been half in love with easeful Death,
Call'd him soft names in many a mused rhyme,
   To take into the air my quiet breath;
Now more than ever seems it rich to die,
   To cease upon the midnight with no pain,
     While thou art pouring forth thy soul abroad
       In such an ecstasy!
   Still wouldst thou sing, and I have ears in vain—
     To thy high requiem become a sod.

618

Thou wast not born for death, immortal Bird!
  No hungry generations tread thee down;
The voice I hear this passing night was heard
  In ancient days by emperor and clown:
Perhaps the self-same song that found a path
  Through the sad heart of Ruth, when, sick for home,
    She stood in tears amid the alien corn;
      The same that oft-times hath
Charm'd magic casements, opening on the foam
  Of perilous seas, in faery lands forlorn.

Forlorn! the very word is like a bell
  To toll me back from thee to my sole self!
Adieu! the fancy cannot cheat so well
  As she is fam'd to do, deceiving elf.
Adieu! adieu! thy plaintive anthem fades
  Past the near meadows, over the still stream,
    Up the hill-side; and now 'tis buried deep
      In the next valley-glades:
Was it a vision, or a waking dream?
  Fled is that music:—Do I wake or sleep?

ODE ON A GRECIAN URN

Thou still unravish'd bride of quietness,
  Thou foster-child of silence and slow time,
Sylvan historian, who canst thus express
  A flowery tale more sweetly than our rhyme:
What leaf-fring'd legend haunts about thy shape
  Of deities or mortals, or of both,
    In Tempe or the dales of Arcady?
What men or gods are these? What maidens loth?
What mad pursuit? What struggle to escape?
    What pipes and timbrels? What wild ecstasy?

Heard melodies are sweet, but these unheard
  Are sweeter; therefore, ye soft pipes, play on;
Not to the sensual ear, but, more endear'd,
  Pipe to the spirit ditties of no tone:

619

Fair youth, beneath the trees, thou canst not leave
  Thy song, nor ever can those trees be bare;
    Bold Lover, never, never canst thou kiss,
Though winning near the goal—yet, do not grieve;
  She cannot fade, though thou hast not thy bliss,
    For ever wilt thou love, and she be fair!

Ah, happy, happy boughs! that cannot shed
  Your leaves, nor ever bid the Spring adieu;
And, happy melodist, unwearied,
  For ever piping songs for ever new;
More happy love! more happy, happy love!
  For ever warm and still to be enjoy'd,
    For ever panting, and for ever young;
All breathing human passion far above,
  That leaves a heart high-sorrowful and cloy'd,
    A burning forehead, and a parching tongue.

Who are these coming to the sacrifice?
  To what green altar, O mysterious priest,
Lead'st thou that heifer lowing at the skies,
  And all her silken flanks with garlands drest?
What little town by river or sea shore,
  Or mountain-built with peaceful citadel,
    Is emptied of this folk, this pious morn?
And, little town, thy streets for evermore
  Will silent be; and not a soul to tell
    Why thou art desolate, can e'er return.

O Attic shape! Fair attitude! with brede
  Of marble men and maidens overwrought,
With forest branches and the trodden weed;
  Thou, silent form, dost tease us out of thought
As doth eternity: Cold Pastoral!
  When old age shall this generation waste,
    Thou shalt remain, in midst of other woe
Than ours, a friend to man, to whom thou say'st,
  "Beauty is truth, truth beauty,"—that is all
    Ye know on earth, and all ye need to know.

620

JOHN KEATS

ODE TO PSYCHE

O Goddess! hear these tuneless numbers, wrung
 By sweet enforcement and remembrance dear,
And pardon that thy secrets should be sung
 Even into thine own soft-conched ear:
Surely I dreamt to-day, or did I see
 The winged Psyche with awaken'd eyes?
I wander'd in a forest thoughtlessly,
 And, on the sudden, fainting with surprise,
Saw two fair creatures, couched side by side
 In deepest grass, beneath the whisp'ring roof
 Of leaves and trembled blossoms, where there ran
  A brooklet, scarce espied:

'Mid hush'd, cool-rooted flowers, fragrant-eyed,
 Blue, silver-white, and budded Tyrian,
They lay calm-breathing on the bedded grass;
 Their arms embraced, and their pinions too;
 Their lips touch'd not, but had not bade adieu,
As if disjoined by soft-handed slumber,
And ready still past kisses to outnumber
 At tender eye-dawn of aurorean love:
  The winged boy I knew;
 But who wast thou, O happy, happy dove?
  His Psyche true!

O latest born and loveliest vision far
 Of all Olympus' faded hierarchy!
Fairer than Phœbe's sapphire-region'd star,
 Or Vesper, amorous glow-worm of the sky;
Fairer than these, though temple thou hast none,
  Nor altar heap'd with flowers;
Nor virgin-choir to make delicious moan
  Upon the midnight hours;
No voice, no lute, no pipe, no incense sweet
 From chain-swung censer teeming;
No shrine, no grove, no oracle, no heat
 Of pale-mouth'd prophet dreaming.

621

O brightest! though too late for antique vows,
    Too, too late for the fond believing lyre,
When holy were the haunted forest boughs,
    Holy the air, the water, and the fire;
Yet even in these days so far retir'd
    From happy pieties, thy lucent fans,
    Fluttering among the faint Olympians,
I see, and sing, by my own eyes inspir'd.
So let me be thy choir, and make a moan
        Upon the midnight hours;
Thy voice, thy lute, thy pipe, thy incense sweet
    From swinged censer teeming;
Thy shrine, thy grove, thy oracle, thy heat
    Of pale-mouth'd prophet dreaming.

Yes, I will be thy priest, and build a fane
    In some untrodden region of my mind,
Where branched thoughts, new grown with pleasant pain,
    Instead of pines shall murmur in the wind:
Far, far around shall those dark-cluster'd trees
    Fledge the wild-ridged mountains steep by steep;
And there by zephyrs, streams, and birds, and bees,
    The moss-lain Dryads shall be lull'd to sleep;

And in the midst of this wide quietness
A rosy sanctuary will I dress
With the wreath'd trellis of a working brain,
    With buds, and bells, and stars without a name,
With all the gardener Fancy e'er could feign,
    Who breeding flowers, will never breed the same:
And there shall be for thee all soft delight
    That shadowy thought can win,
A bright torch, and a casement ope at night,
    To let the warm Love in!

LINES ON THE MERMAID TAVERN

Souls of Poets dead and gone,
What Elysium have ye known,
Happy field or mossy cavern,
Choicer than the Mermaid Tavern?

Have ye tippled drink more fine
Than mine host's Canary wine?
Or are fruits of Paradise
Sweeter than those dainty pies
Of venison?   O generous food!
Drest as though bold Robin Hood
Would, with his maid Marian,
Sup and bowse from horn and can.

I have heard that on a day
Mine host's sign-board flew away,
Nobody knew whither, till
An astrologer's old quill
To a sheepskin gave the story,
Said he saw you in your glory,
Underneath a new old sign
Sipping beverage divine,
And pledging with contented smack
The Mermaid in the Zodiac.

Souls of Poets dead and gone,
What Elysium have ye known,
Happy field or mossy cavern,
Choicer than the Mermaid Tavern?

TO AUTUMN

Season of mists and mellow fruitfulness,
    Close bosom-friend of the maturing sun;
Conspiring with him how to load and bless
    With fruit the vines that round the thatch-eaves run;
To bend with apples the moss'd cottage-trees,
    And fill all fruit with ripeness to the core;
        To swell the gourd, and plump the hazel shells
    With a sweet kernel; to set budding more,
And still more, later flowers for the bees,
Until they think warm days will never cease,
        For Summer has o'er-brimm'd their clammy cells.

Who hath not seen thee oft amid thy store?
   Sometimes whoever seeks abroad may find
Thee sitting careless on a granary floor,
   Thy hair soft-lifted by the winnowing wind;
Or on a half-reap'd furrow sound asleep,
   Drows'd with the fume of poppies, while thy hook
     Spares the next swath and all its twined flowers:
And sometimes like a gleaner thou dost keep
   Steady thy laden head across a brook;
   Or by a cyder-press, with patient look,
     Thou watchest the last oozings hours by hours.

Where are the songs of Spring? Ay, where are they?
   Think not of them, thou hast thy music too,—
While barred clouds bloom the soft-dying day,
   And touch the stubble-plains with rosy hue;
Then in a wailful choir the small gnats mourn
   Among the river sallows, borne aloft
     Or sinking as the light wind lives or dies;
And full-grown lambs loud bleat from hilly bourn;
   Hedge-crickets sing; and now with treble soft
   The red-breast whistles from a garden-croft;
     And gathering swallows twitter in the skies.

ODE ON MELANCHOLY

No, no, go not to Lethe, neither twist
   Wolf's-bane, tight-rooted, for its poisonous wine;
Nor suffer thy pale forehead to be kiss'd
   By nightshade, ruby grape of Proserpine;
Make not your rosary of yew-berries,
   Nor let the beetle, nor the death-moth be
     Your mournful Psyche, nor the downy owl
A partner in your sorrow's mysteries;
   For shade to shade will come too drowsily,
   And drown the wakeful anguish of the soul.

But when the melancholy fit shall fall
   Sudden from heaven like a weeping cloud,
That fosters the droop-headed flowers all,
   And hides the green hill in an April shroud;

624

Then glut thy sorrow on a morning rose,
   Or on the rainbow of the salt sand-wave,
     Or on the wealth of globed peonies;
Or if thy mistress some rich anger shows,
   Emprison her soft hand, and let her rave,
     And feed deep, deep upon her peerless eyes.

She dwells with Beauty—Beauty that must die;
   And Joy, whose hand is ever at his lips
Bidding adieu; and aching Pleasure nigh,
   Turning to Poison while the bee-mouth sips:
Ay, in the very temple of delight
   Veil'd Melancholy has her sovran shrine,
     Though seen of none save him whose strenuous tongue
   Can burst Joy's grape against his palate fine;
His soul shall taste the sadness of her might,
   And be among her cloudy trophies hung.

SONNET

When I have fears that I may cease to be
   Before my pen has glean'd my teeming brain,
Before high-piled books, in charactery,
   Hold like rich garners the full-ripen'd grain;
When I behold, upon the night's starr'd face,
   Huge cloudy symbols of a high romance,
And think that I may never live to trace
   Their shadows, with the magic hand of chance;
And when I feel, fair creature of an hour,
   That I shall never look upon thee more,
Never have relish in the faery power
   Of unreflecting love;—then on the shore
Of the wide world I stand alone, and think
Till love and fame to nothingness do sink.

SONNET

TO HOMER

Standing aloof in giant ignorance,
 Of thee I hear and of the Cyclades,
As one who sits ashore and longs perchance
 To visit dolphin-coral in deep seas.
So thou wast blind;—but then the veil was rent,
 For Jove uncurtain'd Heaven to let thee live,
And Neptune made for thee a spumy tent,
 And Pan made sing for thee his forest-hive;
Aye on the shores of darkness there is light,
 And precipices show untrodden green,
There is a budding morrow in midnight,
 There is a triple sight in blindness keen;
Such seeing hadst thou, as it once befel
To Dian, Queen of Earth, and Heaven, and Hell.

FRAGMENT OF AN ODE TO MAIA

Mother of Hermes! and still youthful Maia!
  May I sing to thee
As thou wast hymned on the shores of Baiæ?
  Or may I woo thee
In earlier Sicilian? or thy smiles
Seek as they once were sought, in Grecian isles,
By bards who died content on pleasant sward,
 Leaving great verse unto a little clan?
O, give me their old vigour, and unheard
 Save of the quiet Primrose, and the span
  Of heaven and few ears,
Rounded by thee, my song should die away
  Content as theirs,
Rich in the simple worship of a day.

626

JOHN KEATS

STANZAS

In a drear-nighted December,
  Too happy, happy tree,
Thy branches ne'er remember
  Their green felicity:
  The north cannot undo them,
  With a sleety whistle through them;
  Nor frozen thawings glue them
    From budding at the prime.

In a drear-nighted December,
  Too happy, happy brook,
Thy bubblings ne'er remember
  Apollo's summer look;
  But with a sweet forgetting,
  They stay their crystal fretting,
  Never, never petting
    About the frozen time.

Ah! would 'twere so with many
  A gentle girl and boy!
But were there ever any
  Writh'd not at passed joy?
  To know the change and feel it,
  When there is none to heal it,
  Nor numbed sense to steel it,
    Was never said in rhyme.

SONNET

TO SLEEP

O soft embalmer of the still midnight,
  Shutting, with careful fingers and benign,
Our gloom-pleas'd eyes, embower'd from the light,
  Enshaded in forgetfulness divine:
O soothest Sleep! if so it please thee, close
  In midst of this thine hymn my willing eyes,

Or wait the "Amen," ere thy poppy throws
   Around my bed its lulling charities.
Then save me, or the passed day will shine
Upon my pillow, breeding many woes,—
   Save me from curious Conscience, that still lords
Its strength for darkness, burrowing like a mole;
   Turn the key deftly in the oiled wards,
And seal the hushed Casket of my Soul.

LA BELLE DAME SANS MERCI

Ah, what can ail thee, wretched wight,
   Alone and palely loitering;
The sedge is wither'd from the lake,
   And no birds sing.

Ah, what can ail thee, wretched wight,
   So haggard and so woe-begone?
The squirrel's granary is full,
   And the harvest's done.

I see a lilly on thy brow,
   With anguish moist and fever dew;
And on thy cheek a fading rose
   Fast withereth too.

I met a lady in the meads
   Full beautiful, a faery's child;
Her hair was long, her foot was light,
   And her eyes were wild.

I set her on my pacing steed,
   And nothing else saw all day long;
For sideways would she lean, and sing
   A faery's song.

I made a garland for her head,
   And bracelets too, and fragrant zone;
She look'd at me as she did love,
   And made sweet moan.

JOHN KEATS

She found me roots of relish sweet,
  And honey wild, and manna dew;
And sure in language strange she said,
  I love thee true.

She took me to her elfin grot,
  And there she gaz'd and sighed deep,
And there I shut her wild sad eyes—
  So kiss'd to sleep.

And there we slumber'd on the moss,
  And there I dream'd, ah woe betide,
The latest dream I ever dream'd
  On the cold hill side.

I saw pale kings, and princes too,
  Pale warriors, death-pale were they all;
Who cry'd—"La belle Dame sans merci
  Hath thee in thrall!"

I saw their starv'd lips in the gloam
  With horrid warning gaped wide,
And I awoke, and found me here
  On the cold hill side.

And this is why I sojourn here
  Alone and palely loitering,
Though the sedge is wither'd from the lake,
  And no birds sing.

SONNET

*(Written on a Blank Page in Shakespeare's Poems,
Facing "A Lover's Complaint.")*

Bright star, would I were stedfast as thou art—
  Not in lone splendour hung aloft the night
And watching, with eternal lids apart,
  Like nature's patient, sleepless Eremite,

The moving waters at their priestlike task
  Of pure ablution round earth's human shores,
Or gazing on the new soft-fallen mask
  Of snow upon the mountains and the moors—
No—yet still stedfast, still unchangeable,
  Pillow'd upon my fair love's ripening breast,
To feel for ever its soft fall and swell,
  Awake for ever in a sweet unrest,
Still, still to hear her tender-taken breath,
And so live ever—or else swoon to death.

Thomas Hood

FAIR INES

O saw ye not fair Ines?
  She's gone into the West,
To dazzle when the sun is down,
  And rob the world of rest:
She took our daylight with her,
  The smiles that we love best,
With morning blushes on her cheek,
  And pearls upon her breast.

O turn again, fair Ines,
  Before the fall of night,
For fear the Moon should shine alone,
  And stars unrivaled bright;
And blessèd will the lover be
  That walks beneath their light,
And breathes the love against thy cheek
  I dare not even write!

Would I had been, fair Ines,
  That gallant cavalier,
Who rode so gaily by thy side,
  And whispered thee so near!

Were there no bonny dames at home,
   Or no true lovers here,
That he should cross the seas to win
   The dearest of the dear?

I saw thee, lovely Ines,
   Descend along the shore,
With bands of noble gentlemen,
   And banners waved before;
And gentle youth and maidens gay,
   And snowy plumes they wore:
It would have been a beauteous dream,—
   If it had been no more!

Alas, alas, fair Ines,
   She went away with song,
With Music waiting on her steps,
   And shoutings of the throng;
But some were sad, and felt no mirth,
   But only Music's wrong,
In sounds that sang Farewell, farewell,
   To her you've loved so long.

Farewell, farewell, fair Ines!
   That vessel never bore
So fair a lady on its deck,
   Nor danced so light before,—
Alas for pleasure on the sea,
   And sorrow on the shore!
The smile that blessed one lover's heart
   Has broken many more!

THE SONG OF THE SHIRT

With fingers weary and worn,
   With eyelids heavy and red,
A woman sat, in unwomanly rags,
   Plying her needle and thread,—

Stitch—stitch—stitch!
In poverty, hunger, and dirt;
    And still with a voice of dolorous pitch
She sang the "Song of the Shirt!"

"Work—work—work
    While the cock is crowing aloof!
And work—work—work
    Till the stars shine through the roof!
It's oh! to be a slave
    Along with the barbarous Turk,
Where woman has never a soul to save,
    If this is Christian work!

"Work—work—work
    Till the brain begins to swim!
Work—work—work
    Till the eyes are heavy and dim!
Seam, and gusset, and band,
  · Band, and gusset, and seam,—
Till over the buttons I fall asleep,
    And sew them on in a dream!

"O men with sisters dear!
    O men with mothers and wives!
It is not linen you're wearing out,
    But human creatures' lives!
        Stitch—stitch—stitch,
    In poverty, hunger, and dirt,—
Sewing at once, with a double thread,
    A shroud as well as a shirt!

"But why do I talk of death,—
    That phantom of grisly bone?
I hardly fear his terrible shape,
    It seems so like my own,—
It seems so like my own
    Because of the fasts I keep;
O God! that bread should be so dear,
    And flesh and blood so cheap!

632

"Work—work—work!
  My labour never flags;
And what are its wages?   A bed of straw,
  A crust of bread—and rags.
That shattered roof—and this naked floor—
  A table—a broken chair—
And a wall so blank my shadow I thank
  For sometimes falling there!

"Work—work—work
  From weary chime to chime!
Work—work—work
  As prisoners work for crime!
Band, and gusset, and seam,
  Seam, and gusset, and band,—
Till the heart is sick and the brain benumbed,
  As well as the weary hand.

"Work—work—work
  In the dull December light!
And work—work—work
  When the weather is warm and bright!
While underneath the eaves
  The brooding swallows cling,
As if to show me their sunny backs,
  And twit me with the Spring.

"Oh but to breathe the breath
  Of the cowslip and primrose sweet,—
With the sky above my head,
  And the grass beneath my feet!
For only one short hour
  To feel as I used to feel,
Before I knew the woes of want
  And the walk that costs a meal!

"Oh but for one short hour,—
  A respite, however brief!
No blessed leisure for love or hope,
  But only time for grief!

A little weeping would ease my heart;
  But in their briny bed
My tears must stop, for every drop
  Hinders needle and thread!"

With fingers weary and worn,
  With eyelids heavy and red,
A woman sat, in unwomanly rags,
  Plying her needle and thread,—
    Stitch—stitch—stitch!
  In poverty, hunger, and dirt:
And still with a voice of dolorous pitch—
Would that its tone could reach the rich!—
  She sang this "Song of the Shirt!"

I REMEMBER, I REMEMBER

I remember, I remember
The house where I was born,
The little window where the sun
Came peeping in at morn;
He never came a wink too soon
Nor brought too long a day;
But now, I often wish the night
Had borne my breath away.

I remember, I remember
The roses, red and white,
The violets, and the lily-cups—
Those flowers made of light!
The lilacs where the robin built,
And where my brother set
The laburnum on his birthday,—
The tree is living yet!

I remember, I remember
Where I was used to swing,
And thought the air must rush as fresh
To swallows on the wing;

634

THOMAS HOOD

My spirit flew in feathers then
That is so heavy now,
The summer pools could hardly cool
The fever on my brow.

I remember, I remember
The fir-trees dark and high;
I used to think their slender tops
Were close against the sky:
It was a childish ignorance,
But now 'tis little joy
To know I'm farther off from Heaven
Than when I was a boy.

IT WAS THE TIME OF ROSES

It was not in the winter
Our loving lot was cast:
It was the time of roses—
We plucked them as we passed!

That churlish season never frowned
On early lovers yet!
O, no—the world was newly crowned
With flowers, when first we met.

'Twas twilight, and I bade you go,
But still you held me fast:
It was the time of roses—
We plucked them as we passed.

RUTH

She stood breast high among the corn,
Clasped by the golden light of morn,
Like the sweetheart of the sun,
Who many a glowing kiss had won.

On her cheek an autumn flush,
Deeply ripened;—such a blush
In the midst of brown was born,
Like red poppies grown with corn.

635

Round her eyes her tresses fell,
Which were blackest none could tell.
But long lashes veiled a light,
That had else been all too bright.

And her hat, with shady brim,
Made her tressy forehead dim;
Thus she stood amid the stooks,
Praising God with sweetest looks.

. . . .

VERSES IN AN ALBUM

Far above the hollow
Tempest, and its moan,
Singeth bright Apollo
In his golden zone,—
Cloud doth never shade him,
Nor a storm invade him,
On his joyous throne.

So when I behold me
In an orb as bright,
How thy soul doth fold me
In its throne of light!
Sorrow never paineth,
Nor a care attaineth,
To that blessed height.

Lord Macaulay

HORATIUS AT THE BRIDGE

Lars Porsena of Clusium
By the Nine Gods he swore
That the great house of Tarquin
Should suffer wrong no more.

By the Nine Gods he swore it,
    And named a trysting-day,
And bade his messengers ride forth,
East and west and south and north,
    To summon his array.

. . . .

Fast by the royal standard,
    O'erlooking all the war,
Lars Porsena of Clusium
    Sat in his ivory car.
By the right wheel rode Mamilius,
    Prince of the Latian name;
And by the left false Sextus,
    That wrought the deed of shame.

But when the face of Sextus
    Was seen among the foes,
A yell that rent the firmament
    From all the town arose.
On the house-tops was no woman
    But spat towards him and hissed,
No child but screamed out curses,
    And shook its little fist.

But the Consul's brow was sad,
    And the Consul's speech was low,
And darkly looked he at the wall,
    And darkly at the foe:
"Their van will be upon us
    Before the bridge goes down;
And if they once may win the bridge,
    What hope to save the town?"

Then out spake brave Horatius,
    The Captain of the Gate:
"To every man upon this earth
    Death cometh soon or late.
And how can man die better
    Than facing fearful odds
For the ashes of his fathers
    And the temples of his Gods,

"And for the tender mother
Who dandled him to rest,
And for the wife who nurses
His baby at her breast,
And for the holy maidens
Who feed the eternal flame,—
To save them from false Sextus
That wrought the deed of shame?

"Hew down the bridge, Sir Consul,
With all the speed ye may;
I, with two more to help me,
Will hold the foe in play.
In yon strait path a thousand
May well be stopped by three:
Now who will stand on either hand,
And keep the bridge with me?"

Then out spake Spurius Lartius,—
A Ramnian proud was he:
"Lo, I will stand at thy right hand,
And keep the bridge with thee."
And out spake strong Herminius,—
Of Titian blood was he:
"I will abide on thy left side,
And keep the bridge with thee."

"Horatius," quoth the Consul,
"As thou sayest so let it be."
And straight against that great array
Forth went the dauntless Three.
For Romans in Rome's quarrel
Spared neither land nor gold,
Nor son nor wife, nor limb nor life,
In the brave days of old.

Then none was for a party;
Then all were for the state;
Then the great man helped the poor,
And the poor man loved the great:

Then lands were fairly portioned;
  Then spoils were fairly sold:
The Romans were like brothers
  In the brave days of old.

Now Roman is to Roman
  More hateful than a foe,
And the Tribunes beard the high,
  And the fathers grind the low.
As we wax hot in faction,
  In battle we wax cold;
Wherefore men fight not as they fought
  In the brave days of old.

.   .   .   .

Was none who would be foremost
  To lead such dire attack;
But those behind cried "Forward!"
  And those before cried "Back!"
And backward now and forward
  Wavers the deep array;
And on the tossing sea of steel
  To and fro the standards reel,
And the victorious trumpet-peal
  Dies fitfully away.

Yet one man for one moment
  Stood out before the crowd;
Well known was he to all the Three,
  And they gave him greeting loud:
"Now welcome, welcome, Sextus!
  Now welcome to thy home!
Why dost thou stay, and turn away?
  Here lies the road to Rome."

Thrice looked he at the city;
  Thrice looked he at the dead;
And thrice came on in fury,
  And thrice turned back in dread;
And, white with fear and hatred,
  Scowled at the narrow way
Where, wallowing in a pool of blood,
  The bravest Tuscans lay.

But meanwhile axe and lever
    Have manfully been plied;
And now the bridge hangs tottering
    Above the boiling tide.
"Come back, come back, Horatius!"
    Loud cried the Fathers all.—
"Back, Lartius! back, Herminius!
    Back, ere the ruin fall!"

Back darted Spurius Lartius;—
    Herminius darted back;
And, as they passed, beneath their feet
    They felt the timbers crack.
But when they turned their faces,
    And on the farther shore
Saw brave Horatius stand alone,
    They would have crossed once more;

But with a crash like thunder
    Fell every loosened beam,
And, like a dam, the mighty wreck
    Lay right athwart the stream:
And a long shout of triumph
    Rose from the walls of Rome,
As to the highest turret-tops
    Was splashed the yellow foam.

And, like a horse unbroken,
    When first he feels the rein,
The furious river struggled hard,
    And tossed his tawny mane,
And burst the curb, and bounded,
    Rejoicing to be free;
And whirling down, in fierce career,
Battlement, and plank, and pier,
    Rushed headlong to the sea.

Alone stood brave Horatius,
    But constant still in mind,—
Thrice thirty thousand foes before,
    And the broad flood behind.

"Down with him!" cried false Sextus,
  With a smile on his pale face;
"Now yield thee," cried Lars Porsena,
  "Now yield thee to our grace."

Round turned he, as not deigning
  Those craven ranks to see;
Naught spake he to Lars Porsena,
  To Sextus naught spake he;
But he saw on Palatinus
  The white porch of his home;
And he spake to the noble river
  That rolls by the towers of Rome:

"O Tiber! Father Tiber!
  To whom the Romans pray,
A Roman's life, a Roman's arms,
  Take thou in charge this day!"
So he spake, and, speaking, sheathed
  The good sword by his side,
And, with his harness on his back,
  Plunged headlong in the tide.

No sound of joy or sorrow
  Was heard from either bank,
But friends and foes in dumb surprise,
With parted lips and straining eyes,
  Stood gazing where he sank;
And when above the surges
  They saw his crest appear,
All Rome sent forth a rapturous cry,
And even the ranks of Tuscany
  Could scarce forbear to cheer.

But fiercely ran the current,
  Swollen high by months of rain;
And fast his blood was flowing,
  And he was sore in pain,
And heavy with his armour,
  And spent with changing blows;
And oft they thought him sinking,
  But still again he rose.

641

Never, I ween, did swimmer,
  In such an evil case,
Struggle through such a raging flood
  Safe to the landing-place;
But his limbs were borne up bravely
  By the brave heart within,
And our good Father Tiber
  Bore bravely up his chin.

"Curse on him!" quoth false Sextus;—
  "Will not the villain drown?
But for this stay, ere close of day
  We should have sacked the town!"
"Heaven help him!" quoth Lars Porsena,
  "And bring him safe to shore;
For such a gallant feat of arms
  Was never seen before."

And now he feels the bottom;
  Now on dry earth he stands;
Now round him throng the Fathers
  To press his gory hands;
And now, with shouts and clapping,
  And noise of weeping loud,
He enters through the River-Gate,
  Borne by the joyous crowd.

  .   .   .   .   .   .

When the oldest cask is opened,
  And the largest lamp is lit;
When the chestnuts glow in the embers,
  And the kid turns on the spit;
When young and old in circle
  Around the firebrands close;
When the girls are weaving baskets,
  And the lads are shaping bows;

When the goodman mends his armour,
  And trims his helmet's plume;
When the goodwife's shuttle merrily
  Goes flashing through the loom;

With weeping and with laughter
   Still is the story told,
How well Horatius kept the bridge
   In the brave days of old.

THE BATTLE OF LAKE REGILLUS

   .   .   .   .

Men said he saw strange visions
   Which none beside might see,
And that strange sounds were in his ears,
   Which none might hear but he.

A woman fair and stately,
   But pale as are the dead,
Oft through the watches of the night
   Sate spinning by his bed.

And as she plied the distaff,
   In a sweet voice and low,
She sang of great old houses,
   And fights fought long ago.

So spun she, and so sang she,
   Until the east was grey,
Then pointed to her bleeding breast,
   And shrieked, and fled away.

   ‘   .   .   .   .

A JACOBITE'S EPITAPH

To my true king I offered, free from stain,
Courage and faith; vain faith, and courage vain.
For him I threw lands, honours, wealth, away,
And one dear hope, that was more prized than they.
For him I languished in a foreign clime,
Grey-haired with sorrow in my manhood's prime;
Heard on Lavernia Scargill's whispering trees,
And pined by Arno for my lovelier Tees;

643

Beheld each night my home in fevered sleep,
Each morning started from the dream to weep;
Till God, who saw me tried too sorely, gave
The resting-place I asked, an early grave.
O thou, whom chance leads to this nameless stone,
From that proud country which was once mine own,
By those white cliffs I never more must see,
By that dear language which I spake like thee,
Forget all feuds, and shed one English tear
O'er English dust.   A broken heart lies here.

Cardinal Newman

LEAD, KINDLY LIGHT

Lead, kindly Light, amid the encircling gloom,
    Lead Thou me on!
The night is dark, and I am far from home—
    Lead Thou me on!
Keep Thou my feet; I do not ask to see
The distant scene,—one step enough for me.

I was not ever thus, nor prayed that Thou
    Shouldst lead me on.
I loved to choose and see my path; but now
    Lead Thou me on!
I loved the garish day, and, spite of fears,
Pride ruled my will: remember not past years.

So long Thy power hath blessed me, sure it still
    Will lead me on,
O'er moor and fen, o'er crag and torrent, till
    The night is gone;
And with the morn those angel faces smile
Which I have loved long since, and lost awhile.

644

THE MONTH OF MARY

The green, green grass, the glittering grove,
    The heaven's majestic dome,
They image forth a tenderer bower,
    A more refulgent home;

They tell us of that Paradise
    Of everlasting rest,
And that high Tree, all flowers and fruit,
    The sweetest, yet the best.

O Mary, pure and beautiful,
    Thou art the Queen of May;
Our garlands wear about thy hair,
    And they will ne'er decay.

Edward Coate Pinkney

A HEALTH

I fill this cup to one made up
    Of loveliness alone,
A woman, of her gentle sex
    The seeming paragon;
To whom the better elements
    And kindly stars have given
A form so fair, that, like the air,
    'Tis less of earth than heaven.

Her every tone is music's own,
    Like those of morning birds,
And something more than melody
    Dwells ever in her words;
The coinage of her heart are they,
    And from her lips each flows
As one may see the burdened bee
    Forth issue from the rose.

645

Affections are as thoughts to her,
    The measures of her hours;
Her feelings have the fragrancy,
    The freshness of young flowers;
And lovely passions, changing oft,
    So fill her, she appears
The image of themselves by turns,—
    The idol of past years!

Of her bright face one glance will trace
    A picture on the brain,
And of her voice in echoing hearts
    A sound must long remain;
But memory, such as mine of her,
    So very much endears,
When death is nigh my latest sigh
    Will not be life's, but hers.

I fill this cup to one made up
    Of loveliness alone,
A woman, of her gentle sex
    The seeming paragon—
Her health! and would on earth there stood
    Some more of such a frame,
That life might be all poetry,
    And weariness a name.

James Clarence Mangan

DARK ROSALEEN

O my dark Rosaleen,
    Do not sigh, do not weep!
The priests are on the ocean green,
    They march along the deep.
There's wine from the royal Pope
    Upon the ocean green,
And Spanish ale shall give you hope,
    My dark Rosaleen!

JAMES CLARENCE MANGAN

My own Rosaleen!
Shall glad your heart, shall give you hope,
Shall give you health, and help, and hope,
   My dark Rosaleen!

Over hills and through dales
   Have I roamed for your sake;
All yesterday I sailed with sails
   On river and on lake.
The Erne, at its highest flood,
   I dashed' across unseen,
For there was lightning in my blood,
   My dark Rosaleen!
   My own Rosaleen!
Oh! there was lightning in my blood,
Red lightning lightened through my blood,
   My dark Rosaleen!

All day long, in unrest,
   To and fro do I move.
The very soul within my breast
   Is wasted for you, love!
The heart in my bosom faints
   To think of you, my Queen,
My life of life, my saint of saints,
   My dark Rosaleen!
   My own Rosaleen!
To hear your sweet and sad complaints,
My life, my love, my saint of saints,
   My dark Rosaleen!

Woe and pain, pain and woe,
   Are my lot, night and noon,
To see your bright face clouded so,
   Like to the mournful moon.
But yet will I rear your throne
   Again in golden sheen;
'Tis you shall reign, shall reign alone
   My dark Rosaleen!

My own Rosaleen!
'Tis you shall have the golden throne,
'Tis you shall reign, and reign alone,
   My dark Rosaleen!

Over dews, over sands,
   Will I fly for your weal:
Your holy, delicate white hands
   Shall girdle me with steel.
At home in your emerald bowers,
   From morning's dawn till e'en,
You'll pray for me, my flower of flowers,
   My dark Rosaleen!
   My own Rosaleen!
You'll think of me through daylight's hours,
My virgin flower, my flower of flowers,
   My dark Rosaleen!

I could scale the blue air,
   I could plough the high hills,
Oh, I could kneel all night in prayer,
   To heal your many ills!
And one beamy smile from you
   Would float like light between
My toils and me, my own, my true,
   My dark Rosaleen!
   My own Rosaleen!
Would give me life and soul anew,
A second life, a soul anew,
   My dark Rosaleen!

Oh! the Erne shall run red
   With redundance of blood,
The earth shall rock beneath our tread,
   And flames wrap hill and wood,
And gun-peal and slogan-cry
   Wake many a glen serene,
Ere you shall fade, ere you shall die,
   My dark Rosaleen!

My own Rosaleen!
The Judgment Hour must first be nigh,
Ere you shall fade, ere you can die,
My dark Rosaleen!

THE NAMELESS ONE

Roll forth, my song, like the rushing river,
   That sweeps along to the mighty sea;
God will inspire me while I deliver
    My soul of thee!

Tell thou the world, when my bones lie whitening
   Amid the last homes of youth and eld,
That once there was one whose veins ran lightning
    No eye beheld.

Tell how his boyhood was one drear night-hour,
   How shone for him, through his griefs and gloom,
No star of all heaven sends to light our
    Path to the tomb.

Roll on, my song, and to after ages
   Tell how, disdaining all earth can give,
He would have taught men, from wisdom's pages,
    The way to live.

And tell how trampled, derided, hated,
   And worn by weakness, disease, and wrong,
He fled for shelter to God, who mated
    His soul with song.

—With song which alway, sublime or vapid,
   Flowed like a rill in the morning beam,
Perchance not deep, but intense and rapid:
    A mountain stream.

Tell how this Nameless, condemned for years long
   To herd with demons from hell beneath,
Saw things that made him, with groans and tears, long
    For even death.

Go on to tell how, with genius wasted,
   Betrayed in friendship, befooled in love,
With spirit shipwrecked, and young hopes blasted,
       He still, still strove;

Till, spent with toil, dreeing death for others
   (And some whose hands should have wrought for him,
If children live not for sires and mothers),
       His mind grew dim;

And he fell far through that pit abysmal,
   The gulf and grave of Maginn and Burns,
And pawned his soul for the devil's dismal
       Stock of returns.

But yet redeemed it in days of darkness,
   And shapes and signs of the final wrath,
When death, in hideous and ghastly starkness,
       Stood on his path.

And tell how now, amid wreck and sorrow,
   And want, and sickness, and houseless nights,
He bides in calmness the silent morrow,
       That no ray lights.

And lives he still, then? Yes! Old and hoary
   At thirty-nine, from despair and woe,
He lives, enduring what future story
       Will never know.

Him grant a grave to, ye pitying noble,
   Deep in your bosoms: there let him dwell!
He, too, had tears for all souls in trouble,
       Here and in hell!

Louisa Macartney Crawford

KATHLEEN MAVOURNEEN

Kathleen Mavourneen! the grey dawn is breaking,
  The horn of the hunter is heard on the hill;
The lark from her light wing the bright dew is shaking,—
  Kathleen Mavourneen! what, slumbering still?
Oh, hast thou forgotten how soon we must sever?
  Oh! hast thou forgotten this day we must part?
It may be for years, and it may be for ever!
  Oh, why art thou silent, thou voice of my heart?
Oh, why art thou silent, Kathleen Mavourneen?

Kathleen Mavourneen, awake from thy slumbers!
  The blue mountains glow in the sun's golden light;
Ah, where is the spell that once hung on my numbers?
  Arise in thy beauty, thou star of my night!
Mavourneen, Mavourneen, my sad tears are falling,
  To think that from Erin and thee I must part!
It may be for years, and it may be for ever!
  Then why art thou silent, thou voice of my heart?
Then why art thou silent, Kathleen Mavourneen?

(This poem is variously ascribed to different women writers of the surname Crawford, but usually credited to Louisa Macartney Crawford.)

Ralph Waldo Emerson

WRITTEN IN EMERSON'S ESSAYS

"O monstrous, dead, unprofitable world,
That thou canst hear, and hearing, hold thy way!
A voice oracular hath peal'd to-day,
To-day a hero's banner is unfurl'd;

651

Hast thou no lip for welcome?"—So I said.
Man after man, the world smiled and pass'd by;
A smile of wistful incredulity
As though one spake of life unto the dead—

Scornful, and strange, and sorrowful, and full
Of bitter knowledge. Yet the will is free;
Strong is the soul, and wise, and beautiful;

The seeds of godlike power are in us still;
Gods are we, bards, saints, heroes, if we will!—
Dumb judges, answer, truth or mockery?

—MATTHEW ARNOLD.

EACH AND ALL

Little thinks, in the field, yon red-cloaked clown
Of thee from the hill-top looking down;
The heifer that lows in the upland farm,
Far-heard, lows not thine ear to charm;
The sexton, tolling his bell at noon,
Deems not that great Napoleon
Stops his horse, and lists with delight,
Whilst his files sweep round yon Alpine height;
Nor knowest thou what argument
Thy life to thy neighbor's creed has lent.
All are needed by each one;
Nothing is fair or good alone.
I thought the sparrow's note from heaven,
Singing at dawn on the alder bough;
I brought him home, in his nest, at even;
He sings the song, but it cheers not now,
For I did not bring home the river and sky;—
He sang to my ear,—they sang to my eye.
The delicate shells lay on the shore;
The bubbles of the latest wave
Fresh pearls to their enamel gave,
And the bellowing of the savage sea
Greeted their safe escape to me.

I wiped away the weeds and foam,
I fetched my sea-born treasures home;
But the poor, unsightly, noisome things
Had left their beauty on the shore
With the sun and the sand and the wild uproar.
The lover watched his graceful maid,
As 'mid the virgin train she strayed,
Nor knew her beauty's best attire
Was woven still by the snow-white choir.
At last she came to her hermitage,
Like the bird from the woodlands to the cage;—
The gay enchantment was undone,
A gentle wife, but fairy none.
Then I said, "I covet truth;
Beauty is unripe childhood's cheat;
I leave it behind with the games of youth:"—
As I spoke, beneath my feet
The ground-pine curled its pretty wreath,
Running over the club-moss burrs:
I inhaled the violet's breath;
Around me stood the oaks and firs;
Pine-cones and acorns lay on the ground;
Over me soared the eternal sky,
Full of light and of deity;
Again I saw, again I heard,
The rolling river, the morning bird;—
Beauty through my senses stole;
I yielded myself to the perfect whole.

THE PROBLEM

. . . .

Not from a vain or shallow thought
His awful Jove young Phidias brought;
Never from lips of cunning fell
The thrilling Delphic oracle;
Out from the heart of nature rolled
The burdens of the Bible old;
The litanies of nations came,
Like the volcano's tongue of flame,

Up from the burning core below,—
The canticles of love and woe:
The hand that rounded Peter's dome
And groined the aisles of Christian Rome
Wrought in a sad sincerity;
Himself from God he could not free;
He builded better than he knew;—
The conscious stone to beauty grew.

· · · · · ·

TO RHEA

Thee, dear friend, a brother soothes,
Not with flatteries, but truths,
Which tarnish not, but purify
The light which dims the morning's eye.
I have come from the spring-woods,
From the fragrant solitudes;—
Listen what the poplar-tree
And murmuring waters counselled me.

If with love thy heart has burned;
If thy love is unreturned;
Hide thy grief within thy breast,
Though it tear thee unexpressed;
For when love has once departed
From the eyes of the false-hearted,
And one by one has torn off quite
The bandages of purple light;
Though thou wert the loveliest
Form the soul had ever dressed,
Thou shalt seem, in each reply,
A vixen to his altered eye;
Thy softest pleadings seem too bold,
Thy praying lute will seem to scold;
Though thou kept the straightest road,
Yet thou errest far and broad.

But thou shalt do as do the gods
In their cloudless periods;

654

For of this lore be thou sure,—
'Though thou forget, the gods, secure,
Forget never their command,
But make the statute of this land.
As they lead, so follow all,
Ever have done, ever shall.
Warning to the blind and deaf,
'Tis written on the iron leaf,
Who drinks of Cupid's nectar cup
Loveth downward, and not up;
He who loves, of gods or men,
Shall not by the same be loved again;
His sweetheart's idolatry
Falls, in turn, a new degree.
When a god is once beguiled
By beauty of a mortal child
And by her radiant youth delighted,
He is not fooled, but warily knoweth
His love shall never be requited.
And thus the wise Immortal doeth,—
'Tis his study and delight
To bless that creature day and night;
From all evils to defend her;
In her lap to pour all splendor;
To ransack earth for riches rare,
And fetch her stars to deck her hair:
He mixes music with her thoughts,
And saddens her with heavenly doubts:
All grace, all good his great heart knows,
Profuse in love, the king bestows,
Saying, "Hearken! Earth, Sea, Air!
This monument of my despair
Build I to the All-Good, All-Fair.
Not for a private good,
But I, from my beatitude,
Albeit scorned as none was scorned,
Adorn her as was none adorned.
I make this maiden an ensample
To Nature, through her kingdoms ample,
Whereby to model newer races,
Statelier forms and fairer faces;

655

To carry man to new degrees
Of power and of comeliness.
These presents be the hostages
Which I pawn for my release.
See to thyself, O Universe!
Thou art better, and not worse."—
And the god, having given all,
Is freed forever from his thrall.

THE WORLD-SOUL

. . . .

He serveth the servant,
  The brave he loves amain;
He kills the cripple and the sick,
  And straight begins again;
For gods delight in gods,
  And thrust the weak aside;
To him who scorns their charities
  Their arms fly open wide.

. . . .

DESTINY

That you are fair or wise is vain,
Or strong, or rich, or generous;
You must add the untaught strain
That sheds beauty on the rose.
There's a melody born of melody,
Which melts the world into a sea.
Toil could never compass it;
Art its height could never hit;
It came never out of wit;
But a music music-born
Well may Jove and Juno scorn.
Thy beauty, if it lack the fire
Which drives me mad with sweet desire,
What boots it? What the soldier's mail,
Unless he conquer and prevail?

RALPH WALDO EMERSON

What all the goods thy pride which lift,
If thou pine for another's gift?
Alas! that one is born in blight,
Victim of perpetual slight:
When thou lookest on his face,
Thy heart saith, "Brother, go thy ways!
None shall ask thee what thou doest,
Or care a rush for what thou knowest,
Or listen when thou repliest,
Or remember where thou liest,
Or how thy supper is sodden";
And another is born
To make the sun forgotten.
Surely he carries a talisman
Under his tongue;
Broad his shoulders are and strong;
And his eye is scornful,
Threatening and young.
I hold it of little matter
Whether your jewel be of pure water,
A rose diamond or a white,
But whether it dazzle me with light.
I care not how you are dressed,
In coarsest weeds or in the best;
Nor whether your name is base or brave:
Nor for the fashion of your behavior;
But whether you charm me,
Bid my bread feed and my fire warm me,
And dress up Nature in your favor.
One thing is forever good;
That one thing is Success,—
Dear to the Eumenides,
And to all the heavenly brood.
Who bides at home, nor looks abroad,
Carries the eagles, and masters the sword.

GOOD-BYE

Good-bye, proud world! I'm going home:
Thou art not my friend, and I'm not thine.
Long through thy weary crowds I roam;
A river-ark on the ocean brine,
Long I've been tossed like the driven foam;
But now, proud world! I'm going home.

Good-bye to Flattery's fawning face;
To Grandeur with his wise grimace;
To upstart Wealth's averted eye;
To supple Office, low and high;
To crowded halls, to court and street;
To frozen hearts and hasting feet;
To those who go, and those who come;
Good-bye, proud world! I'm going home.

I am going to my own hearth-stone,
Bosomed in yon green hills alone,—
A secret nook in a pleasant land,
Whose groves the frolic fairies planned;
Where arches green, the livelong day,
Echo the blackbird's roundelay,
And vulgar feet have never trod
A spot that is sacred to thought and God.

O, when I am safe in my sylvan home,
I tread on the pride of Greece and Rome;
And when I am stretched beneath the pines,
Where the evening star so holy shines,
I laugh at the lore and the pride of man,
At the sophist schools and the learned clan;
For what are they all, in their high conceit,
When man in the bush with God may meet?

RALPH WALDO EMERSON

THE RHODORA:

ON BEING ASKED, WHENCE IS THE FLOWER?

In May, when sea-winds pierced our solitudes,
I found the fresh Rhodora in the woods,
Spreading its leafless blooms in a damp nook,
To please the desert and the sluggish brook.
The purple petals, fallen in the pool,
Made the black water with their beauty gay;
Here might the red-bird come his plumes to cool,
And court the flower that cheapens his array.
Rhodora! if the sages ask thee why
This charm is wasted on the earth and sky,
Tell them, dear, that if eyes were made for seeing,
Then Beauty is its own excuse for being:
Why thou wert there, O rival of the rose!
I never thought to ask, I never knew:
But, in my simple ignorance, suppose
The self-same power that brought me there brought you

THE HUMBLE-BEE

Burly, dozing humble-bee,
Where thou art is clime for me.
Let them sail for Porto Rique,
Far-off heats through seas to seek;
I will follow thee alone,
Thou animated torrid-zone!
Zigzag steerer, desert cheerer,
Let me chase thy waving lines;
Keep me nearer, me thy hearer,
Singing over shrubs and vines.

Insect lover of the sun,
Joy of thy dominion!
Sailor of the atmosphere;
Swimmer through the waves of air;

659

Voyager of light and noon;
Epicurean of June;
Wait, I prithee, till I come
Within earshot of thy hum,—
All without is martyrdom.

When the south wind, in May days,
With a net of shining haze
Silvers the horizon wall,
And with softness touching all,
Tints the human countenance
With a color of romance,
And infusing subtle heats,
Turns the sod to violets,
Thou, in sunny solitudes,
Rover of the underwoods,
The green silence dost displace
With thy mellow, breezy bass.

Hot midsummer's petted crone,
Sweet to me thy drowsy tone
Tells of countless sunny hours,
Long days, and solid banks of flowers;
Of gulfs of sweetness without bound
In Indian wildernesses found;
Of Syrian peace, immortal leisure,
Firmest cheer, and bird-like pleasure.

Aught unsavory or unclean
Hath my insect never seen;
But violets and bilberry bells,
Maple-sap and daffodels,
Grass with green flag half-mast high,
Succory to match the sky,
Columbine with horn of honey,
Scented fern, and agrimony,
Clover, catchfly, adder's-tongue
And brier-roses, dwelt among;
All beside was unknown waste,
All was picture as he passed.

RALPH WALDO EMERSON

Wiser far than human seer,
Yellow-breeched philosopher!
Seeing only what is fair,
Sipping only what is sweet,
Thou dost mock at fate and care,
Leave the chaff, and take the wheat.
When the fierce northwestern blast
Cools sea and land so far and fast,
Thou already slumberest deep;
Woe and want thou canst outsleep;
Want and woe, which torture us,
Thy sleep makes ridiculous.

THE SNOW-STORM

Announced by all the trumpets of the sky,
Arrives the snow, and driving o'er the fields,
Seems nowhere to alight: the whited air
Hides hills and woods, the river, and the heaven,
And veils the farm-house at the garden's end.
The sled and traveller stopped, the courier's feet
Delayed, all friends shut out, the housemates sit
Around the radiant fireplace, enclosed
In a tumultuous privacy of storm.

Come see the north wind's masonry.
Out of an unseen quarry evermore
Furnished with tile, the fierce artificer
Curves his white bastions with projected roof
Round every windward stake, or tree, or door.
Speeding, the myriad-handed, his wild work
So fanciful, so savage, nought cares he
For number or proportion.   Mockingly,
On coop or kennel he hangs Parian wreaths;
A swan-like form invests the hidden thorn;
Fills up the farmer's lane from wall to wall,
Maugre the farmer's sighs; and at the gate
A tapering turret overtops the work.
And when his hours are numbered, and the world
Is all his own, retiring, as he were not,

661

Leaves, when the sun appears, astonished Art
To mimic in slow structures, stone by stone,
Built in an age, the mad wind's night-work,
The frolic architecture of the snow.

WOODNOTES, II

. . . . . .

Speak not thy speech my boughs among:
Put off thy years, wash in the breeze;
My hours are peaceful centuries.
Talk no more with feeble tongue;
No more the fool of space and time,
Come weave with mine a nobler rhyme.
Only thy Americans
Can read thy line, can meet thy glance,
But the runes that I rehearse
Understands the universe;
The least breath my boughs which tossed
Brings again the Pentecost;
To every soul resounding clear
In a voice of solemn cheer,—
"Am I not thine?   Are not these thine?"
And they reply, "Forever mine!"

. . . .

Come learn with me the fatal song
Which knits the world in music strong,
Come lift thine eyes to lofty rhymes,
Of things with things, of times with times,
Primal chimes of sun and shade,
Of sound and echo, man and maid,
The land reflected in the flood,
Body with shadow still pursued.
For Nature beats in perfect tune,
And rounds with rhyme her every rune,
Whether she work in land or sea.
Or hide underground her alchemy.
Thou canst not wave thy staff in air,

662

Or dip thy paddle in the lake,
But it carves the bow of beauty there,
And the ripples in rhymes the oar forsake.
The wood is wiser far than thou;
The wood and wave each other know
Not unrelated, unaffied,
But to each thought and thing allied,
Is perfect Nature's every part,
Rooted in the mighty Heart.

. . . .

FORERUNNERS

Long I followed happy guides,
I could never reach their sides;
Their step is forth, and, ere the day
Breaks up their leaguer, and away.
Keen my sense, my heart was young,
Right good-will my sinews strung,
But no speed of mine avails
To hunt upon their shining trails.
On and away, their hasting feet
Make the morning proud and sweet;
Flowers they strew,—I catch the scent;
Or tone of silver instrument
Leaves on the wind melodious trace;
Yet I could never see their face.
On eastern hills I see their smokes,
Mixed with mist by distant lochs.
I met many travellers
Who the road had surely kept;
They saw not my fine revellers,—
These had crossed them while they slept.
Some had heard their fair report,
In the country or the court.
Fleetest couriers alive
Never yet could once arrive,
As they went or they returned,
At the house where these sojourned.

Sometimes their strong speed they slacken,
Though they are not overtaken;
In sleep their jubilant troop is near,—
I tuneful voices overhear;
It may be in wood or waste,—
At unawares 'tis come and past.
Their near camp my spirit knows
By signs gracious as rainbows.
I thenceforward and long after,
Listen for their harp-like laughter
And carry in my heart, for days,
Peace that hallows rudest ways.

SURSUM CORDA

Seek not the spirit, if it hide
Inexorable to thy zeal:
Trembler, do not whine and chide:
Art thou not also real?
Stoop not then to poor excuse;
Turn on the accuser roundly; say,
"Here am I, here will I abide
Forever to myself soothfast;
Go thou, sweet Heaven, or at thy pleasure stay!"
Already Heaven with thee its lot has cast,
For only it can absolutely deal.

GIVE ALL TO LOVE

Give all to love;
Obey thy heart;
Friends, kindred, days,
Estate, good-fame,
Plans, credit and the Muse,—
Nothing refuse.

'Tis a brave master;
Let it have scope:
Follow it utterly,

Hope beyond hope:
High and more high
It dives into noon,
With wing unspent,
Untold intent;
But it is a god,
Knows its own path
And the outlets of the sky.

It was never for the mean;
It requireth courage stout.
Souls above doubt,
Valor unbending,
It will reward,—
They shall return
More than they were,
And ever ascending.

Leave all for love;
Yet, hear me, yet,
One word more thy heart behoved,
One pulse more of firm endeavor,—
Keep thee to-day,
To-morrow, forever,
Free as an Arab
Of thy beloved.

Cling with life to the maid;
But when the surprise,
First vague shadow of surmise
Flits across her bosom young,
Of a joy apart from thee,
Free be she, fancy-free;
Nor thou detain her vesture's hem,
Nor the palest rose she flung
From her summer diadem.

Though thou loved her as thyself,
As a self of purer clay,
Though her parting dims the day,

665

Stealing grace from all alive;
Heartily know,
When half-gods go,
The gods arrive.

TO EVA

O fair and stately maid, whose eyes
Were kindled in the upper skies
    At the same torch that lighted mine;
For so I must interpret still
Thy sweet dominion o'er my will,
    A sympathy divine.

Ah! let me blameless gaze upon
Features that seem at heart my own;
    Nor fear those watchful sentinels,
Who charm the more their glance forbids,
Chaste-glowing, underneath their lids,
    With fire that draws while it repels.

BACCHUS

Bring me wine, but wine which never grew
In the belly of the grape,
Or grew on vine whose tap-roots, reaching through
Under the Andes to the Cape,
Suffer no savor of the earth to scape.

Let its grapes the morn salute
From a nocturnal root,
Which feels the acrid juice
Of Styx and Erebus;
And turns the woe of Night,
By its own craft, to a more rich delight.

We buy ashes for bread;
We buy diluted wine;
Give me of the true,—

Whose ample leaves and tendrils curled
Among the silver hills of heaven
Draw everlasting dew;
Wine of wine,
Blood of the world,
Form of forms, and mould of statures,
That I intoxicated,
And by the draught assimilated,
May float at pleasure through all natures;
The bird-language rightly spell,
And that which roses say so well.

Wine that is shed
Like the torrents of the sun
Up the horizon walls,
Or like the Atlantic streams, which run
When the South Sea calls.

Water and bread,
Food which needs no transmuting,
Rainbow-flowering, wisdom-fruiting,
Wine which is already man,
Food which teach and reason can.

Wine which Music is,—
Music and wine are one,—
That I, drinking this,
Shall hear far Chaos talk with me;
Kings unborn shall walk with me;
And the poor grass shall plot and plan
What it will do when it is man.
Quickened so, will I unlock
Every crypt of every rock.

I thank the joyful juice
For all I know;—
Winds of remembering
Of the ancient being blo
And seeming-solid w
Open and flow.

Pour, Bacchus! the remembering wine;
Retrieve the loss of me and mine!
Vine for vine be antidote,
And the grape requite the lote!
Haste to cure the old despair,—
Reason in Nature's lotus drenched,
The memory of ages quenched;
Give them again to shine;
Let wine repair what this undid;
And where the infection slid,
A dazzling memory revive;
Refresh the faded tints,
Recut the aged prints,
And write my old adventures with the pen
Which on the first day drew,
Upon the tablets blue,
The dancing Pleiads and eternal men.

SAADI

Behold, he watches at the door!
Behold his shadow on the floor!
Open innumerable doors
The heaven where unveiled Allah pours
The flood of truth, the flood of good,
The Seraph's and the Cherub's food.
Those doors are men: the Pariah hind
Admits thee to the perfect Mind.
Seek not beyond thy cottage wall
Redeemers that can yield thee all:
While thou sittest at thy door
On the desert's yellow floor,
Listening to the gray-haired crones,
Foolish gossips, ancient drones,
Saadi, see! they rise in stature
To the height of mighty Nature,
And the secret stands revealed
Fraudulent Time in vain concealed,—
That blessed gods in servile masks
Plied for thee in household tasks.

RALPH WALDO EMERSON

DIGE

In the long sunny afternoon,
　　The plain was full of ghosts;
I wandered up, I wandered down,
　　Beset by pensive hosts.

The winding Concord gleamed below,
　　Pouring as wide a flood
As when my brothers, long ago,
　　Came with me to the wood.

But they are gone,—the holy ones
　　Who trod with me this lovely vale;
The strong, star-bright companions
　　Are silent, low and pale.

They colored the horizon round;
　　Stars flamed and faded as they bade,
All echoes hearkened for their sound,—
　　They made the woodlands glad or mad.

I touch this flower of silken leaf,
　　Which once our childhood knew;
Its soft leaves wound me with a grief
　　Whose balsam never grew.

Hearken to yon pine-warbler
　　Singing aloft in the tree!
Hearest thou, O traveller,
　　What he singeth to me?

"Go, lonely man," it saith;
　　"They loved thee from their birth;
Their hands were pure, and pure their faith,—
　　There are no such hearts on earth.

"You cannot unlock your heart,
　　The key is gone with them;
The silent organ loudest chants
　　The master's requiem."

669

THRENODY

The South-wind brings
Life, sunshine and desire,
And on every mount and meadow
Breathes aromatic fire;
But over the dead he has no power,
The lost, the lost, he cannot restore;
And, looking over the hills, I mourn
The darling who shall not return.

I see my empty house,
I see my trees repair their boughs;
And he, the wondrous child,
Whose silver warble wild
Outvalued every pulsing sound
Within the air's cerulean round,—
The hyacinthine boy, for whom
Morn well might break and April bloom,—
The gracious boy, who did adorn
The world whereinto he was born,
And by his countenance repay
The favor of the loving Day,—
Has disappeared from the Day's eye;
Far and wide she cannot find him;
My hopes pursue, they cannot bind him.
Returned this day, the south wind searches,
And finds young pines and budding birches;
But finds not the budding man;
Nature, who lost, cannot remake him;
Fate let him fall, Fate can't retake him;
Nature, Fate, men, him seek in vain.

And whither now, my truant wise and sweet,
O, whither tend thy feet?
I had the right, few days ago,
Thy steps to watch, thy place to know:
How have I forfeited the right?
Hast thou forgot me in a new delight?
I hearken for thy household cheer,

RALPH WALDO EMERSON

O eloquent child!
Whose voice, an equal messenger,
Conveyed thy meaning mild.
What though the pains and joys
Whereof it spoke were toys
Fitting his age and ken,
Yet fairest dames and bearded men,
Who heard the sweet request,
So gentle, wise and grave,
Bended with joy to his behest
And let the world's affairs go by,
A while to share his cordial game,
Or mend his wicker wagon-frame,
Still plotting how their hungry ear
That winsome voice again might hear;
For his lips could well pronounce
Words that were persuasions.
Gentlest guardians marked serene
His early hope, his liberal mien;
Took counsel from his guiding eyes
To make this wisdom earthly wise.
Ah, vainly do these eyes recall
The school-march, each day's festival,
When every morn my bosom glowed
To watch the convoy on the road;
The babe in willow wagon closed,
With rolling eyes and face composed;
With children forward and behind,
Like Cupids studiously inclined;
And he the chieftain paced beside,
The center of the troop allied,
With sunny face of sweet repose,
To guard the babe from fancied foes.
The little captain innocent
Took the eye with him as he went;
Each village senior paused to scan
And speak the lovely caravan.
From the window I look out
To mark thy beautiful parade,
Stately marching in cap and coat
To some tune by fairies played;—

A music heard by thee alone
To works as noble led thee on.

Now Love and Pride, alas! in vain,
Up and down their glances strain..
The painted sled stands where it stood;
The kennel by the corded wood;
His gathered sticks to stanch the wall
Of the snow-tower, when snow should fall;
The ominous hole he dug in the sand,
And childhood's castles built or planned;
His daily haunts I well discern,—
The poultry-yard, the shed, the barn,—
And every inch of garden ground
Paced by the blessed feet around,
From the roadside to the brook
Whereinto he loved to look.
Step the meek fowls where erst they ranged;
The wintry garden lies unchanged;
The brook into the stream runs on;
But the deep-eyed boy is gone.

On that shaded day,
Dark with more clouds than tempests are,
When thou didst yield thy innocent breath
In birdlike heavings unto death,
Night came, and Nature had not thee;
I said, "We are mates in misery."
The morrow dawned with needless glow;
Each snowbird chirped, each fowl must crow;
Each tramper started; but the feet
Of the most beautiful and sweet
Of human youth had left the hill
And garden,—they were bound and still.
There's not a sparrow or a wren,
There's not a blade of autumn grain,
Which the four seasons do not tend
And tides of life and increase lend;
And every chick of every bird,
And weed and rock-moss is preferred.

O ostrich-like forgetfulness!
O loss of larger in the less!
Was there no star that could be sent,
No watching in the firmament,
No angel from the countless host
That loiters round the crystal coast,
Could stoop to heal that only child,
Nature's sweet marvel undefiled,
And keep the blossom of the earth,
Which all her harvests were not worth?

Not mine,—I never called thee mine,
But Nature's heir,—if I repine,
And seeing rashly torn and moved
Not what I made, but what I loved,
Grow early old with grief that thou
Must to the wastes of Nature go,—
'Tis because a general hope
Was quenched, and all must doubt and grope.
For flattering planets seemed to say
This child should ills of ages stay,
By wondrous tongue, and guided pen,
Bring the flown Muses back to men.
Perchance not he but Nature ailed,
The world and not the infant failed.
It was not ripe yet to sustain
A genius of so fine a strain,
Who gazed upon the sun and moon
As if he came unto his own,
And, pregnant with his grander thought,
Brought the old order into doubt.
His beauty once their beauty tried;
They could not feed him, and he died,
And wandered backward as in scorn,
To wait an æon to be born.
Ill day which made this beauty waste,
Plight broken, this high face defaced!
Some went and came about the dead;
And some in books of solace read;
Some to their friends the tidings say;
Some went to write, some went to pray;

One tarried here, there hurried one;
But their heart abode with none.
Covetous death bereaved us all,
To aggrandize one funeral.

The eager fate which carried thee
Took the largest part of me:
For this losing is true dying;
This is lordly man's down-lying,
This his slow but sure reclining,
Star by star his world resigning.

O child of paradise,
Boy who made dear his father's home,
In whose deep eyes
Men read the welfare of the times to come,
I am too much bereft.
The world dishonored thou hast left.
O truth's and nature's costly lie!
O trusted broken prophecy!
O richest fortune sourly crossed!
Born for the future, to the future lost!

The deep Heart answered, "Weepest thou?
Worthier cause for passion wild
If I had not taken the child.
And deemest thou as those who pore,
With aged eyes, short way before,—
Think'st Beauty vanished from the coast
Of matter, and thy darling lost?
Taught he not thee—the man of eld,
Whose eyes within his eyes beheld
Heaven's numerous hierarchy span
The mystic gulf from God to man?
To be alone wilt thou begin
When worlds of lovers hem thee in?
To-morrow, when the masks shall fall
That dizen Nature's carnival,
The pure shall see by their own will,
Which overflowing Love shall fill,

'Tis not within the force of fate
The fate-conjoined to separate.
But thou, my votary, weepest thou?
I gave thee sight—where is it now?
I taught thy heart beyond the reach
Of ritual, Bible, or of speech;
Wrote in thy mind's transparent table,
As far as the incommunicable;
Taught thee each private sign to raise
Lit by the supersolar blaze.
Past utterance, and past belief,
And past the blasphemy of grief,
The mysteries of Nature's heart;
And though no Muse can these impart,
Throb thine with Nature's throbbing breast,
And all is clear from east to west.

"I came to thee as to a friend;
Dearest, to thee I did not send
Tutors, but a joyful eye,
Innocence that matched the sky,
Lovely locks, a form of wonder,
Laughter rich as woodland thunder,
That thou might'st entertain apart
The richest flowering of all art:
And, as the great all-loving Day
Through smallest chambers takes its way,
That thou might'st break thy daily bread
With prophet, savior and head;
That thou might'st cherish for thine own
The riches of sweet Mary's Son,
Boy-Rabbi, Israel's paragon.
And thoughtest thou such guest
Would in thy hall take up his rest?
Would rushing life forget her laws,
Fate's glowing revolution pause?
High omens ask diviner guess;
Not to be conned to tediousness.
And know my higher gifts unbind
The zone that girds the incarnate mind.
When the scanty shores are full

With Thought's perilous, whirling pool;
When frail Nature can no more,
Then the Spirit strikes the hour:
My servant Death, with solving rite,
Pours finite into infinite.
Wilt thou freeze love's tidal flow,
Whose streams through nature circling go?
Nail the wild star to its track
On the half-climbed zodiac?
Light is light which radiates,
Blood is blood which circulates,
Life is life which generates,
And many-seeming life is one,—
Wilt thou transfix and make it none?
Its onward force too starkly pent
In figure, bone, and lineament?
Wilt thou, uncalled, interrogate,
Talker! the unreplying Fate?
Nor see the genius of the whole
Ascendant in the private soul,
Beckon it when to go and come,
Self-announced its hour of doom?
Fair the soul's recess and shrine,
Magic-built to last a season;
Masterpiece of love benign,
Fairer that expansive reason
Whose omen 'tis, and sign.
Wilt thou not ope thy heart to know
What rainbows teach, and sunsets show?
Verdict which accumulates
From lengthening scroll of human fates,
Voice of earth to earth returned,
Prayers of saints that inly burned,—
Saying, *What is excellent,*
As God lives, is permanent;
Hearts are dust, hearts' loves remain;
Heart's love will meet thee again.
Revere the Maker; fetch thine eye
Up to his style, and manners of the sky.
Not of adamant and gold
Built he heaven stark and cold;

No, but a nest of bending reeds,
Flowering grass and scented weeds;
Or like a traveller's fleeing tent,
Or bow above the tempest bent;
Built of tears and sacred flames,
And virtue reaching to its aims;
Built of furtherance and pursuing,
Not of spent deeds, but of doing.
Silent rushes the swift Lord
Through ruined systems still restored,
Broadsowing, bleak and void to bless,
Plants with worlds the wilderness;
Waters with tears of ancient sorrow
Apples of Eden ripe to-morrow.
House and tenant go to ground,
Lost in God, in Godhead found."

CONCORD HYMN:

SUNG AT THE COMPLETION OF THE BATTLE MONUMENT, APRIL 19, 1836

By the rude bridge that arched the flood,
  Their flag to April's breeze unfurled,
Here once the embattled farmers stood,
  And fired the shot heard round the world.

The foe long since in silence slept;
  Alike the conqueror silent sleeps;
And Time the ruined bridge has swept
  Down the dark stream which seaward creeps.

On this green bank, by this soft stream,
  We set to-day a votive stone;
That memory may their deed redeem,
  When, like our sires, our sons are gone.

Spirit, that made those heroes dare
  To die, and leave their children free,
Bid Time and Nature gently spare
  The shaft we raise to them and thee.

677

BRAHMA

If the red slayer think he slays,
   Or if the slain think he is slain,
They know not well the subtle ways
   I keep, and pass, and turn again.

Far or forgot to me is near;
   Shadow and sunlight are the same;
The vanished gods to me appear;
   And one to me are shame and fame.

They reckon ill who leave me out;
   When me they fly, I am the wings;
I am the doubter and the doubt,
   And I the hymn the Brahmin sings.

The strong gods pine for my abode,
   And pine in vain the sacred Seven;
But thou, meek lover of the good!
   Find me, and turn thy back on heaven.

DAYS

Daughters of Time, the hypocritic Days,
Muffled and dumb like barefoot dervishes,
And marching single in an endless file,
Bring diadems and fagots in their hands.
To each they offer gifts after his will,
Bread, kingdoms, stars, and sky that holds them all.
I, in my pleached garden, watched the pomp,
Forgot my morning wishes, hastily
Took a few herbs and apples, and the Day
Turned and departed silent. I, too late,
Under her solemn fillet saw the scorn.

RALPH WALDO EMERSON

WALDEINSAMKEIT

I do not count the hours I spend
In wandering by the sea;
The forest is my loyal friend,
Like God it useth me.

In plains that room for shadows make
Of skirting hills to lie,
Bound in by streams which give and take
Their colors from the sky;

Or on the mountain-crest sublime,
Or down the oaken glade,
O what have I to do with time?
For this the day was made.

Cities of mortals woe-begone
Fantastic care derides,
But in the serious landscape lone
Stern benefit abides.

Sheen will tarnish, honey cloy,
And merry is only a mask of sad,
But, sober on a fund of joy,
The woods at heart are glad.

There the great Planter plants
Of fruitful worlds the grain,
And with a million spells enchants
The souls that walk in pain.

Still on the seeds of all he made
The rose of beauty burns;
Through times that wear and forms that fade,
Immortal youth returns.

The black ducks mounting from the lake,
The pigeon in the pines,
The bittern's boom, a desert make
Which no false art refines.

Down in yon watery nook,
Where bearded mists divide,
The gray old gods whom Chaos knew,
The sires of Nature, hide.

Aloft, in secret veins of air,
Blows the sweet breath of song,
O, few to scale those uplands dare,
Though they to all belong!

See thou bring not to field or stone
The fancies found in books;
Leave authors' eyes, and fetch your own,
To brave the landscape's looks.

Oblivion here thy wisdom is,
Thy thrift, the sleep of cares;
For a proud idleness like this
Crowns all thy mean affairs.

TERMINUS

It is time to be old,
To take in sail:—
The god of bounds,
Who sets to seas a shore,
Came to me in his fatal rounds,
And said: "No more!
No farther shoot
Thy broad ambitious branches, and thy root.
Fancy departs: no more invent;
Contract thy firmament
To compass of a tent.
There's not enough for this and that,
Make thy option which of two;
Economize the failing river,
Not the less revere the Giver,
Leave the many and hold the few.
Timely wise accept the terms,
Soften the fall with wary foot;

RALPH WALDO EMERSON

A little while
Still plan and smile,
And,—fault of novel germs,—
Mature the unfallen fruit.
Curse, if thou wilt, thy sires,
Bad husbands of their fires,
Who, when they gave thee breath,
Failed to bequeath
The needful sinew stark as once,
The Baresark marrow to thy bones,
But left a legacy of ebbing veins,
Inconstant heat and nerveless reins,—
Amid the Muses, left thee deaf and dumb,
Amid the gladiators, halt and numb."

As the bird trims her to the gale,
I trim myself to the storm of time,
I man the rudder, reef the sail,
Obey the voice at eve obeyed at prime:
"Lowly faithful, banish fear,
Right onward drive unharmed;
The port, well worth the cruise, is near,
And every wave is charmed."

FRIENDSHIP

A ruddy drop of manly blood
The surging sea outweighs,
The world uncertain comes and goes;
The lover rooted stays.
I fancied he was fled,—
And, after many a year,
Glowed unexhausted kindliness,
Like daily sunrise there.
My careful heart was free again,
O friend, my bosom said,
Through thee alone the sky is arched,
Through thee the rose is red;
All things through thee take nobler form,
And look beyond the earth,

The mill-round of our fate appears
A sun-path in thy worth.
Me too thy nobleness has taught
To master my despair;
The fountains of my hidden life
Are through thy friendship fair.

SACRIFICE

Though love repine, and reason chafe,
There came a voice without reply,—
" 'Tis man's perdition to be safe,
When for the truth he ought to die."

THERE ALWAY, ALWAY SOMETHING SINGS

Let me go where'er I will
I hear a sky-born music still:
It sounds from all things old,
It sounds from all things young,
From all that's fair, from all that's foul,
Peals out a cheerful song.
It is not only in the rose,
It is not only in the bird,
Not only where the rainbow glows,
Nor in the song of woman heard,
But in the darkest, meanest things
There alway, alway something sings.
'Tis not in the high stars alone,
Nor in the cups of budding flowers,
Nor in the redbreast's mellow tone,
Nor in the bow that smiles in showers,
But in the mud and scum of things
There alway, alway something sings.
—THE POET.

682

RALPH WALDO EMERSON

THE BOHEMIAN HYMN

In many forms we try
To utter God's infinity,
But the boundless hath no form,
And the Universal Friend
Doth as far transcend
An angel as a worm.
The great Idea baffles wit,
Language falters under it,
It leaves the learned in the lurch;
Nor art, nor power, nor toil can find
The measure of the eternal Mind,
Nor hymn, nor prayer, nor church.

EROS

They put their finger on their lip,
   The Powers above:
The seas their islands clip,
The moons in ocean dip,
'They love, but name not love.

PHILOSOPHER

Philosophers are lined with eyes within,
And, being so, the sage unmakes the man.
In love, he cannot therefore cease his trade;
Scarce the first blush has overspread his cheek,
He feels it, introverts his learned eye
To catch the unconscious heart in the very act.
His mother died,—the only friend he had,—
Some tears escaped, but his philosophy
Couched like a cat sat watching close behind
And throttled all his passion. Is't not like
That devil-spider that devours her mate
Scarce freed from her embraces?

683

DUTY

So nigh is grandeur to our dust,
    So near is God to man,
When Duty whispers low, "Thou must,"
    The youth replies, "I can."
                            —VOLUNTARIES, III.

URIEL

It fell in the ancient periods
    Which the brooding soul surveys,
Or ever the wild Time coin'd itself
    Into calendar months and days.

This was the lapse of Uriel,
Which in Paradise befell.
Once, among the Pleiads walking,
Sayd overheard the young gods talking;
And the treason, too long pent,
To his ears was evident.
The young deities discuss'd
Laws of form, and metre just,
Orb, quintessence, and sunbeams,
What subsisteth, and what seems.
One, with low tones that decide,
And doubt and reverend use defied,
With a look that solved the sphere,
And stirr'd the devils everywhere,
Gave his sentiment divine
Against the being of a line.
"Line in nature is not found;
Unit and universe are round;
In vain produced, all rays return;
Evil will bless, and ice will burn."
As Uriel spoke with piercing eye,
A shudder ran around the sky;
The stern old war-gods shook their heads;
The seraphs frown'd from myrtle-beds;
Seem'd to the holy festival

The rash word boded ill to all;
The balance-beam of Fate was bent;
The bounds of good and ill were rent;
Strong Hades could not keep his own,
But all slid to confusion.

A sad self-knowledge withering fell
On the beauty of Uriel;
In heaven once eminent, the god
Withdrew that hour into his cloud;
Whether doom'd to long gyration
In the sea of generation,
Or by knowledge grown too bright
To hit the nerve of feebler sight.
Straightway a forgetting wind
Stole over the celestial kind,
And their lips the secret kept,
If in ashes the fire-seed slept.
But, now and then, truth-speaking things
Shamed the angels' veiling wings;
And, shrilling from the solar course,
Or from fruit of chemic force,
Procession of a soul in matter,
Or the speeding change of water,
Or out of the good of evil born,
Came Uriel's voice of cherub scorn,
And a blush tinged the upper sky,
And the gods shook, they knew not why.

MERLIN

I

The trivial harp will never please
Or fill my craving ear;
Its chords should ring as blows the breeze,
Free, peremptory, clear.
No jingling serenader's art,
Nor tinkle of piano strings,
Can make the wild blood start
In its mystic springs.

The kingly bard
Must smite the chords rudely and hard,
As with hammer or with mace;
That they may render back
Artful thunder, which conveys
Secrets of the solar track,
Sparks of the supersolar blaze.
Merlin's blows are strokes of fate,
Chiming with the forest tone,
When boughs buffet boughs in the wood;
Chiming with the gasp and moan
Of the ice-imprisoned flood;
With the pulse of manly hearts;
With the voice of orators;
With the din of city arts;
With the cannonade of wars;
With the marches of the brave;
And prayers of might from martyr's cave.

Great is the art,
Great be the manners, of the bard.
He shall not his brain encumber
With the coil of rhythm and number;
But, leaving rule and pale forethought,
He shall aye climb
For his rhyme.
"Pass in, pass in," the angels say,
"Into the upper doors,
Nor count compartments of the floors,
But mount to paradise
By the stairway of surprise."

Blameless master of the games,
King of sport that never shames,
He shall daily joy dispense
Hid in song's sweet influence.
Forms more cheerly live and go,
What time the subtle mind
Sings aloud the tune whereto
Their pulses beat,
And march their feet,
And their members are combined.

THOMAS WADE

By Sybarites beguiled,
He shall no task decline;
Merlin's mighty line
Extremes of nature reconciled,
Bereaved a tyrant of his will,
And made the lion mild.
Songs can the tempest still,
Scattered on the stormy air,
Mould the year to fair increase,
And bring in poetic peace.

He shall not seek to weave,
In weak, unhappy times,
Efficacious rhymes;
Wait his returning strength.
Bird that from the nadir's floor
To the zenith's top can soar,—
The soaring orbit of the muse exceeds that
    journey's length.
Nor profane affect to hit
Or compass that, by meddling wit,
Which only the propitious mind
Publishes when 'tis inclined.
There are open hours
When the God's will sallies free,
And the dull idiot might see
The flowing fortunes of a thousand years;
Sudden, at unawares,
Self-moved, fly to the doors,
Nor sword of angels could reveal
What they conceal.

Thomas Wade

THE TRUE MARTYR

The Martyr worthiest of the bleeding name
Is he whose life a bloodless part fulfils;
Whom racks nor tortures tear, nor poniard kills,
Nor heat of bigots' sacrificial flame:

687

But whose great soul can to herself proclaim
The fullness of the everlasting ills
With which all pained Creation writhes and thrills,
And yet pursue unblenched her solemn aim;
Who works, all-knowing work's futility;
Creates, all-conscious of ubiquitous death;
And hopes, believes, adores, while Destiny
Points from life's steep to all her graves beneath;
   Whose Thought 'mid scorching woes is found apart—
Perfect amid the flames, like Cranmer's heart!

William Lloyd Garrison

SONNET

(Written While in Prison for Denouncing the Domestic Slave-Trade)

High walls and huge the body may confine,
   And iron gates obstruct the prisoner's gaze,
And massive bolts may baffle his design,
   And vigilant keepers watch his devious ways;
But scorns the immortal mind such base control:
   No chains can bind it and no cell enclose.
Swifter than light it flies from pole to pole,
   And in a flash from earth to heaven it goes.
It leaps from mount to mount; from vale to vale
   It wanders, plucking honeyed fruits and flowers;
It visits home to hear the fireside tale
   And in sweet converse pass the joyous hours;
'Tis up before the sun, roaming afar,
And in its watches wearies every star.

Elizabeth Barrett Browning

SONNETS FROM THE PORTUGUESE

I

I thought once how Theocritus had sung
Of the sweet years, the dear and wish'd-for years,
Who each one in a gracious hand appears
To bear a gift for mortals old or young:
And, as I mused it in his antique tongue,
I saw in gradual vision through my tears
The sweet, sad years, the melancholy years—
Those of my own life, who by turns had flung
A shadow across me.   Straightway I was 'ware,
So weeping, how a mystic Shape did move
Behind me, and drew me backward by the hair;
And a voice said in mastery, while I strove,
"Guess now who holds thee?"—"Death," I said.   But there
The silent answer rang—"Not Death, but Love."

III

Unlike are we, unlike, O princely Heart!
Unlike our uses and our destinies.
Our ministering two angels look surprise
On one another, as they strike athwart
Their wings in passing.   Thou, bethink thee, art
A guest for queens to social pageantries,
With gages from a hundred brighter eyes
Than tears even can make mine, to play thy part
Of chief musician.   What hast thou to do
With looking from the lattice-lights at me—
A poor, tired, wandering singer, singing through
The dark, and leaning up a cypress tree?
The chrism is on thine head—on mine the dew—
And Death must dig the level where these agree.

VI

Go from me. Yet I feel that I shall stand
Henceforward in thy shadow. Nevermore
Alone upon the threshold of my door
Of individual life I shall command
The uses of my soul, nor lift my hand
Serenely in the sunshine as before,
Without the sense of that which I forbore—
Thy touch upon the palm. The widest land
Doom takes to part us, leaves thy heart in mine
With pulses that beat double. What I do
And what I dream include thee, as the wine
Must taste of its own grapes. And when I sue
God for myself, He hears that name of thine,
And sees within my eyes the tears of two.

VIII

What can I give thee back, O liberal
And princely giver, who has brought the gold
And purple of thine heart, unstained, untold,
And laid them on the outside of the wall
For such as I to take or leave withal,
In unexpected largesse? Am I cold,
Ungrateful, that for these most manifold
High gifts, I render nothing back at all?
Not so; not cold,—but very poor instead.
Ask God who knows. For frequent tears have run
The colours from my life, and left so dead
And pale a stuff, it were not fitly done
To give the same as pillow to thy head.
Go farther! let it serve to trample on.

XIV

If thou must love me, let it be for naught
Except for love's sake only. Do not say,
"I love her for her smile—her look—her way
Of speaking gently,—for a trick of thought
690

That falls in well with mine, and certes brought
A sense of pleasant ease on such a day"—
For these things in themselves, Belovèd, may
Be changed, or change for thee—and love, so wrought,
May be unwrought so.   Neither love me for
Thine own dear pity's wiping my cheeks dry:
A creature might forget to weep, who bore
Thy comfort long, and lose thy love thereby!
But love me for love's sake, that evermore
Thou mayst love on, through love's eternity.

XVIII

I never gave a lock of hair away
To a man, Dearest, except this to thee,
Which now upon my fingers thoughtfully
I ring out to the full brown length and say
"Take it."   My day of youth went yesterday;
My hair no longer bounds to my foot's glee,
Nor plant I it from rose or myrtle-tree,
As girls do, any more: it only may
Now shade on two pale cheeks the mark of tears,
Taught drooping from the head that hangs aside
Through sorrow's trick.   I thought the funeral-shears
Would take this first, but Love is justified,—
Take it thou,—finding pure, from all those years,
The kiss my mother left here when she died.

XXII

When our two souls stand up erect and strong,
Face to face, silent, drawing nigh and nigher,
Until the lengthening wings break into fire
At either curving point,—what bitter wrong
Can the earth do us, that we should not long
Be here contented?   Think!   In mounting higher,
The angels would press on us, and aspire
To drop some golden orb of perfect song
Into our deep, dear silence.   Let us stay
Rather on earth, Belovèd—where the unfit

Contrarious moods of men recoil away
And isolate pure spirits, and permit
A place to stand and love in for a day,
With darkness and the death-hour rounding it.

XLIII

How do I love thee?   Let me count the ways.
I love thee to the depth and breadth and height
My soul can reach, when feeling out of sight
For the ends of Being and ideal Grace.
I love thee to the level of every day's
Most quiet need, by sun and candlelight.
I love thee freely, as men strive for Right;
I love thee purely, as they turn from Praise.
I love thee with the passion put to use
In my old griefs, and with my childhood's faith.
I love thee with a love I seemed to lose
With my lost saints,—I love thee with the breath,
Smiles, tears, of all my life!—and, if God choose,
I shall but love thee better after death.

A PORTRAIT

I will paint her as I see her,
    Ten times have the lilies blown,
    Since she looked upon the sun.

And her face is lily-clear,
    Lily-shaped, and dropped in duty
    To the law of its own beauty.

Oval cheeks encoloured faintly,
    Which a trail of golden hair
    Keeps from fading off to air;

And a forehead fair and saintly,
    Which two blue eyes undershine,
    Like meek prayers before a shrine.

692

CHARLES FENNO HOFFMAN

Face and figure of a child,—
  Thought too calm, you think, and tender,
  For the childhood you would lend her.

Yet, child-simple, undefiled,
  Frank, obedient, waiting still
  On the turnings of your will.

        .   .   .   .   .

And if any poet knew her,
  He would sing of her with falls
  Used in lovely madrigals.

And if any painter drew her,
  He would paint her unaware
  With a halo round the hair.

Charles Fenno Hoffman

MONTEREY

We were not many—we who stood
  Before the iron sleet that day—
Yet many a gallant spirit would
Give half his years if he then could
  Have been with us at Monterey.

Now here, now there, the shot, it hailed
  In deadly drifts of fiery spray,
Yet not a single soldier quailed
When wounded comrades round them wailed
  Their dying shout at Monterey.

And on—still on our column kept
  Through walls of flame its withering way;
Where fell the dead, the living stept,
Still charging on the guns which swept
  The slippery streets of Monterey.

The foe himself recoiled aghast,
  When, striking where he strongest lay,
We swooped his flanking batteries past,
And braving full their murderous blast,
  Stormed home the towers of Monterey.

Our banners on those turrets wave;
  And there our evening bugles play;
Where orange boughs above their grave
Keep green the memory of the brave
  Who fought and fell at Monterey.

We are not many,—we who pressed
  Beside the brave who fell that day;
But who of us has not confessed
He'd rather share their warrior rest
  Than not have been at Monterey?

Henry Wadsworth Longfellow

HENRY WADSWORTH LONGFELLOW

"Not to be tuneless in old age!"
Ah! surely blest his pilgrimage,
  Who, in his Winter's snow,
Still sings with note as sweet and clear
As in the morning of the year
  When the first violets blow.

Blest!—but more blest, whom Summer's heat,
Whom Spring's impulsive stir and beat,
  Have taught no feverish lure;
Whose Muse, benignant and serene,
Still keeps his Autumn chaplet green
  Because his verse is pure!

Lie calm, O white and laureate head!
Lie calm, O Dead, that art not dead,
  Since from the voiceless grave,
Thy voice shall speak to old and young
While song yet speaks an English tongue
  By Charles' or Thamis' wave!
                  —Austin Dobson.

694

HENRY WADSWORTH LONGFELLOW

HYMN TO THE NIGHT

I heard the trailing garments of the Night
    Sweep through her marble halls!
I saw her sable skirts all fringed with light
    From the celestial walls!

I felt her presence, by its spell of might,
    Stoop o'er me from above;
The calm, majestic presence of the Night,
    As of the one I love.

I heard the sounds of sorrow and delight,
    The manifold, soft chimes,
That fill the haunted chambers of the Night,
    Like some old poet's rhymes.

From the cool cisterns of the midnight air
    My spirit drank repose;
The fountain of perpetual peace flows there,—
    From those deep cisterns flows.

O holy Night! from thee I learn to bear
    What man has borne before!
Thou layest thy finger on the lips of Care,
    And they complain no more.

Peace! Peace! Orestes-like I breathe this prayer!
    Descend with broad-winged flight,
The welcome, the thrice-prayed for, the most fair,
    The best-beloved Night!

MAIDENHOOD

Maiden! with the meek, brown eyes,
In whose orbs a shadow lies
Like the dusk in evening skies!

Thou whose locks outshine the sun,
Golden tresses, wreathed in one,
As the braided streamlets run!

695

Standing with reluctant feet,
Where the brook and river meet,
Womanhood and childhood fleet!

Gazing, with a timid glance,
On the brooklet's swift advance,
On the river's broad expanse!

Deep and still, that gliding stream
Beautiful to thee must seem,
As the river of a dream.

Then why pause with indecision,
When bright angels in thy vision
Beckon thee to fields Elysian?

Seest thou shadows sailing by,
As the dove, with startled eye,
Sees the falcon's shadow fly?

Hearest thou voices on the shore,
That our ears perceive no more,
Deafened by the cataract's roar?

Oh, thou child of many prayers!
Life hath quicksands,—Life hath snares!
Care and age come unawares!

Like the swell of some sweet tune,
Morning rises into noon,
May glides onward into June.

Childhood is the bough, where slumbered
Birds and blossoms many-numbered;—
Age, that bough with snows encumbered.

Gather, then, each flower that grows,
When the young heart overflows,
To embalm that tent of snows.

Bear a lily in thy hand;
Gates of brass cannot withstand
One touch of that magic wand.

Bear through sorrow, wrong, and ruth,
In thy heart the dew of youth,
On thy lips the smile of truth.

Oh, that dew, like balm, shall steal
Into wounds that cannot heal
Even as sleep our eyes doth seal;

And that smile, like sunshine, dart
Into many a sunless heart,
For a smile of God thou art.

SERENADE

Stars of the summer night!
  Far in yon azure deeps,
Hide, hide your golden light!
  She sleeps!
My lady sleeps!
  Sleeps!

Moon of the summer night!
  Far down yon western steeps,
Sink, sink in silver light!
  She sleeps!
My lady sleeps!
  Sleeps!

Wind of the summer night!
  Where yonder woodbine creeps,
Fold, fold thy pinions light!
  She sleeps!
My lady sleeps!
  Sleeps!

Dreams of the summer night!
  Tell her, her lover keeps
Watch! while in slumbers light
  She sleeps!
My lady sleeps!
  Sleeps!

THE SPANISH GYPSY

CARILLON

In the ancient town of Bruges,
In the quaint old Flemish city,
As the evening shades descended,
Low and loud and sweetly blended,
Low at times and loud at times,
And changing like a poet's rhymes,
Rang the beautiful wild chimes
From the Belfry in the market
Of the ancient town of Bruges.

Then, with deep sonorous clangor
Calmly answering their sweet anger,
When the wrangling bells had ended,
Slowly struck the clock eleven,
And, from out the silent heaven,
Silence on the town descended.
Silence, silence everywhere,
On the earth and in the air,
Save that footsteps here and there
Of some burgher home returning,
By the street lamps faintly burning,
For a moment woke the echoes
Of the ancient town of Bruges.

But amid my broken slumbers
Still I heard those magic numbers,
As they loud proclaimed the flight
And stolen marches of the night;
Till their chimes in sweet collision
Mingled with each wandering vision,
Mingled with the fortune-telling
Gypsy-bands of dreams and fancies,
Which amid the waste expanses
Of the silent land of trances
Have their solitary dwelling;
All else seemed asleep in Bruges,
In the quaint old Flemish city.

And I thought how like these chimes
Are the poet's airy rhymes,
All his rhymes and roundelays,
His conceits, and songs, and ditties,
From the belfry of his brain,
Scattered downward, though in vain,
On the roofs and stones of cities!
For by night the drowsy ear
Under its curtains cannot hear,
And by day men go their ways,
Hearing the music as they pass,
But deeming it no more, alas!
Than the hollow sound of brass.

Yet perchance a sleepless wight,
Lodging at some humble inn
In the narrow lanes of life,
When the dusk and hush of night
Shut out the incessant din
Of daylight and its toil and strife,
May listen with a calm delight
To the poet's melodics,
Till he hears, or dreams he hears,
Intermingled with the song,
Thoughts that he has cherished long;
Hears amid the chime and singing
The bells of his own village ringing,
And wakes, and finds his slumberous eyes
Wet with most delicious tears.

Thus dreamed I, as by night I lay
In Bruges, at the Fleur-de-Blé,
Listening with a wild delight
To the chimes that, through the night,
Rang their changes from the Belfry
Of that quaint old Flemish city.

THE BELFRY OF BRUGES

In the market-place of Bruges stands the belfry old and
brown;
Thrice consumed and thrice rebuilded, still it watches o'er
the town.

699

As the summer morn was breaking, on that lofty tower I
  stood,
And the world threw off the darkness, like the weeds of
  widowhood.

Thick with towns and hamlets studded, and with streams
  and vapors gray,
Like a shield embossed with silver, round and vast the land-
  scape lay.

At my feet the city slumbered. From its chimneys, here and
  there,
Wreaths of snow-white smoke, ascending, vanished, ghost-
  like, into air.

Not a sound rose from the city at that early morning hour,
But I heard a heart of iron beating in the ancient tower.

From their nests beneath the rafters sang the swallows wild
  and high;
And the world, beneath me sleeping, seemed more distant
  than the sky.

Then most musical and solemn, bringing back the olden times,
With their strange, unearthly changes rang the melancholy
  chimes,

Like the psalms from some old cloister, when the nuns sing
  in the choir;
And the great bell tolled among them, like the chanting of a
  friar.

Visions of the days departed, shadowy phantoms filled my
  brain;
They who live in history only seemed to walk the earth
  again;

All the Foresters of Flanders,—mighty Baldwin Bras de Fer,
Lyderick du Bucq and Cressy, Philip, Guy de Dampierre.

I beheld the pageants splendid that adorned those days of old;
Stately dames, like queens attended, knights who bore the
  Fleece of Gold;

700

HENRY WADSWORTH LONGFELLOW

Lombard and Venetian merchants with deep-laden argosies;
Ministers from twenty nations; more than royal pomp and
    ease.

I beheld proud Maximilian, kneeling humbly on the ground;
I beheld the gentle Mary, hunting with her hawk and hound;

And her lighted bridal-chamber, where a duke slept with the
    queen,
And the armèd guard around them, and the sword unsheathed
    between.

I beheld the Flemish weavers, with Namur and Juliers bold,
Marching homeward from the bloody battle of the Spurs of
    Gold;

Saw the fight at Minnewater, saw the White Hoods moving
    west,
Saw great Artevelde victorious scale the Golden Dragon's
    nest.

And again the whiskered Spaniard all the land with terror
    smote;
And again the wild alarum sounded from the tocsin's throat;

Till the bell of Ghent responded o'er lagoon and dike of sand,
"I am Roland! I am Roland! there is victory in the land!"

Then the sound of drums aroused me. The awakened city's
    roar
Chased the phantoms I had summoned back into their graves
    once more.

Hours had passed away like minutes; and, before I was aware,
Lo! the shadow of the belfry crossed the sun-illumined square.

THE ARSENAL AT SPRINGFIELD

This is the Arsenal. From floor to ceiling,
    Like a huge organ, rise the burnished arms;
But from their silent pipes no anthem pealing
    Startles the villages with strange alarms.

701

Ah! what a sound will rise, how wild and dreary,
    When the death-angel touches those swift keys!
What loud lament and dismal Miserere
    Will mingle with their awful symphonies!

I hear even now the infinite fierce chorus,
    The cries of agony, the endless groan,
Which, through the ages that have gone before us,
    In long reverberations reach our own.

On helm and harness rings the Saxon hammer,
    Through Cimbric forest roars the Norseman's song,
And loud, amid the universal clamor,
    O'er distant deserts sounds the Tartar gong.

I hear the Florentine, who from his palace
    Wheels out his battle-bell with dreadful din,
And Aztec priests upon their teocallis
    Beat the wild war-drums made of serpent's skin;

The tumult of each sacked and burning village;
    The shout that every prayer for mercy drowns;
The soldiers' revels in the midst of pillage;
    The wail of famine in beleaguered towns;

The bursting shell, the gateway wrenched asunder,
    The rattling musketry, the clashing blade;
And ever and anon, in tones of thunder
    The diapason of the cannonade.

Is it, O man, with such discordant noises,
    With such accursed instruments as these,
Thou drownest Nature's sweet and kindly voices,
    And jarrest the celestial harmonies?

Were half the power that fills the world with terror,
    Were half the wealth bestowed on camps and courts,
Given to redeem the human mind from error,
    There were no need of arsenals or forts:

HENRY WADSWORTH LONGFELLOW

The warrior's name would be a name abhorrèd!
  And every nation, that should lift again
Its hand against a brother, on its forehead
  Would wear forevermore the curse of Cain!

Down the dark future, through long generations,
  The echoing sounds grow fainter and then cease;
And like a bell, with solemn, sweet vibrations,
  I hear once more the voice of Christ say, "Peace!"

Peace! and no longer from its brazen portals
  The blast of War's great organ shakes the skies!
But beautiful as songs of the immortals,
  The holy melodies of love arise.

THE DAY IS DONE

The day is done, and the darkness
  Falls from the wings of Night,
As a feather is wafted downward
  From an eagle in his flight.

I see the lights of the village
  Gleam through the rain and the mist,
And a feeling of sadness comes o'er me
  That my soul cannot resist:

A feeling of sadness and longing,
  That is not akin to pain,
And resembles sorrow only
  As the mist resembles rain.

Come, read to me some poem,
  Some simple and heartfelt lay,
That shall soothe this restless feeling,
  And banish the thoughts of day.

Not from the grand old masters,
  Not from the bards sublime,
Whose distant footsteps echo
  Through the corridors of Time.

703

For, like strains of martial music,
    Their mighty thoughts suggest
Life's endless toil and endeavor;
    And to-night I long for rest.

Read from some humbler poet,
    Whose songs gushed from his heart,
As showers from the clouds of summer,
    Or tears from the eyelids start;

Who, through long days of labor,
    And nights devoid of ease,
Still heard in his soul the music
    Of wonderful melodies.

Such songs have power to quiet
    The restless pulse of care,
And come like the benediction
    That follows after prayer.

Then read from the treasured volume
    The poem of thy choice,
And lend to the rhyme of the poet
    The beauty of thy voice.

And the night shall be filled with music,
    And the cares, that infest the day,
Shall fold their tents, like the Arabs,
    And as silently steal away.

THE ARROW AND THE SONG

I shot an arrow into the air,
It fell to earth, I knew not where;
For, so swiftly it flew, the sight
Could not follow it in its flight.

I breathed a song into the air,
It fell to earth, I knew not where;
For who has sight so keen and strong,
That it can follow the flight of song?

Long, long afterward, in an oak
I found the arrow, still unbroke;
And the song, from beginning to end,
I found again in the heart of a friend.

EVANGELINE

This is the forest primeval.   The murmuring pines and the
  hemlocks,
Bearded with moss, and in garments green, indistinct in the
  twilight,
Stand like Druids of eld, with voices sad and prophetic,
Stand like harpers hoar, with beards that rest on their bosoms.
Loud from its rocky caverns, the deep-voiced neighboring
  ocean
Speaks, and in accents disconsolate answers the wail of the
  forest.

  This is the forest primeval; but where are the hearts that
    beneath it
Leaped like the roe, when he hears in the woodland the voice
  of the huntsman?
Where is the thatch-roofed village, the home of Acadian
  farmers,—
Men whose lives glided on like rivers that water the wood-
  lands,
Darkened by shadows of earth, but reflecting an image of
  heaven?
Waste are those pleasant farms, and the farmers forever
  departed!
Scattered like dust and leaves, when the mighty blasts of
  October
Seize them, and whirl them aloft, and sprinkle them far o'er
  the ocean.
Naught but tradition remains of the beautiful village of
  Grand-Pré.

    o   o   o   •   o   •   •   •   •

THE BUILDING OF THE SHIP

. . . . .

Thou, too, sail on, O Ship of State!
Sail on, O Union, strong and great!
Humanity with all its fears,
With all the hopes of future years,
Is hanging breathless on thy fate!
We know what Master laid thy keel,
What Workmen wrought thy ribs of steel,
Who made each mast, and sail, and rope,
What anvils rang, what hammers beat,
In what a forge and what a heat
Were shaped the anchors of thy hope!
Fear not each sudden sound and shock,
'Tis of the wave and not the rock;
'Tis but the flapping of the sail,
And not a rent made by the gale!
In spite of rock and tempest's roar,
In spite of false lights on the shore,
Sail on, nor fear to breast the sea!
Our hearts, our hopes, are all with thee,
Our hearts, our hopes, our prayers, our tears,
Our faith triumphant o'er our fears,
Are all with thee,—are all with thee!

SANDALPHON

Have you read in the Talmud of old,
In the Legends the Rabbins have told
    Of the limitless realms of the air,
Have you read it,—the marvellous story
Of Sandalphon, the Angel of Glory,
    Sandalphon, the Angel of Prayer?

How, erect, at the outermost gates
Of the City Celestial he waits,
    With his feet on the ladder of light,
That, crowded with angels unnumbered,
By Jacob was seen, as he slumbered
    Alone in the desert at night?

706

HENRY WADSWORTH LONGFELLOW

The Angels of Wind and of Fire
Chant only one hymn, and expire
  With the song's irresistible stress;
Expire in their rapture and wonder,
As harp-strings are broken asunder
  By music they throb to express.

But serene in the rapturous throng,
Unmoved by the rush of the song,
  With eyes unimpassioned and slow,
Among the dead angels, the deathless
Sandalphon stands listening breathless
  To sounds that ascend from below;—

From the spirits on earth that adore,
From the souls that entreat and implore
  In the fervor and passion of prayer;
From the hearts that are broken with losses,
And weary with dragging the crosses
  Too heavy for mortals to bear.

And he gathers the prayers as he stands,
And they change into flowers in his hands,
  Into garlands of purple and red;
And beneath the great arch of the portal,
Through the streets of the City Immortal
  Is wafted the fragrance they shed.

It is but a legend, I know,—
A fable, a phantom, a show,
  Of the ancient Rabbinical lore;
Yet the old mediæval tradition,
The beautiful, strange superstition,
  But haunts me and holds me the more.

When I look from my window at night,
And the welkin above is all white,
  All throbbing and panting with stars,
Among them majestic is standing
Sandalphon the angel, expanding
  His pinions in nebulous bars.

And the legend, I feel, is a part
Of the hunger and thirst of the heart,
The frenzy and fire of the brain,
That grasps at the fruitage forbidden,
The golden pomegranates of Eden,
To quiet its fever and pain.

DIVINA COMMEDIA

Oft have I seen at some cathedral door
A laborer, pausing in the dust and heat,
Lay down his burden, and with reverent feet
Enter, and cross himself, and on the floor
Kneel to repeat his paternoster o'er;
Far off the noises of the world retreat;
The loud vociferations of the street
Become an undistinguishable roar.
So, as I enter here from day to day,
And leave my burden at this minster gate,
Kneeling in prayer, and not ashamed to pray,
The tumult of the time disconsolate
To inarticulate murmurs dies away,
While the eternal ages watch and wait.

. . . .

NATURE

As a fond mother, when the day is o'er,
Leads by the hand her little child to bed,
Half willing, half reluctant to be led,
And leave his broken playthings on the floor,
Still gazing at them through the open door,
Nor wholly reassured and comforted
By promises of others in their stead,
Which, though more splendid, may not please him more;
So Nature deals with us, and takes away
Our playthings one by one, and by the hand
Leads us to rest so gently, that we go
Scarce knowing if we wish to go or stay,
Being too full of sleep to understand
How far the unknown transcends the what we know.
708

HENRY WADSWORTH LONGFELLOW

KÉRAMOS

Turn, turn, my wheel! Turn round and round
Without a pause, without a sound:
    So spins the flying world away!
This clay, well-mixed with marl and sand,
Follows the motion of my hand;
For some must follow, and some command,
    Though all are made of clay!

Thus sang the Potter at his task
Beneath the blossoming hawthorn-tree,
While o'er his features, like a mask,
The quilted sunshine and leaf-shade
Moved, as the boughs above him swayed,
And clothed him, till he seemed to be
A figure woven in tapestry,
So sumptuously was he arrayed
In that magnificent attire
Of sable tissue flaked with fire.
Like a magician he appeared,
A conjurer without book or beard;
And while he plied his magic art—
For it was magical to me—
I stood in silence and apart,
And wondered more and more to see
That shapeless, lifeless mass of clay
Rise up to meet the master's hand,
And now contract and now expand,
And even his slightest touch obey;
While ever in a thoughtful mood
He sang his ditty, and at times
Whistled a tune between the rhymes,
As a melodious interlude.

Turn, turn, my wheel! All things must change
To something new, to something strange;
    Nothing that is can pause or stay;
The moon will wax, the moon will wane,
The mist and cloud will turn to rain,
The rain to mist and cloud again,
    To-morrow be to-day.

Thus still the Potter sang, and still,
By some unconscious act of will,
The melody and even the words
Were intermingled with my thought,
As bits of colored thread are caught
And woven into nests of birds.
And thus to regions far remote,
Beyond the ocean's vast expanse,
This wizard in the motley coat
Transported me on wings of song,
And by the northern shores of France
Bore me with restless speed along.

What land is this that seems to be
A mingling of the land and sea?
This land of sluices, dikes, and dunes?
This water-net, that tessellates
The landscape? this unending maze
Of gardens, through whose latticed gates
The imprisoned pinks and tulips gaze;
Where in long summer afternoons
The sunshine, softened by the haze,
Comes streaming down as through a screen;
Where over fields and pastures green
The painted ships float high in air,
And over all and everywhere
The sails of windmills sink and soar
Like wings of sea-gulls on the shore?

. . . .

Turn, turn, my wheel!   All life is brief;
What now is bud will soon be leaf,
      What now is leaf will soon decay;
The wind blows east, the wind blows west;
The blue eggs in the robin's nest
Will soon have wings and beak and breast,
      And flutter and fly away.

Now southward through the air I glide,
The song my only pursuivant,
And see across the landscape wide
The blue Charente, upon whose tide

710

The belfries and the spires of Saintes
Ripple and rock from side to side,
As, when an earthquake rends its walls,
A crumbling city reels and falls.

Who is it in the suburbs here,
This Potter, working with such cheer,
In this mean house, this mean attire,
His manly features bronzed with fire,
Whose figulines and rustic wares
Scarce find him bread from day to day?
This madman, as the people say,
Who breaks his tables and his chairs
To feed his furnace fires, nor cares
Who goes unfed if they are fed,
Nor who may live if they are dead?
This alchemist with hollow cheeks
And sunken, searching eyes, who seeks,
By mingled earths and ores combined
With potency of fire, to find
Some new enamel, hard and bright,
His dream, his passion, his delight?

O Palissy! within thy breast
Burned the hot fever of unrest;
Thine was the prophet's vision, thine
The exultation, the divine
Insanity of noble minds,
That never falters nor abates,
But labors and endures and waits,
Till all that it foresees it finds,
Or what it cannot find creates!

Turn, turn, my wheel!   This earthen jar
A touch can make, a touch can mar;
And shall it to the Potter say,
What makest thou?   Thou hast no hand?
As men who think to understand
A world by their Creator planned,
Who wiser is than they.

711

Still guided by the dreamy song,
As in a trance I float along
Above the Pyrenean chain,
Above the fields and farms of Spain,
Above the bright Majorcan isle
That lends its softened name to art,—
A spot, a dot upon the chart,
Whose little towns, red-roofed with tile,
Are ruby-lustred with the light
Of blazing furnaces by night,
And crowned by day with wreaths of smoke.
Then eastward, wafted in my flight
On my enchanter's magic cloak,
I sail across the Tyrrhene Sea
Into the land of Italy,
And o'er the windy Apennines,
Mantled and musical with pines.

The palaces, the princely halls,
The doors of houses and the walls
Of churches and of belfry towers,
Cloister and castle, street and mart,
Are garlanded and gay with flowers
That blossom in the fields of art.
Here Gubbio's workshops gleam and glow
With brilliant, iridescent dyes,
The dazzling whiteness of the snow,
The cobalt blue of summer skies;
And vase and scutcheon, cup and plate,
In perfect finish emulate
Faenza, Florence, Pesaro.
Forth from Urbino's gate there came
A youth with the angelic name
Of Raphael, in form and face
Himself angelic, and divine
In arts of color and design.
From him Francesco Xanto caught
Something of his transcendent grace,
And into fictile fabrics wrought
Suggestions of the master's thought.

Nor less Maestro Giorgio shines
With madre-perl and golden lines
Of arabesques, and interweaves
His birds and fruits and flowers and leaves
About some landscape, shaded brown,
With olive tints on rock and town.

.   .   .   .   .   .

Turn, turn, my wheel! 'Tis nature's plan
The child should grow into the man,
The man grow wrinkled, old, and gray;
In youth, the heart exults and sings,
The pulses leap, the feet have wings;
In age the cricket chirps, and brings
The harvest-home of day.

And now the winds that southward blow,
And cool the hot Sicilian isle,
Bear me away. I see below
The long line of the Libyan Nile,
Flooding and feeding the parched lands
With annual ebb and overflow,
A fallen palm whose branches lie
Beneath the Abyssinian sky,
Whose roots are in Egyptian sands.
On either bank huge water-wheels,
Belted with jars and dripping weeds,
Send forth their melancholy moans,
As if, in their gray mantles hid,
Dead anchorites of the Thebaid
Knelt on the shore and told their beads,
Beating their breasts with loud appeals
And penitential tears and groans.

This city, walled and thickly set
With glittering mosque and minaret,
Is Cairo, in whose gay bazaars
The dreaming traveller first inhales
The perfume of Arabian gales,
And sees the fabulous earthen jars,

713

Huge as were those wherein the maid
Morgiana found the Forty Thieves
Concealed in midnight ambuscade;
And seeing, more than half believes
The fascinating tales that run
Through all the Thousand Nights and One,
Told by the fair Scheherezade.

More strange and wonderful than these
Are the Egyptian deities,
Ammon, and Emeth, and the grand
Osiris, holding in his hand
The lotus; Isis, crowned and veiled;
The sacred Ibis, and the Sphinx;
Bracelets with blue enamelled links;
The Scarabee in emerald mailed,
Or spreading wide his funeral wings;
Lamps that perchance their night-watch kept
O'er Cleopatra while she slept,—
All plundered from the tombs of kings.

Turn, turn, my wheel! The human race,
Of every tongue, of every place,
Caucasian, Coptic, or Malay,
All that inhabit this great earth,
Whatever be their rank or worth,
Are kindred and allied by birth,
And made of the same clay.

O'er desert sands, o'er gulf and bay,
O'er Ganges and o'er Himalay,
Bird-like I fly, and flying sing,
To flowery kingdoms of Cathay,
And bird-like poise on balanced wing
Above the town of King-te-tching,
A burning town, or seeming so,—
Three thousand furnaces that glow
Incessantly, and fill the air
With smoke uprising, gyre on gyre,
And painted by the lurid glare,
Of jets and flashes of red fire.

714

HENRY WADSWORTH LONGFELLOW

As leaves that in the autumn fall,
Spotted and veined with various hues,
Are swept along the avenues,
And lie in heaps by hedge and wall,
So from this grove of chimneys whirled
To all the markets of the world,
These porcelain leaves are wafted on,
Light yellow leaves with spots and stains
Of violet and of crimson dye,
Or tender azure of a sky
Just washed by gentle April rains,
And beautiful with celadon.

Nor less the coarser household wares,
The willow pattern, that we knew
In childhood, with its bridge of blue
Leading to unknown thoroughfares;
The solitary man who stares
At the white river flowing through
Its arches, the fantastic trees
And wild perspective of the view;
And intermingled among these
The tiles that in our nurseries
Filled us with wonder and delight,
Or haunted us in dreams at night.

And yonder by Nankin, behold!
The Tower of Porcelain, strange and old,
Uplifting to the astonished skies
Its ninefold painted balconies,
With balustrades of twining leaves,
And roofs of tile, beneath whose eaves
Hang porcelain bells that all the time
Ring with a soft, melodious chime;
While the whole fabric is ablaze
With varied tints, all fused in one
Great mass of color, like a maze
Of flowers illumined by the sun.

Turn, turn, my wheel!   What is begun
At daybreak must at dark be done,
    To-morrow will be another day;

To-morrow the hot furnace flame
Will search the heart and try the frame,
And stamp with honor or with shame
These vessels made of clay.

Cradled and rocked in Eastern seas,
The islands of the Japanese
Beneath me lie; o'er lake and plain
The stork, the heron, and the crane
Through the clear realms of azure drift,
And on the hillside I can see
The villages of Imari,
Whose thronged and flaming workshops lift
Their twisted columns of smoke on high,
Cloud cloisters that in ruins lie,
With sunshine streaming through each rift,
And broken arches of blue sky.

All the bright flowers that fill the land,
Ripple of waves on rock or sand,
The snow on Fusiyama's cone,
The midnight heaven so thickly sown
With constellations of bright stars,
The leaves that rustle, the reeds that make
A whisper by each stream and lake,
The saffron dawn, the sunset red,
Are painted on these lovely jars;
Again the skylark sings, again
The stork, the heron, and the crane
Float through the azure overhead,
The counterfeit and counterpart
Of Nature reproduced in Art.

Art is the child of Nature; yes,
Her darling child, in whom we trace
The features of the mother's face,
Her aspect and her attitude;
All her majestic loveliness
Chastened and softened and subdued
Into a more attractive grace,
And with a human sense imbued.

716

He is the greatest artist, then,
Whether of pencil or of pen,
Who follows Nature. Never man,
As artist or as artisan,
Pursuing his own fantasies,
Can touch the human heart, or please,
Or satisfy our nobler needs,
As he who sets his willing feet
In Nature's footprints, light and fleet,
And follows fearless where she leads.

Thus mused I on that morn in May,
Wrapped in my visions like the Seer,
Whose eyes behold not what is near,
But only what is far away,
When, suddenly sounding peal on peal,
The church-bell from the neighboring town
Proclaimed the welcome hour of noon.
The Potter heard, and stopped his wheel,
His apron on the grass threw down,
Whistled his quiet little tune,
Not overloud nor overlong,
And ended thus his simple song:

Stop, stop, my wheel! Too soon, too soon
The noon will be the afternoon,
Too soon to-day be yesterday;
Behind us in our path we cast
The broken potsherds of the past,
And all are ground to dust at last,
And trodden into clay!

John Greenleaf Whittier

SNOW-BOUND

The sun that brief December day
Rose cheerless over hills of gray,
And, darkly circled, gave at noon
A sadder light than waning moon.

Slow tracing down the thickening sky
Its mute and ominous prophecy,
A portent seeming less than threat,
It sank from sight before it set.
A chill no coat, however stout,
Of homespun stuff could quite shut out,
A hard, dull bitterness of cold,
That checked, mid-vein, the circling race
Of life-blood in the sharpened face
The coming of the snow-storm told.
The wind blew east; we heard the roar
Of Ocean on his wintry shore,
And felt the strong pulse throbbing there
Beat with low rhythm our inland air.
Meanwhile we did our nightly chores,
Brought in the wood from out of doors,
Littered the stalls, and from the mows
Raked down the herd's-grass for the cows:
Heard the horse whinnying for his corn;
And, sharply clashing horn on horn,
Impatient down the stanchion rows
The cattle shake their walnut bows;
While, peering from his early perch
Upon the scaffold's pole of birch,
The cock his crested helmet bent
And down his querulous challenge sent.

Unwarmed by any sunset light
The gray day darkened into night,
A night made hoary with the swarm
And whirl-dance of the blinding storm,
As zigzag, wavering to and fro,
Crossed and recrossed the wingèd snow:
And ere the early bedtime came
The white drift piled the window-frame,
And through the glass the clothes-line posts
Looked in like tall and sheeted ghosts.
So all night long the storm roared on:
The morning broke without a sun;
In tiny spherule traced with lines
Of Nature's geometric signs,

In starry flake, and pellicle,
All day the hoary meteor fell;
And, when the second morning shone,
We looked upon a world unknown,
On nothing we could call our own.
Around the glistening wonder bent
The blue walls of the firmament,
No cloud above, no earth below,—
A universe of sky and snow!
The old familiar sights of ours
Took marvellous shapes; strange domes and towers
Rose up where sty or corn-crib stood,
Or garden-wall, or belt of wood;
A smooth white mound the brush-pile showed,
A fenceless drift what once was road;
The bridle-post an old man sat
With loose-flung coat and high cocked hat;
The well-curb had a Chinese roof;
And even the long sweep, high aloof,
In its slant splendor, seemed to tell
Of Pisa's leaning miracle.

A prompt, decisive man, no breath
Our father wasted: "Boys, a path!"
Well pleased (for when did farmer boy
Count such a summons less than joy?)
Our buskins on our feet we drew;
With mittened hands, and caps drawn low,
To guard our necks and ears from snow,
We cut the solid whiteness through.
And, where the drift was deepest, made
A tunnel walled and overlaid
With dazzling crystal: we had read
Of rare Aladdin's wondrous cave,
And to our own his name we gave,
With many a wish the luck were ours
To test his lamp's supernal powers.
We reached the barn with merry din,
And roused the prisoned brutes within.
The old horse thrust his long head out,
And grave with wonder gazed about;

The cock his lusty greeting said,
And forth his speckled harem led;
The oxen lashed their tails, and hooked,
And mild reproach of hunger looked;
The hornèd patriarch of the sheep,
Like Egypt's Amun roused from sleep,
Shook his sage head with gesture mute,
And emphasized with stamp of foot.

All day the gusty north-wind bore
The loosening drift its breath before;
Low circling round its southern zone,
The sun through dazzling snow-mist shone.
No church-bell lent its Christian tone
To the savage air, no social smoke
Curled over woods of snow-hung oak.
A solitude made more intense
By dreary-voicèd elements,
The shrieking of the mindless wind,
The moaning tree-boughs swaying blind,
And on the glass the unmeaning beat
Of ghostly finger-tips of sleet.
Beyond the circle of our hearth
No welcome sound of toil or mirth
Unbound the spell, and testified
Of human life and thought outside.
We minded that the sharpest ear
The buried brooklet could not hear,
The music of whose liquid lip
Had been to us companionship,
And, in our lonely life, had grown
To have an almost human tone.

As night drew on, and, from the crest
Of wooded knolls that ridged the west,
The sun, a snow-blown traveller, sank
From sight beneath the smothering bank,
We piled, with care, our nightly stack
Of wood against the chimney-back,—
The oaken log, green, huge, and thick,
And on its top the stout back-stick;

JOHN GREENLEAF WHITTIER

The knotty forestick laid apart,
And filled between with curious art
The ragged brush; then, hovering near,
We watched the first red blaze appear,
Heard the sharp crackle, caught the gleam
On whitewashed wall and sagging beam,
Until the old, rude-furnished room
Burst, flower-like, into rosy bloom;
While radiant with a mimic flame
Outside the sparkling drift became,
And through the bare-boughed lilac-tree
Our own warm hearth seemed blazing free.
The crane and pendent trammels showed,
The Turks' heads on the andirons glowed;
While childish fancy, prompt to tell
The meaning of the miracle,
Whispered the old rhyme: *"Under the tree,*
When fire outdoors burns merrily,
There the witches are making tea."
The moon above the eastern wood
Shone at its full; the hill-range stood
Transfigured in the silver flood,
Its blown snows flashing cold and keen,
Dead white, save where some sharp ravine
Took shadow, or the sombre green
Of hemlocks turned to pitchy black
Against the whiteness at their back.
For such a world and such a night
Most fitting that unwarming light,
Which only seemed where'er it fell
To make the coldness visible.

Shut in from all the world without,
We sat the clean-winged hearth about,
Content to let the north-wind roar
In baffled rage at pane and door,
While the red logs before us beat
The frost-line back with tropic heat;
And ever, when a louder blast
Shook beam and rafter as it passed,

The merrier up its roaring draught
The great throat of the chimney laughed;
The house-dog on his paws outspread
Laid to the fire his drowsy head,
The cat's dark silhouette on the wall
A couchant tiger's seemed to fall;
And, for the winter fireside meet,
Between the andirons' straddling feet,
The mug of cider simmered slow,
The apples sputtered in a row,
And, close at hand, the basket stood
With nuts from brown October's wood.

What matter how the night behaved?
What matter how the north-wind raved?
Blow high, blow low, not all its snow
Could quench our hearth-fire's ruddy glow.
O Time and Change!—with hair as gray
As was my sire's that winter day,
How strange it seems, with so much gone
Of life and love, to still live on!
Ah, brother! only I and thou
Are left of all that circle now,—
The dear home faces whereupon
That fitful firelight paled and shone.
Henceforward, listen as we will,
The voices of that hearth are still;
Look where we may, the wide earth o'er,
Those lighted faces smile no more.
We tread the paths their feet have worn,
    We sit beneath their orchard trees,
    We hear, like them, the hum of bees
And rustle of the bladed corn;
We turn the pages that they read,
    Their written words we linger o'er.
But in the sun they cast no shade,
No voice is heard, no sign is made,
    No step is on the conscious floor!
Yet Love will dream, and Faith will trust
(Since He who knows our need is just),
That somehow, somewhere, meet we must.

JOHN GREENLEAF WHITTIER

Alas for him who never sees
The stars shine through his cypress-trees!
Who, hopeless, lays his dead away,
Nor looks to see the breaking day
Across the mournful marbles play!
Who hath not learned, in hours of faith,
   The truth to flesh and sense unknown,
That Life is ever lord of Death,
   And Love can never lose its own!

We sped the time with stories old,
Wrought puzzles out, and riddles told,
Or stammered from our school-book lore
"The Chief of Gambia's golden shore."
How often since, when all the land
Was clay in Slavery's shaping hand,
As if a far-blown trumpet stirred
The languorous sin-sick air, I heard:
"Does not the voice of reason cry,
   Claim the first right which Nature gave,
From the red scourge of bondage fly,
   Nor deign to live a burdened slave!"
Our father rode again his ride
On Memphremagog's wooded side;
Sat down again to moose and samp
In trapper's hut and Indian camp;
Lived o'er the old idyllic ease
Beneath St. François' hemlock-trees;
Again for him the moonlight shone
On Norman cap and bodiced zone;
Again he heard the violin play
Which led the village dance away,
And mingled in its merry whirl
The grandam and the laughing girl.
Or, nearer home, our steps he led
Where Salisbury's level marshes spread
   Mile-wide as flies the laden bee;
Where merry mowers, hale and strong,
Swept, scythe on scythe, their swaths along
   The low green prairies of the sea.
We shared the fishing off Boar's Head,

And round the rocky Isles of Shoals
The hake-broil on the drift-wood coals;
The chowder on the sand-beach made,
Dipped by the hungry, steaming hot,
With spoons of clam-shell from the pot.
We heard the tales of witchcraft old,
And dream and sign and marvel told
To sleepy listeners as they lay
Stretched idly on the salted hay,
Adrift along the winding shores,
When favoring breezes deigned to blow
The square sail of the gundelow
And idle lay the useless oars.

Our mother, while she turned her wheel
Or run the new-knot stocking-heel,
Told how the Indian hordes came down
At midnight on Cocheco town,
And how her own great-uncle bore
His cruel scalp-mark to fourscore.
Recalling, in her fitting phrase,
So rich and picturesque and free
(The common unrhymed poetry
Of simple life and country ways),
The story of her early days,—
She made us welcome to her home;
Old hearths grew wide to give us room;
We stole with her a frightened look
At the gray wizard's conjuring-book,
The fame whereof went far and wide
Through all the simple country-side;
We heard the hawks at twilight play,
The boat-horn on Piscataqua,
The loon's weird laughter far away;
We fished her little trout-brook, knew
What flowers in wood and meadow grew,
What sunny hillsides autumn-brown
She climbed to shake the ripe nuts down,
Saw where in sheltered cove and bay
The ducks' black squadron anchored lay,

And heard the wild-geese calling loud
Beneath the gray November cloud.
Then, haply, with a look more grave,
And soberer tone, some tale she gave
From painful Sewel's ancient tome,
Beloved in every Quaker home,
Of faith fire-winged by martyrdom,
Or Chalkley's Journal, old and quaint,—
Gentlest of skippers, rare sea-saint!—
Who, when the dreary calms prevailed,
And water-butt and bread-cask failed,
And cruel, hungry eyes pursued
His portly presence, mad for food,
With dark hints muttered under breath
Of casting lots for life or death,
Offered, if Heaven withheld supplies,
To be himself the sacrifice.
Then, suddenly, as if to save
The good man from his living grave,
A ripple on the water grew,
A school of porpoise flashed in view.
"Take, eat," he said, "and be content;
These fishes in my stead are sent
By Him who gave the tangled ram
To spare the child of Abraham."

Our uncle, innocent of books,
Was rich in lore of fields and brooks,
The ancient teachers never dumb
Of Nature's unhoused lyceum.
In moons and tides and weather wise,
He read the clouds as prophecies,
And foul or fair could well divine,
By many an occult hint and sign,
Holding the cunning-warded keys
To all the woodcraft mysteries;
Himself to Nature's heart so near
That all her voices in his ear
Of beast or bird had meanings clear,
Like Apollonius of old,
Who knew the tales the sparrows told,

Or Hermes, who interpreted
What the sage cranes of Nilus said;
A simple, guileless, childlike man,
Content to live where life began;
Strong only on his native grounds,
The little world of sights and sounds
Whose girdle was the parish bounds,
Whereof his fondly partial pride
The common features magnified,
As Surrey hills to mountains grew
In White of Selborne's loving view,—
He told how teal and loon he shot,
And how the eagle's eggs he got,
The feats on pond and river done,
The prodigies of rod and gun;
Till, warming with the tales he told,
Forgotten was the outside cold,
The bitter wind unheeded blew,
From ripening corn the pigeons flew,
The partridge drummed i' the wood, the mink
Went fishing down the river-brink.
In fields with bean or clover gay,
The woodchuck, like a hermit gray,
    Peered from the doorway of his cell;
The muskrat plied the mason's trade,
And tier by tier his mud-walls laid;
And from the shagbark overhead
    The grizzled squirrel dropped his shell.

Next, the dear aunt, whose smile of cheer
And voice in dreams I see and hear,—
The sweetest woman ever Fate
Perverse denied a household mate,
Who, lonely, homeless, not the less
Found peace in love's unselfishness,
And welcome wheresoe'er she went,
A calm and gracious element,
Whose presence seemed the sweet income
And womanly atmosphere of home,—
Called up her girlhood memories,
The huskings and the apple-bees,

The sleigh-rides and the summer sails,
Weaving through all the poor details
And homespun warp of circumstance
A golden woof-thread of romance.
For well she kept her genial mood
And simple faith of maidenhood;
Before her still a cloud-land lay,
The mirage loomed across her way;
The morning dew, that dries so soon
With others, glistened at her noon;
Through years of toil and soil and care,
From glossy tress to thin gray hair,
All unprofaned she held apart
The virgin fancies of the heart.
Be shame to him of woman born
Who hath for such but thought of scorn.

There, too, our elder sister plied
Her evening task the stand beside;
A full, rich nature, free to trust,
Truthful and almost sternly just,
Impulsive, earnest, prompt to act,
And make her generous thought a fact,
Keeping with many a light disguise
The secret of self-sacrifice.
O heart sore-tried! thou hast the best
That Heaven itself could give thee,—rest,
Rest from all bitter thoughts and things!
　How many a poor one's blessing went
　With thee beneath the low green tent
Whose curtain never outward swings!
As one who held herself a part
Of all she saw, and let her heart
　Against the household bosom lean,
Upon the motley-braided mat
Our youngest and our dearest sat,
Lifting her large, sweet, asking eyes,
　Now bathed in the unfading green
And holy peace of Paradise.
Oh, looking from some heavenly hill,

727

Or from the shade of saintly palms,
Or silver reach of river calms,
Do those large eyes behold me still?
With me one little year ago:—
The chill weight of the winter snow
For months upon her grave has lain;
And now, when summer south-winds blow
And brier and harebell bloom again,
I tread the pleasant paths we trod,
I see the violet-sprinkled sod
Whereon she leaned, too frail and weak
The hillside flowers she loved to seek,
Yet following me where'er I went
With dark eyes full of love's content.
The birds are glad; the brier-rose fills
The air with sweetness; all the hills
Stretch green to June's unclouded sky;
But still I wait with ear and eye
For something gone which should be nigh,
A loss in all familiar things,
In flower that blooms, and bird that sings.
And yet, dear heart! remembering thee,
Am I not richer than of old?
Safe in thy immortality,
What change can reach the wealth I hold?
What chance can mar the pearl and gold
Thy love hath left in trust with me?
And while in life's late afternoon,
Where cool and long the shadows grow,
I walk to meet the night that soon
Shall shape and shadow overflow,
I cannot feel that thou art far,
Since near at need the angels are;
And when the sunset gates unbar,
Shall I not see thee waiting stand,
And, white against the evening star,
The welcome of thy beckoning hand?

Brisk wielder of the birch and rule,
The master of the district school

Held at the fire his favored place,
Its warm glow lit a laughing face
Fresh-hued and fair, where scarce appeared
The uncertain prophecy of beard.
He teased the mitten-blinded cat,
Played cross-pins on my uncle's hat,
Sang songs, and told us what befalls
In classic Dartmouth's college halls.
Born the wild Northern hills among,
From whence his yeoman father wrung
By patient toil subsistence scant,
Not competence and yet not want,
He early gained the power to pay
His cheerful, self-reliant way;
Could doff at ease his scholar's gown
To peddle wares from town to town;
Or through the long vacation's reach
In lonely lowland districts teach,
Where all the droll experience found
At stranger hearths in boarding round,
The moonlit skater's keen delight,
The sleigh-drive through the frosty night,
The rustic party, with its rough
Accompaniment of blind-man's-buff,
And whirling-plate, and forfeits paid,
His winter task a pastime made.
Happy the snow-locked homes wherein
He tuned his merry violin,
Or played the athlete in the barn,
Or held the good dame's winding-yarn,
Or mirth-provoking versions told
Of classic legends rare and old,
Wherein the scenes of Greece and Rome
Had all the commonplace of home,
And little seemed at best the odds
'Twixt Yankee pedlers and old gods;
Where Pindus-born Arachthus took
The guise of any grist-mill brook,
And dread Olympus at his will
Became a huckleberry hill.

A careless boy that night he seemed;
   But at his desk he had the look
And air of one who wisely schemed,
   And hostage from the future took
   In trainëd thought and lore of book.
Large-brained, clear-eyed, of such as he
Shall Freedom's young apostles be,
Who, following in War's bloody trail,
Shall every lingering wrong assail;
All chains from limb and spirit strike,
Uplift the black and white alike;
Scatter before their swift advance
The darkness and the ignorance,
The pride, the lust, the squalid sloth,
Which nurtured Treason's monstrous growth,
Made murder pastime, and the hell
Of prison-torture possible;
The cruel lie of caste refute,
Old forms remould, and substitute
For Slavery's lash the freeman's will,
For blind routine, wise-handed skill;
A school-house plant on every hill,
Stretching in radiate nerve-lines thence
The quick wires of intelligence;
Till North and South together brought
Shall own the same electric thought,
In peace a common flag salute,
And, side by side in labor's free
And unresentful rivalry,
Harvest the fields wherein they fought.

Another guest that winter night
Flashed back from lustrous eyes the light.
Unmarked by time, and yet not young,
The honeyed music of her tongue
And words of meekness scarcely told
A nature passionate and bold,
Strong, self-concentered, spurning guide,
Its milder features dwarfed beside
Her unbent will's majestic pride.

730

She sat among us, at the best,
A not unfeared, half-welcome guest,
Rebuking with her cultured phrase
Our homeliness of words and ways.
A certain pard-like, treacherous grace
Swayed the lithe limbs and dropped the lash,
Lent the white teeth their dazzling flash;
And under low brows, black with night,
Rayed out at times a dangerous light;
The sharp heat-lightnings of her face
Presaging ill to him whom Fate
Condemned to share her love or hate.
A woman tropical, intense
In thought and act, in soul and sense,
She blended in a like degree
The vixen and the devotee,
Revealing with each freak or feint
The temper of Petruchio's Kate,
The raptures of Siena's saint.
Her tapering hand and rounded wrist
Had facile power to form a fist;
The warm, dark languish of her eyes
Was never safe from wrath's surprise.
Brows saintly calm and lips devout
Knew every change of scowl and pout;
And the sweet voice had notes more high
And shrill for social battle-cry.
Since then what old cathedral town
Has missed her pilgrim staff and gown,
What convent-gate has held its lock
Against the challenge of her knock!
Through Smyrna's plague-hushed thoroughfares,
Up sea-set Malta's rocky stairs,
Gray olive slopes of hills that hem
Thy tombs and shrines, Jerusalem,
Or startling on her desert throne
The crazy Queen of Lebanon
With claims fantastic as her own,
Her tireless feet have held their way;
And still, unrestful, bowed, and gray,

731

She watches under Eastern skies,
　With hope each day renewed and fresh,
　The Lord's quick coming in the flesh,
Whereof she dreams and prophesies!

Where'er her troubled path may be,
　The Lord's sweet pity with her go!
The outward wayward life we see,
　The hidden springs we may not know.
Nor is it given us to discern
　What threads the fatal sisters spun,
　Through what ancestral years has run
The sorrow with the woman born,
What forged her cruel chain of moods,
What set her feet in solitudes,
　And held the love within her mute,
What mingled madness in the blood,
　A life-long discord and annoy,
　Water of tears with oil of joy,
And hid within the folded bud
　Perversities of flower and fruit.
It is not ours to separate
The tangled skein of will and fate,
To show what metes and bounds should stand
Upon the soul's debatable land,
And between choice and Providence
Divide the circle of events;
But He who knows our frame is just,
Merciful and compassionate,
And full of sweet assurances
And hope for all the language is,
That He remembereth we are dust!

At last the great logs, crumbling low,
Sent out a dull and duller glow,
The bull's-eye watch that hung in view,
Ticking its weary circuit through,
Pointed with mutely warning sign
Its black hand to the hour of nine.
That sign the pleasant circle broke:
My uncle ceased his pipe to smoke,

Knocked from its bowl the refuse gray
And laid it tenderly away;
Then roused himself to safely cover
The dull red brands with ashes over.
And while, with care, our mother laid
The work aside, her steps she stayed
One moment, seeking to express
Her grateful sense of happiness
For food and shelter, warmth and health,
And love's contentment more than wealth,
With simple wishes (not the weak,
Vain prayers which no fulfilment seek,
But such as warm the generous heart,
O'er-prompt to do with Heaven its part)
That none might lack, that bitter night,
For bread and clothing, warmth and light.

Within our beds awhile we heard
The wind that round the gables roared,
With now and then a ruder shock,
Which made our very bedsteads rock.
We heard the loosened clapboards tost,
The board-nails snapping in the frost;
And on us, through the unplastered wall,
Felt the light sifted snow-flakes fall.
But sleep stole on, as sleep will do
When hearts are light and life is new;
Faint and more faint the murmurs grew,
Till in the summer-land of dreams
They softened to the sound of streams,
Low stir of leaves, and dip of oars,
And lapsing waves on quiet shores.

Next morn we wakened with the shout
  Of merry voices high and clear;
  And saw the teamsters drawing near
To break the drifted highways out.
Down the long hillside treading slow
We saw the half-buried oxen go,
Shaking the snow from heads uptost,
Their straining nostrils white with frost.

733

Before our door the straggling train
Drew up, an added team to gain.
The elders threshed their hand a-cold,
   Passed, with the cider-mug, their jokes
   From lip to lip; the younger folks
Down the loose snow-banks, wrestling rolled,
Then toiled again the cavalcade
   O'er windy hill, through clogged ravine,
   And woodland paths that wound between
Low drooping pine-boughs winter-weighed.
From every barn a team afoot,
At every house a new recruit,
Where, drawn by Nature's subtlest law,
Haply the watchful young men saw
Sweet doorway pictures of the curls
And curious eyes of merry girls,
Lifting their hands in mock defence
Against the snow-ball's compliments,
And reading in each missive tost
The charm with Eden never lost.

We heard once more the sleigh-bells' sound;
   And, following where the teamsters led,
The wise old Doctor went his round,
Just pausing at our door to say,
In the brief autocratic way
Of one who, prompt at Duty's call
Was free to urge her claim on all,
   That some poor neighbor sick abed
At night our mother's aid would need.
For, one in generous thought and deed
   What mattered in the sufferer's sight
   The Quaker matron's inward light,
The Doctor's mail of Calvin's creed?
All hearts confess the saints elect
   Who, twain in faith, in love agree,
And melt not in an acid sect
   The Christian pearl of charity!

So days went on: a week had passed
Since the great world was heard from last.

734

The Almanac we studied o'er,
Read and reread our little store
Of books and pamphlets, scarce a score;
One harmless novel, mostly hid
From younger eyes, a book forbid,
And poetry (or good or bad,
A single book was all we had),
Where Ellwood's meek, drab-skirted Muse,
    A stranger to the heathen Nine,
    Sang, with a somewhat nasal whine,
The wars of David and the Jews.
At last the floundering carrier bore
The village paper to our door.
Lo! broadening outward as we read,
To warmer zones the horizon spread;
In panoramic length unrolled
We saw the marvels that it told.
Before us passed the painted Creeks,
    And daft McGregor on his raids
    In Costa Rica's everglades.
And up Taygetos winding slow
Rode Ypsilanti's Mainote Greeks,
A Turk's head at each saddle-bow!
Welcome to us its week-old news,
Its corner for the rustic Muse,
    Its monthly gauge of snow and rain,
Its record, mingling in a breath
The wedding bell and dirge of death:
Jest, anecdote, and love-lorn tale,
The latest culprit sent to jail;
Its hue and cry of stolen and lost,
Its vendue sales and goods at cost,
    And traffic calling loud for gain.
We felt the stir of hall and street,
The pulse of life that round us beat;
The chill embargo of the snow
Was melted in the genial glow;
Wide swung again our ice-locked door,
And all the world was ours once more!

Clasp, Angel of the backward look
  And folded wings of ashen gray
  And voice of echoes far away,
The brazen covers of thy book;
The weird palimpsest old and vast,
Wherein thou hid'st the spectral past;
Where, closely mingling, pale and glow
The characters of joy and woe;
The monographs of outlived years,
Or smile-illumed or dim with tears,
  Green hills of life that slope to death,
And haunts of home, whose vistaed trees
Shade off to mournful cypresses,
  With the white amaranths underneath.
Even while I look, I can but heed
  The restless sands' incessant fall,
Importunate hours that hours succeed
Each clamorous with its own sharp need,
  And duty keeping pace with all.
Shut down and clasp the heavy lids;
I hear again the voice that bids
The dreamer leave his dream midway
For larger hopes and graver fears:
Life greatens in these later years,
The century's aloe flowers to-day!

Yet, haply, in some lull of life,
Some Truce of God which breaks its strife,
The worldling's eyes shall gather dew,
  Dreaming in throngful city ways
Of winter joys his boyhood knew;
And dear and early friends—the few
Who yet remain—shall pause to view
  These Flemish pictures of old days;
Sit with me by the homestead hearth
And stretch the hands of memory forth
  To warm them at the wood-fire's blaze!
And thanks untraced to lips unknown
Shall greet me like the odors blown
From unseen meadows newly mown,

736

Or lilies floating in some pond,
Wood-fringed, the wayside gaze beyond;
The traveller owns the grateful sense
Of sweetness near, he knows not whence,
And, pausing, takes with forehead bare
The benediction of the air.

THE MEETING

. . . .

I ask no organ's soulless breath
To drone the themes of life and death,
No altar candle-lit by day,
No ornate wordsman's rhetoric-play,
No cool philosophy to teach
Its bland audacities of speech
To double-tasked idolaters
Themselves their gods and worshippers,
No pulpit hammered by the fist
Of loud-asserting dogmatist,
Who borrows for the hand of love
The smoking thunderbolts of Jove.
I know how well the fathers taught,
What work the later schoolmen wrought;
I reverence old-time faith and men,
But God is near us now as then;
His force of love is still unspent,
His hate of sin as imminent;
And still the measure of our needs
Outgrows the cramping bounds of creeds;
The manna gathered yesterday
Already savors of decay;
Doubts to the world's child-heart unknown
Question us now from star and stone.

. . . .

VESTA

O Christ of God! whose life and death
  Our own have reconciled,
Most quietly, most tenderly
  Take home Thy star-named child!

Thy grace is in her patient eyes,
  Thy words are on her tongue;
The very silence round her seems
  As if the angels sung.

Her smile is as a listening child's
  Who hears its mother call;
The lilies of Thy perfect peace
  About her pillow fall.

She leans from out our clinging arms
  To rest herself in Thine;
Alone to Thee, dear Lord, can we
  Our well-beloved resign!

Oh, less for her than for ourselves
  We bow our heads and pray;
Her setting star, like Bethlehem's,
  To Thee shall point the way!

CHILD-SONGS

Still linger in our noon of time
  And on our Saxon tongue
The echoes of the home-born hymns
  The Aryan mothers sung.

And childhood had its litanies
  In every age and clime;
The earliest cradles of the race
  Were rocked to poet's rhyme.

Nor sky, nor wave, nor tree, nor flower,
　　Nor green earth's virgin sod,
So moved the singer's heart of old
　　As these small ones of God.

The mystery of unfolding life
　　Was more than dawning morn,
Than opening flower or crescent moon
　　The human soul new-born!

And still to childhood's sweet appeal
　　The heart of genius turns,
And more than all the sages teach
　　From lisping voices learns,—

The voices loved of him who sang,
　　Where Tweed and Teviot glide,
That sound to-day on all the winds
　　That blow from Rydal-side,—

Heard in the Teuton's household songs,
　　And folk-lore of the Finn,
Where'er to holy Christmas hearths
　　The Christ-child enters in!

　·　·　·　·　·　·　·

ICHABOD

So fallen! so lost! the light withdrawn
　　Which once he wore!
The glory from his gray hairs gone
　　Forevermore!

Revile him not,—the Tempter hath
　　A snare for all;
And pitying tears, not scorn and wrath,
　　Befit his fall!

Oh, dumb be passion's stormy rage,
　　When he who might
Have lighted up and led his age,
　　Falls back in night.

Scorn! would the angels laugh, to mark
    A bright soul driven,
Fiend-goaded, down the endless dark,
    From hope and heaven!

Let not the land once proud of him
    Insult him now,
Nor brand with deeper shame his dim,
    Dishonored brow.

But let its humbled sons, instead,
    From sea to lake,
A long lament, as for the dead,
    In sadness make.

Of all we loved and honored, naught
    Save power remains—
A fallen angel's pride of thought,
    Still strong in chains.

All else is gone; from those great eyes
    The soul has fled:
When faith is lost, when honor dies,
    The man is dead!

Then, pay the reverence of old days
    To his dead fame:
Walk backward, with averted gaze,
    And hide the shame!

Edgar Allan Poe

POE'S COTTAGE AT FORDHAM

Here lived the soul enchanted
    By melody of song;
Here dwelt the spirit haunted
    By a demoniac throng;
Here sang the lips elated;
Here grief and death were sated;
Here loved and here unmated
    Was he, so frail, so strong.

740

EDGAR ALLAN POE

Here wintry winds and cheerless
  The dying firelight blew,
While he whose song was peerless
  Dreamed the drear midnight through,
And from dull embers chilling
Crept shadows darkly filling
The silent place, and thrilling
  His fancy as they grew.

Here with brows bared to heaven,
  In starry night he stood,
With the lost star of seven
  Feeling sad brotherhood.
Here in the sobbing showers
Of dark autumnal hours
He heard suspected powers
  Shriek through the stormy wood.

From visions of Apollo
  And of Astarte's bliss,
He gazed into the hollow
  And hopeless vale of Dis,
And though earth were surrounded
By heaven, it still was mounded
With graves. His soul had sounded
  The dolorous abyss.

Poor, mad, but not defiant,
  He touched at heaven and hell.
Fate found a rare soul pliant
  And wrung her changes well.
Alternately his lyre,
Stranded with strings of fire,
Led earth's most happy choir,
  Or flashed with Israfel.

No singer of old story
  Luting accustomed lays,
No harper for new glory,
  No mendicant for praise,

He struck high chords and splendid,
Wherein were finely blended
Tones that unfinished ended
With his unfinished days.

Here through this lonely portal,
Made sacred by his name,
Unheralded immortal
The mortal went and came.
And fate that then denied him,
And envy that decried him,
And malice that belied him,
Here cenotaphed his fame.
—JOHN HENRY BONER.

ROMANCE

Romance, who loves to nod and sing,
With drowsy head and folded wing,
Among the green leaves as they shake
Far down within some shadowy lake,
To me a painted paroquet
Hath been—a most familiar bird—
Taught me by alphabet to say—
To lisp my very earliest word
While in the wild wood I did lie,
A child—with a most knowing eye.

Of late, eternal Condor years
So shake the very Heaven on high
With tumult as they thunder by,
I have no time for idle cares
Through gazing on the unquiet sky.
And when an hour with calmer wings
Its down upon my spirit flings—
That little time with lyre and rhyme
To while away—forbidden things!
My heart would feel to be a crime
Unless it trembled with the strings.

EDGAR ALLAN POE

SONNET. TO SCIENCE

Science! true daughter of Old Time thou art!
  Who alterest all things with thy peering eyes.
Why preyest thou thus upon the poet's heart,
  Vulture, whose wings are dull realities?
How should he love thee? or how deem thee wise,
  Who wouldst not leave him in his wandering
To seek for treasure in the jewelled skies,
  Albeit he soared with an undaunted wing?
Hast thou not dragged Diana from her car?
  And driven the Hamadryad from the wood
To seek a shelter in some happier star?
  Hast thou not torn the Naiad from her flood,
The Elfin from the green grass, and from me
The summer dream beneath the tamarind tree?

TO HELEN

Helen, thy beauty is to me
  Like those Nicæan barks of yore,
That gently, o'er a perfumed sea,
  The weary, wayworn wanderer bore
  To his own native shore.

On desperate seas long wont to roam,
  Thy hyacinth hair, thy classic face,
Thy Naiad airs, have brought me home
  To the glory that was Greece
  And the grandeur that was Rome.

Lo! in yon brilliant window-niche
  How statue-like I see thee stand,
The agate lamp within thy hand!
  Ah, Psyche, from the regions which
  Are Holy Land!

743

ALONE

From childhood's hour I have not been
As others were—I have not seen
As others saw—I could not bring
My passions from a common spring.
From the same source I have not taken
My sorrow; I could not awaken
My heart to joy at the same tone;
And all I lov'd, I lov'd alone.
Then—in my childhood—in the dawn
Of a most stormy life—was drawn
From ev'ry depth of good and ill
The mystery which binds me still:
From the torrent, or the fountain,
From the red cliff of the mountain,
From the sun that 'round me roll'd
In its autumn tint of gold—
From the lightning in the sky
As it pass'd me flying by—
From the thunder and the storm,
And the cloud that took the form
(When the rest of Heaven was blue)
Of a demon in my view.

THE RAVEN

Once upon a midnight dreary,
While I pondered weak and weary,
Over many a quaint and curious
Volume of forgotten lore;
While I nodded, nearly napping,
Suddenly there came a tapping,
As of some one gently rapping—
Rapping at my chamber-door.
" 'Tis some visitor," I muttered,
"Tapping at my chamber-door;
    Only this, and nothing more."

744

EDGAR ALLAN POE

Ah, distinctly I remember,
It was in the bleak December,
And each separate dying ember
Wrought its ghost upon the floor.
Eagerly I wished the morrow;
Vainly I had sought to borrow
From my books surcease of sorrow—
Sorrow for the lost Lenore—
For the rare and radiant maiden
Whom the angels name Lenore—
  Nameless here for evermore.

And the silken, sad, uncertain
Rustling of each purple curtain
Thrilled me—filled me with fantastic
Terrors never felt before;
So that now, to still the beating
Of my heart, I stood repeating,
" 'Tis some visitor entreating
Entrance at my chamber-door;
  This it is, and nothing more."

Presently my soul grew stronger;
Hesitating then no longer,
"Sir," said I, "or, Madam, truly
Your forgiveness I implore;
But the fact is, I was napping,
And so gently you came rapping,
And so faintly you came tapping—
Tapping at my chamber-door,
That I scarce was sure I heard you":
Here I opened wide the door:—
  Darkness there, and nothing more.

Deep into that darkness peering,
Long I stood there wondering, fearing,
Doubting, dreaming dreams no mortals
Ever dared to dream before;
But the silence was unbroken,
And the stillness gave no token,
And the only word there spoken

Was the whispered word "Lenore!"
This I whispered, and an echo
Murmured back the word "Lenore!"
   Merely this, and nothing more.

Back into the chamber turning,
All my soul within me burning,
Soon again I heard a tapping
Something louder than before.
"Surely," said I, "surely that is
Something at my window lattice;
Let me see, then, what thereat is,
And this mystery explore—
Let my heart be still a moment,
And this mystery explore;
   'Tis the wind, and nothing more."

Open here I flung the shutter,
When, with many a flirt and flutter,
In there stepped a stately Raven
Of the saintly days of yore.
Not the least obeisance made he;
Not a minute stopped or stayed he;
But, with mien of lord or lady,
Perched above my chamber-door—
Perched upon a bust of Pallas
Just above my chamber-door—
   Perched, and sat, and nothing more.

Then this ebony bird beguiling
My sad fancy into smiling
By the grave and stern decorum
Of the countenance it wore,
"Though thy crest be shorn and shaven,
Thou," I said, "art sure no craven,
Ghastly, grim, and ancient Raven,
Wandering from the Nightly shore;
Tell me what thy lordly name is
On the Night's Plutonian shore."
   Quoth the Raven, "Nevermore."

EDGAR ALLAN POE

Much I marvelled this ungainly
Fowl to hear discourse so plainly,
Though its answer little meaning,
Little relevancy bore;
For we cannot help agreeing
That no living human being
Ever yet was blessed with seeing
Bird above his chamber-door—
Bird or beast upon the sculptured
Bust above his chamber-door,
    With such name as "Nevermore."

But the Raven, sitting lonely
On that placid bust, spoke only
That one word, as if his soul
In that one word he did outpour.
Nothing farther then he uttered;
Not a feather then he fluttered;
Till I scarcely more than muttered,
"Other friends have flown before;
On the morrow he will leave me,
As my hopes have flown before."
    Then the bird said, "Nevermore."

Startled at the stillness broken
By reply so aptly spoken,
"Doubtless," said I, "what it utters
Is its only stock and store;
Caught from some unhappy master,
Whom unmerciful disaster
Followed fast and followed faster,
Till his songs one burden bore—
Till the dirges of his hope
That melancholy burden bore
    Of 'Never—nevermore.' "

But the Raven still beguiling
All my sad soul into smiling,
Straight I wheeled a cushioned seat

747

In front of bird, and bust, and door;
Then, upon the velvet sinking,
I betook myself to linking
Fancy unto fancy, thinking
What this ominous bird of yore—
What this grim, ungainly, ghastly,
Gaunt, and ominous bird of yore
  Meant in croaking "Nevermore."

This I sat engaged in guessing,
But no syllable expressing
To the fowl, whose fiery eyes
Now burned into my bosom's core;
This and more I sat divining,
With my head at ease reclining
On the cushion's velvet lining
That the lamp-light gloated o'er,
But whose velvet violet lining
With the lamp-light gloating o'er,
  She shall press, ah, nevermore!

Then methought the air grew denser,
Perfumed from an unseen censer
Swung by seraphim whose footfalls
Tinkled on the tufted floor.
"Wretch," I cried, "thy God hath lent thee—
By these angels he hath sent thee
Respite—respite and nepenthe,
From thy memories of Lenore!
Quaff, oh, quaff this kind nepenthe,
And forget this lost Lenore!"
  Quoth the Raven, "Nevermore."

"Prophet!" said I, "thing of evil!—
Prophet still, if bird or devil!—
Whether tempter sent, or whether
Tempest tossed thee here ashore,
Desolate, yet all undaunted,
On this desert land enchanted—
On this home by Horror haunted—
Tell me truly, I implore—
Is there—*is* there balm in Gilead?—

Tell me, tell me, I implore!"
Quoth the Raven, "Nevermore."

"Prophet!" said I, "thing of evil!—
Prophet still, if bird or devil!
By that heaven that bends above us—
By that God we both adore
Tell this soul, with sorrow laden,
If within the distant Aidenn,
It shall clasp a sainted maiden
Whom the angels name Lenore?"
Quoth the Raven, "Nevermore."

"Be that word our sign of parting,
Bird or fiend!" I shrieked, upstarting—
"Get thee back into the tempest
And the Night's Plutonian shore!
Leave no black plume as a token
Of that lie thy soul hath spoken!
Leave my loneliness unbroken!—
Quit the bust above my door!
Take thy beak from out my heart,
And take thy form from off my door!"
Quoth the Raven, "Nevermore."

And the Raven, never flitting,
Still is sitting, still is sitting
On the pallid bust of Pallas,
Just above my chamber-door;
And his eyes have all the seeming
Of a demon's that is dreaming,
And the lamp-light o'er him streaming
Throws his shadow on the floor;
And my soul from out that shadow
That lies floating on the floor
Shall be lifted—nevermore!

LENORE

Ah, broken is the golden bowl! the spirit flown forever!
Let the bell toil!—a saintly soul floats on the Stygian river;
. . . Let a Sabbath song
Go up to God so solemnly the dead may feel no wrong!

The sweet Lenore hath "gone before," with Hope, that flew
    beside,
Leaving thee wild for the dear child that should have been
    thy bride—
For her, the fair and *debonair*, that now so lowly lies,
The life upon her yellow hair but not within her eyes—
The life still there, upon her hair—the death upon her eyes.

"Avaunt! to-night my heart is light. No dirge will I upraise,
"But waft the angel on her flight with a Pæan of old days!
"Let *no* bell toll!—lest her sweet soul, amid its hallowed
    mirth,
"Should catch the note, as it doth float up from the damnèd
    Earth.
"To friends above, from fiends below, the indignant ghost
    is riven—
"From Hell unto a high estate far up within the Heaven—
"From grief and groan, to a golden throne, beside the King
    of Heaven."

TO HELEN

I saw thee once—once only—years ago:
I must not say *how* many—but *not* many.
It was a July midnight; and from out
A full-orbed moon, that, like thine own soul, soaring,
Sought a precipitate pathway up through heaven,
There fell a silvery-silken veil of light,
With quietude, and sultriness, and slumber,
Upon the upturn'd faces of a thousand
Roses that grew in an enchanted garden,
Where no winds dared to stir, unless on tiptoe—
Fell on the upturn'd faces of these roses
That gave out, in return for the love-light,
Their odorous souls in an ecstatic death—
Fell on the upturn'd faces of these roses
That smiled and died in this parterre, enchanted
By thee, and by the poetry of thy presence.
Clad all in white, upon a violet bank
I saw thee half reclining; while the moon
Fell on the upturn'd faces of the roses,
And on thine own, upturn'd—alas, in sorrow!
750

EDGAR ALLAN POE

Was it not Fate, that, on this July midnight—
Was it not Fate, (whose name is also Sorrow,)
That bade me pause before that garden-gate,
To breathe the incense of those slumbering roses?
No footstep stirred: the hated world all slept,
Save only thee and me. (Oh, Heaven!—oh, God!
How my heart beats in coupling those two words!)
Save only thee and me. I paused—I looked—
And in an instant all things disappeared.
(Ah, bear in mind this garden was enchanted!)
The pearly lustre of the moon went out:
The mossy banks and the meandering paths,
The happy flowers and the repining trees,
Were seen no more: the very roses' odors
Died in the arms of the adoring airs.
All—all expired save thee—save less than thou:
Save only the divine light in thine eyes—
Save but the soul in thine uplifted eyes.
I saw but them—they were the world to me.
I saw but them—saw only them for hours—
Saw only them until the moon went down.
What wild heart-histories seemed to lie enwritten
Upon those crystalline, celestial spheres!
How dark a wo! yet how sublime a hope!
How silently serene a sea of pride!
How daring an ambition! yet how deep—
How fathomless a capacity for love!

But now, at length, dear Dian sank from sight,
Into a western couch of thunder-cloud;
And thou, a ghost, amid the entombing trees
Didst glide away. Only thine eyes remained.
They would not go—they never yet have gone.
Lighting my lonely pathway home that night,
They have not left me (as my hopes have) since.
They follow me—they lead me through the years
They are my ministers—yet I their slave.
Their office is to illumine and enkindle—
My duty, to be saved by their bright light,
And purified in their electric fire,
And sanctified in their elysian fire.

751

They fill my soul with Beauty (which is Hope),
And are far up in Heaven—the stars I kneel to
In the sad, silent watches of my night;
While even in the meridian glare of day
I see them still—two sweetly scintillant
Venuses, unextinguished by the sun!

ULALUME

The skies they were ashen and sober;
        The leaves they were crispèd and sere—
        The leaves they were withering and sere;
It was night in the lonesome October
        Of my most immemorial year;
It was hard by the dim lake of Auber,
        In the misty mid region of Weir—
It was down by the dank tarn of Auber,
        In the ghoul-haunted woodland of Weir.

Here once, through an alley Titanic,
        Of cypress, I roamed with my Soul—
        Of cypress, with Psyche, my Soul.
These were days when my heart was volcanic
        As the scoriac rivers that roll—
        As the lavas that restlessly roll
Their sulphurous currents down Yaanek
        In the ultimate climes of the pole—
That groan as they roll down Mount Yaanek
        In the realms of the boreal pole.

Our talk had been serious and sober,
        But our thoughts they were palsied and sere—
        Our memories were treacherous and sere—
For we knew not the month was October,
        And we marked not the night of the year—
        (Ah, night of all nights in the year!)
We noted not the dim lake of Auber—
        (Though once we had journeyed down here)—
Remembered not the dank tarn of Auber,
        Nor the ghoul-haunted woodland of Weir.

752

EDGAR ALLAN POE

And now, as the night was senescent
    And star-dials pointed to morn—
    As the star-dials hinted of morn—
At the end of our path a liquescent
    And nebulous lustre was born,
Out of which a miraculous crescent
    Arose with a duplicate horn—
Astarte's bediamonded crescent
    Distinct with its duplicate horn.

And I said—"She is warmer than Dian:
    She rolls through an ether of sighs—
    She revels in a region of sighs:
She has seen that the tears are not dry on
    These cheeks, where the worm never dies,
And has come past the stars of the Lion
    To point us the path to the skies—
    To the Lethean peace of the skies—
Come up, in despite of the Lion,
    To shine on us with her bright eyes—
Come up through the lair of the Lion,
    With love in her luminous eyes."

But Psyche, uplifting her finger,
    Said—"Sadly this star I mistrust—
    Her pallor I strangely mistrust:—
Oh, hasten!—oh, let us not linger!
    Oh, fly!—let us fly!—for we must."
In terror she spoke, letting sink her
    Wings until they trailed in the dust—
In agony sobbed, letting sink her
    Plumes till they trailed in the dust—
    Till they sorrowfully trailed in the dust.

I replied, "This is nothing but dreaming:
    Let us on by this tremulous light!
    Let us bathe in this crystalline light!
Its Sibyllic splendor is beaming
    With Hope and in Beauty to-night:—
    See!—it flickers up the sky through the night!

Ah, we safely may trust to its gleaming,
    And be sure it will lead us aright—
We safely may trust to a gleaming
    That cannot but guide us aright,
    Since it flickers up to Heaven through the night."

Thus I pacified Psyche and kissed her,
    And tempted her out of her gloom—
    And conquered her scruples and gloom;
And we passed to the end of the vista,
    But were stopped by the door of a tomb—
    By the door of a legended tomb;
And I said—"What is written, sweet sister,
    On the door of this legended tomb?"
    She replied—"Ulalume—Ulalume—
    'Tis the vault of thy lost Ulalume!"

Then my heart it grew ashen and sober
    As the leaves that were crispèd and sere—
    As the leaves that were withering and sere,
And I cried—"It was surely October
    On *this* very night of last year
    That I journeyed—I journeyed down here—
    That I brought a dread burden down here—
    On this night of all nights in the year,
    Ah, what demon has tempted me here?
Well I know, now, this dim lake of Auber—
    This misty mid region of Weir—
Well I know, now, this dank tarn of Auber,
    This ghoul-haunted woodland of Weir."

THE BELLS

Hear the sledges with the bells,
    Silver bells!
What a world of merriment their melody foretells!
    How they tinkle, tinkle, tinkle,
    In the icy air of night!
    While the stars, that oversprinkle
    All the heavens, seem to twinkle
    With a crystalline delight;

Keeping time, time, time,
In a sort of Runic rhyme,
To the tintinnabulation that so musically wells
From the bells, bells, bells, bells,
Bells, bells, bells—
From the jingling and the tinkling of the bells.

Hear the mellow wedding bells,
Golden bells!
What a world of happiness their harmony foretells!
Through the balmy air of night
How they ring out their delight!
From the molten-golden notes,
And all in tune.
What a liquid ditty floats
To the turtle-dove that listens, while she gloats
On the moon!
Oh, from out the sounding cells,
What a gush of euphony voluminously wells!
How it swells!
How it dwells
On the Future! how it tells
Of the rapture that impels
To the swinging and the ringing
Of the bells, bells, bells,
Of the bells, bells, bells, bells,
Bells, bells, bells—
To the rhyming and the chiming of the bells!

Hear the loud alarum bells,
Brazen bells!
What a tale of terror, now, their turbulency tells!
In the startled ear of night
How they scream out their affright!
Too much horrified to speak,
They can only shriek, shriek, shriek,
Out of tune,
In a clamorous appealing to the mercy of the fire,
In a mad expostulation with the deaf and frantic fire,

755

Leaping higher, higher, higher,
With a desperate desire,
And a resolute endeavor
Now—now to sit, or never,
By the side of the pale-faced moon.
Oh, the bells, bells, bells!
What a tale their terror tells
   Of Despair!
How they clang, and clash, and roar!
What a horror they outpour
On the bosom of the palpitating air!
 Yet the ear, it fully knows,
 By the twanging
 And the clanging,
How the danger ebbs and flows;
Yet the ear distinctly tells,
 In the jangling
 And the wrangling,
How the danger sinks and swells,—
By the sinking or the swelling in the anger of the bells,
   Of the bells,
Of the bells, bells, bells, bells,
   Bells, bells, bells—
In the clamor and the clangor of the bells!

Hear the tolling of the bells,
   Iron bells!
What a world of solemn thought their monody compels!
 In the silence of the night
 How we shiver with affright
At the melancholy menace of their tone!
 For every sound that floats
 From the rust within their throats
   Is a groan.
And the people—ah, the people,
They that dwell up in the steeple,
   All alone,
And who, tolling, tolling, tolling,
In that muffled monotone,
Feel a glory in so rolling
On the human heart a stone—

756

EDGAR ALLAN POE

They are neither man nor woman,
They are neither brute nor human,
    They are Ghouls:
And their king it is who tolls;
And he rolls, rolls, rolls,
        Rolls
A pæan from the bells;
And his merry bosom swells
With the pæan of the bells,
And he dances, and he yells:
Keeping time, time, time,
In a sort of Runic rhyme,
To the pæan of the bells,
        Of the bells:
Keeping time, time, time,
In a sort of Runic rhyme,
To the throbbing of the bells,
Of the bells, bells, bells—
To the sobbing of the bells;
Keeping time, time, time,
As he knells, knells, knells,
In a happy Runic rhyme,
To the rolling of the bells,
Of the bells, bells, bells:
To the tolling of the bells,
Of the bells, bells, bells, bells,
        Bells, bells, bells—
To the moaning and the groaning of the bells.

ANNABEL LEE

It was many and many a year ago,
    In a kingdom by the sea,
That a maiden there lived whom you may know
    By the name of Annabel Lee;
And this maiden she lived with no other thought
    Than to love and be loved by me.

I was a child and she was a child,
  In this kingdom by the sea:
But we loved with a love that was more than love—
  I and my Annabel Lee;
With a love that the winged seraphs of heaven
  Coveted her and me.

And this was the reason that, long ago,
  In this kingdom by the sea,
A wind blew out of a cloud, chilling
  My beautiful Annabel Lee;
So that her highborn kinsman came
  And bore her away from me,
To shut her up in a sepulchre
  In this kingdom by the sea.

The angels, not half so happy in heaven,
  Went envying her and me—
Yes!—that was the reason (as all men know,
  In this kingdom by the sea)
That the wind came out of the cloud by night,
  Chilling and killing my Annabel Lee.

But our love it was stronger by far than the love
  Of those who were older than we—
  Of many far wiser than we—
And neither the angels in heaven above,
  Nor the demons down under the sea,
Can ever dissever my soul from the soul
  Of the beautiful Annabel Lee:

For the moon never beams, without bringing me dreams
  Of the beautiful Annabel Lee;
And the stars never rise, but I feel the bright eyes
  Of the beautiful Annabel Lee;
And so, all the night-tide, I lie down by the side
Of my darling—my darling—my life and my bride,
  In the sepulchre there by the sea,
  In her tomb by the sounding sea.

EDGAR ALLAN POE

THE HAUNTED PALACE

In the greenest of our valleys
  By good angels tenanted,
Once a fair and stately palace—
  Radiant palace—reared its head.
In the monarch Thought's dominion—
  It stood there!
Never seraph spread a pinion
  Over fabric half so fair!

Banners yellow, glorious, golden,
  On its roof did float and flow,
(This—all this—was in the olden
  Time long ago,)
And every gentle air that dallied,
  In that sweet day,
Along the ramparts plumed and pallid,
  A wingéd odor went away.

Wanderers in that happy valley,
  Through two luminous windows, saw
Spirits moving musically,
  To a lute's well-tunéd law,
Round about a throne where, sitting
  (Porphyrogene!)
In state his glory well befitting,
  The ruler of the realm was seen.

And all with pearl and ruby glowing
  Was the fair palace door,
Through which came flowing, flowing, flowing
  And sparkling evermore,
A troop of Echoes, whose sweet duty
  Was but to sing,
In voices of surpassing beauty,
  The wit and wisdom of their king.

But evil things, in robes of sorrow,
  Assailed the monarch's high estate.
(Ah, let us mourn!—for never morrow
  Shall dawn upon him desolate!)

759

And round about his home the glory
  That blushed and bloomed,
Is but a dim-remembered story
  Of the old time entombed.

And travellers, now, within that valley,
  Through the red-litten windows see
Vast forms, that move fantastically
  To a discordant melody,
While, like a ghastly rapid river,
  Through the pale door
A hideous throng rush out forever
  And laugh—but smile no more.

THE CONQUEROR WORM

Lo! 'tis a gala night
  Within the lonesome latter years;
An angel throng, bewinged, bedight
  In veils, and drowned in tears,
Sit in a theatre, to see
  A play of hopes and fears,
While the orchestra breathes fitfully
  The music of the spheres.

Mimes, in the form of God on high,
  Mutter and mumble low,
And hither and thither fly—
  Mere puppets they, who come and go
At bidding of vast formless things
  That shift the scenery to and fro,
Flapping from out their Condor wings
  Invisible Wo!

That motley drama—oh, be sure
  It shall not be forgot!
With its Phantom chased for evermore,
  By a crowd that seize it not,

EDGAR ALLAN POE

Through a circle that ever returneth in
  To the self-same spot,
And much of Madness, and more of Sin,
  And Horror the soul of the plot.

But see, amid the mimic rout
  A crawling shape intrude!
A blood-red thing that writhes from out
  The scenic solitude!
It writhes!—it writhes!—with mortal pangs
  The mimes become its food,
And the angels sob at vermin fangs
  In human gore imbued.

Out—out are the lights—out all!
  And, over each quivering form,
The curtain, a funeral pall,
  Comes down with the rush of a storm,
And the angels, all pallid and wan,
  Uprising, unveiling, affirm
That the play is the tragedy, "Man,"
  And its hero the Conqueror Worm.

TO ONE IN PARADISE

Thou wast that all to me, love,
  For which my soul did pine—
A green isle in the sea, love,
  A fountain and a shrine,
All wreathed with fairy fruits and flowers,
  And all the flowers were mine.

Ah, dream too bright to last!
  Ah, starry Hope! that didst arise
But to be overcast!
  A voice from out the Future cries,
"On! on!"—but o'er the Past
  (Dim gulf!) my spirit hovering lies
Mute, motionless, aghast!

For, alas! alas! with me
   The light of Life is o'er!
"No more—no more—no more—"
(Such language holds the solemn sea
   To the sands upon the shore)
Shall bloom the thunder-blasted tree,
   Or the stricken eagle soar!

And all my days are trances,
   And all my nightly dreams
Are where thy dark eye glances,
   And where thy footstep gleams—
In what ethereal dances,
   By what eternal streams.

THE VALLEY OF UNREST

Once it smiled a silent dell
Where the people did not dwell;
They had gone unto the wars,
Trusting to the mild-eyed stars,
Nightly, from their azure towers,
To keep watch above the flowers,
In the midst of which all day
The red sun-light lazily lay.
Now each visitor shall confess
The sad valley's restlessness.
Nothing there is motionless—
Nothing save the airs that brood
Over the magic solitude.
Ah, by no wind are stirred those trees
That palpitate like the chill seas
Around the misty Hebrides!
Ah, by no wind those clouds are driven
That rustle through the unquiet Heaven
Uneasily, from morn till even,
Over the violets there that lie
In myriad types of the human eye—
Over the lilies there that wave
And weep above a nameless grave!

They wave:—from out their fragrant tops
Eternal dews come down in drops.
They weep:—from off their delicate stems
Perennial tears descend in gems.

THE CITY IN THE SEA

Lo! Death has reared himself a throne
In a strange city lying alone
Far down within the dim West,
Where the good and the bad and the worst and the best
Have gone to their eternal rest.
There shrines and palaces and towers
(Time-eaten towers that tremble not!)
Resemble nothing that is ours.
Around, by lifting winds forgot,
Resignedly beneath the sky
The melancholy waters lie.

No rays from the holy heaven come down
On the long night-time of that town;
But light from out the lurid sea
Streams up the turrets silently—
Gleams up the pinnacles far and free—
Up domes—up spires—up kingly halls—
Up fanes—up Babylon-like walls—
Up shadowy long-forgotten bowers
Of sculptured ivy and stone flowers—
Up many and many a marvellous shrine
Whose wreathéd friezes intertwine
The viol, the violet, and the vine.
Resignedly beneath the sky
The melancholy waters lie.
So blend the turrets and shadows there
That all seem pendulous in air,
While from a proud tower in the town
Death looks gigantically down.

There open fanes and gaping graves
Yawn level with the luminous waves

But not the riches there that lie
In each idol's diamond eye—
Not the gaily-jewelled dead
Tempt the waters from their bed;
For no ripples curl, alas!
Along that wilderness of glass—
No swellings tell that winds may be
Upon some far-off happier sea—
No heavings hint that winds have been
On seas less hideously serene.

But lo, a stir is in the air!
The wave—there is a movement there!
As if the towers had thrust aside,
In slightly sinking, the dull tide—
As if their tops had feebly given
A void within the filmy Heaven.
The waves have now a redder glow—
The hours are breathing faint and low—
And when, amid no earthly moans,
Down, down that town shall settle hence,
Hell, rising from a thousand thrones,
Shall do it reverence.

A DREAM WITHIN A DREAM

Take this kiss upon the brow!
And, in parting from you now,
Thus much let me avow—
You are not wrong, who deem
That my days have been a dream:
Yet if hope has flown away
In a night, or in a day,
In a vision, or in none,
Is it therefore the less gone?
All that we see or seem
Is but a dream within a dream.

I stand amid the roar
Of a surf-tormented shore,

And I hold within my hand
Grains of the golden sand—
How few! yet how they creep
Through my fingers to the deep,
While I weep—while I weep!
O God! can I not grasp
Them with a tighter clasp?
O God! can I not save
One from the pitiless wave?
Is all that we see or seem
But a dream within a dream?

DREAM-LAND

By a route obscure and lonely,
Haunted by ill angels only,
Where an Eidolon, named Night,
On a black throne reigns upright,
I have reached these lands but newly
From an ultimate dim Thule—
From a wild weird clime that lieth, sublime,
     Out of Space—out of Time.

Bottomless vales and boundless floods,
And chasms, and caves, and Titan woods,
With forms that no man can discover
For the dews that drip all over;
Mountains toppling evermore
Into seas without a shore;
Seas that restlessly aspire,
Surging, unto skies of fire;
Lakes that endlessly outspread
Their lone waters—lone and dead,—
Their still waters—still and chilly
With the snows of the lolling lily.

By the lakes that thus outspread
Their lone waters, lone and dead,—
Their sad waters, sad and chilly
With the snows of the lolling lily,—

765

By the mountains—near the river
Murmuring lowly, murmuring ever,—
By the gray woods,—by the swamp
Where the toad and the newt encamp,—
By the dismal tarns and pools
　　Where dwell the Ghouls,—
By each spot the most unholy—
In each nook most melancholy,—
There the traveller meets aghast
Sheeted Memories of the Past—
Shrouded forms that start and sigh
As they pass the wanderer by—
White-robed forms of friends long given,
In agony, to the Earth—and Heaven.

For the heart whose woes are legion
'Tis a peaceful, soothing region—
For the spirit that walks in shadow
'Tis—oh, 'tis an Eldorado!
But the traveller, travelling through it,
May not—dare not openly view it;
Never its mysteries are exposed
To the weak human eye unclosed;
So wills its King, who hath forbid
The uplifting of the fringed lid;
And thus the sad Soul that here passes
Beholds it but through darkened glasses.

By a route obscure and lonely,
Haunted by ill angels only,
Where an Eidolon, named Night,
On a black throne reigns upright,
I have wandered home but newly
From this ultimate dim Thule.

ELDORADO

Gaily bedight,
A gallant knight,

EDGAR ALLAN POE

In sunshine and in shadow,
   Had journeyed long,
   Singing a song,
In search of Eldorado.

   But he grew old—
   This knight so bold—
And o'er his heart a shadow
   Fell as he found
   No spot of ground
That looked like Eldorado.

   And, as his strength
   Failed him at length,
He met a pilgrim shadow—
   "Shadow," said he,
   "Where can it be—
This land of Eldorado?"

   "Over the Mountains
   Of the Moon,
Down the Valley of the Shadow,
   Ride, boldly ride,"
   The shade replied,—
"If you seek for Eldorado!"

ISRAFEL

In Heaven a spirit doth dwell
   "Whose heart-strings are a lute";
None sing so wildly well
As the angel Israfel,
And the giddy stars (so legends tell)
Ceasing their hymns, attend the spell
   Of his voice, all mute.

Tottering above
   In her highest noon,
   The enamoured moon
Blushes with love,

While, to listen, the red levin
(With the rapid Pleiads, even,
Which were seven,)
Pauses in Heaven.

And they say (the starry choir
And the other listening things)
That Israfeli's fire
Is owing to that lyre
By which he sits and sings—
The trembling living wire
Of those unusual strings.

But the skies that angel trod,
Where deep thoughts are a duty—
Where Love's a grown up God—
Where the Houri glances are
Imbued with all the beauty
Which we worship in a star.

Therefore, thou art not wrong,
Israfeli, who despisest
An unimpassioned song;
To thee the laurels belong,
Best bard, because the wisest!
Merrily live, and long!

The ecstasies above
With thy burning measures suit—
Thy grief, thy joy, thy hate, thy love,
With the fervor of thy lute—
Well may the stars be mute!

Yes, Heaven is thine; but this
Is a world of sweets and sours;
Our flowers are merely—flowers,
And the shadow of thy perfect bliss
Is the sunshine of ours.

If I could dwell
Where Israfel
   Hath dwelt, and he where I,
He might not sing so wildly well
   A mortal melody,
While a bolder note than this might swell
   From my lyre within the sky.

FOR ANNIE

Thank Heaven! the crisis—
   The danger is past,
And the lingering illness
   Is over at last—
And the fever called "Living"
   Is conquered at last.

Sadly, I know
   I am shorn of my strength,
And no muscle I move
   As I lie at full length—
But no matter!—I feel
   I am better at length.

And I rest so composed,
   Now, in my bed,
That any beholder
   Might fancy me dead—
Might start at beholding me,
   Thinking me dead.

The moaning and groaning,
   The sighing and sobbing,
Are quieted now,
   With that horrible throbbing
At heart:—ah, that horrible,
   Horrible throbbing!

The sickness—the nausea—
   The pitiless pain—
Have ceased, with the fever
   That maddened my brain—
With the fever called "Living"
   That burned in my brain.

And oh! of all tortures
   That torture the worst
Has abated—the terrible
   Torture of thirst
For the naphthaline river
   Of Passion accurst:—
I have drank of a water
   That quenches all thirst:—

Of a water that flows,
   With a lullaby sound,
From a spring but a very few
   Feet under ground—
From a cavern not very far
   Down under ground.

And ah! let it never
   Be foolishly said
That my room it is gloomy
   And narrow my bed;
For man never slept
   In a different bed—
And, to sleep, you must slumber
   In just such a bed.

My tantalized spirit
   Here blandly reposes,
Forgetting, or never
   Regretting its roses—
Its old agitations
   Of myrtles and roses:

For now, while so quietly
   Lying, it fancies
A holier odor
   About it, of pansies—
A rosemary odor,
   Commingled with pansies—
With rue and the beautiful
   Puritan pansies.

And so it lies happily,
  Bathing in many
A dream of the truth
  And the beauty of Annie—
Drowned in a bath
  Of the tresses of Annie.

She tenderly kissed me,
  She fondly caressed,
And then I fell gently
  To sleep on her breast—
Deeply to sleep
  From the heaven of her breast.

When the light was extinguished,
  She covered me warm,
And she prayed to the angels
  To keep me from harm—
To the queen of the angels
  To shield me from harm.

And I lie so composedly,
  Now, in my bed,
(Knowing her love)
  That you fancy me dead—
And I rest so contentedly,
  Now in my bed,
(With her love at my breast)
  That you fancy me dead—
That you shudder to look at me,
  Thinking me dead:—

But my heart it is brighter
  Than all of the many
Stars in the sky.
  For it sparkles with Annie—
It glows with the light
  Of the love of my Annie—
With the thought of the light
  Of the eyes of my Annie.

TO F——

Beloved! amid the earnest woes
   That crowd around my earthly path—
(Drear path, alas! where grows
Not even one lonely rose)—
   My soul at least a solace hath
In dreams of thee, and therein knows
An Eden of bland repose.

And thus thy memory is to me
   Like some enchanted far-off isle
In some tumultuous sea—
Some ocean throbbing far and free
   With storms—but where meanwhile
Serenest skies continually
   Just o'er that one bright island smile.

Edward FitzGerald

RUBÁIYÁT OF OMAR KHAYYÁM

I

Wake! For the Sun who scattered into flight
The Stars before him from the Field of Night,
   Drives Night along with them from Heaven,
     and strikes
The Sultán's Turret with a Shaft of Light.

Before the phantom of False morning died,
Methought a Voice within the Tavern cried,
   "When all the Temple is prepared within,
Why nods the drowsy Worshiper outside?"

. . . . .

Come, fill the Cup, and in the fire of Spring
Your Winter-garment of Repentance fling:
   The Bird of Time has but a little way
To flutter—and the Bird is on the Wing.

EDWARD FITZGERALD

Whether at Naishapúr or Babylon,
Whether the Cup with sweet or bitter run,
   The Wine of Life keeps oozing drop by drop,
The Leaves of Life keep falling one by one.

     .   .   .   .

II

A Book of Verses underneath the Bough,
A Jug of Wine, a Loaf of Bread—and Thou
   Beside me singing in the Wilderness—
Oh, Wilderness were Paradise enow!

Some for the Glories of this World; and some
Sigh for the Prophet's Paradise to come;
   Ah, take the Cash, and let the Credit go,
Nor heed the rumble of a distant Drum!

Look to the blowing Rose about us—"Lo,
Laughing," she says, "into the world I blow,
   At once the silken tassel of my Purse
Tear, and its Treasure on the Garden throw."

And those who husbanded the Golden grain,
And those who flung it to the winds like Rain,
   Alike to no such aureate Earth are turned
As, buried once, Men want dug up again.

The Worldly Hope men set their Hearts upon
Turns Ashes—or it prospers; and anon,
   Like Snow upon the Desert's dusty Face,
Lighting a little hour or two—was gone.

III

Think, in this battered caravanserai
Whose Portals are alternate Night and Day,
   How Sultán after Sultán with his Pomp
Abode his destined Hour, and went his way.

They say the Lion and the Lizard keep
The Courts where Jamshyd gloried and drank deep:
   And Bahrám, that great Hunter—the Wild Ass
Stamps o'er his Head, but cannot break his Sleep.

I sometimes think that never blows so red
The Rose as where some buried Cæsar bled;
   That every Hyacinth the Garden wears
Dropped in her Lap from some once lovely Head.

And this reviving Herb whose tender Green
Fledges the River-Lip on which we lean—
   Ah, lean upon it lightly! for who knows
From what once lovely Lip it springs unseen!

IV

Ah, my Beloved, fill the Cup that clears
To-day of past Regret and future Fears:
   To-morrow!—Why, To-morrow I may be
Myself with Yesterday's Seven thousand Years.

For some we loved, the loveliest and the best
That from his Vintage rolling Time hath pressed,
   Have drunk their Cup a Round or two before,
And one by one crept silently to rest.

And we that now make merry in the Room
They left, and Summer dresses in new bloom,
   Ourselves must we beneath the Couch of Earth
Descend—ourselves to make a Couch—for whom?

Ah, make the most of what we yet may spend,
Before we too into the Dust descend;
   Dust into Dust, and under Dust, to lie,
Sans Wine, sans Song, sans Singer, and—sans End!

V

Why, all the Saints and Sages who discussed
Of the two Worlds so wisely—they are thrust
   Like foolish Prophets forth; their Words to Scorn
Are scattered, and their Mouths are stopped with Dust.

.   .   .   .

With them the seed of Wisdom did I sow,
And with mine own hand wrought to make it grow;
   And this was all the Harvest that I reaped—
"I came like Water, and like Wind I go."

Into this Universe, and *Why* not Knowing
Nor *Whence*, like Water willy-nilly flowing;
   And out of it, as Wind along the Waste,
I know not *Whither*, willy-nilly blowing.

What, without asking, hither hurried *Whence?*
And, without asking, *Whither* hurried hence!
   Oh, many a Cup of this forbidden Wine
Must drown the memory of that insolence!

.   .   .   .

VI

A Hair perhaps divides the False and True;
Yes; and a single Alif were the clue—
   Could you but find it—to the Treasure-house,
And peradventure to The Master too:

Whose secret Presence, through Creation's veins
Running Quicksilver-like eludes your pains;
   Taking all shapes from Máh to Máhi; and
They change and perish all—but He remains;

A moment guessed—then back behind the Fold
Immersed of Darkness round the Drama Rolled
   Which, for the Pastime of Eternity,
He doth Himself contrive, enact, behold.

.   .   .   .

VII

I sent my Soul through the Invisible
Some letter of that After-life to spell:
   And by and by my Soul returned to me,
And answered, "I Myself am Heaven and Hell."

  .   .   .   .

The Ball no question makes of Ayes and Noes,
But Here or There, as strikes the Player, goes;
   And He that tossed you down into the Field,
He knows about it all—He knows—HE knows!

The Moving Finger writes; and, having writ,
Moves on: nor all your Piety nor Wit
   Shall lure it back to cancel half a Line
Nor all your Tears wash out a Word of it.

  .   .   .   .

VIII

What! out of senseless Nothing to provoke
A conscious Something to resent the yoke
   Of unpermitted Pleasure, under pain
Of Everlasting Penalties, if broke!

  .   .   .   .

O Thou, who didst with pitfall and with gin
Beset the Road I was to wander in,
   Thou wilt not with Predestined Evil round
Enmesh, and then impute my Fall to Sin!

Oh Thou, who Man of Baser Earth didst make,
And ev'n with Paradise devise the Snake:
   For all the Sin wherewith the Face of Man
Is blackened—Man's forgiveness give—and take!

  .   .   .   .

IX

Ah, with the Grape my fading Life provide,
And wash the Body whence the Life has died,
   And lay me, shrouded in the living Leaf,
By some not unfrequented Garden-side.

776

EDWARD FITZGERALD

That even my buried Ashes such a snare
Of Vintage shall fling up into the Air
  As not a True-believer passing by
But shall be overtaken unaware.

　　•　　•　　•　　•　　•　　•　　•

X

Yet Ah, that Spring should vanish with the Rose!
That Youth's sweet-scented manuscript should close!
  The Nightingale that in the branches sang,
Ah whence, and whither flown again, who knows!

Would but the Desert of the Fountain yield
One glimpse—if dimly, yet indeed, revealed,
  To which the fainting Traveller might spring,
As springs the trampled herbage of the field!

Would but some winged Angel ere too late
Arrest the yet unfolded Roll of Fate,
  And make the stern Recorder otherwise
Enregister, or quite obliterate!

Ah Love! could you and I with Him conspire
To grasp this sorry Scheme of Things entire,
  Would not we shatter it to bits—and then
Remould it nearer to the Heart's desire!

　　•　　•　　•　　•　　•　　•　　•

XI

Yon rising Moon that looks for us again—
How oft hereafter will she wax and wane;
  How oft hereafter rising look for us
Through this same Garden—and for *one* in vain!

And when like her, oh Sákí, you shall pass
Among the Guests Star-scattered on the Grass,
  And in your joyous errand reach the spot
Where I made One—turn down an empty Glass!

777

THE MEADOWS IN SPRING

'Tis a dull sight
    To see the year dying,
When winter winds
    Set the yellow wood sighing:
        Sighing, oh! sighing.

When such a time cometh,
    I do retire
Into an old room
    Beside a bright fire:
        Oh, pile a bright fire!

And there I sit
    Reading old things,
Of knights and lorn damsels,
    While the wind sings—
        Oh, drearily sings!

I never look out
    Nor attend to the blast;
For all to be seen
    Is the leaves falling fast:
        Falling, falling!

But close at the hearth,
    Like a cricket, sit I,
Reading of summer
    And chivalry—
        Gallant chivalry!

Then with an old friend
    I talk of our youth!
How 'twas gladsome, but often
    Foolish, forsooth:
        But gladsome, gladsome!

Or to get merry
  We sing some old rhyme,
That made the wood ring again
  In summer time—
    Sweet summer time!

Then go we to smoking,
  Silent and snug:
Naught passes between us,
  Save a brown jug—
    Sometimes!

And sometimes a tear
  Will rise in each eye,
Seeing the two old friends
  So merrily —
    So merrily!

And ere to bed
  Go we, go we,
Down on the ashes
  We kneel on the knee,
    Praying together!

Thus, then, live I,
  Till, 'mid all the gloom,
By heaven! the bold sun
  Is with me in the room
    Shining, shining!

Then the clouds part,
  Swallows soaring between;
The spring is alive,
  And the meadows are green!

I jump up, like mad,
  Break the old pipe in twain,
And away to the meadows,
  The meadows again.

Lord Houghton

STRANGERS YET

Strangers yet!
After years of life together,
After fair and stormy weather,
After travel in far lands,
After touch of wedded hands,—
Why thus joined?   Why ever met,
If they must be strangers yet?

Strangers yet!
After childhood's winning ways,
After care and blame and praise,
Counsel asked and wisdom given,
After mutual prayers to Heaven,
Child and parent scarce regret
When they part—are strangers yet.

Strangers yet!
After strife for common ends—
After title of "old friends,"
After passions fierce and tender,
After cheerful self-surrender,
Hearts may beat and eyes be met,
And the souls be strangers yet.

Strangers yet!
Oh! the bitter thought to scan
All the loneliness of man:
Nature, by magnetic laws,
Circle unto circle draws,
But they only touch when met,
Never mingle—strangers yet.

Strangers yet!
Will it evermore be thus—
Spirits still impervious?

Shall we never fairly stand
Soul to soul as hand to hand?
Are the hounds eternal set
To retain us—strangers yet?

Strangers yet!
Tell not Love it must aspire
Unto something other—higher:
God himself were loved the best
Were our sympathies at rest,
Rest above the strain and fret
Of the world of—strangers yet!
Strangers yet!

Alfred, Lord Tennyson

THE DESERTED HOUSE

Life and Thought have gone away
    Side by side,
        Leaving door and windows wide.
Careless tenants they! .

All within is dark as night:
In the windows is no light;
And no murmur at the door,
So frequent on its hinge before.

Close the door, the shutters close,
    Or thro' the windows we shall see
        The nakedness and vacancy
Of the dark deserted house.

Come away: no more of mirth
    Is here or merry-making sound.
The house was builded of the earth,
    And shall fall again to ground.

781

Come away: for Life and Thought
  Here no longer dwell;
    But in a city glorious—
A great and distant city—have bought
  A mansion incorruptible.
    Would they could have stayed with us!

THE LADY OF SHALOTT

PART I

On either side the river lie
Long fields of barley and of rye,
That clothe the wold and meet the sky;
And thro' the field the road runs by
    To many-tower'd Camelot;
And up and down the people go,
Gazing where the lilies blow
Round an island there below,
    The island of Shalott.

Willows whiten, aspens quiver,
Little breezes dusk and shiver
Thro' the wave that runs for ever
By the island in the river
    Flowing down to Camelot.
Four grey walls, and four grey towers,
Overlook a space of flowers,
And the silent isle imbowers
    The Lady of Shalott.

By the margin, willow-veil'd,
Slide the heavy barges trail'd
By slow horses; and unhail'd
The shallop flitteth silken-sail'd
    Skimming down to Camelot:
But who hath seen her wave her hand?
Or at the casement seen her stand?
Or is she known in all the land,
    The Lady of Shalott?

782

Only reapers, reaping early
In among the bearded barley,
Hear a song that echoes cheerly
From the river winding clearly,
  Down to tower'd Camelot:
And by the moon the reaper weary,
Piling sheaves in uplands airy,
Listening, whispers, " 'Tis the fairy
  Lady of Shalott."

PART II

There she weaves by night and day
A magic web with colours gay.
She has heard a whisper say,
A curse is on her if she stay
  To look down to Camelot.
She knows not what the curse may be,
And so she weaveth steadily,
And little other care hath she,
  The Lady of Shalott.

And moving thro' a mirror clear
That hangs before her all the year,
Shadows of the world appear.
There she sees the highway near
  Winding down to Camelot.
There the river eddy whirls,
And there the surly village-churls,
And the red cloaks of market-girls,
  Pass onward from Shalott.

Sometimes a troop of damsels glad,
An abbot on an ambling pad,
Sometimes a curly shepherd-lad,
Or long-hair'd page in crimson clad,
  Goes by to tower'd Camelot;
And sometimes thro' the mirror blue
The knights come riding two and two:
She hath no loyal knight and true,
  The Lady of Shalott.

But in her web she still delights
To weave the mirror's magic sights,
For often thro' the silent nights
A funeral, with plumes and lights,
     And music, went to Camelot:
Or when the moon was overhead,
Came two young lovers lately wed:
"I am half sick of shadows," said
     The Lady of Shalott.

PART III

A bow-shot from her bower-eaves,
He rode between the barley-sheaves,
The sun came dazzling thro' the leaves,
And flamed upon the brazen greaves
     Of bold Sir Lancelot.
A red-cross knight for ever kneel'd
To a lady in his shield,
That sparkled on the yellow field,
     Beside remote Shalott.

The gemmy bridle glitter'd free,
Like to some branch of stars we see
Hung in the golden Galaxy.
The bridle bells rang merrily
     As he rode down to Camelot:
And from his blazon'd baldric slung
A mighty silver bugle hung,
And as he rode his armour rung,
     Beside remote Shalott.

All in the blue unclouded weather
Thick-jewell'd shone the saddle-leather,
The helmet and the helmet-feather
Burned like one burning flame together,
     As he rode down to Camelot.
As often thro' the purple night,
Below the starry clusters bright,
Some bearded meteor, trailing light,
     Moves over still Shalott.

His broad clear brow in sunlight glow'd;
On burnish'd hooves his war-horse trode;
From underneath his helmet flow'd
His coal-black curls as on he rode,
    As he rode down to Camelot.
From the bank and from the river
He flash'd into the crystal mirror,
"Tirra lirra," by the river
    Sang Sir Lancelot.

She left the web, she left the loom,
She made three paces thro' the room,
She saw the water-lily bloom,
She saw the helmet and the plume,
    She look'd down to Camelot.
Out flew the web and floated wide;
The mirror crack'd from side to side;
"The curse is come upon me," cried
    The Lady of Shalott.

PART IV

In the stormy east-wind straining,
The pale yellow woods were waning,
The broad stream in his banks complaining,
Heavily the low sky raining
    Over tower'd Camelot;
Down she came and found a boat
Beneath a willow left afloat,
And round about the prow she wrote
    The Lady of Shalott.

And down the river's dim expanse—
Like some bold seer in a trance,
Seeing all his own mischance—
With a glassy countenance
    Did she look to Camelot.
And at the closing of the day
She loosed the chain, and down she lay;
The broad stream bore her far away,
    The Lady of Shalott.

Lying, robed in snowy white
That loosely flew to left and right—
The leaves upon her falling light—
Thro' the noises of the night
  She floated down to Camelot:
And as the boat-head wound along
The willowy hills and fields among,
They heard her singing her last song,
  The Lady of Shalott.

Heard a carol, mournful, holy,
Chanted loudly, chanted lowly,
Till her blood was frozen slowly,
And her eyes were darken'd wholly,
  Turn'd to tower'd Camelot;
For ere she reach'd upon the tide
The first house by the water-side,
Singing in her song she died,
  The Lady of Shalott.

Under tower and balcony,
By garden-wall and gallery,
A gleaming shape she floated by,
Dead-pale between the houses high,
  Silent into Camelot.
Out upon the wharves they came,
Knight and burgher, lord and dame,
And round the prow they read her name,
  The Lady of Shalott.

Who is this? and what is here?
And in the lighted palace near
Died the sound of royal cheer;
And they cross'd themselves for fear,
  All the knights at Camelot:
But Lancelot mused a little space;
He said, "She has a lovely face;
God in his mercy lend her grace,
  The Lady of Shalott."

ALFRED, LORD TENNYSON

ŒNONE

There lies a vale in Ida, lovelier
Than all the valleys of Ionian hills.
The swimming vapour slopes athwart the glen,
Puts forth an arm, and creeps from pine to pine,
And loiters, slowly drawn.   On either hand
The lawns and meadow-ledges midway down
Hang rich in flowers, and far below them roars
The long brook falling thro' the clov'n ravine
In cataract after cataract to the sea.
Behind the valley topmost Gargarus
Stands up and takes the morning: but in front
The gorges, opening wide apart, reveal
Troas and Ilion's column'd citadel,
The crown of Troas.
              Hither came at noon
Mournful Œnone, wandering forlorn
Of Paris, once her playmate on the hills.
Her cheek had lost the rose, and round her neck
Floated her hair or seem'd to float in rest.
She, leaning on a fragment twined with vine,
Sang to the stillness, till the mountain-shade
Sloped downward to her seat from the upper cliff.

"O mother Ida, many-fountain'd Ida,
Dear mother Ida, harken ere I die.
For now the noonday quiet holds the hill:
The grasshopper is silent in the grass:
The lizard, with his shadow on the stone,
Rests like a shadow, and the cicala sleeps.
The purple flowers droop: the golden bee
Is lily-cradled: I alone awake.
My eyes are full of tears, my heart of love,
My heart is breaking, and my eyes are dim,
And I am all aweary of my life.

"O mother Ida, many-fountain'd Ida,
Dear mother Ida, harken ere I die.

Hear me, O Earth, hear me, O Hills, O Caves
That house the cold crown'd snake! O mountain brooks,
I am the daughter of a River-God,
Hear me, for I will speak, and build up all
My sorrow with my song, as yonder walls
Rose slowly to a music slowly breathed,
A cloud that gather'd shape: for it may be
That, while I speak of it, a little while
My heart may wander from its deeper woe.

"O mother Ida, many-fountain'd Ida,
Dear mother Ida, harken ere I die.
I waited underneath the dawning hills,
Aloft the mountain lawn was dewy-dark,
And dewy-dark aloft the mountain pine,
Beautiful Paris, evil-hearted Paris,
Leading a jet-black goat white-horn'd, white-hooved,
Came up from reedy Simois all alone.

"O mother Ida, harken ere I die.
Far-off the torrent call'd me from the cleft:
Far up the solitary morning smote
The streaks of virgin snow. With down-dropt eyes
I sat alone: white-breasted like a star
Fronting the dawn he moved; a leopard skin
Droop'd from his shoulder, but his sunny hair
Cluster'd about his temples like a God's:
And his cheek brighten'd as the foam-bow brightens
When the wind blows the foam, and all my heart
Went forth to embrace him coming ere he came.

"Dear mother Ida, harken ere I die.
He smiled, and opening out his milk-white palm
Disclosed a fruit of pure Hesperian gold,
That smelt ambrosially, and while I look'd
And listen'd, the full-flowing river of speech
Came down upon my heart.
                    " 'My own Œnone,
Beautiful-brow'd Œnone, my own soul,
Behold this fruit, whose gleaming rind ingrav'n
"For the most fair," would seem to award it thine,
788

As lovelier than whatever Oread haunt
The knolls of Ida, loveliest in all grace
Of movement, and the charm of married brows.'

   "Dear mother Ida, harken ere I die.
He prest the blossom of his lips to mine,
And added, 'This was cast upon the board,
When all the full-faced presence of the Gods
Ranged in the halls of Peleus; whereupon
Rose feud, with question unto whom 'twere due:
But light-foot Iris brought it yester-eve,
Delivering, that to me, by common voice,
Elected umpire, Herè comes to-day,
Pallas and Aphrodite, claiming each
This meed of fairest. Thou, within the cave
Behind yon whispering tuft of oldest pine,
Mayst well behold them unbeheld, unheard
Hear all, and see thy Paris judge of Gods.'

   "Dear mother Ida, harken ere I die.
It was the deep midnoon: one silvery cloud
Had lost his way between the piney sides
Of this long glen. Then to the bower they came,
Naked they came to that smooth-swarded bower,
And at their feet the crocus brake like fire,
Violet, amaracus, and asphodel,
Lotos and lilies: and a wind arose,
And overhead the wandering ivy and vine,
This way and that, in many a wild festoon
Ran riot, garlanding the gnarled boughs
With bunch and berry and flower thro' and thro'.

   "O mother Ida, harken ere I die.
On the tree-tops a crested peacock lit,
And o'er him flow'd a golden cloud, and lean'd
Upon him, slowly dropping fragrant dew.
Then first I heard the voice of her, to whom
Coming thro' Heaven, like a light that grows
Larger and clearer, with one mind the Gods
Rise up for reverence. She to Paris made
Proffer of royal power, ample rule

789

Unquestion'd, overflowing revenue
Wherewith to embellish state, 'from many a vale
And river-sunder'd champaign clothed with corn,
Or labour'd mines undrainable of ore.
Honour,' she said, 'and homage, tax and toll,
From many an inland town and haven large,
Mast-throng'd beneath her shadowing citadel
In glassy bays among her tallest towers.'

"O mother Ida, harken ere I die.
Still she spake on and still she spake of power,
'Which in all action is the end of all;
Power fitted to the season; wisdom-bred
And throned of wisdom—from all neighbour crowns
Alliance and allegiance, till thy hand
Fail from the sceptre-staff. Such boon from me,
From me, Heaven's Queen, Paris, to thee king-born,
A shepherd all thy life but yet king-born,
Should come most welcome, seeing men, in power,
Only, are likest gods, who have attain'd
Rest in a happy place and quiet seats
Above the thunder, with undying bliss
In knowledge of their own supremacy.'

"Dear mother Ida, harken ere I die.
She ceased, and Paris held the costly fruit
Out at arm's-length, so much the thought of power
Flatter'd his spirit; but Pallas where she stood
Somewhat apart, her clear and bared limbs
O'erthwarted with the brazen-headed spear
Upon her pearly shoulder leaning cold,
The while, above, her full and earnest eye
Over her snow-cold breast and angry cheek
Kept watch, waiting decision, made reply.

" 'Self-reverence, self-knowledge, self-control,
These three alone lead life to sovereign power.
Yet not for power, (power of herself
Would come uncall'd for) but to live by law,
Acting the law we live by without fear;
And, because right is right, to follow right
Were wisdom in the scorn of consequence.'

790

"Dear mother Ida, harken ere I die.
Again she said: 'I woo thee not with gifts.
Sequel of guerdon could not alter me
To fairer. Judge thou me by what I am,
So shalt thou find me fairest.
              Yet, indeed,
If gazing on divinity disrobed
Thy mortal eyes are frail to judge of fair,
Unbiass'd by self-profit, oh, rest thee sure
That I shall love thee well and cleave to thee,
So that my vigour, wedded to thy blood,
Shall strike within thy pulses, like a God's,
To push thee forward thro' a life of shocks,
Dangers, and deeds, until endurance grow
Sinew'd with action, and the full-grown will,
Circled thro' all experiences, pure law,
Commeasure perfect freedom.'
              "Here she ceased,
And Paris ponder'd, and I cried, 'O Paris,
Give it to Pallas!' but he heard me not,
Or hearing would not hear me, woe is me!

"O mother Ida, many-fountain'd Ida,
Dear mother Ida, harken ere I die.
Idalian Aphrodite beautiful,
Fresh as the foam, new-bathed in Paphian wells,
With rosy slender fingers backward drew
From her warm brows and bosom her deep hair
Ambrosial, golden round her lucid throat
And shoulder: from the violets her light foot
Shone rosy-white, and o'er her rounded form
Between the shadows of the vine-bunches
Floated the glowing sunlights, as she moved.

"Dear mother Ida, harken ere I die.
She with a subtle smile in her mild eyes,
The herald of her triumph, drawing nigh
Half-whisper'd in his ear, 'I promise thee
The fairest and most loving wife in Greece.'
She spoke and laugh'd: I shut my sight for fear:
But when I look'd, Paris had raised his arm,

And I beheld great Herè's angry eyes,
As she withdrew into the golden cloud,
And I was left alone within the bower;
And from that time to this I am alone,
And I shall be alone until I die.

"Yet, mother Ida, harken ere I die.
Fairest—why fairest wife? am I not fair?
My love hath told me so a thousand times.
Methinks I must be fair, for yesterday,
When I past by, a wild and wanton pard,
Eyed like the evening star, with playful tail
Crouch'd fawning in the weed.   Most loving is she?
Ah me, my mountain shepherd, that my arms
Were wound about thee, and my hot lips prest
Close, close to thine in that quick-falling dew
Of fruitful kisses, thick as Autumn rains
Flash in the pools of whirling Simois.

"O mother, hear me yet before I die.
They came, they cut away my tallest pines,
My dark tall pines, that plumed the craggy ledge
High over the blue gorge, and all between
The snowy peak and snow-white cataract
Foster'd the callow eaglet—from beneath
Whose thick mysterious boughs in the dark morn
The panther's roar came muffled, while I sat
Low in the valley.   Never, never more
Shall lone Œnone see the morning mist
Sweep thro' them; never see them overlaid
With narrow moon-lit slips of silver cloud,
Between the loud stream and the trembling stars.

"O mother, hear me yet before I die.
I wish that somewhere in the ruin'd folds,
Among the fragments tumbled from the glens,
Or the dry thickets, I could meet with her,
The Abominable, that uninvited came
Into the fair Peleïan banquet-hall,
And cast the golden fruit upon the board,
And bred this change; that I might speak my mind,

792

And tell her to her face how much I hate
Her presence, hated both of Gods and men.

"O mother, hear me yet before I die.
Hath he not sworn his love a thousand times,
In this green valley, under this green hill,
Ev'n on this hand, and sitting on this stone?
Seal'd it with kisses? water'd it with tears?
O happy tears, and how unlike to these!
O happy Heaven, how canst thou see my face?
O happy earth, how canst thou bear my weight?
O death, death, death, thou ever-floating cloud,
There are enough unhappy on this earth,
Pass by the happy souls, that love to live:
I pray thee, pass before my light of life,
And shadow all my soul, that I may die.
Thou weighest heavy on the heart within,
Weigh heavy on my eyelids: let me die.

"O mother, hear me yet before I die.
I will not die alone, for fiery thoughts
Do shape themselves within me, more and more,
Whereof I catch the issue, as I hear
Dead sounds at night come from the inmost hills,
Like footsteps upon wool. I dimly see
My far-off doubtful purpose, as a mother
Conjectures of the features of her child
Ere it is born: her child!—a shudder comes
Across me: never child be born of me,
Unblest, to vex me with his father's eyes!

"O mother, hear-me yet before I die.
Hear me, O earth. I will not die alone,
Lest their shrill happy laughter come to me
Walking the cold and starless road of Death
Uncomforted, leaving my ancient love
With the Greek woman. I will rise and go
Down into Troy, and ere the stars come forth
Talk with the wild Cassandra, for she says
A fire dances before her, and a sound

Rings ever in her ears of armed men.
What this may be I know not, but I know
That, wheresoe'er I am by night and day,
All earth and air seem only burning fire."

OF OLD SAT FREEDOM ON THE HEIGHTS

Of old sat Freedom on the heights,
　The thunders breaking at her feet:
Above her shook the starry lights:
　She heard the torrents meet.

There in her place she did rejoice,
　Self-gather'd in her prophet-mind,
But fragments of her mighty voice
　Came rolling on the wind.

Then stept she down thro' town and field
　To mingle with the human race,
And part by part to men reveal'd
　The fullness of her face—

Grave mother of majestic works,
　From her isle-altar gazing down,
Who, God-like, grasps the triple forks,
　And King-like, wears the crown:

Her open eyes desire the truth.
　The wisdom of a thousand years
Is in them.　May perpetual youth
　Keep dry their light from tears;

That her fair form may stand and shine,
　Make bright our days and light our dreams,
Turning to scorn with lips divine
　The falsehood of extremes!

ALFRED, LORD TENNYSON

MORTE D'ARTHUR

. . . .

"The old order changeth, yielding place to new,
And God fulfils himself in many ways,
Lest one good custom should corrupt the world.
Comfort thyself: what comfort is in me!
I have lived my life, and that which I have done
May He within himself make pure! but thou,
If thou shouldst never see my face again,
Pray for my soul. More things are wrought by prayer
Than this world dreams of. Wherefore, let thy voice
Rise like a fountain for me night and day.
For what are men better than sheep or goats
That nourish a blind life within the brain,
If, knowing God, they lift not hands of prayer
Both for themselves and those who call them friend?
For so the whole round earth is every way
Bound by gold chains about the feet of God.
But now farewell. I am going a long way
With these thou seest if indeed I go—
(For all my mind is clouded with a doubt)
To the island-valley of Avilion;
Where falls not hail, or rain, or any snow,
Nor ever wind blows loudly; but it lies
Deep-meadow'd, happy, fair with orchard-lawns
And bowery hollows crown'd with summer sea,
Where I will heal me of my grievous wound."

. . . .

ULYSSES

It little profits that an idle king,
By this still hearth, among these barren crags,
Match'd with an aged wife, I mete and dole
Unequal laws unto a savage race,
That hoard, and sleep, and feed, and know not me.
I cannot rest from travel: I will drink
Life to the lees: all times I have enjoy'd
Greatly, have suffer'd greatly, both with those

That loved me, and alone; on shore, and when
Thro' scudding drifts the rainy Hyades
Vext the dim sea: I am become a name;
For always roaming with a hungry heart
Much have I seen and known; cities of men
And manners, climates, councils, governments,
Myself not least, but honor'd of them all;
And drunk delight of battle with my peers,
Far on the ringing plains of windy Troy.
I am a part of all that I have met;
Yet all experience is an arch wherethro'
Gleams that untravell'd world, whose margin fades
For ever and for ever when I move.
How dull it is to pause, to make an end,
To rust unburnish'd, not to shine in use!
As tho' to breathe were life. Life piled on life
Were all too little, and of one to me
Little remains: but every hour is saved
From that eternal silence, something more,
A bringer of new things; and vile it were
For some three suns to store and hoard myself,
And this grey spirit yearning in desire
To follow knowledge like a sinking star,
Beyond the utmost bound of human thought.
   This is my son, mine own Telemachus,
To whom I leave the sceptre and the isle—
Well-loved of me, discerning to fulfil
This labour, by slow prudence to make mild
A rugged people, and thro' soft degrees
Subdue them to the useful and the good.
Most blameless is he, centred in the sphere
Of common duties, decent not to fail
In offices of tenderness, and pay
Meet adoration to my household gods,
When I am gone. He works his work, I mine.
   There lies the port: the vessel puffs her sail:
There gloom the dark broad seas. My mariners,
Souls that have toil'd, and wrought, and thought with me—
That ever with a frolic welcome took
The thunder and the sunshine, and opposed
Free hearts, free foreheads—you and I are old;

Old age hath yet his honour and his toil;
Death closes all: but something ere the end,
Some work of noble note, may yet be done,
Not unbecoming men that strove with Gods.
The lights begin to twinkle from the rocks:
The long day wanes: the slow moon climbs: the deep
Moans round with many voices. Come, my friends,
'Tis not too late to seek a newer world.
Push off, and sitting well in order smite
The sounding furrows; for my purpose holds
To sail beyond the sunset, and the baths
Of all the western stars, until I die.
It may be that the gulfs will wash us down:
It may be we shall touch the Happy Isles,
And see the great Achilles, whom we knew.
Tho' much is taken, much abides: and tho'
We are not now that strength which in old days
Moved earth and heaven; that which we are, we are;
One equal temper of heroic hearts,
Made weak by time and fate, but strong in will
To strive, to seek, to find, and not to yield.

LOCKSLEY HALL

. . . .

In the Spring a fuller crimson comes upon the robin's breast;
In the Spring the wanton lapwing gets himself another crest;

In the Spring a livelier iris changes on the burnish'd dove;
In the Spring a young man's fancy lightly turns to thoughts
   of love.

. . . .

For I dipt into the future, far as human eye could see,
Saw the Vision of the world, and all the wonder that would
   be;

Saw the heavens fill with commerce, argosies of magic sails,
Pilots of the purple twilight, dropping down with costly bales;

Heard the heavens fill with shouting, and there rain'd a ghastly
   dew
From the nations' airy navies grappling in the central blue;

797

Far along the world-wide whisper of the south-wind rushing
    warm,
With the standards of the peoples plunging thro' the thunder-
    storm;

Till the war-drum throbb'd no longer, and the battle-flags
    were furl'd
In the Parliament of man, the Federation of the world.

There the common sense of most shall hold a fretful realm
    in awe,
And the kindly earth shall slumber, lapt in universal law.

.   .   .   .

Yet I doubt not thro' the ages one increasing purpose runs,
And the thoughts of men are widen'd with the process of the
    suns.

.   .   .   .

Not in vain the distance beacons. Forward, forward let us
    range.
Let the great world spin for ever down the ringing grooves
    of change.

Thro' the shadow of the globe we sweep into the younger
    day:
Better fifty years of Europe than a cycle of Cathay.

.   .   .   .

ST. AGNES' EVE

Deep on the convent-roof the snows
  Are sparkling to the moon:
My breath to heaven like vapour goes:
  May my soul follow soon!
The shadows of the convent-towers
  Slant down the snowy sward,
Still creeping with the creeping hours
  That lead me to my Lord:
Make Thou my spirit pure and clear
  As are the frosty skies,
Or this first snowdrop of the year
  That in my bosom lies.

ALFRED, LORD TENNYSON

As these white robes are soil'd and dark,
  To yonder shining ground;
As this pale taper's earthly spark,
  To yonder argent round;
So shows my soul before the Lamb,
  My spirit before Thee;
So in mine earthly house I am,
  To that I hope to be.
Break up the heavens, O Lord! and far,
  Thro' all yon starlight keen,
Draw me, thy bride, a glittering star,
  In raiment white and clean.

He lifts me to the golden doors;
  The flashes come and go;
All heaven bursts her starry floors,
  And strows her lights below,
And deepens on and up! the gates
  Roll back, and far within
For me the Heavenly Bridegroom waits,
  To make me pure of sin.
The sabbaths of Eternity,
  One sabbath deep and wide—
A light upon the shining sea—
  The Bridegroom with his bride!

A FAREWELL

Flow down, cold rivulet, to the sea,
  Thy tribute wave deliver:
No more by thee my steps shall be,
  For ever and for ever.

Flow, softly flow, by lawn and lea,
  A rivulet then a river:
No where by thee my steps shall be,
  For ever and for ever.

But here will sigh thine alder tree,
  And here thine aspen shiver;
And here by thee will hum the bee,
  For ever and for ever.

799

A thousand suns will stream on thee,
    A thousand moons will quiver;
But not by thee my steps shall be,
    For ever and for ever.

THE EAGLE

He clasps the crag with hookèd hands;
Close to the sun in lonely lands,
Ring'd with the azure world, he stands.

The wrinkled sea beneath him crawls;
He watches from his mountain walls,
And like a thunderbolt he falls.

BREAK, BREAK, BREAK

Break, break, break,
    On thy cold grey stones, O Sea!
And I would that my tongue could utter
    The thoughts that arise in me.

O well for the fisherman's boy,
    That he shouts with his sister at play!
O well for the sailor lad,
    That he sings in his boat on the bay!

And the stately ships go on
    To their haven under the hill;
But O for the touch of a vanish'd hand,
    And the sound of a voice that is still!

Break, break, break,
    At the foot of thy crags, O Sea!
But the tender grace of a day that is dead
    Will never come back to me.

ALFRED, LORD TENNYSON

THE HIGHER PANTHEISM

The sun, the moon, the stars, the seas, the hills and the
plains—
Are not these, O Soul, the Vision of Him who reigns?

Is not the Vision He? tho' He be not that which He seems?
Dreams are true while they last, and do we not live in dreams?

Earth, these solid stars, this weight of body and limb,
Are they not sign and symbol of thy division from Him?

Dark is the world to thee: thyself art the reason why;
For is He not all but thou, that hast power to feel "I am I"?

Glory about thee, without thee; and thou fulfillest thy doom,
Making Him broken gleams, and a stifled splendour and gloom.

Speak to Him thou for He hears, and Spirit with Spirit can
meet—
Closer is He than breathing, and nearer than hands and feet.

God is law, say the wise; O Soul, and let us rejoice,
For if He thunder by law the thunder is yet His voice.

Law is God, say some: no God at all, says the fool;
For all we have power to see is a straight staff bent in a pool;

And the ear of man cannot hear, and the eye of man cannot
see;
But if we could see and hear, this Vision—were it not He?

FLOWER IN THE CRANNIED WALL

Flower in the crannied wall,
I pluck you out of the crannies;—
Hold you here, root and all, in my hand,
Little flower—but if I could understand
What you are, root and all, and all in all,
I should know what God and man is.

801

IN LOVE, IF LOVE BE LOVE

In Love, if Love be Love, if Love be ours,
Faith and unfaith can ne'er be equal powers:
Unfaith in aught is want of faith in all.

It is the little rift within the lute,
That by and by will make the music mute,
And ever widening slowly silence all.

The little rift within the lover's lute
Or little pitted speck in garner'd fruit,
That rotting inward slowly moulders all.

It is not worth the keeping: let it go:
But shall it? answer, darling, answer, no.
And trust me not at all or all in all.
                              —IDYLLS OF THE KING

GARETH AND LYNETTE

.   .   .   .

For truly, as thou sayest, a Fairy King
And Fairy Queens, have built the city, son;
They came from out a sacred mountain-cleft
Toward the sunrise, each with harp in hand,
And built it to the music of their harps.
And, as thou sayest, it is enchanted, son,
For there is nothing in it as it seems,
Saving the King; though some there be that hold
The King a shadow and the city real;
Yet take thou heed of him, for so thou pass
Beneath this archway, then wilt thou become
A thrall to his enchantments, for the king
Will bind thee by such vows as is a shame
A man should not be bound by, yet the which
No man can keep; but so thou dread to swear,
Pass not beneath the gateway, but abide
Without among the cattle of the field.

802

ALFRED, LORD TENNYSON

For, an ye heard a music, like enow
They are building still, seeing the city is built
To music, therefore never built at all,
And therefore built forever.

    •   •   •   •   •   •   •

—IDYLLS OF THE KING

THE PRINCESS

II

As thro' the land at eve we went,
    And pluck'd the ripen'd ears,
We fell out, my wife and I,
O we fell out I know not why,
    And kiss'd again with tears.
And blessings on the falling out
    That all the more endears,
When we fall out with those we love
    And kiss again with tears!
For when we came where lies the child
    We lost in other years,
There above the little grave,
O there above the little grave
    We kiss'd again with tears.

   •   •   •   •   •   •   •   •   •

IV

The splendour falls on castle walls
    And snowy summits old in story:
The long light shakes across the lakes,
    And the wild cataract leaps in glory.
Blow, bugle, blow, set the wild echoes flying,
Blow, bugle; answer, echoes, dying, dying, dying.

O hark, O hear! how thin and clear,
    And thinner, clearer, farther going!
O sweet and far from cliff and scaur
    The horns of Elfland faintly blowing!
Blow, let us hear the purple glens replying:
Blow, bugle; answer, echoes, dying, dying, dying.

803

O love, they die in yon rich sky,
 They faint on hill or field or river:
Our echoes roll from soul to soul,
 And grow for ever and for ever.
Blow, bugle, blow, set the wild echoes flying,
And answer, echoes, answer, dying, dying, dying.

. . . .

 Tears, idle tears, I know not what they mean,
Tears from the depth of some divine despair
Rise in the heart, and gather to the eyes,
In looking on the happy Autumn-fields,
And thinking of the days that are no more.

 Fresh as the first beam glittering on a sail,
That brings our friends up from the underworld,
Sad as the last which reddens over one
That sinks with all we love below the verge;
So sad, so fresh, the days that are no more.

 Ah, sad and strange as in dark summer dawns
The earliest pipe of half-awaken'd birds
To dying ears, when unto dying eyes
The casement slowly grows a glimmering square;
So sad, so strange, the days that are no more.

 Dear as remember'd kisses after death,
And sweet as those by hopeless fancy feign'd
On lips that are for others; deep as love,
Deep as first love, and wild with all regret;
O Death in Life, the days that are no more."

. . . .

 O Swallow, Swallow, flying, flying South,
Fly to her, and fall upon her gilded eaves,
And tell her, tell her, what I tell to thee.

 O tell her, Swallow, thou that knowest each,
That bright and fierce and fickle is the South,
And dark and true and tender is the North.
804

ALFRED, LORD TENNYSON

O Swallow, Swallow, if I could follow, and light
Upon her lattice, I would pipe and trill,
And cheep and twitter twenty million loves.

O were I thou that she might take me in,
And lay me on her bosom, and her heart
Would rock the snowy cradle till I died.

Why lingereth she to clothe her heart with love,
Delaying as the tender ash delays
To clothe herself, when all the woods are green?

O tell her, Swallow, that thy brood is flown:
Say to her, I do but wanton in the South,
But in the North long since my nest is made.

O tell her, brief is life but love is long,
And brief the sun of summer in the North,
And brief the moon of beauty in the South.

O Swallow, flying from the golden woods,
Fly to her, and pipe and woo her, and make her mine,
And tell her, tell her, that I follow thee.

. . . .

VI

Home they brought her warrior dead:
    She nor swoon'd, nor utter'd cry:
All her maidens, watching said,
    "She must weep or she will die."

Then they praised him, soft and low,
    Call'd him worthy to be loved,
Truest friend and noblest foe;
    Yet she neither spoke nor moved.

Stole a maiden from her place,
    Lightly to the warrior stept,
Took the face-cloth from the face;
    Yet she neither moved nor wept.

Rose a nurse of ninety years,
    Set his child upon her knee—
Like summer tempest came her tears—
    "Sweet my child, I live for thee."

.   .   .   .

VII

Ask me no more: the moon may draw the sea;
    The cloud may stoop from heaven and take the shape,
    With fold to fold, of mountain or of cape;
But O too fond, when have I answer'd thee?
            Ask me no more.

Ask me no more: what answer should I give?
    I love not hollow cheek or faded eye:
    Yet, O my friend, I will not have thee die!
Ask me no more, lest I should bid thee live;
            Ask me no more.

Ask me no more: thy fate and mine are seal'd:
    I strove against the stream and all in vain:
    Let the great river take me to the main:
No more, dear love, for at a touch I yield;
            Ask me no more.

.   .   .   .

Come down, O maid, from yonder mountain height:
What pleasure lives in height (the shepherd sang)
In height and cold, the splendour of the hills?
But cease to move so near the Heavens, and cease
To glide a sunbeam by the blasted Pine,
To sit a star upon the sparkling spire;
And come, for Love is of the valley, come,
For Love is of the valley, come thou down
And find him; by the happy threshold, he,
Or hand in hand with Plenty in the maize,
Or red with spirted purple of the vats,
Or foxlike in the vine; nor cares to walk
With Death and Morning on the silver horns,

Nor wilt thou snare him in the white ravine,
Nor find him dropt upon the firths of ice,
That huddling slant in furrow-cloven falls
To roll the torrent out of dusky doors:
But follow; let the torrent dance thee down
To find him in the valley; let the wild
Lean-headed Eagles yelp alone, and leave
The monstrous ledges there to slope, and spill
Their thousand wreaths of dangling water-smoke,
That like a broken purpose waste in air:
So waste not thou; but come; for all the vales
Await thee, azure pillars of the hearth
Arise to thee; the children call, and I
Thy shepherd pipe, and sweet is every sound,
Sweeter thy voice, but every sound is sweet;
Myriads of rivulets hurrying thro' the lawn,
The moan of doves in immemorial elms,
And murmuring of innumerable bees.

. . . .

The woman's cause is man's: they rise or sink
Together, dwarf'd or godlike, bond or free:
For she that out of Lethe scales with man
The shining steps of Nature, shares with man
His nights, his days, moves with him to one goal,
Stays all the fair young planet in her hands.

. . . .

For woman is not undevelopt man,
But diverse: could we make her as the man,
Sweet Love were slain: his dearest bond is this,
Not like to like, but like in difference.
Yet in the long years liker must they grow;
The man be more of woman, she of man;
He gain in sweetness and in moral height,
Nor lose the wrestling thews that throw the world;
She mental breadth, nor fail in childward care,
Nor lose the childlike in the larger mind;
Till at the last she set herself to man,
Like perfect music unto noble words.

. . . .

IN MEMORIAM

Strong Son of God, immortal Love,
   Whom we, that have not seen thy face,
   By faith, and faith alone, embrace,
Believing where we cannot prove;

Thine are these orbs of light and shade;
   Thou madest Life in man and brute;
   Thou madest Death; and lo, thy foot
Is on the skull which thou hast made.

Thou wilt not leave us in the dust:
   Thou madest man, he knows not why;
   He thinks he was not made to die;
And thou hast made him: thou art just.

Thou seemest human and divine,
   The highest, holiest manhood, thou:
   Our wills are ours, we know not how;
Our wills are ours, to make them thine.

Our little systems have their day;
   They have their day and cease to be:
   They are but broken lights of thee,
And thou, O Lord, art more than they.

We have but faith: we cannot know;
   For knowledge is of things we see;
   And yet we trust it comes from thee,
A beam in darkness: let it grow.

Let knowledge grow from more to more,
   But more of reverence in us dwell;
   That mind and soul, according well,
May make one music as before,

But vaster. We are fools and slight;
   We mock thee when we do not fear:
   But help thy foolish ones to bear;
Help thy vain worlds to bear thy light.

ALFRED, LORD TENNYSON

Forgive what seem'd my sin in me;
    What seem'd my worth since I began;
    For merit lives from man to man,
And not from man, O Lord, to thee.

Forgive my grief for one removed,
    Thy creature, whom I found so fair.
    I trust he lives in thee, and there
I find him worthier to be loved.

Forgive these wild and wandering cries,
    Confusions of a wasted youth;
    Forgive them where they fail in truth,
And in thy wisdom make me wise.

I

I held it truth, with him who sings
    To one clear harp in divers tones,
    That men may rise on stepping-stones
Of their dead selves to higher things.

But who shall so forecast the years
    And find in loss a gain to match?
    Or reach a hand thro' time to catch
The far-off interest of tears?

Let Love clasp Grief lest both be drown'd,
    Let darkness keep her raven gloss:
    Ah, sweeter to be drunk with loss,
To dance with death, to beat the ground,

Than that the victor Hours should scorn
    The long result of love, and boast,
    "Behold the man that loved and lost,
But all he was is overworn."

V

I sometimes hold it half a sin
    To put in words the grief I feel;
    For words, like Nature, half reveal
And half conceal the Soul within.

But, for the unquiet heart and brain,
    A use in measured language lies;
    The sad mechanic exercise,
Like dull narcotics, numbing pain.

   ·   ·   ·   ·   ·   ·

IX

Fair ship, that from the Italian shore
    Sailest the placid ocean-plains
    With my lost Arthur's loved remains,
Spread thy full wings, and waft him o'er.

So draw him home to those that mourn
    In vain; a favourable speed
    Ruffle thy mirror'd mast, and lead
Thro' prosperous floods his holy urn.

All night no ruder air perplex
    Thy sliding keel, till Phosphor, bright
    As our pure love, thro' early light
Shall glimmer on the dewy decks.

Sphere all your lights around, above;
    Sleep, gentle heavens, before the prow;
    Sleep, gentle winds, as he sleeps now,
My friend, the brother of my love;

My Arthur, whom I shall not see
    Till all my widow'd race be run;
    Dear as the mother to the son,
More than my brothers are to me.

XI

Calm is the morn without a sound,
    Calm as to suit a calmer grief,
    And only thro' the faded leaf
The chestnut pattering to the ground:

Calm and deep peace on this high wold,
    And on these dews that drench the furze,
    And all the silvery gossamers
That twinkle into green and gold:

Calm and still light on yon great plain
    That sweeps with all its autumn bowers,
    And crowded farms and lessening towers,
To mingle with the bounding main:

Calm and deep peace in this wide air,
    These leaves that redden to the fall;
    And in my heart, if calm at all,
If any calm, a calm despair:

Calm on the seas, and silver sleep,
    And waves that sway themselves in rest,
    And dead calm in that noble breast
Which heaves but with the heaving deep.

                    XII

Lo, as a dove when up she springs
    To bear thro' Heaven a tale of woe,
    Some dolorous message knit below
The wild pulsation of her wings;

Like her I go; I cannot stay;
    I leave this mortal ark behind,
    A weight of nerves without a mind,
And leave the cliffs, and haste away

O'er ocean-mirrors rounded large,
    And reach the glow of southern skies,
    And see the sails at distance rise,
And linger weeping on the marge,

And saying; "Comes he thus, my friend?
    Is this the end of all my care?"
    And circle moaning in the air:
"Is this the end?   Is this the end?"

        .   .   .   .

                    XIII

Tears of the widower, when he sees
    A late-lost form that sleep reveals,
    And moves his doubtful arms, and feels
Her place is empty, fall like these;

                                    811

Which weep a loss for ever new,
　　A void where heart on heart reposed;
　　And, where warm hands have prest and closed,
Silence, till I be silent too.

　　　　•　　•　　•　　•　　•　　•　　•

XXIII

Now, sometimes in my sorrow shut,
　　Or breaking into song by fits,
　　Alone, alone, to where he sits,
The Shadow cloak'd from head to foot,

Who keeps the keys of all the creeds,
　　I wander, often falling lame,
　　And looking back to whence I came,
Or on to where the pathway leads;

And crying, How changed from where it ran
　　Thro' lands where not a leaf was dumb;
　　But all the lavish hills would hum
The murmur of a happy Pan:

When each by turns was guide to each,
　　And Fancy light from Fancy caught,
　　And Thought leapt out to wed with Thought
Ere Thought could wed itself with Speech;

And all we met was fair and good,
　　And all was good that Time could bring,
　　And all the secret of the Spring
Moved in the chambers of the blood;

And many an old philosophy
　　On Argive heights divinely sang,
　　And round us all the thicket rang
To many a flute of Arcady.

XXVII

I envy not in any moods
　　The captive void of noble rage,
　　The linnet born within the cage,
That never knew the summer woods:

812

ALFRED, LORD TENNYSON

I envy not the beast that takes
    His license in the field of time,
    Unfetter'd by the sense of crime,
To whom a conscience never wakes;

Nor, what may count itself as blest,
    The heart that never plighted troth,
    But stagnates in the weeds of sloth;
Nor any want-begotten rest.

I hold it true, whate'er befall;
    I feel it, when I sorrow most;
    'Tis better to have loved and lost
Than never to have loved at all.

L

Be near me when my light is low,
    When the blood creeps, and the nerves prick
    And tingle; and the heart is sick,
And all the wheels of Being slow.

Be near me when the sensuous frame
    Is rack'd with pangs that conquer trust;
    And Time, a maniac scattering dust,
And Life, a Fury slinging flame.

.   .   .   .   .   .

LIII

How many a father have I seen,
    A sober man, among his boys,
    Whose youth was full of foolish noise,
Who wears his manhood hale and green:

And dare we to this fancy give,
    That had the wild oat not been sown,
    The soil, left barren, scarce had grown
The grain by which a man may live?

O, if we held the doctrine sound
    For life outliving heats of youth,
    Yet who would preach it as a truth
To those that eddy round and round?

Hold thou the good: define it well:
  For fear divine Philosophy
  Should push beyond her mark, and be
Procuress to the Lords of Hell.

LIV

O yet we trust that somehow good
  Will be the final goal of ill,
  To pangs of nature, sins of will,
Defects of doubt, and taints of blood;

That nothing walks with aimless feet;
  That not one life shall be destroy'd,
  Or cast as rubbish to the void,
When God hath made the pile complete;

That not a worm is cloven in vain;
  That not a moth with vain desire
  Is shrivell'd in a fruitless fire,
Or but subserves another's gain.

Behold, we know not anything;
  I can but trust that good shall fall
  At last—far off—at last, to all,
And every winter change to spring.

So runs my dream: but what am I?
  An infant crying in the night:
  An infant crying for the light:
And with no language but a cry.

LV

The wish, that of the living whole
  No life may fail beyond the grave,
  Derives it not from what we have
The likest God within the soul?

814

Are God and Nature then at strife,
   That Nature lends such evil dreams?
   So careful of the type she seems,
So careless of the single life;

That I, considering everywhere
   Her secret meaning in her deeds,
   And finding that of fifty seeds
She often brings but one to bear,

I falter where I firmly trod,
   And falling with my weight of cares
   Upon the great world's altar-stairs
That slope thro' darkness up to God,

I stretch lame hands of faith, and grope,
   And gather dust and chaff, and call
   To what I feel is Lord of all,
And faintly trust the larger hope.

LVI

"So careful of the type?" but no,
   From scarped cliff and quarried stone
   She cries, "A thousand types are gone:
I care for nothing, all shall go.

"Thou makest thine appeal to me:
   I bring to life, I bring to death:
   The spirit does but mean the breath
I know no more."   And he, shall be,

Man, her last work, who seem'd so fair,
   Such splendid purpose in his eyes,
   Who roll'd the psalm to wintry skies,
Who built him fanes of fruitless prayer,

Who trusted God was love indeed
   And love Creation's final law—
   Tho' Nature, red in tooth and claw
With ravine, shriek'd against his creed—

Who loved, who suffer'd countless ills,
  Who battled for the True, the Just,
  Be blown about the desert dust,
Or seal'd within the iron hills?

No more?   A monster then, a dream,
  A discord.   Dragons of the prime,
  That tare each other in their slime,
Were mellow music match'd with him.

O life as futile, then, as frail!
  O for thy voice to soothe and bless!
  What hope of answer, or redress?
Behind the veil, behind the veil.

LVII

Peace; come away: the song of woe
  Is after all an earthly song:
  Peace; come away: we do him wrong
To sing so wildly: let us go.

Come; let us go: your cheeks are pale;
  But half my life I leave behind:
  Methinks my friend is richly shrined;
But I shall pass; my work will fail.

Yet in these ears, till hearing dies,
  One set slow bell will seem to toll
  The passing of the sweetest soul
That ever look'd with human eyes.

I hear it now, and o'er and o'er,
  Eternal greetings to the dead;
  And "Ave, Ave, Ave," said,
"Adieu, adieu" for evermore.

LXXV

I leave thy praises unexpress'd
  In verse that brings myself relief,
  And by the measure of my grief
I leave thy greatness to be guess'd;

What practice howsoe'er expert
   In fitting aptest words to things,
   Or voice the richest-toned that sings,
Hath power to give thee as thou wert?

   .   .   .   .   .   .

LXXIX

   .   .   .   .   .

But thou and I are one in kind,
   As moulded like in nature's mint;
   And hill and wood and field did print
The same sweet forms in either mind.

For us the same cold streamlet curl'd
   Thro' all his eddying coves; the same
   All winds that roam the twilight came
In whispers of the beauteous world.

   .   .   .   .   .   .

LXXXV

   .   .   .   .   .

Whatever way my days decline,
   I felt and feel, tho' left alone,
   His being working in mine own,
The footsteps of his life in mine;

A life that all the Muses deck'd
   With gifts of grace, that might express
   All-comprehensive tenderness,
All-subtilising intellect:

   .   .   .   .   .

XCVI

You say, but with no touch of scorn,
   Sweet-hearted, you, whose light-blue eyes
   Are tender over drowning flies,
You tell me, doubt is Devil-born.

I know not: one indeed I knew
   In many a subtle question versed,
   Who touch'd a jarring lyre at first,
But ever strove to make it true:

Perplext in faith, but pure in deeds,
   At last he beat his music out.
   There lives more faith in honest doubt,
Believe me, than in half the creeds.

He fought his doubts and gather'd strength,
   He would not make his judgment blind,
   He faced the spectres of the mind
And laid them: thus he came at length

To find a stronger faith his own;
   And Power was with him in the night,
   Which makes the darkness and the light,
And dwells not in the light alone,

But in the darkness and the cloud,
   As over Sinai's peaks of old,
   While Israel made their gods of gold,
Altho' the trumpet blew so loud.

C

I climb the hill: from end to end
   Of all the landscape underneath,
   I find no place that does not breathe
Some gracious memory of my friend;

No grey old grange, or lonely fold,
   Or low morass and whispering reed,
   Or simple stile from mead to mead,
Or sheepwalk up the windy wold;

Nor hoary knoll of ash and haw
   That hears the latest linnet trill,
   Nor quarry trench'd along the hill,
And haunted by the wrangling daw;

ALFRED, LORD TENNYSON

Nor runlet tinkling from the rock;
　Nor pastoral rivulet that swerves
　To left and right thro' meadowy curves,
That feed the mothers of the flock;

But each has pleased a kindred eye,
　And each reflects a kindlier day;
　And, leaving these, to pass away,
I think once more he seems to die.

CVI

Ring out, wild bells, to the wild sky,
　The flying cloud, the frosty light:
　The year is dying in the night;
Ring out, wild bells, and let him die.

Ring out the old, ring in the new,
　Ring, happy bells, across the snow:
　The year is going, let him go;
Ring out the false, ring in the true.

Ring out the grief that saps the mind,
　For those that here we see no more;
　Ring out the feud of rich and poor,
Ring in redress to all mankind.

Ring out a slowly dying cause,
　And ancient forms of party strife;
　Ring in the nobler modes of life,
With sweeter manners, purer laws.

Ring out the want, the care, the sin,
　The faithless coldness of the times;
　Ring out, ring out my mournful rhymes,
But ring the fuller minstrel in.

Ring out false pride in place and blood,
　The civic slander and the spite;
　Ring in the love of truth and right,
Ring in the common love of good.

Ring out old shapes of foul disease;
   Ring out the narrowing lust of gold;
   Ring out the thousand wars of old,
Ring in the thousand years of peace.

Ring in the valiant man and free,
   The larger heart, the kindlier hand;
   Ring out the darkness of the land,
Ring in the Christ that is to be.

CXXIII

There rolls the deep where grew the tree,
   O earth, what changes hast thou seen!
   There where the long street roars, hath been
The stillness of the central sea.

The hills are shadows, and they flow
   From form to form, and nothing stands;
   They melt like mist, the solid lands,
Like clouds they shape themselves and go.

But in my spirit will I dwell,
   And dream my dream, and hold it true;
   For tho' my lips may breathe adieu,
I cannot think the thing farewell.

CXXVI

Love is and was my Lord and King,
   And in his presence I attend
   To hear the tidings of my friend,
Which every hour his couriers bring.

Love is and was my King and Lord,
   And will be, tho' as yet I keep
   Within his court on earth, and sleep
Encompass'd by his faithful guard,

And hear at times a sentinel
  Who moves about from place to place,
  And whispers to the worlds of space,
In the deep night, that all is well.

CXXVII

And all is well, tho' faith and form
  Be sunder'd in the night of fear;
  Well roars the storm to those that hear
A deeper voice across the storm.

.   .   .   .

But ill for him that wears a crown,
  And him, the lazar, in his rags:
  They tremble, the sustaining crags;
The spires of ice are toppled down,

And molten up, and roar in flood;
  The fortress crashes from on high,
  The brute earth lightens to the sky,
And the great Æon sinks in blood,

And compass'd by the fires of Hell;
  While thou, dear spirit, happy star,
  O'erlook'st the tumult from afar,
And smilest, knowing all is well.

CXXX

Thy voice is on the rolling air;
  I hear thee where the waters run;
  Thou standest in the rising sun,
And in the setting thou art fair.

.   .   .   .

Again the feast, the speech, the glee,
  The shade of passing thought, the wealth
  Of words and wit, the double health,
The crowning cup, the three-times-three,

821

And last the dance;—till I retire:
  Dumb is that tower which spake so loud,
  And high in heaven the streaming cloud,
And on the downs a rising fire:

And rise, O moon, from yonder down
  Till over down and over dale
  All night the shining vapour sail
And pass the silent-lighted town,

The white-faced halls, the glancing rills,
  And catch at every mountain head,
  And o'er the friths that branch and spread
Their sleeping silver thro' the hills;

And touch with shade the bridal doors,
  With tender gloom the roof, the wall;
  And breaking let the splendour fall
To spangle all the happy shores

By which they rest, and ocean sounds,
  And, star and system rolling past,
  A soul shall draw from out the vast
And strike his being into bounds,

And, moved thro' life of lower phase,
  Result in man, be born and think,
  And act and love, a closer link
Betwixt us and the crowning race

Of those that, eye to eye, shall look
  On knowledge; under whose command
  Is Earth and Earth's, and in their hand
Is Nature like an open book;

No longer half-akin to brute,
  For all we thought and loved and did,
  And hoped, and suffer'd, is but seed
Of what in them is flower and fruit;

Whereof the man, that with me trod
  This planet, was a noble type
  Appearing ere the times were ripe,
That friend of mine who lives in God,

That God, which ever lives and loves,
  One God, one law, one element,
  And one far-off divine event,
To which the whole creation moves.

MAUD

PART I

Come into the garden, Maud,
  For the black bat, night, has flown,
Come into the garden, Maud,
  I am here at the gate alone;
And the woodbine spices are wafted abroad,
  And the musk of the roses blown.

For a breeze of morning moves,
  And the planet of Love is on high,
Beginning to faint in the light that she loves
  On a bed of daffodil sky,
To faint in the light of the sun she loves,
  To faint in his light, and to die.

All night have the roses heard
  The flute, violin, bassoon;
All night has the casement jessamine stirr'd
  To the dancers dancing in tune;
Till a silence fell with the waking bird,
  And a hush with the setting moon.

I said to the lily, "There is but one
  With whom she has heart to be gay.
When will the dancers leave her alone?
  She is weary of dance and play."

Now half to the setting moon are gone,
　And half to the rising day;
Low on the sand and loud on the stone
　The last wheel echoes away.

I said to the rose, "The brief night goes
　In babble and revel and wine.
O young lord lover, what sighs are those,
　For one that will never be thine?
But mine, but mine," so I sware to the rose,
　"For ever and ever, mine."

And the soul of the rose went into my blood,
　As the music clash'd in the hall;
And long by the garden lake I stood,
　For I heard your rivulet fall
From the lake to the meadow and on to the wood,
　Our wood, that is dearer than all;

From the meadow your walks have left so sweet
　That whenever a March-wind sighs
He sets the jewel-print of your feet
　In violets blue as your eyes,
To the woody hollows in which we meet
　And the valleys of Paradise.

The slender acacia would not shake
　One long milk-bloom on the tree;
The white lake-blossom fell into the lake
　As the pimpernel dozed on the lea;
But the rose was awake all night for your sake,
　Knowing your promise to me;
The lilies and roses were all awake,
　They sigh'd for the dawn and thee.

Queen rose of the rosebud garden of girls,
　Come hither, the dances are done,
In gloss of satin and glimmer of pearls,
　Queen lily and rose in one;
Shine out, little head, sunning over with curls,
　To the flowers, and be their sun.

There has fallen a splendid tear
  From the passion-flower at the gate.
She is coming, my dove, my dear;
  She is coming, my life, my fate;
The red rose cries, "She is near, she is near."
  And the white rose weeps, "She is late";
The larkspur listens, "I hear, I hear";
  And the lily whispers, "I wait."

She is coming, my own, my sweet;
  Were it ever so airy a tread,
My heart would hear her and beat,
  Were it earth in an earthy bed;
My dust would hear her and beat,
  Had I lain for a century dead;
Would start and tremble under her feet,
  And blossom in purple and red.

PART II

O that 'twere possible
After long grief and pain
To find the arms of my true love
Round me once again!

When I was wont to meet her
In the silent woody places
By the home that gave me birth,
We stood tranced in long embraces
Mixt with kisses sweeter sweeter
Than anything on earth.

A shadow flits before me,
Not thou, but like to thee;
Ah Christ, that it were possible
For one short hour to see
The souls we loved, that they might tell us
What and where they be.

It leads me forth at evening,
It lightly winds and steals
In a cold white robe before me,
When all my spirit reels
At the shouts, the leagues of lights,
And the roaring of the wheels.

Half the night I waste in sighs,
Half in dreams I sorrow after
The delight of early skies;
In a wakeful doze I sorrow
For the hand, the lips, the eyes,
For the meeting of the morrow,
The delight of happy laughter,
The delight of low replies.

'Tis a morning pure and sweet,
And a dewy splendour falls
On the little flower that clings
To the turrets and the walls;
'Tis a morning pure and sweet,
And the light and shadow fleet;
She is walking in the meadow,
And the woodland echo rings;
In a moment we shall meet;
She is singing in the meadow,
And the rivulet at her feet
Ripples on in light and shadow
To the ballad that she sings.

Do I hear her sing as of old,
My bird with the shining head,
My own dove with the tender eye?
But there rings on a sudden a passionate cry,
There is some one dying or dead,
And a sullen thunder is roll'd;
For a tumult shakes the city,
And I wake, my dream is fled;
In the shuddering dawn, behold,
Without knowledge, without pity,
By the curtains of my bed
That abiding phantom cold.

ALFRED, LORD TENNYSON

Get thee hence, nor come again,
Mix not memory with doubt,
Pass, thou deathlike type of pain,
Pass and cease to move about!
'Tis the blot upon the brain
That *will* show itself without.

Then I rise, the eavedrops fall,
And the yellow vapours choke
The great city sounding wide;
The day comes, a dull red ball
Wrapt in drifts of lurid smoke
On the misty river-tide.

Thro' the hubbub of the market
I steal, a wasted frame,
It crosses here, it crosses there,
Thro' all that crowd confused and loud,
The shadow still the same;
And on my heavy eyelids
My anguish hangs like shame.

Alas for her that met me,
That heard me softly call,
Came glimmering thro' the laurels
At the quiet evenfall,
In the garden by the turrets
Of the old manorial hall.

Would the happy spirit descend,
From the realms of light and song,
In the chamber or the street,
As she looks among the blest,
Should I fear to greet my friend
Or to say, "Forgive the wrong,"
Or to ask her, "Take me, sweet,
To the regions of thy rest"?

But the broad light glares and beats,
And the shadow flits and fleets
And will not let me be;
And I loathe the squares and streets,

And the faces that one meets,
Hearts with no love for me:
Always I long to creep
Into some still cavern deep,
There to weep, and weep, and weep
My whole soul out to thee.

   .   .   .   .

THE BROOK

I come from haunts of coot and hern,
   I make a sudden sally
And sparkle out among the fern,
   To bicker down a valley.

By thirty hills I hurry down,
   Or slip between the ridges,
By twenty thorps, a little town,
   And half a hundred bridges.

Till last by Philip's farm I flow
   To join the brimming river,
For men may come and men may go,
   But I go on for ever.

I chatter over stony ways,
   In little sharps and trebles,
I bubble into eddying bays,
   I babble on the pebbles.

With many a curve my banks I fret
   By many a field and fallow,
And many a fairy foreland set
   With willow-weed and mallow.

I chatter, chatter, as I flow
   To join the brimming river,
For men may come and men may go,
   But I go on for ever.

I wind about, and in and out,
  With here a blossom sailing,
And here and there a lusty trout,
  And here and there a grayling,

And here and there a foamy flake
  Upon me, as I travel
With many a silvery waterbreak
  Above the golden gravel,

And draw them all along, and flow
  To join the brimming river,
For men may come and men may go,
  But I go on for ever.

.   .   .   .

I steal by lawns and grassy plots,
  I slide by hazel covers;
I move the sweet forget-me-nots
  That grow for happy lovers.

I slip, I slide, I gloom, I glance,
  Among my skimming swallows;
I make the netted sunbeam dance
  Against my sandy shallows.

I murmur under moon and stars
  In brambly wildernesses;
I linger by my shingly bars;
  I loiter round my cresses;

And out again I curve and flow
  To join the brimming river,
For men may come and men may go,
  But I go on for ever.

.   .   .   .

TITHONUS

The woods decay, the woods decay and fall,
The vapours weep their burden to the ground,
Man comes and tills the field and lies beneath,

829

And after many a summer dies the swan.
Me only cruel immortality
Consumes: I wither slowly in thine arms,
Here at the quiet limit of the world,
A white-hair'd shadow roaming like a dream
The ever silent spaces of the East,
Far-folded mists, and gleaming halls of morn.

Alas! for this grey shadow, once a man—
So glorious in his beauty and thy choice,
Who madest him thy chosen, that he seem'd
To his great heart none other than a God!
I ask'd thee, "Give me immortality."
Then didst thou grant mine asking with a smile,
Like wealthy men who care not how they give.
But thy strong Hours indignant work'd their wills,
And beat me down and marr'd and wasted me,
And tho' they could not end me, left me maim'd
To dwell in presence of immortal youth,
Immortal age beside immortal youth,
And all I was, in ashes. Can thy love,
Thy beauty, make amends, tho' even now,
Close over us, the silver star, thy guide,
Shines in those tremulous eyes that fill with tears
To hear me? Let me go: take back thy gift:
Why should a man desire in any way
To vary from the kindly race of men,
Or pass beyond the goal of ordinance
Where all should pause, as is most meet for all?

A soft air fans the cloud apart; there comes
A glimpse of that dark world where I was born.
Once more the old mysterious glimmer steals
From thy pure brows, and from thy shoulders pure,
And bosom beating with a heart renew'd.
Thy cheek begins to redden thro' the gloom,
Thy sweet eyes brighten slowly close to mine,
Ere yet they blind the stars, and the wild team
Which love thee, yearning for thy yoke, arise,
And shake the darkness from their loosen'd manes,
And beat the twilight into flakes of fire.

830

Lo! ever thus thou growest beautiful
In silence, then before thine answer given
Departest, and thy tears are on my cheek.

Why wilt thou ever scare me with thy tears,
And make me tremble lest a saying learnt,
In days far-off, on that dark earth, be true?
"The Gods themselves cannot recall their gifts."

Ay me! ay me! with what another heart
In days far-off, and with what other eyes
I used to watch—if I be he that watch'd—
The lucid outline forming round thee; saw
The dim curls kindle into sunny rings;
Changed with thy mystic change, and felt my blood
Glow with the glow that slowly crimson'd all
Thy presence and thy portals, while I lay,
Mouth, forehead, eyelids, growing dewy-warm
With kisses balmier than half-opening buds
Of April, and could hear the lips that kiss'd
Whispering I knew not what of wild and sweet,
Like that strange song I heard Apollo sing,
While Ilion like a mist rose into towers.

Yet hold me not for ever in thine East:
How can my nature longer mix with thine?
Coldly thy rosy shadows bathe me, cold
Are all thy lights, and cold my wrinkled feet
Upon thy glimmering thresholds, when the steam
Floats up from those dim fields about the homes
Of happy men that have the power to die,
And grassy barrows of the happier dead.
Release me, and restore me to the ground;
Thou seest all things, thou wilt see my grave:
Thou wilt renew thy beauty morn by morn;
I earth in earth forget these empty courts,
And thee returning on thy silver wheels.

IN THE VALLEY OF CAUTERETZ

All along the valley, stream that flashest white,
Deepening thy voice with the deepening of the night,

All along the valley, where thy waters flow,
I walk'd with one I loved two and thirty years ago.
All along the valley while I walk'd to-day,
The two and thirty years were a mist that rolls away;
For all along the valley, down thy rocky bed
Thy living voice to me was as the voice of the dead,
And all along the valley, by rock and cave and tree,
The voice of the dead was a living voice to me.

EARLY SPRING

Once more the Heavenly Power
      Makes all things new,
And domes the red-plow'd hills
      With loving blue;
The blackbirds have their wills,
      The throstles too.

Opens a door in Heaven;
      From skies of glass
A Jacob's ladder falls
      On greening grass,
And o'er the mountain-walls
      Young angels pass.

Before them fleets the shower,
      And burst the buds,
And shine the level lands,
      And flash the floods;
The stars are from their hands
      Flung thro' the woods,

The woods with living airs
      How softly fann'd,
Light airs from where the deep,
      All down the sand,
Is breathing in his sleep,
      Heard by the land.

832

O follow, leaping blood,
    The season's lure!
O heart, look down and up,
    Serene, secure,
Warm as the crocus cup,
    Like snow-drops, pure!

Past, Future glimpse and fade
    Thro' some slight spell,
Some gleam from yonder vale,
    Some far blue fell,
And sympathies, how frail,
    In sound and smell!

Till at thy chuckled note,
    Thou twinkling bird,
The fairy fancies range,
    And, lightly stirred,
Ring little bells of change
    From word to word.

For now the Heavenly Power
    Makes all things new,
And thaws the cold, and fills
    The flower with dew;
The blackbirds have their wills,
    The poets too.

CROSSING THE BAR

Sunset and evening star,
    And one clear call for me!
And may there be no moaning of the bar,
    When I put out to sea,

But such a tide as moving seems asleep,
    Too full for sound and foam,
When that which drew from out the boundless deep
    Turns again home.

833

Twilight and evening bell,
    And after that the dark!
And may there be no sadness of farewell,
    When I embark;

For tho' from out our bourne of Time and Place
    The flood may bear me far,
I hope to see my Pilot face to face.
    When I have crost the bar.

Oliver Wendell Holmes

THE VOICELESS

We count the broken lyres that rest
    Where the sweet wailing singers slumber,
But o'er their silent sister's breast
    The wild-flowers who will stoop to number?
A few can touch the magic string,
    And noisy Fame is proud to win them:—
Alas for those that never sing,
    But die with all their music in them!

Nay, grieve not for the dead alone
    Whose song has told their hearts' sad story,—
Weep for the voiceless, who have known
    The cross without the crown of glory!
Not where Leucadian breezes sweep
    O'er Sappho's memory-haunted billow,
But where the glistening night-dews weep
    On nameless sorrow's churchyard pillow.

O hearts that break and give no sign
    Save whitening lip and fading tresses,
Till Death pours out his cordial wine
    Slow-dropped from Misery's crushing presses,—
If singing breath or echoing chord
    To every hidden pang were given,
What endless melodies were poured,
    As sad as earth, as sweet as heaven!

OLIVER WENDELL HOLMES

OLD IRONSIDES

(September 14, 1830)

Ay, tear her tattered ensign down!
  Long has it waved on high,
And many an eye has danced to see
  That banner in the sky;
Beneath it rung the battle shout,
  And burst the cannon's roar;—
The meteor of the ocean air
  Shall sweep the clouds no more.

Her deck, once red with heroes' blood,
  Where knelt the vanquished foe,
When winds were hurrying o'er the flood,
  And waves were white below,
No more shall feel the victor's tread,
  Or know the conquered knee;—
The harpies of the shore shall pluck
  The eagle of the sea!

Oh, better that her shattered hulk
  Should sink beneath the wave;
Her thunders shook the mighty deep,
  And there should be her grave;
Nail to the mast her holy flag,
  Set every threadbare sail,
And give her to the god of storms,
  The lightning and the gale!

THE CHAMBERED NAUTILUS

This is the ship of pearl, which, poets feign,
  Sails the unshadowed main,—
  The venturous bark that flings
On the sweet summer wind its purpled wings
In gulfs enchanted, where the Siren sings,
  And coral reefs lie bare,
Where the cold sea-maids rise to sun their streaming hair.

Its webs of living gauze no more unfurl;
　　Wrecked is the ship of pearl!
　　And every chambered cell,
Where its dim dreaming life was wont to dwell,
As the frail tenant shaped his growing shell,
　　Before thee lies revealed,—
Its irised ceiling rent, its sunless crypt unsealed!

Year after year beheld the silent toil
　　That spread his lustrous coil;
　　Still, as the spiral grew,
He left the past year's dwelling for the new,
Stole with soft step its shining archway through,
　　Built up its idle door,
Stretched in his last-found home, and knew the old no more.

Thanks for the heavenly message brought by thee,
　　Child of the wandering sea,
　　Cast from her lap, forlorn!
From thy dead lips a clearer note is born
Than ever Triton blew from wreathèd horn!
　　While on mine ear it rings,
Through the deep caves of thought I hear a voice that sings—

Build thee more stately mansions, O my soul,
　　As the swift seasons roll!
　　Leave thy low-vaulted past!
Let each new temple, nobler than the last,
Shut thee from heaven with a dome more vast,
　　Till thou at length art free,
Leaving thine outgrown shell by life's unresting sea!

L'INCONNUE

　　Is thy name Mary, maiden fair?
　　　Such should, methinks, its music be;
　　The sweetest name that mortals bear
　　　Were best befitting thee;
　　And she to whom it once was given,
　　　Was half of earth and half of heaven.

836

SIR FRANCIS DOYLE

I hear thy voice, I see thy smile,
   I look upon thy folded hair;
Ah! while we dream not they beguile,
   Our hearts are in the snare;
And she who chains a wild bird's wing
Must start not if her captive sing.

So, lady, take the leaf that falls,
   To all but thee unseen, unknown;
When evening shades thy silent walls,
   Then read it all alone;
In stillness read, in darkness seal,
Forget, despise, but not reveal!

Sir Francis Doyle

THE PRIVATE OF THE BUFFS

Last night, among his fellow roughs,
   He jested, quaffed, and swore,
A drunken private of the Buffs,
   Who never looked before.
To-day, beneath the foeman's frown,
   He stands in Elgin's place,
Ambassador from Britain's crown,
   And type of all her race.

Poor, reckless, rude, low-born, untaught,
   Bewildered, and alone,
A heart, with English instinct fraught,
   He yet can call his own.
Aye, tear his body limb from limb,
   Bring cord, or axe, or flame:
He only knows, that not through him
   Shall England come to shame.

Far Kentish hop-fields round him seem'd,
   Like dreams, to come and go;
Bright leagues of cherry-blossom gleam'd,
   One sheet of living snow;

837

The smoke, above his father's door,
　　In grey soft eddyings hung:
Must he then watch it rise no more,
　　Doom'd by himself so young?

Yes, honour calls!—with strength like steel
　　He put the vision by.
Let dusky Indians whine and kneel;
　　An English lad must die.
And thus, with eyes that would not shrink,
　　With knee to man unbent,
Unfaltering on its dreadful brink,
　　To his red grave he went.

Vain, mightiest fleets of iron framed;
　　Vain, those all-shattering guns;
Unless proud England keep, untamed,
　　The strong heart of her sons.
So, let his name through Europe ring—
　　A man of mean estate,
Who died, as firm as Sparta's King,
　　Because his soul was great.

William Makepeace Thackeray

AT THE CHURCH GATE

Although I enter not,
Yet round about the spot
　　Ofttimes I hover;
And near the sacred gate,
With longing eyes I wait,
　　Expectant of her.

The Minster bell tolls out
Above the city's rout,
　　And noise and humming;
They've hushed the Minster bell:
The organ 'gins to swell;
　　She's coming, she's coming!

CHARLES DICKENS

My lady comes at last,
Timid, and stepping fast
    And hastening hither,
With modest eyes downcast;
She comes—she's here—she's past!
    May heaven go with her!

Kneel undisturbed, fair Saint!
Pour out your praise or plaint
    Meekly and duly;
I will not enter there,
To sully your pure prayer
    With thoughts unruly.

But suffer me to pace
Round the forbidden place,
    Lingering a minute,
Like outcast spirits, who wait,
And see, through heaven's gate,
    Angels within it.

Charles Dickens

THE IVY GREEN

Oh, a dainty plant is the Ivy green,
That creepeth o'er ruins old!
Of right choice food are his meals I ween,
In his cell so lone and cold.
The wall must be crumbled, the stone decayed,
To pleasure his dainty whim:
And the mouldering dust that years have made
Is a merry meal for him.
    Creeping where no life is seen,
    A rare old plant is the Ivy green.

Fast he stealeth on, though he wears no wings,
And a staunch old heart has he.
How closely he twineth, how tight he clings
To his friend the huge Oak Tree!

839

And slyly he traileth along the ground,
And his leaves he gently waves,
As he joyously hugs and crawleth round
The rich mould of dead men's graves.
    Creeping where grim death has been,
    A rare old plant is the Ivy green.

Whole ages have fled and their works decayed,
And nations have scattered been;
But the stout old Ivy shall never fade,
From its hale and hearty green.
The brave old plant in its lonely days,
Shall fatten upon the past:
For the stateliest building man can raise,
Is the Ivy's food at last.
    Creeping on where time has been,
    A rare old plant is the Ivy green.
              —PICKWICK PAPERS.

Robert Browning

ROBERT BROWNING

There is delight in singing, though none hear
Beside the singer; and there is delight
In praising, though the praiser sit alone
And see the praised far off him, far above.
Shakespeare is not our poet, but the world's,
Therefore on him no speech! and brief for thee,
Browning! Since Chaucer was alive and hale,
No man hath walked along our roads with step
So active, so inquiring eye, or tongue
So varied in discourse. But warmer climes
Give brighter plumage, stronger wing: the breeze
Of Alpine heights thou playest with, borne on
Beyond Sorrento and Amalfi, where
The Siren waits thee, singing song for song.
          —WALTER SAVAGE LANDOR.

840

ROBERT BROWNING

PIPPA PASSES

.   .   .   .   o

The year's at the spring
And day's at the morn;
Morning's at seven;
The hillside's dew-pearled;
The lark's on the wing;
The snail's on the thorn:
God's in his heaven—
All's right with the world!

.   .   .   .   .

THE LOST LEADER

Just for a handful of silver he left us,
  Just for a riband to stick in his coat—
Found the one gift of which fortune bereft us,
  Lost all the others she lets us devote;
They, with the gold to give, doled him out silver,
  So much was theirs who so little allowed:
How all our copper had gone for his service!
  Rags—were they purple, his heart had been proud!
We that had loved him so, followed him, honoured him,
  Lived in his mild and magnificent eye,
Learned his great language, caught his clear accents,
  Made him our pattern to live and to die!
Shakespeare was of us, Milton was for us,
  Burns, Shelley, were with us,—they watch from their
    graves!
He alone breaks from the van and the freemen,
  —He alone sinks to the rear and the slaves!
We shall march prospering,—not through his presence;
  Songs may inspirit us,—not from his lyre;
Deeds will be done,—while he boasts his quiescence,
  Still bidding crouch whom the rest bade aspire:
Blot out his name, then, record one lost soul more,
  One task more declined, one more footpath untrod,
One more devils'-triumph and sorrow for angels,
  One wrong more to man, one more insult to God!

841

Life's night begins: let him never come back to us!
  There would be doubt, hesitation and pain,
Forced praise on our part—the glimmer of twilight,
  Never glad confident morning again!
Best fight on well, for we taught him—strike gallantly,
  Menace our heart ere we master his own;
Then let him receive the new knowledge and wait us,
  Pardoned in heaven, the first by the throne!

THE FLOWER'S NAME

Down this side of the gravel-walk
  She went while her robe's edge brushed the box:
And here she paused in her gracious talk
  To point me a moth on the milk-white phlox.
Roses, ranged in valiant row,
  I will never think that she passed you by!
She loves you, noble roses, I know;
  But yonder, see, where the rock-plants lie!

This flower she stopped at, finger on lip,
  Stooped over, in doubt, as settling its claim;
Till she gave me, with pride to make no slip,
  Its soft meandering Spanish name:
What a name! Was it love or praise?
  Speech half-asleep or song half-awake?
I must learn Spanish, one of these days,
  Only for that slow sweet name's sake.

Flower, you Spaniard, look that you grow not,
  Stay as you are and be loved forever!
Bud, if I kiss you 'tis that you blow not,
  Mind, the shut pink mouth opens never!
For while it pouts, her fingers wrestle,
  Twinkling the audacious leaves between,
Till round they turn and down they nestle—
  Is not the dear mark still to be seen?

ROBERT BROWNING

MEETING AT NIGHT

The grey sea and the long black land;
And the yellow half-moon large and low;
And the startled little waves that leap
In fiery ringlets from their sleep,
As I gain the cove with pushing prow,
And quench its speed i' the slushy sand.

Then a mile of warm sea-scented beach;
Three fields to cross till a farm appears;
A tap at the pane, the quick sharp scratch
And blue spurt of a lighted match,
And a voice less loud, through its joys and fears,
Than the two hearts beating each to each!

NAY BUT YOU

Nay but you, who do not love her,
  Is she not pure gold, my mistress?
Holds earth aught —speak truth—above her?
  Aught like this tress, see, and this tress,
And this last fairest tress of all,
So fair, see, ere I let it fall?

Because you spend your lives in praising;
  To praise, you search the wide world over:
Then why not witness, calmly gazing,
  If earth holds aught—speak truth—above her?
Above this tress, and this, I touch
But cannot praise, I love so much!

A WOMAN'S LAST WORD

Let's contend no more, Love,
  Strive nor weep:
All be as before, Love,
  —Only sleep!

What so wild as words are?
  I and thou
In debate, as birds are,
  Hawk on bough!

See the creature stalking
  While we speak!
Hush and hide the talking,
  Cheek on cheek!

What so false as truth is,
  False to thee?
Where the serpent's tooth is
  Shun the tree—

Where the apple reddens
  Never pry—
Lest we lose our Edens,
  Eve and I.

Be a god and hold me
  With a charm!
Be a man and fold me
  With thine arm!

Teach me, only teach, Love!
  As I ought
I will speak thy speech, Love,
  Think thy thought—

Meet, if thou require it,
  Both demands,
Laying flesh and spirit
  In thy hands.

That shall be to-morrow,
  Not to-night:
I must bury sorrow
  Out of sight:

—Must a little weep, Love,
  (Foolish me!)
And so fall asleep, Love,
  Loved by thee.

ROBERT BROWNING

A TOCCATA OF GALUPPI'S

O Galuppi, Baldassare, this is very sad to find!
I can hardly misconceive you; it would prove me deaf and
    blind;
But although I take your meaning, 'tis with such a heavy
    mind!

Here you come with your old music, and here's all the good
    it brings.
What, they lived once thus at Venice where the merchants
    were the kings,
Where St. Mark's is, where the Doges used to wed the sea
    with rings?

Ay, because the sea's the street there; and 'tis arched by . . .
    what you call
. . . Shylock's bridge with houses on it, where they kept the
    carnival:
I was never out of England—it's as if I saw it all.

Did young people take their pleasure when the sea was warm
    in May?
Balls and masks begun at midnight, burning ever to mid-day,
When they made up fresh adventures for the morrow, do you
    say?

Was a lady such a lady, cheeks so round and lips so red,—
On her neck the small face buoyant, like a bell-flower on its
    bed,
O'er the breast's superb abundance where a man might base
    his head?

Well, and it was graceful of them—they'd break talk off
    and afford
—She, to bite her mask's black velvet—he, to finger on his
    sword,
While you sat and played Toccatas, stately at the clavichord?

What? Those lesser thirds so plaintive, sixths diminished, sigh on sigh,

Told them something? Those suspensions, those solutions—"Must we die?"

Those commiserating sevenths—"Life might last! we can but try!"

"Were you happy?"—"Yes."—"And are you still as happy?"—"Yes. And you?"

—"Then, more kisses!"—"Did _I_ stop them, when a million seemed so few?"

Hark, the dominant's persistence till it must be answered to!

So, an octave struck the answer. Oh, they praised you, I dare say!

"Brave Galuppi! that was music! good alike at grave and gay!

I can always leave off talking when I hear a master play!"

Then they left you for their pleasure: till in due time, one by one,

Some with lives that came to nothing, some with deeds as well undone,

Death stepped tacitly and took them where they never see the sun.

But when I sit down to reason, think to take my stand nor swerve,

While I triumph o'er a secret wrung from nature's close reserve,

In you come with your cold music till I creep through every nerve.

Yes, you, like a ghostly cricket, creaking where a house was burned:

"Dust and ashes, dead and done with, Venice spent what Venice earned.

The soul, doubtless, is immortal—where a soul can be discerned.

846

"Yours for instance: you know physics, something of geology,
Mathematics are your pastime; souls shall rise in their degree;
Butterflies may dread extinction,—you'll not die, it cannot be!

"As for Venice and her people, merely born to bloom and drop,
Here on earth they bore their fruitage, mirth and folly were
    the crop:
What of soul was left, I wonder, when the kissing had to
    stop?

"Dust and ashes!" So you creak it, and I want the heart to
    scold.
Dear dead women, with such hair, too— what's become of all
    the gold
Used to hang and brush their bosoms? I feel chilly and grown
    old.

HOME-THOUGHTS, FROM ABROAD

Oh, to be in England
Now that April's there,
And whoever wakes in England
Sees, some morning, unaware,
That the lowest boughs and the brush-wood sheaf
Round the elm-tree bole are in tiny leaf,
While the chaffinch sings on the orchard bough
In England—now!

And after April, when May follows,
And the whitethroat builds, and all the swallows!
Hark, where my blossomed pear-tree in the hedge
Leans to the field and scatters on the clover
Blossoms and dewdrops—at the bent spray's edge—
That's the wise thrush; he sings each song twice over,
Lest you should think he never could recapture
The first fine careless rapture!
And though the fields look rough with hoary dew,
All will be gay when noontide wakes anew
The buttercups, the little children's dower
—Far brighter than this gaudy melon-flower!

MY STAR

All that I know
   Of a certain star
Is, it can throw
   (Like the angled spar)
Now a dart of red,
   Now a dart of blue;
Till my friends have said
   They would fain see, too,
My star that dartles the red and the blue!
Then it stops like a bird; like a flower, hangs furled:
   They must solace themselves with the Saturn above it.
What matter to me if their star is a world?
   Mine has opened its soul to me; therefore I love it.

MISCONCEPTIONS

This is a spray the Bird clung to,
   Making it blossom with pleasure,
Ere the high tree-top she sprung to,
   Fit for her nest and her treasure.
   Oh, what a hope beyond measure
Was the poor spray's, which the flying feet hung to,—
So to be singled out, built in, and sung to!

This is a heart the Queen leant on,
   Thrilled in a minute erratic,
Ere the true bosom she bent on,
   Meet for love's regal dalmatic.
   Oh, what a fancy ecstatic
Was the poor heart's, ere the wanderer went on—
Love to be saved for it, proffered to, spent on!

MEMORABILIA

Ah, did you once see Shelley plain,
   And did he stop and speak to you,
And did you speak to him again?
   How strange it seems and new!

848

But you were living before that,
    And also you are living after;
And the memory I started at—
    My starting moves your laughter!

I crossed a moor, with a name of its own
    And a certain use in the world no doubt,
Yet a hand's-breadth of it shines alone
    'Mid the blank miles round about:

For there I picked up on the heather,
    And there I put inside my breast
A moulted feather, an eagle-feather!
    Well, I forget the rest.

A BLOT IN THE 'SCUTCHEON

There's a woman like a dew-drop, she's so purer than the
    purest;
And her noble heart's the noblest, yes, and her sure faith's
    the surest:
And her eyes are dark and humid, like the depth on depth
    of lustre
Hid i' the harebell, while her tresses, sunnier than the wild-
    grape cluster,
Gush in golden-tinted plenty down her neck's rose-misted
    marble:
Then her voice's music . . . call it the well's bubbling, the
    bird's warble!

And this woman says, "My days were sunless and my nights
    were moonless,
Parched the pleasant April herbage, and the lark's heart's out-
    break tuneless,
If you loved me not!" And I who—(ah, for words of
    flame!) adore her,
Who am mad to lay my spirit prostrate palpably before her—
I may enter at her portal soon, as now her lattice takes me,
And by noontide as by midnight make her mine, as hers she
    makes me!

THE LAST RIDE TOGETHER

I said—Then, dearest, since 'tis so,
Since now at length my fate I know,
Since nothing all my love avails,
Since all my life seemed meant for, fails,
    Since this was written and needs must be—
My whole heart rises up to bless
Your name in pride and thankfulness!
Take back the hope you gave,—I claim
Only a memory of the same,
—And this beside, if you will not blame,
    Your leave for one more last ride with me.

My mistress bent that brow of hers;
Those deep dark eyes where pride demurs
When pity would be softening through,
Fixed me a breathing-while or two
    With life or death in the balance: right!
The blood replenished me again;
My last thought was at least not vain:
I and my mistress, side by side
Shall be together, breathe and ride,
So, one day more am I deified,
    Who knows but the world may end to-night?

Hush! if you saw some western cloud
All billowy-bosomed, over-bowed
By many benedictions—sun's
And moon's and evening-star's at once—
    And so, you, looking and loving best,
Conscious grew, your passion drew
Cloud, sunset, moonrise, star-shine too,
Down on you, near and yet more near,
Till flesh must fade for heaven was here!—
Thus leant she and lingered—joy and fear!
    Thus lay she a moment on my breast.

ROBERT BROWNING

Then we began to ride. My soul
Smoothed itself out, a long-cramped scroll
Freshening and fluttering in the wind.
Past hopes already lay behind.
    What need to strive with a life awry?
Had I said that, had I done this,
So might I gain, so might I miss.
Might she have loved me? just as well
She might have hated, who can tell!
Where had I been now if the worst befell?
    And here we are riding, she and I.

Fail I alone, in words and deeds?
Why, all men strive, and who succeeds?
We rode; it seemed my spirit flew,
Saw other regions, cities new,
    As the world rushed by on either side.
I thought,—All labor, yet no less
Bear up beneath their unsuccess.
Look at the end of work, contrast
The petty done, the undone vast,
This present of theirs with the hopeful past!
    I hoped she would love me; here we ride.

What hand and brain went ever paired?
What heart alike conceived and dared?
What act proved all its thought had been?
What will but felt the fleshly screen?
    We ride and I see her bosom heave.
There's many a crown for who can reach.
Ten lines, a statesman's life in each!
The flag stuck on a heap of bones,
A soldier's doing! what atones?
They scratch his name on the Abbey-stones.
    My riding is better, by their leave.

What does it all mean, poet? Well,
Your brains beat into rhythm, you tell
What we felt only; you expressed
You hold things beautiful the best,
    And place them in rhyme so, side by side.

'Tis something, nay 'tis much: but then,
Have you yourself what's best for men?
Are you—poor, sick, old ere your time—
Nearer one whit your own sublime
Than we who never have turned a rhyme?
    Sing, riding's a joy! For me, I ride.

And you, great sculptor—so, you gave
A score of years to Art, her slave,
And that's your Venus, whence we turn
To yonder girl that fords the burn!
    You acquiesce, and shall I repine?
What, man of music, you grown grey
With notes and nothing else to say,
Is this your sole praise from a friend,
"Greatly his opera's strains intend,
But in music we know how fashions end!"
    I gave my youth; but we ride, in fine.

Who knows what's fit for us? Had fate
Proposed bliss here should sublimate
My being—had I signed the bond—
Still one must lead some life beyond,
    Have a bliss to die with, dim-descried.
This foot once planted on the goal,
This glory-garland round my soul,
Could I descry such? Try and test!
I sink back shuddering from the quest.
Earth being so good, would heaven seem best?
    Now, heaven and she are beyond this ride.

And yet—she has not spoke so long!
What if heaven be that, fair and strong
At life's best, with our eyes upturned
Whither life's flower is first discerned,
    We, fixed so, ever should so abide?
What if we still ride on, we two,
With life forever old yet new,
Changed not in kind but in degree,
The instant made eternity,—
And heaven just prove that I and she
    Ride, ride together, forever ride?

ROBERT BROWNING

A GRAMMARIAN'S FUNERAL

Let us begin and carry up this corpse,
 Singing together.
Leave we the common crofts, the vulgar thorpes
 Each in its tether
Sleeping safe on the bosom of the plain,
 Cared-for till cock-crow:
Look out if yonder be not day again
 Rimming 'the rock-row!
That's the appropriate country; there, man's thought,
 Rarer, intenser,
Self-gathered for an outbreak, as it ought,
 Chafes in the censer.
Leave we the unlettered plain its herd and crop;
 Seek we sepulture
On a tall mountain, citied to the top,
 Crowded with culture!
All the peaks soar, but one the rest excels;
 Clouds overcome it;
No! yonder sparkle is the citadel's
 Circling its summit.
Thither our path lies; wind we up the heights;
 Wait ye the warning?
Our low life was the level's and the night's;
 He's for the morning.
Step to a tune, square chests, erect each head,
 'Ware the beholders!
This is our master, famous, calm and dead,
 Borne on our shoulders.

Sleep, crop and herd! sleep, darkling thorpe and croft,
 Safe from the weather!
He, whom we convoy to his grave aloft,
 Singing together,
He was a man born with thy face and throat,
 Lyric Apollo!
Long he lived nameless: how should Spring take note
 Winter would follow?

Till lo, the little touch, and youth was gone!
    Cramped and diminished,
Moaned he, "New measures, other feet anon!
    My dance is finished"?
No, that's the world's way: (keep the mountain-side,
    Make for the city!)
He knew the signal, and stepped on with pride
    Over men's pity;
Left play for work, and grappled with the world
    Bent on escaping:
"What's in the scroll," quoth he, "thou keepest furled?
    Show me their shaping,
Theirs who most studied man, the bard and sage,—
    Give!"—So, he gowned him,
Straight got by heart that book to its last page:
    Learned, we found him.
Yea, but we found him bald too, eyes like lead,
    Accents uncertain:
"Time to taste life," another would have said,
    "Up with the curtain!"
This man said rather, "Actual life comes next?
    Patience a moment!
Grant I have mastered learning's crabbed text,
    Still there's the comment.
Let me know all! Prate not of most or least,
    Painful or easy!
Even to the crumbs I'd fain eat up the feast,
    Ay, nor feel queasy."
Oh, such a life as he resolved to live,
    When he had learned it,
When he had gathered all books had to give!
    Sooner, he spurned it.
Image the whole, then execute the parts—
    Fancy the fabric
Quite, ere you build, ere steel strike fire from quartz,
    Ere mortar dab brick!

(Here's the town-gate reached: there's the market-place
    Gaping before us.)
Yea, this in him was the peculiar grace
    (Hearten our chorus!)

That before living he'd learn how to live—
    No end to learning:
Earn the means first—God surely will contrive
    Use for our earning.
Others mistrust and say, "But time escapes:
    Live now or never!"
He said, "What's time? Leave Now for dogs and apes!
    Man has Forever."
Back to his book then: deeper drooped his head:
    Calculus racked him:
Leaden before, his eyes grew dross of lead:
    Tussis attacked him.
"Now, master, take a little rest!"—not he!
    (Caution redoubled,
Step two abreast, the way winds narrowly!)
    Not a whit troubled,
Back to his studies, fresher than at first,
    Fierce as a dragon
He (soul-hydroptic with a sacred thirst)
    Sucked at the flagon.
Oh, if we draw a circle premature,
    Heedless of far gain,
Greedy for quick returns of profit, sure
    Bad is our bargain!
Was it not great? did not he throw on God,
    (He loves the burthen)—
God's task to make the heavenly period
    Perfect the earthen?
Did not he magnify the mind, show clear
    Just what it all meant?
He would not discount life, as fools do here,
    Paid by instalment.
He ventured neck or nothing—heaven's success
    Found, or earth's failure:
"Wilt thou trust death or not?" He answered "Yes!
    Hence with life's pale lure!"
That low man seeks a little thing to do,
    Sees it and does it:
This high man, with a great thing to pursue,
    Dies ere he knows it.

855

That low man goes on adding one to one,
 His hundred's soon hit:
This high man, aiming at a million,
 Misses an unit.
That, has the world here—should he need the next,
 Let the world mind him!
This, throws himself on God, and unperplexed
 Seeking shall find him.
So, with the throttling hands of death at strife,
 Ground he at grammar;
Still, through the rattle, parts of speech were rife:
 While he could stammer
He settled *Hoti's* business—let it be!—
 Properly based *Oun*—
Gave us the doctrine of the enclitic *De*,
 Dead from the waist down.
Well, here's the platform, here's the proper place:
 Hail to your purlieus,
All ye highfliers of the feathered race,
 Swallows and curlews!
Here's the top-peak; the multitude below
 Live, for they can, there:
This man decided not to Live but Know—
 Bury this man there?
Here—here's his place, where meteors shoot, clouds form,
 Lightnings are loosened,
Stars come and go! Let joy break with the storm.
 Peace let the dew send!
Lofty designs must close in like effects:
 Loftily lying,
Leave him—still loftier than the world suspects,
 Living and dying.

ONE WORD MORE

There they are, my fifty men and women
Naming me the fifty poems finished!
Take them, Love, the book and me together:
Where the heart lies, let the brain lie also.
856

ROBERT BROWNING

Rafael made a century of sonnets,
Made and wrote them in a certain volume
Dinted with the silver-pointed pencil
Else he only used to draw Madonnas:
These, the world might view—but one, the volume.
Who that one, you ask? Your heart instructs you.
Did she live and love it all her lifetime?
Did she drop, his lady of the sonnets,
Die, and let it drop beside her pillow
Where it lay in place of Rafael's glory,
Rafael's cheek so duteous and so loving—
Cheek, the world was wont to hail a painter's,
Rafael's cheek, her love had turned a poet's?
You and I would rather read that volume,
(Taken to his beating bosom by it)
Lean and list the bosom-beats of Rafael,
Would we not? than wonder at Madonnas—

. . . .

Dante once prepared to paint an angel:
Whom to please? You whisper "Beatrice."
While he mused and traced it and retraced it,
(Peradventure with a pen corroded
Still by drops of that hot ink he dipped for,
When, his left-hand i' the hair o' the wicked,
Back he held the brow and pricked its stigma,
Bit into the live man's flesh for parchment,
Loosed him, laughed to see the writing rankle,
Let the wretch go festering through Florence)—
Dante, who loved well because he hated,
Hated wickedness that hinders loving,
Dante standing, studying his angel,—
In there broke the folk of his Inferno.

. . . .

You and I would rather see that angel,
Painted by the tenderness of Dante,
Would we not?—then read a fresh Inferno.

. . . .

God be thanked, the meanest of his creatures
Boasts two soul-sides, one to face the world with,
One to show a woman when he loves her!

This I say of me, but think of you, Love!
This to you—yourself my moon of poets!
Ah, but that's the world's side, there's the wonder,
Thus they see you, praise you, think they know you!
There, in turn I stand with them and praise you—
Out of my own self, I dare to phrase it.
But the best is when I glide from out them,
Cross a step or two of dubious twilight,
Come out on the other side, the novel
Silent silver lights and darks undreamed of,
Where I hush and bless myself with silence.

Oh, their Rafael of the dear Madonnas,
Oh, their Dante of the dread Inferno,
Wrote one song—and in my brain I sing it,
Drew one angel—borne, see, on my bosom!

ABT VOGLER

Would that the structure brave, the manifold music I build,
    Bidding my organ obey, calling its keys to their work,
Claiming each slave of the sound, at a touch, as when Solomon
        willed
    Armies of angels that soar, legions of demons that lurk,
Man, brute, reptile, fly,—alien of end and of aim,
    Adverse, each from the other heaven-high, hell-deep re-
        moved,—
Should rush into sight at once as he named the ineffable Name,
    And pile him a palace straight, to pleasure the princess he
        loved!

        .   .   .   .

All through my keys that gave their sounds to a wish of my
        soul,
    All through my soul that praised as its wish flowed visibly
        forth,
All through music and me! For think, had I painted the
        whole,
    Why, there it had stood, to see, nor the process so wonder-
        worth:

858

Had I written the same, made verse—still, effect proceeds
from cause,
 Ye know why the forms are fair, ye hear how the tale is
told;
It is all triumphant art, but art in obedience to laws,
 Painter and poet are proud in the artist-list enrolled:—

But here is the finger of God, a flash of the will that can,
 Existent behind all laws, that made them and, lo, they are!
And I know not if, save in this, such gift be allowed to man,
 That out of three sounds he frame, not a fourth sound, but
a star.
Consider it well: each tone of our scale in itself is naught:
 It is everywhere in the world—loud, soft, and all is said:
Give it to me to use! I mix it with two in my thought:
 And there! Ye have heard and seen: consider and bow
the head!

 . . . .

All we have willed or hoped or dreamed of good shall exist;
 Not its semblance, but itself; no beauty, nor good, nor
power
Whose voice has gone forth, but each survives for the
melodist
When eternity affirms the conception of an hour.
The high that proved too high, the heroic for earth too hard,
 The passion that left the ground to lose itself in the sky,
Are music sent up to God by the lover and the bard;
 Enough that he heard it once: we shall hear it by and by.

 . . . .

Well, it is earth with me; silence resumes her reign:
 I will be patient and proud, and soberly acquiesce.
Give me the keys. I feel for the common chord again,
 Sliding by semitones till I sink to the minor,—yes,
And I blunt it into a ninth, and I stand on alien ground,
 Surveying awhile the heights I rolled from into the deep;
Which, hark, I have dared and done, for my resting-place is
found,
 The C Major of this life: so, now I will try to sleep.

RABBI BEN EZRA

Grow old along with me!
The best is yet to be,
The last of life, for which the first was made:
Our times are in his hand
Who saith, "A whole I planned,
Youth shows but half; trust God: see all, nor be afraid!"

        .   .   .   .

Then, welcome each rebuff
That turns earth's smoothness rough,
Each sting that bids nor sit nor stand but go!
Be our joys three-parts pain!
Strive, and hold cheap the strain;
Learn, nor account the pang; dare, never grudge the throe!

        .   .   .   .

Not on the vulgar mass
Called "work," must sentence pass,
Things done, that took the eye and had the price;
O'er which, from level stand,
The low world laid its hand,
Found straightway to its mind, could value in a trice:

But all, the world's coarse thumb
And finger failed to plumb,
So passed in making up the main account;
All instincts immature,
All purposes unsure,
That weighed not as his work, yet swelled the man's amount:

Thoughts hardly to be packed
Into a narrow act,
Fancies that broke through language and escaped;
All I could never be,
All, men ignored in me,
This, I was worth to God, whose wheel the pitcher shaped.

        .   .   .   .

So, take and use thy work:
Amend what flaws may lurk,
    860

What strain o' the stuff, what warpings past the aim!
My times be in thy hand!
Perfect the cup as planned!
Let age approve of youth, and death complete the same!

PROSPICE

Fear death?—to feel the fog in my throat,
   The mist in my face,
When the snows begin, and the blasts denote
   I am nearing the place,
The power of the night, the press of the storm,
   The post of the foe;
Where he stands, the Arch Fear in a visible form,
   Yet the strong man must go:
For the journey is done and the summit attained,
   And the barriers fall,
Though a battle's to fight ere the guerdon be gained,
   The reward of it all.
I was ever a fighter, so—one fight more,
   The best and the last!
I would hate that death bandaged my eyes, and forbore,
   And bade me creep past.
No! let me taste the whole of it, fare like my peers
   The heroes of old,
Bear the brunt, in a minute pay glad life's arrears
   Of pain, darkness and cold.
For sudden the worst turns the best to the brave,
   The black minute's at end,
And the elements' rage, the fiend-voices that rave,
   Shall dwindle, shall blend,
Shall change, shall become first a peace out of pain,
   Then a light, then thy breast,
O thou soul of my soul! I shall clasp thee again,
   And with God be the rest!

HERVÉ RIEL

On the sea and at the Hogue, sixteen hundred ninety-two,
  Did the English fight the French,—woe to France!
And, the thirty-first of May, helter-skelter through the blue,
Like a crowd of frightened porpoises a shoal of sharks pursue,
  Came crowding ship on ship to Saint Malo on the Rance,
With the English fleet in view.

'Twas the squadron that escaped, with the victor in full chase;
  First and foremost of the drove, in his great ship, Damfre-
    ville;
    Close on him fled, great and small,
    Twenty-two good ships in all;
And they signalled to the place
"Help the winners of a race!
  Get us guidance, give us harbour, take us quick—or, quicker
    still,
  Here's the English can and will!"

Then the pilots of the place put out brisk and leapt on board;
  "Why, what hope or chance have ships like these to pass?"
    laughed they:
"Rocks to starboard, rocks to port, all the passage scarred and
    scored,
Shall the 'Formidable' here with her twelve and eighty guns
  Think to make the river-mouth by the single narrow way,
Trust to enter where 'tis ticklish for a craft of twenty tons,
    And with flow at full beside?
    Now, 'tis slackest ebb of tide.
  Reach the mooring? Rather say,
While rock stands or water runs,
  Not a ship will leave the bay!"

Then was called a council straight.
Brief and bitter the debate:
"Here's the English at our heels; would you have them take
    in tow
All that's left us of the fleet, linked together stern and bow,
  862

ROBERT BROWNING

For a prize to Plymouth Sound?
Better run the ships aground!"
  (Ended Damfreville his speech).
"Not a minute more to wait!
  Let the Captains all and each
  Shove ashore, then blow up, burn the vessels on the beach!
France must undergo her fate.

"Give the word!" But no such word
Was ever spoke or heard;
  For up stood, for out stepped, for in struck amid all these
—A Captain? A Lieutenant? A Mate—first, second, third?
    No such man of mark, and meet
    With his betters to compete!
    But a simple Breton sailor pressed by Tourville for the
      fleet,
A poor coasting-pilot he, Hervé Riel the Croisickese.

And "What mockery or malice have we here?" cries Hervé
      Riel:
  "Are you mad, you Malouins?   Are you cowards, fools, or
      rogues?
Talk to me of rocks and shoals, me who took the soundings,
    tell
On my fingers every bank, every shallow, every swell
  'Twixt the offing here and Grève where the river disem-
      bogues?
Are you bought by English gold?   Is it love the lying's for?
    Morn and eve, night and day,
    Have I piloted your bay,
Entered free and anchored fast at the foot of Solidor.
  Burn the fleet and ruin France?   That were worse than
      fifty Hogues!
    Sirs, they know I speak the truth!   Sirs, believe me there's
      a way!
Only let me lead the line,
  Have the biggest ship to steer,
  Get this 'Formidable' clear,
Make the others follow mine,
And I lead them, most and least, by a passage I know well,

863

Right to Solidor past Grève,
   And there lay them safe and sound;
   And if one ship misbehave,
   —Keel so much as grate the ground,
Why, I've nothing but my life,—here's my head!" cries
   Hervé Riel.

Not a minute more to wait.
"Steer us in, then, small and great!
   Take the helm, lead the line, save the squadron!" cried its
      chief.
Captains, give the sailor place!
   He is Admiral, in brief.
Still the north-wind, by God's grace!
See the noble fellow's face
As the big ship, with a bound,
Clears the entry like a hound,
Keeps the passage as its inch of way were the wide sea's
      profound!
   See, safe through shoal and rock,
   How they follow in a flock,
Not a ship that misbehaves, not a keel that grates the ground,
   Not a spar that comes to grief!
The peril, see, is past,
All are harboured to the last,
And just as Hervé Riel hollas "Anchor!"—sure as fate,
Up the English come—too late!

So, the storm subsides to calm:
   They see the green trees wave
   On the heights o'erlooking Grève.
Hearts that bled are stanched with balm.
"Just our rapture to enhance,
   Let the English rake the bay,
Gnash their teeth and glare askance
   As they cannonade away!
'Neath rampired Solidor pleasant riding on the Rance!"
How hope succeeds despair on each Captain's countenance!
864

Out burst all with one accord
　"This is Paradise for Hell!
　　Let France, let France's King
　　Thank the man that did the thing!"
What a shout, and all one word,
　"Hervé Riel!"
As he stepped in front once more,
　Not a symptom of surprise
　In the frank blue Breton eyes,
Just the same man as before.

Then said Damfreville, "My friend,
I must speak out at the end,
　Though I find the speaking hard.
Praise is deeper than the lips:
You have saved the King his ships,
　You must name your own reward.
'Faith, our sun was near eclipse!
Demand whate'er you will,
France remains your debtor still.
Ask to heart's content and have! or my name's not Damfre-
　　ville."

Then a beam of fun outbroke
On the bearded mouth that spoke,
As the honest heart laughed through
Those frank eyes of Breton blue:
"Since I needs must say my say,
　Since on board the duty's done,
　And from Malo Roads to Croisic Point, what is it but a
　　run?—
Since 'tis ask and have, I may—
　Since the others go ashore—
Come!　A good whole holiday!
　Leave to go and see my wife, whom I call the Belle
　　Aurore!"
That he asked and that he got,—nothing more.

Name and deed alike are lost:
Not a pillar nor a post

In his Croisic keeps alive the feat as it befell;
Not a head in white and black
On a single fishing-smack,
In memory of the man but for whom had gone to wrack
    All that France saved from the fight whence England
        bore the bell.
Go to Paris: rank on rank
    Search the heroes flung pell-mell
On the Louvre, face and flank!
    You shall look long enough ere you come to Hervé Riel.
So, for better and for worse,
Hervé Riel, accept my verse!
In my verse, Hervé Riel, do thou once more
Save the squadron, honour France, love thy wife the Belle
    Aurore!

THE TWO POETS OF CROISIC

Such a starved bank of moss
    Till, that May-morn,
Blue ran the flash across:
    Violets were born!

Sky—what a scowl of cloud
    Till, near and far,
Ray on ray split the shroud:
    Splendid, a star!

World—how it walled about
    Life with disgrace
Till God's own smile came out:
    That was thy face!

NEVER THE TIME AND THE PLACE

Never the time and the place
    And the loved one all together!
This path—how soft to pace!
    This May—what magic weather!
Where is the loved one's face?

In a dream that loved one's face meets mine,
  But the house is narrow, the place is bleak
Where, outside, rain and wind combine
  With a furtive ear, if I strive to speak,
  With a hostile eye at my flushing cheek,
With a malice that marks each word, each sign!
O enemy sly and serpentine,
  Uncoil thee from the waking man!
    Do I hold the Past
    Thus firm and fast
  Yet doubt if the Future hold I can?
This path so soft to pace shall lead
Through the magic of May to herself indeed!
Or narrow if needs the house must be,
Outside are the storms and strangers: we—
Oh, close, safe, warm sleep I and she,
  —I and she!

WHY I AM A LIBERAL

"Why?" Because all I haply can and do,
  All that I am now, all I hope to be,—
  Whence comes it save from fortune setting free
Body and soul the purpose to pursue,
God traced for both? If fetters, not a few,
  Of prejudice, convention, fall from me,
  These shall I bid men—each in his degree
Also God-guided—bear, and gayly, too?

But little do or can the best of us:
  That little is achieved through Liberty.
Who, then, dares hold, emancipated thus,
  His fellow shall continue bound? Not I,
Who live, love, labour freely, nor discuss
  A brother's right to freedom. That is "Why."

EPILOGUE

At the midnight in the silence of the sleep-time,
    When you set your fancies free,
Will they pass to where—by death, fools think, imprisoned—
Low he lies who once so loved you, whom you loved so,
            —Pity me?

Oh to love so, be so loved, yet so mistaken!
    What had I on earth to do
With the slothful, with the mawkish, the unmanly?
Like the aimless, helpless, hopeless, did I drivel
            —Being—who?

One who never turned his back but marched breast forward,
    Never doubted clouds would break,
Never dreamed, though right were worsted, wrong would
        triumph,
Held we fall to rise, are baffled to fight better,
            Sleep to wake.

No, at noonday in the bustle of man's work-time
    Greet the unseen with a cheer!
Bid him forward, breast and back as either should be,
"Strive and thrive!" cry "Speed,—fight on, fare ever
            There as here!"

Aubrey Thomas De Vere

SORROW

Count each affliction, whether light or grave,
    God's messenger sent down to thee; do thou
With courtesy receive him; rise and bow;
And, ere his shadow pass thy threshold, crave
Permission first his heavenly feet to lave;
    Then lay before him all thou hast; allow
    No cloud of passion to usurp thy brow,
Or mar thy hospitality; no wave
868

Of mortal tumult to obliterate
The soul's marmoreal calmness. Grief should be,
Like joy, majestic, equable, sedate;
　Confirming, cleansing, raising, make free;
Strong to consume small troubles; to commend
Great thoughts, grave thoughts, thoughts lasting to the end.

Charles Mackay

LOVE NEW AND OLD

And were they not the happy days
　When Love and I were young,
When earth was robed in heavenly light,
　And all creation sung?
When gazing in my true love's face,
　Through greenwood alleys lone,
I guessed the secrets of her heart,
　By whispers of mine own.

And are they not the happy days
　When Love and I are old,
And silver evening has replaced
　A morn and noon of gold?
Love stood alone mid youthful joy,
　But now by sorrow tried,
It sits and calmly looks to heaven
　With angels at its side.

Henry David Thoreau

INSPIRATION

If with light head erect I sing,
Though all the Muses lend their force,
From my poor love of anything,
The verse is weak and shallow as its source.

869

But if with bended neck I grope
Listening behind me for my wit,
With faith superior to hope,
More anxious to keep back then forward it,—

Making my soul accomplice there
Unto the flame my heart hath lit,
Then will the verse forever wear,—
Time cannot bend the line which God has writ.

I hearing get, who had but ears,
And sight, who had but eyes before;
I moments live, who lived but years,
And truth discern, who knew but learning's lore.

Now chiefly is my natal hour,
And only now my prime of life;
Of manhood's strength it is the flower,
'Tis peace's end, and war's beginning strife.

It comes in summer's broadest noon,
By a gray wall, or some chance place,
Unseasoning time, insulting June,
And vexing day with its presuming face.

I will not doubt the love untold
Which not my worth nor want hath bought,
Which wooed me young, and wooes me old,
And to this evening hath me brought.

SMOKE

Light-winged Smoke, Icarian bird,
Melting thy pinions in thy upward flight,
Lark without song, and messenger of dawn,
Circling above the hamlets as thy nest;
Or else, departing dream, and shadowy form
Of midnight vision, gathering up thy skirts;
By night star-veiling, and by day
Darkening the light and blotting out the sun;
Go thou my incense upward from this hearth,
And ask the gods to pardon this clear flame.

EMILY BRONTË

MY PRAYER

Great God, I ask thee for no meaner pelf
Than that I may not disappoint myself;
That in my action I may soar as high
As I can now discern with this clear eye.

And next in value, which thy kindness lends,
That I may greatly disappoint my friends,
Howe'er they think or hope that it may be,
They may not dream how thou'st distinguished me.

That my weak hand may equal my firm faith,
And my life practise more than my tongue saith;
   That my low conduct may not show,
     Nor my relenting lines,
   That I thy purpose did not know,
     Or overrated thy designs.

Emily Brontë

THE PRISONER

Still let my tyrants know, I am not doom'd to wear
Year after year in gloom and desolate despair;
A messenger of Hope comes every night to me,
And offers for short life, eternal liberty.

He comes with Western winds, with evening's wandering
    airs,
With that clear dusk of heaven that brings the thickest stars:
Winds take a pensive tone, and stars a tender fire,
And visions rise, and change, that kill me with desire.

Desire for nothing known in my maturer years,
When Joy grew mad with awe, at counting future tears:
When, if my spirit's sky was full of flashes warm,
I knew not whence they came, from sun or thunder-storm.

But first, a hush of peace—a soundless calm descends;
The struggle of distress and fierce impatience ends.
Mute music soothes my breast—unutter'd harmony
That I could never dream, till Earth was lost to me.

Then dawns the Invisible; the Unseen its truth reveals;
My outward sense is gone, my inward essence feels;
Its wings are almost free—its home, its harbour found;
Measuring the gulf, it stoops, and dares the final bound.

O dreadful is the check—intense the agony—
When the ear begins to hear, and the eye begins to see;
When the pulse begins to throb—the brain to think again—
The soul to feel the flesh, and the flesh to feel the chain.

Yet I would lose no sting, would wish no torture less;
The more that anguish racks, the earlier it will bless;
And robed in fires of hell, or bright with heavenly shine,
If it but herald Death, the vision is divine.

LAST LINES

No coward soul is mine,
No trembler in the world's storm-troubled sphere:
I see Heaven's glories shine,
And faith shines equal, arming me from fear.

O God within my breast,
Almighty, ever-present Deity!
Life—that in me has rest,
As I—undying Life—have power in Thee!

Vain are the thousand creeds
That move men's hearts: unutterably vain;
Worthless as wither'd weeds,
Or idlest froth amid the boundless main,

To waken doubt in one
Holding so fast by thine infinity;
So surely anchor'd on
The steadfast rock of immortality.

ARTHUR HUGH CLOUGH

With wide-embracing love
Thy Spirit animates eternal years,
   Pervades and broods above,
Changes, sustains, dissolves, creates, and rears.

   Though earth and man were gone,
And suns and universes ceased to be,
   And Thou were left alone,
Every existence would exist in Thee.

   There is not room for Death,
Nor atom that his might could render void:
   Thou—Thou art Being and Breath,
And what Thou art may never be destroy'd.

THE OLD STOIC

Riches I hold in light esteem,
   And Love I laugh to scorn;
And lust of fame was but a dream,
   That vanished with the morn:

And if I pray, the only prayer
   That moves my lips for me
Is, "Leave the heart that now I bear,
   And give me liberty!"

Yes, as my swift days near their goal,
   'Tis all that I implore;
In life and death a chainless soul,
   With courage to endure.

Arthur Hugh Clough

QUA CURSUM VENTUS

As ships, becalmed at eve, that lay
   With canvas drooping, side by side,
Two towers of sail at dawn of day
   Are scarce long leagues apart descried;

873

When fell the night, upsprung the breeze,
  And all the darkling hours they plied,
Nor dreamt but each the self-same seas
  By each was cleaving, side by side:

E'en so—but why the tale reveal
  Of those, whom year by year unchanged,
Brief absence joined anew to feel,
  Astounded, soul from soul estranged?

At dead of night their sails were filled,
  And onward each rejoicing steered—
Ah, neither blame, for neither willed,
  Or wist, what first with dawn appeared!

To veer, how vain! On, onward strain,
  Brave barks! In light, in darkness too,
Through winds and tides one compass guides—
  To that, and your own selves, be true.

But O blithe breeze! and O great seas,
  Though ne'er, that earliest parting past,
On your wide plain they join again,
  Together lead them home at last.

One port, methought, alike they sought,
  One purpose hold where'er they fare,—
O bounding breeze, O rushing seas!
  At last, at last, unite them there!

SAY NOT, THE STRUGGLE NAUGHT AVAILETH

Say not, the struggle naught availeth,
  The labour and the wounds are vain,
The enemy faints not, nor faileth,
  And as things have been they remain.

If hopes were dupes, fears may be liars;
  It may be, in yon smoke concealed,
Your comrades chase e'en now the fliers,
  And, but for you, possess the field.

874

ARTHUR HUGH CLOUGH

For while the tired waves, vainly breaking,
  Seem here no painful inch to gain,
Far back, through creeks and inlets making,
  Comes silent, flooding in, the main.

And not by eastern windows only,
  When daylight comes, comes in the light;
In front, the sun climbs slow, how slowly,
  But westward, look, the land is bright.

THE STREAM OF LIFE

O stream descending to the sea,
  Thy mossy banks between,
The flowerets blow, the grasses grow,
  The leafy trees are green.

In garden plots the children play,
  The fields the labourers till,
And houses stand on either hand,
  And thou descendest still.

O life descending into death,
  Our waking eyes behold,
Parent and friend thy lapse attend,
  Companions young and old.

Strong purposes our mind possess,
  Our hearts affections fill,
We toil and earn, we seek and learn,
  And thou descendest still.

O end to which our currents tend,
  Inevitable sea,
To which we flow, what do we know,
  What shall we guess of thee?

A roar we hear upon thy shore,
  As we our course fulfil;
Scarce we divine a sun will shine
  And he above us still.

WHERE LIES THE LAND

Where lies the land to which the ship would go?
Far, far ahead, is all her seamen know.
And where the land she travels from? Away,
Far, far behind, is all that they can say.

On sunny noons upon the deck's smooth face,
Linked arm in arm, how pleasant here to pace;
Or, o'er the stern reclining, watch below
The foaming wake far widening as we go.

On stormy nights, when wild north-westers rave,
How proud a thing to fight with wind and wave!
The dripping sailor on the reeling mast
Exults to bear, and scorns to wish it past.

Where lies the land to which the ship would go?
Far, far ahead, is all her seamen know.
And where the land she travels from? Away,
Far, far behind, is all that they can say.

WITH WHOM IS NO SHADOW OF VARIABLENESS

It fortifies my soul to know
That, though I perish, Truth is so:
That, howsoe'er I stray and range,
Whate'er I do, Thou dost not change.
I steadier step when I recall
That, if I slip, Thou dost not fall.

VENICE

How light we go, how soft we skim!
And all in moonlight seem to swim.
In moonlight is it now, or shade?
In planes of sure division made,
By angles sharp of palace walls
The clear light and the shadow falls;

JAMES RUSSELL LOWELL

O sight of glory, sight of wonder!
Seen, a pictorial portent, under,
O great Rialto, the vast round
Of thy thrice-solid arch profound!—
How light we go, how softly!   Ah,
Life should be as the gondola!

COME BACK, COME BACK

Come back, come back, across the flying foam,
We hear faint far-off voices call us home.

.   .   .   .

Come back, come back; and whither back or why?
To fan quenched hopes, forsaken schemes to try;
Walk the old fields; pace the familiar street;
Dream with the idlers, with the bards compete.
      Come back, come back.

Come back, come back; and whither and for what?
To finger idly some old Gordian knot,
Unskilled to sunder, and too weak to cleave,
And with much toil attain to half believe.
      Come back, come back.

.   .   .   .

Come back, come back!
Back flies the foam; the hoisted flag streams back;
The long smoke wavers on the homeward track,
Back fly with winds things which the winds obey,
The strong ship follows its appointed way.

James Russell Lowell

MY LOVE

Not as all other women are
Is she that to my soul is dear;
Her glorious fancies come from far,
Beneath the silver evening-star,
And yet her heart is ever near.

877

Great feelings hath she of her own,
Which lesser souls may never know;
God giveth them to her alone,
And sweet they are as any tone
Wherewith the wind may choose to blow.

Yet in herself she dwelleth not,
Although no home were half so fair;
No simplest duty is forgot,
Life hath no dim and lowly spot
That doth not in her sunshine share.

She doeth little kindnesses,
Which most leave undone, or despise:
For naught that sets one heart at ease,
And giveth happiness or peace,
Is low-esteemed in her eyes.

She hath no scorn of common things,
And, though she seem of other birth,
Round us her heart intwines and clings,
And patiently she folds her wings
To tread the humble paths of earth.

Blessing she is: God made her so,
And deeds of week-day holiness
Fall from her noiseless as the snow,
Nor hath she ever chanced to know
That aught were easier than to bless.

She is most fair, and thereunto
Her life doth rightly harmonize;
Feeling or thought that was not true
Ne'er made less beautiful the blue
Unclouded heaven of her eyes.

She is a woman: one in whom
The spring-time of her childish years
Hath never lost its fresh perfume,
Though knowing well that life hath room
For many blights and many tears.

JAMES RUSSELL LOWELL

I love her with a love as still
As a broad river's peaceful might,
Which, by high tower and lowly mill,
Seems following its own wayward will,
And yet doth ever flow aright.

And, on its full, deep breast serene,
Like quiet isles my duties lie;
It flows around them and between,
And makes them fresh and fair and green,
Sweet homes wherein to live and die.

AN INCIDENT IN A RAILROAD CAR

He spoke of Burns: men rude and rough
    Pressed round to hear the praise of one
Whose heart was made of manly, simple stuff,
    As homespun as their own.

And, when he read, they forward leaned,
    Drinking, with thirsty hearts and ears,
His brook-like songs whom glory never weaned
    From humble smiles and tears.

   .   .   .   .

FREEDOM

   .   .   .   .

We are not free: Freedom doth not consist
In musing with our faces toward the Past,
While petty cares, and crawling interests, twist
Their spider-threads about us, which at last
Grow strong as iron chains, to cramp and bind
In formal narrowness heart, soul, and mind.
Freedom is recreated year by year,
In hearts wide open on the Godward side,
In souls calm-cadenced as the whirling sphere,
In minds that sway the future like a tide.
No broadest creeds can hold her, and no codes;
She chooses men for her august abodes,

Building them fair and fronting to the dawn;
Yet, when we seek her, we but find a few
Light footprints, leading morn-ward through the dew;
Before the day had risen, she was gone.

And we must follow: swiftly runs she on,
And, if our steps should slacken in despair,
Half turns her face, half smiles, through golden hair,
Forever yielding, never wholly won:
That is not love which pauses in the race
Two close-linked names on fleeting sand to trace;
Freedom gained yesterday is no more ours;
Men gather but dry seeds of last year's flowers;
Still there's a charm ungranted, still a grace,
Still rosy Hope, the free, the unattained,
Makes us Possession's languid hand let fall;
'Tis but a fragment of ourselves is gained,—
The Future brings us more, but never all.

· · · · · · · · ·

JUNE

Over his keys the musing organist,
    Beginning doubtfully and far away,
First lets his fingers wander as they list,
    And builds a bridge from Dreamland for his lay:
Then, as the touch of his loved instrument
    Gives hope and fervor, nearer draws his theme,
First guessed by faint auroral flushes sent
    Along the wavering vista of his dream.

    Not only around our infancy
    Doth heaven with all its splendors lie;
    Daily, with souls that cringe and plot,
    We Sinais climb and know it not.

Over our manhood bend the skies;
    Against our fallen and traitor lives
The great winds utter prophecies;
    With our faint hearts the mountain strives;

Its arms outstretched, the druid wood
   Waits with its benedicite;
And to our age's drowsy blood
Still shouts the inspiring sea.

  . . . .

. . . What is so rare as a day in June?
   Then, if ever, come perfect days;
Then Heaven tries earth if it be in tune,
   And over it softly her warm ear lays;
Whether we look, or whether we listen,
We hear life murmur, or see it glisten;
Every clod feels a stir of might,
   An instinct within it that reaches and towers,
And, groping blindly above it for light,
   Climbs to a soul in grass and flowers.

  . . . .

The little bird sits at his door in the sun,
   Atilt like a blossom among the leaves,
And lets his illumined being o'errun
   With the deluge of summer it receives;
His mate feels the eggs beneath her wings,
And the heart in her dumb breast flutters and sings;
He sings to the wide world and she to her nest,—
In the nice ear of Nature which song is the best?

Now is the high-tide of the year,
   And whatever of life hath ebbed away
Comes flooding back with a ripply cheer,
   Into every bare inlet and creek and bay.

  . . . .

           —The Vision of Sir Launfal.

SHE CAME AND WENT

   As a twig trembles, which a bird
      Lights on to sing, then leaves unbent,
  So is my memory thrilled and stirred;—
      I only know she came and went.

As clasps some lake, by gusts unriven,
  The blue dome's measureless content,
So my soul held that moment's heaven;—
  I only know she came and went.

As, at one bound, our swift spring heaps
  The orchards full of bloom and scent,
So clove her May my wintry sleeps;—
  I only know she came and went.

An angel stood and met my gaze,
  Through the low doorway of my tent;
The tent is struck, the vision stays;—
  I only know she came and went.

Oh, when the room grows slowly dim,
  And life's last oil is nearly spent,
One gush of light these eyes will brim,
  Only to think she came and went.

O MOTHER STATE

.   .   .   .

O Mother State, how quenched thy Sinai fires!
  Is there none left of thy staunch Mayflower breed?
No spark among the ashes of thy sires,
  Of Virtue's altar-flame the kindling seed?
Are these thy great men, these that cringe and creep,
  And writhe through slimy ways to place and power?—
How long, O Lord, before thy wrath shall reap
  Our frail-stemmed summer prosperings in their flower?
O for one hour of that undaunted stock
That went with Vane and Sydney to the block!

O for a whiff of Naseby, that would sweep,
  With its stern Puritan besom, all this chaff
  From the Lord's threshing-floor! Yet more than half
The victory is attained when one or two,
  Through the fool's laughter and the traitor's scorn,
  Beside thy sepulchre can abide the morn,
Crucified Truth, when thou shalt rise anew.
                            —To JOHN GORHAM PALFREY.

JAMES RUSSELL LOWELL

TO WILLIAM LLOYD GARRISON

In a small chamber, friendless and unseen,
   Toiled o'er his types one poor, unlearned young man;
The place was dark, unfurnitured, and mean:
   Yet there the freedom of a race began.

.   .   .   .

O Truth! O Freedom! how are ye still born
   In the rude stable, in the manger nursed!
What humble hands unbar those gates of morn
   Through which the splendors of the New Day burst!

.   .   .   .

COMMEMORATION ODE

(Recited at the Harvard Commemoration, June 21, 1865)

.   .   .   .

Life may be given in many ways,
   And loyalty to Truth be sealed
As bravely in the closet as the field,
      So bountiful is Fate;
      But then to stand beside her,
      When craven churls deride her,
To front a lie in arms and not to yield,
      This shows, methinks, God's plan
      And measure of a stalwart man,
      Limbed like the old heroic breeds,
Who stand self-poised on manhood's solid earth,
Not forced to frame excuses for his birth,
Fed from within with all the strength he needs.

      Such was he, our Martyr-Chief,
      Whom late the Nation he had led,
      With ashes on her head,
Wept with the passion of an angry grief:
Forgive me, if from present things I turn
To speak what in my heart will beat and burn,
And hang my wreath on his world-honored urn.

883

Nature, they say, doth dote,
And cannot make a man
Save on some worn-out plan,
Repeating us by rote:
For him her Old-World moulds aside she threw,
And, choosing sweet clay from the breast
Of the unexhausted West,
With stuff untainted shapes a hero new,
Wise, steadfast in the strength of God, and true.
How beautiful to see
Once more a shepherd of mankind indeed,
Who loved his charge, but never loved to lead;
One whose meek flock the people joyed to be,
Not lured by any cheat of birth,
But by his clear-grained human worth,
And brave old wisdom of sincerity!
They knew that outward grace is dust;
They could not choose but trust
In that sure-footed mind's unfaltering skill,
And supple-tempered will
That bent like perfect steel to spring again and thrust.
His was no lonely mountain-peak of mind,
Thrusting to thin air o'er our cloudy bars,
A sea-mark now, now lost in vapor's blind;
Broad prairie rather, genial, level-lined,
Fruitful and friendly for all human kind,
Yet also nigh to heaven and loved of loftiest stars.
Nothing of Europe here,
Or, then, of Europe fronting mornward still,
Ere any names of Serf and Peer
Could Nature's equal scheme deface
And thwart her genial will;
Here was a type of the true elder race,
And one of Plutarch's men talked with us face to face.
I praise him not; it were too late;
And some innative weakness there must be
In him who condescends to victory
Such as the Present gives, and cannot wait,
Safe in himself as in a fate.
So always firmly he;

JAMES RUSSELL LOWELL

He knew to bide his time,
And can his fame abide,
Still patient in his simple faith sublime,
Till the wise years decide.
Great captains, with their guns and drums,
Disturb our judgment for the hour,
But at last silence comes;
These all are gone, and, standing like a tower,
Our children shall behold his fame,
The kindly-earnest, brave, foreseeing man,
Sagacious, patient, dreading praise, not blame,
New birth of our new soil, the first American.

.　.　.　.　.　.　.　.　.

SHIPWRECK

.　.　.　.　.　.　.　.　.

We, who by shipwreck only find the shores
Of divine wisdom, can but kneel at first,
Can but exult to find beneath our feet,
That long stretched vainly down the yielding deeps,
The shock and sustenance of solid earth;
Inland afar we see what temples gleam
Through immemorial stems of sacred groves,
And we conjecture shining shapes therein;
Yet for a space 'tis good to wander here
Among the shells and seaweed of the beach.

.　.　.　.　.　.　.　.　.

—UNDER THE WILLOWS

THE STREET

They pass me by like shadows, crowds on crowds,
Dim ghosts of men, that hover to and fro,
Hugging their bodies round them like thin shrouds
Wherein their souls were buried long ago:
They trampled on their youth, and faith, and love,
They cast their hope of human-kind away,
With Heaven's clear messages they madly strove,
And conquered,—and their spirits turned to clay:

885

Lo! how they wander round the world, their grave,
Whose ever-gaping maw by such is fed,
Gibbering at living men, and idly rave,
"We, only, truly live, but ye are dead."
Alas! poor fools, the anointed eye may trace
A dead soul's epitaph in every face!

Julia Ward Howe

BATTLE-HYMN OF THE REPUBLIC

Mine eyes have seen the glory of the coming of the Lord;
He is trampling out the vintage where the grapes of wrath are
    stored;
He hath loosed the fateful lightning of His terrible swift
    sword;
    His truth is marching on.

I have seen Him in the watch-fires of a hundred circling
    camps;
They have builded Him an altar in the evening dews and
    damps;
I can read his righteous sentence by the dim and flaring lamps;
    His day is marching on.

I have read a fiery gospel, writ in burnished rows of steel:
"As ye deal with my contemners, so with you my grace shall
    deal;
Let the Hero, born of woman, crush the serpent with his
    heel,
    Since God is marching on."

He has sounded forth the trumpet that shall never call retreat;
He is sifting out the hearts of men before His judgment-seat:
Oh, be swift, my soul, to answer Him! be jubilant, my feet!
    Our God is marching on.

In the beauty of the lilies Christ was born across the sea,
With a glory in His bosom that transfigures you and me:
As He died to make men holy, let us die to make men free,
    While God is marching on.

Walt Whitman

O CAPTAIN! MY CAPTAIN!

(Abraham Lincoln, 1809-1865)

O Captain! my Captain! our fearful trip is done,
The ship has weathered every rack, the prize we sought is won,
The port is near, the bells I hear, the people all exulting,
While follow eyes the steady keel, the vessel grim and daring;
But O heart! heart! heart!
O the bleeding drops of red,
Where on the deck my Captain lies,
Fallen cold and dead.

O Captain! my Captain! rise up and hear the bells;
Rise up for you the flag is flung—for you the bugle trills,
For you bouquets and ribboned wreaths—for you the shores
a-crowding,
For you they call, the swaying mass, their eager faces turning;
Here Captain! dear father!
This arm beneath your head!
It is some dream that on the deck
You've fallen cold and dead.

My Captain does not answer, his lips are pale and still,
My father does not feel my arm, he has no pulse nor will,
The ship is anchored safe and sound, its voyage closed and
done,
From fearful trip the victor ship comes in with object won;
Exult O shores, and ring O bells!
But I with mournful tread,
Walk the deck my Captain lies,
Fallen cold and dead.

TO THE MAN-OF-WAR-BIRD

Thou who hast slept all night upon the storm,
Waking renewed on thy prodigious pinions,

887

(Burst the wild storm? above it thou ascended'st,
And rested on the sky, thy slave that cradled thee,)
Now a blue point, far, far in heaven floating,
As to the light emerging here on deck I watch thee,
(Myself a speck, a point on the world's floating vast.)

Far, far at sea,
After the night's fierce drifts have strewn the shore with
    wrecks,
With re-appearing day as now so happy and serene,
The rosy and elastic dawn, the flashing sun,
The limpid spread of air cerulean,
Thou also re-appearest.

Thou born to match the gale, (thou art all wings,)
To cope with heaven and earth and sea and hurricane,
Thou ship of air that never furl'st thy sails,
Days, even weeks untired and onward, through spaces, realms
    gyrating,
At dusk that look'st on Senegal, at morn America,
That sport'st amid the lightning-flash and thunder-cloud,
In them, in thy experiences, hadst thou my soul,
What joys! what joys were thine!

WHEN LILACS LAST IN THE DOORYARD BLOOMED

When lilacs last in the dooryard bloomed,
And the great star early drooped in the western sky in the
    night,
I mourned, and yet shall mourn with ever-returning spring.

Ever-returning spring, trinity sure to me you bring,
Lilac blooming perennial and drooping star in the west,
And thought of him I love.

O powerful western fallen star!
O shades of night—O moody, tearful night!
O great star disappeared—O the black murk that hides the
    star!
O cruel hands that hold me powerless—O helpless soul of me!
O harsh surrounding cloud that will not free my soul!
888

In the dooryard fronting an old farmhouse, near the white-
washed palings,
Stands the lilac-bush tall-growing with heart-shaped leaves of
rich green,
With many a pointed blossom rising delicate, with the per-
fume strong I love,
With every leaf a miracle—and from this bush in the door-
yard,
With delicate-colored blossoms and heart-shaped leaves of
rich green,
A sprig with its flower I break.

In the swamp in secluded recesses,
A shy and hidden bird is warbling a song.

Solitary the thrush,
The hermit withdrawn to himself, avoiding the settlements,
Sings by himself a song.

Song of the bleeding throat,
Death's outlet song of life—(for well, dear brother, I know
If thou wast not gifted to sing thou wouldst surely die).

Over the breast of the spring, the land, amid cities,
Amid lanes and through old woods, where lately the violets
peeped from the ground, spotting the gray debris,
Amid the grass in the fields each side of the lanes, passing the
endless grass,
Passing the yellow-speared wheat, every grain from its shroud
in the dark-brown fields uprisen,
Passing the apple-tree blows of white and pink in the orchards,
Carrying a corpse to where it shall rest in the grave,
Night and day journeys a coffin.
Coffin that passes through lanes and streets,
Through day and night, with the great cloud darkening the
land,
With the pomp of the inlooped flags, with the cities draped
in black,
With the show of the States themselves as of crape-veiled
women standing,
With processions long and winding and the flambeaus of the
night,

889

With the countless torches lit, with the silent sea of faces and
the unbared heads,
With the waiting depot, the arriving coffin, and the somber
faces,
With dirges through the night, with the thousand voices rising
strong and solemn,
With all the mournful voices of the dirges poured around the
coffin,
The dim-lit churches and the shuddering organs—where amid
these you journey,
With the tolling tolling bells' perpetual clang,
Here, coffin that slowly passes,
I give you my sprig of lilac.

(Nor for you, for one alone,
Blossoms and branches green to coffins all I bring,
For fresh as the morning, thus would I chant a song for you,
O sane and sacred death.

All over bouquets of roses,
O death, I cover you over with roses and early lilies,
But mostly and now the lilac that blooms the first,
Copious I break, I break the sprigs from the bushes,
With loaded arms I come, pouring for you,
For you and the coffins all of you, O death.)

O western orb sailing the heaven,
Now I know what you must have meant as a month since I
walked,
As I walked in silence the transparent shadowy night,
As I saw you had something to tell as you bent to me night
after night,
As you drooped from the sky low down as if to my side,
(while the other stars all looked on,)
As we wandered together the solemn night, (for something
I know not what, kept me from sleep,)
As the night advanced, and I saw on the rim of the west how
full you were of woe,
As I stood on the rising ground in the breeze in the cool
transparent night,
As I watched where you passed, and was lost in the nether-
ward black of the night,

As my soul in its trouble dissatisfied sank, as where yon sad
    orb,
Concluded, dropped in the night, and was gone.

Sing on there in the swamp,
O singer bashful and tender, I hear your notes, I hear your
    call,
I hear, I come presently, I understand you,
But a moment I linger, for the lustrous star has detained me,
The star, my departing comrade, holds and detains me.

O how shall I warble myself for the dead one there I loved?
And how shall I deck my song for the large sweet soul that
    has gone?
And what shall my perfume be for the grave of him I love?

Sea-winds blown from east and west,
Blown from the Eastern sea and blown from the Western
    sea, till there on the prairies meeting,
These and with these and the breath of my chant,
I'll perfume the grave of him I love.

O what shall I hang on the chamber walls?
And what shall the pictures be that I hang on the walls,
To adorn the burial-house of him I love?

Pictures of growing spring and farms and homes,
With the Fourth-month eve at sundown, and the gray-smoke
    lucid and bright,
With floods of the yellow gold of the gorgeous, indolent, sink-
    ing sun, burning, expanding the air,
With the fresh spring herbage under foot, and the pale green
    leaves of the trees prolific,
In the distance the flowing glaze, the breast of the river, with
    a wind-dapple here and there,
With ranging hills on the banks, with many a line against the
    sky, and shadows,
And the city at hand with dwellings so dense, and stacks of
    chimneys,
And all the scenes of life and the workshops, and the work-
    men homeward returning.

Lo, body and soul—this land,
My own Manhattan with spires, and the sparkling and hurry-
    ing tides, and the ships,
The varied and ample land, the South and the North in the
    light, Ohio's shores and flashing Missouri,
And ever the far-spreading prairies covered with grass and
    corn.

Lo, the most excellent sun so calm and haughty,
The violet and purple morn with just-felt breezes,
The gentle soft-born measureless light,
The miracle, spreading, bathing all, the fulfilled noon,
The coming eve delicious, the welcome night and the stars,
Over my cities shining all, enveloping man and land.

Sing on, sing on, you gray-brown bird,
Sing from the swamps, the recesses, pour your chant from the
    bushes,
Limitless out of the dusk, out of the cedars and pines.
Sing on, dearest brother, warble your reedy song,
Loud human song, with voice of uttermost woe.

O liquid and free and tender!
O wild and loose to my soul—O wondrous singer!
You only I hear—yet the star holds me, (but will soon
    depart,)
Yet the lilac with mastering odor holds me.

Now while I sat in the day and looked forth,
In the close of the day with its light and the fields of spring,
    and the farmers preparing their crops,
In the large unconscious scenery of my land with its lakes
    and forests,
In the heavenly aerial beauty, (after the perturbed winds and
    the storms,)
Under the arching heavens of the afternoon swift passing,
    and the voices of children and women,
The many-moving sea-tides, and I saw the ships how they
    · sailed,
And the summer approaching with richness, and the fields all
    busy with labor,
892

WALT WHITMAN

And the infinite separate houses, how they all went on, each
    with its meals and minutia of daily usages,
And the streets how their throbbings throbbed, and the cities
    pent—lo, then and there,
Falling upon them all and among them all, enveloping me
    with the rest,
Appeared the cloud, appeared the long black trail,
And I knew death, its thought, and the sacred knowledge of
    death.

Then with the knowledge of death as walking one side of me,
And the thought of death close-walking the other side of me,
And I in the middle as with companions, and as holding the
    hands of companions,
I fled forth to the hiding receiving night that talks not,
Down to the shores of the water, the path by the swamp in the
    dimness,
To the solemn shadowy cedars and ghostly pines so still.
And the singer so shy to the rest received me,
The gray-brown bird I know received us comrades three,
And he sang the carol of death, and a verse for him I love.

From deep secluded recesses,
From the fragrant cedars and the ghostly pines so still,
Came the carol of the bird.

And the charm of the carol rapt me,
As I held as if by their hands my comrades in the night,
And the voice of my spirit tallied the song of the bird.

Come, lovely and soothing death,
Undulate round the world, serenely arriving, arriving,
In the day, in the night, to all, to each,
Sooner or later delicate death.

Praised be the fathomless universe,
For life and joy, and for objects and knowledge curious,
And for love, sweet love—but praise! praise! praise!
For the sure-enwinding arms of cool-enfolding death.

893

Dark mother always gliding near with soft feet,
Have none chanted for thee a chant of fullest welcome?
Then I chant it for thee, I glorify thee above all, bring thee
a song that when thou must indeed come, come un-
falteringly.

Approach, strong deliveress,
When it is so, when thou hast taken them I joyously sing the
dead,
Lost in the loving floating ocean of thee,
Laved in the flood of thy bliss, O death.

From me to thee glad serenades,
Dances for thee I propose, saluting thee, adornments and feast-
ings for thee,
And the sights of the open landscape and the high-spread
sky are fitting,
And life and the fields, and the huge and thoughtful night.

The night in silence under many a star,
The ocean shore and the husky whispering wave whose voice
I know,
And the soul turning to thee, O vast and well-veiled death,
And the body gratefully nestling close to thee.

Over the tree-tops I float thee a song,
Over the rising and sinking waves, over the myriad fields and
the prairies wide,
Over the dense-packed cities all and the teeming wharves and
ways,
I float this carol with joy, with joy to thee, O death.

To the tally of my soul,
Loud and strong kept up the gray-brown bird,
With pure deliberate notes, spreading, filling the night.

Loud in the pines and cedars dim,
Clear in the freshness moist and the swamp-perfume,
And I with my comrades there in the night.

While my sight that was bound in my eyes unclosed,
As to long panoramas of visions.

And I saw askant the armies,
I saw as in noiseless dreams hundreds of battle-flags,
Borne through the smoke of the battles and pierced with mis-
siles I saw them,
And carried hither and yon through the smoke, and torn and
bloody,
And at last but a few shreds left on the staffs, (and all in
silence,)
And the staffs all splintered and broken.

I saw battle-corpses, myriads of them,
And the white skeletons of young men, I saw them,
I saw the debris and debris of all the slain soldiers of the war.
But I saw they were not as was thought,
They themselves were fully at rest, they suffered not,
The living remained and suffered, the mother suffered,
And the wife and the child and the musing comrade suffered,
And the armies that remained suffered.

Passing the visions, passing the night,
Passing, unloosing the hold of my comrades' hands,
Passing the song of the hermit bird, and the tallying song of
my soul,
Victorious song, death's outlet song, yet varying, ever-altering
song,
As low and wailing, yet clear the notes, rising and falling,
flooding the night,
Sadly sinking and fainting, as warning and warning, and yet
again bursting with joy,
Covering the earth and filling the spread of the heaven,
As that powerful psalm in the night I heard from recesses,
Passing, I leave thee, lilac with heart-shaped leaves,
I leave thee there in the dooryard, blooming, returning with
spring.

I cease from my song for thee,
From my gaze on thee in the west, fronting the west, com-
muning with thee,
O comrade lustrous with silver face in the night.

Yet each to keep and all, retrievements out of the night,
The song, the wondrous chant of the gray-brown bird,
And the tallying chant, the echo aroused in my soul,
With the lustrous and drooping star with the countenance full
    of woe,
With the holders holding my hand hearing the call of the bird,
Comrades mine and I in the midst, and their memory ever
    to keep, for the dead I loved so well,
For the sweetest, wisest soul of all my days and lands—and
    this for his dear sake,
Lilac and star and bird twined with the chant of my soul,
There in the fragrant pines and the cedars dusk and dim.

OUT OF THE CRADLE ENDLESSLY ROCKING

．　．　．　．　．　．　．　．　．　．

Once Paumanok,
When the lilac-scent was in the air and Fifth-month grass was
    growing,
Up this seashore in some briers,
Two feather'd guests from Alabama, two together,
And their nest, and four light-green eggs spotted with brown;
And every day the he-bird to and fro near at hand,
And every day the she-bird crouch'd on her nest, silent, with
    bright eyes,
And every day I, a curious boy, never too close, never dis-
    turbing them,
Cautiously peering, absorbing, translating.

Shine! Shine! Shine!
Pour down your warmth, great sun!
While we bask, we two together.

Two together!
Winds blow south, or winds blow north,
Day come white, or night come black,
Home, or rivers and mountains from home,
Singing all time, minding no time,
While we two keep together.

896

Till of a sudden,
Maybe kill'd, unknown to her mate,
One forenoon the she-bird crouch'd not on the nest,
Nor return'd that afternoon, nor the next,
Nor ever appear'd again.

And thenceforward all summer, in the sound of the sea,
And at night under the full of the moon in calmer weather,
Over the hoarse surging of the sea,
Or flitting from brier to brier by day,
I saw, I heard at intervals the remaining one, the he-bird,
The solitary guest from Alabama.

Blow! blow! blow!
Blow up, seawinds, along Paumanok's shore;
I wait and I wait till you blow my mate to me.

Yes, when the stars glisten'd,
All night long on the prong of a moss-scallop'd stake,
Down almost amid the slapping waves,
Sat the lone singer, wonderful, causing tears.
He call'd on his mate,
He pour'd forth the meanings which I of all men know.

Yes, my brother, I know;
The rest might not, but I have treasur'd every note.
For more than once, dimly down to the beach gliding,
Silent, avoiding the moonbeams, blending myself with the
    shadows,
Recalling now the obscure shapes, the echoes, the sounds and
    sights after their sorts,
The white arms out in the breakers tirelessly tossing,
I, with bare feet, a child, the wind wafting my hair,
Listen'd long and long;
Listen'd to keep, to sing, now translating the notes,
Following you, my brother.

Soothe! soothe! soothe!
Close on its wave soothes the wave behind,
And again another behind embracing and lapping, every one
    close;
But my love soothes not me, not me.

Low hangs the moon, it rose late,
It is lagging—O I think it is heavy with love, with love.
O madly the sea pushes upon the land,
With love, with love.

O night! do I not see my love fluttering out among the
*   breakers?*
What is that little black thing I see there in the white?

Loud! Loud! Loud!
Loud I call to you, my love!

High and clear I shoot my voice over the waves;
Surely you must know who is here, is here,
You must know who I am, my love.

Low-hanging moon!
What is that dusky spot in your brown yellow?
O it is the shape, the shape of my mate!
O moon, do not keep her from me any longer.

Land! land! O land!
Whichever way I turn, O I think you could give me my mate
*   back again if you only would.*
For I am almost sure I see her dimly whichever way I
*   look.*

O rising stars!
Perhaps the one I want so much will rise, will rise with some
*   of you.*

O throat! O trembling throat!
Sound clearer through the atmosphere!
Pierce the woods, the earth;
Somewhere listening to catch you must be the one I
*   want.*

Shake out carols!
Solitary here, the night's carols!
Carols of lonesome love! death's carols!
Carols under that lagging, yellow, waning moon!
O under that moon where she droops almost down into the
*   sea!*
O reckless, despairing carols.

But soft! sink low!
Soft; let me just murmur,
And do you wait a moment, you husky-noised sea,
For somewhere I believe I heard my mate responding to me,
So faint, I must be still, be still to listen,
But not altogether still, for then she might not come immedi-
ately to me.

Hither, my love!
Here I am! here!
With this just-sustained note I announce myself to you,
This gentle call is for you, my love, for you.

Do not be decoyed elsewhere:
That is the whistle of the wind, it is not my voice,
That is the fluttering, the fluttering of the spray,
Those are the shadows of leaves.

O darkness! O in vain!—
O I am very sick and sorrowful.

O brown halo in the sky near the moon, drooping upon the
sea!
O troubled reflection in the sea!
O throat! O throbbing heart!
And I singing uselessly, uselessly all the night.

O past! O happy life! O songs of joy!
In the air, in the woods, over fields,
Loved! loved! loved! loved! loved!
But my mate no more, no more with me!
We two together no more.

The aria sinking,
All else continuing, the stars shining,
The winds blowing, the notes of the bird continuous echoing,
With angry moans the fierce old mother incessantly moaning,
On the sands of Paumanok's shore gray and rustling,
The yellow half-moon enlarged, sagging down, drooping, the
face of the sea almost touching,
The boy ecstatic, with his bare feet the waves, with his hair
the atmosphere dallying,
The love in the heart long pent, now loose, now at last
tumultuously bursting,

The aria's meaning, the ears, the soul, swiftly depositing,
The strange tears down the cheeks coursing,
The colloquy there, the trio, each uttering,
The undertone, the savage old mother incessantly crying,
To the boy's soul's questions sullenly timing, some drown'd
    secret hissing,
To the outsetting bard.

Demon or bird! (said the boy's soul)
Is it indeed toward your mate you sing? or is it really to me?
For I, that was a child, my tongue's use sleeping, now I have
    heard you,
Now in a moment I know what I am for, I awake,
And already a thousand singers, a thousand songs, clearer,
    louder and more sorrowful than yours,
A thousand warbling echoes have started to life within me,
    never to die.

O you singers solitary, singing by yourself, projecting me,
O solitary me listening, never more shall I cease perpetuating
    you,
Never more shall I escape, never more the reverberations,
Never more the cries of unsatisfied love be absent from me,
Never again leave me to be the peaceful child I was before
    what there in the night,
By the sea under the yellow and sagging moon,
The messenger there aroused, the fire, the sweet hell within,
The unknown want, the destiny of me.
O give me the clew! (it lurks in the night here somewhere)
O if I am to have so much, let me have more!

A word then, (for I will conquer it)
The word final, superior to all,
Subtle, sent up—what is it?—I listen;
Are you whispering it, and have been all the time, you sea-
    waves?
Is that it from your liquid rims and wet sands?
    900

WALT WHITMAN

Whereto answering, the sea,
Delaying not, hurrying not,
Whispered me through the night, and very plainly before day-
  break,
Lisped to me the low and delicious word death,
And again death, death, death, death,
Hissing melodious, neither like the bird nor like my aroused
  child's heart,
But edging near as privately for me, rustling at my feet,
Creeping thence steadily up to my ears and laving me softly
  all over,
Death, death, death, death, death.

Which I do not forget,
But fuse the song of my dusky demon and brother,
That he sang to me in the moonlight on Paumanok's gray
  beach,
With the thousand responsive songs at random,
My own songs awaked from that hour,
And with them the key, the word up from the waves,
The word of the sweetest song and all songs,
That strong and delicious word which, creeping to my feet,
(Or like some old crone rocking the cradle, swathed in sweet
  garments, bending aside)
The sea whispered me.

A NOISELESS, PATIENT SPIDER

A noiseless, patient spider,
I marked, where, on a little promontory, it stood isolated;
Marked how, to explore the vacant, vast surrounding,
It launched forth filament, filament, filament, out of itself;
Ever unreeling them—ever tirelessly speeding them.

And you, O my Soul, where you stand,
Surrounded, surrounded, in measureless oceans of space,
Ceaselessly musing, venturing, throwing,—seeking the
  spheres, to connect them;
Till the bridge you will need, be formed—till the ductile
  anchor hold;
Till the gossamer thread you fling, catch somewhere, O my
  Soul.

901

JOY, SHIPMATE, JOY!

Joy, shipmate, joy!
(Pleas'd to my soul at death I cry)
Our life is closed, our life begins,
The long, long anchorage we leave,
The ship is clear at last, she leaps!
She swiftly courses from the shore,
Joy, shipmate, joy.

Charles Kingsley

ODE TO THE NORTH-EAST WIND

Welcome, wild North-easter!
    Shame it is to see
Odes to every zephyr;
    Ne'er a verse to thee.
Welcome, black North-easter!
    O'er the German foam;
O'er the Danish moorlands,
    From thy frozen home.
Tired we are of summer,
    Tired of gaudy glare,
Showers soft and steaming,
    Hot and breathless air.
Tired of listless dreaming,
    Through the lazy day:
Jovial wind of winter,
    Turn us out to play.
Sweep the golden reed-beds;
    Crisp the lazy dyke;
Hunger into madness
    Every plunging pike.
Fill the lake with wild-fowl;
    Fill the marsh with snipe;
While on dreary moorlands
    Lonely curlew pipe.

902

Through the black fir-forest
    Thunder harsh and dry,
Shattering down the snow-flakes
    Off the curdled sky.
Hark! the brave North-easter!
    Breast-high lies the scent,
On by bolt and headland,
    Over heath and bent.
Chime, ye dappled darlings,
    Through the sleet and snow.
Who can over-ride you?
    Let the horses go!
Chime, ye dappled darlings,
    Down the roaring blast;
You shall see a fox die
    Ere an hour be past.
Go! and rest to-morrow,
    Hunting in your dreams,
While our skates are ringing
    O'er the frozen streams.
Let the luscious South-wind
    Breathe in lovers' sighs,
While the lazy gallants
    Bask in ladies' eyes.
What does he but soften
    Heart alike and pen?
'Tis the hard grey weather
    Breeds hard English men.
What's the soft South-wester?
    'Tis the ladies' breeze,
Bringing home their true loves
    Out of all the seas:
But the black North-easter,
    Through the snowstorm hurled,
Drives our English hearts of oak
    Seaward round the world.
Come, as came our fathers,
    Heralded by thee,

> Conquering from the eastward,
>   Lords by land and sea.
> Come; and strong within us
>   Stir the Vikings' blood;
> Bracing brain and sinew;
>   Blow, thou wind of God!

George Eliot

TWO LOVERS

Two lovers by a moss-grown spring:
  They leaned soft cheeks together there,
  Mingled the dark and sunny hair,
And heard the wooing thrushes sing.
    O budding time!
    O love's blest prime!

Two wedded from the portal stept:
  The bells made happy carollings,
  The air was soft as fanning wings,
White petals on the pathway slept.
    O pure-eyed bride!
    O tender pride!

Two faces o'er a cradle bent:
  Two hands above the head were locked:
  These pressed each other while they rocked,
Those watched a life that love had sent.
    O solemn hour!
    O hidden power!

Two parents by the evening fire:
  The red light fell about their knees
  On heads that rose by slow degrees
Like buds upon the lily spire.
    O patient life!
    O tender strife!

The two still sat together there,
    The red light shone about their knees;
    But all the heads by slow degrees
Had gone and left that lonely pair.
            O voyage fast!
            O vanished past!

The red light shone upon the floor
    And made the space between them wide;
    They drew their chairs up side by side,
Their pale cheeks joined, and said, "Once more!"
            O memories!
            O past that is!

Frederick Locker-Lampson

THE UNREALISED IDEAL

My only Love is always near,—
    In country or in town
I see her twinkling feet, I hear
    The whisper of her gown.

She foots it ever fair and young,
    Her locks are tied in haste,
And one is o'er her shoulder flung,
    And hangs below her waist.

She ran before me in the meads;
    And down this world-worn track
She leads me on; but while she leads
    She never gazes back.

And yet her voice is in my dreams,
    To witch me more and more;
That wooing voice! Ah me, it seems
    Less near me than of yore.

905

Lightly I sped when hope was high,
    And youth beguiled the chase;
I follow—follow still; but I
    Shall never see her Face.

Jean Ingelow

THE HIGH TIDE ON THE COAST OF LINCOLNSHIRE

. . . .

I shall never hear her more
    By the reedy Lindis shore,
"Cusha! Cusha! Cusha!" calling,
    Ere the early dews be falling;
I shall never hear her song.
    "Cusha! Cusha!" all along
Where the sunny Lindis floweth,
    Goeth, floweth;
From the meads where melick groweth,
Where the water winding down
Onward floweth to the town.

I shall never see her more
Where the reeds and rushes quiver,
    Shiver, quiver;
Stand beside the sobbing river,
Sobbing, throbbing, in its falling
To the sandy, lonesome shore;
I shall never hear her calling,
"Leave your meadow grasses mellow,
    Mellow, mellow;
Quit your cowslips, cowslips yellow;
Come uppe Whitefoot, come uppe Lightfoot;
Quit your pipes of parsley hollow,
    Hollow, hollow;
Come uppe Lightfoot, rise and follow;

906

Lightfoot, Whitefoot,
From your clovers lift the head;
Come uppe Jetty, follow, follow,
Jetty, to the milking shed."

Matthew Arnold

QUIET WORK

One lesson, Nature, let me learn of thee,
One lesson which in every wind is blown,
One lesson of two duties kept at one
Though the loud world proclaim their enmity—

Of toil unsever'd from tranquillity!
Of labour, that in lasting fruit outgrows
Far noisier schemes, accomplish'd in repose,
Too great for haste, too high for rivalry!

Yes, while on earth a thousand discords ring,
Man's fitful uproar mingling with his toil,
Still do thy sleepless ministers move on,

Their glorious tasks in silence perfecting;
Still working, blaming still our vain turmoil,
Labourers that shall not fail, when man is gone.

TO A FRIEND

Who prop, thou ask'st, in these bad days, my mind?—
He much, the old man, who, clearest-soul'd of men,
Saw the Wide Prospect, and the Asian Fen,
And Tmolus hill, and Smyrna bay, though blind.

Much he, whose friendship I not long since won,
That halting slave, who in Nicopolis
Taught Arrian, when Vespasian's brutal son
Clear'd Rome of what most shamed him. But be his

My special thanks, whose even-balanced soul,
From first youth tested up to extreme old age,
Business could not make dull, nor passion wild;

Who saw life steadily, and saw it whole;
The mellow glory of the Attic stage,
Singer of sweet Colonus, and its child.

REQUIESCAT

Strew on her roses, roses,
  And never a spray of yew!
In quiet she reposes;
  Ah, would that I did too!

Her mirth the world required;
  She bathed it in smiles of glee.
But her heart was tired, tired,
  And now they let her be.

Her life was turning, turning,
  In mazes of heat and sound.
But for peace her soul was yearning,
  And now peace laps her round.

Her cabin'd, ample spirit,
  It flutter'd and fail'd for breath.
To-night it doth inherit
  The vasty hall of death.

THE VOICE

As the kindling glances,
  Queen-like and clear,
Which the bright moon lances
From her tranquil sphere
At the sleepless waters
Of a lonely mere,
On the wild whirling waves, mournfully, mournfully,
  Shiver and die.

MATTHEW ARNOLD

As the tears of sorrow
 Mothers have shed—
Prayers that to-morrow
 Shall in vain be sped
When the flower they flow for
 Lies frozen and dead—
Fall on the throbbing brow, fall on the burning breast,
 Bringing no rest,

Like bright waves that fall
 With a lifelike motion
On the lifeless margin of the sparkling Ocean;
A wild rose climbing up a mouldering wall—
A gush of sunbeams through a ruin'd hall—
Strains of glad music at a funeral—
 So sad, and with so wild a start
 To this deep-sober'd heart,
 So anxiously and painfully,
 So drearily and doubtfully,
And oh, with such intolerable change
 Of thought, such contrast strange,
O unforgotten voice, thy accents come,
Like wanderers from the world's extremity,
 Unto their ancient home!

In vain, all, all in vain,
They beat upon mine ear again,
Those melancholy tones so sweet and still.
Those lute-like tones which in the bygone year
 Did steal into mine ear—
Blew such a thrilling summons to my will,
 Yet could not shake it;
Made my tost heart its very life-blood spill,
 Yet could not break it.

THE WORLD'S TRIUMPHS

So far as I conceive the world's rebuke
To him address'd who would recast her new,
Not from herself her fame of strength she took,
But from their weakness who would work her rue.

909

"Behold," she cries, "so many rages lull'd,
So many fiery spirits quite cool'd down;
Look how so many valours, long undull'd,
After short commerce with me, fear my frown!

Thou too, when thou against my crimes wouldst cry,
Let thy foreboded homage check thy tongue!"—
The world speaks well; yet might her foe reply:
"Are wills so weak?—then let not mine wait long!

Hast thou so rare a poison?—let me be
Keener to slay thee, lest thou poison me!"

A QUESTION

TO FAUSTA

Joy comes and goes, hope ebbs and flows
    Like the wave;
Change doth unknit the tranquil strength of men.
    Love lends life a little grace,
    A few sad smiles; and then,
    Both are laid in one cold place,
      In the grave.

Dreams dawn and fly, friends smile and die
    Like spring flowers;
Our vaunted life is one long funeral.
    Men dig graves with bitter tears
    For their dead hopes; and all,
    Mazed with doubts and sick with fears,
      Count the hours.

We count the hours! These dreams of ours,
    False and hollow,
Do we go hence and find they are not dead?
    Joys we dimly apprehend,
    Faces that smiled and fled,
    Hopes born here, and born to end,
      Shall we follow?

MATTHEW ARNOLD

EAST LONDON

'Twas August, and the fierce sun overhead
Smote on the squalid streets of Bethnal Green,
And the pale weaver, through his windows seen
In Spitalfields, look'd thrice dispirited.

I met a preacher there I knew, and said:
"Ill and o'erwork'd, how fare you in this scene?"—
"Bravely!" said he; "for I of late have been
Much cheer'd with thoughts of Christ, *the living bread*."

O human soul! as long as thou canst so
Set up a mark of everlasting light,
Above the howling senses' ebb and flow,

To cheer thee, and to right thee if thou roam—
Not with lost toil thou labourest through the night!
Thou mak'st the heaven thou hop'st indeed thy home.

THE BETTER PART

Long fed on boundless hopes, O race of man,
How angrily thou spurn'st all simpler fare!
"Christ," some one says, "was human as we are;
No judge eyes us from Heaven, our sin to scan;

We live no more, when we have done our span."—
"Well, then, for Christ," thou answerest, "who can care?
From sin, which Heaven records not, why forbear?
Live we like brutes our life without a plan!"

So answerest thou; but why not rather say:
"Hath man no second life?—*Pitch this one high!*
Sits there no judge in Heaven, our sin to see?—

More strictly, then, the inward judge obey!
Was Christ a man like us?—Ah! let us try
If we then, too, can be such men as he!"

IMMORTALITY

Foil'd by our fellow-men, depress'd, outworn,
We leave the brutal world to take its way,
And, *Patience! in another life,* we say,
The world shall be thrust down, and we upborne.

And will not, then, the immortal armies scorn
The world's poor, routed leavings? or will they,
Who fail'd under the heat of this life's day,
Support the fervours of the heavenly morn?

No, no!—the energy of life may be
Kept on after the grave, but not begun;
And he who flagg'd not in the earthly strife,

From strength to strength advancing—only he,
His soul well-knit, and all his battles won,
Mounts, and that hardly, to eternal life.

ISOLATION

TO MARGUERITE

We were apart; yet, day by day,
I bade my heart more constant be.
I bade it keep the world away,
And grow a home for only thee;
Nor fear'd but thy love likewise grew,
Like mine, each day, more tried, more true.

The fault was grave! I might have known,
What far too soon, alas! I learn'd—
The heart can bind itself alone,
And faith may oft be unreturn'd.
Self-sway'd our feelings ebb and swell—
Thou lov'st no more;—Farewell! Farewell!

912

MATTHEW ARNOLD

Farewell!—and thou, thou lonely heart,
Which never yet without remorse
Even for a moment didst depart
From thy remote and spherèd course
To haunt the place where passions reign—
Back to thy solitude again!

Back! with the conscious thrill of shame
Which Luna felt, that summer-night,
Flash through her pure immortal frame,
When she forsook the starry height
To hang over Endymion's sleep
Upon the pine-grown Latmian steep.

Yet she, chaste queen, had never proved
How vain a thing is mortal love,
Wandering in Heaven, far removed.
But thou hast long had place to prove
This truth—to prove, and make thine own:
"Thou hast been, shalt be, art, alone."

Or, if not quite alone, yet they
Which touch thee are unmating things—
Ocean and clouds and night and day;
Lorn autumns and triumphant springs;
And life, and others' joy and pain
And love, if love, of happier men.

Of happier men—for they, at least,
Have *dream'd* two human hearts might blend
In one, and were through faith released
From isolation without end
Prolong'd; nor knew, although not less
Alone than thou, their loneliness.

TO MARGUERITE—CONTINUED

Yes! in the sea of life enisled,
With echoing straits between us thrown,
Dotting the shoreless watery wild,
We mortal millions live alone.

913

The islands feel the enclasping flow,
And then their endless bounds they know.

But when the moon their hollows lights,
And they are swept by balms of spring,
And in their glens, on starry nights,
The nightingales divinely sing;
And lovely notes, from shore to shore,
Across the sounds and channels pour—

Oh! then a longing like despair
Is to their farthest caverns sent;
For surely once, they feel, we were
Parts of a single continent!
Now round us spreads the watery plain—
Oh might our marges meet again!

Who order'd, that their longing's fire
Should be, as soon as kindled, cool'd?
Who renders vain their deep desire?—
A God, a God their severance ruled!
And bade betwixt their shores to be
The unplumb'd, salt, estranging sea.

FRAGMENT OF CHORUS OF A "DEJANEIRA"

O frivolous mind of man,
Light ignorance, and hurrying, unsure thoughts!
Though man bewails you not,
How I bewail you!

Little in your prosperity
Do you seek counsel of the Gods.
Proud, ignorant, self-adored, you live alone.
In profound silence stern,
Among their savage gorges and cold springs,
Unvisited remain
The great oracular shrines.

914

MATTHEW ARNOLD

'Thither in your adversity
Do you betake yourselves for light,
But strangely misinterpret all you hear.
For you will not put on
New hearts with the enquirer's holy robe,
And purged, considerate minds.

And him on whom, at the end
Of toil and dolour untold,
The Gods have said that repose
At last shall descend undisturb'd—
Him you expect to behold
In an easy old age, in a happy home;
No end but this you praise.

But him, on whom, in the prime
Of life, with vigour undimm'd,
With unspent mind, and a soul
Unworn, undebased, undecay'd,
Mournfully grating, the gates
Of the city of death have for ever closed—
Him, I count *him*, well-starr'd.

PHILOMELA

Hark! ah, the nightingale—
The tawny-throated!
Hark, from that moonlit cedar what a burst!
What triumph! hark!—what pain!

O wanderer from a Grecian shore,
Still, after many years, in distant lands,
Still nourishing in thy bewilder'd brain
That wild, unquench'd, deep-sunken, old world pain—
Say, will it never heal?
And can this fragrant lawn
With its cool trees, and night,
And the sweet, tranquil Thames,
And moonshine, and the dew,
To thy rack'd heart and brain
Afford no balm?

Dost thou to-night behold,
Here, through the moonlight on this English grass,
The unfriendly palace in the Thracian wild?
Dost thou again peruse
With hot cheeks and sear'd eyes
The too clear web, and thy dumb sister's shame?
Dost thou once more assay
Thy flight, and feel come over thee,
Poor fugitive, the feathery change
Once more, and once more seem to make resound
With love and hate, triumph and agony,
Lone Daulis, and the high Cephissian vale?
Listen, Eugenia—
How thick the bursts come crowding through the leaves!
Again—thou hearest?
Eternal passion!
Eternal pain!

URANIA

She smiles and smiles, and will not sigh,
While we for hopeless passion die;
Yet she could love, those eyes declare,
Were but men nobler than they are.

Eagerly once her gracious ken
Was turn'd upon the sons of men;
But light the serious visage grew—
She look'd, and smiled, and saw them through.

Our petty souls, our strutting wits,
Our labour'd, puny passion-fits—
Ah, may she scorn them still, till we
Scorn them as bitterly as she!

Yet show her once, ye heavenly Powers,
One of some worthier race than ours!
One for whose sake she once might prove
How deeply she who scorns can love.

916

His eyes be like the starry lights—
His voice like sounds of summer nights—
In all his lovely mien let pierce
The magic of the universe!

And she to him will reach her hand,
And gazing in his eyes will stand,
And know her friend, and weep for glee,
And cry: *Long, long I've look'd for thee.*

Then will she weep; with smiles, till then,
Coldly she mocks the sons of men.
Till then, her lovely eyes maintain
Their pure, unwavering, deep disdain.

SEPARATION

Stop!—not to me, at this bitter departing,
  Speak of the sure consolations of time!
Fresh be the wound, still-renew'd be its smarting,
  So but thy image endure in its prime!

But, if the steadfast commandment of Nature
  Wills that remembrance should always decay—
If the loved form and the deep-cherish'd feature
  Must, when unseen, from the soul fade away—

Me let no half-effaced memories cumber!
  Fled, fled at once, be all vestige of thee!
Deep be the darkness and still be the slumber—
  Dead be the past and its phantoms to me!

Then, when we meet, and thy look strays toward me,
  Scanning my face and the changes wrought there:
Who, let me say, *is this stranger regards me,*
  With the grey eyes, and the lovely brown hair?

DOVER BEACH

The sea is calm to-night.
The tide is full, the moon lies fair
Upon the straits;—on the French coast the light
Gleams and is gone; the cliffs of England stand,
Glimmering and vast, out in the tranquil bay.
Come to the window, sweet is the night-air!
Only, from the long line of spray
Where the sea meets the moon-blanch'd sand,
Listen! you hear the grating roar
Of pebbles which the waves draw back, and fling,
At their return, up the high strand,
Begin, and cease, and then again begin,
With tremulous cadence slow, and bring
The eternal note of sadness in.

Sophocles long ago
Heard it on the Ægean, and it brought
Into his mind the turbid ebb and flow
Of human misery; we
Find also in the sound a thought,
Hearing it by this distant northern sea.

The sea of faith
Was once, too, at the full, and round earth's shore
Lay like the folds of a bright girdle furl'd.
But now I only hear
Its melancholy, long, withdrawing roar,
Retreating, to the breath
Of the night-wind, down the vast edges drear
And naked shingles of the world.

Ah, love, let us be true
To one another! for the world, which seems
To lie before us like a land of dreams,
So various, so beautiful, so new,
Hath really neither joy, nor love, nor light,
Nor certitude, nor peace, nor help for pain;
And we are here as on a darkling plain
Swept with confused alarms of struggle and flight,
Where ignorant armies clash by night.

918

MATTHEW ARNOLD

THE PROGRESS OF POESY

Youth rambles on life's arid mount,
And strikes the rock, and finds the vein,
And brings the water from the fount,
The fount which shall not flow again.

The man mature with labour chops
For the bright stream a channel grand,
And sees not that the sacred drops
Ran off and vanish'd out of hand.

And then the old man totters nigh,
And feebly rakes among the stones.
The mount is mute, the channel dry;
And down he lays his weary bones.

THE LAST WORD

Creep into thy narrow bed,
Creep, and let no more be said!
Vain thy onset! all stands fast.
Thou thyself must break at last.

Let the long contention cease!
Geese are swans, and swans are geese.
Let them have it how they will!
Thou art tired; best be still.

They out-talk'd thee, hiss'd thee, tore thee?
Better men fared thus before thee;
Fired their ringing shot and pass'd,
Hotly charged—and sank at last.

Charge once more, then, and be dumb!
Let the victors, when they come,
When the forts of folly fall,
Find thy body by the wall!

SELF-DEPENDENCE

Weary of myself, and sick of asking
What I am, and what I ought to be,
At this vessel's prow I stand, which bears me
Forwards, forwards, o'er the starlit sea.

And a look of passionate desire
O'er the sea and to the stars I send:
"Ye who from my childhood up have calm'd me,
Calm me, ah, compose me to the end!

Ah, once more," I cried, "ye stars, ye waters,
On my heart your mighty charm renew;
Still, still let me, as I gaze upon you,
Feel my soul becoming vast like you!"

From the intense, clear, star-sown vault of heaven,
Over the lit sea's unquiet way,
In the rustling night-air came the answer:
"Wouldst thou *be* as these are? *Live* as they.

"Unaffrighted by the silence round them,
Undistracted by the sights they see,
These demand not that the things without them
Yield them love, amusement, sympathy.

"And with joy the stars perform their shining,
And the sea its long moon silver'd roll;
For self-poised they live, nor pine with noting
All the fever of some differing soul.

"Bounded by themselves, and unregardful
In what state God's other works may be,
In their own tasks all their powers pouring,
These attain the mighty life you see."

O air-born voice! long since, severely clear,
A cry like thine in mine own heart I hear:
"Resolve to be thyself; and know, that he
Who finds himself, loses his misery!"

920

MATTHEW ARNOLD

MORALITY

We cannot kindle when we will
The fire which in the heart resides;
The spirit bloweth and is still,
In mystery our soul abides.
   But tasks in hours of insight will'd
   Can be through hours of gloom fulfill'd.

With aching hands and bleeding feet
We dig and heap, lay stone on stone;
We bear the burden and the heat
Of the long day, and wish 'twere done.
   Not till the hours of light return,
   All we have built do we discern.

Then, when the clouds are off the soul,
When thou dost bask in Nature's eye,
Ask, how *she* view'd thy self-control,
Thy struggling, task'd morality—
   Nature, whose free, light, cheerful air,
   Oft made thee, in thy gloom, despair.

And she, whose censure thou dost dread,
Whose eye thou wast afraid to seek,
See, on her face a glow is spread,
A strong emotion on her cheek!
   "Ah, child!" she cries, "that strife divine,
   Whence was it, for it is not mine?

"There is no effort on *my* brow—
I do not strive, I do not weep;
I rush with the swift spheres and glow
In joy, and when I will, I sleep.
   Yet that severe, that earnest air,
   I saw, I felt it once—but where?

"I knew not yet the gauge of time,
Nor wore the manacles of space;
I felt it in some other clime,
I saw it in some other place.
   'Twas when the heavenly house I trod,
   And lay upon the breast of God."

THE BURIED LIFE

Light flows our war of mocking words, and yet,
Behold, with tears mine eyes are wet!
I feel a nameless sadness o'er me roll.
Yes, yes, we know that we can jest,
We know, we know that we can smile!
But there's a something in this breast,
To which thy light words bring no rest,
And thy gay smiles no anodyne;
Give me thy hand, and hush awhile,
And turn those limpid eyes on mine,
And let me read there, love! thy inmost soul.

Alas! is even love too weak
To unlock the heart, and let it speak?
Are even lovers powerless to reveal
To one another what indeed they feel?
I knew the mass of men conceal'd
Their thoughts, for fear that if reveal'd
They would by other men be met
With blank indifference, or with blame reproved;
I knew they lived and moved
Trick'd in disguises, alien to the rest
Of men, and alien to themselves—and yet
The same heart beats in every human breast!
But we, my love!—doth a like spell benumb
Our hearts, our voices?—must we too be dumb?

Ah! well for us, if even we,
Even for a moment, can get free
Our heart, and have our lips unchain'd;
For that which seals them hath been deep-ordain'd!

Fate, which foresaw
How frivolous a baby man would be—
By what distractions he would be possess'd,
How he would pour himself in every strife,
And well-nigh change his own identity—
That it might keep from his capricious play
His genuine self, and force him to obey

922

Even in his own despite his being's law,
Bade through the deep recesses of our breast
The unregarded river of our life
Pursue with indiscernible flow its way;
And that we should not see
The buried stream, and seem to be
Eddying at large in blind uncertainty,
Though driving on with it eternally.

But often, in the world's most crowded streets,
But often, in the din of strife,
There rises an unspeakable desire
After the knowledge of our buried life;

A thirst to spend our fire and restless force
In tracking out our true, original course;
A longing to enquire
Into the mystery of this heart which beats
So wild, so deep in us—to know
Whence our lives come and where they go.
And many a man in his own breast then delves,
But deep enough, alas! none ever mines.
And we have been on many thousand lines,
And we have shown, on each, spirit and power;
But hardly have we, for one little hour,
Been on our own line, have we been ourselves—
Hardly had skill to utter one of all
The nameless feelings that course through our breast,
But they course on for ever unexpress'd.
And long we try in vain to speak and act
Our hidden self, and what we say and do
Is eloquent, is well—but 'tis not true!
And then we will no more be rack'd
With inward striving, and demand
Of all the thousand nothings of the hour
Their stupefying power;
Ah yes, and they benumb us at our call!
Yet still, from time to time, vague and forlorn,
From the soul's subterranean depth upborne
As from an infinitely distant land,
Come airs, and floating echoes, and convey
A melancholy into all our day.

Only—but this is rare—
When a belovèd hand is laid in ours,
When, jaded with the rush and glare
Of the interminable hours,
Our eyes can in another's eyes read clear,
When our world-deafen'd ear
Is by the tones of a loved voice caress'd—
A bolt is shot back somewhere in our breast,
And a lost pulse of feeling stirs again.
The eye sinks inward, and the heart lies plain,
And what we mean, we say, and what we would, we know.
A man becomes aware of his life's flow,
And hears its winding murmur, and he sees
The meadows where it glides, the sun, the breeze.

And there arrives a lull in the hot race
Wherein he doth for ever chase
The flying and elusive shadow, rest.
An air of coolness plays upon his face,
And an unwonted calm pervades his breast.
And then he thinks he knows
The hills where his life rose,
And the sea where it goes.

THE FUTURE

A wanderer is man from his birth.
He was born in a ship
On the breast of the river of Time;
Brimming with wonder and joy
He spreads out his arms to the light,
Rivets his gaze on the banks of the stream.

As what he sees is, so have his thoughts been.
Whether he wakes
Where the snowy mountainous pass,
Echoing the screams of the eagles,
Hems in its gorges the bed
Of the new-born clear-flowing stream;
Whether he first sees light

924

MATTHEW ARNOLD

Where the river in gleaming rings
Sluggishly winds through the plain;
Whether in sound of the swallowing sea—
As is the world on the banks,
So is the mind of the man.

Vainly does each, as he glides,
Fable and dream
Of the lands which the river of Time
Had left ere he woke on its breast,
Or shall reach when his eyes have been closed.
Only the tract where he sails
He wots of; only the thoughts,
Raised by the objects he passes, are his.

Who can see the green earth any more
As she was by the sources of Time?
Who imagines her fields as they lay
In the sunshine, unworn by the plough?
Who thinks as they thought,
The tribes who then roam'd on her breast,
Her vigorous, primitive sons?

What girl
Now reads in her bosom as clear
As Rebekah read, when she sate
At eve by the palm-shaded well?
Who guards in her breast
As deep, as pellucid a spring
Of feeling, as tranquil, as sure?

What bard,
At the height of his vision, can deem
Of God, of the world, of the soul,
With a plainness as near,
As flashing as Moses felt,
When he lay in the night by his flock
On the starlit Arabian waste?
Can rise and obey
The beck of the Spirit like him?

925

This tract which the river of Time
Now flows through with us, is the plain.
Gone is the calm of its earlier shore.
Border'd by cities and hoarse
With a thousand cries is its stream.
And we on its breast, our minds
Are confused as the cries which we hear,
Changing and shot as the sights which we see.

And we say that repose has fled
For ever the course of the river of Time.
That cities will crowd to its edge
In a blacker, incessanter line;
That the din will be more on its banks,
Denser the trade on its stream,
Flatter the plain where it flows,
Fiercer the sun overhead.
That never will those on its breast
See an ennobling sight,
Drink of the feeling of quiet again.

But what was before us we know not,
And we know not what shall succeed.

Haply, the river of Time—
As it grows, as the towns on its marge
Fling their wavering lights
On a wider, statelier stream—
May acquire, if not the calm
Of its early mountainous shore,
Yet a solemn peace of its own.

And the width of the waters, the hush
Of the grey expanse where he floats,
Freshening its current and spotted with foam
As it draws to the Ocean, may strike
Peace to the soul of the man on its breast—
As the pale waste widens around him,
As the banks fade dimmer away,
As the stars come out, and the night-wind
Brings up the stream
Murmurs and scents of the infinite sea.

MATTHEW ARNOLD

THE SCHOLAR-GIPSY

Go, for they call you, shepherd, from the hill;
  Go, shepherd, and untie the wattled cotes!
    No longer leave thy wistful flock unfed,
  Nor let thy bawling fellows rack their throats,
    Nor the cropp'd herbage shoot another head.
      But when the fields are still,
  And the tired men and dogs all gone to rest,
  And only the white sheep are sometimes seen
  Cross and recross the strips of moon-blanch'd green.
Come, shepherd, and again renew the quest!

Here, where the reaper was at work of late—
  In this high field's dark corner, where he leaves
    His coat, his basket, and his earthen cruse,
  And in the sun all morning binds the sheaves,
    Then here, at noon, comes back his stores to use—
      Here will I sit and wait,
  While to my ear from uplands far away
  The bleating of the folded flocks is borne,
  With distant cries of reapers in the corn—
All the live murmur of a summer's day.

Screen'd is this nook o'er the high, half-reap'd field,
  And here till sun-down, shepherd! will I be.
    Through the thick corn the scarlet poppies peep,
  And round green roots and yellowing stalks I see
    Pale blue convolvulus in tendrils creep;
      And air-swept lindens yield
  Their scent, and rustle down their perfumed showers
  Of bloom on the bent grass where I am laid,
  And bower me from the August-sun with shade;
And the eye travels down to Oxford's towers.

And near me on the grass lies Glanvil's book—
  Come, let me read the oft-read tale again!
    The story of that Oxford scholar poor,
  Of shining parts and quick inventive brain,
    Who, tired of knocking at preferment's door,
      One summer-morn forsook

927

His friends, and went to learn the gipsy-lore,
 And roam'd the world with that wild brotherhood,
 And came, as most men deem'd, to little good,
But came to Oxford and his friends no more.

But once, years after, in the country-lanes,
 Two scholars, whom at college erst he knew,
 Met him, and of his way of life enquired;
Whereat he answer'd, that the gipsy-crew,
 His mates, had arts to rule as they desired
  The workings of men's brains,
And they can bind them to what thoughts they will.
 "And I," he said, "the secret of their art,
 When fully learn'd, will to the world impart;
But it needs heaven-sent moments for this skill."

This said, he left them, and return'd no more.—
 But rumours hung about the country-side,
 That the lost Scholar long was seen to stray,
Seen by rare glimpses, pensive and tongue-tied,
 In hat of antique shape, and cloak of grey,
  The same the gipsies wore.
Shepherds had met him on the Hurst in spring;
 At some lone alehouse in the Berkshire moors,
 On the warm ingle-bench, the smock-frock'd boors
Had found him seated at their entering.

But, mid their drink and clatter, he would fly.
 And I myself seem half to know thy looks,
 And put the shepherds, wanderer! on thy trace;
And boys who in lone wheatfields scare the rooks
 I ask if thou hast pass'd their quiet place;
  Or in my boat I lie
Moor'd to the cool bank in the summer-heats,
 Mid wide grass meadows which the sunshine fills,
 And watch the warm, green-muffled Cumner hills,
And wonder if thou haunt'st their shy retreats.

For most, I know, thou lov'st retired ground!
 Thee at the ferry Oxford riders blithe,
  Returning home on summer-nights, have met
928

MATTHEW ARNOLD

Crossing the stripling Thames at Bab-lock-hithe,
　Trailing in the cool stream thy fingers wet,
　　As the punt's rope chops round;
And leaning backward in a pensive dream,
　And fostering in thy lap a heap of flowers
　Pluck'd in shy fields and distant Wychwood bowers,
And thine eyes resting on the moonlit stream.

And then they land, and thou art seen no more!—
　Maidens, who from the distant hamlets come
　　To dance around the Fyfield elm in May,
Oft through the darkening fields have seen thee roam,
　Or cross a stile into the public way;
　　Oft thou hast given them store
Of flowers—the frail-leaf'd, white anemony,
　Dark bluebells drench'd with dews of summer eves,
　And purple orchises with spotted leaves—
But none hath words she can report of thee!

And, above Godstow Bridge, when hay-time's here
　In June, and many a scythe in sunshine flames,
　　Men who through those wide fields of breezy grass,
Where black-wing'd swallows haunt the glittering Thames,
　To bathe in the abandon'd lasher pass,
　　Have often pass'd thee near
Sitting upon the river bank o'ergrown;
　Mark'd thine outlandish garb, thy figure spare,
　Thy dark vague eyes, and soft abstracted air—
But, when they came from bathing, thou wast gone!

At some lone homestead in the Cumner hills,
　Where at her open door the housewife darns,
　　Thou hast been seen, or hanging on a gate
To watch the threshers in the mossy barns.
　Children, who early range these slopes and late
　　For cresses from the rills,
Have known thee eying, all an April-day,
　The springing pastures and the feeding kine;
　And mark'd thee, when the stars come out and shine,
Through the long dewy grass move slow away.

929

In autumn, on the skirts of Bagley Wood—
  Where most the gipsies by the turf-edged way
    Pitch their smoked tents, and every bush you see
  With scarlet patches tagg'd and shreds of grey,
    Above the forest-ground called Thessaly—
      The blackbird picking food
  Sees thee, nor stops his meal, nor fears at all;
    So often has he known thee past him stray,
    Rapt, twirling in thy hand a wither'd spray,
  And waiting for the spark from heaven to fall.

And once, in winter, on the causeway chill
  Where home through flooded fields foot-travellers go,
    Have I not pass'd thee on the wooden bridge
  Wrapt in thy cloak and battling with the snow,
    Thy face toward Hinksey and its wintry ridge?
      And thou hast climb'd the hill,
  And gain'd the white brow of the Cumner range;
    Turn'd once to watch, while thick the snowflakes fall.
    The line of festal light in Christ-Church hall—
  Then sought thy straw in some sequester'd grange.

But what—I dream! Two hundred years are flown
  Since first thy story ran through Oxford halls,
    And the grave Glanvil did the tale inscribe
  That thou wert wander'd from the studious walls
    To learn strange arts, and join a gipsy-tribe.
      And thou from earth art gone
  Long since, and in some quiet churchyard laid—
    Some country-nook, where o'er thy unknown grave
    Tall grasses and white flowering nettles wave,
  Under a dark, red-fruited yew-tree's shade.

—No, no, thou hast not felt the lapse of hours!
  For what wears out the life of mortal men?
    'Tis that from change to change their being rolls;
    'Tis that repeated shocks, again, again,
    Exhaust the energy of strongest souls,
      And numb the elastic powers.

930

Till having used our nerves with bliss and teen,
  And tired upon a thousand schemes our wit,
  To the just-pausing Genius we remit
Our well-worn life, and are—what we have been.

Thou hast not lived, why should'st thou perish, so?
  Thou hadst *one* aim, *one* business, *one* desire;
    Else wert thou long since number'd with the dead!
  Else hadst thou spent, like other men, thy fire!
    The generations of thy peers are fled,
      And we ourselves shall go;
  But thou possessest an immortal lot,
    And we imagine thee exempt from age,
    And living as thou liv'st on Glanvil's page,
Because thou hadst—what we, alas! have not.

For early didst thou leave the world, with powers
  Fresh, undiverted to the world without,
    Firm to their mark, not spent on other things;
  Free from the sick fatigue, the languid doubt,
    Which much to have tried, in much been baffled, brings
      O life unlike to ours!
  Who fluctuate idly without term or scope,
    Of whom each strives, nor knows for what he strives,
    And each half lives a hundred different lives;
Who wait like thee, but not, like thee, in hope.

Thou waitest for the spark from heaven! and we,
  Light half-believers of our casual creeds,
    Who never deeply felt, nor clearly will'd,
  Whose insight never has borne fruit in deeds,
    Whose vague resolves never have been fulfill'd;
      For whom each year we see
  Breeds new beginnings, disappointments new;
    Who hesitate and falter life away,
    And lose to-morrow the ground won to-day—
Ah! do not we, wanderer! await it too?

Yes, we await it!—but it still delays,
  And then we suffer! and amongst us one,
    Who most has suffer'd, takes dejectedly

His seat upon the intellectual throne;
    And all his store of sad experience he
      Lays bare of wretched days;
Tells us his misery's birth and growth and signs,
    And how the dying spark of hope was fed,
    And how the breast was soothed, and how the head,
And all his hourly varied anodynes.

This for our wisest! and we others pine,
    And wish the long unhappy dream would end,
      And waive all claim to bliss, and try to bear;
With close-lipp'd patience for our only friend,
    Sad patience, too near neighbour to despair—
      But none has hope like thine!
Thou through the fields and through the woods dost stray,
    Roaming the country-side, a truant boy,
    Nursing thy project in unclouded joy,
And every doubt long blown by time away.

O born in days when wits were fresh and clear,
    And life ran gaily as the sparkling Thames;
      Before this strange disease of modern life,
With its sick hurry, its divided aims,
    Its heads o'ertax'd, its palsied hearts, was rife—
      Fly hence, our contact fear!
Still fly, plunge deeper in the bowering wood!
    Averse, as Dido did with gesture stern
    From her false friend's approach in Hades turn,
Wave us away, and keep thy solitude!

Still nursing the unconquerable hope,
    Still clutching the inviolable shade,
      With a free, onward impulse brushing through,
By night, the silver'd branches of the glade—
    Far on the forest-skirts, where none pursue,
      On some mild pastoral slope
Emerge, and resting on the moonlit pales
    Freshen thy flowers as in former years
    With dew, or listen with enchanted ears,
From the dark dingles, to the nightingales!

932

But fly our paths, our feverish contact fly!
  For strong the infection of our mental strife,
    Which, though it gives no bliss, yet spoils for rest;
  And we should win thee from thy own fair life,
    Like us distracted, and like us unblest.
      Soon, soon thy cheer would die,
  Thy hopes grow timorous, and unfix'd thy powers,
    And thy clear aims be cross and shifting made;
  And then thy glad perennial youth would fade,
  Fade, and grow old at last, and die like ours.

Then fly our greetings, fly our speech and smiles!
  —As some grave Tyrian trader, from the sea,
    Descried at sunrise an emerging prow
  Lifting the cool-hair'd creepers stealthily,
    The fringes of a southward-facing brow
      Among the Ægean isles;
  And saw the merry Grecian coaster come,
    Freighted with amber grapes, and Chian wine,
    Green, bursting figs, and tunnies steep'd in brine—
  And knew the intruders on his ancient home,

The young light-hearted masters of the waves—
  And snatch'd his rudder, and shook out more sail,
    And day and night held on indignantly
  O'er the blue Midland waters with the gale,
    Betwixt the Syrtes and soft Sicily,
      To where the Atlantic raves
  Outside the western straits, and unbent sails
    There where down cloudy cliffs, through sheets of foam,
    Shy traffickers, the dark Iberians come;
  And on the beach undid his corded bales.

THYRSIS

How changed is here each spot man makes or fills!
  In the two Hinkseys nothing keeps the same;
    The village street its haunted mansion lacks,
  And from the sign is gone Sibylla's name,
    And from the roofs the twisted chimney-stacks—
      Are ye too changed, ye hills?

933

See, 'tis no foot of unfamiliar men
  To-night from Oxford up your pathway strays!
  Here came I often, often, in old days—
Thyrsis and I; we still had Thyrsis then.

Runs it not here, the track by Childsworth Farm,
  Past the high wood, to where the elm-tree crowns
  The hill behind whose ridge the sunset flames?
The signal-elm, that looks on Ilsley Downs,
  The Vale, the three lone weirs, the youthful Thames?—
  This winter-eve is warm,
Humid the air! leafless, yet soft as spring,
  The tender purple spray on copse and briers!
  And that sweet city with her dreaming spires,
She needs not June for beauty's heightening,

Lovely all times she lies, lovely to-night!—
  Only, methinks, some loss of habit's power
  Befalls me wandering through this upland dim.
Once pass'd I blindfold here, at any hour;
  Now seldom come I, since I came with him.
  That single elm-tree bright
Against the west—I miss it! is it gone?
  We prized it dearly; while it stood, we said,
  Our friend, the Gipsy-Scholar, was not dead;
While the tree lived, he in these fields lived on.

Too rare, too rare, grow now my visits here,
  But once I knew each field, each flower, each stick;
  And with the country-folk acquaintance made
By barn in threshing-time, by new-built rick.
  Here, too, our shepherd-pipes we first assay'd.
  Ah me! this many a year
My pipe is lost, my shepherd's-holiday!
  Needs must I lose them, needs with heavy heart
  Into the world and wave of men depart,
But Thyrsis of his own will went away.

It irk'd him to be here, he could not rest.
  He loved each simple joy the country yields,
  He loved his mates: but yet he could not keep,
934

For that a shadow lower'd on the fields,
  Here with the shepherds and the silly sheep.
    Some life of men unblest
He knew, which made him droop, and fill'd his head.
  He went; his piping took a troubled sound
  Of storms that rage outside our happy ground;
He could not wait their passing, he is dead.

So, some tempestuous morn in early June,
  When the year's primal burst of bloom is o'er,
  Before the roses and the longest day—
When garden-walks, and all the grassy floor,
  With blossoms red and white of fallen May,
    And chestnut-flowers are strewn—
So have I heard the cuckoo's parting cry,
  From the wet field, through the vext garden-trees,
  Come with the volleying rain and tossing breeze:
The bloom is gone, and with the bloom go I!

Too quick despairer, wherefore wilt thou go?
  Soon will the high Midsummer pomps come on,
  Soon will the musk carnations break and swell,
Soon shall we have gold-dusted snapdragon,
  Sweet-William with his homely cottage-smell,
    And stocks in fragrant blow;
Roses that down the alleys shine afar,
  And open, jasmine-muffled lattices,
  And groups under the dreaming garden-trees,
And the full moon, and the white evening-star.

He hearkens not! light comer, he is flown!
  What matters it? next year he will return,
  And we shall have him in the sweet spring-days,
With whitening hedges, and uncrumpling fern,
  And blue-bells trembling by the forest-ways,
    And scent of hay new-mown.
But Thyrsis never more we swains shall see;
  See him come back, and cut a smoother reed,
  And blow a strain the world at last shall heed—
For Time, not Corydon, hath conquer'd thee!

Alack, for Corydon no rival now!—
But when Sicilian shepherds lost a mate,
   Some good survivor with his flute would go,
Piping a ditty sad for Bion's fate;
   And cross the unpermitted ferry's flow,
      And relax Pluto's brow,
And make leap up with joy the beauteous head
   Of Proserpine, among whose crowned hair
   Are flowers first open'd on Sicilian air,
And flute his friend, like Orpheus, from the dead.

O easy access to the hearer's grace
   When Dorian shepherds sang to Proserpine!
      For she herself had trod Sicilian fields,
   She knew the Dorian water's gush divine,
      She knew each lily white which Enna yields,
         Each rose with blushing face;
   She loved the Dorian pipe, the Dorian strain.
      But ah, of our poor Thames she never heard!
      Her foot the Cumner cowslips never stirr'd;
   And we should tease her with our plaint in vain!

Well! wind-dispersed and vain the words will be,
   Yet, Thyrsis, let me give my grief its hour
      In the old haunt, and find our tree-topp'd hill!
   Who, if not I, for questing here hath power?
      I know the wood which hides the daffodil,
         I know the Fyfield tree,
   I know what white, what purple fritillaries
      The grassy harvest of the river-fields,
      Above by Ensham, down by Sandford, yields,
   And what sedged brooks are Thames's tributaries;

I know these slopes; who knows them if not I?—
   But many a dingle on the loved hillside,
      With thorns once studded, old, white-blossom'd trees,
   Where thick the cowslips grew, and far descried
      High tower'd the spikes of purple orchises,
         Hath since our day put by

The coronals of that forgotten time;
    Down each green bank hath gone the ploughboy's team,
    And only in the hidden brookside gleam
Primroses, orphans of the flowery prime.

Where is the girl, who by the boatman's door,
    Above the locks, above the boating throng,
        Unmoor'd our skiff when through the Wythan flats,
    Red loosestrife and blond meadow-sweet among
        And darting swallows and light water-gnats,
            We track'd the shy Thames shore?
Where are the mowers, who, as the tiny swell
    Of our boat passing heaved the river-grass,
    Stood with suspended scythe to see us pass?—
They all are gone, and thou art gone as well!

Yes, thou art gone! and round me too the night
    In ever-nearing circle weaves her shade.
        I see her veil draw soft across the day,
    I feel her slowly chilling breath invade
        The cheek grown thin, the brown hair sprent with grey;
            I feel her finger light
Laid pausefully upon life's headlong train;—
    The foot less prompt to meet the morning dew,
    The heart less bounding at emotion new,
And hope, once crush'd, less quick to spring again.

And long the way appears, which seem'd so short
    To the less practised eye of sanguine youth;
        And high the mountain-tops, in cloudy air,
    The mountain-tops where is the throne of Truth,
        Tops in life's morning-sun so bright and bare!
            Unbreachable the fort
Of the long-batter'd world uplifts its wall;
    And strange and vain the earthly turmoil grows,
    And near and real the charm of thy repose,
And night as welcome as a friend would fall.

But hush! the upland hath a sudden loss
    Of quiet!—Look, adown the dusk hillside,
        A troop of Oxford hunters going home,

As in old days, jovial and talking, ride!
  From hunting with the Berkshire hounds they come.
    Quick! let me fly, and cross
Into yon farther field!—'Tis done; and see,
  Back'd by the sunset, which doth glorify
  The orange and pale violet evening-sky,
Bare on its lonely ridge, the Tree! the Tree!

I take the omen! Eve lets down her veil,
  The white fog creeps from bush to bush about,
    The west unflushes, the high stars grow bright,
  And in the scatter'd farms the lights come out.
    I cannot reach the signal-tree to-night,
      Yet, happy omen, hail!
  Hear it from thy broad lucent Arno-vale
    (For there thine earth-forgetting eyelids keep
    The morningless and unawakening sleep
  Under the flowery oleanders pale),

Hear it, O Thyrsis, still our tree is there!—
  Ah, vain! These English fields, this upland dim,
    These brambles pale with mist engarlanded,
  That lone, sky-pointing tree, are not for him;
    To a boon southern country he is fled,
      And now in happier air,
  Wandering with the great Mother's train divine
    (And purer or more subtle soul than thee,
    I trow, the mighty Mother doth not see)
  Within a folding of the Apennine,

Thou hearest the immortal chants of old!
  Putting his sickle to the perilous grain
    In the hot cornfield of the Phrygian king,
  For thee the Lityerses-song again
    Young Daphnis with his silver voice doth sing;
      Sings his Sicilian fold,
  His sheep, his hapless love, his blinded eyes—
    And how a call celestial round him rang,
    And heavenward from the fountain-brink he sprang,
  And all the marvel of the golden skies.

938

There thou art gone, and me thou leavest here
   Sole in these fields! yet will I not despair.
     Despair I will not, while I yet descry
   'Neath the soft canopy of English air
     That lonely tree against the western sky.
       Still, still these slopes, 'tis clear,
   Our Gipsy-Scholar haunts, outliving thee!
     Fields where soft sheep from cages pull the hay,
     Woods with anemonies in flower till May,
Know him a wanderer still; then why not me?

A fugitive and gracious light he seeks,
   Shy to illumine; and I seek it too.
     This does not come with houses or with gold,
   With place, with honour, and a flattering crew;
     'Tis not in the world's market bought and sold—
       But the smooth-slipping weeks   .
   Drop by, and leave its seeker still untired;
     Out of the heed of mortals he is gone,
     He wends unfollow'd, he must house alone;
Yet on he fares, by his own heart inspired.

Thou too, O Thyrsis, on like quest was bound!
   Thou wanderedst with me for a little hour!
     Men gave thee nothing; but this happy quest,
   If men esteem'd thee feeble, gave thee power,
     If men procured thee trouble, gave thee rest.
       And this rude Cumner ground,
   Its fir-topped Hurst, its farms, its quiet fields,
     Here cam'st thou in thy jocund youthful time,
     Here was thine height of strength, thy golden prime!
And still the haunt beloved a virtue yields.

What though the music of thy rustic flute
   Kept not for long its happy, country tone;
     Lost it too soon, and learnt a stormy note
   Of men contention-tost, of men who groan,
     Which task'd thy pipe too sore, and tired thy throat—
       It fail'd, and thou wast mute!

939

Yet hadst thou alway visions of our light,
  And long with men of care thou couldst not stay,
  And soon thy foot resumed its wandering way,
Left human haunt, and on alone till night.

Too rare, too rare, grow now my visits here!
  'Mid city-noise, not, as with thee of yore,
    Thyrsis! in reach of sheep-bells is my home.
  —Then through the great town's harsh, heart-wearying
      roar,
    Let in thy voice a whisper often come,
      To chase fatigue and fear:
Why faintest thou? I wander'd till I died.
    Roam on! The light we sought is shining still.
    Dost thou ask proof? Our tree yet crowns the hill,
Our Scholar travels yet the loved hillside.

MEMORIAL VERSES

APRIL, 1850

Goethe in Weimar sleeps, and Greece,
Long since, saw Byron's struggle cease.
But one such death remain'd to come;
The last poetic voice is dumb—
We stand to-day by Wordsworth's tomb.

When Byron's eyes were shut in death,
We bow'd our head and held our breath.
He taught us little; but our soul
Had *felt* him like the thunder's roll.
With shivering heart the strife we saw
Of passion with eternal law;
And yet with reverential awe
We watch'd the fount of fiery life
Which served for that Titanic strife.

When Goethe's death was told, we said:
Sunk, then, is Europe's sagest head.
Physician of the iron age,
Goethe has done his pilgrimage.

He took the suffering human race,
He read each wound, each weakness clear;
And struck his finger on the place,
And said: *Thou ailest here, and here!*
He look'd on Europe's dying hour
Of fitful dream and feverish power;
His eye plunged down the weltering strife,
The turmoil of expiring life—
He said: *The end is everywhere,*
Art still has truth, take refuge there!
And he was happy, if to know
Causes of things, and far below
His feet to see the lurid flow
Of terror, and insane distress,
And headlong fate, be happiness.

And Wordsworth!—Ah, pale ghosts, rejoice!
For never has such soothing voice
Been to your shadowy world convey'd,
Since erst, at morn, some wandering shade
Heard the clear song of Orpheus come
Through Hades, and the mournful gloom.
Wordsworth has gone from us—and ye,
Ah, may ye feel his voice as we!
He too upon a wintry clime
Had fallen—on this iron time
Of doubts, disputes, distractions, fears.
He found us when the age had bound
Our souls in its benumbing round;
He spoke, and loosed our heart in tears.
He laid us as we lay at birth
On the cool flowery lap of earth,
Smiles broke from us and we had ease;
The hills were round us, and the breeze
Went o'er the sun-lit fields again;
Our foreheads felt the wind and rain.
Our youth return'd; for there was shed
On spirits that had long been dead,
Spirits dried up and closely furl'd,
The freshness of the early world.

941

Ah! since dark days still bring to light
Man's prudence and man's fiery might,
Time may restore us in his course
Goethe's sage mind and Byron's force;
But where will Europe's latter hour
Again find Wordsworth's healing power?
Others will teach us how to dare,
And against fear our breast to steel;
Others will strengthen us to bear—
But who, ah! who, will make us feel?
The cloud of mortal destiny,
Others will front it fearlessly—
But who, like him, will put it by?
Keep fresh the grass upon his grave
O Rotha, with thy living wave!
Sing him thy best! for few or none
Hears thy voice right, now he is gone.

HEINE'S GRAVE

"Henri Heine"—'tis here!
That black tombstone, the name
Carved there—no more! and the smooth,
Swarded alleys, the limes
Touch'd with yellow by hot
Summer, but under them still,
In September's bright afternoon,
Shadow, and verdure, and cool.
Trim Montmartre! the faint
Murmur of Paris outside;
Crisp everlasting-flowers,
Yellow and black, on the graves.

Half blind, palsied, in pain,
Hither to come, from the streets'
Uproar, surely not loath
Wast thou, Heine!—to lie
Quiet, to ask for closed
Shutters, and darken'd room,

And cool drinks, and an eased
Posture, and opium, no more;
Hither to come, and to sleep
Under the wings of Renown.

Ah! not little, when pain
Is most quelling, and man
Easily quell'd, and the fine
Temper of genius so soon
Thrills at each smart, is the praise,
Not to have yielded to pain!
No small boast, for a weak
Son of mankind, to the earth
Pinn'd by the thunder, to rear
His bolt-scathed front to the stars;
And, undaunted, retort
'Gainst thick-crashing, insane,
Tyrannous tempests of bale,
Arrowy lightnings of soul.

Hark! through the alley resounds
Mocking laughter! A film
Creeps o'er the sunshine; a breeze
Ruffles the warm afternoon,
Saddens my soul with its chill.
Gibing of spirits in scorn
Shakes every leaf of the grove,
Mars the benignant repose
Of this amiable home of the dead.

Bitter spirits, ye claim
Heine?—Alas, he is yours!
Only a moment I long'd
Here in the quiet to snatch
From such mates the outworn
Poet, and steep him in calm.
Only a moment! I knew
Whose he was who is here
Buried—I knew he was yours!
Ah, I knew that I saw
Here no sepulchre built

In the laurell'd rock, o'er the blue
Naples bay, for a sweet
Tender Virgil! no tomb
On Ravenna sands, in the shade
Of Ravenna pines, for a high
Austere Dante! no grave
By the Avon side, in the bright
Stratford meadows, for thee,
Shakespeare! loveliest of souls,
Peerless in radiance, in joy.

What, then, so harsh and malign,
Heine! distils from thy life?
Poisons the peace of the grave?

I chide with thee not, that thy sharp
Upbraidings often assail'd
England, my country—for we,
Heavy and sad, for her sons,
Long since, deep in our hearts,
Echo the blame of her foes.
We, too, sigh that she flags;
We, too, say that she now—
Scarce comprehending the voice
Of her greatest, golden-mouth'd sons
Of a former age any more—
Stupidly travels her round
Of mechanic business, and lets
Slow die out of her life
Glory, and genius, and joy.

So thou arraign'st her, her foe;
So we arraign her, her sons.

Yes, we arraign her! but she,
The weary Titan, with deaf
Ears, and labour-dimm'd eyes,
Regarding neither to right
Nor left, goes passively by,
Staggering on to her goal;

MATTHEW ARNOLD

Bearing on shoulders immense,
Atlanteän, the load,
Wellnigh not to be borne,
Of the too vast orb of her fate.

But was it thou—I think
Surely it was!—that bard
Unnamed, who, Goethe said,
Had every other gift, but wanted love;
Love, without which the tongue
Even of angels sounds amiss?

Charm is the glory which makes
Song of the poet divine,
Love is the fountain of charm.
How without charm wilt thou draw,
Poet! the world to thy way?
Not by the lightnings of wit—
Not by the thunder of scorn!
These to the world, too, are given;
Wit it possesses, and scorn—
Charm is the poet's alone.
Hollow and dull are the great,
And artists envious, and the mob profane.
We know all this, we know!
Cam'st thou from heaven, O child
Of light! but this to declare?
Alas, to help us forget
Such barren knowledge awhile,
God gave the poet his song!

Therefore a secret unrest
Tortured thee, brilliant and bold!
Therefore triumph itself
Tasted amiss to thy soul.
Therefore, with blood of thy foes,
Trickled in silence thine own.
Therefore the victor's heart
Broke on the field of his fame.

Ah! as of old, from the pomp
Of Italian Milan, the fair
Flower of marble of white
Southern palaces—steps
Border'd by statues, and walks
Terraced, and orange-bowers
Heavy with fragrance—the blond
German Kaiser full oft
Long'd himself back to the fields,
Rivers, and high-roof'd towns
Of his native Germany; so,
So, how often! from hot
Paris drawing-rooms, and lamps
Blazing, and brilliant crowds,
Starr'd and jewell'd, of men
Famous, of women the queens
Of dazzling converse—from fumes
Of praise, hot, heady fumes, to the poor brain
That mount, that madden—how oft
Heine's spirit outworn
Long'd itself out of the din,
Back to the tranquil, the cool
Far German home of his youth!

See! in the May-afternoon,
O'er the fresh, short turf of the Hartz,
A youth, with the foot of youth,
Heine! thou climbest again!
Up, through the tall dark firs
Warming their heads in the sun,
Chequering the grass with their shade—
Up, by the stream, with its huge
Moss-hung boulders, and thin
Musical water half-hid—
Up, o'er the rock-strewn slope,
With the sinking sun, and the air
Chill, and the shadows now
Long on the grey hill-side—
To the stone-roof'd hut at the top!

946

MATTHEW ARNOLD

Or, yet later, in watch
On the roof of the Brocken-tower
Thou standest, gazing!—to see
The broad red sun, over field,
Forest, and city, and spire,
And mist-track'd stream of the wide,
Wide German land, going down
In a bank of vapours—again
Standest, at nightfall, alone!

Or, next morning, with limbs
Rested by slumber, and heart
Freshen'd and light with the May,
O'er the gracious spurs coming down
Of the Lower Hartz, among oaks,
And beechen coverts, and copse
Of hazels green in whose depth
Ilse, the fairy transform'd,
In a thousand water-breaks light
Pours her petulant youth—
Climbing the rock which juts
O'er the valley, the dizzily perch'd
Rock—to its iron cross
Once more thou cling'st; to the Cross
Clingest! with smiles, with a sigh!

Goethe, too, had been there.
In the long-past winter he came
To the frozen Hartz, with his soul
Passionate, eager—his youth
All in ferment!—but he
Destined to work and to live
Left it, and thou, alas!
Only to laugh and to die.

But something prompts me: Not thus
Take leave of Heine! not thus
Speak the last word at his grave!
Not in pity, and not
With half censure—with awe
Hail, as it passes from earth

947

Scattering lightnings, that soul!
The Spirit of the world,
Beholding the absurdity of men—
Their vaunts, their feats—let a sardonic smile,
For one short moment, wander o'er his lips.
That smile was Heine!—for its earthly hour
The strange guest sparkled; now 'tis pass'd away.

That was Heine! and we,
Myriads who live, who have lived,
What are we all, but a mood,
A single mood, of the life
Of the Spirit in whom we exist,
Who alone is all things in one?
Spirit, who fillest us all!
Spirit, who utterest in each
New-coming son of mankind
Such of thy thoughts as thou wilt!
O thou, one of whose moods,
Bitter and strange, was the life
Of Heine—his strange, alas,
His bitter life!—may a life
Other and milder be mine!
May'st thou a mood more serene,
Happier, have utter'd in mine!
May'st thou the rapture of peace
Deep have embreathed at its core;
Made it a ray of thy thought,
Made it a beat of thy joy!

STANZAS IN MEMORY OF THE AUTHOR OF "OBERMANN"

. . . .

Some secrets may the poet tell,
For the world loves new ways;
To tell too deep ones is not well—
It knows not what he says.

MATTHEW ARNOLD

Yet, of the spirits who have reign'd
In this our troubled day,
I know but two, who have attain'd,
Save thee, to see their way.

By England's lakes, in grey old age,
His quiet home one keeps;
And one, the strong much-toiling sage,
In German Weimar sleeps.

But Wordsworth's eyes avert their ken
From half of human fate;
And Goethe's course few sons of men
May think to emulate.

For he pursued a lonely road,
His eyes on Nature's plan;
Neither made man too much a God,
Nor God too much a man.

Strong was he, with a spirit free
From mists, and sane, and clear;
Clearer, how much! than ours—yet we
Have a worse course to steer.

For though his manhood bore the blast
Of a tremendous time,
Yet in a tranquil world was pass'd
His tender youthful prime.

But we, brought forth and rear'd in hours
Of change, alarm, surprise—
What shelter to grow ripe is ours?
What leisure to grow wise?

Like children bathing on the shore,
Buried a wave beneath,
The second wave succeeds, before
We have had time to breathe....

Too fast we live, too much are tried,
Too harass'd, to attain
Wordsworth's sweet calm, or Goethe's wide
And luminous view to gain.

.   .   .   .

EMPEDOCLES ON ETNA

.   .   .   .   .   .

Through the black, rushing smoke-bursts,
Thick breaks the red flame;
All Etna heaves fiercely
Her forest-clothed frame.

Not here, O Apollo!
Are haunts meet for thee.
But, where Helicon breaks down
In cliff to the sea.

Where the moon-silver'd inlets
Send far their light voice
Up the still vale of Thisbe,
O speed, and rejoice!

On the sward at the cliff-top
Lie strewn the white flocks,
On the cliff-side the pigeons
Roost deep in the rocks.

In the moonlight the shepherds,
Soft lull'd by the rills,
Lie wrapt in their blankets
Asleep on the hills.

—What forms are these coming
So white through the gloom?
What garments out-glistening
The gold-flower'd broom?

What sweet-breathing presence
Out-perfumes the thyme?
What voices enrapture
The night's balmy prime?—

'Tis Apollo comes leading
His choir, the Nine.
—The leader is fairest,
But all are divine.

They are lost in the hollows!
They stream up again!
What seeks on this mountain
The glorified train?—

They bathe on this mountain,
In the spring by their road;
Then on to Olympus,
Their endless abode.

—Whose praise do they mention?
Of what is it told?—
What will be forever;
What was from of old.

First hymn they the Father
Of all things; and then,
The rest of immortals,
The action of men.

The day in his hotness,
The strife with the palm;
The night in her silence,
The stars in their calm.

THE PAGAN WORLD

In his cool hall, with haggard eyes,
The Roman noble lay;
He drove abroad, in furious guise,
Along the Appian way.

He made a feast, drank fierce and fast,
And crown'd his hair with flowers—
No easier nor no quicker pass'd
The impracticable hours.

The brooding East with awe beheld
Her impious younger world.
The Roman tempest swell'd and swell'd,
And on her head was hurl'd.

The East bow'd low before the blast
In patient, deep disdain;
She let the legions thunder past,
And plunged in thought again.

So well she mused, a morning broke
Across her spirit grey;
A conquering, new-born joy awoke,
And fill'd her life with day.

"Poor world," she cried, "so deep accurst
That runn'st from pole to pole
To seek a draught to slake thy thirst—
Go, seek it in thy soul!"

She heard it, the victorious West,
In crown and sword array'd!
She felt the void which mined her breast,
She shiver'd and obey'd.

She veil'd her eagles, snapp'd her sword,
And laid her sceptre down;
Her stately purple she abhorr'd,
And her imperial crown.

She broke her flutes, she stopp'd her sports,
Her artists could not please;
She tore her books, she shut her courts,
She fled her palaces;

Lust of the eye and pride of life
She left it all behind,
And hurried, torn with inward strife,
The wilderness to find.

Tears wash'd the trouble from her face!
She changed into a child!
'Mid weeds and wrecks she stood—a place
Of ruin—but she smiled!
—OBERMANN ONCE MORE.

DESTINY

Why each is striving, from of old,
To love more deeply than he can?
Still would be true, yet still grows cold?
—Ask of the Powers that sport with man!

They yoked in him, for endless strife,
A heart of ice, a soul of fire;
And hurled him on the Field of Life,
An aimless unallayed Desire.

THE CANTICLE OF THE SUN

(Translated from St. Francis Di Assisi)

O Most High Almighty Good LORD GOD to Thee belong praise, glory, honour and all blessing.

PRAISED be my LORD GOD with all His creatures and specially our brother the SUN who brings us the day and who brings us the light: fair is he and shines with a very great splendour. O LORD, he signifies to us Thee.

PRAISED be my LORD for our sister the Moon and for the stars the which He has set clear and lovely in heaven.

PRAISED be my LORD for our brother the Wind and for air and cloud, calms and all weather by the which Thou upholdest life in all creatures.

953

PRAISED be my LORD for our sister the Water who is very serviceable unto us and humble and precious and clean.

PRAISED be my LORD for our brother Fire through whom Thou givest us light in the darkness: and he is bright and pleasant and very mighty and strong.

PRAISED be my LORD for our sister the Earth, the which doth sustain us and keep us and bringeth forth divers fruits—and flowers of many colours and grass.

PRAISED be my LORD for all who pardon one another for His love's sake and who endure weakness and tribulation: blessed are they who peaceably endure—for Thou O, Most Highest shall give them a crown.

PRAISED be my LORD for our sister the death of the body from which no man escapeth—Woe to him who dieth in mortal sin. Blessed are they who are found walking by Thy most holy will for the second death shall have no power to do them harm.

PRAISE ye and bless the Lord and give thanks unto Him, and serve Him with great humility.

William (Johnson) Cory

HERACLITUS

They told me, Heraclitus, they told me you were dead,
They brought me bitter news to hear and bitter tears to shed.
I wept as I remember'd how often you and I
Had tired the sun with talking and sent him down the sky.

And now that thou art lying, my dear old Carian guest,
A handful of grey ashes, long, long ago at rest,
Still are thy pleasant voices, thy nightingales, awake;
For Death, he taketh all away, but them he cannot take.

954

WILLIAM (JOHNSON) CORY

OH, EARLIER SHALL THE ROSEBUDS BLOW

Oh, earlier shall the rosebuds blow,
   In after years, those happier years,
And children weep, when we lie low,
   Far fewer tears, far softer tears.

Oh, true shall boyish laughter ring,
   Like tinkling chimes, in kinder times!
And merrier shall the maiden sing:
   And I not there, and I not there.

Like lightning in the summer night
   Their mirth shall be, so quick and free;
And oh! the flash of their delight
   I shall not see, I may not see.

In deeper dream, with wider range,
   Those eyes shall shine, but not on mine:
Unmoved, unblest, by worldly change,
   The dead must rest, the dead shall rest.

MIMNERMUS IN CHURCH

You promise heavens free from strife,
   Pure truth, and perfect change of will;
But sweet, sweet is this human life,
   So sweet, I fain would breathe it still;
Your chilly stars I can forgo,
This warm kind world is all I know.

You say there is no substance here,
   One great reality above:
Back from that void I shrink in fear,
   And child-like hide myself in love:
Show me what angels feel. Till then
I cling, a mere weak man, to men.

You bid me lift my mean desires
  From faltering lips and fitful veins
To sexless souls, ideal quires,
  Unwearied voices, wordless strains:
My mind with fonder welcome owns
One dear dead friend's remember'd tones.

Forsooth the present we must give
  To that which cannot pass away;
All beauteous things for which we live
  By laws of time and space decay.
But O, the very reason why
I clasp them, is because they die.

Coventry Patmore

THE ANGEL IN THE HOUSE

Preludes

UNTHRIFT

Ah, wasteful woman, she that may
  On her sweet self set her own price,
Knowing man cannot choose but pay,
  How has she cheapened paradise;
How given for nought her priceless gift,
  How spoiled the bread, and spilled the wine,
Which, spent with due, respective thrift,
  Had made brutes men, and men divine.

HONOUR AND DESERT

O Queen, awake to thy renown,
  Require what 'tis our wealth to give,
And comprehend and wear the crown
  Of thy despised prerogative!

COVENTRY PATMORE

I, who in manhood's name at length
    With glad songs come to abdicate
The gross regality of strength,
    Must yet in this thy praise abate,
That, through thine erring humbleness
    And disregard of thy degree,
Mainly, has man been so much less
    Than fits his fellowship with thee.

High thoughts had shaped the foolish brow,
    The coward had grasped the hero's sword,
The vilest had been great, hadst thou,
    Just to thyself, been worth's reward.
But lofty honours undersold
    Seller and buyer both disgrace;
And favours that make folly bold
    Banish the light from virtue's face.

THE ROSE OF THE WORLD

Lo, when the Lord made North and South,
    And sun and moon ordainèd, He,
Forthbringing each by word of mouth
    In order of its dignity
Did man from the crude clay express
    By sequence, and all else decreed,
He formed the woman; nor might less
    Than Sabbath such a work succeed.

And still with favour singled out,
    Marred less than man by mortal fall,
Her disposition is devout,
    Her countenance angelical:
The best things that the best believe
    Are in her face so kindly writ
The faithless, seeing her, conceive
    Not only heaven, but hope of it;
No idle thought her instinct shrouds,
    But fancy chequers settled sense,
Like alteration of the clouds
    On noonday's azure permanence.

957

Pure dignity, composure, ease,
  Declare affections nobly fixed,
And impulse sprung from due degrees
  Of sense and spirit sweetly mixed.
Her modesty, her chiefest grace,
  The cestus clasping Venus' side,
How potent to deject the face
  Of him who would affront its pride!

Wrong dares not in her presence speak,
  Nor spotted thought its taint disclose
Under the protest of a cheek
  Outbragging Nature's boast, the rose.
In mind and manners how discreet;
  How artless in her very art;
How candid in discourse; how sweet
  The concord of her lips and heart!

How simple and how circumspect;
  How subtle and how fancy-free;
Though sacred to her love, how decked
  With unexclusive courtesy;
How quick in talk to see from far
  The way to vanquish or evade;
How able her persuasions are
  To prove, her reasons to persuade.

How (not to call true instinct's bent
  And woman's very nature, harm),
How amiable and innocent
  Her pleasure in her power to charm;
How humbly careful to attract,
  Though crowned with all the soul desires,
Connubial aptitude, exact,
  Diversity that never tires!

THE TRIBUTE

Boon Nature to the woman bows;
  She walks in earth's whole glory clad,
And, chiefest far herself of shows,
  All others help her and are glad:

COVENTRY PATMORE

No splendour 'neath the sky's proud dome
    But serves her for familiar wear;
The far-fetched diamond finds its home
    Flashing and smouldering in her hair;
For her the seas their pearls reveal;
    Art and strange lands her pomp supply
With purple, chrome, and cochineal,
    Ochre, and lapis lazuli;
The worm its golden woof presents;
    Whatever runs, flies, dives, or delves,
All doff for her their ornaments,
    Which suit her better than themselves;
And all, by this their power to give,
    Proving her right to take, proclaim
Her beauty's clear prerogative
    To profit so by Eden's blame.

THE MARRIED LOVER

Why, having won her, do I woo?
    Because her spirit's vestal grace
Provokes me always to pursue,
    But, spirit-like, eludes embrace;
Because her womanhood is such
    That, as on court-days subjects kiss
The Queen's hand, yet so near a touch
    Affirms no mean familiarness;
Nay, rather marks more fair the height,
    Which can with safety so neglect
To dread, as lower ladies might,
    That grace could meet with disrespect;
Thus she with happy favour feeds
    Allegiance from a love so high
That thence no false conceit proceeds
    Of difference bridged, or state put by;
Because, although in act and word
    As lowly as a wife can be,
Her manners, when they call me lord,
    Remind me 'tis by courtesy;

959

Not with her least consent of will,
    Which would my proud affection hurt,
But by the noble style that still
    Imputes an unattained desert;
Because her gay and lofty brows,
    When all is won which hope can ask,
Reflect a light of hopeless snows
    That bright in virgin ether bask;
Because, though free of the outer court
    I am, this Temple keeps its shrine
Sacred to heaven; because, in short,
    She's not and never can be mine.

THE TOYS

My little Son, who looked from thoughtful eyes
And moved and spoke in quiet grown-up wise,
Having my law the seventh time disobeyed,
I struck him, and dismissed
With hard words and unkissed,
—His Mother, who was patient, being dead.
Then, fearing lest his grief should hinder sleep,
I visited his bed,
But found him slumbering deep,
With darkened eyelids, and their lashes yet
From his late sobbing wet.
And I, with moan,
Kissing away his tears, left others of my own;
For, on a table drawn beside his head,
He had put, within his reach,
A box of counters and a red-veined stone,
A piece of glass abraded by the beach,
And six or seven shells,
A bottle with bluebells,
And two French copper coins, ranged there with careful art,
To comfort his sad heart.
So when that night I prayed
To God, I wept, and said:
Ah, when at last we lie with trancèd breath,
Not vexing Thee in death,

960

COVENTRY PATMORE

And Thou rememberest of what toys
We made our joys,
How weakly understood
Thy great commanded good,
Then, fatherly not less
Than I whom Thou has moulded from the clay,
Thou'lt leave Thy wrath, and say,
"I will be sorry for their childishness."

DEPARTURE

It was not like your great and gracious ways!
Do you, that have naught other to lament,
Never, my love, repent
Of how, that July afternoon,
You went
With sudden, unintelligible phrase,
And frighten'd eye,
Upon your journey of so many days
Without a single kiss, or a good-bye?
I knew, indeed, that you were parting soon;
And so we sate, within the low sun's rays,
You whispering to me, for your voice was weak,
Your harrowing praise.
Well, it was well
To hear you such things speak,
And I could tell
What made your eyes a growing gloom of love,
As a warm South-wind sombres a March grove.

And it was like your great and gracious ways
To turn your talk on daily things, my Dear,
Lifting the luminous, pathetic lash
To let the laughter flash,
Whilst I drew near,
Because you spoke so low that I could scarcely hear.
But all at once to leave me at the last,
More at the wonder than the loss aghast,

With huddled, unintelligible phrase,
And frighten'd eye,
And go your journey of all days
With not one kiss, or a good-bye,
And the only loveless look the look with which you pass'd:
'Twas all unlike your great and gracious ways.

MAGNA EST VERITAS

Here, in this little Bay,
Full of tumultuous life and great repose,
Where, twice a day,
The purposeless, glad ocean comes and goes,
Under high cliffs, and far from the huge town,
I sit me down.
For want of me the world's course will not fail:
When all its work is done, the lie shall rot;
The truth is great, and shall prevail,
When none cares whether it prevail or not.

Thomas Wentworth Higginson

THE TRUMPETER

I blew, I blew, the trumpet loudly sounding;
I blew, I blew, the heart within me bounding;
The world was fresh and fair, yet dark with wrong,
And men stood forth to conquer at the song—
             I blew! I blew! I blew!

The field is won, the minstrels loud are crying,
And all the world is peace, and I am dying.
Yet this forgotten life was not in vain;
Enough if I alone recall the strain,
             I blew! I blew! I blew!

962

Sydney Dobell

KEITH OF RAVELSTON

The murmur of the mourning ghost
   That keeps the shadowy kine:
"Oh, Keith of Ravelston,
   The sorrows of thy line!"

Ravelston, Ravelston,
   The merry path that leads
Down the golden morning hill
   And through the silver meads;

Ravelston, Ravelston,
   The stile beneath the tree,
The maid that kept her mother's kine,
   The song that sang she!

She sang her song, she kept her kine,
   She sat beneath the thorn,
When Andrew Keith of Ravelston
   Rode through the Monday morn.

His henchmen sing, his hawk-bells ring,
   His belted jewels shine;
Oh, Keith of Ravelston,
   The sorrows of thy line!

Year after year, where Andrew came,
   Comes evening down the glade;
And still there sits a moonshine ghost
   Where sat the sunshine maid.

Her misty hair is faint and fair,
   She keeps the shadowy kine;—
Oh, Keith of Ravelston,
   The sorrows of thy line!

I lay my hand upon the stile,
　　The stile is lone and cold;
The burnie that goes babbling by
　　Says nought that can be told.

Yet, stranger! here, from year to year,
　　She keeps her shadowy kine;—
Oh, Keith of Ravelston,
　　The sorrows of thy line!

Step out three steps where Andrew stood—
　　Why blanch thy cheeks for fear!
The ancient stile is not alone,
　　'Tis not the burn I hear!

She makes her immemorial moan,
　　She keeps her shadowy kine;—
Oh, Keith of Ravelston,
　　The sorrows of thy line.

AMERICA

Nor force nor fraud shall sunder us! Oh ye
Who north or south, on east or western land,
Native to noble sounds, say truth for truth,
Freedom for freedom, love for love, and God
For God; Oh ye who in eternal youth
Speak with a living and creative flood
This universal English, and do stand
Its breathing book; live worthy of that grand
Heroic utterance—parted, yet a whole,
Far, yet unsevered,—children brave and free
Of the great Mother-tongue, and ye shall be
Lords of an Empire wide as Shakespeare's soul,
Sublime as Milton's immemorial theme,
And rich as Chaucer's speech, and fair as Spenser's dream.

Richard Henry Stoddard

THE FLIGHT OF YOUTH

There are gains for all our losses,
    There are balms for all our pain:
But when youth, the dream, departs,
It takes something from our hearts,
    And it never comes again.

We are stronger, and are better,
    Under manhood's sterner reign:
Still we feel that something sweet
Followed youth, with flying feet,
    And will never come again.

Something beautiful is vanished,
    And we sigh for it in vain:
We behold it everywhere,
On the earth, and in the air,
    But it never comes again!

Dante Gabriel Rossetti

THE BLESSED DAMOZEL

The blessed damozel leaned out
    From the gold bar of Heaven;
Her eyes were deeper than the depth
    Of waters stilled at even;
She had three lilies in her hand,
    And the stars in her hair were seven.

Her robe, ungirt from clasp to hem,
    No wrought flowers did adorn,
But a white rose of Mary's gift,
    For service meetly worn;
Her hair that lay along her back
    Was yellow like ripe corn.

965

Herseemed she scarce had been a day
    One of God's choristers;
The wonder was not yet quite gone
    From that still look of hers;
Albeit, to them she left, her day
    Had counted as ten years.

(To one, it is ten years of years.
    . . . Yet now, and in this place,
Surely she leaned o'er me—her hair
    Fell all about my face. . . .
Nothing: the autumn fall of leaves.
    The whole year sets apace.)

It was the rampart of God's house
    That she was standing on;
By God built over the sheer depth
    The which is Space begun;
So high, that looking downward thence
    She scarce could see the sun.

It lies in Heaven, across the flood
    Of ether, as a bridge.
Beneath, the tides of day and night
    With flame and darkness ridge
The void, as low as where this earth
    Spins like a fretful midge.

Around her, lovers, newly met
    'Mid deathless love's acclaims,
Spoke evermore among themselves
    Their heart-remembered names;
And the souls mounting up to God
    Went by her like thin flames.

And still she bowed herself and stooped
    Out of the circling charm;
Until her bosom must have made
    The bar she leaned on warm,
And the lilies lay as if asleep
    Along her bended arm.

DANTE GABRIEL ROSSETTI

From the fixed place of Heaven she saw
    Time like a pulse shake fierce
Through all the worlds. Her gaze still strove
    Within the gulf to pierce
Its path; and now she spoke as when
    The stars sang in their spheres.

The sun was gone now; the curled moon
    Was like a little feather
Fluttering far down the gulf; and now
    She spoke through the still weather.
Her voice was like the voice the stars
    Had when they sang together.

(Ah sweet! Even now, in that bird's song,
    Strove not her accents there,
Fain to be hearkened? When those bells
    Possessed the mid-day air,
Strove not her steps to reach my side
    Down all the echoing stair?)

"I wish that he were come to me,
    For he will come," she said.
"Have not I prayed in Heaven?—on earth,
    Lord, Lord, has he not prayed?
Are not two prayers a perfect strength?
    And shall I feel afraid?

"When round his head the aureole clings,
    And he is clothed in white,
I'll take his hand and go with him
    To the deep wells of light;
As unto a stream we will step down,
    And bathe there in God's sight.

"We two will stand beside that shrine,
    Occult, withheld, untrod,
Whose lamps are stirred continually
    With prayer sent up to God;
And see our old prayers, granted, melt
    Each like a little cloud.

967

"We two will lie i' the shadow of
  That living mystic tree
Within whose secret growth the Dove
  Is sometimes felt to be,
While every leaf that His plumes touch
  Saith His Name audibly.

"And I myself will teach to him,
  I myself, lying so,
The songs I sing here; which his voice
  Shall pause in, hushed and slow,
And find some knowledge at each pause,
  Or some new thing to know."

(Alas! we two, we two, thou say'st!
  Yea, one wast thou with me
That once of old. But shall God lift
  To endless unity
The soul whose likeness with thy soul
  Was but its love for thee?)

"We two," she said, "will seek the groves
  Where the lady Mary is,
With her five handmaidens, whose names
  Are five sweet symphonies,
Cecily, Gertrude, Magdalen,
  Margaret and Rosalys.

"Circlewise sit they, with bound locks
  And foreheads garlanded;
Into the fine cloth white like flame
  Weaving the golden thread,
To fashion the birth-robes for them
  Who are just born, being dead.

"He shall fear, haply, and be dumb:
  Then will I lay my cheek
To his, and tell about our love,
  Not once abashed or weak:
And the dear Mother will approve
  My pride, and let me speak.

"Herself shall bring us, hand in hand,
　　To Him round whom all souls
Kneel, the clear-ranged unnumbered heads
　　Bowed with their aureoles:
And angels meeting us shall sing
　　To their citherns and citoles.

"There will I ask of Christ the Lord
　　Thus much for him and me:—
Only to live as once on earth
　　With Love, only to be,
As then awhile, for ever now
　　Together, I and he."

She gazed and listened and then said,
　　Less sad of speech than mild,—
"All this is when he comes."　She ceased.
　　The light thrilled towards her, filled
With angels in strong level flight.
　　Her eyes prayed, and she smiled.

(I saw her smile.)　But soon their path
　　Was vague in distant spheres:
And then she cast her arms along
　　The golden barriers,
And laid her face between her hands,
　　And wept.　(I heard her tears.)

THE PORTRAIT

This is her picture as she was:
　　It seems a thing to wonder on,
As though mine image in the glass
　　Should tarry when myself am gone.
I gaze until she seems to stir,—
Until mine eyes almost aver
　　That now, even now, the sweet lips part
　　To breathe the words of the sweet heart:—
And yet the earth is over her.

Alas! even such the thin-drawn ray
　　That makes the prison-depths more rude,—
The drip of water night and day
　　Giving a tongue to solitude.
Yet only this, of love's whole prize,
Remains; save what in mournful guise
　　Takes counsel with my soul alone,—
　　Save what is secret and unknown,
Below the earth, above the skies.

In painting her I shrined her face
　　'Mid mystic trees, where light falls in
Hardly at all; a covert place
　　Where you might think to find a din
Of doubtful talk, and a live flame
Wandering, and many a shape whose name
　　Not itself knoweth, and old dew,
　　And your own footsteps meeting you,
And all things going as they came.

A deep dim wood; and there she stands
　　As in that wood that day: for so
Was the still movement of her hands
　　And such the pure line's gracious flow.
And passing fair the type must seem,
Unknown the presence and the dream.
　　'Tis she: though of herself, alas!
　　Less than her shadow on the grass
Or than her image in the stream.

That day we met there, I and she
　　One with the other all alone;
And we were blithe; yet memory
　　Saddens those hours, as when the moon
Looks upon daylight.　And with her
I stooped to drink the spring-water,
　　Athirst where other waters sprang;
　　And where the echo is, she sang,—
My soul another echo there.

970

But when that hour my soul won strength
   For words whose silence wastes and kills,
Dull raindrops smote us, and at length
   Thundered the heat within the hills.
That eve I spoke those words again
Beside the pelted window-pane;
   And there she hearkened what I said,
   With under-glances that surveyed
The empty pastures blind with rain.

Next day the memories of these things,
   Like leaves through which a bird has flown,
Still vibrated with Love's warm wings;
   Till I must make them all my own
And paint this picture. So, 'twixt ease
Of talk and sweet long silences,
   She stood among the plants in bloom
   At windows of a summer room,
To feign the shadow of the trees.

And as I wrought, while all above
   And all around was fragrant air,
In the sick burthen of my love
   It seemed each sun-thrilled blossom there
Beat like a heart among the leaves.
O heart that never beats nor heaves,
   In that one darkness lying still,
   What now to thee my love's great will,
Or the fine web the sunshine weaves?

For now doth daylight disavow
   Those days,—nought left to see or hear.
Only in solemn whispers now
   At night-time these things reach mine ear,
When the leaf-shadows at a breath
Shrink in the road, and all the heath,
   Forest and water, far and wide,
   In limpid starlight glorified,
Lie like the mystery of death.

Last night at last I could have slept,
　　And yet delayed my sleep till dawn,
Still wandering.　Then it was I wept:
　　For unawares I came upon
Those glades where once she walked with me:
And as I stood there suddenly,
　　All wan with traversing the night,
　　Upon the desolate verge of light
Yearned loud the iron-bosomed sea.

Even so, where Heaven holds breath and hears
　　The beating heart of Love's own breast,—
Where round the secret of all spheres
　　All angels lay their wings to rest,—
How shall my soul stand rapt and awed,
When, by the new birth borne abroad
　　Throughout the music of the suns,
　　It enters in her soul at once
And knows the silence there for God!

Here with her face doth memory sit
　　Meanwhile, and wait the day's decline,
Till other eyes shall look from it,
　　Eyes of the spirit's Palestine,
Even than the old gaze tenderer:
While hopes and aims long lost with her
　　Stand round her image side by side,
　　Like tombs of pilgrims that have died
About the Holy Sepulchre.

THE HOUSE OF LIFE

INTRODUCTORY SONNET

A sonnet is a moment's monument,—
Memorial from the Soul's eternity
To one dead deathless hour.　Look that it be,
Whether for lustral rite or dire portent,
Of its own arduous fulness reverent:
Carve it in ivory or in ebony,
As Day or Night may rule; and let Time see
Its flowering crest impearled and orient.

DANTE GABRIEL ROSSETTI

A Sonnet is a coin: its face reveals
The soul,—its converse, to what Power 'tis due:—
Whether for tribute to the august appeals
Of Life, or dower in Love's high retinue,
It serve; or, 'mid the dark wharf's cavernous breath,
In Charon's palm it pay the toll to Death.

I: LOVE ENTHRONED

I marked all kindred Powers the heart finds fair:—
    Truth, with awed lips; and Hope, with eyes upcast;
    And Fame, whose loud wings fan the ashen Past
To signal-fires, Oblivion's flight to scare;
And Youth, with still some single golden hair
    Unto his shoulder clinging, since the last
    Embrace wherein two sweet arms held him fast;
And Life, still wreathing flowers for Death to wear.

Love's throne was not with these; but far above
    All passionate wind of welcome and farewell
He sat in breathless bowers they dream not of;
    Though Truth foreknow Love's heart, and Hope foretell,
    And Fame be for Love's sake desirable,
And Youth be dear, and Life be sweet to Love.

IV: LOVESIGHT

When do I see thee most, belovèd one?
    When in the light the spirits of mine eyes
    Before thy face, their altar, solemnise
The worship of that Love through thee made known?
Or when in the dusk hours, (we two alone,)
    Close-kissed and eloquent of still replies
    Thy twilight-hidden glimmering visage lies,
And my soul only sees thy soul its own?

O love, my love! if I no more should see
Thyself, nor on the earth the shadow of thee,
    Nor image of thine eyes in any spring,—
How then should sound upon Life's darkening slope
The ground-whirl of the perished leaves of Hope,
    The wind of Death's imperishable wing?

V: HEART'S HOPE

By what word's power, the key of paths untrod,
  Shall I the difficult deeps of Love explore,
  Till parted waves of Song yield up the shore
Even as that sea which Israel crossed dryshod?
For lo! in some poor rhythmic period,
  Lady, I fain would tell how evermore
  Thy soul I know not from thy body, nor
Thee from myself, neither our love from God.

Yea, in God's name, and Love's, and thine, would I
  Draw from one loving heart such evidence
As to all hearts all things shall signify;
  Tender as dawn's first hill-fire, and intense
  As instantaneous penetrating sense,
In Spring's birth-hour, of other Springs gone by.

XIII: THE LOVER'S WALK

Sweet twining hedgeflowers wind-stirred in no wise
  On this June day; and hand that clings in hand:—
  Still glades; and meeting faces scarcely fann'd:—
An osier-odoured stream that draws the skies
Deep to its heart; and mirrored eyes in eyes:—
  Fresh hourly wonder o'er the Summer land
  Of light and cloud; and two souls softly spann'd
With one o'erarching heaven of smiles and sighs:—

·Even such their path, whose bodies lean unto
  Each other's visible sweetness amorously,—
Whose passionate hearts lean by Love's high decree
Together on his heart for ever true,
As the cloud-foaming firmamental blue
  Rests on the blue line of a foamless sea.

XXVI: WINGED HOURS

Each hour until we meet is as a bird
  That wings from far his gradual way along
  The rustling covert of my soul,—his song
Still loudlier trilled through leaves more deeply stirr'd:

But at the hour of meeting, a clear word
  Is every note he sings, in Love's own tongue;
    Yet, Love, thou know'st the sweet strain suffers wrong,
Full oft through our contending joys unheard.

What of that hour at last, when for her sake
  No wing may fly to me nor song may flow;
    When, wandering round my life unleaved, I know
The bloodied feathers scattered in the brake,
  And think how she, far from me, with like eyes
Sees through the untuneful bough the wingless skies?

XXXII: HER GIFTS

High grace, the dower of queens; and therewithal
  Some wood-born wonder's sweet simplicity;
    A glance like water brimming with the sky
Or hyacinth-light where forest-shadows fall;
Such thrilling pallor of cheek as doth enthral
    The heart; a mouth whose passionate forms imply
    All music and all silence held thereby;
Deep golden locks, her sovereign coronal;
A round reared neck, meet column of Love's shrine
  To cling to when the heart takes sanctuary;
    Hands which for ever at Love's bidding be,
And soft-stirred feet still answering to his sign:—
These are her gifts, as tongue may tell them o'er.
Breathe low her name, my soul; for that means more.

XXXV: THE DARK GLASS

Not I myself know all my love for thee:
  How should I reach so far, who cannot weigh
    To-morrow's dower by gage of yesterday?
Shall birth and death, and all dark names that be
As doors and windows bared to some loud sea,
  Lash deaf mine ears and blind my face with spray;
    And shall my sense pierce love,—the last relay
And ultimate outpost of eternity?

Lo! what am I to Love, the lord of all?
   One murmuring shell he gathers from the sand,—
   One little heart-flame sheltered in his hand.
Yet through thine eyes he grants me clearest call
And veriest touch of powers primordial
   That any hour-girt life may understand.

XXXVI: THE LAMP'S SHRINE

Sometimes I fain would find in thee some fault,
   That I might love thee still in spite of it:
   Yet how should our Lord Love curtail one whit
Thy perfect praise whom most he would exalt?
Alas! he can but make my heart's low vault
   Even in men's sight unworthier, being lit
   By thee, who thereby show'st more exquisite
Like fiery chrysoprase in deep basalt.

Yet will I nowise shrink; but at Love's shrine
   Myself within the beams his brow doth dart
   Will set the flashing jewel of thy heart
In that dull chamber where it deigns to shine:
   For lo! in honour of thine excellencies
   My heart takes pride to show how poor it is.

XLIX: DEATH-IN-LOVE

There came an image in Life's retinue
   That had Love's wings and bore his gonfalon:
   Fair was the web, and nobly wrought thereon,
O soul-sequestered face, thy form and hue!
Bewildering sounds, such as Spring wakens to,
   Shook in its folds; and through my heart its power
   Sped trackless as the immemorable hour
When birth's dark portal groaned and all was new.

But a veiled woman followed, and she caught
   The banner round its staff, to furl and cling,—
   Then plucked a feather from the bearer's wing,
And held it to his lips that stirred it not,
   And said to me, "Behold, there is no breath:
   I and this Love are one, and I am Death."
976

DANTE GABRIEL ROSSETTI

LIV: WITHOUT HER

What of her glass without her?   The blank grey
  There where the pool is blind of the moon's face.
  Her dress without her?   The tossed empty space
Of cloud-rack whence the moon has passed away.
Her paths without her?   Day's appointed sway
  Usurped by desolate night.   Her pillowed place
  Without her?   Tears, ah me! for love's good grace,
And cold forgetfulness of night or day.

What of the heart without her?   Nay, poor heart,
  Of thee what word remains ere speech be still?
  A wayfarer by barren ways and chill,
Steep ways and weary, without her thou art,
Where the long cloud, the long wood's counterpart,
  Sheds doubled darkness up the labouring hill.

LVII: TRUE WOMAN.   I

Herself

To be a sweetness more desired than Spring;
  A bodily beauty more acceptable
  Than the wild rose-tree's arch that crowns the fell;
To be an essence more environing
Than wine's drained juice; a music ravishing
  More than the passionate pulse of Philomel;—
  To be all this 'neath one soft bosom's swell
That is the flower of life:—how strange a thing!

How strange a thing to be what Man can know
  But as a sacred secret!   Heaven's own screen
Hides her soul's purest depth and loveliest glow;
  Closely withheld, as all things most unseen,—
  The wave-bowered pearl,—the heart-shaped seal of green
That flecks the snowdrop underneath the snow.

LVIII: TRUE WOMAN. 2

Her Love

She loves him; for her infinite soul is Love,
  And he her lodestar. Passion in her is
  A glass facing his fire, where the bright bliss
Is mirrored, and the heat returned. Yet move
That glass, a stranger's amorous flame to prove,
  And it shall turn, by instant contraries,
  Ice to the moon; while her pure fire to his
For whom it burns, clings close i' the heart's alcove.

Lo! they are one. With wifely breast to breast
  And circling arms, she welcomes all command
  Of love,—her soul to answering ardours fann'd:
Yet as morn springs or twilight sinks to rest,
Ah! who shall say she deems not loveliest
  The hour of sisterly sweet hand-in-hand?

LIX: TRUE WOMAN. 3

Her Heaven

If to grow old in Heaven is to grow young,
  (As the Seer saw and said), then blest were he
  With youth for evermore, whose heaven should be
True Woman, she whom these weak notes have sung.
Here and hereafter,—choir-strains of her tongue,—
  Sky-spaces of her eyes,—sweet signs that flee
  About her soul's immediate sanctuary,—
Were Paradise all uttermost worlds among.

The sunrise blooms and withers on the hill
  Like any hillflower; and the noblest troth
  Dies here to dust. Yet shall Heaven's promise clothe
Even yet those lovers who have cherished still
  This test for love:—in every kiss sealed fast
  To feel the first kiss and forbode the last.

978

DANTE GABRIEL ROSSETTI

LXXII: THE CHOICE.   I

Eat thou and drink; to-morrow thou shalt die.
  Surely the earth, that's wise being very old,
  Needs not our help.   Then loose me, love, and hold
Thy sultry hair up from my face; that I
May pour for thee this golden wine, brim-high,
  Till round the glass thy fingers glow like gold.
  We'll drown all hours; thy song, while hours are toll'd,
Shall leap, as fountains veil the changing sky.
Now kiss, and think that there are really those,
  My own high-bosomed beauty, who increase
    Vain gold, vain lore, and yet might choose our way!
    Through many years they toil; then on a day
  They die not,—for their life was death,—but cease;
And round their narrow lips the mould falls close.

LXXIII: THE CHOICE.   2

Watch thou and fear; to-morrow thou shalt die.
  Or art thou sure thou shalt have time for death?
  Is not the day which God's word promiseth
To come man knows not when?   In yonder sky,
Now while we speak, the sun speeds forth: can I
  Or thou assure him of his goal?   God's breath
  Even at this moment haply quickeneth
The air to a flame; till spirits, always nigh
Though screened and hid, shall walk the daylight here.
  And dost thou prate of all that man shall do?
    Canst thou, who hast but plagues, presume to be
    Glad in his gladness that comes after thee?
  Will *his* strength slay *thy* worm in Hell?   Go to:
Cover thy countenance, and watch, and fear.

LXXIV: THE CHOICE.   3

Think thou and act; to-morrow thou shalt die.
  Outstretched in the sun's warmth upon the shore,
  Thou say'st: "Man's measured path is all gone o'er:
Up all his years, steeply, with strain and sigh,

Man clomb until he touched the truth; and I,
    Even I, am he whom it was destined for."
    How should this be?   Art thou then so much more
Than they who sowed, that thou shouldst reap thereby?

Nay, come up hither.   From this wave-washed mound
    Unto the furthest flood-brim look with me;
Then reach on with thy thought till it be drown'd.
    Miles and miles distant though the last line be,
And though thy soul sail leagues and leagues beyond,—
    Still, leagues beyond those leagues, there is more sea.

LXXXVII: LOST DAYS

The lost days of my life until to-day,
What were they, could I see them on the street
Lie as they fell?   Would they be ears of wheat
Sown once for food but trodden into clay?
Or golden coins squandered and still to pay?
Or drops of blood dabbling the guilty feet?
Or such spilt water as in dreams must cheat
The undying throats of Hell, athirst alway?
I do not see them here; but after death
God knows I know the faces I shall see,
Each one a murdered self, with low last breath.
"I am thyself,—what hast thou done to me?"
"And I—and I—thyself," (lo! each one saith,)
"And thou thyself to all eternity!"

CVI: SUDDEN LIGHT

I have been here before,
    But when or how I cannot tell;
I know the grass beyond the door,
    The sweet keen smell,
The sighing sound, the lights around the shore.

DANTE GABRIEL ROSSETTI

You have been mine before,—
How long ago I may not know;
But just when at that swallow's soar
Your neck turned so,
Some veil did fall,—I knew it all of yore.

Has this been thus before?
And shall not thus time's eddying flight
Still with our lives our love restore
In death's despite,
And day and night yield one delight once more?

THE STREAM'S SECRET

What thing unto mine ear
Wouldst thou convey,—what secret thing,
O wandering water ever whispering?
Surely thy speech shall be of her.
Thou water, O thou whispering wanderer,
What message dost thou bring?

Say, hath not Love leaned low
This hour beside thy far well-head,
And there through jealous hollowed fingers said
The thing that most I long to know,—
Murmuring with curls all dabbled in thy flow
And washed lips rosy red?

He told it to thee there
Where thy voice hath a louder tone;
But where it welters to this little moan
His will decrees that I should hear.
Now speak: for with the silence is no fear,
And I am all alone.

Shall Time not still endow
One hour with life, and I and she
Slake in one kiss the thirst of memory?
Say, stream; lest Love should disavow
Thy service, and the bird upon the bough
'Sing first to tell it me.

981

What whisperest thou?   Nay, why
Name the dead hours?   I mind them well:
Their ghosts in many darkened doorways dwell
With desolate eyes to know them by.
That hour must still be born ere it can die:
Of that I'd have thee tell.

. . . .

Let no rebuke find place
In speech of thine: or it shall prove
That thou dost ill expound the words of Love,
Even as thine eddy's rippling race
Would blur the perfect image of his face.
I will have none thereof.

. . . .

Dark as thy blinded wave
When brimming midnight floods the glen,—
Bright as the laughter of thy runnels when
The dawn yields all the light they crave;
Even so these hours to wound and that to save
Are sisters in Love's ken.

Oh sweet her bending grace
Then when I kneel beside her feet;
And sweet her eyes' o'erhanging heaven; and sweet
The gathering folds of her embrace;
And her fall'n hair at last shed round my face
When breaths and tears shall meet.

. . . .

Then by her summoning art
Shall memory conjure back the sere
Autumnal Springs, from many a dying year
Born dead; and, bitter to the heart,
The very ways where now we walk apart
Who then shall cling so near.

And with each thought new-grown,
Some sweet caress or some sweet name
Low-breathed shall let me know her thought the same;
Making me rich with every tone
And touch of the dear heaven so long unknown
That filled my dreams with flame.

982

DANTE GABRIEL ROSSETTI

Pity and love shall burn
In her pressed cheek and cherishing hands;
And from the living spirit of love that stands
Between her lips to soothe and yearn,
Each separate breath shall clasp me round in turn
And loose my spirit's bands.

.   .   .   .

Alas! shall hope be nurs'd
On life's all-succouring breast in vain,
And made so perfect only to be slain?
Or shall not rather the sweet thirst
Even yet rejoice the heart with warmth dispers'd
And strength grown fair again?

Stands it not by the door—
Love's Hour—till she and I shall meet;
With bodiless form and unapparent feet
That cast no shadow yet before,
Though round its head the dawn begins to pour
The breath that makes day sweet?

Its eyes invisible
Watch till the dial's thin-thrown shade
Be born,—yea, till the journeying line be laid
Upon the point that wakes the spell,
And there in lovelier light than tongue can tell
Its presence stand array'd.

Its soul remembers yet
Those sunless hours that passed it by;
And still it hears the night's disconsolate cry,
And feels the branches wringing wet
Cast on its brow, that may not once forget,
Dumb tears from the blind sky.

.   .   .   .

Still silent?   Can no art
Of Love's then move thy pity?   Nay,
To thee let nothing come that owns his sway:
Let happy lovers have no part
With thee; nor even so sad and poor a heart
As thou hast spurned to-day.

To-day? Lo! night is here.
The glen grows heavy with some veil
Risen from the earth or fall'n to make earth pale;
    And all stands hushed to eye and ear,
Until the night-wind shake the shade like fear
        And every covert quail.

        Ah! by another wave
    On other airs the hour must come
Which to thy heart, my love, shall call me home.
    Between the lips of the low cave
Against that night the lapping waters lave,
        And the dark lips are dumb.

        But there Love's self doth stand,
    And with Life's weary wings far flown,
And with Death's eyes that make the water moan,
    Gathers the water in his hand:
And they that drink know nought of sky or land
        But only love alone.

        O soul-sequestered face
    Far off,—O were that night but now!
So even beside that stream even I and thou
    Through thirsting lips should draw Love's grace,
And in the zone of that supreme embrace
        Bind aching breast and brow.

        O water whispering
    Still through the dark into mine ears,—
As with mine eyes, is it not now with hers?—
    Mine eyes that add to thy cold spring,
Wan water, wandering water weltering,
        This hidden tide of tears.

LILITH

Of Adam's first wife, Lilith, it is told
    (The witch he loved before the gift of Eve,)
    That, ere the snake's, her sweet tongue could deceive,
And her enchanted hair was the first gold.

984

DANTE GABRIEL ROSSETTI

And still she sits, young while the earth is old,
  And, subtly of herself contemplative,
  Draws men to watch the bright net she can weave,
Till heart and body and life are in its hold.

The rose and poppy are her flowers; for where
  Is he not found, O Lilith, whom shed scent
And soft-shed kisses and soft sleep shall snare?
  Lo! as that youth's eyes burned at thine, so went
  Thy spell through him, and left his straight neck bent,
And round his heart one strangling golden hair.

THREE SHADOWS

I looked and saw your eyes in the shadow of your hair,
  As a traveller sees the stream in the shadow of the wood;——
And I said, "My faint heart sighs, ah me! to linger there,
  To drink deep and to dream in that sweet solitude."

I looked and saw your heart in the shadow of your eyes,
  As a seeker sees the gold in the shadow of the stream;
And I said, "Ah, me! what art should win the immortal
      prize,
  Whose want must make life cold and Heaven a hollow
      dream?"

I looked and saw your love in the shadow of your heart,
  As a diver sees the pearl in the shadow of the sea;
And I murmured, not above my breath, but all apart,—
  "Ah! you can love, true girl, and is your love for me?"

SIBYLLA PALMIFERA

Under the arch of Life, where love and death,
Terror and mystery, guard her shrine, I saw
Beauty enthroned; and though her gaze struck awe,
I drew it in as simply as my breath.
Hers are the eyes which, over and beneath,
The sky and sea bend on thee,—which can draw,
By sea or sky or woman, to one law,
The allotted bondman of her palm and wreath.

This is that Lady Beauty, in whose praise
Thy voice and hand shake still,—long known to thee
By flying hair and fluttering hem,—the beat
Following her daily of thy heart and feet,
How passionately and irretrievably,
In what fond flight, how many ways and days!

George Meredith

SONG

Love within the lover's breast
Burns like Hesper in the west,
O'er the ashes of the sun,
Till the day and night are done;
Then when dawn drives up her car—
Lo! it is the morning star.

Love! thy love pours down on mine
As the sunlight on the vine,
As the snow-rill on the vale,
As the salt breeze in the sail;
As the song unto the bird,
On my lips thy name is heard.

As a dewdrop on the rose
In thy heart my passion glows,
As a skylark to the sky
Up into thy breast I fly;
As a sea-shell of the sea
Ever shall I sing of thee.

MARIAN

She can be as wise as we,
    And wiser when she wishes;
She can knit with cunning wit,
    And dress the homely dishes.

GEORGE MEREDITH

She can flourish staff or pen,
  And deal a wound that lingers;
She can talk the talk of men,
  And touch with thrilling fingers.

Match her ye across the sea,
  Natures fond and fiery;
Ye who zest the turtle's nest
  With the eagle's eyrie.
Soft and loving is her soul,
  Swift and lofty soaring;
Mixing with its dove-like dole
  Passionate adoring.

Such a she who'll match with me?
  In flying or pursuing,
Subtle wiles are in her smiles
  To set the world a-wooing.
She is steadfast as a star,
  And yet the maddest maiden:
She can wage a gallant war,
  And give the peace of Eden.

WHEN I WOULD IMAGE

When I would image her features,
  Comes up a shrouded head:
I touch the outlines, shrinking;
  She seems of the wandering dead.

But when love asks for nothing,
  And lies on his bed of snow,
The face slips under my eyelids,
  All in its living glow.

Like a dark cathedral city,
  Whose spires, and domes, and towers
Quiver in violet lightnings,
  My soul basks on for hours.

LUCIFER IN STARLIGHT

On a starred night Prince Lucifer uprose.
Tired of his dark dominion swung the fiend
Above the rolling ball in cloud part screened,
Where sinners hugged their spectre of repose.
Poor prey to his hot fit of pride were those.
And now upon his western wing he leaned,
Now his huge bulk o'er Afric's sands careened,
Now the black planet shadowed Arctic snows.
Soaring through wider zones that pricked his scars
With memory of the old revolt from Awe,
He reached the middle height, and at the stars,
Which are the brain of heaven, he looked, and sank.
Around the ancient track marched, rank on rank,
The army of unalterable law.

LOVE IN THE VALLEY

Under yonder beech-tree single on the green-sward,
    Couched with her arms behind her golden head,
Knees and tresses folded to slip and ripple idly,
    Lies my young love sleeping in the shade.
Had I the heart to slide an arm beneath her,
    Press her parting lips as her waist I gather slow,
Waking in amazement she could not but embrace me:
    Then would she hold me and never let me go?
                    *   *   *
Shy as the squirrel and wayward as the swallow,
    Swift as the swallow along the river's light
Circleting the surface to meet his mirrored winglets,
    Fleeter she seems in her stay than in her flight.
Shy as the squirrel that leaps among the pine-tops,
    Wayward as the swallow overhead at set of sun,
She whom I love is hard to catch and conquer,
    Hard, but O the glory of the winning were she won!
                    *   *   *

GEORGE MEREDITH

When her mother tends her before the laughing mirror,
  Tying up her laces, looping up her hair,
Often she thinks, were this wild thing wedded,
  More love should I have, and much less care.
When her mother tends her before the lighted mirror,
  Loosening her laces, combing down her curls,
Often she thinks, were this wild thing wedded,
  I should miss but one for many boys and girls.

                    *   *   *

Heartless she is as the shadow in the meadows
  Flying to the hills on a blue and breezy noon.
No, she is athirst and drinking up her wonder:
  Earth to her is young as the slip of the new moon.
Deals she an unkindness, 'tis but her rapid measure,
  Even as in a dance; and her smile can heal no less:
Like the swinging May-cloud that pelts the flowers with hail-
        stones
  Off a sunny border, she was made to bruise and bless.

                    *   *   *

Lovely are the curves of the white owl sweeping
  Wavy in the dusk lit by one large star.
Lone on the fir-branch, his rattle-note unvaried,
  Brooding o'er the gloom, spins the brown eve-jar.
Darker grows the valley, more and more forgetting:
  So were it with me if forgetting could be willed.
Tell the grassy hollow that holds the bubbling well-spring,
  Tell it to forget the source that keeps it filled.

                    *   *   *

Stepping down the hill with her fair companions,
  Arm in arm, all against the raying West,
Boldly she sings, to the merry tune she marches,
  Brave in her shape, and sweeter unpossessed.
Sweeter, for she is what my heart first awaking
  Whispered the world was; morning light is she.
Love that so desires would fain keep her changeless;
  Fain would fling the net, and fain have her free.

                    *   *   *

Happy, happy time, when the white star hovers
  Low over dim fields fresh with bloomy dew,
Near the face of dawn, that draws athwart the darkness,
  Threading it with colour, like yewberries the yew.

Thicker crowd the shades as the grave East deepens
   Glowing, and with crimson a long cloud swells.
Maiden still the morn is; and strange she is, and secret;
   Strange her eyes; her cheeks are cold as cold sea-shells.

           *   *   *

Sunrays, leaning on our southern hills and lighting
   Wild cloud-mountains that drag the hills along,
Oft ends the day of your shifting brilliant laughter
   Chill as a dull face frowning on a song.
Ay, but shows the South-West a ripple-feathered bosom
   Blown to silver while the clouds are shaken and ascend
Scaling the mid-heavens as they stream, there comes a sunset
   Rich, deep like love in beauty without end.

           *   *   *

When at dawn she sighs, and like an infant to the window
   Turns grave eyes craving light, released from dreams,
Beautiful she looks, like a white water-lily
   Bursting out of bud in havens of the streams.
When from bed she rises clothed from neck to ankle
   In her long nightgown sweet as boughs of May,
Beautiful she looks, like a tall garden lily
   Pure from the night, and splendid for the day.

           *   *   *

Mother of the dews, dark eye-lashed twilight,
   Low-lidded twilight, o'er the valley's brim,
Rounding on thy breast sings the dew-delighted skylark,
   Clear as though the dewdrops had their voice in him.
Hidden where the rose-flush drinks the rayless planet,
   Fountain-full he pours the spraying fountain-showers.
Let me hear her laughter, I would have her ever
   Cool as dew in twilight, the lark above the flowers.

           *   *   *

All the girls are out with their baskets for the primrose;
   Up lanes, woods through, they troop in joyful bands.
My sweet leads: she knows not why, but now she loiters,
   Eyes the bent anemones, and hangs her hands.
Such a look will tell that the violets are peeping,
   Coming the rose: and unaware a cry
Springs in her bosom for odours and for colour,
   Covert and the nightingale; she knows not why.

           *   *   *

GEORGE MEREDITH

Kerchiefed head and chin she darts between her tulips,
    Streaming like a willow grey in arrowy rain:
Some bend beaten cheek to gravel, and their angel
    She will be, she lifts them, and on she speeds again.
Black the driving raincloud breasts the iron gateway:
    She is forth to cheer a neighbour lacking mirth.
So when sky and grass met rolling dumb for thunder
    Saw I once a white dove, sole light of earth.

                    *   *   *

Prim little scholars are the flowers of her garden,
    Trained to stand in rows, and asking if they please.
I might love them well but for loving more the wild ones:
    O my wild ones! they tell me more than these.
You, my wild one, you tell of honied field-rose,
    Violet, blushing eglantine in life; and even as they,
They by the wayside are earnest of your goodness,
    You are of life's, on the banks that line the way.

                    *   *   *

Peering at her chamber the white crowns the red rose,
    Jasmine winds the porch with stars two and three.
Parted is the window; she sleeps; the starry jasmine
    Breathes a falling breath that carries thoughts of me.
Sweeter unpossessed, have I said of her my sweetest?
    Not while she sleeps: while she sleeps the jasmine breathes,
Luring her to love; she sleeps; the starry jasmine
    Bears me to her pillow under white rose-wreaths.

                    *   *   *

Yellow with birdfoot-trefoil are the grass-glades;
    Yellow with cinquefoil of the dew-grey leaf;
Yellow with stonecrop; the moss-mounds are yellow;
    Blue-necked the wheat sways, yellowing to the sheaf.
Green-yellow bursts from the copse the laughing yaffle:
    Sharp as a sickle is the edge of shade and shine:
Earth in her heart laughs looking at the heavens,
    Thinking of the harvest: I look and think of mine.

                    *   *   *

This I may know: her dressing and undressing
    Such a change of light shows as when the skies in sport
Shift from cloud to moonlight; or edging over thunder
    Slips a ray of sun; or sweeping into port
White sails furl; or on the ocean borders

White sails lean along the waves leaping green.
Visions of her shower before me, but from eyesight
   Guarded she would be like the sun were she seen.

      *   *   *

Front door and back of the mossed old farmhouse
   Open with the morn, and in a breezy link
Freshly sparkles garden to stripe-shadowed orchard,
   Green across a rill where on sand the minnows wink.
Busy in the grass the early sun of summer
   Swarms, and the blackbird's mellow fluting notes
Call my darling up with round and roguish challenge:
   Quaintest, richest carol of all the singing throats!

      *   *   *

Cool was the woodside; cool as her white dairy
   Keeping sweet the cream-pan; and there the boys from
      school,
Cricketing below, rushed brown and red with sunshine;
   O the dark translucence of the deep-eyed cool!
Spying from the farm, herself she fetched a pitcher
   Full of milk, and tilted for each in turn the beak.
Then a little fellow, mouth up and on tiptoe,
   Said, "I will kiss you": she laughed and leaned her cheek.

      *   *   *

Doves of the fir-wood walling high our red roof
   Through the long noon coo, crooning through the coo.
Loose droop the leaves, and down the sleepy roadway
   Sometimes pipes a chaffinch; loose droops the blue.
Cows flap a slow tail knee-deep in the river,
   Breathless, given up to sun and gnat and fly.
Nowhere is she seen; and if I see her nowhere,
   Lightning may come, straight rains and tiger sky.

      *   *   *

O the golden sheaf, the rustling treasure-armful!
   O the nutbrown tresses nodding interlaced!
O the treasure-tresses one another over
   Nodding!   O the girdle slack about the waist!
Slain are the poppies that shot their random scarlet
   Quick amid the wheatears: wound about the waist,
Gathered, see these brides of Earth one blush of ripeness!
   O the nutbrown tresses nodding interlaced!

      *   *   *

GEORGE MEREDITH

Large and smoky red the sun's cold disk drops,
  Clipped by naked hills, on violet shaded snow:
Eastward large and still lights up a bower of moonrise,
  Whence at her leisure steps the moon aglow.
Nightlong on black print-branches our beech-tree
  Gazes in this whiteness: nightlong could I.
Here may life on death or death on life be painted.
  Let me clasp her soul to know she cannot die!

*   *   *

Gossips count her faults; they scour a narrow chamber
  Where there is no window, read not heaven or her.
"When she was a tiny," one aged woman quavers,
  Plucks at my heart and leads me by the ear.
Faults she had once as she learnt to run and tumbled:
  Faults of feature some see, beauty not complete.
Yet, good gossips, beauty that makes holy
  Earth and air, may have faults from head to feet.

*   *   *

Hither she comes; she comes to me; she lingers,
  Deepens her brown eyebrows, while in new surprise
High rise the lashes in wonder of a stranger;
  Yet am I the light and living of her eyes.
Something friends have told her fills her heart to brimming
  Nets her in her blushes, and wounds her, and tames.—
Sure of her haven, O like a dove alighting,
  Arms up, she dropped: our souls were in our names.

*   *   *

Soon will she lie like a white-frost sunrise.
  Yellow oats and brown wheat, barley pale as rye,
Long since your sheaves have yielded to the thresher,
  Felt the girdle loosened, seen the tresses fly.
Soon will she lie like a blood-red sunset.
  Swift with the to-morrow, green-winged Spring!
Sing from the South-West, bring her back the truants,
  Nightingale and swallow, song and dipping wing.

*   *   *

Soft new beech-leaves, up to beamy April
  Spreading bough on bough a primrose mountain, you,
Lucid in the moon, raise lilies to the skyfields,
  Youngest green transfused in silver shining through:
Fairer than the lily, than the wild white cherry:

Fair as in image my seraph love appears
Borne to me by dreams when dawn is at my eyelids:
Fair as in the flesh she swims to me on tears.

* * *

Could I find a place to be alone with heaven,
I would speak my heart out: heaven is my need.
Every woodland tree is flushing like the dogwood,
Flashing like the whitebeam, swaying like the reed.
Flushing like the dogwood crimson in October;
Streaming like the flag-reed South-West blown;
Flashing as in gusts the sudden-lighted whitebeam:
All seem to know what is for heaven alone.

SONG IN THE SONGLESS

They have no song, the sedges dry,
And still they sing.
It is within my breast they sing,
As I pass by.
Within my breast they touch a string,
They wake a sigh.
There is but sound of sedges dry;
In me they sing.

S. Weir Mitchell

EVENING

I know the night is near at hand.
The mists lie low on hill and bay,
The autumn sheaves are dewless, dry;
But I have had the day.

Yes, I have had, dear Lord, the day;
When at Thy call I have the night,
Brief be the twilight as I pass
From light to dark, from dark to light.

Christina Georgina Rossetti

HEAVEN OVERARCHES EARTH AND SEA

Heaven overarches earth and sea,
  Earth-sadness and sea-bitterness.
Heaven overarches you and me:
A little while and we shall be—
Please God—where there is no more sea
  Nor barren wilderness.

Heaven overarches you and me,
  And all earth's gardens and her graves.
Look up with me, until we see
The day break and the shadows flee.
What though to-night wrecks you and me,
  If so to-morrow saves?

WHEN I AM DEAD, MY DEAREST

When I am dead, my dearest,
  Sing no sad songs for me;
Plant thou no roses at my head,
  Nor shady cypress-tree:
Be the green grass above me
  With showers and dewdrops wet:
And if thou wilt, remember,
  And if thou wilt, forget.

I shall not see the shadows,
  I shall not feel the rain;
I shall not hear the nightingale
  Sing on, as if in pain:
And dreaming through the twilight
  That doth not rise nor set,
Haply I may remember,
  And haply may forget.

995

UP-HILL

Does the road wind up-hill all the way?
    Yes, to the very end.
Will the day's journey take the whole long day?
    From morn to night, my friend.

But is there for the night a resting-place?
    A roof for when the slow dark hours begin.
May not the darkness hide it from my face?
    You cannot miss that inn.

Shall I meet other wayfarers at night?
    Those who have gone before.
Then must I knock, or call when just in sight?
    They will not keep you standing at that door.

Shall I find comfort, travel-sore and weak?
    Of labour you shall find the sum.
Will there be beds for me and all who seek?
    Yea, beds for all who come.

PASSING AWAY

Passing away, saith the World, passing away:
Chances, beauty and youth sapp'd day by day:
Thy life never continueth in one stay.
Is the eye waxen dim, is the dark hair changing to grey
That hath won neither laurel nor bay?
I shall clothe myself in Spring and bud in May:
Thou, root-stricken, shalt not rebuild thy decay
On my bosom for aye.
Then I answer'd: Yea.

Passing away, saith my Soul, passing away:
With its burden of fear and hope, of labour and play,
Hearken what the past doth witness and say:
Rust in thy gold, a moth is in thine array,
A canker is in thy bud, thy leaf must decay.

996

CHRISTINA GEORGINA ROSSETTI

At midnight, at cockcrow, at morning, one certain day,
Lo, the Bridegroom shall come and shall not delay:
Watch thou and pray.
Then I answer'd: Yea.

Passing away, saith my God, passing away:
Winter passeth after the long delay:
New grapes on the vine, new figs on the tender spray,
Turtle calleth turtle in Heaven's May.
Though I tarry, wait for me, trust me, watch and pray.
Arise, come away; night is past, and lo, it is day;
My love, my sister, my spouse, thou shalt hear me say—
Then I answer'd: Yea.

MIRAGE

The hope I dreamed of was a dream,
   Was but a dream; and now I wake,
Exceeding comfortless, and worn, and old,
   For a dream's sake.

I hang my harp upon a tree,
   A weeping willow in a lake;
I hang my silent harp there, wrung and snapt
   For a dream's sake.

Lie still, lie still, my breaking heart;
   My silent heart, lie still and break:
Life, and the world, and mine own self, are changed
   For a dream's sake.

REMEMBER

Remember me when I am gone away,
   Gone far away into the silent land;
   When you can no more hold me by the hand,
Nor I half turn to go yet turning stay.
Remember me when no more day by day
   You tell me of our future that you planned:
   Only remember me; you understand

997

It will be late to counsel then or pray.
Yet if you should forget me for a while
   And afterwards remember, do not grieve:
   For if the darkness and corruption leave
   A vestige of the thoughts that once I had,
Better by far you should forget and smile
   Than that you should remember and be sad.

REST

O Earth, lie heavily upon her eyes;
Seal her sweet eyes weary of watching, Earth;
Lie close around her: leave no room for mirth
With its harsh laughter, nor for sound of sighs.
She hath no questions, she hath no replies,
Hushed in and curtained with a blessèd dearth
Of all that irked her from the hour of birth;
With stillness that is almost Paradise.
Darkness more clear than noonday holdeth her,
Silence more musical than any song;
Even her very heart has ceased to stir:
Until the morning of Eternity
Her rest shall not begin nor end, but be;
And when she wakes she will not think it long.

THREE SEASONS

"A cup for hope!" she said,
  In springtime ere the bloom was old:
  The crimson wine was poor and cold
By her mouth's richer red.

"A cup for love!" how low,
  How soft the words; and all the while
  Her blush was rippling with a smile
Like summer after snow.

CHRISTINA GEORGINA ROSSETTI

"A cup for memory!"
Cold cup that one must drain alone:
While autumn winds are up and moan
   Across the barren sea.

Hope, memory, love:
Hope for fair morn, and love for day,
And memory for the evening grey
   And solitary dove.

DREAM LAND

Where sunless rivers weep
Their waves into the deep,
She sleeps a charmèd sleep:
   Awake her not.
Led by a single star,
She came from very far
To seek where shadows are
   Her pleasant lot.

She left the rosy morn,
She left the fields of corn,
For twilight cold and lorn
   And water springs.
Through sleep, as through a veil,
She sees the sky look pale,
And hears the nightingale
   That sadly sings.

Rest, rest, a perfect rest
Shed over brow and breast;
Her face is toward the west,
   The purple land.
She cannot see the grain
Ripening on hill and plain;
She cannot feel the rain
   Upon her hand.

999

Rest, rest, for evermore
Upon a mossy shore;
Rest, rest at the heart's core
    Till time shall cease:
Sleep that no pain shall wake;
Night that no morn shall break
Till joy shall overtake
    Her perfect peace.

Emily Dickinson

AUTUMN

The morns are meeker than they were,
The nuts are getting brown;
The berry's cheek is plumper,
The rose is out of town.

The maple wears a gayer scarf,
The field a scarlet gown.
Lest I should be old-fashioned,
I'll put a trinket on.

CHARTLESS

I never saw a moor,
I never saw the sea;
Yet know I how the heather looks,
And what a wave must be.

I never spoke with God,
Nor visited in heaven;
Yet certain am I of the spot
As if the chart were given.

1000

EMILY DICKINSON

CHOICE

Of all the souls that stand create
I have elected one,
When sense from spirit files away
And subterfuge is done;

When that which is and that which was
Apart, intrinsic, stand,
And this brief tragedy of flesh
Is shifted like a sand;

When figures show their royal front
And mists are carved away,—
Behold the atom I preferred
To all the lists of clay!

PARTING

My life closed twice before its close;
    It yet remains to see
If Immortality unveil
    A third event to me,

So huge, so hopeless to conceive,
    As these that twice befell:
Parting is all we know of heaven,
    And all we need of hell.

PEACE

I many times thought peace had come,
When peace was far away;
As wrecked men deem they sight the land
At centre of the sea,

And struggle slacker, but to prove,
As hopelessly as I,
How many the fictitious shores
Before the harbor lie.

SUSPENSE

Elysium is as far as to
The very nearest room,
If in that room a friend await
Felicity or doom.

What fortitude the soul contains,
That it can so endure
The accent of a coming foot,
The opening of a door.

SIMPLICITY

How happy is the little stone
That rambles in the road alone,
And doesn't care about careers,
And exigencies never fears;
Whose coat of elemental brown
A passing universe put on;
And independent as the sun,
Associates or glows alone,
Fulfilling absolute decree
In casual simplicity.

PEDIGREE

The pedigree of honey
Does not concern the bee;
A clover, any time, to him
Is aristocracy.

Thomas Edward Brown

DORA

She knelt upon her brother's grave,
  My little girl of six years old—
He used to be so good and brave,
  The sweetest lamb of all our fold;

He used to shout, he used to sing,
Of all our tribe the little king—
And so unto the turf her ear she laid,
To hark if still in that dark place he play'd.
    No sound! no sound!
    Death's silence was profound;
    And horror crept
    Into her aching heart, and Dora wept.
    If this is as it ought to be,
    My God, I leave it unto Thee.

SALVE!

To live within a cave—it is most good;
    But, if God make a day,
    And some one come, and say,
"Lo! I have gather'd faggots in the wood!"
    E'en let him stay,
And light a fire, and fan a temporal mood!

So sit till morning! when the light is grown
    That he the path can read,
    Then bid the man God-speed!
His morning is not thine: yet must thou own
They have a cheerful warmth—those ashes on the stone.

MY GARDEN

A garden is a lovesome thing, God wot!
    Rose plot,
    Fringed pool,
Fern'd grot—
    The veriest school
    Of peace; and yet the fool
Contends that God is not—
Not God! in gardens! when the eve is cool?
    Nay, but I have a sign:
    'Tis very sure God walks in mine.

1003

Stopford Augustus Brooke

THE EARTH AND MAN

A little sun, a little rain,
  A soft wind blowing from the west—
And woods and fields are sweet again
  And warmth within the mountain's breast.

So simple is the earth we tread,
  So quick with love and life her frame,
Ten thousand years have dawned and fled,
  And still her magic is the same.

A little love, a little trust,
  A soft impulse, a sudden dream,—
And life as dry as desert dust
  Is fresher than a mountain stream.

So simple is the heart of man,
  So ready for new hope and joy;
Ten thousand years since it began
  Have left it younger than a boy.

Edmund Clarence Stedman

VOICE OF THE WESTERN WIND

Voice of the western wind!
  Thou singest from afar,
Rich with the music of a land
  Where all my memories are;
But in thy song I only hear
  The echo of a tone
That fell divinely on my ear
  In days forever flown.

Star of the western sky!
  Thou beamest from afar,
With lustre caught from eyes I knew
  Whose orbs were each a star;
But, oh, those orbs—too wildly bright—
  No more eclipse thine own,
And never shall I find the light
  Of days forever flown!

James Thomson

ART

I

What precious thing are you making fast
  In all these silken lines?
And where and to whom will it go at last?
  Such subtle knots and twines!

I am tying up all my love in this,
  With all its hopes and fears,
With all its anguish and all its bliss,
  And its hours as heavy as years.

I am going to send it afar, afar,
  To I know not where above;
To that sphere beyond the highest star
  Where dwells the soul of my Love.

But in vain, in vain, would I make it fast
  With countless subtle twines;·
For ever its fire breaks out at last,
  And shrivels all the lines.

II

If you have a carrier-dove
  That can fly over land and sea;
And a message for your Love,
  "Lady, I love but thee!"

And this dove will never stir
   But straight from her to you,
And straight from you to her;
   As you know and she knows too.

Will you first ensure, O sage,
   Your dove that never tires
With your message in a cage,
   Though a cage of golden wires?

Or will you fling your dove:
   "Fly, darling, without rest,
Over land and sea to my Love,
   And fold your wings in her breast?"

III

Singing is sweet; but be sure of this,
Lips only sing when they cannot kiss.

Did he ever suspire a tender lay
While her presence took his breath away?

Had his fingers been able to toy with her hair
Would they then have written the verses fair?

Had she let his arm steal round her waist
Would the lovely portrait yet be traced?

Since he could not embrace it flushed and warm
He has carved in stone the perfect form.

Who gives the fine report of the feast?
He who got none and enjoyed it least.

Were the wine really slipping down his throat
Would his song of the wine advance a note?

Will you puff out the music that sways the whirl,
Or dance and make love with a pretty girl?

Who shall the great battle-story write?
Not the hero down in the thick of the fight.

Statues and pictures and verse may be grand,
But they are not the Life for which they stand.

William Morris

LOVE IS ENOUGH

Love is enough: though the World be a-waning,
And the woods have no voice but the voice of complaining,
   Though the sky be too dark for dim eyes to discover
The gold-cups and daisies fair blooming thereunder,
Though the hills be held shadows, and the sea a dark wonder,
   And this day draw a veil over all deeds pass'd over,
Yet their hands shall not tremble, their feet shall not falter;
The void shall not weary, the fear shall not alter
   These lips and these eyes of the loved and the lover.

Samuel Butler

NOT ON SAD STYGIAN SHORE

Not on sad Stygian shore, nor in clear sheen
Of far Elysian plain, shall we meet those
Among the dead whose pupils we have been,
Nor those great shades whom we have held as foes;
No meadow of asphodel our feet shall tread,
Nor shall we look each other in the face
To love or hate each other being dead,
Hoping some praise, or fearing some disgrace.
We shall not argue, saying " 'Twas thus," or "thus,"
Our argument's whole drift we shall forget;
Who's right, who's wrong, 'twill be all one to us;
We shall not even know that we have met.
   Yet meet we shall, and part, and meet again,
   Where dead men meet, on lips of living men.

Algernon Charles Swinburne

IN MEMORY OF SWINBURNE

April whispers—"Canst thou, too, die,
  Lover of life and lover of mine?"
April, queen over earth and sky,
  Yearns, and her trembling lashes shine:
Master in song, good-by, good-by,
  Down to the dim sea-line.

"This is my singing season," he cried,
  "April, what sweet new song do you bring?"
April came and knelt at his side
  Breathing a song too great to sing—
Death!—and the dark cage-door swung wide:
  Seaward the soul took wing.

Sleep, on the breast of thine old-world lover,
  Sleep, by thy "fair green-girdled" sea!
There shall thy soul with the sea-birds hover,
  Free of the deep as their wings are free,
Free; for the grave-flowers only cover
  This, the dark cage of thee.

Thee, the storm-bird, nightingale-souled,
  Brother of Sappho, the seas reclaim!
Age upon age have the great waves rolled
  Mad with her music, fierce and aflame;
Thee, thee too, shall their glory enfold
  Lit with thy snow-winged fame.

April whispers—"Canst thou, too, die,
  Lover of life and lover of mine?"
April, conquering earth and sky,
  Yearns, and her trembling lashes shine:
Master in song, good-by, good-by,
  Down to the dim sea-line.
                                    —ALFRED NOYES.

ALGERNON CHARLES SWINBURNE

ATALANTA IN CALYDON

. . . .

First Chorus
When the hounds of spring are on winter's traces,
  The mother of months in meadow or plain
Fills the shadows and windy places
  With lisp of leaves and ripple of rain;
And the brown bright nightingale amorous
Is half assuaged for Itylus,
For the Thracian ships and the foreign faces,
  The tongueless vigil, and all the pain.

Come with bows bent and with emptying of quivers,
  Maiden most perfect, lady of light,
With a noise of winds and many rivers,
  With a clamour of waters, and with might;
Bind on thy sandals, O thou most fleet,
Over the splendour and speed of thy feet;
For the faint east quickens, the wan west shivers,
  Round the feet of the day and the feet of the night.

Where shall we find her, how shall we sing to her,
  Fold our hands round her knees, and cling?
O that man's heart were as fire and could spring to her,
  Fire, or the strength of the streams that spring!
For the stars and the winds are unto her
As raiment, as songs of the harp-player;
For the risen stars and the fallen cling to her,
  And the southwest-wind and the west-wind sing.

For winter's rains and ruins are over,
  And all the season of snows and sins;
The days dividing lover and lover,
  The light that loses, the night that wins;
And time remember'd is grief forgotten,
And frosts are slain and flowers begotten,
And in green underwood and cover
  Blossom by blossom the spring begins.

1009

The full streams feed on flower of rushes,
    Ripe grasses trammel a travelling foot,
The faint fresh flame of the young year flushes
    From leaf to flower and flower to fruit;
And fruit and leaf are as gold and fire,
And the oat is heard above the lyre,
And the hoofèd heel of a satyr crushes
    The chestnut-husk at the chestnut-root.

And Pan by noon and Bacchus by night,
    Fleeter of foot than the fleet-foot kid,
Follows with dancing and fills with delight
    The Mænad and the Bassarid;
And soft as lips that laugh and hide
The laughing leaves of the trees divide,
And screen from seeing and leave in sight
    The god pursuing, the maiden hid.

The ivy falls with the Bacchanal's hair
    Over her eyebrows hiding her eyes;
The wild vine slipping down leaves bare
    Her bright breast shortening into sighs;
The wild vine slips with the weight of its leaves,
But the berried ivy catches and cleaves
To the limbs that glitter, the feet that scare
    The wolf that follows, the fawn that flies.

   •   •   •   •   •   •   •   •   °

Second Chorus
    Before the beginning of years,
        There came to the making of man
    Time, with a gift of tears;
        Grief, with a glass that ran;
    Pleasure, with pain for leaven;
        Summer, with flowers that fell;
    Remembrance, fallen from heaven;
        And madness, risen from hell;
    Strength, without hands to smite;
        Love, that endures for a breath;
    Night, the shadow of light;
        And life, the shadow of death.

ALGERNON CHARLES SWINBURNE

And the high gods took in hand
  Fire, and the falling of tears,
And a measure of sliding sand
  From under the feet of the years;
And froth and drift of the sea;
  And dust of the labouring earth;
And bodies of things to be
  In the houses of death and of birth;
And wrought with weeping and laughter,
  And fashioned with loathing and love,
With life before and after,
  And death beneath and above,
For a day and a night and a morrow,
  That his strength might endure for a span,
With travail and heavy sorrow,
  The holy spirit of man.

From the winds of the north and the south
  They gathered as unto strife;
They breathed upon his mouth,
  They filled his body with life;
Eyesight and speech they wrought
  For the veils of the soul therein,
A time for labour and thought,
  A time to serve and to sin;
They gave him light in his ways,
  And love, and a space for delight,
And beauty and length of days,
  And night, and sleep in the night.
His speech is a burning fire;
  With his lips he travaileth;
In his heart is a blind desire,
  In his eyes foreknowledge of death;
He weaves, and is clothed with derision;
  Sows, and he shall not reap;
His life is a watch or a vision
  Between a sleep and a sleep.

ITYLUS

Swallow, my sister, O sister swallow,
How can thine heart be full of the spring?
A thousand summers are over and dead.
What hast thou found in the spring to follow?
What hast thou found in thine heart to sing?
What wilt thou do when the summer is shed?

A swallow, sister, O fair swift swallow,
Why wilt thou fly after spring to the south,
The soft south whither thine heart is set?
Shall not the grief of the old time follow?
Shall not the song thereof cleave to thy mouth?
Hast thou forgotten ere I forget?

Sister, my sister, O fleet sweet swallow,
Thy way is long to the sun and the south;
But I, fulfilled of my heart's desire,
Shedding my song upon height, upon hollow,
From tawny body and sweet small mouth
Feed the heart of the night with fire.

I the nightingale all spring through,
O swallow, sister, O changing swallow,
All spring through till the spring be done,
Clothed with the light of the night on the dew,
Sing, while the hours and the wild birds follow,
Take flight and follow and find the sun.

Sister, my sister, O soft light swallow,
Though all things feast in the spring's guest-chamber,
How hast thou heart to be glad thereof yet?
For where thou fliest I shall not follow,
Till life forget and death remember,
Till thou remember and I forget.

Swallow, my sister, O singing swallow,
I know not how thou hast heart to sing.
Hast thou the heart? is it all passed over?
Thy lord the summer is good to follow,
And fair the feet of thy lover the spring;
But what wilt thou say to the spring thy lover?

O swallow, sister, O fleeting swallow,
  My heart in me is a molten ember
    And over my head the waves have met.
But thou wouldst tarry, or I would follow,
  Could I forget or thou remember,
    Couldst thou remember and I forget.

O sweet stray sister, O shifting swallow,
  The heart's division divideth us.
    Thy heart is light as a leaf of a tree;
But mine goes forth among sea-gulls hollow
  To the place of the slaying of Itylus,
    The feast of Daulis, the Thracian sea.

O swallow, sister, O rapid swallow,
  I pray thee sing not a little space.
    Are not the roofs and the lintels wet?
The woven web that was plain to follow,
  The small slain body, the flower-like face,
    Can I remember if thou forget?

O sister, sister, thy first-begotten!
  The hands that cling and the feet that follow,
    The voice of the child's blood crying yet,
Who hath remembered me? Who hath forgotten?
  Thou hast forgotten, O summer swallow,
    But the world shall end when I forget.

RONDEL

These many years since we began to be,
What have the Gods done with us? what with me,
What with my love? They have shown me fates and
    fears,
Harsh springs, and fountains bitterer than the sea,
Grief a fixed star, and joy a vane that veers,
                    These many years.

1013

With her, my Love,—with her have they done well?
But who shall answer for her? who shall tell
Sweet things or sad, such things as no man hears?
May no tears fall, if no tears ever fell,
From eyes more dear to me than starriest spheres,
          These many years!

But if tears ever touched, for any grief,
Those eyelids folded like a white-rose leaf,
Deep double shells where through the eye-flower peers,
Let them weep once more only, sweet and brief,
Brief tears and bright, for one who gave her tears
          These many years!

THE GARDEN OF PROSERPINE

Here, where the world is quiet,
  Here, where all trouble seems
Dead winds' and spent waves' riot
  In doubtful dreams of dreams,
I watch the green field growing
For reaping folk and sowing,
For harvest-time and mowing,
  A sleepy world of streams.

I am tired of tears and laughter,
  And men that laugh and weep;
Of what may come hereafter
  For men that sow to reap:
I am weary of days and hours,
Blown buds of barren flowers,
Desires and dreams and powers,
  And everything but sleep.

Here life has death for neighbour,
  And far from eye or ear
Wan waves and wet winds labour,
  Weak ships and spirits steer;

1014

They drive adrift, and whither
They wot not who make thither;
But no such winds blow hither,
   And no such things grow here.

No growth of moor or coppice,
   No heather-flower or vine,
But bloomless buds of poppies,
   Green grapes of Proserpine,
Pale beds of blowing rushes,
Where no leaf blooms or blushes
Save this whereout she crushes
   For dead men deadly wine.

Pale, without name or number,
   In fruitless fields of corn,
They bow themselves and slumber
   All night till light is born;
And like a soul belated,
In hell and heaven unmated,
By cloud and mist abated
   Comes out of darkness morn.

Though one were strong as seven,
   He too with death shall dwell,
Nor wake with wings in heaven,
   Nor weep for pains in hell;
Though one were fair as roses,
His beauty clouds and closes;
And well though love reposes,
   In the end it is not well.

Pale, beyond porch and portal,
   Crowned with calm leaves, she stands
Who gathers all things mortal
   With cold immortal hands;
Her languid lips are sweeter
Than Love's, who fears to greet her,
To men that mix and meet her
   From many times and lands.

She waits for each and other,
    She waits for all men born;
Forgets the earth her mother,
    The life of fruits and corn;
And spring and seed and swallow
Take wing for her and follow
Where summer song rings hollow
    And flowers are put to scorn.

There go the loves that wither,
    The old loves with wearier wings;
And all dead years draw thither,
    And all disastrous things;
Dead dreams of days forsaken,
Blind buds that snows have shaken,
Wild leaves that winds have taken,
    Red strays of ruined springs.

We are not sure of sorrow,
    And joy was never sure;
To-day will die to-morrow;
    Time stoops to no man's lure;
And Love, grown faint and fretful,
With lips but half regretful
Sighs, and with eyes forgetful
    Weeps that no loves endure.

From too much love of living,
    From hope and fear set free,
We thank with brief thanksgiving
    Whatever gods may be,
That no life lives forever;
That dead men rise up never;
That even the weariest river
    Winds somewhere safe to sea.

Then star nor sun shall waken,
    Nor any change of light:
Nor sound of waters shaken,
    Nor any sound or sight:

Nor wintry leaves nor vernal,
Nor days nor things diurnal;
Only the sleep eternal
In an eternal night.

A FORSAKEN GARDEN

In a coign of the cliff between lowland and highland,
  At the sea-down's edge between windward and lee,
Walled round with rocks as an inland island,
  The ghost of a garden fronts the sea.
A girdle of brushwood and thorn encloses
  The steep, square slope of the blossomless bed
Where the weeds that grew green from the graves of its roses
  Now lie dead.

The fields fall southward, abrupt and broken,
  To the low last edge of the long lone land.
If a step should sound or a word be spoken,
  Would a ghost not rise at the strange guest's hand?
So long have the grey, bare walks lain guestless,
  Through branches and briers if a man make way,
He shall find no life but the sea-wind's, restless
  Night and day.

The dense, hard passage is blind and stifled
  That crawls by a track none turn to climb
To the strait waste place that the years have rifled
  Of all but the thorns that are touched not of Time.
The thorns he spares when the rose is taken;
  The rocks are left when he wastes the plain.
The wind that wanders, the weeds wind-shaken,
  These remain.

Not a flower to be pressed of the foot that falls not;
  As the heart of a dead man the seed-plots are dry;
From the thicket of thorns whence the nightingale calls not,
  Could she call, there were never a rose to reply.

1017

Over the meadows that blossom and wither
    Rings but the note of a sea-bird's song;
Only the sun and the rain come hither
      All year long.

The sun burns sere and the rain dishevels
    One gaunt bleak blossom of scentless breath.
Only the wind here hovers and revels
    In a round where life seems barren as death.
Here there was laughing of old, there was weeping,
    Haply, of lovers none ever will know,
Whose eyes went seaward a hundred sleeping
      Years ago.

Heart handfast in heart as they stood, "Look thither,"
    Did he whisper? "Look forth from the flowers to the sea;
For the foam-flowers endure when the rose-blossoms wither,
    And men that love lightly may die—but we?"
And the same wind sang and the same waves whitened,
    And or ever the garden's last petals were shed,
In the lips that had whispered, the eyes that had lightened,
      Love was dead.

Or they loved their life through, and then went whither?
    And were one to the end—but what end who knows?
Love deep as the sea as a rose must wither,
    As the rose-red seaweed that mocks the rose.
Shall the dead take thought for the dead to love them?
    What love was ever as deep as a grave?
They are loveless now as the grass above them
      Or the wave.

All are at one now, roses and lovers,
    Not known of the cliffs and the fields and the sea.
Not a breath of the time that has been hovers
    In the air now soft with a summer to be.
Not a breath shall there sweeten the seasons hereafter
    Of the flowers or the lovers that laugh now or weep,
When, as they that are free now of weeping and laughter,
      We shall sleep.

1018

Here death may deal not again forever;
  Here change may come not till all change end.
From the graves they have made they shall rise up never,
  Who have left naught living to ravage and rend.
Earth, stones, and thorns of the wild ground growing,
  While the sun and the rain live, these shall be;
Till a last wind's breath, upon all these blowing,
    Roll the sea.

Till the slow sea rise and the sheer cliff crumble,
  Till terrace and meadow the deep gulfs drink,
Till the strength of the waves of the high tides humble
  The fields that lessen, the rocks that shrink;
Here now in his triumph where all things falter,
  Stretched out on the spoils that his own hand spread,
As a god self-slain on his own strange altar,
    Death lies dead.

AVE ATQUE VALE

IN MEMORY OF CHARLES BAUDELAIRE

Nous devions pourtant lui porter quelques fleurs;
Les morts, les pauvres morts, ont de grandes douleurs,
Et quand Octobre souffle, émondeur des vieux arbres,
Son vent mélancolique à l'entour de leurs marbres,
Certe, ils doivent trouver les vivants bien ingrats.
            —LES FLEURS DU MAL.

Shall I strew on thee rose or rue or laurel,
  Brother, on this that was the veil of thee?
  Or quiet sea-flower moulded by the sea,
Or simplest growth of meadow-sweet or sorrel,
  Such as the summer-sleepy dryads weave,
  Waked up by snow-soft sudden rains at eve?
Or wilt thou rather, as on earth before,
  Half-faded fiery blossoms, pale with heat
  And full of bitter summer, but more sweet
To thee than gleanings of a northern shore
  Trod by no tropic feet?

1019

For always thee the fervid languid glories
    Allured of heavier suns in mightier skies;
    Thine ears knew all the wandering watery sighs
Where the sea sobs round Lesbian promontories,
    The barren kiss of piteous wave to wave
    That knows not where is that Leucadian grave
Which hides too deep the supreme head of song.
    Ah, salt and sterile as her kisses were,
    The wild sea winds her and the green gulfs bear
Hither and thither, and vex and work her wrong,
    Blind gods that cannot spare.

Thou sawest, in thine old singing season, brother,
    Secrets and sorrows unbeheld of us:
    Fierce loves, and lovely leaf-buds poisonous,
Bare to thy subtler eye, but for none other
    Blowing by night in some unbreathed-in clime;
    The hidden harvest of luxurious time,
Sin without shape, and pleasure without speech;
    And where strange dreams in a tumultuous sleep
    Make the shut eyes of stricken spirits weep;
And with each face thou sawest the shadow on each,
    Seeing as men sow men reap.

O sleepless heart and sombre soul unsleeping,
    That were athirst for sleep and no more life
    And no more love, for peace and no more strife!
Now the dim gods of death have in their keeping
    Spirit and body and all the springs of song,
    Is it well now where love can do no wrong,
Where stingless pleasure has no foam or fang
    Behind the unopening closure of her lips?
    Is it not well where soul from body slips
And flesh from bone divides without a pang
    As dew from flower-bell drips?

It is enough; the end and the beginning
    Are one thing to thee, who art past the end.
    O hand unclasped of unbeholden friend!
For thee no fruits to pluck, no palms for winning,

1020

ALGERNON CHARLES SWINBURNE

No triumph and no labour and no lust,
   Only dead yew-leaves and a little dust.
O quiet eyes wherein the light saith nought,
   Whereto the day is dumb, nor any night
   With obscure finger silences your sight,
Nor in your speech the sudden soul speaks thought,
   Sleep, and have sleep for light.

Now all strange hours and all strange loves are over,
   Dreams and desires and sombre songs and sweet,
   Hast thou found place at the great knees and feet
Of some pale Titan-woman like a lover,
   Such as thy vision here solicited,
   Under the shadow of her fair vast head,
The deep division of prodigious breasts,
   The solemn slope of mighty limbs asleep,
   The weight of awful tresses that still keep
The savour and shade of old-world pine-forests
   Where the wet hill-winds weep?

Hast thou found any likeness for thy vision?
   O gardener of strange flowers, what bud, what bloom,
   Hast thou found sown, what gathered in the gloom?
What of despair, of rapture, of derision,
   What of life is there, what of ill or good?
   Are the fruits grey like dust or bright like blood?
Does the dim ground grow any seed of ours,
   The faint fields quicken any terrene root,
   In low lands where the sun and moon are mute
And all the stars keep silence?   Are there flowers
   At all, or any fruit?

Alas, but though my flying song flies after,
   O sweet strange elder singer, thy more fleet
   Singing, and footprints of thy fleeter feet,
Some dim derision of mysterious laughter
   From the blind tongueless warders of the dead,
   Some gainless glimpse of Proserpine's veiled head,

Some little sound of unregarded tears
   Wept by effaced unprofitable eyes,
   And from pale mouths some cadence of dead sighs—
These only, these the hearkening spirit hears,
   Sees only such things rise.

Thou art far too far for wings of words to follow,
   Far too far off for thought or any prayer.
   What ails us with thee, who art wind and air?
What ails us gazing where all seen is hollow?
   Yet with some fancy, yet with some desire,
   Dreams pursue death as winds a flying fire,
Our dreams pursue our dead and do not find.
   Still, and more swift than they, the thin flame flies,
   The low light fails us in elusive skies,
Still the foiled earnest ear is deaf, and blind
   Are still the eluded eyes.

Not thee, O never thee, in all time's changes,
   Not thee, but this the sound of thy sad soul,
   The shadow of thy swift spirit, this shut scroll
I lay my hand on, and not death estranges
   My spirit from communion of thy song—
   These memories and these melodies that throng
Veiled porches of a Muse funereal—
   These I salute, these touch, these clasp and fold
   As though a hand were in my hand to hold,
Or through mine ears a mourning musical
   Of many mourners rolled.

I among these, I also, in such station
   As when the pyre was charred, and piled the sods,
   And offering to the dead made, and their gods,
The old mourners had, standing to make libation,
   I stand, and to the gods and to the dead
   Do reverence without prayer or praise, and shed
Offering to these unknown, the gods of gloom,
   And what of honey and spice my seed-lands bear,
   And what I may of fruits in this chilled air,
And lay, Orestes-like, across the tomb
   A curl of severed hair.

ALGERNON CHARLES SWINBURNE

But by no hand nor any treason stricken,
  Not like the low-lying head of Him, the King,
  The flame that made of Troy a ruinous thing,
Thou liest and on this dust no tears could quicken.
  There fall no tears like theirs that all men hear
  Fall tear by sweet imperishable tear
Down the opening leaves of holy poet's pages.
  Thee not Orestes, not Electra mourns;
  But bending us-ward with memorial urns
The most high Muses that fulfil all ages
  Weep, and our God's heart yearns.

For, sparing of his sacred strength, not often
  Among us darkling here the lord of light
  Makes manifest his music and his might
In hearts that open and in lips that soften
  With the soft flame and heat of songs that shine.
  Thy lips indeed he touched with bitter wine,
And nourished them indeed with bitter bread;
  Yet surely from his hand thy soul's food came,
  The fire that scarred thy spirit at his flame
Was lighted, and thine hungering heart he fed
  Who feeds our hearts with fame.

Therefore he too now at thy soul's sunsetting,
  God of all suns and songs, he too bends down
  To mix his laurel with thy cypress crown
And save thy dust from blame and from forgetting.
  Therefore he too, seeing all thou wert and art,
  Compassionate, with sad and sacred heart,
Mourns thee of many his children the last dead,
  And hallows with strange tears and alien sighs
  Thine unmelodious mouth and sunless eyes
And over thine irrevocable head
  Sheds light from the under skies.

And one weeps with him in the ways Lethean,
  And stains with tears her changing bosom chill;
  That obscure Venus of the hollow hill,
That thing transformed which was the Cytherean,

With lips that lost their Grecian laugh divine
Long since, and face no more called Erycine
A ghost, a bitter and luxurious god,
  Thee also with fair flesh and singing spell
  Did she, a sad and second prey, compel
Into the footless places once more trod,
  And shadows hot from hell.

And now no sacred staff shall break in blossom,
  No choral salutation lure to light
  A spirit sick with perfume and sweet night
And love's tired eyes and hands and barren bosom.
  There is no help for these things; none to mend,
  And none to mar; not all our songs, O friend,
Will make death clear, or make life durable.
  Howbeit with rose and ivy and wild vine
  And with wild notes about this dust of thine
At least I fill the place where white dreams dwell
  And wreathe an unseen shrine.

Sleep; and if life was bitter to thee, pardon,
  If sweet, give thanks; thou hast no more to live
  And to give thanks is good, and to forgive.
Out of the mystic and the mournful garden
  Where all day through thine hands in barren braid
  Wove the sick flowers of secrecy and shade,
Green buds of sorrow and sin, and remnants grey,
  Sweet-smelling, pale with poison, sanguine-hearted,
  Passions that sprang from sleep and thoughts that started
Shall death not bring us all as thee one day
  Among the days departed?

For thee, O now a silent soul, my brother,
  Take at my hands this garland, and farewell.
  Thin is the leaf, and chill the wintry smell,
And chill the solemn earth, a fatal mother,
  With sadder than the Niobean womb,
  And in the hollow of her breasts a tomb.

1024

ALGERNON CHARLES SWINBURNE

Content thee, howsoe'er, whose days are done:
    There lies not any troublous thing before,
    Nor sight nor sound to war against thee more,
For whom all winds are quiet as the sun,
    All waters as the shore.

THE TRIUMPH OF TIME

.   .   .   .

I will go back to the great sweet mother,—
    Mother and lover of men, the Sea.
I will go down to her, I and none other,
    Close with her, kiss her, and mix her with me;
Cling to her, strive with her, hold her fast;
O fair white mother, in days long past
Born without sister, born without brother,
    Set free my soul as thy soul is free.

O fair green-girdled mother of mine,
    Sea, that art clothed with the sun and the rain,
Thy sweet hard kisses are strong like wine,
    Thy large embraces are keen like pain.
Save me and hide me with all thy waves,
Find me one grave of thy thousand graves,
Those pure cold populous graves of thine,
    Wrought without hand in a world without stain.

I shall sleep, and move with the moving ships,
    Change as the winds change, veer in the tide;
My lips will feast on the foam of thy lips,
    I shall rise with thy rising, with thee subside;
Sleep, and not know if she be, if she were,
Filled full with life to the eyes and hair;
As a rose is fulfilled to the rose-leaf tips
    With splendid summer and perfume and pride.

This woven raiment of nights and days,
    Were it once cast off and unwound from me,
Naked and glad would I walk in thy ways,
    Alive and aware of thy waves and thee;

1025

Clear of the whole world, hidden at home,
Clothed with the green, and crowned with the foam,
A pulse of the life of thy straits and bays,
    A vein in the heart of the streams of the Sea.

Fair mother, fed with the lives of men,
    Thou art subtle and cruel of heart, men say;
Thou hast taken, and shalt not render again;
    Thou art full of thy dead, and cold as they.
But death is the worst that comes of thee;
Thou art fed with our dead, O Mother, O Sea,
But when hast thou fed on our hearts? or when
    Having given us love, hast thou taken away?

O tender-hearted, O perfect lover,
    Thy lips are bitter, and sweet thine heart.
The hopes that hurt and the dreams that hover,
    Shall they not vanish away and apart?
But thou, thou art sure, thou art older than earth;
Thou art strong for death and fruitful of birth;
Thy depths conceal and thy gulfs discover;
    From the first thou wert; in the end thou art.

CHRISTOPHER MARLOWE

Crowned, girdled, garbed and shod with light and fire,
    Son first-born of the morning, sovereign star!
    Soul nearest ours of all, that wert most far,
Most far off in the abysm of time, thy lyre
Hung highest above the dawn-enkindled quire
    Where all ye sang together, all that are,
    And all the starry songs behind thy car
Rang sequence, all our souls acclaim thee sire.

"If all the pens that ever poets held
    Had fed the feeling of their masters' thoughts,"
    And as with rush of hurtling chariots
The flight of all their spirits were impelled
    Toward one great end, thy glory—nay, not then,
    Not yet might'st thou be praised enough of men.
1026

ALGERNON CHARLES SWINBURNE

WILLIAM SHAKESPEARE

Not if men's tongues and angels' all in one
   Spake, might the word be said that might speak Thee.
   Streams, winds, woods, flowers, fields, mountains, yea, the
       sea,
What power is in them all to praise the sun?
His praise is this,—he can be praised of none.
   Man, woman, child, praise God for him; but he
   Exults not to be worshipped, but to be.
He is; and, being, beholds his work well done.
All joy, all glory, all sorrow, all strength, all mirth,
Are his: without him, day were night on earth.
   Time knows not his from time's own period.
All lutes, all harps, all viols, all flutes, all lyres,
Fall dumb before him ere one string suspires.
   All stars are angels; but the sun is God.

BY THE NORTH SEA

A land that is lonelier than ruin;
   A sea that is stranger than death;
Far fields that a rose never blew in,
   Wan waste where the winds lack breath;
Waste endless and boundless, and flowerless
   But of marsh-blossoms fruitless as free;
Where earth lies exhausted, as powerless
   To strive with the sea.

Far flickers the flight of the swallows,
   Far flutters the weft of the grass
Spun dense over desolate hollows,
   More pale than the clouds as they pass;
Thick woven as the web of a witch is
   Round the heart of a thrall that hath sinned,
Whose youth and the wrecks of its riches
   Are waifs on the wind.

The pastures are herdless and sheepless,
  No pasture or shelter for herds:
The wind is relentless and sleepless,
  And restless and songless the birds;
Their cries from afar fall breathless,
  Their wings are as lightnings that flee;
For the land has two lords that are deathless,—
  Death's self, and the sea.

. . . .

No surety to stand, and no shelter
  To dawn out of darkness but one,
Out of waters that hurtle and welter,
  No succour to dawn with the sun
But a rest from the wind as it passes,
  Where, hardly redeemed from the waves,
Lie thick as the blades of the grasses
  The dead in their graves.

A multitude noteless of numbers,
  As wild weeds cast on an heap:
And sounder than sleep are their slumbers,
  And softer than song is their sleep;
And sweeter than all things, and stranger
  The sense, if perchance it may be,
That the wind is divested of danger,
  And scatheless the sea.

. . . .

As the waves of the numberless waters
  That the wind cannot number who guides,
Are the sons of the shore and the daughters
  Here lulled by the chime of the tides;
And here in the press of them standing
  We know not if these or if we
Live truliest,—or anchored to landing,
  Or drifted to sea.

In the valley he named of decision,
  No denser were multitudes met
When the soul of the seer in her vision
  Saw nations for doom of them set;

Saw darkness in dawn, and the splendour
  Of judgment, the sword and the rod:
But the doom here of death is more tender,
  And gentler the god.

And gentler the wind from the dreary
  Sea-banks by the waves overlapped,
Being weary, speaks peace to the weary,
  From slopes that the tide-stream hath sapped;
And sweeter than all that we call so
  The seal of their slumber shall be
Till the graves that embosom them also
  Be sapped of the sea.

John Burroughs

WAITING

Serene, I fold my hands and wait,
  Nor care for wind, or tide, or sea;
I rave no more 'gainst Time or Fate,
  For, lo! my own shall come to me.

I stay my haste, I make delays,
  For what avails this eager pace?
I stand amid the eternal ways,
  And what is mine shall know my face.

Asleep, awake, by night or day,
  The friends I seek are seeking me;
No wind can drive my bark astray,
  Nor change the tide of destiny.

What matter if I stand alone?
  I wait with joy the coming years;
My heart shall reap where it hath sown,
  And garner up its fruits of tears.

The waters know their own and draw
    The brook that springs in yonder heights;
So flows the good with equal law
    Unto the soul of pure delights.

The stars come nightly to the sky;
    The tidal wave comes to the sea;
Nor time, nor space, nor deep, nor high,
    Can keep my own away from me.

William Edward Hartpole Lecky

HOMEWARD BOUND

.   .   .   .

Thus in the gloom and solitude of thought
I wandered long, till on my lonely path
Thy influence arose. In thee I found
A sacred spot in which the wearied soul
At length might rest—for thou hast been to me
Dear as to night the crystal stars that shine
Like pleasures nestling in her gloomy heart.
From thee, dear wife, I learned how Love can graft
A stronger plume on Life's dishevelled wing—
How, turning to the earth from which it sprang,
The spirit gathers strength, and yet may find
In daily rounds of duty and of love
The sands of life still sparkling as they flow.

TO . . .

'Twas not alone thy beauty's power
    That made thee dear to me;
The quiet of the sunset hour
    Most truly mirrored thee.

'Twas thine to shed a soothing balm
    On doubt and grief and strife,
And make a bright and holy calm
    The atmosphere of life.

FRANCIS BRET HARTE

Thy touch of sympathy could find
    To frozen hearts the key,
The darkened and the arid mind
    Gave light and fruit for thee.

Ah! many a flower unnoticed springs
    On life's most trodden ways,
And common lives and common things
    Grew nobler in thy praise.

UNCONSCIOUS CEREBRATION

Say not that the past is dead.
Though the Autumn leaves are shed,
Though the day's last flush has flown,
Though the lute has lost its tone—
Still within, unfelt, unseen,
Lives the life that once has been;
With a silent power still
Guiding heart or brain or will,
Lending bias, force, and hue
To the things we think and do.
Strange! how aimless looks or words
Sometimes wake forgotten chords,
Bidding dreams and memories leap
From a long unbroken sleep.

Francis Bret Harte

DICKENS IN CAMP

Above the pines the moon was slowly drifting,
        The river sang below;
The dim Sierras, far beyond, uplifting
        Their minarets of snow.

1031

The roaring camp-fire, with rude humor, painted
    The ruddy tints of health
On haggard face and form that drooped and fainted
    In the fierce race for wealth.

Till one arose, and from his pack's scant treasure
    A hoarded volume drew,
And cards were dropped from hands of listless leisure
    To hear the tale anew.

And then, while round them shadows gathered faster,
    And as the firelight fell,
He read aloud the book wherein the Master
    Had writ of "Little Nell."

Perhaps 'twas boyish fancy—for .the reader
    Was youngest of them all—
But, as he read, from clustering pine and cedar
    A silence seemed to fall;

The fir-trees, gathering closer in the shadows,
    Listened in every spray,
While the whole camp with "Nell" on English meadows
    Wandered, and lost their way.

And so in mountain solitudes—o'ertaken
    As by some spell divine—
Their cares drop from them like the needles shaken
    From out the gusty pine.

Lost is that camp, and wasted all its fire;
    And he who wrought that spell?—
Ah, towering pine and stately Kentish spire,
    Ye have one tale to tell!

Lost is that camp! but let its fragrant story
    Blend with the breath that thrills
With hop-vines' incense all the pensive glory
    That fills the Kentish hills.

And on that grave where English oak and holly
    And laurel wreaths entwine,
Deem it not all a too presumptuous folly—
    This spray of Western pine!

RELIEVING GUARD

Came the Relief. "What, Sentry, ho!
How passed the night through the long waking?"
"Cold, cheerless, dark—as may befit
The hour before the dawn is breaking."

"No sight? no sound?" "No; nothing save
The plover from the marshes calling,
And in yon western sky, about
An hour ago, a star was falling."

"A star? There's nothing strange in that."
"No, nothing; but, above the thicket,
Somehow it seemed to me that God
Somewhere had just relieved a picket."

Austin Dobson

URCEUS EXIT

I intended an Ode,
    And it turn'd to a Sonnet.
It began à la mode,
I intended an Ode;
But Rose cross'd the road
    In her latest new bonnet;
I intended an Ode;
    And it turn'd to a Sonnet.

FOR A CHARITY ANNUAL

In Angel-Court the sunless air
    Grows faint and sick; to left and right
    The cowering houses shrink from sight,
Huddled and hopeless, eyeless, bare.

1033

Misnamed, you say?   For surely rare
   Must be the angel-shapes that light
                     In Angel-Court!

Nay! the Eternities are there.
   Death at the doorway stands to smite;
   Life in its garrets leaps to flight;
And Love has climbed that crumbling stair
                     In Angel-Court.

FOR A COPY OF THEOCRITUS

O singer of the field and fold,
Theocritus!   Pan's pipe was thine,—
Thine was the happier Age of Gold.

For thee the scent of new-turned mould,
The bee-hives, and the murmuring pine,
O Singer of the field and fold!

Thou sang'st the simple feasts of old,—
The beechen bowl made glad with wine . .
Thine was the happier Age of Gold.

Thou bad'st the rustic loves be told,—
Thou bad'st the tuneful reeds combine,
O Singer of the field and fold!

And round thee, ever-laughing, rolled
The blithe and blue Sicilian brine . . .
Thine was the happier Age of Gold.

Alas for us!   Our songs are cold;
Our Northern suns too sadly shine:—
O Singer of the field and fold,
Thine was the happier Age of Gold!

IN AFTER DAYS

In after days when grasses high
O'er-top the stone where I shall lie,
   Though ill or well the world adjust
   My slender claim to honoured dust,
I shall not question or reply.

I shall not see the morning sky;
I shall not hear the night-wind sigh;
  I shall be mute, as all men must
    In after days!

But yet, now living, fain were I
That some one then should testify,
  Saying—"He held his pen in trust
  To Art, not serving shame or lust."
Will none?—Then let my memory die
    In after days!

THE SONG OF THE SEA WIND

How it sings, sings, sings,
  Blowing sharply from the sea-line,
With an edge of salt that stings;
  How it laughs aloud, and passes,
  As it cuts the close cliff-grasses;
    How it sings again, and whistles
    As it shakes the stout sea-thistles—
      How it sings!

How it shrieks, shrieks, shrieks,
  In the crannies of the headland,
In the gashes of the creeks;
  How it shrieks once more, and catches
  Up the yellow foam in patches:
    How it whirls it out and over
    To the corn-field and the clover—
      How it shrieks!

How it roars, roars, roars,
  In the iron under-caverns,
In the hollows of the shores;
  How it roars anew, and thunders,
  As the strong hull splits and sunders:
    And the spent ship, tempest driven,
    On the reef lies rent and riven—
      How it roars!

How it wails, wails, wails,
   In the tangle of the wreckage,
In the flapping of the sails;
   How it sobs away, subsiding,
   Like a tired child after chiding;
     And across the ground-swell rolling,
     You can hear the bell-buoy tolling—
       How it wails!

A GREETING

But once or twice we met, touched hands,
To-day between us both expands
   A waste of tumbling waters wide,—
   A waste by me as yet untried,
Vague with the doubt of unknown lands.

Time like a despot speeds his sands:
A year he blots, a day he brands;
   We walked, we talked by Thamis' side
     But once or twice.

What makes a friend? What filmy strands
Are these that turn to iron bands?
   What knot is this so firmly tied
   That naught but fate can now divide?—
Ah, these are things one understands
     But once or twice.

Thomas Hardy

SHELLEY'S SKYLARK

(*The neighbourhood of Leghorn: March,* 1887)

Somewhere afield here something lies
In Earth's oblivious eyeless trust
That moved a poet to prophecies—
A pinch of unseen, unguarded dust:

1036

THOMAS HARDY

The dust of the lark that Shelley heard,
And made immortal through times to be;—
Though it only lived like another bird,
And knew not its immortality:
Lived its meek life; then, one day, fell—
A little ball of feather and bone;
And how it perished, when piped farewell,
And where it wastes, are alike unknown.

Maybe it rests in the loam I view,
Maybe it throbs in a myrtle's green,
Maybe it sleeps in the coming hue
Of a grape on the slope of yon inland scene.

Go find it, faeries, go and find,
That tiny pinch of priceless dust,
And bring a casket silver-lined,
And framed of gold that gems encrust;

And we will lay it safe therein,
And consecrate it to endless time;
For it inspired a bard to win
Ecstatic heights in thought and rhyme.

THE DARKLING THRUSH

I leant upon a coppice gate
    When Frost was spectre-grey,
And Winter's dregs made desolate
    The weakening eye of day.
The tangled bine-stems scored the sky
    Like strings of broken lyres,
And all mankind that haunted nigh
    Had sought their household fires.

The land's sharp features seemed to be
    The Century's corpse outleant,
His crypt the cloudy canopy,
    The wind his death-lament.

The ancient pulse of germ and birth
  Was shrunken hard and dry,
And every spirit upon earth
  Seemed fervourless as I.

At once a voice arose among
  The bleak twigs overhead
In a full-hearted evensong
  Of joy illimited;
An aged thrush, frail, gaunt, and small,
  In blast-beruffled plume,
Had chosen thus to fling his soul
  Upon the growing gloom.

So little cause for carollings
  Of such ecstatic sound
Was written on terrestrial things
  Afar or nigh around,
That I could think there trembled through
  His happy good-night air
Some blessed Hope, whereof he knew
  And I was unaware.

John Addington Symonds

THYSELF

Give me thyself! It were as well to cry:
Give me the splendour of this night of June!
Give me yon star upon the swart lagoon
Trembling in unapproach'd serenity!
Our gondola, that four swift oarsmen ply,
Shoots from the darkening Lido's sandy dune,
Splits with her steel the mirrors of the moon,
Shivers the star-beams that before us fly.
Give me thyself! This prayer is even a knell,
Warning me back to mine own impotence.
1038

Self gives not self; and souls sequester'd dwell
In the dark fortalice of thought and sense,
Where, though life's prisoners call from cell to cell,
Each pines alone and may not issue thence.

LOVE IN DREAMS

Love hath his poppy-wreath,
   Not Night alone.
I laid my head beneath
   Love's lilied throne:
Then to my sleep he brought
   This anodyne—
The flower of many a thought
   And fancy fine:
A form, a face, no more;
   Fairer than truth;
A dream from death's pale shore;
   The soul of youth:
A dream so dear, so deep,
   All dreams above,
That still I pray to sleep—
   Bring Love back, Love!

Edward Rowland Sill

THE FOOL'S PRAYER

The royal feast was done; the King
   Sought some new sport to banish care,
And to his jester cried: "Sir Fool,
   Kneel now, and make for us a prayer!"

The jester doffed his cap and bells,
   And stood the mocking court before;
They could not see the bitter smile
   Behind the painted grin he wore.

1039

He bowed his head, and bent his knee
  Upon the monarch's silken stool;
His pleading voice arose: "O Lord,
  Be merciful to me, a fool!

"No pity, Lord, could change the heart
  From red with wrong to white as wool;
The rod must heal the sin: but, Lord,
  Be merciful to me, a fool!

" 'Tis not by guilt the onward sweep
  Of truth and right, O Lord, we stay;
'Tis by our follies that so long
  We hold the earth from heaven away.

"These clumsy feet, still in the mire,
  Go crushing blossoms without end;
These hard, well-meaning hands we thrust
  Among the heart-strings of a friend.

"The ill-timed truth we might have kept—
  Who knows how sharp it pierced and stung?
The word we had not sense to say—
  Who knows how grandly it had rung?

"Our faults no tenderness should ask,
  The chastening stripes must cleanse them all;
But for our blunders—oh, in shame
  Before the eyes of heaven we fall.

"Earth bears no balsam for mistakes;
  Men crown the knave, and scourge the tool
That did his will; but Thou, O Lord,
  Me merciful to me, a fool!"

The room was hushed; in silence rose
  The King, and sought his gardens cool,
And walked apart, and murmured low,
  "Be merciful to me, a fool!"

TRUTH AT LAST

Does a man ever give up hope, I wonder,—
Face the grim fact, seeing it clear as day?
When Bennen saw the snow slip, heard its thunder
Low, louder, roaring round him, felt the speed
Grow swifter as the avalanche hurled downward,
Did he for just one heart-throb—did he indeed
Know with all certainty, as they swept onward,
There was the end, where the crag dropped away?
Or did he think, even till they plunged and fell,
Some miracle would stop them?   Nay, they tell
That he turned round, face forward, calm and pale,
Stretching his arms out toward his native vale
As if in mute, unspeakable farewell,
And so went down.—'Tis something, if at last,
Though only for a flash, a man may see
Clear-eyed the future as he sees the past,
From doubt, or fear, or hope's illusion free.

Sidney Lanier

EVENING SONG

Look off, dear Love, across the sallow sands,
   And mark yon meeting of the sun and sea,
How long they kiss in sight of all the lands,
   Ah! longer, longer, we.

Now in the sea's red vintage melts the sun,
   As Egypt's pearl dissolved in rosy wine,
And Cleopatra night drinks all.   'Tis done,
   Love, lay thine hand in mine.

Come forth, sweet stars, and comfort heaven's heart;
   Glimmer, ye waves, round else unlighted sands.
O night! divorce our sun and sky apart,
   Never our lips, our hands.

THE MARSHES OF GLYNN

Glooms of the live-oaks, beautiful-braided and woven
With intricate shades of the vines that myriad-cloven
Clamber the forks of the multiform boughs,—
      Emerald twilights,—
      Virginal shy lights,
Wrought of the leaves to allure to the whisper of vows,
When lovers pace timidly down through the green colonnades
Of the dim sweet woods, of the dear dark woods,
  Of the heavenly woods and glades,
That run to the radiant marginal sand-beach within
    The wide sea-marshes of Glynn;—
Beautiful glooms, soft dusks in the noonday fire,—
Wildwood privacies, closets of lone desire,
Chamber from chamber parted with wavering arras of
    leaves,—
Cells for the passionate pleasure of prayer to the soul that
    grieves,
Pure with a sense of the passing of saints through the wood,
Cool for the dutiful weighing of ill with good;—

O braided dusks of the oak and woven shades of the vine,
While the riotous noonday sun of the June-day long did shine,
Ye held me fast in your heart and I held you fast in mine;
But now when the noon is no more, and riot is rest,
And the sun is a-wait at the ponderous gate of the West,
And the slant yellow beam down the wood-aisle doth seem
Like a lane into heaven that leads from a dream,—
Ay, now, when my soul all day hath drunken the soul of the
    oak,
And my heart is at ease from men, and the wearisome sound of
    the stroke
  Of the scythe of time and the trowel of trade is low,
  And belief overmasters doubt, and I know that I know,
  And my spirit is grown to a lordly great compass within,
That the length and the breadth and the sweep of the marshes
    of Glynn

Will work me no fear like the fear they have wrought me
    of yore
When length was fatigue, and when breadth was but bitter-
    ness sore,
And when terror and shrinking and dreary unnamable pain
Drew over me out of the merciless miles of the plain,—

Oh, now, unafraid, I am fain to face
    The vast sweet visage of space.
To the edge of the wood I am drawn, I am drawn,
Where the gray beach glimmering runs, as a belt of the
    dawn,
    For a mete and a mark
    To the forest-dark:—
                So:
Affable live-oak, leaning low,—
Thus—with your favor—soft, with a reverent hand,
(Not lightly touching your person, Lord of the land!)
Bending your beauty aside, with a step I stand
On the firm-packed sand,
              Free
By a world of marsh that borders a world of sea.
    Sinuous southward and sinuous northward the shimmering
        band
Of the sand-beach fastens the fringe of the marsh to the
        folds of the land.
Inward and outward to northward and southward the beach-
        lines linger and curl
As a silver-wrought garment that clings to and follows the
        firm sweet limbs of a girl.
Vanishing, swerving, evermore curving again into sight,
Softly the sand-beach wavers away to a dim gray looping of
        light.
And what if behind me to westward the wall of the woods
        stands high?
The world lies east: how ample, the marsh and the sea and
        the sky!
A league and a league of marsh-grass, waist-high, broad in
        the blade,
Green, and all of a height, and unflecked with a light or a
        shade,

Stretch leisurely off, in a pleasant plain,
To the terminal blue of the main.
Oh, what is abroad in the marsh and the terminal sea?
Somehow my soul seems suddenly free
From the weighing of fate and the sad discussion of sin,
By the length and the breadth and the sweep of the marshes
      of Glynn.

Ye marshes, how candid and simple and nothing-withholding
      and free
Ye publish yourselves to the sky and offer yourselves to the
      sea!
Tolerant plains, that suffer the sea and the rains and the sun,
Ye spread and span like the catholic man who hath mightily
      won
God out of knowledge and good out of infinite pain
And sight out of blindness and purity out of a stain.

As the marsh-hen secretly builds on the watery sod,
Behold I will build me a nest on the greatness of God:
I will fly in the greatness of God as the marsh-hen flies
In the freedom that fills all the space 'twixt the marsh and
      the skies:
By so many roots as the marsh-grass sends in the sod
I will heartily lay me a-hold on the greatness of God:
Oh, like to the greatness of God is the greatness within
The range of the marshes, the liberal marshes of Glynn.

And the sea lends large, as the marsh: lo, out of his plenty
      the sea
Pours fast: full soon the time of the flood tide must be:
Look how the grace of the sea doth go
About and about through the intricate channels that flow
           Here and there,
           Everywhere,
Till his waters have flooded the uttermost creeks and the low-
      lying lanes,
And the marsh is meshed with a million veins,
That like as with rosy and silvery essences flow
In the rose-and-silver evening glow.
          Farewell, my lord Sun!
The creeks overflow: a thousand rivulets run

'Twixt the roots of the sod; the blades of the marsh-grass
     stir;
Passeth a hurrying sound of wings that westward whirr;
Passeth, and all is still; and the currents cease to run;
And the sea and the marsh are one.

How still the plains of the waters be!
The tide is in his ecstasy;
The tide is at his highest height:
               And it is night.
And now from the Vast of the Lord will the waters of sleep
Roll in the souls of men,
But who will reveal to our waking ken
The forms that swim and the shapes that creep
               Under the waters of sleep?
And I would I could know what swimmeth below when the
     tide comes in
On the length and the breadth of the marvelous marshes of
     Glynn.

ACKNOWLEDGMENTS

.   .   .   .

Now at thy soft recalling voice I rise
     Where thought is lord o'er Time's complete estate,
Like as a dove from out the gray sedge flies
     To tree-tops green where cooes his heavenly mate.
From these clear coverts high and cool I see
     How every time with every time is knit,
And each to all is mortised cunningly,
     And none is sole or whole, yet all are fit.
Thus, if this Age but as a comma show
     'Twixt weightier clauses of large-worded years,
My calmer soul scorns not the mark: I know
     This crooked point Time's complex sentence clears
          Yet more I learn while, Friend! I sit by thee:
          Who sees all time, sees all eternity.

A BALLAD OF TREES AND THE MASTER

Into the woods my Master went,
Clean forspent, forspent.
Into the woods my Master came,
Forspent with love and shame.
But the olives they were not blind to Him,
The little gray leaves were kind to Him:
The thorn-tree had a mind to Him
When into the woods He came.

Out of the woods my Master went,
And He was well content.
Out of the woods my Master came,
Content with death and shame.
When Death and Shame would woo Him last,
From under the trees they drew Him last:
'Twas on a tree they slew Him—last
When out of the woods He came.

SONG OF THE CHATTAHOOCHEE

Out of the hills of Habersham,
Down the valleys of Hall,
I hurry amain to reach the plain,
Run the rapid and leap the fall,
Split at the rock and together again,
Accept my bed, or narrow or wide,
And flee from folly on every side
With a lover's pain to attend the plain
Far from the hills of Habersham,
Far from the valleys of Hall.

All down the hills of Habersham,
All down the valleys of Hall,
The rushes cried, *Abide, abide,*
The willful waterweeds held me thrall,
The laving laurel turned my tide,

1046

SIDNEY LANIER

The ferns and the fondling grass said *Stay*,
The dewberry dipped for to work delay,
And the little reeds sighed, *Abide, abide,*
   Here in the hills of Habersham,
   Here in the valleys of Hall.

   High o'er the hills of Habersham,
    Veiling the valleys of Hall,
The hickory told me manifold
Fair tales of shade, the poplar tall
Wrought me her shadowy self to hold,
The chestnut, the oak, the walnut, the pine,
Overleaning, with flickering meaning and sign,
Said, *Pass not, so cold, these manifold*
   Deep shades of the hills of Habersham,
   These glades in the valleys of Hall.

   And oft in the hills of Habersham,
    And oft in the valleys of Hall,
The white quartz shone, and the smooth brook-stone
Did bar me of passage with friendly brawl,
And many a luminous jewel lone
—Crystals clear or a-cloud with mist,
Ruby, garnet and amethyst—
Made lures with the lights of streaming stone,
   In the clefts of the hills of Habersham,
   In the beds of the valleys of Hall.

   But oh, not the hills of Habersham,
    And oh, not the valleys of Hall,
Avail: I am fain for to water the plain.
Downward the voices of Duty call—
Downward, to toil and be mixed with the main.
The dry fields burn, and the mills are to turn,
And a myriad flowers mortally yearn,
And the lordly main from beyond the plain
   Calls o'er the hills of Habersham,
   Calls through the valleys of Hall.

Richard Watson Gilder

ON THE LIFE-MASK OF ABRAHAM LINCOLN

This bronze doth keep the very form and mold
Of our great martyr's face. Yes, this is he:
That brow all wisdom, all benignity;
That human, humorous mouth; those cheeks that hold
Like some harsh landscape all the summer's gold;
That spirit fit for sorrow, as the sea
For storms to beat on; the lone agony
Those silent, patient lips too well foretold.
Yes, this is he who ruled a world of men
As might some prophet of the elder day,—
Brooding above the tempest and the fray
With deep-eyed thought and more than mortal ken.
A power was his beyond the touch of art
Or armèd strength—his pure and mighty heart.

Arthur William O'Shaughnessy

ODE

We are the music-makers,
    And we are the dreamers of dreams,
Wandering by lone sea-breakers,
    And sitting by desolate streams;
World-losers and world-forsakers,
    On whom the pale moon gleams:
Yet we are the movers and shakers
    Of the world for ever, it seems.

With wonderful deathless ditties
We build up the world's great cities,
    And out of a fabulous story
    We fashion an empire's glory:

1048

ARTHUR WILLIAM O'SHAUGHNESSY

One man with a dream, at pleasure,
   Shall go forth and conquer a crown;
And three with a new song's measure
   Can trample a kingdom down.

We, in the ages lying
   In the buried past of the earth,
Built Nineveh with our sighing,
   And Babel itself with our mirth;
And o'erthrew them with prophesying
   To the old of the new world's worth;
For each age is a dream that is dying,
   Or one that is coming to birth.

.   .   .   .

. . . We, with our dreaming and singing,
   Ceaseless and sorrowless we!
The glory about us clinging
   Of the glorious futures we see,
Our souls with high music ringing:
   O men! it must ever be
That we dwell, in our dreaming and singing,
   A little apart from ye.

For we are afar with the dawning
   And the suns that are not yet high,
And out of the infinite morning
   Intrepid you hear us cry—
How, spite of your human scorning,
   Once more God's future draws nigh,
And already goes forth the warning
   That ye of the past must die.

Great hail! we cry to the comers
   From the dazzling unknown shore;
Bring us hither your sun and your summers,
   And renew our world as of yore;
You shall teach us your song's new numbers,
   And things that we dreamed not before:
Yea, in spite of a dreamer who slumbers
   And a singer who sings no more.

HERODIAS

Her long black hair danced round her like a snake
Allured to each charm'd movement she did make;
    Her voice came strangely sweet;
She sang, "O, Herod, wilt thou look on me—
Have I no beauty thy heart cares to see?"
And what her voice did sing her dancing feet
    Seem'd ever to repeat.

She sang, "O, Herod, wilt thou look on me?
What sweet I have, I have it all for thee";
    And through the dance and song
She freed and floated on the air her arms
Above dim veils that hid her bosom's charms:
The passion of her singing was so strong
    It drew all hearts along.

Her sweet arms were unfolded on the air,
They seem'd like floating flowers the most fair—
    White lilies the most choice;
And in the gradual bending of her hand
There lurk'd a grace that no man could withstand;
Yea, none knew whether hands, or feet, or voice,
    Most made his heart rejoice.

KEEPING A HEART

If one should give me a heart to keep,
  With love for the golden key,
The giver might live at ease or sleep;
It should ne'er know pain, be weary, or weep,
  The heart watch'd over by me.

I would keep that heart as a temple fair,
  No heathen should look therein;
Its chaste marmoreal beauty rare
I only should know, and to enter there
  I must hold myself from sin.

1050

ARTHUR WILLIAM O'SHAUGHNESSY

I would keep that heart as a casket hid
   Where precious jewels are ranged,
A memory each; as you raise the lid,
You think you love again as you did
   Of old, and nothing seems changed.

How I should tremble day after day,
   As I touch'd with the golden key,
Lest aught in that heart were changed, or say
That another had stolen one thought away
   And it did not open to me.

But ah, I should know that heart so well,
   As a heart so loving and true,
As a heart that I held with a golden spell,
That so long as I changed not I could foretell
   That heart would be changeless too.

I would keep that heart as the thought of heaven,
   To dwell in a life apart,
My good should be done, my gift be given,
In hope of the recompense there; yea, even
   My life should be led in that heart.

And so on the eve of some blissful day,
   From within we should close the door
On glimmering splendours of love, and stay
In that heart shut up from the world away,
   Never to open it more.

SONG

   Has summer come without the rose,
      Or left the bird behind?
   Is the blue changed above thee,
      O world! or am I blind?
   Will you change every flower that grows,
      Or only change this spot,
   Where she who said, I love thee,
      Now says, I love thee not?

The skies seemed true above thee,
    The rose true on the tree;
The bird seemed true the summer through,
    But all proved false to me.
World! is there one good thing in you,
    Life, love, or death—or what?
Since lips that sang, I love thee,
    Have said, I love thee not?

I think the sun's kiss will scarce fall
    Into one flower's gold cup;
I think the bird will miss me,
    And give the summer up.
O sweet place! desolate in tall
    Wild grass, have you forgot
How her lips loved to kiss me,
    Now that they kiss me not?

Be false or fair above me,
    Come back with any face,
Summer!—do I care what you do?
    You cannot change one place—
The grass, the leaves, the earth, the dew,
    The grave I make the spot—
Here, where she used to love me,
    Here where she loves me not.

SONG

I made another garden, yea,
    For my new Love:
I left the dead rose where it lay
    And set the new above.
Why did my Summer not begin?
    Why did my heart not haste?
My old Love came and walked therein,
    And laid the garden waste.

ARTHUR WILLIAM O'SHAUGHNESSY

She entered with her weary smile,
   Just as of old;
She looked around a little while
   And shivered with the cold:
Her passing touch was death to all,
   Her passing look a blight;
She made the white rose-petals fall,
   And turned the red rose white.

Her pale robe clinging to the grass
   Seemed like a snake
That bit the grass and ground, alas!
   And a sad trail did make.
She went up slowly to the gate,
   And then, just as of yore,
She turned back at the last to wait
   And say farewell once more.

IN THE OLD HOUSE

In the old house where we dwelt
   No care had come, no grief we knew,
No memory of the past we felt,
No doubt assailed us when we knelt;
   It is not so in the new.

In the old house where we grew
   From childhood up, the days were dreams,
   The summers had unwonted gleams,
The sun a warmer radiance threw
   Upon the stair. Alas! it seems
All different in the new!

Our mother still could sing the strain
   In earlier days we listened to;
   The white threads in her hair were few,
She seldom sighed or suffered pain,
Oh, for the old house back again!
   It is not so in the new.

Andrew Lang

SCYTHE SONG

Mowers, weary and brown, and blithe,
  What is the word methinks ye know,
Endless over-word that the Scythe
  Sings to the blades of the grass below?
Scythes that swing in the grass and clover,
  Something, still, they say as they pass;
What is the word that, over and over,
  Sings the Scythe to the flowers and grass?

Hush, ah hush, the Scythes are saying,
  Hush, and heed not, and fall asleep;
Hush, they say to the grasses swaying,
  Hush, they sing to the clover deep!
Hush—'tis the lullaby Time is singing—
  Hush, and heed not, for all things pass.
Hush, ah hush! and the Scythes are swinging
  Over the clover, over the grass!

THE ODYSSEY

As one that for a weary space has lain
  Lulled by the song of Circe and her wine
  In gardens near the pale of Proserpine,
Where that Ææan isle forgets the main,
And only the low lutes of love complain,
  And only shadows of wan lovers pine,
  As such an one were glad to know the brine
Salt on his lips, and the large air again,—
So gladly, from the songs of modern speech
  Men turn, and see the stars, and feel the free
    Shrill wind beyond the close of heavy flowers,
    And through the music of the languid hours,
  They hear like ocean on a western beach
    The surge and thunder of the Odyssey.

1054

Robert Bridges

A PASSER-BY

Whither, O splendid ship, thy white sails crowding,
  Leaning across the bosom of the urgent West,
That fearest nor sea rising, nor sky clouding,
  Whither away, fair rover, and what thy quest?
  Ah! soon, when Winter has all our vales opprest,
When skies are cold and misty, and hail is hurling,
  Wilt thou glide on the blue Pacific, or rest
In a summer haven asleep, thy white sails furling.

I there before thee, in the country that well thou knowest,
  Already arrived am inhaling the odorous air:
I watch thee enter unerringly where thou goest,
  And anchor queen of the strange shipping there,
  Thy sails for awnings spread, thy masts bare;
Nor is aught from the foaming reef to the snow-capped
      grandest
  Peak, that is over the feathery palms more fair
Than thou, so upright, so stately, and still thou standest.

And yet, O splendid ship, unhailed and nameless,
  I know not if, aiming a fancy, I rightly divine
That thou hast a purpose joyful, a courage blameless,
  Thy port assured in a happier land than mine.
  But for all I have given thee, beauty enough is thine,
As thou, aslant with trim tackle and shrouding,
  From the proud nostril curve of a prow's line
In the offing scatterest foam, thy white sails crowding.

ELEGY

The wood is bare: a river-mist is steeping
  The trees that winter's chill of life bereaves:
Only their stiffened boughs break silence, weeping
      Over their fallen leaves;

1055

That lie upon the dank earth brown and rotten,
  Miry and matted in the soaking wet:
Forgotten with the spring, that is forgotten
  By them that can forget.

Yet it was here we walked when ferns were springing,
  And through the mossy bank shot bud and blade:—
Here found in summer, when the birds were singing,
  A green and pleasant shade.

'Twas here we loved in sunnier days and greener;
  And now, in this disconsolate decay,
I come to see her where I most have seen her,
  And touch the happier day.

For on this path, at every turn and corner,
  The fancy of her figure on me falls:
Yet walks she with the slow step of a mourner,
  Nor hears my voice that calls.

So through my heart there winds a track of feeling,
  A path of memory, that is all her own:
Whereto her phantom beauty ever stealing
  Haunts the sad spot alone.

About her steps the trunks are bare, the branches
  Drip heavy tears upon her downcast head;
And bleed from unseen wounds that no sun stanches,
  For the year's sun is dead.

And dead leaves wrap the fruits that summer planted
  And birds that love the South have taken wing.
The wanderer, loitering o'er the scene enchanted,
  Weeps, and despairs of spring.

I HAVE LOVED FLOWERS THAT FADE

  I have loved flowers that fade,
  Within whose magic tents
  Rich hues have marriage made
  With sweet unmemoried scents:

A honeymoon delight,—
A joy of love at sight,
That ages in an hour:—
My song be like a flower!

I have loved airs, that die
Before their charm is writ
Along a liquid sky
Trembling to welcome it.
Notes, that with pulse of fire
Proclaim the spirit's desire,
Then die, and are nowhere:—
My song be like an air!

Die, song, die like a breath,
And wither as a bloom:
Fear not a flowery death,
Dread not an airy tomb!
Fly with delight, fly hence!
'Twas thine love's tender sense
To feast; now on thy bier
Beauty shall shed a tear.

MY DELIGHT AND THY DELIGHT

My delight and thy delight
Walking, like two angels white,
In the gardens of the night:

My desire and thy desire
Twining to a tongue of fire,
Leaping live, and laughing higher;
Thro' the everlasting strife
In the mystery of life.

Love, from whom the world begun,
Hath the secret of the sun.

Love can tell, and love alone,
Whence the million stars were strewn,
Why each atom knows its own,

How, in spite of woe and death,
Gay is life, and sweet is breath:

This he taught us, this we knew,
Happy in his science true,
Hand in hand as we stood
Neath the shadows of the wood,
Heart to heart as we lay
In the dawning of the day.

NIGHTINGALES

Beautiful must be the mountains whence ye come,
And bright in the fruitful valleys the streams wherefrom
Ye learn your song:
Where are those starry woods?   O might I wander there,
Among the flowers, which in that heavenly air
Bloom the year long!

Nay, barren are those mountains and spent the streams:
Our song is the voice of desire, that haunts our dreams,
A throe of the heart,
Whose pining visions dim, forbidden hopes profound,
No dying cadence nor long sigh can sound,
For all our art.

Alone, aloud in the raptured ear of men
We pour our dark nocturnal secret; and then,
As night is withdrawn
From these sweet-springing meads and bursting boughs of
May,
Dream, while the innumerable choir of day
Welcome the dawn.

I LOVE ALL BEAUTEOUS THINGS
I love all beauteous things,
I seek and adore them;
God hath no better praise,
And man in his hasty days
Is honoured for them.

1058

I too will something make
   And joy in the making;
Altho' to-morrow it seem
Like the empty words of a dream
   Remembered on waking.

ELEGY

Clear and gentle stream!
Known and loved so long,
That hast heard the song
And the idle dream
Of my boyish day;
While I once again
Down thy margin stray,
In the selfsame strain
Still my voice is spent,
With my old lament
And my idle dream,
Clear and gentle stream!

Where my old seat was
Here again I sit,
Where the long boughs knit
Over stream and grass
A translucent eaves:
Where back eddies play
Shipwreck with the leaves,
And the proud swans stray,
Sailing one by one
Out of stream and sun,
And the fish lie cool
In their chosen pool.

Many an afternoon
Of the summer day
Dreaming here I lay;
And I know how soon,

Idly at its hour,
First the deep bell hums
From the minster tower,
And then evening comes,
Creeping up the glade,
With her lengthening shade,
And the tardy boon
Of her brightening moon.

Clear and gentle stream!
Ere again I go
Where thou dost not flow,
Well does it beseem
Thee to hear again
Once my youthful song,
That familiar strain
Silent now so long:
Be as I content
With my old lament,
And my idle dream,
Clear and gentle stream!

Eugene Lee-Hamilton

OH, BLESS THE LAW

Oh, bless the law that veils the Future's face;
For who could smile into a baby's eyes,
Or bear the beauty of the evening skies,
If he could see what cometh on apace?
The ticking of the death-watch would replace
The baby's prattle, for the over-wise;
The breeze's murmur would become the cries
Of stormy petrels where the breakers race.
We live as moves the walker in his sleep,
Who walks because he sees not the abyss
His feet are skirting as he goes his way:
If we could see the morrow from the steep
Of our security, the soul would miss
Its footing, and fall headlong from to-day.

EUGENE LEE-HAMILTON

THE RING OF FAUSTUS

There is a tale of Faustus,—that one day
   Lucretia the Venetian, then his love,
   Had, while he slept, the rashness to remove
His magic ring, when fair as a god he lay;

And that a sudden horrible decay
   O'erspread his face; a hundred wrinkles wove
   Their network on his cheek; while she above
His slumber crouched, and watched him shrivel away.

There is upon Life's hand a magic ring—
   The ring of Faith-in-Good, Life's gold of gold;
Remove it not, lest all Life's charm take wing;

Remove it not, lest straightway you behold
   Life's cheek fall in, and every earthly thing
Grow all at once unutterably old.

WHAT THE SONNET IS

Fourteen small broidered berries on the hem
   Of Circe's mantle, each of magic gold;
Fourteen of lone Calypso's tears that roll'd
   Into the sea, for pearls to come of them;

Fourteen clear signs of omen in the gem
   With which Medea human fate foretold;
   Fourteen small drops, which Faustus, growing old,
Craved of the Fiend, to water Life's dry stem.

It is the pure white diamond Dante brought
   To Beatrice; the sapphire Laura wore
When Petrarch cut it sparkling out of thought;

The ruby Shakespeare hewed from his heart's core;
   The dark, deep emerald that Rossetti wrought
For his own soul, to wear for evermore.

John Bannister Tabb

BEETHOVEN AND ANGELO

One made the surging sea of tone
  Subservient to his rod:
One from the sterile womb of stone
  Raised children unto God.

FATHER DAMIEN

O God, the cleanest offering
  Of tainted earth below,
Unblushing to thy feet we bring,—
  "A leper white as snow!"

TO SHELLEY

At Shelley's birth,
The Lark, dawn-spirit, with an anthem loud
  Rose from the dusky earth
  To tell it to the Cloud,
That, like a flower night-folded in the gloom,
  Burst into morning bloom.

At Shelley's death,
The Sea, that deemed him an immortal, saw
  A god's extinguished breath,
  And landward, as in awe,
Upbore him to the altar whence he came,
  And the rekindling flame.

FRATERNITY

I know not but in every leaf
  That sprang to life along with me,
Were written all the joy and grief
  Thenceforth my fate to be.

The wind that whispered to the earth,
  The bird that sang its earliest lay,
The flower that blossomed at my birth—
  My kinsmen all were they.

Ay, but for fellowship with these
  I had not been—nay, might not be;
Nor they but vagrant melodies
  Till harmonized by me.

William Canton

THE COMRADES

In solitary rooms, when dusk is falling,
  I hear from fields beyond the haunted mountains,
  Beyond the irrepenetrable forests,
I hear the voices of my comrades calling
    Home! home! home!

Strange ghostly voices, when the dusk is falling,
  Come from the ancient years; and I remember
  The schoolboy shout, from plain and wood and river,
The signal-cry of scattered comrades, calling
    Home! home! home!

And home we wended when the dusk was falling;
  The pledged companions, talking, laughing, singing,
  Home through the grey French country, no one missing
And now I hear the old-time voices calling
    Home! home! home!

I pause and listen while the dusk is falling;
  My heart leaps back through all the long estrangemen*
  Of changing faith, lost hopes, paths disenchanted;
And tears drop as I hear the voices calling
    Home! home! home!

1063

I hear you while the dolorous dusk is falling;
  I sigh your names—the living—the departed!
  O vanished comrades, is it *yours* the poignant
Pathetic note among the voices calling
        Home! home! home!

Call, and still call me, for the dusk is falling.
  Call, for I fain, I fain would come, but cannot.
  Call, as the shepherd calls upon the moorland.
Though mute, with beating heart I hear your calling,
        Home! home! home!

THROUGH THE AGES

I

O'er the swamp in the forest
  the sunset is red;
And the sad reedy waters,
  in black mirrors spread,
Are aflame with the tall crimson tree-tops o'erhead.

By the swamp in the forest
  the oak-branches groan,
As the Savage primeval,
  with russet hair thrown
O'er his huge naked limbs, swings his hatchet of stone.

By the swamp in the forest
  sings shrilly in glee
The stark forester's lass
  plucking mast in a tree—
And hairy and brown as a squirrel is she!

With the strokes of the flint axe
  the blind woodland rings,
And the echoes laugh back as
  the sylvan girl sings;
And the Sabre-tooth growls in his lair ere he springs!

1064

WILLIAM CANTON

Keen as stars, in green splendour,
    his great eyeballs burn
As he crawls!—Chilled to silence,
    the girl can discern
The fierce pantings which thrill through the fronds of the
    fern.

And the brown frolic face of
    the girl has grown white,
As the large fronds are swayed in
    the weird crimson light,
And she sobs with the strained throbbing dumbness of fright.

With his blue eyes agleam, and
    his wild russet hair
Streaming back, the Man travails,
    unwarned, unaware
Of the lithe shape that crouches, the green eyes that glare.

And now, hark! as he drives with
    a last mighty swing
The stone blade of the axe through
    the oak's central ring,
From the blanched lips what screams of wild agony spring!

There's a rush through the fern-fronds—
    a yell of affright—
And the Savage and Sabre-tooth
    close in fierce fight:—
And the red sunset smoulders and blackens to night.

On the swamp in the forest
    one clear star is shown,
And the reeds fill the night with
    a long troubled moan—
And the girl sits and sobs in the darkness, alone!

II

The great dim centuries of long ago
Sweep past with rain and fire, with wind and snow,
And where the Savage swung his axe of stone
The blue clay silts on Titan trunks o'erthrown,

O'er mammoth's tusks, in river-horse's lair;
And, armed with deer-horn, clad in girdled hair,
A later Savage in his hollow tree
Hunts the strange broods of a primeval sea.

And yet the unstoried centuries again
Sweep past with snow and fire, with wind and rain,
And where that warm primeval ocean rolled
A second forest buds,—blooms broad,—grows old;
And a new race of prehistoric men
Springs from the mystic soil, and once again
Fades like a wood mist through the woodlands hoar.

For lo! the shadowy centuries once more
With wind and fire, with rain and snow sweep by;
And where the forest stood, an empty sky
Arches with lonely blue a lonely land.
The great white stilted storks in silence stand
Far from each other, motionless as stone,
And melancholy leagues of marsh-reeds moan,
And dead tarns blacken 'neath the mournful blue.

The ages speed! And now the skin canoe
Darts with swift paddle through the drear morass,
But ere the painted fisherman can pass,
The brazen horns ring out; a thund'rous throng—
Bronzed faces, tufted helmets—sweeps along,
The silver Eagles flash and disappear
Across the Roman causeway!

                              Year by year
The dim time lapses till that vesper hour
Broods o'er the summer lake with peaceful power,
When the carved galley through the sunset floats.
The rowers, with chains of gold about their throats,
Hang on their dripping oars, and sweet and clear
The sound of singing steals across the mere,
And rising with glad face and outstretched hand,
"Row, Knights, a little nearer to the land,
And let us hear these monks of Ely sing";
Says KNUT, the King.
    1066

WILLIAM CANTON

Now in the fateful years what hour arrives,
And who is this rides Fenward from St. Ives?
A man of massive presence,—bluff and stern.
Beneath their craggy brows his deep eyes burn
With awful thoughts and purposes sublime.
The face is one to abash the front of time,—
Hewn of red rock, so vital, even now
One sees the wart above that shaggy brow.
At Ely there in these idyllic days
His sickles reap, his sheep and oxen graze,
And all the ambition of his sober life
Is but to please Elizabeth his wife,
To drain the Fens—and magnify the Lord.
So in his plain cloth suit, with close-tucked sword,
OLIVER CROMWELL, fated but unknown,
Rides where the Savage swung his axe of stone.

III

In the class-room blue-eyed Phemie
Sits, half listening, hushed and dreamy,
To the grey-haired pinched Professor droning to his class of
girls.

And around her in their places
Rows of arch and sweet young faces
Seem to fill the air with colour shed from eyes and lips and
curls!—

. . . .

Labelled shells suggest the motion,
Moan, and glimmer of that ocean
Where the belemnites dropped spindles and the sand-stars shed
their rays;

Monstrous birds stalk stilted by as
She perceives the slab of Trias
Scrawled with hieroglyphic claw-tracks of the Mesozoic days;

And before her she sees dawn a
Pageant of an awful fauna
While across Silurian ages the Professor's lecture blows.

1067

All the while a soft and pleasant
Rustle of dresses, an incessant
Buzz of smothered frolic rises underneath his meagre nose.

And one pretty plague has during
All the class been caricaturing
Her short-sighted good old Master with a world of wicked
zest;

And the madcaps blush and titter
As they see the unconscious sitter
Sketched as Allophylian Savage—spectacled but much un-
dressed.

But the old man turns the pages
Of the rock-illumined ages,
Tracing from earth's mystic missal the antiquity of Man:

Not six thousand years—but eras,
Ages, eons disappear as
Groping back we touch the system where the Human first
began.

Centuries, as we retrogress, are
Dwarfed to days, the Professor
Says, *our lineage was hoary ere Eve's apple-tree grew green;*

For the Bee, whose drowsy humming
Was prophetic of Man's coming,
Lies in gem-like tomb of amber, buried in the Miocene.

At what point Man came, I know not,
Logic proves not, fossils show not,
But his dim remote existence is a fact beyond dispute.

Look!—And from among some thirty
Arrow barbs of quartz and chert he
Takes the flint head of a hatchet,—and the girls grow hushed
and mute.

1068

WILLIAM CANTON

Old, he says, *art thou, strange stone!   Nor
Less antique thy primal owner!*
*When the Fens were drained this axe was found below two
    forests sunk.*

*Underneath a bed of sea clay
And two forests this relique lay
Where some Allophylian Savage left it in a half-hewn trunk!*

Does the old Professor notice
Large eyes, blue as myosotis,
Raised to him in startled wonder as those fateful words are
    said?

· But for Phemie, through the trees in
Her dream forest, fact and reason
Blend with fancy, and her vision grows complete and clear
    and dread:

By the swamp in the forest
The sylvan girl sings
As his flint-headed hatchet
The wild Woodman swings,
But the hatchet cleaves fast in the trunk he has riven—
The Man stands unarmed as the Sabre-tooth springs!

THE DEATH OF ANAXAGORAS

Of him she banished now let Athens boast;
Let now th' Athenians raise to him they stoned
A statue; *Anaxagoras is dead!*

To you who mourn the Master, called him friend,
Beat back th' Athenian wolves who fanged his throat,
And risked your own to save him,—Pericles—
I now unfold the manner of his end.

The aged man, who found in sixty years
Scant cause for laughter, laughed before he died

And died still smiling:—Athens vexed him not!
Not he, but your Athenians, he would say,
Were banished in his exile!
                              When the dawn
First glimmers white o'er Lesser Asia,
And little birds are twittering in the grass,
While all the sea lies hollow and grey with mist,
And in the streets the ancient watchmen doze,
The Master woke with cold. His feet were chill
And reft of sense; and we who watched him knew
The fever had not wholly left his brain,
For he was wandering, seeking nests of birds—
An urchin from the green Ionian town
Where he was born. We chafed his clay-cold limbs;
And so he dozed, nor dreamed, until the sun
Laughed out—broad day—and flushed the garden gods
Who bless our fruits and vines in Lampsacus.
Feeble, but sane and cheerful, he awoke
And took our hands and asked to feel the sun;
And where the ilex spreads a gracious shade
We placed him, wrapped and pillowed; and he heard
The charm of birds, the social whisper of vines,
The ripple of the blue Propontic sea.
Placid and pleased he lay; but we were sad
To see the snowy hair and silver beard
Like withering mosses on a fallen oak,
And feel that he, whose vast philosophy
Had cast such sacred branches o'er the fields
Where Athens pastures her dull sheep, lay fallen
And never more should know the spring!
                                    Confess,
You too had grieved to see it, Pericles!
But Anaxagoras owned no sense of wrong;
And when we called the plagues of all your gods
On your ungrateful city, he but smiled:
"Be patient, children! Where would be the gain
Of wisdom and divine astronomy,
Could we not school our fretful minds to bear
The ills all life inherits? *I* can smile
To think of Athens! Were they much to blame?
Had I not slain Apollo? Plucked the beard

Of Jove himself?   Poor rabble, who have yet
Outgrown so little the green grasshoppers
From whom they boast descent, are they to blame?
How could they dream,—how credit even when taught—
The sun a red-hot iron ball, in bulk
Not less than Peloponnesus?   How believe
The moon, no silver goddess girt for chace,
But earth and stones, with caverns, hills, and vales?
Poor grasshoppers! who deem the gods absorbed
In all their babble, shrilling in the grass,
What wonder if they rage, should one but hint
That thunder and lightning, born of clashing clouds,
Might happen even with Jove in pleasant mood,—
Not thinking of Athenians at all!"

He paused; and blowing softly from the sea,
The fresh wind stirred the sibilant ilex-leaves;
And lying in the shadow, grieved in mind
That we were grieving, "All my days," he said,
"Hath all my care been fixed on this vast Blue
So still above us; now my days are done,
Let It have care of me!   Be patient; meek;
Not puffed with doctrine!   Nothing can be known;
Nought grasped for certain; sense is circumscribed;
The intellect is weak; and life is short!"

He ceased and mused a little, while we wept.
"And yet be nowise downcast; seek, pursue;
The lover's rapture and the sage's gain
Lie in attainment less than in approach.
Look forward to the time which is to come!
All things are mutable; and change alone
Unchangeable.   But knowledge grows!   The gods
Are drifting from the earth like morning mist;
The days are surely at the doors when men
Shall see but human actions in the world!
Yea, even these hills of Lampsacus shall be
The isles of some new sea, if time not fail!"

And now the reverend fathers of our town
Had heard the Master's end was very near,

And came to do him homage at the close,
And ask what wish of his they might fulfil.
But he, divining that they thought his heart
Might yearn to Athens for a resting-place,
Said gently: "Nay, from everywhere the way
To that dark land you wot of is the same.
I feel no care; I have no wish.   The Greeks
Will never quite forget my Pericles,
And when they think of him will say of me,
'*Twas Anaxagoras taught him!*"
                                        Loath to go,
No kindly office done, yet once again
The reverend fathers pressed him for a wish.
Then laughed the Master: "Nay, if still you urge,
And since 'twere churlish to reject goodwill,
I pray you, every year when time brings back
The month in which I left you, let the boys—
All boys and girls in this your happy town—
Be free of task and school for that one month."
He lay back smiling, and the reverend men
Departed, heavy at heart.   He spoke no more,
But haply musing on his truant days,
Passed from us, and was smiling when he died.

From Lampsacus thus wrote to Pericles
Agis the Lemnian.   How the Master's words,
Wherein he spoke of change unchangeable,
Hold good for things of moment, ill for small;
For lo! six hundred fateful years have sped
And Greece is but a Roman province now,
Whereas through those six centuries, year by year
When summer and the sun brought back the time,
The lads and lasses, free of school and task,
Have held their revelry in Lampsacus,—
A fact so ripe with grave moralities,
That I, Diogenes, have deemed it fit
To note in my *De Vita et Moribus*.

1072

WILLIAM CANTON

THE GOD AND THE SCHOOLBOY

Throughout the land and sea from ancient days
The wonder had been rumoured, that the god
Born on the radiant hills i' the dazzle of dawn—
Asklepios—healed the sick and raised the dead.
The world gave credence gladly. Human faith
With human anguish grew; and, doubtless, God
Was pitiful in heaven, when unaware
Of Whom they sought, men called Asklepios.

Thus, four-and-twenty centuries ago,
At Epidaurus, on that rocky point
Washed north and south with violet sea, the sick
Struck sail. Beyond the vineyards, olive-groves
And hamlets of the Dusty-feet—for so
Our townsmen named the rustic folk who tilled
The sweet brown earth 'twixt mountain-cirque and sea—
A green gorge opened on the beautiful
Still valley in the sunned hills' flowery heart,
Where, throned on gold and ivory, the god—
Chryselephantine, mighty-bearded, ringed
With golden head-rays—held his knotty staff
In one hand, and in one his serpent, wreathed
In shining coils, while near his footstool lay
The first dumb friend man found among the brute.

Oh, marvellous beneath those purple peaks
Glittered the long white marble terrace-walls,
The pillared aisles, the gardens of the god,
The altars white, and white immortal shapes
Half-seen in fragrant bowers of pine and plane.

And hither out of furthest lands and isles
Amid remote dim sea-ways came the blind,
The dumb, the deaf, the palsied, scald, and maimed—
All loathsome shapes of pain and broken strength
And hopeless wasting—if perchance the god
Might heal their stricken bodies.

Shafts of stone
Bore of the midnight vision and the cure
Full many a marvellous record. One who came
From far green-gardened Lampsacus the god
Had graciously made whole; from Halike——
A town whereof none now in all the world
Aught knoweth save the graven name—came one;
And one from cold Torone in the north,
From joyous Mytilene one, and one
From that Hermione, whence Hades-ward
So short the downward way that never coin
Is laid upon the dead man's tongue to pay
The ferry of shadows.

But within the shrine
Hung costly gifts of men made glad to live—
Great vases, gems and mirrors; jewelled eyes,
Fingers of silver, arms and legs of gold;
Rich models of invaluable parts,
And precious images of fleshly ills
From which no quittance were too highly priced;
And, mixed with these, rude gifts of grateful hearts
Whose poverty was not ashamed to give.

Upon a time, among the folk who sought
Surcease of suffering from Asklepios,
Was brought a schoolboy from the white-walled town
Upon the rocky point—Euphanes, frail,
And fever-flushed, and weak with grievous pain;
And as the lad, beneath the clement stars,
Lay wandering in his mind, and dreamed perchance
Of sailing little triremes on the shore,
Or making, it might be, a locust-cage
With reeds and stalks of asphodel beneath
The trellised vines, it seemed as though the god
Stood by him in the holy night and spoke:—
"What wilt thou give me, little playfellow,
If I shall cure thy sickness?" And the lad,
Thinking what pleasure schoolboys have in these,
Replied: "I'll give thee my ten marbles, god!"
Asklepios laughed, right gladdened with the gift,

1074

And said: "Then, truly, I will make thee well!"
And lo! when morning whitened on the hills,
And in the valley's dusk the sacred cock
Clapped wings and sang, the urchin went forth whole!

Full four-and-twenty centuries ago
Euphanes saw the god; and yesterday
The pillar bearing record of the cure
Was dug from wreck of war and drift of years.
" 'Ten marbles!' quoth the child. Asklepios laughed;
But on the morrow forth the lad went whole."
Thus closely had the Greek in ancient times—
Through some prophetic prompting of pure love
God's unfulfilled events divining—drawn
Man's heart unto the human heart in God.

LAUS INFANTIUM

In praise of little children I will say
God first made man, then found a better way
For woman, but His third way was the best.
Of all created things the loveliest
And most divine are children.   Nothing here
Can be to us more gracious or more dear.
And though when God saw all His works were good
There was no rosy flower of babyhood,
'Twas said of children in a later day
That none could enter Heaven save such as they.

The earth, which feels the flowering of a thorn,
Was glad, O little child, when you were born;
The earth, which thrills when skylarks scale the blue,
Soared up itself to God's own Heaven in you;
And Heaven, which loves to lean down and to glass
Its beauty in each dewdrop on the grass—
Heaven laughed to find your face so pure and fair,
And left, O little child, its reflex there!

A NEW POET

I write. He sits beside my chair,
   And scribbles, too, in hushed delight,
He dips his pen in charmèd air:
   What is it he pretends to write?

He toils and toils; the paper gives
   No clue to aught he thinks. What then?
His little heart is glad; he lives
   The poems that he cannot pen.

Strange fancies throng that baby brain;
   What grave, sweet looks! What earnest eyes!
He stops—reflects—and now again
   His unrecording pen he plies.

It seems a satire on myself,—
   These dreamy nothings scrawled in air,
This thought, this work! Oh tricksy elf,
   Wouldst drive thy father to despair?

Despair! Ah, no; the heart, the mind
   Persists in hoping,—schemes and strives
That there may linger with our kind
   Some memory of our little lives.

Beneath his rock in the early world
   Smiling the naked hunter lay,
And sketched on horn the spear he hurled,
   The urus which he made his prey.

Like him I strive in hope my rhymes
   May keep my name a little while,—
O child, who knows how many times
   We two have made the angels smile!

A PHILOSOPHER

Yes, you may let them creep about the rug.
And stir the fire! Aha! that's bright and snug.

1076

WILLIAM CANTON

To think these mites—ay, nurse, unfold the screen!—
Should be as ancient as the Miocene;
That ages back beneath a palm-tree's shade
These rosy little quadrupeds have played,
Have cried for moons or mammoths, and have blacked
Their faces round the Drift Man's fire—in fact,
That ever since the articulate race began
These babes have been the joy and plague of man!

Unnoticed by historian and sage,
These bright-eyed chits have been from age to age
The one supreme majority. I find
Mankind hath been their slaves, and womankind
Their worshippers; and both have lived in dread
Of time and tyrants, toiled and wept and bled,
Because of some quaint elves they called their own.
Had little ones in Egypt been unknown,
No Pharaoh would have had the power, methinks,
To pile the Pyramids or carve the Sphinx.

Take them to bed, nurse; but before she goes
Daddy must toast his little woman's toes.
Strange that such feeble hands and feet as these
Have sped the lamp-race of the centuries!

SUSPIRIUM

These little shoes!—How proud she was of these!
Can you forget how, sitting on your knees,
She used to prattle volubly, and raise
Her tiny feet to win your wondering praise?
Was life too rough for feet so softly shod,
That now she walks in Paradise with God,
Leaving but these—whereon to dote and muse—
     These little shoes?

MOONLIGHT

Sweet moon, endreaming tower and tree,
Is thy pathetic radiance thrown
From ice-cold wealds and cirques of stone—
Hush'd moors where life has ceased to be?

1077

Did grass, long ages back, and flowers
Grow there?   Did living waters run?
Did happy creatures bless the sun
And greet with joy this world of ours?

And, earlier yet, in one starred zone,
Did this bright planet sweep through space—
Glebe of our glebe, race of our race—
A part and parcel of our own?

O moonlight silvering tower and tree!
O part of *my* world torn away,
Part of my life, now lifeless clay,
My dead, shine too—shine down on me.

IN THE SHADOW

Night is the shadow of the Earth, but we
Lose the fine sense through use, nor thank nor praise.
In the hot summer's blue and windless days
Sweet is the grass and dear the shadowing tree,
Whence, stretched at ease, we watch with languid look
Birds, insects, flowers, the cloud, the nut-brown brook.

But all the year and feverish day by day
Earth shadows us; the burden and the heat
Are lifted from us; sweet is night, and sweet
The stars and silvery clouds, and Milky Way.
Use teaches thankfulness a sinful thrift;
We prize the casual, slight the constant gift.

THIS GRACE VOUCHSAFE ME

This grace vouchsafe me for the rhymes I write.
If any last, nor perish quick and quite,
            Lord, let them be
My little images, to stand for me
When I may stand no longer in Thy sight:

1078

Like those old statues of the King who said,
"Carve me in that which needs nor sleep nor bread;
    Let diorite pray,
A King of stone, for this poor King of clay
Who wearies often and must soon be dead!"

Edgar Fawcett

TO AN ORIOLE

How falls it, oriole, thou hast come to fly
In tropic splendor through our Northern sky?

At some glad moment was it nature's choice
To dower a scrap of sunset with a voice?

Or did some orange tulip, flaked with black,
In some forgotten garden, ages back,

Yearning toward Heaven until its wish was heard,
Desire unspeakably to be a bird?

Will Henry Thompson

THE HIGH TIDE AT GETTYSBURG

A cloud possessed the hollow field,
The gathering battle's smoky shield.
Athwart the gloom the lightning flashed,
And through the cloud some horsemen dashed,
And from the heights the thunder pealed.

Then at the brief command of Lee
Moved out that matchless infantry,
With Pickett leading grandly down,
To rush against the roaring crown
Of those dread heights of destiny.

1079

Far heard above the angry guns
A cry across the tumult runs,—
The voice that rang through Shiloh's woods
And Chickamauga's solitudes,
The fierce South cheering on her sons!

Ah, how the withering tempest blew
Against the front of Pettigrew!
A Khamsin wind that scorched and singed
Like that infernal flame that fringed
The British squares at Waterloo!

A thousand fell where Kemper led;
A thousand died where Garnett bled:
In blinding flame and strangling smoke
The remnant through the batteries broke
And crossed the works with Armistead.

"Once more in Glory's van with me!"
 Virginia cried to Tennessee;
"We two together, come what may,
Shall stand upon these works to-day!"
(The reddest day in history.)

Brave Tennessee! In reckless way
Virginia heard her comrade say:
"Close round this rent and riddled rag!"
What time she set her battle-flag
Amid the guns of Doubleday.

But who shall break the guards that wait
Before the awful face of Fate?
The tattered standards of the South
Were shriveled at the cannon's mouth,
And all her hopes were desolate.

In vain the Tennesseean set
His breast against the bayonet!
In vain Virginia charged and raged,
A tigress in her wrath uncaged,
 Till all the hill was red and wet!

WILL HENRY THOMPSON

Above the bayonets, mixed and crossed,
Men saw a gray, gigantic ghost
Receding through the battle-cloud,
And heard across the tempest loud
The death-cry of a nation lost!

The brave went down! Without disgrace
They leaped to Ruin's red embrace.
They only heard Fame's thunders wake,
And saw the dazzling sun-burst break
In smiles on Glory's bloody face!

They fell, who lifted up a hand
And bade the sun in heaven to stand!
They smote and fell, who set the bars
Against the progress of the stars,
And stayed the march of Motherland!

They stood, who saw the future come
On through the fight's delirium!
They smote and stood, who held the hope
Of nations on that slippery slope
Amid the cheers of Christendom.

God lives! He forged the iron will
That clutched and held that trembling hill.
God lives and reigns! He built and lent
The heights for Freedom's battlement
Where floats her flag in triumph still!

Fold up the banners! Smelt the guns!
Love rules. Her gentler purpose runs.
A mighty mother turns in tears
The pages of her battle years,
Lamenting all her fallen sons!

John Vance Cheney

THE MAN WITH THE HOE

A REPLY

Let us a little permit Nature to take her own way: she
better understands her own affairs than we.—*Montaigne*.

Nature reads not our labels, "great" and "small";
Accepts she one and all

Who, striving, win and hold the vacant place;
All are of royal race.

Him, there, rough-cast, with rigid arm and limb,
The Mother moulded him,

Of his rude realm ruler and demigod,
Lord of the rock and clod.

With Nature is no "better" and no "worse,"
On this bared head no curse.

Humbled it is and bowed; so is he crowned
Whose kingdom is the ground.

Diverse the burdens on the one stern road
Where bears each back its load;

Varied the toil, but neither high nor low.
With pen or sword or hoe,

He that has put out strength, lo, he is strong;
Of him with spade or song

Nature but questions,—"This one, shall he stay?"
She answers "Yea," or "Nay,"

"Well, ill, he digs, he sings"; and he bides on,
Or shudders, and is gone.

1082

JOHN VANCE CHENEY

Strength shall he have, the toiler, strength and grace,
So fitted to his place

As he leaned, there, an oak where sea winds blow,
Our brother with the hoe.

No blot, no monster, no unsightly thing,
The soil's long-lineaged king;

His changeless realm, he knows it and commands;
Erect enough he stands,

Tall as his toil.   Nor does he bow unblest:
Labor he has, and rest.

Need was, need is, and need will ever be
For him and such as he;

Cast for the gap, with gnarlèd arm and limb,
The Mother moulded him,—

Long wrought, and moulded him with mother's care,
Before she set him there.

And aye she gives him, mindful of her own,
Peace of the plant, the stone;

Yea, since above his work he may not rise,
She makes the field his skies.

See! she that bore him, and metes out the lot,
He serves her.   Vex him not

To scorn the rock whence he was hewn, the pit
And what was digged from it;

Lest he no more in native virtue stand,
The earth-sword in his hand,

But follow sorry phantoms to and fro,
And let a kingdom go.

ONE

One whitest lily, reddest rose,
None other such the summer knows;
Of bird or brook one perfect tune,
And sung is all the sweet of June.

Once come and gone, the one dear face,
Forever empty is its place;
But one far voice the lover hears,
Calling across the waste of years.

THE HAPPIEST HEART

Who drives the horses of the sun
Shall lord it but a day;
Better the lowly deed were done,
And kept the humble way.

The rust will find the sword of fame,
The dust will hide the crown;
Ay, none shall nail so high his name
Time will not tear it down.

The happiest heart that ever beat
Was in some quiet breast
That found the common daylight sweet,
And left to Heaven the rest.

William Ernest Henley

IN HOSPITAL

BEFORE

Behold me waiting—waiting for the knife.
A little while, and at a leap I storm
The thick, sweet mystery of chloroform,
The drunken dark, the little death-in-life.

1084

WILLIAM ERNEST HENLEY

The gods are good to me: I have no wife,
No innocent child, to think of as I near
The fateful minute; nothing all-too dear
Unmans me for my bout of passive strife.
Yet I am tremulous and a trifle sick,
And, face to face with chance, I shrink a little:
My hopes are strong, my will is something weak.
Here comes the basket? Thank you. I am ready.
But, gentlemen my porters, life is brittle:
You carry Cæsar and his fortunes—steady!

AFTER

Like as a flamelet blanketed in smoke,
So through the anæsthetic shows my life;
So flashes and so fades my thought, at strife
With the strong stupor that I heave and choke
And sicken at, it is so foully sweet.
Faces look strange from space—and disappear.
Far voices, sudden loud, offend my ear—
And hush as sudden. Then my senses fleet
All were a blank, save for this dull, new pain
That grinds my leg and foot; and brokenly
Time and the place glimpse on to me again;
And, unsurprised, out of uncertainty,
I wake—relapsing—somewhat faint and fain,
To an immense, complacent dreamery.

STAFF-NURSE: OLD STYLE

The great masters of the commonplace,
Rembrandt and good Sir Walter—only these
Could paint her all to you: experienced ease
And antique liveliness and ponderous grace;
The sweet old roses of her sunken face;
The depth and malice of her sly, grey eyes;
The broad Scots tongue that flatters, scolds, defies;
The thick Scots wit that fells you like a mace.
These thirty years has she been nursing here,

Some of them under Syme, her hero still.
Much is she worth, and even more is made of her.
Patients and students hold her very dear.
The doctors love her, tease her, use her skill.
They say "The Chief" himself is half-afraid of her.

LADY-PROBATIONER

Some three, or five, or seven, and thirty years;
A Roman nose; a dimpling double-chin;
Dark eyes and shy that, ignorant of sin,
Are yet acquainted, it would seem, with tears;
A comely shape; a slim, high-coloured hand,
Graced, rather oddly, with a signet ring;
A bashful air, becoming everything;
A well-bred silence always at command.
Her plain print gown, prim cap, and bright steel chain
Look out of place on her, and I remain
Absorbed in her, as in a pleasant mystery.
Quick, skilful, quiet, soft in speech and touch . . .
"Do you like nursing?" "Yes, Sir, very much."
Somehow I rather think she has a history.

"THE CHIEF"

His brow spreads large and placid, and his eye
Is deep and bright, with steady looks that still.
Soft lines of tranquil thought his face fulfil—
His face at once benign and proud and shy.
If envy scout, if ignorance deny,
His faultless patience, his unyielding will,
Beautiful gentleness and splendid skill,
Innumerable gratitudes reply.
His wise, rare smile is sweet with certainties,
And seems in all his patients to compel
Such love and faith as failure cannot quell;
We hold him for another Herakles,
Battling with custom, prejudice, disease,
As once the son of Zeus with Death and Hell.

1086

WILLIAM ERNEST HENLEY

SCRUBBER

She's tall and gaunt, and in her hard, sad face
With flashes of the old fun's animation
There lowers the fixed and peevish resignation
Bred of a past where troubles came apace.
She tells me that her husband, ere he died,
Saw seven of their children pass away,
And never knew the little lass at play
Out on the green, in whom he's deified.
Her kin dispersed, her friends forgot and gone,
All simple faith her honest Irish mind,
Scolding her spoiled young saint, she labours on:
Telling her dreams, taking her patients' part,
Trailing her coat sometimes: and you shall find
No rougher, quainter speech, nor kinder heart.

APPARITION

Thin-legged, thin-chested, slight unspeakably,
Neat-footed and weak-fingered: in his face—
Lean, large-boned, curved of beak, and touched with race
Bold-lipped, rich-tinted, mutable as the sea,
The brown eyes radiant with vivacity—
There shines a brilliant and romantic grace,
A spirit intense and rare, with trace on trace
Of passion and impudence and energy.
Valiant in velvet, light in ragged luck,
Most vain, most generous, sternly critical,
Buffoon and poet, lover and sensualist:
A deal of Ariel, just a streak of Puck,
Much Antony, of Hamlet most of all,
And something of the Shorter-Catechist.

IN FISHERROW

A hard north-easter fifty winters long
Has bronzed and shrivelled sere her face and neck;
Her locks are wild and grey, her teeth a wreck;
Her foot is vast, her bowed leg spare and strong.

A wide blue coat, a squat and sturdy throng
Of curt blue coats, a mutch without a speck,
A white vest broidered black, her person deck,
Nor seems their picked, stern, old-world quaintness wrong.
Her great creel forehead-slung, she wanders nigh,
Easing the heavy strap with gnarled, brown fingers
The spirit of traffic watchful in her eye,
Ever and anon imploring you to buy,
As looking down the street she onward lingers,
Reproachful, with a strange and doleful cry.

INVICTUS

Out of the night that covers me,
   Black as the Pit from pole to pole,
I thank whatever gods may be
   For my unconquerable soul.

In the fell clutch of circumstance
   I have not winced nor cried aloud.
Under the bludgeonings of chance
   My head is bloody, but unbowed.

Beyond this place of wrath and tears
   Looms but the Horror of the shade,
And yet the menace of the years
   Finds and shall find me unafraid.

It matters not how strait the gate,
   How charged with punishments the scroll,
I am the master of my fate:
   I am the captain of my soul.

ECHOES

.   .   .   .   .   .

The full sea rolls and thunders
   In glory and in glee.
O, bury me not in the senseless earth
   But in the living sea!

1088

WILLIAM ERNEST HENLEY

Ay, bury me where it surges
  A thousand miles from shore,
And in its brotherly unrest
  I'll range for evermore.

. . . .

MARGARITÆ SORORI

A late lark twitters from the quiet skies;
And from the west,
Where the sun, his day's work ended,
Lingers as in content,
There falls on the old, grey city
An influence luminous and serene,
A shining peace.

The smoke ascends
In a rosy-and-golden haze. The spires
Shine, and are changed. In the valley
Shadows rise. The lark sings on. The sun,
Closing his benediction,
Sinks, and the darkening air
Thrills with a sense of the triumphing night—
Night with her train of stars
And her great gift of sleep.

So be my passing!
My task accomplished and the long day done,
My wages taken, and in my heart
Some late lark singing,
Let me be gathered to the quiet west,
The sundown splendid and serene,
Death.

ON THE WAY TO KEW

On the way to Kew,
By the river old and grey,
Where in the Long Ago
We laughed and loitered so,

1089

I met a ghost to-day,
A ghost that told of you—
A ghost of low replies
And sweet inscrutable eyes,
Coming up from Richmond
As you used to do.

By the river old and grey,
The enchanted Long Ago
Murmured and smiled anew.
On the way to Kew,
March had the laugh of May,
The bare boughs looked aglow,
And old, immortal words
Sang in my breast like birds,
Coming up from Richmond
As I used with you.

With the life of Long Ago
Lived my thought of you.
By the river old and grey
Flowing his appointed way
As I watched I knew
What is so good to know—
Not in vain, not in vain,
Shall I look for you again,
Coming up from Richmond
On the way to Kew.

Edmund Gosse

THE FEAR OF DEATH

Last night I woke and found between us drawn—
  Between us, where no mortal fear may creep—
  The vision of Death dividing us in sleep;
And suddenly I thought, Ere light shall dawn
Some day,—the substance, not the shadow, of Death
  Shall cleave us like a sword. The vision passed,
  But all its new-born horror held me fast,
And till day broke I listened for your breath.

1090

Some day to wake, and find that coloured skies,
  And pipings in the woods, and petals wet,
  Are things for aching memory to forget;
And that your living hands and mouth and eyes
Are part of all the world's old histories!—
  Dear God! a little longer, ah, not yet!

REVELATION

    Into the silver night
      She brought with her pale hand
    The topaz lanthorn-light,
    And darted splendour o'er the land;
      Around her in a band,
  Ringstraked and pied, the great soft moths came flying,
    And flapping with their mad wings, fann'd
  The flickering flame, ascending, falling, dying.

    Behind the thorny pink
      Close wall of blossom'd may,
    I gazed thro' one green chink
    And saw no more than thousands may,—
      Saw sweetness, tender and gay,—
  Saw full rose lips as rounded as the cherry,
    Saw braided locks more dark than bay,
  And flashing eyes decorous, pure, and merry.

    With food for furry friends
      She pass'd, her lamp and she,
    Till eaves and gable-ends
    Hid all that saffron sheen from me:
      Around my rosy tree
  Once more the silver-starry night was shining,
    With depths of heaven, dewy and free,
  And crystals of a carven moon declining.

    Alas! for him who dwells
      In frigid air of thought,
    When warmer light dispels
    The frozen calm his spirit sought;

By life too lately taught
He sees the ecstatic Human from him stealing;
Reels from the joy experience brought,
And dares not clutch what Love was half revealing.

Robert Louis Stevenson

MY WIFE

Trusty, dusky, vivid, true,
With eyes of gold and bramble-dew,
Steel-true, and blade-straight,
The great Artificer
Made my mate.

Honour, anger, valour, fire;
A love that life could never tire,
Death quench or evil stir,
The mighty Master
Gave to her.

Teacher, tender, comrade, wife,
A fellow-farer true through life,
Heart-whole and soul-free
The august Father
Gave to me.

THE CELESTIAL SURGEON

If I have faltered more or less
In my great task of happiness;
If I have moved among my race
And shown no glorious morning face;
If beams from happy human eyes
Have moved me not; if morning skies,
Books, and my food, and summer rain
Knocked on my sullen heart in vain:—
Lord, thy most pointed pleasure take
And stab my spirit broad awake;

ROBERT LOUIS STEVENSON

Or, Lord, if too obdurate I,
Choose thou, before that spirit die,
A piercing pain, a killing sin,
And to my dead heart run them in!

REQUIEM

Under the wide and starry sky
Dig the grave and let me lie.
Glad did I live and gladly die,
   And I laid me down with a will.

This be the verse you grave for me:
Here he lies where he longed to be;
Home is the sailor, home from sea,
   And the hunter home from the hill.

ROMANCE

I will make you brooches and toys for your delight
Of bird-song at morning and star-shine at night.
I will make a palace fit for you and me,
Of green days in forests and blue days at sea.

I will make my kitchen, and you shall keep your room,
Where white flows the river and bright blows the broom,
And you shall wash your linen and keep your body white
In rainfall at morning and dewfall at night.

And this shall be for music when no one else is near,
The fine song for singing, the rare song to hear!
That only I remember, that only you admire,
Of the broad road that stretches and the roadside fire.
                     —Songs of Travel.

IN THE HIGHLANDS

In the highlands, in the country places,
Where the old plain men have rosy faces,

And the young fair maidens
  Quiet eyes;
Where essential silence chills and blesses,
And for ever in the hill-recesses
  Her more lovely music
  Broods and dies—

O to mount again where erst I haunted;
Where the old red hills are bird-enchanted,
  And the low green meadows
  Bright with sward;
And when even dies, the million-tinted,
And the night has come, and planets glinted,
  Lo, the valley hollow
  Lamp bestarr'd!

O to dream, O to awake and wander
There, and with delight to take and render,
  Through the trance of silence,
  Quiet breath!
Lo! for there, among the flowers and grasses,
Only the mightier movement sounds and passes
  Only winds and rivers,
  Life and death.

  —SONGS OF TRAVEL.

ENVOY

Go, little book, and wish to all
Flowers in the garden, meat in the hall,
A bin of wine, a spice of wit,
A house with lawns enclosing it,
A living river by the door,
A nightingale in the sycamore!

Michael Field

GOLD

Yea, gold is son of Zeus: no rust
Its timeless light can stain;
The worm that brings man's flesh to dust
Assaults its strength in vain:

MICHAEL FIELD

More gold than gold the love I sing,
A hard, inviolable thing.

Men say the passions should grow old
With waning years; my heart
Is incorruptible as gold,
'Tis my immortal part:
Nor is there any god can lay
On love the finger of decay.

BELOVED, MY GLORY

Beloved, my glory in thee is not ceased,
Whereas, as thou art waning, forests wane;
Unmoved, as by the victim is the priest,
I pass the world's great altitudes of pain.
But when the stars are gathered for a feast,
Or shadows threaten on a radiant plain,
Or many golden cornfields wave amain,
Oh, then, as one from a filled shuttle weaves,
My spirit grieves.

THE TRAGIC MARY QUEEN OF SCOTS

I could wish to be dead!
Too quick with life were the tears I shed,
Too sweet for tears is the life I led;
And ah, too lonesome my marriage-bed!
I could wish to be dead.

I could wish to be dead,
For just a word that rings in my head;
Too dear, too dear are the words he said,
They must never be rememberèd.
I could wish to be dead.

I could wish to be dead:
The wish to be loved is all mis-read,
And to love, one learns when one is wed,
Is to suffer bitter shame; instead
I could wish to be dead.

1095

Alice Meynell

IN EARLY SPRING

O Spring, I know thee! Seek for sweet surprise
  In the young children's eyes.
But I have learnt the years, and know the yet
  Leaf-folded violet.
Mine ear, awake to silence, can foretell
  The cuckoo's fitful bell.
I wander in a grey time that encloses
  June and the wild hedge-roses.
A year's procession of the flowers doth pass
  My feet, along the grass.
And all you sweet birds silent yet, I know
  The notes that stir you so,
Your songs yet half devised in the dim dear
  Beginnings of the year.
In these young days you meditate your part;
  I have it all by heart.
I know the secrets of the seeds of flowers
  Hidden and warm with showers,
And how, in kindling Spring, the cuckoo shall
  Alter his interval.
But not a flower or song I ponder is
  My own, but memory's.
I shall be silent in those days desired
  Before a world inspired.
O dear brown birds, compose your old song-phrases,
  Earth, thy familiar daisies.

The poet mused upon the dusky height,
  Between two stars towards night,
His purpose in his heart. I watched, a space,
  The meaning of his face:
There was the secret, fled from earth and skies,
  Hid in his gray young eyes.
My heart and all the Summer wait his choice,
  And wonder for his voice.

1096

ALICE MEYNELL

Who shall foretell his songs, and who aspire
    But to divine his lyre?
Sweet Earth, we know thy dimmest mysteries,
    But he is lord of his.

PARTED

Farewell to one now silenced quite,
Sent out of hearing, out of sight,—
    My friend of friends, whom I shall miss.
    He is not banished, though, for this,—
Nor he, nor sadness, nor delight.

Though I shall talk with him no more,
A low voice sounds upon the shore.
    He must not watch my resting-place,
    But who shall drive a mournful face
From the sad winds about my door?

I shall not hear his voice complain,
But who shall stop the patient rain?
    His tears must not disturb my heart,
    But who shall change the years, and part
The world from every thought of pain?

Although my life is left so dim,
The morning crowns the mountain-rim;
    Joy is not gone from summer skies,
    Nor innocence from children's eyes,
And all these things are part of him.

He is not banished, for the showers
Yet wake this green warm earth of ours.
    How can the summer but be sweet?
    I shall not have him at my feet,
And yet my feet are on the flowers.

THE VISITING SEA

As the inhastening tide doth roll,
Home from the deep, along the whole
    Wide shining strand, and floods the caves
      —Your love comes filling with happy waves
The open sea-shore of my soul.

But inland from the seaward spaces,
None knows, not even you, the places
    Brimmed, at your coming, out of sight,
      —The little solitudes of delight
This tide constrains in dim embraces.

You see the happy shore, wave-rimmed,
But know not of the quiet dimmed
    Rivers your coming floods and fills,
    The little pools 'mid happier hills,
My silent rivulets, over-brimmed.

What, I have secrets from you? Yes.
But, visiting Sea, your love doth press
    And reach in further than you know,
    And fills all these; and, when you go,
There's loneliness in loneliness.

RENOUNCEMENT

I must not think of thee; and, tired yet strong,
I shun the thought that lurks in all delight—
The thought of thee—and in the blue Heaven's height,
And in the dearest passage of a song.
Oh, just beyond the fairest thoughts that throng
This breast, the thought of thee waits, hidden yet bright;
But it must never, never come in sight;
I must stop short of thee the whole day long.
But when sleep comes to close each difficult day,
When night gives pause to the long watch I keep,
And all my bonds I needs must loose apart,
Must doff my will as raiment laid away,—
With the first dream that comes with the first sleep
I run, I run, I am gathered to thy heart.

1098

ALICE MEYNELL

A POET OF ONE MOOD

A poet of one mood in all my lays,
   Ranging all life to sing one only love,
   Like a west wind across the world I move,
Sweeping my harp of floods mine own wild ways.

The countries change, but not the west-wind days
   Which are my songs. My soft skies shine above,
   And on all seas the colours of a dove,
And on all fields a flash of silver greys.

I make the whole world answer to my art
   And sweet monotonous meanings. In your ears
I change not ever, bearing, for my part,
   One thought that is the treasure of my years,
A small cloud full of rain upon my heart
   And in mine arms, clasped, like a child in tears.

MATERNITY

One wept whose only child was dead
   New-born, ten years ago.
"Weep not; he is in bliss," they said.
   She answered, "Even so.

"Ten years ago was born in pain
   A child not now forlorn.
But oh, ten years ago, in vain
   A mother, a mother was born."

I AM THE WAY

Thou art the Way.
Hadst Thou been nothing but the goal,
   I cannot say
If Thou hadst ever met my soul.

1099

I cannot see—
I, child of process—if there lies
An end for me,
Full of repose, full of replies.

I'll not reproach
The road that winds, my feet that err.
Access, approach
Art Thou, Time, Way, and Wayfarer.

THE SHEPHERDESS

She walks—the lady of my delight—
A shepherdess of sheep.
Her flocks are thoughts. She keeps them white;
She guards them from the steep.
She feeds them on the fragrant height,
And folds them in for sleep.

She roams maternal hills and bright,
Dark valleys safe and deep.
Into that tender breast at night
The chastest stars may peep.
She walks—the lady of my delight—
A shepherdess of sheep.

She holds her little thoughts in sight,
Though gay they run and leap.
She is so circumspect and right;
She has her soul to keep.
She walks—the lady of my delight—
A shepherdess of sheep.

THE LADY POVERTY

The Lady Poverty was fair:
But she has lost her looks of late,
With change of times and change of air.

1100

ALICE MEYNELL

Ah slattern! she neglects her hair,
Her gown, her shoes. She keeps no state
As once when her pure feet were bare.

Or—almost worse, if worse can be—
She scolds in parlours; dusts and trims,
Watches and counts. Oh, is this she
Whom Francis met, whose step was free,
Who with Obedience carolled hymns,
In Umbria walked with Chastity?

Where is her ladyhood?   Not here,
Not among modern kinds of men;
But in the stony fields, where clear
Through the thin trees the skies appear;
In delicate spare soil and fen,
And slender landscape and austere.

TO SILENCE

Not, Silence, for thine idleness I raise
My silence-bounded singing in thy praise,
But for thy moulding of my Mozart's tune
Thy hold upon the bird that sings the moon,
       Thy magisterial ways.

Man's lovely definite melody-shapes are thine,
Outlined, controlled, compressed, complete, divine;
Also thy fine intrusions do I trace,
Thy afterthoughts, thy wandering, thy grace,
       Within the poet's line.

Thy secret is the song that is to be.
Music had never stature but for thee,
Sculptor! strong as the sculptor Space whose hand
Urged the Discobolus and bade him stand.

.   .   .   .

Man, on his way to Silence, stops to hear and see.

RIVERS UNKNOWN TO SONG

Wide waters in the waste; or, out of reach,
    Rough Alpine falls where late a glacier hung;
Or rivers groping for an alien beach,
    Through continents, unsung.

Nay, not these nameless, these remote, alone;
    But all the streams from all the watersheds—
Peneus, Danube, Nile—are the unknown,
    Young in their ancient beds.

Man has no tale for them. Oh! travellers swift
    From secrets to oblivion! Waters wild
That pass in act to bend a flower or lift
    The bright limbs of a child!

For they are new, they are fresh; there's no surprise
    Like theirs on earth. Oh, strange forevermore!
This moment's Tiber with his shining eyes
    Never saw Rome before.

Man has no word for their eternity—
    Rhine, Avon, Arno, younglings, youth uncrowned!
Ignorant, innocent, instantaneous, free,
    Unwelcomed, unrenowned.

Francis William Bourdillon

EURYDICE

He came to call me back from death
    To the bright world above.
I hear him yet with trembling breath
    Low calling, "O sweet love!
Come back! The earth is just as fair;
The flowers, the open skies are there;
    Come back to life and love!"

Oh! all my heart went out to him,
  And the sweet air above.
With happy tears my eyes were dim;
  I called him, "O sweet love!
I come, for thou art all to me.
Go forth, and I will follow thee,
  Right back to life and love!"

I followed through the cavern black;
  I saw the blue above.
Some terror turned me to look back:
  I heard him wail, "O love!
What hast thou done! What hast thou done!"
And then I saw no more the sun,
  And lost were life and love.

THE NIGHT HAS A THOUSAND EYES

The night has a thousand eyes,
  And the day but one;
Yet the light of the bright world dies
  With the dying sun.

The mind has a thousand eyes,
  And the heart but one;
Yet the light of a whole life dies
  When love is done.

Edwin Markham

THE INVISIBLE BRIDE

The low-voiced girls that go
  In gardens of the Lord,
Like flowers of the field they grow
  In sisterly accord.

1103

Their whispering feet are white
  Along the leafy ways;
They go in whirls of light
  Too beautiful for praise.

And in their band forsooth
  Is one to set me free—
The one that touched my youth—
  The one God gave to me.

She kindles the desire
  Whereby the gods survive—
The white ideal fire
  That keeps my soul alive.

Now at the wondrous hour,
  She leaves her star supreme,
And comes in the night's still power,
  To touch me with a dream.

Sibyl of mystery
  On roads unknown to men,
Softly she comes to me,
  And goes to God again.

A PRAYER

Teach me, Father, how to go
Softly as the grasses grow;
Hush my soul to meet the shock
Of the wild world as a rock;
But my spirit, propt with power,
Make as simple as a flower.
Let the dry heart fill its cup,
Like a poppy looking up;
Let life lightly wear her crown,
Like a poppy looking down,
When its heart is filled with dew,
And its life begins anew.

EDWIN MARKHAM

Teach me, Father, how to be
Kind and patient as a tree.
Joyfully the crickets croon
Under shady oak at noon;
Beetle, on his mission bent,
Tarries in that cooling tent.
Let me, also, cheer a spot,
Hidden field or garden grot—
Place where passing souls can rest
On the way and be their best.

HOW TO GO AND FORGET

I know how to hold
As the lovers of old—
How to cling to you, sing to you,
Let all the world know the song that I bring to you.
But I do not know yet
How to go and forget!

I know how to call
To the God over all—
How to sigh for you, cry for you,
Fight down the terrible dark till I die for you.
But I do not know yet
How to go and forget!

THE NIGHT MOTHS

Out of the night to my leafy porch they came,
A thousand moths. Did He who made the toad
Give them their wings upon the starry road?
Restless and wild, they circle round the flame,
Frail wonder-shapes that man can never tame—
Whirl like the blown flakes of December snows,
Tinted with amber, violet and rose,
Marked with hieroglyphs that have no name.
Out of the summer darkness pours the flight:

Unknown the wild processional they keep.
What lures them to this rush of mad delight?
Why are they called from nothingness and sleep?
Why this rich beauty wandering the night?
Do they go lost and aimless to the deep?

YOUR TEARS

I dare not ask your very all:
　　I only ask a part.
Bring me—when dancers leave the hall—
　　Your aching heart.

Give other friends your lighted face,
　　The laughter of the years:
I come to crave a greater grace—
　　Bring me your tears!

THE MAN WITH THE HOE

*(Written after seeing Millet's world-famous painting of
a brutalized toiler.)*

God made man in his own image,
in the image of God made He him.—*Genesis.*

Bowed by the weight of centuries he leans
Upon his hoe and gazes on the ground,
The emptiness of ages in his face,
And on his back the burden of the world.
Who made him dead to rapture and despair,
A thing that grieves not and that never hopes,
Stolid and stunned, a brother to the ox?
Who loosened and let down this brutal jaw?
Whose was the hand that slanted back this brow?
Whose breath blew out the light within this brain?

Is this the Thing the Lord God made and gave
To have dominion over sea and land;
1106

To trace the stars and search the heavens for power;
To feel the passion of Eternity?
Is this the dream He dreamed who shaped the suns
And markt their ways upon the ancient deep?
Down all the caverns of Hell to their last gulf
There is no shape more terrible than this—
More tongued with censure of the world's blind greed—
More filled with signs and portents for the soul—
More packt with danger to the universe.

What gulfs between him and the seraphim!
Slave of the wheel of labor, what to him
Are Plato and the swing of Pleiades?
What the long reaches of the peaks of song,
The rift of dawn, the reddening of the rose?
Through this dread shape the suffering ages look;
Time's tragedy is in that aching stoop;
Through this dread shape humanity betrayed,
Plundered, profaned and disinherited,
Cries protest to the Powers that made the world,
A protest that is also prophecy.

O masters, lords and rulers in all lands,
Is this the handiwork you give to God,
This monstrous thing distorted and soul-quencht?
How will you ever straighten up this shape;
Touch it again with immortality;
Give back the upward looking and the light;
Rebuild in it the music and the dream;
Make right the immemorial infamies,
Perfidious wrongs, immedicable woes?

O masters, lords and rulers in all lands,
How will the future reckon with this man?
How answer his brute question in that hour
When whirlwinds of rebellion shake all shores?
How will it be with kingdoms and with kings—
With those who shaped him to the thing he is—
When this dumb Terror shall rise to judge the world,
After the silence of the centuries?

1107

LINCOLN, THE MAN OF THE PEOPLE

When the Norn Mother saw the Whirlwind Hour
Greatening and darkening as it hurried on,
She left the Heaven of Heroes and came down
To make a man to meet the mortal need.
She took the tried clay of the common road—
Clay warm yet with the genial heat of Earth,
Dasht through it all a strain of prophecy;
Tempered the heap with thrill of human tears;
Then mixt a laughter with the serious stuff.
Into the shape she breathed a flame to light
That tender, tragic, ever-changing face;
And laid on him a sense of the Mystic Powers,
Moving—all husht—behind the mortal veil.
Here was a man to hold against the world,
A man to match the mountains and the sea.

The color of the ground was in him, the red earth;
The smack and tang of elemental things;
The rectitude and patience of the cliff;
The good-will of the rain that loves all leaves;
The friendly welcome of the wayside well;
The courage of the bird that dares the sea;
The gladness of the wind that shakes the corn;
The pity of the snow that hides all scars;
The secrecy of streams that make their way
Under the mountain to the rifted rock;
The tolerance and equity of light
That gives as freely to the shrinking flower
As to the great oak flaring to the wind—
To the grave's low hill as to the Matterhorn
That shoulders out the sky. Sprung from the West,
He drank the valorous youth of a new world.
The strength of virgin forests braced his mind,
The hush of spacious prairies stilled his soul,
His words were oaks in acorns; and his thoughts
Were roots that firmly gript the granite truth.

1105

EDWIN MARKHAM

Up from log cabin to the Capitol,
One fire was on his spirit, one resolve—
To send the keen ax to the root of wrong,
Clearing a free way for the feet of God,
The eyes of conscience testing every stroke,
To make his deed the measure of a man.
He built the rail-pile as he built the State,
Pouring his splendid strength through every blow;
The grip that swung the ax in Illinois
Was on the pen that set a people free.

So came the Captain with the mighty heart;
And when the judgment thunders split the house,
Wrenching the rafters from their ancient rest,
He held the ridgepole up, and spikt again
The rafters of the Home. He held his place—
Held the long purpose like a growing tree—
Held on through blame and faltered not at praise.
And when he fell in whirlwind, he went down
As when a lordly cedar, green with boughs,
Goes down with a great shout upon the hills,
And leaves a lonesome place against the sky.

THE TESTING

When in the dim beginning of the years,
God mixed in man the raptures and the tears
And scattered through his brain the starry stuff,
He said, "Behold! Yet this is not enough,
For I must test his spirit to make sure
That he can dare the vision and endure.

"I will withdraw my face,
Veil me in shadow for a certain space,
And leave behind only a broken clue,
A crevice where the glory shimmers through,
Some whisper from the sky,
Some footprint in the road to track me by.

1109

"I will leave man to make the fateful guess,
Will leave him torn between the no and yes,
Leave him unresting till he rests in me,
Drawn upward by the choice that makes him free—
Leave him in tragic loneliness to choose,
With all in life to win or all to lose."

VIRGILIA

I

Had we two gone down the world together,
    I had made fair ways for the feet of Song,
And the world's fang been but a foam-soft feather,
    The world that works us wrong.

If you had but stayed when the old sweet wonder
    Was a precious pain in my pulsing side!
Ah, why did you hurry our lives asunder—
    You, born to be my bride?

What sent it upon me—my soul importunes—
    All the grief of the world in a little span,
All the tears and fears, all the fates and fortunes,
    That the heart holds for a man?

Is this then the grief that the first gods kneaded
    Into all joy that the strange world brings?
Did the tears fall into the heap unheeded,
    These tears in mortal things?

But why it was that the whole world wasted,
    This you will know when they count the tears,
After the dust of the grave is tasted,
    After this noise of years.

Yet some things stay though a world lies broken,
    I keep some things that were dear of old—
That first kiss spared and that last word spoken
    And the glint of your hair's dark gold.

Do you mind that hour in the soft sweet morning
   When I held you fast in divine alarms,
When my soul stood up like a god adorning
   His body with bright arms?

Forget it not till the crowns are crumbled
   And the swords of the kings are rent with rust—
Forget it not till the hills lie humbled,
   And the springs of the seas run dust.

II

What was I back in the world's first wonder?—
   An elf-child found on an ocean-reef,
A sea-child nursed by the surge and thunder,
   And marked for the lyric grief.

I mind me well how the waves' edge whitened
   As the shapes of the storm went whirling by—
How I laughed and ran when the loud void lightened,
   And tempest shook the sky.

So I will go down by the way of the willows,
   And whisper it out to the mother Sea,
To the soft sweet shores and the long bright billows,
   The dream that cannot be.

There will be help for the soul's great trouble
   Where the sea's heart sings to the listening ear,
Where the high gray cliff in the pool hangs double,
   And the moon is misting the mere.

'Twas down in the sea that your soul took fashion,
   O strange Love born of the white sea-wave!
And only the sea and her lyric passion
   Can ease the wound you gave.

I will go down to the wide wild places,
   Where the calm cliffs look on the shores around;
I will rest in the power of their great grave faces
   And the gray hush of the ground.

On a cliff's high head a gray gull clamors,
    But down at the base is the Devil's brew,
And the swing of arms and the heave of hammers,
    And the white flood roaring through.

There on the cliff is the sea-bird's tavern,
    And there with the wild things I'll find a home,
Laugh with the lightning, shout with the cavern,
    Run with the feathering foam.

I will climb down where the nests are hanging,
    And the young birds scream to the swinging deep,
Where the rocks and the iron winds are clanging,
    And the long waves lift and leap.

I will thread the shores to the cavern hollows,
    Where the edge of the wave runs white and thin;
I will sing to the surge and the foam that follows
    When the dark tides thunder in.

I will go out where the sea-birds travel,
    And mix my soul with the wind and sea;
Let the green waves weave and the gray rains ravel,
    And the tides go over me.

The Sea is the mother of songs and sorrows,
    And out of her wonder our wild loves come;
And so it will be through the long to-morrows,
    Till all our lips are dumb.

She knows all sighs and she knows all sinning,
    And they whisper out in her breaking wave:
She has known it all since the far beginning,
    Since the grief of that first grave.

She shakes the heart with her stars and thunder
    And her soft low word when the winds are late;
For the sea is Woman, the sea is Wonder—
    Her other name is Fate!

There is daring and dream in her billows breaking—
In the power of her beauty our griefs forget:
She can ease the heart of the long, long aching,
And bury old regret.

III

Will you find rest as our ways dissever?
Will the gladness grow as the days increase?
Howbeit, I leave on your soul forever
The word of the eternal peace.

I will go the road and my song shall save me,
Though grief may stay as the heart's old guest:
I will finish the work that the strange God gave me,
And then pass on to rest.

I will go back to the great world-sorrow,
To the millions bearing the double load—
The fate of to-day and the tear of to-morrow:
I will taste the dust of the road.

I will go back to the pains and the pities
That break the heart of the world with moan;
I will forget in the grief of the cities
The burden of my own.

There in the world-grief my own grief humbles,
My wild hour melts in the days to be,
As the wild white foam of a river crumbles,
Forgotten in the sea.

James Whitcomb Riley

WHEN SHE COMES HOME

When she comes home again! A thousand ways
I fashion, to myself, the tenderness
Of my glad welcome: I shall tremble—yes;
And touch her, as when first in the old days

I touched her girlish hand, nor dared upraise
Mine eyes, such was my faint heart's sweet distress.
Then silence: and the perfume of her dress:
The room will sway a little, and a haze
Cloy eyesight—soul-sight, even—for a space;
And tears—yes; and the ache here in the throat,
To know that I so ill deserve the place
Her arms make for me; and the sobbing note
I stay with kisses, ere the tearful face
Again is hidden in the old embrace.

A PARTING GUEST

What delightful hosts are they—
    Life and Love!
Lingeringly I turn away,
    This late hour, yet glad enough
They have not withheld from me
    Their high hospitality.
So, with face lit with delight
    And all gratitude, I stay
    Yet to press their hands and say,
"Thanks.—So fine a time! Good night."

Edith M. Thomas

EVOE!

"MANY ARE THE WAND-BEARERS, FEW ARE THE TRUE
BACCHANALS."

Many are the wand-bearers;
    Their windy shouts I hear,
Along the hillside vineyard,
    And where the wine runs clear;
They show the vine-leaf chaplet,
    The ivy-wreathen spear;
But the god, the true Iacchus,
    He does not hold them dear.

Many are the wand-bearers,
  And bravely are they clad;
Yes, they have all the tokens
  His early lovers had.
They sing the master passions,
  Themselves unsad, unglad;
And the god, the true Iacchus—
  He knows they are not mad!

Many are the wand-bearers;
  The fawn-skin bright they wear;
There are among them mænads
  That rave with unbound hair.
They toss the harmless firebrand—
  It spends itself in air;
And the god, the true Iacchus,
  He smiles—and does not care.

Many are the wand-bearers;
  And who (ye ask) am I?
One who was born in madness,
  "Evoe!" my first cry—
Who dares, before your spear-points,
  To challenge and defy;
And the god, the true Iacchus,
  So keep me till I die!

Many are the wand-bearers.
  I bear with me no sign;
Yet, I was mad, was drunken,
  Ere yet I tasted wine;
Nor bleeding grape can slacken
  The thirst wherewith I pine;
And the god, the true Iacchus,
  Hears now this song of mine.

THE SECURITY OF DESOLATION

He who hath seen his grain-fields gather blight
  Heeds not the withering of the garden flowers;
He grieves not at the day's withdrawing light
  Who in a dungeon numbers his dim hours;

1115

He feareth not the storm upon his head,
　Whose garments with the rough salt wave are soaked,
And he whose fire within his house is dead,
　Into the outer air will go uncloaked!

So he whose life some weak, loved hand has taken,
　Flies not the shaft of banded myrmidon,
Nor trembles when his citadel is shaken:
　Foretasting all, he hath no more to shun;
The Night, the Cold, the Dearth, the Wound obscure,
　That men call Death, unmoved he shall endure!

PATMOS

All around him Patmos lies,
Who hath spirit-gifted eyes,
Who his happy sight can suit
To the great and the minute.
Doubt not but he holds in view
A new earth and heaven new;
Doubt not but his ear doth catch
Strains nor voice nor reed can match;
Many a silver, sphery note
Shall within his hearing float.

All around him Patmos lies,
Who unto God's priestess flies:
Thou, O Nature, bid him see,
Through all guises worn by thee,
A divine apocalypse.
Manifold his fellowships:
Now the rocks their archives ope;
Voiceless creatures tell their hope
In a language symbol-wrought;
Groves to him sigh out their thought;
Musings of the flower and grass
Through his quiet spirit pass.
'Twixt new earth and heaven new
He hath traced and holds the clue.
Number his delights ye may not;
Fleets the year, but these decay not.

EDITH M. THOMAS

Now the freshets of the rain,
Bounding on from hill to plain,
Show him earthly streams have rise
In the bosom of the skies.
Now he feels the morning thrill,
As upmounts, unseen and still,
Dew the wing of evening drops.
Now the frost, that meets and stops
Summer's feet in tender sward,
Greets him, breathing heavenward.
Hieroglyphics writes the snow,
Through the silence falling slow;
Types of star and petaled bloom
A white missal-page illume.
By these floating symbols fine,
Heaven-truth shall he divine.

All around him Patmos lies,
Who hath spirit-gifted eyes;
He need not afar remove,
He need not the times reprove,
Who would hold perpetual lease
Of an isle in seas of peace.

THE COURAGE OF THE LOST

There be who are afraid to fear,
   The myrmidons of Hope!
Their watchword cannot lend me cheer
   'Gainst that with which I cope!

There is a courage of the lost,
   Who sail uncharted seas,
Past many a firm or flying coast,
   And I must sail with these.

There is a valor of the slain,
   Who strive past mortal sight
While their spent corses strew the plain,
   And I must fight their fight.

Hast thou that courage of the lost,
  Past theirs, that reach their goal?
Whoe'er thou art, I thee accost—
  Thou Comrade of my Soul!

Thou dost not fear to fear—ah, no!
  The depths wilt thou descend;
And when thy planet sinketh low
  Wilt make of Night a friend!

Then come! We two are proof, at last,
  We dare our fears to own—
But had our lot with Hope been cast
  What heart-break had we known!

A CHANT OF THE FOUGHT FIELD

NUNC DIMITTIS

As one who under evening skies
Upon a fought field stricken lies
  (Unknown for stains of blood and grime)
Is fain the mortal shaft to draw
And let life issue through the flaw,
Even so am I, and even so,
Unhand me, Time, and let me go—
    Unhand me, Time!

Upon his clogged and languid sense
Vague cries are borne—he heeds not whence,
  Nor if they utter cheer sublime,
Or fill the air with craven moan;
His spirit's fire is all unblown;
Even so is mine—so faint, so low;
Unhand me, Time, and let me go—
    Unhand me, Time!

For heaven-truth my sword I drew,
With anger keen I did pursue

Not the frail worker but the crime
He framed in glooming ignorance.
Now let who may lift sword and lance,
Or let the rust upon them grow!
Unhand me, Time, and let me go—
    Unhand me, Time!

Or well or ill if I have wrought,
My deed was mated with my thought,
    As bell with bell in tuneful chime.
All things that fall to man's dear lot
I did receive, and faltered not;
Quick come the last! and even so,
Unhand me, Time, and let me go—
    Unhand me, Time!

A dream it was! All that hath been
Now lapseth like some passioned scene
    Played by a well-deceiving mime,
Who most of all himself deceives,
And, waking up, regretless leaves.
I reach for substance past the show—
Unhand me, Time, and let me go—
    Unhand me, Time!

George Edward Woodberry

DIVINE AWE

To tremble, when I touch her hands,
With awe that no man understands;
To feel soft reverence arise
When, lover-sweet, I meet her eyes;
To see her beauty grow and shine
When most I feel this awe divine,—
Whate'er befall me, this is mine;
And where about the room she moves,
My spirit follows her, and loves.

William Sharp

THE WASP

When the ripe pears droop heavily,
　　The yellow wasp hums loud and long
　　His hot and drowsy autumn song:
A yellow flame he seems to be,
　　When darting suddenly from high
　　He lights where fallen peaches lie.

Yellow and black—this tiny thing's
A tiger-soul on elfin wings.

THE WASHER OF THE FORD

There is a lonely stream afar in a lone dim land:
It hath white dust for shore it has, white bones bestrew the
　　　strand:
The only thing that liveth there is a naked leaping sword;
But I, who a seer am, have seen the whirling hand
　　　　Of the Washer of the Ford.
A shadowy shape of cloud and mist, of gloom and dusk, she
　　　stands,
　　　　The Washer of the Ford:
She laughs, at times, and strews the dust through the hollow
　　　of her hands.
She counts the sins of all men there, and slays the red-stained
　　　horde—
The ghosts of all the sins of men must know the whirling
　　　sword
　　　　Of the Washer of the Ford.

She stoops and laughs when in the dust she sees a writhing
　　　limb:
"Go back into the ford," she says, "and hither and thither
　　　swim;
Then I shall wash you white as snow, and shall take you by
　　　the hand,
And slay you here in the silence with this my whirling brand,
1120

And trample you into the dust of this white windless sand"—
    This is the laughing word
    Of the Washer of the Ford
    Along that silent strand.

Oscar Wilde

THE BALLAD OF READING GAOL

I

He did not wear his scarlet coat,
    For blood and wine are red,
And blood and wine were on his hands
    When they found him with the dead,
The poor dead woman whom he loved,
    And murdered in her bed.

He walked amongst the Trial Men
    In a suit of shabby grey;
A cricket cap was on his head,
    And his step seemed light and gay;
But I never saw a man who looked
    So wistfully at the day.

I never saw a man who looked
    With such a wistful eye
Upon that little tent of blue
    Which prisoners call the sky,
And at every drifting cloud that went
    With sails of silver by.

I walked, with other souls in pain,
    Within another ring,
And was wondering if the man had done
    A great or little thing,
When a voice behind me whispered low,
    "That fellow's got to swing."

Dear Christ! the very prison walls
  Suddenly seemed to reel,
And the sky above my head became
  Like a casque of scorching steel;
And, though I was a soul in pain,
  My pain I could not feel.

I only knew what hunted thought
  Quickened his step, and why
He looked upon the garish day
  With such a wistful eye;
The man had killed the thing he loved,
  And so he had to die.

Yet each man kills the thing he loves,
  By each let this be heard,
Some do it with a bitter look,
  Some with a flattering word,
The coward does it with a kiss,
  The brave man with a sword!

Some kill their love when they are young,
  And some when they are old;
Some strangle with the hands of Lust,
  Some with the hands of Gold:
The kindest use a knife, because
  The dead so soon grow cold.

Some love too little, some too long,
  Some sell, and others buy;
Some do the deed with many tears,
  And some without a sigh:
For each man kills the thing he loves,
  Yet each man does not die.

He does not die a death of shame
  On a day of dark disgrace,
Nor have a noose about his neck,
  Nor a cloth upon his face,
Nor drop feet foremost through the floor
  Into an empty space.

1122

OSCAR WILDE

He does not sit with silent men
    Who watch him night and day;
Who watch him when he tries to weep,
    And when he tries to pray;
Who watch him lest himself should rob
    The prison of its prey.

He does not wake at dawn to see
    Dread figures throng his room,
The shivering Chaplain robed in white,
    The Sheriff stern with gloom,
And the Governor all in shiny black,
    With the yellow face of Doom.

He does not rise in piteous haste
    To put on convict-clothes,
While some coarse-mouthed Doctor gloats, and notes
    Each new and nerve-twitched pose,
Fingering a watch whose little ticks
    Are like horrible hammer blows.

He does not know that sickening thirst
    That sands one's throat, before
The hangman with his gardener's gloves
    Slips through the padded door,
And binds one with three leathern thongs,
    That the throat may thirst no more.

He does not bend his head to hear
    The Burial Office read,
Nor, while the terror of his soul
    Tells him he is not dead,
Cross his own coffin, as he moves
    Into the hideous shed.

He does not stare upon the air
    Through a little roof of glass:
He does not pray with lips of clay
    For his agony to pass:
Nor feel upon his shuddering cheek
    That kiss of Caiaphas.

1123

II

Six weeks our guardsman walked the yard,
   In the suit of shabby grey:
His cricket cap was on his head,
   And his step seemed light and gay,
But I never saw a man who looked
   So wistfully at the day.

I never saw a man who looked
   With such a wistful eye
Upon that little tent of blue
   Which prisoners call the sky,
And at every wandering cloud that trailed
   Its ravelled fleeces by.

He did not wring his hands, as do
   Those witless men who dare
To try to rear the changeling Hope
   In the cave of black Despair:
He only looked upon the sun,
   And drank the morning air.

He did not wring his hands nor weep,
   Nor did he peek or pine,
But he drank the air as though it held
   Some healthful anodyne;
With open mouth he drank the sun
   As though it had been wine!

And I and all the souls in pain,
   Who tramped the other ring,
Forgot if we ourselves had done
   A great or little thing,
And watched with gaze of dull amaze
   The man who had to swing.

And strange it was to see him pass
   With a step so light and gay,
And strange it was to see him look
   So wistfully at the day,
And strange it was to think that he
   Had such a debt to pay.

For oak and elm have pleasant leaves
   That in the spring-time shoot:
But grim to see is the gallows-tree,
   With its adder-bitten root,
And, green or dry, a man must die
   Before it bears its fruit!

The loftiest place is that seat of grace
   For which all wordlings try:
But who would stand in hempen band
   Upon a scaffold high,
And through a murderer's collar take
   His last look at the sky?

It is sweet to dance to violins
   When Love and Life are fair:
To dance to flutes, to dance to lutes
   Is delicate and rare:
But it is not sweet with nimble feet
   To dance upon the air!

So with curious eyes and sick surmise
   We watched him day by day,
And wondered if each one of us
   Would end the self-same way,
For none can tell to what red Hell
   His sightless soul may stray.

At last the dead man walked no more
   Amongst the Trial Men,
And I knew that he was standing up
   In the black dock's dreadful pen,
And that never would I see his face
   In God's sweet world again.

Like two doomed ships that pass in storm,
   We had crossed each other's way:
But we made no sign, we said no word,
   We had no word to say;
For we did not meet in the holy night,
   But in the shameful day.

A prison wall was round us both,
  Two outcast men we were:
The world had thrust us from its heart,
  And God from out his care:
And the iron gin that waits for Sin
  Had caught us in its snare.

III

In Debtor's Yard the stones are hard,
  And the dripping wall is high,
So it was there he took the air
  Beneath the leaden sky,
And by each side a Warder walked,
  For fear the man might die.

Or else he sat with those who watched
  His anguish night and day;
Who watched him when he rose to weep,
  And when he crouched to pray;
Who watched him lest himself should rob
  Their scaffold of its prey.

The Governor was strong upon
  The Regulations Act:
The Doctor said that Death was but
  A scientific fact:
And twice a day the Chaplain called,
  And left a little tract.

And twice a day he smoked his pipe,
  And drank his quart of beer:
His soul was resolute, and held
  No hiding-place for fear;
He often said that he was glad
  The hangman's hands were near.

But why he said so strange a thing
  No Warder dared to ask:
For he to whom a watcher's doom
  Is given as his task,
Must set a lock upon his lips,
  And make his face a mask.

Or else he might be moved, and try
  To comfort or console:
And what should Human Pity do
  Pent up in Murderers' Hole?
What word of grace in such a place
  Could help a brother's soul?

With slouch and swing around the ring
  We trod the Fools' Parade!
We did not care: we knew we were
  The Devil's Own Brigade:
And shaven head and feet of lead
  Make a merry masquerade.

We tore the tarry rope to shreds
  With blunt and bleeding nails;
We rubbed the doors, and scrubbed the floors,
  And cleaned the shining rails:
And, rank by rank, we soaped the plank,
  And clattered with the pails.

We sewed the sacks, we broke the stones,
  We turned the dusty drill:
We banged the tins, and bawled the hymns,
  And sweated on the mill:
But in the heart of every man
  Terror was lying still.

So still it lay that every day
  Crawled like a weed-clogged wave:
And we forgot the bitter lot
  That waits for fool and knave,
Till once, as we tramped in from work,
  We passed an open grave.

With yawning mouth the yellow hole
  Gaped for a living thing;
The very mud cried out for blood
  To the thirsty asphalt ring:
And we knew that ere one dawn grew fair,
  Some prisoner had to swing.

Right in we went, with soul intent
   On Death and Dread and Doom:
The hangman, with his little bag,
   Went shuffling through the gloom:
And each man trembled as he crept
   Into his numbered tomb.

That night the empty corridors
   Were full of forms of Fear,
And up and down the iron town
   Stole feet we could not hear,
And through the bars that hide the stars
   White faces seemed to peer.

He lay as one who lies and dreams
   In a pleasant meadow-land,
The watchers watched him as he slept,
   And could not understand
How one could sleep so sweet a sleep
   With a hangman close at hand.

But there is no sleep when men must weep
   Who never yet have wept:
So we—the fool, the fraud, the knave—
   That endless vigil kept,
And through each brain on hands of pain
   Another's terror crept.

Alas! it is a fearful thing
   To feel another's guilt!
For, right within, the sword of Sin
   Pierced to its poisoned hilt,
And as molten lead were the tears we shed
   For the blood we had not spilt.

The Warders with their shoes of felt
   Crept by each padlocked door,
And peeped and saw, with eyes of awe,
   Grey figures on the floor,
And wondered why men knelt to pray
   Who never prayed before.

OSCAR WILDE

All through the night we knelt and prayed,
 Mad mourners of a corse!
The troubled plumes of midnight were
 The plumes upon a hearse:
And bitter wine upon a sponge
 Was the savour of Remorse.

The grey cock crew, the red cock crew,
 But never came the day;
And crooked shapes of terror crouched
 In the corners where we lay:
And each evil sprite that walks by night
 Before us seemed to play.

They glided past, they glided fast,
 Like travellers through a mist:
They mocked the moon in a rigadoon
 Of delicate turn and twist,
And with formal pace and loathsome grace
 The phantoms kept their tryst.

With mop and mow, we saw them go,
 Slim shadows hand and hand:
About, about, in ghostly rout
 They trod a saraband:
And the damned grotesques made arabesques,
 Like the wind upon the sand!

With pirouettes of marionettes
 They tripped on pointed tread:
But with flutes of Fear they filled the ear,
 As their grisly masque they led,
And loud they sang, and long they sang,
 For they sang to wake the dead.

"*Oho!*" they cried, "*The world is wide,
 But fettered limbs go lame!
And once, or twice, to throw the dice
 Is a gentlemanly game,
But he does not win who plays with Sin
 In the Secret House of Shame.*"

No things of air these antics were,
    That frolicked with such glee:
To men whose lives were held in gyves,
    And whose feet might not go free,
Ah! wounds of Christ! they were living things,
    Most terrible to see.

Around, around, they waltzed and wound;
    Some wheeled in smirking pairs;
With the mincing step of a demirep
    Some sidled up the stairs:
And with subtle sneer, and fawning leer,
    Each helped us at our prayers.

The morning wind began to moan,
    But still the night went on;
Through its giant loom the web of gloom
    Crept till each thread was spun:
And, as we prayed, we grew afraid
    Of the Justice of the Sun.

The moaning wind went wandering round
    The weeping prison-wall:
Till like a wheel of turning steel
    We felt the minutes crawl:
O moaning wind! what had we done
    To have such a seneschal?

At last I saw the shadowed bars,
    Like a lattice wrought in lead,
Move right across the whitewashed wall
    That faced my three-planked bed,
And I knew that somewhere in the world
    God's dreadful dawn was red.

At six o'clock we cleaned our cells,
    At seven all was still,
But the sough and swing of a mighty wing
    The prison seemed to fill,
For the Lord of Death with icy breath,
    Had entered in to kill.

OSCAR WILDE

He did not pass in purple pomp,
    Nor ride a moon-white steed.
Three yards of cord and a sliding board
    Are all the gallows' need:
So with rope of shame the Herald came
    To do the secret deed.

We were as men who through a fen
    Of filthy darkness grope:
We did not dare to breathe a prayer,
    Or to give our anguish scope:
Something was dead in each of us,
    And what was dead was Hope.

For Man's grim Justice goes its way,
    And will not swerve aside:
It slays the weak, it slays the strong,
    It has a deadly stride:
With iron heel it slays the strong,
    The monstrous parricide!

We waited for the stroke of eight:
    Each tongue was thick with thirst:
For the stroke of eight is the stroke of Fate
    That makes a man accursed,
And Fate will use a running noose
    For the best man and the worst.

We had no other thing to do,
    Save to wait for the sign to come:
So, like things of stone in a valley lone,
    Quiet we sat and dumb:
But each man's heart beat thick and quick,
    Like a madman on a drum!

With sudden shock, the prison-clock
    Smote on the shivering air,
And from all the jail rose up a wail
    Of impotent despair,
Like the sound that frightened marshes hear
    From some leper in his lair.

And as one sees most dreadful things
  In the crystal of a dream,
We saw the greasy hempen rope
  Hooked to the blackened beam,
And heard the prayer the hangman's snare
  Strangled into a scream.

And all the woe that moved him so
  That he gave that bitter cry,
And the wild regrets, and the bloody sweats,
  None knew so well as I:
For he who lives more lives than one
  More deaths than one must die.

IV

There is no chapel on the day
  On which they hang a man:
The Chaplain's heart is far too sick,
  Or his face is far too wan,
Or there is that written in his eyes
  Which none should look upon.

So they kept us close till nigh on noon,
  And then they rang the bell,
And the Warders with their jingling keys
  Opened each listening cell,
And down the iron stair we tramped,
  Each from his separate Hell.

Out into God's sweet air we went,
  But not in wonted way,
For this man's face was white with fear,
  And that man's face was grey,
And I never saw sad men who looked
  So wistfully at the day.

I never saw sad men who looked
  With such a wistful eye
Upon that little tent of blue
  We prisoners call the sky,
And at every careless cloud that passed
  In happy freedom by.

But there were those amongst us all
  Who walked with downcast head,
And knew that, had each got his due,
  They should have died instead:
He had but killed a thing that lived,
  Whilst they had killed the dead.

For he who sins a second time
  Wakes a dead soul to pain,
And draws it from its spotted shroud,
  And makes it bleed again,
And makes it bleed great gouts of blood,
  And makes it bleed in vain!

Like ape or clown, in monstrous garb
  With crooked arrows starred,
Silently we went round and round
  The slippery asphalt yard;
Silently we went round and round,
  And no man spoke a word.

Silently we went round and round,
  And through each hollow mind
The Memory of dreadful things
  Rushed like a dreadful wind,
And Honour stalked before each man,
  And Terror crept behind.

The Warders strutted up and down,
  And kept their herd of brutes,
Their uniforms were spick and span,
  They wore their Sunday suits,
But we knew the work they had been at,
  By the quicklime on their boots.

For where a grave had opened wide,
  There was no grave at all:
Only a stretch of mud and sand
  By the hideous prison-wall,
And a little heap of burning lime,
  That the man should have his pall.

For he has a pall, this wretched man,
  Such as few men can claim:
Deep down below a prison-yard,
  Naked for greater shame,
He lies, with fetters on each foot,
  Wrapped in a sheet of flame!

And all the while the burning lime
  Eats flesh and bone away,
It eats the brittle bone by night,
  And the soft flesh by day,
It eats the flesh and bone by turns,
  But it eats the heart alway.

For three long years they will not sow
  Or root or seedling there;
For three long years the unblessed spot
  Will sterile be and bare,
And look upon the wondering sky
  With unreproachful stare.

They think a murderer's heart would taint
  Each simple seed they sow.
It is not true!   God's kindly earth
  Is kindlier than men know,
And the red rose would but blow more red,
  The white rose whiter blow.

Out of his mouth a red, red rose!
  Out of his heart a white!
For who can say by what strange way
  Christ brings his will to light,
Since the barren staff the pilgrim bore
  Bloomed in the great Pope's sight?

But neither milk-white rose nor red
  May bloom in prison air;
The shard, the pebble, and the flint,
  Are what they give us there:
For flowers have been known to heal
  A common man's despair.

OSCAR WILDE

So never will wine-red rose or white
    Petal by petal, fall
On that stretch of mud and sand that lies
    By that hideous prison-wall,
To tell the men who tramp the yard
    That God's Son died for all.

Yet though the hideous prison-wall
    Still hems him round and round,
And a spirit may not walk by night
    That is with fetters bound,
And a spirit may but weep that lies
    In such unholy ground,

He is at peace—this wretched man—
    At peace, or will be soon:
There is no thing to make him mad,
    Nor does Terror walk at noon,
For the lampless Earth in which he lies
    Has neither Sun nor Moon.

They hanged him as a beast is hanged:
    They did not even toll
A requiem that might have brought
    Rest to his startled soul,
But hurriedly they took him out,
    And hid him in a hole.

They stripped him of his canvas clothes,
    And gave him to the flies:
They mocked the swollen purple throat,
    And the stark and staring eyes:
And with laughter loud they heaped the shroud
    In which their convict lies.

The Chaplain would not kneel to pray
    By his dishonoured grave:
Nor mark it with that blessed Cross
    That Christ for sinners gave,
Because the man was one of those
    Whom Christ came down to save.

1135

Yet all is well; he has but passed
  To Life's appointed bourne:
And alien tears will fill for him
  Pity's long-broken urn,
For his mourners will be outcast men,
  And outcasts always mourn.

V

I know not whether Laws be right,
  Or whether Laws be wrong;
All that we know who lie in jail
  Is that the wall is strong;
And that each day is like a year,
  A year whose days are long.

But this I know, that every Law
  That men have made for Man,
Since first Man took his brother's life,
  And this sad world began,
But straws the wheat and saves the chaff
  With a most evil fan.

This too I know—and wise it were
  If each could know the same—
That every prison that men build
  Is built with bricks of shame,
And bound with bars lest Christ should see
  How men their brothers maim.

With bars they blur the gracious moon,
  And blind the goodly sun:
And they do well to hide their Hell,
  For in it things are done
That Son of God nor son of Man
  Ever should look upon!

The vilest deeds like poison weeds
  Bloom well in prison-air:
It is only what is good in Man
  That wastes and withers there:
Pale Anguish keeps the heavy gate,
  And the Warder is Despair.

For they starve the little frightened child,
  Till it weeps both night and day:
And they scourge the weak, and flog the fool,
  And gibe the old and grey,
And some grow mad, and all grow bad,
  And none a word may say.

Each narrow cell in which we dwell
  Is a foul and dark latrine,
And the fetid breath of living Death
  Chokes up each grated screen,
And all, but Lust, is turned to dust
  In Humanity's machine.

The brackish water that we drink
  Creeps with a loathsome slime,
And the bitter bread they weigh in scales
  Is full of chalk and lime,
And Sleep will not lie down, but walks
  Wild-eyed, and cries to Time.

But though lean Hunger and green Thirst
  Like asp with adder fight,
We have little care of prison fare,
  For what chills and kills outright
Is that every stone one lifts by day
  Becomes one's heart by night.

With midnight always in one's heart,
  And twilight in one's cell,
We turn the crank, or tear the rope,
  Each in his separate Hell,
And the silence is more awful far
  Than the sound of a brazen bell.

And never a human voice comes near
  To speak a gentle word:
And the eye that watches through the door
  Is pitiless and hard:
And by all forgot, we rot and rot,
  With soul and body marred.

And thus we rust Life's iron chain,
  Degraded and alone:
And some men curse, and some men weep,
  And some men make no moan:
But God's eternal Laws are kind
  And break the heart of stone.

And every human heart that breaks,
  In prison-cell or yard,
Is as that broken box that gave
  Its treasure to the Lord,   .
And filled the unclean leper's house
  With the scent of costliest nard.

Ah! happy they whose hearts can break
  And peace of pardon win!
How else may man make straight his plan
  And cleanse his soul from Sin?
How else but through a broken heart
  May Lord Christ enter in?

And he of the swollen purple throat,
  And the stark and staring eyes,
Waits for the holy hands that took
  The Thief to Paradise;
And a broken and a contrite heart
  The Lord will not despise.

The man in red who reads the Law
  Gave him three weeks of life,
Three little weeks in which to heal
  His soul of his soul's strife,
And cleanse from every blot of blood
  The hand that held the knife.

And with tears of blood he cleansed the hand,
  The hand that held the steel:
For only blood can wipe out blood,
  And only tears can heal:
And the crimson stain that was of Cain
  Became Christ's snow-white seal.

1128

OSCAR WILDE

VI

In Reading gaol by Reading town
   There is a pit of shame,
And in it lies a wretched man
   Eaten by teeth of flame,
In a burning winding-sheet he lies,
   And his grave has got no name.

And there, till Christ call forth the dead,
   In silence let him lie:
No need to waste the foolish tear,
   Or heave the windy sigh:
The man had killed the thing he loved,
   And so he had to die.

And all men kill the thing they love,
   By all let this be heard,
Some do it with a bitter look,
   Some with a flattering word,
The coward does it with a kiss,
   The brave man with a sword!

HÉLAS

To drift with every passion till my soul
Is a stringed lute on which all winds can play,
Is it for this that I have given away
Mine ancient wisdom, and austere control?
Methinks my life is a twice-written scroll
Scrawled over on some boyish holiday
With idle songs for pipe and virelay,
Which do but mar the secret of the whole.
Surely there was a time I might have trod
The sunlit heights, and from life's dissonance
Struck one clear chord to reach the ears of God:
Is that time dead? lo! with a little rod
I did but touch the honey of romance—
And must I lose a soul's inheritance?

REQUIESCAT

Tread lightly, she is near
    Under the snow,
Speak gently, she can hear
    The daisies grow.

All her bright golden hair
    Tarnished with rust,
She that was young and fair
    Fallen to dust.

Lily-like, white as snow,
    She hardly knew
She was a woman, so
    Sweetly she grew.

Coffin-board, heavy stone,
    Lie on her breast;
I vex my heart alone,
    She is at rest.

Peace, Peace, she cannot hear
    Lyre or sonnet,
All my life's buried here,
    Heap earth upon it.

SONNET

ON HEARING THE "DIES IRÆ" SUNG IN THE SISTINE CHAPEL

Nay, Lord, not thus! white lilies in the spring,
    Sad olive-groves, or silver-breasted dove,
    Teach me more clearly of Thy life and love
Than terrors of red flame and thundering.
The hillside vines dear memories of Thee bring:
    A bird at evening flying to its nest
    Tells me of One who had no place of rest:

I think it is of Thee the sparrows sing.
Come rather on some autumn afternoon,
    When red and brown are burnished on the leaves,
    And the fields echo to the gleaner's song,
Come when the splendid fulness of the moon
    Looks down upon the rows of golden sheaves,
    And reap Thy harvest: we have waited long.

Arthur Henry Bullen

BY AVON STREAM

The jonquils bloom round Samarcand.—
    Maybe; but lulled by Avon stream,
By hawthorn-scented breezes fanned,
    'Twere mere perversity to dream
        Of Samarcand.

A very heaven the Javan isle!—
    Fond fancy, whither wilt thou stray?
While bluest skies benignant smile
    On Avon meads, why prate to-day
        Of Javan isle?

The bulbul 'plains by Omar's shrine.—
    But still I hold, and ever must,
Lark's *tirra-lirra* more divine;
    And Stratford Church guards dearer dust
        Than Omar's shrine.

John Davidson

A BALLAD OF A NUN

From Eastertide to Eastertide
    For ten long years her patient knees
Engraved the stones—the fittest bride
    Of Christ in all the diocese.

She conquered every earthly lust;
    The abbess loved her more and more;
And, as a mark of perfect trust,
    Made her the keeper of the door.

High on a hill the convent hung,
    Across a duchy looking down,
Where everlasting mountains flung
    Their shadows over tower and town.

The jewels of their lofty snows
    In constellations flashed at night;
Above their crests the moon arose;
    The deep earth shuddered with delight.

Long ere she left her cloudy bed,
    Still dreaming in the orient land,
On many a mountain's happy head
    Dawn lightly laid her rosy hand.

The adventurous sun took Heaven by storm;
    Clouds scattered largesses of rain;
The sounding cities, rich and warm,
    Smouldered and glittered in the plain.

Sometimes it was a wandering wind,
    Sometimes the fragrance of the pine,
Sometimes the thought how others sinned,
    That turned her sweet blood into wine.

Sometimes she heard a serenade
    Complaining sweetly far away:
She said, "A young man woos a maid";
    And dreamt of love till break of day.

Then would she ply her knotted scourge
    Until she swooned; but evermore
She had the same red sin to purge,
    Poor, passionate keeper of the door!

JOHN DAVIDSON

For still night's starry scroll unfurled,
  And still the day came like a flood:
It was the greatness of the world
  That made her long to use her blood.

In winter-time when Lent drew nigh,
  And hill and plain were wrapped in snow,
She watched beneath the frosty sky
  The nearest city nightly glow.

Like peals of airy bells outworn,
  Faint laughter died above her head
In gusts of broken music borne:
  "They keep the Carnival," she said.

Her hungry heart devoured the town:
  "Heaven save me by a miracle!
Unless God sends an angel down,
  Thither I go though it were Hell."

She dug her nails deep in her breast,
  Sobbed, shrieked, and straight withdrew the bar:
A fledgling flying from the nest,
  A pale moth rushing to a star.

Fillet and veil in strips she tore;
  Her golden tresses floated wide;
The ring and bracelet that she wore
  As Christ's betrothed, she cast aside.

"Life's dearest meaning I shall probe;
  Lo! I shall taste of love at last!
Away!" She doffed her outer robe,
  And sent it sailing down the blast.

Her body seemed to warm the wind;
  With bleeding feet o'er ice she ran:
"I leave the righteous God behind;
  I go to worship sinful man."

She reached the sounding city's gate;
  No question did the warder ask:
He passed her in: "Welcome, wild mate!"
  He thought her some fantastic mask.

Half-naked through the town she went;
  Each footstep left a bloody mark;
Crowds followed her with looks intent;
  Her bright eyes made the torches dark.

Alone and watching in the street
  There stood a grave youth nobly dressed;
To him she knelt and kissed his feet;
  Her face her great desire confessed.

Straight to his house the nun he led:
  "Strange lady, what would you of me?"
"Your love, your love, sweet lord," she said;
  "I bring you my virginity."

He healed her bosom with a kiss;
  She gave him all her passion's hoard;
And sobbed and murmured ever, "This
  Is life's great meaning, dear, my lord.

"I care not for my broken vow;
  Though God should come in thunder soon,
I am sister to the mountains now,
  And sister to the sun and moon."

Through all the towns of Belmarie
  She made a progress like a queen.
"She is," they said, "whate'er she be,
  The strangest woman ever seen.

"From fairyland she must have come,
  Or else she is a mermaiden."
Some said she was a ghoul, and some
  A heathen goddess born again.

1144

But soon her fire to ashes burned;
   Her beauty changed to haggardness;
Her golden hair to silver turned;
   The hour came of her last caress.

At midnight from her lonely bed
   She rose, and said, "I have had my will."
The ragged robe she donned, and fled
   Back to the convent on the hill.

Half-naked as she went before,
   She hurried to the city wall,
Unnoticed in the rush and roar
   And splendour of the Carnival.

No question did the warder ask:
   Her ragged robe, her shrunken limb,
Her dreadful eyes! "It is no mask;
   It is a she-wolf, gaunt and grim!"

She ran across the icy plain;
   Her worn blood curdled in the blast;
Each footstep left a crimson stain;
   The white-faced moon looked on aghast.

She said between her chattering jaws,
   "Deep peace is mine, I cease to strive;
Oh, comfortable convent laws,
   That bury foolish nuns alive!

"A trowel for my passing-bell,
   A little bed within the wall,
A coverlet of stones; how well
   I there shall keep the Carnival!"

Like tired bells chiming in their sleep,
   The wind faint peals of laughter bore;
She stopped her ears and climbed the steep,
   And thundered at the convent door.

It opened straight: she entered in,
  And at the wardress' feet fell prone:
"I come to purge away my sin;
  Bury me, close me up in stone."

The wardress raised her tenderly;
  She touched her wet and fast-shut eyes:
"Look, sister; sister, look at me;
  Look; can you see through my disguise?"

She looked and saw her own sad face,
  And trembled, wondering, "Who art thou?"
"God sent me down to fill your place:
  I am the Virgin Mary now."

And with the word, God's mother shone:
  The wanderer whispered, "Mary, hail!"
The vision helped her to put on
  Bracelet and fillet, ring and veil.

"You are sister to the mountains now,
  And sister to the day and night;
Sister to God." And on the brow
  She kissed her thrice, and left her sight.

While dreaming in her cloudy bed,
  Far in the crimson orient land,
On many a mountain's happy head
  Dawn lightly laid her rosy hand.

Lord Crewe

A HARROW GRAVE IN FLANDERS

Here in the marshland, past the battered bridge,
  One of a hundred grains untimely sown,
Here, with his comrades of the hard-won ridge,
        He rests, unknown.

1146

WILLIAM WATSON

His horoscope had seemed so plainly drawn—
　　School triumphs earned apace in work and play;
Friendships at will; then love's delightful dawn
　　　　And mellowing day;

Home fostering hope; some service to the State;
　　Benignant age; then the long tryst to keep
Where in the yew-tree shadow congregate
　　　　His fathers sleep.

Was here the one thing needful to distil
　　From life's alembic, through this holier fate,
The man's essential soul, the hero will?
　　　　We ask; and wait.

William Watson

LEAVETAKING

Pass, thou wild light,
Wild light on peaks that so
Grieve to let go
　　The day.
Lovely thy tarrying, lovely too is night:
　　Pass thou away.

Pass, thou wild heart,
Wild heart of youth that still
Hast half a will
　　To stay.
I grow too old a comrade, let us part:
　　Pass thou away.

SONG

　　April, April,
　　Laugh thy girlish laughter;
　　Then, the moment after,

Weep thy girlish tears!
April, that mine ears
Like a lover greetest,
If I tell thee, sweetest,
All my hopes and fears,
April, April,
Laugh thy golden laughter,
But, the moment after,
Weep thy golden tears!

INVENTION

I envy not the Lark his song divine,
  Nor thee, O Maid, thy beauty's faultless mould.
Perhaps the chief felicity is mine,
        Who hearken and behold.

The joy of the Artificer Unknown
  Whose genius could devise the Lark and thee—
This, or a kindred rapture, let me own,
        I covet ceaselessly!

IN LALEHAM CHURCHYARD

(*August 18, 1890*)

'Twas at this season, year by year,
The singer who lies songless here
Was wont to woo a less austere,
    Less deep repose,
Where Rotha to Winandermere
    Unresting flows,—

Flows through a land where torrents call
To far-off torrents as they fall,
And mountains in their cloudy pall
    Keep ghostly state,
And Nature makes majestical
    Man's lowliest fate.

1148

WILLIAM WATSON

There, 'mid the August glow, still came
He of the twice-illustrious name,
'The loud impertinence of fame
    Not loth to flee—
Not loth with brooks and fells to claim
    Fraternity.

Linked with his happy youthful lot,
Is Loughrigg, then, at last forgot?
Nor silent peak nor dalesman's cot
    Looks on his grave.
Lulled by the Thames he sleeps, and not
    By Rotha's wave.

'Tis fittest thus! for though with skill
He sang of beck and tarn and ghyll,
The deep, authentic mountain-thrill
    Ne'er shook his page!
Somewhat of worldling mingled still
    With bard and sage.

And 'twere less meet for him to lie
Guarded by summits lone and high
That traffic with the eternal sky
    And hear, unawed,
The everlasting fingers ply
    The loom of God,

Than, in this hamlet of the plain,
A less sublime repose to gain,
Where Nature, genial and urbane,
    To man defers,
Yielding to us the right to reign,
    Which yet is hers.

And nigh to where his bones abide,
The Thames with its unruffled tide
Seems like his genius typified,—
    Its strength, its grace,
Its lucid gleam, its sober pride,
    Its tranquil pace.

But ah! not his the eventual fate
Which doth the journeying wave await—
Doomed to resign its limpid state
    And quickly grow
Turbid as passion, dark as hate,
    And wide as woe.

Rather, it may be, over-much
He shunned the common stain and smutch,
From soilure of ignoble touch
    Too grandly free,
Too loftily secure in such
    Cold purity.

But he preserved from chance control
The fortress of his 'stablisht soul;
In all things sought to see the Whole;
    Brooked no disguise;
And set his heart upon the goal,
    Not on the prize;

And with those few he shall survive
Who seem not to compete or strive,
Yet with the foremost still arrive,
    Prevailing still:
The Elect with whom the stars connive
    To work their will.

Alfred Edward Housman

WITH RUE MY HEART IS LADEN

With rue my heart is laden
    For golden friends I had,
For many a rose-lipt maiden
    And many a lightfoot lad.

By brooks too broad for leaping
    The lightfoot boys are laid;
The rose-lipt girls are sleeping
    In fields where roses fade.

ALFRED EDWARD HOUSMAN

FAR IN A WESTERN BROOKLAND

Far in a western brookland
    That bred me long ago,
The poplars stand and tremble
    By pools I used to know.

There, in the windless night-time,
    The wanderer, marvelling why,
Halts on the bridge to hearken
    How soft the poplars sigh.

He hears: long since forgotten
    In fields where I was known,
Here I lie down in London
    And turn to rest alone.

There, by the starlit fences,
    The wanderer halts and hears
My soul that lingers sighing
    About the glimmering weirs.

LOVELIEST OF TREES

Loveliest of trees, the cherry now
Is hung with bloom along the bough,
And stands about the woodland ride
Wearing white for Eastertide.

Now, of my threescore years and ten,
Twenty will not come again,
And take from seventy springs a score,
It only leaves me fifty more.

And since to look at things in bloom
Fifty springs are little room,
About the woodland I will go
To see the cherry hung with snow.

1185

Ernest Rhys

DAGONET'S CANZONET

A queen lived in the South;
And music was her mouth,
And sunshine was her hair,
By day, and all the night
The drowsy embers there
Remember'd still the light.
My soul, was she not fair!

But for her eyes—they made
An iron man afraid;
Like sky-blue pools they were,
Watching the sky that knew
Itself transmuted there
Light blue, or deeper blue.
My soul, was she not fair!

The lifting of her hands
Made laughter in the lands
Where the sun is, in the South:
But my soul learnt sorrow there
In the secrets of her mouth,
Her eyes, her hands, her hair.
O soul, was she not fair!

LOST IN FRANCE

He had the plowman's strength
In the grasp of his hand.
He could see a crow
Three miles away,
And the trout beneath the stone.
He could hear the green oats growing,
And the sou'-west making rain;
And the wheel upon the hill

When it left the level road.
He could make a gate, and dig a pit,
And plow as straight as stone can fall.
And he is dead.

Francis Thompson

DAISY

Where the thistle lifts a purple crown
   Six foot out of the turf,
And the harebell shakes on the windy hill—
   O the breath of the distant surf!—

The hills look over on the South,
   And southward dreams the sea;
And, with the sea-breeze hand in hand,
   Came innocence and she.

Where 'mid the gorse the raspberry
   Red for the gatherer springs,
Two children did we stray and talk
   Wise, idle, childish things.

She listened with big-lipped surprise,
   Breast-deep 'mid flower and spine:
Her skin was like a grape, whose veins
   Run snow instead of wine.

She knew not those sweet words she spake,
   Nor knew her own sweet way;
But there's never a bird so sweet a song
   Thronged in whose throat that day!

Oh, there were flowers in Storrington
   On the turf and on the spray;
But the sweetest flower on Sussex hills
   Was the Daisy-flower that day!

1153

Her beauty smoothed earth's furrowed face!
    She gave me tokens three:—
A look, a word of her winsome mouth,
    And a wild raspberry.

A berry red, a guileless look,
    A still word,—strings of sand!
And yet they made my wild, wild heart
    Fly down to her little hand.

For, standing artless as the air,
    And candid as the skies,
She took the berries with her hand,
    And the love with her sweet eyes.

The fairest things have fleetest end:
    Their scent survives their close;
But the rose's scent is bitterness
    To him that loved the rose!

She looked a little wistfully,
    Then went her sunshine way:—
The sea's eye had a mist on it,
    And the leaves fell from the day.

She went her unremembering way,
    She went, and left in me
The pang of all the partings gone,
    And partings yet to be.

She left me marvelling why my soul
    Was sad that she was glad;
At all the sadness in the sweet,
    The sweetness in the sad.

Still, still I seemed to see her, still
    Look up with soft replies,
And take the berries with her hand,
    And the love with her lovely eyes.

1154

FRANCIS THOMPSON

Nothing begins, and nothing ends,
  That is not paid with moan;
For we are born in other's pain,
  And perish in our own.

THE HOUND OF HEAVEN

I fled Him, down the nights and down the days;
I fled Him down the arches of the years;
I fled Him, down the labyrinthine ways
  Of my own mind; and in the mist of tears
I hid from Him, and under running laughter.
          Up vistaed hopes I sped;
          And shot, precipitated,
Adown Titanic glooms of chasmèd fears,
From those strong Feet that followed, followed after.
          But with unhurrying chase,
          And unperturbèd pace,
      Deliberate speed, majestic instancy,
          They beat—and a Voice beat
          More instant than the Feet—
"All things betray thee, who betrayest Me."

          I pleaded, outlaw-wise,
By many a hearted casement, curtained red,
  Trellised with intertwining charities;
(For, though I knew His love Who followèd,
          Yet was I sore adread
Lest, having Him, I must have naught beside);
But, if one little casement parted wide,
  The gust of His approach would clash it to.
Fear wist not to evade, as Love wist to pursue.
Across the margent of the world I fled,
  And troubled the gold gateways of the stars,
  Smiting for shelter on their clangèd bars;
          Fretted to dulcet jars
And silvern chatter the pale ports o' the moon.
I said to dawn, Be sudden; to eve, Be soon;
  With thy young skiey blossoms heap me over
          From this tremendous Lover!

Float thy vague veil about me, lest He see!
  I tempted all His servitors, but to find
My own betrayal in their constancy,
In faith to Him their fickleness to me,
  Their traitorous trueness, and their loyal deceit.
To all swift things for swiftness did I sue;
    Clung to the whistling mane of every wind.
      But whether they swept, smoothly fleet,
    The long savannahs of the blue;
        Or whether, Thunder-driven,
     They clanged his chariot 'thwart a heaven
Plashy with flying lightnings round the spurn o' their feet:—
  Fear wist not to evade as Love wist to pursue.
       Still with unhurrying chase,
       And unperturbèd pace,
    Deliberate speed, majestic instancy,
      Came on the following Feet,
      And a Voice above their beat—
"Naught shelters thee, who wilt not shelter Me."

I sought no more that after which I strayed
  In face of man or maid;
But still within the little children's eyes
  Seems something, something that replies;
They at least are for me, surely for me!
I turned me to them very wistfully;
But, just as their young eyes grew sudden fair
  With dawning answers there,
Their angel plucked them from me by the hair.
"Come then, ye other children, Nature's—share
With me" (said I) "your delicate fellowship;
    Let me greet you lip to lip,
    Let me twine with you caresses,
      Wantoning
    With our Lady-Mother's vagrant tresses,
      Banqueting
    With her in her wind-walled palace,
    Underneath her azured daïs,
    Quaffing, as your taintless way is,
      From out a chalice
Lucent-weeping out of the dayspring."

So it was done:
I in their delicate fellowship was one—
Drew the bolt of Nature's secrecies.
I knew all the swift importings
    On the wilful face of skies;
    I knew how the clouds arise
    Spumèd of the wild sea-snortings;
       All that's born or dies
    Rose and drooped with—made them shapers
Of mine own moods, or wailful or divine—
    With them joyed and was bereaven.
    I was heavy with the even,
    When she lit her glimmering tapers
    Round the day's dead sanctities.
    I laughed in the morning's eyes.
I triumphed and I saddened with all weather,
    Heaven and I wept together,
And its sweet tears were salt with mortal mine;
Against the red throb of its sunset-heart
    I laid my own to beat,
    And share commingling heat;
But not by that, by that, was eased my human smart.
In vain my tears were wet on Heaven's grey cheek.
For ah! we know not what each other says,
    These things and I; in sound *I* speak—
Their sound is but their stir, they speak by silences.
Nature, poor stepdame, cannot slake my drouth;
    Let her, if she would owe me,
Drop yon blue bosom-veil of sky, and show me
    The breasts o' her tenderness:
Never did any milk of hers once bless
    My thirsting mouth.
    Nigh and nigh draws the chase,
    With unperturbèd pace,
    Deliberate speed, majestic instancy;
    And past those noisèd Feet
    A voice comes yet more fleet—
"Lo! naught contents thee, who content'st not Me."

Naked I wait Thy love's uplifted stroke!
My harness piece by piece Thou hast hewn from me,
And smitten me to my knee;
I am defenceless utterly.
I slept, methinks, and woke,
And, slowly gazing, find me stripped in sleep.
In the rash lustihood of my young powers,
I shook the pillaring hours
And pulled my life upon me; grimed with smears,
I stand amid the dust o' the mounded years—
My mangled youth lies dead beneath the heap.
My days have crackled and gone up in smoke,
Have puffed and burst as sun-starts on a stream.
Yea, faileth now even dream
The dreamer, and the lute the lutanist;
Even the linked fantasies, in whose blossomy twist
I swung the earth a trinket at my wrist,
Are yielding; cords of all too weak account
For earth with heavy griefs so overplussed.
Ah! is Thy love indeed
A weed, albeit an amaranthine weed,
Suffering no flowers except its own to mount?
Ah! must—
Designer infinite!—
Ah! must Thou char the wood ere Thou canst limn with it?
My freshness spent its wavering shower i' the dust:
And now my heart is as a broken fount,
Wherein tear-drippings stagnate, spilt down ever
From the dank thoughts that shiver
Upon the sighful branches of my mind.
Such is; what is to be?
The pulp so bitter, how shall taste the rind?
I dimly guess what Time in mists confounds;
Yet ever and anon a trumpet sounds
From the hid battlements of Eternity;
Those shaken mists a space unsettle, then
Round the half-glimpsèd turrets slowly wash again.
But not ere him who summoneth
I first have seen, enwound
With glooming robes purpureal, cypress-crowned;

FRANCIS THOMPSON

His name I know, and what his trumpet saith.
Whether man's heart or life it be which yields
  Thee harvest, must Thy harvest fields
  Be dunged with rotten death?

   Now of that long pursuit
   Comes on at hand the bruit;
  That Voice is round me like a bursting sea:
   "And is thy earth so marred,
   Shattered in shard on shard?
  Lo, all things fly thee, for thou fliest Me!
  Strange, piteous, futile thing,
Wherefore should any set thee love apart?
Seeing none but I makes much of naught" (He said),
"And human love needs human meriting:
  How hast thou merited—
Of all man's clotted clay the dingiest clot?
  Alack, thou knowest not
How little worthy of any love thou art!
Whom wilt thou find to love ignoble thee
  Save Me, save only Me?
All which I took from thee I did but take,
  Not for thy harms,
But just that thou might'st seek it in My arms.
  All which thy child's mistake
Fancies as lost, I have stored for thee at home:
  Rise, clasp My hand, and come!"

   Halts by me that footfall:
   Is my gloom, after all,
  Shade of His hand, outstretched caressingly?
   "Ah, fondest, blindest, weakest,
   I am He Whom thou seekest!
Thou dravest love from thee, who dravest Me."

TO A SNOWFLAKE

  What heart could have thought you?—
  Past our devisal
  (O filigree petal!)

1159

Fashioned so purely,
Fragilely, surely,
From what Paradisal
Imagineless metal,
Too costly for cost?
Who hammered you, wrought you,
From argentine vapour?—
"God was my shaper.
Passing surmisal,
He hammered, He wrought me,
From curled silver vapour,
To lust of His mind:—
Thou could'st not have thought me!
So purely, so palely,
Tinily, surely,
Mightily, frailly,
Insculped and embossed,
With His hammer of wind,
And His graver of frost."

DREAM-TRYST

The breaths of kissing night and day
    Were mingled in the eastern Heaven:
Throbbing with unheard melody
    Shook Lyra all its star-chord seven:
        When dusk shrunk cold, and light trod shy,
            And dawn's grey eyes were troubled grey;
        And souls went palely up the sky,
            And mine to Lucidé.

There was no change in her sweet eyes
    Since last I saw those sweet eyes shine;
There was no change in her deep heart
    Since last that deep heart knocked at mine.
        Her eyes were clear, her eyes were Hope's,
            Wherein did ever come and go
        The sparkle of the fountain drops
            From her sweet soul below.

The chambers in the house of dreams
  Are fed with so divine an air,
That Time's hoar wings grow young therein,
  And they who walk there are most fair.
    I joyed for me, I joyed for her,
      Who with the Past meet girt about:
    Where our last kiss still warms the air,
      Nor can her eyes go out.

MESSAGES

What shall I your true-love tell,
  Earth-forsaking maid?
What shall I your true-love tell,
  When life's spectre's laid?

"Tell him that, our side the grave,
  Maid may not conceive
Life should be so sad to have,
  That's so sad to leave!"

What shall I your true-love tell,
  When I come to him?
What shall I your true-love tell—
  Eyes growing dim!

"Tell him this, when you shall part
  From a maiden pined;
That I see him with my heart,
  Now my eyes are blind."

What shall I your true-love tell?
  Speaking-while is scant.
What shall I your true-love tell,
  Death's white postulant?

"Tell him—love, with speech at strife,
  For last utterance saith:
I, who loved with all my life,
  Love with all my death."

CORRELATED GREATNESS

O nothing, in this corporal earth of man,
That to the imminent heaven of his high soul
Responds with colour and with shadow, can
Lack correlated greatness. If the scroll
Where thoughts lie fast in spell of hieroglyph
Be mighty through its mighty habitants;
If God be in His Name; grave potence if
The sounds unbind of hieratic chants;
All's vast that vastness means. Nay, I affirm
Nature is whole in her least things exprest,
Nor know we with what scope God builds the worm.
Our towns are copied fragments from our breast;
And all man's Babylons strive but to impart
The grandeurs of his Babylonian heart.

William Herbert Carruth

EACH IN HIS OWN TONGUE

A Fire-Mist and a planet,—
    A crystal and a cell,—
A jelly-fish and a saurian,
    And caves where the cave-men dwell;
Then a sense of law and beauty,
    And a face turned from the clod,—
Some call it Evolution,
    And others call it God.

A haze on the far horizon,
    The infinite, tender sky,
The ripe, rich tint of the cornfields,
    And the wild geese sailing high,—
And all over upland and lowland
    The charm of the goldenrod,—
Some of us call it Autumn,
    And others call it God.

Like tides on a crescent sea-beach,
    When the moon is new and thin,
Into our hearts high yearnings
    Come welling and surging in,—
Come from the mystic ocean
    Whose rim no foot has trod,—
Some of us call it Longing,
    And others call it God.

A picket frozen on duty,—
    A mother starved for her brood,—
Socrates drinking the hemlock,
    And Jesus on the rood;
And millions who, humble and nameless,
    The straight, hard pathway plod,—
Some call it Consecration,
    And others call it God.

Hamlin Garland

TO A CAPTIVE CRANE

Ho, brother! Art thou prisoned too?
    Is thy heart hot with restless pain?
I heard the call thy bugle blew
    Here by the bleak and chilling main
(Whilst round me shaven parks are spread
    And cindered drives wind on and on);
And at thy cry, thy lifted head,
    My gladdened heart was westward drawn.

O splendid bird! your trumpet brings
To my lone heart the prairie springs.

DO YOU FEAR THE WIND?

Do you fear the force of the wind,
    The slash of the rain?
Go face them and fight them,
    Be savage again.

Go hungry and cold like the wolf,
  Go wade like the crane:
The palms of your hands will thicken,
The skin of your cheek will tan,
You'll grow ragged and weary and swarthy,
  But you'll walk like a man!

THE MOUNTAINS ARE A LONELY FOLK

The mountains they are silent folk,
  They stand afar—alone;
And the clouds that kiss their brows at night
  Hear neither sigh nor groan.
Each bears him in his ordered place
  As soldiers do, and bold and high
They fold their forests round their feet
  And bolster up the sky.

Clinton Scollard

BAG-PIPES AT SEA

Above the shouting of the gale,
  The whipping sheet, the dashing spray,
I heard, with notes of joy and wail,
  A piper play.

Along the dipping deck he trod,
  The dusk about his shadowy form;
He seemed like some strange ancient god
  Of song and storm.

He gave his dim seen pipes a skirl
  And war went down the darkling air;
Then came a sudden subtle swirl,
  And love was there.

1164

CLINTON SCOLLARD

What were the winds that flailed and flayed
  The sea to him, the night obscure?
In dreams he strayed some brackened glade,
  Some heathery moor.

And if he saw the slanting spars,
  And if he watched the shifting track,
He marked, too, the eternal stars
  Shine through the wrack.

And so amid the deep sea din,
  And so amid the wastes of foam,
Afar his heart was happy in
  His highland home!

AS I CAME DOWN FROM LEBANON

As I came down from Lebanon,
Came winding, wandering slowly down
Through mountain passes bleak and brown,
The cloudless day was well-nigh done.
The city, like an opal set
In emerald, showed each minaret
Afire with radiant beams of sun,
And glistened orange, fig, and lime,
Where song-birds made melodious chime,
As I came down from Lebanon.

As I came down from Lebanon,
Like lava in the dying glow,
Through olive orchards far below
I saw the murmuring river run;
And 'neath the wall upon the sand
Swart sheiks from distant Samarcand,
With precious spices they had won,
Lay long and languidly in wait
Till they might pass the guarded gate,
As I came down from Lebanon.

As I came down from Lebanon,
I saw strange men from lands afar,
In mosque and square and gay bazar,
The Magi that the Moslem shun,
And grave Effendi from Stamboul,
Who sherbet sipped in corners cool;
And, from the balconies o'errun
With roses, gleamed the eyes of those
Who dwell in still seraglios,
As I came down from Lebanon.

As I came down from Lebanon,
The flaming flower of daytime died,
And Night, arrayed as is a bride
Of some great king, in garments spun
Of purple and the finest gold,
Outbloomed in glories manifold,
Until the moon, above the dun
And darkening desert, void of shade,
Shone like a keen Damascus blade,
As I came down from Lebanon.

Bliss Carman

LORD OF MY HEART'S ELATION

Lord of my heart's elation,
Spirit of things unseen,
Be thou my aspiration
Consuming and serene!

Bear up, bear out, bear onward,
This mortal soul alone,
To selfhood or oblivion,
Incredibly thine own,—

As the foamheads are loosened
And blown along the sea,
Or sink and merge forever
In that which bids them be.

I, too, must climb in wonder,
Uplift at thy command,—
Be one with my frail fellows
Beneath the wind's strong hand,

A fleet and shadowy column
Of dust or mountain rain,
To walk the earth a moment
And be dissolved again.

Be thou my exaltation
Or fortitude of mien,
Lord of the world's elation,
Thou breath of things unseen!

ROADSIDE FLOWERS

We are the roadside flowers,
    Straying from garden grounds;
Lovers of idle hours,
    Breakers of ordered bounds.

If only the earth will feed us,
    If only the wind be kind,
We blossom for those who need us,
    The stragglers left behind.

And lo, the Lord of the Garden,
    He makes His sun to rise,
And His rain to fall like pardon
    On our dusty paradise.

On us He has laid the duty—
    The task of the wandering breed—
To better the world with beauty,
    Wherever the way may lead.

Who shall inquire of the season,
    Or question the wind where it blows?
We blossom and ask no reason,
    The Lord of the Garden knows.

1167

THE UNRETURNING

The old eternal spring once more
  Comes back the sad eternal way,
With tender rosy light before
  The going-out of day.

The great white moon across my door
  A shadow in the twilight stirs;
But now forever comes no more·
  That wondrous look of Hers.

DAPHNE

I know that face!
  In some lone forest place,
When June brings back the laurel to the hills,
  Where shade and sunlight lace,

Where all day long
  The brown birds make their song—
A music that seems never to have known
  Dismay nor haste nor wrong—

I once before
  Have seen thee by the shore,
As if about to shed the flowery guise
  And be thyself once more.

Dear, shy, soft face,
  With just the elfin trace
That lends thy human beauty the last touch
  Of wild, elusive grace!

Can it be true,
  A god did once pursue
Thy gleaming beauty through the glimmering wood,
  Drenched in the Dorian dew,

BLISS CARMAN

Too mad to stay
His hot and headstrong way,
Demented by the fragrance of thy flight,
Heedless of thy dismay?

But I to thee
More gently fond would be,
Nor less a lover woo thee with soft words
And woodland melody;

Take pipe and play
Each forest fear away;
Win thee to idle in the leafy shade
All the long summer day;

Tell thee old tales
Of love, that still avails
More than all mighty things in this great world,
Still wonder works nor fails;

Teach thee new lore,
How to love more and more,
And find the magical delirium
In joys unguessed before.

I would try over
And over to discover
Some wild, sweet, foolish, irresistible
New way to be thy lover—

New, wondrous ways
To fill thy golden days,
Thy lovely pagan body with delight,
Thy loving heart with praise.

For I would learn,
Deep in the brookside fern,
The magic of the syrinx whispering low
With bubbly fall and turn;

Mock every note
Of the green woodbird's throat,
Till some wild strain, impassioned yet serene,
Should form and float

Far through the hills,
Where mellow sunlight fills
The world with joy, and from the purple vines
The brew of life distils.

Ah, then indeed
Thy heart should have no need
To tremble at a footfall in the brake,
And bid thy bright limbs speed.

But night would come,
And I should make thy home
In the deep pines, lit by a yellow star
Hung in the dark blue dome—

A fragrant house
Of woven balsam boughs,
Where the great Cyprian mother should receive
Our warm unsullied vows.

Wendell Phillips Stafford

INVOCATION

O Thou whose equal purpose runs
In drops of rain or streams of suns,
And with a soft compulsion rolls
The green earth on her snowy poles;
O Thou who keepest in thy ken
The times of flowers, the dooms of men,
Stretch out a mighty wing above—
Be tender to the land we love!

If all the huddlers from the storm
Have found her hearthstone wide and warm;
If she has made men free and glad,
Sharing, with all, the good she had;
If she has blown the very dust
From her bright balance to be just,
Oh, spread a mighty wing above—
Be tender to the land we love!

When in the dark eternal tower
The star-clock strikes her trial hour,
And for her help no more avail
Her sea-blue shield, her mountain-mail,
But sweeping wide, from gulf to lakes,
The battle on her forehead breaks,
Throw Thou a thunderous wing above—
Be lightning for the land we love!

Mary Elizabeth Coleridge

A HUGUENOT

O, a gallant set were they,
As they charged on us that day,
A thousand riding like one!
  Their trumpets crying,
  And their white plumes flying,
And their sabres flashing in the sun.

O, a sorry lot were we,
As we stood beside the sea,
Each man for himself as he stood!
  We were scattered and lonely—
  A little force only
Of the good men fighting for the good.

But I never loved more
On sea or on shore

The ringing of my own true blade,
  Like lightning it quivered,
  And the hard helms shivered,
As I sang, "None maketh me afraid!"

John Jay Chapman

NO PILOTS WE

Would I were one of those who preach no Cause—
Nor guide mankind with meddling fingertips;
But let each star that moves without a pause
Shine as it list—as potent when it dips
Beyond their ken in visual eclipse
As when it blazes in a darkling sky,
Regnant and beautiful, while with mute lips
Men bow the head in worship, or in shy
And inexpressive words admit that God is nigh.

We are no pilots: let us trust our bark,
Miraculous, alert, not made with hands,
That feels a magic impulse through the dark,
And leaps upon the course it understands
From shores unknown to unimagined strands;
Resists the helm we give it, but divines—
Being itself divine—divine commands;
And answers to no compass save the signs
Encircling deepest heaven where the Zodiac shines.

Sir Henry Newbolt

ADMIRAL DEATH

Boys, are ye calling a toast to-night?
  (Hear what the sea-wind saith)
Fill for a bumper strong and bright,
  And here's to Admiral Death!

SIR HENRY NEWBOLT

He's sailed in a hundred builds o' boat,
He's fought in a thousand kinds o' coat,
He's the senior flag of all that float,
    And his name's Admiral Death!

Which of you looks for a service free?
    (Hear what the sea-wind saith)
The rules of the service are but three
    When ye sail with Admiral Death.
Steady your hand in the time o' squalls,
Stand to the last by him that falls,
And answer clear to the voice that calls,
    "Ay, ay! Admiral Death!"

How will ye know him among the rest?
    (Hear what the sea-wind saith)
By the glint o' the stars that cover his breast
    Ye may find Admiral Death.
By the forehead grim with an ancient scar,
By the voice that rolls like thunder far,
By the tenderest eyes of all that are,
    Ye may know Admiral Death.

Where are the lads that sailed before?
    (Hear what the sea-wind saith)
Their bones are white by many a shore,
    They sleep with Admiral Death.
Oh! but they loved him, young and old,
For he left the laggard, and took the bold,
And the fight was fought, and the story's told,
    And they sleep with Admiral Death.

ST. GEORGE'S DAY—YPRES 1915

To fill the gap, to bear the brunt
    With bayonet and with spade,
Four hundred to a four-mile front
    Unbacked and undismayed—
What men are these, of what great race,
    From what old shire or town,
That run with such goodwill to face
    Death on a Flemish down?

1173

Let be! they bind a broken line:
As men die, so die they.
Land of the free! their life was thine,
It is St. George's Day.

Yet say whose ardour bids them stand
    At bay by yonder bank,
Where a boy's voice and a boy's hand
    Close up the quivering rank,
Who under those all-shattering skies
    Plays out his captain's part
With the last darkness in his eyes
    And *Domum* in his heart?

Let be, let be! in yonder line
    All names are burned away.
Land of his love! the fame be thine,
    It is St. George's Day.

Robert Cameron Rogers

THE ROSARY

The hours I spent with thee, dear heart,
    Are as a string of pearls to me;
I count them over, every one apart,
    My rosary.

Each hour a pearl, each pearl a prayer,
    To still a heart in absence wrung;
I tell each bead unto the end and there
    A cross is hung.

Oh memories that bless—and burn!
    Oh barren gain—and bitter loss!
I kiss each bead, and strive at last to learn
    To kiss the cross,
        Sweetheart,
            To kiss the cross.

1174

Richard Hovey

THE SEA GYPSY

I am fevered with the sunset,
I am fretful with the bay,
For the wander-thirst is on me
And my soul is in Cathay.

There's a schooner in the offing,
With her topsails shot with fire,
And my heart has gone aboard her
For the Islands of Desire.

I must forth again to-morrow!
With the sunset I must be
Hull down on the trail of rapture
In the wonder of the sea.

ENVOY

Whose furthest footstep never strayed
Beyond the village of his birth
Is but a lodger for the night
In this old wayside inn of earth.

To-morrow he shall take his pack,
And set out for the ways beyond
On the old trail from star to star,
An alien and a vagabond.

If any record of our names
Be blown about the hills of time,
Let no one sunder us in death,—
The man of paint, the men of rhyme.

Of all our good, of all our bad,
This one thing only is of worth,—
We held the league of heart to heart
The only purpose of the earth.

LOVE IN THE WINDS

When I am standing on a mountain crest,
Or hold the tiller in the dashing spray,
My love of you leaps foaming in my breast,
Shouts with the winds and sweeps to their foray;
My heart bounds with the horses of the sea,
And plunges in the wild ride of the night,
Flaunts in the teeth of tempest the large glee
That rides out Fate and welcomes gods to fight.
Ho, love, I laugh aloud for love of you,
Glad that our love is fellow to rough weather,—
No fretful orchid hothoused from the dew,
But hale and hardy as the highland heather,
Rejoicing in the wind that stings and thrills,
Comrade of ocean, playmate of the hills.

Arthur Symons

MODERN BEAUTY

I am the torch, she saith, and what to me
If the moth die of me?   I am the flame
Of Beauty, and I burn that all may see
Beauty, and I have neither joy nor shame,
But live with that clear light of perfect fire
Which is to men the death of their desire.

I am Yseult and Helen, I have seen
Troy burn, and the most loving knight lies dead.
The world has been my mirror, time has been
My breath upon the glass; and men have said,
Age after age, in rapture and despair,
Love's poor few words, before my image there,

I live, and am immortal; in my eyes
The sorrow of the world, and on my lips
The joy of life, mingle to make me wise;
Yet now the day is darkened with eclipse:

ARTHUR SYMONS

Who is there lives for beauty? Still am I
The torch, but where's the moth that still dares die?

THE LAST MEMORY

When I am old, and think of the old days,
And warm my hands before a little blaze,
Having forgotten love, hope, fear, desire,
I shall see, smiling out of the pale fire,
One face, mysterious and exquisite;
And I shall gaze, and ponder over it,
Wondering, was it Leonardo wrought
That stealthy ardency, where passionate thought
Burns inward, a revealing flame, and glows
To the last ecstasy, which is repose?
Was it Bronzino, those Borghese eyes?
And, musing thus among my memories,
O unforgotten! you will come to seem,
As pictures do, remembered, some old dream.
And I shall think of you as something strange,
And beautiful, and full of helpless change,
Which I beheld and carried in my heart;
But you, I loved, will have become a part
Of the eternal mystery, and love
Like a dim pain; and I shall bend above
My little fire, and shiver, being cold,
When you are no more young, and I am old.

THE RETURN

A little hand is knocking at my heart,
And I have closed the door.
"I pray thee, for the love of God, depart:
Thou shalt come in no more."

"Open, for I am weary of the way.
The night is very black.
I have been wandering many a night and day.
Open. I have come back."

1177

The little hand is knocking patiently;
I listen, dumb with pain.
"Wilt thou not open any more to me?
I have come back again."

"I will not open any more.   Depart.
I, that once lived, am dead."
The hand that had been knocking at my heart
Was still.   "And I?" she said.

There is no sound, save, in the winter air,
The sound of wind and rain.
All that I loved in all the world stands there,
And will not knock again.

MEMORY

As a perfume doth remain
In the folds where it hath lain,
So the thought of you, remaining
Deeply folded in my brain,
Will not leave me: all things leave me:
You remain.

Other thoughts may come and go,
Other moments I may know
That shall waft me, in their going,
As a breath blown to and fro,
Fragrant memories: fragrant memories
Come and go.

Only thoughts of you remain
In my heart where they have lain,
Perfumed thoughts of you, remaining,
A hid sweetness, in my brain.
Others leave me: all things leave me:
You remain.

William Butler Yeats

THE LAND OF HEART'S DESIRE

The wind blows out of the gates of the day,
    The wind blows over the lonely of heart,
And the lonely of heart is withered away,
    While the faeries dance in a place apart,
Shaking their milk-white feet in a ring,
    Tossing their milk-white arms in the air;
For they hear the wind laugh and murmur and sing
    Of a land where even the old are fair,
And even the wise are merry of tongue;
    But I heard a reed of Coolaney say,
"When the wind has laughed and murmured and sung,
    "The lonely of heart must wither away."

THE LAKE ISLE OF INNISFREE

I will arise and go now, and go to Innisfree,
And a small cabin build there, of clay and wattles made;
Nine bean rows will I have there, a hive for the honey bee,
And live alone in the bee-loud glade.

And I shall have some peace there, for peace comes dropping
    slow,
Dropping from the veils of the morning to where the cricket
    sings;
There midnight's all a glimmer, and noon a purple glow,
And evening full of the linnet's wings.

I will arise and go now, for always night and day
I hear lake water lapping with low sounds by the shore;
While I stand on the roadway, or on the pavements grey,
I hear it in the deep heart's core.

1179

THE LOVER TELLS OF THE ROSE IN HIS HEART

All things uncomely and broken, all things worn out and old,
The cry of a child by the roadway, the creak of a lumbering
     cart,
The heavy steps of the ploughman, splashing the wintry
     mould,
Are wronging your image that blossoms a rose in the deeps
     of my heart.

The wrong of unshapely things is a wrong too great to be
     told;
I hunger to build them anew and sit on a green knoll apart,
With the earth and the sky and the water, remade, like a
     casket of gold
For my dreams of your image that blossoms a rose in the
     deeps of my heart.

Herbert Trench

I HEARD A SOLDIER

I heard a soldier sing some trifle
     Out in the sun-dried veldt alone:
He lay and cleaned his grimy rifle
     Idly, behind a stone.

"If after death, love, comes a waking,
     And in their camp so dark and still
The men of dust hear bugles breaking
     Their halt upon the hill,

"To me the slow and silver pealing
     That then the last high trumpet pours,
Shall softer than the dawn come stealing,
     For, with its call, comes yours!"

1180

What grief of love had he to stifle,
   Basking so idly by his stone,
That grimy soldier with his rifle
   Out in the veldt, alone?

COME, LET US MAKE LOVE DEATHLESS

Come, let us make love deathless, thou and I,
   Seeing that our footing on the Earth is brief—
Seeing that her multitudes sweep out to die
   Mocking at all that passes their belief.
For standard of our love not theirs we take;
   If we go hence to-day,
Fill the high cup that is so soon to break
   With richer wine than they!

Ay, since beyond these walls no heavens there be
   Joy to revive or wasted youth repair,
I'll not bedim the lovely flame in thee
   Nor sully the sad splendour that we wear.
Great be the love, if with the lover dies
   Our greatness past recall,
And nobler for the fading of those eyes
   The world seen once for all!

Rudyard Kipling

CITIES AND THRONES AND POWERS

Cities and Thrones and Powers,
   Stand in Time's eye,
Almost as long as flowers,
   Which daily die.
But, as new buds put forth
   To glad new men,
Out of the spent and unconsidered Earth
   The Cities rise again.

This season's Daffodil,
  She never hears
What change, what chance, what chill,
  Cut down last year's:
But with bold countenance,
  And knowledge small,
Esteems her seven days' continuance
  To be perpetual.

So Time that is o'er-kind,
  To all that be,
Ordains us e'en as blind,
  As bold as she:
That in our very death,
  And burial sure,
Shadow to shadow, well persuaded, saith,
  "See how our works endure!"

REBIRTH

If any God should say
  "I will restore
The world her yesterday
  Whole as before
My Judgment blasted it"—who would not lift
Heart, eye, and hand in passion o'er the gift?

If any God should will
  To wipe from mind
The memory of this ill
  Which is mankind
In soul and substance now—who would not bless
Even to tears His loving-tenderness?

If any God should give
  Us leave to fly
These present deaths we live,
  And safely die
In those lost lives we lived ere we were born—
What man but would not laugh the excuse to scorn?

1182

For we are what we are—
    So broke to blood
And the strict works of war—
    So long subdued
To sacrifice, that threadbare Death commands
Hardly observance at our busier hands.

    Yet we were what we were,
        And, fashioned so,
    It pleases us to stare
        At the far show
Of unbelievable years and shapes that flit,
In our own likeness, on the edge of it.

RECESSIONAL

God of our fathers, known of old,
    Lord of our far-flung battle-line,
Beneath whose awful Hand we hold
    Dominion over palm and pine—
Lord God of Hosts, be with us yet,
Lest we forget—lest we forget!

The tumult and the shouting dies;
    The captains and the kings depart:
Still stands Thine ancient sacrifice,
    An humble and a contrite heart.
Lord God of Hosts, be with us yet,
Lest we forget—lest we forget!

Far-called, our navies melt away;
    On dune and headland sinks the fire:
Lo, all our pomp of yesterday
    Is one with Nineveh and Tyre!
Judge of the Nations, spare us yet,
Lest we forget—lest we forget!

If, drunk with sight of power, we loose
    Wild tongues that have not Thee in awe,
Such boasting as the Gentiles use,
    Or lesser breeds without the Law—

Lord God of Hosts, be with us yet,
Lest we forget—lest we forget!

For heathen heart that puts her trust
  In reeking tube and iron shard,
All valiant dust that builds on dust
  And, guarding, calls not Thee to guard,
For frantic boast and foolish word—
Thy Mercy on Thy People, Lord!
                    Amen.

SUSSEX

God gave all men all earth to love,
  But since our hearts are small,
Ordained for each one spot should prove
  Belovèd over all;
That, as He watched Creation's birth,
  So we, in godlike mood,
May of our love create our earth
  And see that it is good.

So one shall Baltic pines content,
  As one some Surrey glade,
Or one the palm-grove's droned lament
  Before Levuka's trade.
Each to his choice, and I rejoice
  The lot has fallen to me
In a fair ground—in a fair ground—
  Yea, Sussex by the sea!

No tender-hearted garden crowns,
  No bosomed woods adorn
Our blunt, bow-headed, whale-backed Downs,
  But gnarled and writhen thorn—
Bare slopes where chasing shadows skim.
  And through the gaps revealed
Belt upon belt, the wooded, dim
  Blue goodness of the Weald.

Clean of officious fence or hedge,
    Half-wild and wholly tame,
The wise turf cloaks the white cliff edge
    As when the Romans came.
What sign of those that fought and died
    At shift of sword and sword?
The barrow and the camp abide,
    The sunlight and the sward.

Here leaps ashore the full Sou'west
    All heavy-winged with brine,
Here lies above the golden crest
    The Channel's leaden line;
And here the sea-fogs lap and cling,
    And here, each warning each,
The sheep-bells and the ship-bells ring
    Along the hidden beach.

We have no waters to delight
    Our broad and brookless vales—
Only the dewpond on the height
    Unfed, that never fails,
Whereby no tattered herbage tells
    Which way the season flies—
Only our close-bit thyme that smells
    Like dawn in Paradise.

Here through the strong unhampered days
    The tinkling silence thrills;
Or little, lost, Down churches praise
    The Lord who made the hills:
But here the Old Gods guard their round,
    And, in her secret heart,
The heathen kingdom Wilfrid found
    Dreams, as she dwells, apart.

Though all the rest were all my share,
    With equal soul I'd see
Her nine-and-thirty sisters fair,
    Yet none more fair than she.

Choose ye your need from Thames to Tweed,
   And I will choose instead
Such lands as lie 'twixt Rake and Rye,
   Black Down and Beachy Head.

I will go out against the sun
   Where the rolled scarp retires,
And the Long Man of Wilmington
   Looks naked towards the shires;
And east till doubling Rother crawls
   To find the fickle tide,
By dry and sea-forgotten walls,
   Our ports of stranded pride.

I will go north about the shaws
   And the deep ghylls that breed
Huge oaks and old, the which we hold
   No more than "Sussex weed";
Or south where windy Piddinghoe's
   Begilded dolphin veers,
And black beside wide-bankèd Ouse
   Lie down our Sussex steers.

So to the land our hearts we give
   Till the sure magic strike,
And Memory, Use, and Love make live
   Us and our fields alike—
That deeper than our speech and thought
   Beyond our reason's sway,
Clay of the pit whence we were wrought
   Yearns to its fellow-clay.

God gives all men all earth to love,
   But since man's heart is small,
Ordains for each one spot shall prove
   Belovèd over all.
Each to his choice, and I rejoice
   The lot has fallen to me
In a fair ground—in a fair ground--
   Yea, Sussex by the sea!

Richard Le Gallienne

THE PASSIONATE READER TO HIS POET

Doth it not thrill thee, Poet,
    Dead and dust though thou art,
To feel how I press thy singing
    Close to my heart?

Take it at night to my pillow,
    Kiss it before I sleep,
And again when the delicate morning
    Beginneth to peep?

See how I bathe thy pages
    Here in the light of the sun;
Through thy leaves, as a wind among roses,
    The breezes shall run.

Feel how I take thy poem
    And bury within it my face,
As I pressed it last night in the heart of a flower
    Or deep in a dearer place.

Think, as I love thee, Poet,
    A thousand love beside,
Dear women love to press thee too
    Against a sweeter side.

Art thou not happy, Poet?
    I sometimes dream that I
For such a fragrant fame as thine
    Would gladly sing and die.

Say, wilt thou change thy glory
    For this same youth of mine?
And I will give my days i' the sun
    For that great song of thine.

SONG

She's somewhere in the sunlight strong,
  Her tears are in the falling rain,
She calls me in the wind's soft song,
  And with the flowers she comes again.

Yon bird is but her messenger,
  The moon is but her silver car;
Yea! sun and moon are sent by her,
  And every wistful waiting star.

SPIRIT OF SADNESS

She loved the Autumn, I the Spring,
Sad all the songs she loved to sing;
And in her face was strangely set
Some great inherited regret.

Some look in all things made her sigh,
Yea! sad to her the morning sky;
"So sad! so sad its beauty seems"—
I hear her say it still in dreams.

But when the day grew grey and old,
And rising stars shone strange and cold,
Then only in her face I saw
A mystic glee, a joyous awe.

Spirit of Sadness, in the spheres
Is there an end of mortal tears?
Or is there still in those great eyes
That look of lonely hills and skies?

THE LONELY DANCER

I had no heart to join the dance,
  I danced it all so long ago—
Ah! light-winged music out of France,
  Let other feet glide to and fro,

RICHARD LE GALLIENNE

Weaving new patterns of romance
  For bosoms of new-fallen snow.

But leave me thus where I may hear
  The leafy rustle of the waltz,
The shell-like murmur in my ear,
  The silken whisper fairy-false
Of unseen rainbows circling near,
  And the glad shuddering of the walls.

Another dance the dancers spin,
  A shadow-dance of mystic pain,
And other partners enter in
  And dance within my lonely brain—
The swaying woodland shod in green,
  The ghostly dancers of the rain;

The lonely dancers of the sea,
  Foam-footed on the sandy bar,
The wizard dance of wind and tree,
  The eddying dance of stream and star;
Yea, all these dancers tread for me
  A measure mournful and bizarre:

An echo-dance where ear is eye,
  And sound evokes the shapes of things,
Where out of silence and a sigh
  The sad world like a picture springs,
As, when some secret bird sweeps by,
  We see it in the sound of wings.

Those human feet upon the floor,
  That eager pulse of rhythmic breath,—
How sadly to an unknown shore
  Each silver footfall hurryeth;
A dance of autumn leaves, no more,
  On the fantastic wind of death.

Fire clasped to elemental fire,
  'Tis thus the solar atom whirls;
The butterfly in aery gyre,
  On autumn mornings, swarms and swirls,
In dance of delicate desire,
  No other than these boys and girls.

The same strange music everywhere,
　　The woven paces just the same,
Dancing from out the viewless air
　　Into the void from whence they came;
Ah! but they make a gallant flare
　　Against the dark, each little flame!

And what if all the meaning lies
　　Just in the music, not in those
Who dance thus with transfigured eyes,
　　Holding in vain each other close;
Only the music never dies,
　　The dance goes on,—the dancer goes.

A woman dancing, or a world
　　Poised on one crystal foot afar,
In shining gulfs of silence whirled,
　　Like notes of the strange music are;
Small shape against another curled,
　　Or dancing dust that makes a star.

To him who plays the violin
　　All one it is who joins the reel,
Drops from the dance, or enters in;
　　So that the never-ending wheel
Cease not its mystic course to spin,
　　For weal or woe, for woe or weal.

TO A BIRD AT DAWN

O bird that somewhere yonder sings,
　　In the dim hour 'twixt dreams and dawn,
Lone in the bush of sleeping things,
　　In some sky sanctuary withdrawn;
Your perfect song is too like pain,
And will not let me sleep again.

I think you must be more than bird,
　　A little creature of soft wings,
Not yours this deep and thrilling word—
　　Some morning planet 'tis that sings;
Surely from no small feathered throat
Wells that august, eternal note.

RICHARD LE GALLIENNE

As some old language of the dead,
  In one resounding syllable,
Says Rome and Greece and all is said—
  A simple word a child may spell;
So in your liquid note impearled
Sings the long epic of the world.

Unfathomed sweetness of your song,
  With ancient anguish at its core,
What womb of elemental wrong,
  With shudder unimagined, bore
Peace so divine—what hell hath trod
This voice that softly talks with God!

All silence in one silver flower
  Of speech that speaks not, save as speaks
The moon in heaven, yet hath power
  To tell the soul the thing it seeks,
And pack, as by some wizard's art,
The whole within the finite part.

To you, sweet bird, one well might feign—
  With such authority you sing
So clear, yet so profound, a strain
  Into the simple ear of spring—
Some secret understanding given
Of the hid purposes of Heaven.

And all my life until this day,
  And all my life until I die,
All joy and sorrow of the way,
  Seem calling yonder in the sky;
And there is something the song saith
That makes me unafraid of death.

Now the slow light fills all the trees,
  The world, before so still and strange,
With day's familiar presences,
  Back to its common self must change,
And little gossip shapes of song
The porches of the morning throng.

1191

Not yours with such as these to vie
  That of the day's small business sing,
Voice of man's heart and of God's sky—
  But O you make so deep a thing
Of joy, I dare not think of pain
Until I hear you sing again.

FLOS ÆVORUM

You must mean more than just this hour,
  You perfect thing so subtly fair,
Simple and complex as a flower,
  Wrought with such planetary care;
How patient the eternal power
  That wove the marvel of your hair.

How long the sunlight and the sea
  Wove and re-wove this rippling gold
To rhythms of eternity;
  And many a flashing thing grew old,
Waiting this miracle to be;
  And painted marvels manifold,

Still with his work unsatisfied,
  Eager each new effect to try,
The solemn artist cast aside,
  Rainbow and shell and butterfly,
As some stern blacksmith scatters wide
  The sparks that from his anvil fly.

How many shells, whorl within whorl,
  Litter the marges of the sphere
With wrack of unregarded pearl,
  To shape that little thing your ear:
Creation, just to make one girl,
  Hath travailed with exceeding fear.

The moonlight of forgotten seas
  Dwells in your eyes, and on your tongue
The honey of a million bees,
  And all the sorrows of all song:
You are the ending of all these,
  The world grew old to make you young.

All time hath traveled to this rose;
    To the strange making of this face
Came agonies of fires and snows;
    And Death and April, nights and days
Unnumbered, unimagined throes,
    Find in this flower their meeting place.

Strange artist, to my aching thought
    Give answer: all the patient power
That to this perfect ending wrought,
    Shall it mean nothing but an hour?
Say not that it is all for nought
    Time brings Eternity a flower.

Lionel Johnson

A FRIEND

All that he came to give,
    He gave and went again:
I have seen one man live,
    I have seen one man reign,
With all the graces in his train.

As one of us, he wrought
    Things of the common hour:
Whence was the charmed soul brought,
    That gave each act such power;
The natural beauty of a flower?

Magnificence and grace,
    Excellent courtesy:
A brightness on the face,
    Airs of high memory:
Whence came all these, to such as he?

Like young Shakespearean kings,
    He won the adoring throng:
And as Apollo sings,
    He triumphed with a song:
Triumphed, and sang, and passed along.

1193

With a light word, he took
The hearts of men in thrall:
And, with a golden look,
Welcomed them, at his call
Giving their love, their strength, their all.

No man less proud than he,
Nor cared for homage less:
Only, he could not be
Far off from happiness:
Nature was bound to his success.

Weary, the cares, the jars,
The lets, of every day:
But the heavens filled with stars,
Chanced he upon the way:
And where he stayed, all joy would stay.

Now when the night draws down,
When the austere stars burn;
Roaming the vast live town,
My thoughts and memories yearn
Toward him, who never will return.

Yet have I seen him live,
And owned my friend, a king:
All that he came to give,
He gave and I, who sing
His praise, bring all I have to bring.

THE PRECEPT OF SILENCE

I know you: solitary griefs,
Desolate passions, aching hours!
I know you: tremulous beliefs,
Agonised hopes, and ashen flowers!

The winds are sometimes sad to me;
The starry spaces full of fear:
Mine is the sorrow on the sea,
And mine the sigh of places drear.

LIONEL JOHNSON

Some players upon plaintive strings
Publish their wistfulness abroad:
I have not spoken of these things,
Save to one man, and unto God.

BEYOND

All was for you: and you are dead.
For, came there sorrow, came there splendour,
You still were mine, and I yours only:
Then on my breast lay down your head,
Triumphant in its dear surrender:
One were we then: though one, not lonely.

Oh, is it you are dead, or I?
Both! both dead, since we are asunder:
You, sleeping: I, for ever walking
Through the dark valley, hard and dry.
At times I hear the mourning thunder:
And voices, in the shadows, talking.

Dear, are there dreams among the dead:
Or is it all a perfect slumber?
But I must dream and dream to madness.
Mine eyes are dark, now yours are fled:
Yet see they sorrows without number,
Waiting upon one perfect sadness.

So long, the melancholy vale!
So full, these weary winds, of sorrow!
So harsh, all things!   For what counts pity?
Still, as each twilight glimmers pale
Upon the borders of each morrow,
I near me to your sleeping city.

GLORIES

Roses from Pæstan rosaries!
More goodly red and white was she:
Her red and white were harmonies,
Not matched upon a Pæstan tree.

1195

Ivories blaunched in Alban air!
She lies more purely blaunched than you:
No Alban whiteness doth she wear,
But death's perfection of that hue.

Nay! now the rivalry is done,
Of red, and white, and whiter still:
She hath a glory from that sun,
Who falls not from Olympus hill.

BY THE STATUE OF KING CHARLES AT CHARING CROSS

TO WILLIAM WATSON

Sombre and rich, the skies;
   Great glooms, and starry plains.
Gently the night wind sighs;
   Else a vast silence reigns.

The splendid silence clings
   Around me: and around
The saddest of all kings
   Crowned, and again discrowned.

Comely and calm, he rides
   Hard by his own Whitehall:
Only the night wind glides:
   No crowds, nor rebels, brawl.

Gone, too, his Court: and yet,
   The stars his courtiers are:
Stars in their stations set;
   And every wandering star.

Alone he rides, alone,
   The fair and fatal king:
Dark night is all his own,
   That strange and solemn thing.

Which are more full of fate·
  The stars; or those sad eyes?
Which are more still and great:
  Those brows; or the dark skies?

Although his whole heart yearn
  In passionate tragedy:
Never was face so stern
  With sweet austerity.

Vanquished in life, his death
  By beauty made amends:
The passing of his breath
  Won his defeated ends.

Brief life, and hapless? Nay:
  Through death, life grew sublime.
Speak after sentence? Yea:
  And to the end of time.

Armoured he rides, his head
  Bare to the stars of doom:
He triumphs now, the dead,
  Beholding London's gloom.

Our wearier spirit faints,
  Vexed in the world's employ:
His soul was of the saints;
  And art to him was joy.

King, tried in fires of woe!
  Men hunger for thy grace:
And through the night I go,
  Loving thy mournful face.

Yet, when the city sleeps;
  When all the cries are still:
The stars and heavenly deeps
  Work out a perfect will.

1197

Ernest Dowson

THEY ARE NOT LONG

They are not long, the weeping and the laughter,
  Love and desire and hate:
I think they have no portion in us after
  We pass the gate.

They are not long, the days of wine and roses:
  Out of a misty dream
Our path emerges for awhile, then closes
  Within a dream.

IN TEMPORE SENECTUTIS

When I am old,
  And sadly steal apart,
Into the dark and cold,
  Friend of my heart!
Remember, if you can,
Not him who lingers, but that other man,
Who loved and sang, and had a beating heart,—
  When I am old!

When I am old,
  And all Love's ancient fire
Be tremulous and cold:
  My soul's desire!
Remember, if you may,
Nothing of you and me but yesterday,
When heart on heart we bid the years conspire
  To make us old.

When I am old,
  And every star above
Be pitiless and cold:
  My life's one love!
Forbid me not to go:
Remember nought of us but long ago,
And not at last, how love and pity strove
  When I grew old!

1198

ERNEST DOWSON

NON SUM QUALIS ERAM BONÆ SUB REGNO CYNARÆ

Last night, ah, yesternight, betwixt her lips and mine
There fell thy shadow, Cynara! thy breath was shed
Upon my soul between the kisses and the wine;
And I was desolate and sick of an old passion,
   Yea, I was desolate and bowed my head:
I have been faithful to thee, Cynara! in my fashion.

All night upon mine heart I felt her warm heart beat,
Night-long within mine arms in love and sleep she lay;
Surely the kisses of her bought red mouth were sweet;
But I was desolate and sick of an old passion,
   When I awoke and found the dawn was grey:
I have been faithful to thee, Cynara! in my fashion.

I have forgot much, Cynara! gone with the wind,
Flung roses, roses riotously with the throng,
Dancing, to put thy pale, lost lilies out of mind;
But I was desolate and sick of an old passion,
   Yea, all the time, because the dance was long:
I have been faithful to thee, Cynara! in my fashion.

I cried for madder music and for stronger wine,
But when the feast is finished and the lamps expire,
Then falls thy shadow, Cynara! the night is thine;
And I am desolate and sick of an old passion,
   Yea, hungry for the lips of my desire:
I have been faithful to thee, Cynara! in my fashion.

VAIN RESOLVES

I said: "There is an end of my desire:
   Now have I sown, and I have harvested,
And these are ashes of an ancient fire,
   Which, verily, shall not be quickened.
Now will I take me to a place of peace,
    Forget mine heart's desire;
In solitude and prayer, work out my soul's release.

"I shall forget her eyes, how cold they were;
   Forget her voice, how soft it was and low,
With all my singing that she did not hear,
   And all my service that she did not know.
I shall not hold the merest memory
      Of any days that were,
Within those solitudes where I will fasten me."

And once she passed, and once she raised her eyes,
   And smiled for courtesy, and nothing said:
And suddenly the old flame did uprise,
   And all my dead desire was quickened.
Yea! as it hath been, it shall ever be,
      Most passionless, pure eyes!
Which never shall grow soft, nor change, nor pity me.

George William Russell

A DREAM OF DEFEATED BEAUTY

All day they played in gardens hid amid golden towers
That made the blue burn deeper above their world of flowers.
Within their flaring gardens the pools drank in the sky
And the light shining figures that flamed or fluttered by.
There lute or harp string sounded from noon to eventide,
And every voice that murmured a mirror was to pride.
All day on play and music the young queen feasted deep:
Her happy heart foretelling of night and love and sleep,
When he unto whose glory the earth made sacrifice
Would give all to make richer the dark of lovely eyes.
Within her palace chamber the purple slumbrous shade
At midnight slowly lightened where the young queen was
      laid;
And moonlight marbled over flower foam and jewel sheen,
And carved in pearl and mystery the white limbs of the
      queen.
The young queen smiled in slumber as if in dream she knew
What dragons chained lay sleeping; what horns for battle
      blew;

1200

And who would bow the genii from thrones of blinding fire
To send their airy children to dance at her desire.
The young queen paled in slumber as if she there had known
Some majesty unbending on some unconquered throne.
Where had she soared in slumber? And who was this who
    came
Making the dusk all starry with plumes of magic flame?
Who mourned in lofty sorrow above the body's pride,
"This Babylon that I have built" and bowed its head and
    sighed.

CARROWMORE

It's a lonely road through bogland to the lake at Carrowmore,
And a sleeper there lies dreaming where the water laps the
    shore;
Though the moth-wings of the twilight in their purples are
    unfurled,
Yet his sleep is filled with music by the masters of the world.

There's a hand is white as silver that is fondling with his hair:
There are glimmering feet of sunshine that are dancing by
    him there:
And half-open lips of faery that were dyed a faery red
In their revels where the Hazel Tree its holy clusters shed.

"Come away," the red lips whisper, "all the world is weary
    now;
'Tis the twilight of the ages and it's time to quit the plough,
Oh, the very sunlight's weary ere it lightens up the dew,
And its gold is changed and faded before it falls to you.

"Though your colleen's heart be tender, a tenderer heart is
    near.
What's the starlight in her glances when the stars are shining
    clear?
Who would kiss the fading shadow when the flower-face
    glows above?
'Tis the beauty of all Beauty that is calling for your love."

Oh! the great gates of the mountain have opened once again,
And the sound of song and dancing falls upon the ears of
    men,
And the Land of Youth lies gleaming, flushed with rainbow
    light and mirth,
And the old enchantment lingers in the honey-heart of earth.

THE TWILIGHT OF EARTH

The wonder of the world is o'er:
    The magic from the sea is gone:
There is no unimagined shore,
    No islet yet to venture on.
The Sacred Hazels' blooms are shed,
The Nuts of Knowledge harvested.

Oh, what is worth this lore of age
    If time shall never bring us back
Our battle with the gods to wage,
    Reeling along the starry track.
The battle rapture here goes by
In warring upon things that die.

Let be the tale of him whose love
    Was sighed between white Deirdre's breasts,
It will not lift the heart above
    The sodden clay on which it rests.
Love once had power the gods to bring
All rapt on its wild wandering.

We shiver in the falling dew,
    And seek a shelter from the storm:
When man these elder brothers knew
    He found the mother nature warm,
A hearth fire blazing through it all,
A home without a circling wall.

We dwindle down beneath the skies,
    And from ourselves we pass away;
The paradise of memories
    Grows ever fainter day by day.

1202

ARTHUR WILLIS COLTON

The shepherd stars have shrunk within,
The world's great night will soon begin.

Will no one, ere it is too late,
    Ere fades the last memorial gleam,
Recall for us our earlier state?
    For nothing but so vast a dream
That it would scale the steeps of air
Could rouse us from so vast despair.

The power is ours to make or mar
    Our fate as on the earliest morn,
The Darkness and the Radiance are
    Creatures within the spirit born.
Yet, bathed in gloom too long, we might
Forget how we imagined light.

Not yet are fixed the prison bars;
    The hidden light the spirit owns
If blown to flame would dim the stars
    And they who rule them from their thrones:
And the proud sceptred spirits thence
Would bow to pay us reverence.

Oh, while the glory sinks within
    Let us not wait on earth behind,
But follow where it flies, and win
    The glow again, and we may find
Beyond the Gateways of the Day
Dominion and ancestral sway.

Arthur Willis Colton

SOMETIME IT MAY BE

Sometime it may be you and I
In that deserted yard shall lie
Where memories fade away;
Caring no more for our old dreams,
Busy with new and alien themes,
The saints and sages say.

1203

But let our graves be side by side,
So passers-by at even-tide
May pause a moment's space:
"Ah, they were lovers who lie here!
Else why these low graves laid so near,
In this forgotten place?"

Stephen Phillips

TO A LOST LOVE

I cannot look upon thy grave,
    Though there the rose is sweet:
Better to hear the long wave wash
    These wastes about my feet!

Shall I take comfort? Dost thou live
    A spirit, though afar,
With a deep hush about thee, like
    The stillness round a star?

Oh, thou art cold! In that high sphere
    Thou art a thing apart,
Losing in saner happiness
    This madness of the heart.

And yet, at times, thou still shalt feel
    A passing breath, a pain;
Disturb'd, as though a door in heaven
    Had oped and closed again.

And thou shalt shiver, while the hymns,
    The solemn hymns shall cease;
A moment half remember me:
    Then turn away to peace.

But oh, for evermore thy look,
    Thy laugh, thy charm, thy tone,
Thy sweet and wayward earthliness,
    Dear trivial things, are gone!

Therefore I look not on thy grave,
　　Though there the rose is sweet;
But rather hear the loud wave wash
　　These wastes about my feet.

Laurence Binyon

NOTHING IS ENOUGH

Nothing is enough!
No, though our all be spent—
Heart's extremest love,
Spirit's whole intent,
All that nerve can feel,
All that brain invent,—
Still beyond appeal
Will Divine Desire
Yet more excellent
Precious cost require
Of this mortal stuff,—
Never be content
Till ourselves be fire.
Nothing is enough.

THINKING OF SHORES

Thinking of shores that I shall never see,
And things that I would know but am forbid
By Time and briefness, treasuries locked from me
In unknown tongue or human bosom hid,

Knowing how unsure is all my knowledge, doled
To sloven memory and to cheated sense,
And to what majesty of stars I hold
My little candle of experience,—

In the vast night, in the untravelled night,
I sigh and seek. And there is answer none,
But in the silence that sure pressure slight
Of your heart beating close beside my own.

O Love, Love, where in you is any bound?
Fool I to seek, who have infinitely found.

TO WOMEN

Your hearts are lifted up, your hearts
That have foreknown the utter price,
Your hearts burn upward like a flame
Of splendour and of sacrifice.

For you, you too, to battle go,
Not with the marching drums and cheers,
But in the watch of solitude
And through the boundless night of fears.

Swift, swifter than those hawks of war,
Those threatening wings that pulse the air,
Far as the vanward ranks are set
You are gone before them, you are there!

And not a shot comes blind with death
And not a stab of steel is pressed
Home, but invisibly it tore
And entered first a woman's breast.

Amid the thunder of the guns,
The lightnings of the lance and sword,
Your hope, your dread, your throbbing pride,
Your infinite passion is outpoured.

From hearts that are as one high heart
Withholding nought from doom and bale,
Burningly offered up,—to bleed,
To bear, to break, but not to fail!

SONG

For Mercy, Courage, Kindness, Mirth,
There is no measure upon earth.
Nay, they wither, root and stem,
If an end be set to them.

Overbrim and overflow,
　　If your own heart you would know;
For the spirit born to bless
　　Lives but in its own excess.

George Sterling

MIRAGE

I well remember that the year was old—
　　A time of fallen leaves and wings departing.
　　Beside our western sea the grass was starting,
And willow buds were eager to unfold.

But all that day the shadowed paths were wet,
　　As tho in cloud had come the waiting vision,
　　And on the sunset altars of transition
Awhile that mournfulness and beauty met.

Long gone the night that held my deathless dream—
　　Its vanished rain long given to the roses;
　　But tho I sleep, no other night discloses
The Three who shone by that delaying Stream.

One was called Evening for her slow caress,
　　And one called Peace because her eyes were tender,
　　(Softly she came, most innocent and slender),
And one called Heart-ache for her loveliness.

They were of slumber and mirage's sky—
　　Frailties of vision, an august illusion,
　　Living a little by the soul's inclusion,
Living in memory as long as I.

Yet did they make the burning stars seem clods—
　　Those shadows of illusion, passing slowly;
　　For on each face a Light fell sad and holy
From tracts I dreamt forbidden save to gods.

A little while, a little while they gleamed,
   Who were not, are not, yet shall haunt me ever,
   Mingling the sorrow of the Once and Never,
To glorify the dream of him that dreamed.

I shall not know them other than they are,
   Who find on paths that memory retraces
   The immortal, mournful beauty of those faces
That haunting, hold me exile of their star.

THE LOST NYMPH

Now whither hast thou flown?
   In what retreat art hid?——
Where falling waters moan
   In shadow, or amid
The rushes of the river, pebble-sown?

'Twas but a breath ago
   I held thy captive hands.
Clearly thy footprints show
   Along the final sands.
Almost I hear thy voice, divinely low.

I do but know thy feet
   Have gone from me—not why.
I do but know them fleet
   As clouds upon the sky.
Ah! gone so soon, whom love hath found so sweet!

Thy loveliness made sure
   Thou wouldst be fled ere long.
No beauty shall endure
   Beyond its shrining song—
However close, however strange and pure.

Afar thy pathway leads,
   Yet will I follow fast,
Hoping, tho day recedes,
   To find thy home at last
And silver of thee 'mid the golden reeds.

GEORGE STERLING

THE MASTER-MARINER

My grandsire sailed three years from home,
  And slew unmoved the sounding whale:
Here on a windless beach I roam
  And watch far out the hardy sail.

The lions of the surf that cry
  Upon this lion-colored shore
On reefs of midnight met his eye:
  He knew their fangs as I their roar.

My grandsire sailed uncharted seas,
  And toll of all their leagues he took:
I scan the shallow bays at ease,
  And tell their colors in a book.

The anchor-chains his music made
  And wind in shrouds and running-gear:
The thrush at dawn beguiles my glade,
  And once, 'tis said, I woke to hear.

My grandsire in his ample fist
  The long harpoon upheld to men:
Behold obedient to my wrist
  A grey gull's-feather for my pen!

Upon my grandsire's leathern cheek
  Five zones their bitter bronze had set:
Some day their hazards I will seek,
  I promise me at times.   Not yet.

I think my grandsire now would turn
  A mild but speculative eye
On me, my pen and its concern,
  Then gaze again to sea—and sigh.

SPRING IN CARMEL

O'er Carmel fields in the springtime the sea-gulls follow the
    plow.
White, white wings on the blue above!
White were your brow and breast, O Love!
   But I cannot see you now.
Tireless ever the Mission swallow
Dips to meadow and poppied hollow;
Well for her mate that he can follow,
   As the buds are on the bough.

By the woods and waters of Carmel the lark is glad in the
       sun.
Harrow! harrow! music of God!
Near to your nest her feet have trod,
   Whose journeyings are done.
Sing, O lover! I cannot sing.
Wild and sad are the thoughts you bring.
Well for you are the skies of spring,
   And to me all skies are one.

In the beautiful woods of Carmel an iris bends to the wind.
O thou far-off and sorrowful flower!
Rose that I found in a tragic hour!
   Rose that I shall not find!
Petals that fell so soft and slowly,
Fragrant snows on the grasses lowly,
Gathered now would I call you holy
   Ever to eyes once blind.

In the pine-sweet valley of Carmel the cream-cups scatter in
    foam.
Azures of early lupin there!
Now the wild lilac floods the air
   Like a broken honey-comb.
So could the flowers of Paradise
Pour their souls to the morning skies;
So like a ghost your fragrance lies
   On the path that once led home.

1210

GEORGE STERLING

On the emerald hills of Carmel the spring and winter have
     met.
Here I find in a gentled spot
The frost of the wild forget-me-not,
   And—I cannot forget.
Heart once light as the floating feather
Borne aloft in the sunny weather,
Spring and winter have come together—
   Shall you and she meet yet?

On the rocks and beaches of Carmel the surf is mighty to-day.
Breaker and lifting billow call
To the high, blue Silence over all
   With the word no heart can say.
Time-to-be, shall I hear it ever?
Time-that-is, with the hands that sever,
Cry all words but the dreadful "Never!"
   And name of her far away!

THE LAST DAYS

The russet leaves of the sycamore
Lie at last on the valley floor—
By the autumn wind swept to and fro
Like ghosts in a tale of long ago.
Shallow and clear the Carmel glides
Where the willows droop on its vine-walled sides.

The bracken-rust is red on the hill;
The pines stand brooding, somber and still;
Grey are the cliffs, and the waters grey,
Where the seagulls dip to the sea-born spray.
Sad November, lady of rain,
Sends the goose-wedge over again.

Wilder now, for the verdure's birth,
Falls the sunlight over the earth;
Killdees call from the fields where now
The banding blackbirds follow the plow;
Rustling poplar and brittle weed
Whisper low to the river-reed.

Days departing linger and sigh;
Stars come soon to the quiet sky;
Buried voices, intimate, strange,
Cry to body and soul of Change;
Beauty, eternal fugitive,
Seeks the home that we cannot give.

OMNIA EXEUNT IN MYSTERIUM

I

The stranger in my gates—lo! that am I,
And what my land of birth I do not know,
Nor yet the hidden land to which I go.
One may be lord of many ere he die,
And tell of many sorrows in one sigh,
But know himself he shall not, nor his woe,
Nor to what sea the tears of wisdom flow,
Nor why one star is taken from the sky.

An urging is upon him evermore,
And tho he bide, his soul is wanderer,
Scanning the shadows with a sense of haste
Where fade the tracks of all who went before—
A dim and solitary traveller
On ways that end in evening and the waste.

II

How dumb the vanished billions who have died!
With backward gaze conjectural we wait,
And ere the invading Shadow penetrate,
The echo from a mighty heart that cried
Is made a sole memorial to pride.
From out that night's inscrutable estate,
A few cold voices wander, desolate
With all that love has lost or grief has sighed.

EDWIN ARLINGTON ROBINSON

Slaves, seamen, captains, councillors and kings,
  Gone utterly, save for those echoes far!
    As they before, I tread a forfeit land,
Till the supreme and ancient silence flings
  Its pall between the dreamer and the star.
    O desert wide! O little grain of sand!

THE BLACK VULTURE

Aloof within the day's enormous dome,
  He holds unshared the silence of the sky.
  Far down his bleak, relentless eyes descry
The eagle's empire and the falcon's home—
Far down, the galleons of sunset roam;
  His hazards on the sea of morning lie;
  Serene, he hears the broken tempest sigh
Where cold sierras gleam like scattered foam.

And least of all he holds the human swarm—
  Unwitting now that envious men prepare
    To make their dream and its fulfillment one,
When, poised above the caldrons of the storm,
  Their hearts, contemptuous of death, shall dare
    His roads between the thunder and the sun.

Edwin Arlington Robinson

FLAMMONDE

The man Flammonde, from God knows where,
With firm address and foreign air,
With news of nations in his talk
And something royal in his walk,
With glint of iron in his eyes,
But never doubt, nor yet surprise,
Appeared, and stayed, and held his head
As one by kings accredited.

1213

Erect, with his alert repose
About him, and about his clothes,
He pictured all tradition hears
Of what we owe to fifty years.
His cleansing heritage of taste
Paraded neither want nor waste;
And what he needed for his fee
To live, he borrowed graciously.

He never told us what he was,
Or what mischance, or other cause,
Had banished him from better days
To play the Prince of Castaways.
Meanwhile he played surpassing well
A part, for most, unplayable;
In fine, one pauses, half afraid
To say for certain that he played.

For that, one may as well forego
Conviction as to yes or no;
Nor can I say just how intense
Would then have been the difference
To several, who, having striven
In vain to get what he was given,
Would see the stranger taken on
By friends not easy to be won.

Moreover, many a malcontent
He soothed and found munificent;
His courtesy beguiled and foiled
Suspicion that his years were soiled;
His mien distinguished any crowd,
His credit strengthened when he bowed;
And women, young and old, were fond
Of looking at the man Flammonde.

There was a woman in our town
On whom the fashion was to frown;
But while our talk renewed the tinge
Of a long-faded scarlet fringe,

1214

The man Flammonde saw none of that,
And what he saw we wondered at—
That none of us, in her distress,
Could hide or find our littleness.

There was a boy that all agreed
Had shut within him the rare seed
Of learning. We could understand,
But none of us could lift a hand.
The man Flammonde appraised the youth,
And told a few of us the truth;
And thereby, for a little gold,
A flowered future was unrolled.

There were two citizens who fought
For years and years, and over nought;
They made life awkward for their friends,
And shortened their own dividends.
The man Flammonde said what was wrong
Should be made right, nor was it long
Before they were again in line,
And had each other in to dine.

And these I mention are but four
Of many out of many more.
So much for them. But what of him—
So firm in every look and limb?
What small satanic sort of kink
Was in his brain? What broken link
Withheld him from the destinies
That came so near to being his?

What was he, when we came to sift
His meaning, and to note the drift
Of incommunicable ways
That make us ponder while we praise?
Why was it that his charm revealed
Somehow the surface of a shield?
What was it that we never caught?
What was he, and what was he not?

How much it was of him we met
We cannot ever know; nor yet
Shall all he gave us quite atone
For what was his, and his alone;
Nor need we now, since he knew best,
Nourish an ethical unrest:
Rarely at once will nature give
The power to be Flammonde and live.

We cannot know how much we learn
From those who never will return,
Until a flash of unforeseen
Remembrance falls on what has been.
We've each a darkening hill to climb;
And this is why, from time to time
In Tilbury Town, we look beyond
Horizons for the man Flammonde.

THE GIFT OF GOD

Blessed with a joy that only she
Of all alive shall ever know,
She wears a proud humility
For what it was that willed it so,—
That her degree should be so great
Among the favored of the Lord
That she may scarcely bear the weight
Of her bewildering reward.

As one apart, immune, alone,
Or featured for the shining ones,
And like to none that she has known
Of other women's other sons,—
The firm fruition of her need,
He shines anointed; and he blurs
Her vision, till it seems indeed
A sacrilege to call him hers.

She fears a little for so much
Of what is best, and hardly dares
To think of him as one to touch
With aches, indignities, and cares;

1216

She sees him rather at the goal,
Still shining; and her dream foretells
The proper shining of a soul
Where nothing ordinary dwells.

Perchance a canvass of the town
Would find him far from flags and shouts,
And leave him only the renown
Of many smiles and many doubts;
Perchance the crude and common tongue
Would havoc strangely with his worth;
But she, with innocence unwrung,
Would read his name around the earth.

And others, knowing how this youth
Would shine, if love could make him great,
When caught and tortured for the truth
Would only writhe and hesitate;
While she, arranging for his days
What centuries could not fulfill,
Transmutes him with her faith and praise,
And has him shining where she will.

She crowns him with her gratefulness,
And says again that life is good;
And should the gift of God be less
In him than in her motherhood,
His fame, though vague, will not be small,
As upward through her dream he fares,
Half clouded with a crimson fall
Of roses thrown on marble stairs.

THE MASTER

LINCOLN

A flying word from here and there
Had sown the name at which we sneered,
But soon the name was everywhere,
To be reviled and then revered:

A presence to be loved and feared,
We cannot hide it, or deny
That we, the gentlemen who jeered,
May be forgotten by and by.

He came when days were perilous
And hearts of men were sore beguiled;
And having made his note of us,
He pondered and was reconciled.
Was ever master yet so mild
As he, and so untamable?
We doubted, even when he smiled,
Not knowing what he knew so well.

He knew that undeceiving fate
Would shame us whom he served unsought;
He knew that he must wince and wait—
The jest of those for whom he fought;
He knew devoutly what he thought
Of us and of our ridicule;
He knew that we must all be taught
Like little children in a school.

We gave a glamour to the task
That he encountered and saw through,
But little of us did he ask,
And little did we ever do.
And what appears if we review
The season when we railed and chaffed?
It is the face of one who knew
That we were learning while we laughed.

The face that in our vision feels
Again the venom that we flung,
Transfigured to the world reveals
The vigilance to which we clung.
Shrewd, hallowed, harassed, and among
The mysteries that are untold,
The face we see was never young
Nor could it wholly have been old.

For he, to whom we had applied
Our shopman's test of age and worth,
Was elemental when he died,
As he was ancient at his birth:
The saddest among kings of earth,
Bowed with a galling crown, this man
Met rancor with a cryptic mirth,
Laconic—and Olympian.

The love, the grandeur, and the fame
Are bounded by the world alone;
The calm, the smouldering, and the flame
Of awful patience were his own:
With him they are forever flown
Past all our fond self-shadowings,
Wherewith we cumber the Unknown
As with inept, Icarian wings.

For we were not as other men:
'Twas ours to soar and his to see;
But we are coming down again,
And we shall come down pleasantly,
Nor shall we longer disagree
On what it is to be sublime,
But flourish in our perigee
And have one Titan at a time.

Frederic Lawrence Knowles

TO MOTHER NATURE

Nature, in thy largess, grant
I may be thy confidant!
Taste who will life's roadside cheer
(Though my heart doth hold it dear—
Song and wine and trees and grass,
All the joys that flash and pass),
I must put within my prayer
Gifts more intimate and rare.

1219

Show me how dry branches throw
Such blue shadows on the snow,—
Tell me how the wind can fare
On his unseen feet of air,—
Show me how the spider's loom
Weaves the fabric from her womb,—
Lead me to those brooks of morn
Where a woman's laugh is born,—
Let me taste the sap that flows
Through the blushes of a rose,
Yea, and drain the blood which runs
From the heart of dying suns,—
Teach me how the butterfly
Guessed at immortality,—
Let me follow up the track
Of Love's deathless Zodiac
Where Joy climbs among the spheres
Circled by her moon of tears,—
Tell me how, when I forget
All the schools have taught me, yet
I recall each trivial thing
In a golden, far-off Spring,—
Give me whispered hints how I
May instruct my heart to fly
Where the baffling Vision gleams
Till I overtake my dreams,
And the impossible be done
When the Wish and Deed grow one!

LOVE TRIUMPHANT

Helen's lips are drifting dust;
Ilion is consumed with rust;
All the galleons of Greece
Drink the ocean's dreamless peace;
Lost was Solomon's purple show
Restless centuries ago;
Stately empires wax and wane—
Babylon, Barbary, and Spain:—

Only one thing, undefaced,
Lasts, though all the worlds lie waste
And the heavens are overturned.
Dear, how long ago we learned!

There's a sight that blinds the sun,
Sound that lives when sounds are done,
Music that rebukes the birds,
Language lovelier than words,
Hue and scent that shame the rose,
Wine no earthly vineyard knows,
Silence stiller than the shore
Swept by Charon's stealthy oar,
Ocean more divinely free
Than Pacific's boundless sea,—
Ye who love have learned it true.
Dear, how long ago we knew!

NATURE: THE ARTIST

Such hints as untaught Nature yields!—
    The calm disorder of the sea,
The straggling splendor of the fields,
    The wind's gay incivility.

O workman with your conscious plan,
    Compass and square are little worth;
Copy (nay, only poets can)
    The artless masonry of earth.

Go watch the windy spring's carouse,
    And mark the winter wonders grow,—
The graceful gracelessness of boughs,
    The careless carpentry of snow!

LAUS MORTIS

Nay, why should I fear Death,
Who gives us life, and in exchange takes breath?

1221

He is like cordial Spring
That lifts above the soil each buried thing;—

Like Autumn, kind and brief—
The frost that chills the branches frees the leaf;—

Like Winter's stormy hours
That spread their fleece of snow to save the flowers.

The lordliest of all things,—
Life lends us only feet, Death gives us wings!

Fearing no covert thrust,
Let me walk onward, armed with valiant trust,

Dreading no unseen knife,
Across Death's threshold step from life to life!

O all ye frightened folk,
Whether ye wear a crown or bear a yoke,

Laid in one equal bed,
When once your coverlet of grass is spread,

What daybreak need you fear?
The Love will rule you there which guides you here!

Where Life, the Sower, stands,
Scattering the ages from his swinging hand

Thou waitest, Reaper lone,
Until the multitudinous grain hath grown;

Scythe-bearer, when thy blade
Harvests my flesh, let me be unafraid!

God's husbandman thou art!—
In His unwithering sheaves, O bind my heart!

1222

William Henry Davies

LEISURE

What is this life if, full of care,
We have no time to stand and stare.

No time to stand beneath the boughs
And stare as long as sheep or cows.

No time to see, when woods we pass,
Where squirrels hide their nuts in grass.

No time to see, in broad daylight,
Streams full of stars, like skies at night.

No time to turn at Beauty's glance,
And watch her feet, how they can dance.

No time to wait till her mouth can
Enrich that smile her eyes began.

A poor life this if, full of care,
We have no time to stand and stare.

THE KINGFISHER

It was the Rainbow gave thee birth,
    And left thee all her lovely Hues;
And, as her mother's name was Tears,
    So runs it in thy blood to choose
For haunts the lonely pools, and keep
In company with trees that weep.

Go you and, with such glorious hues,
    Live with proud Peacocks in green parks;
On lawns as smooth as shining glass,
    Let every feather show its marks;
Get thee on boughs and clap thy wings
Before the windows of proud kings.

1223

Nay, lovely Bird, thou art not vain;
    Thou hast no proud ambitious mind;
I also love a quiet place
    That's green, away from all mankind;
A lonely pool, and let a tree
Sigh with her bosom over me.

SWEET STAY-AT-HOME

Sweet Stay-at-Home, sweet Well-content,
Thou knowest of no strange continent:
Thou hast not felt thy bosom keep
A gentle motion with the deep;
Thou hast not sailed in Indian seas,
Where scent comes forth in every breeze.
Thou hast not seen the rich grape grow
For miles, as far as eyes can go;
Thou hast not seen a summer's night
When maids could sew by a worm's light;
Nor the North Sea in spring send out
Bright hues that like birds flit about
In solid cages of white ice—
Sweet Stay-at-Home, sweet Love-one-place.
Thou hast not seen black fingers pick
White cotton when the bloom is thick,
Nor heard black throats in harmony;
Nor hast thou sat on stones that lie
Flat on the earth, that once did rise
To hide proud kings from common eyes.
Thou hast not seen plains full of bloom
Where green things had such little room
They pleased the eye like fairer flowers—
Sweet Stay-at-Home, all these long hours.
Sweet Well-content, sweet Love-one-place,
Sweet, simple maid, bless thy dear face;
For thou hast made more homely stuff
Nurture thy gentle self enough;
I love thee for a heart that's kind—
Not for the knowledge in thy mind.

1224

WILLIAM HENRY DAVIES

THE TWO CHILDREN

"Ah, little boy! I see
    You have a wooden spade.
Into this sand you dig
    So deep—for what?" I said.
"There's more rich gold," said he,
    "Down under where I stand,
Than twenty elephants
    Could move across the land."

"Ah, little girl with wool!—
    What are you making now?"
"Some stockings for a bird,
    To keep his legs from snow."
And there those children are,
    So happy, small, and proud:
The boy that digs his grave,
    The girl that knits her shroud.

EARLY SPRING

How sweet this morning air in spring,
    When tender is the grass and wet!
I see some little leaves have not
    Outgrown their curly childhood yet;
And cows no longer hurry home,
However sweet a voice cries "Come."

Here, with green Nature all around,
    While that fine bird the skylark sings;
Who now in such a passion is,
    He flies by it, and not his wings;
And many a blackbird, thrush, and sparrow,
Sing sweeter songs than I may borrow.

These watery swamps and thickets wild—
    Called Nature's slums—to me are more
Than any courts where fountains play,
    And men-at-arms guard every door:

For I could sit down here alone,
And count the oak-trees one by one.

THE MOON

Thy beauty haunts me heart and soul,
  O thou fair Moon, so close and bright;
Thy beauty makes me like the child,
  That cries aloud to own thy light:
The little child that lifts each arm
To press thee to her bosom warm.

Though there are birds that sing this night
  With thy white beams across their throats,
Let my deep silence speak for me
  More than for them their sweetest notes:
Who worships thee till music fails
Is greater than thy nightingales.

HAPPY WIND

Oh, happy wind, how sweet
  Thy life must be!
The great, proud fields of gold
  Run after thee:
And here are flowers, with heads
  To nod and shake;
And dreaming butterflies
  To tease and wake.
Oh, happy wind, I say,
To be alive this day.

A GREAT TIME

Sweet Chance, that led my steps abroad,
  Beyond the town, where wild flowers grow—
A rainbow and a cuckoo, Lord,
  How rich and great the times are now!

Know, all ye sheep
And cows, that keep
On staring that I stand so long
In grass that's wet from heavy rain—
A rainbow and a cuckoo's song
May never come together again;
May never come
This side the tomb.

THE EXAMPLE

Here's an example from
A Butterfly;
That on a rough, hard rock
Happy can lie;
Friendless and all alone
On this unsweetened stone.

Now let my bed be hard
No care take I;
I'll make my joy like this
Small Butterfly;
Whose happy heart has power
To make a stone a flower.

THUNDERSTORMS

My mind has thunderstorms,
That brood for heavy hours:
Until they rain me words,
My thoughts are drooping flowers
And sulking, silent birds.

Yet come, dark thunderstorms,
And brood your heavy hours;
For when you rain me words
My thoughts are dancing flowers
And joyful singing birds.

1227

A THOUGHT

When I look into a glass,
  Myself's my only care;
But I look into a pool
  For all the wonders there.

When I look into a glass,
  I see a fool:
But I see a wise man
  When I look into a pool.

Hilaire Belloc

DUNCTON HILL

He does not die that can bequeath
Some influence to the land he knows,
Or dares, persistent, interwreath
Love permanent with the wild hedgerows;
  He does not die, but still remains
  Substantiate with his darling plains.

The spring's superb adventure calls
His dust athwart the woods to flame;
His boundary river's secret falls
Perpetuate and repeat his name.
  He rides his loud October sky
  He does not die. He does not die.

The beeches know the accustomed head
Which loved them, and a peopled air
Beneath their benediction spread
Comforts the silence everywhere;
  For native ghosts return and these
  Perfect the mystery in the trees.

1228

So, therefore, though myself be crosst
The shuddering of that dreadful day
When friend and fire and home are lost,
And even children drawn away—
   The passer-by shall hear me still
   A boy that sings on Duncton Hill.

THE SOUTH COUNTRY

When I am living in the Midlands,
   That are sodden and unkind,
I light my lamp in the evening;
   My work is left behind;
And the great hills of the South Country
   Come back into my mind.

The great hills of the South Country
   They stand along the sea,
And it's there, walking in the high woods,
   That I could wish to be,
And the men that were boys when I was a boy
   Walking along with me.

The men that live in North England
   I saw them for a day:
Their hearts are set upon the waste fells,
   Their skies are fast and grey;
From their castle-walls a man may see
   The mountains far away.

The men that live in West England
   They see the Severn strong,
A-rolling on rough water brown
   Light aspen leaves along.
They have the secret of the Rocks
   And the oldest king of song.

But the men that live in the South Country
   Are the kindest and most wise,
They get their laughter from the loud surf,
   And the faith in their happy eyes

Comes surely from our Sister the Spring
    When over the sea she flies;
The violets suddenly bloom at her feet,
    She blesses us with surprise.

I never get between the pines
    But I smell the Sussex air;
Nor I never come on a belt of sand
    But my home is there.
And along the sky the line of the Downs
    So noble and so bare.

A lost thing could I never find,
    Nor a broken thing mend;
And I fear I shall be all alone
    When I get towards the end.
Who will there be to comfort me
    Or who will be my friend?

I will gather and carefully make my friends
    Of the men of the Sussex Weald;
They watch the stars from silent folds,
    They stiffly plough the field.
By them and the God of the South Country
    My poor soul shall be healed.

If I ever become a rich man,
    Or if ever I grow to be old,
I will build a house with deep thatch
    To shelter me from the cold,
And there shall the Sussex songs be sung
    And the story of Sussex told.

I will hold my house in the high wood,
    Within a walk of the sea,
And the men that were boys when I was a boy
    Shall sit and drink with me.

HILAIRE BELLOC

TO THE BALLIOL MEN STILL IN AFRICA

Years ago when I was at Balliol,
  Balliol men—and I was one—
Swam together in winter rivers,
  Wrestled together under the sun.
And still in the heart of us, Balliol, Balliol,
  Loved already, but hardly known,
Welded us each of us into the others:
  Called a levy and chose her own.

Here is a House that armours a man
  With the eyes of a boy and the heart of a ranger,
And a laughing way in the teeth of the world
  And a holy hunger and thirst for danger:
Balliol made me, Balliol fed me,
  Whatever I had she gave me again:
And the best of Balliol loved and led me.
  God be with you, Balliol men.

I have said it before, and I say it again,
  There never was treason done, and a false word spoken,
And England under the dregs of men,
  And bribes about, and a treaty broken:
But angry, lonely, hating it still,
  I wished to be there in spite of the wrong.
My heart was heavy for Cumnor Hill
  And the hammer of galloping all day long.

Galloping outward into the weather,
  Hands a-ready and battle in all:
Words together and wine together
  And song together in Balliol Hall.
Rare and single! Noble and few! . . .
  Oh! they have wasted you over the sea!
The only brothers ever I knew,
  The men that laughed and quarrelled with me.

    .   .   .   .

Balliol made me, Balliol fed me,
Whatever I had she gave me again:
And the best of Balliol loved and led me,
God be with you, Balliol men.

SONG

INVITING THE INFLUENCE OF A YOUNG LADY UPON THE OPENING YEAR

You wear the morning like your dress
And are with mastery crowned;
Whenas you walk your loveliness
Goes shining all around.
Upon your secret, smiling way
Such new contents were found,
The Dancing Loves made holiday
On that delightful ground.

Then summon April forth, and send
Commandment through the flowers;
About our woods your grace extend
A queen of careless hours.
For oh, not Vera veiled in rain,
Nor Dian's sacred Ring,
With all her royal nymphs in train
Could so lead on the Spring.

Arthur Guiterman

THE IDOL-MAKER PRAYS

Great god whom I shall carve from this gray stone
Wherein thou liest, hid to all but me,
Grant thou that when my art hath made thee known
And others bow, I shall not worship thee.

1232

But, as I pray thee now, then let me pray
    Some greater god,—like thee to be conceived
Within my soul,—for strength to turn away
    From his new altar, when, that task achieved,
He, too, stands manifest. Yea, let me yearn
    From dream to grander dream! Let me not rest
Content at any goal! Still bid me spurn
    Each transient triumph on the Eternal Quest,
Abjuring godlings whom my hand hath made
For Deity, revealed, but unportrayed!

Frances Wells Shaw

WHO LOVES THE RAIN

Who loves the rain
And loves his home,
And looks on life with quiet eyes,
    Him will I follow through the storm;
    And at his hearth-fire keep me warm;
Nor hell nor heaven shall that soul surprise,
    Who loves the rain,
    And loves his home,
And looks on life with quiet eyes.

Ralph Hodgson

EVE

Eve, with her basket, was
Deep in the bells and grass,
Wading in bells and grass
Up to her knees,
Picking a dish of sweet
Berries and plums to eat,
Down in the bells and grass
Under the trees.

1233

Mute as a mouse in a
Corner the cobra lay,
Curled round a bough of the
Cinnamon tall. . . .
Now to get even and
Humble proud heaven and
Now was the moment or
Never at all.

"Eva!" Each syllable
Light as a flower fell,
"Eva!" he whispered the
Wondering maid,
Soft as a bubble sung
Out of a linnet's lung,
Soft and most silverly
"Eva!" he said.
Picture that orchard sprite,
Eve, with her body white,
Supple and smooth to her
Slim finger tips,
Wondering, listening,
Listening, wondering,
Eve with a berry
Half-way to her lips.

Oh, had our simple Eve
Seen through the make-believe!
Had she but known the
Pretender he was!
Out of the boughs he came,
Whispering still her name,
Tumbling in twenty rings
Into the grass.

Here was the strangest pair
In the world anywhere,
Eve in the bells and grass

Kneeling, and he
Telling his story low. . . .
Singing birds saw them go
Down the dark path to
The Blasphemous Tree.

Oh, what a clatter when
Titmous and Jenny Wren
Saw him successful and
Taking his leave!
How the birds rated him,
How they all hated him!
How they all pitied
Poor motherless Eve!

Picture her crying
Outside in the lane,
Eve, with no dish of sweet
Berries and plums to eat,
Haunting the gate of the
Orchard in vain. . . .
Picture the lewd delight
Under the hill to-night—
"Eva!" the toast goes round,
"Eva!" again.

Colonel John McCrae

IN FLANDERS FIELDS

In Flanders fields the poppies blow
Between the crosses, row on row,
   That mark our place; and in the sky
   The larks still bravely singing fly
Scarce heard amid the guns below.

We are the Dead. Short days ago
We lived, felt dawn, saw sunset glow,
   Loved and were loved, and now we lie
      In Flanders fields.

1235

Take up our quarrel with the foe!
To you from failing hands we throw
The torch—be yours to hold it high!
If ye break faith with us who die,
We shall not sleep, though poppies grow
In Flanders fields.

Cale Young Rice

WHEN THE WIND IS LOW

When the wind is low, and the sea is soft,
    And the far heat-lightning plays
On the rim of the west where dark clouds nest
    On a darker bank of haze;
When I lean o'er the rail with you that I love
    And gaze to my heart's content;
I know that the heavens are there above—
    But you are my firmament.

When the phosphor-stars are thrown from the bow
    And the watch climbs up the shroud;
When the dim mast dips as the vessel slips
    Through the foam that seethes aloud;
I know that the years of our life are few,
    And fain as a bird to flee,
That time is as brief as a drop of dew—
    But you are Eternity.

Ford Madox (Hueffer) Ford

FOOTSLOGGERS

TO C. F. G. M.

What is love of one's land? . . .
I don't know very well.
It is something that sleeps
For a year, for a day,

1236

FORD MADOX (HUEFFER) FORD

For a month—something that keeps
Very hidden and quiet and still,
And then takes
The quiet heart like a wave,
The quiet brain like a spell,
The quiet will
Like a tornado; and that shakes
The whole of the soul.

It is omnipotent like love;
It is deep and quiet as the grave,
And it awakes
Like a flame, like a madness,
Like the great passion of your life.
The cold keenness of a tempered knife,
The great gladness of a wedding day,
The austerity of monks who wake to pray
In the dim light,
Who pray
In the darkling grove:
All these and a great belief in what we deem the right
Creeping upon us like the overwhelming sand
Driven by a December gale,—
Make up the love of one's land.

.   .   .   .

L'ENVOI

What is love of one's land?
Ah, we know very well
It is something that sleeps for a year, for a day,
For a month; something that keeps
Very hidden and quiet and still,
And then takes
The quiet heart like a wave,
The quiet brain like a spell,
The quiet will
Like a tornado, and that shakes
The whole being and soul . . .
Aye, the whole of the soul.

1237

Walter de la Mare

THE MIRACLE

Who beckons the green ivy up
  Its solitary tower of stone?
What spirit lures the bindweed's cup
      Unfaltering on?
Calls even the starry lichen to climb
By agelong inches endless Time?

Who bids the hollyhock uplift
  Her rod of fast-sealed buds on high;
Fling wide her petals—silent, swift,
      Lovely to the sky?
Since as she kindled, so she will fade,
Flower above flower in squalor laid.

Ever the heavy billow rears
  All its sea-length in green, hushed wall;
But totters as the shore it nears,
      Foams to its fall;
Where was its mark? on what vain quest
Rose that great water from its rest?

So creeps ambition on; so climb
  Man's vaunting thoughts. He, set on high,
Forgets his birth, small space, brief time,
      That he shall die;
Dreams blindly in his dark, still air;
Consumes his strength; strips himself bare;

Rejects delight, ease, pleasure, hope,
  Seeking in vain, but seeking yet,
Past earthly promise, earthly scope,
      On one aim set:
As if, like Chaucer's child, he thought
All but "O Alma!" nought.

ALL THAT'S PAST

Very old are the woods;
    And the buds that break
Out of the brier's boughs,
    When March winds wake,
So old with their beauty are——
    Oh, no man knows
Through what wild centuries
    Roves back the rose.

Very old are the brooks;
    And the rills that rise
Where snow sleeps cold beneath
    The azure skies
Sing such a history
    Of come and gone,
Their every drop is as wise
    As Solomon.

Very old are we men;
    Our dreams are tales
Told in dim Eden
    By Eve's nightingales;
We wake and whisper awhile,
    But, the day gone by,
Silence and sleep like fields
    Of amaranth lie.

THE STRANGER

Half-hidden in a graveyard,
    In the blackness of a yew,
Where never living creature stirs,
    Nor sunbeam pierces through,

Is a tomb, green and crooked——
    Its faded legend gone——
With but one rain-worn cherub's head
    Of mouldering stone.

1239

There, when the dusk is falling,
  Silence broods so deep
It seems that every wind that breathes
  Blows from the field of sleep.

Day breaks in heedless beauty,
  Kindling each drop of dew,
But unforsaking shadow dwells
  Beneath this lonely yew.

And, all else lost and faded,
  Only this listening head
Keeps with a strange unanswering smile
  Its secret with the dead.

ARABIA

Far are the shades of Arabia,
  Where the Princes ride at noon,
'Mid the verdurous vales and thickets,
  Under the ghost of the moon;
And so dark is that vaulted purple
  Flowers in the forest rise
And toss into blossom 'gainst the phantom stars
  Pale in the noonday skies.

Sweet is the music of Arabia
  In my heart, when out of dreams
I still in the thin clear mirk of dawn
  Descry her gliding streams;
Hear her strange lutes on the green banks
  Ring loud with the grief and delight
Of the dim-silked dark-haired Musicians
  In the brooding silence of night.

They haunt me—her lutes and her forests;
  No beauty on earth I see
But shadowed with that dream recalls
  Her loveliness to me:

Still eyes look coldly upon me,
  Cold voices whisper and say—
"He is crazed with the spell of far Arabia,
  They have stolen his wits away."

THE LISTENERS

"Is there anybody there?" said the Traveller,
  Knocking on the moonlit door;
And his horse in the silence champed the grasses
  Of the forest's ferny floor:
And a bird flew up out of the turret,
  Above the Traveller's head:
And he smote upon the door again a second time;
  "Is there anybody there?" he said.
But no one descended to the Traveller;
  No head from the leaf-fringed sill
Leaned over and looked into his grey eyes,
  Where he stood perplexed and still.
But only a host of phantom listeners
  That dwelt in the lone house then
Stood listening in the quiet of the moonlight
  To that voice from the world of men:
Stood thronging the faint moonbeams on the dark stair,
  That goes down to the empty hall,
Hearkening in an air stirred and shaken
  By the lonely Traveller's call.
And he felt in his heart their strangeness,
  Their stillness answering his cry,
While his horse moved, cropping the dark turf,
  'Neath the starred and leafy sky;
For he suddenly smote on the door, even
  Louder, and lifted up his head:—
"Tell them I came, and no one answered,
  That I kept my word," he said.
Never the least stir made the listeners,
  Though every word he spake
Fell echoing through the shadowiness of the still house
  From the one man left awake:

Ay, they heard his foot upon the stirrup,
   And the sound of iron on stone,
And how the silence surged softly backward,
   When the plunging hoofs were gone.

AN EPITAPH

Here lies a most beautiful lady,
Light of step and heart was she;
I think she was the most beautiful lady
That ever was in the West Country.
But beauty vanishes; beauty passes;
However rare—rare it be;
And when I crumble, who will remember
This lady of the West Country?

THE LINNET

Upon this leafy bush
   With thorns and roses in it,
Flutters a thing of light,
   A twittering linnet.
And all the throbbing world
   Of dew and sun and air
By this small parcel of life
   Is made more fair;
As if each bramble-spray
And mounded gold-wreathed furze,
   Harebell and little thyme,
   Were only hers;
As if this beauty and grace
   Did to one bird belong,
And, at a flutter of wing,
   Might vanish in song.

THE SUNKEN GARDEN

Speak not—whisper not;
Here bloweth thyme and bergamot;

Softly on the evening hour,
Secret herbs their spices shower.
Dark-spiked rosemary and myrrh,
Lean-stalked, purple lavender;
Hides within her bosom, too,
All her sorrows, bitter rue.

Breathe not—trespass not;
Of this green and darkling spot,
Latticed from the moon's beams,
Perchance a distant dreamer dreams;
Perchance upon its darkening air,
The unseen ghosts of children fare,
Faintly swinging, sway and sweep,
Like lovely sea-flowers in its deep;
While, unmoved, to watch and ward,
Amid its gloomed and daisied sward,
Stands with bowed and dewy head
That one little leaden Lad.

THE GHOST

"Who knocks?" "I, who was beautiful,
    Beyond all dreams to restore,
I, from the roots of the dark thorn am hither.
    And knock on the door."

"Who speaks?" "I—once was my speech
    Sweet as the bird's on the air,
When echo lurks by the waters to heed;
    'Tis I speak thee fair."

"Dark is the hour!" "Ay, and cold."
    "Lone is my house." "Ah, but mine?"
"Sight, touch, lips, eyes yearned in vain."
    "Long dead these to thine . . ."

Silence. Still faint on the porch
    Brake the flames of the stars.
In gloom groped a hope-wearied hand
    Over keys, bolts, and bars.

A face peered. All the grey night
In chaos of vacancy shone;
Nought but vast sorrow was there—
The sweet cheat gone.

MUSIC

When music sounds, gone is the earth I know,
And all her lovely things even lovelier grow;
Her flowers in vision flame, her forest trees,
Lift burdened branches, stilled with ecstasies.

When music sounds, out of the water rise
Naiads whose beauty dims my waking eyes,
Rapt in strange dreams burns each enchanted face,
With solemn echoing stirs their dwelling-place.

When music sounds, all that I was I am
Ere to this haunt of brooding dust I came;
While from Time's woods break into distant song
The swift-winged hours, as I hasten along.

A SONG OF ENCHANTMENT

A song of Enchantment I sang me there,
In a green-green wood, by waters fair,
Just as the words came up to me
I sang it under the wild wood tree.

Widdershins turned I singing it low,
Watching the wild birds come and go;
No cloud in the deep dark blue to be seen
Under the thick-thatched branches green.

Twilight came; silence came;
The planet of Evening's silver flame;
By darkening paths I wandered through
Thickets trembling with drops of dew.

But the music is lost and the words are gone
Of the song I sang as I sat alone,
Ages and ages have fallen on me—
On the wood and the pool and the elder tree.

Gilbert Keith Chesterton

THE SWORD OF SURPRISE

Sunder me from my bones, O sword of God,
Till they stand stark and strange as do the trees;
That I whose heart goes up with the soaring woods
May marvel as much at these.

Sunder me from my blood that in the dark
I hear that red ancestral river run,
Like branching buried floods that find the sea
But never find the sun.

Give me miraculous eyes to see my eyes,
Those rolling mirrors made alive in me,
Terrible crystal more incredible
Than all the things they see.

Sunder me from my soul, that I may see
The sins like streaming wounds, the life's brave beat
Till I shall save myself, as I would save
A stranger in the street.

THE PRAISE OF DUST

"What of vile dust?" the preacher said.
    Methought the whole world woke,
The dead stone lived beneath my foot,
    And my whole body spoke.

"You that play tyrant to the dust,
    And stamp its wrinkled face,
This patient star that flings you not
    Far into homeless space,

"Come down out of your dusty shrine
    The living dust to see,
The flowers that at your sermon's end
    Stand blazing silently.

"Rich white and blood-red blossom; stones,
    Lichens like fire encrust;
A gleam of blue, a glare of gold,
    The vision of the dust.

"Pass them all by; till, as you come
    Where, at a city's edge,
Under a tree—I know it well—
    Under a lattice ledge.

"The sunshine falls on one brown head.
    You, too, O cold of clay,
Eater of stones, may haply hear
    The trumpets of that day

"When God to all his paladins
    By his own splendour swore
To make a fairer face than heaven,
    Of dust and nothing more."

TO F. C. IN MEMORIAM PALESTINE

Do you remember one immortal
Lost moment out of time and space,
What time we thought, who passed the portal
Of that divine disastrous place
Where Life was slain and Truth was slandered
On that one holier hill than Rome,
How far abroad our bodies wandered
That evening when our souls came home?

The mystic city many-gated,
With monstrous columns, was your own:
Herodian stones fell down and waited
Two thousand years to be your throne.

1246

GILBERT KEITH CHESTERTON

In the grey rocks the burning blossom
Glowed terrible as the sacred blood:
It was no stranger to your bosom
Than bluebells of an English wood.

Do you remember a road that follows
The way of unforgotten feet,
Where from the waste of rocks and hollows
Climb up the crawling crooked street
The stages of one towering drama
Always ahead and out of sight . . .
Do you remember Aceldama
And the jackal barking in the night?

Life is not void or stuff for scorners:
We have laughed loud and kept our love,
We have heard singers in tavern corners
And not forgotten the birds above:
We have known smiters and sons of thunder
And not unworthily walked with them,
We have grown wiser and lost not wonder;
And we have seen Jerusalem.

A HYMN

O God of earth and altar,
   Bow down and hear our cry,
Our earthly rulers falter,
   Our people drift and die;
The walls of gold entomb us,
   The swords of scorn divide,
Take not thy thunder from us,
   But take away our pride.

From all that terror teaches,
   From lies of tongue and pen,
From all the easy speeches
   That comfort cruel men,
From sale and profanation
   Of honour and the sword,
From sleep and from damnation,
   Deliver us, good Lord!

Tie in a living tether
   The prince and priest and thrall,
Bind all our lives together,
   Smite us and save us all;
In ire and exultation
   Aflame with faith, and free,
Lift up a living nation,
   A single sword to thee.

THE DONKEY

When fishes flew and forests walked,
   And figs grew upon thorn,
Some moments when the moon was blood,
   Then surely I was born;

With monstrous head and sickening cry
   And ears like errant wings,
The devil's walking parody
   On all four-footed things.

The tattered outlaw of the earth,
   Of ancient crooked will;
Starve, scourge, deride me: I am dumb,
   I keep my secret still.

Fools! For I also had my hour;
   One far fierce hour and sweet:
There was a shout about my ears,
   And palms before my feet.

MUSIC

Sounding brass and tinkling cymbal,
   He that made me sealed my ears,
And the pomp of gorgeous noises,
   Waves of triumph, waves of tears,

Thundered empty round and past me,
　Shattered, lost for ever more,
Ancient gold of pride and passion,
　Wrecked like treasure on a shore.

But I saw her cheek and forehead
　Change, as at a spoken word,
And I saw her head uplifted
　Like a lily to the Lord.

Nought is lost, but all transmuted,
　Ears are sealed, yet eyes have seen;
Saw her smiles (O soul be worthy!),
　Saw her tears (O heart be clean!).

Theodosia Garrison

THE TEARS OF HARLEQUIN

To you he gave his laughter and his jest,
His words that of all words were merriest,
　His glad, mad moments when the lights flared high
And his wild song outshrilled the plaudits' din.
　For you that memory, but happier I—
I, who have known the tears of Harlequin.

Not mine those moments when the roses lay
Like red spilled wine on his triumphant way,
　And shouts acclaimed him through the music's beat,
Above the voice of flute and violin.
　But I have known his hour of sore defeat—
I—I have known the tears of Harlequin.

Light kisses and light words, they were not mine—
Poor perquisites of many a Columbine
　Bought with his laughter, flattered by his jest;
But when despair broke through the painted grin,
　His tortured face has fallen on my breast—
I—I have known the tears of Harlequin.

1249

You weep for him, who look upon him dead,
That joy and jest and merriment are fled;
   You weep for him, what time my eyes are dry,
Knowing what peace a weary soul may win
   Stifled by too much masking—even I—
I, who have known the tears of Harlequin.

Amy Lowell

VENUS TRANSIENS

Tell me,
Was Venus more beautiful
Than you are,
When she topped
The crinkled waves,
Drifting shoreward
On her plaited shell?
Was Botticelli's vision
Fairer than mine;
And were the painted rosebuds
He tossed his lady,
Of better worth
Than the words I blow about you
To cover your too great loveliness
As with a gauze
Of misted silver?

For me,
You stand poised
In the blue and buoyant air,
Cinctured by bright winds,
Treading the sunlight.
And the waves which precede you
Ripple and stir
The sands at your feet.

JOHN MASEFIELD

CROWNED

You came to me bearing bright roses,
  Red like the wine of your heart;
You twisted them into a garland
  To set me aside from the mart.
Red roses to crown me your lover,
  And I walked aureoled and apart.

Enslaved and encircled, I bore it,
  Proud token of my gift to you.
The petals waned paler, and shriveled,
  And dropped; and the thorns started through.
Bitter thorns to proclaim me your lover,
  A diadem woven with rue.

John Masefield

A CONSECRATION

Not of the princes and prelates with periwigged charioteers
Riding triumphantly laurelled to lap the fat of the years,—
Rather the scorned—the rejected—the men hemmed in with
    the spears;

The men of the tattered battalion which fights till it dies,
Dazed with the dust of the battle, the din and the cries,
The men with the broken heads and the blood running into
    their eyes.

Not the be-medalled Commander, beloved of the throne,
Riding cock-horse to parade when the bugles are blown,
But the lads who carried the koppie and cannot be known.

Not the ruler for me, but the ranker, the tramp of the road,
The slave with the sack on his shoulders pricked on with the
    goad,
The man with too weighty a burden, too weary a load.

1251

The sailor, the stoker of steamers, the man with the clout,
The chantyman bent at the halliards putting a tune to the
shout,
The drowsy man at the wheel and the tired lookout.

Others may sing of the wine and the wealth and the mirth,
The portly presence of potentates goodly in girth;—
Mine be the dirt and the dross, the dust and scum of the
earth!

THEIRS be the music, the colour, the glory, the gold;
Mine be a handful of ashes, a mouthful of mould.
Of the maimed, of the halt and the blind in the rain and the
cold—
Of these shall my songs be fashioned, my tales be told.
AMEN.

SEA-FEVER

I must go down to the seas again, to the lonely sea and the
sky,
And all I ask is a tall ship and a star to steer her by,
And the wheel's kick and the wind's song and the white sail's
shaking,
And a grey mist on the sea's face and a grey dawn breaking.

I must go down to the seas again, for the call of the running
tide
Is a wild call and a clear call that may not be denied;
And all I ask is a windy day with the white clouds flying,
And the flung spray and the blown spume, and the sea-gulls
crying.

I must go down to the seas again to the vagrant gypsy life,
To the gull's way and the whale's way where the wind's like
a whetted knife;
And all I ask is a merry yarn from a laughing fellow-rover,
And quiet sleep and a sweet dream when the long trick's over.
1252

JOHN MASEFIELD

THE PASSING STRANGE

Out of the earth to rest or range
Perpetual in perpetual change—
The unknown passing through the strange.

Water and saltness held together
To tread the dust and stand the weather
And plough the field and stretch the tether.

To pass the wine-cup and be witty,
Water the sands and build the city,
Slaughter like devils and have pity;

Be red with rage and pale with lust,
Make beauty come, make peace, make trust—
Water and saltness mixed with dust;

Drive over earth, swim under sea,
Fly in the eagle's secrecy,
Guess where the hidden comets be;

Know all the deathy seeds that still
Queen Helen's beauty. Cæsar's will,
And slay them even as they kill;

Fashion an altar for a rood,
Defile a continent with blood,
And watch a brother starve for food;

Love like a madman, shaking, blind,
Till self is burnt into a kind
Possession of another mind;

Brood upon beauty till the grace
Of beauty with the holy face
Brings peace into the bitter place;

Probe in the lifeless granites, scan
The stars for hope, for guide, for plan;
Live as a woman or a man;

Fasten to lover or to friend
Until the heart break at the end,
The break of death that cannot mend;

Then to lie useless, helpless, still,
Down in the earth, in dark, to fill
The roots of grass or daffodil.

Down in the earth, in dark, alone,
A mockery of the ghost in bone,
The strangeness passing the unknown.

Time will go by, that outlasts clocks,
Dawn in the thorps will rouse the cocks,
Sunset be glory on the rocks;

But it, the thing, will never heed
Even the rootling from the seed
Thrusting to suck it for its need.

Since moons decay and suns decline
How else should end this life of mine?
Water and saltness are not wine.

But in the darkest hour of night,
When even the foxes peer for sight,
The byre-cock crows; he feels the light.

So, in this water mixed with dust,
The byre-cock spirit crows from trust
That death will change because it must;

For all things change—the darkness changes,
The wandering spirits change their ranges,
The corn is gathered to the granges.

The corn is sown again, it grows;
The stars burn out, the darkness goes.
The rhythms change, they do not close.

1254

JOHN MASEFIELD

They change; and we, who pass like foam,
Like dust blown through the streets of Rome,
Change ever too; we have no home,

Only a beauty, only a power,
Sad in the fruit, bright in the flower,
Endlessly erring for its hour;

But gathering, as we stray, a sense
Of Life, so lovely and intense,
It lingers when we wander hence;

That those who follow feel behind
Their backs, when all before is blind,
Our joy, a rampart to the mind.

ON GROWING OLD

Be with me, Beauty, for the fire is dying,
My dog and I are old, too old for roving,
Man, whose young passion sets the spindrift flying
Is soon too lame to march, too cold for loving.

I take the book and gather to the fire,
Turning old yellow leaves; minute by minute,
The clock ticks to my heart; a withered wire
Moves a thin ghost of music in the spinet.

I cannot sail your seas, I cannot wander,
Your cornland, nor your hill-land nor your valleys
Ever again, nor share the battle yonder
Where the young knight the broken squadron rallies.

Only stay quiet while my mind remembers
The beauty of fire from the beauty of embers.

Beauty, have pity, for the strong have power,
The rich their wealth, the beautiful their grace,
Summer of man its sunlight and its flower,
Spring time of man all April in a face.

1255

Only, as in the jostling in the Strand,
Where the mob thrusts or loiters or is loud
The beggar with the saucer in his hand

Asks only a penny from the passing crowd.
So, from this glittering world with all its fashion,
Its fire and play of men, its stir, its march,
Let me have wisdom, Beauty, wisdom and passion,
Bread to the soul, rain where the summers parch.

Give me but these, and though the darkness close,
Even the night will blossom as the rose.

Gordon Bottomley

IN MEMORIAM
A. M. W.

SEPTEMBER, 1910

(*For a Solemn Music*)

Out of a silence .
The voice of music speaks.

When words have no more power,
When tears can tell no more,
The heart of all regret
Is uttered by a falling wave
Of melody.

No more, no more
The voice that gathered us
Shall hush us with deep joy;
But in this hush,
Out of its silence,
In the awaking of music,
It shall return.

For music can renew
Its gladness and communion,
Until we also sink,
Where sinks the voice of music,
Into a silence.

Robert Frost

FIRE AND ICE

Some say the world will end in fire,
Some say in ice.
From what I've tasted of desire
I hold with those who favor fire.
But if it had to perish twice,
I think I know enough of hate
To say that for destruction ice
Is also great
And would suffice.

MENDING WALL

Something there is that doesn't love a wall,
That sends the frozen ground-swell under it,
And spills the upper boulders in the sun;
And makes gaps even two can pass abreast.
The work of hunters is another thing:
I have come after them and made repair
Where they have left not one stone on stone,
But they would have the rabbit out of hiding,
To please the yelping dogs. The gaps I mean,
No one has seen them made or heard them made,
But at spring mending-time we find them there.
I let my neighbor know beyond the hill;
And on a day we meet to walk the line
And set the wall between us once again.
We keep the wall between us as we go—
To each the boulders that have fallen to each.
And some are loaves and some so nearly balls
We have to use a spell to make them balance:

1257

"Stay where you are until our backs are turned!"
We wear our fingers rough with handling them.
Oh, just another kind of out-door game,
One on a side—it comes to little more.
There where it is we do not need the wall:
He is all pine and I am apple orchard.
My apple trees will never get across
And eat the cones under his pines, I tell him.
He only says, "Good fences make good neighbors."
Spring is the mischief in me, and I wonder
If I could put a notion in his head:
"*Why* do they make good neighbors? Isn't it
Where there are cows?   But here there are no cows.
Before I built a wall I'd ask to know
What I was walling in or walling out,
And to whom I was like to give offence.
Something there is that doesn't love a wall,
That wants it down."   I could say "Elves" to him,
But it's not elves exactly, and I'd rather
He said it for himself.   I see him there
Bringing a stone grasped firmly by the top
In each hand, like an old-stone savage armed.
He moves in darkness as it seems to me,
Not of woods only and the shade of trees.
He will not go behind his father's saying,
And he likes having thought of it so well
He says again, "Good fences make good neighbors."

MY NOVEMBER GUEST

My Sorrow, when she's here with me,
   Thinks these dark days of autumn rain
Are beautiful as days can be.
She loves the bare, the withered tree;
   She walks the sodden pasture lane.

Her pleasure will not let me stay.
   She talks and I am fain to list:
She's glad the birds are gone away,
She's glad her simple worsted gray
   Is silver now with clinging mist.

The desolate deserted trees,
   The faded earth, the heavy sky—
The beauties she so truly sees—
She thinks I have no eye for these,
   And vexes me for reason why.

Not yesterday I learned to know
   The love of bare November days
Before the coming of the snow;
But it were vain to tell her so,
   And they are better for her praise.

MOWING

There was never a sound beside the wood but one,
And that was my long scythe whispering to the ground.
What was it it whispered?   I knew not well myself;
Perhaps it was something about the heat of the sun,
Something, perhaps, about the lack of sound—
And that was why it whispered and did not speak.
It was no dream of the gift of idle hours,
Or easy gold at the hand of fay or elf:
Anything more than the truth would have seemed too weak
To the earnest love that laid the swale in rows—
Not without feeble-pointed spikes of flowers
(Pale orchises)—and scared a bright green snake.
The fact is the sweetest dream that labor knows.
My long scythe whispered and left the hay to make.

THE AIM WAS SONG

Before man came to blow it right
   The wind once blew itself untaught,
And did its loudest day and night
   In any rough place where it caught.

Man came to tell it what was wrong:
   It hadn't found the place to blow;
It blew too hard—the aim was song.
   And listen—how it ought to go!

He took a little in his mouth,
　And held it long enough for north
To be converted into south,
　And then by measure blew it forth.

By measure.　It was word and note,
　The wind the wind had meant to be—
A little through the lips and throat.
　The aim was song—the wind could see.

THE OFT-REPEATED DREAM

She had no saying dark enough
　For the dark pine that kept
Forever trying the window-latch
　Of the room where they slept.

The tireless but ineffectual hands
　That with every futile pass
Made the great tree seem as a little bird
　Before the mystery of glass!

It never had been inside the room,
　And only one of the two
Was afraid in an oft-repeated dream
　Of what the tree might do.

THE ROAD NOT TAKEN

Two roads diverged in a yellow wood,
And sorry I could not travel both
And be one traveler, long I stood
And looked down one as far as I could
To where it bent in the undergrowth;

Then took the other, as just as fair,
And having perhaps the better claim,
Because it was grassy and wanted wear;
Though as for that the passing there
Had worn them really about the same.

JOEL E. SPINGARN—WILLA S. CATHER

And both that morning equally lay
In leaves no step had trodden black.
Oh, I kept the first for another day!
Yet knowing how way leads on to way,
I doubted if I should ever come back.

I shall be telling this with a sigh
Somewhere ages and ages hence:
Two roads diverged in a wood, and I—
I took the one less traveled by,
And that has made all the difference.

Joel Elias Spingarn

BEAUTY

I found no beauty on the mountain heights;
    I found no beauty where the sea-spray starts;
I found no beauty in God's days and nights;
    I found it only in my heart of hearts.

God I created, and the mountain dawn;
    My scarlet and azure colored all the charts;
Beauty, the goal whence all has come and gone,
    I too created in my heart of hearts.

In wild sea-spray I deified my soul;
    My mountain dawn uplifted all the arts;
In every part I found the glorious Whole—
    All, all, and only, in my heart of hearts.

Willa Sibert Cather

THE PALATINE

IN THE "DARK AGES"

"Have you been with the King to Rome,
    Brother, big brother?"
"I've been there and I've come home,
    Back to your play, little brother."

1261

"Oh, how high is Cæsar's house,
  Brother, big brother?"
"Goats about the doorways browse;
Night-hawks nest in the burnt roof-tree.
Home of the wild bird and home of the bee,
A thousand chambers of marble lie
Wide to the sun and the wind and the sky.
Poppies we find amongst our wheat
Grow on Cæsar's banquet seat.
Cattle crop and neat-herds drowse
On the floors of Cæsar's house."

"But what has become of Cæsar's gold,
  Brother, big brother?"
"The times are bad and the world is old—
Who knows the where of the Cæsar's gold?
Night comes black on the Cæsar's hill;
The wells are deep and the tales are ill;
Fireflies gleam in the damp and mold—
All that is left of the Cæsar's gold.
  Back to your play, little brother."

"What has become of the Cæsar's men,
  Brother, big brother?"
"Dogs in the kennel and wolf in the den
Howl for the fate of the Cæsar's men,
Slain in Asia, slain in Gaul,
By Dacian border and Persian wall.
Rhineland orchard and Danube fen
Fatten their roots on Cæsar's men."

"Why is the world so sad and wide,
  Brother, big brother?"
"Saxon boys by their fields that bide
Need not know if the world is wide.
Climb no mountain but Shire-end hill,
Cross no water but goes to mill.
Ox in the stable and cow in the byre,
Smell of the wood-smoke and sleep by the fire;
Sun-up in seed-time—a likely lad
Hurts not his head that the world is sad.
  Back to your play, little brother."

Percy MacKaye

FRANCE

Half artist and half anchorite,
  Part siren and part Socrates,
Her face —alluring and yet recondite—
  Smiled through her salons and academies

Lightly she wore her double mask,
  Till sudden, at war's kindling spark,
Her inmost self, in shining mail and casque,
  Blazed to the world her single soul—
                    Jeanne d'Arc!

William Ellery Leonard

THE INSULTING LETTER

Thanks for that insult.—I had too much peace:
In the stone tavern down in yonder vale
For a brief space too much of cakes and ale;
Too much of laughter. An ignoble ease
Had lured me from my vows and destinies.
I had forgot the torrent and the gale,
The cliff, the sunrise, and the forest trail,
And how I throve by nature but with these.

Thanks for that insult.—For it was your pen
Stirred the old blood and made me man again.
And crushing your letter with all thought of you,
Inviolate will and fiery dream, I rose;
Struck for the mountains, put my business through,
And stood victorious over larger foes.

1263

Arthur Upson

EX LIBRIS

In an old book at even as I read
    Fast fading words adown my shadowy page,
    I crossed a tale of how, in other age,
At Arqua, with his books around him, sped
The word to Petrarch; and with noble head
    Bowed gently o'er his volume that sweet sage
    To Silence paid his willing seigniorage.
And they who found him whispered, "He is dead!"

Thus timely from old comradeships would I
    To Silence also rise. Let there be night,
Stillness, and only these staid watchers by,
    And no light shine save my low study light—
Lest of his kind intent some human cry
    Interpret not the Messenger aright.

Karle Wilson Baker

DAYS

Some days my thoughts are just cocoons—all cold, and dull, and blind,
They hang from dripping branches in the gray woods of my mind;

And other days they drift and shine—such free and flying things!
I find the gold-dust in my hair, left by their brushing wings.

CREEDS

Friend, you are grieved that I should go
Unhoused, unsheltered, gaunt and free,
My cloak for armor—for my tent
The roadside tree;

1264

And I—I know not how you bear
A roof betwixt you and the blue.
Brother, the creed would stifle me
That shelters you.

Yet, that same light that floods at dawn
Your cloistered room, your cryptic stair,
Wakes me, too—sleeping by the hedge—
To morning prayer!

I SHALL BE LOVED AS QUIET THINGS

I shall be loved as quiet things
Are loved—white pigeons in the sun,
Curled yellow leaves that whisper down
One after one;

The silver reticence of smoke
That tells no secret of its birth
Among the fiery agonies
That turn the earth;

Cloud-islands; reaching arms of trees;
The frayed and eager little moon
That strays unheeded through a high
Blue afternoon.

The thunder of my heart must go
Under the muffling of the dust—
As my gray dress has guarded it
The grasses must;

For it has hammered loud enough,
Clamored enough, when all is said:
Only its quiet part shall live
When I am dead.

James Branch Cabell

GARDEN-SONG

Farewell to Fields and Butterflies
And levities of Yester-year!
For we espy, and hold more dear,
The Wicket of our Destinies.

Whereby we enter, once for all,
A Garden which such Fruit doth yield
As, tasted once, no more afield
We fare where Youth holds carnival.

Farewell, fair Fields, none found amiss
When laughter was a frequent noise
And golden-hearted girls and boys
Appraised the mouth they meant to kiss.

Farewell, farewell! but for a space
We, being young, Afield might stray,
That in our Garden nod and say,
Afield is no unpleasant place.

Ralph M. Jones

BED-TIME

I mind, love, how it ever was this way:
  That I would to my task; and soon I'd hear
Your little fluttering sigh, and you would say,
  "It's bed-time, dear."

So you would go and leave me at my work;
  And I would turn to it with steady will,
And wonder why the room had grown so dark,
  The night so chill.

1266

Betimes I'd hear the whisper of your feet
   Upon the stair; and you would come to me,
All rosy from your dreams, and take your seat
   Upon my knee.

"Poor, tired boy!" you'd say.   But I would miss
   The lonely message of your eyes, and so
Proffer the hasty bribery of a kiss,
   And let you go.

But now, dear heart, that you have scaled the stair
   To that dim chamber far above the sun,
I fumble with my futile task, nor care
   To get it done.

For all is empty since you said good-night
   (So spent you were, and weary with the day!)
And on the hearth the ashes of delight
   Lie cold and grey.

Ah, sweet my love, could I but wish you down
   In that white raiment which I know you wear;
And hear once more the rustle of your gown
   Upon the stair;

Could I but have you, drowsily sweet, to say
   The tender little words that once I knew—
How gaily would I put my work away
   And go with you.

Nicholas Vachel Lindsay

THE DREAMER

"Why do you seek the sun,
In your Bubble-Crown ascending?
Your chariot will melt to mist,
Your crown will have an ending."

"Nay, sun is but a Bubble,
Earth is a whiff of Foam—
To my caves on the coast of Thule
Each night I call them home.
Thence Faiths blow forth to angels
And Loves blow forth to men—
They break and turn to nothing
And I make them whole again:
On the crested waves of chaos
I ride them back reborn:
New stars I bring at evening
For those that burst at morn:
My soul is the wind of Thule
And evening is the sign,
The sun is but a Bubble,
A fragile child of mine."

John Erskine

VALENTINE TO ONE'S WIFE

Hearts and darts and maids and men,
　　Vows and valentines, are here;
Will you give yourself again,
　　Love me for another year?

They who give themselves forever,
　　All contingencies to cover,
Know but once the kind and clever
　　Strategies of loved and lover.

Rather let the year renew
　　Rituals of happiness;
When the season comes to woo,
　　Let me ask, and you say yes.

Brian Hooker

BALLADE OF THE DREAMLAND ROSE

Where the waves of burning cloud are rolled
   On the further shore of the sunset sea,
In a land of wonder that none behold,
   There blooms a rose on the Dreamland Tree
That stands in the Garden of Mystery
   Where the River of Slumber softly flows;
And whenever a dream has come to be,
   A petal falls from the Dreamland Rose.

In the heart of the tree, on a branch of gold,
   A silvern bird sings endlessly
A mystic song that is ages old,
   A mournful song in a minor key,
Full of the glamour of faery;
   And whenever a dreamer's ears unclose
To the sound of that distant melody,
   A petal falls from the Dreamland Rose.

Dreams and visions in hosts untold
   Throng around on the moonlit lea:
Dreams of age that are calm and cold,
   Dreams of youth that are fair and free—
Dark with a lone heart's agony,
   Bright with a hope that no one knows—
And whenever a dream and a dream agree,
   A petal falls from the Dreamland Rose.

ENVOI

Princess, you gaze in a reverie
   Where the drowsy firelight redly glows;
Slowly you raise your eyes to me. . . .
   A petal falls from the Dreamland Rose.

CYRANO'S PRESENTATION OF CADETS

The Cadets of Gascoyne—the defenders
  Of Carbon de Castel-Jaloux:
Free fighters, free lovers, free spenders—
The Cadets of Gascoyne—the defenders
Of old homes, old names, and old splendors—
  A proud and a pestilent crew!
The Cadets of Gascoyne, the defenders
  Of Carbon de Castel-Jaloux.

Hawk-eyed, they stare down all contenders—
  The wolf bares his fangs as they do—
Make way there, you fat money-lenders!
(Hawk-eyed, they stare down all contenders)
Old boots that have been to the menders,
  Old cloaks that are worn through and through—
Hawk-eyed, they stare down all contenders—
  The wolf bares his fangs as they do!

Skull-breakers they are, and sword-benders;
  Red blood is their favorite brew;
Hot haters and loyal befrienders,
Skull-breakers they are, and sword-benders.
Wherever a quarrel engenders,
  They're ready and waiting for you!
Skull-breakers they are, and sword-benders;
  Red blood is their favorite brew!

Behold them, our Gascon defenders
  Who win every woman they woo!
There's never a dame but surrenders—
Behold them, our Gascon defenders!
Young wives who are clever pretenders—
  Old husbands who house the cuckoo—
Behold them—our Gascon defenders
  Who win every woman they woo!

Alfred Noyes

ON REMBRANDT'S PORTRAIT OF A RABBI

He has thought and suffered, but without a cry.
   The wan-hope of this wise old face appears
   To watch, with eyes that hide their own deep tears,
The generations hurrying down to die;
For he can see, beyond our midnight sky
   New griefs arising with the unborn years;
   And, brooding on the riddle of things, he bears
His load of thought, in dreadful innocency.
Children have nestled to him; but all are flown.
   He awaits their homing wings, as old men do
      Across this world's bewildering surge and roar.
An envoy of the Eternal and Unknown;
   An alien to all pride; he faces you,
      In simplest brotherhood, and desires no more.

A FOREST SONG

Who would be a king
That can sit in the sun and sing?
Nay. I have a kingdom of my own.
A fallen oak-tree is my throne.
   Then pluck the strings and tell me true
   If Cæsar in his glory knew
   The worlds he lost in sun and dew.

Who would be a queen
That sees what my love hath seen?—
The blood of myriads vainly shed
To make one royal ruby red!
   Then, tell me, music, why the great
   For quarrelling trumpets abdicate
   This quick, this absolute estate.

1271

Nay.   Who would sing in heaven
Among the choral Seven,
That hears, as Love and I have heard,
The whole sky listening to one bird?
And where's the ruby, tell me where,
Whose crimsons for one breath compare
With this wild rose which all may share?

EPILOGUE

Carol, every violet has
Heaven for a looking-glass!

Every little valley lies
Under many-clouded skies;
Every little cottage stands
Girt about with boundless lands.
Every little glimmering pond
Claims the mighty shores beyond—
Shores no seamen ever hailed,
Seas no ship has ever sailed.

All the shores when day is done
Fade into the setting sun,
So the story tries to teach
More than can be told in speech.

Beauty is a fading flower,
Truth is but a wizard's tower,
Where a solemn death-bell tolls,
And a forest round it rolls.

We have come by curious ways
To the light that holds the days;
We have sought in haunts of fear
For that all-enfolding sphere:
And lo! it was not far, but near.
We have found, O foolish-fond,
The shore that has no shore beyond.

Deep in every heart it lies
With its untranscended skies;
For what heaven should bend above
Hearts that own the heaven of love?

Carol, Carol, we have come
Back to heaven, back to home.
   —THE FLOWER OF OLD JAPAN.

John G. Neihardt

LET ME LIVE OUT MY YEARS

Let me live out my years in heat of blood!
Let me die drunken with the dreamer's wine!
Let me not see this soul-house built of mud
Go toppling to the dust—a vacant shrine.

Let me go quickly, like a candle light
Snuffed out just at the heyday of its glow.
Give me high noon—and let it then be night!
Thus would I go.

And grant that when I face the grisly Thing,
My song may trumpet down the gray Perhaps.
O let me be a tune-swept fiddle string
That feels the Master Melody—and snaps!

PRAYER FOR PAIN

I do not pray for peace nor ease,
 Nor truce from sorrow:
No suppliant on servile knees
 Begs here against to-morrow!

Lean flame against lean flame we flash,
 O Fates that meet me fair;
Blue steel against blue steel we clash—
 Lay on, and I shall dare!

1273

But Thou of deeps the awful Deep,
  Thou Breather in the clay,
Grant this my only prayer—Oh, keep
  My soul from turning gray!

For until now, whatever wrought
  Against my sweet desires,
My days were smitten harps strung taut,
  My nights were slumbrous lyres.

And howso'er the hard blow rang
  Upon my battered shield,
Some lark-like, soaring spirit sang
  Above my battle-field.

And through my soul of stormy night
  The zigzag blue flame ran.
I asked no odds—I fought my fight—
  Events against a man.

But now—at last—the gray mist chokes
  And numbs me. Leave me pain!
Oh, let me feel the biting strokes,
  That I may fight again!

Lascelles Abercrombie

EPILOGUE

What shall we do for Love these days?
How shall we make an altar-blaze
To smite the horny eyes of men
With the renown of our Heaven,
And to the unbelievers prove
Our service to our dear god, Love?
What torches shall we lift above
The crowd that pushes through the mire,
To amaze the dark heads with strange fire?
I should think I were much to blame,
If never I held some fragrant flame

LASCELLES ABERCROMBIE

Above the noises of the world,
And openly 'mid men's hurrying stares,
Worshipped before the sacred fears
That are like flashing curtains furled
Across the presence of our lord Love.
Nay, would that I could fill the gaze
Of the whole earth with some great praise
Made in a marvel for men's eyes,
Some tower of glittering masonries,
Therein such a spirit flourishing
Men should see what my heart can sing:
All that Love hath done to me
Built into stone, a visible glee;
Marble carried to gleaming height
As moved aloft by inward delight;
Not as with toil of chisels hewn,
But seeming poised in a mighty tune.
For of all those who have been known
To lodge with our kind host, the sun,
I envy one for just one thing:
In Cordova of the Moors
There dwelt a passion-minded King,
Who set great bands of marble-hewers
To fashion his heart's thanksgiving
In a tall palace, shapen so
All the wondering world might know
The joy he had of his Moorish lass.
His love, that brighter and larger was
Than the starry places, into firm stone
He sent, as if the stone were glass
Fired and into beauty blown.
　Solemn and invented gravely
In its bulk the fabric stood,
Even as Love, that trusteth bravely
In its own exceeding good
To be better than the waste
Of time's devices; grandly spaced,
Seriously the fabric stood.
But over it all a pleasure went
Of carven delicate ornament,
Wreathing up like ravishment,

Mentioning in sculptures twined
The blitheness Love hath in his mind;
And like delighted senses were
The windows, and the columns there
Made the following sight to ache
As the heart that did them make.
Well I can see that shining song
Flowering there, the upward throng
Of porches, pillars and windowed walls,
Spires like piercing panpipe calls,
Up to the roof's snow-cloud flight;
All glancing in the Spanish light
White as water of arctic tides,
Save an amber dazzle on sunny sides.
You had said, the radiant sheen
Of that palace might have been
A young god's fantasy, ere he came
His serious worlds and suns to frame;
Such an immortal passion
Quivered among the slim hewn stone.
And in the nights it seemed a jar
Cut in the substance of a star,
Wherein a wine, that will be poured
Some time for feasting Heaven, was stored.
  But within this fretted shell,
The wonder of Love made visible,
The King a private gentle mood
There placed, of pleasant quietude.
For right amidst there was a court,
Where always muskèd silences
Listened to water and to trees;
And herbage of all fragrant sort,—
Lavender, lad's-love, rosemary,
Basil, tansy, centaury,—
Was the grass of that orchard, hid
Love's amazements all amid.
Jarring the air with rumour cool,
Small fountains played into a pool
With sound as soft as the barley's hiss
When its beard just sprouting is;

Whence a young stream, that trod on moss,
Prettily rimpled the court across.
And in the pool's clear idleness,
Moving like dreams through happiness,
Shoals of small bright fishes were;
In and out weed-thickets bent
Perch and carp, and sauntering went
With mounching jaws and eyes a-stare;
Or on a lotus leaf would crawl
A brindled loach to bask and sprawl,
Tasting the warm sun ere it dipped
Into the water; but quick as fear
Back his shining brown head slipped
To crouch on the gravel of his lair,
Where the cooled sunbeams, broke in wrack,
Spilt shattered gold about his back.

So within that green-veiled air,
Within that white-walled quiet, where
Innocent water thought aloud,—
Childish prattle that must make
The wise sunlight with laughter shake
On the leafage overbowed,—
Often the King and his love-lass
Let the delicious hours pass.
All the outer world could see
Graved and sawn amazingly
Their love's delighted riotise,
Fixed in marble for all men's eyes;
But only these twain could abide
In the cool peace that withinside
Thrilling desire and passion dwelt;
They only knew the still meaning spelt
By Love's flaming script, which is
God's word written in ecstasies.

And where is now that palace gone,
All the magical skilled stone,
All the dreaming towers wrought
By Love as if no more than thought
The unresisting marble was?
How could such a wonder pass?
Ah, it was but built in vain

1277

Against the stupid horns of Rome,
That pushed down into the common loam
The loveliness that shone in Spain.
But we have raised it up again!
A loftier palace, fairer far,
Is ours, and one that fears no war.
Safe in marvellous walls we are;
Wondering sense like builded fires,
High amazement of desires,
Delight and certainty of love,
Closing around, roofing above
Our unapproached and perfect hour
Within the splendours of love's power.

—EMBLEMS OF LOVE.

Francis Carlin

PERFECTION

Who seeks perfection in the art
Of driving well an ass and cart,
Or painting mountains in a mist,
Seeks God although an Atheist.

HER REVERIE

I wonder how
   'Twill end, should he
Claim father's cow
   Along with me!

Red clouds were ripe
   With dews galore,
When Brian said:
   "Good-night, *asthore!*"
But stars, like whins,
   Grew buds of light
E'er he had kissed

FRANCIS CARLIN

Again good-night;
And Gortin moor
    Had bogged the moon,
Before his last:
    "Good-night, *aroon!*"

I wonder now,
    If such as he
Would claim the cow
    Along with me!

UNDER AN IRISH LARK

When, jars unsealed
And trumpet pealed,
We stir at heaven's quake
To even wake;

And, grade by grade,
We've all obeyed
Our apperceiving past,
As each the blast;

What rapturous
Delight for us,
O bird elect, to be
Love's choice like thee!

To soar on high,
Spurn nether sky,
And laud the Orient
In His descent:

To meet the Slain,
Dawn-red; to gain
The Lover's Side, O lark,
And so Its Mark!

As even thou
But visioned now
Of sun, for having swooned
In Dayspring's Wound.

THE PARISH BARD

Och, would I were deep in Kilbarry
   Where none but the lonely may be,
And the Banshee abroad with her trouble
   As moist as the music in me!

'Tis there I'd be minding your dewy
   Blue eye through a kind violet,
And ye in the midst o' the merry
   With the will and the way to forget.

Dancing you'd be, like the evening
   Ye hobbled my step with your hair,
And neither your voice nor the fiddle's
   With charm to be luring me there.

My grief on the mansion o' music.
   Ye scorned as a magical wile,
And words o' me housing the beauty
   Of dimple enshrining your smile!

There's them that would take to me kindly,
   Nor leave their good luck in the lurch;
Ay, one who would yoke me in chapel
   Were the ring but the key o' the church.

And though I can say it, who shouldn't,
   Small blame on her wish to be known
As the Rose of Rossmire forever
   In song ye are pleased to disown.

Farewell to your chances, *mo cailin;*
   And a bitter good-bye from the bard
On them with their notions to covet
   The fulness of fame ye discard.

For soon I'll be deep in Kilbarry,
   Alone with the lonely, *asthore;*
And dews o' the world dreeping softly
   As snow on the moon in Lough Mor!

Joseph Campbell

THE OLD WOMAN

As a white candle
In a holy place,
So is the beauty
Of an aged face.

As the spent radiance
Of the winter sun,
So is a woman
With her travail done.

Her brood gone from her
And her thoughts as still
As the waters
Under a ruined mill.

Padraic Colum

AN OLD WOMAN OF THE ROADS

O, to have a little house!
  To own the hearth and stool and all!
The heaped-up sods upon the fire,
  The pile of turf against the wall!

To have a clock with weights and chains
  And pendulum swinging up and down!
A dresser filled with shining delph,
  Speckled and white and blue and brown!

I could be busy all the day
  Clearing and sweeping hearth and floor,
And fixing on their shelf again
  My white and blue and speckled store!

I could be quiet there at night
 Beside the fire and by myself,
Sure of a bed, and loth to leave
 The ticking clock and the shining delph!

Och! but I'm weary of mist and dark,
 And roads where there's never a house or bush.
And tired I am of bog and road
 And the crying wind and the lonesome hush!

And I am praying to God on high,
 And I am praying Him night and day,
For a little house—a house of my own—
 Out of the wind's and the rain's way.

THE FURROW AND THE HEARTH

I

Stride the hill, sower,
Up to the sky-ridge,
Flinging the seed,
Scattering, exultant!
Mouthing great rhythms
To the long sea beats
On the wide shore, behind
The ridge of the hillside.

Below in the darkness—
The slumber of mothers—
The cradles at rest—
The fire-seed sleeping
Deep in white ashes!

Give to darkness and sleep:
O sower, O seer!
Give me to the Earth.
With the seed I would enter.
O! the growth thro' the silence
From strength to new strength;

PADRAIC COLUM

Then the strong bursting forth
Against primal forces,
To laugh in the sunshine,
To gladden the world!

II

Who will bring the red fire
Unto a new hearth?
Who will lay the wide stone
On the waste of the earth?

Who is fain to begin
To build day by day?
To raise up his house
Of the moist, yellow clay?

There's clay for the making
Moist in the pit,
There are horses to trample
The rushes thro' it.

Above where the wild duck
Arise up and fly,
There one may build
To the wind and the sky.

There are boughs in the forest
To pluck young and green,
O'er them thatch of the crop
Shall be heavy and clean.

I speak unto him
Who in dead of the night
Sees the red streaks
In the ash deep and white.

While around him he hears
Men stir in their rest,
And stir of the child
That is close to the breast!

1283

He shall arise,
He shall go forth alone.
Lay stone on the earth
And bring fire to the stone.

Witter Bynner

THE NEW WORLD

. . . .

Celia was laughing. Hopefully I said:
"How shall this beauty that we share,
This love, remain aware
Beyond our happy breathing of the air?
How shall it be fulfilled and perfected? . .
If you were dead,
How then should I be comforted?"
    But Celia knew instead:
"He who finds beauty here, shall find it there."
    A halo gathered round her hair.
I looked and saw her wisdom bare
The living bosom of the countless dead.
. . . And there
I laid my head.

James Joyce

STRINGS IN THE EARTH

Strings in the earth and air
    Make music sweet;
Strings by the river where
    The willows meet.

There's music along the river
    For Love wanders there,
Pale flowers on his mantle,
    Dark leaves on his hair.

All softly playing,
  With head to the music bent,
And fingers straying
  Upon an instrument.

James Stephens

HATE

My enemy came nigh,
And I
Stared fiercely in his face.
My lips went writhing back in a grimace,
And stern I watched him with a narrow eye.
Then, as I turned away, my enemy,
That bitter heart and savage, said to me:
"Some day, when this is past,
When all the arrows that we have are cast,
We may ask one another why we hate,
And fail to find a story to relate.
It may seem to us then a mystery
That we could hate each other."
                              Thus said he,
And did not turn away,
Waiting to hear what I might have to say.
But I fled quickly, fearing if I stayed
I might have kissed him as I would a maid.

WHAT TOMAS AN BUILE SAID IN A PUB

I saw God. Do you doubt it?
Do you dare to doubt it?
I saw the Almighty Man. His hand
Was resting on a mountain, and
He looked upon the World and all about it:
I saw Him plainer than you see me now,
You mustn't doubt it.

He was not satisfied;
His look was all dissatisfied.
His beard swung on a wind far out of sight
Behind the world's curve, and there was light
Most fearful from His forehead, and He sighed,
"That star went always wrong, and from the start
I was dissatisfied."

He lifted up His hand—
I say He heaved a dreadful hand
Over the spinning Earth, then I said: "Stay—
You must not strike it, God; I'm in the way;
And I will never move from where I stand."
He said, "Dear child, I feared that you were dead,"
And stayed His hand.

THE WASTE PLACES

I

As a naked man I go
    Through the desert sore afraid,
Holding up my head, although
    I am as frightened as a maid.

The couching lion there I saw
    From barren rocks lift up his eye,
He parts the cactus with his paw,
    He stares at me as I go by.

He would follow on my trace
    If he knew I was afraid,
If he knew my hardy face
    Hides the terrors of a maid.

In the night he rises and
    He stretches forth, he snuffs the air,
He roars and leaps along the sand,
    He creeps and watches everywhere.

His burning eyes, his eyes of bale
    Through the darkness I can see;
He lashes fiercely with his tail,
    He would love to spring at me.

I am the lion in his lair,
    I am the fear that frightens me,
I am the desert of despair,
    And the nights of agony.

Night or day, whate'er befall,
    I must walk that desert land,
Until I can dare to call
    The lion out to lick my hand.

II

As a naked man I tread
    The gloomy forests, ring on ring,
Where the sun that's overhead
    Cannot see what's happening.

There I go: the deepest shade,
    The deepest silence pressing me,
And my heart is more afraid
    Than a maiden's heart would be.

Every day I have to run
    Underneath the demon tree,
Where the ancient wrong is done,
    While I shrink in agony.

There the demon held a maid
    In his arms, and as she, daft,
Screamed again in fear he laid
    His lips upon her lips and laughed.

And she beckoned me to run,
    And she called for help to me.
And the ancient wrong was done
    Which is done eternally.

1287

I am the maiden and the fear,
  I am the sunless shade, the strife,
I the demon lips, the sneer
  Showing under every life.

I must tread that gloomy way
  Until I shall dare to run
And bear the demon with his prey
  From the forest to the sun.

John Drinkwater

INVOCATION

As pools beneath stone arches take
  Darkly within their deeps again
Shapes of the flowing stone, and make
  Stories anew of passing men,

So let the living thoughts that keep,
  Morning and evening, in their kind,
Eternal change in height and deep,
  Be mirrored in my happy mind.

Beat, world, upon this heart, be loud
  Your marvel chanted in my blood.
Come forth, O sun, through cloud on cloud
  To shine upon my stubborn mood.

Great hills that fold above the sea,
  Ecstatic airs and sparkling skies,
Sing out your words to master me—
  Make me immoderately wise.

LAST CONFESSIONAL

For all ill words that I have spoken,
For all clear moods that I have broken,
  For all despite and hasty breath,
  Forgive me, Love, forgive me, Death.

Death, master of the great assize,
Love, falling now to memories,
　　You two alone I need to prove,
　　Forgive me, Death, forgive me, Love.

For every tenderness undone,
For pride when holiness was none
　　But only easy charity,
　　O Death, be pardoner to me.

For stubborn thought that would not make
Measure of love's thought for love's sake,
　　But kept a sullen difference,
　　Take, Love, this laggard penitence.

For cloudy words too vainly spent
To prosper but in argument,
　　When truth stood lonely at the gate,
　　On your compassion, Death, I wait.

For all the beauty that escaped
This foolish brain, unsung, unshaped,
　　For wonder that was slow to move,
　　Forgive me, Death, forgive me, Love.

For love that kept a secret cruse,
For life defeated of its dues,
　　This latest word of all my breath—
　　Forgive me, Love, forgive me, Death.

Thomas S. Jones, Jr.

JOYOUS-GARD

Wind-washed and free, full-swept by rain and wave
　　By tang of surf and thunder of the gale,
　　Wild be the ride yet safe the barque will sail
And past the plunging seas her harbor brave;
Nor care have I that storms and waters rave,
　　I cannot fear since you can never fail—
　　Once have I looked upon the burning grail,
And through your eyes have seen beyond the grave.

1289

I know at last—the strange, sweet mystery,
    The nameless joy that trembled into tears,
        The hush of wings when you were at my side—
For now the veil is rent and I can see,
    See the true vision of the future years,
        As in your face the love of Him who died.

SOMETIMES

Across the fields of yesterday
    He sometimes comes to me,
A little lad just back from play—
    The lad I used to be.

And yet he smiles so wistfully
    Once he has crept within,
I wonder if he hopes to see
    The man I might have been.

Hermann Hagedorn

DOORS

Like a young child who to his mother's door
    Runs eager for the welcoming embrace,
        And finds the door shut, and with troubled face
Calls and through sobbing calls, and o'er and o'er
Calling, storms at the panel—so before
    A door that will not open, sick and numb,
    I listen for a word that will not come,
And know, at last, I may not enter more.

Silence! And through the silence and the dark
    By that closed door, the distant sob of tears
        Beats on my spirit, as on fairy shores
The spectral sea; and through the sobbing—hark!—
    Down the fair-chambered corridor of years,
        The quiet shutting, one by one, of doors.

ARTHUR DAVISON FICKE

BROADWAY

How like the stars are these white, nameless faces—
 These far innumerable burning coals!
This pale procession out of stellar spaces,
 This Milky Way of souls!
Each in its own bright nebulæ enfurled,
Each face, dear God, a world!

I fling my gaze out through the silent night:
 In those far stars, what gardens, what high halls
Has mortal yearning built for its delight,
 What chasms and what walls?
What quiet mansions where a soul may dwell?
What heaven and what hell?

Arthur Davison Ficke

DON QUIXOTE

Dearest of all the heroes! Peerless knight
Whose follies sprang from such a generous blood!
Young, young must be the heart that in thy fight
Beholds no trace of its own servitude.
Young, or else darkened, is the eye that sees
No image of its own fate in thy quest.
The windmills and the swine,—by such as these
Is shaped the doom of those we love the best.
Beloved knight! La Mancha's windows gleam,
Across the plain time makes so chill and gray,
With thy light only. Still thy flambeaux stream
In pomp of one who on his destined day
Put up his spear, his knightly pennon furled,
And died of the unworthiness of the world.

SONNET

This is the burden of the middle years:
To know what things can be, or not be, known;
To find no sunset lovely unto tears;
To pass not with the swallow southward-flown
Toward far Hesperides where gold seas break
Beyond the last horizon round strange isles;
To have forgot Prometheus on his peak;
To know that pilgrim-miles are only miles.
Then death seems not so dreadful with its night
That keeps unstirred a veil of mystery.
Then no acclaimed disaster can affright
Him who is wise in human history
And finds no godhead there to earn his praise
And dreads no horror save his empty days.

SONNET

In the fair picture of my life's estate
Which long ago my yearning fancy drew
From hints of poets, prophets, lords of fate,
What place is there, belovèd one, for you?
How in this edifice of the soaring dome,
Noble, harmonious, lifted towards the stars,
Shall I carve forth a niche to be the home
Of you and of my love that round you wars?
Ah, folly his, who builds him such a house
Too early, by impatient visions led,
Ere he can know what blood shall stain his brows,
And from what troubled streams his heart is fed.
Now must he labor, in late night, alone
To wreck,—and then rebuild it, stone by stone.

Harry Kemp

GOD, THE ARCHITECT

Who thou art I know not,
  But this much I know:
Thou hast set the Pleiades
  In a silver row;

Thou hast sent the trackless winds
  Loose upon their way;
Thou hast reared a colored wall
  Twixt the night and day;

Thou hast made the flowers to blow,
  And the stars to shine;
Hid rare gems of richest ore
  In the tunneled mine—

But, chief of all thy wondrous works,
  Supreme of all thy plan,
Thou hast put an upward reach
  In the heart of Man.

THE HUMMINGBIRD

The sunlight speaks, and its voice is a bird:
It glimmers half-guessed, half-seen, half-heard,
Above the flowerbed, over the lawn . . .
A flashing dip, and it is gone,
And all it lends to the eye is this—
A sunbeam giving the air a kiss.

THE PASSING FLOWER

In Baalbec there were lovers
  Who plucked the passing flower;
In Sidon and Palmyra
  Each flushed, immortal hour

1293

Was gathered in the passing;
In Greece and Rome they knew
That from the living Present
The whitest blossoms grew.

The countless generations
Like Autumn leaves go by:
Love only is eternal,
Love only does not die. . . .

I hear the dying nations
Go by on phantom feet—
But still the rose is fragrant,
And still a kiss is sweet!

BLIND

The Spring blew trumpets of color;
Her Green sang in my brain—
I heard a blind man groping
"Tap—tap" with his cane;

I pitied him in his blindness;
But can I boast, "I see"?
Perhaps there walks a spirit
Close by, who pities me,—

A spirit who hears me tapping
The five-sensed cane of mind
Amid such unguessed glories—
That I am worse than blind.

Sara Teasdale

FOREKNOWN

They brought me with a secret glee
The news I knew before they spoke,
And though they hoped to see me riven,
They found me light as red leaves driven
Before the storm that splits an oak.

For I had learned from many an autumn
The way a leaf can drift and go—
Lightly, lightly, almost gay,
Taking the unreturning way
To mix with winter and the snow.

THE LAMP

If I can bear your love like a lamp before me,
When I go down the long steep Road of Darkness,
I shall not fear the everlasting shadows,
    Nor cry in terror.

If I can find out God, then I shall find Him,
If none can find Him, then I shall sleep soundly,
Knowing how well on earth your love sufficed me,
    A lamp in darkness.

PEACE

Peace flows into me
    As the tide to the pool by the shore;
    It is mine forevermore,
It will not ebb like the sea.

I am the pool of blue
    That worships the vivid sky;
    My hopes were heaven-high,
They are all fulfilled in you.

I am the pool of gold
    When sunset burns and dies—
    You are my deepening skies;
Give me your stars to hold.

James Elroy Flecker

A SHIP, AN ISLE, A SICKLE MOON

A ship, an isle, a sickle moon—
With few but with how splendid stars
The mirrors of the sea are strewn
Between their silver bars!

.   .   .   .

An isle beside an isle she lay,
The pale ship anchored in the bay,
While in the young moon's port of gold
A star-ship—as the mirrors told—
Put forth its great and lonely light
To the unreflecting Ocean, Night.
And still, a ship upon her seas,
The isle and the island cypresses
Went sailing on without the gale:
And still there moved the moon so pale,
A crescent ship without a sail!

IN PHÆACIA

Had I that haze of streaming blue,
    That sea below, the summer faced,
I'd work and weave a dress for you
    And kneel to clasp it round your waist,
And broider with those burning bright
    Threads of the Sun across the sea,
And bind it with the silver light
    That wavers in the olive tree.

Had I the gold that like a river
    Pours through our garden, eve by eve,
Our garden that goes on forever
    Out of the world, as we believe;
Had I that glory on the vine
    That splendour soft on tower and town,
I'd forge a crown of that sunshine,
    And break before your feet the crown.

Through the great pinewood I have been
  An hour before the lustre dies,
Nor have such forest-colours seen
  As those that glimmer in your eyes.
Ah, misty woodland, down whose deep
  And twilight paths I love to stroll
To meadows quieter than sleep
  And pools more secret than the soul!

Could I but steal that awful throne
  Ablaze with dreams and songs and stars
Where sits Night, a man of stone,
  On the frozen mountain spars,
I'd cast him down, for he is old,
  And set my Lady there to rule,
Gowned with silver, crowned with gold,
  And in her eyes the forest pool.

TO A POET A THOUSAND YEARS HENCE

I who am dead a thousand years,
  And wrote this sweet archaic song,
Send you my words for messengers
  The way I shall not pass along.

I care not if you bridge the seas,
  Or ride secure the cruel sky,
Or build consummate palaces
  Of metal or of masonry.

But have you wine and music still,
  And statues and a bright-eyed love,
And foolish thoughts of good and ill,
  And prayers to them who sit above?

How shall we conquer? Like a wind
  That falls at eve our fancies blow,
And old Mæonides the blind
  Said it three thousand years ago.

1297

O friend unseen, unborn, unknown,
   Student of our sweet English tongue,
Read out my words at night, alone:
   I was a poet, I was young.

Since I can never see your face,
   And never shake you by the hand,
I send my soul through time and space
   To greet you.   You will understand.

George Sylvester Viereck

WANDERERS

Sweet is the highroad when the skylarks call,
   When we and Love go rambling through the land.
   But shall we still walk gayly, hand in hand,
At the road's turning and the twilight's fall?
Then darkness shall divide us like a wall,
   And uncouth evil nightbirds flap their wings;
   The solitude of all created things
Will creep upon us shuddering like a pall.
This is the knowledge I have wrung from pain:
We, yea, all lovers, are not one, but twain,
   Each by strange wisps to strange abysses drawn;
But through the black immensity of night
Love's little lantern, like a glow-worm's, bright,
   May lead our steps to some stupendous dawn.

John Collins Squire

IN A CHAIR

The room is full of the peace of night,
   The small flames murmur and flicker and sway,
Within me is neither shadow, nor light,
   Nor night, nor twilight, nor dawn, nor day.

For the brain strives not to the goal of thought,
   And the limbs lie wearied, and all desire
Sleeps for a while, and I am naught
   But a pair of eyes that gaze at a fire.

TREE-TOPS

There beyond my window ledge,
Heaped against the sky, a hedge
Of huge and waving tree-tops stands
With multitudes of fluttering hands.

Wave they, beat they, to and fro,
Never stillness may they know,
Plunged by the wind and hurled and torn
Anguished, purposeless, forlorn.

"O ferocious, O despairing,
In huddled isolation faring
Through a scattered universe,
Lost coins from the Almighty's purse!"

"No, below you do not see
The firm foundations of the tree;
Anchored to a rock beneath
We laugh in the hammering tempest's teeth.

"Boughs like men but burgeons are
On an adamantine star;
Men are myriad blossoms on
A staunch and cosmic skeleton."

THE MARCH

I heard a voice that cried, "Make way for those who died!"
And all the coloured crowd like ghosts at morning fled;
And down the waiting road, rank after rank there strode,
In mute and measured march a hundred thousand dead.

A hundred thousand dead, with firm and noiseless tread,
All shadowy-grey yet solid, with faces grey and ghast,
And by the house they went, and all their brows were bent
Straight forward; and they passed, and passed, and passed,
  and passed.

But O there came a place, and O there came a face,
That clenched my heart to see it, and sudden turned my way;
And in the Face that turned I saw two eyes that burned,
Never-forgotten eyes, and they had things to say.

Like desolate stars they shone one moment, and were gone,
And I sank down and put my arms across my head,
And felt them moving past, nor looked to see the last,
In steady silent march, our hundred thousand dead.

THE LAKE

I am a lake, altered by every wind.
The mild South breathes upon me, and I spread
A dance of merry ripples in the sun.
The West comes stormily and I am troubled,
My waves conflict and black depths show between them
Under the East wind bitter I grow and chill,
Slate-coloured, desolate, hopeless. But when blows
A steady wind from the North my motion ceases,
I am frozen smooth and hard; my conquered surface
Returns the skies' cold light without a comment.
I make no sound, nor can I; nor can I show
What depth I have, if any depth, below.

William Alexander Percy

OVERTONES

I heard a bird at break of day
  Sing from the autumn trees
A song so mystical and calm,
  So full of certainties,

WILLIAM ALEXANDER PERCY

No man, I think, could listen long
    Except upon his knees.
Yet this was but a simple bird,
    Alone, among dead trees.

A VOLUNTEER'S GRAVE

Not long ago it was a bird
    In vacant, lilac skies
Could stir the sleep that hardly closed
    His laughing eyes.

But here, where murdering thunders rock
    The lintels of the dawn,
Although they shake his shallow bed
    Yet he sleeps on.

Another spring with rain and leaf
    And buds serenely red,
And this wise field will have forgot
    Its youthful dead.

And, wise of heart, who loved him best
    Will be forgetting, too,
Even before their own beds gleam
    With heedless dew.

Yet what have all the centuries
    Of purpose, pain, and joy
Bequeathed us lovelier to recall
    Than this dead boy!

THE UNLOVED TO HIS BELOVED

Could I pluck down Aldebaran
And haze the Pleiads in your hair
I could not add more burning to your beauty
Or lend a starrier coldness to your air.

If I were cleaving terrible waters
With death ahead on the visible sands
I could not turn and stretch my hands more wildly,
More vainly turn and stretch to you my hands.

Louis Untermeyer

PRAYER

God, though this life is but a wraith,
   Although we know not what we use,
Although we grope with little faith,
   Give me the heart to fight—and lose.

Ever insurgent let me be,
   Make me more daring than devout;
From sleek contentment keep me free,
   And fill me with a buoyant doubt.

Open my eyes to visions girt
   With beauty, and with wonder lit—
But let me always see the dirt,
   And all that spawn and die in it.

Open my ears to music; let
   Me thrill with Spring's first flutes and drums—
But never let me dare forget
   The bitter ballads of the slums.

From compromise and things half-done,
   Keep me, with stern and stubborn pride;
And when, at last, the fight is won,
   God, keep me still unsatisfied.

MOCKERY

God, I return to You on April days
   When along country roads You walk with me,
   And my faith blossoms like the earliest tree
That shames the bleak world with its yellow sprays—

1302

LOUIS UNTERMEYER

My faith revives, when through a rosy haze
  The clover-sprinkled hills smile quietly,
    Young winds uplift a bird's clean ecstasy . . .
For this, O God, my joyousness and praise!

But now—the crowded streets and choking airs,
  The squalid people, bruised and tossed about;
These, or the over-brilliant thoroughfares,
    The too-loud laughter and the empty shout,
The mirth-mad city, tragic with its cares . . .
  For this, O God, my silence—and my doubt.

ONLY OF THEE AND ME

Only of thee and me the night wind sings,
  Only of us the sailors speak at sea,
The earth is filled with wondered whisperings
  Only of thee and me.

Only of thee and me the breakers chant,
  Only of us the stir in bush and tree;
The rain and sunshine tell the eager plant
  Only of thee and me.

Only of thee and me, till all shall fade;
  Only of us the whole world's thoughts can be—
For we are Love, and God Himself is made
  Only of thee and me.

FEUERZAUBER

I never knew the earth had so much gold—
  The fields run over with it, and this hill
Hoary and old,
  Is young with buoyant blooms that flame and thrill.

Such golden fires, such yellow—lo, how good
  This spendthrift world, and what a lavish God!
This fringe of wood,
  Blazing with buttercup and goldenrod.

1303

You too, beloved, are changed. Again I see
    Your face grow mystical, as on that night
You turned to me,
    And all the trembling world—and you—were white.

Aye, you are touched; your singing lips grow dumb;
    The fields absorb you, color you entire. . . .
And you become
    A goddess standing in a world of fire!

CALIBAN IN THE COAL MINES

God, we don't like to complain—
    We know that the mine is no lark—
But—there's the pools from the rain;
    But—there's the cold and the dark.

God, You don't know what it is—
    You, in Your well-lighted sky,
Watching the meteors whizz;
    Warm, with the sun always by.

God, if You had but the moon
    Stuck in Your cap for a lamp,
Even You'd tire of it soon,
    Down in the dark and the damp.

Nothing but blackness above,
    And nothing that moves but the cars—
God, if You wish for our love,
    Fling us a handful of stars!

HOW MUCH OF GODHOOD

How much of Godhood did it take—
    What purging epochs had to pass,
  Ere I was fit for leaf and lake
    And worthy of the patient grass?

What mighty travails must have been,
　　What ages must have moulded me,
Ere I was raised and made akin
　　To dawn, the daisy and the sea.

In what great struggles was I felled,
　　In what old lives I labored long,
Ere I was given a world that held
　　A meadow, butterflies, and song?

But oh, what cleansings and what fears,
　　What countless raisings from the dead,
Ere I could see Her, touched with tears,
　　Pillow the little weary head.

John Freeman

CATERPILLARS

Of caterpillars Fabre tells how day after day
Around the rim of a vast earth pot they crawled,
Tricked thither as they filed shuffling out one morn
Head to tail when the common hunger called.

Head to tail in a heaving ring day after day,
Night after slow night the starving moments crept,
Each following each, head to tail day after day
An unbroken ring of hunger—then it was snapt.

I thought of you, long-heaving, horned green caterpillars,
As I lay awake. My thoughts crawled each after each,
Crawling at night each after each on the same nerve,
An unbroken ring of thoughts too sore for speech.

Over and over and over and over again
The same hungry thoughts and the hopeless same regrets,
Over and over the same truths, again and again
In a heaving ring returning the same regrets.

1305

Gerald Louis Gould

FALLEN CITIES

I gathered with a careless hand,
    There where the waters night and day
    Are languid in the idle bay,
A little heap of golden sand;
    And, as I saw it, in my sight
    Awoke a vision brief and bright,
A city in a pleasant land.

I saw no mound of earth, but fair
    Turrets and domes and citadels,
    With murmuring of many bells;
The spires were white in the blue air,
    And men by thousands went and came,
    Rapid and restless, and like flame
Blown by their passions here and there.

With careless hand I swept away
    The little mound before I knew;
    The visioned city vanished too,
And fall'n beneath my fingers lay.
    Ah God! how many hast Thou seen,
    Cities that are not and have been,
By silent hill and idle bay!

David Morton

FIELDS AT EVENING

They wear their evening light as women wear
Their pale, proud beauty for a lover's sake,
Too quiet-hearted evermore to care
For moving worlds and musics that they make.

1306

And they are hushed as lonely women are,
So lost in dreams they have no thought to mark
How the wide heavens blossom, star by star,
And the slow dusk is deepening to the dark.
The moon comes like a lover from the hill,
Leaning across the twilight and the trees,
And finds them grave and beautiful and still,
And wearing always, on such nights as these,
A glimmer less than any ghostly light,
As women wear their beauty in the night.

LOVER TO LOVER

Leave me a while, for you have been too long
A nearness that is perilous and sweet:
Loose me a little from the tightening thong
That binds my spirit, eyes and hands and feet.
For there are old communions I would hold,
To mind my heart what field and sky may be:
Earth bears her fruit . . . November has a gold . . .
And stars are still high points in constancy.
Loose me a little, now. . . . I have a need
Of standing in an open, windy place,
Of saying names again, of giving heed
To these companions of man's lonely race . . .
Loose me to these, between one dusk and dawn;—
I shall have need of them, when you are gone.

WHEN THERE IS MUSIC

Whenever there is music, it is you
Who come between me and the sound of strings:
The cloudy portals part to let you through,
Troubled and strange with long rememberings.
Your nearness gathers ghostwise down the room,
And through the pleading violins they play,
There drifts the dim and delicate perfume
That once was you, come dreamily astray.

1307

Behind what thin and shadowy doors you wait
That such frail things as these should set you free!
When all my need, like armies at a gate,
Would storm in vain to bring you back to me;
When in this hush of strings you draw more near
Than any sound of music that I hear.

WHO WALKS WITH BEAUTY

Who walks with Beauty has no need of fear;
The sun and moon and stars keep pace with him,
Invisible hands restore the ruined year,
And time, itself, grows beautifully dim.
One hill will keep the footprints of the moon,
That came and went a hushed and secret hour;
One star at dusk will yield the lasting boon;
Remembered Beauty's white, immortal flower.
Who takes of Beauty wine and daily bread,
Will know no lack when bitter years are lean;
The brimming cup is by, the feast is spread,—
The sun and moon and stars his eyes have seen,
Are for his hunger and the thirst he slakes:
The wine of Beauty and the bread he breaks.

William Rose Benét

THE FALCONER OF GOD

I flung my soul to the air like a falcon flying.
I said: "Wait on, wait on, while I ride below!
  I shall start a heron soon
  In the marsh beneath the moon—
A strange white heron rising with silver on its wings,
    Rising and crying
  Wordless, wondrous things;
  The secret of the stars, of the world's heart-strings,
    The answer to their woe.
Then stoop thou upon him, and grip and hold him so!"
  1308

WILLIAM ROSE BENÉT

My wild soul waited on as falcons hover.
I beat the reedy fens as I trampled past.
  I heard the mournful loon
  In the marsh beneath the moon.
And then, with feathery thunder, the bird of my desire
     Broke from the cover
   Flashing silver fire.
High up among the stars I saw his pinions spire.
     The pale clouds gazed aghast
As my falcon stooped upon him, and gripped and held him
      fast.

My soul dropped through the air—with heavenly plunder?—
Gripping the dazzling bird my dreaming knew?
  Nay! but a piteous freight,
  A dark and heavy weight
Despoiled of silver plumage, its voice forever stilled—
    All of the wonder
   Gone that ever filled
Its guise with glory. O bird that I have killed,
    How brilliantly you flew
Across my rapturous vision when first I dreamed of you!

Yet I fling my soul on high with new endeavor,
And I ride the world below with a joyful mind.
  I shall start a heron soon
  In the marsh beneath the moon—
A wondrous silver heron its inner darkness fledges!
    I beat forever
   The fens and the sedges.
The pledge is still the same—for all disastrous pledges,
    All hopes resigned!
My soul still flies above me for the quarry it shall find!

Shaemas O'Sheel

HE WHOM A DREAM HATH POSSESSED

He whom a dream hath possessed knoweth no more of doubt-
    ing,
For mist and the blowing of winds and the mouthing of
    words he scorns;
Not the sinuous speech of schools he hears, but a knightly
    shouting,
And never comes darkness down, yet he greeteth a million
    morns.

He whom a dream hath possessed knoweth no more of roam-
    ing;
All roads and the flowing of waves and the speediest flight he
    knows,
But wherever his feet are set, his soul is forever homing,
And going, he comes, and coming he heareth a call and goes.

He whom a dream hath possessed knoweth no more of sorrow,
At death and the dropping of leaves and the fading of suns he
    smiles,
For a dream remembers no past and scorns the desire of a
    morrow,
And a dream in a sea of doom sets surely the ultimate isles.

He whom a dream hath possessed treads the impalpable
    marches,
From the dust of the day's long road he leaps to a laughing
    star,
And the ruin of worlds that fall he views from eternal
    arches,
And rides God's battlefield in a flashing and golden car.

JOYCE KILMER

THEY WENT FORTH TO BATTLE, BUT THEY ALWAYS FELL

They went forth to battle, but they always fell;
  Their eyes were fixed above the sullen shields;
Nobly they fought and bravely, but not well,
And sank heart-wounded by a subtle spell.
  They knew not fear that to the foeman yields,
  They were not weak, as one who vainly wields
A futile weapon; yet the sad scrolls tell
How on the hard-fought field they always fell.

It was a secret music that they heard,
  A sad sweet plea for pity and for peace;
And that which pierced the heart was but a word,
Though the white breast was red-lipped where the sword
  Pressed a fierce cruel kiss, to put surcease
  On its hot thirst, but drank a hot increase.
Ah, they by some strange troubling doubt were stirred,
And died for hearing what no foeman heard.

They went forth to battle, but they always fell;
  Their might was not the might of lifted spears;
Over the battle-clamor came a spell
Of troubling music, and they fought not well.
  Their wreaths are willows and their tribute, tears;
  Their names are old sad stories in men's ears;
Yet they shall scatter the red hordes of Hell,
Who went to battle forth and always fell.

Joyce Kilmer

POETS

Vain is the chiming of forgotten bells
  That the wind sways above a ruined shrine.
Vainer his voice in whom no longer dwells
  Hunger that craves immortal Bread and Wine.

Light songs we breathe that perish with our breath
 Out of our lips that have not kissed the rod
They shall not live who have not tasted death.
 They only sing who are struck dumb by God.

TREES

I think that I shall never see
A poem lovely as a tree.

A tree whose hungry mouth is prest
Against the earth's sweet flowing breast;

A tree that looks at God all day,
And lifts her leafy arms to pray;

A tree that may in summer wear
A nest of robins in her hair;

Upon whose bosom snow has lain;
Who intimately lives with rain.

Poems are made by fools like me,
But only God can make a tree.

MARTIN

When I am tired of earnest men,
 Intense and keen and sharp and clever,
Pursuing fame with brush or pen
 Or counting metal disks forever,
Then from the halls of shadowland
 Beyond the trackless purple sea
Old Martin's ghost comes back to stand
 Beside my desk and talk to me.

Still on his delicate pale face
 A quizzical thin smile is showing,
His cheeks are wrinkled like fine lace,
 His kind blue eyes are gay and glowing.

SIEGFRIED SASSOON

He wears a brilliant-hued cravat,
  A suit to match his soft gray hair,
A rakish stick, a knowing hat,
  A manner blithe and debonair.

How good, that he who always knew
  That being lovely was a duty,
Should have gold halls to wander through
  And should himself inhabit beauty.
How like his old unselfish way
  To leave those halls of splendid mirth
And comfort those condemned to stay
  Upon the bleak and sombre earth.

Some people ask: What cruel chance
  Made Martin's life so sad a story?
Martin? Why, he exhaled romance
  And wore an overcoat of glory.
A fleck of sunlight in the street,
  A horse, a book, a girl who smiled,—
Such visions made each moment sweet
  For this receptive, ancient child.

Because it was old Martin's lot
  To be, not make, a decoration
Shall we then scorn him, having not
  His genius of appreciation?
Rich joy and love he got and gave;
  His heart was merry as his dress.
Pile laurel wreaths upon his grave
  Who did not gain, but was, success.

Siegfried Sassoon

AFTERMATH

Have you forgotten yet? . . .
For the world's events have rumbled on since those
  gagged days,
Like traffic checked awhile at the crossing of cityways:

1313

And the haunted gap in your mind has filled with thoughts
    that flow
Like clouds in the lit heavens of life; and you're a man
    reprieved to go,
Taking your peaceful share of Time, with joy to spare.
But the past is just the same—and War's a bloody game . . .
Have you forgotten yet? . . .
Look down, and swear by the slain of the War that you'll
    never forget.

Do you remember the dark months you held the sector
    at Mametz—
The nights you watched and wired and dug and piled sandbags
    on parapets?
Do you remember the rats; and the stench
Of corpses rotting in front of the front-line trench—
And dawn coming, dirty-white, and chill with a hopeless rain?
Do you ever stop and ask, "Is it all going to happen again?"

Do you remember that hour of din before the attack—
And the anger, the blind compassion that seized and shook
    you then
As you peered at the doomed and haggard faces of your men?
Do you remember the stretcher-cases lurching back
With dying eyes and lolling heads—those ashen-grey
Masks of the lads who once were keen and kind and gay?
Have you forgotten yet? . . .
Look up, and swear by the green of the spring that you'll
    never forget.
    March, 1919.

H. D.

LOSS

The sea called—
you faced the estuary,
you were drowned as the tide passed.—
I am glad of this—
at least you have escaped.

1314

H. D.

The heavy sea-mist stifles me.
I choke with each breath—
a curious peril, this—
the gods have invented
curious torture for us.

One of us, pierced in the flank,
dragged himself across the marsh,
he tore at the bay-roots,
lost hold on the crumbling bank—
Another crawled—too late—
for shelter under the cliffs.

I am glad the tide swept you out,
O beloved,
you of all this ghastly host
alone untouched,
your white flesh covered with salt
as with myrrh and burnt iris.

We were hemmed in this place,
so few of us, so few of us to fight
their sure lances,
the straight thrust—effortless
with slight life of muscle and shoulder.

So straight—only we were left,
the four of us—somehow shut off.
And the marsh dragged one back,
and another perished under the cliff,
and the tide swept you out.

Your feet cut steel on the paths,
I followed for the strength
of life and grasp.
I have seen beautiful feet
but never beauty welded with strength.
I marvelled at your height.
You stood almost level
with the lance-bearers
and so slight.

And I wondered as you clasped
your shoulder-strap
at the strength of your wrist
and the turn of your young fingers,
and the lift of your shorn locks,
and the bronze
of your sun-burnt neck.

All of this,
and the curious knee-cap,
fitted above the wrought greaves,
and the sharp muscles of your back
which the tunic could not cover—
the outline
no garment could deface.

I wonder if you knew how I watched,
how I crowded before the spearsmen—
but the gods wanted you,
the gods wanted you back.

John Hall Wheelock

EARTH

Grasshopper, your fairy song
And my poem alike belong
To the dark and silent earth
From which all poetry has birth;
All we say and all we sing
Is but as the murmuring
Of that drowsy heart of hers
When from her deep dream she stirs:
If we sorrow, or rejoice,
You and I are but her voice.

Deftly does the dust express
In mind her hidden loveliness,
And from her cool silence stream
The cricket's cry and Dante's dream;

JOHN HALL WHEELOCK

For the earth that breeds the trees
Breeds cities, too, and symphonies.
Equally her beauty flows
Into a saviour, or a rose,—

Looks down in dream, and from above
Smiles at herself in Jesus' love.
Christ's love and Homer's art
Are but the workings of her heart;
Through Leonardo's hand she seeks
Herself, and through Beethoven speaks
In holy thunderings around
The awful message of the ground.

The serene and humble mould
Does in herself all selves enfold—
Kingdoms, destinies, and creeds,
Great dreams and dauntless deeds,
Science that metes the firmament,
The high, inflexible intent
Of one for many sacrificed—
Plato's brain, the heart of Christ:
All love, all legend, and all lore
Are in the dust forevermore.

Even as the growing grass,
Up from the soil religions pass,
And the field that bears the rye
Bears parables and prophecy.
Out of the earth the poem grows
Like the lily, or the rose;
And all Man is, or yet may be,
Is but herself in agony
Toiling up the steep ascent
Toward the complete accomplishment
When all dust shall be (the whole
Universe,) one conscious soul.

Yea, the quiet and cool sod
Bears in her breast the dream of God.
If you would know what earth is, scan
The intricate, proud heart of man,

Which is the earth articulate,
And learn how holy and how great,
How limitless and how profound
Is the nature of the ground—
How without terror or demur
We may entrust ourselves to her
When we are wearied out, and lay
Our faces in the common clay.

For she is pity, she is love,
All wisdom she, all thoughts that move
About her everlasting breast
Till she gathers them to rest:
All tenderness of all the ages,
Seraphic secrets of the sages,
Vision and hope of all the seers,
All prayer, all anguish, and all tears
Are but the dust, that from her dream
Awakes, and knows herself supreme—
Are but earth when she reveals
All that her secret heart conceals
Down in the dark and silent loam,
Which is ourselves, asleep, at home.

Yea, and this my poem, too,
Is part of her as dust and dew,
Wherein herself she doth declare
Through my lips, and say her prayer.

I DO NOT LOVE TO SEE YOUR BEAUTY FIRE

I do not love to see your beauty fire
The light of eager love in every eye,
Nor the unconscious ardor of desire
Mantle a cheek when you are passing by;
When in the loud world's giddy thoroughfare
Your holy loveliness is noised about—
Lips that my love has prayed to—the gold hair
Where I have babbled all my secrets out—

1318

JOHN HALL WHEELOCK

O then I would I had you in my arms,
Desolate, lonely, broken, and forlorn,
Stripped of your splendor, spoiled of all your charms;
So that my love might prove her haughty scorn—
So I might catch you to my heart, and prove
'Tis not your beauty only that I love!

TO THE MODERN MAN

From mysteries of the Past
  The Future is prophesied.
The Actual comes and goes
  Like shadows on a tide.

Realities come and go
  Like shadows on a pool,—
The leaves are for the wise man,
  The shadows for the fool.

Out of the moment Now
  Rises the god To-Be,
The light upon his brow
  Is from eternity.

Leave dreaming to the fool
  And take things as they are;
All things are in yourself,
  Who stand upon a star

And look upon the stars,
  And yearn with deepening breath—
All things are in yourself—
  Love and Life and Death.

THE LION-HOUSE

Always the heavy air,
  The dreadful cage, the low
Murmur of voices, where
  Some Force goes to and fro
In an immense despair!

1319

As through a haunted brain—
  With tireless footfalls
The Obsession moves again,
  Trying the floor, the walls,
Forever, but in vain.

In vain, proud Force! A might,
  Shrewder than yours, did spin
Around your rage that bright
  Prison of steel, wherein
You pace for my delight.

And O, my heart, what Doom,
  What warier Will has wrought
The cage, within whose room
  Paces your burning thought,
For the delight of Whom?

THE POET TELLS OF HIS LOVE

How shall I sing of Her that is
  My life's long rapture and despair—
Sorrow eternal, Loveliness,
  To whom each heart-beat is a prayer.

Utterly, endlessly, alone
  Possessing me, yet unpossessed—
The dark, the drear Beloved One
  That takes the tribute of this breast.

Dæmon disconsolate, in vain,
  In vain petitioned and implored,
How many a midnight of disdain
  Darkly and dreadfully adored.

Beauty, the virgin, evermore
  Out of these arms with laughter fled—
Vanished . . . a voice by slope and shore
  Haunting the world, Illusion dread!

1320

JOHN HALL WHEELOCK

Most secret Siren, on whose coast
   'Mid spray of perishing song are hurled
All desolate lovers, all the lost
   Soul and half-poets of the world!

Through sleepless nights and lonely days
   In tears and terror served and sought—
Light beyond light, the supreme Face
   That blinds the adoring eyes of Thought!

How long shall I sing of Her! Nay all,
   All song, all sorrow, all silence of
This desperate heart, that is Her Thrall,
   Trembles and tries to tell my love.

PLAINT

Brief is Man's travail here and transitory
   His wrath that soon is spent,
   Brief his lament,
     Lifted in vain against the harsh decrees
    Of the high Destinies
That move not to the measure of his woe:
Even as snow
On sunny meadows, as a lover's story
   Told in an April twilight long ago,
    Brief is he even as these—
His little hour of tumult, or of glory—
    And to what end devised we may not guess,
   Considering, as we go
Toward the same shadows, bearing the same spark,
   His vanity and empty nothingness.
Yet in the mighty Dark
   Dear is the spirit; grievously we know
    Earth has one burden more, one soul the less.

PANTHER! PANTHER!

There is a panther caged within my breast;
  But what his name there is no breast shall know
  Save mine, nor what it is that drives him so,
Backward and forward, in relentless quest:
That silent rage, baffled but unsuppressed,
  The soft pad of those stealthy feet that go
  Over my body's prison to and fro,
Trying the walls forever without rest.

All day I feed him with my living heart;
  But when the night puts forth her dreams and stars,
    The inexorable Frenzy reawakes;
  His wrath is hurled upon the trembling bars,
The eternal passion stretches me apart—
    And I lie silent, but my body shakes.

Joseph M. Plunkett

I SEE HIS BLOOD UPON THE ROSE

I see His blood upon the rose
And in the stars the glory of His eyes,
His body gleams amid eternal snows,
His tears fall from the skies.

I see His face in every flower;
The thunder and the singing of the birds
Are but His voice—and carven by His power
Rocks are His written words.

All pathways by His feet are worn,
His strong heart stirs the ever-beating sea,
His crown of thorns is twined with every thorn,
His cross is every tree.

1322

Robinson Jeffers

JOY

Though joy is better than sorrow joy is not great;
Peace is great, strength is great.
Not for joy the stars burn, not for joy the vulture
Spreads her gray sails on the air
Over the mountain; not for joy the worn mountain
Stands, while years like water
Trench his long sides. "I am neither mountain nor bird
Nor star; and I seek joy."
The weakness of your breed; yet at length quietness
Will cover those wistful eyes.

Rupert Brooke

1914

THE DEAD

Blow out, you bugles, over the rich Dead!
There's none of these so lonely and poor of old,
But, dying, has made us rarer gifts than gold.
These laid the world away; poured out the red
Sweet wine of youth; gave up the years to be
Of work and joy, and that unhoped serene,
That men call age; and those who would have been,
Their sons, they gave, their immortality.
Blow, bugles, blow! They brought us, for our dearth,
Holiness, lacked so long, and Love, and Pain.
Honor has come back, as a king, to earth,
And paid his subjects with a royal wage;
And Nobleness walks in our ways again;
And we have come into our heritage.

THE DEAD

These hearts were woven of human joys and cares,
Washed marvellously with sorrow, swift to mirth.
The years had given them kindness. Dawn was theirs,
And sunset, and the colours of the earth.
These had seen movement, and heard music; known
Slumber and waking; loved; gone proudly friended;
Felt the quick stir of wonder; sat alone;
Touched flowers and furs and cheeks. All this is ended.
There are waters blown by changing winds to laughter
And lit by the rich skies, all day. And after,
Frost, with a gesture, stays the waves that dance
And wandering loveliness. He leaves a white
Unbroken glory, a gathered radiance,
A width, a shining peace, under the night.

THE SOLDIER

If I should die, think only this of me:
That there's some corner of a foreign field
That is forever England. There shall be
In that rich earth a richer dust concealed;
A dust whom England bore, shaped, made aware,
Gave, once, her flowers to love, her ways to roam;
A body of England's, breathing English air,
Washed by the rivers, blest by suns of home.
And think, this heart, all evil shed away,
A pulse in the eternal mind, no less
Gives somewhere back the thoughts by England given;
Her sights and sounds; dreams happy as her day;
And laughter, learnt of friends; and gentleness,
In hearts at peace, under an English heaven.

THE TREASURE

When colour goes home into the eyes,
    And lights that shine are shut again,
With dancing girls and sweet birds' cries
    Behind the gateways of the brain;

1324

ALAN SEEGER

And that no-place which gave them birth, shall close
The rainbow and the rose:—

Still may Time hold some golden space
    Where I'll unpack that scented store
Of song and flower and sky and face,
    And count, and touch, and turn them o'er,
Musing upon them: as a mother, who
Has watched her children all the rich day through,
Sits, quiet-handed, in the fading light,
When children sleep, ere night.

SONNET

Oh! Death will find me, long before I tire
    Of watching you; and swing me suddenly
Into the shade and loneliness and mire
    Of the last land! There, waiting patiently,
One day, I think, I'll feel a cool wind blowing,
    See a slow light across the Stygian tide,
And hear the Dead about me stir, unknowing,
    And tremble. And I shall know that you have died.

And watch you, a broad-browed and smiling dream,
    Pass, light as ever, through the lightless host,
Quietly ponder, start, and sway, and gleam—
    Most individual and bewildering ghost!—

And turn, and toss your brown delightful head
Amusedly, among the ancient Dead.

Alan Seeger

I HAVE A RENDEZVOUS WITH DEATH

I have a rendezvous with Death
At some disputed barricade,
When Spring comes back with rustling shade

1325

And apple-blossoms fill the air—
I have a rendezvous with Death
When Spring brings back blue days and fair.

It may be he shall take my hand
And lead me into his dark land
And close my eyes and quench my breath—
It may be I shall pass him still.
I have a rendezvous with Death
On some scarred slope of battered hill
When Spring comes round again this year
And the first meadow-flowers appear.

God knows 'twere better to be deep
Pillowed in silk and scented down,
Where Love throbs out in blissful sleep,
Pulse nigh to pulse, and breath to breath,
Where hushed awakenings are dear . . .
But I've a rendezvous with Death
At midnight in some flaming town,
When Spring trips north again this year,
And I to my pledged word am true,
I shall not fail that rendezvous.

Scudder Middleton

WISDOM

A wise man holds himself in check,
But fools and poets run ahead.
One must be credulous or sit
Forever with the living dead.

The wise man shuts his door at night
And pulls the bolts and drops the bars.
One must go trustful through the dark
To earn the friendship of the stars.

ALINE KILMER

THE JOURNEY

What matter where the Apple grows?
True heroes never count the miles.
The journey leads to where it leads—
Sargasso or the Western Isles.

No one place holds the dreams of all.
Earth wears a multi-colored robe,
And there are new Hesperides
In every corner of the globe.

Some find the fruit like Hercules—
For such the moon and sun may stop;
Yet never doubt that Sisyphus
Achieved at last the mountain top.

Aline Kilmer

PREVISION

I know you are too dear to stay;
    You are so exquisitely sweet:
My lonely house will thrill some day
    To echoes of your eager feet.

I hold your words within my heart,
    So few, so infinitely dear;
Watching your fluttering hands I start
    At the corroding touch of fear.

A faint, unearthly music rings
    From you to Heaven—it is not far!
A mist about your beauty clings
    Like a thin cloud before a star.

My heart shall keep the child I knew,
    When you are really gone from me,
And spend its life remembering you
    As shells remember the lost sea.

1327

OLIM MEMINISSE JUVABIT

Sometime it may be pleasing to remember
    The curls about your brow,
To talk about your eyes, your smile, your dearness,
    But it is anguish now.

Often I feel that I must speak and tell them
    Of all your golden ways,
How all the words you ever spoke were happy,
    Joy-filled your laughing days.

But though I miss you every empty moment
    Of all my longing years,
How can I speak about your thrilling beauty
    When all my thoughts are tears?

Sometime it may be pleasing to remember
    The curls about your brow,
The way you turned your head, your hands, your laughter,
    But oh, not now, not now!

HAUNTED

Your dying lips were proud and sweet
And when you turned your head away
Against the pillow where you lay
My heart was broken at your feet.
O quivering lips that would be gay,
What was it that you tried to say?
There was a thing you would have said,
There was a word you never spoke;
It rose between us by your bed.
There came a look of hurt surprise
In your unfathomable eyes,
And then it was that my heart broke.

So now wherever I may turn
I see your wistful, following eyes;
I see that anguished question burn
On lips that laugh in Paradise.

1328

ALINE KILMER

If I had been in your dear place
You never would have failed me so!
You always read upon my face
Thoughts that myself could scarcely know.
Oh, how I scorned my fettered soul
Because it could not leap the space
That held me from your lovely goal!

How many a trivial little word
And things you said to me apart,
Strange sayings no one else has heard,
I keep safe buried in my heart.
But the last thing you would have said,
I shall not know it: you are dead.

HILL-COUNTRY

Brown hill I have left behind,
    Why do you haunt me so?
You never were warm and kind
    And I was glad to go.

Is it because there lies,
    Up in your cold brown breast,
One who brought joy to my eyes
    And to my heart brought rest?

Never again shall I see
    The flash in her answering eye.
Never again shall the heart in me
    Stir as she passes by.

Hill, you are proud and cold,
    Haughty and high your face;
Is it, O hill, because you hold
    Her in your grim embrace?

TO A YOUNG AVIATOR

When you go up to die
    Some not far distant day,
I wonder will you try
    To tear your mask away,

And look life in the eyes
For once without disguise?

Behind your mask may hide
What treacherous, covered fires!
What hidden, torturing pride!
What sorrows, what desires!
Whatever there may be
There will be none to see.

Yet I think when you meet
Death coming through the skies,
Calmly his face you'll greet,
Coldly, without surprise;
Then die without a moan,
Still masked although alone.

MY MIRROR

There is a mirror in my room
Less like a mirror than a tomb,
There are so many ghosts that pass
Across the surface of the glass.

When in the morning I arise
With circles round my tired eyes,
Seeking the glass to brush my hair
My mother's mother meets me there.

If in the middle of the day
I happen to go by that way,
I see a smile I used to know—
My mother, twenty years ago.

But when I rise by candlelight
To feed my baby in the night,
Then whitely in the glass I see
My dead child's face look out at me.

CLEMENT WOOD

ATONEMENT

When a storm comes up at night and the wind is crying,
  When the trees are moaning like masts on laboring ships,
I wake in fear and put out my hand to find you
  With your name on my lips.

No pain that the heart can hold is like to this one—
  To call, forgetting, into aching space,
To reach out confident hands and find beside you
  Only an empty place.

This should atone for the hours when I forget you.
  Take then my offering, clean and sharp and sweet,
An agony brighter than years of dull remembrance.
  I lay it at your feet.

TO APHRODITE: WITH A MIRROR

Here, Cyprian, is my jewelled looking-glass,
  My final gift to bind my final vow:
I cannot see myself as I once was;
  I would not see myself as I am now.

Clement Wood

EAGLE SONNETS

III

I have been sure of three things all my life.
The first is that I am—a final one
That yields no room for doubt or windy strife,—
More certain than the blazing of the sun.
The second, that I was—a fainter fact,
Broken by sudden blanks and curious lapses;
A shadow to each living thought and act,
Yet shadowed by a host of vague perhaps.

The third and last of these, that I will be:
A moment leading to a lengthening span,
A fragment formed of continuity,
A child forever growing into man.
Three things are sure. . . . O you who grope for four,
Know, man is sure of three, and never more.

VII

Flower of the dust am I: for dust will flower,
Before its final reckoning is had;
And then this dust, in a hot sudden hour,
Shall stagger, veer, and flounder, in a mad,
Tumultuous plunge into that blazing sun
—Mere dust on fire—that gave it once its birth;
And man and all his doings shall be one
With the charred cinder that was once an earth.
And then again a brief, unhurried cooling,
More flowers that walk and dream, maybe—and then
The agèd sun will end its scanted ruling
As surely as there is an end to men.
The heavens at last will end, as all things must—
To let new heavens ripple out of dust.

IX

O bitter moon, O cold and bitter moon,
Climbing your midnight hillside of bleak sky,
The earth, as you, once knew a blazing noon:
Night brings the silver hour when she will die.
We shall be cold as you are, and as bitter,
Icily circling toward a tepid fire,
Playing at life with our deceitful glitter,
Past joy, past hope, forever past desire.
Yet still the forest lifts its leafy wings,
To flutter for a while before the chill;
And still the careless heart is gay, and sings
In the green temple on the dusty hill;
And the gulls tumble; and the homing ships
Peer for the harbor; and the sand drips.

1332

XI

When down the windy vistas of the years
Has blown the last mad hurricane of being,
When grief has gone, through lack of eyes for tears,
And life is blind, through lack of eyes for seeing;
Only the sluggish soughing of the sea
Moving, of all the bright unrest we know,
Ebbing to final immobility,
While the earth's drowsing spinning note is low,—
That is the hour to weigh each brave endeavor, . . .
The lark of hope sings in our morning air
That life is youth and shall endure forever:
While, in his breast, the maggot of despair
Feeds, in its cool, undeviating lust.
Its silence sings a dusty song of dust.

XIX

I am a tongue for beauty. Not a day,
And not a night, but is a face of her:
The leafy surf of spring, the petal spray;
The nights when snowflakes are too stiff to stir.
She laughs in sunlit waters, and she smiles
In shivering moonlit pools that break the moon;
Her soft face shines above the herded miles
Where slums shrink from the stifling breath of noon.
Her hand is in your hand at every turning;
She slips unseen beside you in the press;
But she will break the brittle heart with yearning,
When, trembling in the glare of loneliness,
You dread to learn you are remote from worth,—
And find you are her shadow on the earth.

XX

We are the singing shadows beauty casts;
Nor shall the shadow live to see its source,
Nor her invisible sun, whose morning lasts
Long after life has spent its feeble force:

1333

No more than waves burned silver by the moon
Shall lift to see their shining silver one,
Or her enkindling sun, whose whitest noon
Shadows some fierier and farther sun.
Trap beauty in your net, she still is flying;
Know her, she is radiantly unknown;
Slay her, she is reborn out of her dying,
To cleave those heights only her wings have flown.
Flee her, till earth ebbs to a vanishing star,
You are her shadow: she is where you are.

John Middleton Murry

SERENITY

I ask no more for wonders: let me be
At peace within my heart, my fever stilled
By the calm circuit of the year fulfilled,
Autumn to follow summer in the tree
Of my new-ordered being. Silently
My leaves shall on the unfretting earth be spilled,
The pride be slowly scattered that shall gild
A windless triumph of serenity.

Vex me no more with dreams; the tortured mind
Hath turned and rent the dreamer. Foreordain
My motions, and my seasons solemn lead
Each to his own perfection whence declined
Their measured sequence promise shall contain,
And my late-opened husk let fall a seed.

Conrad Aiken

MUSIC I HEARD

Music I heard with you was more than music,
And bread I broke with you was more than bread;
Now that I am without you, all is desolate;
All that was once so beautiful is dead.

1334

Your hands once touched this table and this silver,
And I have seen your fingers hold this glass.
These things do not remember you, beloved,—
And yet your touch upon them will not pass.

For it was in my heart you moved among them,
And blessed them with your hands and with your eyes;
And in my heart they will remember always,—
They knew you once, O beautiful and wise.

Harold Vinal

EARTH LOVER

Old loveliness has such a way with me,
    That I am close to tears when petals fall
    And needs must hide my face behind a wall,
When autumn trees burn red with ecstasy.
For I am haunted by a hundred things
    And more than I have seen in April days;
    I have worn stars above my head in praise,
    I have worn beauty as two costly rings.

Alas, how short a state does beauty keep,
    Then let me clasp it wildly to my heart
    And hurt myself until I am a part
Of all its rapture, then turn back to sleep.
    Remembering through all the dusty years
    What sudden wonder brought me close to tears.

Edna St. Vincent Millay

AUTUMN CHANT

Now the autumn shudders
    In the rose's root.
Far and wide the ladders
    Lean among the fruit.

1335

Now the autumn clambers
  Up the trellised frame,
And the rose remembers
  The dust from which it came.

Brighter than the blossom
  On the rose's bough
Sits the wizened orange,
  Bitter berry now;

Beauty never slumbers;
  All is in her name;
But the rose remembers
  The dust from which it came.

FEAST

I drank at every vine.
  The last was like the first.
I came upon no wine
  So wonderful as thirst.

I gnawed at every root.
  I ate of every plant.
I came upon no fruit
  So wonderful as want.

Feed the grape and bean
  To the vintner and monger;
I will lie down lean
  With my thirst and my hunger.

EUCLID ALONE HAS LOOKED

Euclid alone has looked on Beauty bare.
Let all who prate of Beauty hold their peace,
And lay them prone upon the earth and cease
To ponder on themselves, the while they stare

At nothing, intricately drawn nowhere
In shapes of shifting lineage; let geese
. Gabble and hiss, but heroes seek release
From dusty bondage into luminous air.
O blinding hour, O holy, terrible day,
When first the shaft into his vision shone
Of light anatomized! Euclid alone
Has looked on Beauty bare. Fortunate they
Who, though once only and then but far away,
Have heard her massive sandal set on stone.

Herbert S. Gorman

THE LAST FIRE

You saw the last fires burning on the hill
    In that far autumn twilight when we took
The future by the hand through woods as still
    As your heart is to-day, and crossed the brook.

The brook that gurgled through the quietude
    Was just a slender stream that sauntered on.
How were we to know the thing we should—
    That we had crossed our narrow Rubicon?

And after, in the shadow of the leaves,
    When your great eyes grew with the growing night
They left the hollows where the twilight grieves
    And mirrored back the bonfire on the height.

And what quick flame was in your eyes I knew;
    And how the moment caught us on our way
Is Time's own story written for a few
    In dust of ashes in your eyes to-day.

Clark Ashton Smith

IMPRESSION

The silver silence of the moon
Upon the sleeping garden lies;
The wind of evening dies,
As in forgetful dreams a ghostly tune.

How white, how still, the flowers are,
As carved of pearl and ivory!
The pines are ebony,
A sombre frieze on heavens pale and far.

Like mirrors made of lucid stone,
The pools lie calm, and bright, and cold,
Where moon and stars behold,
In some eternal trance, themselves alone.

RECOMPENSE

Ah, more to me than many days and many dreams
And more than every hope, or any memory,
This moment, when thy lips are laid immortally
On mine, and death and time are shadows of old dreams.

Now all the crownless, ruined years have recompense:
In one supreme, undying hour of light and fire,
The many moons and suns have found their one desire—
When in the hour of love, all life has recompense.

TRANSCENDENCE

To look on love with disenamoured eyes;
To see with gaze relentless, rendered clear
Of hope or hatred, of desire and fear,
The inseparable nullity that lies
Behind the veils of various disguise

1338

Which life or death may haply weave; to hear
Forevermore in flute and harp the mere
And all-resolving silence; recognize
The gules of autumn in the greening leaf,
And in the poppy-pod the poppy-flow'r—
This is to be the lord of love and grief,
O'er Time's illusion and thyself supreme,
As, half-aroused in some nocturnal hour,
The dreamer knows and dominates his dream.

Aldous Huxley

DOORS OF THE TEMPLE

Many are the doors of the spirit that lead
   Into the inmost shrine:
    And I count the gates of the temple divine,
    Since the god of the place is God indeed.
And these are the gates that God decreed
   Should lead to His house:—kisses and wine,
Cool depths of thought, youth without rest,
   And calm old age, prayer and desire,
The Lover's and mother's breast,
   The fire of sense and the poet's fire.

But he that worships the gates alone,
   Forgetting the shrine beyond, shall see
   The great valves open suddenly,
Revealing, not God's radiant throne,
   But the fires of wrath and agony.

VILLIERS DE L'ISLE-ADAM

Up from the darkness on the laughing stage
A sudden trap-door shot you unawares,
Incarnate Tragedy, with your strange airs
Of courteous sadness. Nothing could assuage
The secular grief that was your heritage,

Passed down the long line to the last that bears
The name, a gift of yearnings and despairs
Too greatly noble for this iron age.
Time moved for you not in quotidian beats,
But in the long slow rhythm the ages keep
In their immortal symphony. You taught
That not in the harsh turmoil of the streets
Does life consist; you bade the soul drink deep
Of infinite things, saying: "The rest is naught."

Robert Hillyer

TO A SCARLATTI PASSEPIED

Strange little tune, so thin and rare,
Like scents of roses of long ago,
Quavering lightly upon the strings
Of a violin, and dying there
With a dancing flutter of delicate wings;
Thy courtly joy and thy gentle woe,
Thy gracious gladness and plaintive fears
Are lost in the clamorous age we know,
And pale like a moon in the lurid day;
A phantom of music, strangely fled
From the princely halls of the quiet dead,
Down the long lanes of the vanished years,
Echoing frailly and far away.

Edmund Blunden

ALMSWOMEN

At Quincy's moat the squandering village ends,
And there in the almshouse dwell the dearest friends
Of all the village, two old dames that cling
As close as any true loves in the spring.
Long, long ago they passed three-score-and-ten,
1340

And in this doll's house lived together then;
All things they have in common, being so poor,
And their one fear, Death's shadow at the door.
Each sundown makes them mournful, each sunrise
Brings back the brightness in their fading eyes.

Now happy go the rich fair-weather days
When on the roadside folks stare in amaze
At such a honeycomb of fruit and flowers
As mellows round their threshold; what long hours
They gloat upon their steepling hollyhocks,
Bee's balsams, feathery southernwood, and stocks,
Fiery dragon's-mouth, great mallow leaves
For salves, and lemon plants in bushy sheaves,
Shagged Esau's-hands with fine green finger-tips.
Such old sweet names are ever on their lips.
As pleased as little children where these grow,
In cobbled pattens and worn gowns they go,
Proud of their wisdom where on gooseberry shoots
They stuck eggshells to fright from coming fruits
The brisk-billed rascals; pausing still to see
Their neighbor owls saunter from tree to tree,
Or in the hushing half-light mouse the lane
Long winged and lordly.
                          But when those hours wane
Indoors they ponder, scared by the harsh storm
Whose pelting saracens on the window swarm,
And listen for the mail to clatter past
And church clock's deep bay withering on the blast;
They feed the fire that flings a freakish light
On pictured kings and queens grotesquely bright,
Platters and pitchers, faded calendars
And graceful hour-glass trim with lavenders.

Many a time they kiss and cry, and pray
That both be summoned in the selfsame day,
And wiseman linnet tinkling in his cage
End too with them the friendship of the age,
And all together leave their treasured room
Some bell-like evening when the May's in bloom.

George O'Neil

WHERE IT IS WINTER

Now there is frost upon the hill
And no leaf stirring in the wood;
The little streams are cold and still;
Never so still has winter stood.
Never so held as in this hollow,
Beneath these hemlocks dark and low,
Brooding this hour that hours must follow
Burdened with snow. . . .

Now there is nothing, no confusion,
To shield against the silence here;
And spirits, barren of illusion,
To whom all agonies are clear,
Rush on the naked heart and cry
Of every poignant shining thing
Where there is little left to die
And no more Spring.

Edward Davison

SONNET

O Thou in the darkness far beyond the spheres
That seest me, puny, under the night below
Treading through Destiny to Death, forego
Thy triumph and glory for a score of years:
Leave me alive amid my hopes and fears,
The tempest of the mind, the joy, the woe,
That I may battle with myself and know
The worth of life, though be it by bitter tears.
Set not Thy stars against me whether I prove
Evil or good, ere from my inward spirit
Beauty and Truth depart, nor judge me less
In the full storm than in the calm thereof;
Yet from the circle of earth that I inherit
O lift the shadow of this long loneliness!

SONNET

Now that the moonlight withers from the sky
Like hope within my heart, what's left to do
But dream alone until the day I die
On some imagined memory of you?
Believe there was a day when for a space
I looked into your unaverted eyes
To feel my spirit awake at their embrace
Articulate and beautiful and wise;
Or dream I hear your voice in the dim pause
Of dawn, ere birds awake, and feel your hand
Seek mine, when some night-fancy overawes
Your drowsy thoughts, knowing I understand:
Better to falsify you thus and rest
Than know myself forever dispossessed.

George Brandon Saul

ELIZABETH

She has the strange sweet grace of violets
That stand in slender vases in the dusk
When fire-flies weave their unseen fairy nets
About an unreal world of rose and musk.
She has the glad young smile that poppies wear
In quiet gardens when the day comes in
With dewy cobwebs tangled in her hair
And laughing eyes that bid the dance begin!
Her path's a trail of beauty down the years,
And where she steps the dust is touched with flame
A genius, as of hills when night appears,
Clings to her from the silence whence she came.
She passes me, and there remains behind
A sense of flowers drifting down the wind.

1343

Countee Cullen

YET DO I MARVEL

I doubt not God is good, well-meaning, kind,
And did He stoop to quibble could tell why
The little buried mole continues blind,
Why flesh that mirrors Him must some day die,
Make plain the reason tortured Tantalus
Is baited by the fickle fruit, declare
If merely brute caprice dooms Sisyphus
To struggle up a never-ending stair.
Inscrutable His ways are, and immune
To catechism by a mind too strewn
With petty cares to slightly understand
What awful brain compels His awful hand.
Yet do I marvel at this curious thing:
To make a poet black, and bid him sing!

THE SHROUD OF COLOR

"Lord, being dark," I said, "I cannot bear
The further touch of earth, the scented air;
Lord, being dark, forewilled to that despair
My color shrouds me in, I am as dirt
Beneath my brother's heel; there is a hurt
In all the simple joys which to a child
Are sweet; they are contaminate, defiled
By truths of wrongs the childish vision fails
To see; too great a cost this birth entails.
I strangle in this yoke drawn tighter than
The worth of bearing it, just to be man.
I am not brave enough to pay the price
In full; I lack the strength to sacrifice.
I who have burned my hands upon a star,
And climbed high hills at dawn to view the far
Illimitable wonderments of earth,
For whom all cups have dripped the wine of mirth,

For whom the sea has strained her honeyed throat
Till all the world was sea, and I a boat
Unmoored, on what strange quest I willed to float;
Who wore a many-colored coat of dreams,
Thy gift, O Lord—I whom sun-dabbled streams
Have washed, whose bare brown thighs have held the sun
Incarcerate until his course was run,
I who considered man a high-perfected
Glass where loveliness could lie reflected,
Now that I sway athwart Truth's deep abyss,
Denuding man for what he was and is,
Shall breath and being so inveigle me
That I can damn my dreams to hell, and be
Content, each new-born day, anew to see
The streaming crimson vintage of my youth
Incarnadine the altar-slab of Truth?

Or hast Thou, Lord, somewhere I cannot see,
A lamb imprisoned in a bush for me?

Not so? Then let me render one by one
Thy gifts, while still they shine; some little sun
Yet gilds these thighs; my coat, albeit worn,
Still holds its colors fast; albeit torn,
My heart will laugh a little yet, if I
May win of Thee this grace, Lord: on this high
And sacrificial hill 'twixt earth and sky,
To dream still pure all that I loved, and die.
There is no other way to keep secure
My wild chimeras; grave-locked against the lure
Of Truth, the small hard teeth of worms, yet less
Envenomed than the mouth of Truth, will bless
Them into dust and happy nothingness.
Lord, Thou art God; and I, Lord, what am I
But dust? With dust my place. Lord, let me die."

Across the earth's warm, palpitating crust
I flung my body in embrace; I thrust
My mouth into the grass and sucked the dew,
Then gave it back in tears my anguish drew;
So hard I pressed against the ground, I felt
The smallest sandgrain like a knife, and smelt

1345

The next year's flowering; all this to speed
My body's dissolution, fain to feed
The worms. And so I groaned, and spent my strength
Until, all passion spent, I lay full length
And quivered like a flayed and bleeding thing.

So lay till lifted on a great black wing
That had no mate nor flesh-apparent trunk
To hamper it; with me all time had sunk
Into oblivion; when I awoke
The wing hung poised above two cliffs that broke
The bowels of the earth in twain, and cleft
The seas apart. Below, above, to left,
To right, I saw what no man saw before:
Earth, hell, and heaven; sinew, vein, and core.
All things that swim or walk or creep or fly,
All things that live and hunger, faint and die,
Were made majestic then and magnified
By sight so clearly purged and deified.
The smallest bug that crawls was taller than
A tree, the mustard seed loomed like a man.
The earth that writhes eternally with pain
Of birth, and woe of taking back her slain,
Laid bare her teeming bosom to my sight,
And all was struggle, gasping breath, and fight.
A blind worm here dug tunnels to the light,
And there a seed, racked with heroic pain,
Thrust eager tentacles to sun and rain;
It climbed; it died; the old love conquered me
To weep the blossom it would never be.
But here a bud won light; it burst and flowered
Into a rose whose beauty challenged, "Coward!"
There was no thing alive save only I
That held life in contempt and longed to die.
And still I writhed and moaned, "The curse, the curse,
Than animated death, can death be worse?"

"Dark child of sorrow, mine no less, what art
Of mine can make thee see and play thy part?
The key to all strange things is in thy heart."

1346

What voice was this that coursed like liquid fire
Along my flesh, and turned my hair to wire?

I raised my burning eyes, beheld a field
All multitudinous with carnal yield,
A grim ensanguined mead whereon I saw
Evolve the ancient fundamental law
Of tooth and talon, fist and nail and claw.
There with the force of living, hostile hills
Whose clash the hemmed-in vale with clamor fills,
With greater din contended fierce majestic wills
Of beast with beast, of man with man, in strife
For love of what my heart despised, for life
That unto me at dawn was now a prayer
For night, at night a bloody heart-wrung tear
For day again; for *this*, these groans
From tangled flesh and interlockèd bones.
And no thing died that did not give
A testimony that it longed to live.
Man, strange composite blend of brute and god,
Pushed on, nor backward glanced where last he trod.
He seemed to mount a misty ladder flung
Pendant from a cloud, yet never gained a rung
But at his feet another tugged and clung.
My heart was still a pool of bitterness,
Would yield nought else, nought else confess.
I spoke (although no form was there
To see, I knew an ear was there to hear),
"Well, let them fight; they *can* whose flesh is fair."

Crisp lightning flashed; a wave of thunder shook
My wing; a pause, and then a speaking, "Look."

I scarce dared trust my ears or eyes for awe
Of what they heard, and dread of what they saw;
For, privileged beyond degree, this flesh
Beheld God and His heaven in the mesh
Of Lucifer's revolt, saw Lucifer
Glow like the sun, and like a dulcimer
I heard his sin-sweet voice break on the yell

Of God's great warriors: Gabriel,
Saint Clair and Michael, Israfel and Raphael.
And strange it was to see God with His back
Against a wall, to see Christ hew and hack
Till Lucifer, pressed by the mighty pair,
And losing inch by inch, clawed at the air
With fevered wings; then, lost beyond repair,
He tricked a mass of stars into his hair;
He filled his hands with stars, crying as he fell,
"A star's a star although it burns in hell."
So God was left to His divinity,
Omnipotent at that most costly fee.

There was a lesson here, but still the clod
In me was sycophant unto the rod,
And cried, "Why mock me thus?   Am I a god?"

*"One trial more: this failing, then I give
You leave to die; no further need to live."*

Now suddenly a strange wild music smote
A chord long impotent in me; a note
Of jungles, primitive and subtle, throbbed
Against my echoing breast, and tom-toms sobbed
In every pulse-beat of my frame.   The din
A hollow log bound with a python's skin
Can make wrought every nerve to ecstasy,
And I was wind and sky again, and sea,
And all sweet things that flourish, being free.

Till all at once the music changed its key.

And now it was of bitterness and death,
The cry the lash extorts, the broken breath
Of liberty enchained; and yet there ran
Through all a harmony of faith in man,
A knowledge all would end as it began.
All sights and sounds and aspects of my race
Accompanied this melody, kept pace
With it; with music all their hopes and hates
Were charged, not to be downed by all the fates.

1348

COUNTEE CULLEN

And somehow it was borne upon my brain
How being dark, and living through the pain
Of it, is courage more than angels have. I knew
What storms and tumults lashed the tree that grew
This body that I was, this cringing I
That feared to contemplate a changing sky,
This I that grovelled, whining, "Let me die,"
While others struggled in Life's abattoir.
The cries of all dark people near or far
Were billowed over me, a mighty surge
Of suffering in which my puny grief must merge
And lose itself; I had no further claim to urge
For death; in shame I raised my dust-grimed head,
And though my lips moved not, God knew I said,
"Lord, not for what I saw in flesh or bone
Of fairer men; not raised on faith alone;
Lord, I will live persuaded by mine own.
I cannot play the recreant to these;
My spirit has come home, that sailed the doubtful seas."

With a whiz of a sword that severs space,
The wing dropped down at a dizzy pace,
And flung me on my hill flat on my face;
Flat on my face I lay defying pain,
Glad of the blood in my smallest vein,
And in my hands I clutched a loyal dream,
Still spitting fire, bright twist and coil and gleam,
And chiselled like a hound's white tooth.
"Oh, I will match you yet," I cried, "to truth."

Right glad I was to stoop to what I once had spurned,
Glad even unto tears; I laughed aloud; I turned
Upon my back, and though the tears for joy would run,
My sight was clear; I looked and saw the rising sun.

A SONG OF PRAISE

(For one who praised his lady's being fair.)

You have not heard my love's dark throat,
  Slow-fluting like a reed,
Release the perfect golden note
  She caged there for my need.

Her walk is like the replica
  Of some barbaric dance
Wherein the soul of Africa
  Is winged with arrogance.

And yet so light she steps across
  The ways her sure feet pass,
She does not dent the smoothest moss
  Or bend the thinnest grass.

My love is dark as yours is fair,
  Yet lovelier I hold her
Than listless maids with pallid hair,
  And blood that's thin and colder.

You proud-and-to-be-pitied one,
  Gaze on her and despair;
Then seal your lips until the sun
  Discovers one as fair.

SIMON THE CYRENIAN SPEAKS

He never spoke a word to me,
  And yet He called my name;
He never gave a sign to me,
  And yet I knew and came.

At first I said, "I will not bear
  His cross upon my back;
He only seeks to place it there
  Because my skin is black."

COUNTEE CULLEN

But He was dying for a dream,
  And He was very meek,
And in His eyes there shone a gleam
  Men journey far to seek.

It was Himself my pity bought;
  I did for Christ alone
What all of Rome could not have wrought
  With bruise of lash or stone.

FRUIT OF THE FLOWER

My father is a quiet man
  With sober, steady ways;
For simile, a folded fan;
  His nights are like his days.

My mother's life is puritan,
  No hint of cavalier,
A pool so calm you're sure it can
  Have little depth to fear.

And yet my father's eyes can boast
  How full his life has been;
There haunts them yet the languid ghost
  Of some still sacred sin.

And though my mother chants of God,
  And of the mystic river,
I've seen a bit of checkered sod
  Set all her flesh aquiver.

Why should he deem it pure mischance
  A son of his is fain
To do a naked tribal dance
  Each time he hears the rain?

Why should she think it devil's art
  That all my songs should be
Of love and lovers, broken heart,
  And wild sweet agony?

1385

Who plants a seed begets a bud,
    Extract of that same root;
Why marvel at the hectic blood
    That flushes this wild fruit?

Clifford Bax

IN THE TRAIN

Suddenly from a wayside station
In she comes,—a little satchelled
    Country schoolgirl,
Jocund as a field of cowslips.

Looking hard, I think "How goodly
Must have been the stock that bore her . . .
    Down the distant
Georgian days and Jacobean.

What a line of comely maidens,
Bending to avoid the tangled
    Honeysuckle,
Flitted from their fathers' homestead,

Happy-eyed, to wander courting
Through the sunset lighted meadows:
    What upstanding
Sons and sires have wooed and won them. . . .

When she ripens, who shall have her?
Will he know, I wonder? Will he
    Know that, loving
Her, he loves the heart of England?"

Mary Carolyn Davies

REMINISCENCES

The other side of Death, one night,
  Walked out a youth and maid;
And they reviewed (as children might
  A game that they had played)
The battle they had died to fight,
  The cost they both had paid.

"I heard—or seemed to hear," she said
  "Far voices, seemed to see
St. Michael point me to a sword
  To set my country free;
With men, a man, I fought," her head
  Drooped forward wearily.

The boy assented with a nod,
  "Like me," he said, "beguiled.
A dove—a voice from heaven odd
  My fancies were, and wild!
I thought I was the son of God,"
  He said, and, sadly, smiled.

RUST

  Iron, left in the rain
    And fog and dew,
  With rust is covered. Pain
    Rusts into beauty too.

  I know full well that this is so:
  I had a heartbreak long ago.

THE DEAD MAKE RULES

The dead make rules, and I obey.
I too shall be dead some day.

1353

Youth and maid who, past my death,
Have within your nostrils breath,

I pray you, for my own pain's sake,
Break the rules that I shall make!

THE DAY BEFORE APRIL

The day before April
   Alone, alone,
I walked in the woods
   And I sat on a stone.

I sat on a broad stone
   And sang to the birds.
The tune was God's making
   But I made the words.

THE DREAM-BEARER

Where weary folk toil, black with smoke,
   And hear but whistles scream,
I went, all fresh from dawn and dew,
   To carry them a dream.

I went to bitter lanes and dark,
   Who once had known the sky,
To carry them a dream—and found
   They had more dreams than I.

THE GOWN

Beneath the curious gaze of all the dead,
To enter heaven (O my beads unsaid!
Sins unconfessed!)
Dressed
In a gown woven of your fealty!
Oh, poor and lone and frighted I may be,
—But every woman there will look at me.

DOOR-MATS

Women are door-mats and have been,—
The years those mats applaud,—
They keep their men from going in
With muddy feet to God.

May Doney

RUTH

"She stands breast high amid the corn"—
The harvest of her love and tears
And every pain her soul has borne
Through the fulfilling years.

She stoops amid the golden wealth
That drops around her patient feet,
Gathering her suffering and her health—
Her spirit's ripened wheat.

She gleans, unwearied, evermore
The great ears of her joy and grief,
And binds the wonders of her store
Into a little sheaf.

Bruising the grain of all she is,
She kneads a little loaf of bread,
Mingling her life's strange mysteries—
Loins, bosom, heart and head.

And then upon herself she feeds
The life she loves, the lives she bears,
Breaking her passion for their needs,
Her pity for their cares.

1355

So, through her days' allotted span,
  She yields and binds and spends her truth;
The woman God has given to man—
  The everlasting Ruth.

Eleanor Farjeon

THE NIGHT WILL NEVER STAY

The night will never stay,
The night will still go by,
Though with a million stars
You pin it to the sky,
Though you bind it with the blowing wind
And buckle it with the moon,
The night will slip away
Like sorrow or a tune.

Leonora Speyer

DUET

I sing with myself

Out of my sorrow
I'll build a stair,
And every to-morrow
Will climb to me there;

With ashes of yesterday
In its hair.

My fortune is made
Of a stab in the side,
My debts are paid
In pennies of pride;

LEONORA SPEYER

Little red coins
In a heart I hide.

The stones that I eat
Are ripe for my needs,
My cup is complete
With the dregs of deeds;

Clear are the notes
Of my broken reeds.

I carry my pack
Of aches and stings,
Light with the lack
Of all good things;

But not on my back,
Because of my wings!

THE LADDER

I had a sudden vision in the night—
I did not sleep, I dare not say I dreamed—
Beside my bed a pallid ladder gleamed
And lifted upward to the sky's dim height:
And every rung shone strangely in that light,
And every rung a woman's body seemed,
Outstretched, and down the sides her long hair streamed,
And you—you climbed that ladder of delight!
You climbed, sure-footed, naked rung by rung,
Clasped them and trod them, called them by their name,
And my name too I heard you speak at last;
You stood upon my breast the while and flung
A hand up to the next! And then—oh shame—
I kissed the foot that bruised me as it passed.

A NOTE FROM THE PIPES

Pan, blow your pipes and I will be
Your fern, your pool, your dream, your tree!

I heard you play, caught your swift eye,
"A pretty melody!" called I,
"Hail, Pan!"—and sought to pass you by.

Now blow your pipes and I will sing
To your sure lips' accompanying!

Wild god, who lifted me from earth,
Who taught me freedom, wisdom, mirth,
Immortalized my body's worth,

Blow, blow your pipes! And from afar
I'll come—I'll be your bird, your star,
Your wood, your nymph, your kiss, your rhyme,
And all your godlike summer-time!

PIONEERS

Who is the pioneer?
He is the follower here,
Perhaps the last
Of all who passed.

He does not fear nor scorn
To tread
The ventured path, the worn,
Of those ahead;
Nor shall he fail
To blaze his own brave trail
Along the beaten track,
Make of the old a newer way
Of stouter clay,
For others at his back.

He is the pioneer who climbs,
Who dares to climb,
His own high heart,
Although he fall
A thousand times;
Who dares to crawl

1358

On bloody hands and knees
Along its stony ecstasies
Up to the utmost snows;
Nor knows
He stands on these . . .

Or knowing, does not care,
Save to climb on from there!

Who is the pioneer?
He is the follower here,
Dogged and undeterred,
Perhaps the last
Of all who passed.

He passes too,
The heavy bird,
Limping along . . .
Ah, but his song,
His song!

Chester Firkins

ON A SUBWAY EXPRESS

I, who have lost the stars, the sod,
    For chilling pave and cheerless light,
Have made my meeting-place with God
    A new and nether Night—

Have found a fane where thunder fills
    Loud caverns, tremulous;—and these
Atone me for my reverend hills
    And moonlit silences.

A figment in the crowded dark,
    Where men sit muted by the roar,
I ride upon the whirring Spark
    Beneath the city's floor.

1359

In this dim firmament, the stars
    Whirl by in blazing files and tiers;
Kin meteors graze our flying bars,
    Amid the spinning spheres.

Speed! speed! until the quivering rails
    Flash silver where the head-light gleams,
As when on lakes the Moon impales
    The waves upon its beams.

Life throbs about me, yet I stand
    Outgazing on majestic Power;
Death rides with me, on either hand,
    In my communion hour.

You that 'neath country skies can pray,
    Scoff not at me—the city clod;—
My only respite of the Day
    Is this wild ride—with God.

Robin Flower

SAY NOT THAT BEAUTY

Say not that beauty is an idle thing
    And gathered lightly as a wayside flower
That on the trembling verges of the spring
    Knows but the sweet survival of an hour.
For 'tis not so. Through dedicated days
    And foiled adventure of deliberate nights,
We lose and find and stumble in the ways
    That lead to the far confluence of delights.
Not with the earthly eye and fleshly ear,
    But lifted far above mortality,
We see at last the eternal hills, and hear
    The sighing of the universal sea;
And kneeling breathless in the holy place
We know immortal Beauty face to face.

Ivor Gurney

TO THE POET BEFORE BATTLE

Now, youth, the hour of thy dread passion comes:
Thy lovely things must all be laid away;
And thou, as others, must face the riven day
Unstirred by rattle of the rolling drums,
Or bugles' strident cry. When mere noise numbs
The sense of being, the fear-sick soul doth sway,
Remember thy great craft's honour, that they may say
Nothing in shame of poets. Then the crumbs
Of praise the little versemen joyed to take
Shall be forgotten: then they must know we are,
For all our skill in words, equal in might
And strong of mettle as those we honoured; make
The name of poet terrible in just war,
And like a crown of honour upon the fight.

George Rostrevor Hamilton

MULTIPLICITY

When I invade my secret soul
Thinking to find it clean and whole,
There peep at me from cave and den
So many phantoms of half-men
That I, lest those companions gaunt
My laughing work-a-day self should haunt,
Rush out again to the world, to see
A saner multiplicity.

1361

Jessie B. Rittenhouse

TRANSFORMATION

I shall be beautiful when you come back,
  With beauty that is not of lips nor eyes,
  And you will look at me with swift surprise
Seeing in me that loveliness I lack.

And you will wonder how this beauty grew,
  In all the restless clamor of the days,
  Not knowing that I walk in cloistered ways
Bearing within one rapt, still thought of you.

DEBT

My debt to you, Belovèd,
  Is one I cannot pay
In any coin of any realm
  On any reckoning day;

For where is he shall figure
  The debt, when all is said,
To one who makes you dream again
  When all the dreams are dead?

Or where is the appraiser
  Who shall the claim compute
Of one who makes you sing again
  When all the songs were mute?

Margaret Widdemer

THE MASTERS

You have taught me laughter,
  Joyousness and light,
How the day is rosy-wild,
  Star-enthrilled the night:

MARGARET WIDDEMER

Maybe God can teach me
After you are gone
How to bear the blackened night
And the dreadful dawn.

THE DARK CAVALIER

I am the Dark Cavalier; I am the Last Lover:
  My arms shall welcome you when other arms are tired;
I stand to wait for you, patient in the darkness,
  Offering forgetfulness of all that you desired.

I ask no merriment, no pretense of gladness,
  I can love heavy lids and lips without their rose;
Though you are sorrowful you will not weary me;
  I will not go from you when all the tired world goes.

I am the Dark Cavalier; I am the Last Lover;
  I promise faithfulness no other lips may keep;
Safe in my bridal place, comforted by darkness,
  You shall lie happily, smiling in your sleep.

GREEK FOLK SONG

Under dusky laurel leaf,
  Scarlet leaf of rose,
I lie prone, who have known
  All a woman knows.

Love and grief and motherhood,
  Fame and mirth and scorn—
These are all shall befall
  Any woman born.

Jewel-laden are my hands,
  Tall my stone above—
Do not weep that I sleep,
  Who was wise in love.

Where I walk, a shadow gray,
　Through gray asphodel,
I am glad, who have had
　All that life can tell.

Elinor Wylie

THE EAGLE AND THE MOLE

Avoid the reeking herd,
Shun the polluted flock,
Live like that stoic bird,
The eagle of the rock.

The huddled warmth of crowds
Begets and fosters hate;
He keeps, above the clouds,
His cliff inviolate.

When flocks are folded warm
And herds to shelter run,
He sails above the storm,
He stares into the sun.

If in the eagle's track
Your sinews cannot leap,
Avoid the lathered pack,
Turn from the steaming sheep.

If you would keep your soul
From spotted sight or sound,
Live like the velvet mole;
Go burrow underground.

And there hold intercourse
With roots of trees and stones,
With rivers at their source
And disembodied bones.

1364

CHARLOTTE MEW

LET NO CHARITABLE HOPE

Now let no charitable hope
Confuse my mind with images
Of eagle and of antelope:
I am in nature none of these.

I was, being human, born alone;
I am, being woman, hard beset;
I live by squeezing from a stone
The little nourishment I get.

In masks outrageous and austere
The years go by in single file;
But none has merited my fear,
And none has quite escaped my smile.

Charlotte Mew

THE FARMER'S BRIDE

Three Summers since I chose a maid,
    Too young maybe—but more's to do
At harvest-time than bide and woo.
        When us was wed she turned afraid
Of love and me and all things human;
Like the shut of a winter's day.
Her smile went out, and 'twasn't a woman—
    More like a little frightened fay.
        One night, in the Fall, she runned away.

"Out 'mong the sheep, her be," they said,
'Should properly have been abed;
But sure enough she wasn't there
Lying awake with her wide brown stare.
So over seven-acre field and up-along across the down
    We chased her, flying like a hare
    Before our lanterns. To Church-Town
        All in a shiver and a scare

1365

We caught her, fetched her home at last
And turned the key upon her, fast.

She does the work about the house
As well as most, but like a mouse:
Happy enough to chat and play
With birds and rabbits and such as they,
So long as men-folk keep away.
"Not near, not near!" her eyes beseech
When one of us comes within reach.
The women say that beasts in stall
Look round like children at her call.
I've hardly heard her speak at all.

Shy as a leveret, swift as he,
Straight and slight as a young larch tree,
Sweet as the first wild violets, she,
To her wild self. But what to me?
The short days shorten and the oaks are brown,
The blue smoke rises to the low grey sky,
One leaf in the still air falls slowly down,
A magpie's spotted feathers lie
On the black earth spread white with rime,
The berries redden up to Christmas-time.
What's Christmas-time without there be
Some other in the house than we!

She sleeps up in the attic there
Alone, poor maid. 'Tis but a stair
Betwixt us. Oh! my God! the down,
The soft young down of her, the brown,
The brown of her—her eyes, her hair, her hair.

Violet Alleyn Storey

A PRAYER AFTER ILLNESS

Tune me for life again, O quiet Musician.
Strive to adjust my loosened thoughts until,
Made taut, they shall be yielding to Thy Fingers
Gladly as trees to winds that touch this hill.

1366

ANNA HEMPSTEAD BRANCH

Rhyme me with life once more, O silent Poet.
    Out of my weary, fluttering heartbeats make
Cool rhythms, hushed, yet certain as the circling
    Water against the edges of this lake.

Fit me for life again, O patient Artist.
    Paint on my tired soul glad, vivid things.
Splash now upon its dullness beauty's pigments,
    Lovely as pansies and a blue-bird's wings.

Anna Hempstead Branch

TO A NEW YORK SHOP-GIRL DRESSED FOR SUNDAY

To-day I saw the shop-girl go
Down gay Broadway to meet her beau.

Conspicuous, splendid, conscious, sweet,
She spread abroad and took the street.

And all that niceness would forbid,
Superb, she smiled upon and did.

Let other girls, whose happier days
Preserve the perfume of their ways,

Go modestly.   The passing hour
Adds splendor to their opening flower.

But from this child too swift a doom
Must steal her prettiness and bloom,

Toil and weariness hide the grace
That pleads a moment from her face.

So blame her not if for a day
She flaunts her glories while she may.

She half perceives, half understands,
Snatching her gifts with both her hands.

1367

The little strut beneath the skirt
That lags neglected in the dirt,

The indolent swagger down the street—
Who can condemn such happy feet!

Innocent! vulgar—that's the truth!
Yet with the darling wiles of youth!

The bright, self-conscious eyes that stare
With such hauteur, beneath such hair!
Perhaps the men will find me fair!

Charming and charmed, flippant, arrayed,
Fluttered and foolish, proud, displayed,
Infinite pathos of parade!

The bangles and the narrowed waist—
The tinseled boa—forgive the taste!
Oh, the starved nights she gave for that,
And bartered bread to buy her hat!

She flows before the reproachful sage
And begs her woman's heritage.

Dear child, with the defiant eyes,
Insolent with the half surmise
We do not quite admire, I know
How foresight frowns on this vain show!

And judgment, wearily sad, may see
No grace in such frivolity.

Yet which of us was ever bold
To worship Beauty, hungry and cold!

Scorn famine down, proudly expressed
Apostle to what things are best.

Let him who starves to buy the food
For his soul's comfort find her good,

Nor chide the frills and furbelows
That are the prettiest things she knows.

Poet and prophet in God's eyes
Make no more perfect sacrifice.

Who knows before what inner shrine
She eats with them the bread and wine?

Poor waif! One of the sacred few
That madly sought the best they knew!

Dear—let me lean my cheek to-night
Close, close to yours. Ah, that is right.

How warm and near! At last I see
One beauty shines for thee and me.

So let us love and understand—
Whose hearts are hidden in God's hand.

And we will cherish your brief Spring
And all its fragile flowering.

God loves all prettiness, and on this
Surely his angels lay their kiss.

John Myers O'Hara

A FAUN IN WALL STREET

What shape so furtive steals along the dim
    Bleak street, barren of throngs, this day of June;
    This day of rest, when all the roses swoon
In Attic vales where dryads wait for him?
What sylvan this, and what the stranger whim
    That lured him here this golden afternoon;
    Ways where the dusk has fallen oversoon
In the deep canyon, torrentless and grim?

1369

Great Pan is far, O mad estray, and these
    Bare walls that leap to heaven and hide the skies
Are fanes men rear to other deities;
    Far to the east the haunted woodland lies,
And cloudless still, from cyclad-dotted seas,
    Hymettus and the hills of Hellas rise.

Unknown

CUCKOO SONG

Sumer is icumen in,
    Lhude sing cuccu!
Groweth sed, and bloweth med,
    And springth the wude nu—
            Sing cuccu!

Awe bleteth after lomb,
    Lhouth after calve cu;
Bulluc sterteth, bucke verteth,
    Murie sing cuccu!

Cuccu, cuccu, well singes thu, cuccu:
    Ne swike thu naver nu;
Sing cuccu, nu, sing cuccu,
    Sing cuccu, sing cuccu, nu!

THE NUT-BROWN MAID

He. It standeth so; a deed is do',
    Whereof great harm shall grow;
    My destiny is for to die
    A shameful death, I trow;
    Or else to flee: the one must be,
    None other way I know,
    But to withdraw as an outlaw,
    And take me to my bow.

1370

UNKNOWN

Wherefore adieu, my own heart true!
  None other rede I can;
For I must to the green wood go,
  Alone, a banished man.

She. O Lord, what is this world's bliss,
  That changeth as the moon!
My Summer's day in lusty May
  Is darked before the noon.
I hear you say, Farewell: Nay, nay,
  We depart not so soon.
Why say ye so? whither will ye go?
  Alas! what have ye done?
All my welfàre to sorrow and care
  Should change if ye were gone;
For in my mind, of all mankind
  I love but you alone.

He. I can believe, it shall you grieve,
  And somewhat you distrain:
But afterward, your paines hard
  Within a day or twain
Shall soon aslake; and ye shall take
  Comfort to you again.
Why should ye ought, for to make thought?
  Your labour were in vain.
And thus I do, and pray to you,
  As heartily as I can;
For I must to the green wood go,
  Alone, a banished man.

She. Now sith that ye have showed to
  The secret of your mind,
I shall be plain to you again,
  Like as ye shall me find.
Sith it is so that ye will g
  I will not live behin
Shall never be said, t
  Was to her love

1371

Make you ready, for so am I,
 Although it were anon;
For in my mind, of all mankind,
 I love but you alone.

He. I counsel you, remember how
 It is no maiden's law
Nothing to doubt, but to run out
 To wood with an outlàw;
For ye must there in your hand bear
 A bow, ready to draw;
And as a thief, thus must you live,
 Ever in dread and awe.
Whereby to you great harm might grow:
 Yet had I lever than,
That I had to the green wood go,
 Alone, a banished man.

She. I think not nay, but, as ye say,
 It is no maiden's lore:
But love may make me for your sake,
 As I have said before,
To come on foot, to hunt and shoot
 To get us meat in store;
For so that I your company
 May have, I ask no more:
From which to part it makes my heart
 As cold as any stone;
For, in my mind, of all mankind,
 I love but you alone.

Yet take good heed, for ever I dread
 That ye could not sustain
The thorny ways, the deep vallèys,
 The snow, the frost, the rain,
 cold, the heat; for, dry or weet,
 must lodge on the plain;
 above, none other roof
 brake bush or twain:
 should grieve you, I believe,
 ould gladly than
 the green wood go,
 ished man.

UNKNOWN

She.   Sith I have here been partinèr
      With you of joy and bliss,
  I must also part of your wo
      Endure, as reason is.
  Yet I am sure of one pleasùre,
      And, shortly, it is this,
  That, where ye be, me seemeth, pardie,
      I could not fare amiss.
  Without more speech, I you beseech
      That ye were soon agone,
  For, to my mind, of all mankind
      I love but you alone.

He.   If ye go thither, ye must consider,
      When ye have list to dine,
  There shall no meat be for you gete,
      Nor drink, beer, ale, nor wine,
  No sheetes clean, to lie between,
      Made of thread and twine;
  None other house but leaves and boughs,
      To cover your head and mine.
  Oh mine heart sweet, this evil diet,
      Should make you pale and wan;
  Wherefore I will to the green wood go,
      Alone, a banished man.

She.   Among the wild deer, such an archèr,
      As men say that ye be,
  Ye may not fail of good vittail,
      Where is so great plentie.
  And water clear of the rivèr,
      Shall be full sweet to me.
  With which in heal I shall right weel
      Endure, as ye shall see;
  And ere we go, a bed or two
      I can provide anone;
  For, in my mind, of all mankind
      I love but you alone.

He.   Lo yet before, ye must do more,
      If ye will go with me;
  As cut your hair up by your ear,
      Your kirtle to the knee;

With bow in hand, for to withstand
  Your enemies, if need be;
And this same night, before day-light,
  To wood-ward will I flee.
If that ye will all this fulfill,
  Do 't shortly as ye can:
Else will I to the green wood go,
  Alone, a banished man.

She. I shall, as now, do more for you,
  Than 'longeth to womanheed,
To short my hair, a bow to bear,
  To shoot in time of need.
Oh, my sweet mother, before all other
  For you I have most dread;
But now adieu! I must ensue
  Where fortune doth me lead.
All this make ye: Now let us flee;
  The day comes fast upon:
For, in my mind, of all mankind
  I love but you alone.

He. Nay, nay, not so; ye shall not go,
  And I shall tell you why:
Your appetite is to be light
  Of love, I weel espy:
For like as ye have said to me,
  In like wise, hardily,
Ye would answèr whoever it were,
  In way of companỳ.
It is said of old, soon hot, soon cold;
  And so is a woman,
Wherefore I to the wood will go,
  Alone, a banished man.

She. If ye take heed, it is no need
  Such words to say by me;
For oft ye prayed and me assayed,
  Ere I loved you, pardie:
And though that I, of ancestry,
  A baron's daughter be,

1374

Yet have you proved how I you loved,
  A squire of low degree;
And ever shall, whatso befal;
  To die therefore anon;
For, in my mind, of all mankind
  I love but you alone.

He. A baron's child to be beguiled,
  It were a cursed deed!
To be fellàw with an outlaw,
  Almighty God forbid!
It better were, the poor squièr
  Alone to forest yede,
Than I should say, another day,
  That, by my cursed deed,
We were betrayed: wherefore, good maid,
  The best rede that I can,
Is, that I to the green wood go,
  Alone, a banished man.

She. Whatever befal, I never shall,
  Of this thing you upbraid;
But, if ye go, and leave me so,
  Then have ye me betrayed.
Remember weel, how that you deal;
  For if ye, as ye said,
Be so unkind to leave behind,
  Your love, the Nut-Brown Maid,
Trust me truly, that I shall die
  Soon after ye be gone;
For, in my mind, of all mankind
  I love but you alone.

He. If that ye went, ye should repent;
  For in the forest now
I have purveyed me of a maid,
  Whom I love more than you;
Another fairèr than ever ye were,
  I dare it weel avow,
And of you both each should be wroth
  With other, as I trow:

1375

It were mine ease to live in peace;
    So will I, if I can:
Wherefore I to the wood will go,
    Alone, a banished man.

She. Though in the wood I understood
    Ye had a paramour,
All this may not remove my thought,
    But that I will be your.
And she shall find me soft and kind
    And courteous every hour;
Glad to fulfill all that she will
    Command me to my power.
For had ye, lo, an hundred mo,
    Of them I would be one;
For, in my mind, of all mankind
    I love but you alone.

He. Mine own dear love, I see thee prove
    That ye be kind and true;
Of maid and wife, in all my life,
    The best that ever I knew.
Be merry and glad; no more be sad;
    . The case is changèd now;
For it were ruth, that, for your truth,
    Ye should have cause to rue.
Be not dismayed; whatever I said
    To you, when I began;
I will not to the greenwood go,
    I am no banished man.

She. These tidings be more glad to me,
    Than to be made a queen,
If I were sure they would endure:
    But it is often seen,
When men will break promise, they speak
    The wordes on the spleen.
Ye shape some wile me to beguile,
    And steal from me, I ween:
Then were the case worse than it was,
    And I more woe-begone:
For, in my mind, of all mankind
    I love but you alone.

1376

UNKNOWN

He. Ye shall not need further to dread:
    I will not disparàge,
You (God defend!) sith ye descend
    Of so great a lineàge.
Now understand; to Westmoreland,
    Which is mine heritage,
I will you bring; and with a ring,
    By way of marriàge,
I will you take, and lady make,
    As shortly as I can:
Thus have you won an erly's son,
    And not a banished man.

MADRIGAL

Lady, when I behold the roses sprouting,
    Which, clad in damask mantles, deck the arbours,
And then behold your lips, where sweet love harbours,
    My eyes present me with a double doubting:
For viewing both alike, hardly my mind supposes,
Whether the roses be your lips, or your lips the rose

I SAW MY LADY WEEP

    I saw my lady weep,
And Sorrow proud to be advancèd keep.
In those fair eyes where all per
    Her face was full of was more hearts
But such a woe, believe m icing parts.
Than Mirth can do with

    fair,
    Sorrow was th delightful thing;
And passion wise , a wisdom rare;
Silence beyond s to sing,
    She ma so sweet a sadness move
And all th at once both grieve and love.
As made

1377

O fairer than aught else
The world can show, leave off in time to grieve.
Enough, enough! your joyful look excels;
　　Tears kill the heart, believe.
O strive not to be excellent in woe,
Which only breeds your beauty's overthrow.

LOVE AND MAY

Now is the gentle season, freshly flowering,
　　To sing, and play, and dance, while May endureth,
　　And woo, and wed too, that sweet delight procureth.

The fields abroad with spangled flowers are gilded,
　　The meads are mantled, and closes;
　　In May each bush arrayèd, and sweet wild roses.

The nightingale her bower hath gaily builded,
　　And full of kindly lust and loves inspiring,
　　I love, I love, she sings, hark, her mate desiring.

LULLABY

Weep you no more, sad fountains,
　　What need you flow so fast?
Look how the snowy mountains
　　Heaven's sun doth gently waste.
　　my sun's heavenly eyes,
　　w not your weeping,
　Sor now lies sleeping,
　　w softly lies
　　　g.
　　Sleep is
　　A rest　iling,
　Doth not t　e begets;
　　When fa　e smiling
　　Rest you, then　smiling
　　　　　　he sets?
　　　　　　　　eyes,

UNKNOWN

Melt not in weeping,
While she lies sleeping,
Softly, now softly lies
Sleeping.

CUPID AND THE NYMPH

It chanced of late a shepherd's swain,
That went to seek a strayèd sheep,
Within a thicket on the plain
Espied a dainty nymph asleep.

Her golden hair o'erspread her face,
Her careless arms abroad were cast,
Her quiver had her pillow's place,
Her breast lay bare to every blast.

The shepherd stood and gazed his fill,
Nought durst he do, nought durst he say,
When chance, or else perhaps his will,
Did guide the God of Love that way.

The crafty boy that sees her sleep,
Whom if she waked he durst not see,
Behind her closely seeks to creep,
Before her nap should ended be.

There come, he steals her shafts away,
And puts his own into their place;
Ne dares he any longer stay,
But ere she wakes, hies hence apace.

Scarce was he gone when she awakes,
And spies the shepherd standing by;
Her bended bow in haste she takes,
And at the simple swain let fly.

Forth flew the shaft and pierced his heart,
That to the ground he fell with pain;
Yet up again forthwith he start,
And to the nymph he ran amain.

1379

Amazed to see so strange a sight,
She shot, and shot, but all in vain;
The more his wounds, the more his might;
Love yieldeth strength in midst of pain.

Her angry eyes are great with tears,
She blames her hands, she blames her skill;
The bluntness of her shafts she fears,
And try them on herself she will.

Take heed, sweet nymph, try not the shaft,
Each little touch will prick thy heart;
Alas! thou knowest not Cupid's craft,
Revenge is joy, the end is smart.

Yet try she will, and prick some bare;
Her hands were gloved, and next to hand
Was that fair breast, that breast so rare,
That made the shepherd senseless stand.

That breast she prick'd, and through that breast
Love finds an entry to her heart;
At feeling of this new-come guest,
Lord, how the gentle nymph doth start.

She runs not now, she shoots no more;
Away she throws both shafts and bow;
She seeks for that she shunn'd before,
She thinks the shepherd's haste too slow.

Though mountains meet not, lovers may;
So others do, and so do they.
The God of Love sits on a tree,
And laughs that pleasant sight to see.

SISTER, AWAKE!

Sister, awake! close not your eyes!
    The day her light discloses,
And the bright morning doth arise
    Out of her bed of roses.

1380

UNKNOWN

See the clear sun, the world's bright eye,
   In at our window peeping:
Lo, how he blusheth to espy
   Us idle wenches sleeping!

Therefore awake! make haste, I say,
   And let us, without staying,
All in our gowns of green so gay
   Into the Park a-maying!

SUMMER

Cold winter ice is fled and gone,
And summer brags on every tree;
The red-breast peeps among the throng
Of wood-brown birds that wanton be:
Each one forgets what they have been,
And so doth Phyllis, summer's queen.

DEVOTION

Fain would I change that note
To which fond Love hath charm'd me
Long, long to sing by rote,
Fancying that that harm'd me:
Yet when this thought doth come,
"Love is the perfect sum
    Of all delight,"
I have no other choice
Either for pen or voice
    To sing or write.

O Love! they wrong thee much
That say thy sweet is bitter,
When thy rich fruit is such
As nothing can be sweeter.
Fair house of joy and bliss,
Where truest pleasure is,
    I do adore thee:
I know thee what thou art,
I serve thee with my heart,
    And fall before thee.

1381

THERE IS A LADY

There is a lady sweet and kind,
Was never face so pleased my mind;
I did but see her passing by,
And yet I love her till I die.

Her gesture, motion, and her smiles,
Her wit, her voice my heart beguiles,
Beguiles my heart, I know not why,
And yet I love her till I die.

Her free behaviour, winning looks,
Will make a lawyer burn his books;
I touched her not, alas! not I,
And yet I love her till I die.

Had I her fast betwixt mine arms,
Judge you that think such sports were harms
Were't any harm? no, no, fie, fie,
For I will love her till I die.

Should I remain confinèd there
So long as Phœbus in his sphere,
I to request, she to deny,
Yet would I love her till I die.

Cupid is wingèd and doth range,
Her country so my love doth change:
But change she earth, or change she sky,
Yet will I love her till I die.

TWO IN ONE

To ask for all thy love, and thy whole heart,
'Twere madness!
I do not sue
Nor can admit,
Fairest! from you
To have all!
Yet who giveth all, hath nothing to impart
But sadness!

UNKNOWN

He that receiveth all, can have no more
    Than seeing.
      My love, by length
      Of every hour,
    Gathers new strength!
      New growth, new flower!
You must have daily new rewards in store,
    Still being.

You cannot, every day, give me your heart
    For merit!
      Yet, if you will,
      When yours doth go,
    You shall have still
      One to bestow!
For you shall mine, when yours doth part,
    Inherit!

Yet, if you please, I'll find a better way,
    Than change them.
      For so, alone,
      Dearest! we shall
    Be one! and one
      Another's all!
Let us join our hearts, that nothing may
    Estrange them!

LOVE IN THY YOUTH

Love in thy youth, fair maid, be wise;
    Old Time will make thee colder,
And though each morning new arise
    Yet we each day grow older.
Thou as heaven art fair and young,
    Thine eyes like twin stars shining:
But ere another day be sprung,
    All these will be declining.
Then winter comes with all his fears
    And all thy sweets shall borrow;
Too late then wilt thou shower thy tears,
    And I too late shall sorrow.

THE GREAT ADVENTURER

Over the mountains
And over the waves,
Under the fountains
And under the graves;
Under floods that are deepest,
Which Neptune obey;
Over rocks that are steepest,
Love will find out the way.

Where there is no place
For the glow-worm to lie;
Where there is no space
For receipt of a fly;
Where the midge dares not venture
Lest herself fast she lay;
If love come, he will enter,
And soon find out his way.

You may esteem him
A child for his might;
Or you may deem him
A coward from his flight;
But if she whom love doth honour
Be concealed from the day,
Set a thousand guards upon her,
Love will find out the way.

Some think to lose him
By having him confined;
And some do suppose him,
Poor thing, to be blind;
But if ne'er so close ye wall him,
Do the best that you may,
Blind love, if so ye call him,
Will find out his way.

UNKNOWN

You may train the eagle
To stoop to your fist;
Or you may inveigle
The phœnix of the east;
The lioness, ye may move her
To give o'er her prey;
But you'll ne'er stop a lover:
He will find out his way.

If the earth it should part him,
He would gallop it o'er;
If the seas should o'erthwart him,
He would swim to the shore;
Should his love become a swallow,
Through the air to stray,
Love will lend wings to follow,
And will find out the way.

THE KING'S PROGRESS

Yet if his majesty our sovereign lord
Should of his own accord
Friendly himself invite,
And say, "I'll be your guest to-morrow night,"
How should we stir ourselves, call and command
All hands to work!   "Let no man idle stand.
Set me fine Spanish tables in the hall;
See they be fitted all;
Let there be room to eat,
And order taken that there want no meat.
See every sconce and candlestick made bright,
That without tapers they may give a light.
Look to the presence: are the carpets spread,
The dais o'er the head,
The cushions in the chairs,
And all the candles lighted on the stairs?
Perfume the chambers, and in any case
Let each man give attendance in his place!"

1385

Thus if the king were coming would we do,
And 'twere good reason too;
For 'tis a duteous thing
To show all honour to an earthly king,
And after all our travail and our cost,
So he be pleased, to think no labour lost.
But at the coming of the King of Heaven
All's set at six and seven:
We wallow in our sin,
Christ cannot find a chamber in the inn.
We entertain Him always like a stranger,
And as at first still lodge Him in the manger.

HUE AND CRY AFTER CHLORIS

Tell me, ye wand'ring Spirits of the air,
Did you not see a nymph more bright, more fair
Than Beauty's darling, or of looks more sweet
Than stol'n content?   If such an one you meet,
Wait on her hourly wheresoe'er she flies,
And cry, and cry, Amyntor for absence dies.

Go search the vallies; pluck up ev'ry rose,
You'll find a scent, a blush of her in those;
Fish, fish for pearl or coral, there you'll see
How oriental all her colours be;
Go, call the echoes to your aid, and cry
Chloris, Chloris, for that's her name for whom I die.

But stay awhile, I have informed you ill,
Were she on earth, she had been with me still:
Go, fly to Heaven, examine ev'ry sphere:
And try what star hath lately lighted there;
If any brighter than the sun you see,
Fall down, fall down and worship it, for that is she.

THOMAS THE RHYMER

True Thomas lay on Huntlie bank;
   A ferlie he spied wi' his e'e;
And there he saw a lady bright,
   Come riding down by the Eildon Tree.

UNKNOWN

Her skirt was o' the grass-green silk,
  Her mantle o' the velvet fine;
At ilka tett o' her horse's mane
  Hung fifty siller bells and nine.

True Thomas he pu'd aff his cap,
  And louted low down on his knee:
"Hail to thee, Mary, Queen of Heaven!
  For thy peer on earth could never be."

"O no, O no, Thomas!" she said,
  "That name does not belang to me;
I'm but the Queen o' fair Elfland,
  That am hither come to visit thee.

"Harp and carp, Thomas!" she said,
  "Harp and carp along wi' me;
And if ye dare to kiss my lips,
  Sure of your body I will be."

"Betide me weal, betide me woe,
  That weird shall never daunten me."
Syne he has kissed her rosy lips,
  All underneath the Eildon Tree.

"Now, ye maun go wi' me," she said;
  "True Thomas, ye maun go wi' me;
And ye maun serve me seven years,
  Through weal or woe as may chance be."

She's mounted on her milk-white steed;
  She's ta'en true Thomas up behind;
And aye, whene'er her bridle rang,
  The steed gaed swifter than the wind.

O they rade on, and farther on,
  The steed gaed swifter than the wind;
Until they reached a desert wide,
  And living land was left behind.

1387

"Light down, light down now, true Thomas,
    And lean your head upon my knee;
Abide ye there a little space,
    And I will show you ferlies three.

"O see ye not yon narrow road,
    So thick beset wi' thorns and briers?
That is the Path of Righteousness,
    Though after it but few inquires.

"And see ye not yon braid, braid road,
    That lies across the lily leven?
That is the Path of Wickedness,
    Though some call it the Road to Heaven.

"And see ye not yon bonny road,
    That winds about the fernie brae?
That is the Road to fair Elfland,
    Where thou and I this night maun gae.

"But, Thomas, ye sall haud your tongue,
    Whatever ye may hear or see;
For speak ye word in Elfyn-land,
    Ye'll ne'er win back to your ain countrie."

O they rade on, and farther on,
    And they waded rivers abune the knee;
And they saw neither sun nor moon,
    But they heard the roaring of the sea.

It was mirk, mirk night, there was nae starlight,
    They waded through red blude to the knee;
For a' the blude that's shed on earth
    Rins through the springs o' that countrie.

Syne they came to a garden green,
    And she pu'd an apple frae a tree:
"Take this for thy wages, true Thomas;
    It will give thee tongue that can never lee."

1388

UNKNOWN

"My tongue is mine ain," true Thomas, he said;
　"A gudely gift ye wad gie to me!
I neither dought to buy nor sell,
　At fair or tryst where I might be.

"I dought neither speak to prince or peer,
　Nor ask of grace from fair lady!"
"Now haud thy peace!" the lady said,
　"For as I say, so must it be."

He has gotten a coat of the even cloth,
　And a pair o' shoon of the velvet green;
And till seven years were gane and past,
　True Thomas on earth was never seen.

HELEN OF KIRCONNELL

I wish I were where Helen lies,
Night and day on me she cries;
O that I were where Helen lies,
　On fair Kirconnell lea!

Curst be the heart that thought the thought,
And curst the hand that fired the shot,
When in my arms burd Helen dropt,
　And died to succour me!

O think na ye my heart was sair,
When my Love dropp'd and spak nae mair!
There did she swoon wi' meikle care,
　On fair Kirconnell lea.

As I went down the water side,
None but my foe to be my guide,
None but my foe to be my guide,
　On fair Kirconnell lea;

I lighted down my sword to draw,
I hackèd him in pieces sma',
I hackèd him in pieces sma',
　For her sake that died for me.

1389

O Helen fair, beyond compare!
I'll mak a garland o' thy hair,
Shall bind my heart for evermair,
   Until the day I die!

O that I were where Helen lies!
Night and day on me she cries;
Out of my bed she bids me rise,
   Says, "Haste, and come to me!"

O Helen fair! O Helen chaste!
If I were with thee, I'd be blest,
Where thou lies low and taks thy rest,
   On fair Kirconnell lea.

I wish my grave were growing green,
A winding-sheet drawn owre me e'en,
And I in Helen's arms lying,
   On fair Kirconnell lea.

I wish I were where Helen lies!
Night and day on me she cries;
And I am weary of the skies,
   For her sake that died for me.

ON A SHEPHERD LOSING HIS MISTRESS

Stay, Shepherd, prithee shepherd stay!
Didst thou not see her run this way?
Where may she be, must thou not guess?
Alas! I've lost my shepherdess.

I fear some Satyr has betrayed
My pretty lamb unto the shade:
Then, woe is me, for I'm undone,
For in the shade she was my sun.

In summer heat were she not seen,
No solitary vale was green:
The blooming hills, the downy meads,
Bear not a flower but when she treads.

Hushed were the senseless trees when she
Sat but to keep them company:
The silver streams were swelled with pride,
When she sat singing by their side.

The pink, the cowslip and the rose
Strive to salute her where she goes;
And then contend to kiss her show,
The pansy and the daisy too.

But now I wander on the plains,
Forsake my home and fellow-swains,
And must for want of her, I see,
Resolve to die in misery.

LOVE ME NOT FOR COMELY GRACE

Love me not for comely grace,
For my pleasing eye or face,
Nor for any outward part,
No, nor for my constant heart,—
   For those may fail, or turn to ill,
     So thou and I shall sever:
Keep therefore a true woman's eye,
And love me still, but know not why—
   So hast thou the same reason still
     To doat upon me ever!

THE FORSAKEN BRIDE

O waly waly up the bank,
   And waly waly down the brae,
And waly waly yon burn-side
   Where I and my Love wont to gae!
I leant my back unto an aik,
   I thought it was a trusty tree;
But first it bow'd, and syne it brak,
   Sae my true Love did lichtly me.

O waly waly, but love be bonny
    A little time while it is new;
But when 'tis auld, it waxeth cauld
    And fades awa' like morning dew.
O wherefore should I busk my head?
    Or wherefore should I kame my hair?
For my true Love has me forsook,
    And says he'll never loe me mair.

Now Arthur-seat sall be my bed;
    The sheets shall ne'er be prest by me:
Saint Anton's well sall be my drink,
    Since my true Love has forsaken me.
Marti'mas wind, when wilt thou blaw
    And shake the green leaves aff the tree?
O gentle Death, when wilt thou come?
    For of my life I am wearíe.

'Tis not the frost, that freezes fell,
    Nor blawing snaw's inclemencie;
'Tis not sic cauld that makes me cry,
    But my Love's heart grown cauld to me.
When we came in by Glasgow town
    We were a comely sight to see;
My Love was clad in the black velvét,
    And I mysell in cramasie.

But had I wist, before I kist,
    That love had been sae ill to win;
I had locked my heart in a case of gowd
    And pinn'd it with a siller pin.
And, O! if my young babe were born,
    And set upon the nurse's knee.
And I mysell were dead and gane,
    And the green grass growing over me!

PHILLADA FLOUTS ME

O what a plague is love!
    How shall I bear it?
She will inconstant prove,
    I greatly fear it.

UNKNOWN

She so torments my mind
   That my strength faileth,
And wavers with the wind
   As a ship saileth.
Please her the best I may,
She loves still to gainsay;
Alack and well-a-day!
   Phillada flouts me.

At the fair yesterday
   She did pass by me;
She look'd another way
   And would not spy me:
I woo'd for her to dine,
   But could not get her;
Will had her to the wine—
   He might entreat her.
With Daniel she did dance,
On me she look'd askance:
O thrice unhappy chance!
   Phillada flouts me.

Fair maid, be not so coy,
   Do not disdain me!
I am my mother's joy:
   Sweet, entertain me!
She'll give me, when she dies,
   All that is fitting:
Her poultry and her bees,
   And her goose sitting,
A pair of mattrass beds,
And a bag full of shreds;
And yet, for all this guedes,
   Phillada flouts me!

She hath a clout of mine
   Wrought with blue coventry,
Which she keeps for a sign
   Of my fidelity:

1393

But i' faith, if she flinch
    She shall not wear it;
To Tib, my t'other wench,
    I mean to bear it.
And yet it grieves my heart
So soon from her to part:
Death strike me with his dart!
    Phillada flouts me.

Thou shalt eat crudded cream
    All the year lasting,
And drink the crystal stream
    Pleasant in tasting;
Which and whey whilst thou lust,
    And bramble-berries,
Pie-lid and pastry-crust,
    Pears, plums, and cherries.
Thy raiment shall be thin,
Made of a weevil's skin—
Yet all's not worth a pin!
    Phillada flouts me.

In the last month of May
    I made her posies;
I heard her often say
    That she loved roses.
Cowslips and gillyflowers
    And the white lily
I brought to deck the bowers
    For my sweet Philly.
But she did all disdain,
And threw them back again;
Therefore 'tis flat and plain
    Phillada flouts me.

Fair maiden, have a care,
    And in time take me;
I can have those as fair
    If you forsake me:
For Doll the dairy-maid

UNKNOWN

Laugh'd at me lately,
And wanton Winifred
Favours me greatly.
One throws milk on my clothes,
T'other plays with my nose;
What wanting sins are those?
Phillada flouts me.

I cannot work nor sleep
At all in season:
Love wounds my heart so deep
Without all reason.
I 'gin to pine away
In my love's shadow,
Like as a fat beast may,
Penn'd in a meadow.
I shall be dead, I fear,
Within this thousand year:
And all for that my dear
Phillada flouts me.

CHLORIS IN THE SNOW

I saw fair Chloris walk alone,
When feather'd rain came softly down,
As Jove descending from his Tower
To court her in a silver shower:
The wanton snow flew to her breast,
Like pretty birds into their nest,
But, overcome with whiteness there,
For grief it thaw'd into a tear:
    Thence falling on her garments' hem,
    To deck her, froze into a gem.

WILLIE DROWNED IN YARROW

Down in yon garden sweet and gay
    Where bonnie grows the lily,
I heard a fair maid sighing say,
    "My wish be wi' sweet Willie!

1395

"Willie's rare, and Willie's fair,
  And Willie's wondrous bonnie;
And Willie hecht to marry me
  Gin e'er he married ony.

"O gentle wind, that bloweth south
  From where my Love repaireth,
Convey a kiss frae his dear mouth
  And tell me how he fareth!

"O tell sweet Willie to come doun
  And hear the mavis singing,
And see the birds on ilka bush
  And leaves around them hinging.

"The lav'rock there, wi' her white breast
  And gentle throat sae narrow;
There's sport eneuch for gentlemen
  On Leader haughs and Yarrow.

"O Leader haughs are wide and braid
  And Yarrow haughs are bonnie;
There Willie hecht to marry me
  If e'er he married ony.

"But Willie's gone, whom I thought on,
  And does not hear me weeping;
Draws many a tear frae true love's e'e
  When other maids are sleeping.

"Yestreen I made my bed fu' braid,
  The night I'll mak' it narrow,
For a' the live-lang winter night
  I lie twined o' my marrow.

"O came ye by yon water-side?
  Pou'd you the rose or lily?
Or came you by yon meadow green,
  Or saw you my sweet Willie?"

1396

UNKNOWN

She sought him up, she sought him down,
  She sought him braid and narrow;
Syne, in the cleaving of a craig,
  She found him drown'd in Yarrow!

NON NOBIS

Not unto us, O Lord,
Not unto us the rapture of the day,
The peace of night, or love's divine surprise,
High heart, high speech, high deeds 'mid honouring eyes;
For at Thy word
All these are taken away.

Not unto us, O Lord:
To us thou givest the scorn, the scourge, the scar,
The ache of life, the loneliness of death,
The insufferable sufficiency of breath;
And with Thy sword
Thou piercest very far.

Not unto us, O Lord:
Nay, Lord, but unto her be all things given—
My light and life and earth and sky be blasted—
But let not all that wealth of love be wasted:
Let Hell afford
The pavement of her Heaven!

A PRAISE OF HIS LADY

Give place, you ladies, and begone!
  Boast not yourselves at all!
For here at hand approacheth one
  Whose face will stain you all.

The virtue of her lively looks
  Excels the precious stone;
I wish to have none other books
  To read or look upon.

1397

In each of her two crystal eyes
    Smileth a naked boy;
It would you all in heart suffice
    To see that lamp of joy.

I think Nature hath lost the mould
    Where she her shape did take;
Or else I doubt if Nature could
    So fair a creature make.

She may be well compared
    Unto the Phœnix kind,
Whose like was never seen or heard,
    That any man can find.

In life she is Diana chaste,
    In troth Penelopey;
In word and eke in deed steadfast.
    —What will you more we say?

If all the world were sought so far,
    Who could find such a wight?
Her beauty twinkleth like a star
    Within the frosty night.

Her rosial colour comes and goes
    With such a comely grace,
More ruddier, too, than doth the rose,
    Within her lively face.

At Bacchus' feast none shall her meet,
    Ne at no wanton play,
Nor gazing in an open street,
    Nor gadding as a stray.

The modest mirth that she doth use
    Is mix'd with shamefastness;
All vice she doth wholly refuse,
    And hateth idleness.

UNKNOWN

O Lord! it is a world to see
    How virtue can repair,
And deck in her such honesty,
    Whom Nature made so fair.

Truly she doth so far exceed
    Our women nowadays,
As doth the jeliflower a weed;
    And more a thousand ways.

How might I do to get a graff
    Of this unspotted tree?
—For all the rest are plain but chaff,
    Which seem good corn to be.

This gift alone I shall her give;
    When death doth what he can,
Her honest fame shall ever live
    Within the mouth of man.

ENVOY

Go, songs, for ended is our brief, sweet play;
　Go, children of swift joy and tardy sorrow:
And some are sung, and that was yesterday,
　And some unsung, and that may be to-morrow.

Go forth; and if it be o'er stony way,
　Old joy can lend what newer grief must borrow;
And it was sweet, and that was yesterday,
　And sweet is sweet, though purchasèd with sorrow.

Go, songs, and come not back from your far way;
　And if men ask you why ye smile and sorrow,
Tell them ye grieve, for your hearts know to-day;
　Tell them ye smile, for your eyes know to-morrow.
　　　　　　　　　　　　—Francis Thompson.

SUPPLEMENTARY POEMS

SUPPLEMENTARY POEMS

Lizette Woodworth Reese

TEARS

When I consider Life and its few years—
A wisp of fog betwixt us and the sun;
A call to battle, and the battle done
Ere the last echo dies within our ears;
A rose choked in the grass; an hour of fears;
The gusts that past a darkening shore do beat;
The burst of music down an unlistening street—
I wonder at the idleness of tears.
Ye old, old dead, and ye of yesternight,
Chieftains, and bards, and keepers of the sheep,
By every cup of sorrow that you had,
Loose me from tears, and make me see aright
How each hath back what once he stayed to weep;
Homer his sight, David his little lad!

Louise Imogen Guiney

THE KINGS

A man said unto his Angel:
  "My spirits are fallen low,
And I cannot carry this battle:
  O brother! where might I go?

"The terrible Kings are on me
  With spears that are deadly bright;
Against me so from the cradle
  Do fate and my fathers fight."

Then said to the man his Angel:
  "Thou wavering, witless soul,
Back to the ranks! What matter
  To win or to lose the whole,

1403

"As judged by the little judges
    Who hearken not well, nor see?
Not thus, by the outer issue,
    The Wise shall interpret thee.

"Thy will is the sovereign measure
    And only event of things:
The puniest heart, defying,
    Were stronger than all these Kings.

"Though out of the past they gather,
    Mind's Doubt, and Bodily Pain,
And pallid Thirst of the Spirit
    That is kin to the other twain,

"And Grief, in a cloud of banners,
    And ringletted Vain Desires,
And Vice, with the spoils upon him
    Of thee and thy beaten sires,—

"While Kings of eternal evil
    Yet darken the hills about,
Thy part is with broken sabre
    To rise on the last redoubt;

"To fear not sensible failure,
    Nor covet the game at all,
But fighting, fighting, fighting,
    Die, driven against the wall!"

William Vaughn Moody

THE BRUTE

Through his might men work their wills.
They have boweled out the hills
For food to keep him toiling in the cages they have wrought;
And they fling him, hour by hour,
Limbs of men to give him power;
Brains of men to give him cunning; and for dainties to devour

Children's souls, the little worth; hearts of women, cheaply
 bought:
He takes them and he breaks them, but he gives them scanty
 thought.

For about the noisy land,
Roaring, quivering 'neath his hand,
His thoughts brood fierce and sullen or laugh in lust of pride
O'er the stubborn things that he
Breaks to dust and brings to be.
Some he mightily establishes, some flings down utterly.
There is thunder in his stride, nothing ancient can abide,
When he hales the hills together and bridles up the tide.

Quietude and loveliness,
Holy sights that heal and bless,
They are scattered and abolished where his iron hoof is set;
When he splashes through the brae
Silver streams are choked with clay,
When he snorts the bright cliffs crumble and the woods go
 down like hay;
He lairs in pleasant cities, and the haggard people fret
Squalid 'mid their new-got riches, soot-begrimed and desolate.

They who caught and bound him tight
Laughed exultant at his might,
Saying, "Now behold, the good time comes for the weariest
 and the least!
We will use this lusty knave:
No more need for men to slave;
We may rise and look about us and have knowledge ere the
 grave."
But the Brute said in his breast, "Till the mills I grind have
 ceased,
The riches shall be dust of dust, dry ashes be the feast!

"On the strong and cunning few
Cynic favors I will strew;
I will stuff their maw with overplus until their spirit dies;
From the patient and the low
I will take the joys they know;

They shall hunger after vanities and still an-hungered go.
Madness shall be on the people, ghastly jealousies arise;
Brother's blood shall cry on brother up the dead and empty
　　skies.

"I will burn and dig and hack
Till the heavens suffer lack;
God shall feel a pleasure fail Him, crying to his cherubim,
'Who hath flung yon mud-ball there
Where my world went green and fair?'
I shall laugh and hug me, hearing how his sentinels declare,
''Tis the Brute they chained to labor!　He has made the
　　bright earth dim.
Stores of wares and pelf a plenty, but they got no good of
　　him.' "

So he plotted in his rage:
So he deals it, age by age.
But even as he roared hs curse a still small Voice befell;
Lo, a still and pleasant voice bade them none the less rejoice,
For the Brute must bring the good time on; he has no other
　　choice.
He may struggle, sweat, and yell, but he knows exceeding well
He must work them out salvation ere they send him back to
　　hell.

All the desert that he made
He must treble bless with shade,
In primal wastes set precious seed of rapture and of pain;
All the strongholds that he built
For the powers of greed and guilt—
He must strew their bastions down the sea and choke their
　　towers with silt;
He must make the temples clean for the gods to come again,
And lift the lordly cities under skies without a stain.

In a very cunning tether
He must lead the tyrant weather;
He must loose the curse of Adam from the worn neck of the
　　race;
He must cast out hate and fear,
Dry away each fruitless tear,

1406

And make the fruitful tears to gush from the deep heart and
    clear.
He must give each man his portion, each his pride and worthy
    place;
He must batter down the arrogant and lift the weary face,
On each vile mouth set purity, on each low forehead grace.

Then perhaps, at the last day,
They will whistle him away,
Lay a hand upon his muzzle in the face of God, and say,
"Honor, Lord, the Thing we tamed!
Let him not be scourged or blamed,
Even through his wrath and fierceness was thy fierce wroth
    world reclaimed!
Honor Thou thy servants' servant; let thy justice now be
    shown."
Then the Lord will heed their saying, and the Brute come to
    his own,
'Twixt the Lion and the Eagle, by the armpost of the Throne.

Ridgely Torrence

EYE-WITNESS

Down by the railroad in a green valley
By dancing water, there he stayed awhile
Singing, and three men with him, listeners,
All tramps, all homeless reapers of the wind,
Motionless now and while the song went on
Transfigured into mages thronged with visions;
There with the late light of the sunset on them
And on clear water spinning from a spring
Through little cones of sand dancing and fading,
Close beside pine woods where the hermit-thrush
Cast, when love dazzled him, shadows of music
That lengthened, fluting, through the singer's pauses
While the sure earth rolled eastward bringing stars
Over the singer and the men that listened
There by the roadside, understanding all.

1407

A train went by but nothing seemed to be changed.
Some eye at a car window must have flashed
From the plush world inside the glassy Pullman,
Carelessly bearing off the scene for ever,
With idle wonder what the men were doing,
Seeing they were so strangely fixed, and seeing
Torn papers from their smeary dreary meal
Spread on the ground with old tomato cans
Muddy with dregs of lukewarm chicory,
Neglected while they listened to the song.
And while he sang the singer's face was lifted,
And the sky shook down a soft light upon him
Out of its branches where like fruits there were
Many beautiful stars and planets moving,
With lands upon them, rising from their seas,
Glorious lands with glittering sands upon them,
With soils of gold and magic mould for seeding,
The shining loam of lands afoam with gardens
On mightier stars with giant rains and suns
There in the heavens; but on none of all
Was there ground better than he stood upon:
There was no world there in the sky above him
Deeper in promise than the earth beneath him
Whose dust had flowered up in him the singer
And three men understanding every word.

The Tramp Sings:

I will sing, I will go, and never ask me why.
I was born a rover and a passer-by.

I seem to myself like water and sky,
A river and a rover and a passer-by.

But in the winter three years back
We lit us a night fire by the track,

And the snow came up and the fire it flew
And we couldn't find the warming room for two.

One had to suffer, so I left him the fire
And I went to the weather from my heart's desire.

It was night on the line, it was no more fire,
But the zero whistle through the icy wire.

As I went suffering through the snow
Something like a shadow came moving slow.

I went up to it and I said a word;
Something flew above it like a kind of bird.

I leaned in closer and I saw a face;
A light went round me but I kept my place.

My heart went open like an apple sliced;
I saw my Saviour and I saw my Christ.

Well, you may not read it in a book,
But it takes a gentle Saviour to give a gentle look.

I looked in his eyes and I read the news;
His heart was having the railroad blues.

Oh, the railroad blues will cost you dear,
Keeps you moving on for something that you don't see
        here.

We stood and whispered in a kind of moon;
The line was looking like May and June.

I found he was a roamer and a journey man,
Looking for a lodging since the night began.

He went to the doors but he didn't have the pay,
He went to the windows, then he went away.

Says: "We'll walk together and we'll both be fed."
Says: "I will give you the 'other' bread."

Oh, the bread he gave and without money!
O drink, O fire, O burning honey!

It went all through me like a shining storm:
I saw inside me, it was light and warm.

I saw deep under and I saw above,
I saw the stars weighed down with love.

They sang that love to burning birth,
They poured that music to the earth.

I heard the stars sing low like mothers.
He said: "Now look, and help feed others."

I looked around, and as close as touch
Was everybody that suffered much.

They reached out, there was darkness only;
They could not see us, they were lonely.

I saw the hearts that deaths took hold of,
With the wounds bare that were not told of;

Hearts with things in them making gashes;
Hearts that were choked with their dreams' ashes;

Women in front of the rolled-back air,
Looking at their breasts and nothing there;

Good men wasting and trapped in hells;
Hurt lads shivering with the fare-thee-wells.

I saw them as if something bound them;
I stood there but my heart went round them.

I begged him not to let me see them wasted.
Says: "Tell them then what you have tasted."

Told him I was weak as a rained-on bee;
Told him I was lost.—Says: "Lean on me."

Something happened then I could not tell,
But I knew I had the water for every hell.

Any other thing it was no use bringing;
They needed what the stars were singing,

What the whole sky sang like waves of light,
The tune that it danced to, day and night.

Oh, I listened to the sky for the tune to come;
The song seemed easy, but I stood there dumb.

The stars could feel me reaching through them;
They let down light and drew me to them.

I stood in the sky in a light like day,
Drinking in the word that all things say

Where the worlds hang growing in clustered shapes
Dripping the music like wine from grapes.

With "Love, Love, Love," above the pain,
—The vinelike song with its winelike rain.

Through heaven under heaven the song takes root
Of the turning. burning, deathless fruit.

I came to the earth and the pain so near me,
I tried that song but they couldn't hear me.

I went down into the ground to grow,
A seed for a song that would make men know.

Into the ground from my Roamer's light
I went; he watched me sink to night.

Deep in the ground from my human grieving,
His pain ploughed in me to believing.

Oh, he took earth's pain to be his bride,
While the heart of life sang in his side.

For I felt the pain, I took its kiss,
My heart broke into dust with his.

Then sudden through the earth I found life springing;
The dust men trampled on was singing.

Deep in my dust I felt its tones;
The roots of beauty went round my bones.

I stirred, I rose like a flame, like a river,
I stood on the line, I could sing for ever.

Love had pierced into my human sheathing,
Song came out of me simple as breathing.

A freight came by, the line grew colder.
He laid his hand upon my shoulder.

Says, "Don't stay on the line such nights,"
And led me by the hand to the station lights.

I asked him in front of the station-house wall
If he had lodging. Says: "None at all."

I pointed to my heart and looked in his face.—
"Here,—if you haven't got a better place."

He looked and he said: "Oh, we still must roam
But if you'll keep it open, well, I'll call it 'home.' "

The thrush now slept whose pillow was his wing.
So the song ended and the four remained
Still in the faint starshine that silvered them,
While the low sound went on of broken water
Out of the spring and through the darkness flowing
Over a stone that held it from the sea.
Whether the men spoke after could not be told,
A mist from the ground so veiled them, but they waited
A little longer till the moon came up;
Then on the gilded track leading to the mountains,
Against the moon they faded in common gold
And earth bore East with all toward the new morning.

Wilfrid Wilson Gibson

A CATCH FOR SINGING

Said the Old Young Man to the Young Old Man—
Alack and well-a-day!
Said the Young Old Man to the Old Young Man—
The cherry tree's in flourish!

1412

CARL SANDBURG

Said the Old Young Man to the Young Old Man—
The world is growing grey.
Said the Young Old Man to the Old Young Man—
The cherry tree's in flourish!

Said the Old Young Man to the Young Old Man—
Both flower and fruit decay.
Said the Young Old Man to the Old Young Man—
The cherry tree's in flourish!

Said the Old Young Man to the Young Old Man—
Alack and well-a-day!
The world is growing grey,
And flower and fruit decay.
Beware Old Man, beware Old Man!
For the end of life is nearing
And the grave yawns by the way. . . .
Said the Young Old Man to the Old Young Man—
I'm a trifle hard of hearing
And can't catch a word you say . . .
But the cherry tree's in flourish!

Carl Sandburg

PRAYERS OF STEEL

Lay me on an anvil, O God.
Beat me and hammer me into a crowbar.
Let me pry loose old walls.
Let me lift and loosen old foundations.

Lay me on an anvil, O God.
Beat me and hammer me into a steel spike.
Drive me into the girders that hold a skyscraper together.
Take red-hot rivets and fasten me into the central girders.
Let me be the great nail holding a skyscraper through blue
    nights into white stars.

1413

Grace Hazard Conkling

PYTHON

A lithe beautiful fear
Thrusts through the parted canes.
I should have known it near
By the blind blood in my veins.

Here is one way of death,
Though with no threat for me.
Now I have caught my breath,
Now that my brain can see,

Amber pours over the ground,
Darkness of amber too:
Blue of the gulf profound,
Superb and bitter blue

Sharp on the lacquered back.
Gold-corniced groping head,
Bold-swerving diamond back,
Why wish such beauty dead?

Why thwart such will to live?
Better to think twice.
It is I who am fugitive
From Paradise.

Wallace Stevens

THE WORMS AT HEAVEN'S GATE

Out of the tomb, we bring Badroulbadour,
Within our bellies, we her chariot
Here is an eye. And here are, one by one,
The lashes of that eye and its white lid.
Here is the cheek on which that lid declined,
And, finger after finger, here, the hand,

1414.

The genius of that cheek. Here are the lips,
The bundle of the body and the feet.

.   .   .   .   .   .

Out of the tomb we bring Badroulbadour.

Lola Ridge

RÉVEILLE

Come forth, you workers!
Let the fires go cold—
Let the iron spill out, out of the troughs—
Let the iron run wild
Like a red bramble on the floors—
Leave the mill and the foundry and the mine
And the shrapnel lying on the wharves—
Leave the desk and the shuttle and the loom—
Come,
With your ashen lives,
Your lives like dust in your hands.

I call upon you, workers,
It is not yet light
But I beat upon your doors.
You say you await the Dawn
But I say you are the Dawn.
Come, in your irresistible unspent force
And make new light upon the mountains.

You have turned deaf ears to others—
Me you shall hear.
Out of the mouths of turbines,
Out of the turgid throats of engines,
Over the whistling steam,
You shall hear me shrilly piping.
Your mills I shall enter like the wind,
And blow upon your hearts,
Kindling a slow fire.

1415

They think they have tamed you, workers—
Beaten you to a tool
To scoop up hot honor
Till it be cool—
But out of the passion of the red frontiers
A great flower trembles and burns and glows
And each of its petals is a people.

Come forth, you workers—
Clinging to your stable
And your wisp of warm straw—
Let the fires grow cold,
Let the iron spill out of the troughs,
Let the iron run wild
Like a red bramble on the floors. . . .

As our forefathers stood on the prairies
So let us stand in a ring,
Let us tear up their prisons like grass
And beat them to barricades—
Let us meet the fire of their guns
With a greater fire,
Till the birds shall fly to the mountains
For one safe bough.

Humbert Wolfe

THE SOLDIER

I

From "Requiem"

Down some cold field in a world unspoken
   the young men are walking together, slim and tall,
and though they laugh to one another, silence is not broken:
   there is no sound however clear they call.

They are speaking together of what they loved in vain here,
   but the air is too thin to carry the thing they say.
They were young and golden, but they came on pain here,
   and their youth is age now, their gold is grey.

1416

Yet their hearts are not changed, and they cry to one another,
  "What have they done with the lives we laid aside?
Are they young with our youth, gold with our gold, my
      brother?
  Do they smile in the face of death, because we died?"

Down some cold field in a world uncharted
  the young seek each other with questioning eyes.
They question each other, the young, the golden-hearted,
  of the world that they were robbed of in their quiet Paradise.

THE HIGH SONG

From "Requiem"

The high song is over. Silent is the lute now.
  They are crowned for ever and discrowned now.
Whether they triumphed or suffered they are mute now,
  or at the most they are only a sound now.

The high song is over. There is none to complain now.
  No heart for healing, and none to break now
They have gone, and they will not come again now.
  They are sleeping at last, and they will not wake now.

The high song is over. And we shall not mourn now.
  There was a thing to say, and it is said now.
It is as though all these had been unborn now,
  it is as though the world itself were dead now.

The high song is over. Even the echoes fail now;
  winners and losers—they are only a theme now,
their victory and defeat a half-forgotten tale now;
  and even the angels are only a dream now.

There is no need for blame, no cause for praise now.
  Nothing to hide, to change or to discover.
They were men and women. They have gone their ways
      now,
  As men and women must. The high song is over.

1417

John Gould Fletcher

• THE SWAN

Under a wall of bronze,
Where beeches dip and trail
Thin branches in the water,
With red-tipped head and wings,
A beaked ship under sail,
There glides a great black swan.

Under the autumn trees
He goes. The branches quiver,
Dance in the wraith-like water,
Which ripples beneath the sedge
With the slackening furrow that glides
In his wake when he is gone:
The beeches bow dark heads.

Into the windless dusk,
Where in mist great towers stand
Guarding a lonely strand
That is bodiless and dim,
He speeds with easy stride;
And I would go beside,
Till the low brown hills divide
At last, for me and him.

"H. D."

FOURTH SONG FROM CYPRUS

Where is the nightingale,
In what myrrh-wood and dim?
ah, let the night come black,
for we would conjure back
all that enchanted him,
all that enchanted him.

Where is the bird of fire?
in what packed hedge of rose?
In what roofed ledge of flower?
no other creature knows
what magic lurks within,
        what magic lurks within.

Bird, bird, bird, bird, we cry,
hear, pity us in pain:
hearts break in the sunlight,
hearts break in daylight rain,
only night heals again,
        only night heals again.

Lew Sarett

FOUR LITTLE FOXES

Speak gently, Spring, and make no sudden sound;
For in my windy valley, yesterday I found
New-born foxes squirming on the ground . . .
        Speak gently.

Walk softly, March, forbear the bitter blow;
Her feet within a trap, her blood upon the snow,
The four little foxes saw their mother go . . .
        Walk softly.

Go lightly, Spring, oh give them no alarm;
When I covered them with boughs to shelter them from harm,
The thin blue foxes suckled at my arm . . .
        Go lightly.

Step softly, March, with your rampant hurricane;
Nuzzling one another, and whimpering with pain,
The new little foxes are shivering in the rain . . .
        Step softly.

1419

Leonard Bacon

"IO RITORNAI DALLA SANTISSIMA ONDA"

There is dogwood in my soul
The white four-petalled bract,
Pure, virginal, intact,
Gleams in the heart of the whole.
It has taken from the dark
That whiteness manifold.
Warmth trembles through the cold.
From lightlessness a spark
Kindles, and with the kindling
There is a song in my ears
Formed by perpetual spheres
That know no dwindling.
Where the golden-rod and aster
And the sumach flamed,
I saw the Spring unnamed,
And at last am master
Of the pale lordly place,
To which my stricken eyes
Never dared rise
To look on that still face.
Beauty that is content,
The stellar fire
That the soul may not hire,
Nor the wit invent,
Have habitation with me,
Who passing by way of the Grave
Crossed over the sacred wave
Of the Spiritual Sea.

T. S. Eliot

SWEENEY AMONG THE NIGHTINGALES

ὤμοι, πέπληγμαι καιριαν πληγὴν ἔσω

Apeneck Sweeney spreads his knees
Letting his arms hang down to laugh,

The zebra stripes along his jaw
Swelling to maculate giraffe.

The circles of the stormy moon
Slide westward toward the River Plate,
Death and the Raven drift above
And Sweeney guards the horned gate.

Gloomy Orion and the Dog
Are veiled; and hushed the shrunken seas;
The person in the Spanish cape
Tries to sit on Sweeney's knees

Slips and pulls the table cloth
Overturns the coffee-cup,
Reorganized upon the floor
She yawns and draws a stocking up;

The silent man in mocha brown
Sprawls at the window-sill and gapes;
The waiter brings in oranges
Bananas figs and hothouse grapes;

The silent vertebrate in brown
Contracts and concentrates, withdraws;
Rachel *née* Rabinovitch
Tears at the grapes with murderous paws;

She and the lady in the cape
Are suspect, thought to be in league;
Therefore the man with heavy eyes
Declines the gambit, shows fatigue,

Leaves the room and reappears
Outside the window, leaning in.
Branches of wistaria
Circumscribe a golden grin;

The host with someone indistinct
Converses at the door apart,
The nightingales are singing near
The Convent of the Sacred Heart,

And sang within the bloody wood
When Agamemnon cried aloud,
And let their liquid siftings fall
To stain the stiff dishonoured shroud.

John Crowe Ransom

HERE LIES A LADY

Here lies a lady of beauty and high degree.
Of chills and fever she died, of fever and chills,
The delight of her husband, her aunts, an infant of three,
And of medicos marvelling sweetly on her ills.

For either she burned, and her confident eyes would blaze,
And her fingers fly in a manner to puzzle their heads—
What was she making?   Why, nothing; she sat in a maze
Of old scraps of laces, snipped into curious shreds—

Or this would pass, and the light of her fire decline
Till she lay discouraged and cold as a thin stalk white and
blown,
And would not open her eyes, to kisses, to wine;
The sixth of these states was her last; the cold settled down.

Sweet ladies, long may ye bloom, and toughly I hope ye may
thole,
But was she not lucky?   In flowers and lace and mourning,
In love and great honour we bade God rest her soul
After six little spaces of chill, and six of burning.

Edith Sitwell

COLONEL FANTOCK

To Osbert and Sacheverell

Thus spoke the lady underneath the trees:
I was a member of a family
Whose legend was of hunting—(all the rare
And unattainable brightness of the air)—

A race whose fabled skill in falconry
Was used on the small song-birds and a winged
And blinded Destiny. . . . I think that only
Winged ones know the highest eyrie is so lonely.
There in a land, austere and elegant,
The castle seemed an arabesque in music;
We moved in an hallucination born
Of silence, which like music gave us lotus
To eat, perfuming lips and our long eyelids
As we trailed over the sad summer grass,
Or sat beneath a smooth and mournful tree.

And Time passed, suavely, imperceptibly.

But Dagobert and Peregrine and I
Were children then; we walked like shy gazelles
Among the music of the thin flower-bells.
And life still held some promise,—never ask
Of what,—but life seemed less a stranger, then,
Than ever after in this cold existence.
I always was a little outside life,—
And so the things we touch could comfort me;
I loved the shy dreams we could hear and see—
For I was like one dead, like a small ghost,
A little cold air wandering and lost.

All day within the straw-roofed arabesque
Of the towered castle and the sleepy gardens wandered
We; those delicate paladins the waves
Told us fantastic legends that we pondered.

And the soft leaves were breasted like a dove,
Crooning old mournful tales of untrue love.

When night came, sounding like the growth of trees,
My great-grandmother bent to say good-night,
And the enchanted moonlight seemed transformed
Into the silvery tinkling of an old
And gentle music-box that played a tune
Of Circean enchantments and far seas;
Her voice was lulling like the splash of these.

When she had given me her good-night kiss,
There, in her lengthened shadow, I saw this
Old military ghost with mayfly whiskers,—
Poor harmless creature, blown by the cold wind,
Boasting of unseen unreal victories
To a harsh unbelieving world unkind,—
For all the battles that this warrior fought
Were with cold poverty and helpless age—
His spoils were shelters from the winter's rage,
And so for ever through his braggart voice,
Through all that martial trumpet's sound, his soul
Wept with a little sound so pitiful,
Knowing that he is outside life for ever
With no one that will warm or comfort him. . . .
He is not even dead, but Death's buffoon
On a bare stage, a shrunken pantaloon.
His military banner never fell,
Nor his account of victories, the stories
Of old apocryphal misfortunes, glories
Which comforted his heart in later life
When he was the Napoleon of the schoolroom
And all the victories he gained were over
Little boys who would not learn to spell.

All day within the sweet and ancient gardens
He had my childish self for audience—
Whose body flat and strange, whose pale straight hair
Made me appear as thought I had been drowned—
(We all have the remote air of a legend)—
And Dagobert my brother whose large strength,
Great body and grave beauty still reflect
The Angevin dead kings from whom we spring;
And sweet as the young tender winds that stir
In thickets when the earliest flower-bells sing
Upon the boughs, was his just character;
And Peregrine the youngest with a naïve
Shy grace like a faun's, whose slant eyes seemed
The warm green light beneath eternal boughs.
His hair was like the fronds of feathers, life
In him was changing ever, springing fresh
As the dark songs of birds . . . the furry warmth

And purring sound of fires was in his voice
Which never failed to warm and comfort me.

And there were haunted summers in Troy Park
When all the stillness budded into leaves;
We listened, like Ophelia drowned in blond
And fluid hair, beneath stag-antlered trees;
Then, in the ancient park the country-pleasant
Shadows fell as brown as any pheasant,
And Colonel Fantock seemed like one of these.
Sometimes for comfort in the castle kitchen
He drowsed, where with a sweet and velvet lip
The snapdragons within the fire
Of their red summer never tire.
And Colonel Fantock liked our company;
For us he wandered over each old lie,
Changing the flowering hawthorn, full of bees,
Into the silver helm of Hercules,
For us defended Troy from the top stair
Outside the nursery, when the calm full moon
Was like the sound within the growth of trees.

But then one cruel day in deepest June,
When pink flowers seemed a sweet Mozartian tune,
And Colonel Fantock pondered o'er a book,
A gay voice like a honeysuckle nook,—
So sweet,—said, "It is Colonel Fantock's age
Which makes him babble." . . . Blown by winter's rage
The poor old man then knew his creeping fate,
The darkening shadow that would take his sight
And hearing; and he thought of his saved pence
Which scarce would rent a grave . . . that youthful voice
Was a dark bell which ever clanged "Too late"—
A creeping shadow that would steal from him
Even the little boys who would not spell,—
His only prisoners. . . . On that June day
Cold Death had taken his first citadel

Osbert Sitwell

ELEGY FOR MR. GOODBEARE

Do you remember Mr. Goodbeare, the carpenter,
Godfearing and bearded Mr. Goodbeare,
Who worked all day
At his carpenter's tray,
Do you remember Mr. Goodbeare?
Mr. Goodbeare, that Golconda of gleaming fable,
Lived, thin-ground between orchard and stable,
Pressed thus close against Alfred, his rival—
Mr. Goodbeare, who had never been away.

Do you remember Mr. Goodbeare,
Mr. Goodbeare, who never touched a cup?
Do you remember Mr. Goodbeare,
Who remembered a lot?
   Mr. Goodbeare could remember
     When things were properly kept up:
   Mr. Goodbeare could remember
     The christening and the coming-of-age:
   Mr. Goodbeare could remember
     The entire and roasted ox:
   Mr. Goodbeare could remember
     When the horses filled the stable,
And the port-wine-coloured gentry rode after the tawny fox:
   Mr. Goodbeare could remember
     The old lady in her eagle rage,
      Which knew no bounds:
   Mr. Goodbeare could remember
     When the escaped and hungering tiger
Flickered lithe and fierce through Foxton Wood,
When old Sir Nigel took his red-tongued, clamouring
     hounds,
And hunted it then and there,
   As a Gentleman Should.

Do you remember Mr. Goodbeare,
Mr. Goodbeare who never forgot?
  1426

V. SACKVILLE-WEST

Do you remember Mr. Goodbeare,
That wrinkled and golden apricot,
Dear, bearded, godfearing Mr. Goodbeare
Who remembered remembering such a lot?

Oh, do you remember, do you remember,
As *I* remember and deplore,
That day in drear and far-away December
When dear, godfearing, bearded Mr. Goodbeare
Could remember
No more?

V. Sackville-West

SPRING

Fraternity

from "The Land"

The peddler and the reddleman
Go vagrant through the shires.
The peddler tempts the farmer's wife
With all she most admires,
With beads, and boxes made of shells,
With lace and huckaback,
Buckles for shoes and rings for ears,
And Old Moore's Almanack,
With tapes and bobbins, pins and thread,
"What lack you? what d'you lack?"

The reddleman from head to foot
Dyed in his scarlet dye,
Leans like the Devil on the gate,
And grins when children cry.
"Redd for your sheep today, shepherd?
Redd for your yoes and rams?
I never broke a tup's leg yet
Or scared the mothering dams.
You'll find me natty at my job,
And gentle with the lambs."

1427

The tinker and the boggart both
Long since have learned by rote
How cold the rain and sharp the wind
Drive through a ragged coat.
The tinker with his little cart
Hawking his tinny wares,
Puts down his head against the sleet
And whimpers for repairs.
"Kind lady, patch your pots and pans,
And mend your broken chairs?"

The boggart on the frosty ridge,
His sleeveless arms held wide,
Stands gaunt against the wintry sky
Forever crucified,
A raven perched upon his hat,
About his feet the crows.
How bleak December turns the fields,
How desolate the snows,
How long the nights and short the days,
Tatterdemalion knows.

Archibald MacLeish

YOU, ANDREW MARVELL

And here face down beneath the sun
And here upon earth's noonward height
To feel the always coming on
The always rising of the night

To feel creep up the curving east
The earthy chill of dusk and slow
Upon those under lands the vast
And ever climbing shadow grow

And strange at Ecbatan the trees
Take leaf by leaf the evening strange
The flooding dark about their knees
The mountains over Persia change

1428

And now at Kermanshah the gate
Dark empty and the withered grass
And through the twilight now the late
Few travelers in the westward pass

And Baghdad darken and the bridge
Across the silent river gone
And through Arabia the edge
Of evening widen and steal on

And deepen on Palmyra's street
The wheel rut in the ruined stone
And Lebanon fade out and Crete
High through the clouds and overblown

And over Sicily the air
Still flashing with the landward gulls
And loom and slowly disappear
The sails above the shadowy hulls

And Spain go under and the shore
Of Africa the gilded sand
And evening vanish and no more
The low pale light across the land

Nor now the long light on the sea

And here face downward in the sun
To feel how swift how secretly
The shadow of the night comes on. . .

Robert P. Tristram Coffin

CRYSTAL MOMENT

Once or twice this side of death
Things can make one hold his breath.

From my boyhood I remember
A crystal moment of September.

1429

A wooded island rang with sounds
Of church bells in the throats of hounds.

A buck leaped out and took the tide
With jewels flowing past each side.

With his high head like a tree
He swam within a yard of me.

I saw the golden drop of light
In his eyes turned dark with fright.

I saw the forest's holiness
On him like a fierce caress.

Fear made him lovely past belief,
My heart was trembling like a leaf.

He leaned towards the land and life
With need above him like a knife.

In his wake the hot hounds churned,
They stretched their muzzles out and yearned.

They bayed no more, but swam and throbbed,
Hunger drove them till they sobbed.

Pursued, pursuers reached the shore
And vanished.   I saw nothing more.

So they passed, a pageant such
As only gods could witness much,

Life and death upon one tether
And running beautiful together.

Winifred Welles

SILVER FOR MIDAS

Some day, Midas, the daffodils
   Will jangle out of tune,
You will come down from your brassy hills
   Sick and tired of the noon.

To my silver house of birch bark
 You will come down, not asking much,
But feeling through the still dark
 For the things I love to touch.

My cobweb bells that bead the lawn,
 That ring more tinily than tears
Beneath my silver-stepping fawn
 With his pussywillow ears;

My squirrel with his tail curved up
 Like half a silver lyre,
My glassy flowers with stem and cup
 Glazed in a silver fire.

You shall kneel to the star in my pool,
 There your hot cheeks shall be lost,
Your yellow head rise up as cool
 As an aster dipped in frost.

You shall stand in a moonlit place
 As still as sculpture stands,
A look of wonder on your face
 Laid there by my silver hands.

Wilfred Owen

APOLOGIA PRO POEMATE MEO

I, too, saw God through mud,—
 The mud that cracked on cheeks when wretches smiled.
War brought more glory to their eyes than blood,
 And gave their laughs more glee than shakes a child.

Merry it was to laugh there—
 Where death becomes absurd and life absurder.
For power was on us as we slashed bones bare
 Not to feel sickness or remorse of murder.

I, too, have dropped off fear—
 Behind the barrage, dead as my platoon,

1431

And sailed my spirit surging, light and clear
Past the entanglement where hopes lay strewn;

And witnessed exultation—
Faces that used to curse me, scowl for scowl,
Shine and lift up with passion of oblation,
Seraphic for an hour; though they were foul.

I have made fellowships—
Untold of happy lovers in old song.
For love is not the binding of fair lips
With the soft silk of eyes that look and long,

By Joy, whose ribbon slips,—
But wound with war's hard wire whose stakes are strong:
Bound with the bandage of the arm that drips;
Knit in the webbing of the rifle-thong.

I have perceived much beauty
In the hoarse oaths that keep our courage straight;
Heard music in the silentness of duty;
Found peace where shell-storms spouted reddest spate.

Nevertheless, except you share
With them in hell the sorrowful dark of hell,
Whose world is but the trembling of a flare,
And heaven but as the highway for a shell,

You shall not hear their mirth:
You shall not come to think them well content
By any jest of mine.   These men are worth
Your tears.   You are not worth their merriment.

Genevieve Taggard

TRY TROPIC

Of the Properties of Nature for Healing an Illness

Try tropic for your balm,
Try storm,
And after storm, calm.

Try snow of heaven, heavy, soft and slow,
Brilliant and warm.
Nothing will help, and nothing do much harm.

Drink iron from rare springs; follow the sun;
Go far
To get the beam of some medicinal star;
Or in your anguish run
The gauntlet of all zones to an ultimate one.
Fever and chill
Punish you still,
Earth has no zone to work against your ill.

Burn in the jewelled desert with the toad.
Catch lace
Of evening mist across your haunted face;
Or walk in upper air, the slanted road.
It will not lift that load;
Nor will large seas undo your subtle ill.

Nothing can cure and nothing kill
What ails your eyes, what cuts your pulse in two
And not kill you.

Mark Van Doren

WIT

Wit is the only wall
Between us and the dark.
Wit is perpetual daybreak
And skylark
Springing off the unshaken stone
Of man's blood and the mind's bone.

Wit is the only breath
That keeps our eyelids warm,
Facing the driven ice
Of an old storm
That blows as ever it has blown
Against imperishable stone.

1433

Wit is the lighted house
Of our triumphant talk,
Where only weakly comes now
The slow walk
Of outer creatures past the stone,
Moving in a tongueless moan.

Louise Bogan

MEDUSA

I had come to the house, in a cave of trees,
Facing a sheer sky,
Everything moved,—a bell hung ready to strike,
Sun and reflection wheeled by.

When the bare eyes were before me
And the hissing hair,
Held up at a window, seen through a door.
The stiff bald eyes, the serpents on the forehead
Formed in the air.

This is a dead scene forever now.
Nothing will ever stir.
The end will never brighten it more than this,
Nor the rain blur.

The water will always fall, and will not fall,
And the tipped bell make no sound.
The grass will always be growing for hay
Deep on the ground.

And I shall stand here like a shadow
Under the great balanced day,
My eyes on the yellow dust, that was lifting in the wind,
And does not drift away.

Joseph Auslander

STEEL

This man is dead.
Everything you can say
Is now quite definitely said:
This man held up his head
And had his day,
Then turned his head a little to one way
And slept instead.

Young horses give up their pride:
You break them in
By brief metallic discipline
And something else beside . . .
So this man died.

While he lived I did not know
This man; I never heard
His name. Now that he lies as though
He were remembering some word
He had forgotten yesterday or so,
It seems a bit absurd
That his blank lids and matted hair should grow
Suddenly familiar . . . Let him be interred.

Steady now . . . That was his wife
Making that small queer inarticulate sound
Like a knife;
Steady there . . . Let him slip easily into the ground;
Do not look at her,
She is fighting for breath . . .
She is a foreigner . . .
Polak . . . like him . . . she cannot understand . .
It is hard. . . . Leave her alone with death
And a shovelful of sand.

"O the pity of it, the pity of it, Iago!" . . .
Christ, what a hell
Is packed into that line! Each syllable

Bleeds when you say it . . . No matter: Chicago
Is a far cry from Cracow;
And anyhow
What have Poles
To do with such extraneous things as hearts and souls?

There is nothing here to beat the breast over,
Nothing to relish the curious,
Not a smell of the romantic; this fellow
Was hardly your yearning lover
Frustrated; no punchinello;
But just a hunky in a steel mill. Why then fuss
Because his heavy Slavic face went yellow
With the roaring furnace dust? Now that he is in
The cool sweet crush of dirt, to hell with your sobbing violin,
Your sanctimonious 'cello!
Let the mill bellow!

II

If you have ever had to do with steel:
The open-hearth, the blooming-mill, the cranes
Howling under a fifty-ton load, trains
Yowling in the black pits where you reel
Groggily across a sluice of orange fire, a sheet
Tongued from the conduits that bubble blue green; if
Ever you have got a single whiff
Out of the Bessemer's belly, felt the drag
And drip and curdle of steel spit hissing against hot slag;
If ever you have had to eat
One hundred and thirty degrees of solid heat,
Then screwed the hose to the spigot, drowned in steam,
Darted back when the rods kicked up a stream
Of fluid steel and had to duck the ladle that slobbered over,
  and scream
Your throat raw to get your *Goddam!* through—
Then I am talking to you.

Steve did that for ten years with quiet eyes,
And body down to the belt caked wet
With hardening cinder splash and stiffening sweat

And whatever else there is that clots and never utterly dries.
He packed the mud and dolomite, made back-wall,
Herded the heat, and placed his throw in tall
Terrible arcs behind smoked glasses, and watched it fall
Heavy and straight and true,
While the blower kept the gas at a growl and the brew
Yelled red and the melter hollered "Heow!" and you raveled
Her out and the thick soup gargled and you traveled
Like the devil to get out from under. . . . Well, Steve
For ten years of abdominal heft and heave
Worked steel. So much for that. And after
Ten years of night shifts, fourteen hours each,
The Bessemers burn your nerves up, bleach
Rebellion out of your bones; and laughter
Sucked clean out of your guts becomes
More dead than yesterday's feet moving to yesterday's
    drums. . . .
And so they called him "Dummy." The whole gang
From pit boss down to the last mud-slinger cursed
And squirted tobacco juice in a hot and mixed harangue
Of Slovene, Serb, Dutch, Dago, Russian, and—worst—
English as hard and toothless as a skull.
And Steve stared straight ahead of him and his eyes were dull.

Anna was Steve's little woman
Who labored bitterly enough,
Making children of stern and tragic stuff
And a rapture that was hammered rough,
Spilling steel into their spines, yet keeping them wistful and
    human . . .
Anna had her work to do
With cooking and cleaning
And washing the window curtains white as new,
Washing them till they wore through:
For her the white curtains had a meaning—
And starching them white against the savage will
Of the grim dust belching incessantly out of the mill;
Soaking and scrubbing and ironing against that gritty reek
Until her head swam and her knees went weak
And she could hardly speak.
A terrible unbeaten purpose persisted:

Color crying against a colorless world!
White against black at the windows flung up, unfurled!
Candles and candle light!
The flags of a lonely little woman twisted
Out of her hunger for cool clean beauty, her hunger for
    white!—
These were her banners and this was her fight!

No matter how tired she was, however she would ache
In every nerve, she must boil the meat and bake
The bread, and the curtains must go up white—for Steve's
    sake!
One thing was certain:
That John and Stanley and Helen and Mary and the baby
    Steven
Must be kept out of the mills and the mill life, even
If it meant that her man and she would break
Under the brunt of it: she had talked it through with him
A hundred times . . . Let here eyeballs split, her head swim—
The window must have its curtain!

III

Lately Steve had stopped talking altogether
When he slumped in with his dinner pail and heavily
Hunched over his food.
So Anna and the children let him be;
She was afraid to ask him why or whether
As he sat with his eyes glued
On vacancy.
So Anna and the children let him brood.
Only sometimes he would suddenly look at them and her
In a ghastly fixed blur
Till a vast nausea of terror and compassion stood
Blundering in her heart and swarming in her blood—
And she shivered and knew somehow that it was not good.

And then it happened: Spring had come
Like the silver needle-note of a fife,
Like a white plume and a green lance and a glittering knife
And a jubilant drum.

JOSEPH AUSLANDER

But Steve did not hear the earth hum:
Under the earth he could feel merely the fever
And the shock of roots of steel forever;
April had no business with the pit
Or the people—call them people—who breathed in it.
The mill was Steve's huge harlot and his head
Lay between breasts of steel on a steel bed,
Locked in a steel sleep and his hands were riveted.

IV

And then it happened: nobody could tell whose
Fault it was, but a torrent of steel broke loose,
Trapped twenty men in the hot frothy mess . . .
After a week, more or less,
The company, with appropriate finesse,
Having allowed the families time to move,
Expressed a swift proprietary love
By shoving the dump of metal and flesh and shoes
And cotton and cloth and felt
Back in the furnace to remelt.
And that was all, though a dispatch so neat,
So wholly admirable, so totally sweet,
Could not but stick in Steve's dulled brain.
And whether it was the stink or the noise or just plain
Inertia combined with heat,
Steve, one forenoon, on stark deliberate feet,
Let the charging-machine's long iron finger beat
The side of his skull in . . . There was no pain.

For one fierce instant of unconsciousness
Steve tasted the incalculable caress;
For one entire day he slept between
Sheets that were white and cool, embalmed and clean;
For twenty-four hours he touched the hair of death,
Ran his fingers through it, and it was a deep dark green—
And he held his breath.

This man is dead.
Everything you can say
Is now quite definitely said.

1439

Stephen Vincent Benét

THE BALLAD OF WILLIAM SYCAMORE
(1790-1871)

My father, he was a mountaineer,
His fist was a knotty hammer;
He was quick on his feet as a running deer,
And he spoke with a Yankee stammer.

My mother, she was merry and brave,
And so she came to her labor,
With a tall green fir for her doctor grave
And a stream for her comforting neighbor.

And some are wrapped in the linen fine,
And some like a godling's scion;
But I was cradled on twigs of pine
In the skin of a mountain lion.

And some remember a white starched lap
And a ewer with silver handles;
But I remember a coonskin cap
And the smell of bayberry candles.

The cabin logs, with the bark still rough,
And my mother who laughed at trifles,
And the tall, lank visitors, brown as snuff,
With their long, straight squirrel-rifles.

I can hear them dance, like a foggy song,
Through the deepest one of my slumbers,
The fiddle squeaking the boots along
And my father calling the numbers.

The quick feet shaking the puncheon-floor,
And the fiddle squealing and squealing,
Till the dried herbs rattled above the door
And the dust went up to the ceiling.

There are children lucky from dawn till dusk,
But never a child so lucky!

STEPHEN VINCENT BENÉT

For I cut my teeth on "Money Musk"
In the Bloody Ground of Kentucky!

When I grew tall as the Indian corn,
My father had little to lend me,
But he gave me his great, old powder-horn
And his woodsman's skill to befriend me.

With a leather shirt to cover my back,
And a redskin nose to unravel
Each forest sign, I carried my pack
As far as a scout could travel.

Till I lost my boyhood and found my wife,
A girl like a Salem clipper!
A woman straight as a hunting-knife
With eyes as bright as the Dipper!

We cleared our camp where the buffalo feed,
Unheard-of streams were our flagons;
And I sowed my sons like the apple-seed
On the trail of the Western wagons.

They were right, tight boys, never sulky or slow,
A fruitful, a goodly muster.
The eldest died at the Alamo.
The youngest fell with Custer.

The letter that told it burned my hand.
Yet we smiled and said, "So be it!"
But I could not live when they fenced the land,
For it broke my heart to see it.

I saddled a red, unbroken colt
And rode him into the day there;
And he threw me down like a thunderbolt
And rolled on me as I lay there.

The hunter's whistle hummed in my ear
As the city-men tried to move me,
And I died in my boots like a pioneer
With the whole wide sky above me.

Now I lie in the heart of the fat, black soil,
Like the seed of a prairie-thistle;
It has washed my bones with honey and oil
And picked them clean as a whistle.

And my youth returns, like the rains of Spring,
And my sons, like the wild-geese flying;
And I lie and hear the meadow-lark sing
And have much content in my dying.

Go play with the towns you have built of blocks,
The towns where you have bound me!
I sleep in my earth like a tired fox,
And my buffalo have found me.

Horace Gregory

"THROUGH STREETS WHERE CROOKED WICKLOW FLOWS"

Through streets where crooked Wicklow flows
I saw a man with broken nose:
His venomous eyes turned full on me
And cursed the ancient poverty
That scarred his limbs and mired his clothes.

O cursed wind-driven poverty
That breaks the man and mires his clothes.

Beyond the street, beyond the town,
Rose hill and tree and sea and down:
O drear and shadowy green ash-tree,
O hills that neither sleep nor rest
But are like waves in that dark sea
That rides the wind, nor-east, nor-west,

O cursed, wind-driven poverty!

Below the hill, below the town,
Deep, whispering voices everywhere
Break quiet in the morning air
And mount the skies to pierce the sun.

1442

LÉONIE ADAMS

I saw the naked, cowering man
Shrink in the midnight of his eye,
There, to eat bitterness within,
And close the door and hide the sin
That made his withering heart run dry.
O venomous, dark, unceasing eye
That turned on street and town and me,
Between the waves of hill and sea
Until his eyelid closed the sky.

The rain-rilled, shaken, green ash-tree
Spread roots to gather him and me
In downward pull of earth that drains
The blood that empties through men's veins
Under the churchyard, under stone
Until the body lies alone
And will not wake: nor wind, nor sky
Bring sunlight into morning air
And breathe disquiet everywhere
Into the heart of hill and town.

O heart whose heart is like my own
And not to rest or sleep but climb
Wearily out of earth again
To feed again that venomous eye
That is the manhood of my time,
Whether at home or Wicklow town.

This is my street to walk again,
O cursed, wind-driven poverty,
                         I hear the coming of the rain.

Léonie Adams

THE RIVER IN THE MEADOWS

Crystal parting the meads,
A boat drifted up it like a swan.
Tranquil, lovely, its bright front to the waters,
A slow swan is gone.

Full waters, O flowing silver,
Pure, level with the clover,
It will stain drowning a star,
With the moon it will brim over.

Running through lands dewy and shorn,
Cattle stoop at its brink,
And every fawny-colored throat
Will sway its bells and drink.

I saw a boat sailing the river
With a tranced gait. It seemed
Loosed by a spell from its moorings,
Or a thing the helmsman dreamed.

They said it would carry no traveller,
But the vessel would go down,
If a heart were heavy-winged,
Or the bosom it dwelt in stone.

Hart Crane

From "The Dance"

POWHATAN'S DAUGHTER

A cyclone threshes in the turbine crest,
Swooping in eagle feathers down your back;
Know, Maquokeeta, greeting; know death's best;
—Fall, Sachem, strictly as the tamarack!

A birch kneels. All her whistling fingers fly.
The oak grove circles in a crash of leaves;
The long moan of a dance is in the sky.
Dance, Maquokeeta: Pocahontas grieves. . .

And every tendon scurries toward the twangs
Of lightning deltaed down your saber hair.
Now snaps the flint in every tooth; red fangs
And splay tongues thinly busy the blue air. . .

HART CRANE

Dance, Maquokeeta! snake that lives before,
That casts his pelt, and lives beyond!   Sprout, horn!
Spark, tooth!   Medicine-man, relent, restore—
Lie to us,—dance us back the tribal morn!

Spears and assemblies: black drums thrusting on—
O yelling battlements,—I, too, was liege
To rainbows currying each pulsant bone:
Surpassed the circumstance, danced out the siege!

And buzzard-circleted, screamed from the stake;
I could not pick the arrows from my side.
Wrapped in that fire, I saw more escorts wake—
Flickering, sprint up the hill groins like a tide.

I heard the hush of lava wrestling your arms,
And stag teeth foam about the raven throat;
Flame cataracts of heaven in seething swarms
Fed down your anklets to the sunset's moat.

O, like the lizard in the furious noon,
That drops his legs and colors in the sun,
 —And laughs, pure serpent, Time itself, and moon
Of his own fate, I saw thy change begun!

And saw thee dive to kiss that destiny
Like one white meteor, sacrosanct and blent
At last with all that's consummate and free
There, where the first and last gods keep thy tent.

.   .   .   .

Thewed of the levin, thunder-shod and lean,
Lo, through what infinite seasons dost thou gaze—
Across what bivouacs of thine angered slain,
And see'st thy bride immortal in the maize!

Totem and fire-gall, slumbering pyramid—
Though other calendars now stack the sky,
Thy freedom is her largesse, Prince, and hid
On paths thou knewest best to claim her by.

1445

High unto Labrador the sun strikes free
Her speechless dream of snow, and stirred again,
She is the torrent and the singing tree;
And she is virgin to the last of men. . .

West, west and south! winds over Cumberland
And winds across the llano grass resume
Her hair's warm sibilance.   Her breasts are fanned
O stream by slope and vineyard—into bloom!

And when the caribou slant down for salt
Do arrows thirst and leap?   Do antlers shine
Alert, star-triggered in the listening vault
Of dusk?—And are her perfect brows to thine?

We danced, O Brave, we danced beyond their farms,
In cobalt desert closures made our vows. . .
Now is the strong prayer folded in thine arms,
The serpent with the eagle in the boughs.

Richard Hughes

ECSTATIC ODE ON VISION

The Body Speaks:

Low stooped the oaks like eagles
With feathers of green glass.
I saw the coloured sunset
Out of the flowers pass:
The heavenly mask was blushed with colour:
Greyness possessed the grass.

I saw intoxicant Vision
Galloping like a hare
In a fine linear frenzy:
I saw vast beauties there
Curvet on feathered toe;
Thin fell the light, and rare.

1446

RICHARD HUGHES

What wild fury filled that hare!
His blazing eye!   Electric fur!
The fearful flashing of his paws!
The patting of his sparkling claws!
—Lo, the immortal shadow in me,
That pale incubus the Soul,
Faints and fades, and I am free:
Saved are my five senses whole.
Got when God with matter wenched,
Nothing deep in *Thing* entrenched,
Now stripped of his material vest
See the phantom dispossessed:
Whipt with cords of smell and heat,
Lashed with blows of sound and weight,
Before the drumming of those feet,
Before those eyes of flashing light,
Scourged with the scorpions of sight
Flees that viewless parasite.

That fearful hare
With fur of bright glass,
With his bare leaping,
His steps of fine brass,
His hinder feet thudding
And mewing like a bell
By his almighty movement
Possesses World as well:
Sound and Colour sing together
Witness to the shapely earth:
The caterpillar with the weather
Shares his mad, ecstatic mirth:
Running water to the hour
Sings his tones: and every flower
Flies from tree to tree.
Now I have Vision, now I see
The sloping of material Shape:
The cúrving air: the dagger-thrust
Of light, its million-way riposte:
The spraying fountains of the wind
That sparkle veils of musk behind:

The solid hills, their brilliant faces
Spread like nets on living Graces:
Tilted plains: the sky's leaning:
Bellied clouds' abrupt careening:
Trees that like spindles rise to sight
Wound in threads of knotted light:
Flowers drowned in suffused blue
That their delicate bodies show through.

I saw the World's arches,
The spreading roots of light,
The high wordy pillars
That hold all upright,
The deep verbal fundament
Whereon rests sure
The world on thoughtful vaulting,
Interlocked, secure.

And I saw Vision
Grow suddenly still,
So that nothing was moving,
Had moved, or ever will:
I saw the limbs of Vision
Outstretched in Form, where
Intoxicant Vision lay couchant,
Motionless as a hare.

The sunset fades; night falls anon;
The stunted oaks put darkness on
And plovers whistle. Once again
I am mere bodied spirit, fain
To muse on shapeless mysteries;
To shut my eyes on trees.

Roy Campbell

THE ZEBRAS

From the dark woods that breathe of fallen showers,
Harnessed with level rays in golden reins,
The zebras draw the dawn across the plains
Wading knee-deep among the scarlet flowers.

1448

The sunlight, zithering their flanks with fire,
Flashes between the shadows as they pass
Barred with electric tremors through the grass
Like wind along the gold strings of a lyre.
Into the flushed air snorting rosy plumes
That smoulder round their feet in drifting fumes,
With dove-like voices call the distant fillies,
While round the herds the stallion wheels his flight,
Engine of beauty volted with delight,
To roll his mare among the trampled lilies.

Stanley J. Kunitz

LOVERS RELENTLESSLY

Lovers relentlessly contend to be
Superior in their identity:

The compass of the ego is designed
To circumscribe intact a lesser mind

With definition; tender thought would wrest
Each clean protective secret from the breast;

Affection's eyes go deep, make morbid lesion
In pride's tissue, are ferocious with possession;

Love's active hands insistently caress
The quivering body of shy loveliness,

Hands that are desperately moved to own
The subtly reasoned flesh on branching bone;

Lovers regard the simple moon that spills
White magic in a garden, bend their wills

Obliquely on each other; lovers eat
The small ecstatic heart to be complete;

Engaged in complicate analysis
Of passionate destruction, lovers kiss;

1449

In furious involvement they would make
A double meaning single. Some must break

Upon the wheel of love, but not the strange,
The secret lords, whom only death can change.

Edward Doro

THE BOAR AND SHIBBOLETH

I was eleven, hardly more,
When first I saw a crystal boar,
Stretched on the ground in self-admiring fettle,
With purple eyes and snout of golden metal—
Polished by digging roots—and bones of coral.
Looking, I deemed he was a thing immoral,
  Something a boy should never see.
  I turned and ran, precipitously.

A little way, a little way,
  Then my feet would not obey.
The heavy hammers of my memory sang on;
They beat the anvil of my mind, and rang on.
My thoughts, hot, hissing sparks, were defying
My better will. In sharp tones they kept crying,
  'Go, go again, return pellmell
  To that fantastic animal!'

The boar lay on that very place,
  Curled in sleep with bestial grace.
When I came up, I whistled, and he started,
Shaking himself. A noonday nimbus darted
Around his head with tiny beads of glowing,
And I drew back in sudden shyness, knowing
  That I was merely human, and
  Could never wholly understand.

He nosed his snout in my palm,
  Making me comforted and calm

Because I found him for a friendly creature.
Intent, I looked upon his every feature:
The tumbling mane, the purple tusks, the crest
Of wiry hair upon the haunch, the chest
  Covered with downy purple thread,
  The golden cross upon his head,

  The hooves of lapis lazuli.
  Lifting his eyes, he stared at me
And whined. The cry came like a meteor dropping
With wild music, never, never stopping.
Lightly, I sprung upon his back a-straddle,
His spiral tusks for rein, and hide for saddle.
  I laughed. He answered me in style,
  And off we scampered, mile on mile,

  Until we found a sunny field,
  Where I dismounted. The boar heeled
On the corn-red ground and whined in greeting.
I turned about. There stood a maiden beating
Her hands together, overcome with pleasure.
'Wait here awhile, if you have time and leisure,'
  She called; 'the boar, the boar you ride,
  May I have him, to grace my side?'

  'What is your name?' I questioned her.
  Her voice came with a gentle whirr.
'They call me Shibboleth.' 'And what its meaning?'
'An ear of corn, I think, in time of gleaning.
But you, why do you ride? are you in danger?
Tell me your reason in this country, Stranger.'
  Speech would not come. I was possessed,
  Watching the light play on her breast.

  Can I describe the maiden well—
  In other words, a miracle?
Slowly I left her; and my blood was pounding
With a queer rhythm; and her voice was sounding
Full in my eardrums; and the field of corn
That lay behind was, in the wind, a horn
  That delicately mimicked her
  With a voice of gentle whirr.

1451

Homeward at last I somehow went,
  Shaken with my wonderment.
When I confided of the boar that glittered,
The elder people smiled, my sister tittered,
And all my brothers held me in derision.
Their disbelief cut raw, deep in the vision
  And the revelation of my youth,
  Which, I am sure, was gospel truth.

When they heard my tale that way,
  I made a vow never to say
Or breathe the slightest word of my adventure
With the maiden, though meeting her meant sure
That I was thrown for ever in a riot
Of gold and purple thoughts. I wait in quiet.
  Sometimes I say beneath my breath
  The lovely name of Shibboleth.

Elder Olson

ESSAY ON DEITY

God's body is all space.
He is the shifting land
And the lifting seas.
He is the turning wind.
Like waters, all his strange
Substance suffers change
Forever, yet is known
Forever to be one.
Though water dress as blue
Wave or mist or dew
Or ice at the world's end,
It is one element.
Even as waters he
Takes shape of cloud and tree.
I see his essence plain
In transparent rain
And blowing mist: I know
His presence in the snow.

How then, embittered dust
But hostaged unto death,
Thought you to refuse
Your substance to his use?
To every glint of dust,
To every spark of frost,
To every grain of sand
He set his shining hand,
He breathed his shining breath.
How thought you to withstand,
Narrow heart, this power
That touches dimmest star,
That pierces finest seed?
Narrow brain, how thought
Your thinking to shut out
The undimensional Mind?
And you, most narrow sight,
You glass set in the skull,
Reflecting the least leaf,
The littlest flake to fall,
How thought you to lie blind
To the absolute light?

Yet since he everywhere,
In water, land, and air,
Moves as everything—
The gull on stony wing,
The sliding rock, the fish
In the sea's dim mesh—
Then, minute breast of bone,
Behold how all unknown
You drew him home as breath
In crystal lapse and flood.
Heart that refuses God,
You bear him for your blood;
Obdurate mouth, he is
The food that fed your hunger.
Deny him then no longer;
You took him for your bread.
Behold how unaware
In breathing the wild air,

In seeing, being fed,
In knowing even now
These words, this mist and snow,
These birds at the earth's rim,
Whether you will or no,
You have accepted him.

Stephen Spender

"I THINK CONTINUALLY OF THOSE—"

I think continually of those who were truly great.
Who, from the womb, remembered the soul's history
Through corridors of light where the hours are suns
Endless and singing. Whose lovely ambition
Was that their lips, still touched with fire,
Should tell of the Spirit clothed from head to foot in song.
And who hoarded from the Spring branches
The desires falling across their bodies like blossoms.

What is precious is never to forget
The essential delight of the blood drawn from ageless springs
Breaking through rocks in worlds before our earth.
Never to deny its pleasure in the morning simple light
Nor its grave evening demand for love.
Never to allow gradually the traffic to smother
With noise and fog the flowering of the spirit.

Near the snow, near the sun, in the highest fields
See how these names are fêted by the waving grass
And by the streamers of white cloud
And whispers of wind in the listening sky.
The names of those who in their lives fought for life
Who wore at their hearts the fire's centre.
Born of the sun they travelled a short while towards the sun,
And left the vivid air signed with their honour.

AUDREY WURDEMANN

Paul Engle

MARY

You said I would forget you, forget your lithe
Body thrusting the night-black water, lifted
On the long swell of the current, the strong feet beating;
Forget you, brown as the granite-crumbled beach,
Running on the wave-hard sand; forget
The way down river with our paddles flinging
Wild and flashing moonlight.
                               You were wrong,
For always now I see you, always swimming
With body supple as a diving otter's
Churning a wake of pale foam in the torn
And tideless estuaries of my mind
Where the shy fish of memory leap and shatter
The quiet water, their dark scales gleaming.

Audrey Wurdemann

TEXT

Behold this brief hexagonal,
The honey and the honey-cell,
A tower of wax;—a touch, and see
These walls that could sustain a bee
Clinging with clawed and furry feet
Now bend and break and spill their sweet.

Behold, my dear, the dream we saw,
The thing we built without a flaw,
The amber and the agate rime.
The interstitial beat of time,
The microcosmos of our wit,
The sweetness that we sucked from it,
The honeycomb, the holy land
Broken and bleeding in my hand.

1455

INDEXES BY AUTHORS, TITLES AND
FIRST LINES

INDEX BY AUTHORS

Title	*Opening Phrase*	PAGE
ABERCROMBIE, LASCELLES, 1881–		1274
Epilogue	What shall we do for Love	1274
A. E., *see* RUSSELL, GEORGE WILLIAM		
ADDISON, JOSEPH (*England*), 1672–1719		255
Cato	Plato, thou reason'st well	255
AIKEN, CONRAD (*United States*), 1889–		1334
Music I Heard	Music I heard with you	1334
AIKIN, ANNA LETITIA [Mrs. Barbauld] (*England*), 1743–1825		325
Life	Life! we've been long together	325
ARNOLD, MATTHEW (*England*), 1822–1888		907
Austerity of Poetry	That son of Italy who tried	7
Better Part, The	Long fed on boundless hopes	911
Buried Life, The	Light flows our war of mocking	922
Canticle of the Sun, The	O Most High Almighty Good LORD GOD	953
Destiny	Why each is striving	953
Dover Beach	The sea is calm to-night	918
East London	'Twas August, and the fierce sun	911
Empedocles on Etna	Through the black, rushing	950
Epilogue to Lessing's "Laocoön"	One morn as through Hyde Park	1
Fragment of Chorus of a "Dejaneira"	O frivolous mind of man	914
Future, The	A wanderer is man from his birth	924
Heine's Grave	"Henri Heine"—'tis here	942
Immortality	Foil'd by our fellow-men	912
Isolation. To Marguerite	We were apart; yet, day by day	912
Last Word, The	Creep into thy narrow bed	919
Memorial Verses. April, 1850	Goethe in Weimar sleeps	940
Morality	We cannot kindle when we will	921
Pagan World, The	In his cool hall	951
Philomela	Hark! ah, the nightingale	915
Progress of Poesy, The	Youth rambles on life's arid	919
Question, A	Joy comes and goes	910
Quiet Work	One lesson, Nature, let me learn	907
Requiescat	Strew on her roses	908
Scholar-Gipsy, The	Go, for they call you, shepherd	927
Self-Dependence	Weary of myself	920

INDEX BY AUTHORS

Title	*Opening Phrase*	PAGE

ARNOLD, MATTHEW (*continued*):

Separation	Stop!—not to me, at this bitter	917
Shakespeare	Others abide our question	62
Stanzas in Memory of the Author of "Obermann"	Some secrets may the poet tell	948
Thyrsis	How changed is here each spot	933
To a Friend	Who prop, thou ask'st	907
To Marguerite	Yes! in the sea of life enisled	913
Uraria	She smiles and smiles	916
Voice, The	As the kindling glances	908
World's Triumphs, The	So far as I conceive the world's	909
Written in Emerson's Essays	O monstrous, dead, unprofitable	651

ASHBURTON, ROBERT OFFLEY, *see* CREWE, LORD

BAKER, KARLE WILSON (*United States*), 1878–ㅤ1264

Creeds	Friend, you are grieved	1264
Days	Some days my thoughts	1264
I Shall Be Loved as Quiet Things	I shall be loved as quiet things	1265

BARBAULD, MRS., *see* AIKIN, ANNA LETITIA

BARBOUR, JOHN (*Scotland*)ㅤ13

Freedom	A! Fredome is a noble thing!	13

BARNEFIELD, RICHARD (*England*), 1574–1627ㅤ137

Ode, An	As it fell upon a day	137

BARRETT, EATON STANNARD (*Ireland*), 1786–1820ㅤ499

Woman	Not she with traitorous kiss	499

BASSE, WILLIAM (*England*), 1583–1653ㅤ141

Elegy on Mr. William Shakespeare	Renownèd Spenser, lie a thought	141

BAX, CLIFFORDㅤ1352

In the Train	Suddenly from a wayside station	1352

BEAUMONT, FRANCIS (*England*), 1584–1616ㅤ140

Letter to Ben Jonson	What things have we seen	140
On the Tombs in Westminster Abbey	Mortality, behold, and fear	140

BELLOC, HILAIRE (*France*), 1870–ㅤ1228

Duncton Hill	He does not die	1228
Song	You wear the morning	1232
South Country, The	When I am living in the Midlands	1229
To the Balliol Men Still in Africa	Years ago when I was at Balliol	1231

BENÉT, WILLIAM ROSE (*United States*), 1886–ㅤ1308

Falconer of God, The	I flung my soul to the air	1308
Mad Blake	Blake saw a tree-ful of angels	330

BINYON, LAURENCE (*England*), 1869–ㅤ1205

Nothing Is Enough	Nothing is enough!	1205

Title	Opening Phrase	PAGE
BINYON, LAURENCE (*continued*):		
Song	For Mercy, Courage, Kindness	1206
Thinking of Shores	Thinking of shores	1205
To Women	Your hearts are lifted up	1206
BLAKE, WILLIAM (*England*), 1757–1827		330
Ah, Sunflower	Ah, Sunflower, weary of time	335
Clod and the Pebble, The	Love seeketh not itself	334
Divine Image, The	To Mercy, Pity, Peace, and Love	333
Grey Monk, The	But vain the Sword	338
Ideas of Good and Evil	Every night and every morn	335
	To find the Western path	336
	To see a world in a grain	335
London	I wander through each chartered street	337
Love's Prisoner	How sweet I roamed	331
Love's Secret	Never seek to tell thy love	337
Memory, Hither Come	Memory, hither come	332
Milton	And did those feet in ancient	336
Song	My silks and fine array	331
Tiger, The	Tiger, tiger, burning bright	334
To Spring	O Thou with dewy locks	330
To the Muses	Whether on Ida's shady brow	332
Wild-Flower's Song, The	I wandered in the forest	338
BLUNDEN, EDMUND (*England*), 1896–		1340
Almswomen	At Quincy's moat the squandering	1340
BONER, JOHN HENRY (*United States*), 1845–		740
Poe's Cottage at Fordham	Here lived the soul enchanted	740
BOTTOMLEY, GORDON, 1874–		1256
In Memoriam A. M. W.	Out of a silence	1256
BOURDILLON, FRANCIS WILLIAM (*England*), 1852–1921		1102
Eurydice	He came to call me back	1102
Night Has a Thousand Eyes, The	The night has a thousand eyes	1103
BOWLES, WILLIAM LISLE (*England*), 1762–1850		359
Time and Grief	O Time! who know'st a lenient	359
BRANCH, ANNA HEMPSTEAD (*United States*)		1367
To a New York Shop-Girl, Dressed for Sunday	To-day I saw the shop-girl go	1367
BRETON, NICHOLAS (*England*), 1545(?)–1626(?)		22
Phillida and Coridon	In the merry month of May	23
Sweet Pastoral, A	Good Muse, rock me asleep	22
BRIDGES, ROBERT (*England*), 1844–		1055
Elegy	The wood is bare	1055
Elegy	Clear and gentle stream!	1059

INDEX BY AUTHORS

Title	*Opening Phrase*	PAGE

BRIDGES, ROBERT (*continued*):

I Have Loved Flowers That Fade	I have loved flowers that fade	1056
I Love All Beauteous Things	I love all beauteous things	1058
My Delight and Thy Delight	My delight and thy delight	1057
Nightingales	Beautiful must be the mountains	1058
Passer-by, A	Whither, O splendid ship	1055

BRONTË, EMILY (*England*), 1818–1848   871

Last Lines	No coward soul is mine	872
Old Stoic, The	Riches I hold in light esteem	873
Prisoner, The	Still let my tyrants know	871

BROOKE, RUPERT (*England*), 1887–1915   1323

1914
Dead, The	Blow out, you bugles	1323
Dead, The	These hearts were woven	1324
Soldier, The	If I should die	1324
Sonnet	Oh! Death will find me	1325
Treasure, The	When colour goes home	1324

BROOKE, STOPFORD AUGUSTUS (*Ireland*), 1832–1916   1004

Earth and Man, The	A little sun, a little rain	1004

BROWN, THOMAS EDWARD (*England*), 1830–1897   1002

Dora	She knelt upon her brother's	1002
My Garden	A garden is a lovesome thing	1003
Salve!	To live within a cave	1003

BROWNE, WILLIAM (*England*), 1591–1643(?)   163

Elegy on the Countess Dowager of Pembroke	I, hapless soul, that never	165
Epitaph on the Countess of Pembroke	Underneath this sable hearse	164
In Obitum. M. S.	May! Be thou never graced	165
Song	Hearken then awhile to me	165
Welcome, A	Welcome, welcome, do I sing	163

BROWNING, ELIZABETH BARRETT (*England*), 1806–1861   689

Portrait, A	I will paint her as I see her	692
Sonnets from the Portuguese		
I	I thought once how Theocritus	689
III	Unlike are we, unlike	689
VI	Go from me. Yet I feel	690
VIII	What can I give thee back	690
XIV	If thou must love me	690
XVIII	I never gave a lock of hair	691
XXII	When our two souls stand up	691
XLIII	How do I love thee?	692

BROWNING, ROBERT (*England*), 1812–1889   840

Abt Vogler	Would that the structure brave	858

Title	Opening Phrase	PAGE
BROWNING, ROBERT (*continued*):		
Blot in the 'Scutcheon, A	There's a woman like a dewdrop	849
Epilogue	At the midnight in the silence	868
Flower's Name, The	Down this side of the gravelwalk	842
Grammarian's Funeral, A	Let us begin and carry up	853
Hervé Riel	On the sea and at the Hogue	862
Home-Thoughts, from Abroad	Oh, to be in England	847
Last Ride Together, The	I said—Then, dearest	850
Lost Leader, The	Just for a handful of silver	841
Meeting at Night	The grey sea and the long black land	843
Memorabilia	Ah, did you once see Shelley	848
Misconceptions	This is a spray	848
My Star	All that I know	848
Nay But You	Nay but you, who do not love her	843
Never the Time and the Place	Never the time and the place	866
One Word More	There they are, my fifty men	856
Pippa Passes	The year's at the spring	841
Prospice	Fear death?—to feel the fog	861
Rabbi Ben Ezra	Grow old along with me!	860
Toccata of Galuppi's, A	Oh, Galuppi, Baldassarre	845
Two Poets of Croisic, The	Such a starved bank of moss	866
Why I Am a Liberal	"Why?" Because all I haply	867
Woman's Last Word, A	Let's contend no more, Love	843
BRYANT, WILLIAM CULLEN (*United States*), 1794–1878		595
O, Fairest of the Rural Maids	O, fairest of the rural maids	599
Thanatopsis	To him who in the love of Nature	595
To a Waterfowl	Whither, midst falling dew	597
To the Fringed Gentian	Thou blossom bright	598
BULLEN, ARTHUR HENRY, 1857–1920		1141
By Avon Stream	The jonquils bloom	1141
BURNS, ROBERT (*Scotland*), 1759–1796		339
Address to the Unco Guid	Then gently scan your brother man	348
Ae Fond Kiss	Ae fond kiss, and then we sever	351
Auld Lang Syne	Should auld acquaintance be forgot	353
Banks o' Doon, The	Ye banks and braes o' bonie Doon	352
Birks of Aberfeldy, The	Bonie lassie, will ye go	339

INDEX BY AUTHORS

Title	*Opening Phrase*	PAGE

BURNS, ROBERT (*continued*):

Bruce's Address at Bannockburn	Scots, wha hae wi' Wallace bled	355
Ca' the Yowes to the Knowes	Hark, the mavis' e'ening sang	357
Cotter's Saturday Night, The	My lov'd, my honour'd	340
Day Returns, The	The day returns	349
Highland Mary	Ye banks and braes and streams	356
Is There for Honest Poverty	Is there for honest poverty	357
Jean	Of a' the airts the wind can blow	350
John Anderson, My Jo	John Anderson, my jo, John	350
Mally's Meek, Mally's Sweet	As I was walking up the street	354
My Bonie Mary	Go fetch to me a pint o' wine	349
O, Were My Love	O, were my love yon lilac fair	359
Red, Red Rose, A	O, my luve is like a red, red rose	352
Saw Ye Bonie Lesley	O, saw ye bonie Lesley	354
To a Mountain Daisy	Wee, modest, crimson-tippèd	347
To a Mouse	Wee, sleekit, cowrin', tim'rous	345
True Pathos, The	To make a happy fireside	359

BURROUGHS, JOHN (*United States*), 1837–1921 — 1029

Waiting	Serene, I fold my hands	1029

BUTLER, SAMUEL (*England*), 1835–1902 — 1007

Not on Sad Stygian Shore	Not on sad Stygian shore	1007

BYNNER, WITTER (*United States*), 1881– — 1284

New World, The	Celia was laughing	1284

BYRON, GEORGE GORDON, LORD (*England*), 1788–1824 — 500

Childe Harold's Pilgrimage

Canto the Third	There was a sound of revelry	502
	The castled crag of Drachenfels	504
	Clear, placid Leman!	504
	The sky is changed!	505
Canto the Fourth	Oh, Rome! my country!	505
	Simple, erect, severe, austere	506
	There is a pleasure in the pathless	506
	Thy shores are empires	507

Don Juan

Canto the First	Man's love is of man's life	511
Canto the Second	Alas! the love of women	511
Canto the Third	Round her she made an atmosphere	511
	The isles of Greece	511
	Ave Maria! blessed be the hour!	514
Giaour, The	Clime of the unforgotten brave	508
	As rising on its purple wing	509

1464

Title	Opening Phrase	PAGE
BYRON, LORD (*continued*) :		
Ode from the French	There, where death's brief pang	500
Oh! Snatched Away in Beauty's Bloom	Oh! snatched away in beauty's	501
On This Day I Complete My Thirty-sixth Year	'Tis time this heart should be	515
She Walks in Beauty	She walks in beauty	501
Sonnet on Chillon	Eternal Spirit of the chainless	510
Stanzas for Music	There be none of Beauty's daughters	500
CABELL, JAMES BRANCH (*United States*), 1879–		1266
Garden-Song	Farewell to Fields	1266
CAMPBELL, JOSEPH (*Ireland*), 1881–		1281
Old Woman, The	As a white candle	1281
CAMPBELL, THOMAS (*Scotland*), 1777–1844		487
Hallowed Ground	What's hallowed ground?	487
Hohenlinden	On Linden, when the sun was low	490
CAMPION, THOMAS (*England*), 1567(?)–1619		114
Charm, The	Thrice toss these oaken ashes	116
Cherry-Ripe	There is a garden in her face	116
Follow Thy Fair Sun	Follow thy fair sun	114
Follow Your Saint	Follow your saint	117
Jack and Joan	Jack and Joan they think no ill	119
Kind Are Her Answers	Kind are her answers	118
Man of Life Upright, The	The man of life upright	117
Measure of Beauty, The	Give Beauty all her right	ix, 118
Now Winter Nights Enlarge	Now winter nights enlarge	115
When Thou Must Home	When thou must home to shades	120
When to Her Lute Corinna Sings	When to her lute Corinna sings	114
CANTON, WILLIAM (*Island of Chusan, China*), 1845–1926		1063
Comrades, The	In solitary rooms	1063
Death of Anaxagoras, The	Of him she banished	1069
God and the Schoolboy, The	Throughout the land and sea	1073
In the Shadow	Night is the shadow of Earth	1078
Laus Infantium	In praise of little children	1075
Moonlight	Sweet moon, endreaming tower	1077
New Poet, A	I write. He sits beside my chair	1076
Philosopher, A	Yes, you may let them creep	1076
Suspirium	These little shoes!	1077
This Grace Vouchsafe Me	This grace vouchsafe me	1078
Through the Ages	O'er the swamp in the forest	1064
CAREW, THOMAS (*England*), 1595(?)–1639		176
Compliment, The	I do not love thee for that	176
Disdain Returned	He that loves a rosy cheek	177
Song	Ask me no more where Jove	176

Title	*Opening Phrase*	PAGE
CAREY, HENRY (*England*), 1700(?)–1743		279
Sally in Our Alley	Of all the girls that are	279
CARLIN, FRANCIS (*United States*), 1881–		1278
Her Reverie	I wonder how	1278
Parish Bard, The	Och, would I were deep in Kil-barry	1280
Perfection	Who seeks perfection in the art	1278
Under an Irish Lark	When, jars unsealed	1279
CARMAN, WILLIAM BLISS (*Canada*), 1861–		1166
Daphne	I know that face!	1168
Lord of My Heart's Elation	Lord of my heart's elation	1166
Roadside Flowers	We are the roadside flowers	1167
Unreturning, The	The old eternal spring	1168
CARRUTH, WILLIAM HERBERT (*United States*), 1859–		1162
Each in His Own Tongue	A Fire-Mist and a planet	1162
CATHER, WILLA SIBERT (*United States*), 1875–		1261
Palatine, The	Have you been with the King	1261
CHAPMAN, GEORGE (*England*), 1560(?)–1634		53
Her Coming	See where she issues	53
CHAPMAN, JOHN JAY (*United States*), 1862–		1172
No Pilots We	Would I were one of those	1172
CHATTERTON, THOMAS (*England*), 1752–1770		327
Song from Ælla	O sing unto my roundelay	327
CHAUCER, GEOFFREY (*England*), 1340(?)–1400		13
Balade	Hyd, Absolon, thy gilte tresses	14
Canterbury Tales, Prologue to the	Whan that Aprille with his shoures	15
	A Knight ther was	16
	Ther was also a Nonne	16
	A Clerk ther was of Oxenford	17
	With us ther was a Doctour	17
	A good man was ther of re-ligioun	18
Captivity	Your eyën two wol slee me	14
CHENEY, JOHN VANCE (*United States*), 1848–1922		1082
Happiest Heart, The	Who drives the horses of the sun	1084
Man with the Hoe, The (A Reply)	Nature reads not our labels	1082
One	One whitest lily, reddest rose	1084
CHESTERTON, GILBERT KEITH (*England*), 1874–		1245
Donkey, The	When fishes flew	1248
Hymn, A	O God of earth and altar	1247
Music	Sounding brass and tinkling cymbal	1248

Title	*Opening Phrase*	PAGE

CHESTERTON, GILBERT KEITH (*continued*):

Praise of Dust, The	"What of vile dust?"	1245
Sword of Surprise, The	Sunder me from my bones	1245
To F. C. in Memoriam Palestine	Do you remember one immortal	1246

CLOUGH, ARTHUR HUGH (*England*), 1819–1861   873

Come Back, Come Back	Come back, come back	877
Qua Cursum Ventus	As ships, becalmed at eve	873
Say Not, the Struggle Naught Availeth	Say not, the struggle	874
Stream of Life, The	O stream descending to the sea	875
Venice	How light we go	876
Where Lies the Land	Where lies the land	876
With Whom Is No Shadow of Variableness	It fortifies my soul to know	876

COLERIDGE, MARY ELIZABETH (*England*), 1861–1907   1171

| Huguenot, A | O, a gallant set were they | 1171 |

COLERIDGE, SAMUEL TAYLOR (*England*), 1772–1834   446

Christabel	Alas! they had been friends	468
Fancy in Nubibus	O, it is pleasant	475
Kubla Khan	In Xanadu did Kubla Khan	471
Love	All thoughts, all passions	468
Reflections on Having Left a Place of Retirement	Low was our pretty cot	446
Rime of the Ancient Mariner, The	It is an ancient Mariner	449
Song of the Pixies	Hence! thou lingerer, light!	446
Time, Real and Imaginary	On the white level	448
Work Without Hope	All Nature seems at work	473
Youth and Age	Verse, a breeze 'mid blossoms	473

COLLINS, WILLIAM (*England*), 1721–1759   295

Dirge in Cymbeline	The redbreast oft, at evening	300
How Sleep the Brave	How sleep the brave	295
Ode to Evening	If aught of oaten stop	295
Ode to Fear	Thou, to whom the world unknown	301
Passions, The	When Music, heavenly maid	297

COLTON, ARTHUR WILLIS (*United States*), 1868–   1203

| Sometime It May Be | Sometime it may be you and I | 1203 |

COLUM, PADRAIC (*Ireland*), 1881–   1281

| Furrow and the Hearth, The | Stride the hill, sower | 1282 |
| Old Woman of the Roads, An | O, to have a little house! | 1281 |

CORY, WILLIAM [JOHNSON] (*England*), 1823–1892   954

| Heraclitus | They told me, Heraclitus | 954 |
| Mimnermus in Church | You promise heavens | 955 |

Title	Opening Phrase	PAGE

CORY, WILLIAM [JOHNSON] (*continued*):

Oh, Earlier Shall the Rosebuds Blow	Oh, earlier shall the rosebuds	955

COWLEY, ABRAHAM (*England*), 1618–1667 216

Drinking	The thirsty earth soaks up	216
Hymn to Light	Thou, Scythian-like, dost	220
In Defense of the Royal Society	The things which these proud men	219
Life	Life's a name	221
On the Death of Mr. Crashaw	Poet and Saint! to thee alone	217
On the Death of Mr. William Hervey	Say, for you saw us	219
Sport	The merry waves dance up and down	217
Wish, The	Well then, I now do plainly see	218

COWPER, WILLIAM (*England*), 1731–1800 317

Another	Sweet stream, that winds	320
Boadicea. An Ode	When the British Warrior Queen	318
Charity	When one, that holds communion	317
Comparison, A	The lapse of time and rivers	320
My Mary	The twentieth year is wellnigh	320
Task, The		
Book IV	Now stir the fire	323
	Come, Evening, once again	323
Book VI	Books are not seldom talismans	323
	One spirit, His who wore	324
	E'en in the spring and playtime	324
To Mary Unwin	Mary! I want a lyre	322

CRABBE, GEORGE (*England*), 1754–1832 329

Late Wisdom	We've trod the maze of error	329

CRASHAW, RICHARD (*England*), 1613(?)–1649 211

Euthanasia	Wouldst see blithe looks	214
In the Temple	Two went to pray?	212
Saint Teresa	O thou undaunted daughter	211
Wishes for the Supposed Mistress	Whoe'er she be	212

CRAWFORD, LOUISA MACARTNEY (*England*), 18— 651

Kathleen Mavourneen	Kathleen Mavourneen! the grey dawn	651

CRAWFORD, ROBERT (*Scotland*), 1695–1733 278

Bush Aboon Traquair, The	Hear me, ye nymphs	278

CREWE, LORD [Robert Offley Ashburton] (*England*) 1858– 1146

Harrow Grave in Flanders, A	Here in the marshland	1146

CROSS, MARIAN EVANS LEWES, *see* ELIOT, GEORGE

INDEX BY AUTHORS

Title	*Opening Phrase*	PAGE
CULLEN, COUNTEE (*United States*), 1903–		1344
Fruit of the Flower	My father is a quiet man	1351
Shroud of Color, The	"Lord, being dark," I said	1344
Simon the Cyrenian Speaks	He never spoke a word	1350
Song of Praise, A	You have not heard	1350
Yet Do I Marvel	I doubt not God is good	1344
CUNNINGHAM, ALLAN (*Scotland*), 1784–1842		497
Wet Sheet and a Flowing Sea, A	A wet sheet and a flowing sea	497
D., H., 1886–		1314
Loss	The sea called	1314
DANIEL, SAMUEL (*England*), 1562–1619		53
To Delia	Care-charmer Sleep	54
	I must not grieve my Love	53
	Let others sing of Knights	54
	When men shall find thy flower	53
DAVENANT, SIR WILLIAM (*England*), 1606–1668		179
Morning Song	The lark now leaves	179
Praise and Prayer	Praise is devotion	180
DAVIDSON, JOHN (*England*), 1857–1909		1141
Ballad of a Nun, A	From Eastertide to Eastertide	1141
DAVIES, MARY CAROLYN (*United States*)		1353
Day Before April, The	The day before April	1354
Dead Make Rules, The	The dead make rules	1353
Door-Mats	Women are door-mats	1355
Dream-Bearer, The	Where weary folk toil	1354
Gown, The	Beneath the curious gaze	1354
Reminiscences	The other side of Death	1353
Rust	Iron, left in the rain	1353
DAVIES, WILLIAM HENRY (*England*), 1870–		1223
Early Spring	How sweet this morning air	1225
Example, The	Here's an example	1227
Great Time, A	Sweet Chance, that led my steps	1226
Happy Wind	Oh, happy wind, how sweet	1226
Kingfisher, The	It was the Rainbow	1223
Leisure	What is this life	1223
Moon, The	Thy beauty haunts me	1226
Sweet Stay-at-Home	Sweet Stay-at-Home, sweet Well-content	1224
Thought, A	When I look into a glass	1228
Thunderstorms	My mind has thunderstorms	1227
Two Children, The	Ah, little boy! I see	1225
DAVISON, EDWARD, 1898–		1342
Sonnet	Now that the moonlight withers	1343
Sonnet	O Thou in the darkness	1342
DEKKER, THOMAS (*England*), 1570(?)–1641(?)		122
Sweet Content	Art thou poor, yet hast thou	122

1469

Title	*Opening Phrase*	PAGE
DE LA MARE, WALTER (*England*), 1873–		1238
All That's Past	Very old are the woods	1239
Arabia	Far are the shades of Arabia	1240
Epitaph, An	Here lies a most beautiful lady	1242
Ghost, The	"Who knocks?" "I, who	1243
Linnet, The	Upon this leafy bush	1242
Listeners, The	"Is there anybody there?"	1241
Miracle, The	Who beckons the green ivy up	1238
Music	When music sounds	1244
Song of Enchantment, A	A song of Enchantment	1244
Stranger, The	Half-hidden in a graveyard	1239
Sunken Garden, The	Speak not—whisper not	1242
DENHAM, SIR JOHN (*Ireland*), 1615–1669		216
O Could I Flow	O could I flow like thee	216
DE VERE, AUBREY THOMAS (*Ireland*), 1814–1902		868
Sorrow	Count each affliction	868
DICKENS, CHARLES (*England*), 1812–1870		839
Ivy Green, The	Oh, a dainty plant	839
DICKINSON, EMILY (*United States*), 1830–1886		1000
Autumn	The morns are meeker	1000
Chartless	I never saw a moor	1000
Choice	Of all the souls that stand	1001
Parting	My life closed twice	1001
Peace	I many times thought peace	1001
Pedigree	The pedigree of honey	1002
Simplicity	How happy is the little stone	1002
Suspense	Elysium is as far	1002
DOBELL, SYDNEY (*England*), 1824–1874		963
America	Nor force nor fraud shall sunder	964
Keith of Ravelston	The murmur of the mourning ghost	963
DOBSON, AUSTIN (*England*), 1840–1921		1033
For a Charity Annual	In Angel-Court the sunless air	1033
For a Copy of Theocritus	O singer of the field and fold	1034
Greeting, A	But once or twice we met	1036
Henry Wadsworth Longfellow	Not to be tuneless in old age!	694
In After Days	In after days when grasses high	1034
Song of the Sea Wind, The	How it sings, sings, sings	1035
Urceus Exit	I intended an Ode	1033
DONEY, MAY		1355
Ruth	"She stands breast high amid the corn"	1355
DONNE, JOHN (*England*), 1573–1631		132
Absence	Absence, hear thou my protestation	134
Death, Be Not Proud	Death, be not proud	133
Dream, The	Dear love, for nothing less	132
Good Morrow, The	I wonder, by my troth	133

Title	Opening Phrase	PAGE

DONNE, JOHN (*continued*):

Undertaking, The	I have done one braver thing	136
Valediction Forbidding Mourning, A	As virtuous men pass mildly away	134

DOUGLAS, WILLIAM (*Scotland*), 1672(?)–1748 — 255

Annie Laurie	Maxwelton banks are bonnie	255

DOWSON, ERNEST (*England*), 1867–1900 — 1198

In Tempore Senectutis	When I am old	1198
Non Sum Qualis Eram Bonæ sub Regno Cynaræ	Last night, ah, yesternight	1199
They Are Not Long	They are not long, the weeping	1198
Vain Resolves	I said: "There is an end	1199

DOYLE, SIR FRANCIS (*England*), 1810–1888 — 837

Private of the Buffs, The	Last night, among his fellow	837

DRAYTON, MICHAEL (*England*), 1563–1631 — 55

Immortality in Song	How many paltry, foolish	55
Marlowe	Next Marlowe, bathed in Thespian	58
Since There's No Help	Since there's no help, come	56
Some Atheist in Love	Some atheist or vile infidel	56
Summer's Eve, A	Clear had the day been	55

DRINKWATER, JOHN (*England*), 1882– — 1288

Invocation	As pools beneath stone arches	1288
Last Confessional	For all ill words	1288

DRUMMOND, WILLIAM, OF HAWTHORNDEN (*Scotland*), 1585–1649 — 141

I Know That All the Moon Decays	I know that all the moon decays	142
Lessons of Nature, The	Of this fair volume	144
Madrigal	My thoughts hold mortal strife	141
Phœbus, Arise	Phœbus, arise	143
Solitude	Thrice happy he	142
Sonnet: Repent, Repent	The last and greatest herald	142
To His Lute	My lute, be as thou wert	143

DRYDEN, JOHN (*England*), 1631–1700 — 236

Absalom and Achitophel		
Anthony Ashley Cooper, Earl of Shaftesbury	Of these the false Achitophel	240
George Villiers, Duke of Buckingham	A man so various, that he seems	28
Dreams	Dreams are but interludes	50
Life a Cheat	When I consider life	236
Mankind	Men are but children	250
O Souls, in Whom No Heavenly Fire	O souls, in whom no heavenly fire	

INDEX BY AUTHORS

Title — *Opening Phra...*

DRYDEN, JOHN (*continued*):
Power of Music, The — Three poets, in three a...
Song for Saint Cecilia's Day — 'Twas at the royal feas...
On Milton —
Song to a Fair Young Lady — From harmony, from h...
To the Memory of Mrs. Anne — harmony,
Killigrew — Ask not the cause

DYER, SIR EDWARD (*England*) — Thou youngest Virgin-Daug...
My Mind to Me a Kingdom — My mind to me a kingdom is
Is

ELIOT, GEORGE [Marian Evans Lewes Cross] (*Eng-
land*), 1819–1880
Two Lovers — Two lovers by a moss-grown
spring

EMERSON, RALPH WALDO (*United States*), 1803–
1882
Bacchus — Bring me me wine
Bohemian Hymn, The — In many forms we try
Brahma — If the red slayer think he slays   673
Concord Hymn — By the rude bridge   676
Days — Daughters of Time   677
Destiny — That you are fair or wise   678
Dirge — In the long sunny afternoon   656
Duty — So nigh is grandeur to our   669
      dust
Each and All — Little thinks, in the field   684
Eros — They put their finger   652
Forerunners — Long I followed happy guides   683
Friendship — A ruddy drop of manly blood   681
Give All to Love — Give all to love   664
Good-bye — Good-bye, proud world!   658
Humble-Bee, The — Burly, dozing humble-bee   659
Merlin — The trivial harp will never
      please
Philosopher — Philosophers are lined with eyes
Problem, The — Not from a vain or shallow   685
      thought
Rhodora, The — In May, when sea-winds   683
Saad — Behold, he watches at the door!   653
Sacrifice — Though love repine, and reason   659
Snow-Storm, The — Announced by all the trumpets   668
Sursun Corda — Seek not the spirit, if it hide   682
Twins, T...   661
Test, T...   664
There Away, Alway Some- — It is time to be old   680
thing — I hung my verses in the wind
Threnody — Let me go where'er I will   682
To Eva — The South-wind brings   670
To Rhea — O fair and stately maid   666
      Thee, dear friend, a brother   654

1472   8

Title	*Opening Phrase*	PAGE
EMERSON, RALPH WALDO (*continued*):		
Uriel	It fell in the ancient periods	684
Waldeinsamkeit	I do not count the hours	679
Woodnotes, II	Speak not thy speech	662
	Come learn with me	662
World-Soul, The	He serveth the servant	656
ERSKINE, JOHN (*United States*), 1879–		1268
Valentine to One's Wife	Hearts and darts and maids	1268
FARJEON, ELEANOR		1356
Night Will Never Stay, The	The night will never stay	1356
FAWCETT, EDGAR (*United States*), 1847–1904		1079
To an Oriole	How falls it, oriole	1079
FICKE, ARTHUR DAVISON (*United States*), 1883–		1291
Don Quixote	Dearest of all the heroes!	1291
Sonnet	In the fair picture	1292
Sonnet	This is the burden	1292
FIELD, MICHAEL (*England*)		1094
[Katharine Harris Bradley 1846–1914]		
and [Edith Emma Cooper 1862–1913]		
Beloved, My Glory	Beloved, my glory in thee	1095
Gold	Yea, gold is son of Zeus	1094
Tragic Mary Queen of Scots, The	I could wish to be dead!	1095
FIRKINS, CHESTER		1359
On a Subway Express	I, who have lost the stars	1359
FITZGERALD, EDWARD (*England*), 1809–1883		772
Meadows in Spring, The	'Tis a dull sight	778
Rubáiyát of Omar Khayyám	Wake! For the Sun who scattered	772
FLECKER, JAMES ELROY (*England*), 1884–1915		1296
In Phæacia	Had I that haze of streaming blue	1296
Ship, an Isle, a Sickle Moon, A	A ship, an isle, a sickle moon	1296
To a Poet a Thousand Years Hence	I who am dead a thousand years	1297
FLETCHER, JOHN (*England*), 1579–1625		138
God Lyæus	God Lyæus, ever young	139
Man His Own Star	Man is his own star	138
Sleep	Come, Sleep, and with thy	139
Sweetest Melancholy	Hence, all you vain delights	138
FLOWER, ROBIN		1360
Say Not That Beauty	Say not that beauty is an idle thing	1360

1473

INDEX BY AUTHORS

Title	*Opening Phrase*	PAGE

FORD, FORD MADOX [Ford Madox Hueffer] (*England*), 1873– — 1236
Footsloggers — What is love of one's land? — 1236

FREEMAN, JOHN (*England*), 1885– — 1305
Caterpillars — Of caterpillars Fabre tells — 1305

FROST, ROBERT (*United States*), 1875– — 1257
Aim Was Song, The — Before man came to blow — 1259
Fire and Ice — Some say the world will end — 1257
Mending Wall — Something there is that — 1257
Mowing — There was never a sound — 1259
My November Guest — My Sorrow, when she's here — 1258
Oft-Repeated Dream, The — She had no saying dark enough — 1260
Road Not Taken, The — Two roads diverged — 1260

GARLAND, HAMLIN (*United States*), 1860– — 1163
Do You Fear the Wind? — Do you fear the force — 1163
Mountains Are a Lonely Folk, The — The mountains they are — 1164
To a Captive Crane — Ho, brother! Art thou prisoned — 1163

GARRISON, THEODOSIA (*United States*), 1874– — 1249
Tears of Harlequin, The — To you he gave his laughter — 1249

GARRISON, WILLIAM LLOYD (*United States*), 1804–1879 — 688
Sonnet Written in Prison — High walls and huge — 688

GAY, JOHN (*England*), 1688–1732 — 259
Acis and Galatea — Love in her eyes sits playing — 259
 — O ruddier than the cherry — 259
Black-Eyed Susan — All in the Downs the fleet — 260

GILDER, RICHARD WATSON (*United States*), 1844–1909 — 1048
On the Life-Mask of Abraham Lincoln — This bronze doth keep — 1048

GOLDSMITH, OLIVER (*Ireland*), 1728–1774 — 303
Captivity — Fatigued with life, yet loth — 315
Deserted Village, The — Sweet Auburn! loveliest village — 303
Retaliation
  David Garrick — Here lies David Garrick — 316
  Edmund Burke — Here lies our good Edmund — 316
  Sir Joshua Reynolds — Here Reynolds is laid — 316
Traveller, The — Remote, unfriended, melancholy — 314

GORMAN, HERBERT S. (*United States*), 1893– — 1337
Last Fire, The — You saw the last fires burning — 1337

GOSSE, EDMUND (*England*), 1849– — 1090
Fear of Death, The — Last night I woke and found — 1090
Revelation — Into the silver night — 1091

GOULD, GERALD LOUIS (*England*), 1885– — 1306
Fallen Cities — I gathered with a careless hand — 1306

1474

Title	Opening Phrase	PAGE
GRAY, THOMAS (*England*), 1716-1771		283
Elegy Written in a Country Churchyard	The curfew tolls the knell	288
Ode on the Spring, An	Lo! where the rosy-bosomed Hours	286
On a Distant Prospect of Eton College	Ye distant spires, ye antique	283
Progress of Poesy, The	Awake, Æolian lyre, awake	292
GREENE, ROBERT (*England*), 1560–1592		51
Samela	Like to Diana in her summer weed	52
Shepherd's Wife's Song, A	Ah, what is love?	51
GUITERMAN, ARTHUR (*Austria*), 1871–		1232
Idol-Maker Prays, The	Great god whom I shall carve	1232
GURNEY, IVOR		1361
To the Poet Before Battle	Now, youth, the hour of thy dread	1361
HAGEDORN, HERMANN (*United States*), 1882–		1290
Broadway	How like the stars	1291
Doors	Like a young child	1290
HAMILTON, GEORGE ROSTREVOR		1361
Multiplicity	When I invade my secret soul	1361
HARDY, THOMAS (*England*), 1840–		1036
Darkling Thrush, The	I leant upon a coppice gate	1037
Shelley's Skylark	Somewhere afield here something lies	1036
HARTE, FRANCIS BRET (*United States*), 1839–1902		1031
Dickens in Camp	Above the pines the moon	1031
Relieving Guard	Came the Relief	1033
HEMANS, FELICIA DOROTHEA (*England*), 1793–1835		592
England's Dead	Son of the ocean isle!	593
Graves of a Household, The	They grew in beauty	592
HENLEY, WILLIAM ERNEST (*England*), 1846–1903		1084
Echoes	The full sea rolls and thunders	1088
In Fishcrrow	A hard north-easter	1087
In Hospital		
After	Like as a flamelet	1085
Apparition	Thin-legged, thin-chested	1087
Before	Behold me waiting	1084
"Chief, The"	His brow spreads large	1086
Lady-Probationer	Some three, or five, or seven	1086
Scrubber	She's tall and gaunt	1087
Staff-Nurse: Old Style	The great masters	1085
Invictus	Out of the night that covers me	1088
Margaritæ Sorori	A late lark twitters	1089
On the Way to Kew	On the way to Kew	1089

1475

INDEX BY AUTHORS

Title	Opening Phrase	PAGE
HERBERT, GEORGE (*Wales*), 1593–1632		172
Collar, The	I struck the board and cried	175
Discipline	Throw away Thy rod	173
Pulley, The	When God at first made man	172
Quip, The	The merry World did on a day	172
Virtue	Sweet day, so cool, so calm	174
HERRICK, ROBERT (*England*), 1591–1674		150
Cherry-Ripe	Cherry-ripe, ripe, ripe	163
Comfort	What needs complaints	155
Corinna's Going A-Maying	Get up, get up for shame!	156
Delight in Disorder	A sweet disorder in the dress	158
His Theme	I sing of brooks, of blossoms	ix
Litany, The	In the hour of my distress	151
Meditation for His Mistress, A	You are a tulip seen to-day	153
Night-Piece, The	Her eyes the glow-worm	152
Ode for Ben Jonson, An	Ah, Ben! Say how	161
Primrose, The	Ask me why I send you here	153
To Anthea	Now is the time	159
To Blossoms	Fair pledges of a fruitful tree	159
To Daffodils	Fair Daffodils, we weep to see	161
To Daisies	Shut not so soon	154
To Dianeme	Sweet, be not proud	159
To Meadows	Ye have been fresh and green	160
To Music, to Becalm His Fever	Charm me asleep	155
To the Rose	Go, happy rose	163
To the Virgins	Gather ye rosebuds while ye may	162
To Violets	Welcome, maids of honour	150
Upon a Child	Here a pretty baby lies	151
Whenas in Silks My Julia Goes	Whenas in silks my Julia goes	161
HEYWOOD, THOMAS (*England*), 157–(?)–1650		122
Pack, Clouds, Away!	Pack, clouds, away, and welcome	124
Psyche	But Psyche lives	123
Ye Little Birds That Sit and Sing	Ye little birds that sit and sing	122
HIGGINSON, THOMAS WENTWORTH (*United States*), 1823–1911		962
Trumpeter, The	I blew, I blew, the trumpet	962
HILLYER, ROBERT (*United States*), 1895–		1340
To a Scarlatti Passepied	Strange little tune	1340
HODGSON, RALPH (*England*), 1871–		1233
Eve	Eve, with her basket	1233
HOFFMAN, CHARLES FENNO (*United States*), 1806–1884		693
Monterey	We were not many—we who stood	693

Title	Opening Phrase	PAGE
HOGG, JAMES (Scotland), 1770–1835		357
Boy's Song, A	Where the pools are bright	367
Skylark, The	Bird of the wilderness	368
HOLMES, OLIVER WENDELL (United States), 1809–1894		834
Chambered Nautilus, The	This is the ship of pearl	835
L'Inconnue	Is thy name Mary, maiden fair?	836
Old Ironsides	Ay, tear her tattered ensign	835
Voiceless, The	We count the broken lyres	834
HOOD, THOMAS (England) 1799–1845		630
Fair Ines	O saw ye not fair Ines?	630
I Remember, I Remember	I remember, I remember	634
It Was the Time of Roses	It was not in the winter	635
Ruth	She stood breast high	635
Song of the Shirt, The	With fingers weary and worn	631
Verses in an Album	Far above the hollow	636
HOOKER, BRIAN (United States), 1880–		1269
Ballade of the Dreamland Rose	Where the waves of burning cloud	1269
Cyrano's Presentation of Cadets	The Cadets of Gascoyne	1270
HOUGHTON, LORD [Richard Monckton Milnes] (England), 1809–1885		780
Strangers Yet	Strangers yet!	780
HOUSMAN, ALFRED EDWARD (England), 1859–		1150
Far in a Western Brookland	Far in a western brookland	1151
Loveliest of Trees	Loveliest of trees	1151
With Rue My Heart Is Laden	With rue my heart is laden	1150
HOVEY, RICHARD (United States), 1864–1900		1175
Envoy	Whose furthest footstep	1175
Love in the Winds	When I am standing	1176
Sea Gypsy, The	I am fevered with the sunset	1175
HOWARD, HENRY, see SURREY, EARL OF		
HOWE, JULIA WARD (United States), 1819–1910		886
Battle-Hymn of the Republic	Mine eyes have seen the glory	886
HUEFFER, FORD MADOX, see FORD, FORD MADOX		
HUNT, JAMES HENRY LEIGH (England), 1784–1859		496
Abou Ben Adhem	Abou Ben Adhem (may his tribe increase!)	496
Dirge	Blest is the turf, serenely	496
Grasshopper and the Cricket, The	Green little vaulter	497
HUXLEY, ALDOUS (England), 1894–		1339
Doors of the Temple	Many are the doors of the spirit	1339
Villiers de l'Isle-Adam	Up from the darkness	1339
INGELOW, JEAN (England), 1820–1897		906
High Tide on the Coast of		

INDEX BY AUTHORS

Title   *Opening Phrase*   PAGE

INGELOW, JEAN (*continued*):
Lincolnshire, The   I shall never hear her more   906
    JEFFERS, ROBINSON (*United States*), 1887–   1323
Joy   Though joy is better than sor-
                           row   1323
    JOHNSON, LIONEL (*England*), 1867–1902   1193
Beyond   All was for you   1195
By the Statue of King Charles
    at Charing Cross   Sombre and rich, the skies   1196
Friend, A   All that he came to give   1193
Glories   Roses from Pæstan rosaries!   1195
Precept of Silence, The I know you: solitary griefs   1194
    JOHNSON, SAMUEL (*England*), 1709–1784   280
Charles XII   On what foundation stands   281
Poverty   Has Heaven reserved, in pity   280

    JOHNSON-CORY, WILLIAM, *see* CORY, WILLIAM
        (JOHNSON)

    JONES, RALPH M. (*Canada*), 1879   1266
Bed-Time   I mind, love, how it ever   1266
    JONES, THOMAS S., JR. (*United States*), 1882–   1289
Joyous-Gard   Wind-washed and free   1289
Sometimes   Across the fields of yesterday   1290
    JONES, SIR WILLIAM (*England*), 1746-1794   325
What Constitutes a State What constitutes a State?   325
    JONSON, BEN (*England*), 1573–1637   124
Epitaph on Elizabeth L. H. Wouldst thou hear what man
                           can say   126
How Near to Good Is What
    Is Fair   How near to good is what is
                           fair   131
Noble Nature, The   It is not growing like a tree   130
On the Portrait of Shakespeare This figure that thou   127
Picture of the Mind, The A mind so pure, so perfect fine   128
Simplex Munditiis   Still to be neat   129
Slow, Slow, Fresh Fount Slow, slow, fresh fount   131
Song,—To Celia   Drink to me only with thine
                           eyes   130
Song: To Cynthia   Queen and huntress   129
To the Memory of My Be-
    loved Master William
    Shakespeare   Soul of the age!   125
Triumph, The   Have you seen but a bright lily   127
Truth   Truth is the trial of itself   127

    JOYCE, JAMES (*Ireland*), 1882–   1284
Strings in the Earth   Strings in the earth and air   1284
    KEATS, JOHN (*England*), 1795–1821   600
Dedication. To Leigh Hunt,
    Esq.   Glory and loveliness have pass'd   600

INDEX BY AUTHORS

Title	Opening Phrase	PAGE
KEATS, JOHN (*continued*):		
Endymion		
Book I	A thing of beauty is a joy for ever	601
Book IV	O Sorrow, why dost borrow	602
Eve of St. Agnes, The	St. Agnes' Eve—Ah, bitter chill	606
Fragment of an Ode to Maia	Mother of Hermes!	626
La Belle Dame Sans Merci	Ah, what can ail thee	628
Lines on the Mermaid Tavern	Souls of Poets dead and gone	622
Ode on a Grecian Urn	Thou still unravish'd bride	619
Ode on Melancholy	No, no, go not to Lethe	624
Ode to a Nightingale	My heart aches	618
Ode to Psyche	O Goddess! hear these tuneless	621
On First Looking into Chapman's Homer	Much have I travell'd	601
Sonnet on "A Lover's Complaint"	Bright star, would I were stedfast	629
Sonnet	When I have fears	625
Sonnet: To Homer	Standing aloof in giant ignorance	626
Sonnet: To Sleep	O soft embalmer of the still	627
Stanzas	In a drear-nighted December	627
To Autumn	Season of mists	623
To One Who Has Been Long in City Pent	To one who has been long in city	600
KEMP, HARRY (*United States*), 1883–		1293
Blind	The Spring blew trumpets	1294
God, the Architect	Who thou art I know not	1293
Hummingbird, The	The sunlight speaks	1293
Passing Flower, The	In Baalbec there were lovers	1293
KENNEDY, WALTER (*Scotland*), 1460–1508		19
Praise of Age, The	At matin hour, in middis	19
KILMER, ALINE (*United States*), 1888–		1327
Atonement	When a storm comes up at night	1331
Haunted	Your dying lips were proud	1328
Hill-Country	Brown hill I have left behind	1329
My Mirror	There is a mirror in my room	1330
Olim Meminisse Juvabit	Sometime it may be pleasing	1328
Prevision	I know you are too dear to stay	1327
To a Young Aviator	When you go up to die	1329
To Aphrodite: with a Mirror	Here, Cyprian, is my jewelled	1331
KILMER, JOYCE (*United States*), 1886–1918		1311
Martin	When I am tired of earnest men	1312
Poets	Vain is the chiming	1311
Trees	I think that I shall never see	1312

INDEX BY AUTHORS

Title	Opening Phrase	PAGE

KING, HENRY [Bishop of Chichester] (*England*), 1592–1669   167

Contemplation upon Flowers, A   Brave flowers—that I could   168
Dirge, A   What is the existence   167
Elegy, An   Thus kiss I your fair hands   168
Exequy on His Wife   Accept, thou shrine of my   169
Sic Vita   Like to the falling of a star   167

KINGSLEY, CHARLES (*England*), 1819–1875   902
Ode to the North-East Wind   Welcome, wild North-easter!   902

KIPLING, RUDYARD (*India*), 1865–   1181
Cities and Thrones and Powers   Cities and Thrones and Powers   1181
Rebirth   If any God should say   1182
Recessional   God of our fathers, known of old   1183
Sussex   God gave all men all earth   1184

KNOWLES, FREDERIC LAWRENCE (*United States*), 1869–1905   1219
Laus Mortis   Nay, why should I fear Death   1221
Love Triumphant   Helen's lips are drifting dust   1220
Nature: The Artist   Such hints as untaught Nature   1221
On a Fly-leaf of Burns' Songs   These are the best of him   339
To Mother Nature   Nature, in thy largess, grant   1219

LAMB, CHARLES (*England*), 1775–1834   484
Hester   When maidens such as Hester die   486
Old Familiar Faces, The   I have had playmates   485

LANDOR, WALTER SAVAGE (*England*), 1775–1864   477
Child of a Day   Child of a day, thou knowest not   482
Death   Death stands above me   478
Ianthe   From you, Ianthe, little troubles   481
On Catullus   Tell me not what too well I know   481
On Sunium's Height   Wearers of rings and chains   482
One Grey Hair, The   The wisest of the wise   480
Plays   How soon, alas, the hours   482
Resignation   Why, why repine   481
Robert Browning   There is delight in singing   840
Rose Aylmer   Ah, what avails the sceptred   480
Roses and Thorns   Why do our joys depart   479
Separation   There is a mountain and a wood   481
Sweet Was the Song That Youth Sang Once   Sweet was the song that Youth   483
Sympathy   The maid I love ne'er thought   479
To Youth   Where art thou gone   483
Twenty Years Hence   Twenty years hence my eyes   479
Very True, the Linnets Sing   Very true, the linnets sing   484

1480

Title	Opening Phrase	PAGE
LANG, ANDREW (*Scotland*), 1844–1891		1054
Odyssey, The	As one that for a weary space	1054
Scythe Song	Mowers, weary and brown	1054
LANIER, SIDNEY (*United States*), 1842–1881		1041
Acknowledgments	Now at thy soft recalling	1045
Ballad of Trees and the Master, A	Into the woods my Master went	1046
Evening Song	Look off, dear Love	1041
Marshes of Glynn, The	Glooms of the live-oaks	1042
Song of the Chattahoochee	Out of the hills of Habersham	1046
LE GALLIENNE, RICHARD (*England*), 1866–		1187
Flos Ævorum	You must mean more	1192
Lonely Dancer, The	I had no heart to join	1188
Passionate Reader to His Poet, The	Doth it not thrill thee, Poet	1187
Song	She's somewhere in the sunlight	1188
Spirit of Sadness	She loved the Autumn	1188
To a Bird at Dawn	O bird that somewhere yonder sings	1190
LECKY, WILLIAM EDWARD HARTPOLE (*Ireland*), 1838–1903		1030
Homeward Bound	Thus in the gloom and solitude	1030
To ——	'Twas not alone thy beauty's	1030
Unconscious Cerebration	Say not that the past is dead	1031
LEE-HAMILTON, EUGENE (*England*), 1845–1907		1060
Oh, Bless the Law	Oh, bless the law that veils	1060
Ring of Faustus, The	There is a tale of Faustus	1061
What the Sonnet Is	Fourteen small broidered berries	1061
LEONARD, WILLIAM ELLERY (*United States*), 1876–		1263
Indian Summer	O Earth-and-Autumn	9
Insulting Letter, The	Thanks for that insult	1263
LINDSAY, NICHOLAS VACHEL (*United States*), 1879–		1268
Dreamer, The	Why do you seek the sun	1268
LOCKER-LAMPSON, FREDERICK (*England*), 1821–1895		905
Unrealised Ideal, The	My only Love is always near	905
LODGE, THOMAS (*England*), 1558(?)–1625		49
Fair Rosalynd	Like to the clear	49
Phillis	My Phillis hath the morning sun	50
LOGAN, JOHN (*Scotland*), 1748–1788		326
To the Cuckoo	Hail, beauteous stranger	326
LONGFELLOW, HENRY WADSWORTH (*United States*), 1807–1882		694
Arrow and the Song, The	I shot an arrow into the air	704
Arsenal at Springfield, The	This is the Arsenal	701
Building of the Ship, The	Thou, too, sail on, O Ship	706

Title	*Opening Phrase*	PAGE
LONGFELLOW, HENRY WADSWORTH (*continued*):		
Day Is Done, The	The day is done, and the darkness	703
Divina Commedia	Oft have I seen at a cathedral	708
Evangeline	This is the forest primeval	705
Hymn to the Night	I heard the trailing garments	695
Kéramos	Turn, turn, my wheel!	709
Maidenhood	Maiden! with the meek, brown eyes	695
Nature	As a fond mother	708
Sandalphon	Have you read in the Talmud	706
Serenade (*from* The Spanish Student)	Stars of the summer night!	697
Spanish Gypsy, The		
Carillon	In the ancient town of Bruges	698
Belfry of Bruges, The	In the market-place of Bruges	699
LOVELACE, RICHARD (*England*), 1618–1658		215
To Althea, from Prison	When love with unconfinèd wings	215
To Lucasta, Going to the Wars	Tell me not, Sweet	216
LOWELL, AMY (*United States*), 1874–1925		1250
Crowned	You came to me bearing	1251
Venus Transiens	Tell me	1250
LOWELL, JAMES RUSSELL (*United States*), 1819–1891		877
Commemoration Ode	Life may be given in many ways	883
Freedom	We are not free: Freedom doth	879
Incident in a Railroad Car, An	He spoke of Burns	879
June	Over his keys the musing organist	880
My Love	Not as all other women are	877
O Mother State	O Mother State, how quenched	882
She Came and Went	As a twig trembles, which a bird	881
Shipwreck	We, who by shipwreck only find	885
Street, The	They pass me by like shadows	885
To William Lloyd Garrison	In a small chamber, friendless	883
LYLY, JOHN (*England*), 1554(?)–1606		47
Apollo's Song	My Daphne's hair is twisted gold	48
Cupid and My Campaspe Played	Cupid and my Campaspe played	48
Hymn to Apollo	Sing to Apollo, god of day	47
MACAULAY, THOMAS BABINGTON, LORD (*England*), 1800–1859		636
Battle of Lake Regillus, The	Men said he saw strange visions	643
Horatius at the Bridge	Lars Porsena of Clusium	636

Title	Opening Phrase	PAGE
MACAULAY, LORD (*continued*):		
Jacobite's Epitaph, A	To my true king, I offered	643
McCRAE, COLONEL JOHN (*Canada*), 1872–1918		1235
In Flanders Fields	In Flanders fields the poppies blow	1235
MACKAY, CHARLES (*Scotland*), 1814–1889		869
Love New and Old	And were they not the happy days	869
MACKAYE, PERCY (*United States*), 1875–		1263
France	Half artist and half anchorite	1263
MacLEOD, FIONA, *see* SHARP, WILLIAM		
MANGAN, JAMES CLARENCE (*Ireland*), 1803–1849		646
Dark Rosaleen	O my dark Rosaleen	646
Nameless One, The	Roll forth, my song	649
MARKHAM, EDWIN (*United States*), 1852–		1103
How to Go and Forget	I know how to hold	1105
Invisible Bride, The	The low-voiced girls that go	1103
Lincoln, the Man of the People	When the Norn Mother saw	1108
Man with the Hoe, The	Bowed by the weight of centuries	1106
Night Moths, The	Out of the night to my leafy	1105
Prayer, A	Teach me, Father, how to go	1104
Testing, The	When in the dim beginning	1109
Virgilia	Had we two gone down	1110
Your Tears	I dare not ask your very all	1106
MARLOWE, CHRISTOPHER (*England*), 1564–1593		58
Faustus		
Scene XIV	Was this the face that launch'd	59
Scene XVI	O Faustus, now hast thou	60
Hero and Leander	It lies not in our power to love	61
Passionate Shepherd to His Love, The	Come live with me and be my Love	58
Tamburlaine the Great	If all the pens that poets ever	59
MARVELL, ANDREW (*England*), 1621–1678		221
Bermudas	Where the remote Bermudas ride	221
Cromwell in Death	I saw him dead	228
Epitaph, An	Enough; and leave the rest	224
Fair Singer, The	To make a final conquest	228
Garden, A	See how the flowers	227
Garden, The	How vainly men themselves amaze	225
Mower, to Glow-Worms, The	Ye living lamps	230
Nymph Complaining for the Death of Her Faun	The wanton troopers riding by	223
Picture of Little T. C., The	See with what simplicity	231

INDEX BY AUTHORS

Title	*Opening Phrase*	PAGE
MARVELL, ANDREW (*continued*):		
To His Coy Mistress	Had we but world enough	229
MASEFIELD, JOHN (*England*), 1874–		1251
Consecration, A	Not of the princes and prelates	1251
On Growing Old	Be with me, Beauty	1255
Passing Strange, The	Out of the earth to rest	1253
Sea-Fever	I must go down to the seas again	1252
MEREDITH, GEORGE (*England*), 1828–1909		986
Love in the Valley	Under yonder beech-tree	988
Lucifer in Starlight	On a starred night Prince Lucifer	988
Marian	She can be as wise as we	986
Song	Love within the lover's breast	986
Song in the Songless	They have no song, the sedges	994
When I Would Image	When I would image her features	987
MEW, CHARLOTTE		1365
Farmer's Bride, The	Three Summers since I chose	1365
MEYNELL, ALICE (*England*), 1850–1922		1096
I Am the Way	Thou art the Way	1099
In Early Spring	O Spring, I know thee!	1096
Lady Poverty, The	The Lady Poverty was fair	1100
Maternity	One wept whose only child	1099
Parted	Farewell to one now silenced	1097
Poet of One Mood, A	A poet of one mood in all	1099
Renouncement	I must not think of thee	1098
Rivers Unknown to Song	Wide waters in the waste	1102
Shepherdess, The	She walks—the lady of my delight	1100
To Silence	Not, Silence, for thine idleness	1101
Visiting Sea, The	As the inhastening tide	1098
MIDDLETON, SCUDDER (*United States*), 1888–		1326
Journey, The	What matter where the Apple grows?	1327
Wisdom	A wise man holds himself in check	1326
MILLAY, EDNA ST. VINCENT (*United States*), 1892–		1335
Autumn Chant	Now the autumn shudders	1335
Euclid Alone Has Looked	Euclid alone has looked on Beauty	1336
Feast	I drank at every vine	1336
MILNES, RICHARD MONCKTON, *see* HOUGHTON, LORD		
MILTON, JOHN (*England*), 1608–1674		183
Arcades—Song	O'er the smooth enamelled green	201

Title	Opening Phrase	PAGE
MILTON, JOHN (*continued*):		
Comus	Sweet Echo, sweetest Nymph	186
	Sabrina fair, listen where	186
	To the Ocean now I fly	187
Il Penseroso	Hence vain deluding Joys	193
L' Allegro	Hence loathèd Melancholy	197
Lycidas	Yet once more, O ye Laurels	188
Nightingale, The	O Nightingale, that on yon	204
On His Blindness	When I consider how my light	205
On His Deceased Wife	Methought I saw my late espousèd	206
On May Morning	Now the bright morning star	203
On Shakespeare, 1630	What needs my Shakespeare	203
On the Morning of Christ's		
Nativity	This is the month, and this	201
The Hymn	It was the winter wild	202
Paradise Lost		
Book I	Of Man's first disobedience	183
Book III	Hail, holy Light!	184
	With the year seasons return	184
Book IV	O Thou, that with surpassing	184
	Me miserable! which way	185
Book V	These are thy glorious works	185
	Join voices, all ye living	185
	The Seraph Abdiel	186
To the Lady Margaret Ley	Daughter to that good Earl	204
To the Lord General Cromwell	Cromwell, our chief of men	205
MITCHELL, S. WEIR (*United States*), 1829–1914		994
Evening	I know the night is near	991
MONTGOMERY, JAMES (*Scotland*), 1771–1854		445
Falling Leaf, The	Were I a trembling leaf	445
Prayer	Prayer is the soul's sincere	445
MOORE, THOMAS (*Ireland*), 1779–1852		491
As Slow Our Ship	As slow our ship her foamy track	494
Believe Me, If All Those Endearing Young Charms	Believe me, if all those	492
Harp That Once Through Tara's Halls, The	The harp that once through	491
Last Rose of Summer, The	'Tis the last rose of summer	492
Oft, in the Stilly Night	Oft, in the stilly night	495
Oh! Breathe Not His Name	Oh! breathe not his name	491
She Is Far from the Land	She is far from the land	493
MORRIS, WILLIAM (*England*), 1834–1896		1007
Love Is Enough	Love is enough	1007
MORTON, DAVID (*United States*), 1886–		1306
Fields at Evening	They wear their evening	1306

INDEX BY AUTHORS

Title	Opening Phrase	PAGE
MORTON, DAVID (*continued*):		
Lover to Lover	Leave me awhile	1307
When There Is Music	Whenever there is music	1307
Who Walks with Beauty	Who walks with Beauty	1308
MURRY, JOHN MIDDLETON (*England*), 1889–		1334
Serenity	I ask no more for wonders	1334
NEIHARDT, JOHN G. (*United States*), 1881–		1273
Let Me Live Out My Years	Let me live out my years	1273
Prayer for Pain	I do not pray for peace	1273
NEWBOLT, SIR HENRY (*England*), 1862–		1172
Admiral Death	Boys, are ye calling a toast	1172
St. George's Day—Ypres, 1915	To fill the gap	1173
NEWMAN, JOHN HENRY, CARDINAL (*England*), 1801–1890		644
Lead, Kindly Light	Lead, kindly Light	644
Month of Mary, The	The green, green grass	645
NOYES, ALFRED (*England*), 1880–		1271
Epilogue	Carol, every violet has	1272
Forest Song, A	Who would be a king	1271
In Memory of Swinburne	April whispers—"Canst thou	1008
On Rembrandt's Portrait of a Rabbi	He has thought and suffered	1271
O'HARA, JOHN MYERS (*United States*)		1369
Faun in Wall Street, A	What shape so furtive steals	1369
O'NEIL, GEORGE (*United States*), 1897–		1342
Where It Is Winter	Now there is frost upon the hill	1342
O'SHAUGHNESSY. ARTHUR WILLIAM (*England*), 1844–1884		1048
Herodias	Her long black hair danced	1050
In the Old House	In the old house where we dwelt	1053
Keeping a Heart	If one should give me a heart	1050
Ode	We are the music-makers	1048
Song	Has summer come without the rose	1051
Song	I made another garden	1052
O'SHEEL, SHAEMAS (*United States*), 1886–		1310
He Whom a Dream Hath Possessed	He whom a dream hath possessed	1310
They Went Forth to Battle, But They Always Fell	They went forth to battle	1311
PATMORE, COVENTRY (*England*), 1823–1896		956
Angel in the House, The (*Preludes*)		
Honour and Desert	O Queen, awake to thy renown	956
Rose of the World, The	Lo, when the Lord made North	957

1486

Title	*Opening Phrase*	PAGE
PATMORE, COVENTRY (*continued*) :		
Tribute, The	Boon Nature to the woman bows	958
Unthrift	Ah, wasteful woman	956
Departure	It was not like your great	961
Magna est Veritas	Here, in this little Bay	962
Married Lover, The	Why, having won her, do I woo?	959
Toys, The	My little Son, who looked	960
Wind and Wave	The wedded light and heat	7
PEACOCK, THOMAS LOVE (*England*), 1785–1866		498
War Song of Dinas Vawr, The	The mountain sheep are sweeter	498
PERCY, WILLIAM ALEXANDER (*United States*), 1885–		1300
Overtones	I heard a bird at break of day	1300
Unloved to His Beloved, The	Could I pluck down Aldebaran	1301
Volunteer's Grave, A	Not long ago it was a bird	1301
PHILIPS, AMBROSE (*England*), 1675(?)–1749		257
To Miss Charlotte Pulteney	Little gossip, blithe and hale	257
PHILLIPS, STEPHEN (*England*), 1868–1915		1204
To a Lost Love	I cannot look upon thy grave	1204
PINKNEY, EDWARD COATE (*England*), 1802–1828		645
Health, A	I fill this cup to one	645
PLUNKETT, JOSEPH MARY (*Ireland*), 1887–1916		1322
I See His Blood Upon the Rose	I see His blood upon the rose	1322
POE, EDGAR ALLAN (*United States*), 1809–1849		740
Alone	From childhood's hour	744
Annabel Lee	It was many and many a year ago	757
Bells, The	Hear the sledges with the bells	754
City in the Sea, The	Lo! Death has reared himself	763
Conqueror Worm, The	Lo! 'tis a gala night	760
Dream-Land	By a route obscure and lonely	765
Dream Within a Dream, A	Take this kiss upon the brow!	764
Eldorado	Gaily bedight	766
For Annie	Thank Heaven! the crisis	769
Haunted Palace, The	In the greenest of our valleys	759
Israfel	In Heaven a spirit doth dwell	767
Lenore	Ah, broken is the golden bowl!	749
Raven, The	Once upon a midnight dreary	744
Romance	Romance, who loves to nod	742
Sonnet: To Science	Science! true daughter	743
To F——	Beloved! amid the earnest woes	772
To Helen	I saw thee once—once only	750
To Helen	Helen, thy beauty is to me	743
To One in Paradise	Thou wast that all to me	761

1487

INDEX BY AUTHORS

Title	Opening Phrase	PAGE

POE, EDGAR ALLAN (*continued*):

| Ulalume | The skies they were ashen | 752 |
| Valley of Unrest, The | Once it smiled a silent dell | 762 |

POPE, ALEXANDER (*England*), 1688–1744   261

Elegy	What can atone (O ever-injured	264
Epilogue to The Satires	Yes, I am proud; I must be proud	277
Essay on Criticism, An	A *little learning* is a dangerous thing	262
	But most by numbers judge	262

Essay on Man, An

Epistle I	Heaven from all creatures	266
	Lo, the poor Indian!	266
	If plagues or earthquakes	267
	All are but parts of one	267
Epistle II	Know then thyself	267
	Self-love, the spring of motion	268
	Self-love and reason	268
	In lazy apathy let stoics boast	268
	This light and darkness	269
	Vice is a monster	269
	Behold the child	269
Epistle III	Say, where full instinct	269
	For forms of government	270
Epistle IV	O Happiness! our being's end	270
	Shall burning Etna	270
	What nothing earthly gives	271
	Honour and shame from no condition rise	271
	If parts allure thee	271
	See the sole bliss Heaven could	271

Moral Essays

Epistle I	That each from other differs	272
	In vain sedate reflections	272
	In life's low vale	272
	And you, brave Cobham!	273
Epistle II	Come then, the colours	273
	But what are these to great Atossa's	273
	Oh! blest with temper	273
Epistle III	But all our praises	274
	In the worst inn's worst room	274
Epistle V	Statesman, yet friend to truth	275
Ode on Solitude	Happy the man, whose wish and care	261
Prologue. To Mr. Addison's Tragedy of Cato	To wake the soul by tender strokes	265

1488

Title	*Opening Phrase*	PAGE
POPE, ALEXANDER (*continued*):		
Prologue to The Satires	Shut, shut the door, good John!	275
	Why did I write?	276
	Were there one whose fires	276
Rape of the Lock, The		
Canto I	And now, unveil'd	263
Canto II	On her white breast	264
PRIOR, MATTHEW (*England*), 1664–1721		254
Dying Adrian to His Soul, The	Poor, little, pretty	254
Merchant, to Secure His Treasure, The	The merchant, to secure	254
QUARLES, FRANCIS (*England*), 1592–1644		166
On the Life and Death of Man	The world's a theatre	166
Respice Finem	My soul, sit thou a patient	166
RALEIGH, SIR WALTER (*England*), 1552(?)–1618		35
Conclusion, The	Even such is Time	39
His Pilgrimage	Give me my scallop-shell	35
Lie, The	Go, Soul, the Body's guest	36
Nymph's Reply, The	If all the world and love	39
Silent Lover, The	Passions are liken'd to floods	36
Vision Upon Spenser's "Faery Queen," A	Methought I saw the grave	40
RHYS, ERNEST (*England*), 1859–		1152
Dagonet's Canzonet	A queen lived in the South	1152
Lost in France	He had the plowman's strength	1152
RICE, CALE YOUNG (*United States*), 1872–		1236
When the Wind Is Low	When the wind is low, and the sea	1236
RILEY, JAMES WHITCOMB (*United States*), 1852–1916		1113
Parting Guest, A	What delightful hosts are they	1114
When She Comes Home	When she comes home again	1113
RITTENHOUSE, JESSIE B. (*United States*)		1362
Debt	My debt to you, Belovèd	1362
Transformation	I shall be beautiful	1362
ROBINSON, EDWIN ARLINGTON (*United States*), 1869–		1213
Flammonde	The man Flammonde	1213
Gift of God, The	Blessed with a joy that only she	1216
Master, The	A flying word from here and there	1217
ROGERS, ROBERT CAMERON (*United States*), 1862–1912		1174
Rosary, The	The hours I spent with thee	1174
ROGERS, SAMUEL (*England*), 1763–1855		360
Epitaph on a Robin Redbreast	Tread lightly here, for here	361

Title	*Opening Phrase*	PAGE
ROGERS, SAMUEL (*continued*):		
Italian Song	Dear is my little native vale	360
Nature's Gift	Nature denied him much	366
Pæstum	They stand between the mountains	363
Sleeping Beauty, The	Sleep on, and dream of Heaven	366
To . . .	Go—you may call it madness	361
Wish, A	Mine be a cot beside the hill	360
Written in Westminster Abbey	Whoe'er thou art, approach	362
ROSSETTI, CHRISTINA GEORGINA (*England*), 1830–1894		995
Dream Land	Where sunless rivers weep	999
Heaven Overarches Earth and Sea	Heaven overarches earth and sea	995
Mirage	The hope I dreamed of	997
Passing Away	Passing away, saith the World	996
Remember	Remember me when I am gone away	997
Rest	O Earth, lie heavily	998
Three Seasons	"A cup for hope!" she said	998
Up-Hill	Does the road wind up-hill	996
When I Am Dead, My Dearest	When I am dead, my dearest	995
ROSSETTI, DANTE GABRIEL (*England*), 1828–1882		965
Blessed Damozel, The	The blessed damozel leaned out	965
House of Life, The		
Introductory Sonnet	A sonnet is a moment's monument	972
I: Love Enthroned	I marked all kindred Powers	973
IV: Lovesight	When do I see thee most	973
V: Heart's Hope	By what world's power	974
XI: The Portrait	O Lord of all compassionate control	vii
XIII: The Lover's Walk	Sweet twining hedgeflowers	974
XXVI: Winged Hours	Each hour until we meet	974
XXXII: Her Gifts	High grace, the dower of queens	975
XXXV: The Dark Glass	Not I myself know all my love	975
XXXVI: The Lamp's Shrine	Sometimes I fain would find	976
XLIX: Death-in-Love	There came an image	976
LIV: Without Her	What of her glass without her?	977
LVII: True Woman. 1. Herself	To be a sweetness more desired	977
LVIII: True Woman. 2. Her Love	She loves him; for her infinite soul	978
LIX: True Woman. 3. Her Heaven	If to grow old in heaven	978
LXXII: The Choice. 1	Eat thou and drink	979
LXXIII: The Choice. 2	Watch thou and fear	979

Title	Opening Phrase	PAGE
ROSSETTI, DANTE GABRIEL (continued):		
LXXIV: The Choice. 3	Think thou and act	979
LXXXVII: Lost Days	The lost days of my life	980
CVI: Sudden Light	I have been here before	980
Lilith	Of Adam's first wife, Lilith	984
Portrait, The	This is her picture as she was	969
Sibylla Palmifera	Under the arch of Life	985
Stream's Secret, The	What thing unto mine ear	981
Three Shadows	I looked and saw your eyes	985
RUSSELL, GEORGE WILLIAM (Ireland), 1867–		1200
Carrowmore	It's a lonely road	1201
Dream of Defeated Beauty, A	All day they played in gardens	1200
Twilight of Earth, The	The wonder of the world is o'er	1202
SASSOON, SIEGFRIED, 1886–		1313
Aftermath	Have you forgotten yet?	1313
SAUL, GEORGE BRANDON (United States), 1901–		1343
Elizabeth	She has the strange sweet grace	1343
SCOLLARD, CLINTON (United States), 1860–		1164
As I Came Down from Lebanon	As I came down from Lebanon	1165
Bag-Pipes at Sea	Above the shouting of the gale	1164
SCOTT, SIR WALTER (Scotland), 1771–1832		428
Claud Halcro's Song	Farewell to Northmaven	442
Jock of Hazeldean	Why weep ye by the tide, ladie?	439
Lady of the Lake, The		
Canto I	Soldier, rest! thy warfare o'er	433
Canto III	He is gone on the mountain	434
Canto V	Wild as the scream of the curlew	435
Canto VI	Harp of the North, farewell!	435
Lay of the Last Minstrel, The		
Introduction	The way was long, the wind	428
Canto II	If thou wouldst view fair Melrose	429
Canto VI	Breathes there the man	429
	O'er Roslin all that dreary night	430
Lord of the Isles, The		
Canto VI	Rushing, ten thousand horsemen	438
Marmion		
Introduction to Canto I	With more than mortal powers	431
Canto VI	They close, in clouds of smoke	432
	O Woman! in our hours of ease	432
Old Mortality	Sound, sound the clarion	441
	The sun upon the Weirdlaw Hill	441
One Hour with Thee	An hour with thee!	443
Proud Maisie	Proud Maisie is in the wood	442

INDEX BY AUTHORS

Title	*Opening Phrase*	PAGE

SCOTT, SIR WALTER (*continued*):

Rebecca's Hymn — When Israel, of the Lord beloved — 444

Rokeby
Canto III — O Brignal banks are wild and fair — 436
— A weary lot is thine, fair maid — 437

Time — Why sit'st thou by that ruined hall — 440

SEDLEY, SIR CHARLES (*England*), 1639(?)–1701 — 250

Child and Maiden — Ah, Chloris! could I now — 251

Love Still Has Something of the Sea — Love still has something — 250

Phyllis — Phyllis is my only joy — 252

SEEGER, ALAN (*United States*), 1888–1916 — 1325

I Have a Rendezvous with Death — I have a rendezvous with Death — 1325

SHAKESPEARE, WILLIAM (*England*), 1564–1616

As You Like It
Act II, Scene II — Under the greenwood tree — 71
— Who doth ambition shun — 71
Act II, Scene VII — All the world's a stage — 71
— Blow, blow, thou winter wind — 72
Act III, Scene II — Why should this a desert be? — 72
Act V, Scene III — It was a lover and his lass — 73

Crabbèd Age and Youth — Crabbèd Age and Youth cannot live — 113

Cymbeline
Act II, Scene III — Hark! Hark! the lark — 98
Act IV, Scene II — Fear no more the heat o' the sun — 98

Hamlet
Act I, Scene II — O! that this too too solid flesh — 88
— Frailty, thy name is woman! — 88
Act I, Scene III — The chariest maid is prodigal — 89
— I shall th' effect of this good — 89
— Give thy thoughts no tongue — 89
Act I, Scene IV — But to my mind—though I am native — 90
— Angels and ministers of grace — 90
Act I, Scene V — I am thy father's spirit — 91
Act II, Scene II — O! what a rogue and peasant slave — 91
Act III, Scene I — To be, or not to be — 92
Scene II — Since my dear soul was mistress — 93
Scene IV — See, what a grace was seated — 93
Act IV, Scene IV — Sure he that made us — 94

Julius Cæsar
Act I, Scene II — I know that virtue to be in you — 83

1492

Title	*Opening Phrase*	PAGE
SHAKESPEARE, WILLIAM (*continued*):		
Act III, Scene II	Friends, Romans, countrymen	85
Act IV, Scene III	There is a tide in the affairs	85
Act V, Scene V	This was the noblest Roman	86
King Henry the Fourth	O sleep! O gentle sleep!	78
King Henry the Fifth		
Act I, Scene II	So work the honey-bees	79
Act IV, Scene III	I am not covetous for gold	79
	We few, we happy few	80
King Henry the Eighth		
Act III, Scene I	Orpheus with his lute made trees	81
Scene II	Farewell! a long farewell	81
	Love thyself last	82
King John	To gild refinèd gold	76
King Lear	How fearful and dizzy 'tis	94
King Richard the Second		
Act I, Scene III	O! who can hold a fire	76
Act II, Scene I	This royal throne of kings	76
Act III, Scene I	Know'st thou not	77
	Of comfort no man speak	77
King Richard the Third		
Act I, Scene I	Now is the winter of our discontent	80
Scene IV	Methought what pain it was	80
Love's Labour's Lost		
Act IV, Scene III	On a day, alack the day	66
Act V, Scene II	When daisies pied and violets	66
	When icicles hang by the wall	67
Macbeth		
Act I, Scene VII	If it were done when 'tis done	86
Act II, Scene I	Is this a dagger which I see	87
Act III, Scene II	Better be with the dead	87
Act V, Scene II	Canst thou not minister to a mind	88
Scene V	To-morrow, and to-morrow	88
Measure for Measure		
Act II, Scene II	But man, proud man	64
Act III, Scene I	Ay, but to die, and go	64
Act IV, Scene I	Take, O take those lips away	65
Merchant of Venice, The		
Act III, Scene II	Tell me where is fancy bred	69
Act IV, Scene I	The quality of mercy is not	70
Act V, Scene I	How sweet the moonlight sleeps	70
	The man that hath no music	70
Midsummer-Night's Dream, A		
Act I, Scene I	Swift as a shadow	67
Act II, Scene II	You spotted snakes with double tongue	68

INDEX BY AUTHORS

Title	*Opening Phrase*	PAGE
SHAKESPEARE, WILLIAM (*continued*):		
Act V, Scene I	I never may believe	68
Scene II	Now the hungry lion roars	69
Much Ado About Nothing	Sigh no more, ladies	65
Othello		
Act I, Scene III	Most potent, grave, and reverend	95
	Her father lov'd me	95
Act II, Scene I	She that was ever fair	96
Act III, Scene III	Good name in man and woman	97
	Farewell the tranquil mind	97
	Like to the Pontick sea	97
Act V, Scene II	I have done the state some service	97
Pericles		
Act III, Scene I	Thou God of this great vast	99
Romeo and Juliet		
Act I, Scene IV	She is the fairies' midwife	82
Act II, Scene II	He jests at scars that never felt	83
Sonnets		
XII	When I do count the clock	100
XV	When I consider every thing that grows	101
XVII	Who will believe my verse	101
XVIII	Shall I compare thee to a summer's	101
XXIX	When, in disgrace with fortune	102
XXX	When to the sessions of sweet	102
XXXI	Thy bosom is endeared with all	103
XXXIII	Full many a glorious morning	103
XXXIX	O! how thy worth with manners	104
LIV	O! how much more doth beauty	104
LV	Not marble, nor the gilded monuments	104
LVII	Being your slave	105
LX	Like as the waves make towards	105
LXI	Is it thy will thy image should	106
LXV	Since brass, nor stone, nor earth	106
LXXI	No longer mourn for me	107
LXXII	O! lest the world should task you	107
LXXIII	That time of year thou may'st	107
LXXVI	Why is my verse so barren	108
LXXXI	Or I shall live your epitaph to make	108
LXXXIV	Who is it that says most?	109
LXXXVI	Was it the proud full sail	109
LXXXVII	Farewell! thou art too dear	110
LXXXIX	Say that thou didst forsake	110

INDEX BY AUTHORS

Title	Opening Phrase	PAGE

SHAKESPEARE, WILLIAM (*continued*):

XCVII — How like a winter hath my absence — 110

XCVIII — From you have I been absent — 111

XCIX — The forward violet thus did I — 111

CIV — To me, fair friend, you never — 112

CVI — When in the chronicles of wasted time — 112

CXVI — Let me not to the marriage — 113

CXXIX — The expense of spirit in a waste — 113

Tempest, The

Act I, Scene II — Come unto these yellow sands — 63

Act IV, Scene I — Our revels now are ended — 63

Act V, Scene I — Where the bee sucks — 63

Twelfth-Night

Act I, Scene I — If music be the food of love — 74

Act II, Scene III — O mistress mine! where are — 74

Scene IV — Come away, come away, death — 74

She never told her love — 75

Two Gentlemen of Verona — Who is Silvia? what is she? — 64

Venus and Adonis — Hard-favour'd tyrant, ugly — 100

Hadst thou but bid beware — 100

Winter's Tale, The

Act IV, Scene III — O Proserpina! — 75

Lawn as white as driven snow — 75

SHARP, WILLIAM (*England*), 1856–1905 — 1120

Washer of the Ford, The — There is a lonely stream — 1120

Wasp, The — When the ripe pears droop — 1120

SHAW, FRANCES WELLS (*United States*), 1872– — 1233

Who Loves the Rain — Who loves the rain — 1233

SHELLEY, PERCY BYSSHE (*England*), 1792–1822 — 518

Adonais — I weep for Adonais—he is dead! — 525

Alastor — Earth, ocean, air — 519

Cloud, The — I bring fresh showers — 565

Dirge, A — Rough wind, that moanest loud — 591

Dirge for the Year — Orphan Hours, the Year is dead — 576

Fragment: To Music, A — Silver key of the fountain — 546

Fragment: Wedded Souls — I am as a spirit — 564

Fragment on Keats — Here lieth One whose name — 600

Hellas — In the great morning of the world — 539

The world's great age — 540

Hymn of Apollo — The sleepless Hours who watch me — 570

Hymn of Pan — From the forests and highlands — 571

Hymn to Intellectual Beauty — The awful shadow of some unseen — 543

Indian Serenade, The — I arise from dreams of thee — 563

Invocation to Misery — Come, be happy! sit near me — 556

INDEX BY AUTHORS

Title	*Opening Phrase*	PAGE
SHELLEY, PERCY BYSSHE (*continued*):		
Lament, A	O world! O life! O time!	580
Lines Written Among the Euganean Hills	Many a green isle needs must be	546
Love's Philosophy	The fountains mingle with the river	564
Music	I pant for the music	582
Mutability	We are as clouds that veil	542
Ode to the West Wind	O wild West Wind, thou breath	561
Ozymandias	I met a traveller from an antique	546
Prometheus Unbound		
Act I	On a poet's lips I slept	524
Act II	Life of Life! Thy lips enkindle	524
Queen Mab	How wonderful is Death	591
Question, The	I dreamed that, as I wandered	572
Remembrance	Swifter far than summer's flight	580
Revolt of Islam, The	So now my summer task is ended	520
Shelley (*from* Adonais)	Midst others of less note	518
Song	Rarely, rarely, comest thou	578
Song to the Men of England	Men of England, wherefore plough	560
Sonnet	Lift not the painted veil	559
Stanzas—April, 1814	Away! the moor is dark	541
Stanzas. Written in Dejection Near Naples	The sun is warm, the sky	558
Time	Unfathomable Sea! whose waves	578
Time Long Past	Like the ghost of a dear friend	575
To ——	Music, when soft voices die	578
To ——	One word is too often profaned	581
To ——	When passion's trance	581
To a Skylark	Hail to thee, blithe Spirit!	567
To Jane: the Invitation	Best and brightest, come away	584
To Jane: The Keen Stars Were Twinkling	The keen stars were twinkling	590
To Jane: the Recollection	Now the last day of many days	585
To Night	Swiftly walk o'er the western	577
To the Moon	Art thou pale for weariness	575
To Wordsworth	Poet of Nature, thou hast wept	543
Two Spirits, The	O thou, who plumed with strong	573
When the Lamp Is Shattered	When the lamp is shattered	583
With a Guitar, to Jane	Ariel to Miranda:—Take	588
World's Wanderers, The	Tell me, thou Star	575
SHENSTONE, WILLIAM (*England*), 1714–1763		283
Written at an Inn in Henley	To thee, fair freedom!	283
SHIRLEY, JAMES (*England*), 1596–1666		178
Glories of Our Blood and State, The	The glories of our blood	178

Title	*Opening Phrase*	PAGE
SHIRLEY, JAMES (*continued*):		
On Her Dancing	I stood and saw my Mistress	179
Victorious Men of Earth	Victorious men of earth	178
SIDNEY, SIR PHILIP (*England*), 1554–1586		40
Dirge, A	Ring out your bells	44
Doubt You to Whom My Muse	Doubt you to whom my Muse	43
Epitaph on Argalus and Parthenia	His being was in her alone	46
Impatient Lover, The	Be your words made, good Sir	46
Inspiration	I never drank of Aganippe well	42
Look in Thy Heart and Write	Loving in truth and fain in verse	7
My True-Love Hath My Heart	My true-love hath my heart	46
No More, My Dear	No more, my Dear	41
O Fair! O Sweet	O fair! O sweet! when I do look	44
O Happy Thames	O happy Thames that didst	42
Oft Have I Mused	Oft have I mused	47
Philomela	The nightingale, as soon as April	44
Sleep	Come Sleep! O Sleep	41
To the Moon	With how sad steps, O Moon	40
SILL, EDWARD ROWLAND (*United States*), 1841–1887		1039
Fool's Prayer, The	The royal feast was done	1039
Truth at Last	Does a man ever give up hope	1041
Wordsworth	A moonlit desert's yellow sands	369
SKELTON, JOHN (*England*), 1460(?)–1529		21
To Mistress Margery Wentworth	Merry Margaret	21
SMITH, CLARK ASHTON (*United States*), 1893–		1338
Impression	The silver silence of the moon	1338
Recompense	Ah, more to me than many days	1338
Transcendence	To look on love with disenamoured eyes	1338
SOUTHEY, ROBERT (*England*), 1774–1843		475
Curse of Kehama, The	They sin who tell us Love can die	476
My Days Among the Dead Are Passed	My days among the Dead are passed	475
Thalaba	How beautiful is night	476
SPENCER, WILLIAM ROBERT (*England*), 1769–1834		367
To ——	Too late I stayed—forgive	367

Title	Opening Phrase	PAGE
SPENSER, EDMUND (*England*), 1552(?)–1599		28
Amoretti		
XXXIV	Like as a ship	28
LXXII	Oft when my Spirit	29
LXXV	One day I wrote her name	29
LXXXI	Fair is my Love	29
Prothalamion	Calm was the day	30
SPEYER, LEONORA (*United States*)		1356
Duet	Out of my sorrow	1356
Ladder, The	I had a sudden vision	1357
Note from the Pipes, A	Pan, blow your pipes	1357
Pioneers	Who is the pioneer?	1358
SPINGARN, JOEL ELIAS (*United States*), 1875–		1261
Beauty	I found no beauty	1261
SQUIRE, JOHN COLLINS (*England*), 1884–		1298
In a Chair	The room is full of the peace	1298
Lake, The	I am a lake	1300
March, The	I heard a voice that cried	1299
Tree-Tops	There beyond my window ledge	1299
STAFFORD, WENDELL PHILLIPS (*United States*), 1861–		1170
Invocation	O Thou whose equal purpose runs	1170
STEDMAN, EDMUND CLARENCE (*United States*), 1833–1908		1004
Voice of the Western Wind	Voice of the western wind!	1004
STEPHENS, JAMES (*Ireland*), 1882–		1285
Hate	My enemy came nigh	1285
Waste Places, The	As a naked man I go	1286
What Tomas An Buile Said in a Pub	I saw God. Do you doubt it?	1285
STERLING, GEORGE (*United States*), 1869–1926		1207
Black Vulture, The	Aloof within the day's enormous dome	1213
Last Days, The	The russet leaves of the sycamore	1211
Lost Nymph, The	Now whither hast thou flown?	1208
Master-Mariner, The	My grandsire sailed three years	1209
Mirage	I well remember that the year	1207
Omnia Exeunt in Mysterium	The stranger in my gates	1212
Spring in Carmel	O'er Carmel fields	1210
STEVENSON, ROBERT LOUIS (*Scotland*), 1850–1894		1092
Celestial Surgeon, The	If I have faltered more or less	1092
Envoy	Go, little book, and wish	1094
In the Highlands	In the highlands	1093
My Wife	Trusty, dusky, vivid, true	1092

Title	Opening Phrase	PAGE
STEVENSON, ROBERT LOUIS (*continued*):		
Requiem	Under the wide and starry sky	1093
Romance	I will make you brooches	1093
STODDARD, RICHARD HENRY (*United States*), 1825–		
1903		964
Flight of Youth, The	There are gains for all our losses	964
STOREY, VIOLET ALLEYN (*United States*)		1366
Prayer After Illness, A	Tune me for life again	1366
SUCKLING, SIR JOHN (*England*), 1609–1642		206
Ballad Upon a Wedding, A	I tell thee, Dick, where I	206
Constant Lover, The	Why so pale and wan	210
Hast Thou Seen the Down in the Air	Hast thou seen the down	209
I Prithee Send Me Back My Heart	I prithee send me back	209
When, Dearest, I But Think of Thee	When, Dearest, I but think	210
SURREY, EARL OF [Henry Howard] (*England*),		
1517(?)–1547		20
Give Place, Ye Lovers	Give place, ye lovers, here before	20
SWINBURNE, ALGERNON CHARLES (*England*),		
1837–1909		1008
Atalanta in Calydon		
First Chorus	When the hounds of spring	1009
Second Chorus	Before the beginning of years	1010
Ave Atque Vale	Shall I strew on thee rose	1019
Beaumont and Fletcher	An hour ere sudden sunset	137
Ben Jonson	Broad-based, broad-fronted	124
By the North Sea	A land that is lonelier	1027
Christopher Marlowe	Crowned, girdled, garbed	1026
Forsaken Garden, A	In a coign of the cliff	1017
Garden of Proserpine, The	Here, where the world is quiet	1014
In Memory of Walter Savage Landor	Back to the flower-town	477
Itylus	Swallow, my sister	1012
On Lamb's Specimens of Dramatic Poets	If all the flowers	484
Rondel	These many years	1013
Triumph of Time, The	I will go back to the great	1025
William Shakespeare	Not if men's tongues and angels'	1027
SYLVESTER, JOSHUA (*England*), 1563–1618		57
Constancy	Were I as base as is the lowly plain	57
Glorious Stars of Heaven, The	I'll ne'er believe	57

INDEX BY AUTHORS

Title	Opening Phrase	PAGE
SYMONDS, JOHN ADDINGTON (*England*), 1840–1893		1038
Love in Dreams	Love hath his poppy-wreath	1039
Thyself	Give me thyself!	1038
SYMONS, ARTHUR (*Wales*), 1865–		1176
Last Memory, The	When I am old, and think	1177
Memory	As a perfume doth remain	1178
Modern Beauty	I am the torch, she saith	1176
Return, The	A little hand is knocking	1177
TABB, JOHN BANNISTER (*United States*), 1845–1909		1062
Beethoven and Angelo	One made the surging sea	1062
Father Damien	O God, the cleanest offering	1062
Fraternity	I know not but in every leaf	1062
To Shelley	At Shelley's birth	1062
TEASDALE, SARA (*United States*), 1884–		1294
Foreknown	They brought me with a secret glee	1294
Lamp, The	If I can bear your love	1295
Peace	Peace flows into me	1295
ALFRED, LORD TENNYSON (*England*), 1809–1892		781
Break, Break, Break	Break, break, break	800
Brook, The	I come from haunts of coot and hern	828
Crossing the Bar	Sunset and evening star	833
Deserted House, The	Life and Thought have gone away	781
Dream of Fair Women, A	I read, before my eyelids dropt	13
Eagle, The	He clasps the crag with hookèd hands	800
Early Spring	Once more the Heavenly Power	832
Farewell, A	Flow down, cold rivulet	799
Flower in the Crannied Wall	Flower in the crannied wall	801
Gareth and Lynette	For truly, as thou sayest	802
Higher Pantheism, The	The sun, the moon, the stars	801
In Love, If Love Be Love	In Love, if Love be Love	802
In Memoriam	Strong Son of God, immortal love	808
I	I held it truth, with him who sings	809
V	I sometimes hold it half a sin	809
IX	Fair ship, that from the	810
XI	Calm is the morn without a sound	810
XII	Lo, as a dove, when up she springs	811
XIII	Tears of the widower	811
XXIII	Now, sometimes in my sorrow shut	812

Title	*Opening Phrase*	PAGE
ALFRED, LORD TENNYSON (*continued*):		
XXVII	I envy not in any moods	812
L	Be near me when my light is low	813
LIII	How many a father have I seen	813
LIV	O yet we trust that somehow good	814
LV	The wish, that of the living whole	814
LVI	"So careful of the type?" but no	815
LVII	Peace; come away	816
LXXV	I leave thy praises unexpress'd	816
LXXIX	But thou and I are one in kind	817
LXXXV	Whatever way my ways decline	817
XCVI	You say, but with no touch	817
C	I climb the hill	818
CVI	Ring out, wild bells	819
CXXIII	There rolls the deep	820
CXXVI	Love is and was my Lord and King	820
CXXVII	And all is well	821
	But ill for him that wears	821
CXXX	Thy voice is on the rolling air	821
	Again the feast, the speech	821
In the Valley of Cauteretz	All along the valley	831
Lady of Shalott, The	On either side the river lie	782
Locksley Hall	In the Spring a fuller crimson	797
Maud		
Part I	Come into the garden, Maud	823
Part II	O that 'twere possible	825
Morte D'Arthur	The old order changeth	795
Œnone	There lies a vale in Ida	787
Of Old Sat Freedom on the Heights	Of old sat Freedom on the heights	794
Princess, The		
II	As thro' the land at eve	803
IV	The splendour falls on castle walls	803
	Tears, idle tears	804
	O Swallow, Swallow, flying	804
VI	Home they brought her warrior dead	805
VII	Ask me no more: the moon	806
	Come down, O maid, from yonder	806
	The woman's cause is man's	807
	For woman is not undevelopt man	807

INDEX BY AUTHORS

Title	*Opening Phrase*	PAGE

ALFRED, LORD TENNYSON (*continued*):

St. Agnes' Eve — Deep on the convent-roof — 798
Tithonus — The woods decay — 829
Ulysses — It little profits that an idle king — 795

THACKERAY, WILLIAM MAKEPEACE (*India*), 1811–1863

At the Church Gate — Although I enter not — 838

THOMAS, EDITH M. (*United States*), 1854–1925 — 1114

Chant of the Fought Field, A — As one who under evening skies — 1118
Courage of the Lost, The — There be who are afraid — 1117
Evoe! — Many are the wand-bearers — 1114
Patmos — All around him Patmos lies — 1116
Security of Desolation, The — He who hath seen — 1115

THOMPSON, FRANCIS (*England*), 1859–1907 — 1153

Correlated Greatness — O nothing, in this corporal earth — 1162
Daisy — Where the thistle lifts — 1153
Dream-Tryst — The breaths of kissing night — 1160
Envoy — Go songs, for ended is our — 1400
Hound of Heaven, The — I fled Him, down the nights — 1155
Messages — What shall I your true-love tell — 1160
To a Snowflake — What heart could have thought you? — 1159

THOMPSON, WILL HENRY (*United States*), 1848– — 1079

High Tide at Gettysburg, The — A cloud possessed the hollow field — 1079

THOMSON, JAMES (*Scotland*), 1834–1882 — 1005

Art
I — What precious thing are you making fast — 1005
II — If you have a carrier-dove — 1005
III — Singing is sweet; but be sure of this — 1006

THOREAU, HENRY DAVID (*United States*), 1817–1862 — 869

Inspiration — If with light head erect I sing — 869
My Prayer — Great God, I ask thee — 871
Smoke — Light-winged Smoke, Icarian bird — 870

TRENCH, HERBERT (*Ireland*), 1865–1923 — 1180

Come, Let Us Make Love Deathless — Come, let us make love deathless — 1181
I Heard a Soldier — I heard a soldier sing — 1180

1502

Title	Opening Phrase	PAGE
TURBERVILLE, GEORGE (*England*), 1530(?)–1595		21
Lover to His Lady, The	My Girl, thou gazest much	21
UNTERMEYER, LOUIS (*United States*), 1885–		1302
Caliban in the Coal Mines	God, we don't like to complain	1304
Feuerzauber	I never knew the earth	1303
How Much of Godhood	How much of Godhood did it take	1304
Mockery	God, I return to You	1302
Only of Thee and Me	Only of thee and me	1303
Prayer	God, though this life	1302
UPSON, ARTHUR (*United States*), 1877–1908		1264
Ex Libris	In an old book at even	1264
VAUGHAN, HENRY (*Wales*), 1622–1695		232
Anguish	My God and King! to Thee	234
Beyond the Veil	They are all gone into the world	232
Retreat, The	Happy those early days	235
Song to Amoret, A	If I were dead, and, in my place	233
World, The	I saw Eternity the other night	234
VIERECK, GEORGE SYLVESTER (*Germany*), 1884–		1298
Wanderers	Sweet is the highroad	1298
VINAL, HAROLD (*United States*), 1891–		1335
Earth Lover	Old loveliness has such a way	1335
WADE, THOMAS (*England*), 1805–1875		687
True Martyr, The	The Martyr worthiest	687
WALLER, EDMUND (*England*), 1606–1687		180
English Verse	Poets may boast, as safely vain	180
Old Age	The seas are quiet when the winds	181
On a Girdle	That which her slender waist	181
Song	Go, lovely Rose!	182
To a Lady Singing	Chloris, yourself you so excel	181
WATSON, WILLIAM (*England*), 1858–		1147
In Laleham Churchyard	'Twas at this season	1148
Invention	I envy not the Lark his song	1148
Leavetaking	Pass, thou wild light	1147
Song	April, April	1147
Sovereign Poet, The	He sits above the clang	8
WATTS, ISAAC (*England*), 1674–1748		256
Ode to a Schoolmaster	Custom, that Tyranness of Fools	256
True Greatness	Were I so tall to reach the pole	257
WHEELOCK, JOHN HALL (*United States*), 1886–		1316
Earth	Grasshopper, your fairy song	1316

INDEX BY AUTHORS

Title	*Opening Phrase*	PAGE

WHEELOCK, JOHN HALL (*continued*):

I Do Not Love to See Your Beauty Fire	I do not love to see your beauty	1318
Lion-House, The	Always the heavy air	1319
Panther! Panther!	There is a panther caged	1322
Plaint	Brief is Man's travail here	1321
Poet Tells of His Love, The	How shall I sing of Her	1320
To the Modern Man	From mysteries of the Past	1319

WHITE, JOSEPH BLANCO (*Spain*), 1775–1841   487

To Night	Mysterious Night! when our first	487

WHITMAN, WALT (*United States*), 1819–1892   887

Joy, Shipmate, Joy!	Joy, shipmate, joy!	902
Noiseless, Patient Spider, A	A noiseless, patient spider	901
O Captain! My Captain!	O Captain! my Captain!	887
Out of the Cradle Endlessly Rocking	Once Paumanok, when the lilac	896
To the Man-of-War-Bird	Thou who hast slept all night	887
When Lilacs Last in the Dooryard Bloomed	When lilacs last in the dooryard	888

WHITTIER, JOHN GREENLEAF (*United States*), 1807–1892   717

Child-Songs	Still linger in our noon	738
Ichabod	So fallen! so lost!	739
Meeting, The	I ask no organ's soulless breath	737
Snow-bound	The sun that brief December day	717
Vesta	O Christ of God!	738

WIDDEMER, MARGARET (*United States*),   1362

Dark Cavalier, The	I am the Dark Cavalier	1363
Greek Folk Song	Under dusky laurel leaf	1363
Masters, The	You have taught me laughter	1362

WILDE, OSCAR (*Ireland*), 1856–1900   1121

Ballad of Reading Gaol, The	He did not wear his scarlet coat	1121
Hélas	To drift with every passion	1139
Requiescat	Tread lightly, she is near	1140
Sonnet	Nay, Lord, not thus! white lilies	1140

WILMOT, JOHN [Earl of Rochester] (*England*), 1647–1680   252

Constancy	I cannot change, as others do	252
Epitaph on Charles II	Here lies our Sovereign Lord	252
My Light Thou Art	My light thou art	253
Song, A	My dear mistress has	253

WITHER, GEORGE (*England*), 1588–1667   145

For Anniversary Marriage-Days	Lord, living, here are we	145
Lilies Without, Lilies Within	Can I think the Guide of Heaven	145
Marygold, The	When with a serious musing	147

Title	*Opening Phrase*	PAGE
WITHER, GEORGE (*continued*):		
Muse, The	She doth tell me where	149
Shall I, Wasting in Despair	Shall I, wasting in despair	147
WOLFE, CHARLES (*Ireland*), 1791–1823		516
Burial of Sir John Moore		
After Corunna, The	Not a drum was heard	517
To Mary	If I had thought thou couldst	516
WOOD, CLEMENT (*United States*), 1888–		1331
Eagle Sonnets		
III	I have been sure of three things	1331
VII	Flower of the dust am I	1332
IX	O bitter moon, O cold and bitter	1332
XI	When down the windy vistas	1333
XIX	I am a tongue for beauty	1333
XX	We are the singing shadows	1333
WOODBERRY, GEORGE EDWARD (*United States*), 1855–		1119
Divine Awe	To tremble, when I touch	1119
WORDSWORTH, WILLIAM (*England*), 1770–1850		369
After-Thought	I thought of Thee, my partner	423
Character of the Happy Warrior	Who is the happy Warrior?	410
Composed Upon Westminster Bridge	Earth has not anything to show	386
Great Men Have Been Among Us	Great men have been among us	389
Green Linnet, The	Beneath these fruit-tree boughs	395
I Travelled Among Unknown Men	I travelled among unknown men	376
I Wandered Lonely as a Cloud	I wandered lonely as a cloud	402
It Is a Beauteous Evening	It is a beauteous evening	387
It Is Not To Be Thought of	It is not to be thought of	389
Lines. Composed a Few Miles Above Tintern Abbey	Five Years have past	371
Lines Written in Early Spring	I heard a thousand blended notes	370
London, 1802	Milton! thou should'st be living	388
My Heart Leaps Up	My heart leaps up when I behold	379
Nuns Fret Not	Nuns fret not at their convent's	413
O Nightingale! Thou Surely Art	O Nightingale! thou surely art	420
Ode. Intimations of Immortality	There was a time when meadow	414
Ode to Duty	Stern Daughter of the Voice of God	404
On the Departure of Sir Walter Scott	A trouble, not of clouds	428

1505

INDEX BY AUTHORS

Title	*Opening Phrase*	PAGE

WORDSWORTH, WILLIAM (*continued*):

On the Extinction of the Venetian Republic	Once did She hold the gorgeous east	387
On the Subjugation of Switzerland	Two Voices are there	419
Poet, A	A poet!—He hath put his heart	427
Poet's Epitaph, A	But who is He, with modest looks	378
Prelude, The		
Book II	Thus while the days flew by	407
Book III	Her pealing organ was my neighbour	408
	As if awakened, summoned, roused	408
Book XII	O Soul of Nature!	409
Resolution and Independence	There was a roaring in the wind	382
Reverie of Poor Susan, The	At the corner of Wood Street	370
Scorn Not the Sonnet	Scorn not the Sonnet; Critic	424
She Dwelt Among the Untrodden Ways	She dwelt among the untrodden	375
She Was a Phantom of Delight	She was a Phantom of delight	401
Slumber Did My Spirit Seal, A	A slumber did my spirit seal	378
Small Celandine, The	There is a flower, the lesser	403
Solitary Reaper, The	Behold her, single in the field	398
Surprised by Joy	Surprised by joy—impatient	420
Three Cottage Girls, The	How blest the Maid	421
Three Years She Grew in Sun and Shower	Three years she grew	376
To a Highland Girl	Sweet Highland Girl	396
To a Skylark	Up with me! up with me	405
To a Skylark	Ethereal minstrel! pilgrim	423
To a Young Lady	Dear child of Nature	406
To H. C.	O thou! whose fancies from afar	390
To the Cuckoo	O blithe New-Comer! I have heard	400
To the Daisy	In youth from rock to rock	391
To the Same Flower (The Daisy)	With little here to do or see	393
To the Same Flower (The Small Celandine)	Pleasures newly found are sweet	381
To the Small Celandine	Pansies, lilies, kingcups	379
To Toussaint L'Ouverture	Toussaint, the most unhappy man	387
When I Have Borne in Memory	When I have borne in memory	390

Title	Opening Phrase	PAGE
WORDSWORTH, WILLIAM (*continued*):		
World Is Too Much with Us, The	The world is too much with us	413
Written in London	O Friend! I know not	388
Yarrow Revisited	The gallant Youth	424
Yarrow Unvisited	From Stirling castle we had seen	399
Yes, It Was the Mountain Echo	Yes, it was the mountain Echo	412
WOTTON, SIR HENRY (*England*), 1568–1639		120
Character of a Happy Life, The	How happy is he born and taught	121
Elizabeth of Bohemia	You meaner beauties of the night	120
WYATT, SIR THOMAS (*England*), 1503–1542		24
Blame Not My Lute	Blame not my Lute	24
Forget Not Yet	Forget not yet the tried intent	25
My Lute, Awake	My lute, awake, perform the last	26
WYLIE, ELINOR (*United States*)		1364
Eagle and the Mole, The	Avoid the reeking herd	1364
Let No Charitable Hope	Now let no charitable hope	1365
WYNDHAM, SIR CHARLES [Earl of Egremont] (*England*), 1710–1763		282
Fair Thief, The	Before the urchin well could go	282
YEATS, WILLIAM BUTLER (*Ireland*), 1865–		1179
Lake Isle of Innisfree, The	I will arise and go now	1179
Land of Heart's Desire, The	The wind blows out of the gates	1179
Lover Tells of the Rose in His Heart, The	All things uncomely and broken	1180
YOUNG, EDWARD (*England*), 1683–1765		258
Authors and Critics	With fame in just proportion	259
Night Thoughts	Tired Nature's sweet restorer	258
	All promise is poor dilatory man	258
UNKNOWN		1370
Chloris in the Snow	I saw fair Chloris walk alone	1395
Cuckoo Song	Sumer is icumen in	1370
Cupid and the Nymph	It chanced of late a shepherd's	1379
Devotion	Fain would I change that note	1381
Forsaken Bride, The	O waly waly up the bank	1391
Great Adventurer, The	Over the mountains	1384
Helen of Kirconnell	I wish I were where Helen lies	1389
Hue and Cry After Chloris	Tell me, ye wand'ring Spirits	1386
I Saw My Lady Weep	I saw my lady weep	1377
King's Progress, The	Yet if his majesty	1385
Love and May	Now is the gentle season	1378

INDEX BY AUTHORS

Title	Opening Phrase	PAGE
UNKNOWN (*continued*):		
Love in Thy Youth	Love in thy youth, fair maid	1383
Love Me Not for Comely Grace	Love me not for comely grace	1391
Lullaby	Weep you no more	1378
Madrigal	Lady, when I behold the roses	1377
Non Nobis	Not unto us, O Lord	1397
Nut-Brown Maid, The	It standeth so, a deed is do'	1370
On a Shepherd Losing His Mistress	Stay, Shepherd, prithee	1390
Phillada Flouts Me	O what a plague is love!	1392
Praise of His Lady, A	Give place, you ladies	1397
Sister, Awake!	Sister, awake! close not your eyes!	1380
Summer	Cold winter ice is fled and gone	1381
There Is a Lady	There is a lady sweet and kind	1382
Thomas the Rhymer	True Thomas lay on Huntlie bank	1386
Two in One	To ask for all thy love	1382
Willie Drowned in Yarrow	Down in yon garden sweet	1395

INDEX BY TITLES

A

		PAGE
Abou Ben Adhem	*Leigh Hunt*	496
Absalom and Achitophel	*John Dryden*	240
Absence	*John Donne*	134
Abt Vogler	*Robert Browning*	858
Acis and Galatea	*John Gay*	259
Acknowledgments	*Sidney Lanier*	1045
Address to the Unco Guid	*Robert Burns*	348
Admiral Death	*Sir Henry Newbolt*	1172
Adonais	*Percy Bysshe Shelley*	519, 525
Ae Fond Kiss	*Robert Burns*	351
After	*William Ernest Henley*	1085
Aftermath	*Siegfried Sassoon*	1313
After-Thought	*William Wordsworth*	423
Ah, Sunflower	*William Blake*	335
Aim Was Song, The	*Robert Frost*	1259
Alastor	*Percy Bysshe Shelley*	519
All That's Past	*Walter de la Mare*	1239
Almswomen	*Edmund Blunden*	1340
Alone	*Edgar Allan Poe*	744
America	*Sydney Dobell*	964
Amoretti	*Edmund Spenser*	28
Angel in the House, The	*Coventry Patmore*	956
Anguish	*Henry Vaughan*	234
Annabel Lee	*Edgar Allan Poe*	757
Annie Laurie	*William Douglas*	255
Another	*William Cowper*	320
Antiquary, The	*Sir Walter Scott*	440
Apollo's Song	*John Lyly*	48
Apparition	*William Ernest Henley*	1087
Arabia	*Walter de la Mare*	1240
Arcades	*John Milton*	201
Arcadia	*Sir Philip Sidney*	46, 47
Arrow and the Song, The	*Henry Wadsworth Longfellow*	704
Arsenal at Springfield, The	*Henry Wadsworth Longfellow*	701
Art	*James Thomson*	1005
As I Came Down from Lebanon	*Clinton Scollard*	1165
As Slow Our Ship	*Thomas Moore*	494
As You Like It	*William Shakespeare*	71
Astrophel and Stella	*Sir Philip Sidney*	41, 42, 44, 46
At the Church Gate	*William Makepeace Thackeray*	838
Atalanta in Calydon	*Algernon Charles Swinburne*	1009
Atonement	*Aline Kilmer*	1331
Auguries of Innocence	*William Blake*	336
Auld Lang Syne	*Robert Burns*	353
Austerity of Poetry	*Matthew Arnold*	7
Authors and Critics	*Edward Young*	259
Autumn	*Emily Dickinson*	1000
Autumn Chant	*Edna St. Vincent Millay*	1335
Ave Atque Vale	*Algernon Charles Swinburne*	1019

B

Bacchus	*Ralph Waldo Emerson*	666
Bag-Pipes at Sea	*Clinton Scollard*	1164

1509

INDEX BY TITLES

		PAGE
Balade	Geoffrey Chaucer	14
Ballad of a Nun, A	John Davidson	1141
Ballad of Reading Gaol, The	Oscar Wilde	1121
Ballad of Trees and the Master, A	Sidney Lanier	1046
Ballad Upon a Wedding, A	Sir John Suckling	206
Ballade of the Dreamland Rose	Brian Hooker	1269
Banks o' Doon, The	Robert Burns	352
Battle Hymn of the Republic	Julia Ward Howe	886
Battle of Lake Regillus	Lord Macaulay	643
Beaumont and Fletcher	Algernon Charles Swinburne	137
Beauty	Joel Elias Spingarn	1261
Bed-Time	Ralph M. Jones	1266
Beethoven and Angelo	John Bannister Tabb	1062
Before	William Ernest Henley	1084
Believe Me, If All Those Endearing Young Charms	Thomas Moore	492
Bells, The	Edgar Allan Poe	754
Beloved, My Glory	Michael Field	1095
Ben Jonson	Algernon Charles Swinburne	124
Bermudas	Andrew Marvell	221
Better Part, The	Matthew Arnold	911
Beyond	Lionel Johnson	1195
Beyond the Veil	Henry Vaughan	232
Birks of Aberfeldy, The	Robert Burns	339
Black Vulture, The	George Sterling	1213
Black-Eyed Susan	John Gay	260
Blame Not My Lute	Sir Thomas Wyatt	24
Blessed Damozel, The	Dante Gabriel Rossetti	965
Blind	Harry Kemp	1294
Blot in the 'Scutcheon, A	Robert Browning	849
Boadicea. An Ode	William Cowper	318
Bohemian Hymn, The	Ralph Waldo Emerson	683
Boy's Song, A	James Hogg	367
Brahma	Ralph Waldo Emerson	678
Break, Break, Break	Alfred, Lord Tennyson	800
Broadway	Hermann Hagedorn	1291
Brook, The	Alfred, Lord Tennyson	828
Bruce's Address at Bannockburn	Robert Burns	355
Building of the Ship, The	Henry Wadsworth Longfellow	706
Burial of Sir John Moore After Corunna, The	Charles Wolfe	517
Buried Life, The	Matthew Arnold	922
Bush Aboon Traquair, The	Robert Crawford	278
By Avon Stream	Arthur Henry Bullen	1141
By the North Sea	Algernon Charles Swinburne	1027
By the Statue of King Charles at Charing Cross	Lionel Johnson	1196

C

Ca' the Yowes to the Knowes	Robert Burns	357
Caliban in the Coal Mines	Louis Untermeyer	1304
Canterbury Tales, Prologue to the	Geoffrey Chaucer	15
Canticle of the Sun, The	Matthew Arnold	953
Captivity	Geoffrey Chaucer	14
Captivity, The	Oliver Goldsmith	315
Carrowmore	George William Russell	1201
Caterpillars	John Freeman	1305
Cato	Joseph Addison	255
Celebration of Charis, A	Ben Jonson	127
Celestial Surgeon, The	Robert Louis Stevenson	1092
Chambered Nautilus, The	Oliver Wendell Holmes	835
Chant of the Fought Field, A	Edith M. Thomas	1118
Character of a Happy Life, The	Sir Henry Wotton	121

		PAGE
Character of the Happy Warrior	William Wordsworth	410
Charity	William Cowper	317
Charles XII	Samuel Johnson	281
Charm, The	Thomas Campion	116
Chartless	Emily Dickinson	1000
Cherry-Ripe	Thomas Campion	116
Cherry-Ripe	Robert Herrick	163
"Chief, The"	William Ernest Henley	1086
Child and Maiden	Sir Charles Sedley	251
Child of a Day	Walter Savage Landor	482
Child-Songs	John Greenleaf Whittier	738
Childe Harold's Pilgrimage	Lord Byron	502
Chloris in the Snow	Unknown	1395
Choice	Emily Dickinson	1001
Choice, The	Dante Gabriel Rossetti	979
Christabel	Samuel Taylor Coleridge	468
Christopher Marlowe	Algernon Charles Swinburne	1026
Cities and Thrones and Powers	Rudyard Kipling	1181
City in the Sea, The	Edgar Allan Poe	763
Claud Halcro's Song	Sir Walter Scott	442
Clod and the Pebble, The	William Blake	334
Cloud, The	Percy Bysshe Shelley	565
Collar, The	George Herbert	175
Come Back, Come Back	Arthur Hugh Clough	877
Come, Let Us Make Love Deathless	Herbert Trench	1181
Comfort	Robert Herrick	155
Commemoration Ode	James Russell Lowell	883
Comparison, A	William Cowper	320
Compliment, The	Thomas Carew	176
Composed Upon Westminster Bridge	William Wordsworth	386
Comrades, The	William Canton	1063
Comus	John Milton	186
Conclusion, The	Sir Walter Raleigh	39
Concord Hymn	Ralph Waldo Emerson	677
Conqueror Worm, The	Edgar Allan Poe	760
Consecration, A	John Masefield	1251
Constancy	Joshua Sylvester	57
Constancy	John Wilmot	252
Constant Lover, The	Sir John Suckling	210
Contemplation Upon Flowers, A	Henry King	168
Corinna's Going A-Maying	Robert Herrick	156
Correlated Greatness	Francis Thompson	1162
Cotter's Saturday Night, The	Robert Burns	340
Courage of the Lost	Edith M. Thomas	1117
Crabbèd Age and Youth	William Shakespeare	113
Creeds	Karle Wilson Baker	1264
Cromwell in Death	Andrew Marvell	228
Crossing the Bar	Alfred, Lord Tennyson	833
Crowned	Amy Lowell	1251
Cuckoo Song	Unknown	1370
Cupid and My Campaspe Played	John Lyly	48
Cupid and the Nymph	Unknown	1379
Curse of Kehama, The	Robert Southey	476
Cymbeline	William Shakespeare	98
Cynthia's Revels	Ben Jonson	130, 131
Cyrano's Presentation of Cadets	Brian Hooker	1270

D

| Dagonet's Canzonet | Ernest Rhys | 1152 |
| Daisy | Francis Thompson | 1153 |

INDEX BY TITLES

		PAGE
Daphne	Bliss Carman	1168
Dark Cavalier, The	Margaret Widdemer	1363
Dark Glass, The	Dante Gabriel Rossetti	975
Dark Rosaleen	James Clarence Mangan	646
Darkling Thrush, The	Thomas Hardy	1037
Day Before April, The	Mary Carolyn Davies	1354
Day Is Done, The	Henry Wadsworth Longfellow	703
Day Returns, The	Robert Burns	349
Daybreak	William Blake	336
Days	Karle Wilson Baker	1264
Days	Ralph Waldo Emerson	678
Dead, The	Rupert Brooke	1323
Dead, The	Rupert Brooke	1324
Dead Make Rules, The	Mary Carolyn Davies	1353
Death	Walter Savage Landor	478
Death of Anaxagoras, The	William Canton	1069
Death-in-Love	Dante Gabriel Rossetti	976
Debt	Jessie B. Rittenhouse	1362
Dedication. To Leigh Hunt, Esq.	John Keats	600
Delight in Disorder	Robert Herrick	158
Departure	Coventry Patmore	961
Deserted House, The	Alfred, Lord Tennyson	781
Deserted Village, The	Oliver Goldsmith	305
Destiny	Matthew Arnold	953
Destiny	Ralph Waldo Emerson	656
Devotion	Unknown	1381
Dickens in Camp	Bret Harte	1031
Dirge	Ralph Waldo Emerson	669
Dirge	Leigh Hunt	496
Dirge, A	Henry King	167
Dirge, A	Percy Bysshe Shelley	591
Dirge, A	Sir Philip Sidney	44
Dirge for the Year	Percy Bysshe Shelley	576
Dirge in Cymbeline	William Collins	300
Discipline	George Herbert	173
Disdain Returned	Thomas Carew	177
Divina Commedia	Henry Wadsworth Longfellow	708
Divine Awe	George Edward Woodberry	1119
Divine Image, The	William Blake	333
Do You Fear the Wind?	Hamlin Garland	1163
Don Juan	Lord Byron	511
Don Quixote	Arthur Davison Ficke	1291
Donkey, The	Gilbert Keith Chesterton	1248
Door-Mats	Mary Carolyn Davies	1355
Doors	Hermann Hagedorn	1290
Doors of the Temple	Aldous Huxley	1339
Dora	Thomas Edward Brown	1002
Doubt You to Whom My Muse	Sir Philip Sidney	43
Dover Beach	Matthew Arnold	918
Dream, The	John Donne	132
Dream-Bearer, The	Mary Carolyn Davies	1354
Dream-Land	Edgar Allan Poe	765
Dream Land	Christina Georgina Rossetti	999
Dream of Defeated Beauty, A	George William Russell	1200
Dream of Fair Women, A	Alfred, Lord Tennyson	13
Dream Within a Dream, A	Edgar Allan Poe	764
Dream-Tryst	Francis Thompson	1160
Dreamer, The	Nicholas Vachel Lindsay	1267
Dreams	John Dryden	250
Drinking	Abraham Cowley	216
Duet	Leonora Speyer	1356
Duncton Hill	Hilaire Belloc	1228

1512

		PAGE
Duty	Ralph Waldo Emerson	684
Dying Adrian to His Soul, The	Matthew Prior	254

E

Each and All	Ralph Waldo Emerson	652
Each in His Own Tongue	William Herbert Carruth	1162
Eagle, The	Alfred, Lord Tennyson	800
Eagle and the Mole, The	Elinor Wylie	1364
Eagle Sonnets	Clement Wood	1331
Early Spring	William Henry Davies	1225
Early Spring	Alfred, Lord Tennyson	832
Earth	John Hall Wheelock	1316
Earth and Man, The	Stopford Augustus Brooke	1004
Earth Lover	Harold Vinal	1335
East London	Matthew Arnold	911
Echoes	William Ernest Henley	1088
Eldorado	Edgar Allan Poe	766
Elegy	Robert Bridges	1055
Elegy	Robert Bridges	1059
Elegy	Alexander Pope	264
Elegy, An	Henry King	168
Elegy on Mr. Wm. Shakespeare	William Basse	141
Elegy on the Countess·Dowager of Pembroke	William Browne	165
Elegy ˙Written in a Country Churchyard	Thomas Gray	288
Elizabeth	George Brandon Saul	1343
Elizabeth of Bohemia	Sir Henry Wotton	120
Emblems of Love	Lascelles Abercrombie	1278
Empedocles on Etna	Matthew Arnold	950
Endymion	John Keats	601
England's Dead	Felicia Dorothea Hemans	593
English Verse	Edmund Waller	180
Envoy	Richard Hovey	1175
Envoy	Robert Louis Stevenson	1094
Envoy	Francis Thompson	1400
Epilogue	Lascelles Abercrombie	1274
Epilogue	Robert Browning	868
Epilogue	Alfred Noyes	1272
Epilogue to Lessing's "Laocoön"	Matthew Arnold	1
Epilogue to the Satires	Alexander Pope	277
Epistle to Dr. Blacklock	Robert Burns	359
Epistle to Pope	Edward Young	259
Epitaph, An	Walter de la Mare	1242
Epitaph, An	Andrew Marvell	224
Epitaph on a Robin Redbreast, An	Samuel Rogers	361
Epitaph on Argalus and Parthenia	Sir Philip Sidney	46
Epitaph on Charles II	John Wilmot	252
Epitaph on Elizabeth L. H.	Ben Jonson	126
Epitaph on the Countess of Pembroke	William Browne	164
Eros	Ralph Waldo Emerson	683
Essay on Criticism	Alexander Pope	262
Essay on Man, An	Alexander Pope	266
Euclid Alone Has Looked	Edna St. Vincent Millay	1336
Eurydice	Francis William Bourdillon	1102
Euthanasia	Richard Crashaw	214
Evangeline	Henry Wadsworth Longfellow	705
Eve	Ralph Hodgson	1233
Eve of St. Agnes, The	John Keats	606
Evening	S. Weir Mitchell	994

INDEX BY TITLES

		PAGE
Evening Song	Sidney Lanier	1041
Evoe !	Edith M. Thomas	1114
Ex Libris	Arthur Upson	1264
Example, The	William Henry Davies	1227
Exequy on His Wife	Henry King	169

F

Fair Ines	Thomas Hood	630
Fair Maid of the Exchange, The	Thomas Heywood	123
Fair Rosalynd	Thomas Lodge	49
Fair Singer, The	Andrew Marvell	228
Fair Thief, The	Sir Charles Wyndham	282
Falconer of God, The	William Rose Benét	1308
Fallen Cities	Gerald Louis Gould	1306
Falling Leaf, The	James Montgomery	445
Fancy in Nubibus	Samuel Taylor Coleridge	475
Far in a Western Brookland	Alfred Edward Housman	1151
Farewell, A	Alfred, Lord Tennyson	799
Farmer's Bride, The	Charlotte Mew	1365
Father Damien	John Bannister Tabb	1062
Faun in Wall Street, A	John Myers O'Hara	1369
Faustus	Christopher Marlowe	59
Fear of Death, The	Edmund Gosse	1090
Feast	Edna St. Vincent Millay	1336
Feuerzauber	Louis Untermeyer	1303
Fields at Evening	David Morton	1306
Fire and Ice	Robert Frost	1257
Flammonde	Edwin Arlington Robinson	1213
Flight of Youth, The	Richard Henry Stoddard	965
Flos Ævorum	Richard Le Gallienne	1192
Flower in the Crannied Wall	Alfred, Lord Tennyson	801
Flower of Old Japan, The	Alfred Noyes	1273
Flower's Name, The	Robert Browning	842
Follow Thy Fair Sun	Thomas Campion	114
Follow Your Saint	Thomas Campion	117
Fool's Prayer, The	Edward Rowland Sill	1039
Footsloggers	Ford Madox Ford	1236
For a Charity Annual	Austin Dobson	1033
For a Copy of Theocritus	Austin Dobson	1034
For Annie	Edgar Allan Poe	769
For Anniversary Marriage-Days	George Wither	145
Foreknown	Sara Teasdale	1294
Forerunners	Ralph Waldo Emerson	663
Forest Song, A	Alfred Noyes	1271
Forget Not Yet	Sir Thomas Wyatt	25
Forsaken Bride, The	Unknown	1391
Forsaken Garden, A	Algernon Charles Swinburne	1017
Fragment : To Music, A	Percy Bysshe Shelley	546
Fragment : Wedded Souls	Percy Bysshe Shelley	564
Fragment of an Ode to Maia	John Keats	626
Fragment of Chorus of a "De-janeira"	Matthew Arnold	914
Fragment on Keats	Percy Bysshe Shelley	600
France	Percy MacKaye	1263
Fraternity	John Bannister Tabb	1062
Freedom	John Barbour	13
Freedom	James Russell Lowell	879
Friend, A	Lionel Johnson	1193
Friendship	Ralph Waldo Emerson	681
Fruit of the Flower	Countee Cullen	1351
Furrow and the Hearth, The	Padraic Colum	1282
Future, The	Matthew Arnold	924

1514

G

		PAGE
Garden, A	Andrew Marvell	227
Garden, The	Andrew Marvell	225
Garden of Proserpine, The	Algernon Charles Swinburne	1014
Garden-Song	James Branch Cabell	1266
Gareth and Lynette	Alfred, Lord Tennyson	802
Ghost, The	Walter de la Mare	1243
Giaour, The	Lord Byron	508
Gift of God, The	Edwin Arlington Robinson	1216
Give All to Love	Ralph Waldo Emerson	664
Give Place, Ye Lovers	Earl of Surrey	20
Glories	Lionel Johnson	1195
Glories of Our Blood and State, The	James Shirley	178
Glorious Stars of Heaven, The	Joshua Sylvester	57
God and the Schoolboy, The	William Canton	1073
God Lyæus	John Fletcher	139
God, the Architect	Harry Kemp	1293
Gold	Michael Field	1094
Good-bye	Ralph Waldo Emerson	658
Good Morrow, The	John Donne	133
Gown, The	Mary Carolyn Davies	1354
Grammarian's Funeral, A	Robert Browning	853
Grasshopper and the Cricket, The	Leigh Hunt	497
Graves of a Household, The	Felicia Dorothea Hemans	592
Great Adventurer, The	Unknown	1384
Great Men Have Been Among Us	William Wordsworth	389
Great Time, A	William Henry Davies	1226
Greek Folk Song	Margaret Widdemer	1363
Green Linnet, The	William Wordsworth	395
Greeting, A	Austin Dobson	1036
Grey Monk, The	William Blake	338
Guy Mannering	Sir Walter Scott	440

H

Hallowed Ground	Thomas Campbell	487
Hamlet	William Shakespeare	88
Happiest Heart, The	John Vance Cheney	1084
Happy Wind	William Henry Davies	1226
Harp That Once Through Tara's Halls, The	Thomas Moore	491
Harrow Grave in Flanders, A	Lord Crewe	1146
Hast Thou Seen the Down in the Air	Sir John Suckling	209
Hate	James Stephens	1285
Haunted	Aline Kilmer	1328
Haunted Palace, The	Edgar Allan Poe	759
He Whom a Dream Hath Possessed	Shaemas O'Sheel	1310
Health, A	Edward Coate Pinkney	645
Heart of Midlothian, The	Sir Walter Scott	442
Heart's Hope	Dante Gabriel Rossetti	974
Heaven Overarches Earth and Sea	Christina Georgina Rossetti	994
Heine's Grave	Matthew Arnold	942
Hélas	Oscar Wilde	1139
Helen of Kirconnel	Unknown	1389
Hellas	Percy Bysshe Shelley	539
Henry Wadsworth Longfellow	Austin Dobson	694
Her Coming	George Chapman	53
Her Gifts	Dante Gabriel Rossetti	975
Her Heaven	Dante Gabriel Rossetti	978
Her Love	Dante Gabriel Rossetti	978
Her Reverie	Francis Carlin	1278

INDEX BY TITLES

PAGE

Heraclitus — William (Johnson) Cory — 954
Hero and Leander — Christopher Marlowe — 61
Herodias — Arthur O'Shaughnessy — 1050
Herself — Dante Gabriel Rossetti — 977
Hervé Riel — Robert Browning — 862
Hester — Charles Lamb — 486
High Tide at Gettysburg, The — Will Henry Thompson — 1079
High Tide on the Coast of Lincolnshire, The — Jean Ingelow — 906
Higher Pantheism, The — Alfred, Lord Tennyson — 801
Highland Mary — Robert Burns — 356
Hill-Country — Aline Kilmer — 1329
His Pilgrimage — Sir Walter Raleigh — 35
His Theme — Robert Herrick — ix
Hohenlinden — Thomas Campbell — 490
Holy Sonnets — John Donne — 133
Home-Thoughts, from Abroad — Robert Browning — 847
Homeward Bound — W. E. H. Lecky — 1030
Honest Man's Fortune, The — John Fletcher — 138
Honour and Desert — Coventry Patmore — 956
Horatius at the Bridge — Lord Macaulay — 636
Hound of Heaven, The — Francis Thompson — 1155
House of Life, The — Dante Gabriel Rossetti — 972
How Much of Godhood — Louis Untermeyer — 1304
How Sleep the Brave — William Collins — 295
How to Go and Forget — Edwin Markham — 1105
Hue and Cry After Chloris — Unknown — 1386
Huguenot, A — Mary Elizabeth Coleridge — 1171
Humble-Bee, The — Ralph Waldo Emerson — 659
Hummingbird, The — Harry Kemp — 1293
Hymn, A — Gilbert Keith Chesterton — 1247
Hymn of Apollo — Percy Bysshe Shelley — 570
Hymn of Pan — Percy Bysshe Shelley — 571
Hymn to Apollo — John Lyly — 47
Hymn to Intellectual Beauty — Percy Bysshe Shelley — 543
Hymn to Light — Abraham Cowley — 220
Hymn to the Night — Henry Wadsworth Longfellow — 695

I

I Am the Way — Alice Meynell — 1099
I Do Not Love to See Your Beauty Fire — John Hall Wheelock — 1318
I Have a Rendezvous with Death — Alan Seeger — 1325
I Have Loved Flowers That Fade — Robert Bridges — 1056
I Heard a Soldier — Herbert Trench — 1180
I Know That All the Moon Decays — William Drummond — 142
I Love All Beauteous Things — Robert Bridges — 1058
I Prithee Send Me Back My Heart — Sir John Suckling — 209
I Remember, I Remember — Thomas Hood — 634
I Saw My Lady Weep — Unknown — 1377
I See His Blood Upon the Rose — Joseph Mary Plunkett — 1322
I Shall Be Loved as Quiet Things — Karle Wilson Baker — 1265
I Travelled Among Unknown Men — William Wordsworth — 376
I Wandered Lonely As a Cloud — William Wordsworth — 402
Ianthe — Walter Savage Landor — 481
Ichabod — John Greenleaf Whittier — 739
Idea — Michael Drayton — 56
Ideas of Good and Evil — William Blake — 335
Idol-Maker Prays, The — Arthur Guiterman — 1232
Idylls of the King — Alfred, Lord Tennyson — 802, 803
Il Penseroso — John Milton — 193
Immortality — Matthew Arnold — 912
Immortality in Song — Michael Drayton — 55

PAGE

Impatient Lover, The   Sir Philip Sidney   46
Impression   Clark Ashton Smith   1338
In a Chair   John Collins Squire   1298
In After Days   Austin Dobson   1034
In Defense of the Royal Society   Abraham Cowley   219
In Early Spring   Alice Meynell   1096
In Fisherrow   William Ernest Henley   1087
In Flanders Fields   Colonel John McCrae   1235
In Hospital   William Ernest Henley   1084
In Laleham Churchyard   William Watson   1148
In Love, If Love Be Love   Alfred, Lord Tennyson   802
In Memoriam   Gordon Bottomley   1256
In Memoriam A. M. W.   Alfred, Lord Tennyson   808
In Memory of Swinburne   Alfred Noyes   1008
In Memory of Walter Savage Landor   Algernon Charles Swinburne   477
In Obitum. M. S.   William Browne   165
In Phæacia   James Elroy Flecker   1296
In Tempore Senectutis   Ernest Dowson   1198
In the Highlands   Robert Louis Stevenson   1093
In the Old House   Arthur O'Shaughnessy   1053
In the Shadow   William Canton   1078
In the Temple   Richard Crashaw   212
In the Train   Clifford Bax   1352
In the Valley of Cauteretz   Alfred, Lord Tennyson   831
Incident in a Railroad Car, An   James Russell Lowell   879
Indian Serenade, The   Percy Bysshe Shelley   563
Indian Summer   William Ellery Leonard   9
Inspiration   Sir Philip Sidney   42
Inspiration   Henry David Thoreau   869
Insulting Letter, The   William Ellery Leonard   1263
Invention   William Watson   1148
Invictus   William Ernest Henley   1088
Invisible Bride, The   Edwin Markham   1103
Invocation   John Drinkwater   1288
Invocation   Wendell Phillips Stafford   1170
Invocation to Misery   Percy Bysshe Shelley   556
Is There for Honest Poverty   Robert Burns   357
Isolation   Matthew Arnold   912
Israfel   Edgar Allan Poe   767
It Is a Beauteous Evening   William Wordsworth   387
It Is Not to Be Thought Of   William Wordsworth   389
It Was the Time of Roses   Thomas Hood   635
Italian Song   Samuel Rogers   360
Italy—A Farewell   Samuel Rogers   366
Itylus   Algernon Charles Swinburne   1012
Ivanhoe   Sir Walter Scott   445
Ivy Green, The   Charles Dickens   839

J

Jack and Joan   Thomas Campion   119
Jacobite's Epitaph, A   Lord Macaulay   643
Jean   Robert Burns   350
Jock of Hazeldean   Sir Walter Scott   439
John Anderson, My Jo   Robert Burns   350
Journey, The   Scudder Middleton   1327
Joy   Robinson Jeffers   1323
Joy, Shipmate, Joy!   Walt Whitman   902
Joyous-Gard   Thomas S. Jones, Jr.   1289
Julius Cæsar   William Shakespeare   83
June   James Russell Lowell   880

INDEX BY TITLES

K

		PAGE
Kathleen Mavourneen	*Louisa Macartney Crawford*	651
Keeping a Heart	*Arthur O'Shaughnessy*	1050
Keith of Ravelston	*Sydney Dobell*	963
Kéramos	*Henry Wadsworth Longfellow*	709
Kind Are Her Answers	*Thomas Campion*	118
King Henry IV	*William Shakespeare*	78
King Henry V	*William Shakespeare*	79
King Henry VIII	*William Shakespeare*	81
King John	*William Shakespeare*	76
King Lear	*William Shakespeare*	94
King Richard II	*William Shakespeare*	76
King Richard III	*William Shakespeare*	80
Kingfisher, The	*William Henry Davies*	1223
King's Progress, The	*Unknown*	1385
Kubla Khan	*Samuel Taylor Coleridge*	471

L

La Belle Dame Sans Merci	*John Keats*	628
Ladder, The	*Leonora Speyer*	1357
Lady of Shalott, The	*Alfred, Lord Tennyson*	782
Lady of the Lake, The	*Sir Walter Scott*	433
Lady Poverty, The	*Alice Meynell*	1100
Lady-Probationer	*William Ernest Henley*	1086
Lake, The	*John Collins Squire*	1300
Lake Isle of Innisfree, The	*William Butler Yeats*	1179
L'Allegro	*John Milton*	197
Lament, A	*Percy Bysshe Shelley*	580
Lamp, The	*Sara Teasdale*	1295
Lamp's Shrine, The	*Dante Gabriel Rossetti*	976
Land of Heart's Desire, The	*William Butler Yeats*	1179
Last Confessional	*John Drinkwater*	1288
Last Days, The	*George Sterling*	1211
Last Fire, The	*Herbert S. Gorman*	1337
Last Lines	*Emily Brontë*	872
Last Memory, The	*Arthur Symons*	1177
Last Ride Together, The	*Robert Browning*	850
Last Rose of Summer, The	*Thomas Moore*	492
Last Word, The	*Matthew Arnold*	919
Late Wisdom	*George Crabbe*	329
Laus Infantium	*William Canton*	1075
Laus Mortis	*Frederic Lawrence Knowles*	1221
Lay of the Last Minstrel, The	*Sir Walter Scott*	428
Lead, Kindly Light	*Cardinal Newman*	644
Leavetaking	*William Watson*	1147
Legend of Good Women, The	*Geoffrey Chaucer*	15
Leisure	*William Henry Davies*	1223
Lenore	*Edgar Allan Poe*	749
Lessons of Nature, The	*William Drummond*	144
Let Me Live Out My Years	*John G. Neihardt*	1273
Let No Charitable Hope	*Elinor Wylie*	1365
Letter to Ben Jonson	*Francis Beaumont*	140
Lie, The	*Sir Walter Raleigh*	36
Life	*Anna Letitia Aikin*	325
Life	*Abraham Cowley*	221
Life a Cheat	*John Dryden*	236
Lilies Without, Lilies Within	*George Wither*	145
Lilith	*Dante Gabriel Rossetti*	984
Lincoln, the Man of the People	*Edwin Markham*	1108
L'Inconnue	*Oliver Wendell Holmes*	836
Lines. Composed a Few Miles Above Tintern Abbey	*William Wordsworth*	372

1518

INDEX BY TITLES

		PAGE
Lines on the Mermaid Tavern	John Keats	622
Lines Written Among the Euganean Hills	Percy Bysshe Shelley	546
Lines Written in Early Spring	William Wordsworth	370
Linnet, The	Walter de la Mare	1242
Lion-House, The	John Hall Wheelock	1319
Listeners, The	Walter de la Mare	1241
Litany, The	Robert Herrick	151
Locksley Hall	Alfred, Lord Tennyson	797
London	William Blake	337
London	Samuel Johnson	280
London, 1802	William Wordsworth	388
Lonely Dancer, The	Richard Le Gallienne	1188
Look in Thy Heart and Write	Sir Philip Sidney	7
Lord of My Heart's Elation	Bliss Carman	1166
Lord of the Isles, The	Sir Walter Scott	438
Loss	H. D.	1314
Lost Days	Dante Gabriel Rossetti	980
Lost in France	Ernest Rhys	1152
Lost Leader, The	Robert Browning	841
Lost Nymph, The	George Sterling	1208
Love	Samuel Taylor Coleridge	468
Love and May	Unknown	1378
Love Enthroned	Dante Gabriel Rossetti	973
Love Freed from Ignorance and Folly	Ben Jonson	131
Love in Dreams	John Addington Symonds	1039
Love in the Valley	George Meredith	988
Love in the Winds	Richard Hovey	1176
Love in Thy Youth	Unknown	1383
Love is Enough	William Morris	1007
Love Me Not for Comely Grace	Unknown	1391
Love New and Old	Charles Mackay	869
Love Still Has Something of the Sea	Sir Charles Sedley	250
Love Triumphant	Frederic Lawrence Knowles	1220
Loveliest of Trees	Alfred Edward Housman	1151
Lover Tells of the Rose in His Heart, The	William Butler Yeats	1180
Lover to His Lady, The	George Turberville	21
Lover to Lover	David Morton	1307
Lover's Walk, The	Dante Gabriel Rossetti	974
Love's Labour's Lost	William Shakespeare	66
Love's Philosophy	Percy Bysshe Shelley	564
Love's Prisoner	William Blake	331
Love's Secret	William Blake	337
Lovesight	Dante Gabriel Rossetti	973
Lucifer in Starlight	George Meredith	988
Lullaby	Unknown	1378
Lycidas	John Milton	188

M

Macbeth	William Shakespeare	86
Mad Blake	William Rose Benét	330
Madrigal	William Drummond	141
Madrigal	Unknown	1377
Magna Est Veritas	Coventry Patmore	962
Maidenhood	Henry Wadsworth Longfellow	695
Mally's Meek, Mally's Sweet	Robert Burns	354
Man His Own Star	John Fletcher	138
Man of Life Upright, The	Thomas Campion	117
Man with the Hoe, The	Edwin Markham	1106

INDEX BY TITLES

		PAGE
Man with the Hoe, The (A Reply)	John Vance Cheney	1082
Mankind	John Dryden	250
March, The	John Collins Squire	1299
Margaritæ Sorori	William Ernest Henley	1089
Marian	George Meredith	986
Marlowe	Michael Drayton	58
Marmion	Sir Walter Scott	431
Married Lover, The	Coventry Patmore	959
Marshes of Glynn, The	Sidney Lanier	1042
Martin	Joyce Kilmer	1312
Marygold, The	George Wither	147
Master, The	Edwin Arlington Robinson	1217
Master-Mariner, The	George Sterling	1209
Masters, The	Margaret Widdemer	1362
Maternity	Alice Meynell	1099
Maud	Alfred, Lord Tennyson	823
Meadows in Spring, The	Edward FitzGerald	778
Measure for Measure	William Shakespeare	64
Measure of Beauty, The	Thomas Campion	ix, 118
Meditation for His Mistress, A	Robert Herrick	153
Meeting, The	John Greenleaf Whittier	737
Meeting at Night	Robert Browning	843
Memorabilia	Robert Browning	848
Memorial Verses	Matthew Arnold	940
Memory	Arthur Symons	1178
Memory, Hither Come	William Blake	332
Mending Wall	Robert Frost	1257
Merchant of Venice, The	William Shakespeare	69
Merchant, to Secure His Treasure, The	Matthew Prior	254
Merciles Beaute	Geoffrey Chaucer	14
Merlin	Ralph Waldo Emerson	685
Messages	Francis Thompson	1161
Midsummer-Night's Dream, A	William Shakespeare	67
Milton	William Blake	336
Mimnermus in Church	William (Johnson) Cory	955
Miracle, The	Walter de la Mare	1238
Mirage	Christina Georgina Rossetti	997
Mirage	George Sterling	1207
Misconceptions	Robert Browning	848
Mockery	Louis Untermeyer	1302
Modern Beauty	Arthur Symons	1176
Monterey	Charles Fenno Hoffman	693
Month of Mary, The	Cardinal Newman	645
Moon, The	William Henry Davies	1226
Moonlight	William Canton	1077
Moral Essays	Alexander Pope	272
Morality	Matthew Arnold	921
Morning Song	Sir William Davenant	179
Morte D'Arthur	Alfred, Lord Tennyson	795
Mountains Are a Lonely Folk, The	Hamlin Garland	1164
Mower, to Glow-Worms, The	Andrew Marvell	230
Mowing	Robert Frost	1259
Much Ado About Nothing	William Shakespeare	65
Multiplicity	George Rostrevor Hamilton	1361
Muse, The	George Wither	149
Music	Gilbert Keith Chesterton	1248
Music	Walter de la Mare	1244
Music	Percy Bysshe Shelley	582
Music I Heard	Conrad Aiken	1334
Mutability	Percy Bysshe Shelley	542
My Bonie Mary	Robert Burns	349
My Days Among the Dead Are Passed	Robert Southey	475

PAGE

My Delight and Thy Delight — Robert Bridges — 1057
My Garden — Thomas Edward Brown — 1003
My Heart Leaps Up — William Wordsworth — 379
My Light Thou Art — John Wilmot — 253
My Love — James Russell Lowell — 877
My Lute, Awake — Sir Thomas Wyatt — 26
My Mary — William Cowper — 320
My Mind to Me a Kingdom Is — Sir Edward Dyer — 27
My Mirror — Aline Kilmer — 1330
My November Guest — Robert Frost — 1258
My Prayer — Henry David Thoreau — 871
My Star — Robert Browning — 848
My True Love Hath My Heart — Sir Philip Sidney — 46
My Wife — Robert Louis Stevenson — 1092

N

Nameless One, The — James Clarence Mangan — 649
Nature — Henry Wadsworth Longfellow — 708
Nature: The Artist — Frederic Lawrence Knowles — 1221
Nature's Gift — Samuel Rogers — 366
Nay But You — Robert Browning — 843
Never the Time and the Place — Robert Browning — 866
New Poet, A — William Canton — 1076
New World, The — Witter Bynner — 1284
Nice Valour, The — John Fletcher — 139
Night Has a Thousand Eyes, The — Francis William Bourdillon — 1103
Night Moths, The — Edwin Markham — 1105
Night Thoughts — Edward Young — 258
Night Will Never Stay, The — Eleanor Farjeon — 1356
Night-Piece, The — Robert Herrick — 152
Nightingale, The — John Milton — 204
Nightingales — Robert Bridges — 1058
1914 — Rupert Brooke — 1323
No More, My Dear — Sir Philip Sidney — 41
No Pilots We — John Jay Chapman — 1172
Noble Nature, The — Ben Jonson — 130
Noiseless, Patient Spider, A — Walt Whitman — 901
Non Nobis — Unknown — 1397
Non Sum Qualis Eram Bonæ sub Regno Cynaræ — Ernest Dowson — 1199
Not on Sad Stygian Shore — Samuel Butler — 1007
Note from the Pipes, A — Leonora Speyer — 1357
Nothing Is Enough — Laurence Binyon — 1205
Now Winter Nights Enlarge — Thomas Campion — 115
Nuns Fret Not at Their Convent's Narrow Room — William Wordsworth — 413
Nut-Brown Maid, The — Unknown — 1370
Nymph Complaining for the Death of Her Fawn, The — Andrew Marvell — 223
Nymph's Reply, The — Sir Walter Raleigh — 39

O

O Captain, My Captain! — Walt Whitman — 885
O Could I Flow — Sir John Denham — 216
O Fair! O Sweet! — Sir Philip Sidney — 44
O, Fairest of the Rural Maids — William Cullen Bryant — 599
O Happy Thames — Sir Philip Sidney — 42
O Mother State — James Russell Lowell — 882
O Nightingale! Thou Surely Art — William Wordsworth — 420
O Souls in Whom No Heavenly Fire — John Dryden — 236

INDEX BY TITLES

		PAGE
O Were My Love	Robert Burns	359
Obermann Once More	Matthew Arnold	953
Ode	Arthur O'Shaughnessy	1048
Ode, An	Richard Barnefield	137
Ode for Ben Jonson, An	Robert Herrick	161
Ode from the French	Lord Byron	500
Ode: Intimations of Immortality	William Wordsworth	414
Ode on a Grecian Urn	John Keats	619
Ode on Melancholy	John Keats	624
Ode on Solitude	Alexander Pope	261
Ode on the Spring, An	Thomas Gray	286
Ode to a Nightingale	John Keats	617
Ode to a Schoolmaster	Isaac Watts	256
Ode to Duty	William Wordsworth	404
Ode to Evening	William Collins	295
Ode to Fear	William Collins	301
Ode to Psyche	John Keats	621
Ode to the North-East Wind	Charles Kingsley	902
Ode to the West Wind	Percy Bysshe Shelley	561
Odyssey, The	Andrew Lang	1054
Œnone	Alfred, Lord Tennyson	787
Of Old Sat Freedom on the Heights	Alfred, Lord Tennyson	794
Oft Have I Mused	Sir Philip Sidney	47
Oft in the Stilly Night	Thomas Moore	495
Oft-Repeated Dream, The	Robert Frost	1260
Oh, Bless the Law	Eugene Lee-Hamilton	1060
Oh! Breathe Not His Name	Thomas Moore	491
Oh, Earlier Shall the Rosebuds Blow	William (Johnson) Cory	955
Oh! Snatched Away in Beauty's Bloom	Lord Byron	501
Old Age	Edmund Waller	181
Old Familiar Faces, The	Charles Lamb	485
Old Ironsides	Oliver Wendell Holmes	835
Old Mortality	Sir Walter Scott	441
Old Stoic, The	Emily Brontë	873
Old Woman, The	Joseph Campbell	1281
Old Woman of the Roads, An	Padraic Colum	1281
Olim Meminisse Juvabit	Aline Kilmer	1328
Omnia Exeunt in Mysterium	George Sterling	1212
On a Distant Prospect of Eton College	Thomas Gray	283
On a Fly-leaf of Burns' Songs	Frederic Lawrence Knowles	339
On a Girdle	Edmund Waller	181
On a Shepherd Losing His Mistress	Unknown	1390
On a Subway Express	Chester Firkins	1359
On Catullus	Walter Savage Landor	481
On First Looking Into Chapman's Homer	John Keats	601
On Growing Old	John Masefield	1255
On Her Dancing	James Shirley	179
On His Blindness	John Milton	205
On His Deceased Wife	John Milton	206
On Lamb's Specimens of Dramatic Poets	Algernon Charles Swinburne	484
On May Morning	John Milton	203
On Milton	John Dryden	183
On Rembrandt's Portrait of a Rabbi	Alfred Noyes	1271
On Shakespeare	John Milton	203
On Sunium's Height	Walter Savage Landor	482
On the Death of Mr. Crashaw	Abraham Cowley	217

PAGE

On the Death of Mr. William Her-
vey   *Abraham Cowley*   219
On the Departure of Sir Walter
Scott   *William Wordsworth*   428
On the Extinction of the Venetian
Republic   *William Wordsworth*   387
On the Life and Death of Man   *Francis Quarles*   166
On the Life-Mask of Abraham
Lincoln   *Richard Watson Gilder*   1048
On the Morning of Christ's Na-
tivity   *John Milton*   201
On the Portrait of Shakespeare   *Ben Jonson*   127
On the Subjugation of Switzer-
land   *William Wordsworth*   419
On the Tombs in Westminster Ab-
bey   *Francis Beaumont*   140
On the Way to Kew   *William Ernest Henley*   1089
On This Day I Complete My
Thirty-sixth Year   *Lord Byron*   515
One   *John Vance Cheney*   1084
One Grey Hair, The   *Walter Savage Landor*   480
One Hour with Thee   *Sir Walter Scott*   443
One Word More   *Robert Browning*   856
Only of Thee and Me   *Louis Untermeyer*   1303
Othello   *William Shakespeare*   95
Out of the Cradle Endlessly
Rocking   *Walt Whitman*   896
Overtones   *William Alexander Percy*   1300
Ozymandias   *Percy Bysshe Shelley*   546

P

Pack, Clouds, Away!   *Thomas Heywood*   124
Pæstum   *Samuel Rogers*   363
Pagan World, The   *Matthew Arnold*   951
Palatine, The   *Willa Sibert Cather*   1261
Panther! Panther!   *John Hall Wheelock*   1322
Paradise Lost   *John Milton*   183
Parish Bard, The   *Francis Carlin*   1280
Parted   *Alice Meynell*   1097
Parting   *Emily Dickinson*   1001
Parting Guest, A   *James Whitcomb Riley*   1114
Passer-by, A   *Robert Bridges*   1055
Passing Away   *Christina Georgina Rossetti*   996
Passing Flower, The   *Harry Kemp*   1293
Passing Strange, The   *John Masefield*   1253
Passionate Pilgrim, The   *William Shakespeare*   114
Passionate Reader to His Poet,
The   *Richard Le Gallienne*   1187
Passionate Shepherd to His Love,
The   *Christopher Marlowe*   58
Passions, The   *William Collins*   297
Patient Grissel   *Thomas Dekker*   122
Patmos   *Edith M. Thomas*   1116
Peace   *Emily Dickinson*   1001
Peace   *Sara Teasdale*   1295
Pedigree   *Emily Dickinson*   1002
Perfection   *Francis Carlin*   1278
Pericles   *William Shakespeare*   99
Phillada Flouts Me   *Unknown*   1392
Phillida and Coridon   *Nicholas Breton*   23
Phillis   *Thomas Lodge*   50
Philomela   *Matthew Arnold*   915

		PAGE
Philomela	Sir Philip Sidney	44
Philosopher	Ralph Waldo Emerson	683
Philosopher, A	William Canton	1076
Phœbus, Arise	William Drummond	143
Phyllis	Sir Charles Sedley	252
Pickwick Papers	Charles Dickens	840
Picture of Little T. C., The	Andrew Marvell	231
Picture of the Mind, The	Ben Jonson	128
Pioneers	Leonora Speyer	1358
Pippa Passes	Robert Browning	841
Pirate, The	Sir Walter Scott	443
Plaint	John Hall Wheelock	1321
Plays	Walter Savage Landor	482
Poe's Cottage at Fordham	John Henry Boner	740
Poet, A	William Wordsworth	427
Poet, The	Ralph Waldo Emerson	682
Poet of One Mood, A	Alice Meynell	1099
Poet Tells of His Love, The	John Hall Wheelock	1320
Poets	Joyce Kilmer	1311
Poet's Epitaph, A	William Wordsworth	378
Portrait, A	Elizabeth Barrett Browning	692
Portrait, The: "This Is Her Picture"	Dante Gabriel Rossetti	969
Portrait, The: "O Lord of All"	Dante Gabriel Rossetti	vii
Poverty	Samuel Johnson	280
Power of Music, The	John Dryden	236
Praise and Prayer	Sir William Davenant	180
Praise of Age, The	Walter Kennedy	19
Praise of Dust, The	Gilbert Keith Chesterton	1245
Praise of His Lady, A	Unknown	1397
Prayer	James Montgomery	445
Prayer	Louis Untermeyer	1302
Prayer, A	Edwin Markham	1104
Prayer After Illness, A	Violet Alleyn Storey	1366
Prayer for Pain	John G. Neihardt	1273
Precept of Silence, The	Lionel Johnson	1194
Prelude, The	William Wordsworth	407
Prevision	Aline Kilmer	1327
Primrose, The	Robert Herrick	153
Princess, The	Alfred, Lord Tennyson	803
Prisoner, The	Emily Brontë	871
Private of the Buffs, The	Sir Francis Doyle	837
Problem, The	Ralph Waldo Emerson	653
Progress of Poesy, The	Matthew Arnold	919
Progress of Poesy, The	Thomas Gray	292
Prologue. To Mr. Addison's Tragedy of Cato	Alexander Pope	265
Prologue to the Satires	Alexander Pope	275
Prometheus Unbound	Percy Bysshe Shelley	524
Prospice	Robert Browning	861
Prothalamion	Edmund Spenser	30
Proud Maisie	Sir Walter Scott	442
Psyche	Thomas Heywood	123
Pulley, The	George Herbert	172

Q

Qua Cursum Ventus	Arthur Hugh Clough	873
Queen Mab	Percy Bysshe Shelley	591
Question, A	Matthew Arnold	910
Question, The	Percy Bysshe Shelley	572
Quiet Work	Matthew Arnold	907
Quip, The	George Herbert	172

R

		PAGE
Rabbi Ben Ezra	Robert Browning	860
Rape of Lucrece, The	Thomas Heywood	124
Rape of the Lock, The	Alexander Pope	263
Raven, The	Edgar Allan Poe	744
Rebecca's Hymn	Sir Walter Scott	444
Rebirth	Rudyard Kipling	1182
Recessional	Rudyard Kipling	1183
Recompense	Clark Ashton Smith	1338
Red, Red Rose, A	Robert Burns	352
Reflections on Having Left a Place of Retirement	Samuel Taylor Coleridge	446
Relieving Guard	Bret Harte	1033
Remember	Christina Georgina Rossetti	997
Remembrance	Percy Bysshe Shelley	580
Reminiscences	Mary Carolyn Davies	1353
Renouncement	Alice Meynell	1098
Requiem	Robert Louis Stevenson	1093
Requiescat	Matthew Arnold	908
Requiescat	Oscar Wilde	1140
Resignation	Walter Savage Landor	481
Resolution and Independence	William Wordsworth	382
Respice Finem	Francis Quarles	166
Rest	Christina Georgina Rossetti	998
Retaliation	Oliver Goldsmith	316
Retreat, The	Henry Vaughan	235
Return, The	Arthur Symons	1177
Revelation	Edmund Gosse	1091
Reverie of Poor Susan, The	William Wordsworth	370
Revolt of Islam, The	Percy Bysshe Shelley	520
Rhodora, The	Ralph Waldo Emerson	659
Rime of the Ancient Mariner, The	Samuel Taylor Coleridge	449
Ring of Faustus, The	Eugene Lee-Hamilton	1061
Rivers Unknown to Song	Alice Meynell	1102
Road Not Taken, The	Robert Frost	1260
Roadside Flowers	Bliss Carman	1167
Robert Browning	Walter Savage Landor	840
Rokeby	Sir Walter Scott	436
Romance	Edgar Allan Poe	742
Romance	Robert Louis Stevenson	1093
Romeo and Juliet	William Shakespeare	80
Rondel	Algernon Charles Swinburne	1013
Rosary, The	Robert Cameron Rogers	1174
Rose Aylmer	Walter Savage Landor	480
Rose of the World, The	Coventry Patmore	957
Roses and Thorns	Walter Savage Landor	479
Rubáiyát of Omar Khayyám	Edward FitzGerald	772
Rust	Mary Carolyn Davies	1353
Ruth	May Doney	1355
Ruth	Thomas Hood	635

S

Saadi	Ralph Waldo Emerson	668
Sacrifice	Ralph Waldo Emerson	682
St. Agnes' Eve	Alfred, Lord Tennyson	798
St. George's Day—Ypres, 1915	Sir Henry Newbolt	1173
Saint Teresa	Richard Crashaw	211
Sally in Our Alley	Henry Carey	279
Salve!	Thomas Edward Brown	1003
Samela	Robert Greene	52
Sandalphon	Henry Wadsworth Longfellow	706
Saw Ye Bonie Lesley	Robert Burns	354

INDEX BY TITLES

		PAGE
Say Not That Beauty	Robin Flower	1360
Say Not, the Struggle Naught Availeth	Arthur Hugh Clough	874
Scholar-Gipsy, The	Matthew Arnold	927
Scorn Not the Sonnet	William Wordsworth	424
Scrubber	William Ernest Henley	1087
Scythe Song	Andrew Lang	1054
Sea Gypsy, The	Richard Hovey	1175
Sea-Fever	John Masefield	1252
Security of Desolation, The	Edith M. Thomas	1115
Self-Dependence	Matthew Arnold	920
Separation	Matthew Arnold	917
Separation	Walter Savage Landor	481
Serenade	Henry Wadsworth Longfellow	697
Serenity	John Middleton Murry	1334
Shakespeare	Matthew Arnold	62
Shall I, Wasting in Despair	George Wither	147
She Came and Went	James Russell Lowell	881
She Dwelt Among the Untrodden Ways	William Wordsworth	375
She Is Far from the Land	Thomas Moore	493
She Walks in Beauty	Lord Byron	501
She Was a Phantom of Delight	William Wordsworth	401
Shelley (From "Adonais")	Percy Bysshe Shelley	518
Shelley's Skylark	Thomas Hardy	1036
Shepherdess, The	Alice Meynell	1100
Shepherd's Wife's Song, The	Robert Greene	51
Ship, an Isle, a Sickle Moon, A	James Elroy Flecker	1296
Shipwreck	James Russell Lowell	885
Shroud of Color, The	Countee Cullen	1344
Sibylla Palmifera	Dante Gabriel Rossetti	985
Sic Vita	Henry King	167
Sidera	Sir Philip Sidney	47
Silent Lover, The	Sir Walter Raleigh	36
Silent Woman, The	Ben Jonson	129
Simon the Cyrenian Speaks	Countee Cullen	1350
Simplex Munditiis	Ben Jonson	129
Simplicity	Emily Dickinson	1002
Since There's No Help	Michael Drayton	56
Sister, Awake!	Unknown	1380
Skylark, The	James Hogg	368
Sleep	John Fletcher	139
Sleep	Sir Philip Sidney	41
Sleeping Beauty, The	Samuel Rogers	366
Slow, Slow, Fresh Fount	Ben Jonson	131
Slumber Did My Spirit Seal, A	William Wordsworth	378
Small Celandine, The	William Wordsworth	403
Smoke	Henry David Thoreau	870
Snow-bound	John Greenleaf Whittier	717
Snow-storm, The	Ralph Waldo Emerson	661
Soldier, The	Rupert Brooke	1324
Solitary Reaper, The	William Wordsworth	398
Solitude	William Drummond	142
Some Atheist in Love	Michael Drayton	56
Sometime It May Be	Arthur Willis Colton	1203
Sometimes	Thomas S. Jones, Jr.	1290
Song, A	John Wilmot	253
Song: "April, April"	William Watson	1147
Song: "Ask me no more"	Thomas Carew	176
Song: "For Mercy, Courage"	Laurence Binyon	1206
Song: "Go, lovely Rose"	Edmund Waller	182
Song: "Has summer come"	Arthur O'Shaughnessy	1051
Song: "Heaken then"	William Browne	165
Song: "I made another garden"	Arthur O'Shaughnessy	1052

PAGE

Song: "Love within the lover's breast"	George Meredith	986
Song: "My silks and fine array"	William Blake	331
Song: "Rarely, rarely comest thou"	Percy Bysshe Shelley	578
Song: "She's somewhere in the sunlight"	Richard Le Gallienne	1188
Song: "You wear the morning"	Hilaire Belloc	1232
Song for Saint Cecilia's Day	John Dryden	248
Song from Ælla	Thomas Chatterton	327
Song in the Songless	George Meredith	994
Song of Enchantment, A	Walter de la Mare	1244
Song of Praise, A	Countee Cullen	1350
Song of the Chattahoochee	Sidney Lanier	1046
Song of the Pixies	Samuel Taylor Coleridge	446
Song of the Sea Wind, The	Austin Dobson	1035
Song of the Shirt, The	Thomas Hood	631
Song to a Fair Young Lady	John Dryden	247
Song to Amoret, A	Henry Vaughan	233
Song—To Celia	Ben Jonson	130
Song: To Cynthia	Ben Jonson	129
Song to the Men of England	Percy Bysshe Shelley	560
Songs of Travel	Robert Louis Stevenson	1093, 1094
Sonnet, The	Dante Gabriel Rossetti	972
Sonnet: "In the fair picture"	Arthur Davison Ficke	1292
Sonnet: "Lift not the painted veil"	Percy Bysshe Shelley	559
Sonnet: "Nay, Lord, not thus"	Oscar Wilde	1140
Sonnet: "Now that the moonlight"	Edward Davison	1343
Sonnet: "O Thou in the darkness"	Edward Davison	1342
Sonnet: "Oh! Death will find me"	Rupert Brooke	1325
Sonnet: Repent, Repent!	William Drummond	142
Sonnet: "This is the burden"	Arthur Davison Ficke	1292
Sonnet: To Homer	John Keats	626
Sonnet: To Science	Edgar Allan Poe	743
Sonnet: To Sleep	John Keats	627
Sonnet: "When I have fears"	John Keats	625
Sonnet. Written While in Prison	William Lloyd Garrison	688
Sonnet on "A Lover's Complaint"	John Keats	629
Sonnet on Chillon	Lord Byron	510
Sonnets	William Shakespeare	100
Sonnets from the Portuguese	Elizabeth Barrett Browning	609
Sorrow	Aubrey Thomas de Vere	868
South Country, The	Hilaire Belloc	1228
Sovereign Poet, The	William Watson	8
Spanish Gypsy, The	Henry Wadsworth Longfellow	698
Spirit of Sadness	Richard Le Gallienne	1188
Sport	Abraham Cowley	217
Spring in Carmel	George Sterling	1210
Staff-Nurse: Old Style	William Ernest Henley	1085
Stanzas	John Keats	627
Stanzas—April, 1814	Percy Bysshe Shelley	541
Stanzas for Music	Lord Byron	500
Stanzas in Memory of the Author of "Obermann"	Matthew Arnold	948
Stanzas. Written in Dejection, Near Naples	Percy Bysshe Shelley	558
Stranger, The	Walter de la Mare	1239
Strangers Yet	Lord Houghton	780
Stream of Life, The	Arthur Hugh Clough	875
Stream's Secret, The	Dante Gabriel Rossetti	981
Street, The	James Russell Lowell	885
Strings in the Earth	James Joyce	1284

INDEX BY TITLES

		PAGE
Sudden Light	*Dante Gabriel Rossetti*	980
Summer	*Unknown*	1381
Summer's Eve, A	*Michael Drayton*	55
Sunken Garden, The	*Walter de la Mare*	1242
Surprised by Joy	*William Wordsworth*	420
Sursum Corda	*Ralph Waldo Emerson*	664
Suspense	*Emily Dickinson*	1002
Suspirium	*William Canton*	1077
Sussex	*Rudyard Kipling*	1184
Sweet Content	*Thomas Dekker*	122
Sweet Pastoral, A	*Nicholas Breton*	22
Sweet Stay-at-Home	*William Henry Davies*	1224
Sweet Was the Song That Youth Sang Once	*Walter Savage Landor*	483
Sweetest Melancholy	*John Fletcher*	138
Sword of Surprise, The	*Gilbert Keith Chesterton*	1245
Sympathy	*Walter Savage Landor*	479

T

Tamburlaine the Great	*Christopher Marlowe*	59
Task, The	*William Cowper*	323
Tears of Harlequin, The	*Theodosia Garrison*	1249
Tempest, The	*William Shakespeare*	63
Terminus	*Ralph Waldo Emerson*	680
Test, The	*Ralph Waldo Emerson*	8
Testing, The	*Edwin Markham*	1109
Thalaba	*Robert Southey*	476
Thanatopsis	*William Cullen Bryant*	595
There Alway, Alway Something Sings	*Ralph Waldo Emerson*	682
There Is a Lady	*Unknown*	1382
They Are Not Long	*Ernest Dowson*	1198
They Went Forth to Battle But They Always Fell	*Shaemas O'Sheel*	1311
Thinking of Shores	*Laurence Binyon*	1205
This Grace Vouchsafe Me	*William Canton*	1078
Thomas the Rhymer	*Unknown*	1386
Thought, A	*William Henry Davies*	1228
Three Cottage Girls, The	*William Wordsworth*	421
Three Seasons	*Christina Georgina Rossetti*	998
Three Shadows	*Dante Gabriel Rossetti*	985
Three Years She Grew in Sun and Shower	*William Wordsworth*	376
Threnody	*Ralph Waldo Emerson*	670
Through the Ages	*William Canton*	1064
Thunderstorms	*William Henry Davies*	1227
Thyrsis	*Matthew Arnold*	933
Thyself	*John Addington Symonds*	1038
Tiger, The	*William Blake*	334
Time	*Sir Walter Scott*	440
Time	*Percy Bysshe Shelley*	578
Time and Grief	*William Lisle Bowles*	359
Time Long Past	*Percy Bysshe Shelley*	575
Time, Real and Imaginary	*Samuel Taylor Coleridge*	448
Tithonus	*Alfred, Lord Tennyson*	829
To ———	*W. E. H. Lecky*	1030
To ———	*Samuel Rogers*	361
To ———: "Music, when soft"	*Percy Bysshe Shelley*	578
To ———: "One word is too often"	*Percy Bysshe Shelley*	581
To ———: "When passion's trance"	*Percy Bysshe Shelley*	581
To ———	*William Robert Spencer*	367
To a Bird at Dawn	*Richard Le Gallienne*	1190

		PAGE
To a Captive Crane	Hamlin Garland	1163
To a Friend	Matthew Arnold	907
To a Highland Girl	William Wordsworth	396
To a Lady Singing	Edmund Waller	181
To a Lost Love	Stephen Phillips	1204
To a Mountain Daisy	Robert Burns	347
To a Mouse	Robert Burns	345
To a New York Shop-Girl Dressed for Sunday	Anna Hempstead Branch	1367
To a Poet a Thousand Years Hence	James Elroy Flecker	1297
To a Scarlatti Passepied	Robert Hillyer	1340
To a Skylark	Percy Bysshe Shelley	567
To a Skylark: "Ethereal Minstrel"	William Wordsworth	423
To a Skylark: "Up with me!"	William Wordsworth	405
To a Snowflake	Francis Thompson	1159
To a Waterfowl	William Cullen Bryant	597
To a Young Aviator	Aline Kilmer	1329
To a Young Lady	William Wordsworth	406
To Althea, From Prison	Richard Lovelace	215
To an Oriole	Edgar Fawcett	1079
To Anthea	Robert Herrick	159
To Aphrodite: With a Mirror	Aline Kilmer	1331
To Autumn	John Keats	623
To Blossoms	Robert Herrick	159
To Daffodils	Robert Herrick	161
To Daisies	Robert Herrick	154
To Delia	Samuel Daniel	53
To Dianeme	Robert Herrick	159
To Eva	Ralph Waldo Emerson	666
To F——	Edgar Allan Poe	772
To F. C. In Memoriam Palestine	Gilbert Keith Chesterton	1246
To H. C.	William Wordsworth	390
To Helen: "Helen, thy beauty"	Edgar Allan Poe	743
To Helen: "I saw thee once"	Edgar Allan Poe	750
To His Coy Mistress	Andrew Marvell	229
To His Lute	William Drummond	143
To Jane: The Invitation	Percy Bysshe Shelley	584
To Jane: The keen stars were twinkling	Percy Bysshe Shelley	590
To Jane: The Recollection	Percy Bysshe Shelley	585
To John Gorham Palfrey	James Russell Lowell	882
To Lucasta, Going to the Wars	Richard Lovelace	216
To Marguerite	Matthew Arnold	913
To Mary	Charles Wolfe	516
To Mary Unwin	William Cowper	322
To Meadows	Robert Herrick	160
To Miss Charlotte Pulteney	Ambrose Philips	257
To Mistress Margery Wentworth	John Skelton	21
To Mother Nature	Frederic Lawrence Knowles	1219
To Music, To Becalm His Fever	Robert Herrick	155
To Night	Percy Bysshe Shelley	577
To Night	Joseph Blanco White	487
To One in Paradise	Edgar Allan Poe	761
To One Who Has Been Long in City Pent	John Keats	600
To Rhea	Ralph Waldo Emerson	654
To Shelley	John Bannister Tabb	1062
To Silence	Alice Meynell	1101
To Spring	William Blake	330
To the Balliol Men Still in Africa	Hilaire Belloc	1231
To the Cuckoo	John Logan	326
To the Cuckoo	William Wordsworth	400

INDEX BY TITLES

		PAGE
To the Daisy	William Wordsworth	391
To the Fringed Gentian	William Cullen Bryant	598
To the Lady Margaret Ley	John Milton	204
To the Lord General Cromwell	John Milton	205
To the Man-of-War-Bird	Walt Whitman	887
To the Memory of Mrs. Anne Killigrew	John Dryden	242
To the Memory of My Beloved Master William Shakespeare	Ben Jonson	125
To the Modern Man	John Hall Wheelock	1319
To the Moon	Percy Bysshe Shelley	575
To the Moon	Sir Philip Sidney	40
To the Muses	William Blake	332
To the Poet Before Battle	Ivor Gurney	1361
To the Rose	Robert Herrick	163
To the Same Flower (The Daisy)	William Wordsworth	393
To the Same Flower (The Small Celandine)	William Wordsworth	381
To the Small Celandine	William Wordsworth	379
To the Virgins	Robert Herrick	162
To Toussaint L'Ouverture	William Wordsworth	387
To Violets	Robert Herrick	150
To William Lloyd Garrison	James Russell Lowell	883
To Women	Laurence Binyon	1206
To Wordsworth	Percy Bysshe Shelley	543
To Youth	Walter Savage Landor	483
Toccata of Galuppi's, A	Robert Browning	845
Toys, The	Coventry Patmore	960
Tragic Mary Queen of Scots, The	Michael Field	1095
Transcendence	Clark Ashton Smith	1338
Transformation	Jessie B. Rittenhouse	1362
Traveller, The	Oliver Goldsmith	314
Treasure, The	Rupert Brooke	1324
Tree-Tops	John Collins Squire	1299
Trees	Joyce Kilmer	1312
Tribute, The	Coventry Patmore	958
Triumph, The	Ben Jonson	127
Triumph of Time, The	Algernon Charles Swinburne	1025
True Greatness	Isaac Watts	257
True Martyr, The	Thomas Wade	687
True Pathos, The	Robert Burns	359
True Woman	Dante Gabriel Rossetti	977
Trumpeter, The	Thomas Wentworth Higginson	962
Truth	Ben Jonson	127
Truth at Last	Edward Rowland Sill	1041
Twelfth-Night	William Shakespeare	74
Twenty Years Hence	Walter Savage Landor	479
Twilight of Earth, The	George William Russell	1202
Two Children, The	William Henry Davies	1225
Two Gentlemen of Verona, The	William Shakespeare	64
Two in One	Unknown	1382
Two Lovers	George Eliot	904
Two Poets of Croisic, The	Robert Browning	866
Two Spirits, The	Percy Bysshe Shelley	573

U

Ulalume	Edgar Allan Poe	752
Ulysses	Alfred, Lord Tennyson	795
Unconscious Cerebration	W. E. H. Lecky	1031
Under an Irish Lark	Francis Carlin	1279
Under the Willows	James Russell Lowell	885
Undertaking, The	John Donne	136
Unknown Eros, The	Coventry Patmore	7

		PAGE
Unloved to His Beloved, The	*William Alexander Percy*	1301
Unrealised Ideal, The	*Frederick Locker-Lampson*	905
Unreturning, The	*Bliss Carman*	1168
Unthrift	*Coventry Patmore*	956
Up-Hill	*Christina Georgina Rossetti*	996
Upon a Child	*Robert Herrick*	151
Urania	*Matthew Arnold*	916
Urceus Exit	*Austin Dobson*	1033
Uriel	*Ralph Waldo Emerson*	684

V

Vain Resolves	*Ernest Dowson*	1199
Valediction Forbidding Mourning, A	*John Donne*	134
Valentine to One's Wife	*John Erskine*	1268
Valentinian	*John Fletcher*	139
Valley of Unrest, The	*Edgar Allan Poe*	762
Vanity of Human Wishes, The	*Samuel Johnson*	281
Venice	*Arthur Hugh Clough*	876
Venus and Adonis	*William Shakespeare*	100
Venus Transiens	*Amy Lowell*	1250
Verses in an Album	*Thomas Hood*	636
Very True, the Linnets Sing	*Walter Savage Landor*	484
Vesta	*John Greenleaf Whittier*	738
Victorious Men of Earth	*James Shirley*	178
Villiers de L'Isle-Adam	*Aldous Huxley*	1339
Virgilia	*Edwin Markham*	1110
Virtue	*George Herbert*	174
Vision of Sir Launfal, The	*James Russell Lowell*	881
Vision Upon Spenser's "Faery Queen," A	*Sir Walter Raleigh*	40
Visiting Sea, The	*Alice Meynell*	1098
Voice, The	*Matthew Arnold*	908
Voice of the Western Wind	*Edmund Clarence Stedman*	1004
Voiceless, The	*Oliver Wendell Holmes*	834
Voluntaries, III	*Ralph Waldo Emerson*	684
Volunteer's Grave, A	*William Alexander Percy*	1301

W

Waiting	*John Burroughs*	1070
Waldeinsamkeit	*Ralph Waldo Emerson*	679
Wanderers	*George Sylvester Viereck*	1298
War Song of Dinas Vawr, The	*Thomas Love Peacock*	498
Washer of the Ford, The	*William Sharp*	1120
Wasp, The	*William Sharp*	1120
Waste Places, The	*James Stephens*	1286
Welcome, A	*William Browne*	163
Wet Sheet and a Flowing Sea, A	*Allan Cunningham*	497
What Constitutes a State?	*Sir William Jones*	325
What the Sonnet Is	*Eugene Lee-Hamilton*	1061
What Tomas An Buile Said in a Pub	*James Stephens*	1285
When, Dearest, I But Think of Thee	*Sir John Suckling*	210
When I Am Dead, My Dearest	*Christina Georgina Rossetti*	995
When I Have Borne in Memory	*William Wordsworth*	390
When I would Image	*George Meredith*	987
When Lilacs Last in the Dooryard Bloomed	*Walt Whitman*	888
When She Comes Home	*James Whitcomb Riley*	1113
When the Lamp Is Shattered	*Percy Bysshe Shelley*	582

		PAGE
When the Wind Is Low	Cale Young Rice	1236
When There Is Music	David Morton	1307
When Thou Must Home	Thomas Campion	120
When to Her Lute Corinna Sings	Thomas Campion	114
Whenas in Silks My Julia Goes	Robert Herrick	161
Where It Is Winter	George O'Neil	1342
Where Lies the Land	Arthur Hugh Clough	876
Who Loves the Rain	Frances Wells Shaw	1233
Who Walks with Beauty	David Morton	1308
Why I Am a Liberal	Robert Browning	867
Wild-Flower's Song, The	William Blake	338
William Shakespeare	Algernon Charles Swinburne	1027
Willie Drowned in Yarrow	Unknown	1395
Wind and Wave	Coventry Patmore	7
Winged Hours	Dante Gabriel Rossetti	974
Winter's Tale, The	William Shakespeare	75
Wisdom	Scudder Middleton	1326
Wish, A	Samuel Rogers	360
Wish, The	Abraham Cowley	218
Wishes for the Supposed Mistress	Richard Crashaw	212
With a Guitar, to Jane	Percy Bysshe Shelley	588
With Rue My Heart Is Laden	Alfred Edward Housman	1150
With Whom Is No Shadow of Variableness	Arthur Hugh Clough	876
Without Her	Dante Gabriel Rossetti	977
Woman	Eaton Stannard Barrett	499
Woman-Hater, The	John Fletcher	139
Woman's Last Word, A	Robert Browning	843
Woodnotes, II	Ralph Waldo Emerson	662
Woodstock	Sir Walter Scott	444
Wordsworth	Edward Rowland Sill	369
Work Without Hope	Samuel Taylor Coleridge	473
World, The	Henry Vaughan	234
World Is too Much with Us, The	William Wordsworth	413
World-Soul, The	Ralph Waldo Emerson	656
World's Triumphs, The	Matthew Arnold	909
World's Wanderers, The	Percy Bysshe Shelley	575
Written at an Inn at Henley	William Shenstone	283
Written in Emerson's Essays	Matthew Arnold	651
Written in London	William Wordsworth	388
Written in Westminster Abbey	Samuel Rogers	362

Y

Yarrow Revisited	William Wordsworth	424
Yarrow Unvisited	William Wordsworth	399
Ye Little Birds That Sit and Sing	Thomas Heywood	122
Yes, It Was the Mountain Echo	William Wordsworth	412
Yet Do I Marvel	Countee Cullen	1344
Your Tears	Edwin Markham	1106
Youth and Age	Samuel Taylor Coleridge	473

INDEX BY FIRST LINES

A

	PAGE
A Clerk ther was of Oxenford also	17
A cloud possessed the hollow field	1079
"A cup for hope!" she said	998
A Fire-Mist and a planet	1162
A flying word from here and there	1217
A! Fredome is a noble thing	13
A garden is a lovesome thing, God wot!	1003
A good man was ther of religioun	18
A hard north-caster fifty winters long	1087
A Knight ther was, and that a worthy man	16
A land that is lonelier than ruin	1027
A late lark twitters from the quiet skies	1089
A little hand is knocking at my heart	1177
A *little learning* is a dangerous thing	262
A little sun, a little rain	1004
A man so various, that he seemed to be	241
A mind so pure, so perfect fine	128
A moonlit desert's yellow sands	369
A noiseless, patient spider	901
A Poet!—He hath put his heart to school	427
A poet of one mood in all my lays	1099
A queen lived in the South	1152
A ruddy drop of manly blood	681
A ship, an isle, a sickle moon	1296
A slumber did my spirit seal	378
A song of Enchantment I sang me there	1244
A sonnet is a moment's monument	972
A sweet disorder in the dress	158
A thing of beauty is a joy for ever	601
A trouble, not of clouds, or weeping rain	428
A wanderer is man from his birth	924
A weary lot is thine, fair maid	437
A wet sheet and a flowing sea	497
A wise man holds himself in check	1326
Abou Ben Adhem (may his tribe increase!)	496
Above the pines the moon was slowly drifting	1031
Above the shouting of the gale	1164
Absence, hear thou my protestation	134
Accept, thou shrine of my dead saint	169
Across the fields of yesterday	1290
Ae fond kiss, and then we sever	351
Again the feast, the speech, the glee	821
Ah Ben!	161
Ah, broken is the golden bowl! the spirit flown forever!	749
Ah, Chloris! could I now but sit	251
Ah, did you once see Shelley plain	848
Ah, little boy! I see	1225
Ah, more to me than many days and many dreams	1338
Ah, Sunflower, weary of time	335
Ah, wasteful woman, she that may	956
Ah, what avails the sceptred race	480
Ah, what can ail thee, wretched wight	628
Ah, what is love? It is a pretty thing	51
Alas! the love of women! it is known	511
Alas! they had been friends in youth	468

INDEX BY FIRST LINES

	PAGE
All along the valley, stream that flashest white	831
All are but parts of one stupendous whole	267
All around him Patmos lies	1116
All day they played in gardens hid amid golden towers	1200
All in the Downs the fleet was moored	260
All Nature seems at work. Slugs leave their lair	473
All promise is poor dilatory man	258
All that he came to give	1193
All that I know	848
All the world's a stage	71
All things uncomely and broken, all things worn out and old	1180
All thoughts, all passions, all delights	468
All was for you: and you are dead	1195
Aloof within the day's enormous dome	1213
Although I enter not	838
Always the heavy air	1319
An hour ere sudden sunset fired the west	137
An hour with thee!—When earliest day	445
And all is well, tho' faith and form	821
And did those feet in ancient time	336
And now, unveil'd, the toilet stands displayed	263
And were they not the happy days	869
And you, brave Cobham! to the latest breath	273
Angels and ministers of grace defend us!	90
Announced by all the trumpets of the sky	661
April, April	1147
April whispers—"Canst thou, too, die	1008
Ariel to Miranda:—Take	588
Art thou pale for weariness	575
Art thou poor, yet hast thou golden slumbers?	122
As a fond mother, when the day is o'er	708
As a naked man I go	1286
As a perfume doth remain	1178
As a twig trembles, which a bird	881
As a white candle	1281
As I came down from Lebanon	1165
As I was walking up the street	354
As if awakened, summoned, roused, constrained	408
As it fell upon a day	137
As one that for a weary space has lain	1054
As one who under evening skies	1118
As pools beneath stone arches take	1288
As rising on its purple wing	509
As ships, becalmed at eve, that lay	873
As slow our ship her foamy track	494
As the inhastening tide doth roll	1098
As the kindling glances	908
As thro' the land at eve we went	803
As virtuous men pass mildly away	134
Ask me no more: the moon may draw the sea	806
Ask me no more where Jove bestows	176
Ask me why I send you here	153
Ask not the cause why sullen Spring	247
At matin hour, in middis of the night	19
At Quincy's moat the squandering village ends	1340
At Shelley's birth	1062
At the corner of Wood Street, when daylight appears	370
At the midnight in the silence of the sleep-time	868
Ave Maria! blessed be the hour!	514
Avoid the reeking herd	1364
Awake, Æolian lyre, awake	292
Away! the moor is dark beneath the moon	541
Ay, but to die, and go we know not where	64
Ay, tear her tattered ensign down!	835

1534

B

	PAGE
Back to the flower-town, side by side	477
Be near me when my light is low	813
Be with me, Beauty, for the fire is dying	1255
Be your words made, good Sir, of Indian ware	46
Beautiful must be the mountains whence ye come	1058
Before man came to blow it right	1259
Before the beginning of years	1010
Before the urchin well could go	282
Behold, he watches at the door!	668
Behold her, single in the field	398
Behold me waiting—waiting for the knife	1084
Behold the child, by nature's kindly law	269
Being your slave, what should I do but tend	105
Believe me, if all those endearing young charms	492
Beloved! amid the earnest woes	772
Beloved, my glory in thee is not ceased	1095
Beneath the curious gaze of all the dead	1354
Beneath these fruit-tree boughs that shed	395
Best and brightest, come away!	584
Bird of the wilderness	368
Better be with the dead	87
Blake saw a tree-ful of angels at Peckham Rye	330
Blame not my Lute! for he must sound	24
Blessed with a joy that only she	1216
Blest is the turf, serenely blest	496
Blow, blow, thou winter wind	72
Blow out, you bugles, over the rich Dead!	1323
Bonie lassie, will ye go	339
Books are not seldom talismans and spells	323
Boon Nature to the woman bows	958
Bowed by the weight of centuries he leans	1106
Boys, are ye calling a toast to-night?	1172
Brave flowers—that I could gallant it like you	168
Break, break, break	800
Breathes there the man, with soul so dead	429
Brief is Man's travail here and transitory	1321
Bright star, would I were stedfast as thou art	629
Bring me wine, but wine which never grew	666
Broad-based, broad-fronted, bounteous, multiform	124
Brown hill I have left behind	1330
Burly, dozing humble-bee	659
But all our praises why should lords engross?	274
But ill for him that wears a crown	821
But man, proud man	64
But most by numbers judge a poet's song	262
But once or twice we met, touched hands	1036
But Psyche lives, and on her breath attend	123
But thou and I are one in kind	817
But to my mind,—though I am native here	90
But vain the Sword and vain the Bow	338
But what are these to great Atossa's mind?	273
But who is He, with modest looks	378
By a route obscure and lonely	765
By the rude bridge that arched the flood	677
By what word's power, the key to paths untrod	974

C

Calm is the morn without a sound	810
Calm was the day, and through the trembling air	30
Came the Relief. "What, Sentry, ho!	1033
Can I think the Guide of Heaven	145

INDEX BY FIRST LINES

PAGE

Canst thou not minister to a mind diseas'd 88
Care-charmer Sleep, son of the sable Night 54
Carol, every violet has 1272
Celia was laughing. Hopefully I said 1284
Charm me asleep, and melt me so 155
Cherry-ripe, ripe, ripe, I cry 163
Child of a day, thou knowest not 482
Chloris, yourself you so excel 181
Cities and Thrones and Powers 1181
Clear and gentle stream! 1059
Clear had the day been from the dawn 55
Clear, placid Leman! thy contrasted lake 504
Clime of the unforgotten brave! 508
Cold winter ice is fled and gone 1381
Come away, come away, death 74
Come back, come back, across the flying foam 877
Come, be happy!—sit near me 556
Come down, O maid, from yonder mountain height . . . 806
Come, Evening, once again, season of peace 323
Come into the garden, Maud 823
Come learn with me the fatal song 662
Come, let us make love deathless, thou and I 1181
Come live with me and be my Love 58
Come, Sleep, and with thy sweet deceiving 139
Come, Sleep! O Sleep, the certain knot of peace 41
Come then, the colours and the ground prepare 273
Come unto these yellow sands 63
Could I pluck down Aldebaran 1301
Count each affliction, whether light or grave 868
Crabbèd Age and Youth cannot live together 113
Creep into thy narrow bed 919
Cromwell, our chief of men, who through a cloud . . . 205
Crowned, girdled, garbed and shod with light and fire . . 1026
Cupid and my Campaspe played 48
Custom, that Tyranness of Fools 256

D

Daughter to that good Earl, once President 204
Daughters of Time, the hypocritic Days 678
Dear Child of Nature, let them rail! 406
Dear is my little native vale 360
Dear love, for nothing less than thee 132
Dearest of all the heroes! Peerless knight 1291
Death, be not proud, though some have callèd thee . . . 133
Death stands above me, whispering low 478
Deep on the convent-roof the snows 798
Do you fear the force of the wind 1163
Do you remember one immortal 1246
Does a man ever give up hope, I wonder 1041
Does the road wind up-hill all the way? 996
Doth it not thrill thee, Poet 1187
Doubt you to whom my Muse these notes intendeth . . . 43
Down in yon garden sweet and gay 1395
Down this side of the gravel-walk 842
Dreams are but interludes which Fancy makes 250
Drink to me only with thine eyes 130

E

Each hour until we meet is as a bird 974
Earth has not anything to show more fair 386
Earth, ocean, air, belovèd brotherhood! 519
Eat thou and drink; to-morrow thou shalt die 979

	PAGE
E'en in the spring and playtime of the year	324
Elysium is as far as to	1002
Enough; and leave the rest to fame	224
Eternal Spirit of the chainless Mind!	510
Ethereal minstrel! pilgrim of the sky!	423
Euclid alone has looked on Beauty bare	1336
Eve, with her basket, was	1233
Even such is Time, that takes in trust	39
Every night and every morn	335

F

Fain would I change that note	1381
Fair Daffodils, we weep to see	161
Fair is my Love, when her fair golden hairs	29
Fair pledges of a fruitful tree	159
Fair ship, that from the Italian shore	810
Far above the hollow	636
Far are the shades of Arabia	1240
Far in a western brookland	1151
Farewell! a long farewell, to all my greatness!	81
Farewell the tranquil mind; farewell content!	97
Farewell! thou art too dear for my possessing	110
Farewell to Fields and Butterflies	1266
Farewell to Northmaven	442
Farewell to one now silenced quite	1097
Fatigued with life, yet loth to part	315
Fear death?—to feel the fog in my throat	861
Fear no more the heat o' the sun	98
Five years have past; five summers, with the length	371
Flow down, cold rivulet, to the sea	799
Flower in the crannied wall	801
Flower of the dust am I: for dust will flower	1332
Foil'd by our fellow-men, depress'd, outworn	912
Follow thy fair sun, unhappy shadow	114
Follow your saint. Follow, with accents sweet!	117
For all ill words that I have spoken	1288
For forms of government let fools contest	270
For Mercy, Courage, Kindness, Mirth	1206
For truly, as thou sayest, a Fairy King	802
For woman is not undevelopt man	807
Forget not yet the tried intent	25
Fourteen small broidered berries on the hem	1061
Frailty, thy name is woman!	88
Friend, you are grieved that I should go	1264
Friends, Romans, countrymen, lend me your ears	85
From childhood's hour I have not been	744
From Eastertide to Eastertide	1141
From harmony, from heavenly harmony	248
From mysteries of the Past	1319
From Stirling castle we had seen	399
From the forests and highlands	571
From you have I been absent in the spring	111
From you, Ianthe, little troubles pass	481
Full many a glorious morning have I seen	103

G

Gaily bedight	766
Gather ye rosebuds while ye may	162
Get up, get up for shame! The blooming morn	156
Give all to love	664

INDEX BY FIRST LINES

PAGE

Give Beauty all her right . . . . ix, 118
Give me my scallop-shell of quiet 35
Give me thyself! It were as well to cry 1038
Give place, ye lovers, here before 20
Give place, you ladies, and begone! 1397
Give thy thoughts no tongue 89
Glooms of the live-oaks, beautiful-braided and woven . . . 1042
"Glory and loveliness have pass'd away" 600
Go fetch to me a pint o' wine 349
Go for they call you, shepherd, from the hill 927
Go from me. Yet I feel that I shall stand 690
Go, happy rose, and interwove 163
Go, little book, and wish to all 1094
Go, lovely Rose! 182
Go, songs, for ended is our brief, sweet play 1400
Go. Soul, the Body's guest 36
Go—you may call it madness, folly 361
God gave all men all earth to love 1184
God, I return to You on April days 1302
God Lyæus, ever young 139
God of our fathers, known of old 1183
God, though this life is but a wraith 1302
God, we don't like to complain 1304
Goethe in Weimar sleeps, and Greece 940
Good Muse, rock me asleep 22
Good name in man or woman, dear my lord 97
Good-bye, proud world! I'm going home 658
Grasshopper, your fairy song 1316
Great God, I ask thee for no meaner pelf 871
Great god whom I shall carve from this gray stone . . . 1232
Great men have been among us; hands that penned . . . 389
Green little vaulter in the sunny grass 497
Grow old along with me! 860

H

Had I that haze of streaming blue 1296
Had we but world enough, and time 229
Had we two gone down the world together 1110
Hadst thou but bid beware, then he had spoke 100
Hail, beauteous stranger of the grove! 326
Hail, holy Light! offspring of heaven first-born! . . . 184
Hail to thee, blithe spirit! 567
Half artist and half anchorite 1263
Half-hidden in a graveyard 1239
Happy the man, whose wish and care 261
Happy those early days, when I 235
Hard-favour'd tyrant, ugly, meagre, lean 100
Hark! ah, the nightingale 915
Hark! hark! the lark at heaven's gate sings 98
Hark, the mavis' e'ening sang 357
Harp of the North, farewell! The hills grow dark . . . 435
Has Heaven reserved, in pity to the poor 280
Has summer come without the rose 1051
Hast thou seen the down in the air 209
Have you been with the King to Rome 1261
Have you forgotten yet? 1313
Have you read in the Talmud of old 706
Have you seen but a bright lily grow 127
He came to call me back from death 1102
He clasps the crag with hookèd hands 800
He did not wear his scarlet coat 1121
He does not die that can bequeath 1228
He had the plowman's strength 1152

INDEX BY FIRST LINES

PAGE

He has thought and suffered, but without a cry 1271
He is gone on the mountain 434
He jests at scars, that never felt a wound 83
He never spoke a word to me 1350
He serveth the servant 656
He sits above the clang and dust of Time 8
He spoke of Burns: men rude and rough 879
He that loves a rosy cheek 177
He who hath seen his grain-fields gather blight 1115
He whom a dream hath possessed knoweth no more of doubting . 1310
Hear me, ye nymphs, and every swain 278
Hear the sledges with the bells 754
Hearken then awhile to me 165
Hearts and darts and maids and men 1268
Heaven from all creatures hides the book of fate 266
Heaven overarches earth and sea 995
Helen, thy beauty is to me 743
Helen's lips are drifting dust 1220
Hence, all you vain delights 138
Hence loathèd Melancholy 197
Hence! thou lingerer, light! 446
Hence vain deluding Joys 193
"Henri Heine"—'tis here! 942
Her eyes the glow-worm lend thee 152
Her father lov'd me; oft invited me 95
Her long black hair danced round her like a snake . . . 1050
Her pealing organ was my neighbour too 408
Here a pretty baby lies 151
Here, Cyprian, is my jewelled looking-glass 1331
Here in the marshland, past the battered bridge 1146
Here, in this little Bay 962
Here lies a most beautiful lady 1242
Here lies David Garrick, describe me who can 316
Here lies our good Edmund, whose genius was such . . . 316
Here lies our Sovereign Lord the King 252
"Here lieth One whose name was writ on water" 600
Here lived the soul enchanted 740
Here Reynolds is laid, and, to tell you my mind 316
Here, where the world is quiet 1014
Here's an example from 1227
High grace, the dower of queens; and therewithal . . . 975
High walls and huge the body may confine 688
His being was in her alone 46
His brow spreads large and placid, and his eye 1086
Ho, brother! Art thou prisoned too? 1163
Home they brought her warrior dead 805
Honour and shame from no condition rise 271
How beautiful is night! 476
How blest the Maid whose heart —yet free 421
How changed is here each spot man makes or fills! . . . 933
How do I love thee? Let me count the ways 692
How falls it, oriole, thou hast come to fly 1079
How fearful and dizzy 'tis 94
How happy is he born and taught 121
How happy is the little stone 1002
How it sings, sings, sings 1035
How light we go, how soft we skim! 876
How like a winter hath my absence been 110
How like the stars are these white, nameless faces . . . 1291
How many a father have I seen 813
How many paltry, foolish, painted things 55
How much of Godhood did it take 1304
How near to good is what is fair! 131

INDEX BY FIRST LINES

	PAGE
How shall I sing of Her that is	1320
How sleep the brave, who sink to rest	295
How soon, alas, the hours are over	482
How sweet I roamed from field to field	331
How sweet the moonlight sleeps upon this bank!	70
How sweet this morning air in spring	1225
How vainly men themselves amaze	225
How wonderful is Death	591
Hyd, Absolon, thy gilte tresses clere	14

I

I am a lake, altered by every wind	1300
I am a tongue for beauty. Not a day	1333
I am as a spirit who has dwelt	564
I am fevered with the sunset	1175
I am not covetous for gold	79
I am the Dark Cavalier; I am the Last Lover	1363
I am the torch, she saith, and what to me	1176
I am thy father's spirit	97
I arise from dreams of thee	563
I ask no more for wonders: let me be	1334
I ask no organ's soulless breath	737
I blew, I blew, the trumpet loudly sounding	962
I bring fresh showers for the thirsting flowers	565
I cannot change, as others do	252
I cannot look upon thy grave	1204
I climb the hill: from end to end	818
I come from haunts of coot and hern	828
I could wish to be dead!	1095
I dare not ask your very all	1106
I do not count the hours I spend	679
I do not love thee for that fair	176
I do not love to see your beauty fire	1318
I do not pray for peace nor ease	1273
I doubt not God is good, well-meaning, kind	1344
I drank at every vine	1336
I dreamed that, as I wandered by the way	572
I envy not in any moods	812
I envy not the Lark his song divine	1148
I fill this cup to one made up	645
I fled Him, down the nights and down the days	1155
I flung my soul to the air like a falcon flying	1308
I found no beauty on the mountain heights	1261
I gathered with a careless hand	1306
I had a sudden vision in the night	1357
I had no heart to join the dance	1188
I, hapless soul, that never knew a friend	165
I have a rendezvous with Death	1325
I have been here before	980
I have been sure of three things all my life	1331
I have done one braver thing	136
I have done the state some service, and they know't	97
I have had playmates, I have had companions	485
I have loved flowers that fade	1056
I heard a bird at break of day	1300
I heard a soldier sing some trifle	1180
I heard a thousand blended notes	370
I heard a voice that cried, "Make way for those who died!"	1299
I heard the trailing garments of the Night	695
I held it truth, with him who sings	809
I hung my verses in the wind	8
I intended an Ode	1033
I know how to hold	1105

	PAGE
I know not but in every leaf	1062
I know that all the moon decays	142
I know that face!	1168
I know that virtue to be in you, Brutus	83
I know the night is near at hand	994
I know you are too dear to stay	1327
I know you: solitary griefs	1194
I leant upon a coppice gate	1037
I leave thy praises unexpress'd	816
I looked and saw your eyes in the shadow of your hair	985
I love all beauteous things	1058
I made another garden, yea	1052
I many times thought peace had come	1001
I marked all kindred Powers the heart finds fair	973
I met a traveller from an antique land	546
I mind, love, how it ever was this way	1266
I must go down to the seas again, to the lonely sea and the sky	1252
I must not grieve my Love, whose eyes would read	53
I must not think of thee; and, tired yet strong	1098
I never drank of Aganippe well	42
I never gave a lock of hair away	691
I never knew the earth had so much gold	1303
I never may believe	68
I never saw a moor	1000
I pant for the music which is divine	582
I prithee send me back my heart	209
I read, before my eyelids dropt their shade	13
I remember, I remember	634
I said—Then, dearest, since 'tis so	850
I said: "There is an end of my desire	1199
I saw Eternity the other night	234
I saw fair Chloris walk alone	1395
I saw God. Do you doubt it?	1285
I saw him dead: a leaden slumber lies	228
I saw my lady weep	1377
I saw thee once—once only—years ago	750
I see His blood upon the rose	1322
I shall be beautiful when you come back	1362
I shall be loved as quiet things	1265
I shall never hear her more	906
I shall th' effect of this good lesson keep	89
I shot an arrow into the air	704
I sing of brooks, of blossoms, birds and bowers	ix
I sometimes hold it half a sin	809
I stood and saw my Mistress dance	179
I struck the board and cried, No more	175
I tell thee, Dick, where I have been	206
I think that I shall never see	1312
I thought of Thee, my partner and my guide	423
I thought once how Theocritus had sung	689
I travelled among unknown men	376
I wander through each chartered street	337
I wandered in the forest	338
I wandered lonely as a cloud	402
I weep for Adonais—he is dead!	525
I well remember that the year was old	1207
I who am dead a thousand years	1297
I, who have lost the stars, the sod	1359
I will arise and go now, and go to Innisfree	1179
I will go back to the great sweet mother	1025
I will make you brooches and toys for your delight	1093
I will paint her as I see her	692
I wish I were where Helen lies	1385

PAGE

I wonder, by my troth, what thou and I 133
I wonder how 1278
I write. He sits beside my chair 1076
I'll ne'er believe that the Arch-Architect 57
If all the flowers of all the fields on earth 484
If all the pens that ever poets held 59
If all the world and love were young 39
If any God should say 1182
If aught of oaten stop, or pastoral song 295
If I can bear your love like a lamp before me 1295
If I had thought thou couldst have died 516
If I have faltered more or less 1092
If I should die, think only this of me 1324
If I were dead, and, in my place 233
If it were done when 'tis done, then 'twere well . . . 86
If music be the food of love, play on 74
If one should give me a heart to keep 1050
If parts allure thee, think how Bacon shined 271
If plagues or earthquakes break not Heav'n's design . . . 267
If the red slayer think he slays 678
If thou must love me, let it be for naught 690
If thou would'st view fair Melrose aright 429
If to grow old in Heaven is to grow young 978
If with light head erect I sing 869
If you have a carrier-dove 1005
In a coign of the cliff between lowland and highland . . 1017
In a drear-nighted December 627
In a small chamber, friendless and unseen 883
In after days when grasses high 1034
In an old book at even as I read 1264
In Angel-Court the sunless air 1033
In Baalbec there were lovers 1293
In Flanders fields the poppies blow 1235
In Heaven a spirit doth dwell 767
In his cool hall, with haggard eyes 951
In lazy apathy let stoics boast 268
In life's low vale, the soil the virtues like 272
In Love, if Love be Love, if Love be ours 802
In many forms we try 683
In May, when sea-winds pierced our solitudes 659
In praise of little children I will say 1075
In solitary rooms, when dusk is falling 1063
In the ancient town of Bruges 698
In the fair picture of my life's estate 1292
In the great morning of the world 539
In the greenest of our valleys 759
In the highlands, in the country places 1093
In the hour of my distress 151
In the long sunny afternoon 669
In the market-place of Bruges stands the belfry old and brown 699
In the merry month of May 23
In the old house where we dwelt 1053
In the Spring a fuller crimson comes upon the robin's breast . 797
In the worst inn's worst room, with mat half-hung . . . 274
In vain, sedate reflections we would make 272
In Xanadu did Kubla Khan 471
In youth from rock to rock I went 391
Into the silver night 1091
Into the woods my Master went 1046
Iron, left in the rain 1353
Is it thy will thy image should keep open 106
"Is there anybody there?" said the Traveller 1241
Is there for honest poverty 357
Is this a dagger which I see before me 87

PAGE

Is thy name Mary, maiden fair? 836
It chanced of late a shepherd's swain 1379
It fell in the ancient periods 684
It fortifies my soul to know 876
It is a beauteous evening, calm and free 387
It is an ancient Mariner 449
It is not growing like a tree 130
It is not to be thought of that the Flood 389
It is time to be old 680
It lies not in our power to love or hate 61
It little profits that an idle king 795
It standeth so; a deed is do' 1370
It was a lover and his lass 73
It was many and many a year ago 757
It was not in the winter 635
It was not like your great and gracious ways! . . . 961
It was the Rainbow gave thee birth 1223
It was the winter wild 202
It's a lonely road through bogland to the lake at Carrowmore . . 1201

J

Jack and Joan they think no ill 119
John Anderson, my jo, John 350
Join voices, all ye living souls, ye birds 185
Joy comes and goes, hope ebbs and flows 910
Joy, shipmate, joy! 902
Just for a handful of silver he left us 841

K

Kathleen Mavourneen! the grey dawn is breaking . . . 651
Kind are her answers 118
Know then thyself, presume not God to scan 267
Know'st thou not that when the searching eye 77

L

Lady, when I behold the roses sprouting 1377
Lars Porsena of Clusium 636
Last night, ah, yesternight, betwixt her lips and mine . . 1199
Last night, among his fellow roughs 837
Last night I woke and found between us drawn . . . 1090
Lawn as white as driven snow 75
Lead, kindly Light, amid the encircling gloom 644
Leave me awhile, for you have been too long 1307
Let me go where'er I will 682
Let me live out my years in heat of blood! 1273
Let me not to the marriage of true minds 113
Let others sing of Knights and Paladines 54
Let us begin and carry up this corpse 853
Let's contend no more, Love 843
Life and Thought have gone away 781
Life may be given in many ways 883
Life of Life! thy lips enkindle 524
Life! we've been long together 325
Life's a name 221
Lift not the painted veil which those who live . . . 559
Light flows our war of mocking words, and yet . . . 922
Light-winged Smoke, Icarian bird 870
Like a young child who to his mother's door 1290
Like as a flamelet blanketed in smoke 1085
Like as a ship, that through the ocean wide 28

PAGE

Like as the waves make towards the pebbled shore 105
Like the ghost of a dear friend dead 575
Like to Diana in her summer weed 52
Like to the clear in highest sphere 49
Like to the falling of a star 167
Like to the Pontick sea 97
Little gossip, blithe and hale 257
Little thinks, in the field, yon red-cloaked clown 652
Lo, as a dove when up she springs 811
Lo! Death has reared himself a throne 763
Lo, the poor Indian! whose untutor'd mind 266
Lo! 'tis a gala night 760
Lo, when the Lord made North and South 957
Lo! where the rosy-bosomed Hours 286
Long fed on boundless hopes, O race of man 911
Long I followed happy guides 663
Look off, dear Love, across the sallow sands 1041
"Lord, being dark," I said, "I cannot bear 1344
Lord, living, here are we 145
Lord of my heart's elation 1166
Love hath his poppy-wreath 1039
Love in her eyes sits playing 259
Love in thy youth, fair maid, be wise 1383
Love is and was my Lord and King 820
Love is enough: though the World be a-waning 1007
Love me not for comely grace 1391
Love seeketh not itself to please 334
Love still has something of the sea 250
Love thyself last: cherish those hearts that hate thee . . . 82
Love within the lover's breast 986
Loveliest of trees, the cherry now 1151
Loving in truth, and fain in verse my love to show . . . 7
Low was our pretty Cot: our tallest rose 446

M

Maiden! with the meek, brown eyes 695
Man is his own star; and the soul that can 138
Man's love is of man's life a thing apart 511
Many a green isle needs must be 546
Many are the doors of the spirit that lead 1339
Many are the wand-bearers 1114
Mary! I want a lyre with other strings 322
Maxwelton banks are bonnie 255
May! Be thou never graced with birds that sing . . . 165
Me miserable! which way shall I fly 185
Memory, hither come 332
Men are but children of a larger growth 250
Men of England, wherefore plough 560
Men said he saw strange visions 643
Merry Margaret 21
Methought I saw my late espousèd saint 206
Methought I saw the grave where Laura lay 40
Methought what pain it was to drown 80
Midst others of less note, came one frail Form 518
Milton! thou should'st be living at this hour 383
Mine be a cot beside the hill 360
Mine eyes have seen the glory of the coming of the Lord . . 886
Mortality, behold, and fear 140
Most potent, grave, and reverend signiors 95
Mother of Hermes! and still youthful Maia! 626
Mowers, weary and brown, and blithe 1054
Much have I travell'd in the realms of gold 601
Music I heard with you was more than music 1334

PAGE

Music, when soft voices die 578
My Daphne's hair is twisted gold 48
My days among the Dead are passed 475
My dear mistress has a heart 253
My debt to you, Belovèd 1362
My delight and thy delight 1057
My enemy came nigh 1285
My father is a quiet man 1351
My Girl, thou gazest much 21
My God and King! to Thee 234
My grandsire sailed three years from home 1209
My heart aches, and a drowsy numbness pains 617
My heart leaps up when I behold 379
My life closed twice before its close 1001
My light thou art, without thy glorious sight 253
My little Son, who looked from thoughtful eyes 960
My lov'd, my honour'd, much respected friend 340
My lute, awake, perform the last 26
My lute, be as thou wert when thou didst grow 143
My mind has thunderstorms 1227
My mind to me a kingdom is 27
My only Love is always near 905
My Phillis hath the morning sun 50
My silks and fine array 331
My Sorrow, when she's here with me 1258
My soul, sit thou a patient looker-on 166
My thoughts hold mortal strife 141
My true-love hath my heart, and I have his 46
Mysterious Night! when our first parent knew 487

N

Nature denied him much 366
Nature, in thy largess, grant 1219
Nature reads not our labels, "great" and "small" . . . 1082
Nay but you, who do not love her 843
Nay, Lord, not thus! white lilies in the spring 1140
Nay, why should I fear Death 1221
Never seek to tell thy love 337
Never the time and the place 866
Next Marlowe, bathed in the Thespian springs 58
Night is the shadow of the Earth, but we 1078
No coward soul is mine 872
No longer mourn for me when I am dead 107
No more, my Dear, no more these counsels try 41
No, no, go not to Lethe, neither twist 624
Nor force nor fraud shall sunder us! Oh ye 964
Not a drum was heard, not a funeral note 517
Not as all other women are 877
Not from a vain or shallow thought 653
Not I myself know all my love for thee 975
Not if men's tongues and angels' all in one 1027
Not long ago it was a bird 1301
Not marble, nor the gilded monuments 104
Not of the princes and prelates with periwigged charioteers . . 1251
Not on sad Stygian shore, nor in clear sheen 1007
Not she with traitorous kiss her Saviour stung 499
Not, Silence, for thine idleness I raise 1101
"Not to be tuneless in old age!" 694
Not unto us, O Lord 1397
Nothing is enough! 1205
Now at thy soft recalling voice I rise 1045
Now is the gentle season, freshly flowering 1378

INDEX BY FIRST LINES

	PAGE
Now is the time, when all the lights wax dim	159
Now is the winter of our discontent	80
Now let no charitable hope	1365
Now, sometimes in my sorrow shut	812
Now stir the fire, and close the shutters fast	323
Now that the moonlight withers from the sky	1343
Now the autumn shudders	1335
Now the bright morning star, day's harbinger	203
Now the hungry lion roars	69
Now the last day of many days	585
Now there is frost upon the hill	1342
Now whither hast thou flown?	1208
Now winter nights enlarge	115
Now, youth, the hour of thy dread passion comes	1361
Nuns fret not at their convent's narrow room	413

O

O, a gallant set were they	1171
O bird that somewhere yonder sings	1190
O bitter moon, O cold and bitter moon	1332
O blithe New-Comer! I have heard	400
O Brignal banks are wild and fair	436
O Captain! my Captain! our fearful trip is done	887
O Christ of God! whose life and death	738
O could I flow like thee, and make thy stream	216
O Earth, lie heavily upon her eyes	998
O Earth-and-Autumn of the setting sun	9
O fair and stately maid, whose eyes	666
O fair! O sweet! when I do look on thee	44
O, fairest of the rural maids	599
O Faustus	60
O Friend! I know not which way I must look	388
O frivolous mind of man	914
O Galuppi, Baldassare, this is very sad to find!	845
O God of earth and altar	1247
O God, the cleanest offering	1062
O Goddess! hear these tuneless numbers, wrung	621
O Happiness! our being's end and aim!	270
O happy Thames that didst my Stella bear!	42
O! how much more doth beauty beauteous seem	104
O! how thy worth with manners may I sing	104
O, it is pleasant, with a heart at ease	475
O! lest the world should task you to recite	107
O Lord of all compassionate control	vii
O mistress mine! where are you roaming?	74
O monstrous, dead, unprofitable world	651
O Most High Almighty Good Lord God	953
O Mother State, how quenched thy Sinai fires!	882
O my dark Rosaleen	646
O, my luve is like a red, red rose	352
O Nightingale, that on yon bloomy spray	204
O Nightingale! thou surely art	420
O nothing, in this corporal earth of man	1162
O Proserpina!	75
O Queen, awake to thy renown	956
O ruddier than the cherry!	259
O, saw ye bonie Lesley	354
O saw ye not fair Ines?	630
O sing unto my roundelay	327
O singer of the field and fold	1034
O sleep! O gentle sleep!	78
O soft embalmer of the still midnight	627
O Sorrow, why dost borrow	602

PAGE

O Soul of Nature! excellent and fair! 409
O souls, in whom no heavenly fire is found 236
O Spring, I know thee! Seek for sweet surprise 1096
O stream descending to the sea 875
O Swallow, Swallow, flying, flying South 804
O! that this too too solid flesh would melt 88
O that 'twere possible 825
O Thou in the darkness far beyond the spheres 1342
O Thou, that with surpassing glory crowned 184
O Thou undaunted daughter of desires! 211
O Thou, who plumed with strong desire 573
O Thou whose equal purpose runs 1170
O Thou! whose fancies from afar are brought 390
O thou with dewy locks, who lookest down 330
O Time! who know'st a lenient hand to lay 359
O, to have a little house! 1281
O waly waly up the bank 1391
O, were my love yon lilac fair 359
O what a plague is love! 1392
O! what a rogue and peasant slave am I 91
O! who can hold a fire in his hand 76
O wild West Wind, thou breath of Autumn's being 561
O Woman! in our hours of ease 432
O world! O life! O time! 580
O yet we trust that somehow good 814
Och, would I were deep in Kilbarry 1280
O'er Carmel fields in the springtime the sea-gulls follow the plow . 1210
O'er Roslin all that dreary night 430
O'er the smooth enamelled green 201
O'er the swamp in the forest 1064
Of a' the airts the wind can blaw 350
Of Adam's first wife, Lilith, it is told 984
Of all the girls that are so smart 279
Of all the souls that stand create 1001
Of caterpillars Fabre tells how day after day 1305
Of comfort no man speak 77
Of him she banished now let Athens boast 1069
Of Man's first disobedience, and the fruit 183
Of old sat Freedom on the heights 794
Of these the false Achitophel was first 240
Of this fair volume which we World do name 144
Oft have I mused, but now at length I find 47
Oft have I seen at some cathedral door 708
Oft in the stilly night 495
Oft when my spirit doth spread her bolder wings 29
Oh, a dainty plant is the Ivy green 839
Oh, bless the law that veils the Future's face 1060
Oh! blest with temper, whose unclouded ray 273
Oh! breathe not his name, let it sleep in the shade 491
Oh! Death will find me, long before I tire 1325
Oh, earlier shall the rosebuds blow 955
Oh, happy wind, how sweet 1226
Oh Rome! my country! city of the soul! 505
Oh! snatched away in beauty's bloom 501
Oh, to be in England 847
Old loveliness has such a way with me 1335
On a day, alack the day! 66
On a poet's lips I slept 524
On a starred night Prince Lucifer uprose 988
On either side the river lie 782
On her white breast a sparkling cross she wore 264
On Linden, when the sun was low 490
On the sea and at the Hogue, sixteen hundred ninety-two . . . 862

INDEX BY FIRST LINES

PAGE

On the way to Kew 1089
On the wide level of a mountain's head 448
On what foundation stands the warrior's pride 281
Once did She hold the gorgeous east in fee 387
Once it smiled a silent dell 762
Once more the Heavenly Power 832
Once Paumanok 896
Once upon a midnight dreary 744
One day I wrote her name upon the strand 29
One lesson, Nature, let me learn of thee 907
One made the surging sea of tone 1062
One morn as through Hyde Park we walk'd 1
One spirit, His who wore the platted thorns 324
One wept whose only child was dead 1099
One whitest lily, reddest rose 1084
One word is too often profaned 581
Only of thee and me the night wind sings 1303
Or I shall live your epitaph to make 108
Orphan Hours, the Year is dead 576
Orpheus with his lute made trees 81
Others abide our question. Thou art free 62
Our revels now are ended. These our actors 63
Out of a silence 1256
Out of my sorrow 1356
Out of the earth to rest or range 1253
Out of the hills of Habersham 1046
Out of the night that covers me 1088
Out of the night to my leafy porch they came 1105
Over his keys the musing organist 880
Over the mountains 1384

P

Pack, clouds, away! and welcome, day! 124
Pan, blow your pipes and I will be 1357
Pansies, lilies, kingcups, daisies 379
Pass, thou wild light 1147
Passing away, saith the World, passing away 996
Passions are liken'd best to floods and streams 36
Peace; come away: the song of woe 816
Peace flows into me 1295
Phœbus, arise 143
Philosophers are lined with eyes within 683
Phyllis is my only joy 252
Plato, thou reason'st well 255
Pleasures newly found are sweet 381
Poet and Saint! to thee alone are given 217
Poet of Nature, thou hast wept to know 543
Poets may boast, as safely vain 180
Poor, little, pretty, fluttering thing 254
Praise is devotion fit for mighty minds 180
Prayer is the soul's sincere desire 445
Proud Maisie is in the wood 442

Q

Queen and huntress, chaste and fair 129

R

Rarely, rarely comest thou 578
Remember me when I am gone away 997
Remote, unfriended, melancholy, slow 314
Renownèd Spenser, lie a thought more nigh . . . : . 141

PAGE

Riches I hold in light esteem 873
Ring out, wild bells, to the wild sky 819
Ring out your bells, let mourning shews be spread 44
Roll forth, my song, like the rushing river 649
Romance, who loves to nod and sing 742
Roses from Pæstan rosaries! 1195
Rough wind, that moanest loud 591
Round her she made an atmosphere of life 511
Rushing, ten thousand horsemen came 438

S

Sabrina fair, listen where thou art sitting 186
St. Agnes' Eve—Ah, bitter chill it was! 606
Say, for you saw us, ye immortal lights 219
Say not that beauty is an idle thing 1360
Say not that the past is dead 1031
Say not, the struggle naught availeth 874
Say that thou didst forsake me for some fault 110
Say, where full instinct is the unerring guide 269
Science! true daughter of Old Time thou art! 743
Scorn not the Sonnet; Critic, you have frowned 424
Scots, wha hae wi' Wallace bled 355
Season of mists and mellow fruitfulness 623
See how the flowers, as at parade 227
See the sole bliss Heaven could on all bestow! 271
See, what a grace was seated on this brow 93
See where she issues in her beauty's pomp 53
See with what simplicity 231
Seek not the spirit, if it hide 664
Self-love and reason to one end aspire 268
Self-love, the spring of motion, acts the soul 268
Serene, I fold my hands and wait 1029
Shall burning Etna, if a sage requires 270
Shall I compare thee to a summer's day? 101
Shall I strew on thee rose or rue or laurel 1019
Shall I, wasting in despair 147
She can be as wise as we 986
She doth tell me where to borrow 149
She dwelt among the untrodden ways 375
She had no saying dark enough 1260
She has the strange sweet grace of violets 1340
She is far from the land where her young hero sleeps . . . 493
She is the fairies' midwife, and she comes 82
She knelt upon her brother's grave 1002
She loved the Autumn, I the Spring 1188
She loves him; for her infinite soul is Love 978
She never told her love 75
She smiles and smiles, and will not sigh 916
"She stands breast high amid the corn" 1355
She stood breast high among the corn 635
She that was ever fair and never proud 96
She walks in beauty, like the night 501
She walks—the lady of my delight 1100
She was a Phantom of delight 401
She's somewhere in the sunlight strong 1188
She's tall and gaunt, and in her hard, sad face 1087
Should auld acquaintance be forgot 353
Shut not so soon; the dull-eyed night 154
Shut, shut the door, good John! fatigued I said 275
Sigh no more, ladies, sigh no more 65
Silver key of the fountain of tears 546
Simple, erect, severe, austere, sublime 506

INDEX BY FIRST LINES

	PAGE
Since brass, nor stone, nor earth, nor boundless sea	106
Since my dear soul was mistress of her choice	93
Since there's no help, come, let us kiss and part	56
Sing to Apollo, god of day	47
Singing is sweet; but be sure of this	1006
Sister, awake! close not your eyes!	1380
Sleep on, and dream of Heaven awhile	366
Slow, slow, fresh fount, keep time with my salt tears	131
"So careful of the type?" but no	815
So fallen! so lost! the light withdrawn	739
So far as I conceive the world's rebuke	909
So nigh is grandeur to our dust	684
So now my summer task is ended, Mary	520
So work the honey-bees	79
Soldier, rest! thy warfare o'er	433
Sombre and rich, the skies	1196
Some atheist or vile infidel in love	56
Some days my thoughts are just cocoons—all cold, and dull, and blind	1264
Some say the world will end in fire	1257
Some secrets may the poet tell	948
Some three, or five, or seven, and thirty years	1086
Something there is that doesn't love a wall	1257
Sometime it may be pleasing to remember	1328
Sometime it may be you and I	1203
Sometimes I fain would find in thee some fault	976
Somewhere afield here something lies	1036
Son of the ocean isle!	593
Soul of the age!	125
Souls of Poets dead and gone	622
Sound, sound the clarion, fill the fife!	441
Sounding brass and tinkling cymbal	1248
Speak not thy speech my boughs among	662
Speak not—whisper not	1242
Standing aloof in giant ignorance	626
Stars of the summer night!	697
Statesman, yet friend to truth! of soul sincere	275
Stay, Shepherd, prithee shepherd stay!	1390
Stern Daughter of the Voice of God!	404
Still let my tyrants know, I am not doom'd to wear	871
Still linger in our noon of time	738
Still to be neat, still to be dressed	129
Stop!—not to me, at this bitter departing	917
Strange little tune, so thin and rare	1340
Strangers yet!	780
Strew on her roses, roses	908
Stride the hill, sower	1282
Strings in the earth and air	1284
Strong Son of God, immortal Love	808
Such a starved bank of moss	866
Such hints as untaught Nature yields!	1221
Suddenly from a wayside station	1352
Sumer is icumen in	1370
Sunder me from my bones, O sword of God	1245
Sunset and evening star	833
Sure he that made us with such large discourse	94
Surprised by joy—impatient as the Wind	420
Swallow, my sister, O sister swallow	1012
Sweet Auburn! loveliest village of the plain	303
Sweet, be not proud of those two eyes	159
Sweet Chance, that led my steps abroad	1226
Sweet day, so cool, so calm, so bright	174
Sweet Echo, sweetest Nymph that liv'st unseen	186
Sweet Highland Girl, a very shower	396

PAGE

Sweet is the highroad when the skylarks call 1298
Sweet moon, endreaming tower and tree 1077
Sweet Stay-at-Home, sweet Well-content 1224
Sweet stream, that winds through yonder glade 320
Sweet twining hedgeflowers wind-stirred in no wise 974
Sweet was the song that Youth sang once 483
Swift as a shadow, short as any dream 67
Swifter far than summer's flight 580
Swiftly walk o'er the western wave 577

T

Take, O take those lips away 65
Take this kiss upon the brow! 764
Teach me, Father, how to go 1104
Tears, idle tears, I know not what they mean 804
Tears of the widower, when he sees 811
Tell me not, Sweet, I am unkind 216
Tell me not what too well I know 481
Tell me, thou Star, whose wings of light 575
Tell me, was Venus more beautiful 1250
Tell me where is fancy bred 69
Tell me, ye wand'ring Spirits of the air 1386
Thank Heaven! the crisis 769
Thanks for that insult.—I had too much peace 1263
That each from other differs, first confess 272
That son of Italy who tried to blow 7
That time of year thou may'st in me behold 107
That which her slender waist confined 181
That you are fair or wise is vain 656
The awful shadow of some unseen Power 543
The blessed damozel leaned out 965
The breaths of kissing night and day 1160
The Cadets of Gascoyne—the defenders 1270
The castled crag of Drachenfels 504
The chariest maid is prodigal enough 89
The curfew tolls the knell of parting day 288
The day before April 1354
The day is done, and the darkness 703
The day returns, my bosom burns 349
The dead make rules, and I obey 1353
The expense of spirit in a waste of shame 113
The forward violet thus did I chide 111
The fountains mingle with the river 564
The full sea rolls and thunders 1088
The gallant Youth, who may have gained 424
The glories of our blood and state 178
The great masters of the commonplace 1085
The green, green grass, the glittering grove 645
The grey sea and the long black land 843
The harp that once through Tara's halls 491
The hope I dreamed of was a dream 997
The hours I spent with thee, dear heart 1174
The isles of Greece, the isles of Greece! 511
The jonquils bloom round Samarcand 1141
The keen stars were twinkling 590
The Lady Poverty was fair 1100
The lapse of time and rivers is the same 320
The lark now leaves his watery nest 170
The last and greatest herald of heaven's King 142
The lost days of my life until to-day 980
The low-voiced girls that go 1103
The maid I love ne'er thought of me 479

PAGE

The man Flammonde, from God knows where 1213
The man of life upright 117
The man that hath no music in himself 70
The Martyr worthiest of the bleeding name 687
The merchant, to secure his treasure 254
The merry waves dance up and down and play 217
The merry World did on a day 172
The morns are meeker than they were 1000
The mountain sheep are sweeter 498
The mountains they are silent folk 1164
The murmur of the mourning ghost . . . . . . ° 963
The night has a thousand eyes 1103
The night will never stay 1356
The nightingale, as soon as April bringeth 44
The old eternal spring once more 1168
The old order changeth, yielding place to new 795
The other side of Death, one night 1353
The pedigree of honey 1002
The quality of mercy is not strain'd 70
The redbreast oft, at evening hours 300
The room is full of the peace of night 1298
The royal feast was done; the King 1039
The russet leaves of the sycamore 1211
The sea called 1314
The sea is calm to-night 918
The seas are quiet when the winds give o'er 181
The seraph Abdiel, faithful found 186
The silver silence of the moon 1338
The skies they were ashen and sober 752
The sky is changed!—and such a change! Oh night . . . 505
The sleepless Hours who watch me as I lie 570
The South-wind brings 670
The splendour falls on castle walls 803
The Spring blew trumpets of color 1294
The stranger in my gates—lo! that am I 1212
The sun is warm, the sky is clear 558
The sun that brief December day 717
The sun, the moon, the stars, the seas, the hills and the plains . 801
The sun upon the Weirdlaw Hill 441
The sunlight speaks, and its voice is a bird 1293
The things which these proud men despise, and call . . . 219
The thirsty earth soaks up the rain 216
The trivial harp will never please 685
The twentieth year is wellnigh past 320
The wanton troopers riding by 223
The way was long, the wind was cold 428
The wedded light and heat 7
The wind blows out of the gates of the day 1179
The wisest of the wise 480
The wish, that of the living whole 814
The woman's cause is man's: they rise or sink 807
The wonder of the world is o'er 1202
The wood is bare: a river-mist is steeping 1055
The woods decay, the woods decay and fall 829
The world is too much with us; late and soon 413
The world's a theatre. The earth, a stage 166
The world's great age begins anew 540
The year's at the spring 841
Thee, dear friend, a brother soothes 654
Then gently scan your brother man 348
Ther was also a Nonne, a Prioress 16
There are gains for all our losses 965
There be none of Beauty's daughters 500
There be who are afraid to fear 1117

	PAGE
There beyond my window ledge	1299
There came an image in Life's retinue	976
There is a flower, the lesser Celandine	403
There is a garden in her face	116
There is a lady sweet and kind	1382
There is a lonely stream afar in a lone dim land	1120
There is a mirror in my room	1330
There is a mountain and a wood between us	481
There is a panther caged within my breast	1322
There is a pleasure in the pathless woods	506
There is a tale of Faustus,—that one day	1061
There is a tide in the affairs of men	85
There is delight in singing, though none hear	840
There lies a vale in Ida, lovelier	787
There rolls the deep where grew the tree	820
There they are, my fifty men and women	856
There was a roaring in the wind all night	382
There was a sound of revelry by night	502
There was a time when meadow, grove, and stream	414
There was never a sound beside the wood but one	1259
There, where death's brief pang was quickest	500
There's a woman like a dew-drop, she's so purer than the purest	849
These are the best of him	339
These are thy glorious works, Parent of good	185
These hearts were woven of human joys and cares	1324
These little shoes!—How proud she was of these!	1077
These many years since we began to be	1013
They are all gone into the world of light	232
They are not long, the weeping and the laughter	1198
They brought me with a secret glee	1294
They close, in clouds of smoke and dust	432
They grew in beauty, side by side	592
They have no song, the sedges dry	991
They pass me by like shadows, crowds on crowds	885
They put their finger on their lip	683
They sin who tell us Love can die	476
They stand between the mountains and the sea	363
They told me, Heraclitus, they told me you were dead	954
They wear their evening light as women wear	1306
They went forth to battle, but they always fell	1311
Thin-legged, thin-chested, slight unspeakably	1087
Think thou and act; to-morrow thou shalt die	979
Thinking of shores that I shall never see	1205
This bronze doth keep the very form and mold	1048
This figure that thou here seest put	127
This grace vouchsafe me for the rhymes I write	1078
This is a spray the Bird clung to	848
This is her picture as she was	969
This is the Arsenal. From floor to ceiling	701
This is the burden of the middle years	1292
This is the forest primeval. The murmuring pines and the hem- locks	705
This is the month, and this the happy morn	201
This is the ship of pearl, which, poets feign	835
This light and darkness in our chaos join'd	269
This royal throne of kings, this scepter'd isle	76
This was the noblest Roman of them all	86
Thou art the Way	1099
Thou blossom bright with autumn dew	598
Thou God of this great vast, rebuke these surges	99
Thou, Scythian-like, dost round thy lands above	220
Thou still unravish'd bride of quietness	619
Thou, to whom the world unknown	301

INDEX BY FIRST LINES

PAGE

Thou, too, sail on, O Ship of State! 706
Thou wast that all to me, love 761
Thou who hast slept all night upon the storm 887
Thou youngest Virgin-Daughter of the skies 242
Though joy is better than sorrow joy is not great 1323
Though love repine, and reason chafe 682
Three poets, in three distant ages born 183
Three Summers since I chose a maid 1365
Three years she grew in sun and shower 376
Thrice happy he who by some shady grove 142
Thrice toss these oaken ashes in the air 116
Through the black, rushing smoke-bursts 950
Throughout the land and sea from ancient days 1073
Throw away Thy rod 173
Thus in the gloom and solitude of thought 1030
Thus kiss I your fair hands, taking my leave 168
Thus while the days flew by, and years passed on . . . 407
Thy beauty haunts me heart and soul 1226
Thy bosom is endeared with all hearts 103
Thy shores are empires, changed in all save thee 507
Thy voice is on the rolling air 821
Tiger, tiger, burning bright 334
Tired Nature's sweet restorer, balmy Sleep 258
'Tis a dull sight 778
'Tis the last rose of summer 492
'Tis time this heart should be unmoved 515
To ask for all thy love, and thy whole heart 1382
To be a sweetness more desired than Spring 977
To be, or not to be: that is the question 92
To drift with every passion till my soul 1139
To fill the gap, to bear the brunt 1173
To find the Western path 336
To gild refinèd gold, to paint the lily 76
To him who in the love of Nature holds 595
To live within a cave—it is most good 1003
To look on love with disenamoured eyes 1338
To make a final conquest of all me 228
To make a happy fireside clime 359
To me, fair friend, you never can be old 112
To Mercy, Pity, Peace and Love 333
To my true king I offered, free from stain 643
To one who has been long in city pent 600
To see a world in a grain of sand 335
To the Ocean now I fly 187
To thee, fair freedom! I retire 283
To tremble, when I touch her hands 1119
To wake the soul by tender strokes of art 265
To you he gave his laughter and his jest 1249
To-day I saw the shop-girl go 1367
To-morrow, and to-morrow, and to-morrow 88
Too late I stayed—forgive the crime 367
Toussaint, the most unhappy man of men! 387
Tread lightly here, for here, 'tis said 361
Tread lightly, she is near 1140
True Thomas lay on Huntlie bank 1386
Trusty, dusky, vivid, true 1092
Truth is the trial of itself 127
Tune me for life again, O quiet Musician 1366
Turn, turn, my wheel! Turn round and round 709
'Twas at the royal feast for Persia won 236
'Twas at this season, year by year 1148
'Twas August, and the fierce sun overhead 911
'Twas not alone thy beauty's power 1030
Twenty years hence my eyes may grow 479

INDEX BY FIRST LINES

	PAGE
Two lovers by a moss-grown spring	904
Two roads diverged in a yellow wood	1260
Two Voices are there; one is of the sea	419
Two went to pray? oh, rather say	212

U

Under dusky laurel leaf	1363
Under the arch of Life, where love and death	985
Under the greenwood tree	71
Under the wide and starry sky	1093
Under yonder beech-tree single on the green-sward	988
Underneath this sable hearse	164
Unfathomable Sea! whose waves are years	578
Unlike are we, unlike, O princely Heart!	689
Up from the darkness on the laughing stage	1339
Up with me! up with me into the clouds!	405
Upon this leafy bush	1242

V

Vain is the chiming of forgotten bells	1311
Verse, a breeze 'mid blossoms straying	473
Very old are the woods	1239
Very true, the linnets sing	484
Vice is a monster of so frightful mien	269
Victorious men of earth, no more	178
Voice of the western wind!	1004

W

Wake! For the Sun who scattered into flight	772
Was it the proud full sail of his great verse	109
Was this the face that launch'd a thousand ships	59
Watch thou and fear; to-morrow thou shalt die	979
We are as clouds that veil the midnight moon	542
We are not free: Freedom doth not consist	879
We are the music-makers	1048
We are the roadside flowers	1167
We are the singing shadows beauty casts	1333
We cannot kindle when we will	921
We count the broken lyres that rest	834
We few, we happy few, we band of brothers	60
We were apart; yet, day by day	912
We were not many —we who stood	693
We who by shipwreck only find the shores	885
We've trod the maze of error round	329
Wearers of rings and chains	482
Weary of myself, and sick of asking	920
Wee, modest, crimson-tippèd flow'r	347
Wee, sleekit, cowrin, tim'rous beastie	345
Weep you no more, sad fountains	1378
Welcome, maids of honour	150
Welcome, welcome, do I sing	163
Welcome, wild North-easter!	902
Well then, I now do plainly see	218
Were I a trembling leaf	445
Were I as base as is the lowly plain	57
Were I so tall to reach the pole	257
Were there one whose fires	276
Whan that Aprille with his shoures sote	15
What can atone (O ever-injured shade!)	264
What can I give thee back, O liberal	690

PAGE

What constitutes a State? 325
What delightful hosts are they 1114
What heart could have thought you? 1159
What is love of one's land? 1236
What is the existence of man's life 167
What is this life if, full of care 1223
What matter where the Apple grows? 1327
What needs complaints 155
What needs my Shakespeare for his honoured bones . . 203
What nothing earthly gives, or can destroy 271
What of her glass without her? The blank grey . . . 977
"What of vile dust?" the preacher said 1245
What precious thing are you making fast 1005
What shall I your true-love tell 1161
What shall we do for Love these days? 1274
What shape so furtive steals along the dim 1369
What thing unto mine ear 981
What things have we seen 140
What's hallowed ground? Has earth a clod . . . 487
Whatever way my days decline 817
When a storm comes up at night and the wind is crying . . 1331
When colour goes home into the eyes 1324
When daisies pied and violets blue 66
When, dearest, I but think of thee 210
When do I see thee most, belovèd one? 973
When down the windy vistas of the years 1333
When fishes flew and forests walked 1248
When God at first made man 172
When I am dead, my dearest 995
When I am living in the Midlands 1229
When I am old 1198
When I am old, and think of the old days 1177
When I am standing on a mountain crest 1176
When I am tired of earnest men 1312
When I consider every thing that grows 101
When I consider how my light is spent 205
When I consider life, 'tis all a cheat 236
When I do count the clock that tells the time . . . 100
When I have borne in memory what has tamed . . . 390
When I have fears that I may cease to be 625
When I invade my secret soul 1361
When I look into a glass 1228
When I would image her features 987
When icicles hang by the wall 67
When, in disgrace with fortune and men's eyes . . . 102
When in the chronicle of wasted time 112
When in the dim beginning of the years 1109
When Israel, of the Lord beloved 444
When, jars unsealed 1279
When lilacs last in the dooryard bloomed 888
When Love with unconfinèd wings 215
When maidens such as Hester die 486
When men shall find thy flower, thy glory pass . . . 53
When Music, heavenly maid, was young 297
When music sounds, gone is the earth I know . . . 1244
When one, that holds communion with the skies . . . 317
When our two souls stand up erect and strong . . . 691
When passion's trance is overpast 581
When she comes home again! A thousand ways . . . 1113
When the British Warrior Queen 318
When the hounds of spring are on winter's traces . . 1009
When the lamp is shattered 583
When the Norn Mother saw the Whirlwind Hour . . 1108
When the ripe pears droop heavily 1120

	PAGE
When the wind is low, and the sea is soft	1236
When thou must home to shades of underground	120
When to her lute Corinna sings	114
When to the sessions of sweet silent thought	102
When with a serious musing I behold	147
When you go up to die	1329
Whenas in silks my Julia goes	161
Whenever there is music, it is you	1307
Where art thou gone, light-ankled Youth?	483
Where lies the land to which the ship would go?	876
Where sunless rivers weep	999
Where the bee sucks, there suck I	63
Where the pools are bright and deep	367
Where the remote Bermudas ride	221
Where the thistle lifts a purple crown	1153
Where the waves of burning cloud are rolled	1269
Where weary folk toil, black with smoke	1354
Whether on Ida's shady brow	332
Whither, midst falling dew	597
Whither, O splendid ship, thy white sails crowding	1055
Who beckons the green ivy up	1238
Who doth ambition shun	71
Who drives the horses of the sun	1084
Who is it that says most? which can say more	109
Who is Silvia? what is she?	64
Who is the happy Warrior? Who is he	410
Who is the pioneer?	1358
"Who knocks?" "I, who was beautiful	1243
Who loves the rain	1233
Who prop, thou ask'st, in these bad days, my mind?	907
Who seeks perfection in the art	1278
Who thou art I know not	1293
Who walks with Beauty has no need of fear	1308
Who will believe my verse in time to come	101
Who would be a king	1271
Whoe'er she be	213
Whoe'er thou art, approach, and, with a sigh	362
Whose furthest footstep never strayed	1175
"Why?" Because all I haply can and do	867
Why did I write? what sin to me unknown	276
Why do our joys depart	479
Why do you seek the sun	1267
Why each is striving, from of old	953
Why, having won her, do I woo?	959
Why is my verse so barren of new pride	108
Why should this a desert be?	72
Why sit'st thou by that ruined hall	440
Why so pale and wan, fond lover?	210
Why weep ye by the tide, ladie?	439
Why, why repine, my pensive friend	481
Wide waters in the waste; or, out of reach	1102
Wild as the scream of the curlew	435
Wind-washed and free, full-swept by rain and wave	1289
With fame in just proportion envy grows	259
With fingers weary and worn	631
With how sad steps, O Moon, thou climb'st the skies!	40
With little here to do or see	393
With more than mortal powers endow'd	431
With rue my heart is laden	1150
With the year seasons return	184
With us ther was a Doctour of Phisyk	17
Women are door-mats and have been	1355
Would I were one of those who preach no Cause	1172

INDEX BY FIRST LINES

PAGE

Would that the structure brave, the manifold music I build . . 858
Wouldst see blithe looks, fresh cheeks beguile 214
Wouldst thou hear what man can say 126

Y

Ye banks and braes and streams around 356
Ye banks and braes o' bonie Doon 352
Ye distant spires, ye antique towers 283
Ye have been fresh and green 160
Ye little birds that sit and sing 122
Ye living lamps, by whose dear light 230
Yea, gold is son of Zeus: no rust 1094
Years ago when I was at Balliol 1231
Yes, I am proud, I must be proud to see 277
Yes! in the sea of life enisled 913
Yes, it was the mountain Echo 412
Yes, you may let them creep about the rug 1076
Yet if his majesty our sovereign lord 1385
Yet once more, O ye Laurels, and once more 188
You are a tulip seen to-day 153
You came to me bearing bright roses 1251
You have not heard my love's dark throat 1350
You have taught me laughter 1362
You meaner beauties of the night 120
You must mean more than just this hour 1192
You promise heavens free from strife 955
You saw the last fires burning on the hill 1337
You say, but with no touch of scorn 817
You spotted snakes with double tongue 68
You wear the morning like your dress 1232
Your dying lips were proud and sweet 1328
Your eyën two wol slee me sodenly 14
Your hearts are lifted up, your hearts 1206
Youth rambles on life's arid mount 919

SUPPLEMENTARY INDEX
BY AUTHORS, TITLES AND FIRST LINES

INDEX BY AUTHORS

Title	Opening Phrase	PAGE
ADAMS, LÉONIE (U.S.A.), 1899		1443
The River in the Meadows	Crystal parting the meads	1443
AUSLANDER, JOSEPH (U.S.A.), 1897-		1435
Steel	This man is dead	1435
BACON, LEONARD (U.S.A.), 1887-		1420
"Io Ritornai Dalla Santissima Onda"	There is dogwood in my soul	1420
BENÉT, STEPHEN VINCENT (U.S.A.), 1898-		1440
The Ballad of William Sycamore	My father, he was a mountaineer	1440
BOGAN, LOUISE (U.S.A.), 1897-		1434
Medusa	I had come to the house, in a cave of trees	1434
CAMPBELL, ROY (South Africa), 1901-		1448
The Zebras	From the dark woods that breathe of fallen showers	1448
COFFIN, ROBERT P. TRISTRAM (U.S.A.), 1892-		1429
Crystal Moment	Once or twice this side of death	1429
CONKLING, GRACE HAZARD (U.S.A.), 1878-		1414
Python	A lithe beautiful fear	1414
CRANE, HART (U.S.A.), 1899-1932		1444
Powhatan's Daughter	A cyclone threshes in the turbine crest	1444
"D., H." (U.S.A.), 1886-		1418
Fourth Song from Cyprus	Where is the nightingale	1418
DORO, EDWARD (U.S.A.)		1450
The Boar and Shibboleth	I was eleven, hardly more	1450
ELIOT, T. S. (U.S.A.), 1888-		1420
Sweeney Among the Nightingales	Apeneck Sweeney spreads his knees	1420
ENGLE, PAUL (U.S.A.), 1909-		1455
Mary	You said I would forget you, forget your lithe	1455
FLETCHER, JOHN GOULD (U.S.A.), 1886-		1418
The Swan	Under a wall of bronze	1418
GIBSON, WILFRID WILSON (England), 1878-		1412
A Catch For Singing	Said the Old Young Man to the Young Old Man—	1412

1561

INDEX BY AUTHORS

Title	*Opening Phrase*	PAGE
GREGORY, HORACE (U.S.A.), 1898-		1442
"Through Streets Where Crooked Wicklow Flows"	Through streets where crooked Wicklow flows	1442
GUINEY, LOUISE IMOGEN (U.S.A.), 1861-1920		1403
The Kings	A Man said unto his Angel:	1403
HUGHES, RICHARD (England), 1900-		1446
Ecstatic Ode on Vision	Low stooped the oaks like eagles	1446
KUNITZ, STANLEY J. (U.S.A.),		1449
Lovers Relentlessly	Lovers relentlessly contend to be	1449
MACLEISH, ARCHIBALD (U.S.A.), 1892-		1428
You, Andrew Marvell	And here face down beneath the sun	1428
MOODY, WILLIAM VAUGHN (U.S.A.), 1869-1910		1404
The Brute	Through his might men work their wills	1404
OLSON, ELDER (U.S.A.),		1452
Essay on Deity	God's body is all space	1452
OWEN, WILFRED (England), 1893-1918		1431
Apologia Pro Poemate Meo	I, too, saw God through mud,—	1431
RANSOM, JOHN CROWE (U.S.A.), 1888-		1422
Here Lies a Lady	Here lies a lady of beauty and high degree	1422
REESE, LIZETTE WOODWORTH (U.S.A.), 1856-1935		1403
Tears	When I consider Life and its few years—	1403
RIDGE, LOLA (Ireland), 1884-		1415
Réveille	Come forth, you workers!	1415
SANDBURG, CARL (U.S.A.), 1878-		1413
Prayers of Steel	Lay me on an anvil, O God	1413
SARETT, LEW (U.S.A.), 1886-		1419
Four Little Foxes	Speak gently, Spring, and make no sudden sound;	1419
SITWELL, EDITH (England), 1890-		1422
Colonel Fantock	Thus spoke the lady underneath the trees:	1422
SITWELL, OSBERT (England), 1892-		1426
Elegy for Mr. Goodbeare	Do you remember Mr. Goodbeare, the carpenter	1426
SPENDER, STEPHEN (England), 1909-		1454
"I Think Continually of Those—"	I think continually of those who were truly great	1454
STEVENS, WALLACE (U.S.A.), 1879-		1414
The Worms at Heaven's Gate	Out of the tomb, we bring Badroulbadour	1414

INDEX BY AUTHORS

Title	Opening Phrase	PAGE
TAGGARD, GENEVIEVE (U.S.A.), 1894-		1432
Try Tropic	Try tropic for your balm	1432
TORRENCE, RIDGLEY (U.S.A.), 1875-		1407
Eye-Witness	Down by the railroad in a green valley	1407
VAN DOREN, MARK (U.S.A.), 1894-		1433
Wit	Wit is the only wall	1433
WELLES, WINIFRED (U.S.A.), 1893-		1430
Silver for Midas	Some day, Midas, the daffodils	1430
WEST, V. SACKVILLE- (England), 1892-		1427
Spring	The peddler and the reddleman	1427
WOLFE, HUMBERT (England), 1885-		1416
The Soldier	Down some cold field in a world unspoken	1416
The High Song	The high song is over. Silent is the lute now	1417
WURDEMANN, AUDREY (U.S.A.), 1911-		1455
Text	Behold this brief hexagonal	1455

INDEX BY TITLES

A

		PAGE
A Catch for Singing	*Wilfrid Wilson Gibson*	1412
Apologia Pro Poemate Meo	*Wilfred Owen*	1431

C

Colonel Fantock	*Edith Sitwell*	1422
Crystal Moment	*Robert P. Tristram Coffin*	1429

E

Ecstatic Ode on Vision	*Richard Hughes*	1446
Elegy for Mr. Goodbeare	*Osbert Sitwell*	1426
Essay on Deity	*Elder Olson*	1452
Eye-Witness	*Ridgely Torrence*	1407

F

Four Little Foxes	*Lew Sarett*	1419
Fourth Song From Cyprus	*"H.D."*	1418

H

Here Lies a Lady	*John Crowe Ransom*	1422

I

"Io Ritornai Dalla Santissima Onda"	*Leonard Bacon*	1420
"I Think Continually of Those—"	*Stephen Spender*	1454

L

Lovers Relentlessly	*Stanley J. Kunitz*	1449

M

Mary	*Paul Engle*	1455
Medusa	*Louise Bogan*	1434

P

Powhatan's Daughter	*Hart Crane*	1444
Prayers of Steel	*Carl Sandburg*	1413
Python	*Grace Hazard Conkling*	1414

R

Réveille	*Lola Ridge*	1415

INDEX BY TITLES

S

		PAGE
Silver for Midas	Winifred Welles	1430
Spring	V. Sackville-West	1427
Steel	Joseph Auslander	1435
Sweeney Among the Nightingales	T. S. Eliot	1420

T

Tears	Lizette Woodworth Reese	1403
Text	Audrey Wurdemann	1455
The Ballad of William Sycamore	Stephen Vincent Benét	1440
The Boar and Shibboleth	Edward Doro	1450
The Brute	William Vaughn Moody	1404
The High Song	Humbert Wolfe	1417
The Kings	Louise Imogen Guiney	1403
The River in the Meadows	Léonie Adams	1443
The Soldier	Humbert Wolfe	1416
The Swan	John Gould Fletcher	1418
The Worms at Heaven's Gate	Wallace Stevens	1414
The Zebras	Roy Campbell	1448
"Through Streets Where Crooked Wicklow Flows"	Horace Gregory	1442
Try Tropic	Genevieve Taggard	1432

W

Wit	Mark Van Doren	1433

Y

You, Andrew Marvell	Archibald MacLeish	1428

INDEX BY FIRST LINES

A

	PAGE
A cyclone threshes in the turbine crest	1444
A lithe beautiful fear	1414
A man said unto his Angel	1403
And here face down beneath the sun	1428
Apeneck Sweeney spreads his knees	1420

B

Behold this brief hexagonal	1455

C

Come forth, you workers!	1415
Crystal parting the meads	1443

D

Down by the railroad in a green valley	1407
Down some cold field in a world unspoken	1416
Do you remember Mr. Goodbeare, the carpenter	1426

F

From the dark woods that breathe of fallen showers	1448

G

God's body is all space	1452

H

Here lies a lady of beauty and high degree	1422

I

I had come to the house, in a cave of trees	1434
I think continually of those who were truly great	1454
I, too, saw God through mud,—	1431
I was eleven, hardly more	1450

L

Lay me on an anvil, O God	1413
Lovers relentlessly contend to be	1449
Low stooped the oaks like eagles	1446

M

My father, he was a mountaineer	1440

INDEX BY FIRST LINES

O

	PAGE
Once or twice this side of death	1429
Out of the tomb, we bring Badroulbadour	1414

S

Said the Old Young Man to the Young Old Man—	1412
Some day, Midas, the daffodils	1430
Speak gently, Spring, and make no sudden sound	1419

T

The high song is over. Silent is the lute now	1417
The peddler and the reddleman	1427
There is dogwood in my soul	1420
This man is dead	1435
Through his might men work their wills	1404
Through streets where crooked Wicklow flows	1442
Try tropic for your balm	1432
Thus spoke the lady underneath the trees	1422

U

Under a wall of bronze	1418

W

When I consider life and its few years—	1403
Where is the nightingale	1418
Wit is the only wall	1433

Y

You said I would forget you, forget your lithe	1455